HMH SCIENCE DIMENSIONS™

Teacher Edition • Grade 4

Acknowledgments for Covers

Front cover: model car ©GIPhotoStock/Science Source

Back cover: Mars Rover ©NASA/JPL/Cornell University/Maas Digital

Copyright © 2018 by Houghton Mifflin Harcourt Publishing Company

All rights reserved. No part of this work may be reproduced or transmitted in any form or by any means, electronic or mechanical, including photocopying or recording, or by any information storage and retrieval system, without the prior written permission of the copyright owner unless such copying is expressly permitted by federal copyright law. Requests for permission to make copies of any part of the work should be submitted through our Permissions website at https://customercare.hmhco.com/contactus/Permissions.html or mailed to Houghton Mifflin Harcourt Publishing Company, Attn: Intellectual Property Licensing, 9400 Southpark Center Loop, Orlando, Florida 32819-8647.

Common Core State Standards © Copyright 2010. National Governors Association Center for Best Practices and Council of Chief State School Officers. All rights reserved.

This product is not sponsored or endorsed by the Common Core State Standards Initiative of the National Governors Association Center for Best Practices and the Council of Chief State School Officers.

Printed in the U.S.A.

ISBN 978-0-544-71339-0

3 4 5 6 7 8 9 10 0877 25 24 23 22 21 20 19 18 17

4500964517   A B C D E F G

If you have received these materials as examination copies free of charge, Houghton Mifflin Harcourt Publishing Company retains title to the materials and they may not be resold. Resale of examination copies is strictly prohibited.

Possession of this publication in print format does not entitle users to convert this publication, or any portion of it, into electronic format.

Teacher Edition Contents

About the Program

Authors and Reviewers	**T4**
About HMH Science Dimensions	**T7**
NGSS and HMH Science Dimensions	**T22**
Program Scope and Sequence	**T36**
Program Pacing	**T38**
Program Author Articles:	
Why NGSS?	**T44**
Evidence Notebooks	**T50**
ELA Connections	**T53**
College and Career Readiness	**T56**
Every Student, Every Standard	**T59**
EQuIP Rubric	**T60**
Student Edition Contents	**T64**
Safety in Science	**T71**

Units

Unit 1—Engineering and Technology	1
Unit 2—Energy	65
Unit 3—Waves and Information Transfer	141
Unit 4—Plant Structure and Function	229
Unit 5—Animal Structure and Function	281
Unit 6—Changes to Earth's Surface	349
Unit 7—Rocks and Fossils	453
Unit 8—Natural Resources and Hazards	523

Resources

Reading in the Science Content Area	**TR2**
English Language Arts Correlations	**TR6**
Math Correlations	**TR10**
ScienceSaurus Correlations	**TR12**
Student Edition Interactive Glossary	**TR16**
Index	**TR24**

Program Authors

Michael A. DiSpezio

Global Educator
North Falmouth, Massachusetts

Michael DiSpezio has authored many HMH instructional programs for Science and Mathematics. He has also authored numerous trade books and multimedia programs on various topics and hosted dozens of studio and location broadcasts for various organizations in the U.S. and worldwide. Most recently, he has been working with educators to provide strategies for implementing the Next Generation Science Standards, particularly the science and engineering practices, cross-cutting concepts, and the use of Evidence Notebooks. To all his projects, he brings his extensive background in science, his expertise in classroom teaching at the elementary, middle, and high school levels, and his deep experience in producing interactive and engaging instructional materials.

Marjorie Frank

Science Writer and Content-Area Reading Specialist
Brooklyn, New York

An educator and linguist by training, a writer and poet by nature, Marjorie Frank has authored and designed a generation of instructional materials in all subject areas, including past HMH Science programs. Her other credits include authoring science issues of an award-winning children's magazine, writing game-based digital assessments, developing blended learning materials for young children, and serving as instructional designer and co-author of pioneering school-to-work software. In addition, she has served on the adjunct faculty of Hunter, Manhattan, and Brooklyn Colleges, teaching courses in science methods, literacy, and writing. For *HMH Science Dimensions*™, she has guided the development of our K-2 strands and our approach to making connections between NGSS and Common Core ELA/literacy standards.

Michael R. Heithaus, Ph.D.

Dean, College of Arts, Sciences & Education
Professor, Department of Biological Sciences
Florida International University
Miami, Florida

Mike Heithaus joined the FIU Biology Department in 2003, has served as Director of the Marine Sciences Program and Executive Director of the School of Environment, Arts, and Society, which brings together the natural and social sciences and humanities to develop solutions to today's environmental challenges. He now serves as Dean of the College of Arts, Sciences & Education. His research focuses on predator-prey interactions and the ecological importance of large marine species. He has helped to guide the development of Life Science content in *HMH Science Dimensions*™, with a focus on strategies for teaching challenging content as well as the science and engineering practices of analyzing data and using computational thinking.

Cary I. Sneider, Ph.D.

Associate Research Professor
Portland State University
Portland, Oregon

While studying astrophysics at Harvard, Cary Sneider volunteered to teach in an Upward Bound program and discovered his real calling as a science teacher. After teaching middle and high school science in Maine, California, Costa Rica, and Micronesia, he settled for nearly three decades at Lawrence Hall of Science in Berkeley, California, where he developed skills in curriculum development and teacher education. Over his career Cary directed more than 20 federal, state, and foundation grant projects, and was a writing team leader for the Next Generation Science Standards. He has been instrumental in ensuring *HMH Science Dimensions*™ meets the high expectations of the NGSS and provides an effective three-dimensional learning experience for all students.

Advisors and Reviewers

Program Advisors

Paul D. Asimow, PhD
Eleanor and John R. McMillan Professor of Geology and Geochemistry
California Institute of Technology
Pasadena, California

Eileen Cashman, PhD
Professor
Humboldt State University
Arcata, California

Mark B. Moldwin, PhD
Professor of Space Sciences and Engineering
University of Michigan
Ann Arbor, Michigan

Kelly Y. Neiles, PhD
Assistant Professor of Chemistry
St. Mary's College of Maryland
St. Mary's City, Maryland

Sten Odenwald, PhD
Astronomer
NASA Goddard Spaceflight Center
Greenbelt, Maryland

Bruce W. Schafer
Director of K-12 STEM Collaborations, retired
Oregon University System
Portland, Oregon

Barry A. Van Deman
President and CEO
Museum of Life and Science
Durham, North Carolina

Kim Withers, PhD
Assistant Professor
Texas A&M University-Corpus Christi
Corpus Christi, Texas

Adam D. Woods, PhD
Professor
California State University, Fullerton
Fullerton, California

Classroom Reviewers

Michelle Barnett
Lichen K-8 School
Citrus Heights, California

Brandi Bazarnik
Skycrest Elementary
Citrus Heights, California

Kristin Wojes-Broetzmann
Saint Anthony Parish School
Menomonee Falls, Wisconsin

Andrea Brown
District Science and STEAM Curriculum TOSA
Hacienda La Puente Unified School District
Hacienda Heights, California

Denice Gayner
Earl LeGette Elementary
Fair Oaks, California

Emily Giles
Elementary Curriculum Consultant
Kenton County School District
Ft. Wright, Kentucky

Crystal Hintzman
Director of Curriculum, Instruction and Assessment
School District of Superior
Superior, Wisconsin

Roya Hosseini
Junction Avenue K-8 School
Livermore, California

Cynthia Alexander Kirk
Classroom Teacher, Learning Specialist
West Creek Academy
Valencia, California

Marie LaCross
Fair Oaks Ranch Community School
Santa Clarita, California

Emily Miller
Science Specialist
Madison Metropolitan School District
Madison, Wisconsin

Monica Murray, EdD
Principal
Bassett Unified School District
La Puente, California

Carolyn Quigley
Ironia Elementary
Randolph, New Jersey

Wendy Savaske
Director of Instructional Services
School District of Holmen
Holmen, Wisconsin

Tina Topoleski
District Science Supervisor
Jackson School District
Jackson, New Jersey

Advisors and Reviewers continued

Educator Advisory Panel Members

Dr. C. Alex Alvarez
Director of STEM and Curriculum
Valdosta City Schools
Valdosta, Georgia

Kerri Angel
Science Teacher
Department Chair
Churchill County School District
Churchill County Middle School
Fallon, Nevada

Maria Blue
Teacher
Emblem Academy
Saugus Union School District
Saugus, California

Regina Brinker
STEM Coordinator
Livermore Valley Joint Unified School District
Livermore, California

Andrea Brown
District Science and STEAM Curriculum TOSA
Hacienda La Puente Unified School District
Hacienda Heights, California

Conni Crittenden
4th and 5th Grade Classroom Teacher
Williamston Community Schools
Williamston, Michigan

Ronald M. Durso, Ed.S.
District Science Supervisor
Fair Lawn Public Schools
Fair Lawn, New Jersey

Cheryl Frye
NGSS/STEM Coordinator
Menifee Union School District
Menifee, California

Brandon A. Gillette, Ph.D
Middle School Science Teacher
The Pembroke Hill School
Kansas City, Missouri

Susan L. Kallewaard, M.A. Ed., NBCT
Fifth Grade Teacher
Haverhill Elementary School
Portage, Michigan

John Labriola
Middle School Science Teacher, Science Content Coordinator
Charities Middle School
Wood River Junction, Rhode Island

Gilbert J. Luna
K-12 Science Curriculum Specialist
Vancouver Public Schools
Vancouver, Washington

Jennifer Su Mataele
PreK-12 Technology, STEAM TOSA
Hacienda La Puente Unified School District
Hacienda Heights, California

Shawna Metcalf
Science Teacher Specialist
Glendale Unified School District
Glendale, California

Erica Rose Motamed
Science Teacher
Lake Center Middle School
Santa Fe Springs, California

Monica Murray, EdD
Principal
Bassett Unified School District
La Puente, California

Stefanie Pechan
5th Grade Teacher, STEM Coordinator, PAEMST
Robert Down Elementary
Pacific Grove, California

Christie Purdon
K-12 Science Coordinator
Blue Valley School District
Overland Park, Kansas

Stephen J. Rapa
Science Department Chair
Worcester Public Schools
Worcester, Massachusetts

Alison L. Riordan
Science Curriculum Coordinator, K-12
Plymouth Public Schools
Plymouth, Massachusetts

Greta Trittin Smith
Academic Coach--Science
Garvey School District
Rosemead, California

Marsha Veninga
8th Grade Science Teacher
Bloomington Junior High School
Bloomington District 87
Bloomington, Illinois

HMH SCIENCE DIMENSIONS
ENGINEERED for the NEXT GENERATION

Program Overview
GRADES K–5

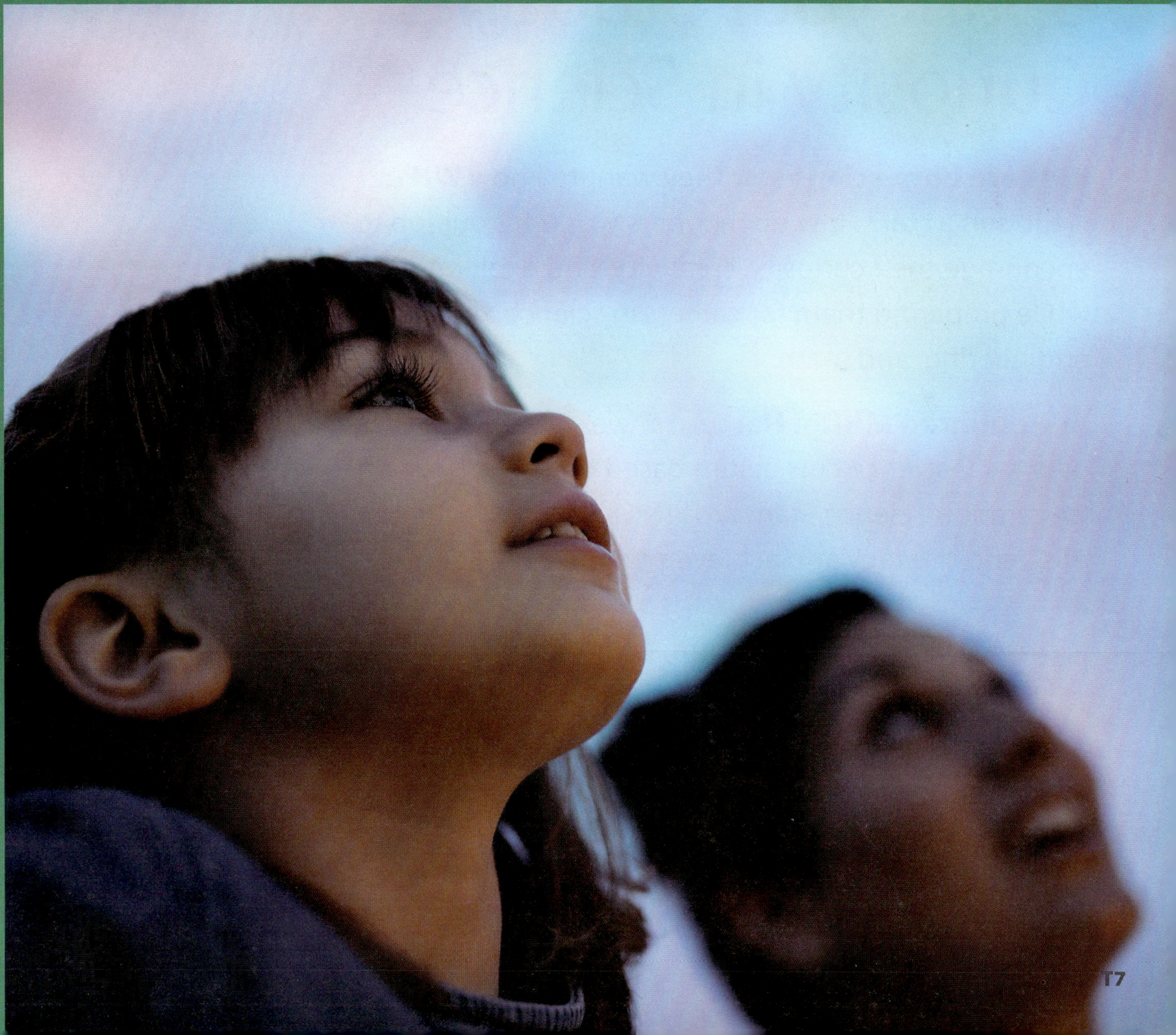

Introducing…

HMH SCIENCE DIMENSIONS™

Spark your Students' Curiosity in Science

Kids are born scientists. They want to know **WHY**: Is the sun a star? How do magnets work? It's our job to encourage their curiosity, creativity, and exploration while preparing them for careers in science, technology, engineering, and math.

At **Houghton Mifflin Harcourt**® we've created a brand new K–12 science curriculum based off of the Next Generation Science Standards (NGSS)* to raise the level of science literacy and achievement in our students.

A brand-new K–12 program, built from the ground up specifically for NGSS that:

- engages students
- promotes active learning and deeper thinking
- sparks an interest in science and science-related careers
- creates enduring understanding
- builds problem-solving skills
- creates lifelong learners

…better than any other program.

An **all-new**, complete solution for NGSS: Digital, print, and hands-on

HMH Science Dimensions is thoughtfully crafted to incorporate the Three Dimensions of Learning and Performance Expectations (PEs) of NGSS* into every lesson, every activity, every video—every piece!

What sets ***HMH Science Dimensions*** apart?

Three-Dimensional Learning. Designed—not aligned—around the Three Dimensions of Science Learning: Disciplinary Core Ideas (DCIs), Crosscutting Concepts (CCCs), and Science and Engineering Practices (SEPs)

Professional Support from HMH®. Simplifying your transition to an NGSS curriculum every step of the way

Active Learning. Activities, investigation, and evidence-gathering at the foundation of every lesson

Integrated Engineering & STEM. Developing students who are experts in the engineering design process

Digital-First Flexibility. Immersive learning experiences that engage students in doing science

Embedded Assessment. Preparing students to succeed on high-stakes performance-based assessments

*Next Generation Science Standards and logo are registered trademarks of Achieve. Neither Achieve nor the lead states and partners that developed the Next Generation Science Standards was involved in the production of, and does not endorse, this product.

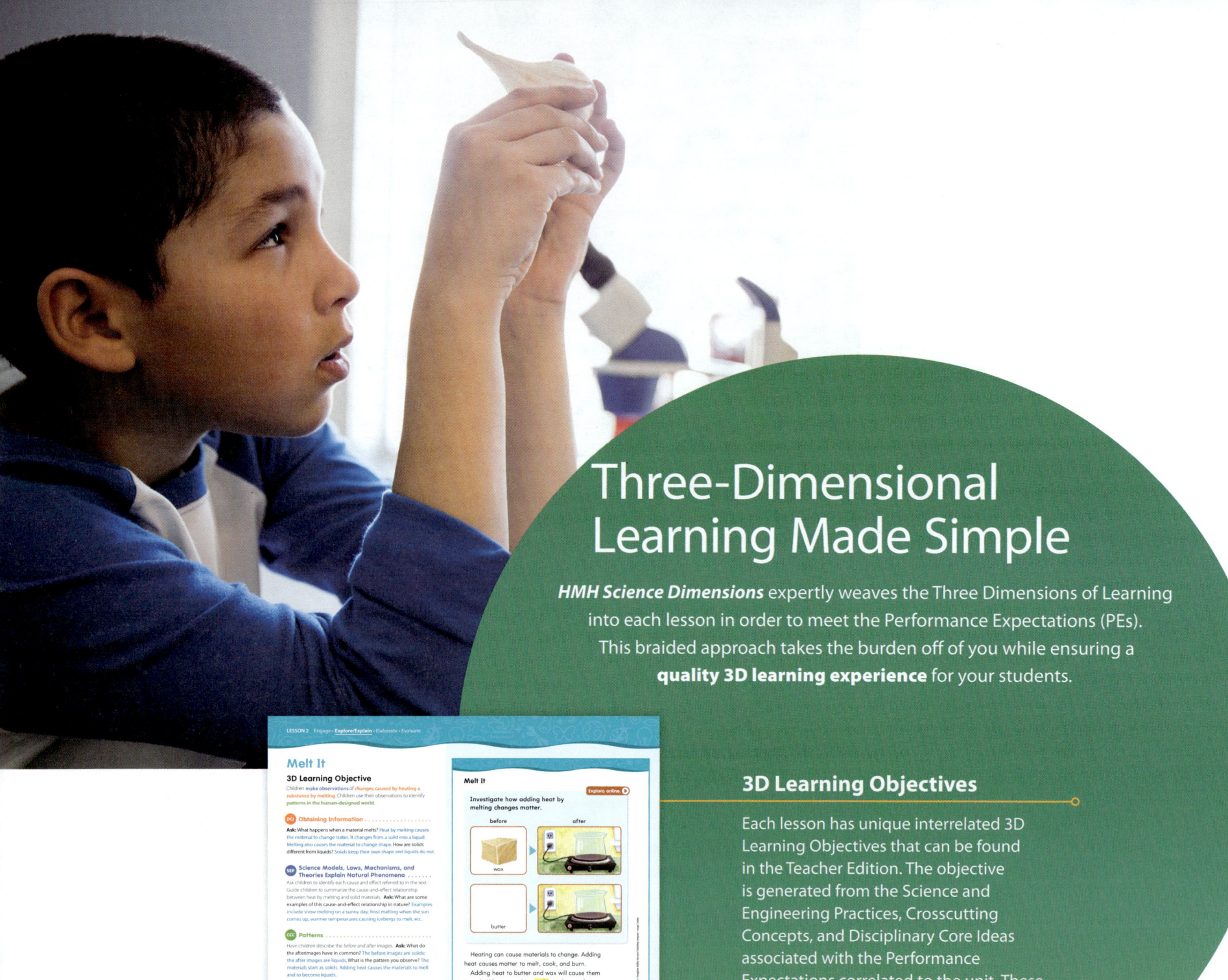

Three-Dimensional Learning Made Simple

HMH Science Dimensions expertly weaves the Three Dimensions of Learning into each lesson in order to meet the Performance Expectations (PEs). This braided approach takes the burden off of you while ensuring a **quality 3D learning experience** for your students.

Grade 2 Teacher Edition

3D Learning Objectives

Each lesson has unique interrelated 3D Learning Objectives that can be found in the Teacher Edition. The objective is generated from the Science and Engineering Practices, Crosscutting Concepts, and Disciplinary Core Ideas associated with the Performance Expectations correlated to the unit. These **custom stepping-stone objectives** ensure that the lessons cover 100% of the NGSS* material associated with the PEs.

Clearly Labeled NGSS References

- The NGSS labeling in the Teacher Edition clearly identifies all the PEs, SEPs, DCIs, and CCCs of NGSS, including the math and ELA connections. This helps educators **identify the standards** that are being covered in any given lesson.

- Additionally, throughout the **HMH Science Dimensions** Teacher Edition, you will find features to help you orient toward the critical dimensions of the **EQuIP Rubric**. These features will demonstrate the best practices of NGSS summarized by this evaluation instrument.

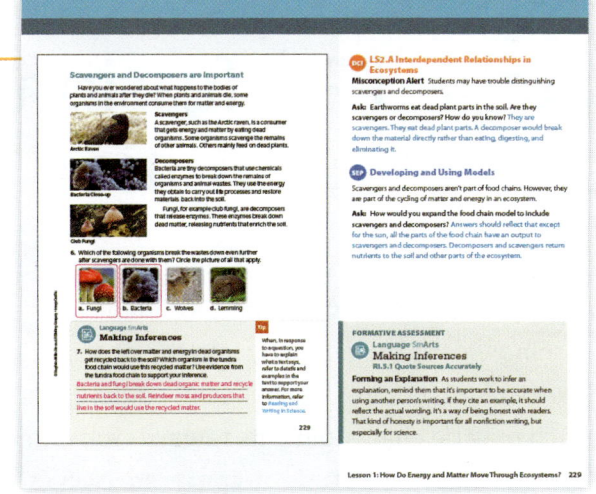

Grade 5 Teacher Edition

Follow the NGSS Story Through the Entire Curriculum!

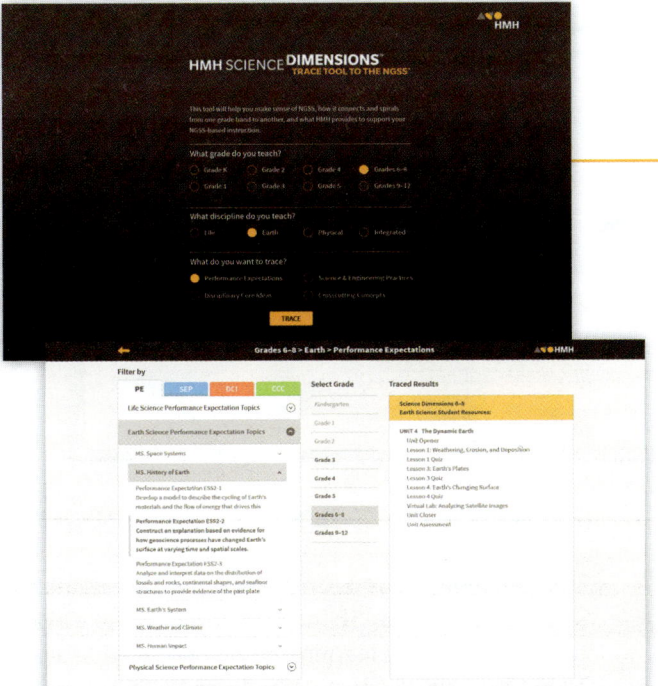

- The **HMH Science Dimensions Trace Tool to the NGSS** helps you make sense of the standards, understand how they connect and spiral from one grade to another, and **identify HMH resources** to support your NGSS-based instruction.

- You can **trace the standards** by PEs, SEPs, CCCs, or DCIs. When you click on a standard, you can view where in the program that standard is covered.

- But the **Trace Tool** is more powerful than a typical correlation—it also shows you **how each standard** and **dimension spirals** throughout the entire K–12 sequence. It's a snap to see what students should know already, and what you're preparing them for.

English Language Arts and Math Connections

Strong math and reading skills are essential to ensuring STEM learning and science literacy. **HMH Science Dimensions** offers Common Core **Math and ELA connections** throughout the curriculum.

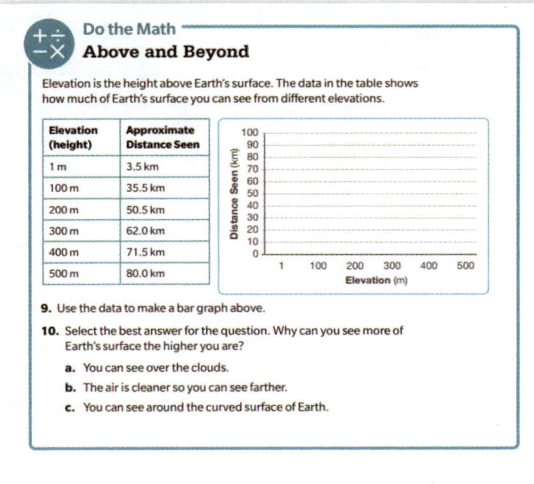

Grade 5 Print Student Edition *"Do the Math"*

*Next Generation Science Standards and logo are registered trademarks of Achieve. Neither Achieve nor the lead states and partners that developed the Next Generation Science Standards was involved in the production of, and does not endorse, this product.

Unmatched Professional Support to Help You Transition with Ease

HMH Science Dimensions invests as much in teachers as it does in students. With a thoughtfully structured Teacher Edition, professional development courses focused on NGSS* best practices, and professional learning videos built directly into the core curriculum, teachers have more support than ever. An NGSS curriculum requires a significantly different approach to teaching science, and although this new approach may be challenging, its **rewards** are immediate. HMH provides the support you need to make the transition to a **student-centered**, NGSS style of teaching.

Grade 2 Teacher Edition

Understand Where Your Instruction Fits

- The **Teacher Edition** (online and print) is organized around the familiar **5E instructional model**. This helps to lower the learning curve and provide a solid foundation upon which to build an NGSS curriculum.

- Additional Collaboration, Differentiate Instruction, Formative Assessment, and Claims, Evidence, and Reasoning suggestions provide a wealth of support and resources to help you **enrich the learning experience** for everyone.

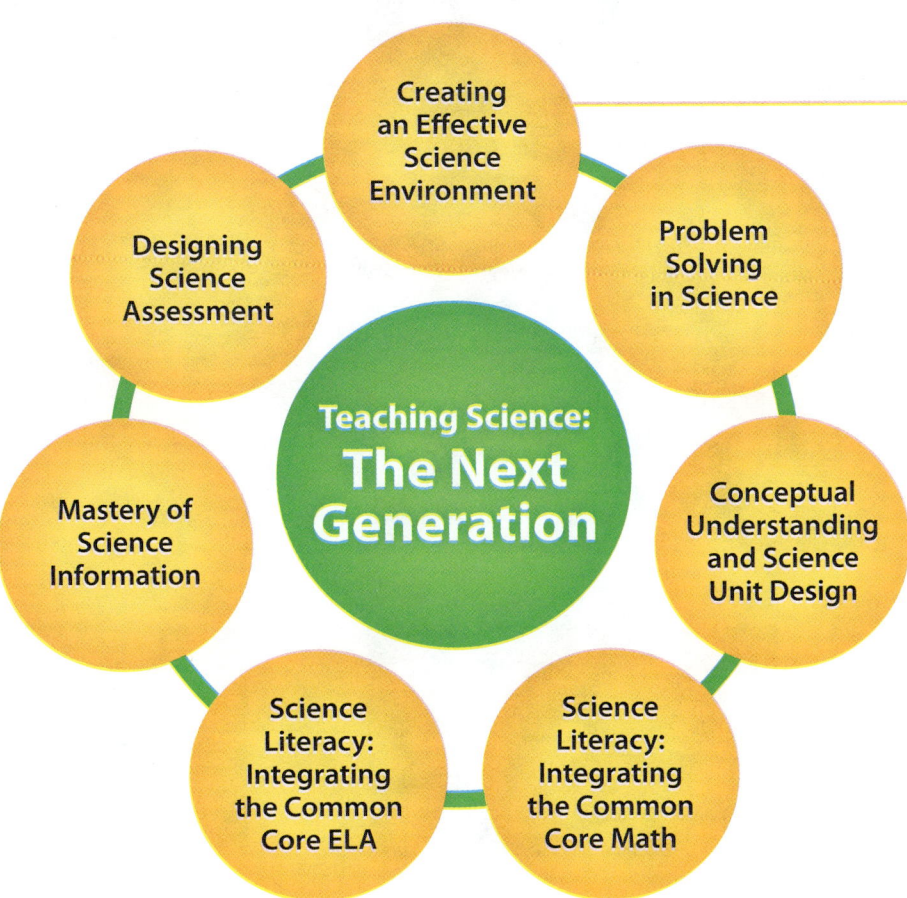

Professional Development to Build Your Confidence

- HMH offers 8 separate **best practices** courses that can help you transition to an NGSS curriculum with or without *HMH Science Dimensions*.

- Start with ***Teaching Science: The Next Generation***, and follow it up with one or more additional modules as either a preparation to or support for your adoption of NGSS. Our expert consultant staff will introduce you to the new science standards, and explain how they have been designed and organized across disciplines and grades to provide all students an internationally benchmarked science education.

PROFESSIONAL SUPPORT

See NGSS in Action

Embedded professional development videos help teachers better prepare for this new approach to science education. Just-in-time videos featuring our **dynamic consulting authors** guide teachers through the key approaches that ensure NGSS success.

» **FOUNDATION** videos help educators and parents better understand the NGSS, as well as the background that led up to their development.

» **ENGINEERING** videos support educators as they incorporate the design process into their classrooms.

» **CHALLENGING Content** videos for Grades 4–12 help educators know how to address specific content areas that students tend to struggle with in an NGSS curriculum.

» **HANDS-ON Activity** videos for Grades K–2 model what the hands-on activities within the curriculum should look like when implemented. These help ensure a more successful implementation of an NGSS solution.

Professional Development Video

*Next Generation Science Standards and logo are registered trademarks of Achieve. Neither Achieve nor the lead states and partners that developed the Next Generation Science Standards was involved in the production of, and does not endorse, this product.

Build Student Confidence with Authentic Investigations

Students are more engaged and learn more meaningfully through investigative inquiry. **HMH Science Dimensions** is built on this approach. Your students will learn to conduct hands-on investigations, define questions and objectives, make claims, and identify evidence—in short, to **take charge** and **fully engage** in their learning!

Every Lesson Is an Activity

- Each lesson begins with **Can You Explain It?**— a **problem to solve or discrepant event to explain**. This lesson-leading feature provides intrinsic motivation to spark curiosity and serves as the context for the three-dimensional learning and hands-on activities throughout the lessons. Students are motivated to think critically and construct explanations of *how* and *why*.

- The program is built around **active learning**. Rather than receive content passively, students are asked to **solve problems** or explain phenomena, by stating **claims**, gathering **evidence**, and providing explanations through **reasoning**.

Grade 5 Online Student Edition

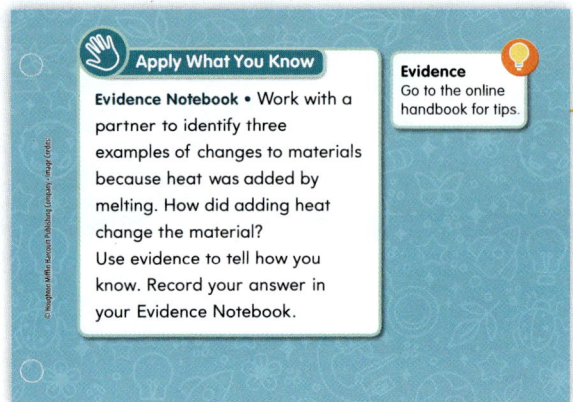

Grade 2 Print Student Edition

Science Notebooking to Strengthen Writing Skills

Many of the lessons in **HMH Science Dimensions** support the use of **Evidence Notebooks**. **Helpful prompts** have been inserted throughout the lessons to guide students on when to use these notebooks. Students will love creating their own study guides that can be taken into the next grade, and teachers will love the extra writing practice!

ACTIVITY-DRIVEN

Drive Student Learning with Hands-On Investigations

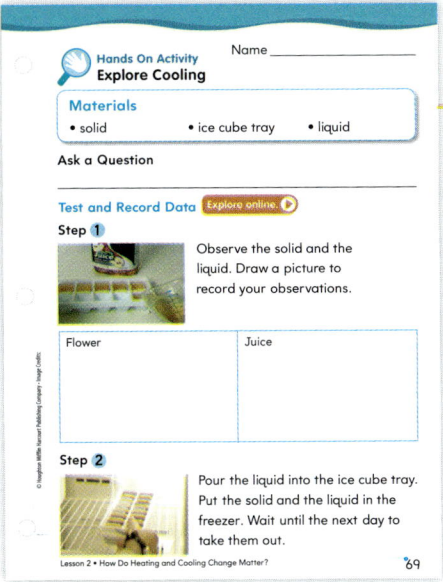

Grade 2 Print Student Edition

- **Hands-On Activities** are integrated into many of the lessons. These are built with teachers' busy schedules in mind. Each activity uses **easily sourced materials**.

- Students get to actively "do science;" they **think critically** about their observations, practice gathering evidence, and defend their claims.

Cultivate Collaboration

Working as a team is an essential part of developing **21st-century skills**. **HMH Science Dimensions** provides ample opportunities for students to participate in groups to complete activities and partner with their peers to discuss their findings.

Grade 5 Print Student Edition

Save Prep Time with Equipment Kits

- **Equipment Kits** provide the **consumable** and **non-consumable** materials you need to complete most of the hands-on activities so you have all the materials you need right at your fingertips.

- The **Safety Kit** provides the materials you need to address **classroom safety** while performing the program activities.

T15

The Students of Today Will Solve the Technology Challenges of Tomorrow!

NGSS* has raised the engineering design process to the same level as scientific inquiry. In **HMH Science Dimensions**, science, technology, engineering, and math are considered an **integral** part of the curriculum. Lessons are designed for students to explore science the same way real-life scientists do. Watch your students' eyes **light up** as they brainstorm solutions, share their ideas, and experiment to find solutions.

ENGINEERING AND STEM

Elevate Engineering

In **HMH Science Dimensions,** engineering and STEM are carried throughout every unit and not just treated as an ancillary. This approach elevates engineering design to the same level as scientific literacy. Each Unit includes a **Performance Task**, offering students multiple opportunities throughout the program to apply the **engineering design process** by defining a problem and designing a solution.

Grade 5 Print Student Edition

Provide Extra Support for Students Who Need It

The **Science and Engineering Practices Online Handbook** will help students achieve a higher level of understanding and skill as they build their experience applying the **Science and Engineering Practices** of NGSS.

Build Literacy and Science Content Knowledge

- The program includes print and online access to **Science and Engineering Leveled Readers** for Grades K–5. These colorful, fun, and interesting Readers provide three levels of readability for students: **On-Level, Extra Support,** and **Enrichment**.

- The accompanying **Teacher Guide** provides **activities** and **support** for before reading, during reading, and during response to reading.

*Next Generation Science Standards and logo are registered trademarks of Achieve. Neither Achieve nor the lead states and partners that developed the Next Generation Science Standards was involved in the production of, and does not endorse, this product.

Engage with Meaningful Technology

HMH Science Dimensions is a truly digital-first program. The curriculum leverages the advantages of technology while prioritizing a **student-centered learning model**. Students can view videos and animations, interact with instructional images and text, enter responses, pursue their intellectual interests by choosing lesson paths, and enjoy simulation-based learning. All of these features help you maintain an **integrated three-dimensional approach** to learning science.

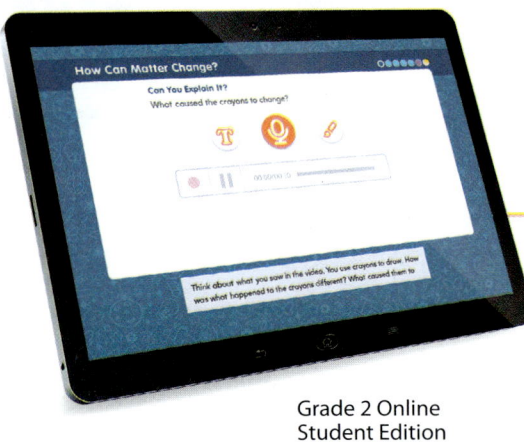

Grade 2 Online Student Edition

Immersive Digital Curriculum

Online lessons are enriched above and beyond the print lessons with educational videos, learning interactivities, and places to save student work as **responses** and **technology-enhanced item choices**. Vocabulary is highlighted and clickable, with point-of-use pop-up definitions.

Maximize Student Choice

The **Take It Further** feature at the end of each lesson maximizes the opportunity for students to elaborate further on what they have learned so far. By leveraging the power of technology, students can continue to go in depth on **topics of their choice**, to learn more and create stronger, more personal links to their learning.

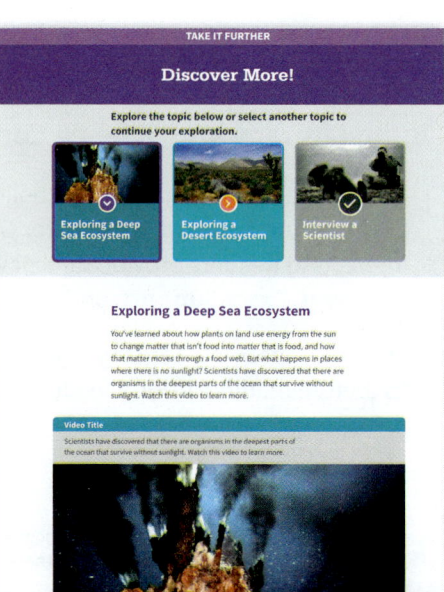

Grade 5 Online Student Edition

Deepen Understanding with Open-Ended Simulations

Unique **You Solve It** simulations provide completely **open-ended opportunities** for students to demonstrate their ability to problem solve and perform at the level described by the NGSS* Performance Expectations. The program encourages students to explore multiple answers to a problem and learn to develop explanations and defend their answers.

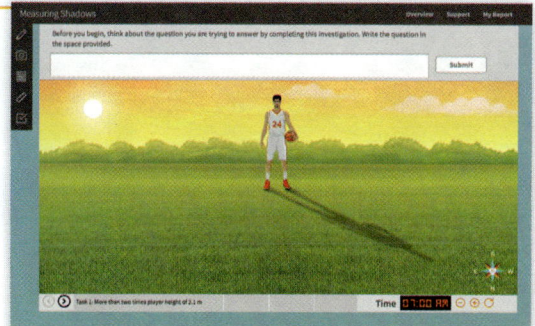

Grade 5 *You Solve It*

DIGITAL FIRST

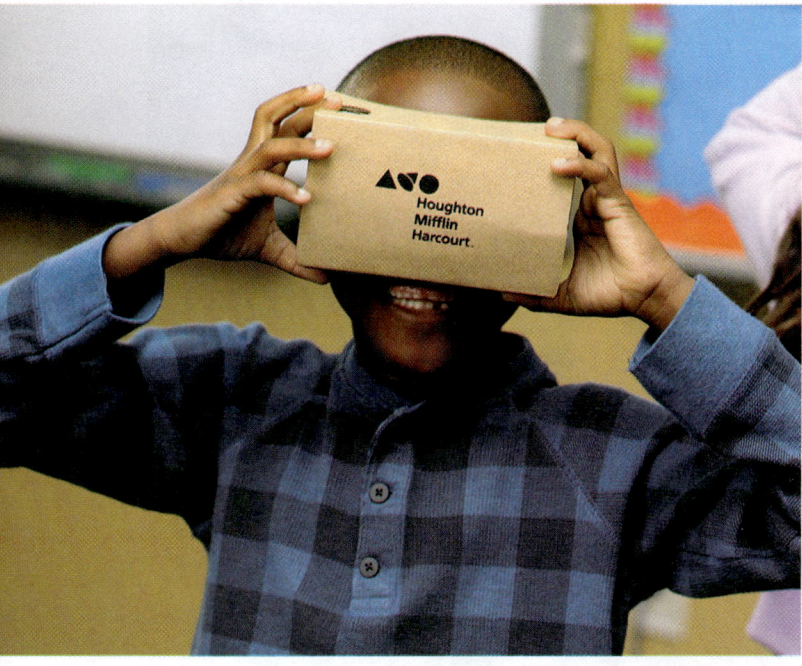

Explore Immersive Virtual Worlds

- As a Google® content partner, HMH has developed field trips for Google Expeditions.

HMH Field Trips
powered by

Google Expeditions

Using a simple Google Cardboard™ device and a smartphone, students are swept away into **3D, 360-degree experiences** in fascinating locations, directly tied to science content!

- An HMH **Teacher Guide** provides ideas for incorporating the Expeditions into your lessons, as well as tips on how to **guide** and **customize** the experience.

The Ultimate Online and Offline Program Experience

- Teachers can look forward to accessing **HMH Science Dimensions** through a new online learning system that supports integration with LMS solutions. This **flexible system** allows teachers to seamlessly embed the program's resources into their instruction.

- Additionally, program content can be accessed offline through the **HMH Player**® app. This allows for **maximum compatibility** in 1:1 or **Bring Your Own Device** learning environments and with the wide variety of technology that students have at home. No matter what, **HMH Science Dimensions** will be accessible.

*Next Generation Science Standards and logo are registered trademarks of Achieve. Neither Achieve nor the lead states and partners that developed the Next Generation Science Standards was involved in the production of, and does not endorse, this product.

Let Students Show What They Know

For the first time ever, through NGSS,* science standards now include specific **measureable learning outcomes**. These Performance Expectations guide test developers and teachers in understanding how to measure student learning. *HMH Science Dimensions* offers flexible assessment tools in a variety of formats to help you assess both formative and summative student learning according to NGSS.

Authentic Performance Assessment

Performance-Based Assessments help you ensure that your students can perform the science and engineering practices called for by NGSS. And they also guide students toward making connections across Performance Expectations.

Grade 5 Performance-Based Assessment

T20

Assess on All Dimensions

- Formal assessment questions **aligned to multiple dimensions** provide you with a complete picture of student understanding.

- A unique **3D Evaluation Rubric** helps you evaluate open-ended student responses and identify the underlying cause of student misunderstanding so that you can target remediation where it's most needed.

Grade 5 Online Student Edition

Reflect on Evidence Gathered

At the end of a lesson, the **Lesson Self-Check** encourages students to reflect on the evidence they gathered throughout the lesson. They have another chance to respond to the discrepant phenomenon or central question of the lesson with **open-ended response** questions.

Prepare for High-Stakes Tests

Technology-enhanced assessment items prepare your students for modern **computer-based high-stakes tests**. Parallel print assessments ensure that your students are challenged in the same way both on- and offline.

Kindergarten Online Assessment

*Next Generation Science Standards and logo are registered trademarks of Achieve. Neither Achieve nor the lead states and partners that developed the Next Generation Science Standards was involved in the production of, and does not endorse, this product.

NGSS and *HMH Science Dimensions*

4-PS3 Energy

	Print and Digital Resources	
	Supporting Learning Experiences	**Assessment & Performance**

Performance Expectation
4-PS3-1
Use evidence to construct an explanation relating the speed of an object to the energy of that object.
	Unit 2
	Lesson 1 and **Hands-On Activity**
	Lesson 3 and **Hands-On Activity**
		Unit 2
		Unit Project
		You Solve It (digital only)
		Unit Performance Task
		Assessment Guide and Online
		    Lesson Quizzes
		    Unit Test
		    Performance-Based Assessment
		    End-of-Year Test

Disciplinary Core Idea (DCI)	**PS3.A Definitions of Energy** The faster a given object is moving, the more energy it possesses.
Science and Engineering Practices	**Constructing Explanations and Designing Solutions** Use evidence (e.g., measurements, observations, patterns) to construct an explanation.
Crosscutting Concept	**Energy and Matter** Energy can be transferred in various ways and between objects.

T22   Resources

4-PS3 Energy continued

Print and Digital Resources

	Supporting Learning Experiences	Assessment & Performance
Performance Expectation **4-PS3-2** Make observations to provide evidence that energy can be transferred from place to place by sound, light, heat, and electric currents.	Unit 2 Lesson 1 and **Hands-On Activity** Lesson 2 and **Hands-On Activity** Lesson 3 and **Hands-On Activity**	Unit 2 Unit Project You Solve It (digital only) **Unit Performance Task** Assessment Guide and Online Lesson Quizzes Unit Test **Performance-Based Assessment** End-of-Year Test
Disciplinary Core Idea (DCI)	**PS3.A Definitions of Energy** Energy can be moved from place to place by moving objects or through sound, light, or electric currents. **PS3.B Conservation of Energy and Energy Transfer** Energy is present whenever there are moving objects, sound, light, or heat. When objects collide, energy can be transferred from one object to another, thereby changing their motion. In such collisions, some energy is typically also transferred to the surrounding air; as a result, the air gets heated and sound is produced. Light also transfers energy from place to place. Energy can also be transferred from place to place by electric currents, which can then be used locally to produce motion, sound, heat, or light. The currents may have been produced to begin with by transforming the energy of motion into electrical energy.	
Science and Engineering Practices	**Planning and Carrying Out Investigations** Make observations to produce data to serve as the basis for evidence for an explanation of a phenomenon or test a design solution.	
Crosscutting Concept	**Energy and Matter** Energy can be transferred in various ways and between objects.	

NGSS and *HMH Science Dimensions*

4-PS3 Energy

		Print and Digital Resources	
		Supporting Learning Experiences	**Assessment & Performance**

Performance Expectation
 4-PS3-3
 Ask questions and predict outcomes about the changes in energy that occur when objects collide.
		Unit 2
		 Lesson 3 and **Hands-On Activity**
			Unit 2
			 Unit Project
			 Unit Performance Task
			 Assessment Guide and Online
			     Lesson Quizzes
			     Unit Test
			 Performance-Based Assessment
			 End-of-Year Test

Disciplinary Core Idea (DCI)	**PS3.A Definitions of Energy** Energy can be moved from place to place by moving objects or through sound, light, or electric currents. **PS3.B Conservation of Energy and Energy Transfer** Energy is present whenever there are moving objects, sound, light, or heat. When objects collide, energy can be transferred from one object to another, thereby changing their motion. In such collisions, some energy is typically also transferred to the surrounding air; as a result, the air gets heated and sound is produced. **PS3.C Relationship Between Energy and Forces** When objects collide, the contact forces transfer energy so as to change the objects' motions.		
Science and Engineering Practices	**Asking Questions and Defining Problems** Ask questions that can be investigated based on patterns such as cause and effect relationships.		
Crosscutting Concept	**Energy and Matter** Energy can be transferred in various ways and between objects.		

NGSS and *HMH Science Dimensions*

4-PS3 Energy continued

Performance Expectation

4-PS3-4
Apply scientific ideas to design, test, and refine a device that converts energy from one form to another.

Print and Digital Resources	
Supporting Learning Experiences	**Assessment & Performance**
Unit 2	Unit 2
Lesson 1 and **Hands-On Activity**	Unit Project
Lesson 2 and **Hands-On Activity**	You Solve It (digital only)
Lesson 3 and **Hands-On Activity**	**Unit Performance Task**
	Assessment Guide and Online
	Lesson Quizzes
	Unit Test
	Performance-Based Assessment
	End-of-Year Test

Disciplinary Core Idea (DCI)

PS3.B Conservation of Energy and Energy Transfer Energy is present whenever there are moving objects, sound, light, or heat. When objects collide, energy can be transferred from one object to another, thereby changing their motion. In such collisions, some energy is typically also transferred to the surrounding air; as a result, the air gets heated and sound is produced.

PS3.D Energy in Chemical Processes and Everyday Life The expression "produce energy" typically refers to the conversion of stored energy into a desired form for practical use.

ETS1.Defining Engineering Problems Possible solutions to a problem are limited by available materials and resources (constraints). The success of a designed solution is determined by considering the desired features of a solution (criteria). Different proposals for solutions can be compared on the basis of how well each one meets the specified criteria for success or how well each takes the constraints into account.

Science and Engineering Practices

Asking Questions and Defining Problems Define a simple problem that can be solved through the development of a new or improved object or tool.

Crosscutting Concept

Energy and Matter Energy can be transferred in various ways and between objects.

Influence of Engineering, Technology, and Science on Society and the Natural World Engineers improve existing technologies or develop new ones.

Science is a Human Endeavor Most scientists and engineers work in teams.

Science is a Human Endeavor Science affects everyday life.

Resources **T25**

NGSS and *HMH Science Dimensions*

4-PS4 Waves and Their Applications in Technologies for Information Transfer

	Print and Digital Resources	
	Supporting Learning Experiences	**Assessment & Performance**

Performance Expectation
4-PS4-1
Develop a model of waves to describe patterns in terms of amplitude and wavelength and that waves can cause objects to move.
	Unit 3
	Lesson 1 and **Hands-On Activity**
		Unit 3
		Unit Project
		You Solve It (digital only)
		Unit Performance Task
		Assessment Guide and Online
		    Lesson Quizzes
		    Unit Test
		    Performance-Based Assessment
		    End-of-Year Test

Disciplinary Core Idea (DCI)	**PS4.A Wave Properties** Waves, which are regular patterns of motion, can be made in water by disturbing the surface. When waves move across the surface of deep water, the water goes up and down in place; there is no net motion in the direction of the wave except when the water meets a beach. **Wave Properties** Waves of the same type can differ in amplitude (height of the wave) and wavelength (spacing between wave peaks).	
Science and Engineering Practices	**Developing and Using Models** Develop a model using an analogy, example, or abstract representation to describe a scientific principle. **Scientific Knowledge is Based on Empirical Evidence** Science findings are based on recognizing patterns.	
Crosscutting Concept	**Patterns** Similarities and differences in patterns can be used to sort, classify, and analyze simple rates of change for natural phenomena.	

T26   Resources

4-PS4 Waves and Their Applications in Technologies for Information Transfer
continued

Print and Digital Resources

	Supporting Learning Experiences	Assessment & Performance

Performance Expectation
4-PS4-2
Develop a model to describe that light reflecting from objects and entering the eye allows objects to be seen.
	Unit 3
	Lesson 2 and **Hands-On Activity**
		Unit 3
		Unit Project
		You Solve It (digital only)
		Unit Performance Task
		Assessment Guide and Online
		    Lesson Quizzes
		    Unit Test
		    Performance-Based Assessment
		    End-of-Year Test

Disciplinary Core Idea (DCI)	**PS4.B Electromagnetic Radiation** An object can be seen when light reflected from its surface enters the eyes.
Science and Engineering Practices	**Developing and Using Models** Develop a model to describe phenomena.
Crosscutting Concept	**Cause and Effect** Cause and effect relationships are routinely identified.

	Supporting Learning Experiences	Assessment & Performance

Performance Expectation
4-PS4-3
Generate and compare multiple solutions that use patterns to transfer information.
	Unit 3
	Lesson 1 and **Hands-On Activity**
	Lesson 3 and **Hands-On Activity**
		Unit 3
		Unit Project
		You Solve It (digital only)
		Unit Performance Task
		Assessment Guide and Online
		    Lesson Quizzes
		    Unit Test
		    Performance-Based Assessment
		    End-of-Year Test

Disciplinary Core Idea (DCI)	**PS4.C Information Technologies and Instrumentation** Digitized information can be transmitted over long distances without significant degradation. High-tech devices, such as computers or cell phones, can receive and decode information—convert it from digitized **ETS1.C Optimizing the Design Solution** Different solutions need to be tested in order to determine which of them best solves the problem, given the criteria and the constraints.
Science and Engineering Practices	**Constructing Explanations and Designing Solutions** Generate and compare multiple solutions to a problem based on how well they meet the criteria and constraints of the design SOLUTION.
Crosscutting Concept	**Patterns** Similarities and differences in patterns can be used to sort and classify designed products. **Interdependence of Science, Engineering, and Technology** Knowledge of relevant scientific concepts and research findings is important in engineering.

NGSS and *HMH Science Dimensions*

4-LS1 From Molecules to Organisms: Structures and Processes

Performance Expectation

4-LS1-1

Construct an argument that plants and animals have internal and external structures that function to support survival, growth, behavior, and reproduction.

Print and Digital Resources	
Supporting Learning Experiences	**Assessment & Performance**
Unit 4	Unit 4
Lesson 1 and **Hands-On Activity**	Unit Project
Lesson 2 and **Hands-On Activity**	You Solve It (digital only)
Unit 5	**Unit Performance Task**
Lesson 1 and **Hands-On Activity**	Assessment Guide and Online
Lesson 2 and **Hands-On Activity**	Lesson Quizzes
Lesson 3 and **Hands-On Activity**	Unit Test
	Performance-Based Assessment
	End-of-Year Test
	Unit 5
	Unit Project
	You Solve It (digital only)
	Unit Performance Task
	Assessment Guide and Online
	Lesson Quizzes
	Unit Test
	Performance-Based Assessment
	End-of-Year Test

Disciplinary Core Idea (DCI)	**LS1.A Structure and Function** Plants and animals have both internal and external structures that serve various functions in growth, survival, behavior, and reproduction.
Science and Engineering Practices	**Engaging in Argument from Evidence** Construct an argument with evidence, data, and/or a model.
Crosscutting Concept	**Systems and System Models** A system can be described in terms of its components and their interactions.

4-LS1 From Molecules to Organisms: Structures and Processes continued

Print and Digital Resources	
Supporting Learning Experiences	**Assessment & Performance**

Unit 5
Lesson 1 and **Hands-On Activity**
Lesson 2 and **Hands-On Activity**
Lesson 3 and **Hands-On Activity**
	Unit 5
	Unit Project
	You Solve It (digital only)
	Unit Performance Task
	Assessment Guide and Online
	    Lesson Quizzes
	    Unit Test
	Performance-Based Assessment
	End-of-Year Test

Performance Expectation

4-LS1-2

Use a model to describe that animals receive different types of information through their senses, process the information in their brain, and respond to the information in different ways.

Disciplinary Core Idea (DCI)	**LS1.D Information Processing** Different sense receptors are specialized for particular kinds of information, which may be then processed by the animal's brain. Animals are able to use their perceptions and memories to guide their actions.
Science and Engineering Practices	**Constructing Explanations and Designing Solutions** Use a model to test interactions concerning the functioning of a natural system.
Crosscutting Concept	**Systems and System Models** A system can be described in terms of its components and their interactions.

4-ESS1 Earth's Place in the Universe

Print and Digital Resources	
Supporting Learning Experiences	**Assessment & Performance**

Unit 7
Lesson 1 and **Hands-On Activity**
Lesson 2 and **Hands-On Activity**
Lesson 3 and **Hands-On Activity**
	Unit 7
	Unit Project
	You Solve It (digital only)
	Unit Performance Task
	Assessment Guide and Online
	    Lesson Quizzes
	    Unit Test
	Performance-Based Assessment
	End-of-Year Test

Performance Expectation

4-ESS1-1

Identify evidence from patterns in rock formations and fossils in rock layers to support an explanation for changes in a landscape over time.

Disciplinary Core Idea (DCI)	**ESS1.C The History of Planet Earth** Local, regional, and global patterns of rock formations reveal changes over time due to earth forces, such as earthquakes. The presence and location of certain fossil types indicate the order in which rock layers were formed.
Science and Engineering Practices	**Constructing Explanations and Designing Solutions** Identify the evidence that supports particular points in an explanation.
Crosscutting Concept	**Patterns** Patterns can be used as evidence to support an explanation. **Scientific Knowledge Assumes an Order and Consistency in Natural Systems** Science assumes consistent

NGSS and *HMH Science Dimensions*

4-ESS2 Earth's Systems

	Print and Digital Resources	
	Supporting Learning Experiences	**Assessment & Performance**

Performance Expectation
4-ESS2-1
Make observations and/or measurements to provide evidence of the effects of weathering or the rate of erosion by water, ice, wind, or vegetation.
	Unit 6
	Lesson 1 and **Hands-On Activity**
	Lesson 2 and **Hands-On Activity**
		Unit 6
		Unit Project
		You Solve It (digital only)
		Unit Performance Task
		Assessment Guide and Online
		    Lesson Quizzes
		    Unit Test
		Performance-Based Assessment
		End-of-Year Test

Disciplinary Core Idea (DCI)	**ESS2.A Earth Materials and Systems** Rainfall helps to shape the land and affects the types of living things found in a region. Water, ice, wind, living organisms, and gravity break rocks, soils, and sediments into smaller particles and move them around.	
Science and Engineering Practices	**Biogeology** Living things affect the physical characteristics of their regions. **Engaging in Argument from Evidence** Construct an argument with evidence.	
Crosscutting Concept	**Cause and Effect** Cause and effect relationships are routinely identified, tested, and used to explain change.	

Performance Expectation
4-ESS2-2
Analyze and interpret data from maps to describe patterns of Earth's features.
	Unit 6
	Lesson 1 and **Hands-On Activity**
	Lesson 2 and **Hands-On Activity**
	Lesson 3 and **Hands-On Activity**
	Lesson 4 and **Hands-On Activity**
		Unit 6
		Unit Project
		You Solve It (digital only)
		Unit Performance Task
		Assessment Guide and Online
		    Lesson Quizzes
		    Unit Test
		Performance-Based Assessment
		End-of-Year Test

Disciplinary Core Idea (DCI)	**ESS2.B Plate Tectonics and Large-Scale System Interactions** The locations of mountain ranges, deep ocean trenches, ocean floor structures, earthquakes, and volcanoes occur in patterns. Most earthquakes and volcanoes occur in bands that are often along the boundaries between continents and oceans. Major mountain chains form inside continents or near their edges. Maps can help locate the different land and water features areas of Earth.	
Science and Engineering Practices	**Analyzing and Interpreting Data** Analyze and interpret data to make sense of phenomena using logical reasoning.	
Crosscutting Concept	**Patterns** Patterns can be used as evidence to support an explanation.	

4-ESS3 Earth and Human Activity

Print and Digital Resources

Supporting Learning Experiences	Assessment & Performance

Unit 8
Lesson 1 and **Hands-On Activity**
Lesson 2 and **Hands-On Activity**
	Unit 8
	Unit Project
	You Solve It (digital only)
	Unit Performance Task
	Assessment Guide and Online
	    Lesson Quizzes
	    Unit Test
	    Performance-Based Assessment
	    End-of-Year Test

Performance Expectation

4-ESS3-1

Obtain and combine information to describe that energy and fuels are derived from natural resources and their uses affect the environment.

Disciplinary Core Idea (DCI)
ESS3.A Natural Resources Energy and fuels that humans use are derived from natural sources, and their use affects the environment in multiple ways. Some resources are renewable over time, and others are not.

Science and Engineering Practices
Obtaining, Evaluating, and Communicating Information Obtain and combine information from books and other reliable media to explain phenomena.

Crosscutting Concept
Cause and Effect Cause and effect relationships are routinely identified and used to explain change.

Interdependence of Science, Engineering, and Technology Knowledge of relevant scientific concepts and research findings is important in engineering.

Influence of Engineering, Technology, and Science on Society and the Natural World Over time, people's needs and wants change, as do their demands for new

NGSS and *HMH Science Dimensions*

4-ESS3 Earth and Human Activity
continued

	Print and Digital Resources	
	Supporting Learning Experiences	**Assessment & Performance**

Performance Expectation
4-ESS3-2
Generate and compare multiple solutions to reduce the impacts of natural Earth processes on humans.
	Unit 8
	Lesson 3 and **Hands-On Activity**
	Lesson 4 and **Hands-On Activity**
		Unit 8
		Unit Project
		You Solve It (digital only)
		Unit Performance Task
		Assessment Guide and Online
		    Lesson Quizzes
		    Unit Test
		    Performance-Based Assessment
		    End-of-Year Test

Disciplinary Core Idea (DCI)	**ESS3.B Natural Hazards** A variety of hazards result from natural processes (e.g., earthquakes, tsunamis, volcanic eruptions). Humans cannot eliminate the hazards but can take steps to reduce their impacts. **ETS1.B Designing Solutions to Engineering Problems** Testing a solution involves investigating how well it performs under a range of likely conditions.
Science and Engineering Practices	**Constructing Explanations and Designing Solutions** Generate and compare multiple solutions to a problem based on how well they meet the criteria and constraints of the design solution.
Crosscutting Concept	**Cause and Effect** Cause and effect relationships are routinely identified, tested, and used to explain change. **Influence of Engineering, Technology, and Science on Society and the Natural World** Engineers improve existing technologies or develop new ones to increase their benefits, to decrease known risks, and to meet societal demands.

3-5 ETS1 Engineering Design

Performance Expectation

3-5-ETS1-1

Define a simple design problem reflecting a need or a want that includes specified criteria for success and constraints on materials, time, or cost.

Print and Digital Resources

Supporting Learning Experiences	Assessment & Performance
Unit 1	Unit 1
Lesson 1 and **Hands-On Activity**	Unit Project
Lesson 2 and **Hands-On Activity**	You Solve It (digital only)
Lesson 3 and **Hands-On Activity**	**Unit Performance Task**
Unit 2	Assessment Guide and Online
Lesson 1 and **Hands-On Activity**	Lesson Quizzes
	Unit Test
	Performance-Based Assessment
	End-of-Year Test

Disciplinary Core Idea (DCI)	**ETS1.A Defining and Delimiting Engineering Problems** Possible solutions to a problem are limited by available materials and resources (constraints). The success of a designed solution is determined by considering the desired features of a solution (criteria). Different proposals for solutions can be compared on the basis of how well each one meets the specified criteria for success or how well each takes the constraints into account.
Science and Engineering Practices	**Asking Questions and Defining Problems** Define a simple design problem that can be solved through the development of an object, tool, process, or system and includes several criteria for success and constraints on materials, time, or cost.
Crosscutting Concept	**Influence of Science, Engineering, and Technology on Society and the Natural World** People's needs and wants change over time, as do their demands for new and improved technologies.

NGSS and *HMH Science Dimensions*

3-5 ETS1 Engineering Design continued

Print and Digital Resources

	Supporting Learning Experiences	Assessment & Performance

Performance Expectation
3-5-ETS1-2
Generate and compare multiple possible solutions to a problem based on how well each is likely to meet the criteria and constraints of the problem.
	Unit 1
	Lesson 1 and **Hands-On Activity**
	Lesson 2 and **Hands-On Activity**
	Unit 8
	Lesson 3 and **Hands-On Activity**
	Lesson 4 and **Hands-On Activity**
		Unit 1
		Unit Project
		You Solve It (digital only)
		Unit Performance Task
		Assessment Guide and Online
		   Lesson Quizzes
		   Unit Test
		   Performance-Based Assessment
		   End-of-Year Test

Disciplinary Core Idea (DCI)	**ETS1.B Developing Possible Solutions** Research on a problem should be carried out before beginning to design a solution. Testing a solution involves investigating how well it performs under a range of likely conditions. **Developing Possible Solutions** At whatever stage, communicating with peers about proposed solutions is an important part of the design process, and shared ideas can lead to improved designs.
Science and Engineering Practices	**Constructing Explanations and Designing Solutions** Generate and compare multiple solutions to a problem based on how well they meet the criteria and constraints of the design problem.
Crosscutting Concept	**Influence of Science, Engineering, and Technology on Society and the Natural World** Engineers improve existing technologies or develop new ones to increase their benefits, decrease known risks, and meet societal demands.

	Supporting Learning Experiences	Assessment & Performance

Performance Expectation
3-5-ETS1-3
Plan and carry out fair tests in which variables are controlled and failure points are considered to identify aspects of a model or prototype that can be improved.
	Unit 1
	Lesson 1 and **Hands-On Activity**
	Lesson 2 and **Hands-On Activity**
	Lesson 3 and **Hands-On Activity**
	Unit 3
	Lesson 2 and **Hands-On Activity**
		Unit 1
		Unit Project
		You Solve It (digital only)
		Unit Performance Task
		Assessment Guide and Online
		   Lesson Quizzes
		   Unit Test
		   Performance-Based Assessment
		   End-of-Year Test

Disciplinary Core Idea (DCI)	**ETS1.B Developing Possible Solutions** Tests are often designed to identify failure points or difficulties, which suggest the elements of the design that need to be improved. **ETS1.C Optimizing the Design Solution** Different solutions need to be tested in order to determine which of them best solves the problem, given the criteria and the constraints.
Science and Engineering Practices	**Planning and Carrying Out Investigations** Plan and conduct an investigation collaboratively to produce data to serve as the basis for evidence, using fair tests in which variables are controlled and the number of trials considered

Teacher Notes

Program Scope and Sequence

	Grade K-2	Grade 3-5
Engineering and Design	GK Unit 1 Engineering and Technology* G1 Unit 1 Engineering and Technology* G2 Unit 1 Engineering Design Process*	G3 Unit 1 Engineering * **G4 Unit 1 Engineering and Technology*** G5 Unit 1 Engineering and Technology*

Physical Science	GK Unit 2 Forces and Motion
	G1 Unit 2 Sound
	    Unit 3 Light
	G2 Unit 2 Matter
		G3 Unit 2 Forces
		    Unit 3 Motion
		G4 Unit 2 Energy
		    Unit 3 Waves and Information Transfer
		G5 Unit 2 Matter

Life Science	GK Unit 3 Plants and Animals
	G1 Unit 4 Plant and Animal Structures
	    Unit 5 Living Things and Their Young
	G2 Unit 3 Environments for Living Things
		G3 Unit 4 Life Cycles and Inherited Traits
		    Unit 5 Organisms and Their Environment
		    Unit 6 Fossils
		G4 Unit 4 Plant Structure and Function
		    Unit 5 Animal Structure and Function
		G5 Unit 3 Energy and Matter in Organisms
		    Unit 4 Energy and Matter in Ecosystems

Earth and Space Sciences	GK Unit 4 Sun Warms Earth
	    Unit 5 Weather
	    Unit 6 Earth's Resources
	G1 Unit 6 Objects and Patterns in the Sky
	G2 Unit 4 Earth's Surface
	    Unit 5 Changes to Earth's Surface
		G3 Unit 7 Weather and Patterns
		G4 Unit 6 Changes to Earth's Surface
		    Unit 7 Rocks and Fossils
		    Unit 8 Natural Resources and Hazards
		G5 Unit 5 Systems in Space
		    Unit 6 Earth's Systems
		    Unit 7 Earth and Human Activities

*Engineering strand is embedded throughout other units and strands.   Included in this Teacher Edition

Grade 6-8

Engineering and Design

Module A Engineering and Science*
- Unit 1 Introduction to Engineering and Science
- Unit 2 The Practices of Engineering

Physical Science

Module I Energy and Energy Transfer
- Unit 1 Energy and Matter
- Unit 2 Energy Transfer

Module J Chemistry
- Unit 1 The Structure of Matter
- Unit 2 States of Matter and Changes of State
- Unit 3 Chemical Processes and Equations
- Unit 4 The Chemistry of Materials

Module K Forces, Motion, and Fields
- Unit 1 Forces and Motion
- Unit 2 Electric and Magnetic Forces

Module L Waves and Their Applications
- Unit 1 Waves
- Unit 2 Information Transfer

Life Science

Module B Cells and Heredity
- Unit 1 Cells
- Unit 2 Organisms as Systems
- Unit 3 Reproduction, Heredity, and Growth

Module C Ecology and the Environment
- Unit 1 Matter and Energy in Living Systems
- Unit 2 Relationships in Ecosystems
- Unit 3 Ecosystem Dynamics

Module D The Diversity of Living Things
- Unit 1 The History of Life on Earth
- Unit 2 Evolution
- Unit 3 Human Influence on Inheritance

Earth and Space Sciences

Module E Earth's Water and Atmosphere
- Unit 1 Circulation of Earth's Air and Water
- Unit 2 Weather and Climate

Module F Geologic Processes and History
- Unit 1 The Dynamic Earth
- Unit 2 Earth Through Time

Module G Earth and Human Activity
- Unit 1 Earth's Natural Hazards
- Unit 2 Resources in Earth's Systems
- Unit 3 Using Resources
- Unit 4 Human Impacts on Earth Systems

Module H Space Science
- Unit 1 Patterns in the Solar System
- Unit 2 The Solar System and Universe

Trace Tool to the NGSS
Go online to view how the standards apply to your grade level, and to trace connections to prior and subsequent grades.

Program Scope and Sequence T37

Pacing Guide

The following Pacing Guide recommends days for the core instructional elements of each unit. You have options for covering lesson materials: you may choose to follow the comprehensive path or you may choose the core path. You may also customize your Pacing Guide based on your classroom schedule and needs.

Pressed for Time? Follow the faster-paced core schedule.

	Core	Comprehensive 45 minute class	Customize Your Pacing Guide
Unit 1 Engineering and Technology			
Unit 1 Project		2 days	
Lesson 1 **Engineer It** • How Do Engineers Define Problems?	3 days	4 days	
Lesson 2 **Engineer It** • How Do Engineers Design Solutions?	3 days	4 days	
Lesson 3 **Engineer It** • How Do Engineers Test and Improve Prototypes?	3 days	4 days	
You Solve It		1 day	
Unit 1 Performance Task		1 days	
Performance-Based Assessment		1 days	
Unit 1 Review and Unit 1 Test	2 days	2 days	
Total Days for Unit 1	11 days	19 days	
Unit 2 Energy			
Unit 2 Project		2 days	
Lesson 1 What Is Energy?	3 days	4 days	

T38 Pacing Guide

Pacing Guide

	Core	Comprehensive 45 minute class	Customize Your Pacing Guide
Unit 2 Energy continued			
Lesson 2 How Is Energy Transferred?	3 days	4 days	
Lesson 3 How Do Collisions Show Energy?	3 days	4 days	
You Solve It		1 day	
Unit 2 Performance Task		1 days	
Performance-Based Assessment		1 days	
Unit 2 Review and 2 Unit Test	2 days	2 days	
Total Days for Unit 2	11 days	19 days	
Unit 3 Waves and Information Transfer			
Unit 3 Project		2 days	
Lesson 1 What Are Waves?	3 days	4 days	
Lesson 2 How Does Light Reflect?	3 days	4 days	
Lesson 3 How Is Information Transferred from Place to Place?	3 days	4 days	
You Solve It		1 day	
Unit 3 Performance Task		1 days	
Performance-Based Assessment		1 days	
Unit 3 Review and Unit 3 Test	2 days	2 days	
Total Days for Unit 3	11 days	19 days	

Pacing Guide

	Core	Comprehensive 45 minute class	Customize Your Pacing Guide
Unit 4 Plant Structure and Function			
Unit 4 Project		2 days	
Lesson 1 What Are Some Plant Parts and How Do They Function?	3 days	4 days	
Lesson 2 **Engineer It** • How Do Plants Grow and Reproduce?	3 days	4 days	
You Solve It		1 day	
Unit 4 Performance Task		1 days	
Performance-Based Assessment		1 days	
Unit 4 Review and Unit 4 Test	2 days	2 days	
Total Days for Unit 4	8 days	15 days	
Unit 5 Animal Structure and Function			
Unit 5 Project		2 days	
Lesson 1 **Engineer It** • What Are Some External Structures of Animals?	3 days	4 days	
Lesson 2 What Are Some Internal Structures of Animals?	3 days	4 days	
Lesson 3 How Do Senses Work?	3 days	4 days	
You Solve It		1 day	
Unit 5 Performance Task		1 days	
Performance-Based Assessment		1 days	
Unit 5 Review and Unit 5 Test	2 days	2 days	

Pacing Guide

	Core	Comprehensive 45 minute class	Customize Your Pacing Guide
Unit 5 Animal Structure and Function continued			
Total Days for Unit 5	11 days	19 days	
Unit 6 Changes to Earth's Surface			
Unit 6 Project		2 days	
Lesson 1 How Does Water Shape Earth's Surface?	3 days	4 days	
Lesson 2 What Other Factors Shape Earth's Surface?	3 days	4 days	
Lesson 3 **Engineer It** • How Can Maps Help Us to Learn About Earth's Surface?	3 days	4 day	
Lesson 4 What Patterns Do Maps Show Us?	3 days	4 day	
You Solve It		1 day	
Unit 6 Performance Task		1 days	
Performance-Based Assessment		1 days	
Unit 6 Review and Unit 6 Test	2 days	2 days	
Total Days for Unit 6	14 days	23 days	
Unit 7 Rocks and Fossils			
Unit 7 Project		2 days	
Lesson 1 How Do Rock Layers Change?	3 days	4 days	
Lesson 2 What Do Fossils Tell Us About Ancient Environments?	3 days	4 days	
Lesson 3 What Are Some Patterns Fossils Show Us?	3 days	4 days	

Pacing Guide

	Core	Comprehensive 45 minute class	Customize Your Pacing Guide
Unit 7 Rocks and Fossils continued			
You Solve It		1 days	
Unit 7 Performance Task		1 days	
Performance-Based Assessment		1 days	
Unit 7 Review and Unit 7 Test	2 days	2 days	
Total Days for Unit 7	11 days	19 days	
Unit 8 Natural Resources and Hazards			
Unit 8 Project		2 days	
Lesson 1 What Non-Renewable Resources Are Used for Energy?	3 days	4 days	
Lesson 2 **Engineer It** • What Renewable Resources Are Used for Energy?	3 days	4 days	
Lesson 3 How Can People Reduce the Impact of Land-Based Hazards?	3 days	4 day	
Lesson 4 **Engineer It** • How Can People Reduce the Impact of Water-Based Hazards?	3 days	4 day	
You Solve It		1 day	
Unit 8 Performance Task		1 days	
Performance-Based Assessment		1 days	
Unit 8 Review and Unit 8 Test	2 days	2 days	
Total Days for Unit 8	14 days	23 days	

Teacher Notes

The Next Generation Science Standards: A Reason to Cheer

Cary I. Sneider, Ph.D.

Change is rarely welcomed with open arms. A few weeks ago I was helping a colleague facilitate a team of teacher-leaders develop a district plan to implement the Next Generation Science Standards (NGSS). During a break two of the teachers asked to speak with me. They were upset and nearly in tears. One of the teachers explained that they had spent the past 20 years developing the best possible science program for their school. The kids and parents loved it. The principal was proud of what they had accomplished. But now they would be asked to start all over because they would be assigned to teach science units they had never taught before.

It helped that the district leaders were listening and willing to consider some changes that these teachers recommended, although the leaders were quite firm about implementing the NGSS. It was also helpful for these teachers to learn that they would be helping other teachers by sharing the great ideas and resources that they had developed for their own students, so their creativity and hard work wouldn't be wasted. Even more important, I believe, was the gradual realization, over the next couple of days, that the profound changes called for by the NGSS were not simply a change in when different science topics would be taught but rather a change in how they would be taught—in ways that these excellent teacher-leaders valued and had established with their own students.

> **"...the profound changes called for by the NGSS were not simply a change in when different science topics would be taught but rather a change in how they would be taught."**

What follows is a brief summary of the ways that the NGSS is similar to but also different from science as it has been taught for the past 20 years. I won't compare it with "traditional" science education, because the method of having students read and answer questions at the end of the chapter is (thankfully) rarely done these days. But the changes called for by the NGSS can be surprising even for teachers who are comfortable with a hands-on inquiry approach that has come to characterize the best of science teaching. And I'll admit some of these changes have been hard for me to get used to, after nearly 50 years as a science educator and as a member of the NGSS writing team.

Disciplinary Core Ideas

With respect to the disciplinary core ideas (what we used to call the "content") of the new standards, at least 80% are unchanged. Students still need to learn about Newton's Laws of Motion and the Periodic Table of Elements. Some topics in the Earth and space sciences have been updated—such as by the addition of a greater focus on human impacts on the environment—so that topics that many teachers introduced as a way to enrich the curriculum with contemporary issues are now mainstream.

Crosscutting concepts

Crosscutting concepts should also be familiar to teachers who appreciate the nature of scientific thinking. The purpose of these seven concepts is to help students see the commonalities among the science and engineering fields. They include the idea that patterns we observe in nature are clues to some underlying process. For example, the monthly pattern of moon phases can best be understood in terms of systems and system models by manipulating a model of the Earth-sun-moon system. The crosscutting concept of cause and effect grows from our human instinct to know why things occur as they do, and the concepts of energy and matter are fundamental to all fields of science and engineering. The crosscutting concept of structure and function is useful in understanding how the structure of molecules affect the macroscopic behavior of a substance, as well as understanding how the structure of an organ enables it to carry out its function in the body. As students mature they are more able to study the world by applying the concepts of scale, proportion, and quantity. And finally, the need to explain stability and change is at the root of our conservation laws in physics, chemical reactions in chemistry, and the theory of evolution in biology. By introducing these crosscutting concepts at appropriate times, teachers can help their students gain perspective on the study of various topics in science and see how they all—in a very important sense—reflect the same scientific way of thinking.

Emphasizing Technology and Engineering

Despite these similarities, the NGSS is very different from what has come before. One way it differs from prior standards is in the prominent role of technology and engineering. Although the idea that students should learn about technology and engineering has been around since the beginning of the standards movement[1], they have rarely been woven into the natural sciences as they are in the NGSS. Technology in

> "Technology in the NGSS is portrayed as the application of science to the development of various products, processes, and systems to meet human needs..."

---

[1] American Association for the Advancement of Science. (1990). *Project 2061: Science for all Americans.* London: Oxford University Press.

the NGSS is portrayed as the application of science to the development of various products, processes, and systems to meet human needs, such as the application of wave phenomena to communication technologies. Engineering is positioned both as a core idea about defining and solving problems and as a means of applying the natural sciences to a wide variety of issues of both societal and environmental importance. And along with engineering comes a new set of skills for students to learn, such as defining problems by identifying criteria and constraints, applying tradeoffs to find the best acceptable solution, and learning to appreciate failure as a valuable aspect of the iterative design process.

Science and Engineering Practices

Some of the practices of science and engineering in the NGSS will be familiar to teachers, and some will seem quite different. What is especially different is that all of these practices are useful for scientific inquiry and engineering design. Table 1 illustrates why they are called practices of science and engineering.

It has taken me some time to fully appreciate what it means to help students develop skills in using these practices, since most of my career has focused on teaching concepts. I empathized with the two teachers whom I referred to in my opening paragraph because I've been in a similar position. My favorite subject is astronomy, and I've developed some really effective ways for students to use models so they can understand phenomena such as moon phases and seasons. I hated to give those methods up! But if students are to learn to develop and use models, then they are the ones who need to figure out how to use models to explain the phenomena. Telling them how to use the models just doesn't cut it. I should add that it's fine to illustrate how to use a model so they can learn how it's done, but at some point the students need to pick up the pieces as a means for figuring out why the moon goes through phases and how phases are different from eclipses. Another way to think about this is to consider who is doing the science. If the teacher is doing all of the explaining and asking all of the questions, the teacher—not the student—is doing the science.

Performance Expectations

Perhaps the most unusual aspect of the NGSS is the way these three dimensions are assembled—in single statements called Performance Expectations (PEs). They are called that because the NGSS is a set of assessment

> "Perhaps the most unusual aspect of the NGSS is the way these three dimensions are assembled—in single statements called Performance Expectations."

Table 1. Science and Engineering Practices

Practices	Science	Engineering
1. Asking Questions and Defining Problems	A basic practice of science is to ask questions about the world that can be answered by gathering data.	Engineering begins by defining a problem in terms of criteria for a successful solution, and constraints or limits.
2. Developing and Using Models	Science often involves the construction and use of models to help answer questions about natural phenomena.	Engineering makes use of models to analyze existing systems or to test possible solutions to a new problem.
3. Planning and Carrying Out Investigations	Scientific investigation can be controlled experiments to test predictions, attempts to identify correlations, or taxonomic identifications of species.	Engineers use investigations both to gain data essential for their design and to test the designs they develop.
4. Analyzing and Interpreting Data	Scientific investigations generally produce data that must be analyzed in order to derive meaning.	Engineers analyze and interpret data to determine how well each meets specific design criteria.
5. Using Mathematics and Computational Thinking	In science, mathematics and computers are used for a range of tasks from constructing models to analyzing data, and expressing relationship between variables.	In engineering, mathematics and computers are integral parts of the engineering design process.
6. Constructing Explanations and Designing Solutions	The goal of science is to explain phenomena in the natural world.	The goal of engineering is to solve meaningful problems.
7. Engaging in Argument From Evidence	In science, reasoning, argument, and participating actively in a community of peers is essential for finding explanations for natural phenomena.	In engineering, reasoning and argument are essential for finding the best possible solutions to problems.
8. Obtaining, Communicating and Presenting Information	A major practice of science is to communicate ideas and results of scientific inquiry and to obtain and evaluate findings reported by others.	Engineering needs to start by finding out how similar problems have been solved in the past and communicating ideas clearly and persuasively.

> **"The NGSS describes which practices students of various ages are expected to use in order to demonstrate their understanding of a specific core idea and crosscutting concept."**

standards. That is, they describe what students should be able to do at the end of instruction—not just what they know, but what they can do with what they know. That means achievement of these standards cannot be assessed with a multiple-choice test alone. Performance assessments of some sort will be necessary. The challenge for curriculum developers and teachers is to figure out what experiences they can provide so that their students will be able to meet these Performance Expectations not just at the end of class, but several months or even years later.

If all this seems daunting, keep in mind that the NGSS requires students to learn fewer core ideas than prior standards do so that teachers have time to teach those that remain in depth. When our writing team circulated drafts for public comment, we were told that there were too many standards to reasonably expect students to learn; so in the final round we cut the number of standards by one third. We did not "cheat" by combining standards—we actually cut the number of core ideas.

Another major advantage of the NGSS is that the standards are specific. I recall a project a few years ago, when I was helping to facilitate a team of teachers and other instructional leaders in the state of Washington to revise the state's standards. The Director of Science and I were meeting groups at various locations in the state to gather feedback on a draft. I recall one teacher who stood up to complain that the state test had questions that were impossible to anticipate because the standards were too vague. "Just tell us what the tests will be about," he said, "and we can help our students succeed!" The Next Generation Science Standards will not be subject to that objection. The NGSS describes which practices students of various ages are expected to use in order to demonstrate their understanding of a specific core idea and crosscutting concept. Each PE is followed by an additional clarification of the specific experiences that are referred to in the PE and also a list of performances that would not be assessed at that grade level.

So, to sum up: The great majority of core ideas in the NGSS are the same core ideas we've been teaching for years, with the addition of a few updates, especially related to societal and environmental issues. Although crosscutting concepts may sound new, they represent well-known features of scientific thinking. A new feature of the NGSS is that technology and engineering are woven deeply into the fabric of the document so that students are expected to develop skills that are quite new to most science teachers. And finally, the core ideas are fewer in number than prior standards in order to allow teachers more time to teach to mastery. The standards are also more specific to enable students to have greater success on tests by making it easier to align curriculum, instruction, and assessment. These last qualities alone are a reason for science teachers to cheer the NGSS.

Building an NGSS Curriculum

It's especially important for curriculum developers to keep in mind that the NGSS is sparse for a reason and to avoid including lessons just because they were there before and teachers expected to see them. Studies that have attempted to explain why U.S. students do poorly on international examinations have faulted textbooks in this country for being "a mile wide and an inch deep."[2] In light of that finding, I've been very impressed with the new **HMH Science Dimensions** textbook series. As a consulting author I've been pleased to see it develop as an entirely new curriculum that sticks to the PEs at each grade level, with rich science content and activities involving practices and core ideas but without extraneous material that would take up valuable instructional time.

It's hard to say what impact the NGSS will have, but I'm hopeful. For the past two years I've worked with middle school teachers in one school district in Oregon, which was one of the first states to adopt the NGSS. The teachers were given the task of designing units to match the sequence of PEs that their state recommended. I asked the teachers who had the most experience teaching a unit to design it for the district, even if they were not going to be teaching it in the fall. Initially some of the teachers protested having to spend a week during the summer preparing lessons they would not be teaching. One veteran teacher saved the day by saying, "Let's think of this as a barn raising. We'll all pitch in to help one group of teachers, and later they'll pitch in to help us."

Change is rarely embraced, but in the long run it has the advantage of keeping us on our toes. Science teachers are among the most creative people I know. With the support of their school and district leaders I know they will rise to the challenge, even if it means giving up some of their most treasured lessons. Their students will certainly be the beneficiaries of renewed instructional ideas and materials, especially as those students become the ones doing the science in the classroom.

> "Science teachers are among the most creative people I know. With the support of their school and district leaders I know they will rise to the challenge."

[2] Schmidt, W. H., McKnight, C., & Raizen, S. (Eds.). (1997). A splintered vision: An investigation of U.S. science and mathematics education (Vol. 1). Dordrecht, The Netherlands: Kluwer Academic Publishers.

Evidence Notebooks

by Michael A. DiSpezio

In **HMH Science Dimensions** you'll discover references to a brand-new type of tool—the evidence notebook—designed to support and reinforce the three-dimensional learning so central to NGSS pedagogy. Evidence notebook may be a new term to you. So what is it and how does it differ from a traditional lab notebook or science journal? Great questions. As you are about to discover, the evidence notebook is a critical part of an NGSS approach to effective science education.

Think back to science notebooks that you maintained throughout your student experience. There's a good chance that these were a linear chronology of your learning accomplishments. In the earlier grades, they were bound records of classroom experience. For the most part, these entries were limited to lab observations; data collection tables; and answers to specific, prepackaged questions. By the time you reached middle school, the role of the lab notebook often segued into worksheet-and-lab-report repository.

Typically, all notebooks were organized in the same manner. There was little opportunity for individuality, personal voice, or indication of a student's interests. Often, they were used as summative assessment based on the expected homogenization of entries.

With the Next Generation Science Standards' revolutionary approach to pedagogy, the role and organization of what had been a record-keeping device has evolved. No longer a landscape on which to record prescriptive responses, the evidence notebook assumes the role of conceptual "scratch-pad." Like computer RAM, this is where the higher processing occurs.

With this evolution to a much more interactive role for the evidence notebook, let's examine the nuts and bolts of creating and maintaining it. The first thing to consider is that the notebook is student directed. Remember, it's primarily for the students—not for you! With that in mind, it is organized according to each student's learning style, personal interests, questions, observations, and interaction with the three dimensions of science.

Using evidence notebooks, students can

- assume an increased role and responsibility for their own learning
- direct or create their own learning path by recording, selecting, and pursuing questions of interest
- organize their thinking
- record and analyze observations
- compare/contrast passive information to higher-level thinking and critical analysis
- better commit ideas to long-term memory through the writing process
- perfect language skills in an authentic learning experience
- communicate understanding and competency
- record and evaluate evidence both from within the classroom and outside of the classroom in a Claims/Evidence/Reasoning model

EVIDENCE NOTEBOOK

Beyond the Classroom Walls

The evidence notebook travels both literally and figuratively beyond the physical school boundary. Not limited to recording classroom experiences and prescribed assignments, it assumes the role of interactive diary. Students record relevant thoughts and observations of the world around them in their notebooks. For example, if studying runoff, they might write about or photograph neighborhood gullies or storm-drainage systems. Entries can then be examined in a context of active learning using these meaningful examples from students' immediate world.

Spreading It Out

One way in which students might organize their notebooks is based upon right- and left-side pages of a spread. The left side of the page spread might incorporate the higher-level thinking process associated with an investigation. The posed question, evolving thoughts, and critical-thinking analysis would form this page's content. The facing right-hand page might include more of the prescribed and quantitative thought processes, such as the steps, data collection, and observations.

Claims/Evidence/ Reasoning Connection

Claims/Evidence/Reasoning, or CER for short, is a strategy for getting students to go beyond memorization and construct explanations. The evidence notebook is the ideal landscape on which to address all three of the CER components. First, students can record and further distill their claims into testable hypotheses. Then, based upon a student-directed investigation, they can collect and record data as evidence. Finally, the students can illustrate the logic they used in arriving at a reasoned explanation.

Evidence for Assessment

Don't overlook the role that the evidence notebook can play in formative assessment. By reviewing student notebooks, the instructor gains insight into each student's qualitative thinking. The instructor can then offer targeted feedback to help students improve their evidence notebook's organization and entries.

> "The evidence notebook travels both literally and figuratively beyond the physical school boundary."

From Data to Thinking About Data

As you know, "thinking about one's thinking" is a key element to successful learning. However, prior to evidence notebooks, students lacked a classroom tool adapted to metacognition. Now, within evidence notebooks, students can record and analyze their thinking processes. By reflecting on how best they learn, they can assume more control of personal learning. Not only does this awareness result in richer understanding, but it also evolves the organization and content of the evidence notebook to its most effective design.

Organizing the Evidence Notebook

By now, perhaps you are wondering what makes up the specific content and organization of an effective evidence notebook? The definitive answer is "it depends." That's because it varies from student to student. Although all notebooks should have a sequential format, the nature of each notebook's specific content and organization depends upon individual learning styles.

That said, effective evidence notebooks may include

- student interests and related questions
- a record of prior knowledge
- evidence collected from student-directed explorations
- short essays that address concepts and a student's personal thinking process
- graphic organizers such as concept maps and Venn diagrams
- drawings and embedded digital photographs
- observations that go beyond the classroom's physical boundaries
- reflections on understanding
- thinking and processes that address claims, evidence, and reasoning

21st Century Tools

Exploit the technology! As the installed base of tablets and PCs broadens, there are increasing opportunities for creating electronic evidence notebooks. Strategies in *HMH Science Dimensions* print and electronic student editions offer the opportunity for open-ended student input. Students can also construct an evidence notebook using appropriate apps and software. In addition to accepting written input, electronic versions can include embedded media such as digital photos, video clips, and sound files.

Dynamic, Not Static

Unlike its traditional counterpart, the evidence notebook is not a static record. It is a work in progress on which understanding is continually constructed. Students update its content on a daily basis, not just around investigations and lab reports. So remind students to keep it current and use it as a foundation on which to construct understanding.

How *HMH Science Dimensions* Supports an Evidence Notebook

Throughout both the Electronic Student Edition and the student text of *HMH Science Dimensions* are evidence-notebook writing prompts. They are designed to introduce and reinforce the skills that you've just read about. But these should be considered only the beginning. Let your imagination run wild, but most of all, encourage your students to use this important tool in ways that foster their own learning and understanding of science and engineering and their connections to everyday life.

Aligning English Language Arts and Science

By Marjorie Frank

As educators, we often think in terms of disciplines: I teach English. I'm a science teacher. I'm a math coach. While these may be useful distinctions, they obscure an important consideration: Our brain has no such distinctions.

The Brain and Learning

No special region is active during science class and inactive during English or math. Or, vice versa. Yet, we often operate as if it were. Most science teachers don't focus deeply on reading or writing skills; English and math teachers aren't greatly concerned with science concepts. Yet, the cognitive processes in all these—and other—disciplines are pretty much the same. We just talk about them differently . . . and sometimes, we don't even do that. For example, citing evidence to support a claim is central to science. Explaining how an author uses evidence to support particular points is central to English language study. How different are these phenomena, really?

Which Standards?

Here's a short activity to test this idea. The sentences below are from science and English language arts standards. Except for giveaway words such as science and nonfiction, which I've deleted, the standards are reproduced here verbatim. See if you can tell which are science standards and which are ELA standards. [Answers are at the end of this article.]

1. Obtain information using various texts, text features (e.g. headings, tables of contents, glossaries, electronic menus, icons), and other media that will be useful in answering a question.

2. Ask questions based on observations to find more information. . . .

3. Write arguments to support claims . . . using valid reasoning and relevant and sufficient evidence.

4. Construct an argument with evidence to support a claim.

5. Ask questions to clear up any confusion. . . .

6. Know and use various text features (e.g. headings, tables of contents, glossaries, electronic menus, icons) to locate key facts or information. . . .

7. Obtain and combine information from books and/or other reliable media to explain phenomena or solutions . . . to a design problem.

8. Integrate information from several texts on the same topic. . . .

This confluence of interdisciplinary realities is embodied in the Next Generation Science Standards.

Curriculum Crossover in NGSS

Released in April 2013, the Next Generation Science Standards are, I believe, the only standards to date that recognize and embrace the natural crossover of disciplines. If you were to print the standards, each page would include a set of Science and Engineering Practices, a set of Disciplinary Core Ideas, a set of Crosscutting Concepts, and sets of ELA and Mathematics standards—formalizing what is true naturally: they all work together.

> "Much of the time, you may be engaging in cross-disciplinary practices without even realizing it."

Much of the time, you may be engaging in cross-disciplinary practices without even realizing it. In English class, your students participate in exchanges that require close reading of a text. They cite evidence from the reading to support their responses to questions. Is this really different from asking students to cite evidence in support of a science claim? In science class, your students communicate solutions to a design problem via posters or verbal presentations. Is this all that different from reporting on a topic or engaging in collaborative discussions? Perhaps the expression a distinction without a difference applies here.

If your students are doing science, and I do mean doing science, they are likely to be engaging in crossover English language arts skills coincidentally.

HMH Science Dimensions takes the coincidence out of the crossover.

HMH Science Dimensions and Integrated Learning

The instructional design and lesson plans of the student-facing materials for all levels of **HMH Science Dimensions** facilitate English language arts in ways that are both subtle and explicit. Prompts throughout a lesson lead learners to collaborate, ask questions, summarize, explain, analyze. Frequent opportunities connected to students' Evidence Notebooks integrate writing into the process. You need only scroll through a digital lesson or page through the print to find evidence of these approaches.

Something else you'll find in the student-facing materials for young learners is a system of light-bulb icons and headings that identify an extensive structure of online handbooks containing tips and strategies for developing science, math, and language arts skills. Some of the language skills that receive attention include asking and answering questions, doing research, collaborating, using visuals, and describing problems.

For the youngest learners is a robust feature in the student-facing materials called Read, Write, Share! Here, children are guided to practice asking and answering questions, collaborating, drawing, writing, and presenting ideas to others. And throughout the teacher-facing materials you will find suggestions for collaboration, a quintessentially language-based endeavor.

For older learners you'll find a lesson feature called Language SmArts. These are activities that integrate language arts skills into the science learning process. Some Language SmArts activities appear in the student-facing materials; others appear only in the teacher-facing components. Examples of activities include those connected to making inferences, conducting research, and using visuals in multimedia displays among others. In all cases, they represent another way in which **HMH Science Dimensions** helps facilitate the alignment of English language arts and the Next Generation Science Standards.

In the end, if your goal is to help learners draw upon their full complement of natural abilities to gain ownership of science, you can relax knowing that you've come to the right place: **HMH Science Dimensions**.

“...all levels of *HMH Science Dimensions* facilitate English language arts in ways that are both subtle and explicit.”

Answers:

1. NGSS standard; **2.** NGSS standard; **3.** English language arts standard; **4.** NGSS standard; **5.** English language arts standard; **6.** English language arts standard; **7.** NGSS standard; **8.** English language arts standard.

NGSS and College and Career Readiness

by Michael R. Heithaus, Ph.D.

Improving STEM education at every level—from K–12 through university—is a national priority. Distinction in STEM fields is critical to ensuring the ability of the United States to compete in international markets and to actualize intellectual goals, and jobs in STEM fields are projected to grow at higher rates than in other professions. Yet at the university and career levels, there is seemingly not enough interest or achievement in STEM fields. How we prepare students for college and career is a growing concern. The Next Generation Science Standards are built to ensure readiness.

What is college and career readiness?

At the simplest level, being college ready means that students are able to succeed in college classes without remediation. Being career ready means that graduates are prepared to obtain and succeed in entry-level positions. Sounds simple, but as STEM fields evolve and change, so do requirements related to content-area knowledge. For that reason, NGSS and **HMH Science Dimensions** focus on students demonstrating that they have mastered important skills more than specific knowledge or facts. Through formative assessments, evidence notebooks, and summative assessments, including critical performance-based assessments, teachers are supplied with the tools they need to understand student performance. Strategies throughout this Teacher Edition provide means of addressing many deficiencies.

When students have mastered skills and understand the underlying connections between STEM fields and other curriculum areas, they will not only have the background knowledge they need but also be prepared to fill in gaps in their understanding independently, without the need for remediation or extensive on-the-job training. And although college and career readiness might seem like qualities for students to master in high school, NGSS brings a greater coherence across grade levels: students from primary grades through high school have the opportunity to work on these skills and learn to apply them in everyday life.

According to the NGSS, career and college-ready students should be able to

- make sense of the world and approach novel problems, phenomena, and information using a blend of science and engineering practices, disciplinary core ideas, and crosscutting concepts
- use valid research strategies
- be self-directed in planning, monitoring, and evaluation
- flexibly apply knowledge across disciplines (through continued exploration of Science and Engineering Practices, crosscutting concepts, and Disciplinary Core Ideas)

Not included in this list are some other skills that students should master to succeed in today's college classroom and workplace. First, students need to be

- comfortable working in diverse groups and with peers with different perspectives
- able to support their claims with logical arguments while being respectful and constructive in dealing with those who don't agree
- able to think critically and creatively
- able to communicate effectively in multiple settings and via diverse media

New teaching methods and a new role for teachers

The new focus on skills rather than content knowledge alone has led to big changes, backed by research, in how we teach science at universities and in K–12 classrooms. We know that active learning from student-centered activities that include group work and problem solving enhance student success.

There is no question that implementing NGSS requires teachers to shift both what and how they teach. For much of the instruction, the teacher's role in the classroom is different. Because NGSS integrates the practices of science and engineering with content-area knowledge, there is an increasing focus on students being scientists in the discovery process and leading their own investigations. Does this mean teachers are less important? Not by a long shot. In fact, teachers are probably more important than ever! It will take a bit of work to adapt your course to active learning and to integrate NGSS-style learning, but believe me, it will be worth it for you and your students.

Some things to keep in mind:

- Think about questions. Asking the right questions can be critical to getting students on—or back to—the right track to discovering material for themselves and making connections between concepts that are critical to NGSS. Pose questions to get students to think deeply about the nature and strength of evidence used to support a claim.

- Facilitate team learning. Science and engineering are all about teams, and students need to be comfortable working in groups with peers. Team learning can help students at very different levels benefit from the same course of investigation. I have found that strong students gain better mastery of concepts when they help students who are having trouble. On the flip side, some students actually learn better from a peer than a teacher! Pay attention to group dynamics, but facilitate cooperative teams wherever you can.

- Moderate discussions and peer critiques purposefully.

- Remember that NGSS can help improve math skills. Throughout **HMH Science Dimensions**, you'll find opportunities to practice age- and discipline-appropriate math practices to support science

> "There is no question that implementing NGSS requires teachers to shift both what and how they teach. For much of the instruction, the teacher's role in the classroom is different."

investigations and learning. Find ways to bring math into investigations. Math is critical to science and engineering, and science and engineering can make math more accessible and exciting to students!

- Help students make connections continuously. The **HMH Science Dimensions** Teacher Edition provides many strategies to assist students in making those connections. There is plenty of evidence that multiple opportunities to associate pieces of information in different contexts facilitate retention. NGSS is built so that particular standards can be blended with others and integrated throughout a year and across grade levels. Online resources facilitate this blending—and you will find them already integrated in HMH Science Dimensions!

- Collaborate! Whether you teach kindergarten or college, you are not alone in applying NGSS innovations in science education. When you talk to your colleagues and look online for best ideas and practices, you are serving as a role model for your students.

As you move into teaching NGSS and preparing students for college and career, look for the many strategies and opportunities for assessment embedded in both the student-facing materials and the Teacher materials of your **HMH Science Dimensions** program. These will facilitate implementation of best practices in NGSS pedagogy. Even if your students won't be entering STEM fields, solid science education at this point will help students prepare for the coming years by inculcating the critical thinking skills necessary for science literacy and making informed, reasonable, evidence-backed decisions in all facets of life.

> **"Whether you teach kindergarten or college, you are not alone in applying NGSS innovations in science education."**

All Students, All Standards

NGSS has a sharp emphasis on teaching all standards to all students. One of the challenges of teaching using NGSS pedagogy is reteaching. The three dimensions of science would seem to present challenges that you haven't encountered before. But there is good news: two of the dimensions are self-reteaching!

Both the Science and Engineering Practices and the Crosscutting Concepts are revisited time and again throughout the year. Strategies for teaching these occur within the teacher margin materials.

While you may need to remind children (about CCs) or monitor closely (for SEPs), multiple exposures to a concept in different contexts have been shown to be the most effective reteaching possible.

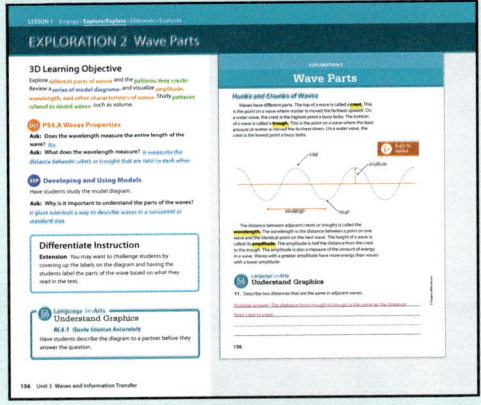

And for reteaching Disciplinary Core Ideas, **HMH Science Dimensions™** has you covered.

Key Science concepts are recontextualized in the *Science and Engineering Readers*. These readers present the same concepts at two different levels and provide additional concepts and advanced reading for children who are easily mastering the concepts.

Sciencesaurus provides a quick, in depth, visual reference at suitable readabilities for students. The engaging writing and illustrations help to present the content in another context and in slightly different ways so as to reinforce key DCIs and recontextualize the Science Dimensions student-facing materials. Recontextualization and easier reading are both shown to improve comprehension of difficult, but important, science concepts.

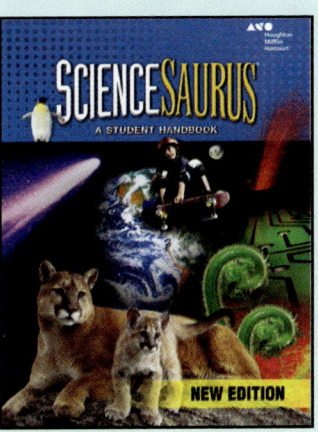

The *Interactive Worktext* and the *Interactive Online Student Edition* present the same content in different ways. The *Interactive Online Student Edition* provides additional interactions and voice over to reinforce and reteach the content in ways that enable children with reading deficits to learn the core science concepts. It also provides children with immediate feedback on many interactivities to reinforce learning.

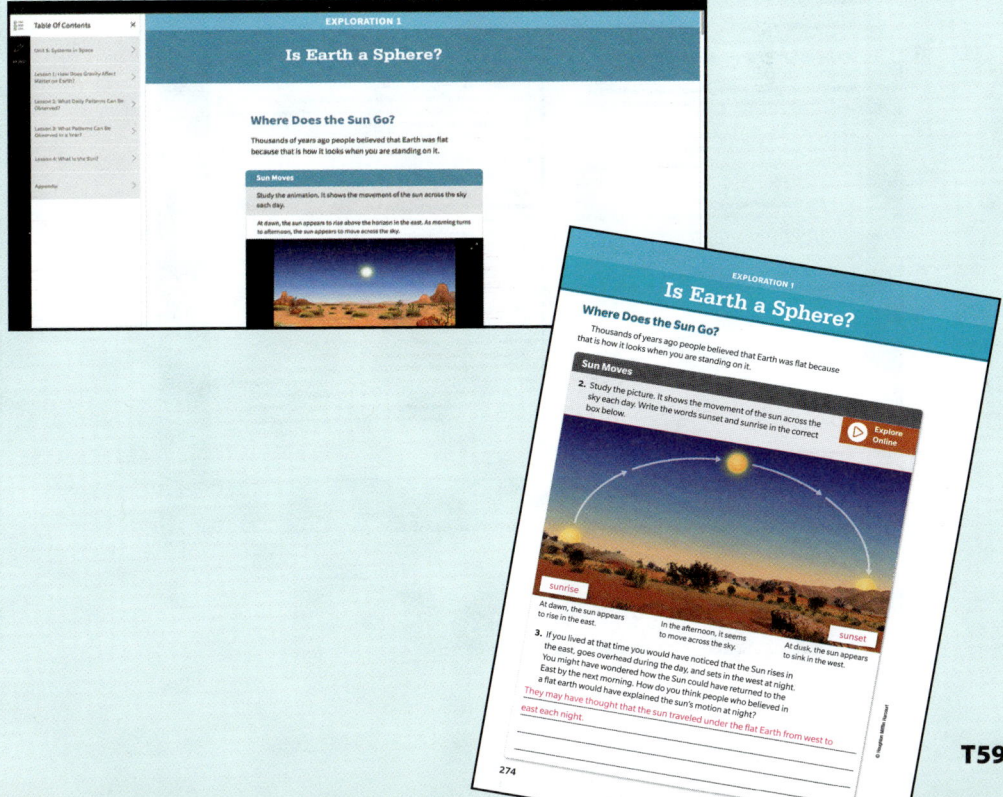

T59

HMH Science Dimensions™ and the EQuIP Rubric

The **EQuIP Rubric** is an instrument for evaluating a curriculum's conformance with the contours of an authentic NGSS program. As such, one needs to bear in mind the known limitations and proper usages of the rubric:

- The rubric is intended to be applied to lessons or units, not to entire curricula.
- The rubric itself indicates that it is unlikely that a single lesson will lead to mastery of a Performance Expectation. High-Quality Units may do so.
- The evaluation process is intended to be done in a group, not by an individual.
- The rubric requires familiarity with the Performance Expectation and its supporting Dimensions of Learning. The **HMH Science Dimensions™ Trace Tool to the NGSS** can help provide this orientation.

Throughout the **HMH Science Dimensions Teacher Edition,** you will find features to help you orient toward the critical dimensions of the EQuIP Rubric. Using the book, you are well beyond the evaluation phase of considering a program, but these features will demonstrate the best practices of NGSS summarized by the evaluation instrument. Highlights of critical EQuIP Rubric evaluation points are summarized in the reduced page you see here.

Unit Planning Pages

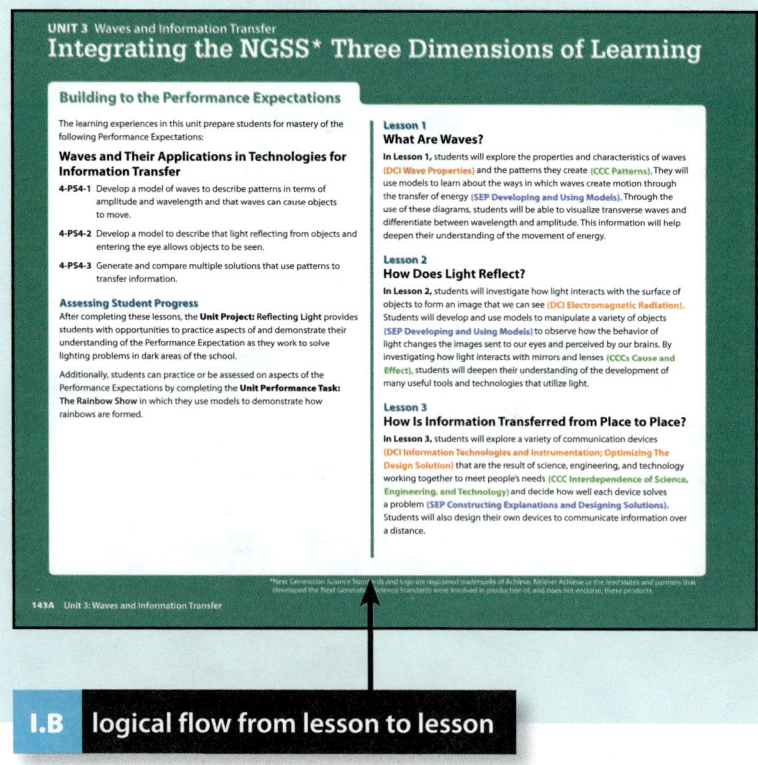

I.B logical flow from lesson to lesson

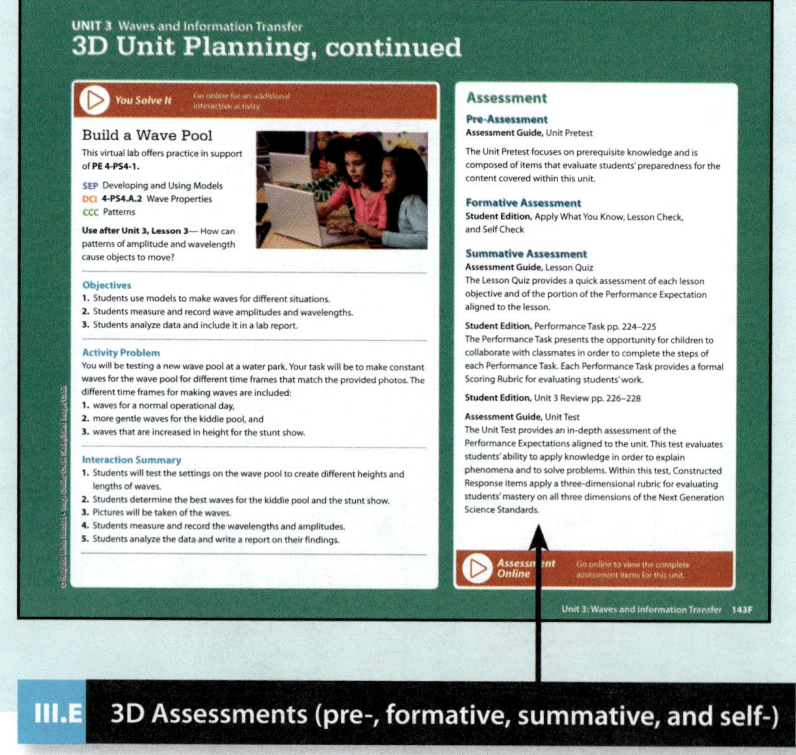

III.E 3D Assessments (pre-, formative, summative, and self-)

T60

Lesson Planning Pages

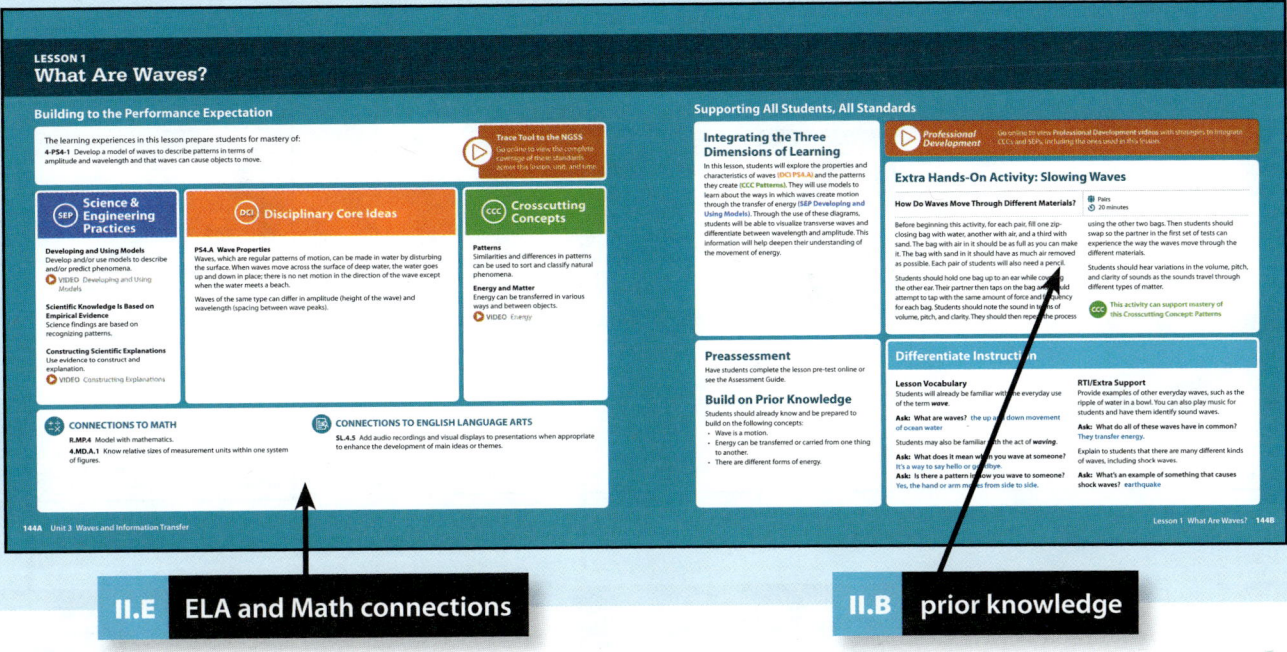

II.E ELA and Math connections

II.B prior knowledge

Lesson Opener Pages

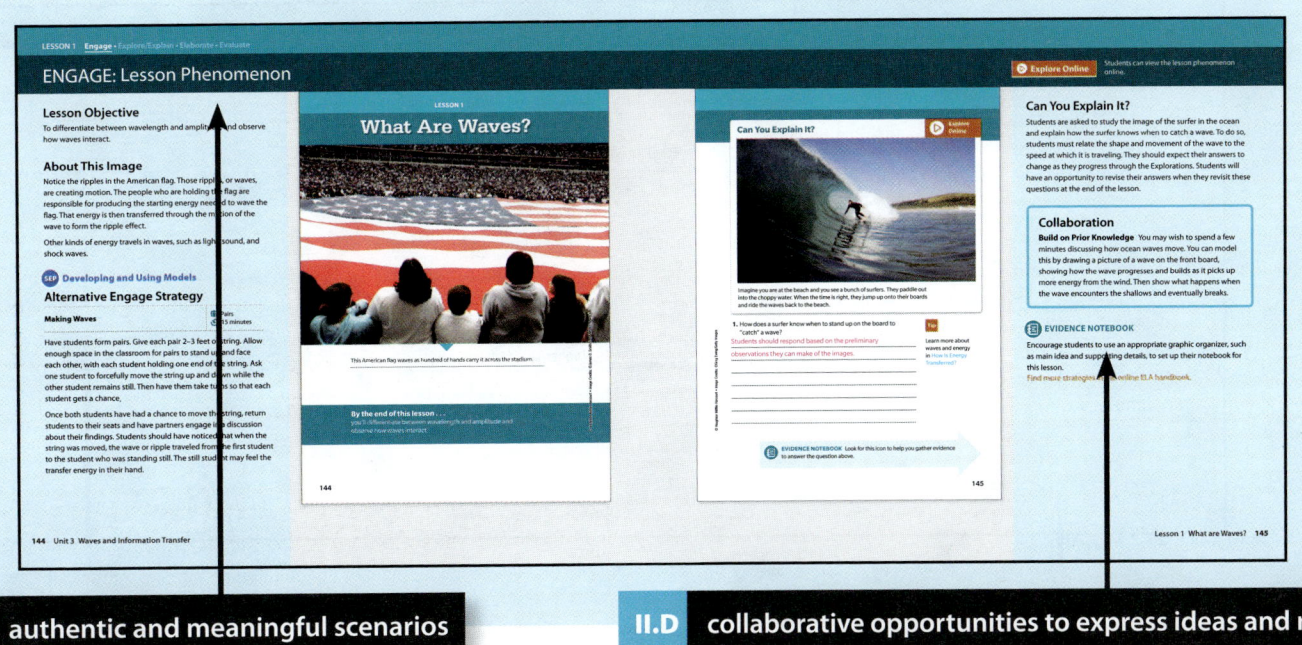

II.A authentic and meaningful scenarios

II.D collaborative opportunities to express ideas and respond

HMH Science Dimensions™ and the EQuIP Rubric

Lesson Pages

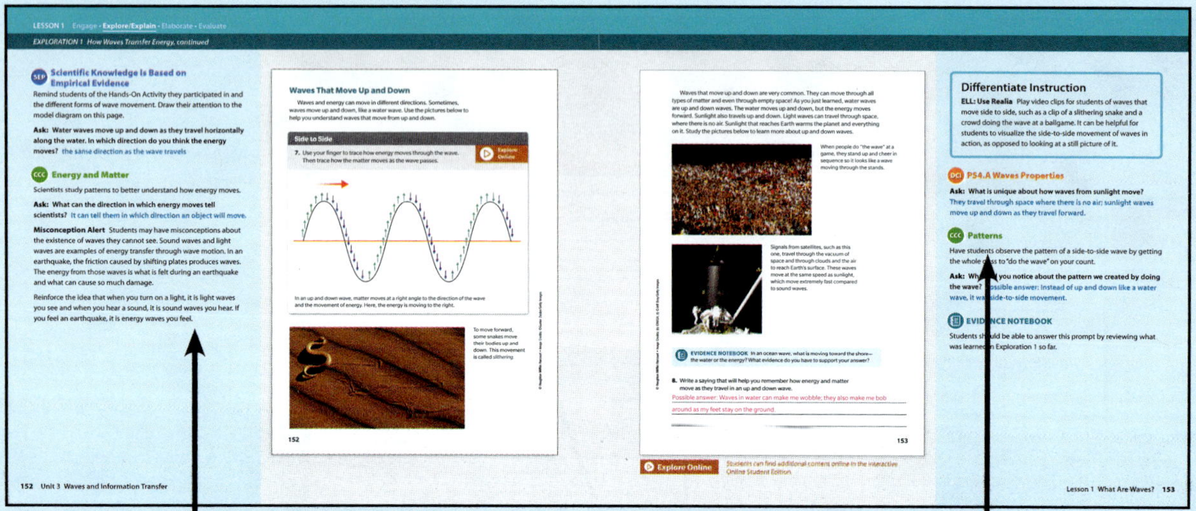

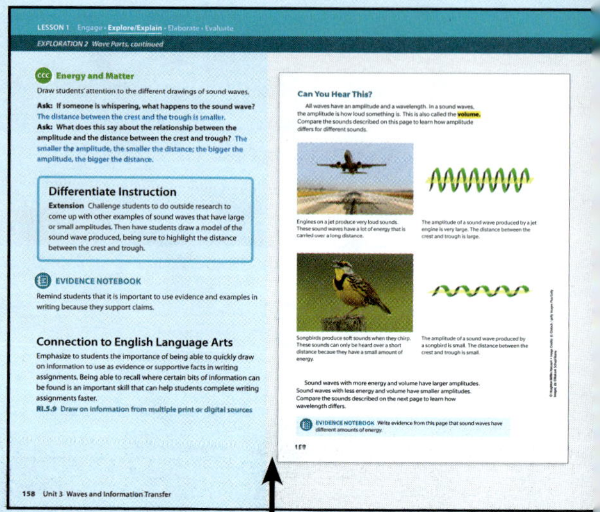

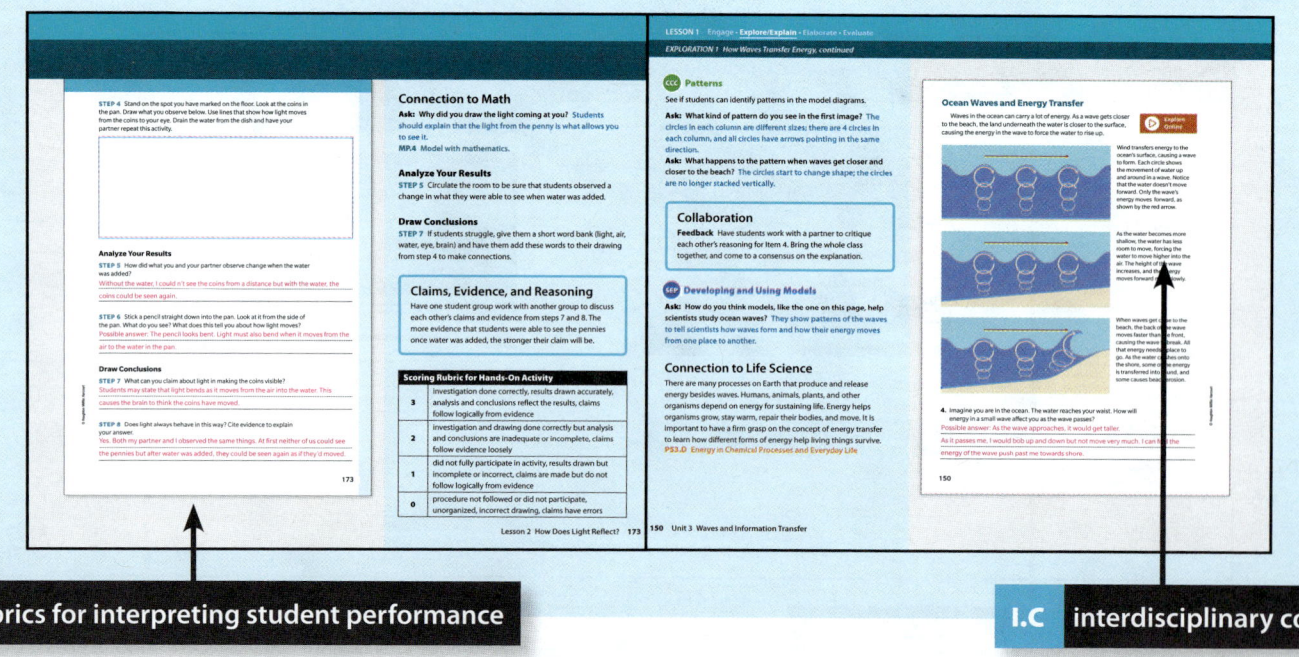

- **I.A.i-iii** 3D learning
- **II.E** differentiating instruction
- **II.C** scientifically accurate and grade-appropriate content

Lesson Pages

- **III.C** rubrics for interpreting student performance
- **I.C** interdisciplinary connections

Lesson Closer Pages

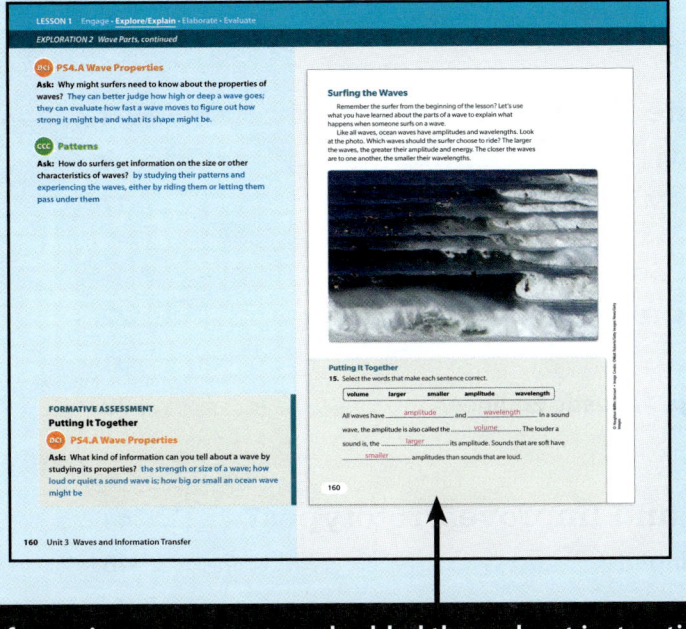

III.B formative assessments embedded throughout instruction

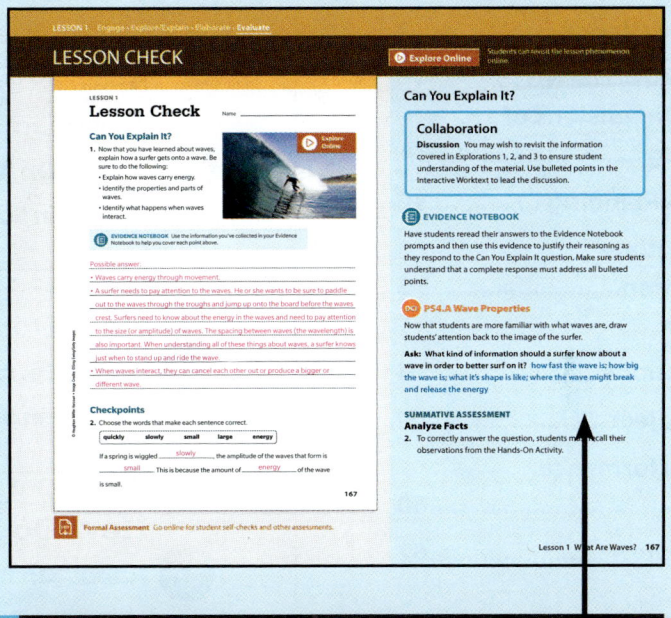

III.A eliciting direct observable evidence of 3D learning

Unit Closer Pages

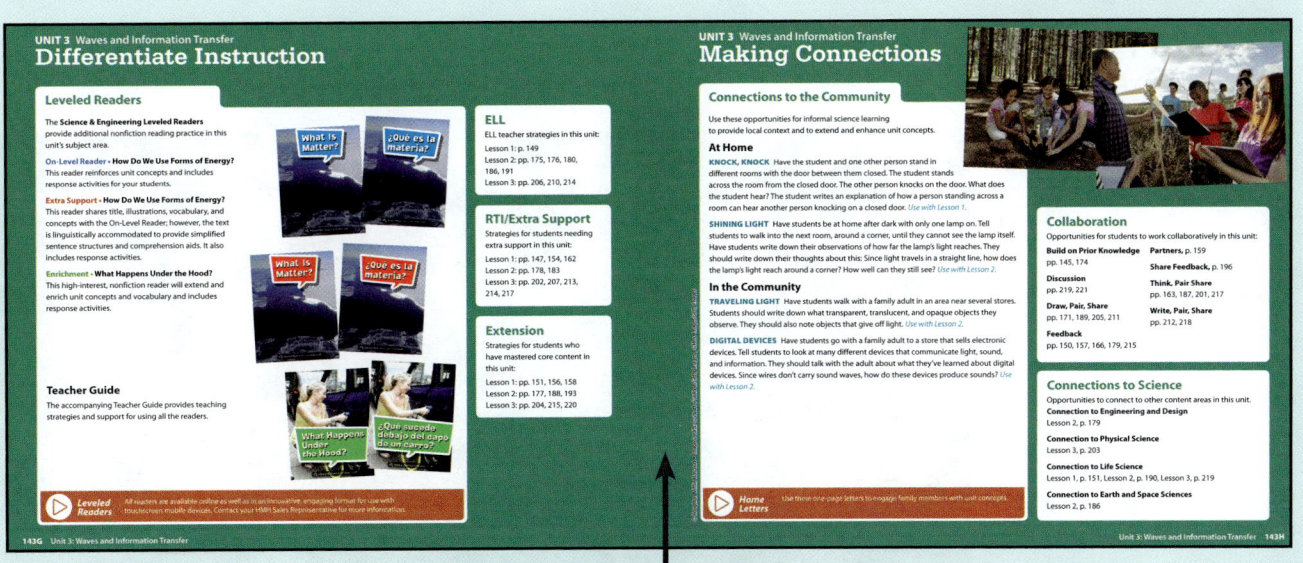

I.D developing connections

T63

Unit 1
Engineering and Technology

Unit at a Glance	2
Integrating the NGSS Three Dimensions of Learning	3A
3D Unit Planning	3C
Differentiate Instruction	3G
Making Connections	3H
Unit Project	3I
Unit Performance Task	60
Unit Review	62

UNIT 1 Engineering and Technology

Engineering and Technology 1

ENGINEER IT Lesson 1
How Do Engineers Define Problems? 4
- **Hands-On Activity:** Menu Planning 9
- **People in Science & Engineering:** Marion Downs 17

ENGINEER IT Lesson 2
How Do Engineers Design Solutions? 22
- **Hands-On Activity:** Design It! 31
- **Careers in Science & Engineering:** Acoustic Engineer 39

ENGINEER IT Lesson 3
How Do Engineers Test and Improve Prototypes? 44
- **Hands-On Activity:** Testing, Testing! 46

UNIT 1 PERFORMANCE TASK 60
UNIT 1 REVIEW 62

T64 Contents

UNIT 2 Physical Science

Energy 65

Lesson 1
What Is Energy? 68
Hands-On Activity: Light the Bulb 76
People in Science & Engineering: Mary Artiles 83

ENGINEER IT **Lesson 2**
How Is Energy Transferred? 88
Hands-On Activity: Design and Test a Solar Cooker ... 99
Careers in Science & Engineering: HVAC Tech 109

Lesson 3
How Do Collisions Show Energy? 114
Hands-On Activity: Test It! Stored Energy in a Rubberband ... 122
People in Science & Engineering: Amanda Steffy 131

UNIT 2 PERFORMANCE TASK 136
UNIT 2 REVIEW 138

Unit 2
Energy

Unit at a Glance 66
Integrating the NGSS Three Dimensions of Learning 67A
3D Unit Planning 67C
Differentiate Instruction 67G
Making Connections 67H
Unit Project 67I
Unit Performance Task 136
Unit Review 138

Unit 3
Waves and Information Transfer

Unit at a Glance	142
Integrating the NGSS Three Dimensions of Learning	143A
3D Unit Planning	143C
Differentiate Instruction	143G
Making Connections	143H
Unit Project	143I
Unit Performance Task	224
Unit Review	226

UNIT 3
Waves and Information Transfer 141

Lesson 1
What Are Waves? 144
- **Hands-On Activity:** Let's Make Waves 146
- **People in Science & Engineering:** Christian Doppler, Debra Fischer 165

Lesson 2
How Does Light Reflect? 170
- **Hands-On Activity:** Disappearing Coins 172
- **Hands-On Activity:** Reflecting on Angles 182
- **Careers in Science & Engineering:** Optics Researcher 195

Lesson 3
How Is Information Transferred from Place to Place? 200
- **Hands-On Activity:** Pixels to Pictures 208

UNIT 3 PERFORMANCE TASK 224
UNIT 3 REVIEW 226

UNIT 4 Life Science

Plant Structure and Function 229

Lesson 1
What Are Some Plant Parts and How Do They Function? 232
- **Hands-On Activity:** Hold the Soil 243
- **People in Science & Engineering:** Clayton Anderson 249

ENGINEER IT Lesson 2
How Do Plants Grow and Reproduce? 254
- **Hands-On Activity:** Flying High 268
- **Careers in Science & Engineering:** Pomologist 271

UNIT 4 PERFORMANCE TASK 276
UNIT 4 REVIEW 278

UNIT 5

Animal Structure and Function 281

ENGINEER IT Lesson 1
What Are Some External Structures of Animals? 284
- **Hands-On Activity:** Staying Warm 296
- **Careers in Science & Engineering:** Mimicking Animal Movement 299

Lesson 2
What Are Some Internal Structures of Animals? 304
- **Hands-On Activity:** Pump It Up! 311
- **People in Science & Engineering:** Henry Gray, Vanessa Ruiz 319

Lesson 3
How Do Senses Work? 324
- **Hands-On Activity:** Touch Test 330

UNIT 5 PERFORMANCE TASK 344
UNIT 5 REVIEW 346

xiii

Unit 4
Plant Structure and Function

Unit at a Glance 230
Integrating the NGSS Three Dimensions of Learning 231A
3D Unit Planning 231C
Differentiate Instruction 231G
Making Connections 231H
Unit Project 231I
Unit Performance Task 276
Unit Review 278

Unit 5
Animal Structure and Function

Unit at a Glance 282
Integrating the NGSS Three Dimensions of Learning 283A
3D Unit Planning 283C
Differentiate Instruction 283G
Making Connections 283H
Unit Project 283I
Unit Performance Task 344
Unit Review 346

Contents T67

Unit 6
Changes to Earth's Surface

Unit at a Glance 350

Integrating the NGSS Three Dimensions of Learning 351A

3D Unit Planning 351C

Differentiate Instruction 351G

Making Connections 351H

Unit Project 351I

Unit Performance Task 448

Unit Review 450

UNIT 6 Earth and Space Science

Changes to Earth's Surface 349

Lesson 1
How Does Water Shape Earth's Surface? 352
- Hands-On Activity: The Rate of Change 366
- People in Science & Engineering: Anjali Fernandes 373

Lesson 2
What Other Factors Shape Earth's Surface? 378
- Hands-On Activity: Finding Change 392
- ENGINEER IT Slowing Change 399

ENGINEER IT **Lesson 3**
How Can Maps Help Us Learn About Earth's Surface? . 404
- Hands-On Activity: Park Designer 419
- Careers in Science & Engineering: City Planner 422

Lesson 4
What Patterns Do Maps Show Us? 428
- Hands-On Activity: Tracking Quakes 440
- People in Science & Engineering: Lewis and Clark 443

UNIT 6 PERFORMANCE TASK 448
UNIT 6 REVIEW 450

UNIT 7

Rocks and Fossils 453

Lesson 1
How Do Rock Layers Change? 456
Hands-On Activity: Modeling How Rocks Can Form and Change 468
People in Science & Engineering: Bernard Hubbard 477

Lesson 2
What Do Fossils Tell Us About Ancient Environments? 482
Hands-On Activity: Old and New 486

Lesson 3
What Are Some Patterns Fossils Show Us? 500
Hands-On Activity: Layer By Layer 502
People in Science & Engineering: Edward Cope, Mary Ann Mantell, Louis Walter Alvarez, Patricia Vickers-Rich, Don Zhiming 513

UNIT 7 PERFORMANCE TASK 518
UNIT 7 REVIEW 520

Unit 7
Rocks and Fossils

Unit at a Glance 454
Integrating the NGSS Three Dimensions of Learning 455A
3D Unit Planning 455C
Differentiate Instruction 455G
Making Connections 455H
Unit Project 455I
Unit Performance Task 518
Unit Review 520

Unit 8
Natural Resources and Hazards

Unit at a Glance 524
Integrating the NGSS Three Dimensions of Learning 525A
3D Unit Planning 525C
Differentiate Instruction 525G
Making Connections 525H
Unit Project 525I
Unit Performance Task 620
Unit Review 622

UNIT 8

Natural Resources and Hazards 523

Lesson 1
What Non-Renewable Resources Are Used for Energy? 526
- Hands-On Activity: Catch That Dirt 540
- Careers in Science & Engineering: Geologist, Chemist, Climatologist, Marine Biologist 543

ENGINEER IT Lesson 2
What Renewable Resources Are Used for Energy? 548
- Hands-On Activity: Running on Sunshine 562
- People in Science & Engineering: Elon Musk 567

ENGINEER IT Lesson 3
How Can People Reduce the Impact of Land-Based Hazards? 572
- Hands-On Activity: Reduce the Risk 586
- People in Science & Engineering: Lucy Jones 591

ENGINEER IT Lesson 4
How Can People Reduce the Impact of Water-Based Hazards? 596
- Hands-On Activity: Is It Safe? 612

UNIT 8 PERFORMANCE TASK 620
UNIT 8 REVIEW 622

Glossary R1
Index R16

Safety in the Lab

Doing science is a lot of fun. But, a science lab can be a dangerous place. Falls, cuts, and burns can happen easily. **Know the safety rules and listen to your teacher.**

- ☐ **Think ahead.** Study the investigation steps so you know what to expect. If you have any questions, ask your teacher. Be sure you understand all caution statements and safety reminders.
- ☐ **Be neat and clean.** Keep your work area clean. If you have long hair, pull it back so it doesn't get in the way. Roll or push up long sleeves to keep them away from your activity.
- ☐ **Oops!** If you spill or break something, or get cut, tell your teacher right away.
- ☐ **Watch your eyes.** Wear safety goggles anytime you are directed to do so. If you get anything in your eyes, tell your teacher right away.
- ☐ **Yuck!** Never eat or drink anything during a science activity.
- ☐ **Don't get shocked.** Be careful if an electric appliance is used. Be sure that electric cords are in a safe place where you can't trip over them. Never use the cord to pull a plug from an outlet.
- ☐ **Keep it clean.** Always clean up when you have finished. Put everything away and wipe your work area. Wash your hands.
- ☐ **Play it safe.** Always know where to find safety equipment, such as fire extinguishers. Know how to use the safety equipment around you.

xvii

Safety in Science

Indoors

Use the following discussion points to emphasize key safety rules for indoor science activities.

Ask: Why is it important to understand safety reminders before you begin an activity? You may get hurt because you don't notice the reminders during the activity.

Ask: Why do you need to keep long sleeves and hair out of the way during science activities? Hair and clothes can snag equipment and get stained. They can also catch fire.

Ask: Tell me what you would do if you spilled some water. Students should mention informing the teacher and helping clean up.

Ask: What could happen if the spill wasn't cleaned up? Students should realize that water makes the floor slippery and increases the risk of falls.

Ask: First, put on a pair of safety goggles. What are the differences between safety goggles and ordinary glasses? Students should recognize the sturdy material and protection all around the sides of the lenses.

Ask: Why are these differences important during science activities? The lenses are less likely to break. The protection on the sides keeps liquid and objects from getting into your eyes.

Ask for a student volunteer. Tell them to walk up to and point at a piece of safety equipment in the classroom, then tell the class when and how you would use it.

Safety in Science

Outdoors

Use the following discussion points to emphasize key safety rules for outdoor science activities.

Ask: How does your clothing affect your safety outdoors? Covering up your arms and legs protects you from scratches and from the sun.

Ask: Why do you think open-toed or dressy shoes are poor choices for exploring outdoors? Sturdy shoes can protect your feet from sharp objects, plants, and biting insects.

Ask: Why is it unsafe to taste anything outdoors? Many plants and animals are poisonous. Even adults can be fooled.

Ask: Why is it important to stay with your group and stay on marked trails? With a group, someone will be there to help if you get hurt or have a problem. Marked trails are safer; walking through wild areas may damage habitats.

Ask: Why are running and horseplay riskier outdoors? You don't know the area. The ground level may change quickly. If you're moving fast, it's easier to fall and get hurt before you can stop.

Ask: Why is it especially important to wash your hands when you come back indoors? It helps keep you from getting sick and from rubbing grit into your eyes by accident.

T72   Safety in Science

Safety in the Field

Lots of science research happens outdoors. It's fun to explore the wild! But, you need to be careful. The weather, the land, and the living things can surprise you.

☐ **Think ahead.** Study the investigation steps so you know what to expect. If you have any questions, ask your teacher. Be sure you understand all caution statements and safety reminders.

☐ **Dress right.** Wear appropriate clothes and shoes for the outdoors. Cover up and wear sunscreen and sunglasses for sun safety.

☐ **Clean up the area.** Follow your teacher's instructions for when and how to throw away waste.

☐ **Oops!** Tell your teacher right away if you break something or get hurt.

☐ **Watch your eyes.** Wear safety goggles when directed to do so. If you get anything in your eyes, tell your teacher right away.

☐ **Yuck!** Never taste anything outdoors.

☐ **Stay with your group.** Work in the area as directed by your teacher. Stay on marked trails.

☐ **"Wilderness" doesn't mean go wild.** Never engage in horseplay, games, or pranks.

☐ **Always walk.** No running!

☐ **Play it safe.** Know where safety equipment can be found and how to use it. Know how to get help.

☐ **Clean up.** Wash your hands with soap and water when you come back indoors.

xviii

Safety Symbols

To highlight important safety concerns, the following symbols are used in a Hands-On Activity. Remember that no matter what safety symbols you see, all safety rules should be followed at all times.

Dress Code

- Wear safety goggles as directed.
- If anything gets into your eye, tell your teacher immediately
- Do not wear contact lenses in the lab.
- Wear appropriate protective gloves as directed.
- Tie back long hair, secure loose clothing, and remove loose jewelry.

Glassware and Sharp Object Safety

- Do not use chipped or cracked glassware.
- Notify your teacher immediately if a piece of glass breaks.
- Use extreme care when handling all sharp and pointed instruments.
- Do not cut an object while holding the object in your hands.
- Cut objects on a suitable surface, always in a direction away from your body.

Electrical Safety

- Do not use equipment with frayed electrical cords or loose plugs.
- Do not use electrical equipment near water or when clothing or hands are wet.
- Hold the plug when you plug in or unplug equipment.

Chemical Safety

- If a chemical gets on your skin, on your clothing, or in your eyes, rinse it immediately, and tell your teacher.
- Do not clean up spilled chemicals unless your teacher directs you to do so.
- Keep your hands away from your face while you are working on any activity.

Heating and Fire Safety

- Know your school's evacuation-fire routes.
- Never leave a hot plate unattended while it is turned on or while it is cooling.
- Allow equipment to cool before storing it.

Plant and Animal Safety

- Do not eat any part of a plant.
- Do not pick any wild plant unless your teacher instructs you to do so.
- Treat animals carefully and respectfully.
- Wash your hands throughly after handling any plant or animal.

Cleanup

- Clean all work surfaces and protective equipment as directed by your teacher.
- Wash your hands throughly before you leave the lab or after any activity.

Safety in Science

Safety Symbols

Safety symbols will appear in the instructions for each Hands-On Activity to emphasize important notes of caution. Make sure students learn what they represent and understand the appropriate precautions to take.

Use the following discussion points to emphasize key safety rules for each Hands-On Activity.

Ask: How are safety goggles different from regular eyeglasses? Safety goggles are made of sturdy material and have protection around the sides of the lenses.

Ask: Why should you tie back long hair? Loose long hair could obstruct the materials in the activity or become contaminated.

Ask: If chemicals get on your skin, clothing, or in your eyes, why is it important to rinse it immediately? Chemicals can burn or stain skin or clothing. Rinsing immediately help to reduce the impact of the chemicals.

Ask: Why should you wash your hands thoroughly after each activity? Hands can get contaminated from the materials in the activity. Washing hands helps to ensure that materials from the activity are not ingested when eating. Washing hands also keeps you from rubbing things into your eyes.

Safety in Science

Student Safety Quiz

Use this quiz to check student understanding of lab safety practices and procedures.

It is important that students take responsibility for their safety and the safety of others. Be sure to discuss with students each question and answer to help them understand the importance of safe conduct during an activity.

Safety Quiz

Name _____

Circle the letter of the BEST answer.

1. Before starting an activity, you should
   a. try an experiment of your own.
   b. open all containers and packages.
   (c.) read all directions and make sure you understand them.
   d. handle all the equipment to become familiar with it.

2. At the end of any activity you should
   (a.) wash your hands thoroughly before leaving the lab.
   b. cover your face with your hands.
   c. put on your safety goggles.
   d. leave the materials where they are.

3. If you get hurt or injured in any way, you should
   (a.) tell your teacher immediately.
   b. find bandages or a first aid kit.
   c. go to your principal's office.
   d. get help after you finish the activity.

4. If your equipment is chipped or broken, you should
   a. use it only for solid materials.
   (b.) give it to your teacher for recycling or disposal.
   c. put it back.
   d. increase the damage so that it is obvious.

5. If you have unused liquids after finishing an activity, you should
   a. pour them down a sink or drain.
   b. mix them all together in a bucket.
   c. put them back into their original containers.
   (d.) dispose of them as directed by your teacher.

6. When working with materials that might fly into the air and hurt someone's eye, you should wear
   (a.) goggles.
   b. an apron.
   c. gloves.
   d. a hat.

7. If you get something in your eye you should
   a. wash your hands immediately.
   b. put the lid back on the container.
   c. wait to see if your eye becomes irritated.
   (d.) tell your teacher right away.

UNIT 1 Engineering and Technology

UNIT 1

Engineering and Technology

Unit Project: Extend a Sense
How can you extend your sense of sight, smell, or touch? You will conduct an investigation with your team. Ask your teacher for details.

When a new rocket is designed, it must be tested.

Unit Overview
In this unit, students will . . .
- explore how engineers define problems and solutions.
- learn about the importance of prototypes.
- use models to examine how prototypes are tested and improved.

About This Image
A rocket is a great example of a type of space technology. Engineers designed rockets to launch into outer space, leaving Earth's atmosphere in a safe and effective way. In order to design rockets that work, engineers have had to explore processes to identify problems and solutions. They also needed to build prototypes that were tested. Sometimes those tests failed. Engineers used failed tests to come up with ways to improve the designs. Space engineering and technology continues to evolve and advance. Today, we have much more sophisticated rocket designs than we did years ago.

Unit Project
As students work through the unit lessons, have them research, plan, and write down notes about the design process for extending your sense of sight, smell, or touch.

To begin learning about the design process, draw students' attention to the various parts of a rocket that could potentially cause problems or need improvements, or challenge the class to use online or media center resources to find other types of space technology, such as orbiting satellites, and have them perform the same process of identifying potential problems and solutions. More support for the Unit Project can be found on pp. 3I–3L.

UNIT 1 Engineering and Technology

The learning experiences in this unit prepare students for the mastery of:

Performance Expectations

3-5-ETS1-1 Define a simple design problem reflecting a need or a want that includes specified criteria for success and constraints on materials, time, or cost.

3-5-ETS1-2 Generate and compare multiple possible solutions to a problem based on how well each is likely to meet the criteria and constraints of the problem.

3-5-ETS1-3 Plan and carry out fair tests in which variables are controlled and failure points are considered to identify aspects of a model or prototype that can be improved.

▶ Explore Online

In addition to the print resources, the following resources are available online to support this unit.

Unit Pretest
Lesson 1 How Do Engineers Define Problems?
- Online Student Edition
- Lesson Quiz

Lesson 2 How Do Engineers Design Solutions?
- Online Student Edition
- Lesson Quiz

Lesson 3 How Do Engineers Test and Improve Prototypes?
- Online Student Edition
- Lesson Quiz

You Solve It
Unit Performance Task
Unit Test

UNIT 1

At a Glance

LESSON 1
How Do Engineers Define Problems? 4

LESSON 2
How Do Engineers Design Solutions? 22

LESSON 3
How Do Engineers Test and Improve Prototypes? 44

Unit Review 60

Vocabulary Game: Guess the Word

Materials
- Kitchen timer or online computer timer

Directions
1. Take turns to play.
2. To take a turn, choose a vocabulary word. Do not tell the word to the other players.
3. Set the timer for one minute.
4. Give a one-word clue about your word. Point to a player. That player has one chance to guess your word.
5. Repeat step 4 with other players until a player guesses the word or time runs out. Give a different one-word clue each time.
6. The first player to guess the word gets 1 point. If the player can then use the word in a sentence, he or she gets 1 more point. Then that player chooses the next word.
7. The first player to score 5 points wins.

criteria: The desirable features of a solution.

optimize: To make a solution as good as possible.

Unit Vocabulary

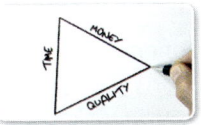
constraint: A real world limit on a solution, for example, safety needs, time, money, or materials.

criteria: The desirable features of a solution.

engineering: The process of designing new or improved techology.

failure analysis: Figuring out what went wrong with a solution and why.

fair test: A test that does not give any advantage to the conditions or objects being tested.

optimize: To make a solution as good as possible.

Unit Vocabulary

Students can explore all lesson vocabulary terms in the **Online Glossary**.

Vocabulary Strategies

Have students review the terms individually. Then pair up and share an example of one term with their partner and tell why they think it's an example. Have each pair write down their examples to check during the unit.

Differentiate Instruction

RTI/Extra Support Have struggling readers find the vocabulary words within the unit. Have students use context clues to infer definitions and then share with a partner.

Extension Have students pick two terms and then work in small groups to illustrate and explain the terms for a second- or third-grade student.

ELL Pronounce each term and have students repeat it. Then pair up students by native language and have them explain each term in their native language.

Vocabulary Game: Guess the Word

Preparation
Use a timer on your smartphone or tablet, if that is more convenient than a kitchen timer or online computer timer.

Game Play
- Students choose a word card and give clues about their word for other players to guess.
- Encourage students to use a different clue each time.

UNIT 1 Engineering and Technology
Integrating the NGSS* Three Dimensions of Learning

Building to the Performance Expectations

The learning experiences in this unit prepare students for mastery of the following Performance Expectations:

Engineering Design

3-5-ETS1-1 Define a simple design problem reflecting a need or a want that includes specified criteria for success and constraints on materials, time, or cost.

3-5-ETS1-2 Generate and compare multiple possible solutions to a problem based on how well each is likely to meet the criteria and constraints of the problem.

3-5-ETS1-3 Plan and carry out fair tests in which variables are controlled and failure points are considered to identify aspects of a model or prototype that can be improved.

Assessing Student Progress

After completing these lessons, the **Unit Project: Extend a Sense** provides students with opportunities to practice aspects of and demonstrate their understanding of the Performance Expectation as they apply engineering and design concepts to come up with a device that would enhance one of their senses.

Additionally, students can practice or be assessed on aspects of the Performance Expectations by completing the **Unit Performance Task: Designing a Portable Chair**, in which they apply design and engineering concepts to make a model of a portable chair.

Lesson 1
How Do Engineers Define Problems?

In Lesson 1, students will learn introductory concepts of engineering and technology. They will explore engineering problems **(DCI Defining and Delimiting Engineering Problems)** and develop solutions based on criteria and constraints **(SEP Asking Questions and Defining Problems).** By investigating problems and solutions, students will gain a deeper understanding of engineering and technology's impacts on society **(CCC Influence of Engineering, Technology, and Science on Society and the Natural World).**

Lesson 2
How Do Engineers Design Solutions?

In Lesson 2, students will explore the ways engineers come up with solutions to problems **(DCI Developing Possible Solutions).** They will learn about how these solutions are then integrated into technology that affects society and the environment **(CCC Influence of Engineering, Technology, and Science on Society and the Natural World).** They will come up with explanations and design solutions of their own **(SEP Constructing Explanations and Designing Solutions)** and learn about the processes that engineers go through, including using constraints and criteria.

Lesson 3
How Do Engineers Test and Improve Prototypes?

In Lesson 3, students will plan, design, and test possible solutions **(SEP Planning and Carrying Out Investigations)** for a prototype to determine which design best solves a problem within the given criteria and constraints **(DCI Optimizing the Design Solution).** Students will then identify failure points or difficulties with a design and suggest and implement changes that improve it **(DCI Developing Possible Solutions).** Students learn that engineers must communicate in order to share observations, gain insight, and optimize future solutions and designs **(CCC Influence of Science, Engineering, and Technology on Society and the Natural World).**

*Next Generation Science Standards and logo are registered trademarks of Achieve. Neither Achieve or the lead states and partners that developed the Next Generation Science Standards were involved in production of, and does not endorse, these products.

NGSS Across this Unit

Explore Online! Online only.

Next Generation Science Standard	Unit Project	Lesson 1	Lesson 2	Lesson 3	Unit Performance Task	You Solve It!
SEP Planning and Carrying Out Investigations				•		
SEP Constructing Explanations and Designing Solutions	•		•			
SEP Asking Questions and Defining Problems	•	•			•	•
DCI ETS1.A Defining and Delimiting Engineering Solutions	•	•			•	•
DCI ETS1.B Developing Possible Solutions	•		•	•	•	
DCI ETS1.C Optimizing the Design Solution				•	•	
CCC Influence of Science, Engineering, and Technology on Society and the Natural World	•	•	•	•	•	•

NGSS Across the Grades

Before	Grades 3–5	After
Engineering Design K-2-ETS1-1 K-2-ETS1-2 K-2-ETS1-3	**Engineering Design** 3-5-ETS1-1 3-5-ETS1-2 3-5-ETS1-3	**Engineering Design** MS-ETS1-1 MS-ETS1-2 MS-ETS1-3 MS-ETS1-4

Trace Tool to the NGSS™ Go online to view the complete coverage of these standards across this grade level and time.

UNIT 1 Engineering and Technology
3D Unit Planning

Lesson 1 How Do Engineers Define Problems pp. 4–21

Overview

Objective Define a design problem and identify the constraints and criteria for a design solution.

SEP Asking Questions and Defining Problems
DCI ETS1.A Defining and Delimiting Engineering Problems
CCC Influence of Engineering, Technology, and Science on Society and the Natural World
Math and **English Language Arts** standards and features are detailed on lesson planner pages.

Print and Online Student Editions — Explore Online!

ENGAGE
Lesson Phenomenon pp. 4–5
Can You Solve It? Can you come up with a design for a wearable hearing-enhancing device that does not rely on batteries?
Can You Solve It! Video

EXPLORE/EXPLAIN
What Is Technology? pp. 6–13
What Do You See?
 Apply What You Know Engineered?
What Is the Problem?
 **HANDS-ON** Menu Planning
HANDS-ON Worksheet

Real-World Limits pp. 14–16
Limited Limits
 Apply What You Know Paper Building

ELABORATE
Take It Further pp. 17–18
People in Science: Improving Hearing
Take It Further — Writing Within Constraints
Take It Further — Limits in Nature

EVALUATE
Lesson Check pp. 19–20
Lesson Roundup p. 21
Lesson Quiz

HANDS-ON ACTIVITY PLANNING

Apply What You Know

Engineered?
- 10 minutes
- Individuals

Materials
- 5 or more nonliving things that are not engineered
- 5 or more nonliving things that are engineered

Preparation/Tip Let students wander around the classroom to inspect objects that have been engineered. Give students a few minutes to do this, and then have them return to their seat to complete the list.

Paper Building
- 10 minutes
- Small groups

Materials
- 10 index cards
- 10 cm of adhesive tape

Preparation/Tip Set some parameters and provide tips on how to manipulate the cards to build a strong structure. For example, discuss folding cards to make angular shapes.

HANDS-ON

Menu Planning
- 1 class period
- Pairs

Materials
- recipe cards

Objective Students ask questions and define problems related to food to plan menus. They will analyze constraints to come up with criteria.

Preparation/Tip Have recipe cards and any additional materials ready for students to use with their partners.

Lesson 2 How Do Engineers Design Solutions? pp. 22–43

Overview

Objective Research and design possible solutions to a problem, and investigate how well your solution performs.

SEP Constructing Explanations and Designing Solutions
DCI ETS1.B Developing Possible Solutions
CCC Influence of Engineering, Technology, and Science on Society and the Natural World

Math and **English Language Arts** standards and features are detailed on lesson planner pages.

Print and Online Student Editions — **Explore Online!**

ENGAGE	**Lesson Phenomenon** pp. 22–23 **Can You Solve It?** Can you elaborate on the design of your hearing-enhancing device based on criteria and constraints?	Can You Solve It! Video
EXPLORE/ EXPLAIN	**Research Matters** pp. 24–27 Ears to You Targeting Sounds	HANDS-ON Worksheet
	Past Hearing Helpers pp. 28–33 Looking Back to Look Forward **Apply What You Know** Hear Here **HANDS-ON** Design It!	
	Passing the Test pp. 34–37 Testing, Testing, 1, 2, 3 More Testing Fair Tests Your Fair Test	

ELABORATE	**Take It Further** pp. 38–40
	Careers In Science & Engineering
	Acoustic Engineer
		Take It Further
		   Hearing Aid History
		Take It Further
		   Don't Make a Move

EVALUATE	**Lesson Check** pp. 41–42 **Lesson Roundup** p. 43	Lesson Quiz

HANDS-ON ACTIVITY PLANNING

Apply What You Know

Hear Here

- 10 minutes
- Pairs

Preparation/Tip Find a space in which pairs of students will be able to focus their hearing on each other and not get distracted by other sounds.

HANDS-ON

Design It!

- 1 class period
- Pairs

Objective Students work in pairs to design hearing-enhancing devices based on constraints and criteria. They must identify the problem and solve for it through this activity.

Materials
- plastic and/or paper cups
- cloth scraps
- duct tape
- masking tape
- wire clothes hangers
- string
- rubber tubing
- plastic headband
- scissors
- baseball or painter's cap

Preparation/Tip Prepare for this activity by making the materials available to students and rearranging the room to make space for pairs of students to spread out their designs and materials.

Unit 1 Engineering and Technology 3D

UNIT 1 Engineering and Technology
3D Unit Planning, continued

Lesson 3 How Do Engineers Test and Improve Prototypes? pp. 44–59

Overview

Objective Plan, design, and test possible solutions for a prototype to determine which design best solves a problem within given criteria and constraints; identify failure points or difficulties with a design and suggest and implement changes that improve it; communicate in order to share observations, gain insight, and optimize future solutions and designs.

SEP Planning and Carrying Out Investigations
DCI ETS1.B Developing Possible Solutions
DCI ETS1.C Optimizing the Design Solutions
CCC Influence of Engineering, Technology, and Science on Society and the Natural World

Math and **English Language Arts** standards and features are detailed on lesson planner pages.

	Print and Online Student Editions	Explore Online!
ENGAGE	**Lesson Phenomenon** pp. 44–45 **Can You Solve It?** Can you use collaboration and communication to improve your design?	Can You Solve It! Video
EXPLORE/ EXPLAIN	HANDS-ON Class Collaboration pp. 46–48 **Things Fail and Improve** pp. 49–51 Try, Try Again Apply What You Know Tissue Rope Cakes Done Right! **Getting Better** pp. 52–54 Talking to the Team Apply What You Know Sharing Feedback	HANDS-ON Worksheet
ELABORATE	**Take It Further** pp. 55–56 Sense Extenders for Science	Take It Further Ear Areas Take It Further High or Low?
EVALUATE	**Lesson Check** pp. 57–58 **Lesson Roundup** p. 59	Lesson Quiz

HANDS-ON ACTIVITY PLANNING

Apply What You Know

Tissue Rope
- 15 minutes
- Pairs

Materials
- 6 feet of toilet tissue

Preparation/Tip Point out to students that this activity works best if one student reads the directions to the other, who will try to follow them.

Sharing Feedback
- 10 minutes
- Trios

Preparation/Tip Remind students to make kind, thoughtful, helpful design critiques. Model this process for them by critiquing one group's design.

HANDS-ON

Class Collaboration
- 1 class period
- Small groups

Materials
See materials list for Lesson 2 Hands-On

Objective Students further develop their final design sketch to build their hearing enhancement device from the previous lessons.

Preparation/Tip

UNIT 1 Engineering and Technology
3D Unit Planning, continued

 **You Solve It** Go online for an additional interactive activity.

Keeping It Warm and Cool

This virtual lab offers practice in support of **PE 3-5-ETS1-1 and ETS1.A.**

SEP Asking Questions and Defining Problems

DCI **ETS1.A** Defining and Delimiting Engineering Solutions

CCC Influence of Engineering, Technology, and Science on Society and the Natural World

Use after Unit 1, Lesson 3— What materials keep a home cool in a hot, humid climate and warm in a cold climate?

Objectives
1. Students observe that heat is transferred between the inside and outside of a house from a higher temperature to a lower temperature material.
2. Students will analyze the pros and cons of insulating materials.

Activity Problem
Your job is to find the optimal insulator choices for houses in two different climates. The criteria and constraints are as follows:
1. Heat loss is reduced inside the house in a cold climate, and
2. The house is cool in a hot and humid climate.

Interaction Summary
1. Students test different insulation materials in the lab.
2. Then they select a climate zone to test the insulation materials.
3. Students collect data in a table for each insulation material.
4. They use the data to write a lab report.

Assessment

Pre-Assessment
Assessment Guide, Unit Pretest

The Unit Pretest focuses on prerequisite knowledge and is composed of items that evaluate students' preparedness for the content covered within this unit.

Formative Assessment
Student Edition, Apply What You Know, Lesson Check, and Self Check

Summative Assessment
Assessment Guide, Lesson Quiz
The Lesson Quiz provides a quick assessment of each lesson objective and of the portion of the Performance Expectation aligned to the lesson.

Student Edition, Performance Task pp. 60–61
The Performance Task presents the opportunity for children to collaborate with classmates in order to complete the steps of each Performance Task. Each Performance Task provides a formal Scoring Rubric for evaluating students' work.

Student Edition, Unit 1 Review pp. 62–64

Assessment Guide, Unit Test
The Unit Test provides an in-depth assessment of the Performance Expectations aligned to the unit. This test evaluates students' ability to apply knowledge in order to explain phenomena and to solve problems. Within this test, Constructed Response items apply a three-dimensional rubric for evaluating students' mastery on all three dimensions of the Next Generation Science Standards.

UNIT 1 Engineering and Technology
Differentiate Instruction

Leveled Readers

The **Science & Engineering Leveled Readers** provide additional nonfiction reading practice in this unit's subject area.

On-Level Reader • What is the Engineering Process?
This reader reinforces unit concepts and includes response activities for your students.

Extra Support • What is the Engineering Process?
This reader shares title, illustrations, vocabulary, and concepts with the On-Level Reader; however, the text is linguistically accommodated to provide simplified sentence structures and comprehension aids. It also includes response activities.

Enrichment • City Water Tunnel 3
This high-interest, nonfiction reader will extend and enrich unit concepts and vocabulary and includes response activities.

Teacher Guide

The accompanying Teacher Guide provides teaching strategies and support for using all the readers.

ELL

ELL teacher strategies in this unit:

Lesson 1: p. 10
Lesson 2: p. 26
Lesson 3: p. 50

RTI/Extra Support

Strategies for students needing extra support in this unit:

Lesson 1: p. 6
Lesson 2: pp. 32, 35, 36, 39
Lesson 3: p. 56

Extension

Strategies for students who have mastered core content in this unit:

Lesson 1: p. 13
Lesson 2: pp. 25, 29, 36
Lesson 3: p. 52

 **Leveled Readers** — All readers are available online as well as in an innovative, engaging format for use with touchscreen mobile devices. Contact your HMH Sales Representative for more information.

UNIT 1 Engineering and Technology
Making Connections

Connections to the Community

Use these opportunities for informal science learning to provide local context and to extend and enhance unit concepts.

At Home

TECHNOLOGY AT HOME Have students look around their homes and write down ten examples of technology. For each of these, students will also identify the problem that this item was engineered to solve. How do they think people handled this problem before this device was engineered? *Use with Lesson 1.*

PERSONAL ROBOT Have students look around their home and imagine they are going to build their own personal robot. What would be their criteria for what the robot could do? What would be constraints on its size, weight, and actions? *Use with Lesson 2.*

In the Community

LOTS OF GADGETS Have students go with a family adult to visit a hardware store. Tell them to look at a number of different gadgets and discuss what problem each one was engineered to solve. What criteria and constraints did the engineers probably work with? *Use with Lesson 1.*

IT PASSED THE TEST Tell students to go with a family adult to a store selling home furnishings and supplies. Have the students select several items to think about. Students should talk with their family adult about some characteristics each item probably was tested for and how the test might have been done. *Use with Lesson 3.*

Collaboration

Opportunities for students to work collaboratively in this unit:

Brainstorm p. 55	**Partners** p. 15
Build on Prior Knowledge pp. 5, 23, 53	**Pathways** pp. 17, 38
Discussion pp. 19, 41, 57	**Think, Pair Share** pp. 25, 37, 39
Feedback pp. 7, 29, 35	**Write, Pair, Share** p. 51

Connections to Science

Opportunities to connect to other content areas in this unit.

Connection to Life Science
Lesson 2, p. 26

Lesson 3, p. 56

Connection to Earth and Space Sciences
Lesson 1, p. 16

Lesson 3, p. 54

Home Letters Use these one-page letters to engage family members with unit concepts.

UNIT 1 Engineering and Technology
Unit Project

Unit Project: Extend a Sense 👥 Small Groups ⏱ 2 class periods

For this task, small groups of students will work together to use technology to design a device that will improve one of the human senses. They will ask questions and identify a problem to solve related to the sense and then engineer a possible solution to the problem. Students may have limited knowledge of the potential of the human senses. Provide background, instruction, and assistance as needed.

3D Learning Objective

- Ask questions to identify a limitation of one of the human senses.
- Identify criteria and constraints in developing solutions to the human senses problem.
- Design a possible solution to the problem.

Skills and Standards Focus

This project supports building student mastery of **Performance Expectation 3-5-ETS1-1 and -2.**

SEP Asking Questions and Defining Problems
SEP Constructing Explanations and Designing Solutions
DCI **ETS1.A** Defining and Delimiting Engineering Problems
DCI **ETS1.B** Developing Possible Solutions
CCC Influence of Engineering, Technology, and Science on Society and the Natural World

Suggested Materials

- drawing paper
- drawing utensils
- print and electronic references for human senses

Preparation and Planning Tips

Ensure that each group understands it can select one of the five human senses: sight, hearing, taste, touch, smell to extend. Review the characteristics of each sense and the descriptive words related to the senses before students begin. For example:

- taste: salty, sweet, bitter, sour
- sound: sound wavelength and frequency, intensity, direction, pitch, duration, loudness, location
- sight: color, brightness, detail
- touch: texture, sharp, smooth, hot, cool, itchy
- smell: odor, fragrance, aroma, musky, floral, minty, pungent

Differentiate Instruction

RTI/Extra Support To provide background on senses, discuss students' experience with each sense, including favorite sights, sounds, smells, tastes, and things to touch. Provide different sounds, pictures, textures, smells, and tastes and survey student preferences. Have students determine if one of their senses is stronger than another.

Extension Have students research animals that have different sense perception than humans. For example, dogs and cats can see in the dark. Bears have the most sensitive sense of smell. Owls have a highly sensitive sense of hearing. Encourage students to consider animal senses as they design their sense devices.

Go online to access the Unit Project downloadable worksheet for students.

Explore Online

Name _____

UNIT PROJECT
Extend a Sense

Think of the many different senses you have. If you could improve any of your senses to a super-power level, which sense would it be? How would your sense work differently and be better? For this project, you will work with your team to come up with a design for a device that can be used to enhance your sense of sight, smell, or touch. Then, you will present your design concept to the class.

Write a question that you will consider as you come up with your sense-enhancing designs.

Students should write a question concerning enhancing the sense of sight, smell, or touch.

Materials

Think about how you will need to perform this investigation. What materials will you need?

Materials can include drawing paper and utensils and references (print or electronic).

As a team, decide on the sense you wish to focus on. Think about selecting a sense based on your interest. Which sense did you select, and why?

Accept any response. Possible response: We selected the sense of touch so that we could feel microorganisms that are not visible to the naked eye.

3

UNIT 1 PROJECT
Extend a Sense

DCI ETS1.A Defining and Delimiting Engineering Problems

Before students begin the task, check their understanding of key concepts.

Ask: What do engineers do? **Possible answer: Identify problems and design solutions to address problems and meet needs and wants.**

Refer students to Lesson 1, Exploration 1, *Defining Engineering Problems,* for concept support.

ESSENTIAL QUESTIONS Ask the following questions before students begin to plan their activity.

- What is the problem?
- What are the constraints and criteria?

CCC Influence of Engineering, Technology, and Science on Society and the Natural World

Discuss the sense improvement devices students know of and how they were engineered to solve problems. For example: eyeglasses, hearing aids, earplugs, oven mitts, masks, special cookware

Ask: What is your strongest and weakest sense? **Possible answer: I am very sensitive to sound. I have no sense of smell.**

Ask: How do people's needs change over time for improved sense perception? **Possible answer: As people age, their senses of hearing and sight are not the same, and they may need glasses or hearing aids.**

SEP Asking Questions and Defining Problems

Discuss one sense. Have students ask questions about the limitations of the sense and the advantages of enhancing the sense.

Research and Plan

Students should decide which sense they will try to improve.

Ask: What problem are you trying to solve? Possible answer: being able to see in the dark

Ask: What devices are already available to solve this problem? Possible answer: flashlights, night vision goggles, headlamps

Ask: How would your device be different from the ones currently available? Possible answer: less expensive and easier to use

 Asking Questions and Defining Problems

Criteria and Constraints

Ask: What is the criteria? improve one of the senses

Ask: What constraints do you have? Possible answer: We are limited in cost and the materials we can use.

 Influence of Engineering, Technology, and Science on Society and the Natural World

Engineering

Have students describe the limitations of the sense they have selected. They may consider the following.

- What sense limitations do humans have?
- What device could improve this sense?
- How could the device be designed so it is easy to use?
- Why and how would the device work?

 ETS1.B Developing Possible Solutions

Possible Solutions

Have groups brainstorm solutions to see if they can help solve the problem. Then have them settle on one solution to develop and sketch the design.

Research and Plan

Plan your research. Consider the following:

- What is the problem that you are trying to solve?
- What is the solution?
- What are the criteria?
- What are the constraints?

Students should list the problem, solution, criteria, and constraints associated with their chosen sense.
Possible response: the problem is that we cannot feel all the things there are to feel in life. We need to be able to enhance our sense of touch. The solution is to design a special glove that allows us to have more feeling in our fingertips. Our criteria are that the design must be able to be worn by people of all ages and sizes, it must be safe to use, and it must be comfortable. The constraints are money and resources.

Review your design with your team and look for possible areas for improvement. Will you make any modifications to your design? Why or why not?

Accept all responses.

Analyze Your Results

Using your design, make two observations about how your selected sense will be enhanced.

Possible response: the extra sensors in the tips of the gloves make it possible for people to feel more things – things they cannot even see.

Restate Your Question

Write the question you investigated.

Students should identify the question created at the beginning of the project.

Claims, Evidence, and Reasoning

Make a claim that answers your question.

Possible response: It is possible to enhance your senses with the right technology and designs.

What evidence from your analysis supports your claim?

Students should cite evidence from their analyses to support their claims.

Discuss your reasoning with a partner.

5

Analyze Your Results

 Constructing Explanations and Designing Solutions

Have students present their design to the rest of the class and explain its purpose and how and why it will work. Have them identify any new problems that need to be solved.

DCI ETS1.C Optimizing the Design Solution

Review with students what it means to make a claim. Guide them to understand that they will use the evidence from their tests to support their claim.

Claims, Evidence, and Reasoning

Students should claim that devices can be designed to improve a sense.

Ask: What claim can you make? **Possible answer: Your sense of sight at night can be improved by eyeglasses that have reflecting lights.**

How does your evidence support your claim? **My/Our evidence supports this because we compared different solutions to the problem.**

Encourage students to discuss their reasoning.

Scoring Rubric for Hands-On Activity	
3	States a claim supported with ample, detailed evidence that their device will meet the criteria and address the constraints of enhancing a sense.
2	States a claim that is somewhat supported with evidence that their device will enhance a sense.
1	States a claim that is not supported by evidence.
0	Does not state a claim.

Unit 1 Engineering and Technology 3L

LESSON 1
How Do Engineers Define Problems?

Building to the Performance Expectation

The learning experiences in this lesson prepare students for mastery of:
3-5-ETS1-1 Define a simple design problem reflecting a need or a want that includes specified criteria for success and constraints on materials, time, or cost.

Trace Tool to the NGSS
Go online to view the complete coverage of these standards across this lesson, unit, and time.

Science & Engineering Practices

Disciplinary Core Ideas

Crosscutting Concepts

Asking Questions and Defining Problems
Define a simple design problem that can be solved through the development of an object, tool, process, or system and includes several criteria for success and constraints on materials, time, or cost.

▶ VIDEO Science and Engineering Practice: Asking Questions and Defining Problems

ETS1.A Defining and Delimiting Engineering Problems
Possible solutions to a problem are limited by available materials and resources (constraints). The success of a designed solution is determined by considering the desired features of a solution (criteria). Different proposals for solutions can be compared on the basis of how well each one meets the specified criteria for success or how well each takes the constraints into account.

Influence of Science, Engineering, and Technology on Society and the Natural World
People's needs and wants change over time, as do their demands for new and improved technologies. (3-5-ETS1-1)

CONNECTIONS TO MATH

MP.2 Reason abstractly and quantitatively
MP.4 Model with mathematics
MP.5 Use appropriate tools strategically

CONNECTIONS TO ENGLISH LANGUAGE ARTS

W.5.7 Conduct short research projects that use several sources to build knowledge through investigation of different aspects of a topic.

W.5.8 Recall relevant information from experiences or gather relevant information from print and digital sources; summarize or paraphrase information in notes and finished work, and provide a list of sources.

W.5.9 Draw evidence from literary or informational texts to support analysis, reflection, and research.

Supporting All Students, All Standards

Integrating the Three Dimensions of Learning

In this lesson, students will learn about introductory concepts related to engineering and technology. They will explore engineering problems **(DCI ETS1.A)**, and use the information to learn how to develop solutions based on criteria and constraints. **(SEP Asking Questions and Defining Problems)**. By investigating problems and solutions, students will gain a deeper understanding of how engineering and technology impacts society and people on a daily basis **(CCCs Influence of Engineering, Technology, and Science on Society and the Natural World)**.

Professional Development Go online to view **Professional Development videos** with strategies to integrate CCCs and SEPs, including the ones used in this lesson.

Extra Hands-On Activity: Build a Better Bookshelf

Can You Build a Better Bookshelf?

👥 Small groups
🕐 30–40 minutes for two days

Have students find an area in the classroom where a bookshelf already is or where one could be placed. They should then design a new bookshelf or brainstorm ways to improve the existing bookshelf, such as redesigning it or making it easier to reach.

Students can draw their designs, listing the constraints and criteria of their designs. Additionally, you may wish to have them create models or full-size bookshelves if time allows. Each group should then assess the design of at least one other group, comparing what they see as the criteria and constraints of that bookshelf to help the designers of it improve on the design. If time allows, groups should do one more redesign based on the feedback they have received.

 SEP This activity can support mastery of this Science and Engineering Practice: Asking Questions and Defining Problems

Preassessment

Have students complete the unit pre-test online or see the Assessment Guide.

Build on Prior Knowledge

Students should already know and be prepared to build on the following concepts:
- Engineering is a field of study that uses math, science, and other areas of knowledge to design and build things.
- Criteria and constraints are used in the engineering design process to define a problem prior to creating a solution.

Differentiate Instruction

Lesson Vocabulary
- criteria
- engineering

Students may be more familiar with the everyday use of *problem*.

Ask: What does it mean when you have a problem? I need help. Something is wrong.

Connect students' answers to the use of problems in science, technology, and engineering. Give students an example of an engineering problem.

RTI/Extra Support

Give students a series of scenarios that involve problems. For each scenario . . .

Ask: What is the problem? Answers will vary.

Ask: What is the opposite of a problem? a solution

LESSON 1   **Engage** • Explore/Explain • Elaborate • Evaluate

ENGAGE: Lesson Phenomenon

Lesson Objective
To define a design problem and identify the constraints and criteria for a design solution.

About This Image
Animals in the wild, such as rabbits, need to find or hunt for their own food. Some animals use tools or strategies for gathering and hunting.

Animals rely on sight and sound to survive in the wild. If an animal is missing its sight or hearing, this is a problem that may prevent the animal from finding food.

Each animal has its own unique ability to survive in the wild. Plants, such as the grasses seen in the image, can be a source of food for certain species.

 **Asking Questions and Defining Problems**

Alternative Engage Strategy

How Do You Eat? | 👥 Small groups
                     | ⏱ 15 minutes

Ask students where they get their food (grocery store). Then place students into small groups and ask teams to come up with a list of technologies that make it possible for food to be provided in grocery stores. Ask a volunteer from each group to share results and discuss them as a whole class.

LESSON 1

How Do Engineers Define Problems?

Animals that live in the wild have to catch their own food if they want to eat. A hunter often can hear the prey. The prey often can hear the hunter coming. Think about the ways in which these animals hear the world around them.

By the end of this lesson . . .
you'll be able to define a design problem and identify the constraints and criteria for a design solution.

Unit 1 Engineering and Technology

Can You Solve It?

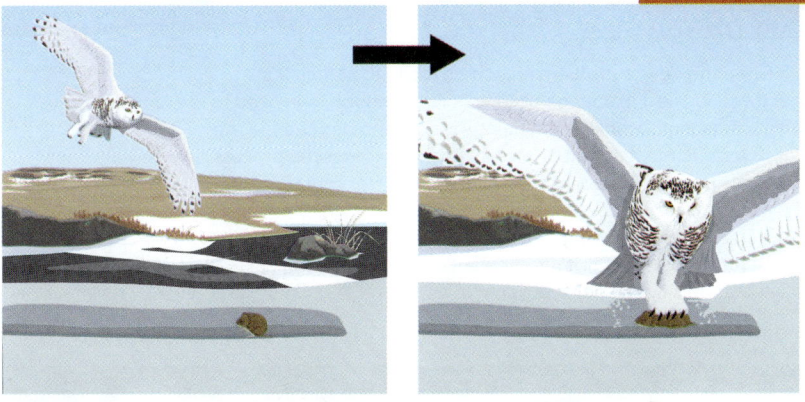

What sounds do you think the vole make that the owl could hear? What helps the animals on these two pages find food and protect themselves from being eaten?

1. Think of the sounds living things including birds make. Imagine that your class is going on a nature hike to observe and identify these sounds. As part of your nature hike, you need to design a lightweight hearing-enhancing device that you can wear. It can't use batteries. How would you define this problem?

Students should respond based on the text details and preliminary ideas based on the images.
_____
_____
_____
_____
_____
_____

 EVIDENCE NOTEBOOK Look for this icon to help you gather evidence to answer the questions above.

Can You Solve It?

Students are asked to record their observations of the vole and owl from the images. They must think of a solution to the problem of "noise." To do so, students must understand what batteries are and what kinds of alternatives there are to using them. Urge students not to worry about whether their answers are correct. They should expect their ideas to change as they progress through the Explorations. They will have an opportunity to revise their answers when they revisit these questions at the end of the lesson.

Collaboration

Build on Prior Knowledge Students who have never been on a nature hike, or who do not know much about wild animals, may have a difficult time participating in this Engage activity. You may wish to discuss the images as a whole class first, and then give students a chance to record their responses individually.

EVIDENCE NOTEBOOK

Encourage students to use an appropriate graphic organizer, such as main idea and supporting details, to set up their notebook for this lesson.

Find more strategies in the online ELA handbook.

LESSON 1   Engage • **Explore/Explain** • Elaborate • Evaluate

EXPLORATION 1 What Is Technology?

3D Learning Objective

Learn how to identify an engineering problem by **asking questions** about **possible solutions based on constraints and criteria**. Use the collected data to analyze lists of needs and wants according to **society and the natural world.**

 Asking Questions and Defining Problems

Students must think about the types of materials needed to construct a paper airplane.

Ask: What is the need or want when building a paper airplane?
to make it fly

Ask: What kinds of problems might you run into when trying to build a paper airplane? not enough materials; not knowing how to put it together; the airplane doesn't fly

---

Differentiate Instruction

RTI/Extra Support Make sure students understand the contents of the image as they will need to understand the technology shown to determine how engineers played a role in meeting the want or need. Some students may not recognize the microwave oven mounted over the stove.

Unit 1 Engineering and Technology

EXPLORATION 1

What Is Technology?

What Do You See?

The hearing device problem may seem too hard at first. It's easier if you tackle it in an organized way. First, though, you need to learn a little about techology. Techology is how humans change the natural world to meet a want or a need. **Engineering** is the process of designing new or improved technology. Engineers are the people who do engineering.

The first part of designing a solution is describing what the solution must do. How will it meet a want or need? Examining familiar technology can help you learn to do that.

Kitchen Tech

2. Think about how each technology you see meets a want or need. How did engineers play a role in the technology shown in the picture?

6

> **Explore Online** Review the digital resource for additional source content.

HANDS-ON Apply What You Know
Engineered?

3. In the first column, write the name of five non-living things you see in your classroom that are engineered. In the other column, write the name of five non-living things you see in your classroom that are not engineered. Turn to a partner, and justify your choices for each column.

Engineered	Not engineered
Students should cite familiar examples such as a desk, a door, a pencil, a clock, and a backpack as non-living things that were engineered.	Non-living things that are not engineered are harder to identify. Examples might include rocks, clouds, and water.

Match the engineering contributions with the technology in the picture.
a. Designed tools to melt and form glass. Made a process to cut glass and assemble a frame.
b. Designed tools to cut, fold, and glue sheets of cardboard into containers.
c. Designed electric circuits, mechanical parts, and an easy-to-use control panel.

4. Look at the kitchen scene again, and identify three more examples of technology and the problems they solve. How do you know that these are examples of technology?

Possible answer: The paper towel holder, keeps roll in one place; the stove, cooks food; and the sink faucet, controls water flow. They are examples of technology because they satisfy a want or need.
_____
_____
_____
_____
_____
_____

7

HANDS-ON Apply What You Know
Engineered?
Students work on this activity independently, but you might wish to let students wander around the classroom to inspect objects that have been engineered. Give students a few minutes to do this, and then have them return to their seats to complete the list.

Influence of Engineering, Technology, and Science on Society and the Natural World
Emphasize the concept of how engineering and technology are based on the needs and wants of people in society. In addition, explain how engineering and technology also shape the way society works. You might explain that the invention of the dishwasher was based on a need or want, but it also changed the way people wash dishes in certain parts of the world.

Ask: What was the need or want for inventing the refrigerator? To keep food cold and safe to eat.
Ask: Why is it important to keep food cold? Food lasts longer that way.
Ask: How has that shaped society? People can keep more food in their homes and it stays fresher longer.

Connection to English Language Arts
Students use information from the print images of the kitchen technology to respond to the prompt.
W.5.8 Recall relevant information from experiences or gather relevant information from print and digital sources; summarize or paraphrase information in notes and finished work, and provide a list of sources.

LESSON 1   Engage • **Explore/Explain** • Elaborate • Evaluate

EXPLORATION 1   What Is Technology?, continued

 ETS1.A Defining and Delimiting Engineering Problems

Emphasize for students the importance of finding problems and coming up with workable solutions in engineering. Make sure students grasp the concept of criteria. Provide more relatable examples of criteria if necessary.

Ask: Why is it important for engineers to understand the criteria for their designs? **so they know what the design is supposed to do**

EVIDENCE NOTEBOOK

Students may need assistance with the concept of criteria. If necessary, turn this Evidence Notebook activity into a whole-class activity and make a class list of the criteria for hearing enhancers. Then give students time to record the information in their notebook.

FORMATIVE ASSESSMENT

 Language SmArts
Cite Evidence for Criteria
W.5.9 Draw evidence from texts

Defining a Problem This activity is an opportunity for students to observe everyday objects and apply engineering practices to them to better understand the process of defining problems and coming up with criteria for solutions or improvements. If students are stuck, ask how they would know that a solution works well (desirable features, criteria).

What Is the Problem?

View the image of the kitchen again. After you have thought about the specific parts of technology in the kitchen, pick three items in the kitchen that you think best meet a want or need.

5. Write the name of each item in the left-hand column. Write out the need or want that is met by the item in the right-hand column.

Technology item	Need or want met
1. Students should identify how their chosen technologies are useful.	
2.	
3.	

You have learned that when a need or want is met, engineers have worked to meet the criteria. **Criteria** are desirable features of the solution. For example, you want rags can soak up liquids. Paper towels were an improvement on rags. Paper towels meet a new criterion—they are made to be thrown away. They still soak up liquids.

A paper towel is designed to be absorbent and strong so it can soak up liquids without ripping.

 EVIDENCE NOTEBOOK   What are the criteria for your hearing enhancer?

 Language SmArts
Cite Evidence for Criteria

6. Pick an everyday object, such as a backpack or lunchbox, that you would like to improve. Give the criteria for a successful improvement.

Possible answer: My backpack needs improving. It needs to hold a water bottle. The criterion is "hold at least one water bottle," so the solution could be a small pocket on the side of the backpack or a hook-on bottle.

Tip
The English Language Arts Handbook can provide help with understanding how to cite evidence to explain your ideas.

Unit 1   Engineering and Technology

HANDS-ON ACTIVITY

Menu Planning

Objective
Collaborate Engineering solutions can be a plan or process, too. Suppose that you need to plan three main dishes for dinner on three different nights, nine meals all together. Each night, you must analyze your meal options in order to meet a constraint. A **constraint** is a limit on possible solutions. On the first night, you have a constraint that the budget is $35.00.

For each night, choose a main dish from the recipe cards. The constraints for each set of meals are listed in the steps below. Your goal is a set of three main dishes that meet all the constraints.

When you are faced with a problem or situation that needs a solution, how can thinking carefully about the criteria and constraints help you develop one?

Possible answer: They make you focus on the wants and needs that are most important and identify resource limits.

Materials
- recipe cards

Procedure
STEP 1 Think of what you would consider a good meal. It may be that the meal is healthy for you, contains well-balanced ingredients, or looks and smells tasty. Write down three criteria for what makes a good meal.

Criteria

1.	*Possible answer: It's easy to make. It's tasty. It's not expensive.*
2.	
3.	

9

HANDS-ON ACTIVITY Pairs 1 class period
Menu Planning

3D Learning Objective

SEP **Asking Questions and Defining Problems**

Students ask questions and define problems related to food to plan menus. They will analyze constraints to come up with criteria.

Materials
The materials listed in the student edition are a starting point. Other suggested materials: writing utensils, magazine pictures, or other images of foods/meals to inspire students.

Preparation
Have recipe cards and any additional materials ready for students to use with their partners.

DCI **ETS1.A Defining and Delimiting Engineering Problems**

Constraints are limitations, but they are similar to problems. They require students to consider them, and then work around them to satisfy criteria. Explain to students that engineers and those who design and build technology often have many constraints that limit possible solutions.

Ask: What kinds of constraints do you think engineers must work with? *tools, resources, money, people, rules/laws, standards/regulations*

Ask: How do you think engineers are able to manage all of those constraints to design or build things? *They have to make checklists and make sure all of the constraints are considered.*

STEP 1 Check that students have a proper understanding of food that is healthful. Keep in mind that students of all ethnicities and cultures may have their own unique understanding of what healthy or well balanced"meals are, as they may be used to eating certain kinds of foods that are traditional in their culture.

Lesson 1 How Do Engineers Define Problems? 9

LESSON 1 Engage • **Explore/Explain** • Elaborate • Evaluate

EXPLORATION 1 HANDS-ON ACTIVITY, *continued*

CCC **Influence of Engineering, Technology, and Science on Society and the Natural World**

Have students pause for a moment to think about the food industry and the kinds of engineering and technology that goes into it. Tell students that technology is not the only thing that can be engineered: food can be engineered, too!

Ask: What do you think it means for food to be engineered? **It means it was grown, mixed, or made in a special way.**

Explain that engineers and scientists can grow food in a special way. They do that by making a controlled environment for the food.

> ## Differentiate Instruction
>
> **ELL: Support** Students whose primary language is not English may find it challenging to translate foods from their culture to words that describe the similar foods in English. Provide additional support by using pictures, if necessary, to help students make sure they are thinking correctly about the types of foods they want to make as part of the Hands-On Activity.

STEP 2 Circulate the room and make sure students fill out all boxes in the table and come up with the correct total cost. If the total cost exceeds $35.00, prompt students to reconsider the meals.

STEP 3 Help students connect the criteria to real-world scenarios, such as managing a restaurant.

Ask: What kinds of criteria do chefs have when preparing meals for patrons? **How much the food costs; how much food to serve; what is healthy; what is tasty**

Ask: What do you think happens if a customer at a restaurant has an allergy to a certain food, such as pasta?

Ask: What can a chef do to work around that constraint or that problem? **The chef can give the customer something else instead.**

STEP 2 Plan out the first set of meals. Choose from the list of recipe cards that meet the constraint of a budget of $35.00. Enter the recipes and costs in the table below. Don't forget to check your math.

	Recipe card	Cost
Meal 1	Student choices for the combined cost of three meals should not exceed $35.	
Meal 2		
Meal 3		
Total cost		

STEP 3 Now apply the three criteria you picked to the three meals you have put together. Evaluate the quality of the meals using the three criteria. Enter your evaluation below.

Possible answer: They are not easy to make, but they are tasty and inexpensive.

STEP 4 Now plan out a second set of meals for the next three nights, choosing from all 12 recipe cards. For this set of meals, your constraints are that you have a budget of $35.00 and a total of 100 minutes to prepare all three meals. The meals must be prepared one at a time. Enter the recipes, costs, and times in the table below.

	Recipe card	Cost	Prep time
Meal 1	Student choices for the combined prep time of meals should not exceed 100 minutes.		
Meal 2			
Meal 3			
Total cost			
Time to prepare all three meals			

STEP 5 Now apply the three criteria you picked before to the three meals you have put together. Evaluate the quality of the meals using the three criteria. Write your evaluation below.

Possible answer: They are easy to make and tasty but they are more expensive than the first set.

STEP 6 Last, plan out a third set of meals for the last three nights using all 12 recipe cards. Your constraints for this meal are that you have a budget of $35.00, you have a total of 100 minutes to prepare all three meals, and some of your guests are vegetarians. Enter your recipes and the constraints below.

	Recipe card	Cost	Prep time	Vegetarian option
Meal 1	Menu must include vegetarian options to meet the constraint.			
Meal 2				
Meal 3				
Total Cost				
Time to prepare all three meals				
Number of meal options for vegetarian guests				

STEP 7 Now apply the three criteria you picked before to the three meals you have put together. Evaluate the quality of the meals using the three criteria. Enter your evaluation below.

Possible answer: They are not as easy to make and not as tasty, and they are more expensive than the other nights.

Explore Online Review the digital resource for additional source content.

ETS1.A Defining and Delimiting Engineering Problems

Explain to students that people in any industry face problems that they need to find solutions for. Remind students of the example of the chef. The chef may run into a problem if a customer is allergic to a type of food that comes with a meal. The chef can find a solution by offering the customer a substitute food. Engineers need to work around problems in a similar way, but instead of dealing with food allergies, they are usually dealing with technology.

Asking Questions and Defining Problems

Prompt students to evaluate their meals using the following questions:

Did they meet all of the criteria?

Are there still any constraints?

What problems remain?

Influence of Engineering, Technology, and Science on Society and the Natural World

STEP 7 After students complete their responses to step 7, ask them to describe if they are satisfied with the end result of their dishes; why, or why not? Then relate students' responses to engineering and technology.

Ask: What do you think happens when engineers are not fully satisfied with the technology they design? Sometimes they can't change it if they had to build it a certain way. They may try to improve the next time.

Conclude by explaining to students that sometimes engineers, just like chefs, can only do the best with the constraints they must meet and the criteria they work toward.

LESSON 1 Engage • **Explore/Explain** • Elaborate • Evaluate

EXPLORATION 1 HANDS-ON ACTIVITY, continued

Analyze Your Results

STEP 8 Circulate the room and help students come up with different plans if they get stuck.

Draw Conclusions

Invite students to work in pairs for this part of the activity. Students can share their responses with a partner based on two things they would use to guide the other student during the activity.

> ### Claims, Evidence, and Reasoning
> Have students work with a partner to critique each other's meal plans. Ask each pair to be prepared to share one way that they changed their constraints and how it changed the recipe selection.

Scoring Rubric for Hands-On Activity	
3	Completes the activity fulfilling all constraints and meeting all criteria.
2	Completes the activity fulfilling most constraints and meeting most criteria.
1	Completes the activity fulfilling some constraints and meeting some criteria.
0	Fails to complete any constraints or criteria.

Analyze Your Results

STEP 8 Which constraint was easiest to plan around? Which constraint was hardest? In both cases, tell how you might have planned differently. Enter your answers in the table below.

Best	Possible answer: The easiest was the cost constraint. It would be easy to substitute another dish. The hardest was the vegetarian constraint, plus
Worst	the constraints on time and money. It was hard to find recipes that were tasty. I would have eaten the same inexpensive thing every night.

Draw Conclusions

STEP 9 What was the goal of the activity? How did your solution help achieve that goal?
Possible answer: The goal was to make choices that meet criteria and constraints. My solutions were different based on the different criteria and constraints.

STEP 10 Say that another student wants to complete this activity for the first time. What are two things you would tell this student to guide him or her during the activity?
Possible answer: Pay attention to the costs and the prep time. You can't just choose the recipes you like.

STEP 11 Change one of your criteria. How would this change your recipe selections?
Possible answer: Change the criterion for tastiness to simple ingredients. Then we wouldn't choose recipes that are expensive and take a lot of time.

Recipe Cards

1 Chicken and Spinach with Penne Pasta
Cost: $15 **Prep Time:** 30 minutes
Ingredients:
• boneless chicken • butter
• spinach • olive oil
• penne pasta

2 Cheeseburgers with French Fries
Cost: $11 **Prep Time:** 40 minutes
Ingredients:
• American sliced cheese • ground beef
• buns • french fries

3 Chicken Noodle Soup with a Grilled Cheese Sandwich

Cost: $13   **Prep Time:** 25 minutes
Ingredients:
- canned chicken noodle soup
- sandwich bread
- sliced cheese
- butter

4 Shrimp with Rice, Tomatoes, and Olives

Cost: $17   **Prep Time:** 35 minutes
Ingredients:
- large Gulf shrimp
- wild rice
- cherry tomatoes
- black and green olives

5 Steak with Mixed Vegetables

Cost: $15   **Prep Time:** 30 minutes
Ingredients:
- 8 oz. sirloin steak
- mixed vegetables

6 Chicken with Broccoli

Cost: $14   **Prep Time:** 30 minutes
Ingredients:
- 8 oz. chicken breast
- broccoli

7 Salmon and Rice

Cost: $17   **Prep Time:** 40 minutes
Ingredients:
- 8 oz. salmon
- brown rice
- olive oil, basil

8 Tomato Soup with Grilled Cheese (Vegetarian Option)

Cost: $10   **Prep Time:** 25 minutes
Ingredients:
- canned tomato and basil soup
- sliced sandwich bread
- sliced cheese, butter

9 Vegetable Pizza (Vegetarian Option)

Cost: $14   **Prep Time:** 35 minutes
Ingredients:
- pizza dough
- olive oil
- squash
- goat cheese
- tomato sauce
- green onions
- red peppers

10 Tofu Cheeseburgers with French Fries (Vegetarian Option)

Cost: $13   **Prep Time:** 40 minutes
Ingredients:
- tofu mix
- buns
- sliced cheese
- french fries

11 Beans and Cheese Quesadillas (Vegetarian Option)

Cost: $12   **Prep Time:** 25 minutes
Ingredients:
- black or pinto beans
- shredded cheese
- small tortillas

12 Spaghetti and Marinara Sauce (Vegetarian Option)

Cost: $13   **Prep Time:** 25 minutes
Ingredients:
- marinara sauce
- spaghetti pasta

Differentiate Instruction

Extension This activity can be extended by having students research the food values such as calories, fat content, protein, carbohydrate, and vitamins found in each recipe. They can then determine the criteria of the meals based on meeting nutritional values. Additionally, students can determine what type of constraints would apply to the activity.

LESSON 1   Engage • **Explore/Explain** • Elaborate • Evaluate

EXPLORATION 2 Real-World Limits

3D Learning Objective

Develop a deeper understanding of how to identify **constraints.** Learn how to **ask questions** to identify constraints, which is how engineering problems are **defined and delimited.** Through the use of a bicycle as an example, see how **engineering and technology influences society,** such as transportation.

DCI ETS1.A Defining and Delimiting Engineering Problems

Help students see and define the types of problems that could occur with the bicycle. To get this activity started, **ask:** What are some problems you've had or heard about for bikes? *tire got flat, pedal came loose, brake didn't work*

Tell students that engineers have to dig deeper when it comes to looking at problems, because they need to understand the cause of the problem. For instance, if a pedal became loose, engineers might ask, "Why did the pedal come loose? What caused it?" Then they would study the bike and break it down to figure out the true reason.

Connection to Math

Draw students' attention to the bicycle and prompt them to think about some of the features of a bike using abstract math. For instance, the price of all the parts of the bike may add up to be expensive. Therefore, cost of materials can be a constraint of building your own bike.

MP.2 Reason abstractly and quantitatively

EXPLORATION 2

Real-World Limits

Limited Limits

Part of defining engineering problems is identifying the constraints. A constraint is a limit on possible solutions. Examples of constraints include money, time, and materials. Some safety constraints are by law.

Bike Tech

7. Match the safety constraints described to the bike parts.

14

---

14 Unit 1 Engineering and Technology

Explore Online — Have students explore more about bike parts online.

HANDS-ON Apply What You Know
Paper Building 10 • 10 • 10

8. You have 10 index cards and 10 cm of tape. In 10 minutes, work as a team to build the tallest stucture you can. It should support at least one book. In the space below, list the constraints and tell which was the hardest to meet and why.

   Possible answer: The constraints were 10 minutes time, 10 cards, and 10 cm of tape. It was hardest to have a solution within the time limit.

a. It helps control speed. Safety regulations say that a 68 kg (150 lb.) bicycle rider moving at 24 km/hr (15 mph) must be able to use them to stop within 4.5 m (15 ft).

b. It undergoes great force as you pedal. Grit from the road causes wear, and water rusts it. Safety regulations say it must withstand a pull of 818 kg (1800 pounds) before breaking.

c. This part supports your weight while you ride. Its height is adjustable. Safety regulation say it must support a weight of 68 kg (150 lb.) without moving down.

9. Describe another possible constraint for bicycle. Look back at the bicycle image for different ideas. Enter your answer below.

   Possible answer: The handlebar tightness is a possible safety constraint. The handlebars must not turn while the front wheel is held steady.

15

HANDS-ON Apply What You Know
Paper Building 10 • 10 • 10

Students work on this activity in small groups. Students should report that there was a limit to how tall they could construct a building made of cards that could support the weight of a book.

Scoring Guidelines

Students should construct the model and be able to identify the constraints.

Collaboration

Partners Have students get into pairs to come up with other possible constraints for the design of a bicycle. You may wish to pass out other images of bicycles (such as close ups of the pedals or chains) to help prompt student responses.

SEP Asking Questions and Defining Problems

Help students think about the types of questions to ask for defining problems, such as "How does this part work?" or "How could this part easily break?" or "What could make this part work better?"

DCI ETS1.A Defining and Delimiting Engineering Problems

Help students relate the process of asking questions and defining problems to engineering.

Ask: How do engineers use information about problems? to decide what to make to satisfy needs or wants while staying within the limits of constraints

Lesson 1 How Do Engineers Define Problems?   15

LESSON 1   Engage • Explore/Explain • Elaborate • Evaluate

EXPLORATION 2 Real-World Limits, continued

 Influence of Engineering, Technology, and Science on Society and the Natural World

Help students connect the concept of improvements with engineering and technology. Talk about how improvements benefit society or the natural world. Ask students to give examples beyond the text of the student edition.

Connection to Earth Science

Engineers apply the same principles of criteria and constraints when designing tools and technologies that address natural hazards. Although people cannot control natural events, such as hurricanes, earthquakes, or volcanic eruptions, engineers and scientists can work together to come up with designs for technologies that will help keep people safer.

ESS3.B Natural Hazards

EVIDENCE NOTEBOOK

Students should be able to identify at least one constraint now. Make sure students have a proper understanding of constraints.

FORMATIVE ASSESSMENT

Give students an opportunity to go back through their print and digital sources to find information that will help them describe a classroom object that could be improved.

Ask: What are some criteria for improving the object?

Ask: What are likely constraints on possible solutions (improvements)?

Improvements

Engineers improve solutions all the time. A new solution may not work for everyone, though. Some people may have constraints, such as money or available space, on the solutions they can decide to buy or use.

laundry basket

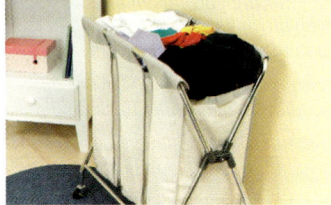
three-bin laundry basket

10. Look at the laundry baskets. How is the three-bin basket an improvement? What constraints might a buyer have that would keep them from using the improved solution?

Possible answer: The three-bin hamper allows you to sort dirty laundry one by one as you put it in. A buyer might not have room for the larger three-bin system or it might cost too much.

 EVIDENCE NOTEBOOK Think back to your hearing enhancer. What constraints are there on your solution?

11. Remember, criteria are features of a desirable solution, while constraints are limits that must be met in order to be acceptable. In the following lists of criteria and constraints, draw a star next to each constraint.

A new pair of shoes	A homework assignment
comfortable	neatly written
resists water	shows originality
attractive	completed by tomorrow's class ★
costs less than $35 ★	good grammar

16

16 Unit 1 Engineering and Technology

LESSON 1 Engage • Explore/Explain • **Elaborate** • Evaluate

TAKE IT FURTHER

 **Explore Online** — Students can explore all three Take It Further paths online

TAKE IT FURTHER
Discover More

Check out this path . . . or go online to choose one of these other paths.

People in Science → • Writing within Constraints • Limits in Nature

Improving Hearing

Marion Downs was an audiologist, a doctor specializing in hearing. She helped many thousands of children to speak and hear better by noticing and solving a problem.

Infants born with hearing problems can't hear their own voice or the voices of others. So, they can't develop language skills. Infants can't talk at first, anyway. So, before the 1960s, it took two or three years to notice an infant's hearing problem.

Dr. Downs engineered a hearing test that didn't require infants to talk. Instead, a doctor watched them respond to sounds, such as a rattles. A second part of the solution was to change what doctors do nationwide. Now, doctors screen all six-month-old infants to see if they might need hearing aids.

One type of hearing aid infants receive is a cochlear implant. This hearing aid is implanted under the skin behind the ear. It converts sounds to electrical signals that are sent to the inner ear.

Although Dr. Downs was not an engineer, she engineered a solution to a serious gap in our nation's health system.

Marion Downs, audiologist

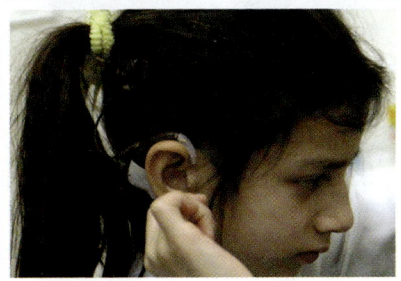
Cochlear implant

Collaboration

Pathways You may choose to assign this activity or to direct students online to the Interactive Worktext where they can explore and choose from all three paths. These activities can be assigned individually, to pairs, or to small groups.

People in Science

Students will learn about Marion Downs, an audiologist who had an important impact on hearing enhancement. Emphasize for students that this is an example of a scientist who identified a problem that children had and came up with a solution.

ETS1.A Defining and Delimiting Engineering Problems
W.5.8 Recall relevant information from experiences or gather relevant information from print and digital sources

DCI ETS1.A Defining and Delimiting Engineering Problems

Marion Downs defined a problem and came up with a solution that helps children hear better.

CCC Influence of Engineering, Technology, and Science on Society and the Natural World

The problem and solution focus by Marion Downs improved the quality of life of young students. Help students make the connection that this is an example of how technology and science had a positive impact on society.

LESSON 1 Engage • Explore/Explain • **Elaborate** • Evaluate

TAKE IT FURTHER, continued

SEP Asking Questions and Defining Problems

In order for people to design new medical tools, they must ask and answer a series of questions, such as "What do people need?" or "What would help them?" More specific questions are then asked to identify details, and problems are defined. In the case of hearing and noise, scientists probably started with a question such as "What causes hearing loss?" Noise is one of those answers. Then, scientists may have asked, "How can we block or reduce noise?" From there, the development of the ear plug may have come to light. Now, ear plugs are a small and convenient means of blocking or limiting sound. They are also effective. In this example, scientists were able to define a problem and solve it by asking a series of questions that led them to a design solution.

▶ Explore Online

Students can explore these additional topics online

Writing Within Constraints
Students participate in a writing activity that has constraints that they must fulfill. *(No outside research required.)*

Limits in Nature
Student groups carry out research about the types of technologies and tools that are available to address limits in nature. They can explore existing tools/technologies, or come up with their own ideas for them based on the needs and wants. *(Outside research required.)*

Protecting Hearing

Noise is a major cause of hearing loss later in life. The loss can be temporary after being exposed to a loud noise, such as a firecracker. It might take a day or more to recover. A person can have permanent hearing loss if he or she is exposed to loud noises for long periods of time. Loud music, jet engine noise, and gunfire can cause permanent hearing loss.

Musicians, construction workers, or others who have jobs in loud noise environments can protect their sense of hearing from permanent damage. Devices like over-the-ear hearing protectors block loud noises from damaging the sense of hearing.

Dense foam ear plugs also protect the ear from loud noises. They are flexible and fit snugly in the ear canal.

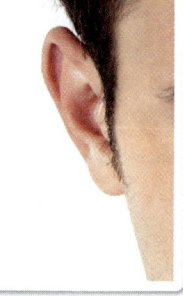
Dense foam ear plugs

Over-ear hearing protectors

12. What are some criteria for hearing aids? for hearing protectors? What are some constraints?

Possible answer: Hearing aid criteria: lightweight, comfortable, clear sound. Hearing protector criteria: lowers sound volume, comfortable. Constraints for both—nontoxic, safe to use

13. Research how people have their hearing tested. Summarize what you find below. Include an idea that you want to explore more. Be prepared to share your findings.

Students should identify differences between hearing checks for children and those for adults.

18

18 Unit 1 Engineering and Technology

LESSON 1
Engage • Explore/Explain • Elaborate • **Evaluate**

LESSON CHECK

 **Explore Online** — Students can revisit the lesson phenomenon online.

LESSON 1
Lesson Check

Name _____

Can You Solve It?

1. In the next lesson you will develop a device to enhance your ability to hear sounds in the wild.
   - What does your hearing enhancer need to do? What are the limits on its design?
   - Make sure to use the words *criteria* and *constraints*.

EVIDENCE NOTEBOOK Use the information you've collected in your Evidence Notebook to help you cover each point above.

Possible answer:
- Criteria—Enhances hearing and is comfortable to wear, lightweight, and durable.
- Constraints—Uses only materials provided by my teacher, costs less than a certain amount, must be finished in a week or less.

Checkpoints
Answer the questions that follow about how engineers define problems.

2. Choose all the statements that are correct.
   - **a. Solutions meet a want or need.**
   - b. Solutions are separate from engineering.
   - **c. Solutions are the technology all around us.**
   - **d. Solutions come in different forms because they help solve problems.**
   - e. Solutions must be complicated in order to work.

19

Formal Assessment Go online for student self-checks and other assessments.

Can You Solve It?

> **Collaboration**
> **Discussion** You may wish to revisit the information covered in Explorations 1 and 2 to ensure student understanding of the material. Use bulleted points in the student edition to lead the discussion.

EVIDENCE NOTEBOOK
Have students reread their answers to the Evidence Notebook prompts, and then use this evidence to justify their reasoning as they respond to the Can You Solve It question. Make sure students understand that a complete response must address all bulleted points.

DCI ETS1.A Defining and Delimiting Engineering Problems
Draw students' attention back to the image of the owl and the vole. Now that students are more familiar with the terms *constraint* and *criteria*, have them think about the scenario in the image using these concepts.

Ask: What are some of the constraints on the vole? **size, can't fly**

SUMMATIVE ASSESSMENT
Analyze Problem-Defining Processes
2. To correctly answer the question, students must have a clear understanding of the **Crosscutting Concept Influence of Engineering, Technology, and Science on Society and the Natural World**. Make sure to review this concept with students if necessary

Lesson 1 How Do Engineers Define Problems? 19

LESSON 1 Engage • Explore/Explain • Elaborate • **Evaluate**

LESSON CHECK, continued

3. This question asks students to focus on the concept of criteria. Students should be able to answer this question by referring back to the paper airplane and bicycle.

4. Students will be able to answer this question if they are familiar with lunchboxes. Students may be more familiar with bagged lunches or school-supplied lunches. Assess the students in the classroom to make sure this question is accessible to all students. If some students struggle, help them by providing other examples if you can.

5. In Exploration 2, students have more practice with constraints. Have them recall their activity putting together the food menu. Students can correctly answer this question by thinking about constraints as limitations.

6. To help students answer this question, you may need to remind them that without these objects of technology, there may be problems. And engineers focus on problems to lead to—solutions!

Using Representations to Assess Proficiency

7. Explorations 1 and 2 focus on these terms and their meanings. Encourage students to refer back to the Exploration pages for a review.

8. Remind students that they have seen this image before. Earlier, they were evaluating the bicycle. Now, for this question, they are looking at the whole picture. Make sure students do not just focus on the bicycle or else they may not be able to answer the question correctly.

---

3. Which statement is true of solutions?
   a. Solutions do not meet a want or need.
   b. Solutions can be tested.
   c. Solutions are the limitations of a problem.
   d. Solutions are the technology of a problem.

4. Janet is trying to improve the design of her lunchbox. Choose all of following statements that are good criteria for her to keep in mind.
   a. The lunchbox can't be too heavy to hold for a long time.
   b. The lunchbox should have sharp corners and rough edges.
   c. The lunchbox could use a special pocket for water bottles.
   d. The lunchbox could keep food colder.

5. Identify all the likely constraints faced when designing and building a two-room treehouse.
   a. time   d. sunlight
   b. budget   **e. tree size**
   c. materials   **f. number of rooms**

6. Choose the correct word to complete the sentence.

   In a room full of objects, we can think of different technology objects as ___solutions___ because they help satisfy a want or need.

   | criteria |
   | solutions |
   | constraints |
   | problems |

7. Draw lines to match each word to its description.

engineering	desired features of a solution
constraints	identification of a want or need
criteria	using technology to design solutions to solve problems
problem	absolute limits on a solution

8. Write the name of the item from the picture that uses technology to fill each need or want.
   a. keep warm ___vest___
   b. protect the head ___helmet___
   c. improve vision ___glasses___
   d. adjust speed and force ___gears___

20

---

20 Unit 1 Engineering and Technology

LESSON 1
Lesson Roundup

A. Choose the best words from the word bank to complete the sentences.

| a specific weight | imitations | requirements |
| criteria | solutions | |

Good criteria tell __requirements__ an engineering solution should meet.

Constraints are the __limitations__ on an engineering solution.

B. Choose the best words from the word bank to complete the sentences.

| solutions | criteria | constraints | weather and day of the week |
| materials and budget | brand of bike and criteria | | |

Omar is going to try to improve his bicycle. He first looks to see what his limitations, or __constraints__, are. He knows that the biggest limit is how much money he can spend. He also must have the bike ready to ride in a race in two weeks. His constraints are __a budget and a time limit__.

C. Choose the best words from the word bank to complete the sentences.

| solutions | other materials | books | design |
| solution | requirements | limitations | criteria |

Engineering __solutions__ have different criteria and constraints.

These criteria describe __requirements__. The constraints describe the __limitations__ for the engineering solution.

Lesson Roundup

DCI ETS1.A Defining and Delimiting Engineering Problems

This lesson summary enables students to quickly revisit key points and prepare for tests.

A. To clarify students' understanding of the terms and phrases in the word bank, have them revisit Exploration 1. You may also remind students of how all of these terms work together. Let them know that not every term or phrase from the word bank will be used. Alternatively, write your own additional fill-in-the-blank sentences so that all the terms and phrases in the word bank are used to assess student knowledge. **ETS1.A**

B. Students may wish to scan the image of the bicycle from Exploration 2 to help them fill in the missing terms/phrases. For the first sentence, help students understand that the missing word or phrase is another way for saying "limitations." For the second sentence, help students understand that the missing word or phrase is asking for examples of constraints. **ETS1.A**

C. Students have spent a lot of time studying these terms in Explorations 1 and 2. If students need additional support, help them understand that the second sentence is asking for another term for the word "need." In the third sentence, have students think about what term describes "limitations." Students can easily refer back to B to see the inverse form of this sentence. **ETS1.A**

LESSON 2
How Do Engineers Design Solutions?

Building to the Performance Expectations

The learning experiences in this lesson prepare students for mastery of:

3-5-ETS1-2 Generate and compare multiple possible solutions to a problem based on how well each is likely to meet the criteria and constraints of the problem.

Trace Tool to the NGSS
Go online to view the complete coverage of these standards across this lesson, unit, and time.

 **Science & Engineering Practices**

 Disciplinary Core Ideas

 **Crosscutting Concepts**

Constructing Explanations and Designing Solutions
Generate and compare multiple solutions to a problem based on how well they meet the criteria and constraints of the design problem.

▶ **VIDEO** Constructing Scientific Explanations

ETS1.B Developing Possible Solutions
Research on a problem should be carried out before beginning to design a solution. Testing a solution involves investigating how well it performs under a range of likely conditions. At whatever stage, communicating with peers about proposed solutions is an important part of the design process, and shared ideas can lead to improved designs. (3-5-ETS1-2)

Influence of Engineering, Technology, and Science on Society and the Natural World
Engineers improve existing technologies or develop new ones to increase their benefits, decrease known risks, and meet societal demands.

 CONNECTIONS TO MATH

MP.2 Reason abstractly and quantitatively.
MP.4 Model with mathematics.
MP.5 Use appropriate tools strategically.
3-5.OA Operations and Algebraic Thinking

 CONNECTIONS TO ENGLISH LANGUAGE ARTS

RI.5.1 Quote accurately from a text when explaining what the text says explicitly and when drawing inferences from the text.

RI.5.7 Draw on information from multiple print or digital sources, demonstrating the ability to locate an answer to a question quickly or to solve a problem efficiently.

RI.5.9 Integrate information from several texts on the same topic in order to write or speak about the subject knowledgeably.

22A Unit 1 Engineering and Technology

Supporting All Students, All Standards

Integrating the Three Dimensions of Learning

In this lesson, students will explore the ways engineers come up with solutions to problems **(DCI ETS1.B)**. They will learn about how these solutions are then integrated into technology that has an important impact on society and the environment **(CCC Influence of Engineering, Technology, and Science on Society and the Natural World)**. They will participate in a variety of activities and use various print and digital sources to come up with explanations and design solutions of their own **(SEP Constructing Explanations and Designing Solutions)**, as well as learn about the processes that engineers go through, including using constraints and criteria.

 **Professional Development** — Go online to view **Professional Development videos** with strategies to integrate CCCs and SEPs, including the ones used in this lesson.

Extra Hands-On Activity: Defining Sound Constraints

What Kinds of Sounds Can Be Heard?

Small groups
30–45 minutes

Have students work in small groups to determine the limits of sound that can be heard, in terms of pitch, volume, and distance from the source. Since they will be exploring methods to augment hearing, they should account for constraints different types of sound will cause for their hearing aids.

Have them design a method of testing that qualifies as a fair test with standard sounds. They should perform tests to determine the sound levels that can be heard as the volume, pitch, and distance are modified.

At least two different members of a group should be tested to determine what they can and cannot hear.

Students should find that there are lower limits to the volume a sound can be and still be heard by humans. They should also observe that different people can hear different volumes, pitches, and distances.

 This activity can support mastery of this Crosscutting Concept: Systems and Models

Preassessment

Have students complete the unit pre-test online or see the Assessment Guide.

Build on Prior Knowledge

Students should already know and be prepared to build on the following concepts:
- Problems are what engineers want to solve for.
- Criteria are the desirable features of designs or solutions.
- Constraints are absolute limits on possible solutions.

Differentiate Instruction

Lesson Vocabulary
- fair test

Students will already be familiar with the everyday use of the words *fair* and *test*.

Ask: What is a test? a check of what works or what you know
Ask: What does it mean to be fair? not play favorites, be unbiased

Connect students' answers to the concept of how engineers make fair tests of solutions.

RTI/Extra Support
Demonstrate a fair test to find which toy car is fastest (same test conditions, same timer, test more than once).

Ask: What did we just do? made a fair test of speed
Ask: Why was it fair? same conditions for each car
Ask: Can you rely on the results? yes

Explain to students that there are many different kinds of tests. And that both scientists and engineers want to carry out fair tests so they can rely on the results.

Lesson 2 How Do Engineers Design Solutions? 22B

LESSON 2   **Engage** • Explore/Explain • Elaborate • Evaluate

ENGAGE: How Do Engineers Design Solutions?

Lesson Objective

Research and design possible solutions to a problem, and investigate how well your solution performs.

About This Image

The song a bird sings is a regular part of nature's soundtrack. While there is nothing wrong with the song itself, there are, however, problems that can be associated with trying to hear and/or record these songs clearly. Being able to hear the song clearly over ambient sounds and being able to record the song are two problems that engineers might be able to solve.

 Constructing Explanations and Designing Solutions

Alternative Engage Strategy

Problems in Nature	👥 Small groups ⏱ 10-15 min

Ask students to think of one potential problem that may be associated with observing or recording data about organisms in an outdoor, natural setting, such as a park, garden, or wetland. (Students should not use the example of a bird's song).

Then, ask students to think about how they could solve the problem. Have them explain their solution in a form of their choice, such as writing about an idea for a type of machine or technology or drawing a picture of it. Ask volunteers to share their proposed solutions with the class.

Think about the bird calls and other sounds you might hear on a nature walk. Observing and identifying those sounds can be a challenge.

By the end of this lesson . . .
you'll research and design possible solutions to a problem and investigate how well your solution performs.

Unit 1   Engineering and Technology

Can You Solve It?

Recall the nature hike scenario that you read about in the last lesson. You thought about the criteria and constraints for a hearing-enhancing device. This device would help you and others better hear the wildlife on your walk.

1. What might your hearing-enhancing device look like? Why? How will the constraints and criteria affect its appearance? Enter your answers below.

   Students should respond based on the preliminary
   observations they can make of the images.
   _____
   _____
   _____
   _____
   _____
   _____

   Tip
   For more information about what engineers do, review How Do Engineers Define Problems?

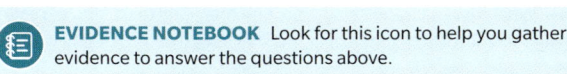 **EVIDENCE NOTEBOOK** Look for this icon to help you gather evidence to answer the questions above.

▶ **Explore Online** Students can view the lesson phenomenon online.

Can You Solve It?

Students are asked to study the image and come up with a description of a hearing-enhancing device. To do so, students must be sure to relate the hearing-enhancing device to the kinds of appropriate criteria and constraints they may need to work with. They should expect their answers to change as they progress through the Explorations. Students will have an opportunity to revise their answers when they revisit these questions at the end of the lesson.

Collaboration

Build on Prior Knowledge Have students work in small groups to review what they have learned about constraints, criteria, and problems. Remind students that engineers must consider and work with criteria and constraints all the time. Based on prior knowledge, have student groups share examples of criteria and constraints that engineers may encounter when designing technology.

 EVIDENCE NOTEBOOK

Encourage students to use an appropriate graphic organizer, such as main idea and supporting details, to set up their notebook for this lesson.

Find more strategies in the online ELA handbook.

LESSON 2   Engage • **Explore/Explain** • Elaborate • Evaluate

EXPLORATION 1 Research Matters!

3D Learning Objective

Explore the **processes for coming up with solutions to problems** by studying how animals use their hearing in the wild. Draw on images of animal ears, and **explain how their ears work to keep them safe and fed**. Compare and contrast the different songs that birds sing, and consider how these songs, as well as animal ears, can **influence engineers** as they work on their designs.

DCI ETS1.B Developing Possible Solutions

This page tells about some of the steps students can take when coming up with a solution to a problem.

Ask: What kinds of problems do the animals' ears and good hearing solve? *keep them from going hungry; keep them safe from danger*

Ask: All of these animals have something in common: their large ears! Does this mean that they can all hear the same way or that their ears have the same features? *No; the rabbit's ears are longer than any of the other animals' shown; the mule deer's and aye-aye's ears are farther apart than the fox's and the rabbit's ears.*

Ask: How can the environments in which these animals live help explain the differences among these animals' ears? *Their ears are adapted to specific living conditions or problems.*

CCC Influence of Engineering, Technology, and Science on Society and the Natural World

Ask: What kinds of technology can you think of that mimic how some of these animals on the page use their ears? *technology for listening to the vibrations in the ground to detect earthquakes; hearing-aid technology*

EXPLORATION 1

Research Matters!

Ears to You!

Designing a solution can be tough. Depending on the situation, there can be many different steps. One important first step is to learn more about the problem before you start to design a solution.

Your challenge is to design a hearing-enhancing device to use on a nature walk. Where should you start? You might want to start by learning how different animals use hearing to solve their problems. View each image below and read the captions to explore how some animals use hearing to solve different problems.

The fox is an excellent hunter. It uses its hearing to locate small mammals that burrow underground. When the fox figures out where an animal is, it will dig it up.

Mule deer are common in the western United States. These animals have large ears that allow them to hear sounds such as those made by predators, which can pose dangers.

Aye-ayes live on Madagascar. They tap on tree bark with their long fingers and use their ears to listen for moving larva. When they hear the larva, they use their fingers to pry them out of the bark and eat them.

Wild rabbits live in many temperate environments. These animals can independently rotate their ears to pick up the softest of sounds. Rabbits use their hearing to identify possible predators.

24

Look again at the photos on the previous page and recall what you read. Use this information to complete the table below. Then answer the question to explain how animals can use hearing to solve problems.

Ears, Ears, Ears

2. In the table, make a detailed drawing of each animal's ear.

Type of animal	Shape of ear
Red fox	Drawings should approximate the different types of ears shown on the previous page.
Mule deer	
Aye-aye	
Wild rabbit	

3. How do the ears of these animals differ? How are they the same? How can looking at these animals' ears help you design your hearing-enhancing device?

Some students may have said that each of the ears has the same general shape—looks like a funnel, but that the ears are different sizes. Looking at the ear shapes can help students decide on a possible shape for their devices.

Differentiate Instruction

Extension Challenge students to take this activity one step further by writing a brief summary of the features of the ear that allow the animal to hear so well, next to each of the drawings of the ears.

Collaboration

Think, Pair, Share Have students work with a partner to share each other's drawings and explanations. Call on pairs of students to share their drawings and explanations with the rest of the class.

SEP Constructing Explanations and Designing Solutions

Ask: What can scientists and engineers learn by studying the ears of animals? how to model or design and build hearing-enhancing devices; how to get the best hearing

LESSON 2   Engage • **Explore/Explain** • Elaborate • Evaluate

EXPLORATION 1 *Research Matters!, continued*

CCC Influence of Engineering, Technology, and Science on Society and the Natural World

When people listen to birds tweeting and chirping, we call the sounds songs. However, in the animal kingdom, these songs are an important form of communication among birds.

Ask: Do you think listening to songbirds can help engineers with their designs? Explain your answer. **Yes; by listening to the songs, they can hear the complexity of the song and try to design listening or recording devices that can pick up the pitch, tone, and composition of the songs.**

Connection to Life Science

Animals are adapted to their environments in different ways, and sometimes those ways are physical. By studying the physical characteristics of animals, scientists can make inferences about the types of traits that are most important for the animals' survival. Traits can also change and evolve over time if there are long-term changes to the abiotic or biotic factors in an environment.

LS3.A Inheritance of Traits

Differentiate Instruction

ELL: Use Realia Students learning English may struggle with the word representations that people use to identify what the different songbirds sound like. Play a clip for them of different bird songs. Ask them to think about how they could represent the song in words, such as "drink you tea," which is used to represent the song of the Eastern towhee.

Targeting Sounds

As you have just learned, hearing is an important sense for many animals. It helps them to survive in their environments. It helps them find food and avoid predators or other dangers. View the photos on these pages and think about the sounds each songbird makes. How could your hearing enhancer help you hear differences between the songs?

North American Songbirds

The black-capped chickadee is a songbird often found near wooded areas. Its most often heard song is short whistled two or three note 'fee-bee" or "fee-bee-bee."

The American robin is a common songbird. It often sings just before daylight. Some describe its song as "cheerily cheer-up cheer-up cheerily cheer-up."

26

Unit 1 Engineering and Technology

The northern cardinal is often found near dense, bushy areas. Its song can be described as a quick and lively "birdie birdie birdie." It signals danger with a loud, short "chip".

The yellow warbler lives in dense woody areas and swamps. Its song sounds like, "sweet sweet sweet, I'm so sweet."

 EVIDENCE NOTEBOOK Apply what you read on this page to possible features of your hearing-enhancing device.

Wildlife, including songbirds, use sounds to communicate and survive in their environments. Think about the similarities and differences between the songs of the North American songbirds that you just read about and answer the question below.

 Language SmArts
Comparing and Contrasting

Tip
The English Language Arts Handbook can provide help with understanding how to compare and contrast.

4. What is the same about the birds' songs? What is different? What else might you need to help you determine what type of bird you are listening to?

Students might state that each bird's song has different notes but that some of the patterns and rhythms sound the same. Students might say recordings of sounds from different types of birds may help them identify the birds they are listening to.

 **Explore Online** Review the digital resource for additional source content.

 ETS1.B Developing Possible Solutions

Engineers look for clues in nature when designing technology.

Ask: What kinds of clues do you think are important for engineers, and what can they help them with? Patterns can help them figure out if something can be repeated or not, and relationships between organisms or between organisms and their environment can help them figure out if something works well in the environment or not.

 EVIDENCE NOTEBOOK

Students should be able to apply the various sounds of songbirds to their hearing-enhancing technologies.

FORMATIVE ASSESSMENT

 Language SmArts
Comparing and Contrasting
RI.5.7 Draw on information from multiple print or digital sources

Studying Similarities and Differences As students work to respond to the prompt, remind them that it's important to be able to locate and use information from a variety of sources. As students work through their Explorations, encourage them to make notes of where to find certain information if they ever need to go back to it again. This is a good habit for study and research skills.

LESSON 2   Engage • **Explore/Explain** • Elaborate • Evaluate

EXPLORATION 2 Past Hearing Helpers

3D Learning Objective

Explore how engineers often **study past designs of devices to help them come up with ideas for new technologies**. Learn about some of the kinds of devices related to sound and hearing and the **influence that the advances in technology have had on humans**. Students will also have an opportunity to participate in a sound demonstration and **explain why sounds and hearing can be amplified by changing the shape of the ears**.

DCI ETS1.B Developing Possible Solutions

This page tells students about how looking at past devices can help engineers design new solutions.

Ask: What do you think engineers are looking for when studying devices from the past? how something works; how well it works; what it doesn't do well; what can be improved

CCC Influence of Engineering, Technology, and Science on Society and the Natural World

Ask: What kind of impact has the design of a stethoscope had on society? It helps doctors and nurses find out more about a person's heart and lungs without being invasive; by listening to a person's heart and lungs with a stethoscope, a healthcare professional can determine if the heart and lungs are functioning properly or if a person is sick and what type of illness they have.

EXPLORATION 2

Past Hearing Helpers

Looking Back to Look Forward

Solutions to problems can have many different parts. Looking at others' solutions can often help improve an existing design. In other words, we can learn from past solutions to help us with new and better solutions.

Many hearing-enhancing devices have been made over time. Most are not perfect solutions, though. Engineers continue to build on and work to improve solutions like these hearing aids from the past and present.

This early ear trumpet collected and directed sound waves to the listener's ear. The device worked best when the sounds were nearby.

Ear trumpets with longer tubes helped amplify sounds, too. They were easier to hold and direct toward the sound.

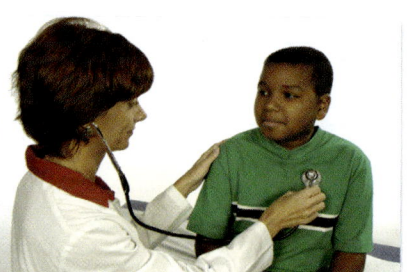

A stethoscope is often used in medicine. Sound travels from the person to the cup, which increases the volume of the sound. The sound moves through the tubes to the user's ears.

This concrete listening post collects and focuses sounds like a curved mirror. Before radar, it was used to listen for approaching enemy planes.

28

Unit 1 Engineering and Technology

Listen and Learn!

5. Look again at the photos on the previous page. In the table below, describe each device in your own words. Then tell how you think you could change the device to improve it.

Description	How I might improve device
Ear-Trumpet	Students' device descriptions should be similar to the information given in the captions. Students might say that each of the hearing devices has a funnel or funnel-like shape that concentrates sound into a smaller area. They might suggest improving each device by increasing the size of the funnel or collection surface.
Ear-Trumpet with a long tube	
Stethoscope	
British acoustic mirror listening post	

6. How might you use what you've learned here to design your hearing-enhancing device?

Possible answer: I could use cardboard or paper or plastic cups to funnel sound to my ears. I might use plastic tubing, too, to channel the sound from the funnels to my ears. The concrete listening post is too heavy, but the shape may be useful.

Differentiate Instruction

Extension Challenge students to take this activity further by having them perform outside research on one other device that has been improved upon from the past. Examples include eyeglasses, magnifying glasses, and microscopes. Students should think about the kind of impact the device has had on society or the environment. Then, call on volunteers to share their findings with the class.

SEP Constructing Explanations and Designing Solutions

After students have completed the table on the page, have them turn their attention back to the external research they did on their computer or mobile device.

Ask: In what way(s) do you think your device could be improved? Responses will vary.

Collaboration

Feedback Have students respond to Item 6 individually and then pair up with a partner to critique each other's answers. Encourage a discussion between partners, and invite students to share their answers with the class. Use an engaging prompt for students to respond to, such as:

- What kinds of criteria would apply to your design?
- What kinds of constraints might limit possible solutions?

LESSON 2 Engage • **Explore/Explain** • Elaborate • Evaluate

EXPLORATION 2 *Past Hearing Helpers, continued*

HANDS-ON Apply What You Know
Hear Here
Students should be able to tell a difference in the ability to hear their partners when their hands are cupped over their ears.

Scoring Guidelines
A strong performance in this activity involves active participation and awareness of the various sounds.

DCI ETS1.B Developing Possible Solutions

Ask: When you cup your hands around your ears, which animal does this remind you of? Which animal has similarly shaped ears that allow them to hear this way? **rabbits; bats; the aye-aye**

 **EVIDENCE NOTEBOOK**

Students should think about what they just learned about cupping their ears and relate it to what they learned about animals' ears from Exploration 1.

FORMATIVE ASSESSMENT

DCI ETS1.B Developing Possible Solutions

Ask: If you were to design a human-like robot, what kind of ears would you design for it and why? **Answers will vary but should demonstrate understanding that they have the opportunity to design ears that can hear better than the human ear.**

 HANDS-ON Apply What You Know

Hear Here

7. Work with a partner. Stand about 3 meters apart. Turn so that your ear is pointing toward your partner. Close your eyes. Have your partner whisper your name. Have your partner whisper your name again, but cup your hands to your ears. Compare the two sounds. Trade roles with your partner so that he or she can observe your whispering. Describe the sounds below. Why did they sound different? Can cupping your hands to your ears make it easier to locate a faint sound? Test and see.

Possible answer: The second whisper was louder than the first. This happened because cupping our hands near our ears redirected more sound to the ear, which made it seem louder.

 EVIDENCE NOTEBOOK How can your results from this activity help you design your device?

Putting It Together

8. How does studying others' hearing-enhancing solutions help you with your possible design? How does looking at different types of animals' ears help you with your design?

Students might have mentioned that others' solutions give them ideas as to which types of designs work well and which do not. Looking at animals' ears also helps because they show real-world examples of solutions that can be adapted and modified.

EXPLORATION 3 Passing the Test

EXPLORATION 3

Passing the Test

Testing, Testing, 1, 2, 3

Engineers design many things that people depend on. It's not enough for an engineer to say that a design works. It needs to be tested to ensure it solves the problem. Each design starts out as a prototype, or early version for testing. Prototypes must be thoroughly tested to be sure they're safe and work correctly. Often, it takes many prototypes to get one that is ideal. Most types of engineering solutions are like this. They need to be tested and improved many times before they meet criteria and satisfy contraints of safety, time, money, or materials.

Anechoic means "no echoes." An *anechoic chamber* is used to test speakers, headphones, and microphones. The walls in the chamber are designed to absorb sound waves.

3D Learning Objective

Learn about the importance of **testing designs**. Explore a variety of testing environments, and get a sense for how testing can help find flaws and lead engineers to **redesign their products to make something even better**. Relate the concept of testing devices to the **benefit it has on society**.

DCI ETS1.B Developing Possible Solutions

Remind students that there are many kinds of engineers and each is trained and experienced in searching for specific problems and designing possible solutions.

Ask: Why do you think it's important for engineers to use anechoic chambers when testing speakers, headphones, and microphones? **so they can hear how they work without any interruptions to the sound**

CCC Influence of Engineering, Technology, and Science on Society and the Natural World

As a whole class, think about other uses for anechoic technology.
Ask: How do you think anechoic technology has had an influence on society? **It can help engineers produce better quality products.**

LESSON 2 Engage • **Explore/Explain** • Elaborate • Evaluate

EXPLORATION 3 Passing the Test, continued

Differentiate Instruction

RTI/Extra Support Students may find the image of aquadynamic testing confusing. Provide additional support by labeling the badminton birdie on the image.

SEP Constructing Explanations and Designing Solutions

Have students study the image of the eye-tracking rig.

Ask: What kinds of problems do you think engineers identified in order to come up with the idea or need for an eye-tracking rig?
Software and webpage designs were not allowing people to read them efficiently; athletes were not tracking a ball efficiently

Collaboration

Feedback Have students complete item 9 independently and then team up with a partner to review each other's work and provide constructive feedback. One of the terms from the word bank, *final design*, is not included as one of the correct answers. Give the pairs of students an extra assignment to use that term in a complete sentence, in the context of engineering. Students can take turns saying the term in a sentence to their partner.

More Testing

Look at photos below. Then read the captions to learn more about some other engineering designs and how they are tested.

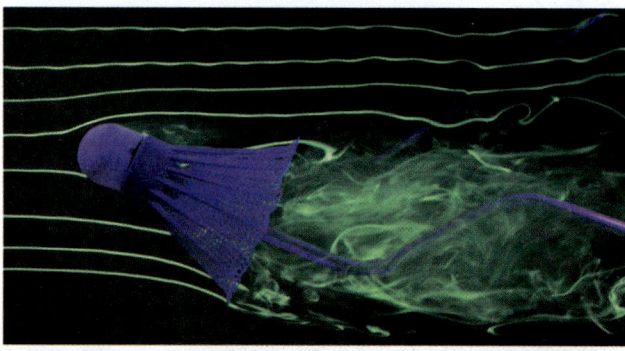

An *aquadynamic* testing facility is similar to a wind tunnel. It is used to test vehicles and objects that move through water to make sure they are safe and do not leak. It is also used to model movement through air.

This is an eye-tracking rig. It keeps a record of eye movements while a person uses software or a web page. Portable, wearable devices are used in sports to see if players are really keeping their eyes on the ball!

9. Choose the word or words that correctly complete each sentence.

| anechoic chamber | eye-tracking rig | final design |
| improve | prototype | |

A _**prototype**_ is an early version of a design solution. These versions are tested to help _**improve**_ a design solution. An _**anechoic chamber**_ might be tested by a rock band to help with their recordings. Video gamers might use an _**eye-tracking rig**_ to test and improve their gaming skills.

32

Unit 1 Engineering and Technology

Fair Tests

Testing and retesting solutions is important. A **fair test** is one that doesn't give any advantage to the conditions or objects being tested. For a fair test, engineers observe and measure the effects of changing only one thing at a time. Changing many things at once seems faster. However, then there is no way to know what causes the results.

Here's an example of a fair test. Supposed you want to find the fastest way to walk home. You'd need to time each route walking at roughly the same speed on similar days. You would not compare walking the first route, running the second, and carrying a heavy backpack on the third. The same is true for the results on a slippery, icy day and on a warm, dry day.

Learn More About Sound Tests

Look at the sound system test room below. You may have seen one like it in a store. Read each caption to find out more about different parts. Then answer the question on the next page.

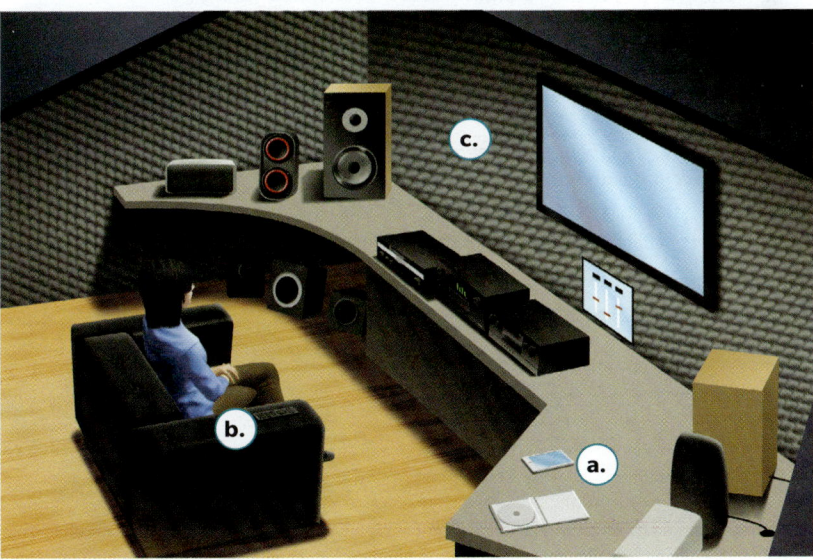

a. **Sound source**
A CD, smartphone, TV, or radio is a possible source of test sounds.

b. **Remote control**
A remote control adjusts loudness and chooses the speakers being tested.

c. **Wall lining**
The wall lining helps keep outside sounds from interfering with the music.

DCI ETS1.B Developing Possible Solutions

Remind students that engineers always have an objective: a goal they are trying to reach or a problem they are trying to solve.

Ask: What do you think engineers are trying to design or solve when using audio-testing systems? *how to reproduce sound that is clearer or crisper; how to get better quality sound*

Differentiate Instruction

RTI/Extra Support You can provide extra support to students by adding labels onto the image next to the hotspot letters.

Extension For a challenge, have students use the Internet to research additional testing facilities that are similar to anechoic chambers. Have them present their findings as a presentation to the class, using visual aids.

CCC Influence of Engineering, Technology, and Science on Society and the Natural World

Technology is constantly evolving in order to enhance the way humans interact with the world.

Ask: Who or what might benefit from better sound quality? *musicians and recording artists; people who want to listen to music*

LESSON 2   Engage • **Explore/Explain** • Elaborate • Evaluate

EXPLORATION 3 Passing the Test, continued

> ## Collaboration
> **Think, Pair, Share** Have students respond to item 10 independently and then share their responses with a neighbor. Encourage students to discuss their answers together, and then invite them to share their ideas with the class. Urge students to provide as many details as possible for their steps.

 Constructing Explanations and Designing Solutions

Ask: What kinds of issues do you think you might find by performing a fair test? **The sound isn't as clear as it should be; the distance for the sound is too short**

 EVIDENCE NOTEBOOK

Have students think back to the Hands-On Activity and the criteria they came up with for that. Students should draw upon that activity to answer the prompt in their notebooks.

FORMATIVE ASSESSMENT

CCC **Influence of Engineering, Technology, and Science on Society and the Natural World**

Ask: What is the benefit of redesigning and retesting the device? **It helps makes sure the device will work the best that it can.**

Ask: How might this better influence society? **People can wear the device comfortably and travel with it easily; people can buy it for a better price because it is made with fewer materials and resources.**

Your Fair Test

10. What steps would you take to make a fair test of a the speakers shown in the sound system test room?

    Possible answer: I would test only one speaker system at a time. I would use the same sound source (CD, smartphone), sit or stand in the same place, listen at the same loudness, and keep the rest of the room set up as similar as possible each time.

EVIDENCE NOTEBOOK Explain how the criteria for your hearing-enhancing device affect what you will test.

Putting It Together

11. What factors will your team need to think about and address in order to make a fair test of your hearing-enhancing device?

    Possible answers: using a consistent source of nature sounds or bird calls, testing at consistent distances and positions, keeping the background noise level as close to the same as possible.

34

34 Unit 1 Engineering and Technology

HANDS-ON ACTIVITY
Design It!

Objective

Collaborate with a team to design your own hearing-enhancing device. Make sure you use the design criteria and constraints as you construct your device. Also use what you've learned about past solutions, animals' ears, and fair tests. Be safe—don't put *anything* in your ears.

What problem will you solve to meet this objective?
Possible answer: How can I make a hearing-enhancing device that satisfies the constraints and criteria?

Possible Materials
- plastic cups
- paper cups
- cloth scraps
- duct tape
- masking tape
- wire clothes hangers
- string
- rubber tubing
- plastic head bands
- scissors
- baseball or painter's cap

Procedure

STEP 1 Handle and examine the materials available to you. Brainstorm ideas with your team. Choose the best one. Then, make a rough sketch in the box of how you think your device will look and work.

What is the constraint? ___no batteries___

What are your criteria? ___enhances hearing, comfortable, durable, lightweight___

Check student sketches to see how they address constraints and criteria.

35

Student Lab Worksheet and complete Teacher Support available online.

HANDS-ON ACTIVITY Pairs 1 class period
Design It!

3D Learning Objective

SEP **Constructing Explanations and Designing Solutions**

Students work in pairs to design hearing-enhancing devices based on constraints and criteria. They must identify the problem and solve for it through this activity.

Materials
The materials listed in the student edition are a starting point. You may wish to add cardboard to this list as well. Be sparing. Part of the purpose of the activity is to have students learn how to work within constraints; in this case, a limited amount of resources.

Preparation
Prepare for this activity by making the materials available to students and rearranging the room to make space for pairs of students to spread out their designs and materials. Before you begin, remind students not to put **anything** in their ears.

DCI **ETS1.B Developing Possible Solutions**

This activity asks students to design a hearing-enhancing device.

Ask: What are your criteria for this device? **It must enhance hearing.**

Ask: What are the constraints? **time, materials, and resources**

Procedure

STEP 1 Have students work independently to complete this step. Emphasize to them that they can only design their devices using the materials they have, so it's important to think strategically about how to make the materials work together.

Lesson 2 How do Engineers Design Solutions? 35

LESSON 2   Engage • **Explore/Explain** • Elaborate • Evaluate

EXPLORATION 3   Passing the Test, continued

STEP 2 Students should complete this step independently. This step has two parts: listing the materials and explaining how the materials will help meet the criteria of the design. Make sure students complete both parts of the step.

STEP 3 Circulate around the room, and help students add notes to their tables if they get stuck.

CCC Influence of Engineering, Technology, and Science on Society and the Natural World

Remind students that engineers often study designs of the past to learn about ways to improve future devices.

Ask: What kinds of devices can you think of from the past that will help you come up with ideas for ways to improve your design? **Responses will vary.**

Differentiate Instruction

RTI/Extra Support Some students may not think that their designs need to be improved, but encourage them to come up with two more possible designs that would allow their hearing-enhancing devices to work effectively. If students are unable to come up with improvement ideas for their designs, provide them with prompts such as the following:

- Is there a way to improve the structure?
- Is there a way to build the device with fewer materials?
- Are those the best materials to use for the design?
- Is there a way to make the design simpler?

STEP 2 Identify the materials from those available that you will use to make your design come to life. Write your list in the first box below. Also write how the materials will help to meet the criteria.

First Design Notes

Ensure that materials that students have selected are appropriate and safely utilized. Verify that nothing is inserted into ears and observe head lice precautions.

STEP 3 With your team, build and test your device. Use the test results to improve the device. Stop testing and improving when you are satisfied that it meets the constraints and criteria. In the space below, keep a record of the design changes you make. Include a reason for each change.

Additional Design Notes

Check to make sure materials and notes capture design changes and improvements.

Unit 1 Engineering and Technology

STEP 4 When you are satisfied that it meets the constraints and criteria, think of a different design that might work even better. If there is time, build and text a second device that is different in some way.

STEP 5 Use the final design and your notes to answer the questions in the table below.

a.	Why did you choose each material? How did they help your design?	Possible answer: I chose cups based on my observations of animal ears. I chose the tubing based on designs of other devices used to enhance hearing. I chose the hat and tape to allow me to wear the finished device. The cups and tubing help collect and magnify sound waves.
b.	Why did you pick this design?	I picked this design because it was lightweight and easy to carry and wear.
c.	How well did your design meet the criteria and constraints? Explain.	Students should identify how the design met the criteria and constraints.

Analyze Your Results

STEP 6 Did your design meet the goals of this activity? Support your claim with evidence and reasoning.
If methodically planned, tested, and improved, students' designs will have met the goal.

STEP 7 Explain why you choose two of your materials.
Possible answer: I chose the cups to collect sound waves. I used the hat to support the device and to make it easily removable.

Draw Conclusions

STEP 8 If other students looked at your final design, what improvements did they suggest? Why?
Possible answer: Others might suggest that I use different materials, make the device larger or smaller, or figure out a different way to wear the device.

37

 Review the digital resource for additional source content.

CCC Influence of Engineering, Technology, and Science on Society and the Natural World

Analyze Your Results
STEP 5 Help students connect their designs to real-world problems and solutions. Have them focus back on the problem they are trying to solve and how it will help society.

Draw Conclusions
Give students an opportunity to showcase their designs. Leave some time at the end of the activity for students to walk around and view each other's work. Then, have students complete Step 8. Students can draw on the feedback they might want to give to their peers to figure out the types of suggestions their peers may give to them.

> ## Claims, Evidence, and Reasoning
> Have students cite evidence to support their claims in Step 5. Call on volunteers to share their explanations with the whole class.

Scoring Rubric for Hands-On Activity	
3	Completes the design using a set of criteria and constraints; provides an explanation well supported by evidence and reasoning.
2	Completes the design using a set of criteria and constraints; provides an explanation without evidence or reasoning.
1	Participates in the activity but does not make conclusions or provide explanations.
0	does not participate completely in the activity

Lesson 2 How Do Engineers Design Solutions? 37

LESSON 2   Engage • Explore/Explain • **Elaborate** • Evaluate

TAKE IT FURTHER Discover More

Collaboration

Pathways You may choose to assign this activity or to direct students online to the Interactive Online Student Edition where they can explore and choose from all three paths. These activities can be assigned individually, to pairs, or to small groups.

Careers in Science & Engineering: Acoustic Engineer

Students will learn about the careers of acoustic engineers. They will explore the types of problems acoustic engineers solve, as well as the tools they use to test the devices to ensure they work properly.

ETS1.B Developing Possible Solutions

DCI ETS1.B Developing Possible Solutions

Direct students to study the image of the concert hall. Be sure to point out the shape of it, the design, the number of rows of seats, the use of fabrics and materials, and other details you can find within the image.

Ask: What kinds of things do you think acoustic engineers must consider when designing concert halls? materials (fabric, concrete, stone); size; shape; ceiling height; distance from seats to the stage

---

TAKE IT FURTHER

Discover More

Check out this path . . . or go online to choose one of these other paths.

Careers in Science & Engineering
- Hearing Aid History
- Don't Make a Move . . .

Acoustic Engineer

Engineers work in many fields. An acoustic engineer solves problems related to sound or hearing. From concert halls to quiet cars, acoustic engineers design sound-related objects and systems. They study engineering, physics, and math to be successful. The tools of their trade are microphones, computers, and their ears.

An acoustic engineer might work with concert hall designers to ensure that the venue will absorb and reflect sounds so that the concertgoers enjoy the performances.

an acoustic test lab

38

Unit 1 Engineering and Technology

Acoustic engineers can design concert halls so the sounds that come from the stage sound great no matter where you sits. Like all engineers, they make and test multiple solutions until they are the best they can be within the design constraints and criteria.

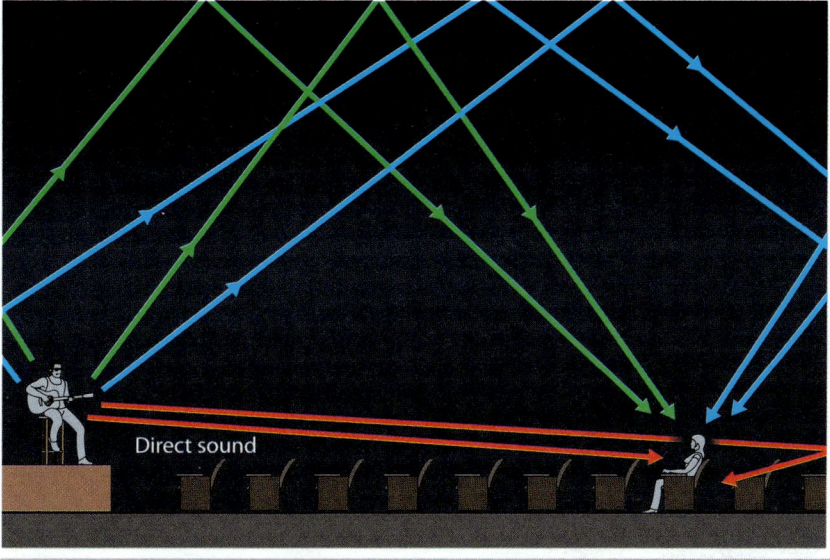

This shows the paths of sound reflection in an auditorium.

12. Describe two or three problems that an acoustic engineer might help solve.
Student examples might include that acoustic engineers create concert halls and theaters that provide quality concerts and plays for spectators. These engineers can also design microphones and speakers to record and project sounds.

Differentiate Instruction

RTI/Extra Support If students find the image confusing, redraw the image on the board, giving students the chance to follow the directions of the sounds to better comprehend the concept of sound reflection. Or as an alternative, students can redraw the images themselves to gain practice in seeing how the sound travels.

Ask: What do you find unique about the way sound travels?
Sample answers: It bounces off of the ceiling; it can curve back around toward the person.

SEP Constructing Explanations and Designing Solutions

Direct students to study the image on the page or the one you draw on the board.

Ask: What kind of explanation might an engineer give for the movement and reflection of the sound? The sound is bouncing (reflecting) off of various materials so that it can end up where it is supposed to be focused.

Collaboration

Think, Pair, Share Once students have responded to the prompt individually, have them pair up with a partner to review each other's responses and provide feedback. As a whole class, see if any students came up with different responses. Tell students that their responses do not have to be limited to concert halls.

LESSON 2 Engage • Explore/Explain • **Elaborate** • Evaluate

TAKE IT FURTHER, *continued*

 Influence of Engineering, Technology, and Science on Society and the Natural World

Different materials have their own characteristic sounds that they make.

Ask: How can the sounds that materials make, or the effects they produce, be used to help society or the environment? Responses will vary but should demonstrate that students understand the relationship between materials and how they are applied to things such as cars, buildings, and entertainment.

> **Do The Math**
> **Measuring Sound**
>
> **5.NBT.A.2** Explain patterns in the number of zeros of the product when multiplying a number by powers of 10….
>
> **MP.4** Model with mathematics.
>
> Students should demonstrate the ability to perform these calculations based on knowledge of place value. Encourage students to write out their work. Suggest that they count zeros in each row to reinforce the pattern.

> ▶ **Explore Online**
>
> Students can explore these additional topics online.
>
> ### Hearing Aid History
>
> Students explore the history of hearing aids and how their technology has developed over the years. *(Outside research required.)*
>
> ### Don't Make a Move
>
> Students carry out research about engineering technology and movement. *(Outside research required.)*

Make Some Sound Observations

13. Look around the room you are in. List at least three different materials that the room itself and objects within it are made of. Write the materials on the lines in the table. Speak softly with your mouth about three inches away from the material. Listen for differences in the sound of your voice. Record your observations.

Material	Observations
Possible answers: glass	clear
fabric	muffled
paper	fluttery

14. Based on your observations of how the materials affected the sound of your voice, Which materials would you use in a music hall? Which materials would you avoid? Why?

Possible answer: In a music hall, I would use materials that absorb sound such as foam or insulated wallboard or tile. I would also use metal, wood, or glass if not enough sound was reflected.

 Do the Math
Measuring Sound

15. Human hearing is amazingly sensitive. We can hear sounds from a pin dropping to a landslide. Sound is measured in decibels (dB). A sound that you can barely hear is 0 dB. A quiet whisper that is 10 times louder is 10 dB. A sound that is 100 times louder is 20 dB. A sound that is 1,000 times louder is 30 dB. Complete the table.

Sound	Decibels	Times Louder
whisper	10 dB	10 times
country sounds	20 dB	100 times
city sounds	30 dB	1,000 times
big truck	90 dB	1,000,000,000 times
rock band	100 dB	10,000,000,000 times

Unit 1 Engineering and Technology

LESSON 2 Engage • Explore/Explain • Elaborate • **Evaluate**

LESSON CHECK

 **Explore Online** — Students can revisit the lesson phenomenon online.

LESSON 2

Lesson Check

Name _____

Can You Solve It?

1. Recall the imaginary nature hike and your proposed solution for a hearing-enhancing device. Use what you've learned to do the following:
   - Explain the importance of researching previous solutions to the same problem.
   - Explain how solutions are designed.
   - Describe how and why potential design solutions are tested.

EVIDENCE NOTEBOOK Use the information you've collected in your Evidence Notebook to help you cover each point above.

Possible answer:
- Students might state that knowing about previous solutions can help you come up with new solutions to a problem.
- Engineering solutions are made given a set of criteria and constraints.
- Solutions are tested and retested to make sure the solutions meet the design goals.

Checkpoints

2. Choose the word or words that correctly complete each sentence.

| solutions | problems | audio |
| acoustics | fair tests | old prototypes |

Engineers design ___**solutions**___ to help solve problems. They perform ___**fair tests**___ to help them design new devices.

41

Formal Assessment Go online for student self-checks and other assessments.

Can You Solve It?

> ### Collaboration
> **Discussion** You may wish to revisit and discuss the image as a group to assess students' understanding of the material. Use the bulleted points in the Interactive Worktext to lead the discussion.

EVIDENCE NOTEBOOK

Have students reread their answers to the Evidence Notebook prompts and then use this evidence to justify their reasoning as they respond to the Can You Solve It question. Make sure students understand that a complete response must address all bulleted points.

DCI ETS1.B Developing Possible Solutions

Draw students' attention back to the image of the birder with a microphone. Now that students are more familiar with sound and sound technology,

Ask: What kinds of problems might this birder have with the microphone technology he is using? The sound might not be focused enough; the materials might not be weatherproof; the cord between the microphone and the headphones might not work; the whole apparatus is large and bulky, so the birder may not be able to move quickly if he needs to follow birds.

SUMMATIVE ASSESSMENT
Analyze Facts

2. To correctly answer the question, students must recall information they learned in Explorations 1, 2, and 3.

Lesson 2 How Do Engineers Design Solutions? **41**

LESSON 2 Engage • Explore/Explain • Elaborate • **Evaluate**

LESSON CHECK, *continued*

3. If students get stuck on this question because they find the diagram confusing, redraw the diagram for them so that they can list the steps in the design process into columns for *Good* and *Bad*.

4. Students should be able to answer this question based on information learned in Exploration 3. Make sure students read each answer choice as a part of the complete sentence to see whether it makes sense as read.

5. Students should be able to answer this question based on information learned in Exploration 1. Have them also use images to help them arrive at the correct answers.

6. The words *test* and *retest* could both be considered correct for the first fill-in-the-blank. The words *testing* and *retesting* could also both be considered correct for the second fill-in-the-blank.

3. Draw lines to sort each of the following descriptions of the engineering design process into the correct category—**Good Design Practice** or **Poor Design Practice**.

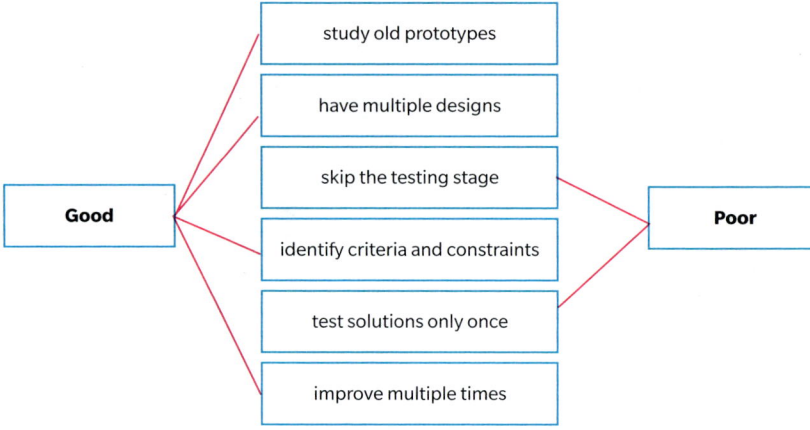

4. Select all of the choices that correctly complete this sentence.

   Engineers _____

   a. test solutions to design problems more than once.
   b. don't waste time learning about other solutions to their problems.
   c. don't try to improve others' solutions or their own solutions.
   d. create more than one solution to the same problem.

   (a and d are circled)

5. You've learned that animals use their hearing to solve problems. Which of these problems can they solve using this sense? Select all that apply.

   a. finding food
   b. swimming faster or slower
   c. locating dangerous predators
   d. sleeping well at night

   (a and c are circled)

6. Choose words from the word bank to complete the sentences.

many tries	retest	retesting
test	testing	one try

   Engineers ___test___ designs because it's important to be sure a solution works. Usually ___retesting___ happens because it takes ___many tries___ to get a working prototype.

42

42 Unit 1 Engineering and Technology

LESSON 2

Lesson Roundup

A. A new student just joined your class and needs to get caught up on this lesson. What should she do to begin designing her hearing-enhancing device?

- a. research careers in acoustic engineering
- **b. study the devices already made by other students** ✓
- c. learn how different birds sing different types of songs
- d. ask for materials other than those available

B. Which of these should the new student learn more about at this point? Select all that apply.

- **a. ear trumpets** ✓
- b. light and mirrors
- **c. stethoscopes** ✓
- **d. sound waves** ✓

C. It's your job to tutor the new student so that she quickly catches up. Pretend that you will give her the paragraph below to help her. Choose the words to correctly complete the sentences that she will read.

| one part | many parts | no prototype |
| multiple prototypes | test them only once | retest them many times |

Like actual engineers, we are solving a problem. Thus, we should create _multiple prototypes_ of our hearing-enhancing devices. Then we should _retest them many times_. During our tests, we should change _one part_ of the design at a time.

D. What do professional engineers do during the design process? Select all that apply.

- **a. use prototypes** ✓
- b. test each design only once
- c. come up with a single solution
- **d. research on existing solutions** ✓
- e. change multiple things when testing
- **f. meet all of the constraints and as many criteria as possible** ✓

Lesson Roundup

DCI ETS1.B Developing Possible Solutions

This lesson summary enables students to quickly revisit key points and prepare for tests.

A. Students should be able to draw on what they learned about an engineering design process to answer this question correctly. For a bit of guidance, encourage students to revisit Exploration 2 and scan the material. **ETS1.B**

B. Options A, C, and D all have to do with sounds and ears. Option B has to do with the eyes. Students should be able to detect this distinction. However, if they get stuck, you can clue them to think about the answer choices according to senses. **EST1.B**

C. Exploration 3 focuses on testing designs. Students may refer to it to refresh their memory. Certain phrases and tenses should help them eliminate the distractors from the word bank. **ETS1.B**

D. Give students a chance to scan Explorations 1, 2, and 3 in order to piece together the total design process learned in the lesson. If they need scaffolding support, begin by reminding them that they may need to combine information from all Explorations to find the correct answers. **EST1.B**

LESSON 3
How Do Engineers Test and Improve Prototypes?

Building to the Performance Expectation

The learning experiences in this lesson prepare students for mastery of:

3-5-ETS1-3 Plan and carry out fair tests in which variables are controlled and failure points are considered to identify aspects of a model or prototype that can be improved.

Trace Tool to the NGSS
Go online to view the complete coverage of these standards across this lesson, unit, and time.

Science & Engineering Practices

Planning and Carrying Out Investigations
Plan and conduct an investigation collaboratively to produce data to serve as the basis for evidence, using fair tests in which variables are controlled and the number of trials considered.

▶ VIDEO Planning and Carrying Out Investigations

Disciplinary Core Ideas

ETS1.B Developing Possible Solutions
Tests are often designed to identify failure points or difficulties, which suggest the elements of the design that need to be improved.

ETS1.C Optimizing the Design Solution
Different solutions need to be tested in order to determine which of them best solves the problem, given the criteria and the constraints.

Crosscutting Concepts

Influence of Science, Engineering, and Technology on Society and the Natural World
All human activity draws on natural resources and has both short- and long-term consequences, positive as well as negative, for the health of people and the natural environment.

The uses of technologies and limitations on their use are driven by individual or societal needs, desires, and values; by the findings of scientific research; and by differences in such factors as climate, natural resources, and economic conditions.

CONNECTIONS TO MATH

MP.2 Reason abstractly and quantitatively.
MP.4 Model with mathematics.
MP.5 Use appropriate tools strategically.

CONNECTIONS TO ENGLISH LANGUAGE ARTS

W.5.7 Conduct short research projects that use several sources to build knowledge through investigation of different aspects of a topic.

W.5.8 Recall relevant information from experiences or gather relevant information from print and digital sources; summarize or paraphrase information in notes and finished work, and provide a list of sources.

W.5.9 Draw evidence from literary or informational texts to support analysis, reflection, and research.

Supporting All Students, All Standards

Integrating the Three Dimensions of Learning

In this lesson, students will plan, design, and test possible solutions **(SEP Planning and Carrying Out Investigations)** for a prototype to determine which design best solves a problem within the given criteria and constraints **(DCI ETS1.C)**. Students will then identify failure points or difficulties with a design and suggest and implement changes that improve it **(DCI ETS1.B)**. Students learn that engineers must communicate in order to share observations, gain insight, and optimize future solutions and designs **(CCC Influence of Science, Engineering, and Technology on Society and the Natural World)**.

Professional Development — Go online to view **Professional Development videos** with strategies to integrate CCCs and SEPs, including the ones used in this lesson.

Extra Hands-On Activity: How Do Engineers Test and Improve Prototypes?

How Are Variables Controlled?

- Small groups
- 30–45 minutes

Have students control the variables in paper airplanes. Start the activity by having every student make a paper airplane. Provide students with different types of paper to use for their airplane, as well as other materials to use to augment their airplanes. Students should throw each airplane from the same height and same starting place to determine which will go farthest. They should identify the weight and types of paper used and evaluate how the plane's design played a role in its flight.

Have them choose two variables to investigate, and perform flight tests again. Once they have their flight data, they should redesign the paper airplanes, reducing the variables down to one, and retest.

DCI This activity can support mastery of this Disciplinary Core Idea:
ETS1.B Developing Possible Solutions

Preassessment

Have students complete the unit pre-test online or see the Assessment Guide.

Build on Prior Knowledge

Students should already know and be prepared to build on the following concepts:
- A prototype is a first, typical, or preliminary model of something, from which other forms are developed or copied.
- A prototype is not the final copy or design.
- Products and machines go through many stages of development, including testing and multiple redesigns.

Differentiate Instruction

Lesson Vocabulary
- failure analysis
- optimize

Students will be aware of words related to the term *optimize*, such as optimistic.

Ask: If I told you that you had the *optimum* amount of fish for the size of your fish tank, what would you guess *optimize* meant? make best or most favorable

ELL: Use Realia

Provide additional assistance to English-language learners by demonstrating how to optimize something, such as the design of an object. The object can be something simple, such as a ball or a paperweight.

Lesson 3 How Do Engineers Test and Improve Prototypes? **44B**

LESSON 3 **Engage** • Explore/Explain • Elaborate • Evaluate

ENGAGE: Lesson Phenomenon

Lesson Objective

Plan, design, and test possible solutions for a prototype to determine which design best solves a problem within given criteria and constraints; identify failure points or difficulties with a design and suggest and implement changes that improve it; communicate in order to share observations, gain insight, and optimize future solutions and designs.

About This Image

Engineers link scientific discoveries (such as crash dummies) with the commercial applications that meet the needs of society (such as auto safety). Highway safety agencies around the world rely on the crash-worthiness test to observe damage and generate data about a car's performance. Crash dummies were developed in 1949 by the U.S. Air Force for testing aircraft ejection seats. Crash dummies are made to look like and respond like human bodies, but they are loaded with special instrumentation.

 SEP Planning and Carrying Out Investigations

Alternative Engage Strategy

Build a Boat

 Pairs
30–50 min

Give each student pair a ball of modeling clay or dough and a container of water (the size of a shoebox). Have the student pairs plan a boat design that they think will successfully float without sinking. Then, have them discuss and make improvements to the boat. Tell students that it may take four or five trials before they have a boat design they like. Have them modify and make improvements as time permits.

LESSON 3

How Do Engineers Test and Improve Prototypes?

Crash dummies test what happens to humans in car crashes. Since the 1950s, the dummies have gotten smarter! Some early dummies were much smaller than average humans. Others didn't collect good data. Testing and redesign have made today's crash dummies more effective than those in the past.

By the end of this lesson...
you'll collaborate to improve your hearing device and determine a deign that best solves the problem.

44

44 Unit 1 Engineering and Technology

Can You Solve It?

Early rocket designs often failed with their first tests. They ended with crashes and fiery explosions. Future designs were improved to solve those problems.

1. How can collaboration and communication lead to improving your hearing-enhancing device prototype?
   Students should respond based on the preliminary observations they can make of the images.

Tip

In this lesson you'll work on the hearing device you've been designing. For more information about what engineers do, review How Do Engineers Define Problems?

EVIDENCE NOTEBOOK Look for this icon to help you gather evidence to answer the question above.

▶ **Explore Online**   Students can view the lesson phenomenon online.

Can You Solve It?

Students are asked to consider the benefits of testing their hearing-enhancing device prototype. Students should be able to guess that when you test a prototype, sometimes you find things that fail or that need improvement. The test provides you with the data you need to make the design better. In this case, testing the device will ensure that it works to improve hearing on a nature walk. Even though the question asks about the hearing-enhancing device, the benefits of testing a design solution are the same no matter what object or product you are testing. Urge students not to worry about whether their answers are correct, but just to write down their initial thoughts. They should expect their ideas to expand as they progress through the explorations. They will have an opportunity to revise their answers when they revisit these questions at the end of the lesson.

DCI ETS1.B Developing Possible Solutions

In order to develop solutions and create designs that best solve problems, engineers require a specific set of abilities. Engineers apply the principles of science and mathematics to develop economical solutions to technical problems.

Tell students that the word *engineer* comes from a Latin word meaning "cleverness."

Ask: What sort of skills should engineers have? a desire to make a difference in the world, a desire to think through complex problems, strength in math and science, like to solve puzzles, like a challenge, like computers, a curiosity about how things work

EVIDENCE NOTEBOOK

Encourage students to use an appropriate graphic organizer, such as main idea and supporting details, to set up their notebook for this lesson.
Find more strategies in the online ELA handbook.

Lesson 3 How Do Engineers Test and Improve Prototypes?

LESSON 3   Engage • **Explore/Explain** • Elaborate • Evaluate

EXPLORATION 1 Things Fail and Improve

HANDS-ON ACTIVITY Small groups   1 class period
Class Collaboration

3D Learning Objective

 Planning and Carrying Out Investigations

Students collaborate to improve the design of their hearing-enhancement device from the previous lessons.

Materials
The list of possible materials is fairly comprehensive, but consider having students turn in a wish list of materials a few days before the activity so that you can acquire objects they might like to try. You could also have students bring in some objects from home.

Preparation
Have materials set out in labeled bins in a common supply area, but place a pair of scissors and some tape at each individual work station, since each group will most likely need them.

Procedure
STEP 1 Encourage students not to skip this step. Prioritizing criteria is often needed in order to focus on key improvements.

 ETS1.B Developing Possible Solutions

Encourage students to watch and listen respectfully as others demonstrate. They should pay attention to find possible design flaws or ways that a model can be improved.

HANDS-ON ACTIVITY
Class Collaboration

Objective
In the past two lessons, you learned how to define engineering problems and design engineering solutions. You have also learned how to apply these skills to designing a hearing-enhancing device. Recall that the purpose of this device is to help someone observe and identify natural sounds during a nature walk.

Collaborate Work with your class to further improve your team's design from the previous lesson. First, collect your team's device or gather the materials you need to rebuild it.

What problem will you solve to meet this objective?
Possible answer: How can I build an even better hearing-enhancing device?
_____

Possible Materials
- safety goggles
- plastic cups
- paper cups
- cloth scraps
- duct tape
- masking tape
- wire clothes hangers
- string
- rubber tubing
- plastic head bands
- scissors
- baseball or painter's cap

Procedure
STEP 1 Recall your design criteria and constraints. List them on the lines below. Rank the criteria in order of importance. Remember them as your class works to improve your designs.
Students should provide the list of criteria and constraints they developed.
_____
_____
_____
_____

46

Student Lab Worksheet and complete Teacher Support available online.

46   Unit 1   Engineering and Technology

STEP 2 Demonstrate and explain your team's design for your class. Tell which features and materials worked best. As the other teams demonstrate, take notes below. List features that you might use to improve your team's design.

Notes from demonstations
Check student notes to confirm capture of other teams' good design features.

STEP 3 Choose one feature to improve based on your notes in Step 2. It should support one of your top-ranked criteria. Plan and build your improved device.

STEP 4 As a team, plan a fair test of your improved design. Write down the test procedure you will use in the table below. Test your design. Record your test results. If you need to, keep revising and testing your design until you are satisfied with the improvement.

Test plan and results
Test plan   Check student procedure and test results to confirm that a fair test was designed and carried out.   **Test results**

47

STEP 2 Help students prepare orderly presentations—what works, why materials were chosen, and how it is used.

STEP 3 Students might choose, "Make the device more wearable." Remind students to check their prioritized criteria and constraints list.

STEP 4 Before students fill in this table, review the concept of a *fair test*.

CCC Influence of Science, Engineering, and Technology on Society and the Natural World

Remind students that many inventions were created thousands of years ago and that each invention is created to have some sort of influence on society, or the people who use the devices. It can be difficult to know if there were prototypes and improvements. Sometimes scientists get lucky and find text that describes design solutions from long ago. This is how we know about the Greco-Egyptian engineer Heron of Alexandria who created countless machines in the late first century CE. Also known as *mekanicos* (machine man), Heron was famous for designing a steam engine, a coin-operated slot machine, and automatic doors.

Ask: Can you think of an item that we use today that was invented by many different civilizations at the same time? Accept all guesses, but tell students that mirrors were used by almost every civilization—some used polished volcanic glass, and some used polished bronze or copper.

Lesson 3 How Do Engineers Test and Improve Prototypes? 47

LESSON 3   Engage • **Explore/Explain** • Elaborate • Evaluate

EXPLORATION 1 *Things Fail and Improve, continued*

Analyze Your Results

STEP 5 Some students might have different opinions about what is most important for a successful design. It is acceptable to have more than one correct answer here.

 ETS1.C Optimizing the Design Solution

STEP 7 After students answer this question, offer them the chance to answer it all over again with the condition that unlimited supplies were available.

Draw Conclusions

STEP 8 Some student groups may have performed more than one test. Have students specify the test they performed when answering this question.

Claims, Evidence, and Reasoning

Have one student group work with another group to discuss each other's claims and evidence from Step 8. Allow them 5–10 minutes to tell each other about their designs.

Scoring Rubric for Hands-On Activity	
3	has prioritized list of criteria and constraints; performs fair tests; completes test procedures and results table; analyzes and concludes the results; and cites evidence
2	has a partly prioritized list of criteria and constraints; performs some fair tests; completes most test procedures and results table; analyzes and concludes the results; and cites some evidence
1	2 or 3 of the points above need improvement or are incomplete
0	4 or 5 of the points above need improvement or are incomplete

48   Unit 1 Engineering and Technology

Analyze Your Results

STEP 5 What improvement did your team add and why did you choose it?
Possible answer: Because comfort was our top criterion, we added a padded support band. Responses should include a feature detail and a rationale.

STEP 6 Did your team's design pass your test? Explain.
Possible answer: Yes, because the device was more comfortable and we could still identify tapping and soft conversations from a distance.

STEP 7 If you could add or change another feature to improve your design, what would it be? Why?
Possible answer: Another team strongly recommended larger earpieces, so we'd like to see how much they help in identifying sounds from a greater distance.

Draw Conclusions

STEP 8 State a claim about your improved design and how it tested. Cite evidence from the activity to support your claim.
Possible answer: We claim that our device was improved because it was more comfortable and still met the other criteria. It was sturdy and amplified sounds from a distance.

STEP 9 If you could start over with designing your hearing-enhancing device, how would you do it? Explain.
Possible answer: We'd start by combining the best features of all the successful teams' designs. We already know that those features work, although they may not work well together.

STEP 10 What questions came to you about the task of designing and testing prototypes?
Possible answer: How do other hearing devices work? How are they tested? Are there easier ways to plan and carry out fair tests?

48

EXPLORATION 1

Things Fail and Improve

Try, Try Again!

You've learned that engineering solutions are designed and built to solve a problem. Often, perhaps like what happened with your hearing-enhancing device, a first design doesn't work. For example, a design might work okay, but testing suggests that it can work a lot better. Or the design might meet almost all of the criteria but be unsafe. When this happens, engineers head back to the drawing board to improve their designs.

Designs can also improve bit by bit as engineers learn more about the materials they're using. Small positive changes build up as engineers test and add them to the design. The end result is the ideal, or best, design possible within the constraints of time, materials, and budget.

HANDS-ON Apply What You Know
Tissue Rope

2. Look at the rope shown here. Suppose you need to make your own, but out of toilet paper.
   - Your goal is to work with a partner to find the best toilet-paper rope-making technique you can. You are limited to 15 minutes to explore and build. A loop of your product will be tested to see how much weight it will support.
   - Get two arm-lengths of toilet paper from your teacher.
   - Wait for your teacher to say "start." Then, with your partner, figure out the best way to turn the paper into a rope.
   - Try lots of ideas! When you are happy with your technique, get more paper from your teacher and make your test sample. Be sure to budet time for this.

Was your final product better or worse than your first attempt? Tell how your rope-making technique changed as you tried different ideas.

Possible answer: The final rope was better. The first idea we tried was weak, but it got better as we figured out how to twist and braid strands.

49

3D Learning Objective

Plan and carry out investigations to **identify failure points or difficulties** and **suggest needed improvements** for a design or design process. **Test** to **figure out which of them best solves the problem.** Relate this information to **how society uses new technologies**.

SEP Planning and Carrying Out Investigations

To ensure that a test is fair, that all variables are controlled, and that the number of trials is adequate, sometimes scientists will write up an investigation but then collaborate with others to be sure there are no missing steps or parts.

Ask: What is collaboration? working with one or more other people toward a common goal

HANDS-ON Apply What You Know
Tissue Rope

Pair students for this activity. Point out to students that this activity works best if one student reads the directions to the other, who will try to follow them.

Scoring Guideline

An excellent group result is a strong rope and a demonstrated understanding of improving bit by bit through innovation.

CCC Influence of Engineering, Technology, and Science on Society and the Natural World

Discuss with students the ways in which knots have influenced society.

Ask: What can people do with knots? What are they used for? tying things together for boating, fishing, hiking, and many other purposes

Lesson 3 How Do Engineers Test and Improve Prototypes? **49**

LESSON 3 Engage • **Explore/Explain** • Elaborate • Evaluate

EXPLORATION 1 *Things Fail and Improve, continued*

Connection to Math

Have students study the cake recipes on the page, paying careful attention to the baking times. Have students form pairs and discuss the variables of baking a cake, such as temperature, timing, etc. Call on groups to share their answers as to why the baking times differ. This requires use of abstract mathematical concepts.

MP.2 Reason abstractly and quantitatively

Differentiate Instruction

ELL: Mirroring Pair ELL students with confident English speakers. Have one student read the first bullet point instruction under the "Just Right!" recipe. Then, have the second student mirror the first student by reading the same instruction under the "Too High!" recipe. Have students continue this way, one reading an instruction and the next reading the same instruction in another recipe. When the text the two students are reading differs, they know they have found the culprit! Have them circle the recipe step that caused the recipe to fail.

SEP Planning and Carrying Out Investigations

Pair students, and explain that they will perform a penny-drops experiment to determine how many drops of water you can fit on a penny. Each student group will need three droppers, one penny, and three small cups—one with water, one with rubbing alcohol, and one with vegetable oil. Describe the experiment verbally, but do not give them written instructions. Check for understanding. Have each pair write simple instructions for the lab. Then, have groups trade instructions and see how the investigation goes following another group's instructions. During the investigation, students should look for instructions that fail in order to change them to yield the correct results.

50 Unit 1 Engineering and Technology

Cakes Done Right!

Engineers test their designs many times to get the best solution. Tests help them figure out what went wrong and why. This process is called **failure analysis.** It requires thinking carefully about causes and effects, especially for more complex devices or systems.

3. Review the process of testing your hearing-enhancing device. Use your testing and results to complete a failure analysis on your solution. Use the table below to record your thoughts and ideas.

What didn't work?	Why I think it didn't work.	How can I fix or improve it?	How critical it is to fix the solution?
Possible answer: the earpieces	They were too heavy and put pressure on the head.	The solution might be to use a lighter material.	The change is critical because people might not be able to use the device if it hurts to wear.

Engineers improve designs by careful testing, one system part at a time. They work this way to zero in on an ideal solution for given criteria—the best bicycle, the clearest window, or even the best tasting cake. Read below about recreating Grandma's famous yellow cake.

Too high, too low, too dry . . . just right!

4. Look at the test bake pictures and the information for each test cake. Then write in the likely ideal recipe choices below.

Grandma's Ideal Cake

You're trying to match this cake's taste and look. Based on the test cakes, what are these recipe details?

Use __2 teaspoons__ of baking powder.

Bake for __30 minutes__ minutes.

50

- This test cake tastes about right. It has 3 teaspoons of baking powder to make it puff up. It baked for 30 minutes at 350°F.
- How does it compare to the ideal cake you're trying to match?

- This test cake also tastes okay, although it's a little chewy. It has 1 teaspoon of baking powder and baked for 25 minutes at 350°F.
- How does it compare to the ideal cake you're trying to match?

- This test cake tastes about right. It's dry and crumbly, though. It baked for 35 minutes at 350°F. 2 teaspoons of baking powder were used to make this cake.
- How does it compare to the ideal cake you're trying to match?

 EVIDENCE NOTEBOOK Summarize your response to Question 3 in your Evidence Notebook.

Putting it Together

5. Choose the correct word to complete each sentence.

| destroy | failure | imperfect | improve | problem solving | perfect |

Most prototypes are **imperfect**. When testing a design solution, it is critical to go through a **failure** analysis. This helps **improve** a solution.

Collaboration

Write, Pair, Share Encourage students to write each and every failure with their designs in a table. Tell them they can expand the table if they need to. Each element of a design that doesn't work should be examined. That way, when the model is reworked, the different solutions can be retested to be sure that the changes worked better to solve the problem. Have students fill out the tables on their own and then pair together to share ideas and add to their tables.

 EVIDENCE NOTEBOOK

Once students work through the table accompanying item 3 collaboratively, have each student summarize the information in writing in their notebooks. This will allow them the time to think through things on their own. It will also give you an opportunity to spot misconceptions. Sometimes students might disagree in whether or not a particular fix is critical, and writing independently gives each student the freedom to their own opinions and ideas.

FORMATIVE ASSESSMENT

 ETS1.B Developing Possible Solutions

Once you have gone through these answers together as a class, ask students to suggest sentences that put together concepts from the lesson thus far that use the words that were NOT chosen from the word bank. In other words, use the unused words to create their own fill-in-the-blanks. This can be challenging!

LESSON 3   Engage • **Explore/Explain** • Elaborate • Evaluate

EXPLORATION 2 Getting Better

3D Learning Objective

Develop an understanding of how **communication plays an important role in the design of new technologies**. Explore how communication **impacts everyday things that they experience**. Learn more about the **process for designing solutions**.

> ### Differentiate Instruction
>
> **Extension** Have students do some research and look for famous inventions that were the direct result of a collaboration of a few or many different engineers. Have them share the results of their research with the class.

DCI ETS1.B Developing Possible Solutions

Explain to students that tests are designed to identify failure points or difficulties, which suggest the elements of the design that need to be improved.

Ask: How does this relate back to the volleyball team? Sometimes teams have weaknesses. It could be a particular person not carrying their weight, or it could be a skill they need more work on, or they could be out of shape or not flexible enough. Teams need to evaluate their weaknesses and then work to improve them.

EXPLORATION 2

Getting Better

Talking to the Team

When engineers work on design solutions, team members often communicate with each other. They share their observations to help improve what they are working on and to perhaps gain insight on future solutions.

Communication is an important part of most situations. Like an engineering team, a volleyball team needs to communicate. By talking or giving each other signals during practice, players work as a team and will likely play better during a game.

Explore Online

a. Players communicate what the next play will be. The player who plans to hit the ball first calls, "Got it!"

b. Players signal so everyone knows where the ball is going. The second player is ready and waiting to make the second hit.

52

Unit 1 Engineering and Technology

c. The third player is in motion and ready to return the ball over the net.

After a game, volleyball players may talk about what worked well and what didn't work so well. They also may talk about what they plan on doing better during their next practice or game. Likewise, engineers communicate after testing solutions to try to **optimize,** or make as good as possible, their solutions and designs. Good communication and teamwork help improve any team's final results.

7. How is communication important to both sports and engineering?

Possible answer: Communication helps people consider more than one possible solution or strategy. It can help improve a design or plan, and perhaps give insight on future solutions or plans. Good communication and teamwork help improve any team's final results.

8. Which of these do you think are ways to improve communication among team members? Circle all that apply.
   a. Tell a team member that her design is well done and suggest an improvement.
   b. Tell a team member her project is bad, and she shouldn't even test it.
   c. Give a team member some suggestions for alternative materials.
   d. Yell at a team member until he agrees with your viewpoint.
   e. Talk to others about the way they tested their project and suggest more good tests.
   f. Tell a team member he used the materials wrong, even though his design tested well.

DCI ETS1.C Optimizing the Design Solution

Engineers work hard on designing solutions and even on improving upon their designs. But engineers don't often make or manufacture their ideas by themselves. They draw them! Engineers make detail drawings.

Ask: What should detail drawings contain? labeled parts, a scale, measurements, multiple angles

Optimizing design solutions is all about making the best design possible at a given time and then allowing that design to develop over time. If you look at technologies from long ago, they were the best from that time, and engineers have improved upon them to make them what they are today. Take cars for example—where did they begin? Leonardo da Vinci sketched a horseless mechanical cart in the 1500s. About 200 years later, a French inventor built a steam engine cart.

Ask: How do cars run today? Sample answer: engines fueled by gasoline or diesel

Connection to English Language Arts

Have each student choose a technology that has seen great change over time. If you can reserve time in the media center, have them find something that interests them. Each student should gather information from several sources on a different invention. Encourage products that they use every day, such as cellular phones or tablets or MP3 players or sporting equipment. Some students may be more interested in the development of toys or cargo ships or airplane travel. Put students into groups of four, and have them share their research with one another. Then, mix up the groups so that students get to hear a variety of ideas. If time permits, have them present to the class.

W.5.7 Conduct short research projects that use several sources

LESSON 3   Engage • **Explore/Explain** • Elaborate • Evaluate

EXPLORATION 2 Getting Better, continued

HANDS-ON Apply What You Know
Sharing Feedback

Remind students to make kind, thoughtful, helpful design critiques. Model this process for them by critiquing one group's design.

Scoring Guidelines

If you don't want written feedback, you can assign participation points for being engaged and helpful.

Connection to Earth Science

Relate the diagram of the engineering process to Earth's systems. Explain to students that the engineering process follows a specific process, similar to how Earth's processes work, such as the water cycle. Have a discussion about these parallels and what they might infer.

ESS2.A Earth's Materials and Systems

 EVIDENCE NOTEBOOK

At this point, students should have a solid foundation on the topic of optimizing design solutions. Ask them to tell you what *optimize* means and then what the process of optimization is, followed by why it is so important in the field of engineering. They should write about why engineers should always work to optimize design solutions. The best response will include an example of a design and how it has been optimized over time.

FORMATIVE ASSESSMENT

 Language SmArts
Recalling Relevant Information
W.5.8 Recall relevant information

Students should include two major topics in their response: what they learned themselves (sometimes from their mistakes) and what they learned from their collaborators. Complete responses show a mature reflection of their design solutions.

 HANDS-ON Apply What You Know
Sharing Feedback

9. Now that you've learned about the importance of communication, team up with two other students and take turns giving feedback on each of your designs. After you have considered one another's feedback, make a plan to retest and improve your hearing-enhancing device.

10. These steps show a process for designing solutions. Write an *A* by steps you learned about in Lesson 1, a *B* for Lesson 2, and a *C* for Lesson 3.

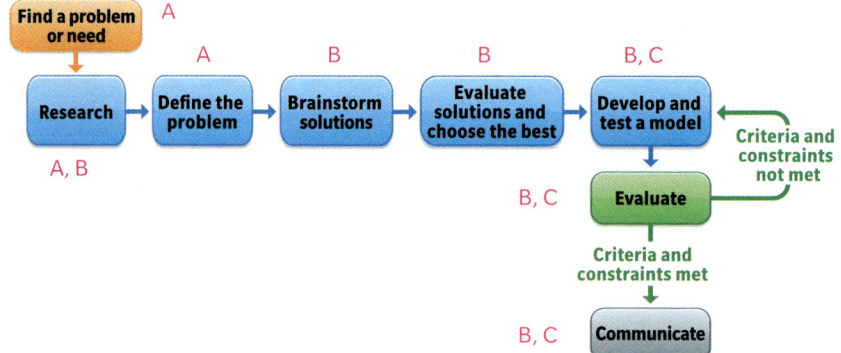

 EVIDENCE NOTEBOOK Use what you've learned in this lesson to describe how you can optimze your solution.

 Language SmArts
Recalling Relevant Information

11. Think about what you learned during the testing of your device. Also think about the feedback you got from others. Use this relevant information to explain what you've learned about the last few steps of an engineering design process.

Possible answer: Testing allows you to see what works and what doesn't work. Communication and feedback from others can give you new ideas and help you figure out ways to improve your design.

Tip

The English Language Arts Handbook can provide help with understanding how to find and use relevant information to answer questions.

54

---

54   Unit 1 Engineering and Technology

TAKE IT FURTHER Discover More

Check out this path . . . or go online to choose one of these other paths.

- Sense Extenders for Science
- Ear Areas
- High or Low?

Sense Extenders for Science

Scientists and engineers use many different types of tools to extend their senses. Some tools enhance their ability to see objects that are very far away or too small to see with the unaided eye. Other tools amplify sound or allow their users to see what's inside the human body. Some tools produce images that can be studied at a later time.

All of the tools shown on these two pages have been redesigned over time to extend human senses.

The first telescopes were invented in the early 17th century. **Refracting telescopes,** such as this one, use lenses to magnify objects. Over time, these tools were improved to make their lenses larger and clearer.

Hydrophones are underwater microphones. The earliest ones were used in the 1920s by ship captains to communicate. Today, hydrophones have many uses, including listening to whales communicate.

In 1667, Robert Hooke used a simple **light microscope** to observe tiny living things. Today, complex light microscopes are used in many fields of science, including biology and geology.

Sense Extenders for Science

In this activity, students learn about the different tools and technology that have been created, designed, and redesigned by scientists and engineers over time to help extend human senses. Science creates the need for tools. Technology is created by engineers for science. Tools and technology expand and help open up our senses to more discoveries.

DCI ETS1.B Developing Possible Solutions

Light microscopes have come a long way since their invention, with the help of science, technology, and engineering.

Ask: How are you able to magnify microscopic objects with a light microscope? A light at the bottom of the microscope reflects light rays up to the object through a hole in the stage. Objective lenses magnify the image, which is made even larger when it is seen through the lens of the eyepiece.

Collaboration

Brainstorm Hydrophones were used in World War I to detect submarines and to allow submarines to locate targets without coming to the surface. A hydrophone began as a microphone extended through the bottom of the vessel. But it didn't take long for engineers to figure out that several microphones faced in different directions separated by a few feet and attached by a bar would yield way better results! Make a list of two objects you use in your everyday life that you think can be improved upon. Work with your partners to discuss some ideas about how you would improve them.

LESSON 3 Engage • Explore/Explain • **Elaborate** • Evaluate

TAKE IT FURTHER, continued

Connection to Life Science

Like a thermographic camera, mosquitoes have special sensory structures to detect humans! Mosquitoes are attracted by the odor of the carbon dioxide gas that humans and other animals exhale. Mosquitoes also pick up other cues that signal a human is nearby. They use their vision to spot a host and thermal sensory information to detect heat rising from our bodies.

LS1.D Information Processing

 Planning and Carrying Out Investigations

Have students design a simple animal sketch showing a structure for getting food. It can be real or imagined. Then, have them trade drawings with a partner and optimize each other's design solutions.

 **Influence of Engineering, Technology, and Science on Society and the Natural World**

Scientific discoveries about the natural world can often lead to new and improved technologies, which are developed through the engineering design process.

 Explore Online

Students can explore these additional topics online.

Ear Areas

Students examine how the physical characteristics of different ears affect how they work. *(Outside research required.)*

High or Low?

Students examine how ears are helpful in determining what is going on around us. *(Outside research required.)*

Thermographic cameras produce images using infrared radiation. Such cameras were first used in the early 1900s to help soldiers see at night. Today, these cameras are used to study rocks that could cause earthquakes, to study galaxies that are far away, to determine if farm animals are sick, to identify dangerous pollutants in the environment, and to inspect buildings and other structures for damage or poor construction.

12. How would you use a thermographic camera?

Possible answer: to see at night in the woods

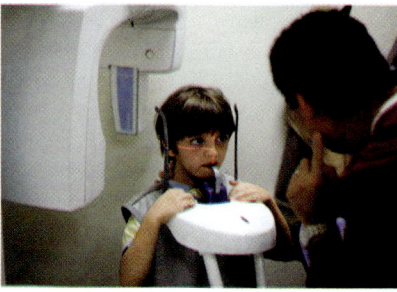

X-rays were discovered in 1895. These rays can pass through skin and tissue but not denser materials, such as teeth and bones. X-rays are used to determine if teeth are healthy, bones are broken, or tumors are present in the body. They can also be used to treat some cancerous tumors.

X-rays are also used at airports to screen for dangerous materials inside suitcases, to learn about the minerals that make up rocks, and even to study objects in space.

13. Research one of the tools on these pages. Or find another tool that extends other senses. Draw the tool and show how it works. Describe how an engineer might use the tool to solve a problem or test a solution.

Check student drawings and descriptions to evaluate how the senses are extended.

Lesson 3   Engage • Explore/Explain • Elaborate • **Evaluate**

LESSON CHECK

Explore Online — Students can revisit the lesson phenomenon online.

LESSON 3

Lesson Check

Name _____

Can You Solve It?

1. Now that you know about the importance of testing prototypes, apply what you've learned to the rocket example. Be sure to do the following:
   - Explain why multiple solutions should be developed and tested.
   - Discuss the importance of identifying failure points.
   - Describe why communication is critical to any team of people working together.

EVIDENCE NOTEBOOK Use the information you've collected in your Evidence Notebook to help you cover each point above.

Possible answer:
- An engineering design solution might not actually work when tested. Thus, it is important to try several alternatives to improve the chances of success.
- Identifying what doesn't work helps engineers improve a prototype.
- Communication is critical to any team because hearing others' feedback can lead to fresh ideas.

Checkpoints

2. How is communication an important part of designing solutions? Choose all of the statements that are correct.
   a. **Communication helps people talk about improvement.**
   b. **Communication helps identify problems.**
   c. Communication only causes arguments.
   d. **Communication creates a sense of teamwork.**
   e. Communication is critical only if everyone agrees.

57

Formal Assessment Go online for student self-checks and other assessments.

Can You Solve It?

Collaboration

Discussion You may wish to revisit and discuss the image as a group to assess students' understanding of the material. Use the bulleted points in the Interactive Worktext to lead the discussion.

EVIDENCE NOTEBOOK

Have students reread their answers to the Evidence Notebook prompts and then use this evidence to justify their reasoning as they respond to the Can You Solve It question. Make sure students understand that a complete response must address all bulleted points.

CCC Influence on Engineering, Technology, and Science on Society and the Natural World

Ask students to think about how the design process affects society and the environment. When a design process fails, sometimes that can help engineers and scientists understand what needs to be done to improve something. And in the end, society and the natural world may benefit.

SUMMATIVE ASSESSMENT

DCI ETS1.C Optimizing the Design Solution

Analyzing Processes

2. Once students complete this question, you can help them with a strategy. Note how the two answers that are incorrect have the word *only* in them. Tell students that in multiple-choice questions, absolutes are often incorrect because they don't take a wide variety of situations into account. Discuss and review how communication builds teams.

Lesson 3 How Do Engineers Test and Improve Prototypes?   57

LESSON 3 Engage • Explore/Explain • Elaborate • **Evaluate**

LESSON CHECK, continued

3. The Hands-On Activity at the beginning of this lesson is all about testing design solutions. Students should be able to fill in the three blanks correctly, but struggling students could review Exploration 2 for a discussion of optimizing design solutions with teamwork and the steps for the engineering design process that was developed over the course of three lessons.

4. Remind students that the best strategy for answering a multiple-choice question if they are unsure is to eliminate the answer choices that are definitely not correct. Since answer choices d and e here include the negative aspects of being a good communicator, students should be able to identify them as wrong answer choices since communication was identified as a vital skill for engineers.

5. This question gets at the heart of what engineers do and combines both of the disciplinary core ideas about developing solutions and then optimizing design solutions. Students should be able to identify that the engineer needs to try other options to figure out what went wrong and realize that that is a normal part of the process.

6. If students need some reminders or hints about giving feedback, they can review the section on sharing feedback in Exploration 2. Examples are given for athletes and engineers.

---

3. Choose the correct words to complete each sentence.

not build	test	throw away
multiple times	once	once and then stop
mistakes	testing	original problem

When building and designing an engineering solution, it is always important to ___**test**___ the solution. Good engineers will always try to test a solution ___**multiple times**___. It is important to keep in mind the ___**original problem**___ that the solution was meant to solve when designing and testing a solution.

4. Circle the letter of each correct statement.
   a. **Making good observations is important.**
   b. **Making good observations helps to figure out what needs to be improved.**
   c. **Making good observations shows you what to test next.**
   d. Making good observations is not important because it slows down the process.
   e. Making good observations can be distracting and should be stopped when it happens.

5. An engineer is testing a solution. The solution is failing. What should she do? Select all that apply.
   a. **She should consider using other materials for the same design.**
   b. **She should figure out what didn't go right with her design.**
   c. **She should understand that sometimes things don't work as planned.**
   d. She should not try to develop other solutions to this problem.

6. Feedback is important in solving any problem. Select the best example of how to give good feedback.
   a. Tell the other person that his or her project is a good example of what not to do.
   b. Tell the person that his or her design is poorly built. Do not suggest any improvements.
   c. **Tell the person that his or her design is built well but still suggest some possible improvements.**
   d. Ignore the person if he or she isn't listening to you.

LESSON 3
Lesson Roundup

A. Which of these describes a good approach to solving an engineering problem? Select all that apply.
   a. Research, revise, and repeat.
   b. Give up if your first solution fails so that you don't waste any more of your time.
   c. Failure marks the end of the process.
   (d. If at first you don't succeed, try, try again.)

B. Explain why an engineering design solution that does not pass testing can be considered a successful solution.

Possible answer: Often, learning what doesn't work is just as important as seeing what does work in a design solution. Learning from mistakes can provide information on what not to do in future designs.

C. Below are steps that you might follow to solve an engineering problem. Add numbers to put them in order.
   a. Test the prototype. __6__
   b. Perform failure analysis. __7__
   c. Identify criteria and constraints. __3__
   d. Test final design. __9__
   e. Create the prototype. __5__
   f. Identify the problem that needs solving. __1__
   g. Choose materials for the prototype. __4__
   h. Improve prototype. __8__
   i. Research information about the problem. __2__

Lesson Roundup

DCI ETS1.B Developing Possible Solutions
ETS1.C Optimizing the Design Solution

This lesson summary enables students to quickly revisit key points and prepare for tests.

A. Point out to students that this question gets to the heart of the characteristics that engineers must possess. Engineers need to be curious problem solvers, and this theme was consistent throughout the lessons in this unit. Help struggling students eliminate incorrect answer choices by reminding them that engineers have a goal of optimizing their design solutions. **ETS1.B, ETS1.C**

B. Remind students that a failure analysis is an integral part of the design process and that it in fact is helpful in order to make designs even better so that they function the best they can. Tell them that it is better to find a flaw during development rather than after the product is released to the public. **ETS1.B, ETS1.C**

C. This question provides a great opportunity for visual learners to show understanding and competency by labeling parts of the engineering design process. Struggling students can revisit Exploration 2 to revisit the steps in the diagram.
ETS1.B, ETS1.C

UNIT 1 Performance Task

ENGINEER IT! small groups · 1 class period
Designing a Portable Chair

3D Assessment Goal
Students **develop models** of a more comfortable chair. They analyze the **problems** and come up with **solutions** for their new designs, to demonstrate understanding of **ETS1.A, ETS1.B, and EST1.C** in support of **ETS1-1**.

Materials
- paper
- pencil

Preparation
Schedule class time in the computer lab or ensure all small groups have access to the computer in the classroom.

CCC Influence of Science, Engineering, and Technology on Society and the Natural World
Students will design portable chairs that provide more comfort to the people who sit in them. From this activity, students can learn that even something as simple as a chair has an impact on society.
Ask: What are some features of a chair?

Research
Review how to properly cite resources.
Print: title, author, copyright date, page number
Online: webpage title, URL, date visited
If students are doing their own research on the Internet, remind them how to search for reliable sources that can be trusted.

Brainstorm
Remind students that the brainstorming group is just to come up with ideas. Each of them will be individually responsible for coming up with an idea of how to design chairs to be more comfortable.

60 Unit 1 Engineering and Technology

UNIT 1   UNIT PERFORMANCE TASK

ENGINEER IT!
Designing a Portable Chair

You work for a company that builds seating for large events. Clients are complaining that the portable chairs you make are not comfortable. It is your team's task to learn about portable chairs and design one that your clients will like.

Clients don't like sitting on this.

STATING YOUR GOAL: How will you know that you have completed your assignment?

Sample answer: when we have designed portable seats that are comfortable to use

Review the checklist at the end of this Unit Performance Task. Keep those requirements in mind as you proceed.

RESEARCH: Study the portable chairs that are currently on the market. Find out which are the most popular. Note their features. Examine several online or library resources, and cite them.

Student should note popular chair features and cite sources.

BRAINSTORM: Brainstorm three or more ideas with your team that might fit with your goal. Evaluate the ideas, and choose the best based on the criteria of the project.

Student should list at least three desirable features for a new portable chair.

60

MAKE A PLAN: Plan a design for your chair by considering the questions below.

1. What materials will you use for your chair and why?
2. What are your standards for using or rejecting materials or features?
3. What features from other chairs, if any, will you use for your chair?
4. What original features, if any, will you use for your chair?

Student should provide a general description of the chair and its features, including materials needed and why.

_____

_____

_____

_____

_____

VISUALIZE: Draw a sketch and make a construction paper model of your chair. Name and describe all of your chair's parts and features.

EVALUATE AND REDESIGN: How close have you come to reaching your goal? Are there ways to improve your design? If so, what are they?

_____

_____

COMMUNICATE: Make improvements if necessary, and present and describe your chair to your class.

Checklist

Review your project and check off each completed item.

_____ Includes information about considered features and why each was included or rejected.

_____ Includes citation of multiple sources used in your research.

_____ Includes a sketch or model of your completed chair, along with written descriptions of its parts and features.

_____ Includes an evaluation of the chair's design and descriptions of any improvements made.

Make a Plan

SEP Asking Questions and Defining Problems

Ask: What might people find uncomfortable about the current design for the chairs?

Evaluate and Redesign

Students may have limited ideas for improvements and redesigning their chairs. Consider having student partners critique each other's designs and reasoning. Use sentence frames to guide their discussions:

- I don't understand why you chose _____.
- How will _____ get the _____ to be more comfortable?

Scoring Rubric for Performance Task	
3	• complete resources, clear reasoning, multiple sources • complete, detailed, accurate chair design and problems with solutions • presentation engaging, accurate, supported by drawing and description
2	• most resources, adequate reasoning and sources • most parts present in the chair design, and problems with solutions • presentation mostly accurate, has a drawing and description
1	• some key resources and reasoning, a few sources • some description, mixed accuracy of chair design and problem with solution • presentation inaccurate, has either a drawing or a description but not both
0	• few key resources, no reasons, minimal sources • little description, inaccurate details of chair design and problem with no solution • presentation incomplete

UNIT 1 Review

SUMMATIVE ASSESSMENT

1. Students can correctly answer this question by thinking about engineering. They should recall the definition of *criteria* and not be confused by the fact that the doors/windows are showing the view of nature. A review can be found in Lesson 1, Exploration 1.

2. Students should understand this basic concept of engineering. Information about criteria can be revisited in Lesson 1, Exploration 1. They can recall how constraints are used by looking at the *Hands-On Activity* in Lesson 1.

3. Students should generalize the content from Lesson 1 to correctly answer this question. To review, have students review the parts of an engineering project. They should read the sentences out loud to check for sense.

UNIT 1

Unit Review

1. Which statements are true of the object shown here? Circle all that apply.

   a. **It meets a want or need.**
   b. It can be found in nature.
   c. It meets no specified criteria.
   d. **It was designed by engineers.**
   e. **It is an example of technology.**

2. Which pair of factors defines any engineering problem? Circle the correct choice.
   a. wants and needs
   b. time and expense
   c. nature and technology
   d. **criteria and constraints**

3. Fill in the blank with the correct word to complete each sentence.

A set of criteria	A budget	materials
A list of constraints	criteria	constraints

   _____*A set of criteria*_____ states the desirable features of a solution.

   Limits on solving a problem are called _____*constraints*_____.

62

Unit 1 Engineering and Technology

4. You are faced with the situation shown here, a filthy pet, and decide to confront it using technology.
Using the numbers 1–8, arrange these steps to show one way you could proceed.

   __5__ Evaluate test results.

   __3__ Design a prototype to solve the problem.

   __1__ Identify the problem to be solved.

   __7__ Retest the modified prototype.

   __8__ Construct a final design.

   __2__ Research existing related technology.

   __4__ Build and test the prototype.

   __6__ Modify the prototype.

5. Which steps from the previous exercise are likely to be taken more than once? Circle all that apply.

   a. (Evaluate test results.)
   b. (Improve the prototype.)
   c. Construct a final design.
   d. (Retest improved prototype.)
   e. Identify the problem to be solved.

6. Fill in the blank with the correct word to complete each sentence.

a single thing	several things at once
improve their designs	develop their criteria

   Testing a prototype works best when the engineer observes and measures the effects of changing __a single thing__.

   Engineers test and retest to __improve their designs__.

---

4. Students are asked to place the steps in correct order. Have students refer back to Lesson 3, Explorations 1 and 2 as a refresher on prototypes.

5. Students must refer back to the complete process in order to answer this item correctly. Encourage them to revisit Lesson 3.

6. Encourage students to whisper the sentences out loud to themselves, using each answer choice in the sentence. This can help them hear the correct or incorrect options. Lesson 3 can provide a good review for students on prototyping.

Unit 1 Engineering and Technology

UNIT 1 Review, continued

7. Students will need to apply their knowledge of engineering to the answer choices to answer this question correctly. Have students revisit information about solutions in Lesson 2.
8. Have students think not only about engineering itself but also how it impacts society. They can review information about engineering testing in Lessons 1 and 2.
9. Failure analysis is specifically discussed in Lesson 3, Exploration 1. Have students use all answer choices in the sentence and say them out loud to arrive at the correct answers.
10. Students can recall their *Hands-On Activities* in this unit, which required brainstorming and collaboration.

3D Item Analysis	1	2	3	4	5	6	7	8	9	10
SEP Asking Questions and Defining Problems		•	•		•	•		•	•	•
SEP Constructing Explanations and Designing Solutions			•	•	•	•	•		•	•
DCI Defining and Delimiting Engineering Problems			•		•	•	•		•	•
DCI Developing Possible Solutions				•	•	•	•	•	•	•
DCI Optimizing the Design Solution					•	•	•	•	•	•
CCC Influence of Science, Engineering, and Technology on Society and the Natural World			•		•		•			

7. What makes crash test dummies useful substitutes for human beings? Circle the correct choice.
   a. They are able to avoid collisions.
   b. They have been used since the 1950s.
   c. They contain sensors that collect data.
   d. They are smaller than average humans.

8. Which of the following name good reasons for repeated engineering testing? Circle all that apply.
   a. to ensure safety
   b. to solve problems
   c. to reduce feedback
   d. to eliminate criteria
   e. to develop a final product

9. Fill in the blank with the correct word to complete each sentence.

   | failure points | results | prototypes |
   | working solutions | design difficulties | breakthroughs |

   An engineer can find things needing improvement by isolating _____failure points_____.

   That term refers to _____design difficulties_____.

10. Fill in the blank with the correct word to complete each sentence.

    | collaboration | failure | research |
    | a prototype | peer pressure | brainstorming |

    _____Brainstorming_____ gets you a lot of ideas quickly.
    However, we say that "_____Collaboration_____ leads to optimization."
    Because sharing successes often helps make the best engineering solution.

64 Unit 1 Engineering and Technology

UNIT 2 Energy

UNIT 2

Energy

Unit Project: Truck Pull
How can you use elastic energy or a spring to move a truck? You will design and test a truck with your team. Ask your teacher for details.

Explore Online

Bumper cars show how physical contact transfers energy.

65

Unit Overview

In this unit, students will . . .
- discover what energy is and how it is transferred.
- explore how collisions show energy.

About This Image

Bumper cars use electricity to move around the rink. The electricity is delivered through the long pole on the bumper car. As the bumper car moves around, the top of the pole moves along a ceiling grid. As a bumper car collides with another bumper car, energy is transferred. The impact of the collision makes this a thrilling ride that is less dangerous than some other rides because of the rubber bumper. This amusement park ride is an example of Newton's third law of motion.

Unit Project

As students work through the unit lessons, have them start thinking about ways to move a truck using elastic or spring energy.

Draw students' attention to the bumper cars and how they move in different directions. Challenge students to research or test their team truck to understand how the team truck can move in different directions, like the bumper cars. More support for the Unit Project can be found on pp. 67I–67L.

Unit 2 Energy 65

UNIT 2 Energy

The learning experiences in this unit prepare students for the mastery of:

Performance Expectations

4-PS3-1 Use evidence to construct an explanation relating the speed of an object to the energy of that object.

4-PS3-2 Make observations to provide evidence that energy can be transferred from place to place by sound, light, heat, and electric currents.

4-PS3-3 Ask questions and predict outcomes about the changes in energy that occur when objects collide.

4-PS3-4 Apply scientific ideas to design, test, and refine a device that converts energy from one form to another.

▶ Explore Online

In addition to the print resources, the following resources are available online to support this unit.

Unit Pretest
Lesson 1 What Is Energy?
- Online Student Edition
- Lesson Quiz

Lesson 2 How Is Energy Transferred?
- Online Student Edition
- Lesson Quiz

Lesson 3 How Do Collisions Show Energy?
- Online Student Edition
- Lesson Quiz

You Solve It Crash Course
Unit Performance Task
Unit Test

UNIT 2
At a Glance

LESSON 1
What Is Energy? 68

LESSON 2
How Is Energy Transferred? 88

LESSON 3
How Do Collisions Show Energy? 114

Unit Review 136

Vocabulary Game: Guess the Word

Materials
- Kitchen timer or online computer timer

Directions
1. Take turns to play.
2. To take a turn, choose a vocabulary word. Do not tell the word to the other players.
3. Set the timer for one minute.
4. Give a one-word clue about your word. Point to a player. That player has one chance to guess your word.
5. Repeat step 4 with other players until a player guesses the word or time runs out. Give a different one-word clue each time.
6. The first player to guess the word gets 1 point. If the player can then use the word in a sentence, he or she gets 1 more point. Then that player chooses the next word.
7. The first player to score 5 points wins.

vibrate
To move back and forth.

energy
The ability to do work and cause changes in matter.

Unit Vocabulary

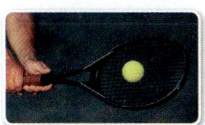
collision: The result of two objects bumping into each other.

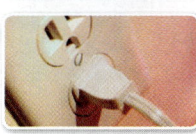
electric current: The flow of electric charges along a path.

energy: The ability to do work and cause changes in matter.

energy transfer: The movement of energy from place to place or from one object to another.

energy transformation: A change in energy from one form to another.

heat: The energy that moves between objects of different temperatures.

vibrate: To move back and forth.

Unit Vocabulary

Students can explore all lesson vocabulary terms in the **Online Glossary**.

Vocabulary Strategies

Have students review the terms individually. Then pair up and have pairs choose two terms and write a detailed sentence using both terms accurately.

Differentiate Instruction

RTI/Extra Support Have students use context clues to infer definitions.

Extension Have students use the terms and then work in small groups to illustrate and explain the terms for a third-grade student.

ELL Pronounce each term and have students repeat it. Then have students explain how they think the image relates to the definition.

Vocabulary Game: Guess the Word

Preparation
Use a timer on your smartphone or tablet, if that is more convenient than a kitchen timer or online computer timer.

Game Play
- Students choose a word card and give clues about their word for other players to guess.
- Encourage students to use a different clue each time.

UNIT 2 Energy
Integrating the NGSS* Three Dimensions of Learning

Building to the Performance Expectations

The learning experiences in this unit prepare students for mastery of the following Performance Expectations:

Energy

4-PS3-1 Use evidence to construct an explanation relating the speed of an object to the energy of that object.

4-PS3-2 Make observations to provide evidence that energy can be transferred from place to place by sound, light, heat, and electric currents.

4-PS3-4 Apply scientific ideas to design, test, and refine a device that converts energy from one form to another.

Assessing Student Progress

After completing these lessons, the **Unit Project: Truck Pull** provides students with opportunities to practice aspects of and demonstrate their understanding of the Performance Expectations as they use spring or elastic energy to move an object.

Additionally, students can practice or be assessed on aspects of the Performance Expectations by completing the **Unit Performance Task: Energy Transfer All Around** in which they apply concepts of energy transfer to an investigation using real-world objects.

Lesson 1
What Is Energy?

In Lesson 1, students define energy and explore ways it can be transferred between objects **(DCI Definitions of Energy; PS3.B Conservation of Energy and Energy Transfer).** They recognize ways people use energy **(DCI Energy in Chemical Processes and Everyday Life)** and the impact it has on society and nature **(CCC Influence of Engineering, Technology, and Science on Society and the Natural World).** They observe and participate in activities requiring strategic thinking about design solutions to problems **(SEP Planning and Carrying Out Investigations; Constructing Explanations and Designing Solutions).**

Lesson 2
How Is Energy Transferred?

In Lesson 2, students collect evidence for energy storage, learn ways energy moves in waves and how it transfers through the addition or subtraction of heat **(DCI Definitions of Energy; Conservation of Energy and Energy Transfer; Energy in Chemical Processes and Everyday Life; Defining Engineering Problems).** They plan and build a cooker to transfer the sun's energy into food **(SEP Planning and Carrying Out Investigations, Constructing Explanations and Designing Solutions).** By looking at how energy transfers, students develop a greater understanding of how it can be used to effect changes in matter **(CCC Energy and Matter).**

Lesson 3
How Do Collisions Show Energy?

In Lesson 3, students learn that every object contains energy. When objects collide, they transfer that energy **(DCI Definitions of Energy; Conservation of Energy and Energy Transfer; Relationship Between Energy and Forces).** They observe this by experimenting with rubber bands and toys **(SEP Asking Questions and Defining Problems; Constructing Explanations and Designing Solutions).** They visualize how potential energy can become stored energy and can be transferred through impacts **(CCCs Energy and Matter).**

*Next Generation Science Standards and logo are registered trademarks of Achieve. Neither Achieve or the lead states and partners that developed the Next Generation Science Standards were involved in production of, and does not endorse, these products.

NGSS Across this Unit

Explore Online! Online only.

Next Generation Science Standard	Unit Project	Lesson 1	Lesson 2	Lesson 3	Unit Performance Task	You Solve It!
SEP Planning and Carrying Out Investigations	•	•	•		•	•
SEP Constructing Explanations and Designing Solutions	•	•		•		•
SEP Asking Questions and Defining Problems	•	•		•		•
DCI PS3.A Definitions of Energy		•	•			•
DCI PS3.B Conservation of Energy and Energy Transfer	•	•	•	•	•	•
DCI PS3.C Relationship Between Energy and Forces	•			•	•	•
DCI PS3.D Energy in Chemical Processes and Everyday Life		•	•	•		
DCI EST1.A Defining and Delimiting Engineering Problems		•	•			
CCC Energy and Matter	•	•	•	•	•	•
CCC Influence of Engineering, Technology, and Science on Society and the Natural World		•	•	•		
CCC Science is a Human Endeavor		•	•	•	•	

NGSS Across the Grades

Before	Grade 4	After
Energy	**Energy**	**Energy**
K-PS3-1	4-PS3-1	MS-PS3-1
K-PS3-2	4-PS3-2	MS-PS3-2
	4-PS3-4	MS-PS3-4

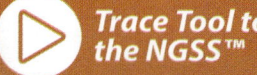
Trace Tool to the NGSS™ Go online to view the complete coverage of these standards across this grade level and time.

Unit 2: Energy 67B

UNIT 2 Energy
3D Unit Planning

Lesson 1 What Is Energy? pp. 68–87

Overview

Objective
Recognize common transformations of electrical energy.

SEP Planning and Carrying Out Investigations, Constructing Explanations, Asking Questions and Defining Problems
DCI PS3.A, PS3.B, PS3.D, ETS1.A
CCC Energy and Matter, Influence of Engineering, Technology, and Science on Society, Science is a Human Endeavor
Math and **English Language Arts** standards and features are detailed on lesson planner pages.

Print and Online Student Editions   ▶ **Explore Online!**

ENGAGE
Lesson Phenomenon pp. 68–69
Can You Explain It? Where did the energy come from to make the heavy train move? And when it stopped, where did that energy go?
▶ Can You Explain It! Video

EXPLORE/ EXPLAIN
Energy is All Around pp. 70–77
✋ **Apply What You Know** Energy Near You
Where Does Our Energy Come From?
 ENGINEER IT! Energy from Algae
Saving It for Later
✋ **Apply What You Know** Testing, Testing
✋ **HANDS-ON** Light the Bulb
Energy Transfer pp. 78–82

HANDS-ON Worksheet

ELABORATE
Take It Further pp. 83–84
Mayra Artiles, Car Engineer

Take It Further
Vampire Appliances
Take It Further
Potato Power

EVALUATE
Lesson Check pp. 85–86
Lesson Roundup p. 87

Lesson Quiz

✋ HANDS-ON ACTIVITY PLANNING

Apply What You Know

Energy Near You
⏱ 5 minutes
👥 Individuals

Preparation/Tip Before students get started, you may want to create a list on the board of the various ways to group energy, such as movement, heat, light, and so on.

Testing, Testing
⏱ 5 minutes
👥 Individuals

Preparation/Tip You may want to show some examples of batteries, including their terminals, so students can devise ways of creating circuits to test them.

HANDS-ON

Light the Bulb
⏱ 1 class period
👥 Pairs

Objective Students ask questions related to circuits and light bulbs. Explain to them that scientists and engineers ask questions and define problems on a regular basis when planning investigations.

Materials
- size D battery with holder
- light bulb
- three lengths of wire
- switch

Preparation/Tip Preassemble the materials so that each pair of students can pick up their box of materials and be ready to start the activity. Go over safety precautions of not placing batteries in or near mouths and for students to alert you immediately if a bulb is broken or breaks.

Overview

Objective Understand and observe energy transfer involving light, sound, and heat and provide evidence illustrating the changes that result.

SEP Planning and Carrying Out Investigations, Constructing Explanations
DCI PS3.A, PS3.B, PS3.D, ETS1.A
CCC Energy and Matter, Influence of Engineering, Technology, and Science on Society, Science is a Human Endeavor
Math and **English Language Arts** standards and features are detailed on lesson planner pages.

Print and Online *Student Editions* • Explore Online!

ENGAGE
Lesson Phenomenon pp. 88–89
Can You Explain It? What is different about the sound of a power drill and the sound of someone whispering? What accounts for the difference?
▶ Can You Explain It! Video

EXPLORE/ EXPLAIN
Heat pp. 90–94
 ENGINEER IT! Thermal Imaging
HANDS-ON Worksheet

Here Comes the Sun pp. 95–101
 **HANDS-ON** Design and Test a Solar Cooker

Seeing Sound pp. 102–108

👋 **Apply What You Know** Make Vibrations

👋 **Apply What You Know** Tune In

ELABORATE
Take It Further pp. 109–110
Career in Science: HVAC Tech
Take It Further Keep It Cold
Take It Further The Paynes and Fast-Traveling Whale Songs

EVALUATE
Lesson Check pp. 111–112
Lesson Roundup p. 113
Lesson Quiz

👋 HANDS-ON ACTIVITY PLANNING

Apply What You Know

Make Vibrations
⏱ 15 minutes
👥 Small groups

Materials
- wax paper
- empty container
- rubber band
- grains of sand, rice, or confetti

Preparation/Tip If they do not have a small drum and one is not available from the school, instruct each student to bring a clean, empty can from home, along with some rice or confetti.

Tune In
⏱ 5 minutes
👥 Small groups

Materials
- tuning fork
- metal and wooden rails or similar objects

Preparation/Tip Find a suitable spot in the classroom or school for the Hands-On Activity to take place. (You may be more likely to find a metal railing outside and a wooden railing inside.)

HANDS-ON

Design and Test a Solar Cooker
⏱ 20 minutes and several hours to test cooker in sunlight
👥 Small groups

Materials
- aluminum foil
- cooker or pot with glass top

Objective Students will observe energy transfer and provide evidence illustrating the changes by designing and testing a solar cooker.

Preparation/Tip The amount of time students need to prepare their experiments will depend on the materials chosen and the procedure decided upon.

Unit 2: Energy 67D

UNIT 2 Energy
3D Unit Planning, continued

Lesson 3 How Do Collisions Show Energy? pp. 114–135

Overview

Objective Observe energy transfers and recognize the correlation between speed and the amount of energy an object possesses, and identify collisions as a form of motion energy transfer.

SEP Asking Questions and Defining Problems, Constructing Explanations and Designing Solutions
DCI PS3.A, PS3.B, PS3.C
CCC Energy and Matter

Math and **English Language Arts** standards and features are detailed on lesson planner pages.

	Print and Online Student Editions	 Explore Online!
ENGAGE	**Lesson Phenomenon** pp. 114–115 **Can You Explain It?** When someone "breaks" in a game of pool, how do the cue ball and the balls it strikes react?	Can You Explain It! Video
EXPLORE/ EXPLAIN	**Things That Move Have Energy** pp. 116–124 **Apply What You Know** Bang a Gong The Faster They Are Hit, the Harder They Fall **Apply What You Know** Flour Power **HANDS-ON** Test It! Stored Energy in a Spring **Wonderful Springs** pp. 125–127 **ENGINEER IT!** Shocking **Collisions** pp. 128–130 **Apply What You Know** Rebounce	HANDS-ON Worksheet
ELABORATE	**Take It Further** pp. 131–132 Careers in Science: Amanda Steffys	Take It Further Bump! Take It Further Collision Game!
EVALUATE	**Lesson Check** pp. 133–134 **Lesson Roundup** p. 135	Lesson Quiz

HANDS-ON ACTIVITY PLANNING

Apply What You Know

Bang a Gong ⏱ 10 minutes 👥 Individuals or pairs	**Materials** • gonglike object, such as metal pot lid

Preparation/Tip Have each student bring an empty tin can from home to use as a gong or cymbal.

Flour Power ⏱ 5 minutes 👥 Small groups	**Materials** • ping-pong ball • baking dish • flour

Preparation/Tip Students may opt to replace the foam ball with something lighter or heavier. If heavier, ask them to use an object that will not result in damage to any surfaces.

Rebounce ⏱ 5 minutes 👥 Pairs	**Materials** • meterstick • tennis ball

Preparation/Tip You can expand this activity by having students bounce the balls on surfaces of different elasticity.

HANDS-ON

Test It! Stored Energy in a Spring ⏱ 1 class period 👥 Small groups	**Materials** • safety goggles • giant rubber band • chair • tape • ruler • toy car or truck • meterstick

Objective Observe energy transfer involving motion, and provide evidence illustrating the changes.

Preparation/Tip As a safety precaution, instruct all students to remain behind or to the side of the chairs.

UNIT 2 Energy
3D Unit Planning, continued

 **You Solve It** — Go online for an additional interactive activity.

Crash Course

This virtual lab offers practice in support of **PE 4-PS3-1, 4-PS3-2,** and **4-PS3-3.**

SEP Constructing Explanations, Planning and Carrying Out Investigations, Asking Questions and Defining Problems

DCI **4-PS3.A.1, 4-PS3.A.2, 4-PS3.B.2, 4-PS3.C.1**

CCC Energy and Matter

Use after Unit 2, Lesson 3—Can you predict how objects will act when they collide?

Objectives
1. Students will predict the changes in energy that occur when objects collide.
2. Students determine the speed in which a moving car can scatter materials.
3. Students will analyze how energy will change when materials collide.

Activity Problem
You will be a tester for a toy manufacturer. The task is to test a new toy car launcher. The criteria and constraints are as followed:
1. the car must propel forward,
2. the car must have enough energy to scatter at least five of the foam bricks, and
3. all of the foam bricks must stay within the circle.

Interaction Summary
1. Students will practice using the launcher to determine how the car reacts to different speeds.
2. Students choose the speed to have the car propel forward and knock down at least five foam bricks. Five trial tests are completed.
3. Observations and data are recorded.
4. Tests continue until at least five foam bricks are knocked over and all the foam bricks are within the circle.
5. Students analyze the data and write a report on their findings.

Assessment

Pre-Assessment
Assessment Guide, Unit Pretest

The Unit Pretest focuses on prerequisite knowledge and is composed of items that evaluate students' preparedness for the content covered within this unit.

Formative Assessment
Student Edition, Apply What You Know, Lesson Check, and Self Check

Summative Assessment
Assessment Guide, Lesson Quiz
The Lesson Quiz provides a quick assessment of each lesson objective and of the portion of the Performance Expectation aligned to the lesson.

Student Edition, Performance Task pp. 136–137
The Performance Task presents the opportunity for children to collaborate with classmates in order to complete the steps of each Performance Task. Each Performance Task provides a formal Scoring Rubric for evaluating students' work.

Student Edition, Unit 2 Review pp. 138–140

Assessment Guide, Unit Test
The Unit Test provides an in-depth assessment of the Performance Expectations aligned to the unit. This test evaluates students' ability to apply knowledge in order to explain phenomena and to solve problems. Within this test, Constructed Response items apply a three-dimensional rubric for evaluating students' mastery on all three dimensions of the Next Generation Science Standards.

 **Assessment Online** — Go online to view the complete assessment items for this unit.

Unit 2: Energy **67F**

UNIT 2 Energy
Differentiate Instruction

Leveled Readers

The **Science & Engineering Leveled Readers** provide additional nonfiction reading practice in this unit's subject area.

On-Level Reader • How Do We Generate and Use Electricity?
This reader reinforces unit concepts and includes response activities for your students.

Extra Support • How Do We Generate and Use Electricity?
This reader shares title, illustrations, vocabulary, and concepts with the On-Level Reader; however, the text is linguistically accommodated to provide simplified sentence structures and comprehension aids. It also includes response activities.

Enrichment • Energy on Demand: Making Electricity
This high-interest, nonfiction reader will extend and enrich unit concepts and vocabulary and includes response activities.

Teacher Guide

The accompanying Teacher Guide provides teaching strategies and support for using all the readers.

ELL
ELL teacher strategies in this unit:
Lesson 1: p. 81
Lesson 2: pp. 91, 96, 110
Lesson 3: pp. 118, 128

RTI/Extra Support
Strategies for students needing extra support in this unit:
Lesson 1: p. 72
Lesson 2: pp. 90, 94, 97, 102, 103, 106, 108
Lesson 3: p. 116

Extension
Strategies for students who have mastered core content in this unit:
Lesson 1: pp. 79, 82
Lesson 2: pp. 92, 104, 105, 108
Lesson 3: pp. 117, 119, 125, 127, 132

 **Leveled Readers** All readers are available online as well as in an innovative, engaging format for use with touchscreen mobile devices. Contact your HMH Sales Representative for more information.

UNIT 2 Energy
Making Connections

Connections to the Community

Use these opportunities for informal science learning to provide local context and to extend and enhance unit concepts.

At Home

TOY ENERGY Remind students that different forms of energy include sound, light, motion, heat, and electrical energy. Have students make a chart listing ten of their favorite toys and identifying the type or types of energy used or produced by each toy. *Use with Lesson 1.*

SOUND ENERGY TRANSFER Explain to students that they can use an echo to observe how sound can be transferred through air, carrying energy with it. Instruct students to find a safe location where they can stand as far as possible from the side of their home or a tall building. Then have them clap several times and listen for the echo. *Use with Lesson 3.*

In the Community

SOLAR ENERGY Have students look around their community and make a list of as many homes or buildings as possible that have solar panels on the roofs. *Use with Lesson 1.*

COLLISIONS IN THE COMMUNITY Challenge students to make a chart listing five activities they observe in the community that involve objects colliding. For each activity on the list, have students list the types of energy transfer involved in the collision. Allot class time for students to share and discuss their observations with the class. *Use with Lesson 3.*

Home Letters Use these one-page letters to engage family members with unit concepts.

Collaboration

Opportunities for students to work collaboratively in this unit:

Build on Prior Knowledge
p. 69

Feedback
pp. 70, 75, 80, 118

Discussion
pp. 85, 111, 133

Think, Pair Share
pp. 92, 106, 109

Draw, Pair, Share
pp. 89, 102, 115, 129

Write, Pair, Share
p. 98

Connections to Science

Opportunities to connect to other content areas in this unit:

Connection to Life Science
Lesson 1, p. 72

Connection to Earth and Space Sciences
Lesson 1, p. 78

Unit 2: Energy 67H

UNIT 2 Energy
Unit Project

Unit Project: Truck Pull 👥 Small groups 🕐 2 class periods

For this task, small groups of students will learn how energy transfers from one object to another. They will research energy transfer, then design a model to transfer spring or elastic energy from one object to another. Students should understand that there are different types of energy and that objects have stored energy. They should also understand the relationship between energy and mass/matter; the larger the mass, the more energy needed to move it.

3D Learning Objective

- Understand the relationship between energy and matter
- Plan and carry out an investigation into energy transfer from one object into another
- Test a design, asking questions and designing solutions when it does not work as it should

Skills and Standards Focus

This project supports building student mastery of **Perfomance Expectations 4-PS3-2, 4-PS3-3, 4-PS3-4**	**SEP** Planning and Carrying Out Investigations **SEP** Asking Questions and Defining Problems **DCI** PS3.B Conservation of Energy and Energy Transfer **CCC** Energy and Matter

Suggested Materials

- rubber bands
- large and small springs
- toy truck
- cardboard
- marbles
- references—print (books, magazines), electronic (websites)

Preparing and Planning Tips

Ensure that each group has a set of print resources or list of URLs for websites you have previously reviewed. Have them select the material that they will transfer energy into, such as a toy truck or marble. Then have them research types of energy that can help move objects. Guide them to understand that springs and rubber bands contain different kinds of stored energy, each of which can be used to move another object through a transfer of energy.

Unit Project: Truck Pull
How can you use elastic energy or a spring to move a truck? You will design and test a truck with your team. Ask your teacher for details.

Differentiate Instruction

ELL Some students may have difficulty understanding words related to energy transfer. Provide a diagram with arrows showing stored energy converted into motion. The diagram should show spring or elastic energy transferring into other objects, making them move.

Extension Ask students to draw a diagram of their model with the spring/rubber band and toy truck/marble labeled. They should include arrows showing how energy is transferred from the spring/rubber band to toy truck/marble.

Name _____

UNIT PROJECT
Truck Pull

What makes things move? How can you move an object, like a toy? For this project, you will work in teams to design a way to use spring or elastic energy to move a toy truck across a surface.

Think about how energy is transferred from one object to another. Write a question that you will consider as you work on your designs.

Students should write a question concerning the transfer of energy to the truck to move it forward.

Materials

Think about how you will make your design work during testing. What materials will you need?

Materials can include rubber bands, springs (small and large), toy truck, cardboard, marbles.

For your design, start by thinking about the type of energy you will use. What kind of energy will you design to move the toy truck?

Accept all responses. We will use spring energy to move the truck – we will test whether the small or large spring works best.

UNIT 2 PROJECT
Truck Pull

PS3.B Conservation of Energy and Energy Transfer

Before students begin the task, check their understanding of key concepts.

Ask: What kind of energy is stored in the spring or rubber band? potential energy/spring or elastic energy

What kind of energy will the toy truck or marble use when moving? kinetic energy

Refer students to Lesson 3, Explorations 1, 2, and 3 for concept support.

ESSENTIAL QUESTIONS Ask the following questions before students begin to plan their activity.

- Which type of energy will you use for your model: spring or elastic?
- What happens when a moving object collides into an object at rest?
- How will you test your model, and what do you expect your model to show?

CCC Energy and Matter

Remind students that any time two objects come into contact, energy is transferred.

Ask: When two objects collide, what happens to the energy in the first object? Possible answer: Most of the energy of the first object is transferred into the second object, causing it to move. The remainder of the energy is converted into heat and sound.

Research and Plan

Students should carefully consider the energy transfer and object they will model.

Ask: How will you select your energy and object? Possible answer: My/Our group will discuss the two types of energy, spring and elastic, and the two types of objects, toy truck or marble, to determine which type of energy will best transfer into which type of object.

Research

Groups will then research the type of energy they selected. Students should understand the differences between the two types of energy and how each is stored as potential energy. They should consider ways in which their type of energy can be converted into kinetic energy and how much kinetic energy it might take to move the object they selected. They will then draft a model showing how they will convert the energy from the spring or rubber band into the toy truck or marble.

Ask: What problems do you expect to encounter as you plan your model? Possible answer: My/Our object (spring or rubber band) may not have enough stored energy to convert into kinetic energy to move the second object (toy truck or marble). I/We need to test our models, then make adjustments to increase the potential energy if necessary.

Finding a Solution

Students may not realize the connection between mass and energy: the larger the mass, the more energy it contains. This is just as true of springs and rubber bands. Larger springs and rubber bands will contain more energy than smaller springs and rubber bands. Therefore, if a smaller spring or rubber band does not contain enough energy to move the toy truck or marble, then students should use the larger ones. If this still does not work, students should brainstorm ways to combine the energy from more than one spring or rubber band.

Plan and Design

Make a plan for the research you will need to do and how you will test your model. As you make your plan, consider the following:

- The amount of energy needed to transfer between the objects
- The size of the force transferring the energy to the toy truck
- The role of collision energy
- Criteria and constraints for moving the truck

Students should describe their approach to using energy to move the truck, touching on these various points. Answers will vary depending on whether students are using spring or elastic energy.

Test your design! Describe any modifications you want to make.

Accept all responses.

Possible response: We need to redo our design because the force of energy was not strong enough to move the truck

Analyze Your Results

Look for patterns in your data. Make two observations about energy transfer.

Possible responses: more energy is needed to move the truck because the truck has a lot of mass; a compressed small spring does not have as much energy as a compressed large spring

Restate Your Question

Write the question you investigated.

Students should identify the question created at the beginning of the project.

Claims, Evidence, and Reasoning

Make a claim that answers your question.

Possible answers: the large spring was better at moving the truck.

Review your design. What evidence from your design supports your claim?

Students should cite evidence from their designs to support the claim.

Discuss your reasoning with a partner.

Analyze Your Results

SEP Asking Questions and Defining Problems

Students should consider the following questions as they interpret their research data and test results: How much spring or elastic energy will it take to move our object? How can we increase the amount of energy transferred from the spring or rubber band? How many times should we test our model to determine the results?

SEP Planning and Carrying Out Investigations

Scientists do not arrive at a conclusion based on a single test. They make repeated tests with the same input to see if they get the same results. Sometimes they change the input to see how those changes affect the results. Students, too, should conduct their tests more than once, recording their data and the results each time.

Claims, Evidence, and Reasoning

Students should state a specific claim related to energy transfer between the two objects they chose.

Ask: What claim can you make? Possible claim: The large spring was better at moving the truck.

How does your evidence support your claim? Students should cite the results of their tests to support their claim.

Encourage students to discuss their reasoning.

Scoring Rubric for Hands-On Activity	
3	States a claim about energy transfer and supports it with ample, detailed evidence.
2	States a claim about energy transfer and somewhat supports it with evidence.
1	States a claim that is not supported by evidence.
0	Does not state a claim.

LESSON 1
What Is Energy?

Building to the Performance Expectations

The learning experiences in this lesson prepare students for mastery of:

4-PS3-2 Make observations to provide evidence that energy can be transferred from place to place by sound, light, heat, and electric currents.

4-PS3-4 Apply scientific ideas to design, test, and refine a device that converts energy from one form to another.

 **Trace Tool to the NGSS** Go online to view the complete coverage of these standards across this lesson, unit, and time.

 Science & Engineering Practices

Disciplinary Core Ideas

 Crosscutting Concepts

Planning and Carrying Out Investigations
Plan and conduct an investigation…
▶ **VIDEO** Planning and Carrying Out Investigations

Constructing Explanations and Designing Solutions
Use evidence to construct or support an explanation…
▶ **VIDEO** Constructing Scientific Explanations

Asking Questions and Defining Problems
Ask questions that can be investigated, and predict reasonable outcomes…
▶ **VIDEO** Asking Questions and Defining Problems

PS3.A Definitions of Energy
Energy can be moved from place to place by moving objects or through sound, light, or electric currents.

PS3.B Conservation of Energy and Energy Transfer
- Energy is present whenever there are moving objects, sound, light, or heat.
- Energy can also be transferred from place to place by electric currents, which can then be used locally to produce motion, sound, heat, or light. The currents may have been produced to begin with by transforming the energy of motion into electrical energy.

PS3.D Energy in Chemical Processes and Everyday Life
The expression "produce energy" typically refers to the conversion of stored energy into a desired form for practical use.

ETS1.A Defining and Delimiting Engineering Problems
Possible solutions to a problem are limited by available materials and resources (constraints). The success of a designed solution is determined by considering the desired features of a solution (criteria). Different proposals for solutions can be compared on the basis of how well each one meets the specified criteria for success or how well each takes the constraints into account.

Energy and Matter
Energy can be transferred in various ways and between objects.

Influence of Engineering, Technology, and Science on Society and the Natural World
- Engineers improve existing technologies or develop new ones.

Science is a Human Endeavor
Most scientists and engineers work in teams. Science affects everyday life.

 CONNECTIONS TO MATH

MP.2 Reason abstractly and quantitatively.
MP.4 Model with mathematics.

 CONNECTIONS TO ENGLISH LANGUAGE ARTS

W.4.7 Conduct short research projects that build knowledge through investigation of different aspects of a topic.

W.4.8 Recall relevant information from experiences or gather relevant information from sources; take notes and categorize information, and provide a list of sources.

Supporting All Students, All Standards

Integrating the Three Dimensions of Learning

In this lesson, students will define energy and explore the ways in which energy can be transferred or moved from one thing to another **(DCI PS3.A, PS3.B)**. They will learn to recognize the ways people rely on energy for everyday life **(DCI PS3.D)** and the impact energy has on society and natural worlds **(CCC Influence of Engineering, Technology, and Science on Society and the Natural World)**. Students will gain a deeper understanding of these concepts through observation, as well as by participating in activities that require them to think strategically and creatively about design solutions to problems that meet specific criteria **(SEPs Planning and Carrying Out Investigations Constructing Explanations and Designing Solutions)**.

 **Professional Development** Go online to view **Professional Development videos** with strategies to integrate CCCs and SEPs, including the ones used in this lesson.

Extra Hands-On Activity: Hybrid Car Case Study

How Do Hybrid Cars Use Energy?

👥 Small groups
⏱ 30 minutes

Using classroom and media resources, have students visit auto manufacturers' webpages to gather information on hybrid cars and the technology being used to harness and convert energy into motion. Groups should generate research questions. Each group chooses three questions from the list to research and share with the class what they have learned. If you are allowing Internet research, discuss information that may have a particular bias. For example, sites sponsored by a manufacturer would likely highlight a car's benefits rather than drawbacks.

Students will find that most hybrid cars use both gasoline and electricity to operate. Hybrid cars also have advanced aerodynamics to reduce drag, have special tires, and are made of lightweight materials. Drivers can save on gas costs by replacing a traditional car with a hybrid. Hybrids get better gas mileage than cars with a gas-only engine and don't generate as many harmful emissions, though the batteries and electronics also create future disposal issues.

 This activity can support mastery of this Crosscutting Concept: Influence of Engineering, Technology, and Science on Society

Preassessment

Have students complete the lesson pre-test online or see the Assessment Guide.

Build on Prior Knowledge

Students should already know and be prepared to build on the following concepts:
- In science and engineering, there are often problems that need to be solved (solutions), which lead to inventions and discoveries.
- Scientists and engineers work with criteria and constraints to come up with design solutions.

Differentiate Instruction

Lesson Vocabulary
- energy
- energy transfer
- energy transformation

Students may be more familiar with the everyday use of **energy**.

Ask: What does it mean if you have a lot of energy? *I feel awake; I am active; I want to do things.*

RTI/Extra Support

Show students examples of energy in the classroom, or offer demonstrations.

Ask: Does this light use energy? (Flick the classroom lights on and off.) *yes*

Ask: What kind of energy does it use? *electricity*

Show students a plant.

Ask: What kind of energy makes the plant grow when it is outside? *sun/sunshine*

Lesson 1 What Is Energy? **68B**

LESSON 1 **Engage** • Explore/Explain • Elaborate • Evaluate

ENGAGE: Lesson Phenomenon

Lesson Objective
Recognize common transformations of electrical energy.

About This Image
This is an image of something students see on a daily basis. In fact, students can probably point out an electrical cord in the classroom. Electrical cords transfer electricity from one source to another. Electricity provides the energy to power something, such as a lamp or a computer. There are many different types of electrical cords.

Many students believe that electric charges "flow" through an electrical cord like a water flows through a hose. Have students line up with their hands on the shoulders of the person in front of them. Lightly push the student at the back of the line so that the student tips slightly forward and pushes the next student in line. Point out that the energy of the push passes through the line without the people in the line physically moving from one end to the other.

SEP Planning and Carrying Out Investigations

Alternative Engage Strategy

Where Does Energy Come from? Small groups 10 min

Ask students where they think energy comes from. Then place students into small groups and ask teams to come up with a list of energy sources. Ask a volunteer from each group to share results and discuss them as a whole class.

LESSON 1

What Is Energy?

If you follow an electrical cord from the wall socket, it might lead to a lamp, television, hair dryer, or vacuum cleaner. Many devices use electrical energy to give us other forms of energy, such as heat, light, sound, and motion.

By the end of this lesson . . .
you'll be able to recognize common transformations of electrical energy.

> **▶ Explore Online** Students can view the lesson phenomenon online.

Can You Explain It?

Students are asked to study the image and explain where the energy comes from. To do so, students must pay close attention to the details. Urge students not to worry about whether their answers are correct. They should expect their ideas to change as they progress through the Explorations. They will have an opportunity to revise their answers when they revisit these questions at the end of the lesson.

> ### Collaboration
> **Build on Prior Knowledge** You may wish to spend a few minutes discussing how trains work in order to build on prior knowledge that will help students better understand the energy source in the image. You may also find it necessary to build on students' prior knowledge of energy to help them apply characteristics of energy to the Engage activity.

 EVIDENCE NOTEBOOK

Encourage students to use an appropriate graphic organizer, such as main idea and supporting details, to set up their notebook for this lesson.

Find more strategies in the online ELA handbook.

Can You Explain It?

▶ Explore Online

Energy makes things change. Energy in a toaster produces heat, and the heat toasts a slice of bread. Your body's energy might pedal a bicycle so that it goes faster or slows down. Heavy trains need energy to stop and go.

1. Where did the energy come from to make the heavy train speed along the track? When the train stopped, where did the energy go?

Students should respond based on the preliminary observations they can make of the images.

 EVIDENCE NOTEBOOK Look for this icon to help you gather evidence to answer the questions above.

Lesson 1 What Is Energy

LESSON 1   Engage • **Explore/Explain** • Elaborate • Evaluate

EXPLORATION 1 Energy is All Around

3D Learning Objective

Learn the **definition of energy** and how it can be **moved through electric currents**. **Ask questions** about how energy can be **transferred from one object to another**. Apply this knowledge to **plan and carry out an investigation** to find out how to light up a bulb.

DCI PS3.A Definitions of Energy

The image on the page shows different forms of energy.

Ask: What do all the forms of energy have in common? Possible answer: They cause something to happen.

Differentiate Instruction

ELL: Using Realia Help students grasp the concept of what is and is not energy by bringing in some items seen in the picture and doing a demonstration. Examples include turning on a radio, waving a fan, or gently throwing a ball in the classroom.

SEP Asking Questions and Defining Problems

Help students identify patterns related to energy. Encourage students to think about cause-and-effect relationships by using the outdoor image.

Collaboration

Feedback Have students review and critique each other's answers for the items that are or are not energy. Allow students to work in pairs to complete the sentences using the words in the word bank. Encourage a discussion among pairs related to the sentences.

---

70   Unit 2 Energy

EXPLORATION 1

Energy Is All Around

Sound? Light? Heat? Motion? ENERGY!

You use energy every day. With energy from your muscles, you move. You pick up a book, open a door, and toss a ball. Using energy from devices, you might talk on the phone, watch a program, or go to school.

Energy is the ability to cause change in matter. Heat energy can dry clothes in a dryer or cook food in the oven. Energy stored in a battery can run a computer. Wind energy can turn a windmill or push a sailboat.

Ways Energy Moves

2. The picture shows different forms of energy. What do you see moving? What energy makes it move? What sends out sound energy? Where is there light or heat energy? On the next page, label each image *energy* or *not energy*.

70

a. brightly shining sun
___energy___

d. radio
___energy___

c. empty shell on the beach
___not energy___

b. rolling water waves
___energy___

3. Name another example of energy you see in the picture. What kind of energy is it?
___Possible answer: The running children have motion energy.___

4. Choose the best words to complete the sentences.

| light   sound   heat |

Energy is a measure of the ability to cause change in matter. You can see ___light___ energy, you can hear ___sound___ energy, and you can feel ___heat___ energy.

Tip
The English Language Arts Handbook can provide help with understanding how to identify cause and effect.
Reading and Writing in Science

 5. **Language SmArts** Choose one of the energy examples above. Describe the effect the energy causes.
___Possible answer: Energy from the rolling water waves crashes on the beach. The effect is the sand is moved.___

HANDS-ON Apply What You Know
Energy Near You

6. Find five examples of energy in your classroom. Write them below. Group them by the kind of energy they show.
___Possible answers: light from light bulbs and from the sun through the windows; sound from a video and from students' voices; motion of people moving around the room___

71

 Energy and Matter

Emphasize the concepts of how energy can be transferred, or moved, between objects. Energy causes some form of change to another object. Energy can also cause processes.

Ask: What is an example of a process that energy is a part of?
Possible answers: water cycle; photosynthesis

> **Language SmArts**
> **W.4.8** Recall relevant information from experiences or gather relevant information from print and digital sources
>
> Students will now get to apply concepts of cause and effect by using the image to gather information to write a statement about energy.

HANDS-ON Apply What You Know
Energy Near You

Students should work independently and explore the room to identify examples of energy. Before students get started, you may want to create a list on the board of the various ways to group energy, such as movement, heat, light, and so on. Then students can look for at least one example of energy for each of the groups.

Scoring Guidelines
Good scores are based on participation and the ability to find five examples of energy in the classroom.

 PS3.B Conservation of Energy and Energy Transfer

Students will learn from this Hands-On activity that energy is all around them, particularly when there is some sort of movement.
Ask: What are some of the things that are powered by energy in this class? Possible answers: the lights, the computer, the monitor, the air conditioner, the heater

Lesson 1 What Is Energy?   71

LESSON 1 Engage • **Explore/Explain** • Elaborate • Evaluate

EXPLORATION 1 Energy is All Around, continued

DCI **PS3.D Energy in Chemical Processes and Everyday Life**

Emphasize for students that energy helps create scientific processes that people need for sustaining life on Earth.

Ask: How is the electricity that runs through a wire to turn on your TV similar to how plants get energy from the sun? **Possible answer: Both forms of energy cause something to happen.**
What is the difference between them? **Possible answer: The wire creates a direct path for the electricity to travel.**

Connection to Life Science

Energy takes many forms. Food is an example of a substance that provides energy to us. For example, it gives us energy to move around.

Ask: What happens when you are low on energy? **Possible answers: I feel tired.**
What do you do when you are tired? **Possible answers: I rest or eat some food.**

LS1.C Organization for matter and energy flow in organisms

Differentiate Instruction

RTI/Extra Support If the image of the coal burning power plant confuses students, use a highlighter to show the flow through the various parts of the plant.

CCC **Influence of Engineering, Technology, and Science on Society and the Natural World**

There are many natural forms of energy. Engineers have invented ways to harvest and direct energy to where it needs to go. Technologies that focus on energy have made a big difference in society.

Ask: What are some technologies that rely on energy? **Possible answers: cars, refrigerators, televisions**

Where Does Our Energy Come From?

When you turn on a television, you see pictures and hear sound. Where do the light and sound energy come from?

You can see a wire connecting a wall socket to the television. That wire carries electric current. Electric current is a flow of electric charges along a path. Each photo shows one step in how the energy gets to your home.

Hundreds of millions of years ago, plants took in the sun's energy, just as they do now. After the plants died, a long, slow change turned them into coal. Some of the energy the plants got from the sun is now in that coal. That stored energy is called chemical energy.

a. At the energy generating station, the coal is burned. Burning changes the coal's chemical energy into heat energy.

b. Next, that heat energy makes water become steam, and the steam makes a turbine spin.

c. The spinning of magnets in the generator produces electrical energy.

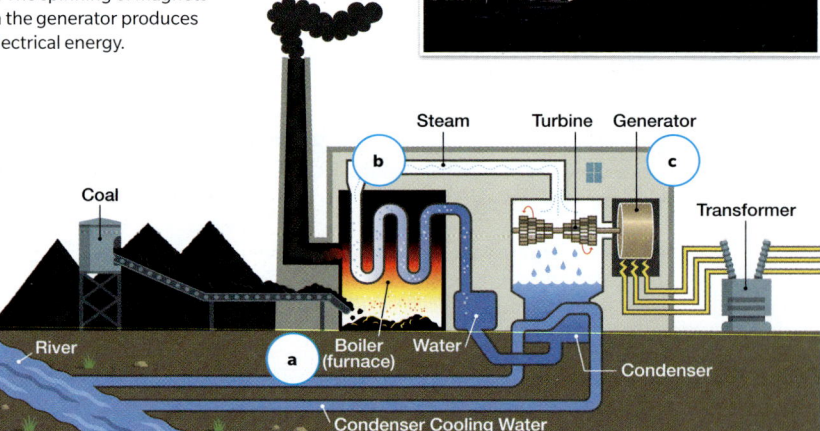

72

72 Unit 2 Energy

How does that electrical energy get to your home?

How do you use electrical energy?

7. Where does the energy in coal come from?
Energy from the sun was stored in plants, which died and transformed into coal over a long period of time.

Engineer It!
Energy from Algae

Scientists and engineers are always looking for alternative forms of energy for people to use. A new source of energy being developed is the harvesting of algae.

Algae use a gas called carbon dioxide to make energy and release clean oxygen as a byproduct. Algae farmed for this purpose becomes an oil that is then converted into fuel. These renewable algae fuels are an alternative to fossil fuels such as coal or oil.

Algae is grown in this farm facility.

8. Explain how algae farming can help make air quality better.
Possible answer: Burning oil from algae might produce less smoke than burning coal.

EVIDENCE NOTEBOOK Describe alternative energy, and explain why it is important to have different forms of it.

73

Explore Online Have students explore online to learn more about the forms of energy they may encounter every day.

Engineer It!
Energy from Algae

SEP Constructing Explanations and Designing Solutions

Students use the image and facts in the Engineer It section to answer Item 7. They can answer the question by drawing on what they already know about the atmosphere and applying it to the image and facts about algae.

Connection to English Language Arts

Assign students to perform some light research on algae and the different ways in which it is being grown and used for energy. Direct students to take notes on what they read and be sure to cite their sources.

W.4.8 Gather relevant information from print and digital sources; take notes and categorize information, and provide a list of sources.

EVIDENCE NOTEBOOK

Students should be able to understand the meaning of "alternative energy" by now. If students struggle with this concept, remind them of some of the more mainstream forms of energy.

Lesson 1 What Is Energy? **73**

LESSON 1 Engage • **Explore/Explain** • Elaborate • Evaluate

EXPLORATION 1 Energy is All Around, continued

DCI PS3.A Definitions of Energy

Help students grasp the concept of the various ways in which energy changes or creates changes. When teaching students about how batteries work, it may be helpful to draw a diagram on the board to provide a visual for students to see how chemical energy changes into electrical energy.

Ask: What are some devices that require batteries? *Possible answers: TV remote, remote-controlled cars or helicopters*
Why do batteries need to be replaced or recharged? *Possible answer: They can run out of chemical energy.*

Differentiate Instruction

ELL: Using Realia If students struggle to determine which battery is used for each device, show students samples of the actual batteries and pass them around the class. Seeing the sizes and shapes of the batteries may help students complete the chart. Make sure the battery samples are new and free of corrosion, and remind students not to place the batteries near or in their mouth.

Connection to Math

Assign students to research a comparison of the battery size and weight to the voltage and amperes it can produce. Have them put their data in a line graph or bar graph and look for patterns.
MP.2 Reason abstractly and quantitatively.

Saving It for Later

A battery stores chemical energy. When a device uses the battery, the chemical energy inside the battery changes into electrical energy. The device changes the electrical energy into motion, sound, or other forms of energy. There are many types and sizes of batteries for different purposes.

Batteries

9. Learn more about different types of batteries. Then answer the question below.

Button batteries are named for their size and shape. They are small and reliable for devices that use small amounts of energy very slowly.

AA batteries are used in many devices. They come in both single-use and rechargeable forms.

9V batteries are useful in devices that change stored energy into other energy. They are a reliable energy source for safety devices.

What type of battery goes in these devices?

AA batteries 9V battery button battery

74

74 Unit 2 Energy

Do the Math

Calculate Energy Units

10. Your portable DVD player uses rechargable AA batteries. They last 48 hours before needing to be recharged. In the space below, calculate how many two-hour movies you can watch on your DVD player with fully charged batteries. How many times will the batteries need to be recharged in a 30 day month?

    48 ÷ 2 = 24 — 24 movies
    30 ÷ 2 = 15 — 15 times

HANDS-ON Apply What You Know

Testing, Testing

11. Suppose you have a battery and you want to know whether it still has energy stored in it. Design a way to test whether the battery still works. Describe your design below.

    Possible answer: Put the batteries in a flashlight to see if the flashlight turns on.

Putting It Together

12. Choose the words that make the sentences most correct.

    | sound | matter | batteries | current |

    Energy is a measure of the ability to cause change in ___matter___. You can feel some heat energy and hear some ___sound___ energy. An electric ___current___ is a flow of electric charge. Two ways that energy is stored are coal and ___batteries___.

    75

Have students explore online to learn more about batteries and energy output.

Do the Math

Calculate Energy Units

MP.4 Model with mathematics.

Students apply concepts of division to calculate the answer. If students are having difficulties dividing, suggest they use repeat subtraction.

HANDS-ON Apply What You Know

Testing, Testing

Students must think abstractly to come up with a response to the question prompt.

 Planning and Carrying Out Investigations

Students are not physically testing the batteries. They should describe a way in which they could reasonably carry out the investigation to come up with a new design for testing batteries. Remind students that batteries transfer energy, converting it from chemical to electrical energy.

Collaboration

Feedback Once students have come up with their design solution for the battery tests, have students pair up and review each other's responses. Allow students to change or improve on their design solutions based on the critique of their peers.

FORMATIVE ASSESSMENT

Putting it Together

Before students work on completing the sentences,

Ask: What is energy? It is the measure of the ability to cause change in matter.

Lesson 1 What Is Energy? 75

LESSON 1 Engage • **Explore/Explain** • Elaborate • Evaluate

EXPLORATION 1 Energy is All Around, continued

HANDS-ON ACTIVITY Pairs 1 class period
Light the Bulb

3D Learning Objective

SEP Asking Questions and Defining Problems

Students ask questions related to circuits and light bulbs. Explain to them that scientists and engineers ask questions and define problems on a regular basis when planning investigations.

Materials
The materials listed are a starting point. You may also want to have extra bulbs and batteries.

Preparation
Preassemble the materials so that each pair of students can pick up their box of materials and be ready to start the activity. Go over safety precautions of not placing batteries in or near mouths and of alerting you immediately if a bulb is broken or breaks.

DCI ETS1.A Defining Engineering Problems

This investigation has some constraints. Constraints are limitations. They require students to consider them and then work around them to meet the criteria. Explain that engineers and those who design and build technology often have many constraints to work with.

Ask: What kinds of constraints do you have for this activity?
materials; time

Procedure
STEP 1 Monitor students to be sure they have a proper investigation plan in place.

STEPS 2–3 Circulate the room, and help students if they get stuck. Remind them that Step 2 is based on their plan from Step 1. You may want to suggest to students that since they are working in pairs, one student should connect the parts and the other should record the connections and order of connecting.

Light the Bulb

Objective
In a flashlight or other electrical device, a battery may be connected in a circuit. A **circuit** is a closed path or loop that an electric charge flows through.

What question will you investigate to meet this objective?
Possible question: How can you build a simple circuit that will let you light up a bulb?

Materials
- battery (size D) with holder
- light bulb with holder
- three lengths of wire
- switch

Procedure
STEP 1 Start by asking questions and sharing ideas. How should you connect the materials you have to make the bulb light up? Plan a simple investigation to find out. Write your plan below, and show your plan to your teacher.

Possible answer: We plan different tests using different ways to connect the batteries and the wire to see which arrangement works.

STEP 2 Lay out the parts in the order you think will make the bulb light up.

STEP 3 Connect the parts to test your plan. How did you connect the parts?
Students should describe the order in which they connected the pieces.

76

 Student Lab Worksheet and complete Teacher Support available online.

76 Unit 2 Energy

STEP 4 Does the bulb light up? If not, keep working until you "see the light"! What did you change about your arrangement?

Students should describe what changes they made and how that enabled the bulb to light up.

Analyze Your Results

STEP 5 After you've built a circuit that works, draw a picture of it. Show how the parts are connected.

> Student drawings should show a complete circuit. They should cite evidence from their experiment.

STEP 6 What occurred when the battery was connected to the light bulb and switch?

The bulb lit up.

STEP 7 What caused the bulb to light up?

energy from the battery

STEP 8 What questions do you have about circuits?

Possible questions: How can I make a circuit that works to power other devices? Do all electrical devices need circuits to work?

Draw Conclusions

STEP 9 Make a claim about bulbs. Cite evidence to support your claim.

Without a circuit, energy doesn't flow to light up the bulb.

Analyze Your Results

STEP 5 Part of the process of carrying out investigations of new technology is drawing pictures of the designs. Encourage students to draw their designs with as much detail and accuracy as possible.

STEPS 6–7 Demonstrate the correct way to light the bulb in case pairs of students were not able to achieve that result. Help students apply concepts of lighting up the bulb to other real-world issues.

Ask: What happens when energy runs out? **Possible answer: Objects can no longer be powered.**

STEP 8 You may wish to group students with similar questions to research or experiment to identify the answers.

Draw Conclusions

Invite students to complete this final step independently.

STEP 9 Make sure students understand the importance of the circuit. Without the circuit, the batteries would not light up the bulb.

> ### Claims, Evidence, and Reasoning
>
> To emphasize the importance of the circuit,
>
> **Ask:** What is a statement that could be used to explain why the scenario in Step 9 will not work? **Possible answer: The bulb needs energy from the battery and a circuit to light up.**

Scoring Rubric for Hands-On Activity	
3	Completes the activity by getting the bulb to light up.
2	Completes the activity, but the bulb does not light up.
1	Does not complete the activity.

LESSON 1   Engage • **Explore/Explain** • Elaborate • Evaluate

EXPLORATION 2 Energy Transfer

3D Learning Objective

Develop a deeper understanding of how energy **transfers and changes forms**. Learn how to **ask questions** to identify the cause-and-effect relationship that energy has with devices. Examine a series of images that depict devices that use energy. Become familiar with the importance and presence of **energy in everyday life**.

DCI PS3.B Conservation of Energy and Energy Transfer

The images on the page tell students about the transfer of energy.
Ask: Think about a television. How does the transfer of energy work for a television? *The energy comes through a wire with a circuit and provides electricity that the television uses. Then, the television displays the image and sound.*

CCC Energy and Matter

Emphasize the concept of energy as being something that changes forms and can be stronger or weaker than other forms of energy.
Ask: What is an example of a strong source of energy? *Possible answer: the sun*
What is an example of a weak source of energy? *Possible answer: a candle*

Connection to Earth Science

The transfer of energy is also something that occurs naturally on Earth. Have students think about the ways in which energy cycles through various parts of ecosystems, such as the air, soil, and water.

Ask: How can energy found in soil end up in the air? *Possible answer: Animals may consume energy and matter found in soil. It is then released and absorbed into the atmosphere as a gas.*
LS2.B Cycles of Matter and Energy Transfer in Ecosystems

EXPLORATION 2

Energy Transfer

Transfer to Transform

You walk into a dark room and flip a switch, and suddenly light shines out of a lamp. How does electrical energy become light energy?

The switch allows electric charges to flow through the lamp cord and into the lamp. This is an **energy transfer**, a movement of energy from place to place or from one object to another.

Inside the lamp, another energy transfer moves the electrical energy to the light bulb. The bulb transforms the electrical energy into light energy. **Energy transformation** is a change in energy from one form to another.

A battery is a source of electrical energy. The electrical energy transfers to the flashlight. The electrical energy transforms into light energy.

Electrical energy transfers into the cell phone. The electrical energy transforms into sound energy, which allows you to have a conversation.

Electrical energy from the battery transfers into the mini-drone. The electrical energy transforms into motion energy when it flies away!

Energy from the sun transfers to the solar panels. The solar energy transforms into electrical energy, and the electrical energy becomes heat energy to warm water for bathing and washing dishes.

 13. Language SmArts Describe the energy transformation that occurs with an everyday task such as listening to the radio. On a piece of paper, draw a diagram to match your description. Label it.

Possible answer: Electrical energy is transformed to sound energy when a radio is turned on.

 EVIDENCE NOTEBOOK When the bell rings signaling the end of class, what evidence would you say proves that energy has been transferred?

Constructing Explanations and Designing Solutions

Have students observe the image of the solar panels on the roof.

Ask: What would happen to a solar-powered house on cloudy days? There wouldn't be as much immediate power.

What can engineers do when they design solar panels to make sure there is always power? Possible answer: Design a way to store unused power so there are energy reserves for cloudy days.

Differentiate Instruction

Extension For a challenge, have students research alternative power sources, such as wind turbines or water turbines. Small groups can do the research. Have students write and perform a brief commercial on their findings.

Language SmArts
W.4.8 Recall relevant information from experiences or gather relevant information from sources.

Forming an Explanation When writing explanations, students should call on experience, prior knowledge, and facts. The more facts they can use to support their explanations, the better. Encourage students to go back through Exploration 1 to identify and cite information that supports their claims.

EVIDENCE NOTEBOOK

Students should be able to make the connection between the bell ringing at school and the transfer of energy. Allow students time to review what they have learned so far before recording their responses.

LESSON 1 Engage • **Explore/Explain** • Elaborate • Evaluate

EXPLORATION 2 Energy Transfer, continued

PS3.B Conservation of Energy and Energy Transfer

Energy does not necessarily need to be transferred to only one thing at a time. Sometimes, energy can come from one source and be used to power multiple devices. Similarly, it is possible for an object to use energy in more than one way.

Ask: What forms of energy do you see or hear coming from a lawn mower? Possible answers: It cuts grass; it makes noise; some of them have lights; it moves.

> ## Collaboration
>
> **Feedback** After students have answered the questions on these two pages, have them work with a partner to provide feedback on each other's responses. Bring the whole class together, and make sure students understand the differences between heat, motion, light, and sound energy.

SEP Asking Questions and Defining Problems

Help students think about the types of questions to ask when they need to identify how energy is transferred.

Ask: What is an example of a question you can ask yourself when trying to figure out how energy is transferred? Possible answers: What is the cause? What is the effect?

Many from One

When you turn on a television, electrical energy transfers through the electrical cord into the television. Inside the television, the electrical energy transforms to light and sound energy as well as heat energy.

In the same way, a vacuum cleaner turns electrical energy into motion, sound, and some heat energy. When electrical energy transfers into a device, it usually transforms into more than one form of energy.

Energy Transformations

14. Look at each photo. Write the form of energy the electrical energy changes into after it transfers into each device.

a. When this microwave is running, you hear sounds and see lights and movement. What kind of energy is cooking the broccoli from the inside?

heat

b. The mini-drone is moving. In addition to energy of motion, what form of energy do you hear?

sound

80 Unit 2 Energy

c. The electrical energy transferring into this blender changes into several different types of energy. Which type spins the blade?

motion

d. A hair dryer produces sound and other forms of energy. What kind of energy helps dry your hair?

heat and air motion

15. Write the name of each object into each energy form that is present when the object is turned on. Each object will have at least two forms of energy.

| blender | toy drone | lamp |
| hair dryer | clothes iron | microwave |

Sound	Light	Motion	Heat
Possible answers: blender hair dryer toy drone microwave	Possible answers: microwave toy drone lamp	Possible answers: blender toy drone microwave hair dryer	Possible answers: hair dryer clothes iron lamp microwave

16. **Language SmArts** How can electrical energy be transformed? Conduct research, and list the types or ways electrical energy can transform. Turn your list and research sources in to your teacher.

81

Influence of Engineering, Technology, and Science on Society and the Natural World

Scientists and engineers have found ways to use energy in new technologies.

Ask: Do the different forms of energy have to exist together? Or can a device use motion energy without light energy? Answers may vary but should reflect student understanding that some forms of energy can exist without the other. Other forms might not. For instance, motion can create heat. Therefore, sometimes objects that create a lot of fast motion can also create heat as an effect.

Differentiate Instruction

RTI/Extra Support If students have difficulties understanding the terms in the word box, you may want to show images of the devices to help students have a proper understanding of the terms.

Language SmArts
W.4.7 Conduct short research projects that build knowledge through investigation of different aspects of a topic.

Give students time to research how energy can be transformed. Remind students of good research skills, including the use of reputable and reliable web pages, using citations, avoiding plagiarism, and finding evidence that is factual.

Lesson 1 What Is Energy? 81

LESSON 1   Engage • **Explore/Explain** • Elaborate • Evaluate

EXPLORATION 2   Energy Transfer, continued

DCI PS3.A Definitions of Energy

Engineers are often tasked with the job of finding solutions such as making batteries last longer or reducing the noise a machine makes. Many times this has to do with the use or application of energy.

Ask: What might an engineer do when trying to figure out how to make a battery last longer? Possible answers: find out why the battery keeps dying; find out what is draining the battery; come up with a way to stop the battery from being drained

SEP Constructing Explanations and Designing Solutions

There are different ways that batteries can be preserved so that they do not die as quickly.

Ask: What are some solutions to making batteries last longer? Possible answers: shutting the device off when it's not being used; taking the batteries out of the device when it's not being used; recharging the batteries once they get low

---

Differentiate Instruction

Extension Have students perform research on the concept of energy usage. Give students prompts, such as "What devices use large amounts of energy?" or "What devices use up very little amounts of energy?" Have students work in small teams of mixed ability, and encourage them to share their answers with the whole class in a discussion.

FORMATIVE ASSESSMENT
Putting it Together

Before students work on completing the sentences,
Ask: What senses could you use to detect motion energy? Explain your choices. Possible answer: touch, feeling the motion of the wind; sight, seeing the motion happen

---

Changing Forms of Energy

Have you ever been using a cell phone and had the battery "die"? Why do cell phone batteries need to be recharged so often?

Every time a cell phone is active, its stored energy is getting used. Calls use some energy. Using the Internet takes much more energy. Playing games can use up a great deal of energy.

Right after being recharged, the battery indicator shows a full charge.

After the cell phone has been used a lot, the energy stored in the battery is nearly gone.

17. Think of an example from your life of a battery running out of energy. What do you do to conserve battery energy?

Possible answer: My flashlight did not work when I needed it while camping. To conserve battery life, now I make sure I don't leave it on when I am using it.

___

Putting It Together

18. Choose the best words to complete each sentence.

| light   sound   motion   heat |

When a hair dryer is turned on, you can feel the blowing breeze caused by its ____motion____ energy and the drying warmth from its ____heat____ energy. You can hear the whir of its ____sound____ energy.

Tip Think of how you use your senses to detect each kind of energy.

82   Unit 2 Energy

LESSON 1   Engage • Explore/Explain • **Elaborate** • Evaluate

TAKE IT FURTHER Discover More

 **Explore Online**   Students can explore all three Take It Further paths online.

TAKE IT FURTHER
Discover More

Check out this path... or go online to choose one of these other paths.

| People in Engineering | • Vampire Appliances
• Potato Power |

Mayra Artiles, Car Engineer

Explore Online

Have you ever thought of becoming an automobile engineer? Mayra Artiles did, and now she's an engineer working on hybrid electric vehicles. She enjoys designing, building, and testing cars. She even gets to program software into the cars. She likes the teamwork with other engineers, and she also likes getting out to test-drive the cars.

Mayra Artiles pays close attention to transfer of energy. Like any automobile engineer, she knows that the energy of the car's motion affects the battery. Batteries are also sensitive to outdoor temperatures during a hot summer day or in the cold of winter.

Mayra Artiles driving a hybrid car

19. What forms of energy do you notice when a car's engine is turned on?
Students might identify heat and sound energy any time the engine is turned on, motion energy of car vibrations when it is parked, as well as movement while it is being driven.

83

Collaboration

Pathways You may choose to assign this activity or to direct students online to the eSE where they can explore and choose from all three paths. These activities can be assigned individually, to pairs, or to small groups.

People in Engineering: Mayra Artiles, Car Engineer

DCI **ETS1.A Defining and Delimiting Engineering Problems**

Students will learn about Mayra Artiles, an automobile engineer who has an interesting career designing and testing hybrid cars. Mayra uses what scientists and engineers know about energy to improve how automobiles function. When making such improvements, it is necessary for engineers, such as Mayra, to identify the problems and constraints. Examples of constraints are weather, cost, battery longevity, and limited resources.

Make sure students understand the meaning of *hybrid*. Emphasize for students that this is an example of an engineer who spends her work life identifying problems, developing solutions, and using energy in ways that have an impact on society and the natural world.

CCC **Influence of Engineering, Technology, and Science on Society and the Natural World**

Mayra Artiles has an impact on society and the natural world. By working with teams of engineers, she helps design hybrid automobiles that can reduce toxic gas emissions caused by fossil fuels such as gasoline. Instead, she and her teammates design cars to run off alternative energy sources that are better for the environment.

Lesson 1 What Is Energy?   83

LESSON 1 Engage • Explore/Explain • **Elaborate** • Evaluate

TAKE IT FURTHER, continued

SEP Asking Questions and Defining Problems

In order for people to design new technology, they must ask and answer a series of questions, such as "What do people need?" or "What would help the environment?" From there, more specific questions are asked until most of the details are identified and problems are defined.

Ask: What kind of question did Marcus Lehmann probably ask when he started building the wave carpet? **Possible answer: How can the waves from the ocean be used to create power?**

Differentiate Instruction

ELL: Using Realia Show a video clip of ocean waves. Have students pay attention and identify the kind of energy the movement of the waves shows. Students should be able to grasp a simple concept that the motion of the waves produces energy, which can be directed toward the device that needs energy.

▶ Explore Online

Students can explore these additional topics online.

Vampire Appliances
Vampire appliances can use energy, or power, even when they are not turned on. *(Outside research required.)*

Potato Power
Students learn about the power and type of energy that potatoes can generate. Students identify projects using potatoes to light up a bulb. *(Outside research required.)*

Dr. Marcus Lehmann

Did you know that people can use the power of ocean waves to generate electricity and fresh water?

The ocean is a fascinating sight for many people. Dr. Marcus Lehmann was so intrigued by the ocean, he decided to use its waves to produce electrical energy.

Lehmann, along with his team of engineers at the University of California, Berkeley, built the wave carpet.

Dr. Marcus Lehmann

A wave carpet will transform ocean waves into usable energy.

20. Think of an engineering project. What could you design to protect a battery from hot and cold weather? Remember that the protected battery still has to work. It also has to be able to give off some heat while it's working.

   Possible answer: Build a small shelter box with an electric light bulb to use batteries in cold weather. Build a reflective shade to protect them from sun during hot weather.

84

84 Unit 2 Energy

LESSON 1

LESSON CHECK

LESSON 1

Lesson Check

Name _____

Can You Explain It?

1. You have learned about energy and how one form can change into another. Think back to the photo of the train. Where do you think the energy came from to make the heavy train speed along the track?
   - When the train stopped, where did the energy go?
   - Describe how energy causes change.
   - Explain how energy changes form.

 EVIDENCE NOTEBOOK Use the information you've collected in your Evidence Notebook to help you cover each point above.

- The train carried stored energy as fuel to make it move.
- When the train stopped, it stopped using that stored fuel.
- The energy of motion of the train transformed into sound and heat energy as the train slowed and stopped.

_____
_____
_____
_____

Checkpoints

2. Which of these shows energy?
   a. a car that has tires
   b. **a car that begins to move**
   c. a car parked in a garage
   d. a picture of a new car

85

Formal Assessment Go online for student self-checks and other assessments.

Can You Explain It?

Collaboration

Discussion You may wish to revisit the information covered in Explorations 1 and 2 to ensure student understanding of the material. Use bulleted points in the student edition to lead the discussion.

EVIDENCE NOTEBOOK

Have students reread their answers to the Evidence Notebook prompts and then use this evidence to justify their reasoning as they respond to the Can You Explain It? Make sure students understand that a complete response must address all bulleted points.

PS3.B Conservation of Energy and Energy Transfer

Draw students' attention back to the image of the train. Now that students are more familiar with the concept of energy, have them think about the kind of energy being used by the train.

Ask: What kind of energy is present while the train is stopping? motion, heat, light, and sound when it blows the whistle

SUMMATIVE ASSESSMENT
Analyze Problem-Defining Processes

2. To correctly answer the question, students must have a clear understanding of the Crosscutting Concept Energy and Matter. They must also recall that energy creates something to happen.

Lesson 1 What Is Energy?   85

LESSON 1 Engage • Explore/Explain • Elaborate • **Evaluate**

LESSON CHECK, continued

3. You may suggest that students first determine which of the choices are devices that use energy, and then have them decide which choices are forms of energy.

4. Make sure students understand what a turbine is. Provide an image of a turbine, if possible. Students may become confused by the answer choices, as answers "b" and "d" both use the term *motion energy*. Help students understand the difference between the two answer choices.

5. Students can recall the activity they participated in, in which they needed to light the bulb and write down the process and materials they used and in the correct order. Remind students of the importance of order when it comes to how energy works.

6. Remind students to recall the light bulb activity to remember the importance of a circuit and the function it plays in transferring energy.

---

3. Which of these is a form of energy? Circle all correct answers.
   a. **heat**
   b. oven
   c. **electricity**
   d. **light**
   e. lamp
   f. microwave oven
   g. **sound**
   h. **motion**
   i. popcorn maker
   j. **chemical**

4. What would happen at an electricity generating station if the turbines did not spin?
   a. Coal would not burn.
   b. **Motion energy would not generate electric energy.**
   c. Chemical energy would not change into heat energy.
   d. Heat energy would not make motion energy.

5. Number these sentences in the order in which they occur.
   __2__ Electric energy transfers through the cord.
   __4__ Electric energy transforms to light energy.
   __1__ You turn on a light switch.
   __3__ Electric energy transfers into the lamp.

6. If there is not a complete circuit between a battery and a lamp, what will be the result?
   a. The lamp will turn on, but it will not turn off.
   b. **The lamp will turn off, but it will not turn on.**
   c. The lamp will both turn on and turn off.
   d. The wires will get very hot.

LESSON 1

Lesson Roundup

A. Which of these devices does NOT change electrical energy into motion energy? Choose the best answer.
   a. DVD player
   b. clock
   c. clothes dryer
   d. electric stove ✓

B. Which form of energy can be observed in all of these: a washing machine, a printer, and a radio? Choose the best answer.
   a. sound ✓
   b. motion
   c. light
   d. heat

C. Write each word beneath the intended energy form that is present when the object is turned on. Some objects will have more than one form of energy.

   blender   toy drone
   hair dryer   clothes iron

Sound	Light	Motion	Heat
blender, toy drone, hair dryer	clothes iron	blender, toy drone, hair dryer	hair dryer, clothes dryer, toy drone, blender

D. Choose the best answer.
   A cell phone battery will last longest if the phone is mostly used to _____.
   a. text or call. ✓
   b. use the Internet.
   c. play games.
   b. watch movies.

Lesson Roundup

 PS3.B Conservation of Energy and Energy Transfer

This lesson summary enables students to quickly revisit key points and prepare for tests.

A. Have students revisit Exploration 1 to recall how energy is transferred into motion. Students should also recall the different forms of energy to help them respond correctly to this question. **PS3.B**

B. To correctly answer this question, students need to find the similarities between the washing machine, printer, and radio. From there, students should consider the different forms of energy from Explorations 1 and 2. Finally, students must conclude the form of energy that all the devices have in common. **PS3.B**

C. Students have spent a lot of time studying the forms of energy in Explorations 1 and 2. If students need additional support, guide them to think about how each device in the word bank functions. If necessary, provide images of a blender, hair dryer, toy drone, and clothes iron for students to recall the intended purpose of each device when turned on. **PS3.B**

D. To answer this question correctly, students must recall what they learned in Exploration 2 regarding what kinds of activities drain batteries the fastest. **PS3.B**

LESSON 2
How Is Energy Transferred?

Building to the Performance Expectations

The learning experiences in this lesson prepare students for mastery of:

4-PS3-2 Make observations to provide evidence that energy can be transferred from place to place by sound, light, heat, and electric currents.

4-PS3-4 Apply scientific ideas to design, test, and refine a device that converts energy from one form to another.

Trace Tool to the NGSS
Go online to view the complete coverage of these standards across this lesson, unit, and time.

 **Science & Engineering Practices**

 Disciplinary Core Ideas

 **Crosscutting Concepts**

Planning and Carrying Out Investigations
Make observations and measurments to produce data to serve as the basis for evidence for an explanation of a phenomenon.

Constructing Explanations and Designing Solutions
Identify the evidence that supports particular points in an explanation. Apply scientific ideas to solve design problems.

 VIDEO Planning and Carrying Out Investigations and Constructing Scientific Explanations

PS3.A Definitions of Energy
Energy can be moved from place to place by moving objects or through sound, light, or electric currents.

PS3.B Conservation of Energy and Energy Transfer
- Energy is present whenever there are moving objects, sound, light, or heat.
- Light also transfers energy from place to place.
- Energy can also be transferred from place to place by electric currents, which can then be used locally to produce motion, sound, heat, or light.

PS3.D Energy in Chemical Processes and Everyday Life
The expression "produce energy" typically refers to the conversion of stored energy into a desired form for practical use.

ETS1.A Defining Engineering Problems
Possible solutions to a problem are limited by available materials and resources (constraints). The success of a designed solution is determined by considering the desired features of a solution (criteria). Different proposals for solutions can be compared on the basis of how well each one meets the specified criteria for success or how well each takes the constraints into account.

Energy and Matter
Energy can be transferred in various ways and between objects.

Influence of Engineering, Technology, and Science on Society and the Natural World
Engineers improve existing technologies or develop new ones.

Science is a Human Endeavor
- Most scientists and engineers work in teams.
- Science affects everyday life.

 VIDEO Energy and Matter

 CONNECTIONS TO MATH

4.OA.C.5 Generate a number or shape pattern that follows a given rule. Identify apparent features of the pattern that were not explicit in the rule itself.

 CONNECTIONS TO ENGLISH LANGUAGE ARTS

W.4.8 Recall relevant information from experiences or gather relevant information from print and digital sources; take notes and categorize information...

Supporting All Students, All Standards

Integrating the Three Dimensions of Learning

In this lesson, students collect evidence for the storage of energy, learn ways energy moves in waves, and learn how energy transfers through the addition or subtraction of heat **(DCI PS3.A, PS3.B, PS3.D, and ETS1.A)**. Working as a team, students plan and build a solar cooker, which they use to transfer the sun's energy into food, thereby cooking it **(SEP Planning and Carrying Out Investigations, Constructing Explanations and Designing Solutions)**. By looking at how energy transfers through matter, students develop a greater understanding of how the application of energy can be used to effect changes in matter **(CCC Energy and Matter)**.

 **Professional Development** Go online to view **Professional Development videos** with strategies to integrate CCCs and SEPs, including the ones used in this lesson.

Extra Hands-On Activity: Hot and Cold

How Does Heat Transfer?

 Whole class
10 minutes

Heat transfers from warmer objects into cooler objects. To demonstrate this, place before students two glasses, each about 1/3 filled with water. The water in one glass should be fairly hot; the water in the other should be fairly cool. Have students use a thermometer to take the temperature of the water in each glass. They should then write the two temperatures on a sheet of paper.

Explain to students that you are going to mix the two glasses of water, and ask them what they think will happen to the temperature when you do. Have students predict the temperature of the mixed water.

Proceed to mix the two glasses of water. Do not shake the glass, and do not wait too long to complete the next step. Have students again take the temperature and write it on a sheet of paper. Did students' predictions come true about how the temperature of the water would change? Have students explain what happened to the water when it was mixed and why.

 This activity can support mastery of this Crosscutting Concept: Energy and Matter

Preassessment

Have students complete the lesson pre-test online or see the Assessment Guide.

Build on Prior Knowledge

Students should already know and be prepared to build on the following concepts:
- Energy is a measure of the ability to cause change in matter, and can take the form of sound, light, heat, and motion.
- Energy moves in waves and can be changed or transferred.
- Energy can be stored in batteries and then used at a later time.

Differentiate Instruction

Lesson Vocabulary
- heat
- sound
- vibrate

Remind students that there are many words that convey the same or similar meanings as *heat*.

Ask: What are other words for heat?
Possible answers: hot, warm, warmth, temperature

Point out that there are many things heat can do, such as cook food, burn skin, cause sweating, and so on.

ELL/ELD Strategy
Point out that the word *vibrate* comes from a Latin word (*vibrare*) meaning "wave."

Ask: What is something that makes a wave? water

Explain to students that waves are how energy travels. Water waves happen when energy moves through water. Energy also moves through other material in waves.

Lesson 2 How Is Energy Transferred? **88B**

LESSON 2 **Engage** • Explore/Explain • Elaborate • Evaluate

ENGAGE: Lesson Phenomenon

Lesson Objective

To understand and observe energy transfer involving light, sound, and heat, and provide evidence illustrating the changes that result.

About This Image

When a person presses down on and/or strums the strings of an electric guitar, the strings vibrate, sending an electric current through a wire and to an amplifier. When a drumstick hits a drumhead, the drumhead vibrates, moving the air around it and causing a sound wave. When people talk, they release bursts of air through the larynx that vibrates their vocal chords, producing sound. Microphones convert energy from one form to another. When a person speaks or sings into a microphone, the sound waves he or she makes strike the microphone's diaphragm, which then vibrates. These vibrations cause other parts of the microphone to vibrate as well, which becomes an electric current.

 SEP **Planning and Carrying Out Investigations**

Alternative Engage Strategy

Hearing Waves	👥 pairs ⏱ 10 min

Explain to students that they need to speak to each other from a distance but they cannot let others hear them. Tell them that they have two open tin cans, one for each student, and a single string to stretch between them. Ask students to sketch how they might be able to talk to each other in a whisper using the two tin cans and the string. Then bring the whole class together, and ask students to relate their drawings and answer the following questions as a group discussion: How might you use the tin cans and string to speak to each other? What would happen to the sound from your mouths? Name two ways in which that sound would transfer.

LESSON 2

How Is Energy Transferred?

A band produces sound energy that is transformed in different ways. Motion energy in an electric guitar, for example, transforms into to electric current through wires. This electric energy transforms into sound energy through speakers. The sound transfers through air to reach your ears.

By the end of this lesson . . .
you'll be able to explain energy transfers of light, sound, and heat.

Unit 2 Energy

> **Explore Online** Students can view the lesson phenomenon online.

Can You Explain It?

Wow! Electric drills transfer enough energy to break apart brick walls. People who use electric drills must wear ear protection.

Whispers, on the other hand, can be hard to hear. When people whisper, they have to be close to each other to hear.

1. What is the difference between the sounds in the photos? What do you think makes each sound loud or soft? Explain how energy transfer from loud sounds is different from soft sounds.

   Students should respond based on the preliminary observations they can make of the images.

   Tip
   Learn more about energy and how it is transferred in *What Is Energy?*

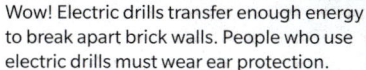 **EVIDENCE NOTEBOOK** Look for this icon to help you gather evidence to answer the questions above.

89

Can You Explain It?

Students are asked to compare sounds as illustrated in two photographs. In the first, a road construction crew member is using a pheumatic drill on a brick wall. In the second, one girl is whispering to another. The sounds are different in the photos because a different amount of sound energy is being transferred. In the first photo, a high amount of sound energy is being transferred from the pneumatic drill into the wall, where it is breaking apart the brick. Sound is transferring to motion. In the second image, much less energy is being used to transfer sound from one girl's mouth to the other girl's ear, which might make it more difficult for the second girl to hear what the first girl is saying.

Collaboration

Draw, Pair, Share Find images in magazines, books, or newspapers, and bring them to class. Put students into pairs, instructing each to have a sheet of paper and a writing utensil handy. Hold up each image, and ask each pair of students to discuss between themselves what is making sound in the image. Then have them sketch the item and draw an arrow showing in which direction the sound is moving. Give students time to finish their sketches, and then move on to another image. If there is a receiver for the sound, such as a person or an animal, have students sketch the receiver as well and draw an arrow from the item producing the sound to the receiver's ear(s).

EVIDENCE NOTEBOOK

Encourage students to use an appropriate graphic organizer, such as main idea and supporting details, to set up their notebook for this lesson.
Find more strategies in the online ELA handbook.

Lesson 2 How Is Energy Transferred? 89

LESSON 2   Engage • **Explore/Explain** • Elaborate • Evaluate

EXPLORATION 1 Heat

3D Learning Objective

Students **carry out investigations** to learn that heat is a measurement of temperature and that it describes how **energy transfers** between **matter** of uneven temperatures. They develop an understanding of the ways energy transfers heat up or cool down objects and sometimes change the structures of matter.

> ## Differentiate Instruction
>
> **RTI/Extra Support** Provide students with different types of materials, from metal objects to fabrics. Do not provide the same exact material to more than one student. Ask each student to touch the object. Then ask the students to describe whether the object was cool or warm. Engage in a class discussion about why each object feels the way it does.

SEP Planning and Carrying Out Investigations

The evidence on this page discusses how changes in temperature can change the structure of matter.

Ask: What is one way you can tell whether an object is warm or cool? Possible answers: touch it; place your hand near it; see it burning; see it frozen

Place a cool metal object in front of students, and ask each one to touch it one by one. Ask each student whether the object is warm or cool. The first students to touch it should say that it's cool; the last students to touch it might say that it's warm.

Ask: Why did the last students to touch the object find it warmer than the first students? Heat energy was transferred from students' fingertips/hands to the metal object, causing it to become warmer.

EXPLORATION 1
Heat

Hot or Not?

How do we know if something is cold or hot? Sometimes, we can see clues. Other times, we can feel whether something is hot or cold. The terms *hot* and *cold* are ways to describe temperature. Temperature is a measurement of heat. **Heat** is energy that transfers, or moves, between objects with different temperatures. Look at these photos that show evidence of energy transfer as heat.

Glassblowing involves high temperatures. Glass is heated by a glassblower to the point that it becomes molten. It can then be shaped. This often involves using a blowpipe to insert air into the glass.

Dry ice is actually a solid form of carbon dioxide. Freezing carbon dioxide takes an extremely cold temperature, much colder than that needed to freeze water. Because dry ice is so cold, it is dangerous to touch.

2. Look at the two pictures. How would you describe the differences? What details in each picture gave you clues?

Possible answer: The first image shows extremely hot. There is fire, and it is orange and warm. The second shows extremely cold. It is blue and icy.

We use words such as *hot*, *cold*, *warmer*, and *cooler* to describe temperature without being exact. To get an exact measurement of temperature, we use a tool called a *thermometer*. Temperature can be measured using different scales in degrees. The thermometer below has two scales, Celsius (C) and Fahrenheit (F).

Differences in Degrees

3. This thermometer shows measurements in Celsius (C) and Fahrenheit (F). The symbol that looks like a little *o* stands for "degrees." Write a letter in each circle to identify the temperatures shown in the pictures.

Explore Online

The girl's clothes trap heat near her body. Her jacket slows down energy transfer to the cold air. The girl stays warm while playing in the snow in temperatures as low as 0 °C (32 °F) or below.

The water coming from this shower head is hotter than the air near it. We know this because of the steam. The temperature of this shower water is 42 °C (108 °F).

The inside of a refrigerator must be kept cold so food doesn't spoil. If it is too cold, fresh food freezes. The ideal temperature is a little below 4 °C (38 °F).

Heat moves from the stove to a tea kettle, then from the kettle to the water, and finally from the water vapor to the air. Water boils at 100 °C (212 °F).

91

LESSON 2 Engage • **Explore/Explain** • Elaborate • Evaluate

EXPLORATION 1 Heat, continued

Collaboration

Think, Pair, Share Engage in a class discussion about energy transfers. Calling students' attention to the images in their textbooks, explain that heat can be used to change the structures of food other than pancakes. Separate students into pairs, and have them brainstorm foods that change by being cooked. After pairs have been given ample time to brainstorm, call everyone together, and have pairs share their ideas with the class.

Ask: What types of food can be cooked with heat?
Possible answers: meats, breads, eggs

Ask: What might happen to some matter if heat is removed from it? It might grow cold or freeze.

DCI PS3.D Energy in Chemical Processes and Everyday Life

Chemical processes occur when heat changes the structure of matter, and that change cannot be undone. For example, once wood has burned to ash and released chemicals in the form of smoke, that ash and smoke cannot be put back together to form wood. These chemical processes can produce energy that can be exploited for human use.

Ask: What are some examples of heat being applied to an object to release energy that can be used by people? Possible answers: Burning wood can be used to heat a house; cooking food can result in people being fed.

Differentiate Instruction

Extension Have students write a short essay describing how heat can be added to or removed from an object to change its state or structure. They should explain how the transfer occurs and give examples.

Hot by Contact

Remember that heat is energy that transfers between objects with different temperatures. Heat energy sometimes transfers easily between objects that are touching. When objects of two different temperatures touch, heat energy moves from the warmer object to the cooler object.

How does this energy transfer work when cooking a pancake? A pancake griddle starts out at room temperature. When the stove burner is hot, it transfers heat to the bottom of the griddle. The heat spreads through the whole griddle. The heat energy in the hot griddle then transfers to the cooler pancake batter. As the batter heats, the pancake cooks.

Energy is transferred as heat moves from a stove burner toward a pancake griddle.

Energy is also transferred as heat moves from the hot griddle to the colder pancake batter.

4. Select the best words to complete each sentence.

| batter | burner | cooler | energy |
| faster | griddle | slower | warmer |

Heat is ____energy____ that moves from a ____warmer____ object to a ____cooler____ object. A pancake cooks when energy transfers from the ____burner____ to the ____griddle____ to the ____batter____. The last pancake in the batch cooks ____faster____ than the first pancake because the griddle is hotter.

Distant Heat

Pancakes cook because objects are in contact. Heat energy can also transfer between objects that are not touching each other.

Study each picture to figure out the source of heat energy. That is, determine where you think the heat is coming from. Then locate the objects the heat is transferring to.

The flame of a gas burner heats the air above the burner. The hot air rises and fills the balloon. Heat transfers into the balloon. Soon the whole balloon is full of hot air.

The space heater transfers heat to the air around it. This makes the air in the room gain heat energy and become warmer. Soon, the room is nice and cozy.

 EVIDENCE NOTEBOOK Sound and heat are both forms of energy. What evidence have you gathered so far to help you explain how sound energy is transferred?

 5. Language SmArts Complete the chart by writing the cause and effect from each example.

Heat Transfer without Touch		
Example	Heat source	What heat transfers to
marshmallows roasting over a campfire	fire	marshmallows
heat lamp incubating hatching chicks	heat lamp	baby chicks
snow melting on a sidewalk on a sunny day	sun	snow

93

 PS3.A Definitions of Energy

Students should understand that there is no such thing as cold energy, only heat energy. Cold occurs when heat energy transfers out of an object or place. For example, water freezes when temperatures drop below a certain level; this means that heat energy is leaving the water. Once the amount of heat energy drops below a certain level, the state of water changes from liquid to solid (ice). When heat energy returns, the water will change from solid back to liquid. If enough heat energy is added, the liquid will change state to a gas (vapor).

Ask: What causes cold? **Possible answer: heat energy leaving a place or object**

 EVIDENCE NOTEBOOK

Students may say that their evidence so far indicates that energy can travel through the air. As heat energy can transfer through a distance, so too can sound energy.

Language SmArts
W.4.8 Categorize Information

The chart is an opportunity not only to reinforce students' basic understanding of cause and effect, but also to show them how to categorize information. Explain to students that when they categorize, they place blocks of similar information together. For example, in the table, one column features causes, and another features effects. Remind students that causes are what make things happen and effects are what happens as the results of causes. You may wish to have students come up with additional examples of cause and effect from the Exploration.

Lesson 2 How Is Energy Transferred? 93

LESSON 2   Engage • **Explore/Explain** • Elaborate • Evaluate

EXPLORATION 1 Heat, continued

 Engineer It!
Thermal Imaging

CCC Science Is a Human Endeavor

Scientists have developed thermal imaging in ways that help people. In addition to the example in the student edition, thermal imaging can help police officers find fugitives when they are on the run at night, or it can help locate people lost at sea. It can even identify heat signatures in the structures of walls and reveal hidden compartments.

Separate students into small groups or pairs. Then have them brainstorm other ways in which thermal imaging can help people.

Ask: What are some other ways thermal imaging might be able to help people? *Possible answers: It can help with search-and-rescue missions at night. It can help locate the path a person has taken. It can help locate evidence of recent activity or movement.*

Differentiate Instruction

RTI/Extra Support If the activity in item 6 proves too difficult for some students, use the following fill-in-the-blank sentence instead. Objects with different **temperatures** show up in different colors on a thermal image. Thus, one object must be **warmer (or cooler)** than the other to be detected.

FORMATIVE ASSESSMENT
Putting it Together

Ask: How does heat energy move between objects?
Give one example of heat energy transfer. Possible answer: Heat energy transfers from warmer objects to cooler objects. One example is heat transferring from a flame into wood; another is heat transferring from a hot plate to a pan to the food within the pan.

94 Unit 2 Energy

 **Engineer It!**
Thermal Imaging

Thermal imaging devices can "see" how hot or cold air moves into and out of a house. By knowing how energy is being transferred, people can insulate areas of the houses to help them stay warmer or cooler.

Thermal imaging devices are also used by fire departments. When there is fire in a house, there is a lot of heat and smoke. Because firefighters cannot see through the smoke, they cannot see if anyone is trapped in a house. By using a thermal imaging device, they can see the cooler bodies in all the hot smoke. This helps the firefighters rescue people and pets from the fires.

Thermal imaging of buildings can help save energy.

6. Two objects on a thermal image are different colors. What must be true of these objects?

Objects with different temperatures show up in different colors on a thermal image. Thus, one object must be warmer than the other.

Putting it Together

7. Select the best words to complete each sentence.

| a different | cooler | does not move | do not touch |
| transfers | the same | touch | warmer |

Heat is energy that __transfers__ when objects have __a different__ temperature. Heat energy always moves from a __warmer__ to a __cooler__ object. A pancake cooks when objects __touch__. Heaters warm an area even though they __do not touch__ objects.

94

EXPLORATION 2 Here Comes the Sun

EXPLORATION 2

Here Comes the Sun

Lighting Up Life

The sun is a star that gives off light and heat. These forms of energy are important to Earth and the things that live on it.

8. What else do you know about energy from the sun? Brainstorm a list of ways in which the sun's energy affects Earth and living things.

Possible answer: The sun's rays warm Earth; the sun's energy makes us warm when we are in the sun's light; the sun shining during rain makes a rainbow; light from the sun helps plants make food; sunlight is what causes it to be day.

All life on Earth depends on light and heat from the sun. The sun heats Earth's atmosphere, making Earth warm enough for water to be liquid and for living things to survive.

Sunlight makes it possible for plants to grow and provide the oxygen we breathe. Plants also provide us with some of our food. The sun's heating of Earth's atmosphere sets the water cycle in motion. Energy from the sun causes wind and weather patterns, too.

Solar panels like these transform light energy into electrical energy that can be used to heat buildings. Solar panels can also change light energy into energy that heats the water used in buildings.

9. Solar panels are evidence for which of these statements?
   a. Light can be transformed into other energy forms.
   b. Heat energy moves toward warmer objects.
   c. Sound transfers heat energy.
   d. Life on Earth depends on sunlight.

3D Learning Objective

Students will **carry out investigations** to learn about other types of energy and conclude that **energy transfers** from place to place through light and other types of waves as well as through **chemical processes**. Using this information, they come to an understanding that **science is a human endeavor** and study specific examples of the **influence of engineering, technology, and science on society and the natural world**.

CCC Influence of Engineering, Technology, and Science on Society and the Natural World

Solar panels are one example of ways that scientists are using technology to transfer energy for the benefit of humans.

Ask: What are other examples of ways that humans are transferring energy to benefit people? Possible answers: Wind turbines transfer motion energy into electrical energy for homes and businesses. Large plants burn waste products to transfer heat energy into electrical energy for homes and businesses. Nuclear plants turn water into steam to generate electricity for homes and businesses.

DCI PS3.B Conservation of Energy and Energy Transfer

Light moves energy from place to place. Light from the sun moves energy from the sun to Earth. Solar panels focus that light and trap it and then transfer the energy so that it can be used by people. The solar panels in the images are located outside and generate electricity. However, not all solar panels generate electricity; some absorb heat and transfer it to buildings.

Ask: Where might you find solar panels that generate heat?
Possible answers: homes, businesses, schools

LESSON 2 Engage • **Explore/Explain** • Elaborate • Evaluate

EXPLORATION 2 *Here Comes the Sun, continued*

DCI PS3.A Definitions of Energy

Some waves require a medium through which to travel, such as air, water, or earth. Seismic waves, for example, travel through earth and sometimes water. Such waves are known as mechanical waves. Other types of waves do not need a medium. They can travel through a vacuum. These are known as electromagnetic waves. Light is one example of an electromagnetic wave.

Ask: Which types of waves are shown by this scale?
electromagnetic waves

Build on Prior Knowledge

Light is not the only type of energy wave produced by the sun. Light is one type of electromagnetic wave. The sun releases many types of electromagnetic energy waves, including x-rays, infrared rays, ultraviolet rays, microwaves, and radio waves.

Differentiate Instruction

ELL: Use Realia English-language learners may have a difficult time understanding what timelines or scales are. Explain that a scale such as the one in this spread shows things in relation to other things that are similar. Show several examples of scales to students.

Ask: What is one purpose of a scale? Possible answer: to show how things are related to each other

---

A Family of Waves

Light from the sun is a form of energy we can see. These waves travel outward in all directions from the sun and spread out as they move. Other kinds of waves are not visible but also carry energy as they travel and spread out. These other types of energy waves include radio waves, microwaves, and x-rays.

View each image and read the captions to learn about different types of energy waves. Each type of wave has a certain level of energy. The five types of energy waves discussed here are arranged in order of lowest energy (radio waves) to highest energy (x-rays).

Energy Rays

Have you used a microwave oven to heat food? **Microwaves** are higher in energy than radio waves. They have less energy than visible light waves. Images of rain and storm patterns on the weather news online or on TV are also often made using microwaves.

Lowest energy

Radio waves spread out and travel from a broadcast tower to radio receivers such as car radios. Radio waves have low energy compared to other waves.

Visible light is in the middle of the range of energy waves. Visible light includes all the colors we see. A rainbow shows a range of colors, from red to violet. What we see as red light has the lowest energy of visible light waves. Violet has the highest energy.

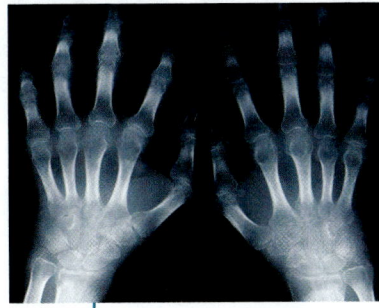

X-rays have much more energy when compared to visible light and radio waves. Have you ever seen an x-ray image of your teeth at your dentist's office? A dentist uses x-rays to better see the health of a person's teeth. X-rays are passed through the body and processed to make images of bones and tissues.

Ultraviolet light is invisible light. Ultraviolet, or UV, light is higher in energy than the range of light humans can see. But some insects can see UV light! The Hubble Space Telescope senses UV light. Images from the telescope show us the UV light given off by many different objects in space.

Highest energy →

 EVIDENCE NOTEBOOK What evidence do you have that visible light is made of all colors?

 Language SmArts
Energy Experience

10. Which of the energy waves shown on these pages have you experienced? What evidence do you have of each type of energy?

Students might say that they listened to the radio and that the sounds are evidence of radio waves. Or they may say that they or someone in their families used a microwave oven, citing the cooked product as evidence of these energy waves. Students also may have seen weather images on a computer or on TV. These images are evidence of microwave energy. Some students might state that seeing colors is evidence of visible light energy.

DCI PS3.A Definitions of Energy

X-rays are the most powerful form of electromagnetic ray shown on this scale. Because they're so powerful, they can pass through many solid objects. X-rays can also be dangerous to humans.

Ask: Why are x-rays more dangerous to people than other types of electromagnetic rays? **X-rays are far more powerful than many other types.**

CCC Influence of Engineering, Technology, and Science on Society and the Natural World

The Hubble Space Telescope was sent into space in April 1990 and since that time has taken many photographs. Without the haze of our atmosphere to obstruct its view, Hubble can detect many things that we cannot see with our naked eyes. In fact, it can see things that we can't see even with the most powerful telescopes on Earth. Among its many features is the ability to find different kinds of light, include ultraviolet light.

Ask: How does the Hubble Space Telescope reflect the natural world in "seeing" ultraviolet light? **In the natural world, some insects can see ultraviolet light.**

 EVIDENCE NOTEBOOK

Students may point to rainbows as evidence or say they can see a variety of colors with their own eyes.

 Language SmArts
Energy Experience
W.4.8 Recall relevant information from experiences

Using evidence: Tell students to use evidence as they recall experiences with different types of energy waves. Emphasize to students that evidence is used to support ideas and information when writing.

LESSON 2   Engage • **Explore/Explain** • Elaborate • Evaluate

EXPLORATION 2 Here Comes the Sun, continued

PS3.D Energy in Chemical Processes and Everyday Life

There are different kinds of changes that can happen to matter. A physical change happens when the state of matter changes as a result of energy being applied to it. For example, heat energy can melt ice into liquid water or evaporate liquid water into water vapor. A chemical change also requires energy and changes matter's physical state. However, it also changes the very structure of the matter, and that change cannot be undone. Wood burning into ash and smoke or egg yolk frying in a pan are examples of chemical changes.

Ask: Is a melting candle an example of a physical or a chemical change? **A melting candle shows a both a physical change in the melting wax, and a chemical change because the wick is converted into heat and light and cannot be changed back.**

Collaborate

Write, Pair, Share Ask students to write down other examples of stored energy being released when heat energy is added to an object. Then separate them into pairs. Ask each student to share his or her examples with his or her partner. Pairs should be encouraged to discuss their examples with the class.

FORMATIVE ASSESSMENT

LSA3.A Definitions of Energy

Ask: How do electromagnetic rays travel, and where do they come from? **Possible answer: Electromagnetic rays travel in waves, and many of them come from the sun. Others can come from objects on Earth, such as radio towers, light bulbs, microwave machines, and x-ray machines.**

Enhancing Energy

What kinds of energy transformations happen as the candle burns? Recall that batteries contain stored energy. A candle has stored energy, too. How do we know this? As a candle burns, energy stored in the wick transforms to heat and light. The stored energy changes form. Heat and light are evidence that the candle contained stored energy.

When a candle burns, energy from the wax and wick transforms into heat and light.

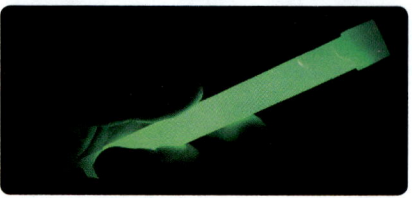
When a glow stick is activated, chemical reactions inside the stick cause the stored energy to transform into light.

11. Choose the best answer to complete the sentences below.

less	microwaves	more	stored energy
ultraviolet light	visible light	x-rays	

Visible light waves have ___**more**___ energy than radio waves and ___**less**___ energy than x-rays. One type of energy wave that people cannot see but some insects can is ___**ultraviolet light**___. ___**Microwaves**___ can be used to make weather maps. ___**X-rays**___ can be used to study bones and teeth. Candles transform ___**stored**___ energy to heat and light.

Putting it Together

12. Choose one type of energy wave, describe its energy level in relation to other waves, and explain one way it is used in everyday life.

Possible answer: Radio waves are one type of energy waves. They have lower energy than microwaves and visible light rays. Radios transform radio waves into sound energy that we can hear.

Tip

When a question asks you to explain something, use details and examples from the text to support your explanation.
Reading and Writing in Science

98

98   Unit 2 Energy

HANDS-ON ACTIVITY
Design and Test a Solar Cooker

Objective

Collaborate to design and test a cooker that uses energy from the sun.

Design criteria the desired features of a solution. They can include using only certain materials. Or they can be specific to what your solution must do.

Describe the problem that you will try to solve in this activity. How will your solution be helpful in everyday life? What will your solar cooker need to do in order to be a success?

Possible answer: The problem we will try to solve is to design a cooker that could be used to cook basic foods or heat water. This device could be helpful when camping. To be successful, we think our cooker should be able to heat up at least 2 °C every 3 minutes.

Materials
Discuss with your group what you think you will need to build your cooker. Do some research if needed.

Students should identify the materials they will need.

Procedure

STEP 1 List the materials your group plans to use in the **Materials** box above.

STEP 2 Make a sketch of your design for your solar cooker in the box.

Drawings should incorporate space to contain food and a method for concentrating the sun's energy into that space.

HANDS-ON ACTIVITY 👥 Small groups 🕐 1 class period

Design and Test a Solar Cooker

3D Learning Objective

SEP Planning and Carrying Out Investigations & Constructing Explanations and Designing Solutions

Students will observe energy transfer involving light and heat and provide evidence illustrating the changes.

Materials

As part of the process of constructing explanations and designing solutions, students are expected to come up with a list of materials they will need for their experiment. Possible materials may include an actual cooker with a glass top to allow sunlight into it, but to keep pests out, or aluminum foil to focus the sun's energy.

Preparation

The amount of time students need to prepare their experiments will depend on the materials chosen and the procedure decided upon. Most cookers shouldn't take more than 10 minutes to prepare.

SEP Planning and Carrying Out Investigations & Constructing Explanations and Designing Solutions

Students are expected to design and test a solar cooker. They begin by planning and designing their cookers and then carry out their investigation, constructing an explanation for how it works as they go.

Procedure

STEP 1 Circulate among student groups, and listen as they discuss which materials they will need to build their solar cookers.

Ask: What have you seen other people cook food in? cookers, pots, pans

Lesson 2 How Is Energy Transferred? 99

LESSON 2   Engage • **Explore/Explain** • Elaborate • Evaluate

EXPLORATION 2 HANDS-ON ACTIVITY, *continued*

DCI ETS1.A Defining Engineering Problems

The activity on these pages asks students to solve an engineering problem—cooking food or drink using only energy from the sun—with materials they provide.

Ask: Why might someone use a solar cooker to cook food rather than a conventional oven or stove? **Possible answers: He or she might not have access to electricity. He or she may want to save on the cost of electricity.**

STEP 3 Once students have finished their step-by-step plans, look them over, offering advice on how to make them better.

STEP 4 Observe as students use their solar cookers. Be sure that they handle their cookers safely and wash their hands after handling any food. Note that cookers may be hot after being in the sunlight and should be handled with care.

Ask: Why is it important to handle the cookers with care and to wash your hands after you handle food? **Possible answers: You could get burned; you could get food poisoning.**

STEP 5 Circulate among students as they complete their data tables, answering any questions they may have.

STEP 3 Make a step-by-step plan to build and test the solar cooker.

Record the steps your group has agreed upon to build the solar cooker.
Plans should include multiple steps for execution.

STEP 4 Build your solar cooker according to your group's plan. Place the completed cooker in direct sunlight to test it. Use a thermometer to measure how quickly your solar cooker heats up.

Record Your Results

STEP 5 Record temperature changes in your cooker in the data table below.
CAUTION: Do not touch any foil you may have used in your solar cooker when it is in the sunlight.

Solar Cooker Test in Direct Sunlight

Time	Temperature (°C)
0 minutes	(starting temperature)
at 3 minutes	*Check student responses. They should note an increase of temperature over time.*
at 6 minutes	
at 9 minutes	
at 12 minutes	
at 15 minutes	

Analyze Your Results

STEP 6 What was the highest temperature reached in your solar cooker? By how many degrees did the temperature change from the start of the test to the end?

Possible answer: The highest temperature reached by our cooker was 28 °C. Our starting temperature was 20 °C, so the temperature increased by 8 °C.

STEP 7 Did your solar cooker meet all of the design criteria you listed on page 99? How well did it succeed in solving the problem you stated? Did all steps of the plan go as expected?

Possible answer: My group's cooker met all of our design criteria, but it was not as efficient as some of the other groups' designs. The steps did go as planned.

Draw Conclusions

STEP 8 What do you think your group could do to improve the design of your solar cooker? Be specific.

Possible answer: Some of the materials were difficult to work with, and the results did not come out as we had expected. We might be able to improve our design by using more foil to make the cooker more efficient as well as trying to make the cooker more air-tight to prevent energy loss.

STEP 9 Make a claim about energy transfer from the sun. Cite evidence from your test to support your claim.

Claims should focus on the ability of the sun to warm objects. Temperature measurements provide evidence.

STEP 10 List another question you would like to ask about energy transfers.

Possible answer: What happens to the heat in the solar cooker as it cools off?

101

 Energy and Matter

Point out to students that heat energy from the sun's light is transferring into the cooker. As a result, the food or liquid inside the cooker is undergoing a chemical change.

Analyze Your Results

STEPS 6–7 Help students connect what they have learned in their experiment to the real world.

Ask: What does this activity tell you about the sun's energy?
Possible answer: The sun's energy is strong enough to cook food.

Draw Conclusions

Ask: What else can the sun's energy do? Possible answers: It can be used to heat homes. It can be used to generate electricity.

Claims, Evidence, and Reasoning

Have students work with a partner to critique each other's claims and evidence. Ask each pair to be prepared to share one way that they changed or improved their claim on the basis of evidence. Discuss responses as a class.

Ask: What is the most reliable evidence about solar cookers that you gathered during this investigation? Why? Students may cite information they researched or observations made during the activity.

Scoring Rubric for Hands-On Activity	
3	Students' cooker cooks the food/liquid inside it and reaches the required temperature.
2	Students' cooker warms up the food/liquid inside it but does not reach the required temperature.
1	Students' cooker does not warm up the food/liquid inside it.

LESSON 2 Engage • **Explore/Explain** • Elaborate • Evaluate

EXPLORATION 3 Seeing Sound

3D Learning Objective

Students develop an understanding of how energy is transferred through sound waves. Students **plan and carry out an investigation** to learn that **energy moves through sound**, transferring between **matter**. Sound originates as vibrations, which move in waves through the air, transferring from the vibrating object to other objects.

Differentiate Instruction

RTI/Extra Support If necessary, engage students in a class discussion about objects that produce sounds, such as televisions, radios, phones, and so on. Then ask them to draw one of these in the box, next to a person's ear, with arrows showing where the sound is coming from and where it is going.

Ask: Which part of your body picks up sound waves? How do you know? **The ear; this is how most people detect sounds.**

Collaborate

Draw, Pair, Share After students have completed their drawings, have them trade their art with a partner. Ask each pair to discuss the accuracy of their drawings. Then have them share their findings with the class.

 EVIDENCE NOTEBOOK

Students should take away from the lesson the idea that loud sounds require more energy while soft sounds require less energy. The louder the sound, the more energy it takes to produce it. Students may also state that loud sounds involve greater vibrations and therefore have larger waves than soft sounds do.

102 Unit 2 Energy

EXPLORATION 3

Seeing Sound

Good Vibrations

Sounds are all around you. But what is sound? **Sound** is energy that travels in vibrations. To **vibrate** means to move back and forth. Sound vibrations come from an object or organism that starts the vibration. Then, the vibration travels through the air or surrounding objects. When a sound vibration reaches your ear, you sense the sound. Soft sounds have smaller waves than louder sounds.

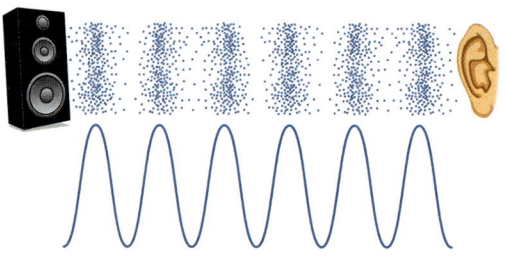

You can't see sound waves. But the small particles that make up all kinds of matter vibrate as sound waves strike objects.

13. Draw a picture to show how sound might move from an object to your ear.

a simple drawing that includes arrows to show sound moving from an object to a person's ear

 EVIDENCE NOTEBOOK Use the information on these pages to help you explain how a loud sound is different from a soft sound.

102

When you pluck a string of a guitar, it vibrates back and forth. If you pluck it hard, you transfer a lot of energy to the string. The sound is loud. If you pluck it softly, you transfer less energy. The sound is soft. If the string vibrates faster, the sound gets higher in pitch. If the string vibrates slowly, the sound gets lower in pitch.

Telephones, televisions, radios, computers, and sound systems all have speakers. Speakers transfer electrical energy into sound energy. When you listen to recorded music or a video, sound vibrations travel through a speaker. The speaker vibrates and transfers sound vibrations to the air, which then spread outward to your ear.

HANDS-ON Apply What You Know
Make Vibrations

Can make sound you can see? Design a musical instrument that allows you to observe vibrations. Below is an example of what you could make.

Use the rubber band to hold a piece of waxed paper around the top of an empty container. The paper should be fairly tight and flat across the top of the container. Place the small objects on top of the waxed paper. Tap the surface of the drum. Observe what happens to the objects.

Materials
- materials of your choosing to make an instrument

OR
- waxed paper
- empty container
- rubber band
- small objects such as grains of sand, rice, or confetti

14. Describe what happened with the instrument you made. What kind of energy transfer did you observe?

Possible answer: I observed the objects move up and down or "dance" around on the waxed paper when I tapped on the surface of the drum. Tapping on the paper made it vibrate. This was the first energy transfer. Then vibrations of the paper transferred energy to the objects and made the objects vibrate, too.

Differentiate Instruction

RTI/Extra Support Does your band or band room have an acoustic guitar? Discuss the caption from the first image with students. Invite a member of the band or the band instructor to class; have him or her illustrate each fact in the caption on an actual acoustic guitar.

Pluck a string on the guitar softy.
Ask: What is happening to the string? It is vibrating softy.

Pluck a string on the guitar hard.
Ask: What is happening to the string? It is vibrating with more energy.

HANDS-ON Apply What You Know
Make Vibrations

If they do not have a small drum, and one is not available from the school, instruct each student to bring a clean, empty can from home, along with some rice or confetti. Have them follow the directions in the activity. Circulate among students as they make their small drumheads, answering questions and directing them as needed.

Ask: Why is it important that the wax paper be tight over the top of the can? If the wax paper is too loose, it will not vibrate when struck.

Scoring Guidelines
The most effective drumheads will result in the objects on the wax paper moving as the paper vibrates. The least effective drumheads will result in no movement of the objects on the wax paper.

Lesson 2 How Is Energy Transferred?

LESSON 2   Engage • **Explore/Explain** • Elaborate • Evaluate

EXPLORATION 3 *Seeing Sound, continued*

CCC Science Is a Human Endeavor

Airplanes are loud. If you've ever been in one, or been near an airport during takeoff, you know that this is true. But why are airplanes loud? Because it takes a powerful engine and lots of energy to get the airplane off the ground. As the engine revs up for takeoff, the noise gets louder. However, by looking at nature, scientists have been able to make airplanes less loud than they used to be. For example, they've invented turbo fan engines, which use a different kind of airflow through the engine, making it less noisy. They've also modeled parts of airplane wings after the wings of birds. Movable slats in wings are now "brush-like," imitating birds' feathers.

DCI PS3.B Conservation of Energy and Energy Transfer

There are three ways instruments make sound: by vibrating a string (think plucking a string), by vibrating the air (think blowing into something), and by vibrating a surface (think striking something).

Ask: Name one instrument for each type of sound vibration.
Possible answers: guitar=vibrating a string; tuba=vibrating the air; drums=vibrating a surface

> ## Differentiate Instruction
>
> **Extension** Show students the images without the accompanying text. Ask them to identify what appears in each and to tell whether it has a soft or a loud sound and whether the energy is high or low.

Loud and Soft, High and Low

Sounds are everywhere. Some sounds, like whispers, are soft. Other sounds, like jet planes, are very loud. Why do sounds differ? It's the energy transfer. If a lot of energy is transferred from or to an object, the sound is loud. If less energy is transferred from or to an object, the sound is softer. Loud sounds have more energy than softer sounds.

Loud sounds cause particles to vibrate vigorously with much energy. Soft sounds cause them to vibrate with less energy.

Sound Off!

15. Look at the photos. Decide if each sound is soft or loud. Then decide if each has low energy or high energy. Circle your answers.

A plane's engines roar as the plane takes off and touches down.

The airplane makes a (soft **(loud)**) sound, which has (**(high)** low) energy.

A mouse is a small animal that makes squeaky sounds.

A mouse makes a (**(soft)** loud) sound when it squeaks, which has (high **(low)**) energy.

104

104   Unit 2 Energy

When fireworks explode, they transfer both sound and light energy.

Exploding fireworks make (soft / **loud**) sounds, which have (**high** / low) energy.

A gentle breeze from an open window can cause curtains to move.

Curtains moving like this make a (**soft** / loud) sound, which has (high / **low**) energy.

Dripping water makes a sound when it hits the floor or ground.

The dripping faucet makes a (**soft** / loud) sound, which has (high / **low**) energy.

16. Select another object or organism that makes sound. Draw it in the box, and describe it as a soft or loud sound, and whether it has high or low energy.

Possible answer: An electric guitar makes a loud sound with high energy.

SEP Constructing Explanations and Designing Solutions

Have students stretch a rubber band between their thumb and their forefinger. The rubber band should not be too tight. Ask students to pluck their rubber band softly.

Ask: What do you see? The rubber band vibrates.
What do you hear? a soft sound

Then have students pluck the rubber band harder.

Ask: What do you see? The rubber band vibrates even more.
What do you hear? a louder sound
What relationship does the exercise demonstrate? How loud a sound is depends on how much it vibrates.

DCI PS3.B Conservation of Energy and Energy Transfer

When fireworks explode, there is a transfer of energy. Stored energy inside the fireworks turns to sound, light, and heat energy. When a firework explodes, you hear a loud sound. You also see beautiful lights. If you are close enough, you may feel heat from the explosion.

Ask: What are the three forms of energy that result from a fireworks explosion? sound, light, heat

Differentiate Instruction

Extension Show students the images without the accompanying text. Ask them to identify what appears in each and to tell whether it has a soft or a loud sound and whether the energy is high or low.

LESSON 2 Engage • *Explore/Explain* • Elaborate • Evaluate

EXPLORATION 3 *Seeing Sound, continued*

Collaborate

Think, Pair, Share Have students examine the three images at the top of the page. Then separate students into pairs, and have them discuss with each other what they have learned from the images. After they have been given ample time to discuss their findings, have them share their thoughts with the class.

Do the Math
Compare the Speed of Sound

4.OA.C.5 Generate a number or shape pattern that follows a given rule. Identify apparent features of the pattern that were not explicit in the rule itself.

First, students must order the sounds from slowest to fastest. Then they must identify why sound traveled through some mediums faster than it did through others. Sound is energy, and it moves from particle to particle. When particles are closer together, the sound has less space to "jump." Because of this, it moves much more quickly when there are more particles closer together. The particles of solid objects are closer together than those of non-solid objects.

Differentiate Instruction

RTI/Extra Support On a separate sheet of paper, have students list in one column the materials and the speed at which sound moved through them. Then, in a second column, have students write the numbers 1 through 6. Have them draw a line from the fastest speed to the 1 and so on until they are done. Alternately, because some students may find it easier to order the speeds from slowest to fastest, have them begin with the slowest speed and draw a line from it to the 6.

Energy on the Move

Sound vibrations can transmit through any substance. As you can see in the picture below, sound transmits faster through solid materials than through liquids or gases such as air. This is because the particles in solids are closer together than the particles in liquids or gases.

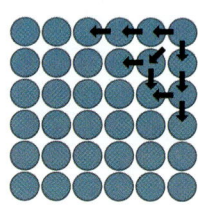 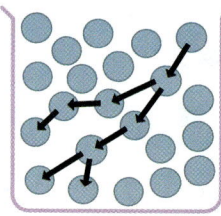 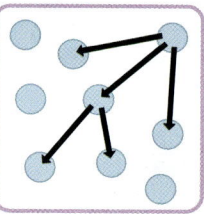

Notice how sound moves in a solid (left), a liquid (middle), and a gas (right). Describe the effect the distance between particles makes.

Do the Math
Compare the Speed of Sound

16. Analyze the data in the table. Order the speeds from fastest to slowest. Then draw a conclusion about the data.

Speed of Sound in Different Materials

Order	Material at 0 °C	Speed of sound (m/s)
5	Air	331
2	Copper	4,600
4	Fresh water	1,433
6	Rubber	60
3	Silver	3,650
1	Steel	6,100

Using these data, I can conclude that sound travels fastest through solid metal (steel, silver, and copper), slower through liquids (fresh water), and slowest through gases (air). Sound moves slowly through rubber.

Unit 2 Energy

Tuned In!

A tuning fork is a tool that is used to tune musical instruments. When struck, the fork vibrates. When struck, the sound does not travel very far in the air. The sound travels much farther through a solid, because the particles are closer together.

The tuning fork is vibrating in the air.

Here the fork is vibrating against a metal railing.

HANDS-ON Apply What You Know
Tune In

17. Work with a group to test how sound travels through different materials. If you don't have a tuning fork, use something else to make a sound along a metal railing. On the lines below, list the materials you will use. Describe the steps you will do to carry out the test. Record your results.

Possible answer: We used a tuning fork and struck it against a metal rail and a wooden rail. When the fork was struck against the rails, it vibrated faster than it did when it vibrated in the air.

18. Which of these is true? Circle the answer.
    a. Sound vibrations travel faster through air than through metal.
    b. Sound vibrations travel faster through water than through wood.
    c. Sound vibrations travel faster through solids than through gases.
    d. Sound vibrations travel through wood, metal, and air at the same speed.

Explore Online — Have students go online to learn more about how tuning forks work.

Content Background

Musician John Shore invented the tuning fork in 1711. Up until that time, musicians had to rely on pitch pipes to tune their instruments. Unfortunately, pitch pipes were made out of wood, which meant that when it was hot and humid, their shape and pitch would change. Shore was a trumpeter and instrument maker who wanted something more reliable with which to tune his instruments. Because of its shape and material, a tuning fork is not affected by most changes in temperature or environment. The result is greater accuracy and reliability. Today, electronic tuners are often used for convenience.

HANDS-ON Apply What You Know
Tune In

Find a suitable spot in the classroom or school for the Hands-On Activity to take place. (You may be more likely to find a metal railing outside and a wooden railing inside.) Have students follow the directions in the activity. Circulate among students, answering questions and directing them as needed.

Ask: In addition to the metal and wooden rails, what are some other materials you might test? stone walls, hard earth
What outcomes would you expect with those tests? The fork would vibrate more against the stone wall than against the hard earth.

Scoring Guidelines

The tuning fork vibrates faster against hard surfaces than against soft ones.

LESSON 2   Engage • **Explore/Explain** • Elaborate • Evaluate

EXPLORATION 3 Seeing Sound, continued

 PS3.B Conservation of Energy and Energy Transfer

The photo shows several examples of energy transfers in a kitchen. Find other photos that show energy transfers. They can be of sports games or construction crews building a structure. Or they can be of the sun or moon shining on a beautiful landscape.

Ask: What energy transfers does this photo show? *Answers will vary based on the photos selected.*

Differentiate Instruction

RTI/Extra Support Make a list of the energy transfers shown in the photos. Then ask students to tell what kind of energy each shows (light, heat, sound, etc.). Note that some may show more than one type of energy.

Extension Have students find photos in a magazine or newspaper. Ask them to make a list of the energy transfers shown in each.

FORMATIVE ASSESSMENT

 PS3.A Definitions of Energy

There are different types of energy, and not all of them transfer the same way. Some energy travels in waves, while other energy travels in straight lines. Some energies need a medium, while others can travel through a vacuum.

Ask: How is sound energy different from light energy? *Sound energy vibrates through the medium of air, in waves from the object that made it. Unlike light, it cannot travel through empty space.*

Energy Bands

You've learned that energy transfer takes place all around us all the time. And a busy kitchen is no exception! Pots and pans bumping against counters, stove burners aglow, and cookies baking are just a few examples of energy transfer in a kitchen.

Look at the photo to find as many examples as you can of energy transferring.

Energy Transfers in a Busy Kitchen

19. Fill in the chart with all the evidence you found in the photo of energy transfers that involve sound, light, and heat in a kitchen. Can you think of others that are not shown in the photo? Add those to the table, too.

Energy Transfers in a Busy Kitchen		
Sound	Light	Heat
Possible answers: Energy transfers into heat when people in a kitchen use the stove or the oven. Energy transfers into light through the flames on the stove burners and electric lights in the room. Energy transfers that involve sound might include a timer beeping, bacon sizzling or frying on the stove, and the sounds of knives chopping or forks hitting plates.		

Putting it Together

20. Use the following words to write a short paragraph about sound: *vibrations, solids, liquids, gases, soft, loud, more energy,* and *less energy.*

Sound is energy vibrations that can move through all types of matter. Sounds travel faster through solids than through liquids. Sounds transfer energy slowest in gases. Soft sounds are quiet. Loud sounds transfer more energy than soft sounds.

Tip

When you write about things that are different, it is useful to use words such as *than, more,* and *less*. Words ending in *–er* and *–est* are also used in comparisons.

Reading and Writing in Science

TAKE IT FURTHER

Discover More

Check out this path . . . or go online to choose one of these other paths.

- Career in Science: HVAC Tech
- Keep It Cold
- The Paynes and Fast-Traveling Whale Songs

What does a heating, ventilation, and air conditioning (HVAC) system do? Many buildings have central heating or air conditioning systems. This means a large fan or pump system blows heated or cooled air through the whole home. But what happens when the system breaks or needs to be serviced? Most people call in an HVAC technician, or HVAC tech for short.

Explore Online

HVAC techs travel around an area to maintain and fix problems in HVAC systems. In cold climates, people need their heating source to work well, especially in winter. The same with cooling systems in a hot climate. When their HVAC system breaks down, people want it fixed fast! An HVAC tech's job involves knowing how to install and fix electrical and plumbing parts of the system.

HVAC systems move air throughout entire buildings.

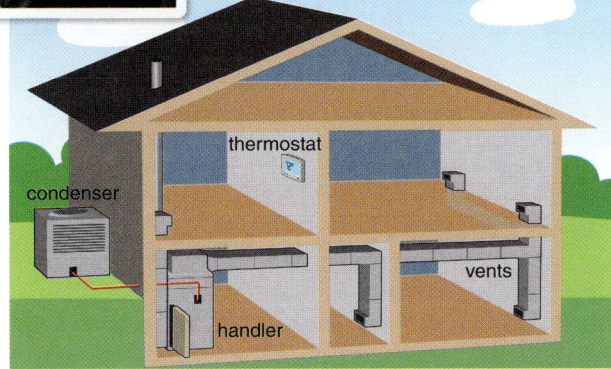

109

Lesson 2 How Is Energy Transferred? **109**

LESSON 2 Engage • Explore/Explain • **Elaborate** • Evaluate

TAKE IT FURTHER, continued

CCC Science Is a Human Endeavor

Explain that HVAC systems are the products of science and that they affect people's everyday lives. In the United States, most homes, apartments, schools, and businesses are equipped with heating and cooling systems to keep them warm in winter and cool in summer.

Ask: How is an HVAC system the product of science as a human endeavor? *Possible answer: HVAC systems were invented by scientists to make people's lives easier. They involve the science of energy transfer and technology.*

Differentiate Instruction

ELL: Use Realia For item 21, take English-language learners on a brief tour of your school's HVAC system. Invite your HVAC tech to discuss with them what the system does and how he or she sees to it that the system runs smoothly. Encourage students to ask questions.

▶ Explore Online

Students can explore these additional topics online.

Keep It Cold
Students learn how to keep cold drinks cool when in a warm environment. *(Outside research required.)*

The Paynes and Fast-Traveling Whale Songs
Students learn how whale songs travel through water. *(No outside research required.)*

Look at the drawing at the bottom of the previous page. It shows how an HVAC system works. The main unit for the system may be in the basement or in its own closet. The main air conditioning unit may be outdoors or on the roof. A large fan or pump pushes heated or cooled air through sheet metal air ducts or passageways.

An HVAC system may also be used as a fan, by blowing air through the ducts without heating or cooling it. The air ducts guide the air from the main unit to vents leading into each room. The ducts are mostly behind walls, under floors, or above ceilings.

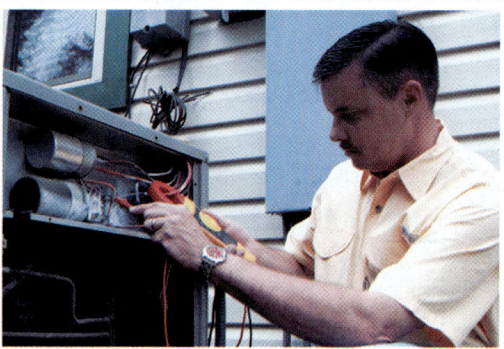

To become an HVAC tech, a person must attend school to get a certificate or be trained by an expert HVAC specialist. Community colleges may offer courses on HVAC systems. Some HVAC courses may be taken online.

21. Suppose you had the chance to interview an HVAC tech. Write three or four questions you would want to ask on the lines below.
Possible questions: What do you like best about your job? What do you like least about your job? What does an HVAC tech do in the course of a day? How did you get your training?

22. Interview an HVAC tech or do research to help you answer the questions you wrote above. Write the answers on the lines below.
Possible answer: I really like trying to figure out how to solve problems with HVAC systems, and I like talking to customers. I don't like the long hours I usually work in summer and winter. On a typical day, I follow a schedule to fix and service HVAC systems in a certain area of the city. I got trained on the job by an HVAC specialist. I also take classes once a year to improve my knowledge of these systems.

LESSON 2   Engage • **Explore/Explain** • Elaborate • **Evaluate**

LESSON CHECK

▶ **Explore Online**   Students can revisit the lesson phenomenon online.

LESSON 2

Lesson Check

Name _____

Can You Explain It?

1. Now that you've learned about energy transfer, explain how sounds transfer energy. Be sure to do the following:
   - Define *sound*.
   - Explain how energy relates to the loudness of a sound.
   - Describe energy transfers in the sounds from an electric drill.

 EVIDENCE NOTEBOOK Use the information you've collected in your Evidence Notebook to help you cover each point above.

Possible answer:
- Sound is energy that travels in vibrations.
- Some sounds are loud. Others are soft. This is because when a lot of energy transfers into sound, the sound is louder. Less energy transfers into a softer sound.
- The sound from an electric drill is loud. The energy from the drill smashing into a brick wall transfers to the air as sound.

Checkpoints

2. Which of the following produce energy from a stored form by transferring it to a useful form? Select all of the correct answers.
   - **a. battery**
   - **b. candle**
   - **c. glow stick**
   - d. thermometer

111

Formal Assessment Go online for student self-checks and other assessments.

Can You Explain It?

Collaboration

Discussion You may wish to revisit the image as a group activity to assess students' understanding of the material. Use the bulleted points in the student edition to lead the discussion.

 EVIDENCE NOTEBOOK

Have students reread their answers to the Evidence Notebook prompts and then use that evidence to justify their reasoning as they respond to the Can You Explain It question. Make sure students understand that a complete response addresses all bulleted points.

 PS3.A Definitions of Energy

Have students look back at the two images in the Engage. Have them reread the captions. If students have difficulty responding, draw arrows showing the transfer of sound energy from the object that is vibrating to the ear of the person hearing it.

Ask: If the construction worker does not wear ear plugs, what could happen to his ears after repeated use of the jackhammer? Explain your answer. The jackhammer vibrates hard and fast, which means that it produces a lot of sound energy. Too much sound energy could damage the man's hearing.

SUMMATIVE ASSESSMENT

2. Batteries, candles, and glow sticks all contain stored energy. When a battery is used, a candle is burned, or a glow stick is bent and waved, that energy is transferred into electricity, light and heat, and light, respectively. Thermometers, on the other hand, do transfer energy, but not from stored energy. Rather, heat energy from the atmosphere causes the mercury in the thermometer to expand.

Lesson 2 How Is Energy Transferred?   111

LESSON 2 Engage • **Explore/Explain** • Elaborate • Evaluate

LESSON CHECK, continued

3. You may have to remind students that thermometers contain mercury, and mercury is affected by heat. Also, heat transfers out of warmer objects into cooler ones rather than the other way around. If necessary, have students revisit the information about heat energy transfers in Exploration 1.

4. Remind students that sound energy is energy they can hear. They can eliminate the incorrect answers by asking themselves, "Is that a sound I can hear?" They can revisit this information about sound energy in Exploration 3.

5. For examples of energy transfers that involve more than one energy, students can reread Explorations 1, 2, and 3. Students can also ask themselves, "Does this object give off light or absorb light?" If the answer is "give off light," then the energy is converted to light energy.

6. Remind students that sound travels faster through harder surfaces because their particles are closer together. Have them look at each option and ask which has the particles that are the farthest apart.

---

3. Select the words that correctly complete the sentences in the paragraph.

| cooler | decreasing | distance |
| increasing | temperature | warmer |

A thermometer shows the __temperature__ of an object. When temperature rises, it is evidence that heat energy is __increasing__. When a pancake cooks, energy transfers from the __warmer__ griddle to the __cooler__ batter.

4. Which are evidence of energy transfer involving sound? Select all of the correct answers.
   a. a burning candle
   (b.) an airplane taking off
   (c.) water dripping
   (d.) orchestra playing music
   e. solar cooker
   (f.) plucking of a guitar string
   (g.) kids whispering
   h. Hubble telescope

5. Energy can transfer *to* or *from* different types of energy. Which of the following involve a transfer of energy *to* light energy? Select all of the correct answers.
   a. electric light
   (b.) tuning fork
   c. solar cooker
   d. solar panels
   (e.) burning candle
   (f.) glow stick

6. Circle the type of matter through which sound travels the slowest.
   a. wood
   b. steel
   (c.) air
   d. water

112

Unit 2 Energy

LESSON 2
Lesson Roundup

A. Decide which kinds of energy transfer are involved in each example below. Sort each example into the correct column in the table. Some examples might fall into more than one category.

orchestra   tea kettle   solar panels   fireworks

sound	light	heat
orchestra	solar panels	tea kettle
tea kettle	fireworks	solar panels
fireworks		fireworks

B. Select the best answer to complete this sentence. A good way to transfer light energy to heat energy is to use a _____.
  a. microwave oven   c. hand warmer
  b. battery   **d. solar cooker**

C. Sound will travel fastest through _____.
  a. fog   c. salt water
  b. air   **d. metal railing**

D. Choose the words that make the sentences correct.

cooler   warmer   high   low

When a warmer object touches a cooler object, heat transfers from the __warmer__ object to the __cooler__ object. The sound of a jackhammer transfers __high__ energy, while a whisper transfers __low__ energy.

113

Lesson Roundup

 PS3.A Definitions of Energy
PS3.B Conservation of Energy and Energy Transfer
PS3.D Energy in Chemical Processes and Everyday Life

This lesson summary enables students to quickly revisit key points and prepare for tests.

A. To clarify students' understanding of energy transfers involving heat, light, and sound, have them revisit Explorations 1, 2, and 3. You may also remind students that light energy is energy they see, sound energy is energy they hear, and heat energy is energy they feel. Sometimes, light energy and heat energy are closely related, as in the case of fire. Have students look at each option and ask themselves: *Do I feel heat from it? Do I see light from it? Do I hear sound from it?* **PS3.A**

B. If students struggle with this question, have them reflect on the Hands-On Activity, in which they turned light into heat energy to cook food or heat up liquid. Light energy can be converted into heat to cook food or warm homes, businesses, and school. Point out that only one option does one of those things. **PS3.B, PS3.D**

C. Students may wish to revisit Exploration 3, which covers sound energy and how it is transferred. Remind students that, unlike light, sound energy cannot travel through a vacuum, or empty space. It must have a medium. The closer the particles of the medium, the faster sound will travel through it. Have students ask themselves which medium is the hardest, with the most compact particles? **PS3.A**

D. If students grapple with this question, you may wish to direct them to Explorations 1 and 3, which deal with heat energy and sound energy. If necessary, explain that heat energy tends to move from hot to cold and that the amount of energy in a sound is proportional to how loud the sound will be. The faster an object vibrates, the more energy it has to make sound. That will directly affect how soft or how loud the sound is. **PS3.B**

Lesson 2 How Is Energy Transferred? 113

LESSON 3
How Do Collisions Show Energy?

Building to the Performance Expectations

The learning experiences in this lesson prepare students for mastery of:

4-PS3-1 Use evidence to construct an explanation relating the speed of an object to the energy of that object.

4-PS3-3 Ask questions and predict outcomes about the changes in energy that occur when objects collide.

4-PS3-4 Apply scientific ideas to design, test, and refine a device that converts energy from one form to another.

Trace Tool to the NGSS
Go online to view the complete coverage of these standards across this lesson, unit, and time.

Science & Engineering Practices

Asking Questions and Defining Problems
Ask questions that can be investigated and predict reasonable outcomes based on patterns such as cause-and-effect relationships.

▶ VIDEO Asking Questions and Defining Problems

Constructing Explanations and Designing Solutions
Identify the evidence that supports particular points in an explanation. Apply scientific ideas to solve design problems

▶ VIDEO Constructing Scientific Explanations

Disciplinary Core Ideas

PS3.A Definitions of Energy
The faster a given object is moving, the more energy it possesses.

Energy can be moved from place to place by moving objects or through sound, light, or electric currents.

PS3.B Conservation of Energy and Energy Transfer
When objects collide, energy can be transferred from one object to another, thereby changing their motion. In such collisions, some energy is typically also transferred to the surrounding air; as a result, the air gets heated and sound is produced.

PS3.C Relationship Between Energy and Forces
When objects collide, the contact forces transfer energy so as to change the objects' motions.

PS3.D Energy in Chemical Processes and Everyday Life
The expression "produce energy" typically refers to the conversion of stored energy into a desired form for practical use.

Crosscutting Concepts

Energy and Matter
Energy can be transferred in various ways and between objects.

▶ VIDEO Energy
▶ VIDEO Matter

Influence of Engineering, Technology, and Science on Society and the Natural World
Engineers improve existing technologies or develop new ones.

Science Is a Human Endeavor
Most scientists and engineers work in teams. Science affects everyday life.

 CONNECTIONS TO MATH

4.OA.A.3 Solve multistep word problems posed with whole numbers and having whole-number answers using the four operations, including problems in which remainders must be interpreted.

4.MD.A.1 Know relative sizes of measurement units within one system of units. Express measurements in a larger unit in terms of a smaller unit.

 CONNECTIONS TO ENGLISH LANGUAGE ARTS

RI.4.5 Describe the overall structure of events, ideas, concepts, or information in a text or part of a text.

RI.5.7 Draw on information from multiple…sources.

W.4.2 Write informative/explanatory texts…

W.4.8 Recall relevant information from experiences.

Supporting All Students, All Standards

Integrating the Three Dimensions of Learning

In this lesson, students learn that every object contains energy. When objects collide, they transfer that energy **(DCIs PS3A, PS3.B, and PS3.C)**. Students observe this concept in action by experimenting with rubber bands and toy automobiles **(SEPs Asking Questions and Defining Problems, Constructing Explanations and Designing Solutions)** and applying the knowledge they gain to situations involving collisions between objects. Students begin to visualize how potential energy can become stored energy and can then be transferred through impacts **(CCCs Energy and Matter)**. Students' investigations lead them to an understanding that the size and speed of moving objects affects how much energy they have and can transfer, and when objects collide with the ground, some of their energy transfers to the ground.

 **Professional Development** Go online to view **Professional Development videos** with strategies to integrate CCCs and SEPs, including the ones used in this lesson.

Extra Hands-On Activity: Crash Bang Boom

Which Is The Bigger Collision?

Small groups
30–45 minutes

Each group of students will need materials for a simple ramp, a meter stick, a balance with masses, and four different-size and different-mass balls. Students should build a ramp for testing how far one ball will move after it has been hit with another ball.

Students should set up their ramp so the descending ball collides with the other ball at the same place every time. They should record how far the second ball moves from the collision point. Have students make a chart showing the mass of the descending ball, the mass of the ball being hit, and how far the second ball moved. Students can then try out different combinations of balls to see how mass affects the distance a ball moves due to a collision. In summing up their data, students should see that there are patterns of motion to the balls as a result of the mass of the balls.

 SEP This activity can support mastery of this Science and Engineering Practice: Constructing Explanations and Designing Solutions

Preassessment

Have students complete the lesson pre-test online or see the Assessment Guide.

Build on Prior Knowledge

Students should already know and be prepared to build on the following concepts:
- Energy is a measure of the ability to cause change in matter.
- There are many different types of energy, including light, motion, heat, and electrical among others.
- When an object is heated up, energy is transferred into it. When an object is cooled down, energy is transferred out of it.

Differentiate Instruction

Lesson Vocabulary
- collision
- energy
- motion

Explain that some other words for **collision** are *bump* and *crash*. When things bump into each other, very little energy is transferred. When things crash into each other, much more energy is transferred.

Ask: What is an example of something bumping into something else? *students bumping into each other*

Explain that when things bump into each other, energy moves from each into the other; for example, from elbow to desk and desk to elbow.

Extension
Show students a video of things crashing into each other, such as a baseball into a catcher's mitt.

Ask: How is this similar to a person bumping his or her elbow into a desk? How is it different? *Energy is transferred from the baseball into the mitt and from the mitt into the baseball. The amount of energy being transferred is greater.*

Collisions occur every day. When we walk, our feet collide with the ground. Have students share other examples of minor everyday collisions.

Lesson 3 How Do Collisions Show Energy? **114B**

LESSON 3   **Engage** • Explore/Explain • Elaborate • Evaluate

ENGAGE: Lesson Phenomenon

Lesson Objective

Observe energy transfers and recognize the correlation between speed and the amount of energy an object possesses, and identify collisions as a form of motion energy transfer.

About This Image

Bubble balls are designed to collide with each other with a minimum amount of energy transfer. Because there is so little energy transfer, the person inside a bubble ball is unlikely to get hurt. Bubble balls are a safe way to learn about energy transfer.

 SEP Asking Questions and Defining Problems

Alternative Engage Strategy

| **What Happened to the Pencils?** | Whole class
 5 min |

Ask students what happens when pencils roll into each other. Have students retrieve two pencils from their desks. Ask them to lay the two pencils parallel to each other about three inches apart. Then direct each student to gently apply enough force to one pencil so that it will roll into the other. Ask students why the first pencil came to a stop when it hit the second pencil and why the second pencil began to move when it was hit. Engage in a class discussion, inviting students to participate by raising their hands, asking questions, and answering questions.

LESSON 3

How Do Collisions Show Energy?

These bubble balls allow bumping game players to bump, roll, and flip over without getting hurt.

By the end of this lesson . . .
you'll be able to explain how energy changes when objects in motion collide.

Can You Explain It?

Picture in your mind what happens when the cue ball hits the group of balls at the other end of the table. What happens in a collision?

1. When one ball hits a group of balls, what do you think will happen to the cue ball? What about the balls that were racked up at the other end of the table?

   Students should respond based on the preliminary observations they can make of the image.

   Tip
   Learn more about energy in What Is Energy? and How Is Energy Transferred?

 EVIDENCE NOTEBOOK Look for this icon to help you gather evidence to answer the questions above.

Can You Explain It?

Students are asked to explain what happened to both the cue ball and the racked balls when they collide. To do so, students must understand that energy from the cue ball's motion will be transferred into the racked balls. When this happens, the cue ball will likely stop while the other balls start to move. The energy does not transfer from the cue ball to the other balls all at once, however; it moves from each ball as that ball touches another ball nearby. Most students will not yet understand what is happening, but assure them that this is okay. Their knowledge will grow as they move through the lesson's Explorations. They will have an opportunity to revise their answers when they revisit these questions at the end of the lesson.

Collaboration

Draw, Pair, Share Have students watch the video and then draw what they saw. Alternately, you can show the transfer of energy by using a group of tennis balls and rolling a single tennis ball into the others. Have students place arrows on their drawing, showing the movement of energy between balls. Then separate students into pairs. Ask each pair to exchange their drawings, comparing and contrasting where their arrows are located on the balls. Have them discuss with each other why those chose the directions for their arrows. Stress that their answers will not be graded.

 EVIDENCE NOTEBOOK

Encourage students to use an appropriate graphic organizer, such as cause and effect, to set up their notebook for this lesson.
Find more strategies in the online ELA handbook.

LESSON 3 Engage • *Explore/Explain* • Elaborate • Evaluate

EXPLORATION 1 Things That Move Have Energy

3D Learning Objective

Recognize the relationship between speed and the **amount of energy an object possesses**. Investigate the relationship between energy and matter by observing objects in motion and **asking questions** about their energy. **Construct explanations** that the faster an object is moving, the more energy it has; and the bigger an object is, the more energy it can contain. Understand the **relationship between energy and forces** and between **energy and matter**.

SEP Construction Explanations and Designing Solutions

The evidence on the page tells us that when we move, or are in motion, we have energy.

Ask: If you are not moving, do you have energy? **Yes, stationary objects have potential energy.**

Differentiate Instruction

RTI/Extra Support If the questions are too difficult for students, ask yes or no questions that specifically identify the location of the roller coaster's cars. For example: Does this roller coaster have energy when the cars are sitting on top of the hill? Does it have energy when they are moving down the hill?

EXPLORATION 1

Things That Move Have Energy

Energy and Things That Move!

Imagine riding on a huge roller coaster with lots of drops and turns. Are you excited? Are you nervous? Think about inching slowly up the hills—and plunging to the valleys below! But what does this all have to do with energy? Think about the roller coaster and energy in this photo.

The coaster is still as the passengers buckle their seat belts, but it's getting ready to move. As the coaster climbs the hill, it slows down. At the top, there's a pause. As the coaster starts to nudge over the top of the hill, it moves faster. The riders can feel the whoosh of air on their faces as the coaster drops. The coaster's speed changes as it climbs and drops.

2. Does this roller coaster have energy? When does it have energy? How do you know?

Possible answer: Yes, I know the roller coaster has energy when it is moving. It also has energy when it is at the top of the hill about to move.

What do a moving car, a stretched rubber band being released, and a rolling ball have in common? They all have motion energy! Anything that is moving has motion energy. Objects can also have stored energy, like the roller coaster on the hill, because of their position. That energy beomes motion when it races down!

116

116 Unit 2 Energy

There might be a dish on the edge of a shelf, ready to fall. Even before the dish falls, it has energy, because of its position up on the shelf.

When you swing on a swing set, you have motion energy. At the top of each swing, you stop moving but have stored energy to move again.

When an archer pulls back on the string to shoot an arrow, energy is being stored. What will happen when the archer lets go of the string?

A rolling soccer ball has motion energy. Kicking it adds to that energy, making it move even faster, and scoring a goal!

3. Choose the best phrase to complete the sentences.

| have motion energy | become motion energy | speed up |

The objects that are moving _have motion energy_. The objects that are about to move have energy that can _become motion energy_.

Science Is a Human Endeavor

Point out that unlike other animals, humans have a conception of the natural world around them and are always trying to better understand it, especially through science. Discuss how science informs the design of the things shown in the images.

Ask: How do you think science influenced the design of the dishes on the shelf? **Sample answer: figuring out what materials are strongest, not too heavy, easy to clean**
How do you think science influenced the design of the bow? **Sample answer: determining a material and design that would be flexible but also strong enough to snap back and shoot the arrow with the greatest speed and accuracy**

PS3.D Energy in Chemical Processes and Everyday Life

The images are all examples of energy in everyday life.

Ask: What kind of energy do you see in each photo? **potential energy, motion energy**

Differentiate Instruction

Extension Have students answer Item 3, and give examples of objects that have motion energy (a rolling ball, a moving car, a falling glass, and so on). Then have students give examples of objects that do not have motion energy but could (a stationary ball, a parked car, a cup sitting on a table, and so on).

LESSON 3   Engage • **Explore/Explain** • Elaborate • Evaluate

EXPLORATION 1 Things That Move Have Energy, continued

Collaboration

Feedback Bring a clean, dry, empty paint can to class or to an area of the school where loud sounds will not disturb others. Turn the paint can upside down on the floor. Have each student hit the paint can with a drumstick or a long, thin piece of wood. Engage students in a discussion as to why they think some hits on the paint can were louder than others.

CCC Energy and Matter

Explain to students that a gong is an example of matter. When a gong is struck, energy passes from the object striking the gong into the gong, creating a sound.

Ask: What type of matter is the gong? solid
What other types of matter are there? liquids, gases

Differentiate Instruction

ELL: Use Realia Students learning English may struggle with the idea that energy can be stronger or weaker depending on how hard something is struck. Provide each student with a party horn. Have them blow gently into the horns. A mild sound will issue from the horn. Have them blow hard into the horns, to produce a stronger, louder sound. Explain that the difference in volume is based on difference in energy.

HANDS-ON Apply What You Know
Bang a Gong
Have each student bring an empty tin can from home to use as a gong or cymbal. Following closely the Collaboration above, have each student perform the experiment and answer the questions in the activity.

118   Unit 2 Energy

Swifter and Stronger!

Do you think the speed of an object affects its energy? Look at the pictures. In one, a slow-moving ball strikes a gong. In the other, a fast-moving ball strikes a gong. The more the gong moves, the more energy the ball transfers to the gong.

Is the ball swung slowly or quickly? How does the gong react?

Is the ball swung slowly or quickly? How does the gong react this time?

4. Choose the best words to complete the sentences about objects of the same weight.

all	faster	slower
can	cannot	never

_____Faster_____ objects transfer more energy to the object they hit.

_____Slower_____ moving objects transfer less energy to the object they hit.

The speed of an object _____can_____ show(s) the amount of energy in the object.

 HANDS-ON Apply What You Know

Bang a Gong

5. Gather materials to experiment with what you have seen in the pictures. Set up the materials and test. Tell how your setup was the same and how it was different. How were the results the same, and how were they different? What does this show you about the relationship between speed and energy?

118

The Faster They Are Hit, the Harder They Fall

You noticed that the faster you threw a ball, the more energy it had. The increased energy made the gong move more. Now think back to the pool game. If the cue ball moved slowly toward the group of balls at the end, what would happen? What if the cue ball were moving very fast?

A game of bowling is a lot like a pool game. You roll the bowl toward the pins, trying to knock down as many as you can. How does energy change your bowling score? Let's find out!

Slide a bowling ball slowly toward the pins.

When the ball hits the pins, how many pins fall down? Do they topple over or fly from the other pins?

Now move the ball more quickly. How many pins fall?

What else do you notice about the pins when a ball thrown quickly hits them?

6. Use the slow and fast bowling ball example to explain the relationship between speed and energy.

A faster ball has more energy and strikes the pins with greater force than a slower ball.

Content Background

Speed and Energy Speed is the distance an object moves in a certain amount of time. For example, a car may move 1 mile in 1 minute. If the car continued at that rate, it would have moved 60 miles in 1 hour. Therefore, the car's speed can be stated as "60 miles per hour." There are different ways to measure and express speed: miles per hour, kilometers per hour, meters per second, and more. The faster an object's speed, the more energy it contains.

Differentiate Instruction

Extension Some students may struggle with writing a short essay in response to item 6. If this is the case, ask short, simple questions instead.

Ask: If the bowling ball hits the pins at a slower rate of speed, what will happen? Fewer pins will fall.
If the bowling ball hits the pints at a higher rate of speed, what will happen? More pins will fall.
Which contains more energy, the slower-moving ball or the faster-moving ball? Why? the faster-moving ball, because it has more energy

DCI PS3.A Definitions of Energy

Remind students that energy is a force that can cause objects or matter to change.

Ask: What is energy doing in the images? Energy is being transferred from the bowling ball into one or more pins, and from those pins into other pins. This results in the pins being knocked over.

LESSON 3   Engage • **Explore/Explain** • Elaborate • Evaluate

EXPLORATION 1 Things That Move Have Energy, continued

Influence of Engineering, Technology, and Science on Society and the Natural World

Everything is made up of particles that the eye cannot see. On a very small level invisible to us, particles often collide. When they do, they can release large amounts of energy. To help us understand the impact of particle collisions and what can result from them, scientists have built a huge machine, the Large Hadron Collider (LHC), to observe particle collisions and their results safely. The reason the LHC is so large is because scientists want the particles to accelerate so they collide at the highest controllable energy. The faster the speed, the greater the energy released, or transferred, upon impact. A very long beam with the gentlest possible curve is required to allow the particles to accelerate without flying off course.

PS3.B Conservation of Energy and Energy Transfer

Engage in a discussion about the first two images (the car and the semi truck) on the page. One is large and one is small.

Ask: If two objects are moving the same speed, does size affect their energy? yes
Which vehicle will have more energy? the semi truck
What happens to the energy from the semi truck? It transfers into the car.
What happens to the energy in the car? It transfers into the semi truck.

HANDS-ON Apply What You Know
Flour Power

Students may opt to replace the foam ball with something lighter or heavier. If heavier, ask them to use an object that will not result in damage to any surfaces. Students may opt to replace the flour with water or another substance. Instruct students to complete the activity on a surface that is easy to clean, regardless of the substance used. If students are completing the activity at home, have them do so under a parent or guardian's supervision.

Motion Energy and Size: It's a Big Deal!

You already know that the speed of an object affects its energy. But what about size? If you wanted to knock down bowling pins, would you use a bowling ball or a tennis ball? That's right! You'd use a bowling ball because it's heavier. The heavier ball will have more energy than a lighter ball and will knock down more pins.

Look at the two vehicles. Imagine that they are both moving at 80 km/h (about 50 mph). Which do you think has more energy? If the speed is the same, how does one have more energy than the other?

 **HANDS-ON** Apply What You Know
Flour Power

7. Try the lab you just saw in the pictures. Change one thing you saw. Repeat what was done in the picture and record your results. How were the results the same, and how were they different? What does this show you about the relationship between speed and energy?

EVIDENCE NOTEBOOK Explain what would happen to the flour if the balls you used were heavier. Explain what would happen if the balls were lighter.

Language SmArts
Cause and Effect

8. Explain how weight can affect collisions.
A heavier object has more energy than a lighter object if the objects are traveling at the same speed.

120

120   Unit 2 Energy

Notice the ping pong ball above the pan of flour. What happens when the ball hits the flour? Only a little of the flour moves. The ball didn't have much energy to transfer to the flour.

This baseball is dropped from the same height but is heavier than the ping pong ball. It also falls at the same speed. The crater left by the baseball is larger than the crater left by the ping pong ball. That's because the heavier ball had more energy to transfer.

Putting it Together

9. Explain why there is more damage when objects moving quickly collide than when they are moving slowly.

Possible answer: Moving objects have energy based on their motion. If an object is moving more slowly, it has less motion energy. If an object is moving faster, it has more motion energy. When objects collide, they transfer energy. The more motion energy there is to transfer, the bigger the collision.

 EVIDENCE NOTEBOOK

Students should note that when the balls were heavier, more flour was moved from the pan. When the balls were lighter, less flour was moved from the pan. This is because the amount of energy transferred from the balls to the flour is different. A heavier ball transfers more energy; a lighter ball transfers less energy.

 Language SmArts
Cause and Effect
W.4.2 Write informative/explanatory texts

As students explain how weight influences collisions, remind them that their explanation needs to be clear and concise. This means writing in complete sentences that are to the point. Writing about science especially calls for clarity so that other scientists can repeat experiments or convey the same information accurately.

FORMATIVE ASSESSMENT
Putting it Together

 PS3.C Relationship Between Energy and Forces

Ask: How are speed, size, and energy related? When objects move at a faster speed, they have more energy. When objects are larger, they have more energy. When these objects collide with something, more energy is transferred than would be if they were slower and/or smaller.

LESSON 3 Engage • **Explore/Explain** • Elaborate • Evaluate

EXPLORATION 1 Things That Move Have Energy, continued

HANDS-ON ACTIVITY Small groups 1 class period

Test It! Stored Energy in a Spring

3D Learning Objective

DCI **PS3.B Conservation of Energy and Energy Transfer**
PS3.C Relationship Between Energy and Forces

Observe energy transfer involving motion, and provide evidence illustrating the changes.

Materials
The materials listed in the student edition are a starting point. If toy cars or trucks are not available, other objects may be substituted. Safety googles should be worn when stretched elastics are used.

Preparation
Clear a space in the floor large enough for students to conduct their experiments. As a safety precaution, instruct all students to remain behind or to the side of the chairs from which the toy cars/trucks will be launched.

CCC **Energy and Matter**

Remind students that all objects are made up of matter and that all matter has potential, or stored, energy in it.

Ask: What represents matter in this experiment? **Sample answers: the rubber band, the toy cars/trucks**

SEP **Asking Questions and Defining Problems**

All experimentation begins with a problem and a question.

Ask: What problem is this experiment trying to solve? **Sample answer: The problem here is to determine how much energy is stored in a stretched rubber band.**

HANDS-ON ACTIVITY

Test It! Stored Energy in a Rubber Band

Objective

Collaborate to compare amounts of stored energy. You know that energy is stored in a rubber band—but how much energy?

Materials
- safety goggles
- giant rubber band
- chair
- tape
- ruler
- toy car or truck
- meterstick

What question will you investigate to meet this objective?

Possible question: How can I test a rubber band for stored energy?

Procedure

STEP 1 CAUTION: Wear safety goggles. Cut a giant rubber band in half, and tie the ends around the legs of a chair. Place two metersticks in front of the chair. They should be 20 cm apart and in parallel lines to serve as a track for the toy.

What roll does the rubber band play in this investigation?

The rubber band will transfer the energy to the toy.

STEP 2 Tape an index card to the floor behind the rubber band. Mark lines on the card that are 2 cm and 4 cm behind the rubber band. Choose a third distance and mark it on the card.

What do the marks represent?

The marks will represent different amounts of energy that the stretched rubber band will store.

122

Student Lab Worksheet and complete Teacher Support available online.

122 Unit 2 Energy

STEP 3 Place a toy car or truck against the rubber band. Pull the toy back to the 2 cm mark, and release it. Measure the distance the toy travels. Record the data. Repeat this step two more times.

Why do you repeat this step at the 2 cm mark?
Repeating this step provides data that can be averaged to show what generally happens when the rubber band is stretched back 2 cm.

STEP 4 Repeat Step 3 using the 4 cm mark, and the third distance you selected. How might your result change if the 4 cm mark had been measured incorrectly and it was actually 6 cm?

How might your result change if the 4 cm mark had been measured incorrectly and it was actually 6 cm?
The measurement of the vehicle's distance will more accurately reflect the stored energy in the rubber band.

STEP 5 Record your results in the table.

Distance Toy Travels					
Rubber band stretched 2 cm		Rubber band stretched 4 cm		Rubber band stretched ___ cm	
Trial	Distance (cm)	Trial	Distance (cm)	Trial	Distance (cm)
1		1		1	
2		2		2	
3		3		3	

Procedure

STEP 1 Monitor students closely as they attach the rubber bands to the chair legs. Because large rubber bands, when pulled taut, can slip and rebound, they can hurt someone. Keep a close eye on students to make sure they are attaching their rubber bands safely and securely.

Connection to Math

Throughout this activity, students are expected to measure distance using the metric system. Measuring distance helps students understand the amount of energy in an object based on its size and speed. The bigger the object is, the shorter distance it will go. The faster an object is, the farther distance it will go.

As you circulate among students, be sure to answer any questions they have about how to measure and record their data.

Ask: Why is learning to measure distances and volumes important in real life? **Sample answer: We measure distances as part of our everyday lives, such as when we're hanging pictures or gauging how far we can go on a tank of gas. We measure volumes when we are preparing or making food or pouring concrete.**

4.MD.A.1 Solve problems involving measurement and conversion of measurements

DCI PS3.D Energy in Chemical Processes and Everyday Life

As with basic math applications as discussed above, energy is important in everyday life. Without out, we wouldn't live. Energy fuels every aspect of our lives, from the way our bodies break down food and converts it to energy or the way we warm our houses.

Ask: What is one way we use elastic energy, such as that found in a rubber band, in our everyday lives? **Sample answer: Vehicles have springs that make going over bumps or potholes easier. Wind-up clocks have springs that help us tell what time it is. Tennis racket strings and tennis balls are elastic.**

Lesson 3 How Do Collisions Show Energy?

LESSON 3   Engage • **Explore/Explain** • Elaborate • Evaluate

EXPLORATION 1 HANDS-ON ACTIVITY, continued

Analyze Results

Step 6 Ask different pairs or groups to come together to compare and contrast their results. Then have them share their results with the class, discussing how factors differed and were alike and why the results of some groups were different than those of others.

Draw Conclusions

Students may have other questions about energy than the one they express in Step 8. Have them write their questions down and exchange them with other students. Then ask the other students to see whether they can answer the questions. If not, allow the students time on the Internet or in the library to research the questions they have.

> ## Claims, Evidence, and Reasoning
>
> Have students work with a partner to critique each other's claims and evidence in Step 7. Ask each pair to be prepared to share one way that they changed or improved their claim or the evidence decided. Discuss responses as a class.
>
> **Ask:** Using what you have learned in this experiment, name some other objects that contain elastic energy.
> Sample answer: yo-yos, springs, bows, trampolines, bungee cords, rubber balls, slingshots

Scoring Rubric for Hands-On Activity	
3	Student followed all procedures and recorded and analyzed the results correctly.
2	Student followed all procedures and recorded the results correctly but had difficult analyzing those results.
1	Student followed most procedures but had difficulty recording and analyzing the results correctly.
0	Student did not follow procedures or record results correctly and came to the wrong conclusions.

Analyze Your Results

STEP 6 Use the data you collected to answer these questions. Write your answers in the table.

Were your results similar for all the trials with the rubber band stretched back 2 cm? What about 4 cm and the distance you chose?	Students should note similar results for repeated trials at each distance.
If your results were inconsistent across the trials, what do you think caused those differences?	Students should cite differences in their stretching techniques.
With which of the stretching distances did the toy travel the longest distance?	The toy should consistently travel farther the longer the rubber band is stretched.
Compare your data with the data of another group. Are the other data the same? If not, why do you think they are different?	Student data will differ because of the ways they attach and stretch their rubber bands.

Draw Conclusions

STEP 7 Make a claim about how much stored energy exists in a rubber band based on your experiment. Cite evidence.

Students may claim that there are different amounts of stored energy in a rubber band depending on how it is stretched. They should cite evidence from their tables.

STEP 8 Compare the third distance you selected with the other groups in your class. What conclusions can you draw about the distances selected?

Possible answer: If the distance the rubber band was stretched was too small, there would not be enough stored energy to move the toy very far.

STEP 9 What is one question you have about stored energy?
Possible question: How does gravity affect stored energy?

EXPLORATION 2 Wonderful Springs

EXPLORATION 2

Wonderful Springs

Ready to GO!

Earlier, you found out that anything that is moving has energy. A ball on top of a hill has the potential to move. When it does, it has energy of motion. You know that if you pull a rubber band back farther and farther, you can let it go—and it will go far! Energy is stored in the rubber band.

Many objects with bands and springs have stored energy that can be released to make them move!

Springtime!

10. Circle the picture that has no stored energy.

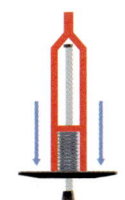
At the bottom of the jump, the spring is fully compressed. All the energy is stored in the spring.

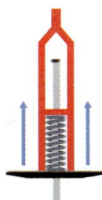
As the pogo stick goes up, the energy in the spring is released and becomes motion energy.

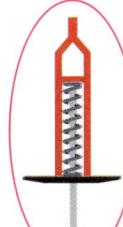
At the top of the jump, the spring has transferred all the energy that was stored in it to motion energy.

As the pogo stick compresses, energy is being stored in the spring. The spring has the potential to push up and become motion.

125

3D Learning Objective

Construct explanations about **energy and the movement of matter** in the context of bands and a spring, supporting a general understanding of how **energy can be transferred between objects**.

SEP Constructing Explanations and Designing Solutions

The evidence on this page tells about the storage and release of energy.

Ask: What is the most important part of explaining how a pogo stick works? **telling how its spring stores and releases energy**

Ask: What provides the energy stored by the pogo stick? **the weight and motion of the user**

Differentiate Instruction

Extension Have students answer item 10 and then describe what a spring with no stored energy would be like. (It would not be compressed.) Then have them describe what a rubber band with no stored energy would be like. (It would not be stretched.)

LESSON 3   Engage • **Explore/Explain** • Elaborate • Evaluate

EXPLORATION 2   *Wonderful Springs, continued*

CCC Energy and Matter

Emphasize that a moving object's energy will transfer to any matter it touches. Point out that a rolling ball touches both the ground and the air around it. Also point out that the amount of energy needed to compress a spring varies according to the size and strength of the spring.

Ask: What happens to a moving object when its energy transfers to other matter? **It is left with less energy.**
What eventually happens to any moving object that touches other matter? **It stops moving.**
Which ball will touch more ground and air as it rolls—a large one or a small one? **a large one**
Which needs more energy to compress it—a small spring or a large spring? **a large spring**
Would a compressed small spring or a compressed large spring have more stored energy? **a compressed large spring**

Differentiate Instruction

ELL: Use Realia Students may have trouble connecting the mass of an object with the amount of energy needed to move the object. To help them gain an understanding, have a variety of similar size balls or cubes of different masses. Have them hold one object in each hand and lightly heft the object so they can feel the difference in mass between the two objects.

The Bigger, the Better

In the hands-on investigation, you saw that the farther you pulled back the rubber band, the more energy you released to move the car. But what if you replaced the small car with a larger car or one made of heavier steel? How far would the car travel then?

Mass and Energy

11. Take a look at these spring setups. Consider the relative masses of the balls and the relative amounts of stored energy in the springs. Then predict which balls will travel the least distance, the middle distance, and the greatest distance.

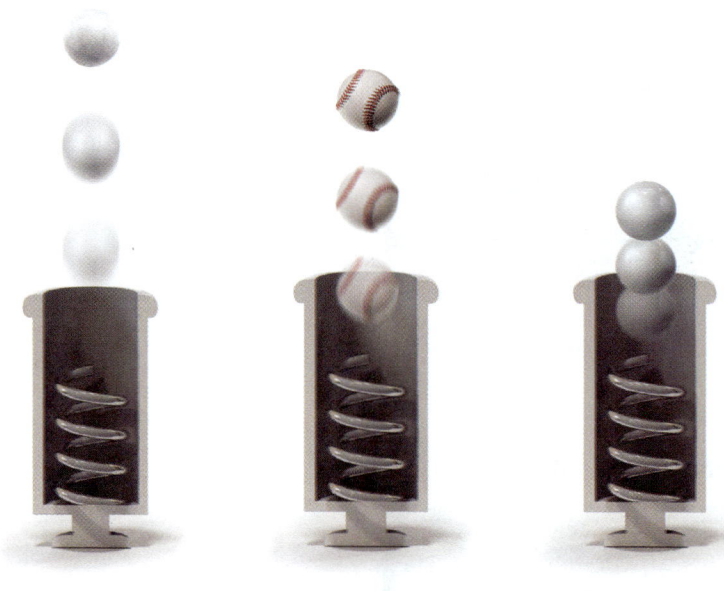

foam ball — The correct prediction is that this setup will propel the ball the farthest.

baseball — The correct prediction is that this setup will propel the ball the medium distance.

steel ball — The correct prediction is that this setup will propel the ball the shortest distance.

126

126   Unit 2   Energy

Engineer It!
Shocking

Buckle up! It's going to be a bumpy ride! When an uneven path causes a vehicle to bounce into the air, the vehicle experiences a collision every time it hits the ground. The motion energy from those collisions jolts the vehicle and the riders inside.

Cars and trucks have springs near the tires. When a spring is compressed, it absorbs and stores energy. The springs in an off-road truck are big and can store a lot of collision energy. That cuts down on the amount of energy that gets transferred to the riders every time the truck hits the ground after bouncing into the air.

12. Describe what it would feel like to ride on a bumpy path in a car that did not have springs to absorb energy.

Possible answer: An off-road ride in a vehicle without springs would be rough and even dangerous. The body cannot withstand collisions the way rubber and metal can.

Language SmArts
Recall from Experience

13. Considering the examples you have seen so far, identify another object that is able to absorb and store energy that is useful to you.

Students might name springs in furniture or the rubber soles of shoes.

Putting It Together

14. Choose the best word or phrase to complete each sentence in the paragraph.

stored energy	energy of motion	no energy at all	
more compressed	less compressed	lighter	heavier

A compressed spring or a rubber band stretched out both have **stored energy**.

An object will travel farther when the compression energy launching it is **more compressed**. If two objects are launched by a rubber band with the same amount of compression, the object that is **lighter** will travel farther.

127

Engineer It!
Shocking

PS3.A Definitions of Energy

The evidence on the page tells about energy being moved from place to place by the motion of springs.

Ask: What happens to the energy that the "shock absorbers" absorb? **It is released back in the direction it came from.**

Connection to English Language Arts

Because "spring" is a term that students may be more familiar with as related to seasons, make sure they understand what is meant by a "spring" that is used in vehicles for movement. Offer some examples of where else students may see or use springs.

W.3.8 Recall information from experiences

Language SmArts
Recall from Experience

W.4.8 Recall relevant information

As students work to recall an example, remind them that what they are learning about absorbed and released energy applies to countless things in everyday life. Science is learned in the classroom, but it can be used anywhere.

FORMATIVE ASSESSMENT

Putting it Together

Ask: What is similar about springs and rubber bands, and what is the biggest way they are different? **Springs and rubber bands both store energy. Springs store it by being compressed, and rubber bands store it by being stretched.**

Lesson 3 How Do Collisions Show Energy? 127

LESSON 3 Engage • Explore/Explain • Elaborate • Evaluate

EXPLORATION 3 Collisions

3D Learning Objective

Study images illustrating collisions to learn that energy is not only transferred upon impact, it sometimes changes form due to conservation of energy and energy transfers. Construct explanations of observed phenomena utilizing a variety of methods, such as performing basic experiments that involve energy and matter.

Differentiate Instruction

ELL: Building Background English language learners may have a difficult time understanding the word *collision*. Explain that another word for *collision* is *crash*, but not all collisions are destructive, noisy, or violent.

Ask: Can you think of examples of crashes, or collisions, that happen every day? **Sample answer: striking a ball with a bat, racket, stick, or other object**

Language SmArts
Cause and Effect
RI.4.5 Describe overall structure

As students describe how a collision between two objects causes a transfer of energy that sets other objects in motion, remind them that this is a cause-and-effect relationship.

Ask: What are some examples of cause and effect that you have seen today? **Sample answer: I ate breakfast, which gave me energy for the morning.**

EVIDENCE NOTEBOOK

Students witness collisions every day. They may list more obvious examples of collisions, such as people bumping into each other, or less obvious examples, such as people or animals walking.

EXPLORATION 3

Collisions

Scatter!

What is a collision? A **collision** happens when two objects bump into each other. Think about a game of pool. When the cue ball hits the other balls, there are collisions. When these happen, energy is transferred. The total energy of all the balls is the same, but energy transfers to make the balls move in different directions. When a cue ball hits one of the balls, its motion slows. It transfers energy to the other balls and then moves in a different direction.

Language SmArts
Cause and Effect

15. Describe what happens to the other balls that are cued up when the cue ball hits them. Explain the transfer of energy.

The balls move outward. Energy is transferred from one ball to the next and to the next with each collision.

If you were going to collide with something, would you rather collide with something moving quickly or slowly? A slow-moving object has less energy, so the collision has less of an impact. A fast-moving object has more energy—so the object it collides with moves fast, too! You can see this in sports. If you want a soccer ball to go fast, you kick it hard!

 EVIDENCE NOTEBOOK You see collisions every day. List some examples in your evidence notebook.

128

128 Unit 2 Energy

What Happens Next?

Take a look at these images, and think about them. Does a ball move faster and farther in a bunt or with a full swing? What do these images tell you about speed in collisions? View each image to see what happens before, during, and after a baseball collision.

The pitcher sends the ball hurtling toward the plate. The batter puts his bat out to bunt the ball, hoping to make the ball collide with the bat.

The ball has collided with the bat, causing the ball to change direction. It still has motion energy, but the motion of the ball has changed.

The batter has hit the ball. The collision has changed the direction of the ball. The collision has also added more motion energy to the ball.

The outfielder can only watch the ball soar far overhead because the batter has hit a mighty home run.

16. Look at the players catching the baseballs. Which collision between the ball and the mitt has the least amount of energy?

Possible answer: The bunt wasn't hit as hard, so it probably hits the mitt with less energy.

DCI PS3.B A Definitions of Energy

The images illustrate the steps in a collision, from the objects moving toward each other, to their coming into contact with each other, to their changes in motion. A bunt is when a baseball batter lightly lets a pitched ball strike his bat instead of swinging at it. The result is that the ball doesn't travel very far. However, when the batter hits the ball with his bat using all the energy he can muster, a collision occurs that can send the ball much farther away.

Ask: Which will transfer the most energy—a bunt or a full swing? **full swing**

Collaboration

CCC Energy and Matter

Draw, Pair, Share Have students study the images. On a blank piece of paper, have students draw a collision from a sport other than baseball, which they can choose. In their drawing, they should place arrows to show the direction in which the energy is moving. Then separate students into pairs. Partners should share their drawings, comparing and contrasting the sport they chose and examining the arrows closely to see whether they are correctly placed. After they are done, pairs should share their findings about their chosen sports with the rest of the class.

SEP Constructing Explanations and Designing Solutions

As students construct their explanations for how the players should throw the ball, have them consider what they have learned so far in terms of the relationship between energy and the motion of objects.

EXPLORATION 3 Collisions, continued

PS3.B Conservation of Energy and Energy Transfer

When objects collide in the atmosphere, they don't just transfer energy between them, causing a change in motion. They also transfer energy into the air. One result of this energy transference is sound. Think about what it is like to smack the palm of your hand against a hard surface. A loud sound is produced. The harder you smack that flat surface, the louder the sound is. That's because more energy produces louder sounds. You would also notice that your hand becomes warm. Why? Another result of energy transference is that heat is produced.

Ask students to give specific examples of energy transfers that result in loud sounds or heat.

HANDS-ON Apply What You Know
Rebounce

As with springs and rubber bands, many balls contain elastic energy. This is what causes them to bounce when they are dropped. Depending on how much elastic energy it has, a ball may bounce only a few or many times. With each bounce, it loses some of its energy, which is why each bounce is shorter than the one before it. Eventually, it will lose enough energy so that it will cease to bounce and become motionless. What happens is that each bounce transfers energy out of the ball and into the object with which it is colliding.

Ask: What do balls collide with? **the ground**

FORMATIVE ASSESSMENT
Putting it Together

 Energy and Matter

When matter comes into contact, or collides, with other matter, energy is exchanged.

Ask: What are three ways energy is transferred between objects? **heat, sound, change in motion**

Too Hot to Handle!

Have you ever hit a nail with a hammer? That collision makes a lot of noise! What else did you notice about the nail—besides the fact that it went into the wood? If you had touched the nail, it would have been warm. The hammer would be warm, too! What causes the nail and hammer to heat up?

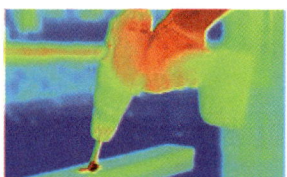

When a screw and wood collide, energy is transferred. Thermal imaging shows a difference in temperature. As the drill pushes the screw, it causes motion and heat energy!

What Happens to Energy in a Drop?

If you took a steel ball and dropped it, some of the energy would go right into the ground. A steel ball isn't springy—it won't bounce much. A tennis ball will. Look at what happens to the energy in a bouncing ball.

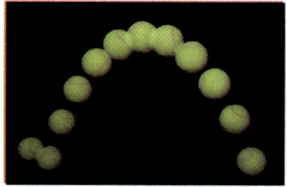

A tennis ball dropped toward the ground bounces back high, but not as high as the height from which it was dropped. Why? Some of the energy is transferred to the ground, and the rest to heat and sound energy.

 HANDS-ON Apply What You Know
Rebounce

Hold a meterstick perpendicular to the ground. Have a partner hold a tennis ball parallel to the meterstick and drop it. Observe the ball as it bounces. Take turns doing this several times. Where does the energy go when the ball collides with the ground?

Putting it Together

17. What conclusion can you draw about energy transfer based on what you observed with the tennis ball?

Each time the ball hit the ground, the ground absorbed some of its energy, causing it to slow down.

130

130 Unit 2 Energy

LESSON 3   Engage • Explore/Explain • **Elaborate** • Evaluate

TAKE IT FURTHER Discover More

▶ **Explore Online**   Students can explore all three Take It Further paths online.

TAKE IT FURTHER

Discover More

Check out this path . . . or go online to choose one of these other paths.

Careers in Science
- Bump!
- Collision Game!

Amanda Steffy

When we drive on roads, we think about the interaction of the tires with the ground. How do we design tires that don't heat up too much? How do we handle roads that aren't perfectly flat?

Now imagine that you design tires for a vehicle on Mars. That's what Amanda Steffy does! She is an engineer for NASA's Jet Propulsion Laboratory (JPL). Her team tests the wheels and tires of the Mars rovers in different conditions. To do this, Steffy and team had to recreate the surface of Mars in California!

Amanda Steffy works for NASA's Jet Propulsion Laboratory.

The tires of the Mars Rover were designed for rough terrain.

131

Collaboration

You may choose to assign this activity or to direct students online to the Interactive Online Student Edition, where they can explore and choose from all three paths. These activities can be assigned individually, to pairs, or to small groups.

Careers in Science

Students learn about the science of making tires that will survive the harsh conditions on Mars. Amanda Steffy and her team test tires to failure to find one that will hold up to the weather and rock conditions found on Mars, which includes extreme cold and sharp or loose rocks. Encourage students to go online to watch all the videos to learn about how energy transfers when objects bump or collide.

PS3.B Conservation of Energy and Energy Transfer
RI.5.7 Draw on information from multiple print or digital sources

🔶 **PS3.C Relationship Between Energy and Forces**
DCI

Tires must be somewhat resistant to the heat energy generated by friction. Friction results when two objects move against each other. Have you ever had a rug burn? This is caused by your skin moving across a carpet or rug; the resulting friction generated heat, which 'burned' you. Tires move rapidly across the ground. Because neither the tire nor the ground are perfectly smooth, tiny ridges or bumps (or large ones, in some cases) cause the two objects to resist each other, resulting in the objects slowing down. When these surfaces come into contact, they also generate heat. Tires must be able to withstand this heat, as well as to depress or expand in response to ridges or bumps in the surface over which they travel.

Lesson 3 How Do Collisions Show Energy?   131

LESSON 3   Engage • Explore/Explain • **Elaborate** • Evaluate

TAKE IT FURTHER, continued

DCI PS3.A Definitions of Energy

Misconception Alert Some students may believe that all friction is caused by rough or bumpy spots between two surfaces moving in opposition to each other. However, even some smooth surfaces may have friction when rubbed against each other. Scientists believe it's due to the electromagnetic attraction between the charged particles of the two surfaces that are touching.

SEP Constructing Explanations and Designing Solutions

Ask: How does testing tires on similar surfaces help scientists design solutions to reduce tire wear on rover type vehicles? *By testing the tires on similar surfaces, scientists can design tires that should hold up to the similar surfaces on other planets.*

Differentiate Instruction

Extension Have students research the Mars Exploration Rover Mission. Have them tell what a Mars Rover is and how it moves on the surface of Mars. Students should give a brief history of the mission, name some hazards rovers face, explain how NASA has overcome these hazards, and describe what the mission has accomplished.

▶ Explore Online

Students can explore these additional topics online.

Bump!
Students research how the bumpers of cars have changed over time. *(No outside research required.)*

Collision Game!
Student design and build a game that uses the stored energy in a spring as a focal point of the game. *(Outside research required.)*

The surface of Mars is different than what scientists believed it to be. Some of the rocks are sharp and can cut the tires. Some rocks are held tight to the ground while other rocks are very loose.

When a rover tire hits a loose rock, the tire spins faster, but if it hits a sharp rock held tight to the ground, the sharp rock can damage the tire. Amanda tests tires until they fail to find those designs that will hold up on the rough surface of Mars. Understanding these collisions on Earth helps scientists guide the rover on Mars.

Rovers are tested on rough terrain similar to that on Mars.

18. What factors do Amanda Steffy and other scientists who work on vehicles like the Mars rovers need to consider about the energy of motion as they work?

The surface of Mars and its gravity determine what the ride of the rover will be like and how much energy the tires need to be able to absorb.

19. How is Amanda Seffy's work related to collisions? Write a few ideas below.

Possible answer: A moving vehicle on a bumpy path is having collisions with the ground. Those collisions transfer energy between the ground and the vehicle.

LESSON CHECK

LESSON 3

Lesson Check

Name _____

Can You Explain It?

1. What will happen when the ball hits the group of balls? Write a few sentences below to explain what happens to all the balls on the pool table. Be sure to do the following:
   - Describe the motion and collisions.
   - Identify energy transfers.
   - Mention heat or sound.

EVIDENCE NOTEBOOK Use the information you've collected in your Evidence Notebook to help you cover each point above.

- When the one ball hits the other balls on the table, all balls will be set in motion. The more speed an object has, the more motion of energy the object has.
- When two or more objects collide, energy is transferred between the objects.
- When energy is transferred between two or more objects, the energy can be transformed into other forms of energy, such as sound or heat.

Checkpoints

2. A soccer ball sits in the grass. A girl pulls her leg back to kick the soccer ball. She kicks! What happens next? Circle all the correct answers.
   a. The ball travels in one direction while the leg continues to travel.
   b. The ball travels in one direction while the leg stops.
   c. The collision of the leg and ball makes the ball travel quickly.
   d. The collision of the leg and ball produces a noise.
   e. The ball travels in one direction while the leg moves backwards.

Formal Assessment Go online for student self-checks and other assessments.

Can You Explain It?

Collaboration

You may wish to revisit the image from the beginning of the lesson as a group activity to assess students' understanding of what it shows. Use the bulleted points in the Interactive Worktext to lead the discussion.

EVIDENCE NOTEBOOK

Have students reread their answers to the Evidence Notebook prompts and then use this evidence to justify their reasoning as they respond to the Can You Explain It question. Make sure students understand that a complete response must address all bulleted points.

PS3.B Conservation of Energy and Energy Transfer

Focus students on the image of the billiard balls. The cue ball is moving quickly toward a group of racked balls.

Ask: How will energy be transferred from the cue ball to the remainder of the balls? When the cue ball strikes the first ball in the group, its energy will transfer into that ball, knocking it into the others. When that ball collides with other balls, its energy transfers into them, and so on, until the energy has transferred into the last remaining balls. Once energy has transferred out of the balls, they roll to a stop.

SUMMATIVE ASSESSMENT

Engage in Argument from Evidence

2. Though students did not learn about soccer balls in the lesson, they follow the same principles as other balls in motion. To understand this, students should recall what they learned in Explorations 1 and 3.

Lesson 3 How Do Collisions Show Energy?

LESSON 3   Engage • Explore/Explain • Elaborate • **Evaluate**

LESSON CHECK, continued

3. Remind students that when a ball bounces, the height at which it bounces gets lower with each bounce. The reason is that some of the ball's energy is being transferred. Ask them what it is they see, hear, or feel when a collision occurs. If they need additional help in answering the question, direct them to re-read Explorations 1–3.

4. Explain that energy of motion is energy that comes from movement. If students continue to have a hard time understanding energy of motion, direct them to revisit Exploration 1.

5. Note that motionless objects have potential energy. If necessary, point students to Exploration 1 to learn what potential is and objects have it.

6. Remind students that there are a number of factors that affect how far and how fast an object will move. If they continue to struggle with the concept, direct them to re-read Exploration 2.

---

3. A child plays hopscotch. When she jumps on the ground, which of the following things happen? Circle all the correct answers.
   a. **The ground absorbs some of the energy.**
   b. The collision produces light energy.
   c. **The collision produces heat energy.**
   d. **The collision produces sound energy.**
   e. The girl continues to bounce, going higher each time.

4. Which of the following have energy of motion? Circle all the correct answers.
   a. an electric lamp that has just been plugged in
   b. **a child jumping on a trampoline**
   c. **a fish swimming in an aquarium**
   d. the warmth of the sun
   e. **a baseball player hitting a ball with a bat**

5. A roller coaster moves to the top of a hill where it stops. What happens to the energy when the coaster stops?
   a. The energy becomes motion energy.
   b. **The energy is stored energy.**
   c. The energy converts to heat energy.
   d. The weight of the roller coaster causes it to collide with another car.

6. An archer is shooting an arrow with a bow. He pulls the string far back, lets the arrow go, and watches it fly far. On his second try, he uses a lighter arrow while pulling the string on the bow back a distance equal to his first try. Tell what happens next. How do you know?

   The lighter arrow should travel farther when the same amount of energy is transferred to it from an equally stretched bow. (Students should know this from the examples they have looked at so far.)

134

134   Unit 2   Energy

LESSON 3

Lesson Roundup

A. You and a friend are sitting on the ground a few meters apart. You each have a basketball and roll them toward each other. The ball that your friend rolls is moving faster. Write a few sentences to tell what happens next.

Possible answer: The balls will collide. The ball that is moving faster will transfer the most energy to the other object in the collision, so it will knock the other ball out of the way.

B. Which of these types of energy changes in a collision? Circle all that are correct.
- (**a.** heat)
- (**b.** sound)
- (**c.** motion)
- **d.** stored
- **e.** electrical

C. Which of these is a collision? Circle all the answers you think are correct.
- (**a.** a baseball player bunting the ball)
- **b.** a rubber band snapping
- **c.** a ball player missing a catch as the ball sails overhead
- (**d.** a hockey player hitting a hockey puck with a stick)
- **e.** two cars driving down a highway
- (**f.** a mallet hitting a croquet ball)

D. Choose the phrase that makes the sentence correct.

| tennis ball   bowling ball   table tennis ball |

If a spring is compressed at the same compression and is used to launch a table tennis ball, a tennis ball, and a bowling ball on the same flat surface, the _table tennis ball_ will go the farthest distance.

135

Lesson Roundup

 PS3.A Defintions of Energy
PS3.B Conservation of Energy and Energy Transfer
PS3. C Relationship Between Energy and Forces

This lesson summary enables students to quickly revisit key points and prepare for tests.

A. Have students revisit Explorations 1 and 2. Remind students that speed and size are factors in the energy transfer of a collision. If two objects are the same size, moving at different speeds, then the faster object will have more energy to transfer. If two objects are different sizes, moving at the same speed, the larger object will have more energy to transfer. If the objects are both different sizes and moving at different speeds, the size and speed of each has to be considered. **PS3.A, PS3.B, PS3.C**

B. Tell students that Exploration 3 will help them understand and answer the question. Students should think about what they see, hear, and feel during a collision. This will help them arrive at two of the correct answers (sound and motion), while thinking about the results of energy transfers will help them arrive at the other correct answer (heat). Students have learned that when energy is transferred to an object, that object gets warmer. **PS3.A, PS3.B**

C. Remind students they can find the definition of the word *collision* in Exploration 3, but there are many different examples of collisions in the other Explorations in this lesson. A collision occurs when two objects bump or crash into one another. How powerful a collision is depends on the amount of energy found in each of the objects that are colliding. **PS3.A, PS3.B, PS3.C, PS3.D**

D. A spring carries elastic (or potential elastic) energy. Students who are struggling with understanding how elastic energy works may revisit Exploration 2. Students should also think about the look and feel of a table tennis ball, a tennis ball, and a bowling ball. The smallest, lightest objects will be launched the farthest. **PS3.C, PS3.D**

Lesson 3 How Do Collisions Show Energy? 135

UNIT 2 Performance Task

ENGINEER IT!  small groups 2–3 class periods
Energy Transfers All Around

3D Assessment Goal
Students **work in teams** to **plan and carry out investigations** to demonstrate their understanding of **PS3.B** and **PS3.C** in support of **4-PS3-1, 4-PS3-3,** and **4-PS3-4**.

Materials
- paper
- pencil
- variety of objects for demonstrating transfer of energy
- resources
- camera or electronic device for presentation

Preparation
Arrange computer access time. Make the checklist as a chart to hang up during the activity.

PS3.C Relationship Between Energy and Forces

The objects that teams choose will determine the type of data they will be able to collect. **Ask: How will you collect data to demonstrate how objects transfer energy?**

Research
Review how to properly cite resources.
Print: title, author, copyright date, page number
Online: webpage title, URL, date visited

Brainstorm
Have students roll a number cube to choose a recorder, highest roll records. Remind students that the brainstorming group is just to come up with ideas. Each of them will be individually responsible for their own part of the design, testing, and presentation.

UNIT 2   UNIT PERFORMANCE TASK

ENGINEER IT!
Energy Transfers All Around

The publisher you work for is putting together a book called "Energy Transfers All Around." Your team has been assigned to write a section about how objects transfer energy. To do that, you'll need to set up some experiments, run them, and collect and analyze their data. Then you'll create a multimedia presentation that reports on your procedures, results, and conclusions.

This shows one way to investigate energy transfer. Can you find others?

DEFINE YOUR TASK: What form will your completed project take?

Sample answer: It will be a multimedia presentation that explains how objects transfer energy.

Before beginning, review the checklist at the end of this Unit Performance Task. Keep those items in mind as you proceed.

RESEARCH: Use online or library resources to learn about the principle of physical energy transfer. Search the Internet for simple experiments that explore that principle. Describe and cite your sources.

Student should cite sources as instructed.

EXAMINE DATA: Examine the experiments you have found for ideas your team can use to investigate energy transfer. Focus on simple activities using marbles, model cars, or other rolling objects. Tell which approaches seem best to you, and state why.

Student should describe one or two effective experimental approaches found through research.

PLAN YOUR PROCEDURE: Consider the questions below as you plan your procedure and presentation.

1. What materials will you need, and how will you use them?
2. How will your experiment be set up?
3. What will the basic steps of your procedure be?
4. What variables (size and number of rolling objects, speed of movement, etc.) will you introduce into your procedure? How?
5. How will you record, compare, and chart your results?
6. What will be the content, approach, and organization of your multimedia presentation?

Student should name the materials that will be needed for the experiment, summarize its steps, and explain how procedures and results will be recorded, analyzed, and presented.

_____

_____

_____

PERFORM AND RECORD: Execute your procedures as planned, and record and analyze your results.

COMMUNICATE: Prepare and give a multimedia presentation that describes your team's research, procedures, results, and conclusions.

☑ Checklist

Review your project and check off each completed item.

_____ Includes a clear statement of your task.

_____ Includes a list of cited sources.

_____ Includes a description of your procedure and the materials used in conducting it.

_____ Includes results and analysis of those results.

_____ Includes a multimedia report about your team's research, procedures, results, and conclusions.

137

Plan Your Procedure

SEP Planning and Carrying Out Investigations

Remind students that even well-planned designs can fail. Have them think about what could go wrong and make adjustments to their experiment, if needed. **Ask: How will you know if your design is a success?**

Communicate

Students may benefit from writing out a script of what each person will do and say during the presentation. Suggest students rehearse their presentation before delivering it in front of the class.

Scoring Rubric for Performance Task	
3	• statement of the task is clear and precise • sources are complete and cited correctly • descriptions and materials are included/complete • results are complete; analysis matches results • presentation is well-organized and engaging
2	• statement of the task is included • most sources are included but not cited accurately • descriptions and materials lack specifics • results are included; analysis is not specific to results • presentation supports experiment; lacks enthusiasm
1	• statement of the task is incomplete • sources are incomplete or not cited properly • procedure descriptions and materials are incomplete • results and analysis are incomplete • presentation is inaccurate
0	• statement of the task is missing • sources are missing • procedure descriptions and materials are missing • results and analysis are missing • presentation is missing

Unit 2 Energy

UNIT 2 Review

SUMMATIVE ASSESSMENT

1. For students to answer this question, they will need to understand the different types of energy. Suggest students review Lesson 1, Exploration 1 before attempting this question.

2. Students should use process of elimination to cross out any choices that they know are not correct. If they are still having trouble answering the question, suggest they review the sections *Where Does Our Energy Come From?* and *Saving It for Later* in Lesson 1.

3. Students should recall that energy is the ability to cause change in matter, and their definitions should be similar. Point out to students that this a multi-step problem. Remind them to use complete sentences.

UNIT 2

Unit Review

1. Which statement best describes the energy transfer shown here? Circle the correct choice.
   a. electrical energy into light and heat
   b. sound and motion into light and heat
   c. light and heat into sound and motion
   d. electrical energy into sound and motion

2. Which of these are forms of stored energy? Circle all that apply.
   a. coal
   b. gasoline
   c. a toaster
   d. a battery
   e. an automobile

3. In your own words, define *energy*. Then name some examples of energy you see every day.

   Possible answer: Energy is the ability to change matter. Motion, sound, light, and heat are examples of energy I see every day.

4. Classify each fuel source as a fossil fuel (F) or an alternative fuel (A).

   __A__ Solar
   __F__ Coal
   __F__ Oil
   __A__ Wind
   __A__ Algae
   __F__ Natural gas

5. An archer shoots an apple from a tree. Number these statements so that they explain the role of energy in that action.

   __5__ The arrow hits the apple.
   __2__ The string and bow store the energy.
   __3__ The archer releases the string.
   __7__ The apple is forced from the tree.
   __1__ The archer pulls back on the string.
   __6__ The arrow transfers energy to the apple.
   __4__ The arrow's energy moves it through the air.

6. Which choices describe the temperature in the pot above? Circle all that apply.

   a. 0 °C
   b. 32 °F
   (c. 100 °C)
   (d. 212 °F)

139

4. Students can correctly answer this question by knowing the difference between fossil fuels and alternative fuels. Fossil fuels and alternative fuels can be reviewed in Lesson 1, Exploration 1.

5. Students should be able to answer this question if they have a strong understanding of how energy is transferred. Some students may find it easier to sequence the role of energy from the last step backward to the first step.

6. Students will need to know certain temperatures of common situations, such as a child sledding on a cold winter day or melting ice. They can review differences in degrees in Lesson 2, Exploration 1.

Unit 2 Energy 139

UNIT 2 Review, continued

7. Students explored collisions of cue balls in Lesson 3. If they have difficulties answering this question, suggest they go back to the *Can You Explain It?* in Lesson 3 to review.

8. Students should recall that some of the energy is transferred to the ground when a ball is dropped. Suggest that students go back to the section *What Happens to Energy in a Drop?* in Lesson 3 if they are having difficulties answering this question.

9. Students need a strong understanding of the difference in energy transfer and energy transformation to answer this question. They can review these concepts in Lesson 2.

10. Students should recall from Lesson 2, Exploration 1 that heat is energy that transfers between objects of different temperatures.

3D Item Analysis	1	2	3	4	5	6	7	8	9	10
SEP Constructing Explanations and Designing Solutions						•	•			
DCI Definitions of Energy		•		•	•	•		•	•	
DCI Conservation of Energy and Energy Transfer		•		•	•	•	•	•	•	•
DCI Energy in Chemical Processes and Everyday Life			•							
DCI Relationship Between Energy and Forces					•		•	•	•	
CCC Energy and Matter		•		•	•	•	•	•	•	•

---

7. What happens to a cue ball when it collides with another ball during a pool game? Circle all that apply.
   a. **It changes direction.**
   b. It gains stored energy.
   c. It gains energy of motion.
   d. **It loses some of its energy.**

8. When a ball is dropped on the ground, it ___loses___ energy with each bounce and eventually becomes ___still___.

9. Write the sentences in the correct columns.

   > Heat moves from a burner to a pot of water.
   > Motion energy moves from a hand to a baseball.
   > Electrical energy changes into light energy in a lamp.
   > Light energy from the sun changes into electrical energy in solar panels.
   > Motion energy changes to sound energy in a weather radio.
   > Heat moves from a hand warmer packet to a person.

Energy transfer	Energy transformation
Heat moves from a burner to a pot of water. Motion energy moves from a hand to a baseball. Heat moves from a hand warmer packet to a person.	Electrical energy changes into light energy in a lamp. Light energy from the sun changes into electrical energy in solar panels. Motion energy changes to sound energy in a weather radio.

10. Write the correct words to complete the sentence.

    > heat   temperature

    In this picture, ___temperature___ is moving between objects of different temperatures.

140

UNIT 3 Waves and Information Transfer

Unit Project: Reflecting Light
How can you bring more sunlight into dark areas in your school? You will plan a method with your team. Ask your teacher for details.

Cell phones are everywhere! How does your pictures travel from your phone to a phone hundreds of miles away?

Unit Overview

In this unit, students will . . .
- discover the different parts of waves.
- explore how light can be reflected.
- examine and describe how information is transferred from place to place.

About This Image

Wow, technology has changed a lot! We can now take a picture and send it to someone across the nation in a matter of seconds. Smartphones, such as the one in this image, use signals. Although smartphones can do many functions, such as take pictures, surf the Internet, send texts, and make calls, they need to have the hardware to do these things. Codes are used to send texts, emails, and photos electronically.

Unit Project

As students work through the unit lessons, have them research, plan, and write down notes about how they can possibly bring more sunlight into dark areas of the school. For their Unit Projects, they will need to design a way to bring in more light.

Challenge students to research more about light and inventions that use light. More support for the Unit Project can be found on pp. 143I–143L.

UNIT 3 Waves and Information Transfer

The learning experiences in this unit prepare students for the mastery of:

Performance Expectations

4-PS4-1 Develop a model of waves to describe patterns in terms of amplitude and wavelength and that waves can cause objects to move.

4-PS4-2 Develop a model to describe that light reflecting from objects and entering the eye allows objects to be seen.

4-PS4-3 Generate and compare multiple solutions that use patterns to transfer information.* *[Clarification Statement: Examples of solutions could include drums sending coded information through sound waves, using a grid of 1s and 0s representing black and white to send information about a picture, and using Morse code to send text.]*

Explore Online

In addition to the print resources, the following resources are available online to support this unit.

Unit Pretest
Lesson 1 What Are Waves?
- Online Student Edition
- Lesson Quiz

Lesson 2 How Does Light Reflect?
- Online Student Edition
- Lesson Quiz

Lesson 3 How Is Information Transferred from Place to Place?
- Online Student Edition
- Lesson Quiz
- **You Solve It** Build a Wave Pool

Unit Performance Task
Unit Test

UNIT 3
At a Glance

LESSON 1
What Are Waves? **144**

LESSON 2
How Does Light Reflect? **170**

LESSON 3
How is Information Transferred from Place to Place? **200**

Unit Review **224**

Vocabulary Game: Picture It

Materials
- Kitchen timer or online computer timer
- Sketch pad

Directions
1. Take turns to play.
2. To take a turn, choose a vocabulary word. Do not tell the word to the other players.
3. Set the timer for one minute.
4. Draw pictures on the sketch pad to give clues about the word. Draw only pictures and numbers. Do not write words.
5. The first player to guess the vocabulary word gets 1 point. If that player can use the word in a sentence, he or she gets 1 more point. Then that player gets a turn to choose a word.
6. The first player to score 5 points wins.

Unit Vocabulary

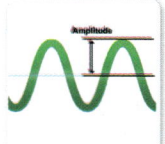
amplitude: A measure of the amount of energy in a wave.

transparent: Letting all light through.

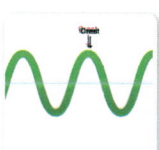
crest: The top part of a wave.

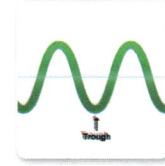
trough: The bottom part of a wave.

opaque: Not letting any light through.

volume: How loud or soft a sound is.

reflection: The bouncing of light waves when they encounter an obstacle.

wave: The up-and-down movement of surface water. It can also be a disturbance that carries energy through space.

translucent: Letting some light through.

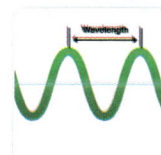
wavelength: The distance between a point on one wave and the identical point on the next wave.

Unit Vocabulary

Students can explore all lesson vocabulary terms in the **Online Glossary**.

Vocabulary Strategies

Have students review the terms individually. Then pair up and share an example of one term with their partner and tell why they think it's an example. Have each pair write down their examples to check during the unit.

Differentiate Instruction

RTI/Extra Support Have struggling readers find the vocabulary words within the unit. Have students use context clues to infer definitions and then share with a partner.

Extension Have students pick two terms and then work in small groups to define those terms using illustrations and labels.

ELL Pronounce each term and have students repeat it. Have students describe the terms in their native language. Suggest they use the images for context clues.

Vocabulary Game: Picture It

Preparation
Use a timer on your smartphone or table, if that is more convenient than a kitchen timer or online computer timer.

Game Play
- Students draw pictures of the words and other students guess the word being drawn.

UNIT 3 Waves and Information Transfer
Integrating the NGSS* Three Dimensions of Learning

Building to the Performance Expectations

The learning experiences in this unit prepare students for mastery of the following Performance Expectations:

Waves and Their Applications in Technologies for Information Transfer

4-PS4-1 Develop a model of waves to describe patterns in terms of amplitude and wavelength and that waves can cause objects to move.

4-PS4-2 Develop a model to describe that light reflecting from objects and entering the eye allows objects to be seen.

4-PS4-3 Generate and compare multiple solutions that use patterns to transfer information.

Assessing Student Progress

After completing these lessons, the **Unit Project: Reflecting Light** provides students with opportunities to practice aspects of and demonstrate their understanding of the Performance Expectation as they work to solve lighting problems in dark areas of the school.

Additionally, students can practice or be assessed on aspects of the Performance Expectations by completing the **Unit Performance Task: The Rainbow Show** in which they use models to demonstrate how rainbows are formed.

Lesson 1
What Are Waves?

In Lesson 1, students will explore the properties and characteristics of waves **(DCI Wave Properties)** and the patterns they create **(CCC Patterns)**. They will use models to learn about the ways in which waves create motion through the transfer of energy **(SEP Developing and Using Models)**. Through the use of these diagrams, students will be able to visualize transverse waves and differentiate between wavelength and amplitude. This information will help deepen their understanding of the movement of energy.

Lesson 2
How Does Light Reflect?

In Lesson 2, students will investigate how light interacts with the surface of objects to form an image that we can see **(DCI Electromagnetic Radiation)**. Students will develop and use models to manipulate a variety of objects **(SEP Developing and Using Models)** to observe how the behavior of light changes the images sent to our eyes and perceived by our brains. By investigating how light interacts with mirrors and lenses **(CCCs Cause and Effect)**, students will deepen their understanding of the development of many useful tools and technologies that utilize light.

Lesson 3
How Is Information Transferred from Place to Place?

In Lesson 3, students will explore a variety of communication devices **(DCI Information Technologies and Instrumentation; Optimizing The Design Solution)** that are the result of science, engineering, and technology working together to meet people's needs **(CCC Interdependence of Science, Engineering, and Technology)** and decide how well each device solves a problem **(SEP Constructing Explanations and Designing Solutions)**. Students will also design their own devices to communicate information over a distance.

*Next Generation Science Standards and logo are registered trademarks of Achieve. Neither Achieve or the lead states and partners that developed the Next Generation Science Standards were involved in production of, and does not endorse, these products.

NGSS Across this Unit

Explore Online! Online only.

Next Generation Science Standard	Unit Project	Lesson 1	Lesson 2	Lesson 3	Unit Performance Task	You Solve It!
SEP Scientific Knowledge Is Based on Empirical Evidence		•				
SEP Constructing Explanations and Designing Solutions	•			•		
SEP Developing and Using Models		•	•		•	•
DCI PS4.A Wave Properties		•				•
DCI PS4.B Electromagnetic Radiation	•		•		•	
DCI PS4.C Information Technologies and Instrumentation				•		
DCI ETS1.C Optimizing the Design Solution				•		
CCC Patterns		•		•	•	•
CCC Interdependence of Science, Engineering, and Technology				•		
CCC Cause and Effect	•		•			

NGSS Across the Grades

Before
Waves and Their Applications in Technologies for Information Transfer
1-PS4-1
1-PS4-2
1-PS4-3
1-PS4-4

Grade 4
Waves and Their Applications in Technologies for Information Transfer
4-PS4-1
4-PS4-2
4-PS4-3

After
Waves and Their Applications in Technologies for Information Transfer
MS-PS4-1
MS-PS4-2
MS-PS4-3

Trace Tool to the NGSS™ Go online to view the complete coverage of these standards across this grade level and time.

UNIT 3 Waves and Information Transfer
3D Unit Planning

Lesson 1 What Are Waves pp. 144–169

Overview

Objective Differentiate between wavelength and amplitude, and observe how waves interact.

SEP Developing and Using Models, Scientific Knowledge Is Based on Empirical Evidence
DCI PS4.A
CCC Patterns

Math and **English Language Arts** standards and features are detailed on lesson planner pages.

	Print and Online *Student Editions*	*Explore Online!*
ENGAGE	**Lesson Phenomenon** pp. 144–145 **Can You Explain It?** How does a surfer know when to stand up on the board and "catch" a wave?	Can You Explain It! Video
EXPLORE/ EXPLAIN	**How Waves Transfer Energy** pp. 149–155 **Apply What You Know** Bobbing and Waving Waves That Move Up and Down Shake Like a Quake! 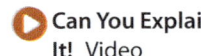 **HANDS-ON** Let's Make Waves **Wave Parts** pp. 156–160 **Waves Interact!** pp. 161–164	**HANDS-ON** Worksheet
ELABORATE	**Take It Further** pp. 165–166 People in Science: Christian Doppler And Debra Fischer	**Take It Further** Seismic Waves and Earthquakes Theater Acoustics
EVALUATE	**Lesson Check** pp. 167–168 **Lesson Roundup** p. 169	**Lesson Quiz**

HANDS-ON ACTIVITY PLANNING

Apply What You Know

Bobbing and Waving
- 10 minutes
- Small groups

Materials
- bucket
- water
- cork

Preparation/Tip Set up buckets half full of water on a surface that won't be damaged by spilled water.

HANDS-ON

Let's Make Waves
- 1 class period
- Pairs

Materials
- safety goggles
- yarn
- coiled spring toy
- meterstick
- stopwatch

Objective Students work in pairs to model how energy moves through waves. They will create waves with certain materials and measure the transfer of energy with other materials.

Preparation/Tip Preassemble the materials so that each pair of students can pick up their box of materials and be ready to start the activity.

Lesson 2 How Does Light Reflect? pp. 170–199

Overview

Objective Describe the effects of matter on light, identify how light interacts with mirrors, lenses, prisms, and non-reflective surfaces due to their unique properties.

SEP Developing and Using Models
DCI PS4.B
CCC Cause and Effect

Math and **English Language Arts** standards and features are detailed on lesson planner pages.

	Print and Online Student Editions	▶ *Explore Online!*
ENGAGE	**Lesson Phenomenon** pp. 170–171 **Can You Explain It?** How does a telescope let us see things that are millions of kilometers away?	Can You Explain It! Video
EXPLORE/ EXPLAIN	**HANDS-ON** Disappearing Coins pp. 172–173 **Reflection and Our Eyes** pp. 174–184 Apply What You Know Seeing Color **HANDS-ON** Reflecting on Angles **Refraction and Lenses** pp. 185–194 Apply What You Know Read This! **ENGINEER IT!** Designed for Safety	**HANDS-ON** Worksheet
ELABORATE	**Take It Further** pp. 195–196 Optics Engineers	**Take It Further** Light and Art **Take It Further** Lighthouses and Lenses
EVALUATE	**Lesson Check** pp. 197–198 **Lesson Roundup** p. 199	**Lesson Quiz**

✋ HANDS-ON ACTIVITY PLANNING

Apply What You Know

Seeing Color ⏱ 10 minutes 👥 Whole class	**Materials** • flashlight • colored gels

Preparation/Tip Plan which surfaces you will use for this demonstration, such as a desk, the floor, paper, or a wall.

Read This! ⏱ 10 minutes 👥 Pairs	**Materials** • lens set (concave and convex) • printed materials

Preparation/Tip Have pairs take turns using the different lenses.

HANDS-ON

Disappearing Coins ⏱ 20 minutes 👥 Partners **Objective** Students use a model to investigate how images differ when light interacts with air and water.	**Materials** • pennies • shallow baking pan • masking tape • water

Preparation/Tip Make sure each station has a piece of masking tape (or electrical tape, or painter's tape) to mark the floor.

Reflecting on Angles ⏱ 1 class period 👥 Pairs **Objective** Students make their own model of reflected objects to investigate how the angles of reflection affect light.	**Materials** • piece of cardboard • small mirror • modeling clay • 3 pushpins • labels • metric ruler • protractor

Preparation/Tip Gather the materials for this activity ahead of time, as it may be challenging to get a class set of small mirrors.

Unit 3: Waves and Information Transfer   **143D**

UNIT 3 Waves and Information Transfer
3D Unit Planning, continued

Lesson 3 How Is Information Transferred from Place to Place? pp. 200–223

Overview

Objective Explore and compare patterns in multiple methods of transferring information, and actually transfer information using codes and a pixilated image.

SEP Constructing Explanations and Designing Solutions
DCI PS4.C
CCC Patterns, Interdependence of Science, Engineering, and Technology

Math and **English Language Arts** standards and features are detailed on lesson planner pages.

Print and Online Student Editions   ▶ Explore Online!

ENGAGE	**Lesson Phenomenon** pp. 200–201 **Can You Explain It?** How has the way we receive information changed over the years?	▶ Can You Explain It! Video
EXPLORE/ EXPLAIN	**History of Information Transfer** pp. 202–209 Apply What You Know Make a Scytale HANDS-ON Pixels to Pictures **Bits and Bytes** pp. 210–218 Apply What You Know Make Your Own Code Code, Computers, and Networks Sounds in the Air Apply What You Know The Phone Is for You! Apply What You Know Make a Wave Bits of Color	HANDS-ON Worksheet
ELABORATE	**Take It Further** pp. 219–220 Elephant Communication	Take It Further People in Science Wave That Flag
EVALUATE	**Lesson Check** pp. 221–222 **Lesson Roundup** p. 223	Lesson Quiz

✋ HANDS-ON ACTIVITY PLANNING

Apply What You Know

Make a Scytale
⏱ 30 minutes
👥 Pairs

Materials
- cardboard tubes
- scissors
- paper
- adhesive tape
- pencils

Preparation/Tip Stress that pairs must choose tubes of the same size, or they will not be able to read the messages.

Make Your Own Code
⏱ 15 minutes
👥 Pairs

Materials
- index cards

Preparation/Tip Circulate to make sure they are putting the correct number of dots on their cards.

Make a Wave
⏱ 10 minutes
👥 Pairs

Materials
- spring toy

Preparation/Tip Provide a binary code message that students must translate for each other.

HANDS-ON

Pixels to Pictures
⏱ 1 class period
👥 Small groups

Materials
- pencil or pen
- markers
- paper
- ruler

Objective Students create a pixelated message using binary code, and discuss the constraints of the design.

Preparation/Tip Preassemble materials bundles for students. Distribute to begin the activity.

143E Unit 3: Waves and Information Transfer

UNIT 3 Waves and Information Transfer
3D Unit Planning, continued

 **You Solve It** — Go online for an additional interactive activity.

Build a Wave Pool

This virtual lab offers practice in support of **PE 4-PS4-1**.

SEP Developing and Using Models
DCI 4-PS4.A.2 Wave Properties
CCC Patterns

Use after Unit 3, Lesson 3— How can patterns of amplitude and wavelength cause objects to move?

Objectives
1. Students use models to make waves for different situations.
2. Students measure and record wave amplitudes and wavelengths.
3. Students analyze data and include it in a lab report.

Activity Problem
You will be testing a new wave pool at a water park. Your task will be to make constant waves for the wave pool for different time frames that match the provided photos. The different time frames for making waves are included:
1. waves for a normal operational day,
2. more gentle waves for the kiddie pool, and
3. waves that are increased in height for the stunt show.

Interaction Summary
1. Students will test the settings on the wave pool to create different heights and lengths of waves.
2. Students determine the best waves for the kiddie pool and the stunt show.
3. Pictures will be taken of the waves.
4. Students measure and record the wavelengths and amplitudes.
5. Students analyze the data and write a report on their findings.

Assessment

Pre-Assessment
Assessment Guide, Unit Pretest

The Unit Pretest focuses on prerequisite knowledge and is composed of items that evaluate students' preparedness for the content covered within this unit.

Formative Assessment
Student Edition, Apply What You Know, Lesson Check, and Self Check

Summative Assessment
Assessment Guide, Lesson Quiz
The Lesson Quiz provides a quick assessment of each lesson objective and of the portion of the Performance Expectation aligned to the lesson.

Student Edition, Performance Task pp. 224–225
The Performance Task presents the opportunity for children to collaborate with classmates in order to complete the steps of each Performance Task. Each Performance Task provides a formal Scoring Rubric for evaluating students' work.

Student Edition, Unit 3 Review pp. 226–228

Assessment Guide, Unit Test
The Unit Test provides an in-depth assessment of the Performance Expectations aligned to the unit. This test evaluates students' ability to apply knowledge in order to explain phenomena and to solve problems. Within this test, Constructed Response items apply a three-dimensional rubric for evaluating students' mastery on all three dimensions of the Next Generation Science Standards.

 **Assessment Online** — Go online to view the complete assessment items for this unit.

UNIT 3 Waves and Information Transfer
Differentiate Instruction

Leveled Readers

The **Science & Engineering Leveled Readers** provide additional nonfiction reading practice in this unit's subject area.

On-Level Reader • How Do We Use Forms of Energy?
This reader reinforces unit concepts and includes response activities for your students.

Extra Support • How Do We Use Forms of Energy?
This reader shares title, illustrations, vocabulary, and concepts with the On-Level Reader; however, the text is linguistically accommodated to provide simplified sentence structures and comprehension aids. It also includes response activities.

Enrichment • What Happens Under the Hood?
This high-interest, nonfiction reader will extend and enrich unit concepts and vocabulary and includes response activities.

Teacher Guide
The accompanying Teacher Guide provides teaching strategies and support for using all the readers.

ELL
ELL teacher strategies in this unit:
Lesson 1: p. 149
Lesson 2: pp. 175, 176, 180, 186, 191
Lesson 3: pp. 206, 210, 214

RTI/Extra Support
Strategies for students needing extra support in this unit:
Lesson 1: pp. 147, 154, 162
Lesson 2: pp. 178, 183
Lesson 3: pp. 202, 207, 213, 214, 217

Extension
Strategies for students who have mastered core content in this unit:
Lesson 1: pp. 151, 156, 158
Lesson 2: pp. 177, 188, 193
Lesson 3: pp. 204, 215, 220

 **Leveled Readers** All readers are available online as well as in an innovative, engaging format for use with touchscreen mobile devices. Contact your HMH Sales Representative for more information.

UNIT 3 Waves and Information Transfer
Making Connections

Connections to the Community

Use these opportunities for informal science learning to provide local context and to extend and enhance unit concepts.

At Home

KNOCK, KNOCK Have the student and one other person stand in different rooms with the door between them closed. The student stands across the room from the closed door. The other person knocks on the door. What does the student hear? The student writes an explanation of how a person standing across a room can hear another person knocking on a closed door. *Use with Lesson 1.*

SHINING LIGHT Have students be at home after dark with only one lamp on. Tell students to walk into the next room, around a corner, until they cannot see the lamp itself. Have students write down their observations of how far the lamp's light reaches. They should write down their thoughts about this: Since light travels in a straight line, how does the lamp's light reach around a corner? How well can they still see? *Use with Lesson 2.*

In the Community

TRAVELING LIGHT Have students walk with a family adult in an area near several stores. Students should write down what transparent, translucent, and opaque objects they observe. They should also note objects that give off light. *Use with Lesson 2.*

DIGITAL DEVICES Have students go with a family adult to a store that sells electronic devices. Tell students to look at many different devices that communicate light, sound, and information. They should talk with the adult about what they've learned about digital devices. Since wires don't carry sound waves, how do these devices produce sounds? *Use with Lesson 2.*

 **Home Letters** Use these one-page letters to engage family members with unit concepts.

Collaboration

Opportunities for students to work collaboratively in this unit:

Build on Prior Knowledge pp. 145, 174

Discussion pp. 219, 221

Draw, Pair, Share pp. 171, 189, 205, 211

Feedback pp. 150, 157, 166, 179, 215

Partners, p. 159

Share Feedback, p. 196

Think, Pair Share pp. 163, 187, 201, 217

Write, Pair, Share pp. 212, 218

Connections to Science

Opportunities to connect to other content areas in this unit.

Connection to Engineering and Design Lesson 2, p. 179

Connection to Physical Science Lesson 3, p. 203

Connection to Life Science Lesson 1, p. 151, Lesson 2, p. 190, Lesson 3, p. 219

Connection to Earth and Space Sciences Lesson 2, p. 186

UNIT 3 Waves and Information Transfer
Unit Project

Unit Project: Reflecting Light 👥 Small groups ⏱ 3 class periods

For this task, small groups of students will study the school building and create a design to add more natural sunlight to dark areas. Students should understand how light waves from the sun affect indoor lighting throughout the day, which involves a general knowledge of Earth's rotation. They will also need to understand how light waves are obstructed by opaque objects such as walls, buildings, and trees.

3D Learning Objective

- Understand properties of the sun's light waves
- Design a solution to improve natural lighting
- Identify cause-and-effect relationships in lighting problems

Skills and Standards Focus

This project supports building student mastery of **Perfomance Expectations 4-PS4-1, 4-PS4-2, 4-PS4-3**	**SEP** Constructing Explanations and Designing Solutions **DCI** PS4.B: Electromagnetic Radiation **CCC** Cause and Effect

Suggested Materials

- drawing paper and utensils
- poster board
- rulers
- colored markers or pencils
- references—print (books, magazines), electronic (websites)

Preparation and Planning Tips

Ensure that each group has a set of print resources or list of URLs for websites you have previously reviewed that describe how light waves reflect and enable people to see. Prepare to have them visit locations in the school to study the amount of sunlight at different times of the day. Guide them to understand that Earth's rotation affects the amount of sunlight in a location.

Differentiate Instruction

Extra Support Have students draw a simple picture of the school. Then have them draw pictures of the sun's light waves reflecting off the school at three times of the day: early morning, midday, and afternoon to show the amount of light coming in. Western and eastern window exposures will be different at different times of the day. Discuss how the brightness changes in different locations of the school throughout the day when the sun is shining.

Extension Challenge students to consider controlling glare when increasing the sun's light. Glare can be particularly distracting and annoying in educational settings.

Name _____

UNIT PROJECT
Reflecting Light

Think about the different parts of your school, from the hallways, to the cafeteria, to the library, to the auditorium. Which parts of the school are lit with natural light? Which parts of the school are dark or gloomy? For this project, you will work in teams to come up with a design for bringing more sunlight into dark areas of your school.

Write a question that you will consider as you come up with your designs.

Students should write a question concerning adding more sunlight into the school.

_____

Materials

Think about how you will redesign the school to allow more sunlight into dark areas. What materials will you need?

Materials can include drawing paper and utensils, poster board, rulers, colorful markers or pencils, online/print resources.

_____

_____

To make your design, identify the area of the school you wish to focus on. Which part of the school needs more natural sunlight? What are some initial ideas you have for bringing more sunlight to that area?

Possible response: The hallway needs more sunlight because it is dark and gloomy now. My initial idea is to create skylights in the ceiling to let more natural light in from the sky, since we cannot add windows, because the walls are lined with lockers.

143

Explore Online Go online to access the Unit Project downloadable worksheet for students.

UNIT 3 PROJECT
Reflecting Light

DCI PS4.B: Electromagnetic Radiation

Before students begin the task, check their understanding of key concepts.

Ask: How is light a form of electromagnetic radiation? Light waves travel through space moving energy from one place to another.

Ask: How are we able to see? Objects can be seen when light reflected from their surfaces enters our eyes.

Refer students to Lesson 2, Exploration 1 for concept support.

ESSENTIAL QUESTIONS
Ask the following questions before students begin to plan their activity.

- How are light waves from the sun reflected?
- How do opaque objects obstruct light waves?
- How will your design increase the amount of the sun's light waves in a particular location in the school?

Review Lesson 2, *How Does Light Reflect?* so that students have a fresh understanding of electromagnetic radiation.

CCC Cause and Effect

Encourage students to identify the causes that have the effect of dark areas in the school. It could be lack of windows, skylights, or blockages of light.

Ask: What causes darkness? Possible answer: Light waves are not available or they are being blocked by opaque objects.

Unit 3 Waves and Information Transfer 143J

Research and Plan

Teams should brainstorm where dark locations in the school may be and plan to visit different locations of the school at different times of the day for observation.

Ask: How will you select the location for your design? Possible answer: My/Our group will look for a place that is dark at some times and light at other times of the day.

How will you determine why the location is dark? Possible answer: My/Our group will look for obstructions to light waves from the sun.

Lighting

Groups should collect their data and return to the class to analyze it. Have them develop criteria and constraints for their designs.

Ask: What is the criteria for your design? Possible answer: Increase the amount of sunlight in a dark location.

What problems do you expect to encounter as you create your design? Possible answer: The location may be a place where the sun's light waves cannot reach without great difficulty.

What are the constraints of your design? Possible answer: materials, and costs

Lighting Design

As teams develop their designs, encourage them to show how the amount of light will be affected at different times of the day and during different seasons.

Plan and Design

Make a plan for the research you will need to do and how you will come up with your predictions. As you make your plan, consider the following:

- Where will the sun be positioned during different times of the day? Will this affect how much sunlight the area gets?
- Consider other structures around the school that could get in the way of sunlight, such as other tall buildings, trees, mountains, etc.
- What are the criteria for designing a way to get more sunlight?
- What are the constraints for getting more sunlight?

Students should demonstrate consideration to the position of the sun at various times and various seasons, as this can affect how much sunlight their area gets and whether or not their designs are effective. They should list criteria and constraints to their designs.

Swap designs with another team, and provide constructive feedback. Then, swap your designs back and think about the feedback you received on your design. Will you make any modifications to your design? Why or why not?

Accept all responses.

Analyze Your Results

Look for patterns in your design. Make two observations about adding sunlight into your school.

Possible responses: the best way to add sunlight to the school is by creating skylights in the ceiling. This is so that the light from the sun can shine down into the school. The school is surrounded by other tall buildings, so windows would not likely help make the areas lighter.

Restate Your Question

Write the question you investigated.

Students should identify the question created at the beginning of the project.

Claims, Evidence, and Reasoning

Make a claim that answers your question.

Possible response: The best way to get natural sunlight into the school is by adding skylights into the ceiling.

What evidence from your analysis supports your claim?

Students should cite evidence from their designs to support their claims.

Possible response: The sun will be at its highest point in the middle of the day. Sunrise starts before school starts, and sunset starts after school ends. Therefore, adding a skylight should allow the most amount of light through the school.

Discuss your reasoning with a partner.

143

Analyze Your Results

 Constructing Explanations and Designing Solutions

Have teams share their designs with the class and compare and contrast different designs for the same locations in the school.

Ask: What are the most effective solutions from each design? Possible answers: a mirror to reflect light from one place to another, a skylight, a tube of light

How does each design meet the criteria within the constraints? Students should evaluate each team in terms of the criteria to increase sunlight in an area within the constraints.

Could we combine designs to create a more effective solution? Students should select elements from each design to create a potentially more effective solution.

Claims, Evidence, and Reasoning

Students should state a specific claim related to increasing electromagnetic radiation in a location in the school and discuss their reasoning.

Ask: What claim can you make? Possible claim: We can increase electromagnetic radiation by installing a wall of windows.

How does your evidence support your claim? Students should review their designs to support their claim.

Scoring Rubric for Hands-On Activity	
3	States a claim about electromagnetic radiation and supports it with ample, detailed evidence.
2	States a claim about electromagnetic radiation and somewhat supports it with evidence.
1	States a claim that is not supported by evidence.
0	Does not state a claim.

LESSON 1
What Are Waves?

Building to the Performance Expectation

The learning experiences in this lesson prepare students for mastery of:

4-PS4-1 Develop a model of waves to describe patterns in terms of amplitude and wavelength and that waves can cause objects to move.

Trace Tool to the NGSS
Go online to view the complete coverage of these standards across this lesson, unit, and time.

 **Science & Engineering Practices**

 **Disciplinary Core Ideas**

 Crosscutting Concepts

Developing and Using Models
Develop and/or use models to describe and/or predict phenomena.
 VIDEO Developing and Using Models

Scientific Knowledge Is Based on Empirical Evidence
Science findings are based on recognizing patterns.

Constructing Scientific Explanations
Use evidence to construct and explanation.
 VIDEO Constructing Explanations

PS4.A Wave Properties
Waves, which are regular patterns of motion, can be made in water by disturbing the surface. When waves move across the surface of deep water, the water goes up and down in place; there is no net motion in the direction of the wave except when the water meets a beach.

Waves of the same type can differ in amplitude (height of the wave) and wavelength (spacing between wave peaks).

Patterns
Similarities and differences in patterns can be used to sort and classify natural phenomena.

Energy and Matter
Energy can be transferred in various ways and between objects.
 VIDEO Energy

 CONNECTIONS TO MATH

R.MP.4 Model with mathematics.
4.MD.A.1 Know relative sizes of measurement units within one system of figures.

 CONNECTIONS TO ENGLISH LANGUAGE ARTS

SL.4.5 Add audio recordings and visual displays to presentations when appropriate to enhance the development of main ideas or themes.

Supporting All Students, All Standards

Integrating the Three Dimensions of Learning

In this lesson, students will explore the properties and characteristics of waves **(DCI PS4.A)** and the patterns they create **(CCC Patterns)**. They will use models to learn about the ways in which waves create motion through the transfer of energy **(SEP Developing and Using Models)**. Through the use of these diagrams, students will be able to visualize transverse waves and differentiate between wavelength and amplitude. This information will help deepen their understanding of the movement of energy.

 **Professional Development** — Go online to view **Professional Development videos** with strategies to integrate CCCs and SEPs, including the ones used in this lesson.

Extra Hands-On Activity: Slowing Waves

How Do Waves Move Through Different Materials?

 Pairs
20 minutes

Before beginning this activity, for each pair, fill one zip-closing bag with water, another with air, and a third with sand. The bag with air in it should be as full as you can make it. The bag with sand in it should have as much air removed as possible. Each pair of students will also need a pencil.

Students should hold one bag up to an ear while covering the other ear. Their partner then taps on the bag and should attempt to tap with the same amount of force and frequency for each bag. Students should note the sound in terms of volume, pitch, and clarity. They should then repeat the process using the other two bags. Then students should swap so the partner in the first set of tests can experience the way the waves move through the different materials.

Students should hear variations in the volume, pitch, and clarity of sounds as the sounds travel through different types of matter.

 This activity can support mastery of this Crosscutting Concept: Patterns

Preassessment

Have students complete the lesson pre-test online or see the Assessment Guide.

Build on Prior Knowledge

Students should already know and be prepared to build on the following concepts:
- Wave is a motion.
- Energy can be transferred or carried from one thing to another.
- There are different forms of energy.

Differentiate Instruction

Lesson Vocabulary

Students will already be familiar with the everyday use of the term *wave*.

Ask: What are waves? *the up and down movement of ocean water*

Students may also be familiar with the act of *waving*.

Ask: What does it mean when you wave at someone? *It's a way to say hello or goodbye.*

Ask: Is there a pattern in how you wave to someone? *Yes, the hand or arm moves from side to side.*

RTI/Extra Support

Provide examples of other everyday waves, such as the ripple of water in a bowl. You can also play music for students and have them identify sound waves.

Ask: What do all of these waves have in common? *They transfer energy.*

Explain to students that there are many different kinds of waves, including shock waves.

Ask: What's an example of something that causes shock waves? *earthquake*

Lesson 1 What Are Waves? **144B**

LESSON 1 **Engage** • Explore/Explain • Elaborate • Evaluate

ENGAGE: Lesson Phenomenon

Lesson Objective

To differentiate between wavelength and amplitude, and observe how waves interact.

About This Image

Notice the ripples in the American flag. Those ripples, or waves, are creating motion. The people who are holding the flag are responsible for producing the starting energy needed to wave the flag. That energy is then transferred through the motion of the wave to form the ripple effect.

Other kinds of energy travels in waves, such as light, sound, and shock waves.

SEP **Developing and Using Models**

Alternative Engage Strategy

Making Waves

- Pairs
- 15 minutes

Have students form pairs. Give each pair 2–3 feet of string. Allow enough space in the classroom for pairs to stand up and face each other, with each student holding one end of the string. Ask one student to forcefully move the string up and down while the other student remains still. Then have them take turns so that each student gets a chance.

Once both students have had a chance to move the string, return students to their seats and have partners engage in a discussion about their findings. Students should have noticed that when the string was moved, the wave or ripple traveled from the first student to the student who was standing still. The still student may feel the transfer energy in their hand.

LESSON 1

What Are Waves?

This American flag waves as hundred of hands carry it across the stadium.

By the end of this lesson...
you'll differentiate between wavelength and amplitude and observe how waves interact.

144

Unit 3 Waves and Information Transfer

 **Explore Online** Students can view the lesson phenomenon online.

Can You Explain It?

Imagine you are at the beach and you see a bunch of surfers. They paddle out into the choppy water. When the time is right, they jump up onto their boards and ride the waves back to the beach.

1. How does a surfer know when to stand up on the board to "catch" a wave?

   Students should respond based on the preliminary observations they can make of the images.

   Tip
   Learn more about waves and energy in How Is Energy Transferred?

 EVIDENCE NOTEBOOK Look for this icon to help you gather evidence to answer the question above.

145

Can You Explain It?

Students are asked to study the image of the surfer in the ocean and explain how the surfer knows when to catch a wave. To do so, students must relate the shape and movement of the wave to the speed at which it is traveling. They should expect their answers to change as they progress through the Explorations. Students will have an opportunity to revise their answers when they revisit these questions at the end of the lesson.

Collaboration

Build on Prior Knowledge You may wish to spend a few minutes discussing how ocean waves move. You can model this by drawing a picture of a wave on the front board, showing how the wave progresses and builds as it picks up more energy from the wind. Then show what happens when the wave encounters the shallows and eventually breaks.

 EVIDENCE NOTEBOOK

Encourage students to use an appropriate graphic organizer, such as main idea and supporting details, to set up their notebook for this lesson.

Find more strategies in the online ELA handbook.

Lesson 1 What are Waves?

LESSON 1   Engage • **Explore/Explain** • Elaborate • Evaluate

EXPLORATION 1 How Waves Transfer Energy

HANDS-ON ACTIVITY Pairs   1 class period
Let's Make Waves!

3D Learning Objective

SEP Developing and Using Models

Students work in pairs to model how energy moves through waves. They will create waves with certain materials and measure the transfer of energy with other materials.

Materials
The materials listed in the student edition are a starting point. Yarn may be traded out with fabric ribbon or thick string.

Preparation
Preassemble the materials so that each pair of students can pick up their box of materials and be ready to start the activity.

DCI PS4.A Wave Properties

This activity asks students to consider the properties of waves in order to understand how they are able to transfer energy.

Ask: What do you think helps waves be able to transfer energy?
the patterns of how they move

Procedure
STEP 1 Make sure students are assembling their materials correctly. If students do not properly tie the yarn to the spring toy, they might not get accurate results.

STEP 2 Make sure students have enough space to perform the activity in the classroom. You may need to rearrange some of the desks or tables to allow students to stand 4 meters apart.

HANDS-ON ACTIVITY
Let's Make Waves!

Objective
Collaborate to model the energy transfer that takes place in waves using a coiled spring toy.

Materials
- safety goggles
- yarn
- coiled spring toy
- meterstick
- stopwatch

What question will you investigate to meet this objective?
Possible answer: How does energy move through a spring toy?

Procedure

STEP 1 Tie a piece of yarn to the center of the coiled spring toy as shown in the photo above.

Why do you think the yarn is needed?
Possible answer: Energy is invisible, so we need the yarn to observe how energy will affect the spring coil.

STEP 2 Put on safety goggles. Take one end of the coiled spring toy and have your partner take the other. Move so that you are about 4 meters apart.

146

Student Lab Worksheet and complete Teacher Support available online.

146   Unit 3 Waves and Information Transfer

STEP 3 While you partner holds the end still, slowly wiggle your end of the spring from side to side. In the data table, record how long it takes the wave to get to your partner. Repeat this procedure, wiggling the spring at medium speed and then at a faster speed.

Speed	Time
Slow	
Medium	Check data for reasonable responses.
Fast	

STEP 4 Hold one end of the spring still. Hold the other end and gather 10 coils of the spring toy together. Hold onto the last coil and release the extra coils you gathered. Use the stopwatch to record how long it takes for the wave to reach your partner. Record your data in the first row of the table.

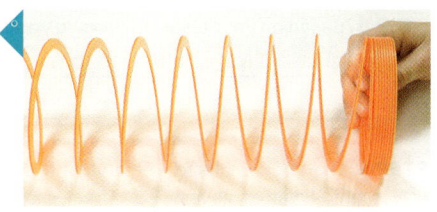

Number of Coils	Time
10	Check data for reasonable responses.

STEP 5 Repeat Step 4 using different numbers of coils. Record the number of coils you gathered and your results in the table under the first row.

How does the number of coils change how long it takes for the energy to reach your partner?
Possible answer: When I held fewer coils, the speed of the waves was slower than when I held more coils.

147

CCC Patterns

As students perform the demonstration with the spring toy, they will notice patterns in the toy's movement.

Ask: What kinds of patterns are being created by the spring toy? There is a back and forth motion.

STEP 3 Circulate and help students add data to their tables if they get stuck.

Differentiate Instruction

RTI/Extra Support If students get confused by the table, model for them how to fill the table out. Some students may think that they need to put the actual speed into the speed column, whereas they only need to indicate fast, medium, or slow. Also, take this time to remind students to pay attention to the timer so that accurate time data are collected.

STEPS 4–5 Make sure students are performing the activity safely. When performing this step, it is possible for fingers to get caught in the coils of the spring toy if students are not careful or not paying attention. Remind students of proper safety precautions.

Connection to Math

Students must be able to look at the table and conceptualize the data. If data is collected correctly, students should be able to reproduce the same results when the test is repeated.
MP.4 Model with mathematics

SEP Developing and Using Models

Ask: How does modeling the pattern of waves help you better understand how energy is transferred? Energy is not always transferred in the same way. The transfer depends on the wave.

Lesson 1 What are Waves? **147**

LESSON 1 Engage • **Explore/Explain** • Elaborate • Evaluate

EXPLORATION 1 How Waves Transfer Energy, continued

Analyze Your Results

STEP 6 Ask: Do you think the spring toy wave pattern would continue forever? It would eventually run out of energy and stop.

STEP 7 Ask: Why do you think the amount of coils impacts the speed of the waves? It changes the transfer of energy.

 **Patterns**

Ask: How can studying energy patterns relate to wave properties? Different kinds of waves will produce unique patterns of energy.

Draw Conclusions

Invite students to complete steps 8, 9, and 10 independently.

> ## Claims, Evidence, and Reasoning
> Have students cite evidence to support their claims in step 9 and share their explanations with the whole class.

Scoring Rubric for Hands-On Activity	
3	completes activity; provides an explanation well supported by evidence and reasoning
2	completes activity; provides an explanation without evidence or reasoning
1	participates in the activity but does not make conclusions or provide explanations

Analyze Your Results

STEP 6 How did energy move in your first test?
Possible answer: We observed that the waves in the first test moved back and forth. When we wiggled the spring faster, the waves got faster.

STEP 7 How did energy move in your second test?
Possible answer: When I held fewer coils, the speed was slower than it was when I held more coils.

Draw Conclusions

STEP 8 Based on your tests, how would you define a wave?
Possible answer: Waves with more energy cause matter to move more quickly.

STEP 9 Use your results to write a claim that relates energy in a wave to the way in which matter moves.
Possible answer: When we wiggled one end of the spring, we observed waves moving back and forth. When we held the coils and let them go, we saw waves moving along the spring. We also saw that the yarn moved higher and lower when we applied more force to set the spring in motion.

STEP 10 Use evidence from this activity to answer the following questions: How do waves move? What affects wave movement?
Possible answer: Do waves move the same way through other materials?

STEP 11 What is moving along the spring: waves or matter? How does the yarn provide evidence for your answer?
The spring waves moves energy, not matter. The coils shake, but they don't move down the wave like the energy does., or else the yarn would have moved too.

148

148 Unit 3 Waves and Information Transfer

EXPLORATION 1
How Waves Transfer Energy

Waves 101

You may see or experience waves every day. A wave can be the up and down movement of water. Wind can make a flag wave. In science, a **wave** is a disturbance that carries energy, such as sound or light.

2. List some other examples of waves in everyday life. How do you know if a wave is strong or weak?

Possible answer: I see waves in swimming pools and use microwaves to cook food. A wave is strong if it has a lot of energy or makes food very hot.

Have you ever thrown a rock into a pond? Once the rock hits the water, it creates a bunch of ripples on the surface. Ripples form because energy from the rock is transferred to the water. Waves are evidence that energy is transferred.

The size of a wave is related to the amount of energy transferred. The rock that was dropped into the pond in the photo was small.

3. What would happen to the waves in this same pond if a larger rock were dropped into the water?
   a. The waves would be closer together.
   b. The waves would be smaller in size.
   c. There would be fewer waves with less energy.
   d. There would be larger waves with more energy.

3D Learning Objective

Explore the **properties of waves**, including how energy is transferred, by looking at a series of **model diagrams** that represent movements and **patterns** of waves. Students will also learn about the **direction in which waves travel** and how that affects energy transfer.

DCI PS4.A Wave Properties

This page tells about some of the properties of waves as related to movement, strength, and size.

Ask: What can you tell about a really large wave in the ocean? It has a lot of energy and strength.

Ask: Does a strong wave carry more energy than a weak wave? Yes.

Differentiate Instruction

ELL: Making Comparisons This page presents several comparisons (strong vs. weak; big vs. small). Help students clearly understand these comparisons through the use of images. For instance, when discussing small or large waves, show students images of small and large waves. Use these visuals as students work through the page activities.

LESSON 1 Engage • **Explore/Explain** • Elaborate • Evaluate

EXPLORATION 1 *How Waves Transfer Energy, continued*

CCC Patterns

See if students can identify patterns in the model diagrams.

Ask: What kind of pattern do you see in the first image? *The circles in each column are different sizes; there are 4 circles in each column, and all circles have arrows pointing in the same direction.*

Ask: What happens to the pattern when waves get closer and closer to the beach? *The circles start to change shape; the circles are no longer stacked vertically.*

> ## Collaboration
> **Feedback** Have students work with a partner to critique each other's reasoning for Item 4. Bring the whole class together, and come to a consensus on the explanation.

SEP Developing and Using Models

Ask: How do you think models, like the one on this page, help scientists study ocean waves? *They show patterns of the waves to tell scientists how waves form and how their energy moves from one place to another.*

Connection to Life Science

There are many processes on Earth that produce and release energy besides waves. Humans, animals, plants, and other organisms depend on energy for sustaining life. Energy helps organisms grow, stay warm, repair their bodies, and move. It is important to have a firm grasp on the concept of energy transfer to learn how different forms of energy help living things survive.

PS3.D Energy in Chemical Processes and Everyday Life

Ocean Waves and Energy Transfer

Waves in the ocean can carry a lot of energy. As a wave gets closer to the beach, the land underneath the water is closer to the surface, causing the energy in the wave to force the water to rise up.

 Explore Online

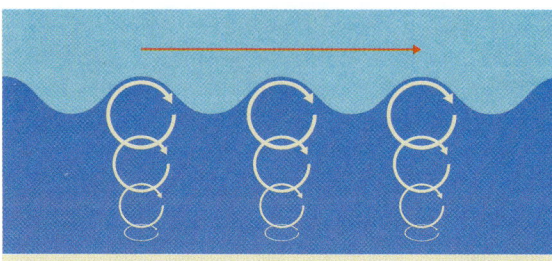

Wind transfers energy to the ocean's surface, causing a wave to form. Each circle shows the movement of water up and around in a wave. Notice that the water doesn't move forward. Only the wave's energy moves forward, as shown by the red arrow.

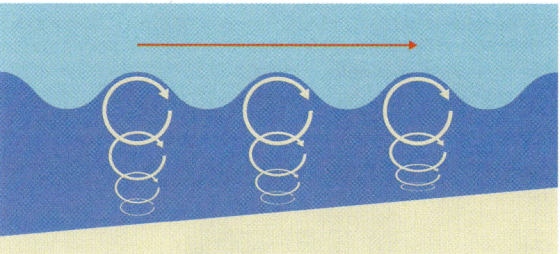

As the water becomes more shallow, the water has less room to move, forcing the water to move higher into the air. The height of the wave increases, and the energy moves forward more slowly.

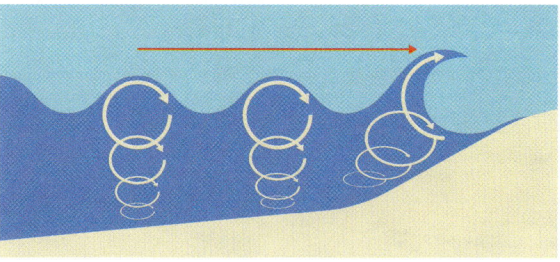

When waves get close to the beach, the back of the wave moves faster than the front, causing the wave to break. All that energy needs a place to go. As the water crashes onto the shore, some of the energy is transferred into sound, and some causes beach erosion.

4. Imagine you are in the ocean. The water reaches your waist. How will energy in a small wave affect you as the wave passes?

Possible answer: As the wave approaches, it would get taller. As it passes me, I would bob up and down but not move very much. I can feel the energy of the wave push past me towards shore.

If there is a lot of wind or a heavy storm, there is a lot of energy in ocean waves. When they get close to shore, all of that energy is released. Sometimes, out at sea, strong winds create large waves. These waves can travel great distances until they find a place to "break." Surfers often look for places like this so that they can make their way back to shore atop one of these waves.

Buoys are often used as channel markers or as data collection places. While these objects do move up and down with the waves, they do not move forward from their spot. They are often anchored to the sea floor.

Waves crashing along a sandy beach can change the land. Waves add sand to the beach as they come ashore but also erode it and carry it out to sea.

5. Select the best word to complete this sentence.

| energy | motion | buoy |

When ocean waves hit the beach, ____energy____ is released.

HANDS-ON Apply What You Know
Bobbing and Waving

6. Get a bucket and a cork from your teacher. Fill the bucket up part of the way with water, and then drop the cork into it. Notice what happens. Then gently rock the bucket side to side to add more energy to the water. Record your observations of the water in the bucket in terms of energy.

151

 Students can find additional content online in the Interactive Online Student Edition.

DCI PS4.A Wave Properties

This page tells about other properties of waves, such as how waves release energy.

Ask: How do you think buoys help scientists study waves? **They can tell scientists how strong or big the waves are, depending on how much they move up and down.**

Differentiate Instruction

Extension Challenge students to take the study of waves further by researching how waves have enough energy and strength to change landforms. For instance, students may wonder how waves have sculpted rock formations over time, or pushed back the seashore. Allow students time to perform this outside research and invite them to share findings with the whole class.

HANDS-ON Apply What You Know
Bobbing and Waving

Have students complete this activity in small groups, and make sure to have enough materials prepared for students to carry out the tests. Leave students enough time at the end for them to record their findings and invite groups to share their observations with the whole class.

Scoring Guideline

Exceptional activity results will show a detailed record of observations and an explanation of how the cork reacted to waves in the pail.

Lesson 1 What Are Waves? 151

LESSON 1 Engage • **Explore/Explain** • Elaborate • Evaluate

EXPLORATION 1 How Waves Transfer Energy, continued

SEP Scientific Knowledge Is Based on Empirical Evidence

Remind students of the Hands-On Activity they participated in and the different forms of wave movement. Draw their attention to the model diagram on this page.

Ask: Water waves move up and down as they travel horizontally along the water. In which direction do you think the energy moves? *the same direction as the wave travels*

CCC Energy and Matter

Scientists study patterns to better understand how energy moves.

Ask: What can the direction in which energy moves tell scientists? *It can tell them in which direction an object will move.*

Misconception Alert Students may have misconceptions about the existence of waves they cannot see. Sound waves and light waves are examples of energy transfer through wave motion. In an earthquake, the friction caused by shifting plates produces waves. The energy from those waves is what is felt during an earthquake and what can cause so much damage.

Reinforce the idea that when you turn on a light, it is light waves you see and when you hear a sound, it is sound waves you hear. If you feel an earthquake, it is energy waves you feel.

Waves That Move Up and Down

Waves and energy can move in different directions. Sometimes, waves move up and down, like a water wave. Use the pictures below to help you understand waves that move from up and down.

Side to Side

7. Use your finger to trace how energy moves through the wave. Then trace how the matter moves as the wave passes.  Explore Online

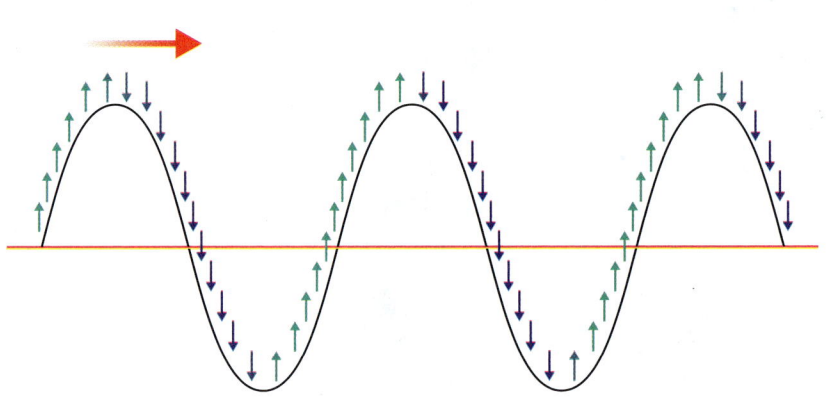

In an up and down wave, matter moves at a right angle to the direction of the wave and the movement of energy. Here, the energy is moving to the right.

To move forward, some snakes move their bodies up and down. This movement is called *slithering*.

152

152 Unit 3 Waves and Information Transfer

Waves that move up and down are very common. They can move through all types of matter and even through empty space! As you just learned, water waves are up and down waves. The water moves up and down, but the energy moves forward. Sunlight also travels up and down. Light waves can travel through space, where there is no air. Sunlight that reaches Earth warms the planet and everything on it. Study the pictures below to learn more about up and down waves.

When people do "the wave" at a game, they stand up and cheer in sequence so it looks like a wave moving through the stands.

Signals from satellites, such as this one, travel through the vacuum of space and through clouds and the air to reach Earth's surface. These waves move at the same speed as sunlight, which move extremely fast compared to sound waves.

 EVIDENCE NOTEBOOK In an ocean wave, what is moving toward the shore—the water or the energy? What evidence do you have to support your answer?

8. Write a saying that will help you remember how energy and matter move as they travel in an up and down wave.

Possible answer: Waves in water can make me wobble; they also make me bob around as my feet stay on the ground.

153

 **Explore Online** Students can find additional content online in the Interactive Online Student Edition.

Differentiate Instruction

ELL: Use Realia Play video clips for students of waves that move side to side, such as a clip of a slithering snake and a crowd doing the wave at a ballgame. It can be helpful for students to visualize the side-to-side movement of waves in action, as opposed to looking at a still picture of it.

DCI PS4.A Waves Properties

Ask: What is unique about how waves from sunlight move? They travel through space where there is no air; sunlight waves move up and down as they travel forward.

CCC Patterns

Have students observe the pattern of a side-to-side wave by getting the whole class to "do the wave" on your count.

Ask: What did you notice about the pattern we created by doing the wave? Possible answer: Instead of up and down like a water wave, it was side-to-side movement.

EVIDENCE NOTEBOOK

Students should be able to answer this prompt by reviewing what was learned in Exploration 1 so far.

Lesson 1 What Are Waves? 153

LESSON 1   Engage • **Explore/Explain** • Elaborate • Evaluate

EXPLORATION 1   How Waves Transfer Energy, *continued*

SEP Developing and Using Models

Ask: What does this model tell you about the movement of sound waves? **Sound waves can travel in either direction.**

Ask: What do the energy and matter of sound waves have in common? **They both move in the same direction.**

> ### Differentiate Instruction
>
> **RTI/Extra Support** Students may have a difficult time interpreting the diagram of the sound waves. Feel free to walk students through each segment of the waves before tracing the entire pattern. Alternatively, you might want to label the diagram, particularly the arrows, so students can clearly visualize the movement of the waves and energy.
>
> **ELL: Use Realia** Demonstrate for students the sound waves that are produced by a drum. Bring a small drum into the classroom, or borrow one from the music room. Then pass it around the room so each student has a chance to strike the drum and observe how the the drum vibrates.

CCC Patterns

Ask: What patterns do all types of waves share? **a pattern of movement that transfers energy**

Shake Like a Quake!

BOOM! A firework goes off! There's a bright flash of light followed by the sound of the explosion. Light and sound are both waves. But unlike light, energy in sound waves travels back and forth parallel to the wave.

Back and Forth

9. Use your finger to find the 3 points where the wave is the most compressed. This is the energy of the wave moving to the right.

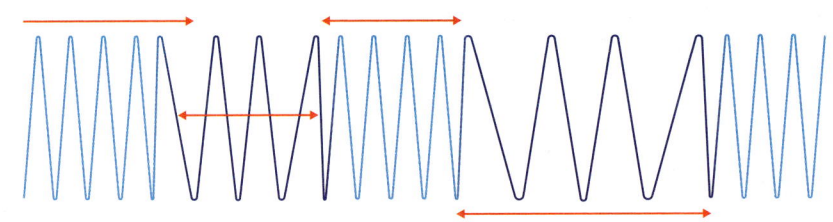

Some waves move back and forth. Energy in these waves moves in the direction in which the wave moves. The matter also moves in the same direction as the energy does.

When a drum is struck, its skin vibrates. You hear the sound because the air above the drum moves in the same direction that the energy moves.

154

Unit 3   Waves and Information Transfer

Sound is one example of a wave in which energy and matter move in the same direction. Unlike light, sound can only travel through matter. Sound travels better through water than through air. Because of this, animals that live in the ocean can hear sounds that are far away from them.

Another type of wave that moves bak and forth is one of the waves generated during an earthquake. When the ground starts to shake during a quake, different waves move through the rocks in the ground. These waves are used to figure out how strong an earthquake is. Look at the pictures below to find out more about waves that travel back and forth.

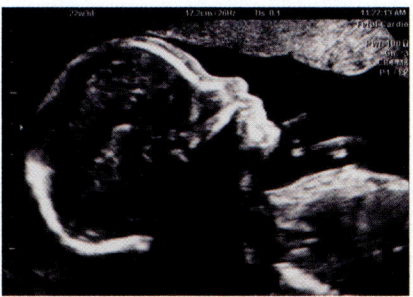

Ultrasound can be used to look inside of things—even people! These sounds move slowly and can't be heard by humans. The sound waves bounce around to form images of objects.

Some earthquake waves make rocks move in the same direction in which the waves are moving. This movement of matter and energy makes the ground shake, and buildings to crumble.

EVIDENCE NOTEBOOK What types of waves are sound waves? How do they move matter and energy?

Language SmArts
Classifying

10. Classify the examples by writing "up" before the up and down waves and "bf" before the back and forth waves.

    __bf__ guitar being played
    __up__ sunlight coming through a window
    __up__ boat bobbing in the water
    __bf__ ultrasound of a human heart
    __up__ crowd doing "the wave" at a basketball game
    __bf__ bell being rung
    __up__ communication satellite in space

Tip

The English Language Arts Handbook can provide help with understanding how to classify groups of items.

155

 **Explore Online** Students can go online to take a closer look at the movement of energy through a wave.

DCI PS4.A Waves Properties

This page tells students about the characteristics of sound waves and earthquake waves.

Ask: What are the properties of ultrasound waves? **slow; bounce around; cannot be heard by humans; can be used to create images**

What are the properties of earthquake waves? **move in and out; make rocks move; makes the ground shake**

EVIDENCE NOTEBOOK

Students should think back to when they learned about water waves. This was the very first type of wave they learned about.

FORMATIVE ASSESSMENT

SEP Language SmArts
Classifying

RI.5.7 Draw on information from multiple print or digital sources, demonstrating the ability to locate an answer to a question quickly or to solve a problem efficiently.

Classifying Information As students work to classify the examples according to the type of wave, remind them that it's important to draw on what they learned from both text and images throughout the section. Pictures can be just as informative as text. This information can help them answer the questions more quickly and accurately.

Ask: What type of wave moves in and out? **sound**

Lesson 1 What Are Waves?

LESSON 1   Engage • **Explore/Explain** • Elaborate • Evaluate

EXPLORATION 2 Wave Parts

3D Learning Objective

Explore **different parts of waves** and the **patterns they create**. Review a **series of model diagrams**, and visualize **amplitude, wavelength, and other characteristics of waves**. Study **patterns related to sound waves**, such as volume.

DCI   PS4.A Waves Properties

Ask: Does the wavelength measure the entire length of the wave? **No.**

Ask: What does the wavelength measure? **It measures the distance between crests or troughs that are next to each other.**

SEP   Developing and Using Models

Have students study the model diagram.

Ask: Why is it important to understand the parts of the waves? **It gives scientists a way to describe waves in a consistent or standard way.**

Differentiate Instruction

Extension You may want to challenge students by covering up the labels on the diagram and having the students label the parts of the wave based on what they read in the text.

Language SmArts
Understand Graphics
RI.5.1 Quote Sources Accurately

Have students describe the diagram to a partner before they answer the question.

EXPLORATION 2
Wave Parts

Hunks and Chunks of Waves

Waves have different parts. The top of a wave is called a **crest.** This is the point on a wave where matter is moved the farthest upward. On a water wave, the crest is the highest point a buoy bobs. The bottom of a wave is called a **trough.** This is the point on a wave where the least amount of matter is moved the farthest down. On a water wave, the crest is the lowest point a buoy bobs.

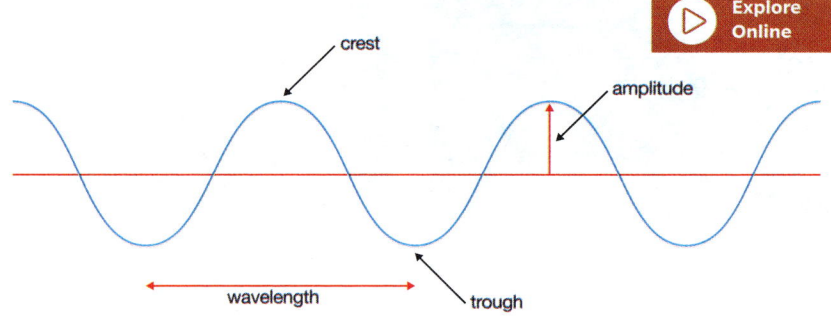

The distance between adjacent crests or troughs is called the **wavelength.** The wavelength is the distance between a point on one wave and the identical point on the next wave. The height of a wave is called its **amplitude.** The amplitude is half the distance from the crest to the trough. The amplitude is also a measure of the amount of energy in a wave. Waves with a greater amplitude have more energy than waves with a lower amplitude.

Language SmArts
Understand Graphics

11. Describe two distances that are the same in adjacent waves.

Possible answer: The distance from trough to trough is the same as the distance from crest to crest.

156

High and Low . . . Long and Short

12. Use the drawings to compare each set of waves. Choose the correct words from the word bank to complete the sentences.

| amplitude | wavelength | more | less | shorter | longer |

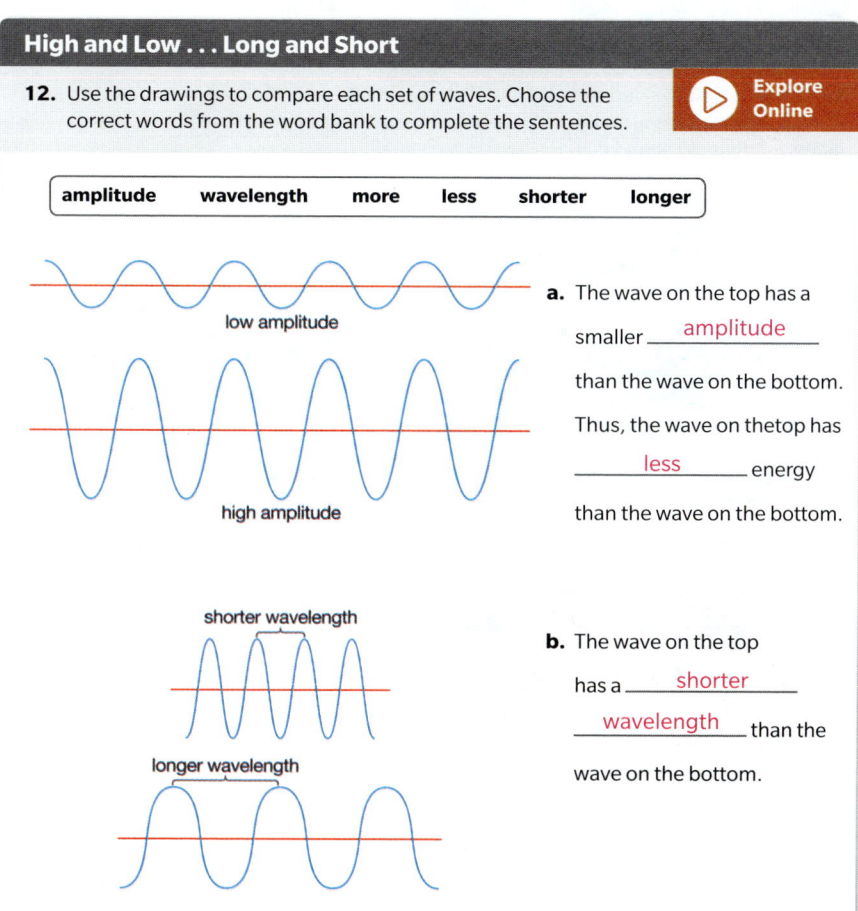

a. The wave on the top has a smaller __amplitude__ than the wave on the bottom. Thus, the wave on the top has __less__ energy than the wave on the bottom.

b. The wave on the top has a __shorter__ __wavelength__ than the wave on the bottom.

13. Select the word or words that make each sentence correct.

| crest | trough | wavelength | amplitude |

a. The top of a wave is called the __crest__.

b. The bottom of a wave is called the __trough__.

c. The distance between two crests is a wave's __wavelength__.

d. A wave with much energy has a large __amplitude__.

LESSON 1 Engage • **Explore/Explain** • Elaborate • Evaluate

EXPLORATION 2 *Wave Parts, continued*

 Energy and Matter

Draw students' attention to the different drawings of sound waves.

Ask: If someone is whispering, what happens to the sound wave? The distance between the crest and the trough is smaller.

Ask: What does this say about the relationship between the amplitude and the distance between the crest and trough? The smaller the amplitude, the smaller the distance; the bigger the amplitude, the bigger the distance.

Differentiate Instruction

Extension Challenge students to do outside research to come up with other examples of sound waves that have large or small amplitudes. Then have students draw a model of the sound wave produced, being sure to highlight the distance between the crest and trough.

EVIDENCE NOTEBOOK

Remind students that it is important to use evidence and examples in writing because they support claims.

Connection to English Language Arts

Emphasize to students the importance of being able to quickly draw on information to use as evidence or supportive facts in writing assignments. Being able to recall where certain bits of information can be found is an important skill that can help students complete writing assignments faster.

RI.5.9 Draw on information from multiple print or digital sources

158 Unit 3 Waves and Information Transfer

Can You Hear This?

All waves have an amplitude and a wavelength. In a sound waves, the amplitude is how loud something is. This is also called the **volume**. Compare the sounds described on this page to learn how amplitude differs for different sounds.

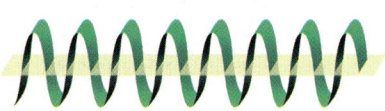

Engines on a jet produce very loud sounds. These sound waves have a lot of energy that is carried over a long distance.

The amplitude of a sound wave produced by a jet engine is very large. The distance between the crest and trough is large.

Songbirds produce soft sounds when they chirp. These sounds can only be heard over a short distance becaue they have a small amount of energy.

The amplitude of a sound wave produced by a songbird is small. The distance between the crest and trough is small.

Sound waves with more energy and volume have larger amplitudes. Sound waves with less energy and volume have smaller amplitudes. Compare the sounds described on the next page to learn how wavelength differs.

 EVIDENCE NOTEBOOK Write evidence from this page that sound waves have different amounts of energy.

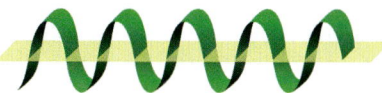

A dog whistle produces sound waves that only some animals, such as dogs, can hear.

The wavelength of a sound produced by a dog whistle is short. The distance between two neighboring crests is small.

A flute produces a variety of sound waves that humans can hear.

The wavelength of a sound produced by a flute is longer than the wavelength produced by a dog whistle.

 Do the Math
Relative Measures

14. Decide which sounds have higher and lower amplitude. Then write each sound in your order of higher to lower amplitude in each column. Be prepared to defend your choices.

    a. lion roaring
    b. train whistle
    c. cat meowing
    d. water dripping
    e. fireworks exploding
    f. flag snapping in the wind
    g. trumpet blowing
    h. fire crackling

High amplitude	Low amplitude
fireworks exploding train whistle trumpet blowing lion roaring	flag snapping in a strong wind cat meowing fire crackling water dripping

---

DCI PS4.A Waves Properties

Some sounds can only be heard by other animals. Before students have a chance to read the page, discuss dog whistles.

Ask: If a dog whistle is so high that it can only be heard by dogs and not humans, then what do you think its sound wave looks like? **The wavelength is short, and the distance between neighboring crests and neighboring troughs is small.**

> ## Collaboration
>
> **Partners** Have students work in pairs to answer Item 14. Then encourage them to think of five more examples, not on the page, for sounds with long wavelengths (low pitch) and sounds with short wavelengths (high pitch). When all pairs have finished, invite students to share their new examples with the whole class.

SEP Developing and Using Models

Have students select two of the examples and individually draw the model of the waves to represent those examples. Make sure the waves are appropriately drawn to represent the amplitude of each sound.

 Do the Math
Relative Measures

MD.A.1 Know relatives sizes of measurement units within one system of units.

Students identify relative sizes of measurement units by sorting high and low amplitude. Discuss the relative measurements within each group by sorting the sounds from loudest to softest. This will be difficult in some cases and provides for good discussion and understanding of amplitude.

EXPLORATION 2 Wave Parts, continued

DCI PS4.A Wave Properties

Ask: Why might surfers need to know about the properties of waves? *They can better judge how high or deep a wave goes; they can evaluate how fast a wave moves to figure out how strong it might be and what its shape might be.*

CCC Patterns

Ask: How do surfers get information on the size or other characteristics of waves? *by studying their patterns and experiencing the waves, either by riding them or letting them pass under them*

FORMATIVE ASSESSMENT
Putting It Together

DCI PS4.A Wave Properties

Ask: What kind of information can you tell about a wave by studying its properties? *the strength or size of a wave; how loud or quiet a sound wave is; how big or small an ocean wave might be*

Surfing the Waves

Remember the surfer from the beginning of the lesson? Let's use what you have learned about the parts of a wave to explain what happens when someone surfs on a wave.

Like all waves, ocean waves have amplitudes and wavelengths. Look at the photo. Which waves should the surfer choose to ride? The larger the waves, the greater their amplitude and energy. The closer the waves are to one another, the smaller their wavelengths.

Putting It Together

15. Select the words that make each sentence correct.

| volume | larger | smaller | amplitude | wavelength |

All waves have __amplitude__ and __wavelength__. In a sound wave, the amplitude is also called the __volume__. The louder a sound is, the __larger__ its amplitude. Sounds that are soft have __smaller__ amplitudes than sounds that are loud.

160

Unit 3 Waves and Information Transfer

EXPLORATION 3 Waves Interact

EXPLORATION 3
Waves Interact

Harmony!

Waves can interact with each other. If waves combine in pleasing ways, they are said to be in harmony. Look at the photos on this page to see what happens when sound and light waves interact.

If you have ever been to a concert, you've heard waves that are in harmony. The musicians here are playing instruments that make different sounds. When the sounds combine, music is produced.

Music is a collection of different sound waves interacting. If you listen carefully to music, you can pick out sounds and notes from each instrument in a band.

If you've been to a theater, you might have seen a dark stage at the beginning of a show. You also may have seen different lights come on, one by one, until the entire stage is lit up.

Like sound waves, light waves can interact, and when many people are seen on a stage and many lights are on, all of the light waves are interacting to show the actors.

16. What are some other examples of waves interacting that you may have seen or heard?

Students might mention seeing and hearing water waves combine and crash onto the shore. They might also mention an orchestra made up of many types of musical instruments being played together.

3D Learning Objective

Explore how **waves interact with each other**. Analyze **diagrams that show the different ways waves can be combined**, both to produce a new wave or to cancel each other out. Find **patterns related to the ways that waves interact**.

DCI PS4.A Wave Properties

An interesting property of waves is that they work harmoniously.

Ask: Do waves, such as sound and light waves, always work in harmony with each other? *no*
What do you think happens when sound or light waves do not interact in an agreeable way? *colors clash; music is not harmonious or in rhythm*

LESSON 1   Engage • **Explore/Explain** • Elaborate • Evaluate

EXPLORATION 3 Waves Interact, continued

CCC Patterns

Ask: What kinds of patterns can you identify from the examples of waves on the page? **The two waves are being combined (added together) to create a new wave.**

SEP Constructing Scientific Explanations

Ask: In what way do you think scientists and engineers use information about combined waves? **to make predictions about the new wave that will be formed.**

Ask: What can this help them discover? **how fast something can move; how light or loud something will be; how much energy will be transferred**

Differentiate Instruction

RTI/Extra Support Students may be confused by the diagram of the waves being added together. Help break down this model diagram by adding labels to remind students of the parts of the waves. You might also reproduce the diagram on the board and work through the equation of combining both waves to produce the new wave, including showing how the two waves overlap.

Crossing Invisible Paths

When two waves come together, they can combine to form a larger wave. Or they can cancel each other out. Waves can also combine to form a new wave with different characteristics than either of the source waves. Study the pictures and captions on these pages to see what happens when waves combine or cancel each other out.

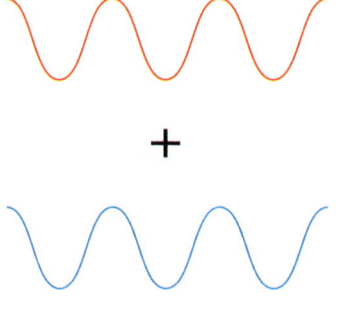
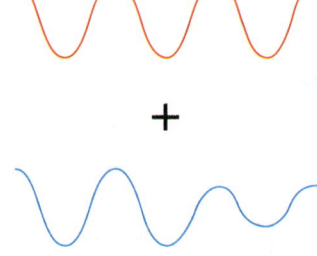
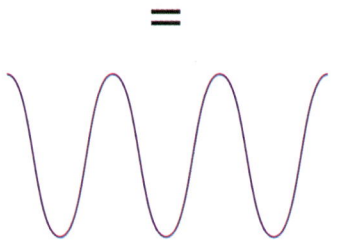
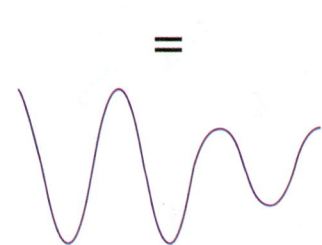

Sometimes waves join together to produce a larger or louder wave. Think about a rock band. When multiple sound waves from the instruments combine, they can create a sound with a loud volume. Waves that are able to combine in this way often have the similar or same wavelength and amplitude.

Waves can also join together to form a completely different wave. The crest of one wave might join with the crest of another wave and create a wave with twice the amplitude. Or the crest of one wave might join with another wave on its way to the trough to form a wave with a much smaller amplitude at that point.

162

162 Unit 3 Waves and Information Transfer

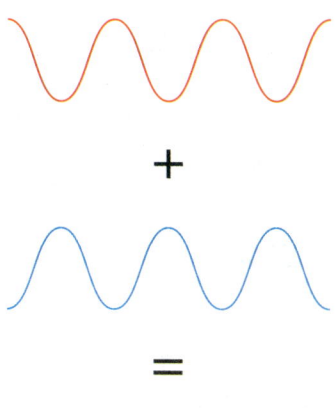

Sometimes waves can work against each other. When this happens, they can cancel each other out. Waves that cancel each other out are often opposite in amplitude. Then when the two waves join, the lows cancel out the highs to produce a neutral wave.

Noise-canceling headphones are a type of technology that uses wave cancellation. A small microphone outside the headphones picks up background sounds. The headphones then generate a wave with the opposite characteristics. The two waves then cancel each other out. This produces a quiet environment for the user.

EVIDENCE NOTEBOOK Apply what you've learned on these two pages to ocean waves and surfing.

17. What would happen if two opposite sound waves combined? Choose the correct answer.

    a. The sound would get a lot louder.
    b. The waves would cancel each other out.
    c. The amplitude of the waves would increase.
    d. The wavelength of the waves would get shorter.

163

DCI PS4.A Wave Properties

Remind students of what they predicted would happen if sound or light waves did not get along in a harmonious way.

Ask: Look at the picture on the page of the man wearing noise-canceling headphones. Waves can be cancelled. What other things can you do with waves? You can block them (an example might be the lead aprons you wear when getting x-rays) or deflect them.

EVIDENCE NOTEBOOK

Help students summarize the information on the two pages. They should be able to relate the content to ocean waves and surfing.

Collaboration

Think, Pair, Share Have students answer item 17 individually, and then pair up with the partner to review and discuss. Engage students in a whole class discussion about the correct and incorrect answers.

Lesson 1 What Are Waves? 163

LESSON 1 Engage • **Explore/Explain** • Elaborate • Evaluate

EXPLORATION 3 Waves Interact, continued

 SEP Developing and Using Models

Ask: When tuning an instrument, what would the model of the waves look like? *The sound wave of the tuned note and the sound wave of the note that needs tuning would not look the same, but after the note that needs tuning is tuned, both sound waves would match.*

 CCC Patterns

Ask: What do the music instruments that can go out of tune have in common? *They rely on some kind of material that can be either too tight (sharp) or too loose (flat).*

FORMATIVE ASSESSMENT
Putting It Together

 DCI PS4.A Wave Properties

Students recall the properties of waves that they learned about in Exploration 3. Inform students that some words from the word bank will not be used as answers.

Ask: What do noise-canceling headphones do? *They produce a sound wave that is the opposite of a sound wave that needs to be canceled out.*

Hear the Beat

Do you own a musical instrument? If so, then chances are you know that you need to tune it on occasion. There is nothing worse than trying to play a song and having all the notes sound weird. Read on to learn how a piano is tuned.

A piano tuner uses eight tuning forks to match the notes from each series of eight keys on the piano to the notes made by the tuning forks. An out-of-tune piano creates a sound known as a beat. This wave is usually larger than the wave of the note. The tuner's ear hears the difference in the sounds.

To fix the problem, the tuner also uses tuning forks. Each fork creates a particular note, or sound wave, that will match the same note, or sound wave, on the piano. The tuner hits the fork and listens to the note it makes. It is then matched up to the piano strings to see if it is the same. If it is different, the piano tuner adjusts the piano strings to make the two notes match.

Tuning forks are mechanical.

Some instruments are tuned with electronic tuners.

18. When piano tuners tune pianos using tuning forks, what are they trying to do? Choose the correct answer.

   a. Increase the volume of the instrument.
   b. Decrease the volume of the instrument.
   c. Match the two sound waves.
   d. Cancel the two sound waves out.

Putting It Together

19. Select the words from the word bank to make each sentence correct.

| amplitude | louder | quieter | combine | cancel out |

Noise-canceling headphones work when sound waves ___**combine**___.

The headphones ___**amplitude**___ unwanted sounds with small ___**cancel out**___ so they cannot be heard. At concerts, waves can combine to form ___**louder**___ sounds.

164

Unit 3 Waves and Information Transfer

TAKE IT FURTHER Discover More

Check out this path . . . or go online to choose one of these other paths.

- People in Science
- Seismic Waves and Earthquakes
- Theater Acoustics

Christian Doppler and Debra Fischer

Why does the siren of an ambulance or fire truck sound different as it gets closer to you? It's the Doppler effect, of course!

Christian Doppler was an Austrian physicist and mathematician. He discovered that sound waves appear to have a higher pitch as your approach the object making the sound. Pitch is the highness or lowness of a sound. When an object giving off a sound wave is moving away from you, the sound will appear to have a lower pitch. This is called the Doppler effect.

Christian Doppler

Imagine a fire truck is approaching you, siren blaring. As the truck passes you, the siren will have a lower pitch. The reason is the time it takes for the wave crests to reach you increases when the truck is moving away. So, from your point of view, the wavelength is longer and the pitch is higher.

Collaboration

You may choose to assign this activity or to direct students to the Interactive Online Student Edition where they can explore and choose from all three paths. These activities can be assigned individually, to pairs, or to small groups.

People in Science: Christian Doppler and Debra Fischer

Students will learn about the Doppler effect, including its origin and applications. They will also read about how Debra Fischer applied the Doppler effect to astronomy and what she discovered in doing so. Make sure to connect the information in this section to students' understanding of the properties of waves.

DCI PS4.A Wave Properties

According to the Doppler effect, sounds get higher or lower in pitch according to proximity and speed.

Ask: What if you are standing still, and a fire truck passes you with its siren on. As the fire truck gets farther away, what will happen to the sound coming from the siren? **It will get lower in pitch.**

LESSON 1 Engage • Explore/Explain • **Elaborate** • Evaluate

TAKE IT FURTHER, continued

CCC Patterns

People often refer to weather *patterns*. Thanks to Doppler's ideas, weather is not only tracked and forecast, its patterns can also be studied so that meteorologists and other scientists have an idea of what kind of weather to predict or expect in the future. Doppler radar uses colors to represent certain types of weather patterns. You may be familiar with seeing Doppler radar images if you watch the weather on the news or view it streaming from your phone, tablet, or computer.

> **Collaboration**
>
> **Feedback** Once students have responded to the prompt individually, have them pair up with a partner to review each other's responses and provide feedback. Give students time to make improvements on their ideas based on feedback. Call on volunteers to share their ideas with the whole class.

▶ Explore Online

Students can explore these additional topics online.

Seismic Waves and Earthquakes

Students explore the definition of seismic waves and learn about how this information is applied to the study of earthquakes. They can learn about the careers of seismologists. *(Outside research required.)*

Theater Acoustics

Students carry out research about design of acoustics in theatres and how acoustics are used to magnify and increase the range of sound waves. *(Outside research required.)*

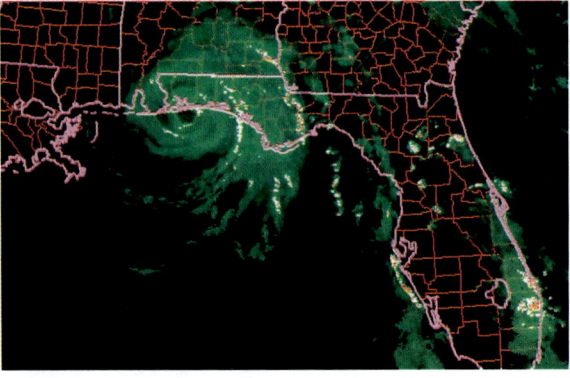

Doppler's ideas are used by weather forecasters to predict oncoming storms. Using Doppler radar, they are able to see how fast storms are moving. They can also determine where the storms are going and what types of precipitation are going to fall.

There are many uses for the Doppler effect. The Doppler effect helps identify and predict the movement of storms. It helps locate new planets, too! Although you can see stars all over the sky, you cannot see planets orbiting them.

Dr. Debra Fischer, an astrophysicist, thought that the Doppler effect could be used to find stars with planets orbiting them. Dr. Fischer looked at the way waves were emitted from different stars. In some cases, the waves would change a little. It turns out that as planets orbit a star, the gravity between them causes changes in waves emitted by the star.

Dr. Fischer used what we know about the Doppler effect to not only prove that planets orbit stars we see in the sky, but also to calculate the size of those planets.

Dr. Debra Fischer

20. On the lines below, describe the Doppler effect.

Students might say sound has a higher pitch as an object approaches and a lower pitch as it moves away.

166

Unit 3 Waves and Information Transfer

LESSON 1   Engage • Explore/Explain • Elaborate • **Evaluate**

LESSON CHECK

▶ **Explore Online**   Students can revisit the lesson phenomenon online.

LESSON 1

Lesson Check

Name _____

Can You Explain It?

1. Now that you have learned about waves, explain how a surfer gets onto a wave. Be sure to do the following:
   • Explain how waves carry energy.
   • Identify the properties and parts of waves.
   • Identify what happens when waves interact.

 EVIDENCE NOTEBOOK Use the information you've collected in your Evidence Notebook to help you cover each point above.

Possible answer:
• Waves carry energy through movement.
• A surfer needs to pay attention to the waves. He or she wants to be sure to paddle out to the waves through the troughs and jump up onto the board before the waves crest. Surfers need to know about the energy in the waves and need to pay attention to the size (or amplitude) of waves. The spacing between waves (the wavelength) is also important. When understanding all of these things about waves, a surfer knows just when to stand up and ride the wave.
• When waves interact, they can cancel each other out or produce a bigger or different wave.

Checkpoints

2. Choose the words that make each sentence correct.

| quickly | slowly | small | large | energy |

If a spring is wiggled ___slowly___, the amplitude of the waves that form is ___small___. This is because the amount of ___energy___ of the wave is small.

167

 Formal Assessment Go online for student self-checks and other assessments.

Can You Explain It?

 Collaboration

Discussion You may wish to revisit the information covered in Explorations 1, 2, and 3 to ensure student understanding of the material. Use bulleted points in the Interactive Worktext to lead the discussion.

EVIDENCE NOTEBOOK

Have students reread their answers to the Evidence Notebook prompts and then use this evidence to justify their reasoning as they respond to the Can You Explain It question. Make sure students understand that a complete response must address all bulleted points.

DCI PS4.A Wave Properties

Now that students are more familiar with what waves are, draw students' attention back to the image of the surfer.

Ask: What kind of information should a surfer know about a wave in order to better surf on it? how fast the wave is; how big the wave is; what it's shape is like; where the wave might break and release the energy

SUMMATIVE ASSESSMENT
Analyze Facts

2. To correctly answer the question, students must recall their observations from the Hands-On Activity.

Lesson 1 What Are Waves? 167

LESSON 1 Engage • Explore/Explain • Elaborate • **Evaluate**

LESSON CHECK, continued

3. If students get stuck on this question, remind them of the parts, or structures, of a wave. They will need that basic understanding to recall what the amplitude is.

4. Students should be able to answer this question based on information learned in Explorations 1 and 2. You may need to remind students of the relationship between wavelengths and what determines their size.

5. This item may be tricky for some students. Provide assistance by helping students think through each of the examples listed.

6. One of the terms in the word bank will not be used. Students should be able to answer this question by recalling information learned in Exploration 3.

---

3. Write *high* or *low* on each line to correctly describe the amplitude of each sound.

    high   low   low   high

4. In the second column of the table, write *long* or *short* to correctly describe the wavelength of each wave.

surfing wave	long
seismic wave	long
tuba	long
dog whistle	short

5. Which of the following are examples of wave interactions? Select all that apply.
   a. **a full orchestra playing a song**
   b. moving a spring back and forth quickly
   c. **having two spotlights on a performer**
   d. **watching a movie in surround sound**
   e. tuning a piano to the correct notes
   f. **wearing noise canceling headphones on an airplane**

6. Choose the words or phrases that make each sentence correct.

| cancel | separate | noise-canceling headphones | theater spotlights |

__Noise-canceling headphones__ are devices that __cancel__ out unwanted sounds. __Theater spotlights__ are devices that also show how waves can interact. When only one of these objects is used, waves do not combine.

168

168 Unit 3 Waves and Information Transfer

LESSON 1

Lesson Roundup

A. Which of these are evidence that ocean waves have energy? Select all of the correct answers.
  a. They can combine or cancel each other out.
  b. They need a medium in which to move.
  c. They make things wet.
  d. They crash when they hit shore.

B. Which of these are true? Select all of the correct answers.
  a. All waves move from up and down.
  b. Some waves don't need a medium in which to travel.
  c. Some waves lack troughs and crests.
  d. All waves move back and forth.
  e. Some waves transfer energy and some transfer matter.

C. Label each part of the wave.
  a. crest
  b. trough
  c. wavelength
  d. amplitude

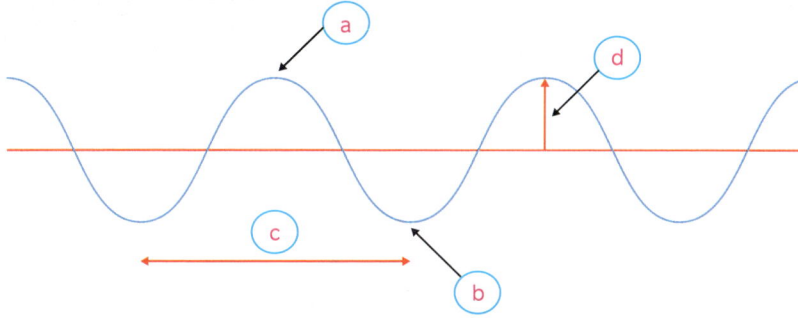

D. What else have you learned about waves in this lesson?
Possible answer: Sound waves have volume, but light waves do not. Sound is a wave that can be heard but not seen. Waves can join to form larger or louder waves. Or they can cancel each other out. Energy in some waves moves in the same direction as the matter through which the waves pass. Energy in other waves moves at right angles to the movement of the matter.

Lesson Roundup

DCI PS4.A Waves Properties

This lesson summary enables students to quickly revisit key points and prepare for tests.

A. To clarify students' understanding of the properties of waves, have them revisit Explorations 1, 2, and 3. You may also remind students that more information regarding ecosystems and their effects can be found in Exploration 2.

It may also be necessary to remind students that waves do not just refer to the waves from the ocean so that they do not become confused or stumped by the distractor. **PS4.A**

B. Students may wish to scan Explorations 1 and 2 before responding. Remind students to visualize the parts of a wave by recalling how the diagrams of waves were labeled. **PS4.A**

C. Students have spent a lot of time studying the parts of a wave in Explorations 2 and 3. If students need additional support, encourage them to think about the names for the parts of the waves and see whether the names themselves can provide some clues. Use guiding questions to help them if they get stuck. **PS4.A**

D. Give students a chance to scan Explorations 1, 2, and 3 and pick out information that was not covered in the rest of the questions on the page. **PS4.A**

LESSON 2
How Does Light Reflect?

Building to the Performance Expectation

The learning experiences in this lesson prepare students for mastery of:

4-PS4-2 Develop a model to describe that light reflecting from objects and entering the eye allows objects to be seen.

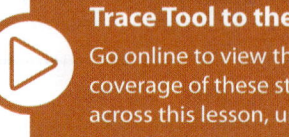

Trace Tool to the NGSS
Go online to view the complete coverage of these standards across this lesson, unit, and time.

 **Science & Engineering Practices**

 Disciplinary Core Ideas

 **Crosscutting Concepts**

Developing and Using Models
Develop and/or use models to describe and/or predict phenomena.
▶ VIDEO Developing and Using Models

Constructing Scientific Explanations
Use evidence to construct and explanation.
▶ VIDEO Constructing Explanations

PS4.B Electromagnetic Radiation
An object can be seen when light reflected from its surface enters the eyes.

Cause and Effect
Cause-and-effect relationships are routinely identified.

Energy and Matter
Energy can be transferred in various ways and between objects.
▶ VIDEO Energy

 CONNECTIONS TO MATH

MP.4 Model with mathematics.

4.G.A.1 Draw points, lines, line segments, rays, angles (right, acute, obtuse), and perpendicular and parallel lines. Identify these in two-dimensional figures.

4.MD.A.1 Solve problems involving measurement and conversion of measurements.

 CONNECTIONS TO ENGLISH LANGUAGE ARTS

L.4.4.B Use common, grade-appropriate Greek and Latin affixes and roots as clues to the meaning of a word (e.g., telegraph, photograph, autograph).

L.4.4.C Consult reference materials (e.g., dictionaries, glossaries, thesauruses), both print and digital, to find the pronunciation and determine or clarify the precise meaning of key words and phrases.

RI.4.2 Determine the main idea of a text and explain how it is supported by key details; summarize the text.

SL.4.5 Add audio recordings and visual displays to presentations when appropriate to enhance the development of main ideas or themes.

170A Unit 3 Waves and Information Transfer

Supporting All Students, All Standards

Integrating the Three Dimensions of Learning

In this lesson, students will investigate how light interacts with the surface of objects to form an image that we can see **(DCI PS4.B)**. Students will develop and use models to manipulate a variety of objects **(SEP Developing and Using Models)** in order to observe how the behavior of light changes the images sent to our eyes and perceived by our brains. By investigating how light interacts with mirrors and lenses **(CCC Cause and Effect)**, students will deepen their understanding of the development of many useful tools and technologies that utilize light. Students do so by asking and answering questions, carrying out investigations, analyzing and interpreting data, and communicating information.

 **Professional Development** Go online to view professional development videos with strategies to integrate CCCs and SEPs, including the ones used in this lesson.

Extra Hands-On Activity: Looking Around a Corner

How Can Reflection Help Someone See?

Pairs
40–50 minutes

Before beginning this activity, gather a variety of materials for students to use when they build their periscopes, such as small plastic mirrors, modeling clay, masking tape, scissors, one-quart milk and juice cartons, and an assortment of cardboard and cardboard boxes. Have mirrors available beforehand to students so that they can explore how mirrors reflect light and images.

Students should design a method to use at least two mirrors and the materials to develop an instrument that enables them to see around a corner or over a taller space, such as the top of a bookshelf. You may wish to assign conditions to the design project, such as their design must be able to be worn or the user must be able to read text in the reflection of the mirrors. Students should be able to use their periscopes to see around a corner without being seen themselves.

 This activity can support mastery of this Science and Engineering Practice: **Developing and Using Models**

Preassessment

Have students complete the lesson pre-test online or see the Assessment Guide.

Build on Prior Knowledge

Students should already know and be prepared to build on the following concepts:
- When light is present, people can see objects.
- There are many sources of light, but the initial energy for all light sources comes from the sun.
- Light travels through space in straight lines as waves of energy.

Differentiate Instruction

Lesson Vocabulary
- energy
- light
- transparent
- opaque
- shadow

Students may not know the term *transparent*, but they may have seen the word associated with transparent tape.

Ask: What would you use transparent tape for? *to join together the two edges of a piece of paper that has ripped*

Ask: Why is it important for the tape to be transparent? *If the tape is transparent, you can see through it and you won't be able to tell that the paper was ripped.*

ELL/ELD Strategy

Give students ripped paper, newspaper, magazine articles and tell them to try and tape them back together as best they can so that you can't tell where they were ripped. This can only be done if the tape is *transparent*.

Ask: Is plastic wrap transparent? Why/why not? *Yes, plastic wrap is transparent because you can see through it.*

Lesson 2 How Does Light Reflect? **170B**

LESSON 2   **Engage** • Explore/Explain • Elaborate • Evaluate

ENGAGE: Lesson Phenomenon

Lesson Objective

To describe the effects of matter on light, identify how light interacts with mirrors, lenses, prisms, and non-reflective surfaces due to their unique properties.

About This Image

Light exists and reflects in space! If something has a reflective surface, such as a mirror, then light can bounce off of it. The reflection of light is not just limited to Earth.

 SEP **Developing and Using Models**

Alternative Engage Strategy

Now You See It; Now You Don't 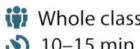 Whole class
⏱ 10–15 min

Each student should have a piece of paper and pencil or pen. Then ask students to close their eyes. If there are window coverings in the room, be sure they are closed. Turn off computer monitors (or anything that gives off light) and turn off the lights. Place a series of random objects on your desk or at some place in the front of the room that is visible to all. The objects can be anything that wasn't there before—a bag of marbles, a poster, a banana, a frying pan, etc. Ask students to be still and on the count of three, open their eyes and jot down objects they can see on your desk that weren't there before. Only give them 3–5 seconds (not enough time for their eyes to adjust to the dark). Now turn on the lights. Again, tell them to open their eyes and jot down objects they can see on your desk that weren't there before.

Ask: Which of your lists is longer—what you saw in the dark, or what you saw in the light? *The light list should be longer.*

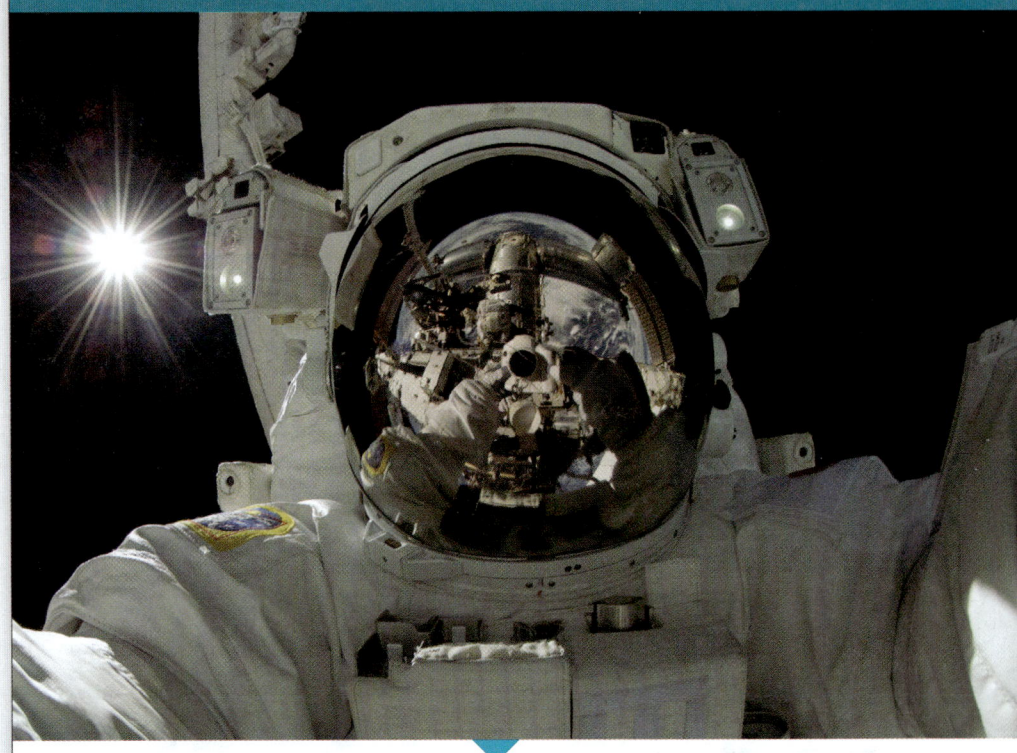

LESSON 2

How Does Light Reflect?

Even astronauts take selfies! All visible light, bounces off certain surfaces, such as mirrors. Light bouncing off our eyes allows us to read these words.

By the end of this lesson . . .
you'll be able to explain how light interacts with different surfaces and why people can see the things they do.

170

Unit 3 Waves and Information Transfer

Can You Explain It?

Telescopes like this one can be used to capture light from objects in space. This nebula, which is a cloud of dust and gases, is millions of kilometers from Earth. So how can we see it?

1. How does a telescope allow us to see things that are millions of kilometers away from us?

   Students should respond based on the preliminary observations they can make of the images.

Tip

Learn more about waves in What Are Waves? and how energy transfers through waves in How Is Energy Transferred?

 EVIDENCE NOTEBOOK Look for this icon to help you gather evidence to answer the question above.

171

Can You Explain It?

Students are asked to consider a telescope and a nebula in order to form some hypotheses about how telescopes work. To do so, students must rely on some prior knowledge about lenses and mirrors in telescopes and how they work together to allow us to see objects millions of kilometers from Earth. Students may or may not know at this point that telescopes capture the light from a nebula, for example, and then manipulate the light in order to form an image. Urge students not to worry about whether their answers are correct but just to write down their initial thoughts. They should expect their ideas to expand as they progress through the explorations. They will have an opportunity to revise their answers when they revisit these questions at the end of the lesson.

Collaboration

Draw, Pair, Share Put students together at a table or station in groups of 3–4. Put a light microscope in front of each group, or one in front of the class for everyone to see. If microscopes aren't available, a picture of a light microscope will suffice. Have students draw some individual microscope parts and annotate their drawings. Tell them to sketch their ideas about the parts of a microscope that may be similar to a telescope. Have them pair up and share their ideas about how these technologies allow us to see objects that are microscopic and far away.

EVIDENCE NOTEBOOK

Encourage students to use an appropriate graphic organizer, such as main idea and supporting details, to set up their notebook for this lesson.

Find more strategies in the online ELA handbook.

Lesson 2 How Does Light Reflect? 171

LESSON 2   Engage • **Explore/Explain** • Elaborate • Evaluate

EXPLORATION 1 Reflection and Our Eyes

HANDS-ON ACTIVITY Pairs 15-20 mins
Disappearing Coins

3D Learning Objective

SEP Developing and Using Models

Students use pennies in a pan as a model to investigate how images differ when light interacts with air and water.

DCI PS4.B Electromagnetic Radiation

An object can be seen when light reflected from its surface enters the eyes. Students will draw conclusions about why they were able to see the pennies in a pan with water but not without.

Materials
In addition to the materials listed in the student edition, each student group will need a pitcher with water to add to their pan. Have paper towels handy to clean up spills. Also put a ruler at each station so students can draw straight lines to show how light moves.

Preparation
Set up stations ahead of time so that the activity runs smoothly. Make sure each station has a piece of masking tape (or duct tape, electrical tape, or painter's tape) to mark the floor.

Procedure
STEP 2 For safety, be sure each student group has a clear path. Ask each student to look out for his or her partner and issue a gentle warning if something is in the way.

STEP 3 Tell students to notice the position of each penny before they start pouring water in. You might need to remind them to use proper vocabulary. If they don't use the word *variable* in their answer, prompt them to add it by reminding them that in order to get accurate data, all *variables* except the one you are testing should remain the same in an experiment.

Objective
Collaborate to investigate light's affect on objects. Have you ever tossed coins into a fountain and made a wish? If so, then you have probably noticed that sometimes you can see the coins in the water and sometimes you can't. Is this magic? Not really. It has to do with how you see light and how it can bend.

Materials
• pennies
• shallow baking pan
• masking tape
• water

What question will you investigate to meet this objective?
Possible answer: How does light allow me to see or prevent me from seeing coins in a pan of water?

Procedure

STEP 1 Place a few pennies into a shallow baking dish.

STEP 2 Slowly walk backwards while keeping an eye on the pennies. Stop when you can no longer see them over the side of the pan. Mark your spot on the floor with masking tape.

What is the masking tape for?
Possible answer: The masking tape shows where you should stand. If you stand in the wrong place, you may be able to still see the pennies.

STEP 3 Slowly add water to the pan until it is just about full. Make sure the coins stay in the same place.

Why do the coins need to remain in the same spot?
All variables, except one, must be kept the same to gather accurate data.

172

Student Lab Worksheet and complete Teacher Support available online.

172 Unit 3 Waves and Information Transfer

STEP 4 Stand on the spot you have marked on the floor. Look at the coins in the pan. Draw what you observe below. Use lines that show how light moves from the coins to your eye. Drain the water from the dish and have your partner repeat this activity.

[drawing space]

Analyze Your Results

STEP 5 How did what you and your partner observe change when the water was added?

Without the water, I couldn't see the coins from a distance but with the water, the coins could be seen again.

STEP 6 Stick a pencil straight down into the pan. Look at it from the side of the pan. What do you see? What does this tell you about how light moves?

Possible answer: The pencil looks bent. Light must also bend when it moves from the air to the water in the pan.

Draw Conclusions

STEP 7 What can you claim about light in making the coins visible?

Students may state that light bends as it moves from the air into the water. This causes the brain to think the coins have moved.

STEP 8 Does light always behave in this way? Cite evidence to explain your answer.

Yes. Both my partner and I observed the same things. At first neither of us could see the pennies but after water was added, they could be seen again as if they'd moved.

173

Connection to Math

Ask: Why did you draw the light coming at you? Students should explain that the light from the penny is what allows you to see it.

MP.4 Model with mathematics.

Analyze Your Results

STEP 5 Circulate the room to be sure that students observed a change in what they were able to see when water was added.

Draw Conclusions

STEP 7 If students struggle, give them a short word bank (light, air, water, eye, brain) and have them add these words to their drawing from step 4 to make connections.

Claims, Evidence, and Reasoning

Have one student group work with another group to discuss each other's claims and evidence from steps 7 and 8. The more evidence that students were able to see the pennies once water was added, the stronger their claim will be.

Scoring Rubric for Hands-On Activity	
3	investigation done correctly, results drawn accurately, analysis and conclusions reflect the results, claims follow logically from evidence
2	investigation and drawing done correctly but analysis and conclusions are inadequate or incomplete, claims follow evidence loosely
1	did not fully participate in activity, results drawn but incomplete or incorrect, claims are made but do not follow logically from evidence
0	procedure not followed or did not participate, unorganized, incorrect drawing, claims have errors

Lesson 2 How Does Light Reflect? 173

LESSON 2   Engage • **Explore/Explain** • Elaborate • Evaluate

EXPLORATION 1   Reflection and Our Eyes, continued

3D Learning Objective

Learn how light moves from place to place as a wave, either passing through or bouncing off of objects. **Develop and use models** in order to see **cause-and-effect** relationships between light and the objects it comes in contact with. Understand how eyes are adapted to collect light, and **objects can be seen when light reflected from their surfaces enters the eyes.** Examine how colors are due to which wavelengths of light are absorbed or reflected by a given object.

Build on Prior Knowledge

Before students can start thinking about how light behaves, they should be reminded of the basic properties of light. Remind students that light moves very quickly, and that light rays move in one direction until they hit an object.

Ask: What are some natural sources of light? sunlight, fire, lightning, and stars

DCI PS4.B Electromagnetic Radiation

When you are sitting in a dark room with the blinds closed, you are not exposed to any natural light coming from the sun or stars. If you turn on your computer in the room, suddenly you can see.

Ask: Why can you see in a dark room when you turn on an electrical device such as a tablet or computer? These devices give off light.

EXPLORATION 1

Reflection and Our Eyes

What Do You See?

Imagine you are in a windowless room. There are no lights. Can you see anything? Of course not! Why? You need light to see. Light travels from place to place as a wave. It may come from the sun, a candle, or a flashlight. Once light reaches its target, it might pass through the target. Or it may bounce back. Read these pages to find out more about light.

Most people close the window blinds in their bedrooms at night to make the room darker. By not letting light into the room, many people can sleep through the night.

When window blinds are open, light can enter the room. People need light to see things. With the blinds open, much of the outside light can enter the room.

2. Why can't you see outside with the blinds closed?
Students should be able to deduce that sunlight cannot pass through closed blinds. Light is needed to see.

174

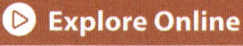 Students can learn more about reflection online.

174   Unit 3 Waves and Information Transfer

This box allows light to pass through it. The box is **transparent,** which means light can pass through it. A car window can be transparent also.

This box allows some, but not all, light to pass through it. The box is **translucent,** meaning some light can pass through it. Waxed paper is also translucent.

This box prevents any light from passing through it. The box is **opaque,** which means light cannot pass through it. Most window blinds are opaque.

All, Some, None

3. On the lines, identify each material as *opaque, translucent,* or *transparent.*

opaque

transparent

translucent

transparent

opaque

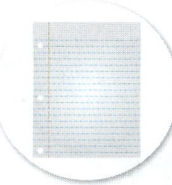
translucent

EVIDENCE NOTEBOOK What type of material is a telescope mirror? How does it interact with light?

SEP Developing and Using Models

Ask: Name something that is transparent. Accept all reasonable responses like windows or air.

> ### Differentiate Instruction
> **ELL: Use of Realia** Have students work in small groups of 3 or 4. Turn off the lights in the room and give each student group a variety of items (some transparent, some translucent, and some opaque) and a flashlight. Have students shine the light through the objects and then classify them as *transparent, translucent,* or *opaque.*

CCC Cause and Effect

Have students make a cause-and-effect table, similar to the one below, to practice with the terms *transparent, translucent,* and *opaque.*

CAUSE	EFFECT
Windows are transparent.	Light passes through windows.
Tomatoes are opaque.	Light does not pass through tomatoes.
Waxed paper is translucent.	Some light can pass through waxed paper.

EVIDENCE NOTEBOOK

Students should reason that light bounces off mirrors in a telescope. The mirrors are simply smooth surfaces with shiny, dark backgrounds that reflect very well. The dark surface makes it opaque, which means that light cannot pass through it.

Lesson 2 How Does Light Reflect?

LESSON 2 Engage • **Explore/Explain** • Elaborate • Evaluate

EXPLORATION 1 Reflection and Our Eyes, continued

CCC Cause and Effect

Reflectors are a perfect example of a cause-and-effect relationship. Waves bounce off when they hit a reflective object or obstacle (cause) and a reflection can be seen (effect)!

Ask: Why do people put solar panels on their homes? *to collect light and produce energy to power their homes*

Differentiated Instruction

ELL: Word Discovery Solar cells are small devices that convert solar energy into electricity. Many solar cells make up a solar panel. Solar cells are also called photovoltaic cells. The terms *solar* and *photovoltaic* are important concepts to help learn about reflection, but they will make even more sense in each student's primary language. Be sure to relate the following terms with their French and Spanish versions and allow students to say them in their primary language during classroom discussions:

ENGLISH	SPANISH	FRENCH
solar	solar	solaire
photovoltaic cell	celda fotovoltaica	cellule photovoltaique

You might also want to point out the root words:
photo = light
voltaic = electricity

Misconception Alert Many students think that only shiny objects they can see themselves in reflect light. Be sure to discuss how light can be reflected off of any object. While many reflective surfaces are shiny, even ones that are opaque can reflect light.

Bouncing Waves

Look in the mirror. What do you see? Your reflection looking back at you! A **reflection** is the bouncing of waves when they hit an obstacle. Anything you can see is either a light source or is reflecting light. In the case of your reflection, the obstacle is the back surface of the mirror.

So how does a mirror work? A piece of glass is polished, and then painted with shiny silver paint on one side. When light hits the layer of paint, it is reflected. Many other things can reflect light, too.

Common Reflectors

4. View the images and read the captions to learn more about some surfaces that reflect.

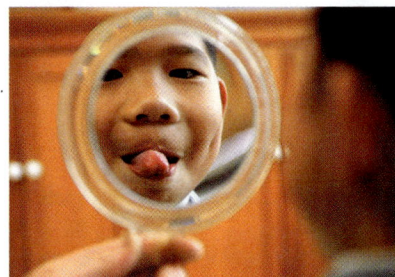 

Mirrors cause light to bounce off them. The image in a mirror is backwards because of the way the light reflects from the mirror.

A disco ball is made of many tiny mirrors. When light hits them, it reflects and makes colored spots on the walls.

Some of the sunlight that hits solar panels is absorbed and some is reflected. Solar panels change sunlight into electricity.

Water is a good reflector of light. Sunlight is bouncing off water in this lake. When the lake is perfectly still, the water can act like a mirror.

Not all reflective surfaces are flat. This sculpture is called Cloud Gate. It is located in Chicago, Illinois. Even though it is not flat, it is very smooth, and light can still bounce off its surface.

As you have read, light can be reflected off of different surfaces. And the surface does not have to be flat to reflect light.

The color of an object can also impact how light is reflected. Dark objects usually do not reflect as much light as light-color objects. If you are out after dark, you want to be sure to wear light-color clothing. This way, car headlights will reflect off your clothes and allow drivers to see you.

5. Identify three other things that reflect light. How do you know they are reflecting light waves?

Possible answer: A chrome bumper on a car reflects light, causing the light to bounce off the bumper. This makes the bumper appear shiny. My hand also reflects light. I know this because I can see it. A metal spoon reflects light because I can see a reflection of myself in it.

SEP Constructing Scientific Explanations

Cloud Gate is a sculpture, a model that was created to reflect the beautiful sky and famous skyline of Chicago, Illinois. People have been visiting it for years to observe the beauty of reflection. Some people have imagined what the sculpture would look like if the artist Anish Kapoor painted Cloud Gate with the darkest black paint available.

Ask: Do you think Cloud Gate would still reflect the skyline? Why or why not? No, it wouldn't reflect the skyline because the newly black surface would absorb most of the light instead of reflecting it.

> ## Differentiate Instruction
>
> **Extension** Students that are curious or those that have an interest in art may want to do some additional research about outdoor art that takes advantage of scientific principles for their effect. You may give them some suggestions, like Burke's Quantum Stream or The Extreme Water Cycle.

DCI PS4.B Electromagnetic Radiation

Objects can be seen when light reflected from their surfaces enters our eyes. But the color of an object also has an impact on how light is reflected. Since white does not absorb a lot of light, it reflects it back at you. So white is a good color to wear if you are out after dark.

If you have ever been to a play, you might have noticed that the stage technicians (people that deal with props, changing scenes, sound, etc.) wear black.

Ask: Why do stage technicians wear black? Black absorbs the most light and reflects very little. Stage technicians wear black so that they are not seen and can change scenery and props between scenes. The black clothing helps them blend in with the darkness.

Lesson 2 How Does Light Reflect?

LESSON 2   Engage • **Explore/Explain** • Elaborate • Evaluate

EXPLORATION 1   Reflection and Our Eyes, continued

SEP Developing and Using Models

The four pictures on these pages serve as visual models that will help students understand that some objects reflect a lot of light and some objects reflect a little light, and this variation is not just due to whether the objects are transparent, translucent, or opaque. The texture of an object can also make a difference.

> ## Differentiated Instruction
>
> **RTI/Extra Support** It can be very difficult for students to comprehend what objects look like on a microscopic level. The pictures in the book may not seem real to them. Obtain a light microscope and some small, thin samples of objects for them to look at. Some great examples would be thin cloth, foil, or newspaper. Let them see for themselves that when something appears smooth, it can have bumps and ridges at a microscopic level.

DCI PS4.B Electromagnetic Radiation

An object can be seen when light reflected from its surface enters the eyes. During the day, the sun illuminates objects and reflected light allows us to see them. The retina in your eyes detects light waves and sends signals to your brain.

Ask: Have you ever wondered why space is black, even though the sun's rays travel throughout it? *Some students might know that space is black because there are so few objects in space to reflect light in large enough amounts for you to detect it that it appears dark.*

Smooth Waves Ahead

You've learned that many surfaces are smooth and reflective. However, not all smooth things reflect light. There are some surfaces that look smooth to the eyes and even feel smooth to the touch. But when those surfaces are magnified, you can see they are very bumpy. This may impact the surface's ability to reflect light.

Look at the photos on these pages to see how some everyday objects look under a microscope. Even though some objects may appear smooth, their surfaces are really bumpy. The bumps scatter light in different directions making an object less reflective.

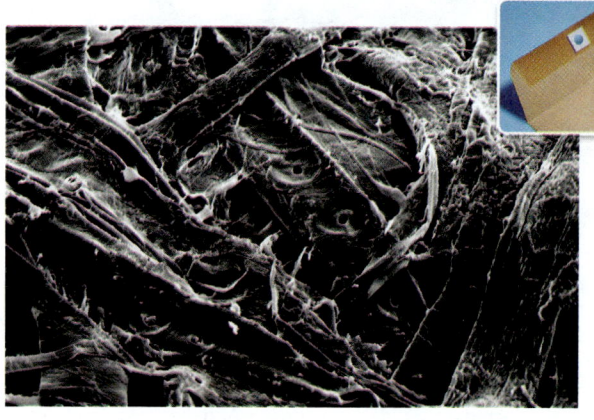
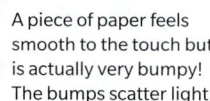

A piece of paper feels smooth to the touch but is actually very bumpy! The bumps scatter light.

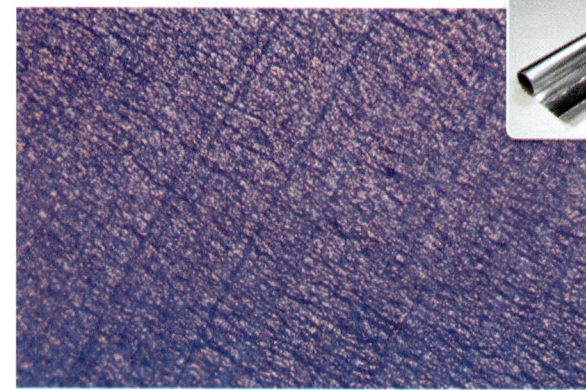

Aluminum is a metal that is used for many things, including foil used in the kitchen. It has a very reflective surface.

Hook and loop fasteners helps objects stick together. It is not reflective.

Gold is a metal often used to make jewelry. The surface of gold is usually reflective.

6. Which three objects will *best* reflect light?
   a. a mirror
   b. a black T-shirt
   c. a brown piece of paper
   d. a stapler
   e. a piece of aluminum foil
   f. a gold necklace

Collaboration

Feedback Have students work with a partner to discuss their answers to Item 6. Some students may think of staplers as metallic items and put stapler as the correct answer. staplers do reflect light, mirrors, a piece of aluminum foil, and a gold necklace are the *best* answers. A black T-shirt and a brown piece of paper reflect the least amount of light. Shiny surfaces are the most reflective. Have students explain to each other why they believe their answers are correct.

CCC Cause and Effect

Give students the following objects: a mirror, a balled-up piece of aluminum foil, a bumpy golf ball, and a flat sheet of paper. Have them make quick sketches of each object, and then ask them to sketch rays of light coming into each object at an angle and then reflecting off the object.

Ask: How are the rays of light coming off the surface of a smooth object different from those coming off a bumpy surface? Light rays coming off a smooth surface always bounce off at the same angle they hit the surface. Light rays coming off a bumpy surface reflect off in many directions.

Connection to Engineering

Tell students that NASA engineers also use gold to make astronaut helmet visors and other equipment. In space, the sun radiates heat to astronauts and their equipment. To help control the surface temperature of any object that is exposed to the sun's heat waves, NASA wraps equipment in metal that will best reflect the heat away and keep the equipment from getting too hot. Gold, just like the diagram on this page, is a great choice for reflecting infrared radiation.

ETS1.C Optimizing the Design Solution

LESSON 2   Engage • **Explore/Explain** • Elaborate • Evaluate

EXPLORATION 1 Reflection and Our Eyes, continued

DCI PS4.B Electromagnetic Radiation

Ask: How do shadows form? If light shines onto an object, and the object blocks the light, a shadow forms in the area behind the object where the light cannot reach.

> ## Differentiate Instruction
>
> **ELL: Modeling** Stage a demonstration of how shadows work using classroom materials. Involve students in the activity so they get a hands-on understanding of shadows and light. Ask students to observe what they see.

HANDS-ON Apply What You Know
Seeing Color
This demonstration focuses on colored filters. Plan ahead by getting theatrical gels for spotlights. Call on many students to participate in this activity so you get a wide range of colors. Students can create charts individually or in small groups, or you can create a chart as a whole class on the front board.

Scoring Guideline
An excellent score consists of participation and involvement in the charting exercise.

From the Sun to Your Eyes

You know that to see something, there has to be light. Your eyes are specially adapted to collect as much light as possible. Imagine you're outside on a sunny day, playing catch with a friend. You can see your friend standing a few meters away. You can see the object she's tossing to you. All of this is possible because light is bouncing off everything and entering your eyes.

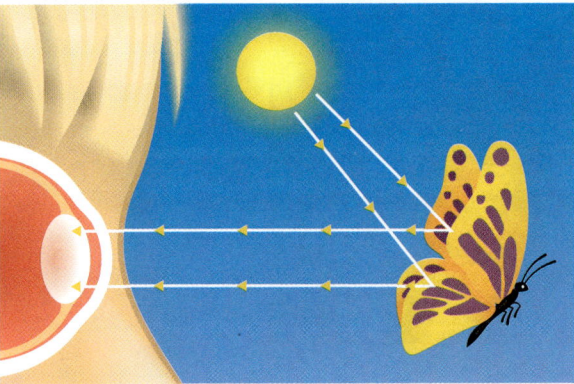

In order to see an object, it must be emitting light, like the sun, or light needs to bounce off it. What happens on a sunny day? Light from the sun reaches Earth. The light reflects off an object. Then, the light hits the surface of the eye.

7. What would happen to the path of light if it hit a transparent surface like a glass window?
   a. The light would change direction.
   b. The light would reflect off it.
   c. The light would pass through it.
   d. The light would scatter all around.

>
> **HANDS-ON** Apply What You Know
> ### Seeing Color
>
> 8. How do colored filters change the way we see? Using colored theatrical gels for spotlights, observe the clothing of your classmates. What does a red shirt look like through a red gel filter? Does a green shirt appear the same through the same red filter? Make a chart to describe what different colors look like through the gels. What patterns do you see in your data?

180

Let's Make Colors!

Light is made up of many different colors all blended together. Each color of the rainbow has a different wavelength. As a result, you see a red apple as red because the red wavelengths are being reflected by the apple's skin. The other wavelengths are absorbed by the apple.

These four objects are reflecting and absorbing light differently. The bowling ball is absorbing all wavelengths of visible light. The blue balloon is reflecting blue wavelengths but absorbing all the others. The volleyball is reflecting all wavelengths. The orange is reflecting orange wavelengths but absorbing other wavelengths of light.

9. Look at the object to the right. Explain how it is absorbing and reflecting visible light.

A lemon looks yellow because it reflects yellow wavelengths of light and absorbs red, orange, green, blue, and violet wavelengths.

Putting It Together

10. Select the words to correctly complete each sentence.

| white   black   opaque   transparent |

Light reflects from ___opaque___ surfaces and passes through ___transparent___ ones. ___White___ objects reflect all wavelengths of light. ___Black___ objects absorb all visible light.

SEP Constructing Scientific Explanations

The four objects shown act as models to illustrate the concept that visible light looks white but really contains many different colors blended together. When an object appears red, it is because red is the wavelength of light being reflected back at you. The red object is absorbing all other wavelengths.

Misconception Alert Many students believe that color is a property of an object, separate from light. Be sure you explain that color is a property that is perceived by the "receiver" of the image. Color is determined by which wavelengths of light are absorbed or reflected, so color and light go hand in hand!

CCC Cause and Effect

Reflection of certain wavelengths of light (cause) form color (effect). When students answer item 9, be sure their answer includes not only that yellow light is being reflected, but also that all other wavelengths of light are being absorbed. Encourage students to always think about light entering and leaving an object.

FORMATIVE ASSESSMENT

These questions will help you determine whether or not it is time to move on. If students really understand the reflection of light, they will use the terms *opaque* and *transparent* correctly, and they will be able to distinguish between black and white objects.

Ask: Imagine you step inside a closet with no light and close the door. Open your eyes. What is the "color" you see? You wouldn't see any color. It would appear black because no light is available to reflect off of any objects.

Lesson 2 How Does Light Reflect?   181

LESSON 2 Engage • **Explore/Explain** • Elaborate • Evaluate

EXPLORATION 1 Reflection and Our Eyes, continued

HANDS-ON ACTIVITY Pairs   1 class period
Reflecting on Angles

3D Learning Objective

SEP **Developing and Using Models**

Students make their own model of reflected objects to investigate how the angles of reflection affect light.

Materials
You can get small mirrors in convenience stores and online teaching resource stores, or you can substitute "mirror sheets" or "mirror boards" available at craft stores. You can also substitute map tacks, map pins, or thumbtacks for the pushpins.

Preparation
Gather the materials for this activity ahead of time, as it may be challenging to get a class set of small mirrors. It would be ideal for each student to complete this activity on their own, but student pairs will suffice if there aren't enough supplies or if you want specific student grouping.

Procedure
STEP 2 Students may have difficulty answering this question because it might not be clear why the position of the pushpins matters.

Ask: Once we put in all of the pushpins, what do we hope to find out in this activity? **This activity will show us the angles of light reflection. Changing the placement of the pushpins will change the angles of reflection.**

Reflecting on Angles

Consider This Have you ever been to a carnival that had a fun house? Sometimes these places have fun mirrors. When you look into them, your reflection can be squashed, stretched out, or even pencil thin. How do these mirrors work? Well it all has to do with the reflection of light. These mirrors are bent in a certain way. This bending changes the angle at which light hits them to make the funny images you see.

Materials
- 10 cm × 10 cm piece of cardboard
- small mirror
- modeling clay
- 3 pushpins of different colors
- labels
- metric ruler
- protractor

Objective

Collaborate to investigate how angles of reflection affect light.

What question will you answer during your investigation?
Possible answer: How does changing the angle at which light strikes a surface affect light?

Procedure

STEP 1 Stand the mirror up at the end of the cardboard using the clay.

STEP 2 Label the pushpins PP1, PP2, and PP3. Place PP1 and PP2 into the cardboard 5 cm from the mirror.

Why does the position of the pushpins matter?
Possible answer: The pushpins will be used for finding angles of reflections.

STEP 3 Position yourself so that PP1 lines up with the reflection of PP2.

182

Student Lab Worksheet and complete Teacher Support available online.

Unit 3 Waves and Information Transfer

STEP 4 Put PP3 into the cardboard at the end of the mirror in front of PP2's reflection. PP1, PP3, and the reflection of PP2 should make a straight line.

STEP 5 Draw lines on the cardboard to connect PP3 with PP1 and PP2.

STEP 6 Draw lines along the front of the mirror and then remove it.

STEP 7 Use a protractor to measure the angles between each of the PP lines and the mirror line.

Why did you remove the mirror during this step of the investigation?

The reflection has been recorded, so it will be easier to use the protractor with the mirror no longer on the table.

STEP 8 Draw a picture of your cardboard as seen from above. Include the point each pin forms as well as the angle formed by the pins.

Check students' drawings. They should show two identical angles.

Differentiate Instruction

RTI/Extra Support Pair students according to mixed ability so students can support each other during the activity and then again during the analysis. Some students may not have extensive experience with protractors, and working with a partner that has used protractors takes the pressure off.

CCC Cause and Effect

Make sure students understand that the angle of reflection is caused by the position of the pushpin on the cardboard.

STEP 4 Ask students to stop at this point and check in with you if PP1, PP3, and the reflection of PP2 do not make a straight line. Make adjustments before they start to draw and measure angles.

DCI PS4.B Electromagnetic Radiation

Remind students that a key factor in reflection is a smooth surface. When light coming from the pushpins strikes the smooth surface of the mirror, the light rays bounce back at the same angle. That is why the pushpins were clearly visible in the mirror.

Connection to Math

Students use rulers and protractors in this activity to draw lines of reflection and then measure the angles they make as they place pushpins in the cardboard. Discuss *accuracy* with the students.

Ask: What does it mean to be accurate in an activity? It means nearness to the actual value.

4.G.A.1 Draw points, lines, line segments, rays, angles (right, acute, obtuse), and perpendicular and parallel lines.

Lesson 2 How Does Light Reflect?

LESSON 2 Engage • **Explore/Explain** • Elaborate • Evaluate

EXPLORATION 1 Reflection and Our Eyes, continued

Analyze Your Results

STEP 10 Pull the class together and discuss the answer to this question to be sure that all students understand the point of getting an initial straight line to form one ray needed for the angle.

> ### Claims, Evidence, and Reasoning
> Some students might say that light traveled in a straight line. Try to get them to expand their reasoning and make a specific claim—in this case, the light traveled from the pin to the mirror to their eyes.
>
> **Ask:** What evidence do you have that light was reflected? If there was no light, you would not be able to see the pushpins, and there would be no reflection in the mirror.

Draw Conclusions

STEP 12 Have students go back and change their models by moving one pushpin farther from the mirror to see how it affects the angle, and then moving the same pushpin closer to the mirror to observe the difference in the angle.

Scoring Rubric for Hands-On Activity	
3	investigation done correctly, results drawn accurately, analysis and conclusions reflect the results, claims follow logically from evidence
2	investigation and drawing done correctly but analysis and conclusions are inadequate or incomplete, claims follow evidence loosely
1	did not fully participate in activity, results drawn but incomplete or incorrect, claims are made but do not follow logically from evidence
0	procedure not followed or did not participate, unorganized, incorrect drawing, claims have errors

184 Unit 3 Waves and Information Transfer

Analyze Your Results

STEP 9 What shape did the lines make when you recorded their angles? Why?
The lines are straight. This is because light travels in a straight line before it is reflected from a surface.

STEP 10 Why was it important to start this activity with PP1 and the reflection of PP2 in the same line?
Students should state that this was important to get an initial straight line to form one ray needed for making an angle.

Draw Conclusions

STEP 11 Use evidence from this activity to make a claim about how light travels and behaves when it strikes an object.
Students might have said that based on their observations, light travels in straight lines until it strikes an object and bounces off it to move in another straight line.

STEP 12 What effect would moving one of the pushpins farther from the mirror have on the angle?
Students should deduce that the angle between the two rays would get smaller and smaller the farther one pushpin was moved away from the mirror.

STEP 13 What are some other questions you have about how light reflects from a surface?
Possible questions: What would happen to the light if the mirror was curved? What would happen if I move the mirror farther from the light? What would happen if the pushpins were closer to each other?

EXPLORATION 2 Refraction and Lenses

EXPLORATION 2

Refraction and Lenses

Seeing Light

Light moves faster than any other wave or object, but its speed can change. Light moves much faster in air than it does in the water. When light hits a liquid like water it bends.

The sun is millions of kilometers away from Earth. Thus, it takes time for its light to reach us. The sunlight you see at any time left the sun eight minutes before you see it!

White light is made of different colors of light. So when white light shines through a prism or passes through raindrops, it is separated into the colors of the rainbow.

Do the Math

Convert Units of Time

11. The sun is millions of kilometers from Earth. When light leaves the sun, it takes eight minutes to reach Earth. It takes sunlight 12 minutes and 40 seconds to reach Mars. How much longer, in seconds does it take sunlight to reach Mars?

    60 seconds/~~minute~~ × 8 ~~minutes~~ = 480 seconds
    60 seconds/~~minute~~ × 12 ~~minutes~~ = 720 seconds
    720 seconds + 40 seconds = 760 seconds
    760 seconds − 480 seconds = 280 seconds

3D Learning Objective

Develop and use models to examine how lenses are used to alter the behavior of light. Students investigate the **cause-and-effect relationship** between light passing from one material into another and the bending of light waves. Students will also investigate how different types of lenses are incorporated into devices that help us use **the reflection and refraction of light** to our advantage.

 Energy and Matter

Less and less light can penetrate as you go deeper and deeper down in the ocean because sunlight that enters the ocean slows down when it transitions from air to water, and much of it gets absorbed by the water.

 PS4.B Electromagnetic Radiation

Ask: If you are scuba diving deep in the ocean, are objects visible? Why or why not? Yes, you can see objects because light can penetrate down in the ocean to the depth scuba divers can go.

 Do the Math

Convert Units of Time

4.MD.A.1 Solve problems involving measurement and conversion of measurements.

Ensure students know relative sizes of measurement units for time.

Ask: How many seconds are there in a minute? 60
Ask: How many minutes are there in an hour? 60

Remind students that when they are doing conversions, they should always ask themselves if the results of their conversions make sense. For example, when converting from one unit to its subunit, the result should be larger.

Lesson 2 How Does Light Reflect?

LESSON 2   Engage • **Explore/Explain** • Elaborate • Evaluate

EXPLORATION 2 Refraction and Lenses, continued

CCC Cause and Effect

The bending of light waves as they go from one medium to another causes the effect known as refraction.

> ### Differentiate Instruction
>
> **ELL: Use Realia** Demonstrate refraction, or give students the materials to demonstrate refraction themselves. Give student pairs a small glass or clear plastic container of water (the size of a drinking glass) and have them model refraction with a pencil, a ruler, or a straw. Have them look straight down into the glass and then from the side. Have the partners explain the phenomenon of refraction to one another using the words *light, bend, refraction, medium, speed,* and *direction.*
>
> **Ask:** Name a place outside where there is a change from air to water.   **the beach, a lake, a pond, a river**

DCI PS4.B Electromagnetic Radiation

Remember that an object can be seen when light reflected from its surface enters the eyes. Refraction can make objects appear bent to our eyes, but it's just an optical illusion!

Connection to Earth Science

The archerfish has visual adaptations to see and hunt insects outside and above the water, helping the archerfish get food from an area where other fish cannot! This ability gives archerfish an advantage.

LS4.C Adaptation

Breaking Straws

The next time you drink with a straw, take a closer look at it. If you look straight down into the glass, the straw will look straight. But from certain angles, it will appear as if the straw is broken. This is an optical illusion caused by refraction.

Refraction is the bending of light waves as they pass from one material to another. Light changes direction and speed when it hits a barrier. Look at the photos to see how refraction can affect how things appear.

12. Why does the straw in the photo appear to be bent?

Light changes both speed and direction as it travels from the air into the liquid. These changes in the light waves make the straw appear to be bent.

An archerfish is able to see insects on plants that are above the water. When the fish hunts for food, it watches an insect to set up its attack. To capture its prey, the fish squirts water out of its mouth, at just the right angle to account for refraction. The water hits the insect and knocks it into the water.

186

Unit 3 Waves and Information Transfer

To better understand refraction, think about the following. A group of students is walking in a straight line and at a fast pace.

When the students reach a line drawn on the ground, they slow down, which also causes them to change direction. Every time a student crosses the line, he or she does this.

These students represent light waves. The line on the ground is the boundary between any two materials. The shift is the refraction caused when the waves change direction and speed.

Language SmArts
Using Word Parts

13. Use a dictionary to divide the words *reflection* and *refraction* into parts. Write original definitions for each word using the definitions of its parts.

Re- means back, *frac* means to break, and *–tion* means the act of. Refraction means the act of breaking something back. *Flec* means to bend, so reflection means the act of bending back.

14. Chose the words to correctly complete each sentence.

| broken | medium | refraction |

_____Refraction_____ is the bending of a light wave. This happens when the wave changes _____medium_____. This interaction can make objects appear _____broken_____.

SEP Developing and Using Models

Actually seeing refraction can help students connect the word with the process. Try the collaboration below to encourage students to create their own models of refraction. Some students may want to sketch their ideas, and others might want to explain them aloud.

Collaboration

Think, Pair, Share Pair students and ask them to consider the student model of refraction shown on the student page. This would adequately provide a visual representation of what happens to light waves when they transition from one medium to another. Provide students time to brainstorm and develop their own models for refraction. Encourage them to come up with as many ideas as possible and write them down. Then come together as a class to share ideas. Give them an example to get them started. **A remote controlled toy car is driving across hardwood floors, and it rolls at an angle onto carpet. The toy changes direction because of a change in medium.**

Language SmArts
Using Word Parts
L.4.4.B Greek and Latin Roots
L.4.4.C Clarify Meaning

As students work to determine the meaning of the word parts of *reflection* and *refraction*, point out that the words have different roots, *flec* and *frac*, but they have the same prefix, *re-*, and the same suffix, *-tion*. Discuss with the class how the prefix and the suffix change the meaning of each root word.

Lesson 2 How Does Light Reflect?

LESSON 2 Engage • **Explore/Explain** • Elaborate • Evaluate

EXPLORATION 2 *Refraction and Lenses, continued*

 Cause and Effect

Because of the development and utilization of the lens, we can now see things that were not accessible to us before.

Ask: What do we mean when we say "cannot be seen with the unaided eye?" **It means only your eye, not aided by an optical device.**

> **Differentiate Instruction**
>
> **Extension** Some students might be interested in the history of the camera. Tell them that the very first camera was the pinhole camera that was used as far back as the year 1500. Have students research and then draw a timeline from 1500 to present time, showing how cameras developed.

DCI PS4.B Electromagnetic Radiation

Since mirrors are some of the best reflectors of light, it should not be surprising that mirrors are used in cameras to reflect the light that enters through the lenses. It is an interesting fact to note that the mirror flips up just before a picture is taken.

Ask: How do you think film works to save an image? **Film is coated with special light-sensitive chemicals. The light that comes into the camera causes a chemical reaction on the film that stores the image you are seeing.**

 EVIDENCE NOTEBOOK

Students should comment on how mirrors are flat, shiny surfaces, which are the best kind of objects for reflection of light waves. When light waves hit the mirror, the mirror reflects the light back at the same angle, creating the mirror image we see.

188 Unit 3 Waves and Information Transfer

Lenses

Some objects, such as cells, are too small to see with the unaided eye. Other objects, such as stars, are too far away. Over time, many tools have been invented to help people look at objects they otherwise would not be able to see.

Many of these tools contain lenses. A lens is a piece of plastic or glass that magnifies an object. Some lenses are curved; others are flat. Read on to find out more about how lenses have helped us.

Smile!

15. As you read about this camera, underline key phrases to help you remember how a camera such as this one works.

Have you ever used a camera? If so, you may know that it has several important parts. Cameras need light to take pictures. This light gets manipulated by the lenses in the camera. After the light comes through the lenses, it bounces off a mirror, reflects two more times inside a prism, and then forms an image in the eye piece.

The lens of this camera is a collection of curved pieces of glass that magnify an image. Larger lenses are able to refract more light than smaller lenses.

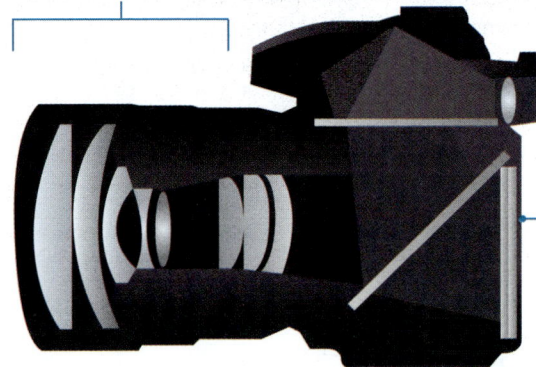

The mirror in this camera reflects the light that enters through the lenses and moves it toward the viewfinder. The mirror flips up just before a picture is taken.

EVIDENCE NOTEBOOK How do lenses and mirrors affect light?

188

Imagine you are out at sea on a boat. You see something in the distance but can't make out what it is. You take out your binoculars to get a better look. Binoculars are useful for seeing things that are far away. They use a series of lenses to collect and bend light to magnify an object. They work a lot like telescopes but are not as powerful.

Now imagine being at the park. You find a small pebble that has a bunch of shiny flecks in it. You want to get a better look at them, so you pull out your hand lens. Hand lenses are sometimes called magnifying glasses. They're great tools to use to see small things. They have curved lenses that change how the light goes through them to make things look bigger.

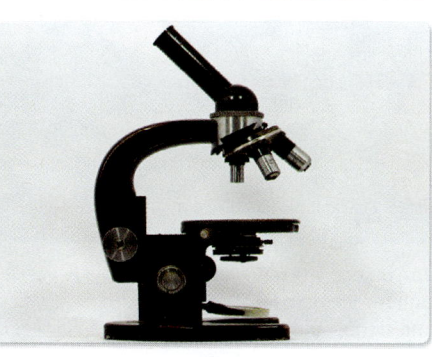

You know that there are many creatures on Earth too small to see with an unaided eye. But did you know that there are parts of these creatures that are really, really small? To see these small creatures and their parts, you could use a microscope. Like binoculars and hand lenses, microscopes use lenses to make objects look larger than they really are.

16. Which of the following refract light to produce images of objects? Select all that apply.

a. binoculars
b. hand lenses
c. windows in a house
d. car windshields
e. microscopes
f. mirrors

189

Connection to English Language Arts

It is easy to figure out what different optical devices do if you look up their root words. For example, the word *camera* comes from the Latin *camera obscura,* which describes a black box with a lens that could project images of external objects. Have students look up the root words and clarify the meanings of *microscope* and *binoculars.*

L.4.4.B Greek and Latin Roots
L.4.4.C Clarify Meaning

SEP Developing and Using Models

If you have access to a light microscope, review the parts with the students to show them the path of the light to the object you are viewing. This can just as easily be done with a labeled diagram if a microscope isn't available. Make sure students know that light has to pass through the object in order to see it, so objects under a light microscope must be very thin.

Collaboration

Draw, Pair Share Give each pair of students hand lenses or magnifying lenses and some objects to observe. Choose a field of view for everyone to use, for example, a 4 cm by 4 cm square. Have students draw what they see of the object with the naked eye and then draw the same object magnified with the lens. Then have students pair together to share their observations. The point here is just to let them observe how curved lenses change how the light goes through them to make images bigger.

LESSON 2 Engage • **Explore/Explain** • Elaborate • Evaluate

EXPLORATION 2 Refraction and Lenses, continued

DCI PS4.B Electromagnetic Radiation

We can see because of light. Your eye is actually very similar to a camera, and it has similar parts.

Ask: When light enters the eye, it is passing from air into a different medium. What happens to the light? It is refracted.

After light passes through, it travels through a thick, gel-like fluid called the *vitreous humour*. *Vitreous* means glassy and *humour* means fluid. The fluid provides support for other important parts of the eye. Vitreous humour is a clear fluid.

Ask: Why must this humour, or fluid, be clear? so light can pass through it
What is another name we give to objects that light can pass through? transparent

Light passes through the lens of your eye and is recorded on the back of your eye on a structure called the *retina*. The retina turns the message into an electrical signal that your brain can understand.

Connection to Life Science

Like all of the internal and external structures in our bodies, the structure of our eyes is uniquely and perfectly adapted to collect as much light as possible in order to enable vision.
LS1.A Structure and Function

Cause and Effect

Tell students that the relationship between structure and function, as seen in the structure of human lenses, is a cause-and-effect relationship. Because of the structure of our eye, we are able to collect light and interpret images in the world around us.

Ask: What is another structure/function or cause/effect relationship in the human body you can think of that allows us to sense the world around us? Our ears are specially designed with specific structures for hearing, and our tongue is designed with specific structures for tasting.

Human Lenses

You know that to see something, there needs to be light. Your eyes have special parts that collect visible light so that you can see the world around you. Just like a camera or a telescope, each of your eyes has a lens. The job of the lens is to focus the light.

Remember that light travels in a straight line to your eyes. Once the light enters your eyes, it goes through different parts of your eyes and brain before you see an image. Since light moves so fast, this process happens nearly instantly.

From the Sun to You

17. Use the information above, the drawing, and the information below to answer the question.

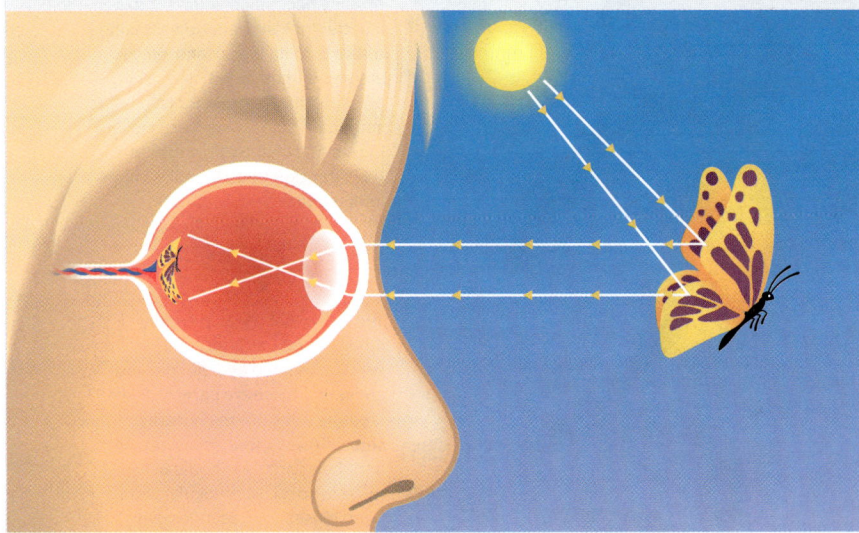

Light leaves the sun and then reflects off of an object. The reflected light hits the surface of the eye and travels through the lens to a focal point inside the eye. There the light is changed into signals and sent to the brain. The brain figures out the signals and you understand what you see.
What happens at the focal point inside the eye?

Light is converted to signals and sent to the brain.

190

190 Unit 3 Waves and Information Transfer

18. Write or diagram the process that produces vision into a flow chart showing six steps.

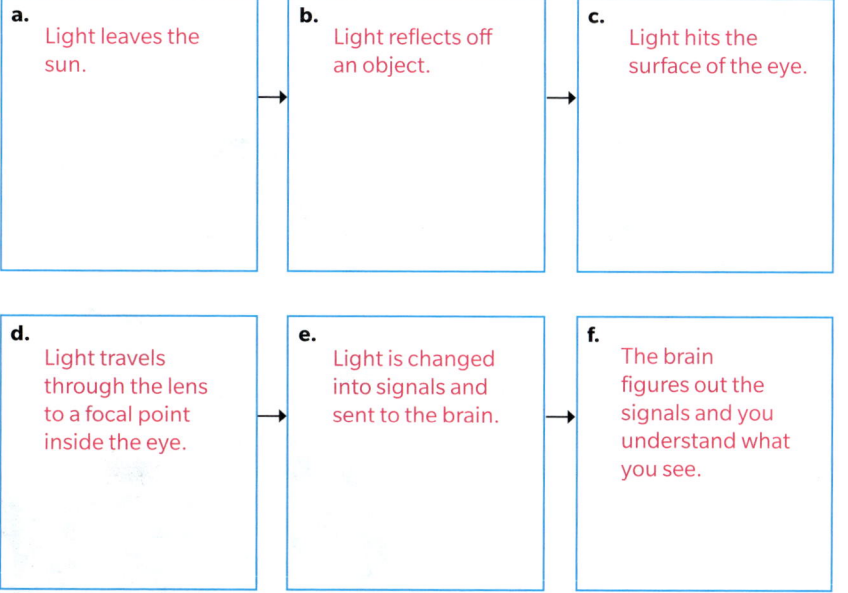

a. Light leaves the sun.
b. Light reflects off an object.
c. Light hits the surface of the eye.
d. Light travels through the lens to a focal point inside the eye.
e. Light is changed into signals and sent to the brain.
f. The brain figures out the signals and you understand what you see.

19. Choose the words to correctly complete each sentence.

| air | brain | eyes | light |
| spine | reflects | refracts | |

In order to see, __light__ must be present. Light __reflects__ off of objects and enters the __eyes__.

There it is changed into a signal that is passed to the __brain__. The signals are used to produce an image.

This is how you see things.

EVIDENCE NOTEBOOK How does the lens in your eye work to produce an image?

 Constructing Scientific Explanations

Flow charts allow students to put their ideas down in a logical order to show their understanding and possible misconceptions about a topic. Some students might express their understanding a little differently and, therefore, not use all of the boxes or even have need of additional boxes. Be available to show them how they can restructure their ideas if needed and undo their misconceptions to fine-tune their understanding of the process that produces vision.

Differentiate Instruction

ELL: Modeling Use a model to illustrate the process of how the eye works to enable vision. A 3D plastic model of the human eye would be best, but there are cheaper, paper alternatives that are 2D and will do the trick. If no models are available, pair students, give them printed color pictures of the eye that are not labeled, and have them work together to label any parts they know and annotate the path of light into the eye to ultimately form an image. Be sure to give students time and structure for thinking, enabling them to formulate individual ideas and share these ideas with a peer. Student pairs may volunteer to share with the class.

EVIDENCE NOTEBOOK

Students will write what they know about the how lenses work, and they may relate the lens in a human eye to a camera lens or the lens in a telescope, binoculars, or microscope. Be sure they know the main function of the lens—that it focuses light onto the back of the eye. It is not important at this point that they know the term *retina*. Remind them that the lens changes shape to make sure that the image on the back of the eye is as clear as possible.

Lesson 2 How Does Light Reflect? 191

LESSON 2   Engage • **Explore/Explain** • Elaborate • Evaluate

EXPLORATION 2   Refraction and Lenses, continued

CCC Cause and Effect

Lenses with different shapes have different effects on light rays. Eyeglasses use lenses of different shapes to bend light rays and correct vision.

DCI PS4.B Electromagnetic Radiation

We know that an object can be seen when light reflected from its surface enters the eyes. Students may not know what exactly goes wrong in a person's eyes when they need glasses. Tell them that usually people need glasses because the shape of their eyeball causes the light rays to bend in a different way. Some people have eyeballs that are too short, some are too long, and some are irregularly shaped.

Ask: What does it mean to be nearsighted? People have difficulty seeing objects that are far away.
What does it mean to be farsighted? People have difficulty seeing objects that are near.

Connection to English Language Arts

The compare and contrast table on this page is an excellent visual display for students to organize their knowledge about concave and convex lenses. Watch out for misunderstandings and statements that might be listed in the wrong column. Have students check each other's tables for correctness and ask questions if they need to. If you have a way to make an audio recording, have students work in pairs and take turns narrating and explaining how convex and concave lenses are different. Tell them to keep their explanations under a minute. Use their recordings along with some slides showing convex and concave lenses. They will love hearing their own voices!

SL.4.5 Add audio recordings and visual displays to presentations when appropriate to enhance the development of main ideas or themes.

Super Lenses

You probably know a few people who wear glasses to help them see. Eyeglasses are lenses used to correct vision problems. The two main types of lenses used in glasses are convex lenses and concave lenses. Both lenses allow light to pass into them, but each interacts with light in different ways. Study the drawings to see how these lenses compare.

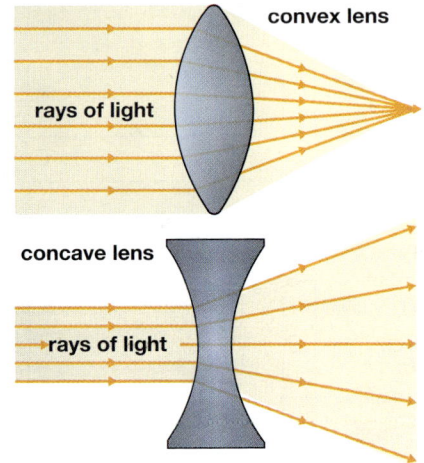

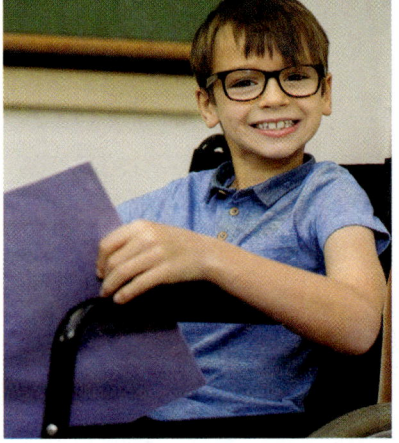

Convex lenses are curved outwards. Concave lenses are curved inwards. Notice how these differences cause light to behave once it enters the lenses.

Eyeglasses are often used to correct vision problems. Some people do not have to wear glasses until they are older. Others start when they are young.

20. Use the information and drawings to complete the table below to compare and contrast convex and concave lenses.

Convex	Both	Concave
curved outwards	collect and focus light	curved inwards
thicker in middle than on edges	used to correct vision problems	thinner in middle than on edges
cause light to come together at a single point		cause light rays to spread out

192

HANDS-ON Apply What You Know

Read This!

21. Get a convex and a concave lens from your teacher. Use each lens to look at different types of printed materials. Place one lens over the words on a worksheet or this book page. Note whether the words appear larger or smaller. Then use the other lens and do the same thing.

    How does the print look different with the different lenses?

    <u>The convex lens made the print look larger. The concave lens made it</u>
    <u>look smaller.</u>

Telescopes can be used to see things that are millions and millions of kilometers from Earth. A refracting telescope has a curved primary lens that gathers light and bends it. It then sends the light waves to another lens called the eyepiece. This is the part through which you look. A refracting telescope bends light to produce a magnified image of a distant object.

22. Choose the word or phrase to correctly complete each sentence.

| bend | bounce off | concave |
| convex | far away | close up |

<u>Convex</u> lenses focus light into a single point.
<u>Concave</u> lenses cause light to spread out. Refracting telescopes cause light to <u>bend</u> and are used to view objects that are <u>far away</u>.

193

HANDS-ON Apply What You Know
Read This!
Students use different lenses to observe print materials.

Ask: What do you expect the image will look like through a concave lens? **the image will be smaller**
What do you expect the image will look like through a convex lens? **the image will be larger**

Scoring Guidelines
An excellent score involves active participation in the activity and predictions about the observations.

 Developing and Using Models

In 1609, Galileo was the first to use a telescope to make observations of objects in space. You can imagine that the telescope he used was very different from the kind of telescopes we have today. Galileo's telescope created fuzzy images. Scientists continued to develop models and through trial and error built telescopes that are stronger and more advanced and help us learn more about the universe.

Differentiate Instruction

Extension Some students may be fascinated with astronomy and will want to know more. Have them research and find the goals of the Hubble Space Telescope. Print out some Hubble images and discuss what they show students. Tell students that scientists are constantly working on telescopes that can produce clearer images and see farther into space. Have students research and report on recent advancements in telescope technology.

LESSON 2   Engage • **Explore/Explain** • Elaborate • Evaluate

EXPLORATION 2 *Refraction and Lenses, continued*

Engineer It!
Designed for Safety

Point out to students that engineers and scientists use scientific principles to make people's lives easier. In this case, mirrors add a necessary component to motor vehicles.

Ask: What other piece of technology uses mirrors to create a simpler or better or safer piece of equipment to make our lives easier? solar power (solar panels), telescopes, more efficient lightbulbs that use nanomirror technology

Energy and Matter

Just like the mirrors that make driving safer, the mirrors in a funhouse are designed to make images of you that aren't real and are slightly distorted.

Ask: What principle of light is in action in a funhouse mirror? reflection

Funhouse mirrors make people look different by tilting or curving different pieces or parts of the mirror. This changes the angle at which light hits the mirror and your eyes. Because of this, the image seems distorted.

FORMATIVE ASSESSMENT

Language SmArts
Identifying Main Ideas and Details

RI.4.2 Identify Main Ideas and Details

Now that they have more information about how mirrors work, help them connect the details of what car mirrors are used for and how they help drivers stay safe in a car. Be sure that students can explain why the safety warning is written on mirrors: "Objects in the mirror are closer than they appear."

Engineer It!
Designed for Safety

Have you ever noticed words printed on the passenger-side mirror of a car? The message says: *Objects in mirror are closer than they appear*. What does this message mean?

These side mirrors might appear flat, but if you examine them very closely, you can see that they have a curved surface. They are slightly convex.

The driver in a car is sitting several feet away from the passenger-side mirror. The mirror is in a fixed position so that it reflects just a section of what is on that side of the car for the driver to see. A convex mirror reflects *more* of the view on that side of the car than a flat mirror surface would. But the tradeoff for seeing more is that the driver doesn't perceive the distance to the objects in the mirror accurately.

Why does this matter? One of the things a driver uses mirrors for is backing up a vehicle. If a driver is backing a car *toward* an object in the mirror, it is important to know that the object is closer than his or her eyes might think!

23. If a convex car mirror makes objects appear closer than they really are, what do you think the reflection in a concave mirror would look like?

A concave mirror would make objects appear farther away, or even upside down.

Language SmArts
Identifying Main Ideas and Details

24. Identify the main idea of the passage on this page. Then write down at least three details that support this idea.

Main idea: Mirrors are safety features on cars. Details: Mirrors reflect light to form images of objects near the car. Mirrors allow the driver to see around the car. Mirrors help the driver judge distances to objects.

Tip

The English Language Arts Handbook can provide help with understanding how to identify the main idea.

TAKE IT FURTHER Discover More

TAKE IT FURTHER
Discover More

Check out this path . . . or go online to choose one of these other paths.

- **People in Engineering**
- Light and Art
- Lighthouses and Lenses

Optics Engineers

Microscopes, telescopes, and lasers are all tools that make use of light, mirrors, and lenses. Without knowing how light behaves, none of these would have been invented.

People who design tools that use light are called *optical engineers*. They investigate how light refracts and reflects. They use this knowledge to invent tools that can be used in many different fields. For example, lasers are beams of light that can be used to carry out a delicate surgery. Lasers are also used to scan products at the checkout counter or produce a light show at a rock concert.

Optical engineers, like Dr. Kristopher Davis, use knowledge of light and lenses to help engineers design useful tools, such as video projectors, laser printers, or even the Hubble Space Telescope.

Optical engineers at the University of Central Florida developed technology to test the efficiency, or the ability to produce electrical energy with less waste, of solar cells like this.

Explore Online
Students can explore all three Take It Further paths online.

Collaboration
You may choose to assign this activity or to direct students online to the Interactive Online Student Edition where they can explore and choose from all three paths. These activities can be assigned individually, to pairs, or to small groups.

People in Engineering: Optics Engineers

DCI PS4.B Electromagnetic Radiation

Light behaves in predictable ways. We know that objects can be seen when light from the object's surface enters our eyes. It is important to point out to students that without observations and knowledge about the behavior of light, computers, lasers, microscopes, telescopes—many of the things that help us learn about and manipulate the world around us—would not have been possible.

Build on Prior Knowledge

Make sure students understand what an engineer does. Understanding optical engineering will be more effective with a stronger background on general engineering. Remind students that engineers identify problems and look for solutions.

LESSON 2 Engage • Explore/Explain • **Elaborate** • Evaluate

TAKE IT FURTHER, continued

SEP Developing and Using Models

Scientists use computers to design models and run tests.

Ask: What is a computer model? **A computer-based model is a computer program that is designed to simulate what might happen in a situation.**

Collaboration

Share Feedback Students work together to discuss the specific classes and skills necessary to become an optical engineer. Pairs will create a set of future job interview questions for an optical engineer position. Have them work together to create the best list and then answer the questions themselves if time permits.

▷ Explore Online

Students can explore these additional topics online.

Light and Art

Students explore an application of wavelengths of light by studying the color palette of an artist. (*Outside research required.*)

Lighthouses and Lenses

Students here are introduced to the Fresnel lens and the Fresnel lamps, concepts used today not only in lighthouses, but also in car headlights and theatres. (*Outside research required.*)

196 Unit 3 Waves and Information Transfer

Like with most fields of research today, optical engineers commonly use computers to design models. They also use computers to test their models. In this field, it is important to have a very strong background in both math and science.

A few of the latest discoveries coming out of this engineering field include a communications cable that can carry 22 times more signal than regular cables. Another discovery is flexible glass that can be used in the fields of communications and energy exploration. These discoveries, along with many, many others, will lead the way as the technology and optics age continues.

Dr. Davis and the UCF optics team use LEDs with different wavelengths of light attached to a system of fiber optic cables to test solar cell efficiency. By understanding how efficient a solar cell is, optical engineers can alter and improve their design, so they produce more electrical energy.

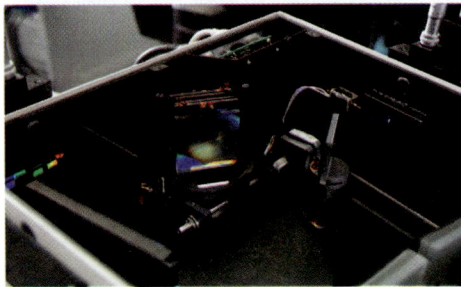

Optical engineers at UCF also conduct research on lasers like this one, fiber optics, and optical imagery for medical fields. The goal of each research field is to improve our every day lives with optical materials that are stronger, faster, and more efficient.

25. Research other aspects of optical engineering. What kind of training does someone need to become an optical engineer? Would you enjoy working in this field? Why?

Possible answer: To become an optical engineer, training in science is necessary. Since the behavior of light can be measured, having a strong background in math also is important. Understanding how light behaves is essential to building and testing tools that harness this energy. I would like to work in this field because I am good in math and like to try and invent things.

196

LESSON CHECK

LESSON 2
Lesson Check

Name _____

Can You Explain It?

1. Now that you know about lenses and how they interact with light, explain how a telescope, which has just a few mirrors inside it, allows us to see things millions of kilometers away. Be sure to do the following:
   - Describe how light moves.
   - Explain how light reflects and refracts.
   - Detail how light allows you to see objects.

 EVIDENCE NOTEBOOK Use the information you've gathered in your Evidence Notebook to help you cover each point above.

Possible answer:
- Light moves very quickly as waves.
- Mirrors inside the telescope capture and reflect the light from objects far away. Reflection is when light bounces off a mirror or object. Refraction is when light bends when passing through a lens or other object.
- This light travels to our eyes when we look into the eyepiece. The lenses in our eyes focus the light, sending signals to the brain that allow us to form images of the objects.

Checkpoints

2. You shine a light into a dark container. The light shines back at you. Which of these terms describe the container and behavior of the light? Select all that apply.
   a. reflection
   b. refraction
   c. opaque
   d. transparent
   e. translucent

 Formal Assessment Go online for student self-checks and other assessments.

Can You Explain It?

> ### Collaboration
> **Discussion** You may wish to revisit and discuss the images as a group to assess students' understanding of the material. Use the bulleted points in the student edition to lead the discussion.

 EVIDENCE NOTEBOOK

Have students reread their answers to the Evidence Notebook prompts, and then use this evidence to justify their reasoning as they respond to the Can You Explain It? Make sure students understand that a complete response must address all bulleted points.

CCC Cause and Effect

Ask: What happens if you shine a light into a transparent container instead of a dark one? **Most of the light will pass through a transparent container.**

Tell students that some substances are opaque but become more translucent as their temperature changes.

Ask: Can you think of a substance that becomes translucent as the temperature increases? **candle wax, butter**

SUMMATIVE ASSESSMENT

2. Students should be able to correctly identify the terms that go along with the scenario presented here. A black container signifies that the container is opaque, not transparent or translucent. Since the light is shining "back at you," students should recognize this as reflection. If a student response is incorrect, then it might just be a case of confusing terms. Have students make flashcards together to review the terms *reflection* versus *refraction,* and *opaque* versus *transparent* and *translucent.*

LESSON 2 Engage • Explore/Explain • Elaborate • **Evaluate**

LESSON CHECK, continued

3. This question asks students to correctly apply terms associated with the refraction of light. Remind students to review the Hands-On Activity from the beginning of the lesson. Remind them that coins can appear to be in different positions based upon the viewpoint of the observer due to the refraction (bending) of light waves.

4. Students will remember that refraction is the bending of light, but be sure they also remember why light bends. When light waves transition from one medium to another, the speed of the light changes. The change in speed causes the light rays to change direction if they enter the new medium at an angle.

5. The key phrase in this question is "bounces off." Students will recognize that when rays of light bounce off something, the rays are being reflected. They should recall from Exploration 1 that soda is translucent, meaning that some light rays bounce off it and some pass through.

6. To help students respond, have some sample items handy to represent each of the three types of objects—transparent, translucent, and opaque. Some items that are easy to show before students answer the question are: a glass or plastic wrap (transparent), a colored glass jar or wax paper (translucent), and a piece of foil or foam (opaque).

---

3. Choose the word or phrase that correctly completes each sentence.

bend	destroy	stay in place	move
angles	heights	eye	brain

Water can ____**bend**____ light. Coins thrown into a fountain look like they ____**move**____ when looked at from different ____**angles**____. This is because the water creates an illusion. Your ____**eye**____ is tricked into thinking the coins have moved.

4. You put a spoon into a clear glass of water. When you look at the spoon, it appears bent. Which of these describes the glass of water and the behavior of the light? Select all that apply.
   a. reflection
   (b. refraction)
   c. opaque
   (d. transparent)
   e. translucent

5. You shine a flashlight into a glass of apple juice. Some of the light bounces off the liquid. Some of it passes through it. Which of these describe the soda and the light behavior? Select all that apply.
   (a. reflection)
   b. refraction
   c. opaque
   d. transparent
   (e. translucent)

6. Label each object as *opaque*, *transparent*, or *translucent*.

____**transparent**____   ____**translucent**____   ____**opaque**____

198

Unit 3 Waves and Information Transfer

LESSON 2

Lesson Roundup

A. You throw a penny into a fountain. You see where it lands. Your little brother cannot. He is standing next to you. Which of these explains why this is so? Select all that apply.
  a. Light was reflected.
  b. Light was refracted.
  c. He's at the wrong angle.
  d. The water is opaque.
  e. The water is too cold.
  f. The penny is reflecting light.

B. Order the steps to show how light from the sun allows you to see an object.

  __6__ You see the object.
  __4__ Light is changed into a signal.
  __1__ Light leaves the sun.
  __5__ Signal enters the brain
  __2__ Light reflects off of an object.
  __3__ Light enters the lens in your eye.

C. Choose the word or words that correctly describe each object and how light behaves in the situation.

| reflection | refraction | passes through |
| opaque | transparent | translucent |

opaque, reflection | transparent, passes through, and refraction | translucent, reflection, and passes through

D. Which of these describes a lens that causes light to spread out when it focuses it?
  a. translucent
  b. opaque
  c. concave
  d. convex

199

Lesson Roundup

DCI PS4.B Electromagnetic Radiation

This lesson summary enables students to quickly revisit key points and prepare for tests.

A. The distractors here could be a temptation for students that do not fully grasp the concepts in this lesson. If students comprehend the lesson vocabulary and concepts, they should now recognize the penny scenario as an example of refraction and be able to determine that your little brother cannot see the penny because of his position. Remind struggling students of the "Disappearing Coins" activity at the beginning of the lesson. **PS4.B**

B. Encourage students to use a pencil to draw a flow chart or number the steps given here off to the side before filling in the actual answers. Have them confirm the correct answers on the side in rough draft form before they fill in the correct order of steps. If a student is having trouble getting started, ask them where most light energy comes from and point them in the direction of light leaving the sun. **PS4.B**

C. Tell students to choose the words to describe each object first. It is more logical and perhaps easier if students first consider the object and then how light would behave in each case. Tell them that the words in the word bank can be used more than once. **PS4.B**

D. Have students think back to their activity with the lenses, and recall what they learned from Explorations 1 and 2 to answer the question. If time permits, you might also allow students to test the lenses again to see for themselves. **PS4.B**

LESSON 3
How Is Information Transferred from Place to Place?

Building to the Performance Expectation

The learning experiences in this lesson prepare students for mastery of:

4-PS4-3 Generate and compare multiple solutions that use patterns to transfer information.

Trace Tool to the NGSS
Go online to view the complete coverage of these standards across this lesson, unit, and time.

 **Science & Engineering Practices**

 Disciplinary Core Ideas

 **Crosscutting Concepts**

Constructing Explanations and Designing Solutions
Generate and compare multiple solutions to a problem based on how well they meet the criteria and constraints of the design solution.

▶ **VIDEO** Constructing Explanations and Designing Solutions

PS4.C Information Technologies and Instrumentation
Digitized information can be transmitted over long distances without significant degradation. High-tech devices, such as computers or cell phones, can receive and decode information—convert it from digitized form to voice—and vice versa.

ETS1.C Optimizing The Design Solution
Different solutions need to be tested in order to determine which of them best solves the problem, given the criteria and the constraints.

Patterns
Similarities and differences in patterns can be used to sort and classify designed products.

Interdependence of Science, Engineering, and Technology
Knowledge of relevant scientific concepts and research findings is important in engineering.

 CONNECTIONS TO MATH

4.OA.C.5 Generate and analyze patterns.

 CONNECTIONS TO ENGLISH LANGUAGE ARTS

W.4.2.D Use precise language and domain-specific vocabulary to inform about or explain the topic.

W.4.7 Conduct short research projects that build knowledge…

RI.4.5 Determine the overall structure of events, ideas, concepts, or information…

SL.4.2 Paraphrase portions of text read aloud or information presented in diverse media formats…

Supporting All Students, All Standards

Integrating the Three Dimensions of Learning

In this lesson, students will explore a variety of communication devices **(DCI PS4.C and ETS1.C)** that are the result of science, engineering, and technology working together to meet people's needs **(CCC Interdependence of Science, Engineering, and Technology)**, and decide how well each device solves a problem **(SEP Constructing Explanations and Designing Solutions)**. Students will also design their own devices to communicate information over a distance.

 **Professional Development** Go online to view professional development videos with strategies to integrate CCCs and SEPs, including the ones used in this lesson.

Extra Hands-On Activity: Create a Code

What Information Can a Code Transfer?

Small groups
45 minutes

Each group will develop a code to transmit information over a set distance and test it to find out how effective it is. Groups will then trade codes, and attempt to use the other group's code. Start by giving each group a different card with a simple statement, a color name, and a simple math equation on it. Tell students they need to create a code that will allow them to communicate the information on their card across the gym or down a hallway, without using words. Their code can be unique symbols, repurposed letters, or any other symbols that can make up a code.

After developing and recording its code, each group should test it among themselves to see how well it works over the distance given. Once groups feel their codes are refined enough, have them swap codes. Then have each group test the others' code over the same distance to determine its effectiveness.

 This activity can support mastery of this Crosscutting concept: Patterns

Preassessment

Have students complete the lesson pre-test online or see the Assessment Guide.

Build on Prior Knowledge

Students should already know and be prepared to build on the following concepts:
- Tools are used to do things better or more easily.
- Scientists design new technologies to meet the needs of society.
- The design process involves describing a problem, designing a solution, and testing it.
- Waves are regular patterns of motion; sound and light move in waves.

Differentiate Instruction

Lesson Vocabulary
Write the definition of *technology* on the board: the use of science knowledge to solve problems. Stress that science, engineering, and technology go hand-in-hand.
Say: If you want to design a new computer chip, you need to know the electrical properties of materials, and to invent a drug to cure cancer, you need to understand how the body functions. Then ask students to name an example of technology in their homes, such as a microwave oven, vacuum, or TV, and explain how that technology solves problems.

ELL Strategy
To help bridge understanding, point out cognates of key terms in the lesson, such as: *satellite/el satélite, technology/la tecnología, pictograph/pictografía, hieroglyphics/jeroglíficos, telegraph/el telégrafo,* and *binary code/código binario.* Spotlight the similarities and discuss the differences, such as including a definite article before some nouns and having the adjective following the noun it modifies. Pronounce each word in English, and have students repeat it.

Lesson 3 How Is Information Transferred from Place to Place? **200B**

LESSON 3 **Engage** • Explore/Explain • Elaborate • Evaluate

ENGAGE: Lesson Phenomenon

Lesson Objective

Explore and compare patterns in multiple methods of transferring information, and actually transfer information using codes and a pixilated image.

About This Image

A satellite is a machine launched into space to orbit Earth. Satellites are used mostly for communications, sending TV signals and phone calls around the world. The solar panels on the satellite turn sunlight into electricity to run the machine; the antenna on top sends and receives information to and from Earth. Some communication satellites are geostationary; they orbit Earth in the same amount of time it takes Earth to revolve once. These satellites always appear above the same area of Earth.

Constructing Explanations and Designing Solutions

Alternative Engage Strategy

Let's Communicate | Whole Class | 10 min

Remind students that communication is the sending and receiving of information. Then gesture for students to stand, wait a moment, and then gesture for them to sit down.

Ask: How did I communicate information about whether you should stand or sit? **with body language**
Would this be a good way of communicating with someone who was in another room or another town? **No, they couldn't see what you gestured.**

Have students work in small groups to create lists of different ways people can send or receive information over a distance. Ask a volunteer from each group to share results, then discuss the lists as a whole class.

200 Unit 3 Waves and Information Transfer

LESSON 3

How Is Information Transferred from Place to Place?

This satellite sends information to Earth from space. The information is coded into waves of energy.

By the end of this lesson . . .
you'll be able to describe ways that codes and signals are used to transfer information.

Can You Explain It?

How times have changed! 30 years ago, televisions were large pieces of furniture and telephones had wires. Today, we have televisions that have hundreds of channels, and phones that can take photos and surf the web.

1. How has the way we receive information changed over the years?

Students should respond based on the preliminary observations they can make of the images.

Tip
Learn more about energy transfer in *What Are Waves?*

_____
_____
_____
_____
_____
_____
_____
_____

EVIDENCE NOTEBOOK Look for this icon to help you gather evidence to answer the question above.

 **Explore Online** Students can view the lesson phenomenon online.

Can You Explain It?

Students are asked to record their initial thoughts about two illustrations that compare the use of communication technology in the past and the present. To do so, students must think about the many ways people communicate. Encourage students to record the first thoughts that come into their minds. Point out that their ideas might change as they work through the Explorations and Hands-On Activities. Explain that they will have another opportunity to answer the same questions at the end of the lesson.

Collaboration

Think, Pair, Share Pair students and have them discuss how the way we rely on information has changed over the years. Call on pairs to share their ideas with the class. Use this discussion to gauge students' prior knowledge of the topic and to identify possible misconceptions they may have.

DCI PS4.C Information Technologies and Instrumentation

The images on this page focus on information technologies. Help students understand that as society changes, new technologies come along to meet people's needs.

Ask: How is the phone you use today like the phone your grandparents used at your age? *both are used to communicate information*

EVIDENCE NOTEBOOK

Encourage students to use an appropriate graphic organizer, such as main idea and supporting details, to set up their notebook for this lesson.
Find more strategies in the online ELA handbook.

Lesson 3 How Is Information Transferred from Place to Place? **201**

LESSON 3   Engage • **Explore/Explain** • Elaborate • Evaluate

EXPLORATION 1 History of Information Transfer

3D Learning Objective

Compare and contrast a variety of **communication devices** that have been used over time as **new technologies were designed** to meet the needs of society. **Design devices** to transmit codes.

 PS4.C Information Technologies and Instrumentation

Students read about some ways humans communicated long ago.

Ask: Why did ancient humans draw pictographs on cave walls?
to have a record of something that happened to them

 Constructing Explanations and Designing Solutions

Differentiate Instruction

RTI/Extra Support To help students who might have difficulties, read in small segments. For example, have students read one caption on this page, then stop and discuss what they read. Repeat the procedure with the other three captions.

 Language SmArts
RI.4.1 Drawing Inferences

Give pairs of students two minutes to discuss the question. Then call on different pairs to share their ideas with the class.

Ask: How do we use images and symbols on signs today so that everyone can understand, no matter what language they speak? sign for a train station; signs on restroom doors; traffic signs; direction arrows

---

EXPLORATION 1

History of Information Transfer

The Old Ways

Humans always have needed to communicate. Before talking, ancient people probably sent messages by pointing, grunting, or hand gestures. As different groups of people spread out, they needed to communicate over distances. Also, it became common for ancient cultures to record their histories using pictures.

One of the earliest recorded forms of communication used *pictographs*. These drawings are often painted in caves. They are very fragile but have lasted because they are painted in places that are protected from the weather. Pictographs recorded events, such as important ceremonies and good hunting areas.

Ancient Egyptians communicated using *hieroglyphics*. Hieroglyphics are symbols for ideas, words, or letters. For example, a drawing of a lion might represent the letter L. Egyptians made papyrus, an early form of paper, so ideas were not limited to the size of a wall. They passed on information about ceremonies. Because hieroglyphics could be written on paper, they could be carried from place to place.

 2. Language SmArts Interview an older adult. How have the ways they communicated changed over time?
Possible answer: My grandparents remember placing telephone calls by speaking to an operator. They also had only black and white television sets.

202

Unit 3 Waves and Information Transfer

How can people send messages long distances without making any noise? In ancient China, there were often battles that involved soldiers from faraway places. Soldiers used smoke signals to communicate across long distances.

Native Americans on the plains in the Midwest also used smoke to send signals. The smoke signals served as a "universal language" between the tribes.

A talking drum has two heads. It can be tuned to different notes, but usually produce low wavelengths. Drums were used to tell stories, send messages, and lead ceremonies. Drums are an ancient form of communication, but they are still important to the cultures of West Africa.

"One if by land. Two if by sea." So goes the story from Paul Revere's ride, letting people know the British were coming. Using the lanterns in the Old North Church, colonists were able to send simple messages to many people at once.

3. Choose the words or phrases that make each sentence correct.

| hieroglyphics | lanterns | talking drums | smoke signals |

One of the earliest ways of sending messages was through the use of ___hieroglyphics___. This involved drawing pictures on paper. To send signals across long distances, the ancient Chinese used ___smoke signals___ to alert the troops that enemies were coming.

203

Connection to Physical Science

The images and information on this spread address how science affects everyday life. Humans needed ways to communicate with one another; humans, using science, came up with solutions. Have students speculate.

Ask: How do you use pictographs or hieroglyphics technology in your everyday life? as emoticons in emails and texts

4-PS3-4 Science Is a Human Endeavor

Collaboration

Feedback Have students review and critique each other's answers for item 2. Allow students to change their answers if they listed something incorrectly. Encourage discussion about why the other answer choices are not correct.

CCC Patterns

Explain to students that patterns were important when communicating with smoke signals or drums. For example, when Native Americans sent up two puffs of smoke, it was usually a sign that everything was okay; three puffs signaled that something was wrong. Drum patterns of loud or soft, fast or slow, and high or low sounds sent different messages, imitating the phrasing and tones of the drummer's home language.

Lesson 3 How Is Information Transferred from Place to Place? 203

LESSON 3   Engage • **Explore/Explain** • Elaborate • Evaluate

EXPLORATION 1 History of Information Transfer, continued

SEP **Constructing Explanations and Designing Solutions**

Students read about the telegraph. Discuss how a pattern of coded dots (short electrical signals) and dashes (long electrical signals) created words and messages. Ask students to refer to the code as you transmit two short bursts (*i*), pause, then three short bursts (*s*), by tapping a ruler on your desk or clapping your hands.

CCC **Interdependence of Science, Engineering, and Technology**

Point out that inventors, such as Morse, need prior scientific knowledge and engineering know-how when creating new technologies.

Ask: What scientific and engineering knowledge did Morse need to invent the telegraph? Possible answers: how sound travels; how electricity works; how to manufacture a transmitter.

Differentiate Instruction

Extension Challenge students to integrate the information on Morse code as an activity. Students can work in pairs or small groups to attempt to communicate by drawing out the Morse codes and having another group or pair attempt to decipher their messages.

 Language SmArts

W.4.7 Conduct short research projects that build knowledge through investigation of different aspects of a topic.

Remind students that part of performing research involves citing evidence, facts, or examples as much as possible. Have students include an example of miscommunication as part of their answers.

204 Unit 3 Waves and Information Transfer

Newer Ways

With the discovery of electricity, signals could be sent over much greater distances, thousands of miles away. A device called the *telegraph* was invented that allowed information to travel all over the world along wires. The telegraph was invented in the 1830s. A man named Samuel Morse invented a "language" that could be used to send messages using the telegraph.

Character	Morse Code	Character	Morse Code	Number	Morse Code
A	·—	N	—·	1	·————
B	—···	O	———	2	··———
C	—·—·	P	·——·	3	···——
D	—··	Q	——·—	4	····—
E	·	R	·—·	5	·····
F	··—·	S	···	6	—····
G	——·	T	—	7	——···
H	····	U	··—	8	———··
I	··	V	···—	9	————·
J	·———	W	·——	0	—————
K	—·—	X	—··—		
L	·—··	Y	—·——		
M	——	Z	——··		

The telegraph code is called *Morse code*. It is a series of dots and dashes, each making up a letter. An operator in one place taps out a message. It travels through wires to another location. A second operator decodes the message. Operators needed to be skills so messages could be sent quickly and accurately.

 4. Language SmArts Telegraph messages were very popular, but not always reliable. Research how telegraphs were sent. Name some ways a message might be miscommunciated or misunderstood.

If the operator encodes a letter wrong, or the second operator decodes a letter wrong, the message could be miscommunicated.

204

By using the telegraph, messages have been sent all over the world. When it was first invented, cables were laid across the Atlantic Ocean to Europe. This was beneficial during the World Wars to keep track of the enemies. The last telegraph was sent in 2013.

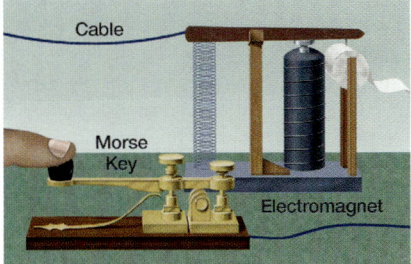

A battery, an electromagnet, a telegraph key, and a cable make up a telegraph. By tapping the key, an electric pulse is sent through the cable.

The telegraph operator uses a code called Morse code. It is a series of dots and dashes, each making up a letter.

The signal moves along the cable to a machine on the other end.

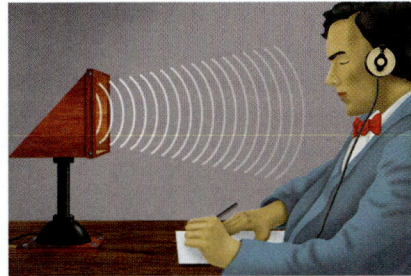

The electric pulse is transformed into sound. The operator listens and decodes the dots and dashes and makes words from them.

5. In the space below, write your name in Morse Code.

Review students' codes for accuracy.

205

PS4.C Information Technologies and Instrumentation

Refer students to the opening paragraph. Have students speculate.

Ask: In what other ways do you think the connection to Europe by telegraph cables might have been important? Possible answers: businesses in the United States could get messages to businesses in Europe faster; people could keep in touch with friends or family in Europe; scientists from many countries could collaborate easier.

Connection to English Language Arts

The step-by-step illustrations on this page show the sequence of events, from the operator transmitting the message to its decoding by another operator. Discuss the sequence with students.

Ask: What do the illustrations show? Sample answer: They show what happens after someone hits a key to send a message by telegraph.

How do the illustrations help you better understand what you read in the text? Sample answer: They show me exactly what the text tells.

RI.4.7 Integration of Knowledge and Ideas

Collaboration

Draw, Pair, Share Ask partners to write and illustrate each step in sending and receiving a telegraph on a card. Then have pairs number the cards in order, and create a flow chart by gluing the cards to a poster and drawing lines to connect them to show the sequence. Invite pairs to share their posters with the class.

LESSON 3 Engage • **Explore/Explain** • Elaborate • Evaluate

EXPLORATION 1 History of Information Transfer, continued

DCI ETS1.C Optimizing the Design Solution

The text and photos on the page are about the criteria for choosing a particular code to use.

Ask: What is the most important thing to consider when choosing a code to use? Sample answer: will the person I send it to understand the message.

Connection to Math

Cracking codes and secret messages involves a lot of math, from simple number work to logical thinking. Tell students that thousands of years ago, Julius Caesar used a special code to communicate battle plans to his soldiers without the enemy finding out. Instead of writing the letter *a*, he wrote the alphabet letter three places further on (*d*). When he got to the end of the alphabet, he went back to the beginning. Instead of *x*, he wrote *a*, and so on. Ask students to write a short message using this Caesar code, then have a partner decode it.

4.OA.C.5 Generate and analyze patterns

Differentiate Instruction

ELL: Reading To support English language learners, read the question aloud and allow students to reply in their native language. Then write their answers in English on the board in complete sentences, and have students echo-read them with you.

 EVIDENCE NOTEBOOK

Students should demonstrate ability to relate the information in this Exploration to historical events.

Codes

Think about sending a signal. Each message needs a sender and a receiver. Chances are you talk to or text your friends using the phone. Or you have a face to face chat in the lunchroom at school.

How do you make your message clear? Sometimes, using text messages does not always get the correct message across. If you use shorthand like symbols or emojis, the receiver may not know what you mean.

Sometimes you want to send a message that's meant for only one person. How do you keep it a secret? In this case, you want to be sure only the receiver can understand the message. To do this, you could use a secret code. Secret codes have been around for hundreds of years. They are really useful to protect important information, like bank accounts or personal information on websites.

6. Can you think of some times in history when a secret code would have been needed? What makes a good code?

Possible answer: During wartime, secret codes are needed. This keeps the enemy from learning about top secret plans and missions. A good code is one that is hard to break. It has several different parts that only trained receivers will understand.

During World War II, the United States government needed a way to encode special messages. They recruited Americans who spoke little known Navajo as code talkers.

Another tool used to send secret messages is the *Enigma machine,* a device that looks a lot like an old typewriter with a keyboard and some wheels sticking out of the top. The Germans developed the Enigma during World War II.

 EVIDENCE NOTEBOOK Why was the Navajo language perfect for a code to use against the Japanese in World War II? Record your answer in your Evidence Notebook.

As you have seen, there are many different codes. Codes and different ways to send codes have been around for thousands of years. But codes don't have to be very complicated, and they can be fun to use. Look at the images to see some more codes.

Flags can be used to relay coded messages, especially between ship and shore, or two people too far away to hear each other.

A **scytale** is another tool that can be used to send a coded message. A strip is wrapped around a tube. A message will be added, then the tube removed.

HANDS-ON Apply What You Know
Make a Scytale

7. Get some paper, scissors, tape, pencil, and paper towel tube from your teacher. Cut the paper into long strips. Tape one end of the strip to the side of the tube. Wrap the rest of the strip around the tube. Write a message from one end of the tube to the other. Then add a bunch of other letters around the ones you wrote to fill in the space. Take off the strip of paper and trade it with a classmate to see if they can figure out what you wrote.

Putting It Together

8. Suppose you wanted to send a secret message using Morse code. Circle the things you need to send a complete message. Select all that apply.
   a. (a sender)
   b. a microphone
   c. (a series of dots and dashes)
   d. a pile of papers
   e. a tablet
   f. (a receiver)

HANDS-ON Apply What You Know
Make a Scytale

DCI ETS1.C Optimizing The Design Solution

Gather paper, scissors, tape, pencils, and different-size paper towel tubes for students. Have students work in pairs. As a student chooses a paper tube, stress that the partner must choose a tube of the same size, or else he or she cannot read the message. Before students begin making the scytale, you may wish to download visuals of the activity. A successful scytale can be read by the partner. Have pairs share their code tools with the class. Encourage discussion about why some codes worked better than others.

Scoring Guidelines
An excellent score on this activity involves active participation and a true attempt to decode the message.

Differentiate Instruction

RTI/Extra Support Model for students how to construct a scytale, and how to decode the message. Talk about what decisions must be made when writing the code on the strips and the reasons for one choice or another.

FORMATIVE ASSESSMENT
Putting It Together

SEP Constructing Explanations and Designing Solutions

Make sure students understand that the question asks them only what they need to send a message; they do not need a receiver just to send it.

LESSON 3 Engage • **Explore/Explain** • Elaborate • Evaluate

EXPLORATION 1 History of Information Transfer, continued

HANDS-ON ACTIVITY Small groups   1 class period
Pixels to Pictures

3D Learning Objective
Students create a pixilated message using binary code and discuss the constraints of the design.

 **Patterns**

Write *pixel* on the board, and underline the letters *pix*. Explain that they are a short way of saying "pictures." Circle the letters *el* and explain that they stand for "element." Clarify that every digital photograph is made up of picture elements, or pixels—the smallest unit of information that makes up an image. Add that the pattern of pixel placement creates the image you see.

Materials
The materials listed in the student edition are a starting point. You may wish to include graph paper with adequate size boxes so that students will have ready-made supplies for the activity and for making other binary-code examples.

Preparation
Preassemble materials bundles for students. Distribute to begin the activity.

Procedure
STEP 1 Circulate as students draw the grids. Make sure boxes are all the same size. Offer help as needed.

STEP 2 Monitor as students write in the zeroes and ones. Remind them to double check to make sure they marked each box correctly. Explain that the activity will not work unless the procedure is followed correctly.

208 Unit 3 Waves and Information Transfer

HANDS-ON ACTIVITY
Pixels to Pictures

Objective
Have you ever looked closely at a picture using a magnifying glass? If so, you may have seen that the image was made up of millions of tiny dots. Each dot that makes a picture is called a *pixel*. When there are a lot of pixels in an image, it will be very sharp. If there are few pixels, the image will be blurry.

Materials
- pencil/pen
- paper
- ruler
- markers

Discover how pixels work.

What question will you investigate to meet this objective?
How can pixels form a picture?
_____

Procedure
STEP 1 Use the ruler to draw a grid on the paper. It should have 7 columns and 11 rows.

STEP 2 Fill in the boxes with ones and zeros as seen in the illustration on page 209.

208

Student Lab Worksheet and complete Teacher Support available online.

STEP 3 Color in the boxes that have ones in them to see what the message says.

STEP 4 What does the message say?
Hi

0	0	0	0	0	0	0
0	0	0	0	0	0	0
0	1	0	1	0	1	0
0	1	0	1	0	0	0
0	1	0	1	0	1	0
0	1	1	1	0	1	0
0	1	0	1	0	1	0
0	1	0	1	0	1	0
0	1	0	1	0	1	0
0	0	0	0	0	0	0
0	0	0	0	0	0	0

Analyze Your Results

STEP 5 Each box in the grid represents one pixel. What was the hardest part about making an image using pixels? What was the easiest?
Possible answer: The hardest part was filling in each spot on the grid correctly with the proper color. The easiest part was filling in the rest of the grid with zeros.

STEP 6 How are the ones in your grid used to represent something else?
Possible answer: The ones told you where to color dark pixels that formed lines to make letters.

STEP 7 Using a new grid, make a message for a friend to decode. To show more details, should you include more boxes in the same size grid or fewer?
Possible answer: You would need a grid with more boxes to show greater detail.

Draw Conclusions

STEP 8 The pictures on a computer or television screen are made of pixels of colored light. What has to happen to those pixels for the pictures to show things that look like they are in motion?
Possible answer: The pixels need to change colors very fast.

STEPS 3–4 Circulate as students fill in their boxes. Check each grid and have the student answer the question. If a student's result was different, have him or her review the process with another student, who got the right result, and make changes.

Analyze Your Results

STEP 7 Demonstrate or use models to show students how larger or smaller pixels change the way an image looks.

Draw Conclusions

STEP 8 requires making an inference—an educated guess based on evidence and reasoning.

Ask: Which design would work best, smaller boxes or larger boxes? Guide students to understand that with the constraint of paper size, smaller boxes would allow for more pixels.

Claims, Evidence, and Reasoning

Have students discuss the question and come to a consensus for a response based on valid reasoning.

Ask: How is this idea similar to a flipbook? Sample answer: you show movement by making small changes.

Scoring Rubric for Hands-On Activity	
3	follows directions, outcome correct, analysis reflects understanding of pixels, forms logical conclusion
2	follows directions, outcome correct, analysis inconsistent, forms a conclusion
1	follows some directions, but outcome incorrect, analysis lacking, no conclusion

LESSON 3   Engage • **Explore/Explain** • Elaborate • Evaluate

EXPLORATION 2 Bits and Bytes

3D Learning Objective

Explore how digital **information devices,** such as television, computers, and cellphones, are **designed** using **binary code patterns** that create a universal, digital, language.

DCI PS4.C Information Technologies and Instrumentation

Point to the word *digital* in the first sentence. Write the word on the board and underline the root *digit*. Explain that it is from the Latin *digitus*, meaning "finger," but it also refers to counting, as when people count on their digits, or fingers. We use *digital* to refer to numbers used in computer technology.

Differentiate Instruction

ELL: Modeling Challenge English-speaking volunteers to pantomime or draw pictures to convey the meanings of phrases such as *a little tricky* and *get the hang of it*. Encourage students acquiring English to pronounce the English phrases, then give the equivalent (on something similar) in their own language.

HANDS-ON Apply What You Know
Make Your Own Code

Have construction paper and scissors, or index cards, available for students. Circulate to make sure they are putting the correct number of dots on their cards. Provide guidance, as needed. Explain that students will use the cards after reading the next page, which shows examples of binary cards.

Scoring Guideline

Students should be scored on their ability to follow the directions.

EXPLORATION 2
Bits and Bytes

Bits of Code

In our digital world, everything needs to be changed into code. Pictures, words, and numbers on our devices are converted into codes of ones and zeros that can be sent as electronic signals. This collection of ones and zeros is called *binary code*. Each number of the code is a bit. This is the smallest piece of information that can be stored by a computer. Binary code is a little tricky at first. However, once you get the hang of it, it is pretty easy.

Binary code

Binary code is needed to store information in a computer. If you were to look at the software that runs your phone, gaming system, or laptop, you would find nothing but a very, VERY long chain of ones and zeros.

 HANDS-ON Apply What You Know
Make Your Own Code

9. Using what you learn about binary code on page 211, make your own set of binary cards. Get index cards from your teacher and then draw a different number of dots on each one. The first card should have one dot. The second card should have two, and so on, up to 16. With a partner make binary code for a number and then decode what it is.

210

---

210   Unit 3 Waves and Information Transfer

Learn Binary Code

1

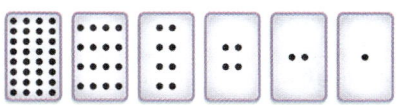

Look at the cards. Starting with one on the right, the next card would be two, then four, then eight, then 16, then 32, then 64, and so on.

2

If the first card is showing its dot, it is a one. If the card is not, it is a zero. An example with four digits of a binary code would 0001.

3

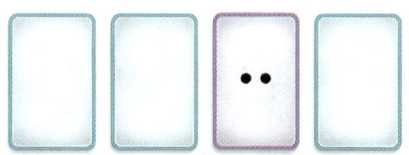

The binary number for two would be 0010. Here, the two-dot card would be flipped over showing its dots. All the others are hidden.

4

The binary number for three would be 0011. Here, both the two-dot card and the one-dot card are flipped.

Do the Math
Code Blue

10. In the table below, turn each blue number into binary code.

	Number of "dots" per bit					
Number	**16**	**8**	**4**	**2**	**1**	**Binary Code**
1	0	0	0	0	1	00001
3	0	0	0	1	1	00011
5	0	0	1	0	1	00001
10	0	1	0	1	0	00011
13	0	1	1	0	1	01101
19	1	0	0	1	1	10011
21	1	0	1	0	1	10101

Patterns

Explain to students that another way of thinking about binary code is to imagine light bulbs that can be turned on or off. Each bulb would have a number value, double the value of the bulb next to it, right to left (1, 2, 4, 8, and so on). If a bulb is off, its value is 0. As you write equations on the board, **say:** "Imagine a pattern of three bulbs. If all three are off, the pattern would be $0 + 0 + 0 = 0$. If the first bulb is on, the second off, and the third on, the pattern would be (right to left) $4 + 0 + 1 = 5$. Add another bulb, turn it on, and we have $8 + 4 + 0 + 1 = 13$. In binary code we write this using only ones (on) and zero (off), so we say 1101 binary = 13."

Ask: What would the number values and binary be if the first bulb were off, the second on, the third off, and the fourth on?
$8 + 0 + 2 + 0 = 10$, or 1010 binary

Collaboration

Draw, Pair, Share Have student pairs use the binary cards they drew to make binary code patterns for their partners to decode. Remind partners to take turns.

Do the Math
Code Blue
4.OA.C.5 Generate and analyze patterns

Remind students of the patterns you wrote on the board as they figure out the binary code for 1 and 3. Make sure students understand the relationship between the number value and the on/off binary code.

Ask: How do you represent the numeral 1 if you are using light bulbs? off, off, off, off, on

LESSON 3 Engage • **Explore/Explain** • Elaborate • Evaluate

EXPLORATION 2 Bits and Bytes, continued

SEP Constructing Explanations and Designing Solutions

Remind students that with most things, there are two sides, good news and bad news. The good news about cell phones: they are light and easy to take with you wherever you go. The bad news: cell phone use can be constrained by signal strength and battery capacity.

Ask: Have you heard about a cell phone helping to save a life? Have you ever had a cell phone not work when you needed it? What happened? *Answers will vary; let students share technological experiences.*

Connection to English Language Arts

Have students make idea webs for the term *wireless technology*. Tell them to write four things the term brings to mind, then connect them in a web. If students have difficulty getting started, prompt them with a hint, such as *remote control, cordless,* or *Wi-Fi*. Have students share their finished webs in a class discussion.

W.4.2.D Use precise language and domain-specific vocabulary to inform about or explain the topic.

Collaboration

Write, Pair, Share Give students 2-3 minutes for a quick partner discussion before answering item 11. Then have them share their response with the class, explaining why they made the choices they did. Allow students to amend their answers with any new information gleaned from the discussion.

Connecting the World

Today, a lot of what we do is made easier by wireless technology. We are able to talk on a cell phone. We can "stream" movies to our TVs from wireless Internet modems or to our handheld devices. We can even listen to music that is relayed as signals from satellites.

All of these things rely on electronic signals transferring bits of code from one place to another. However, these signals can be interrupted. If you have ever had a dropped cell phone call or an Internet video that would not play, you have experienced an interrupted digital code.

The number of bits a device can move or process is a constraint. If a signal has too much information for the network to move, it slows down or stops. This is why you hear about the need for an Internet connection to be high speed.

Today we listen to music on our phones and other small devices.

11. What types of things can cause the picture to buffer on the computer or TV?
Possible answer: Internet speed could be the cause. If the signal coming across the Internet is very slow, then it will take a long time to reach your machine. It will only come in small packets. This results in only tiny parts of the video being able to be viewed at a time.

 12. Language SmArts Think about two criterion and two constraints to a device that can surf the Internet.
Possible answer: The device needs to be able to move a lot of information fast, and the device should also connect to a network easily. One constraint would be affordability. If it is too expensive, few people would be able to use it. Another constraint would be the amount of battery energy used. A device that uses up the battery too quickly would not be very useful.

What is happening here? Error messages appear often on computers and tablets. Sometimes it means there was a communication problem between parts of the system. Other times it means that the stream of bits of code needs to catch up.

Find the Cause

13. Draw a line from the issue to the possible cause. Find a cause for each issue.

- error message
  - too much traffic online
  - too far from cell tower
  - computer speed is too slow
  - too many phones being used at once
- lost signal

EVIDENCE NOTEBOOK How do you know when your cell phone signal strength is low? What can you do to improve it?

PS4.C Information Technologies and Instrumentation

Discuss the photograph and the caption with students. Explain that the computer has a buffer—an area where data is stored temporarily while being moved from one place to another. When the computer downloads information faster than it can play it, some of the data is kept in the buffer until it can be moved to, or played on, the screen. That's why a "loading" message may appear as the computer moves the digital data from the buffer to the screen. Ask students to relate their personal experiences with buffering problems, such as long pauses right in the middle of a song or video.

Differentiate Instruction

RTI/Extra Support Remind students that things do not just happen, someone or something causes them to happen. Whoever or whatever makes something happen is the cause; what happens is the effect. Let student pairs work together to match the cause(s) for each issue in item 12. Next, have each pair review and critique answers with another pair. Allow students to change their responses if they marked something incorrectly. Encourage discussion about why an answer choice was not correct.

EVIDENCE NOTEBOOK

Students should record that they know the signal strength is low if there are no bars on the cell phone. To improve things, students might say they need to move around until they get bars on the phone.

LESSON 3 Engage • **Explore/Explain** • Elaborate • Evaluate

EXPLORATION 2 *Bits and Bytes, continued*

CCC Interdependence of Science, Engineering, and Technology

As students read the text, clarify that a modem is an electronic hardware device that is engineered to convert signals from one computer into signals that another computer can read. The photos and illustrations on this page follow a message from one computer to another.

Ask: What happens after Kesha hits the send key on his computer? *Her message goes to the modem.*

Ask: What happens next? *The message is translated into code signals and goes out through a cable to Grandma's modem.*

> ## Differentiate Instruction
>
> **RTI/Extra Support** Make sure students understand the sequence of events from Kesha typing the message to Grandma reading it. Have students act out the sequence, if necessary, to help them remember how a modem sends and receives code.
>
> **ELL: Reading** Pair students acquiring English with strong English-speaking students as you read and discuss the text and visuals. Circulate to make sure that English-speaking partners are helping the English-language learners understand how a modem works to convert messages into code and back again.

Code, Computers, and Networks

Humans communicate with words, letters, numbers, and pictures. Computers and other devices do not know what these are. Instead, they need to translate them into code (remember binary code?).

Now picture how signals are sent between computers. First, you input the words on the keyboard. Then, the computer translates them into binary code. If you are sending an email or a text to a friend, the computer needs to be able to "talk" to the Internet. The way computers talk to the rest of the world is with a device called a modem.

The modem sends the signals to and from your computer. When you send an email, the pathway goes from your computer to the modem. It then goes to another modem and then to your friend's computer.

Kesha just sent an email to her grandma. The signal goes from the computer to the modem. It goes across the lines to grandma's modem and then to her computer.

Grandma is waiting for Kesha's email. To get to her, the signal comes from her modem. It takes very little time for the message to be received.

How Computers Help Us Communicate

Suppose you want to send a email. How does it work? The sending computer translates a message into codes that can be sent.

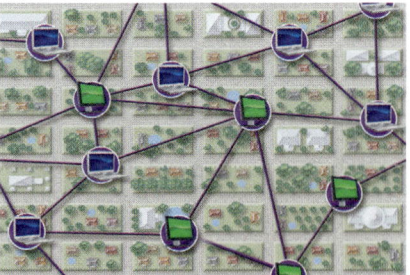
The codes are first sent through your local area network, or LAN, made up of all the modems in a virtual neighborhood.

214

214 Unit 3 Waves and Information Transfer

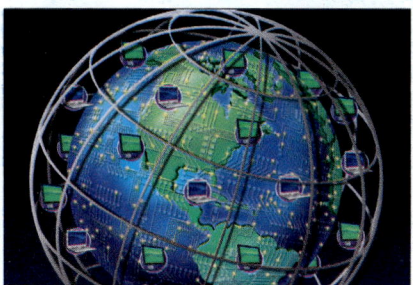

The LAN sends the signals to all the computer networks to the internet.

The signals containing coded words and pictures are decoded clearly by the receiver. Your message can now be read.

14. **Language SmArts** Put these steps in order of how a message would get from Kesha's computer to Grandma's computer.

Kesha's modem	keyboard	Grandma's modem
third	first	fourth

Grandma's computer	Kesha's computer
fifth	second

15. Choose the correct words to complete each sentence. You may use a term more than once.

> binary code   modem   computer

When signals are sent from a computer, they need to be in _binary code_. The computer sends the digitized signal to a _modem_. This puts the signal on the Internet. The message first comes to the receiver's _modem_ before it gets to their _computer_.

CCC Patterns

Remind students that communication relies on the use of patterns. Have them think about kinds of patterns they see in various forms of communication. If they require prompting, urge them to think about senders and receivers of information.

Collaboration

Feedback Have students review and critique each other's responses to items 13 and 14. Allow students to change their answers to correct errors or add newly gleaned information.

Differentiate Instruction

Extension Challenge students to create a game to test knowledge about computers, binary code, modems, and networks. Let students work in small groups to research information and then make a board game or a quiz show patterned after a TV game. For a game show, have students write the questions on note cards and take turns being the host. Groups can play their game with another group while the rest of the class acts as the audience. A board game can be played by small groups with assistance from the inventors.

Language SmArts
RI.4.5 Sequencing

Have students mark the sequence of events in the scenario. If necessary, let students revisit the photos on the previous page to refresh their memories.

LESSON 3 Engage • **Explore/Explain** • Elaborate • Evaluate

EXPLORATION 2 Bits and Bytes, continued

Misconception Alert Some students may think that telephone wires carry sound waves. Clarify that landline telephone wires carry electrical impulses with coded information. Cell phones carry radio waves that send coded information. The code is decoded at the other end of the call and reproduced as sound.

SEP Constructing Explanations and Designing Solutions

HANDS-ON Apply What You Know
The Phone Is For You!

 **Patterns**

When playing the telephone game, make sure the story is written before students start passing the information along. This will provide verification as to what should have been said. The game works better with more people. Students will hopefully observe that the phrase coming out of the last student's mouth is NOT what went into the first student's ears.

Ask: What did you hear from the person who told you the story?
Answers will vary depending on the story and what an individual student heard.

Scoring Guidelines
An excellent score involves active student participation. Those who do not want to participate should not receive full credit.

HANDS-ON Apply What You Know
Make a Wave

Place students into pairs and give each group a spring to use for the activity. Make sure they are writing down the numbers to arrive at the correct message.

Scoring Guidelines
An excellent score involves active student participation. Those who do not want to participate should not receive full credit.

Sounds in the Air

When you talk on a cell phone, you use radio waves. A cell phone converts your voice (sound waves) into radio waves. These waves then get sent to a cell tower. From here, the waves are relayed to other towers. Finally, a tower sends the radio waves to a receiving phone. This entire process happens almost instantly.

HANDS-ON Apply What You Know
The Phone Is for You!

16. Choose one classmate to be the leader. The leader should write down a message before telling it to the first student. The first student tells the second student the message. The second student tells the third student the story. This is repeated until all the students have heard the message. After the final student has been told, they should say the message aloud. Compare it to what was written down.

HANDS-ON Apply What You Know
Make a Wave

17. Can you use a spring toy to send a message? Using binary code, send a short message to a classmate. "0" is represented by moving the spring back and forth. "1" is represented by moving the spring up and down. Have your classmate say the message aloud. Compare it to what was written down. Are they the same? What might improve your ability to send a message more accurately?

Possible answer: The messages were not the same. Taking my time would keep the message clear. I could also make my movements larger.

Unit 3 Waves and Information Transfer

How Cell Phones Help Us Communicate

1

When you talk on a cell phone, the sound waves of your voice are converted into digital code. The code is then sent as radio waves through the air.

2

The sender's radio waves reach cell phone towers, which exist in a network around the world.

3

The waves bounce from tower to tower to satellites and then to other towers.

4

The radio waves are received by a cell phone which converts them back into sound.

18. Choose the correct words to complete each sentence.

| sound waves | light wave | radio waves |
| microwaves | tower | trough |

Cells phones convert __sound waves__ into __radio waves__. They are then sent to a cell __tower__. From here, they relay to other towers. They eventually arrive at a __tower__ near another phone.

217

PS4.C Information Technologies and Instrumentation

The illustrations and captions on this page reinforce the concepts introduced on the previous page. Focus students' attention on the order of the images.

Ask: What happens when the radio waves reach the first tower closest to the sender? *The waves bounce from tower to tower, to satellites, and onto other towers until they get to the receiver's device.*

Differentiate Instruction

RTI/Extra Support Tell students that choral reading can help them build fluency. Add that fluent readers can better see relationships between ideas and remember what they read. Model reading aloud the text under the first illustration, then have students reread it chorally. Next ask students to paraphrase the text to exhibit understanding. Repeat the procedure with the rest of the text.

Collaboration

Think, Pair, Share Let students work in pairs to complete item 16. Then have partners discuss their response with another pair of students. Have students explain why they made the choices they did, and why the other choices were incorrect. In order to make connections, ask students to discuss why cell phones are important in their lives.

LESSON 3 Engage • **Explore/Explain** • Elaborate • Evaluate

EXPLORATION 2 *Bits and Bytes, continued*

Collaboration

Write, Pair, Share Have student pairs explore online to learn more about how we see low and high resolution images, and why high resolution is better. Ask each pair to summarize its findings for the class, complete with images drawn to represent low and high resolutions.

DCI ETS1.C Optimizing the Design Solution

Ask: What is the difference between low and high resolution of an image? **Possible answer: Low resolution has fewer pixels than high resolution, so a low resolution picture is not as clear.**

FORMATIVE ASSESSMENT
Putting It Together

DCI PS4.C Information Technologies and Instrumentation

Finding the Main Idea This activity is an opportunity to assess students' ability to find the main idea of a selection. Before students fill in the blanks, remind them that the main idea is what a selection is mostly about. Facts, or details, in the selection support the main idea. Add that sometimes the main idea is stated directly, but sometimes it is not. To find the main idea in that case, you have to put all the details together.

Ask: What is the main idea of this Exploration? **Possible answer: Digital devices such as cell phones, computers, and TVs use binary code to transmit signals.**
What questions do you need to ask to better understand how digital devices work? **Answers will vary. Where could you find answers to your questions? Possible answer: in an encyclopedia or on the Internet.**

Bits of Color

Pixels are important. Remember that each picture or image you see on a screen is made of pixels. The more pixels there are, the clearer and more crisp the image will be. Back in the 1980s, videogames and TVs had lower resolution than today. This means that the number of pixels on the screen was smaller. With today's TVs, there are many more pixels. This makes the pictures much clearer and the colors brighter. This is called high resolution, or high definition. You might have heard it called HD.

Does this image really look like an apple? This image has very low resolution. This means there are very few pixels that make it up. The edges look fuzzy. And the texture of the picture looks grainy. This is how television and computer pictures looked many years ago.

Here is an image with higher resolution. Notice how much clearer it is. The image also looks much smoother and more realistic. Most people today like to see high resolution images. This is because they look much more realistic than low resolution.

Putting It Together

19. Choose the correct words to complete each sentence.

| light pulses | a system of ones and zeros |
| Morse | binary |

An image on a TV is like the image made in the grid activity because both rely on ___a system of ones and zeroes___ to create images. All digital devices use ___binary___ code to transmit signals.

TAKE IT FURTHER

Discover More

Check out this path . . . or go online to choose one of these other paths.

Elephant Communication → • People in Science • Wave That Flag

Elephant Stomp Sounds

There are all kinds of sounds. All sound waves have amplitude and wavelength. As humans, we can only hear things that are within a certain wavelength. Some animals can hear sounds that we cannot. Elephants have adapted to generate and hear sounds with longer wavelengths than humans can hear. These sounds are called *infrasounds*. These sounds can travel over great distances. This is very helpful to elephant herds. The sounds can alert them of dangers. They can alert them of a new food source. Being able to hear in this range has been extensively studied in three species of elephants.

Elephants are the largest land animals. Their size makes them fairly safe from predators. They live in large social groups and are constantly "talking" to each other. Most of their sounds are made with their trunks. However, they are able to make rumbling noises from within their bodies. These rumbles cannot be heard by humans.

Elephants may be able to hear through their feet as well as their ears.

LESSON 3   Engage • Explore/Explain • **Elaborate** • Evaluate

TAKE IT FURTHER, continued

Connection to English Language Arts

Read the text and discuss the diagrams with students. Then ask them to paraphrase the information. Remind them that to paraphrase, we retell the most important information in our own words. Point out to students that paraphrasing can not only help them remember what they read, but also help them prepare to write reports about a topic.

SL.4.2 Paraphrase portions of a text read aloud or information presented in diverse media and formats, including visually, quantitatively, and orally.

Differentiate Instruction

Extension Challenge interested student pairs to research other animals that communicate through the ground. For example, a kangaroo thumps its tail, the blind mole rat thumps its head, and even tiny termites head-drum to communicate. Have each pair plan a presentation for classmates, complete with visuals.

▶ Explore Online

Students can explore these additional topics online.

People in Science

Students learn how both Alexander Graham Bell and actress Hedy Lamarr helped to change communication technology. *(No outside research required.)*

Wave That Flag

Students discover how semaphores are used by a lifeguard at the beach to inform people and keep them safe. *(No outside research required.)*

It has been found that these sounds, called *infrasonic,* are felt by the elephants. They are used as a form of long distance communication.

Think about where elephants live. Living on the open savannah has many challenges. Infrasonic calls are ideal for living here. Being able to avoid danger is important. Using infrasonic calls lets the elephants stay in touch even if they are not close. Since the signals are heard and felt, scientists believe the elephants take them in through their feet as well as their ears.

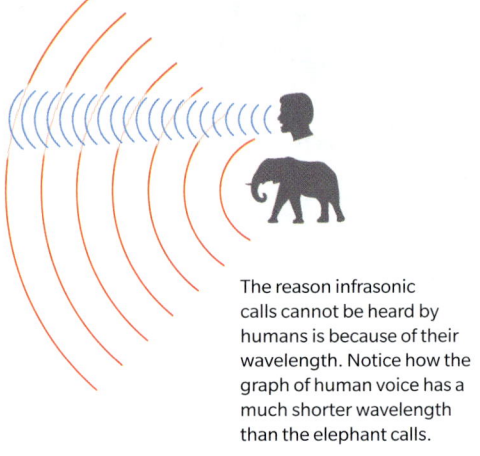

The reason infrasonic calls cannot be heard by humans is because of their wavelength. Notice how the graph of human voice has a much shorter wavelength than the elephant calls.

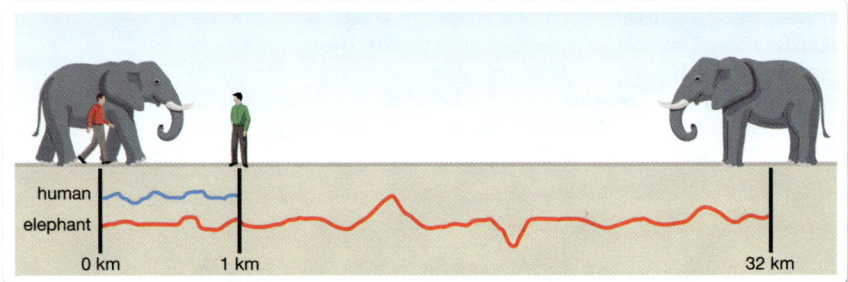

An infrasound made by an elephant can travel large distances. Human speech has shorter wavelengths that don't travel nearly as far.

19. How is the way elephants use infrasonic sounds to communicate alike and different from the way we use cell phones?

Possible answer: The way elephants communicate with infrasounds is like the way humans communicate with cell phones because both can travel long distances. They are different because one method uses naturally made sounds, and the other method uses the technology of a phone to communicate. Cell phone signals travel through the air, while the elephants' infrasonic signals travel through the air and ground.

220

---

220   Unit 3 Waves and Information Transfer

LESSON 3 Engage • Explore/Explain • Elaborate • **Evaluate**

LESSON CHECK

 **Explore Online** Students can revisit the lesson phenomenon online.

LESSON 3
Lesson Check

Name _____

Can You Explain It?

1. How has the way we rely on information transfer changed over the years? Be sure to discuss the following:
   • Ways information has been transferred historically.
   • How energy transfer plays a role in information transfer.
   • How information is encoded, moved long distances, and then decoded without losing any of the information.
   • Criteria and constraints of information technology.

 EVIDENCE NOTEBOOK Use the information you've collected in your Evidence Notebook to help answer the question.

• Possible answer: Pictures were drawn on cave walls to tell stories and record history. Smoke signals and lanterns were used to send messages over distances.
• Energy transfer like electricity led to the development of the telegraph and Morse code. The invention of the telephone could carry voice signals over a wire.
• Messages are translated into binary code and then sent by waves to devices where they are decoded.
• Technology is smaller but relies on signals and devices that can decode them.

Checkpoints

2. Which of these methods use technology to transfer information? Select all that apply.
   a. Morse code
   b. using flags
   c. creating a scytale
   d. infrasonic elephant sounds
   e. texting a friend using your phone

221

Formal Assessment Go online for student self-checks and other assessments.

Can You Explain It?

> ### Collaboration
> **Discussion** You may wish to revisit and discuss the image as a group to assess students' understanding of the material. Use the bulleted points in the Interactive Worktext to lead the discussion.

 EVIDENCE NOTEBOOK

Have students reread their answers to the Evidence Notebook prompts, and then use this evidence to justify their reasoning as they respond to the Can You Explain It question. Make sure they understand that a complete response must address all bulleted points.

 PS4.C Information Technologies and Instrumentation

Focus students on the many advances in communication technology by asking them to speculate.

Ask: If Paul Revere and the colonists were alive today, how do you think they would get out the message "the British are coming" without the enemy knowing?

Let students turn and tell a partner how they think the message would best be transferred. Encourage the use of evidence from the text to support the idea. Have pairs share their ideas with the class.

Checkpoints
SUMMATIVE ASSESSMENT

2. This question asks students which methods use technology. Check that students analyze each possible answer before choosing. If necessary, let students skim Explorations 1 and 2 and the Take It Further article.

Lesson 3 How Is Information Transferred from Place to Place? **221**

LESSON 3   Engage • Explore/Explain • Elaborate • **Evaluate**

LESSON CHECK, continued

Using Representations to Assess Proficiency

3. In Exploration 1, students learned how people communicate by using patterns of signals from drums. Allow students to revisit the information to refresh their memories.

4. This concept was covered in Exploration 2. If students have difficulty with the question, have them go back and reread information relating to these forms of technology.

5. This concept was covered in Exploration 2. Let students having difficulty check their Evidence Notebook and the Exploration for clues.

6. To solve the secret message, students need to figure out that each letter of the alphabet is represented by its numerical value: 1 = A, 2 = B, and so on. The six-word message is "I learned many things about signals."

---

3. Suppose you wanted to describe African drums to a classmate. You want to tell them how they are used as a form of sending signals. Which of these would you say? Select all that apply.
   a. The drums send signals you can hear. ✓
   b. The drums have a very high wavelength.
   c. The drums have a very low wavelength. ✓
   d. The drums are used for religious ceremonies. ✓

4. Choose the correct words to complete each of the sentences. The ancient Egyptians used __hieroglyphics__ as means of story telling and recording their history. Soldiers in ancient China used __smoke signals__ to send silent messages a long distance. The most famous use of __lantern__ signals was during Paul Revere's ride. The "one if by land, two if by sea" signals told the colonists the British were coming.

   | hieroglyphics |
   | Morse code |
   | drums |
   | smoke signals |
   | lantern |

5. Put these steps in order of how a message would get from your cell phone to your friend's cell phone.

tower near your friend's cell phone	tower close to your cell phone	friend's cell phone
4	2	5

your cell phone	relay
1	3

6. Use the code key below to decode the message (hint: it is six words long). The message is:
   9 12 5 1 18 14 5 4 13 1 14 25 20 8 9 14 7 19 1 2 15 21 20 19 9 7 14 1 12 19

1	2	3	4	5	6	7	8	9	10	11	12	13
A	B	C	D	E	F	G	H	I	J	K	L	M
14	15	16	17	18	19	20	21	22	23	24	25	26
N	O	P	Q	R	S	T	U	V	W	X	Y	Z

   I LEARNED MANY THINGS ABOUT SIGNALS

222

222   Unit 3   Waves and Information Transfer

LESSON 3
Lesson Roundup

A. Which of these describe the use of hieroglyphics and pictographs in ancient times? Select all that apply.
   a. They were often drawn on walls.
   b. They are a form of signal that can be heard.
   c. They record events and cultural histories.
   d. They were made using modern art tools.

B. How are cell phone signals transferred? Select the best answer for the question.
   a. They go from the tower to the phone to another phone.
   b. They go from the receiver's phone to the sender's phone.
   c. They go from sender to tower to relay to tower to receiver.
   d. They go from tower to receiver to sender to relay back to the receiver.

C. Decide if each phrase is describing signal transfer using coded or uncoded communication. Some may go into more than one category.

D. Why are codes used to relay messages? Select all that apply.
   a. They do not depend on understanding a language.
   b. Everyone can understand them.
   c. They can be encoded and decoded digitally and sent by waves.
   d. They are short.

Lesson Roundup

 PS4.C Information Technologies and Instrumentation

This lesson summary enables students to quickly revisit key points and prepare for tests.

A. To clarify students' understanding of early methods of communication, have them revisit Exploration 1. Teach students to look for clues within the distractors, words such as *modern*. Students can often use the process of elimination for multiple choice questions by looking for words in the answer choices that stand out as incorrect. **PS4.C**

B. Students may wish to scan Exploration 2 before responding. If students need support, begin by reminding them of where a telephone message begins (with a sender) and where it ends (when someone receives it). You can remind them of the patterns they studied in terms of communicating messages. **PS4.C**

C. This question asks students to use common sense to know the difference between coded and uncoded communication. If any student is unsure, explain that when we talk face to face, we say what we mean; we don't need a code. If this diagram confuses students, help them interpret the same information using a different format. Also be sure to tell students that some choices can go into more than one category. **PS4.C**

D. Students should be able to answer this question easily. If necessary, point out that codes are not decodable by everyone, only the people allowed to decode them. **PS4.C**

UNIT 3 Performance Task

👥 small groups   🕐 2 class periods

The Rainbow Show

Students **use models** to demonstrate how to make a rainbow through research and observing **patterns.** They demonstrate their understanding of **PS4.B** in support of **4-PS4-2** and **4-LS1-2**.

Materials
- paper
- pencil
- colored pencils
- resource materials
- prisms
- light source
- camera or electronic device for presentation

Preparation
Arrange computer access time. Make the checklist as a chart to hang up during the activity.

🟠 DCI PS4.B Electromagnetic Radiation

Students may find it useful to watch some informational videos of how rainbows form. **Ask: What makes a rainbow?**

Research
Review with students appropriate resource materials to use during research. You may want to provide a number of websites that students can use.

Print: title, author, copyright date, page number
Online: webpage title, URL, date visited

Demonstration Preparation
Have students observe a prism and discuss their observations. Suggest students explore different ways one and two prisms make rainbows.

224   Unit 3 Waves and Information Transfer

UNIT 3   **UNIT PERFORMANCE TASK**

The Rainbow Show

Your task is to prepare and give a three-part educational presentation about rainbows. In Part One, you'll tell your class all about rainbows, what they are, and how they form. In Part Two, you'll dazzle your class by making a rainbow appear before their eyes. Then in Part Three, you'll wrap it all up by taking your rainbow and sending it back to where it came from.

Rainbows occur all the time in nature. But did you know that you can make your own?

UNDERSTAND YOUR GOAL: Describe a successful "Rainbow Show."

Sample answer: It will give good information about rainbows. It will be interesting and entertaining. It will show the class things they have never seen.

Review the checklist at the end of this Unit Performance Task. Keep those requirements in mind as you proceed.

RESEARCH: Use online and library sources to collect information about rainbows. Find out how rainbows form, what colors they contain, and other facts about them. Consider adding entertainment value to your presentation by finding a short poem about rainbows or some interesting rainbow trivia. Examine several sources, and cite the ones you choose. Describe your findings.

Student should describe planned content and cite sources.

DEMONSTRATION PREPARATION: Use online and library sources to find out how a prism can create a rainbow. Then investigate how a second prism can turn the rainbow's colors back into white light. Describe your findings, and cite your sources.

Student should summarize planned content and cite sources.

224

ARRANGE YOUR INFORMATION: Consider the questions below as you organize and script your show.

1. How can multimedia help you present your information?
2. What information do you want to include?
3. In what order do you want to place your information?
4. What can you add to make your speech entertaining?
5. What materials will you need for your demonstration, and how will you use them?

Student should list needed materials and the reasons they are needed, along with other relevant thoughts and ideas.

_____
_____
_____
_____

PREPARE: Script your show. Remember that Part One is for giving information, and Parts Two and Three are for giving demonstrations.

EDITING AND REVISION: Does your planned presentation accomplish the goal that you set for it? Are there ways to improve it? If so, how? Make any changes necessary to improve it.

COMMUNICATE: Present your "Rainbow Show" to your class.

✅ Checklist

Review your project and check off each completed item.

____ Includes a statement of the presentation's goal.

____ Includes description of the presentation's content, along with cited sources.

____ Includes a list of materials needed for the demonstration portions of the presentation.

____ Includes a script, outlining all three parts of the show.

____ Includes a hands-on, three-part presentation to the class.

Arrange Your Information

 Using Models

Ask: What materials will you use for your presentation of a rainbow?

Editing and Revision

Many students find it difficult to edit their own work. Suggest teams pair up to offer suggestions on how to improve their presentations.

Scoring Rubric for Performance Task	
3	• statement of the goal is clear and precise • sources are complete and cited correctly • descriptions and materials included and complete • all parts of the script are complete and precise • hands-on presentation is well organized and engaging
2	• statement of the goal is included • most sources are included but not cited accurately • descriptions and materials included but incomplete • all parts of the script are included but incomplete • hands-on presentation lacks enthusiasm
1	• statement of the goal is incomplete • sources are incomplete or not cited properly • descriptions and materials are incomplete • the show's script is incomplete • hands-on presentation is inaccurate
0	• statement of the goal is missing • sources are missing • descriptions and materials are missing • the show's script is missing • hands-on presentation is missing

UNIT 3 Review

SUMMATIVE ASSESSMENT

1. To answer this question, students need a strong understanding of the different types of waves. Students can review them in Lesson 1. Suggest students study the image and identify the types of waves being shown.

2. Students can use the process of elimination to cross out any choices that they know are not correct. If they are still having trouble answering the question, suggest they review the parts of a wave in Lesson 1, Exploration 2.

3. Instruct students to refer back to the section *Codes* in Lesson 3, Exploration 1 to help them answer this question correctly. Remind them to use complete sentences when answering the question.

UNIT 3

Unit Review

1. What two types of waves are produced by this performance? Circle the correct choices.
   a. **light waves**
   b. water waves
   c. **sound waves**
   d. seismic waves

2. Which choice names two parts of a wave? Circle the correct choice.
   a. size and speed
   b. **crest and trough**
   c. amplitude and volume
   d. wavelength and reflection

3. Why were Navajo soldiers important during World War II?
   Navajo soldiers sent messages in code for the United States. The code was never broken.

4. Classify each item as an example of back and forth waves (B) or up and down waves (U).

   __B__ Music
   __U__ Light from stars
   __U__ Satellite signals
   __B__ Earthquake tremors

5. What qualities is a reflective surface likely to have? Circle all that apply.
   a. **It is likely to be shiny.**
   b. It is likely to be clear.
   c. It is likely to be dark.
   d. **It is likely to be opaque.**

6. What sort of object is each recipe box? Write a word from the Word Bank on each line.

   | transparent   translucent   opaque |

   transparent   translucent   opaque

7. Which of these made the telegraph possible? Select all that apply.
   a. **the discovery of electricity**
   b. the discovery of radio waves
   c. **the development of Morse code**
   d. the development of flag semaphore

227

4. Students should recall that waves move in different directions. Have them review the section *Waves That Move Like Snakes* in Lesson 1, Exploration 1 before attempting to classify the items.

5. Students should recall from Lesson 2 that a reflection is the bouncing of waves when they hit an obstacle. Students may find it helpful to eliminate any choices they know to be incorrect first.

6. For students to sort these terms correctly, they need a strong understanding of *transparent, translucent,* and *opaque*. They can review these terms and definitions in Lesson 2, Exploration 1.

7. Students discovered a lot of different ways of communication in Lesson 3. Have them review the section *Newer Ways* in Exploration 1 if they are having difficulties answering this question.

UNIT 3 Review, continued

8. Students discovered the meaning of each of these terms in Lesson 3. Suggest students use the strategy of trying each term in the sentence and then deciding which one is correct.

9. Students should recall from Lesson 1 the different parts of a wave. Suggest students review the section *Hunks and Chucks of Waves* in Lesson 1, Exploration 2 before attempting to answer this problem. Recommend they study the diagrams in this section carefully.

10. Students explored how our eyes see objects in the section *Human Lenses* in Lesson 2, Exploration 2. Remind students to answer the question in a sequence and to write in complete sentences.

3D Item Analysis	1	2	3	4	5	6	7	8	9	10
SEP Obtaining, Evaluating, and Communicating Information			•		•					•
DCI Waves Properties		•	•		•	•			•	
DCI Electromagnetic Radiation						•	•		•	•
DCI Information Technologies and Instrumentation				•				•	•	
CCC Patterns			•		•			•	•	
CCC Cause and Effect				•		•	•	•		•

---

8. Select a word from the word bank to complete the sentence.

   | pixels | scythes | bits |

   A picture looks like a single image, but it is really millions of tiny dots called ___pixels___ .

9. Match the word with its definition

   wavelength — the distance between two crests
   amplitude — the height of a wave
   volume — the loudness of a sound
   crest — the highest point of a wave
   trough — the lowest point of a wave

10. Describe how our eyes see. Use the image below to help you.

Possible answer: Light from the sun or some other light source reaches a object, such as a shoe or a hamburger. Light reflects off of the object and them moves to our eyes. The image refracts off the lenses of our eyes and then is transferred to our brains as a signal. Our brain then interprets the signal as a shoe or a hamburger.

228

228 Unit 3 Waves and Information Transfer

UNIT 4 Plant Structure and Function

UNIT 4

Plant Structure and Function

Unit Project: Plant and Animal Partnerships
How does the structure and function of plants and animals work together for pollination? Ask your teacher for details.

Explore Online

Apples are tasty, but they are also vital to the reproduction of apple trees. Plants, like animals, are made of individual structures that serve a specific purpose.

229

Unit Overview
In this unit, students will . . .
- explore the functions of internal and external plant structures and how they aid in growth, survival, behavior and reproduction.
- learn how different plant structures work together as a system.

About This Image
Apples, like all other fruits and living things, are made up of special parts that have their own structure and function. There are certain parts of the apple, such as seeds, that are vital to the fruit's viability. The structure of the apple is such that its most important structures are kept safe and hidden inside the apple's core. The skin of the apple protects the inside structures. Each part of the apple serves a unique purpose.

Unit Project
As students work through the unit lessons, have them take notes on the structure and function of plant and animal partnerships, paying particular attention to pollination. This information will be useful for the Unit Project, in which students will show how plants and animals work together to make pollination possible.

Draw students' attention to the picture of the apple, or bring in an apple for students to examine. Hold a whole class discussion on how the fruit came to be. Discuss the factors that made the fruit possible. You can also challenge the class to use online or media center resources to find other types of fruit, or you can bring in other types of fruit as realia, and have them perform the same process for things like bananas, oranges, or peaches. More support for the Unit Project can be found on pp. 231I–231L.

UNIT 4 Plant Structure and Function

The learning experience in this unit prepares children for the mastery of:

Performance Expectation

4-LS1-1 Construct an argument that plants and animals have internal and external structures that function to support survival, growth, behavior, and reproduction.

> **Explore Online**

In addition to the print resources, the following resources are available online to support this unit.

Unit Pretest
Lesson 1 What Are Some Plant Parts and How Do They Function?
- Online Student Edition
- Lesson Quiz

Lesson 2 How Do Plants Grow and Reproduce?
- Online Student Edition
- Lesson Quiz

You Solve It Growing Plants in Different Biomes
Unit Performance Task
Unit Test

UNIT 4

At a Glance

LESSON 1
What Are Some Plant Parts and How Do They Function? 232

LESSON 2
How Do Plants Grow and Reproduce? 254

Unit Review 276

Vocabulary Game: Concentration

Materials
- 1 set of word cards

Setup
- Mix up the cards.
- Place the cards face down on a table in even rows. No card should touch another card.

Directions
1. Take turns to play.
2. Choose two cards. Turn the cards face up.
   - If the cards match, keep the pair and take another turn.
   - If the cards do not match, turn them back over.
3. The game is over when all cards have been matched. The player with the most matched pairs wins.

Unit Vocabulary

fertilization: The process when male and female reproductive parts join together.

leaf: The part of a plant that makes food using air, light, and water.

pollination: The transfer of pollen in flowers or cones.

reproduction: To have young, or more living things of the same kind.

root: A plant part that is usually underground and absorbs water and minerals from the soil.

seed: The part of a plant that contains a new plant.

spore: A reproductive structure of some plants, such as mosses and ferns, that can form a new plant.

stem: The part of a plant that holds it up and has tubes that carry water, minerals, and nutrients through the plant.

Unit Vocabulary

Students can explore all lesson vocabulary terms in the **Online Glossary**.

Vocabulary Strategies

Have students review the terms individually. Then pair up and have pairs choose two terms and write a detailed sentence using both terms accurately.

Differentiate Instruction

RTI/Extra Support Have struggling readers find the vocabulary words within the unit. Bring in leaves, roots, and seeds to use as realia so students can visualize the vocabulary terms.

Extension Have students pick two terms and then work in small groups to illustrate and explain the terms for a younger student.

ELL Pronounce each term and have students repeat it. Then pair up students by native language and have them explain each term in their native language. Use realia wherever appropriate.

Vocabulary Game: Concentration

Preparation
Have the cards prepared and shuffled so that the pairs are not placed near each other.

Game Play
- The game is over when all cards have been matched.

UNIT 4 Plant Structure and Function
Integrating the NGSS* Three Dimensions of Learning

Building to the Performance Expectation

The learning experiences in this unit prepare students for mastery of the following Performance Expectation:

From Molecules to Organisms: Structures and Processes

4-LS1-1 Construct an argument that plants and animals have internal and external structures that function to support survival, growth, behavior, and reproduction.

Assessing Student Progress

After completing these lessons, the **Unit Project: Plant and Animal Partnerships** provides students with opportunities to practice aspects of and demonstrate their understanding of the Performance Expectations as they research an example of a plant-and-animal pair whose structures are adapted to each other.

Additionally, students can practice or be assessed on aspects of the Performance Expectations by completing the **Unit Performance Task: Flower Parts** in which they study images of flowering plants and determine how the parts constitute the whole.

Lesson 1
What Are Some Plant Parts and How Do They Function?

In Lesson 1, students will gather evidence about the function of internal and external plant parts **(DCI LS1.A)** to construct an argument **(SEP Engaging in Argument from Evidence)** that these parts work together to form a system **(CCC Systems and System Models)** used for growth, survival, reproduction, and behavior. Students also investigate how plants move, and they design and build a system to grow a plant in water rather than soil.

Lesson 2
How Do Plants Grow and Reproduce?

In Lesson 2, students develop an understanding of how the internal and external structures of both flowering and non-flowering plants function to support survival, growth, and reproduction **(DCI LS1.A).** Students will construct arguments from evidence **(SEP Engaging in Argument from Evidence)** to explain the components and interactions of systems **(CCCs Cause and Effect, Systems and System Models)** and how they work together to enable reproduction.

*Next Generation Science Standards and logo are registered trademarks of Achieve. Neither Achieve or the lead states and partners that developed the Next Generation Science Standards were involved in production of, and does not endorse, these products.

NGSS Across the Unit

Explore Online!
Online only.

Next Generation Science Standards	Unit Project	Lesson 1	Lesson 2	Unit Performance Task	You Solve It!
SEP Engaging in Argument from Evidence	•	•	•		•
SEP Analyzing and Interpreting Data			•	•	•
SEP Asking Questions and Defining Problems	•		•		•
DCI LS1.A Structure and Function	•	•	•	•	•
CCC Systems and System Models	•	•	•	•	•
CCC Cause and Effect			•		•

NGSS Across the Grades

Before
From Molecules to Organisms: Structures and Processes
3-LS1-1

Grade 4
From Molecules to Organisms: Structures and Processes
4-LS1-1

After
From Molecules to Organisms: Structures and Processes
5-LS1-1 Support and argument that plants get the materials they need for growth chiefly from air and water.

Trace Tool to the NGSS™ — Go online to view the complete coverage of these standards across this grade level and time.

Unit 4: Plant Structure and Function   231B

UNIT 4 Plant Structure and Function
3D Unit Planning

Lesson 1 What Are Some Plant Parts and How Do They Function? pp. 232–253

Overview

Objective To gather evidence about the function and structure of plant parts in order to construct an argument that these parts are used for survival, growth, reproduction, and behavior.

SEP Engaging in Argument from Evidence
DCI **LS1.A** Structure and Function
CCC Systems and System Models
CCC Influence of Engineering, Technology, and Science

Math and **English Language Arts** standards and features are detailed on lesson planner pages.

	Print and Online Student Editions	▶ **Explore Online!**
ENGAGE	**Lesson Phenomenon** pp. 232–233 **Can You Explain It?** Why do the plants in the picture bend one way or another?	▶ Can You Explain It! Video
EXPLORE/ EXPLAIN	**Plant Dissection** pp. 234–238 Do Parts Serve Purposes? **What's Inside?** pp. 239–245 Slurp! 🛡 **ENGINEER IT!** Green Roofs ✋ **Apply What You Know** Modeling Water Flow in Plants ✋ **HANDS-ON** Hold the Soil **Can Plants Move?** pp. 246–248 Move and Groove ✋ **Apply What You Know** Plant Response	HANDS-ON Worksheet
ELABORATE	**Take It Further** pp. 249–250 **People in Science & Engineering:** Clayton Anderson	Take It Further Burrr! Take It Further How Unusual!
EVALUATE	**Lesson Check** pp. 251–252 **Lesson Roundup** p. 253	Lesson Quiz

✋ HANDS-ON ACTIVITY PLANNING

Apply What You Know

Modeling Water Flow in Plants
⏱ 30 minutes
👥 Pairs

Materials
- plastic straws
- small bits of plastic tubing
- scissors
- masking tape
- paper clips

Preparation/Tip You might want to have students begin the activity by drawing a design of their 3D models before building them.

Plant Response
⏱ 20 minutes
👥 Individual

Materials
- drawing paper
- drawing utensils

Preparation/Tip Allow students some creative freedom for the captions they write, but make sure the captions are plant-related.

HANDS-ON

Hold the Soil
⏱ 1 class period/4 weeks
👥 Small groups

Objective Students will test the function of roots as they build a system to grow plants in water rather than soil. Then students make a claim about the effectiveness of their process based on their evidence.

Materials
- 5 bean seeds
- plastic cup or bottle
- paper towel
- gravel
- vermiculite
- cotton balls
- foam pellets
- liquid nutrients
- aluminum foil
- plastic wrap
- metric ruler
- water

Preparation/Tip Students do not need to use all of the materials, but they can choose the ones they want to use.

Lesson 2 How Do Plants Grow and Reproduce? pp. 254–275

Overview

Objective Describe the process of pollination and fertilization in both flowering and non-flowering plants. Identify the basic reproductive structures of plants and how the parts form a system for reproduction.

SEP Analyzing and Interpreting Data
SEP Engaging in Argument from Evidence
SEP Asking Questions and Defining Problems
DCI LS1.A Structure and Function
CCC Cause and Effect
CCC Systems and System Models

Math and **English Language Arts** standards and features are detailed on lesson planner pages.

Print and Online Student Editions · Explore Online!

ENGAGE	**Lesson Phenomenon** pp. 254–255 **Can You Explain It?** How did the flower turn into fruit? Why didn't the other flowers turn into fruits?	Can You Explain It! Video
EXPLORE/ EXPLAIN	**Why Do Plants Have Flowers?** pp. 256–260 Flower Power 👐 **Apply What You Know** Pollination Models **What If Plants Don't Produce Flowers?** pp. 261–264 Flowerless 👐 **Apply What You Know** Pinecone Parts **On The Move** pp. 265–270 How Do Seeds Get Around? 👐 **HANDS-ON** Flying High	HANDS-ON Worksheet
ELABORATE	**Take It Further** pp. 271–272 **Careers In Science & Engineering:** Pomologist	**Take It Further** Wait, There's More! **Take It Further** It's What's On the Inside
EVALUATE	**Lesson Check** pp. 273–274 **Lesson Roundup** p. 275	Lesson Quiz

👐 HANDS-ON ACTIVITY PLANNING

Apply What You Know

Pollination Models
⏱ 20 minutes
👥 Pairs

Materials
- clear plastic cups
- cotton balls, pipe cleaners
- different colored powders

Preparation/Tip Offer guidance to students by telling what some of the materials should be used to represent in their models.

Pinecone Parts
⏱ 20 minutes
👥 Pairs

Materials
- pinecone and paper plate
- drawing paper and utensils

Preparation/Tip As students dissect and explore the pinecone, warn them to be careful that they do not pinch their fingers in the pinecone parts.

HANDS-ON

Flying High
⏱ 1 class period
👥 Small groups

Objective Students will design and test a device that disperses seeds using wind.

Materials
- corn kernels for seeds
- balloons and a meterstick
- box of tissues & a paper bag
- paper clips and tape
- rubber bands
- straws and a fan
- yarn and ribbon
- aluminum foil & cotton balls
- popsicle sticks & pipe cleaners

Preparation/Tip Allow students to modify their designs and swap out different materials throughout the activity, as long as they stay within their budget.

Unit 4: Plant Structure and Function   231D

UNIT 4 Plant Structure and Function
3D Unit Planning, continued

 **You Solve It**   Go online for an additional interactive activity.

Plant Structure and Function

This virtual lab offers practice in support of **PE 4-LS1-1**.

- **SEP** Scientific Investigations Use a Variety of Methods
- **SEP** Scientific Knowledge Is Based on Empirical Evidence
- **SEP** Science Models, Laws, Mechanisms, and Theories Explain Natural Phenomena
- **DCI** **4-LS1.A** Structure and Function
- **CCC** Cause and Effect
- **CCC** Patterns
- **CCC** Systems and System Models

Use after Unit 4, Lesson 2— What plants grow best in certain biomes?

Objectives
1. Students will determine the characteristics of different biomes.
2. Students interpret data to decide what plants grow best in certain biomes.

Activity Problem
You are going to choose plants that grow well in a particular area. Your tasks include:
1. learning characteristics about your particular area,
2. choosing plants that will grow well in your area, and
3. recording data and analyzing how the plants grew in a report.

Interaction Summary
1. Students collect information about different biomes.
2. They choose plants that will survive well in the different biomes.
3. Photos are taken of the chosen plants.
4. Plants growth and survival are recorded.

Assessment

Pre-Assessment
Assessment Guide, Unit Pretest

The Unit Pretest focuses on prerequisite knowledge and is composed of items that evaluate students' preparedness for the content covered within this unit.

Formative Assessment
Student Edition, Apply What You Know, Lesson Check, and Self Check

Summative Assessment
Assessment Guide, Lesson Quiz
The Lesson Quiz provides a quick assessment of each lesson objective and of the portion of the Performance Expectation aligned to the lesson.

Student Edition, Performance Task pp. 276–277
The Performance Task presents the opportunity for children to collaborate with classmates in order to complete the steps of each Performance Task. Each Performance Task provides a formal Scoring Rubric for evaluating students' work.

Student Edition, Unit 4 Review pp. 278–280

Assessment Guide, Unit Test
The Unit Test provides an in-depth assessment of the Performance Expectations aligned to the unit. This test evaluates students' ability to apply knowledge in order to explain phenomena and to solve problems. Within this test, Constructed Response items apply a three-dimensional rubric for evaluating students' mastery on all three dimensions of the Next Generation Science Standards.

 **Assessment Online**   Go online to view the complete assessment items for this unit.

Teacher Notes

UNIT 4 Plant Structure and Function
Differentiated Instruction

Leveled Readers

The **Science & Engineering Leveled Readers** provide additional nonfiction reading practice in this unit's subject area.

On-Level Reader • How Do Plants and Animals Reproduce and Adapt?
This reader reinforces unit concepts and includes response activities for your students.

Extra Support • How Do Plants and Animals Reproduce and Adapt?
This reader shares title, illustrations, vocabulary, and concepts with the On-Level Reader; however, the text is linguistically accommodated to provide simplified sentence structures and comprehension aids. It also includes response activities.

Enrichment • Exploring the Galapagos Islands
This high-interest, nonfiction reader will extend and enrich unit concepts and vocabulary and includes response activities.

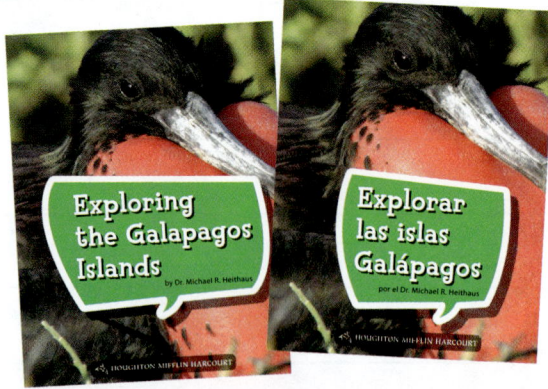

Teacher Guide

The accompanying Teacher Guide provides teaching strategies and support for using all the readers.

ELL
ELL teacher strategies in this unit:
Lesson 1: pp. 236, 247
Lesson 2: p. 255

RTI/Extra Support
Strategies for students needing extra support in this unit:
Lesson 1: pp. 235, 237, 239, 241, 246
Lesson 2: pp. 256, 260, 267

Extension
Strategies for students who have mastered core content in this unit:
Lesson 1: pp. 244, 247, 249
Lesson 2: p. 262

 **Leveled Readers** All readers are available online as well as in an innovative, engaging format for use with touchscreen mobile devices. Contact your HMH Sales Representative for more information.

UNIT 4 Plant Structure and Function
Making Connections

Connections to the Community

Use these opportunities for informal science learning to provide local context and to extend and enhance unit concepts.

At Home

DIFFERENT TYPES OF PLANT PARTS Have each student collect and bring in one example each of a root, a stem, a leaf, and a flower from around their home. Instruct students that each should be from a different type of plant. Then have students share their plant parts with the class and describe the type of plant each came from. Use the activity as an opportunity to point out to students that there is a wide variety of each type of plant part. *Use with Lesson 1.*

FRUIT SEEDS Have students work with a responsible adult to cut open one or more types of fruit and collect the seeds inside. Provide class time for students to show their seeds to other students. *Use with Lesson 2.*

In the Community

PLANT PICTURES Have students, along with a responsible adult, look around the community for examples of interesting trees or other types of plants. Then have them choose several plants and draw pictures of them, labeling each of their parts. *Use with Lesson 1.*

CARING FOR PLANTS Contact a local master gardener and arrange a hands-on presentation in which students learn about different types of plants, how they reproduce, and how to care for them. *Use with Lesson 2.*

 **Home Letters** Use these one-page letters to engage family members with unit concepts.

Collaboration
Opportunities for students to work collaboratively in this unit:

Discussion
pp. 251, 273

Think, Pair Share
pp. 233, 236, 239, 246

Draw, Pair, Share
p. 241

Write, Pair, Share
p. 255

Feedback
p. 234

Connections to Science
Opportunities to connect to other content areas in this unit:

Connection to Physical Science
Lesson 1, p. 236

Lesson 2, p. 264

UNIT 4 Plant Structure and Function
Unit Project

Unit Project: Plant and Animal Partnerships
👥 Small groups 🕐 2 class periods

For this task, small groups of students will research and then present ways that plant and animal structures work together to allow pollination to occur. They will need to select and agree on a plant and animal that work together for pollination. Students are encouraged but not required to research plants and animals in their area. They may be unfamiliar with these, so provide guidance and instruction as needed.

3D Learning Objective

- Collect and analyze data about the structures of plants and animals
- Identify plant and animal systems that allow them to pollinate
- Analyze research material to determine how plants and animals pollinate

Skills and Standards Focus

This project supports building student mastery of **Perfomance Expectation 4-LS1-1.**

- **SEP** Analyzing and Interpreting Data
- **SEP** Engaging in Argument from Evidence
- **DCI** LS1.A: Structure and Function
- **CCC** Systems and System Models

Suggested Materials

- drawing paper
- drawing utensils
- references—print (books, magazines), electronic (websites)

Preparation and Planning Tips

Ensure that each group has a set of print resources or list of URLs for websites you have previously reviewed. Make sure students understand that in order to research effectively, they must have a clear idea of which plant and animal they are researching. Specifically, students should have chosen a plant and an animal that act together to pollinate. If necessary, provide students with a list of plants and pollinators to choose from.

Differentiate Instruction

RTI/Extra Support When supplying a list of plants and pollinators, match each plant with a pollinator so that students don't have to spend too much time researching this themselves. This will allow each group to focus on the structure of the animal's body parts and how they work with the structure of the plant to make pollination easier.

Extension To account for their observations, have students draw a diagram relating how the animal's structures work with the plant's structures to pollinate. For example, they may draw an insect with a long proboscis that perfectly fits into the flower.

Name _____

UNIT PROJECT
Plant and Animal Partnerships

Have you ever seen a hummingbird drink nectar from a flower, and notice that its beak is the perfect shape and length for reaching the sweet nectar it wants? For this project, you will investigate how the structure and function of plants and animals work together for pollination, and present your findings to the class.

Write a question that you will investigate as you perform your analysis of plant and animal structures and functions, related to pollination.

Students should write a question concerning how the structures of plants and animals support their function, thus allowing pollination to occur.

Materials

Think about how you will need to perform this investigation. What materials will you need?

Materials can include drawing paper, drawing utensils, and references (print or electronic).

To carry out this investigation, as a team, decide on the plant and animal you wish to focus on. Think about selecting plants and animals based on your interest, or based on the ones that are native to your area (although you are not limited to this). Which plant and animal did your team decide on?

Accept any response so long as the structure and parts of the plants and animals result in pollination. Check to make sure students' selections support this.

UNIT 4 PROJECT
Plant and Animal Partnerships

DCI **LS1.A Structure and Function**

Before students begin the task, check their understanding of key concepts.

Ask: What is the purpose of pollination? *Pollination moves pollen from one plant to another so that the plants can reproduce.*

Refer students to Lesson 2, Exploration 1 for concept support.

ESSENTIAL QUESTIONS Ask the following questions before students begin to plan their activity.

- What is needed for pollination to occur?
- What kinds of animals can help plants pollinate?

Provide students with a list of animal body parts that can help spread pollen. The list should include noses, mouths, and feet among others parts, and explain how each helps in pollination. Instruct students that their research should focus on how the body structures and features of the animal they chose help the pollination process.

CCC **Systems and System Models**

Though some flowering plants may appear very different to the naked eye, they have similar features when it comes to reproduction. Because plants cannot move from place to place, sexual reproduction must be carried out with the help of outside forces. Pollen must be carried from one plant to another by external means. These can include wind and water as well as other animals.

Ask: Why do flowering plants need help when reproducing? *They cannot move from place to place; therefore, their pollen must be carried by outside forces.*

Research and Plan

Students should carefully consider the plants and animals they will use.

Ask: How will you select your organism? We will do an initial round of research to see which animals feed from which plants. Then we will select a plant and animal that works together.

Research and Plan

Groups will then research the plants and animals they chose and create a presentation about how the animals' structures, such as noses or feet, help spread pollen from one plant to another to aid in reproduction.

Ask: Which specific structures did you look for in the animals that might aid in pollination? Possible answer: We looked for structures that might touch the pollen as the animal feeds on the nectar. These included legs, mouths, noses, and wings.

Some students'/groups' conclusions may focus on the features of the animal while excluding the features of the plant that aid in pollination. Remind them that pollinators are usually adapted to certain plants. For example, a long proboscis in an animal may be adapted to a long pistil in a plant. Both the proboscis and the pistil are important structures needed for pollination to occur.

Analyze Your Results

SEP Analyzing and Interpreting Data

Students should consider the following questions as they interpret their research data: What kind of plants require the help of pollinators? Do all animals transfer pollen from one plant to another in the same way? How are different animals adapted to different plants?

Research and Plan

Make a plan for how you will carry out your research investigation. As you make your plan, consider the following:

- What are the structures and functions of the animal body parts?
- What are the structures and functions of the plant body parts?
- Do the structures and functions work together to result in pollination?

Students should list the structures and functions of the animal body parts and plant body parts, and then describe how the structures and functions of both work together to support pollination.

Review your research as a group. Write a conclusion about the structures and functions of animal and plant body parts, and how they work together support pollination.

Student conclusions should reflect understanding of how plant and animal body structures work together to function towards pollination. Possible responses could include a discussion of pollinators and their role in spreading pollen. Make sure students accurately identify animals that are pollinators.

231

231K Unit 4 Plant Structure and Function

Analyze Your Results

Look for patterns in the data you found. Using your investigation, make an observation about animal and plant body parts and pollination.

Possible response: For some plants pollination is only possible with the help of pollinators. The external structures of animals and plants have to be compatible. This is why some animals have longer beaks or the ability to get close to flowers.

Restate Your Question

Write the question you investigated.

Students should identify the question created at the beginning of the project.

Claims, Evidence, and Reasoning

Make a claim that answers your question.

Possible answers: For many flowers pollination depends on animals that feed on pollen. Only certain types of animals feed on pollen because of how their external and internal body structures work.

Review your investigation. What evidence from your investigation supports your claim?

Students should cite evidence from their investigation to support their claims.

Discuss your reasoning with a partner.

SEP Engaging in Argument from Evidence

Review with students what it means to make a claim. Guide them to understand that they will use their research of plants and pollinators as evidence to support their claim.

Claims, Evidence, and Reasoning

Students should claim that the structures of plants and animals work together to help pollination, or the reproduction of some plants, to occur.

Ask: What claim can you make? **Possible claim: My/Our pollinator's feet pick up the pollen from the plant and transfer it to other plants of the same species.**

Ask: How does your evidence support your claim? **Possible answer: My/Our research shows that the only feature in my/our animal able to transfer pollen is the feet. It has tiny hairs to catch the pollen. The other features are not adapted to transfer pollen.**

Encourage students to discuss their reasoning.

Scoring Rubric for Hands-On Activity	
3	States a claim supported with ample, detailed evidence that the pollinator and plant's features are adapted to transfer pollen from one plant to another.
2	States a claim that is somewhat supported with evidence that the pollinator and plant's features are adapted to transfer pollen from one plant to another.
1	States a claim that is not supported by evidence.
0	Does not state a claim.

LESSON 1
What Are Some Plant Parts and How Do They Function?

Building to the Performance Expectation

The learning experiences in this lesson prepare students for mastery of:

4-LS1-1 Construct an argument that plants and animals have internal and external structures that function to support survival, growth, behavior, and reproduction.

Trace Tool to the NGSS
Go online to view the complete coverage of these standards across this lesson, unit, and time.

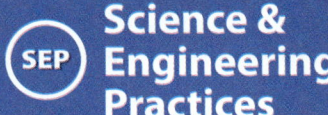 **Science & Engineering Practices**

 Disciplinary Core Ideas

 **Crosscutting Concepts**

Engaging in Argument from Evidence
Construct an argument with evidence, data, and/or a model.

LS1.A Structure and Function
Plants and animals have both internal and external structures that serve various functions in growth, survival, behavior, and reproduction. (4-LS1-1)

Systems and System Models
A system can be described in terms of its components and their interactions.
 VIDEO System Models

Influence of Engineering, Technology and Science
Engineers improve existing technologies or develop new ones to increase their benefits, to decrease known risks, and to meet societal demands.

 CONNECTIONS TO MATH

4.G.A.3 Recognize a line of symmetry for a two-dimensional figure as a line across the figure such that the figure can be folded across the line into matching parts. Identify line-symmetric figures and draw lines of symmetry.

MP.2 Reason abstractly and quantitatively.

 CONNECTIONS TO ENGLISH LANGUAGE ARTS

W.4.1 Write opinion pieces on topics or texts, supporting a point of view with reasons and information. (4-LS1-1)

RI.4.8 Explain how an author uses reasons and evidence to support particular points in a text.

RI.4.7 Interpret information presented visually, orally, or quantitatively

RI.4.9 Integrate information from two texts on the same topic in order to write or speak about the subject knowledgeably.

Supporting All Students, All Standards

Integrating the Three Dimensions of Learning

In this lesson, students will gather evidence about the function of internal and external plant parts **(DCI LS1.A)** to construct an argument **(SEP Engaging in Argument from Evidence)** that these parts work together to form a system **(CCC Systems and System Models)** used for growth, survival, reproduction, and behavior.

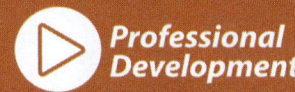

Professional Development — Go online to view **Professional Development videos** with strategies to integrate CCCs and SEPs, including the ones used in this lesson.

Extra Hands-On Activity: Plant Parts

How Many Plant Parts Can You Find?

 Pairs
30-45 minutes

Survey the area on and near school grounds for a place where students can dig up weeds for direct observation. Select a place with no poison ivy if that plant is common in your region! As an added precaution, provide photos to help students be on the lookout for poison ivy, and caution them against touching the plant. Equip students with disposable food prep gloves, hand lenses, and small garden shovels or sturdy plastic spoons.

Supervise an expedition in which students select small weed plants and carefully remove them from the earth, attempting to keep the root system as intact as possible.

Instruct students to brush away as much soil as they can and spread their plants on white paper to examine them closely with hand lenses. Have students draw in their Evidence Notebooks, with details of the structures they observe. Encourage students to break apart the plant and illustrate cross sections as well. Finally, instruct students to add descriptive text labels to their illustrations. As students learn about plant parts throughout the lesson, they can add details to their text.

 This activity can support mastery of this Crosscutting Concept: Systems and System Models

Preassessment

Have students complete the unit pre-test online or see the Assessment Guide.

Build on Prior Knowledge

Students should already know and be prepared to build on the following concepts:
- All organisms have external parts that they use to perform daily functions.
- Plants depend on water and light to grow and also depend on animals for pollination or to move their seeds around.

Differentiate Instruction

Lesson Vocabulary
- leaf
- root
- spore
- stem

Write the key terms on the board, and discuss their definitions. Have students use the words to ask one another yes/no questions, with the reply restating a definition.

Ask: Do *spores* really grow new plants? Yes, some plants have spores instead of seeds.

ELL/ELD Strategy
Point out cognates of key terms from students' home languages, such as *spores/esporas,* to bridge understanding. Pronounce each word in English, and have students repeat it. Ask other students to share the same words in their home languages.

Lesson 1 What Are Some Plant Parts and How Do They Function? **232B**

LESSON 1 **Engage** • Explore/Explain • Elaborate • Evaluate

ENGAGE: Lesson Phenomenon

Lesson Objective
To gather evidence about the function and structure of plant parts in order to construct an argument that these parts are used for survival, growth, reproduction, and behavior.

About This Image
Plants include everything from blades of grass to cultivated flowers to giant trees. Flowers are an example of a plant part used in reproduction.

 SEP Engaging in Argument from Evidence

Alternative Engage Strategy

What's Your Opinion? 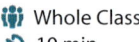 Whole Class 10 min

Ask students to list the numbers 1 through 3 on paper. Have students think about all the plants they've seen, from huge trees to tiny flowers.

Read each statement listed below. Tell students to write *Agree* or *Disagree* for each.

1. All plants have the same parts. (false)
2. Plants cannot move on their own. (false)
3. Plants get food from soil. (false)

Keep the slips until the end of the lesson. Then have students revisit their choices.

LESSON 1

What Are Some Plant Parts and How Do They Function?

Different plants have different types of structures. The structures function in ways that enable the plants to survive.

By the end of this lesson...
you'll be able to identify the different parts of plants and the functions of these parts.

232

232 Unit 4 Plant Structure and Function

Can You Explain It?

Have you ever seen a plant that is bent over to one side? If there are indoor plants in your home or at school, you may have noticed a plant that leans in one direction instead of growing straight up.

1. Why do you think the plants in the pictures bend in the directions that they do? How would this behavior help the plant grow and survive?

Students should answer based on the preliminary observations they can make of the images.

EVIDENCE NOTEBOOK Look for this icon to help you gather evidence to answer the questions above.

233

Explore Online Students can view the lesson phenomenon online.

Can You Explain It?

Students are asked to record their initial thoughts about why plants in the pictures are bending in a certain direction. To do so, students must begin to think about the different parts of plants and how they function to help the plant grow and survive. Encourage students to record the first thoughts that come into their minds. Point out that their ideas might change as they work through the Explorations and Hands-On Activities. Explain that they will have another opportunity to answer the same questions at the end of the lesson.

Collaboration

Think, Pair, Share Pair students, and have them discuss their ideas about the leaning plants. Circulate to gauge students' prior knowledge about plant parts and their functions. To help you identify any possible misconceptions students may have, Ask each pair to paraphrase the case of the leaning plants and how that helps the plants survive.

EVIDENCE NOTEBOOK

Encourage students to use an appropriate graphic organizer, such as main idea and supporting details, to set up their notebook for this lesson.

Find more strategies in the online ELA handbook.

Lesson 1 What Are Some Plant Parts and How Do They Function? 233

LESSON 1   Engage • **Explore/Explain** • Elaborate • Evaluate

EXPLORATION 1 Plant Dissection

3D Learning Objective

In this lesson, students will gather evidence about the **functions of external plant parts:** which specific **parts of a plant's system** help it grow, help it survive, and help it reproduce. Then students **write an argument** about which is the most important part for growth.

CCC Systems and System Models

The diagram on this page shows the parts of a plant, which like all systems, can only work through the interaction of its components. As students read and answer the questions, stress that a *function* is a job, or what a plant part does for the whole.

Ask: What familiar plant parts do you see in the diagram? *stem, leaves, roots, flower*
Ask: How does the stem support the flower? *It holds it up so it can get sunlight. The stem helps transport water and food.*

SEP Engaging in Argument from Evidence

Have pairs of students share their answers on this and the following page, and explain why they gave that answer. Remind students to give valid reasons for their choices. Review that when making an argument, they should explain their reasoning but listen to the other person's views as well. Then they should try to come to a consensus of opinions.

Ask: What evidence do you have to support that roots are needed for surival? *Roots take in water from the soil. Plants need water to survive.*

EXPLORATION 1
Plant Dissection

Do Parts Serve Purposes?

You can tell from a quick glance at a plant that it has different parts. Most plants have certain parts in common that perform the same functions.

Functions of Plant Parts

2. Complete each description then label the plant parts with the correct letter.

| root | stem | leaf | flower |

a. ____root____ This part of the plant grows down into soil.

b. ____leaf____ This part of the plant captures sunlight.

c. ____stem____ This part of the plant grows away from the ground and helps keep the plant upright.

d. ____flower____ This part of the plant attracts insects.

3. Fill in the chart below to explain how you think each of these parts helps a plant survive.

Plant part	How does it help the plant survive?
Root	Possible answer: The roots of a plant hold it in place.
Stem	Possible answer: The stem holds the plant upright and directs leaves toward light.
Leaf	Possible answer: Leaves take in sunlight so the plant can make food.
Flower	Possible answer: Flowers enable the plant to reproduce.

234

Part by Part

Different parts of plants serve different purposes. Read about the functions of these plant parts and how they help the different types of plants survive.

Thorns are sharp, pointed parts on some plants. Thorns protect a plant from being eaten by animals. **Flowers** attract insects and are involved in reproduction so the plant can make new plants.

Cones are involved in the reproduction of certain kinds of plants. **Bark**, a tree's woody covering, protects it from cold temperatures and from animal damage.

Cacti live in dry areas and have **spines** instead of wide, flat leaves. Not having flat leaves reduces water loss. Spines also protect the cactus from animals.

Plants such as ferns and mosses produce **spores**, which are released into the air. When spores land in a spot where conditions are right for growth, a new plant will start to grow.

Roots help hold a plant in place. They also absorb water and nutrients from the soil. These materials are needed for a plant to survive and grow.

Leaves capture sunlight and use it to make food in the form of sugar. Plants use the food to grow. Plant **stems** support leaves and help plants stay upright.

4. How are thorns on a flower and spines on a cactus similar? Select the correct answer.
   a. Both reduce water loss.
   b. Both protect plants from animals.
   c. Both absorb water from soil.
   d. Both hold plants upright.

5. Which function do roots *not* perform?
   a. absorb water from soil
   b. anchor a plant in place
   c. develop seeds for reproduction
   d. absorb nutrients from soil

DCI LS1.A Structure and Function

The images and text on this page are about different plant parts and their functions.

Ask: How are bark and spines alike? They both protect a plant.

Invite students to play "What Am I?" Let them take turns describing a plant part's functions in riddle form and having the rest of the group guess what it is. For example: I protect the outside of a tree from an animal's claws. What am I? (bark)

Misconception Alert Because students see raindrops on leaves, they may think the leaves are taking in water for the plant. Explain that roots take in water for the plant, not the leaves.

Ask: How does a plant get water? through its roots

Differentiate Instruction

RTI/Extra Support If the information about all six plant parts distracts students as they read, have them cover five of the entries with paper and focus on just one at a time. Suggest that they read the information, reread it, and then ask questions, if necessary, to make sure they understand what each plant part is and what its job, or function, is.

Connection to English Language Arts

Remind students that it is important to provide valid evidence when making a claim.

Ask: What evidence supports the claim that roots help a plant survive? Roots hold a plant in place and absorb water and nutrients from the soil that the plant needs to survive.
RI.4.8 Explain how an author uses reasons and evidence to support particular points in a text.

LESSON 1   Engage • **Explore/Explain** • Elaborate • Evaluate

EXPLORATION 1 *Plant Dissection, continued*

DCI LS1.A Structure and Function

Differentiate Instruction

ELL: Miming/Drawing Pair up proficient English-speaking students with students acquiring English as you read and discuss the different plant parts that have similar functions. The English-speaking student mimes or draws to convey any unknown word or concept; the student acquiring English responds by miming or drawing while saying the word(s) in English to demonstrate understanding.

Connection to Physical Science

Remind students that energy can be transferred between matter. Light energy transmitted from the sun helps plants on Earth make food. Tiny parts of a plant's leaves use light energy to turn carbon dioxide and water into food in a process called *photosynthesis*.

Ask: What would happen to the plants if the leaves could not capture the sun's light energy? The plant would not be able to make its own food.
PS3-2 Energy Transfer

Collaboration

Think, Pair, Share Have students work in pairs to compare the differences in the two root types. Have them think about why one plant may need a fibrous root to survive while another needs a taproot to survive. If time allows, let students research the reasons for these adaptations. Continue for leaves and stems.

Similar but Different

When you look around at different plants, you see that they often have the same parts—roots, stems, leaves, flowers, and more. But these parts do not look exactly the same in all plants. Leaves and flowers differ in shape, size, and color. Some plants have thorns. Others do not.

Different Parts, Similar Jobs

6. Compare how the plant parts in each set of photographs function. Write whether the parts most support protection, growth, or reproduction.

A. **A taproot,** such as a carrot or radish, absorbs water and also stores food and water for the plant.

B. **Fibrous roots** absorb water and minerals from the soil. These materials move through the roots up into the plant.

_____growth_____

C. This large, **flat leaf** captures sunlight. Having lots of large leaves in spring and summer helps the plant absorb more sunlight and make more food.

D. The **needles** of evergreens such as pine trees gather sunlight for the plant to make food. Their shape and waxy coating reduce water loss during dry weather.

_____growth_____

E. **Woody stems** help plants such as trees and shrubs stay upright in strong winds. They can help trees become very tall. Tall plants get more sunlight.

F. Other plants, such as dandelions and sunflowers, have **green stems.** These stems can also capture sunlight while they hold the plants up and support branches, leaves, and other parts.

_____growth_____

G. Plants such as pine trees make **cones** instead of flowers. Male cones release pollen that pollinates female cones. Female cones then hold seeds until they are ready to be released. New plants grow from seeds that land in places with the right conditions.

H. Other types of plants use **spores** to reproduce. Once spores are released, they are carried by wind. If spores land in a place with the right conditions, new plants will grow.

I. Plants such as dandelions and apple trees produce **flowers**. A flower has different parts that are involved in reproduction, including petals and the pollen-producing stamen. Many flowers attract animals that move pollen from one plant to another.

reproduction
_____

J. Some plants, such as roses, have **thorns** with sharp, pointed ends that can injure an animal that tries to eat the plant.

K. Tough, thick **bark** prevents many animals from eating trees and shrubs. It also helps reduce infections caused by fungi or bacteria getting into a plant.

L. Plants, such as cacti, that live in dry areas have leaves shaped like **spines**. An animal that tries to eat a spiny plant will likely be injured.

protection
_____

237

CCC Systems and System Models

As students continue to discover plant parts with similar functions, stress that all the parts together make up a system.

Ask: What would happen if there were no plant parts to help with reproduction? The plant would become extinct.

Ask: What might happen if all the thorns on a rosebush fell off? An animal would eat the plant.

SEP Engaging in Argument from Evidence

Reinforce the concept of valid evidence to support a claim.

Ask: What evidence could you use to support the claim that animals help flowers reproduce? Some animals move pollen from one plant to another.

Ask: What evidence could you use to support the claim that cactus spines are a kind of protection for the plant? Animals don't try to eat the cactus, because they would get stuck by sharp spikes.

Differentiate Instruction

Extention Advanced students can research additional ways plants protect themselves. They can then make a presentation on how humans can protect themselves from being injured by a plant.

Lesson 1 What Are Some Plant Parts and How Do They Function? **237**

LESSON 1 Engage • **Explore/Explain** • Elaborate • Evaluate

EXPLORATION 1 *Plant Dissection, continued*

🟠 DCI **LS1.A Structure and Function**

Allow students to scan the material again, if necessary, to refresh their memories about the different plant parts.

Ask: What is another plant part that has more than one function? **bark, green stems, spines**

🟢 CCC **Systems and System Models**

As students think about the different plant parts, remind them that all the parts work together to keep the plant alive. Prepare students for the writing assignment.

Ask: Do you think any one part of a plant is the most important?
Possible answer: No, all parts have different necessary functions.

EVIDENCE NOTEBOOK

Students should have recorded that the leaves use light from the sun. The leaves use the light to help make food.

FORMATIVE ASSESSMENT

Language SmArts
Writing Opinion Pieces
W.4.1 Write Opinion Pieces

Remind students that an opinion piece is a point of view supported by facts. The claim in an opinion piece should be debatable—other people may disagree with it. Using valid evidence to support the claim can help to persuade others to agree with the claim. Review proper debate etiquette. Students should not interrupt when others are talking. If they have questions, they should write them and ask when the person is finished talking. If a student disagrees with another student, they need to be respectful. No one should be mocked for his or her opinion.

Think of the functions of the different plant parts you have learned about. Recall that some plant parts have more than one function. For example, roots absorb water and minerals from the soil, but they also anchor a plant in place.

 EVIDENCE NOTEBOOK Which part of the plant uses light? What does it use light for? Record your explanation in your Evidence Notebook.

Language SmArts
Writing Opinion Pieces

7. Make a claim about which plant part you think is most important overall for plant growth. Use three facts to provide evidence to support your claim. You can use facts from this lesson. You may also need to do additional research.

Record your claim and your evidence in the table below. Then debate your claim with your classmates.

Claim	Evidence
I think that the _____ is the most important part for plant growth.	Fact 1: *Students should supply facts from research that support the claim for the plant part they have identified.* Fact 2: _____ Fact 3: _____

238

238 Unit 4 Plant Structure and Function

EXPLORATION 2 What's Inside?

Slurp!

You have already learned that the roots of a plant absorb water and minerals from soil. How does the plant use the water?

Before

Explore Online

You've seen a stalk of celery like this before.

After

If you put a stalk of celery that has been cut in colored water, it will look like this.

8. Why do the leaves become the same color as the colored water? How do you think this happens?

Possible answer: The plant takes in the water, which travels inside the plant to the leaves.

LESSON 1 Engage • **Explore/Explain** • Elaborate • Evaluate

EXPLORATION 2 *What's Inside?*, continued

DCI LS1.A Structure and Function

The text and images on the page are about the tube system inside plants that transports the food and water to help the plant survive and grow. After reading the text and answering the questions, have students speculate further.

Ask: What, if anything, might happen to the plant if one or more of the tubes were broken or crushed? **The plant would get less water or food; the tubes that were left could not send enough water or food, and the plant could die.**

CCC Systems and System Models

Remind students that the tubes are part of the plant's whole system and that parts of a system must work together.

Ask: What other parts help give a plant water and food? **the roots that get the water from the soil and the leaves that make the food**

> **Language SmArts**
> **RI.4.7 Interpret Information Presented Visually**
>
> The diagrams on this page illustrate how water and food move through a plant's tube systems to deliver life-giving water and/or food. Discuss what students learned about the tubes.
>
> **Ask:** How do the diagrams help you understand what happens to the water and food? **Possible response: the diagrams use arrows to show the direction of the movement of water and/or food in the tubes.**
>
> **Ask:** How do the diagrams help you better understand the text? **Possible response: the diagrams show what the text tells.**

240 Unit 4 Plant Structure and Function

It's What's Inside That Counts

To learn why the celery's appearance changed when it was placed in colored water, take a closer look at the inside of the stems in the two plants below. Each one will show a different system of tubes that helps the plant survive and grow.

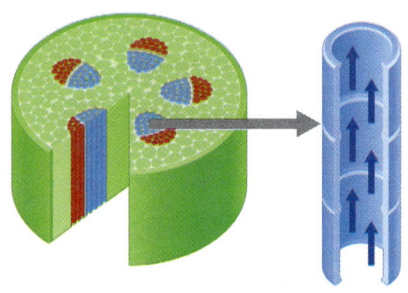 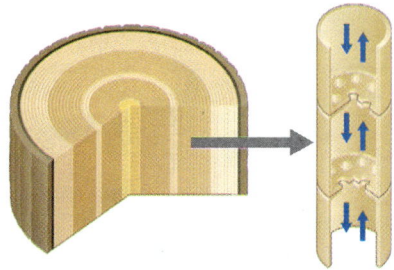

Inside a plant stem is a system of **water-carrying tubes**. Water, taken in from the roots, moves through the tubes into the plant's leaves so the leaves can use the water to make food.

Sugar made in a plant's leaves moves through a system of **food-carrying tubes**. These tubes travel from the leaves, throughout the plant, and down to the roots. Some plant roots, like carrots, store extra sugar produced by the plant.

9. Language SmArts Briefly describe the two different tube systems in a plant.

Food moves from the leaves to all parts of a plant through food-carrying tubes. Water moves from the roots to all parts of a plant through water-carrying tubes.

_____

_____

10. Write the words in the order in which food moves from one plant part to the next.

| roots | tubes | leaves |

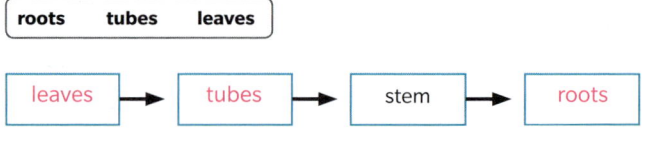

leaves → tubes → stem → roots

240

Engineer It!
Green Roofs

Growing grass and plants on the rooftops of buildings in cities helps solve two problems. First, it allows more space to grow plants in cities that have limited space. Second, a grass layer reduces the heating of the building on hot summer days.

In winter, heat from inside the building keeps the grass warmer, which means it can grow for a longer part of the year.

- Vegetation
- Growing medium
- Drainage
- Water and root barrier
- Thermal insulation
- Roof surface

To grow grass on rooftops successfully, you need different layers of materials. To protect the roof and the plants, you need a layer of insulation and then a layer of waterproof material to keep roots from growing into the the roof. Next is a layer of material that will allow water to drain away from the roof. On the top layer are the soil and growing plants.

11. What are some advantages and disadvantages of green roofs? Do additional research if needed.

Possible answer: advantages: More plants grow in cities, and buildings are cooler in summer; disadvantages: requires care such as mowing grass and could cause damage to buildings

241

 **Explore Online** Have students explore online to learn more about growing plants on top of buildings.

Engineer It!
Green Roofs

CCC **Influence of Engineering, Technology and Science**

Explain to students that green roofs are a great example of the influence of science on engineering.

Ask: In order to make green roofs work, what did engineers need to study? How plants grow

SEP **Engage in Argument from Evidence**

Discuss the photograph with students, and help them understand how the rooftop garden is set up to get the advantage of the plant coverage without damage to the roof. Read the opening text, and then discuss the author's claims.

Ask: What problems does the author claim a rooftop garden can solve? It provides more space to grow plants in cities with limited space, and the grass cuts down heating of the building on hot summer days.

Collaboration

Draw, Pair, Share Have student pairs explore online to learn more about the benefits of growing grass on the rooftops of buildings. Ask each pair to then make an advertising poster promoting the idea. Remind students that ads often use words and phrases such as *new*, *save*, *proven*, *8 out of 10 prefer it*, *guaranteed*, *long-lasting benefit*, *be the first*, and *special*. Have pairs share their posters with the class.

LESSON 1   Engage • **Explore/Explain** • Elaborate • Evaluate

EXPLORATION 2 What's Inside?, continued

 Systems and System Models

HANDS-ON Apply What You Know
Modeling Water Flow in Plants

Students are asked to make a 3D model of a plant's water system. Have students work in pairs to complete the activity. Make arts and crafts materials available to students, including some straws, clay or small bits of plastic tubing. Remind students that this does not have to be a working model.

Assessment Rubric
Exemplary activity results will accurately show a model of the internal water tubes.

SEP Engage in Argument from Evidence

Have pairs present their 3-D models to the class. Encourage classmates to critique the design by asking questions about the device and how it will function and suggesting any possible improvements.

Ask: What evidence do you have that supports your claim that this represents a plant's water system? **Accept all reasonable responses.**

 EVIDENCE NOTEBOOK

Students should record that the leaf system needs light in order to produce the food that it transports throughout the plant.

FORMATIVE ASSESSMENT

 SEP Engage in Argument from Evidence

Make sure students understand that different structures have different functions.

Ask: What is the function of the tubes in a plant's system?
to transport water and food to all parts of the plant

 HANDS-ON Apply What You Know
Modeling Water Flow in Plants

12. Using what you can infer about water moving in celery, make a 3D model of a plant's water system. Your model does not need to function, but do use different arts and crafts materials to represent the different types of materials in the plant.

 EVIDENCE NOTEBOOK Think about the tube systems in plants and the leaning plants pictured at the beginning of the lesson. Which tube system needs light to do its function or job?

Putting It Together

13. What color do you see in the celery besides its normal green color? What does this suggest?

The color blue. The colored water is making its way inside the plant.

14. Use the celery investigation to support the following claim with evidence. "A celery plant has a tube system that carries water through the plant." Select all evidence statements that apply.

   a. I can see the tubes when the celery is cut open.
   b. I can see the color of the tubes is the same color as the water when the celery is cut open.
   c. The color of water in the bowl got lighter. This means water must have been absorbed by the celery.
   d. I can see that the leaves turned the same color as the water.

HANDS-ON ACTIVITY
Hold the Soil

Objective
Collaborate to build a system to grow plants in water instead of soil.

Growing plants in water instead of soil is called hydroponics. As long as plants have the sunlight, space, water, and nutrients they need added to the water, they can grow without soil.

Imagine a company has hired you to grow hydroponic plants. Use your knowledge of plant parts and their functions to design such a system. What will be your goal for the activity?
to grow several bean plants from a small number of seeds using inexpensive materials.

Materials	Cost
• 5 bean seeds	$3
• plastic cup or bottle	$1 for 1 or $2 for 3
• paper towel	$1 for 2 or $2 for 5
• gravel	$2 per 113 g
• vermiculite	$2 per 113 g
• cotton balls	$1 for 3 or $2 for 10
• foam pellets	$1 per 113 g
• liquid nutrients	$2 per 50 g
• aluminum foil	$1 per ¼ sq. m
• plastic wrap	$1 per ¼ sq. m
• metric ruler	$0
• water	$0

Find a Problem What question will you investigate to meet this objective?
Possible answer: How can I grow a plant without soil?

Procedure
STEP 1 Research with your group how to grow seeds in water instead of soil.

STEP 2 Brainstorm ideas for your system in which to grow seeds. Keep the following criteria and constraints in mind.

Criteria	Constraints
☐ Your system should use water in place of soil.	☐ Your system cannot be larger than 30 cm x 15 cm x 15 cm.
☐ Your system should provide the seeds with what they need to sprout and grow.	☐ The total budget for your system must not be greater than $12.

243

Student Lab Worksheet and complete Teacher Support available online.

HANDS-ON ACTIVITY Small groups 1 class period/four weeks
Hold the Soil

3D Learning Objective
 SEP Engaging in Argument from Evidence

Students test the function of roots as they build a system to grow plants in water rather than soil. Then students make a claim about the effectiveness of their process, based on their evidence.

Preparation
Place all available materials in a common area so groups can choose which they want to use. Be sure that each group has an area in which to assemble and/or track their hydroponic plants.

Materials
The materials listed in the student edition are a starting point. You may wish to add newspaper (to cover work areas), goggles, gloves, and a camera (to document plant growth).

Connection to Math
Remind groups of the constraint: their systems must not cost more than $12. Encourage students not to spend their whole budget. This allows them to purchase more items later if needed. Circulate as groups decide what to choose.

Ask: Which materials did you choose? What was your final cost? *Possible response: seeds ($3), cups (2 for $2), water ($0), gravel ($2), towel ($1), liquid nutrients ($2), ruler ($0), cotton ball ($1), and plastic wrap ($1); total $12*
MP.2 Reason abstractly and quantitatively.

Procedure
STEP 2 Circulate as groups brainstorm to be sure they have a proper understanding of the criteria and constraints that must be met. If their total cost exceeds $12, prompt them to reconsider materials.

Lesson 1 What Are Some Plant Parts and How Do They Function? 243

LESSON 1 Engage • **Explore/Explain** • Elaborate • Evaluate

EXPLORATION 2 HANDS-ON ACTIVITY, continued

DCI LS1.A Structure and Function

Remind students that plants need nutrients to grow and that for plants to grow in water, nutrients must be added to the water.

Ask: How will the roots in your system get nutrients? The roots will absorb nutrients we put into the water.

STEP 4 Monitor groups to make sure students add liquid nutrients according to the directions on the product. Help students figure out the amount to add; too much can impair the growth of the plant. Remind students of safety during all experiments, such as wearing gloves and goggles when adding the liquid nutrients to the water.

STEP 6 Set a schedule for recording plant growth twice a week. Circulate each time to observe and assist students as needed as they record results. If possible, let students record photographically as well. Model how to complete the table for students if necessary.

Differentiate Instruction

Extension Challenge students to repeat the activity with different materials and then compare results. Encourage students to make graphs to compare the statistics. As students share their graphs with the class, encourage them to explain what caused the differences in results. To challenge students even more, have them do side-by-side experiments planting one seed in soil and one in water and then compare those results.

Systems and System Models

Circulate as students analyze their results.

Ask: How does having a record of your observations help you evaluate the effectiveness of your bean system? We can tell how effective our plan was over time.

STEP 3 **Plan** your system. Make a drawing or blueprint on a piece of paper. Draw and label each part of your system.

Explain how you made sure you met the criteria and constraints in your system.
Possible answer: We are using 10 seeds, cups, water, and nutrients that are within cost

STEP 4 **Build** your system.

STEP 5 **Test** your system
Write out the steps.
Possible answer: 1. Plant seeds. 2. Check water. 3. Observe daily.

STEP 6 Observe your system. Record results at least two times a week for four weeks. Use a ruler as a tool to measure the growth of the plants.

Observation Table

Date	Seed/plant growth (cm)	Other observations
Students should complete chart with dates and growth measurements.		

244

---

244 Unit 4 Plant Structure and Function

Analyze Your Results

STEP 7 How many of your bean seeds sprouted? Of those plants, how many survived four weeks or more? How much did they grow?

Responses should reflect results in the data table.

STEP 8 Evaluate and Redesign your device. How well did you meet the criteria and constraints? What improvements could you make to your system's design?

Students should identify at least one physical functional detail they would change to improve.

Draw Conclusions

STEP 9 Communicate to compare your hydroponic system and results with other groups. Did another group's seeds grow better than yours? Why or why not?

Students should make valid comparisons based on their observations and data.

STEP 10 Make a claim based on the question you investigated. Support your claim with evidence from this activity.

Evidence to support claims should relate clearly to recorded observations.

STEP 11 Think of other questions you would like to ask about designing systems to grow plants.

Possible answer: Would it be possible to design hydroponic systems big enough to grow all of people's food?

Analyze Your Results

STEP 8 As groups evaluate their designs, remind them to measure their success against the given criteria and constraints. Did their seeds grow and sprout? Did they stay in budget? Etc.

Draw Conclusions

STEP 9 Invite students to compare and contrast with other groups to discuss what worked or did not work with the systems.

> ### Claims, Evidence, and Reasoning
>
> For Step 10, have group members come to a consensus for a valid claim they could make, based on their results. Remind the group that there should be adequate evidence to convince others that the claim is valid.
>
> **Ask:** Is there enough valid evidence to support your claim? Answers will vary, depending on the evidence.

Scoring Rubric for Hands-On Activity	
3	meets all criteria and constraints; works collaboratively with group; keeps accurate data, analyzes all data for redesign improvements
2	meets most criteria and constraints; generally works collaboratively with group; keeps mostly accurate data, analyzes most data for redesign improvements
1	does not meet most criteria and constraints; has trouble working collaboratively; data is inaccurate, improvements are not based on data
0	little or no attempt to meet the requirements above

Lesson 1 What Are Some Plant Parts and How Do They Function?

LESSON 1   Engage • **Explore/Explain** • Elaborate • Evaluate

EXPLORATION 3 Can Plants Move?

3D Learning Objective

Students investigate how **parts of a plant system** **move in response to their environment**, and they **make a claim** about how this helps the plant survive.

Collaboration

Think, Pair, Share Assign student pairs to discuss the questions and their ideas. At this point students are making predictions based on prior knowledge of plant parts and their functions.

CCC Systems and System Models

Remind students that the parts of a plant's system work together to help it survive.

Ask: How do the plant's movements help it survive? Roots move to get life-giving water; stem moves to get light so leaves can produce food; leaves move to protect the plant from damage.

Differentiate Instruction

RTI/Extra Support If students struggle with the questions, review the parts of a plant. Make sure students can identify the leaves, stem, and roots. Ask them which part moved and what the function of that part is. Help them tie the two together to make a prediction.

EXPLORATION 3

Can Plants Move?

Move and Groove

Have you ever seen a vine grow up the side of a house or wrap around a fence post? What happens if a potted plant gets knocked over on its side and keeps growing? Plants have certain behaviors that help them to grow and survive.

Explore Online

a

b

c

15. In picture **a,** the plant was knocked over on its side and grew in one direction. Why do you think this occurred?

Possible answer: The stem bends so the plant still grows upward.

16. In picture **b,** the plant was placed by a window and grew in one direction. Why do you think this occurred?

Possible answer: The plant grew toward the available light.

17. In picture **c,** the leaves of the mimosa folded inward when it was touched. Why do you think this happened?

Possible answer: The plant is protecting itself from harm.

Oh, Behave!

In nature, plants live in environments where conditions change constantly. The sun is not visible all day. The temperature can change drastically. A herd of animals may rumble through the environment. Whatever the conditions, plants have to absorb sunlight, make food, grow, and survive.

How Do You Grow?

18. Read about plant behaviors below and complete the activity.

Plants **respond to light**. Plants need sunlight to make food, so a house plant that sits in front of a window will grow toward the light. If the plant is not turned regularly, it will become very lopsided. Circle the image that shows what will happen if this plant is left in the window.

The roots of plants grow down toward the center of Earth in **response to gravity**. The stem of a plant grows in the opposite direction, away from the center of Earth. This usually results in the stem growing upward. Circle the image that shows what will happen if this plant is knocked over.

Some plants respond to touch. A leaf might curl up to protect a plant from damage or from being eaten. A Venus flytrap clasps its leaves closed if an insect touches the fine hairs on the inside of the leaves. For plants that eat insects, this is an important **response to touch**. Circle the image that shows what will happen when the fly lands on the leaf.

247

SEP Engage in Argument from Evidence

Remind students that humans respond to their environments, too. If someone feels in danger, the person reacts by moving away—the brain sends a message to the leg muscles to run!

Ask: What evidence is there that a plant is trying to protect itself from damage? The leaf curls up when touched.

DCI LS1.A Structure and Function

Ask: How does the structure of a plant allow it to bend? The stem is flexible and long.

Differentiate Instruction

Extension Challenge students to find out more about the Venus flytrap and its habitat. Have students report their findings to the class. Encourage the use of visuals, such as downloaded images or a poster showing a Venus flytrap's parts up close. Students might also research other carnivorous plants, such as pitcher plants or sundews.

Connections to English Lanuage Arts

Have students work in teams to write an opinion piece with evidence to argue which one of these behaviors is the most important for survival. Have students debate their ideas with the whole class. Remind students of proper debate etiquette. Determine the winner of the debate by keeping score of the teams. The team that provides the most scientific evidence wins.

W.4.1 Write Opinion Pieces

LESSON 1   Engage • **Explore/Explain** • Elaborate • Evaluate

EXPLORATION 3 *Can Plants Move?*, continued

 EVIDENCE NOTEBOOK

Students should record that the top photos, showing how the plant moves toward the light, are most like the bending behaviors shown in the Engage section. Both plants were reaching for the sunlight.

HANDS-ON Apply What You Know
Plant Response

Students work on this activity independently. Circulate to make sure students understand that they are to show the action of a plant's response. Students may use additional paper if needed. Have students share their comic strips. Discuss the drawings and captions.

Assessment Rubric
An excellent response includes drawings and captions that clearly explains a plant's behavior.

FORMATIVE ASSESSMENT

Multiple Sources
RI.4.9 Synthesize Multiple Sources

As students construct their claim about how plant responses help plant survival, remind them to cite the numbers of the pages where they found the facts they used to develop their arguments. Then, have students share their claims and, as a class, evaluate each to see if there is enough evidence given to support the claim.

Ask: Is there enough valid evidence to support the claim that plant behavior helps the plant survive and grow? Why or why not? **Answers will vary, depending on the student's evidence.**

 EVIDENCE NOTEBOOK Which photo on the previous page shows a plant's bending behavior similar to what you saw at the beginning of the lesson? Describe the similarities in your Evidence Notebook.

 HANDS-ON Apply What You Know
Plant Response

19. Choose one of the ways a plant responds to its environment. Draw a comic strip with at least three panels showing one of the plant behaviors you learned about. Write captions for each panel you draw.

Check for comics to show an understanding of plant behaviors.

 Language SmArts
Multiple Sources

20. Using multiple sources, explain how plant behavior helps plants survive. Cite your sources.

Student answers should reflect information about plant responses to light, gravity, and touch from different cited sources.

Tip
The English Language Arts Handbook can provide help with understanding how to use and cite multiple sources.

248

---

248   Unit 4 Plant Structure and Function

TAKE IT FURTHER Discover More

Discover More

Check out this path... or go online to choose one of these other paths.

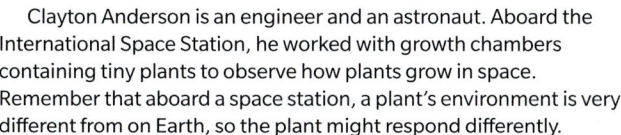

Clayton Anderson

Clayton Anderson is an engineer and an astronaut. Aboard the International Space Station, he worked with growth chambers containing tiny plants to observe how plants grow in space. Remember that aboard a space station, a plant's environment is very different from on Earth, so the plant might respond differently.

While there is gravity in space, people and things on the space station experience it differently than we do on Earth. Everything appears to be floating. Think about how this affects plants in ways such as keeping soil in a container or watering a plant. It takes some problem solving to sprout seeds in space.

When a plant grows on Earth, its stem grows away from Earth while its roots grow toward Earth. If a potted plant is knocked onto its side, the sideways stem will grow up at an angle, and the roots will grow down.

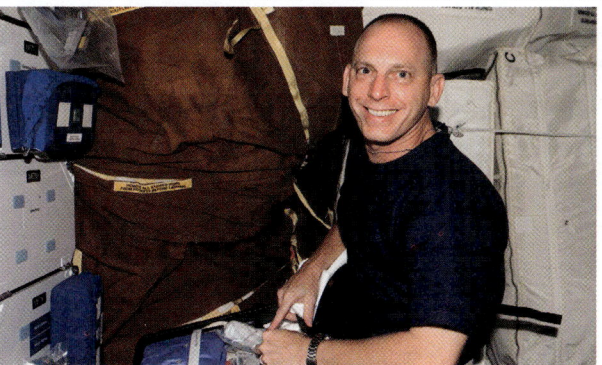

Clayton Anderson, engineer and astronaut

Collaboration

You may choose to assign this activity or to direct student pairs online to the eSE where they can explore and choose from all three paths. These activities can be assigned individually, to pairs, or to small groups.

People in Science & Engineering: Clayton Anderson

DCI LS1.A Structure and Function

When the STS-118 space shuttle launched into space in August of 2007, 10 million cinnamon basil seeds went along for the ride. Nearly all the seeds returned to Earth for students to grow, but 16 seeds were left behind on the International Space Station for an in-orbit experiment. Flight Engineer Clayton Anderson used the seeds to grow plants, testing how gravity would affect the structure and function of the plants' parts. He documented the plants' growth by photographing them every other day. The 20-day in-orbit plant investigation was a success. A veteran of two space flights, the one in 2007 and another in 2010, Anderson has logged 167 days in space.

Differentiate Instruction

Extension Challenge interested student pairs to find out more about this experiment and others that have taken place aboard International Space Station. Encourage students to check out NASA's webpage www.nasa.com, as well as encyclopedias and other Internet sources. Have each pair plan a presentation for classmates, complete with visuals, and explain how experiments are done in space.

LESSON 1 Engage • Explore/Explain • **Elaborate** • Evaluate

TAKE IT FURTHER, continued

Engineer It!
Upside Down Plants

CCC Systems and System Models

Remind students that the more they understand about plant systems, the better they can understand the types of problems that may need to be solved involving plants.

Ask: How can engineers use information about plant systems? to design technologies that mimic plants to solve a problem

SEP Engaging in Argument from Evidence

After students have made their devices and monitored the effectiveness, plan a group discussion. Have students compare their results and any photos they may have taken. Then have them argue for the success of their claim that the device would work.

Ask: Why was your design successful? The soil stayed in and allowed the roots to grow down and the plant to grow up.

▶ Explore Online

Students can explore these additional topics online.

Burrr!
Students explore what happens to make some plants to survive the winter. *(No outside research required.)*

How Unusual!
Students learn about botanist Jenny Xiang and an unusual plant, the corpse flower. Provide a list of a few other unusual plants for groups of students to research, such as sundews, night-blooming cereus, mistletoe, Indian pipe, century plant, or welwitschia. *(Outside research required.)*

Engineer It!
Upside Down Plants

21. Suppose you are a scientist who has been hired by a science museum. Your job is to make a device to hang a plant upside down to teach young children about how plants respond to the force of gravity.

Procedure

A. Find a Problem to solve.
How can I build a device to teach about plant's response to gravity?

B. Brainstorm ideas with your team on how to build your device. Keep in mind the following criteria and constraints:

Criteria	Constraints
☐ The device must cause the plant to hang upside down.	☐ Not including the plant and soil, you can only use five materials to build it.
☐ The stem and the roots must be able to grow out of the device.	☐ The device must be made of 50% recycled materials
☐ Minimal soil should fall from the device when it hangs upside down.	

C. Plan your device. Make a drawing. Then, have your teacher approve your design, including whatever equipment may be needed to hang the device.

D. Build your device.

E. Test your device by placing soil and a plant in it. Observe the plant's response over time to being flipped upside down, and keep data about your observations.

F. Evaluate and Redesign your device. How did you meet the criteria and constraints? How could you improve your device?
Possible answer: Our device lost a lot of soil. Group B used a lid with a hole in it, which kept the soil in.

G. Communicate your findings with your classmates. Compare and contrast the results.

250

Unit 4 Plant Structure and Function

LESSON 1 Engage • Explore/Explain • Elaborate • **Evaluate**

LESSON CHECK

▶ **Explore Online** — Students can revisit the lesson phenomenon online.

LESSON 1
Lesson Check

Name _____

Can You Explain It?

1. Now that you've learned more about plant parts and the functions they perform, explain why a plant bends as its light source moves. Be sure to do the following:
   - Explain the relationship between sunlight and food in plants.
   - Identify the role of each plant part in picking up and using sunlight.
   - Describe how growth and food relate to better chances of survival for a plant.

 EVIDENCE NOTEBOOK Use the information you've collected in your Evidence Notebook to help you cover each point above.

Possible answer:
- Plants need food to grow and survive. They need light to make food.
- Leaves are the plant parts that take in the most light and make the food. Stems hold leaves and carry food made in leaves to roots. Roots store food.
- Having leaves face the sun for the most time they can each day allows the plant to make more food.

Checkpoints

2. Which parts of a plant help protect it from animals? Select all that apply.
   - **a. bark**
   - b. leaves
   - **c. spines**
   - **d. thorns**

251

 Formal Assessment Go online for student self-checks and other assessments.

Can You Explain It?

> ### Collaboration
> **Discussion** You may wish to revisit and discuss the images as a group to assess students' understanding of the material. Use the bulleted points in the student edition to lead the discussion.

 EVIDENCE NOTEBOOK

Have students reread their answers to the Evidence Notebook prompts and then use this evidence to justify their reasoning as they respond to the Can You Explain It question. Make sure students understand that a complete response must address all bulleted points.

DCI **LS1.A Structure and Function**

Focus students on the function of a plant's structure by having them reread the caption beneath the images in the Engage.

Ask: How does the stem help the leaves do their job? The stem leans toward the sunlight so the leaves can use the sun's energy to make food.

SUMMATIVE ASSESSMENT

2. This question asks students to choose the three plant parts that protect it from harm. Check that students reason through each one of these answer choices before choosing. If necessary, have them revisit the information about plant protection in Exploration 1.

LESSON 1 Engage • Explore/Explain • Elaborate • **Evaluate**

LESSON CHECK, *continued*

Using Representations to Assess Proficiency
In Exploration 2, students discovered that a tube system in a plant carries water and food throughout the plant to ensure survival. Allow students to revisit the information to refresh their memories.

3. Make sure students study and compare the images to note the differences between them. To answer the question, they must recall what they learned about plant systems. If students struggle, label the parts of the plant. This concept was covered most directly in Exploration 2, but was also important for the Hands-On Apply What You Know. If students have difficulty with the question, have them go back and look at photos and captions relating to internal tubes.

4. If students get stuck on this question, draw a plant on the front board and, as a whole class, label the parts of the plant, including the roots. This visual may help students answer the question. This concept was covered most directly in Exploration 1, but was also a part of Exploration 2. Students can check their Evidence Notebook and the Exploration for clues.

5. If students get stuck on this question, draw a plant on the front board and, as a whole class, label the parts of the plant, including the leaves. This visual may help students answer the question. Students must be able to relate all parts of the plant and their functions in order to understand the system of plants. Invite students to review Explorations 1 through 3.

6. Tell students that each word from the word bank will be used only once for this item. Encourage students to read the sentences aloud, but to themselves, to hear which answers sound the best. Plant response was covered in Exploration 3. Students can check the photos and text for clues to the answers for the fill-in.

---

3. Study the parts of the image. Write the letter of the correct label for the material that is carried by the system of tubes in each image. All labels may not apply.

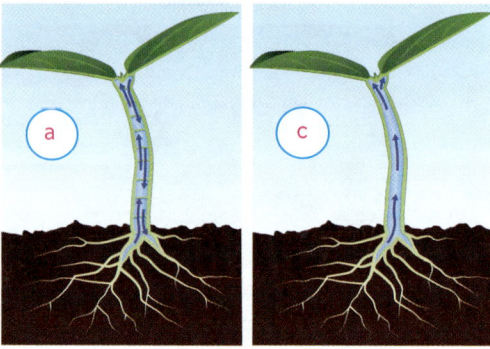

   a. food
   b. soil
   c. water
   d. heat

4. How do roots help plants grow?
   a. **Roots absorb water, which plants need to make food.**
   b. Roots capture sunlight, which gives plants a source of energy for making food.
   c. Roots help protect plants from animals.
   d. Roots help plants reproduce.

5. How do the leaves of a plant help it grow and survive?
   a. Leaves absorb water, which plants need to make food.
   b. **Leaves capture sunlight, which plants need to make the food that is essential for growth and survival.**
   c. Leaves help protect plants from animals.
   d. Leaves help plants reproduce by attracting animals that transfer pollen from one plant to another.

6. Plants respond to ___light___ when they make food. Some plants respond to ___touch___ when they trap food. In response to ___gravity___, plant parts bend so each part is in the right position to do its special job.

   | gravity |
   | light |
   | touch |

252

---

252 Unit 4 Plant Structure and Function

LESSON 1
Lesson Roundup

Plant Parts

A. Write the main function of each plant part.

growth   reproduction   protection

stem — growth
roots — growth
flower — reproduction
spines — protection

Internal Systems

B. Choose the correct descriptions.
   a. **Water moves from the roots of a plant to the rest of the plant through a system of tubes.**
   b. Food moves from the roots of a plant to the rest of the plant through a system of leaves.
   c. **Food moves from the leaves of a plant to the rest of the plant through a system of tubes.**
   d. Water moves from the leaves of a plant to the rest of the plant through a system of tubes.

Plant Behavior

C. Write the letter of the type of response that each picture shows.

 c
 b
 a

a. response to touch
b. response to gravity
c. response to light

Lesson Roundup

DCI LS1.A Structure and Function

This lesson summary enables students to quickly revisit key points and prepare for tests.

Using Representations to Assess Proficiency

A. Tell students that in order to answer the question, they need to study the images and apply those images to the terms in the word bank. Let students know that one of the words in the word bank will be used more than once. Encourage students to focus on the function of the plant, based on the parts that are shown. To clarify students' understanding of key terms, have them revisit Exploration 1 to look for definitions. **LS1.A**

B. Tell students that there is more than one correct answer to this question. If students struggle, draw a plant on the front board and label the parts. It may help students to see a visual of a plant with the parts labeled to answer this question. Students may wish to scan Exploration 2 before responding. If students need scaffolded support, begin by reminding them that they may need to combine information to find the answer. If necessary, ask guiding questions to help students find pertinent information. **LS1.A**

C. Make sure students understand what is being asked of them in this question. They are focusing on the type of response being shown in each image. Have them think about the function of each part that has responded to its environment. Roots need water, so they grow down to retrieve water from the ground. If necessary, allow students to skim the text and images in Exploration 3 to confirm the different responses plants have to their environment. **LS1.A**

LESSON 2
How Do Plants Grow and Reproduce?

Building to the Performance Expectation

The learning experiences in this lesson prepare students for mastery of:

4-LS1-1 Construct an argument that plants and animals have internal and external structures that function to support survival, growth, behavior, and reproduction.

Trace Tool to the NGSS
Go online to view the complete coverage of these standards across this lesson, unit, and time.

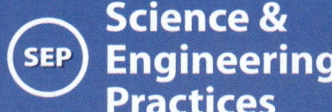  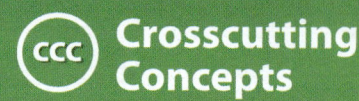

Science & Engineering Practices

Analyzing and Interpreting Data
Analyze and interpret data to make sense of phenomena using logical reasoning.

Engaging in Argument from Evidence
Construct an argument with evidence, data, and/or a model.

▶ **VIDEO** Analyzing Data Using Mathematics and Computational Skills

Asking Questions and Defining Problems
Ask questions that can be investigated and predict reasonable outcomes based on patterns such as cause-and-effect relationships.

▶ **VIDEO** Asking Questions and Defining Problems

Disciplinary Core Ideas

LS1.A Structure and Function
Plants and animals have both internal and external structures that serve various functions in growth, survival, behavior, and reproduction.

Crosscutting Concepts

Cause and Effect
Cause-and-effect relationships are routinely identified, tested, and used to explain change.

Systems and System Models
A system can be described in terms of its components and interactions.

▶ **VIDEO** System Models

 CONNECTIONS TO MATH

4.G.A.3 Recognize a line of symmetry for a two-dimensional figure as a line across the figure such that the figure can be folded across the line into matching parts. Identify line-symmetric figures and draw lines of symmetry.

 CONNECTIONS TO ENGLISH LANGUAGE ARTS

W.4.9 Draw evidence from literary or informational texts to support analysis, reflection, and research.

R.I.4.2 Write informative/explanatory texts to examine a topic and convey ideas and information clearly.

W.4.7 Conduct short research projects that build knowledge.

Supporting All Students, All Standards

Integrating the Three Dimensions of Learning

In this lesson, students develop an understanding of how the internal and external structures of both flowering and non-flowering plants function to support survival, growth, and reproduction **(DCI LS1.A)**. Students will construct arguments from evidence **(SEP Engaging in Argument from Evidence)** to explain the components and interactions of systems **(CCCs Cause and Effect, Systems and System Models)** and how they work together to enable reproduction.

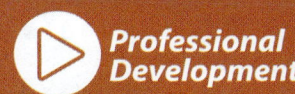 **Professional Development** Go online to view **Professional Development videos** with strategies to integrate CCCs and SEPs, including the ones used in this lesson.

Extra Hands-On Activity: Seed Journey

How Do Seeds Travel?

- Groups of three
- 50 minutes

Prepare seed sets for each group. Include seeds that are dispersed by water, wind, animals, and bursting. Provide small dishes of water, fans, and scissors or a plasstic knife.

Have students make a classification chart for their seeds in their notebooks. Have them test each type of seed using water and wind (fan). Finally, have them dissect each seed, and predict how each seed is dispersed.

For the second part, have students conduct research on types of seeds and how they travel. They should use this information to reclassify their seeds as needed. Come together as a class and have student groups use evidence to back their claims of how seeds are dispersed in specific ways.

 SEP This activity can support mastery of this Science and Engineering Practice: Engaging in Argument from Evidence

Preassessment

Have students complete the unit pre-test online or see the Assessment Guide.

Build on Prior Knowledge

Students should already know and be prepared to build on the following concepts:
- Plant life cycles and tropisms are necessary for the survival of each plant type.
- There are common patterns in many plants' life cycles.
- All organisms have external parts that they use to perform daily functions.
- External structures of plants include roots, stems, leaves, thorns, flowers, cones, and bark.

Differentiate Instruction

Lesson Vocabulary
- pollinators
- fertilization
- reproduction
- spores

Explain that flowers produce pollen, a yellow or green dust. **Pollinators** are animals that transfer pollen from one flower to another. The pollen grows a tube down to the ovule (female part or structure of a plant). When this happens, fertilization occurs. **Fertilization** is the process when reproductive cells join to form a new cell. A seed is formed, and it will grow into a new plant. This means the original plant has **reproduced**.

ELL/ELD Strategy
Show students illustrated plant life cycle diagrams and carefully explain the different steps. Help students form sentences of the various steps using the key vocabulary and write them on the board. Leave them there for the duration of the lesson.

Ask: What other cycles in nature do you know about? Sample answer: the cycles of seasons, the water cycle, cycles of matter

LESSON 2 **Engage** • Explore/Explain • Elaborate • Evaluate

ENGAGE: Lesson Phenomenon

Lesson Objective

Describe the process of pollination and fertilization in both flowering and non-flowering plants. Identify the basic reproductive structures of plants, and how the parts form a system for reproduction.

About This Image

This photo shows various types of seeds. Under the right conditions (adequate water, sun, and nutrients), these seeds will grow into different kinds of plants.

 SEP **Engaging in Argument from Evidence**

Alternative Engage Strategy

Seed Differences	👥 Whole class ⏱ 10 min

Bring a variety of different types of fruit to class. Separate the class into small groups and give each group the same collection of different fruit. Have students discuss and list each fruit's characteristics and predict the process that the fruit went through to become a fruit.

Have groups share their descriptions and predictions and compare notes. Then confirm the correct predictions.

LESSON 2

How Do Plants Grow and Reproduce?

As with animals, plants also grow and reproduce. Whether the plant is a tree, a kind of grass, or a flower, it begins its life as a seed. Under the right conditions, the seeds in this picture will grow into different kinds of plants.

By the end of this lesson . . .
you'll be able to explain how plants grow and reproduce.

254

Unit 4 Plant Structure and Function

Can You Explain It?

Explore Online

Madison was excited about a fruit tree in the backyard of her new home. As spring began, she observed the tree every day, and noticed several bees near the tree.

A couple of months later, Madison noticed some of the flowers started to swell, while others began to wither and turn brown. She wondered what was happening.

Gradually the bulges left over from the flowers got bigger. Slowly but surely the fruit grew and grew. Eventually, the tree was covered in ripe apples.

1. How did the one flower turn into fruit? Why did some of the other flowers not turn into fruit?

Students should respond based on the preliminary observations they can make of the images.

Tip
To recall the names of many parts of plants, read What Are Some External Structures of Plants?.

EVIDENCE NOTEBOOK Look for this icon to help you gather evidence to answer the questions above.

Explore Online
Students can view the lesson phenomenon online.

Can You Explain It?

Students are asked to record their initial thoughts about how the flower from the fruit tree turned into fruit and why the other flowers didn't. Urge students not to worry about whether their answers are correct. They should expect their ideas to change as they progress through the Explorations. They will have an opportunity to revise their answers when they revisit these questions at the end of the lesson.

Collaborate

Write, Pair, Share Have students work in pairs to write down their ideas about why some flowers turn into fruit and others don't. In this way, you can more accurately gauge students' prior ability to make sense of the phenomenon by applying knowledge gained through previous experience about plants and reproduction.

EVIDENCE NOTEBOOK

Encourage students to use an appropriate graphic organizer, such as main idea and supporting details, to set up their notebook for this lesson.

Find more strategies in the online ELA handbook.

LESSON 2   Engage • **Explore**/Explain • Elaborate • Evaluate

EXPLORATION 1 Why Do Plants Have Flowers?

3D Learning Objective

Develop an understanding of the **structure and function** of flowering plants and, by **gathering evidence**, understand how they form a **reproductive system**.

DCI LS1.A Structure and Function

Explain to students that a flower has many parts or structures, each with its own function. Male and female structures have important roles in reproduction.

Ask: What are the female parts of the flower? the pistil, which contains the ovary and the ovule

Ask: What are the male parts of the flower? the stamen and its anther

Ask: How is a seed produced? when the pollen produced from the anther comes into contact with an ovule

The function of two other parts of the flower do not have a direct role in reproduction, but they aid in reproduction.

Ask: What is the function of the sepal and petals? It covers and protect the flower bud. Their color and scent attracts insects and birds that help pollinate the plants.

Differentiated Instruction

RTI/Extra Support Bring in several plants and arrange students in groups to locate various parts and explain their functions.

 Systems and System Models

Ask: How is the diagram helpful in your understanding of a plant and its flower? It shows where the different parts are located and what they look like up close.

256   Unit 4 Plant Structure and Function

EXPLORATION 1

Why Do Plants Have Flowers?

Flower Power

Have you ever looked closely at a flower? There are structures inside a flower that help the plant reproduce. View the illustration below to learn more about the names and functions of these structures.

The **anther** is part of the stamen. This male structure sits on top of the long filament and produces pollen. When pollen comes into contact with the ovule, a seed is produced.

The **stamen** is a male part of a flower that contains the anther and filament.

The **pistil** is a female part of the flower that contains the ovary and the ovule.

The **ovule,** also called an *egg,* is inside the ovary. If pollen reaches the ovule, a seed is produced. It is a female structure.

The **sepals** are the outer parts of a flower that cover the flower bud. They protect the flower while it is developing.

The **petals** make up the outside of a flower. Petals are often brightly colored and scented to attract insects and birds to help pollinate the plants.

2. Choose the correct words from the diagram that complete the sentences. The ___sepals___ cover and protect the flower bud. The ___anther___ is where pollen is produced. If pollen comes into contact with the ___ovule___, a seed is produced.

256

Where Did the Pollen Go?

You know that flowers produce pollen. You have likely seen yellow dust floating in the air or coating the top of a car during the spring or summer. This is pollen. If you are allergic to pollen, you know exactly when flowers are producing it in high amounts! Pollen is necessary for the reproduction of plants.

Pollination is the transfer pollen from one flower to another. Animals, like hummingbirds, are attracted to the flowers to feed on their sweet, sugary nectar. As an animal, like this hummingbird, feeds on the nectar, some of the pollen gets stuck on its body.

After the hummingbird moved to the next flower to feed, some of the pollen on its body fell off onto the new flower. The pollen grew a tube down to the ovule and fertilization occured. **Fertilization** is the process when male and female reproductive parts join together.

3. **Language SmArts** Summarize the process a flowering plant goes through for fertilization using the words *pollination* and *fertilization*.

Fertilization happens when pollen is carried from one flower to another by an animal. The pollen grows a tube down to the ovule and a seed forms.

When a plant **reproduces,** it makes another plant. For example, when pollen reaches an ovule, a seed begins to develop. Eventually, the seed will be moved from the flower to a new location. If the new location has the right conditions, the seed will grow into a new plant. This means that the original plant has reproduced.

257

DCI LS1.A Structure and Function

Remind students that pollen is necessary for plants to reproduce.

Ask: What does pollen look like? It is a somewhat thick yellow powder.

Have students study the two images closely and describe what they see.

Explain that some animals are pollinators. They are drawn to flowers to feed on their sweet nectar. As they feed, they collect pollen from the flowers' anthers.

Ask: How do pollinators spread pollen? After they feed from one flower, they move on to feed from another, and some of the pollen they've collected on their bodies gets transferred.
Ask: How does fertilization occur? When the pollen the pollinator spreads to the second flower reaches its ovule, fertilization takes place.
Ask: What is fertilization? It is a process that takes place when reproductive cells join and form a new cell.

Remind students that the word *reproduces* means to make another plant. Discuss with students what other things reproduce, such as animals and humans. At the end of the discussion, be sure to remind students that all living things as a whole reproduce.

Language SmArts
W.4.9 Draw evidence from informational texts

Encourage students to draw diagrams to supplement their summaries. When students have finished, separate them into pairs and have them share their drawings with each other, discussing their similarities and differences and comparing them against the summary.

Lesson 2 How Do Plants Grow and Reproduce? 257

LESSON 2 Engage • **Explore/Explain** • Elaborate • Evaluate

EXPLORATION 1 Why Do Plants Have Flowers?, continued

 Analyzing and Evaluating Data

We know that animals such as hummingbirds are pollinators.

Ask: What other animals are pollinators? Birds, bees, butterflies, and bats are pollinators.

Explain that like hummingbirds, these animals are attracted to the sweet smell of the flower. They eat or gather the nectar of the flower and in the process, the pollen sticks to their faces or bodies. As they move from flower to flower, they transfer that pollen.

Explain that not only sweet-smelling flowers attract pollinators.

Ask: How do you think skunk cabbage got its name? Sample answer: Skunks make a foul smell and perhaps skunk cabbage does, too.

Ask: What kind of animals are attracted to skunk cabbage? flies

Flies that normally lay their eggs on rotting meat are attracted to the foul-smelling skunk cabbage that has the odor of rotting meat.

Ask: Other than pollinators, are there are other ways pollen is spread? wind

Collaboration

Jigsaw Divide the class into 4-5 groups. Assign each person in a group a different way flowers are pollinated, for example, wind, hummingbird, butterfly, etc. Then divide students by topic to join together to become experts on their assigned pollination method. For example all the bat students form a group. Have groups research their assigned pollination method. Then the experts return to their original groups to teach others what they learned.

In More Ways Than One

You've already read about one way that pollen can be moved from one plant to another with help from animals. View the images to learn other ways pollination can take place.

Some plants are pollinated by animals called pollinators. These animals are attracted to the nectar by the sweet smell of the flower. When they eat, pollen sticks to their faces or bodies. As they move from one flower to another, the pollen is also transferred.

Unlike most sweet-smelling flowers, the skunk cabbage in this photo smells like rotting meat. This stinky plant attracts flies. The flies land on the flowers, get pollen on their bodies, and move pollen from flower to flower as they fly around.

Some plants do not depend on animals for pollination. Instead, their pollen is moved by the wind. This plant releases pollen that drifts in the wind. If the pollen lands on the same type of plant, fertilization can occur.

258

258 Unit 4 Plant Structure and Function

Some flowers can self-pollinate. This means that the pollen made by the anther is the same pollen that fertilizes the ovule. The pollen does not come from another plant.

4. Which choices are ways pollen can move from one flower to another? Select all that apply.

 **a.** insects   **b.** birds   **c.** rain   **d.** wind

 EVIDENCE NOTEBOOK Now that you've learned how pollination occurs, think about the image from the beginning of the lesson. What pollinators did you see? What were they doing to the flower? How does the flower change as a result of their visit?

 HANDS-ON Apply What You Know

Pollination Models

5. Make two models of flowers using cups to represent the flowers. Place a cotton ball in each to represent the stamen. Sprinkle some powder on one of the cotton balls to represent pollen. Using a pipe cleaner to represent a bee's leg, how can you model moving pollen from one flower to the other? Try it!

How did you model pollination? What is another way you could model pollination using these materials?

Students should describe what they did with their models, and then describe another way to move material from one place to another, such as wind.

 LS1.A Structure and Function

Although the structure of many flowering plants look different, their functions are similar.

Ask: Besides pollinators and wind, what else could move pollen from one flower to another? Sample answer: water

Explain that the pollen of some plants made by its anther is the same pollen that fertilizes its ovule. These type of plants are called self pollinators.

 EVIDENCE NOTEBOOK

Evidence should include: Plants can become pollinated by pollinators such as birds, bees, butterflies, and bats that are attracted to sweet-smelling flowers. The apple tree had bees around it. These pollinators collected pollen on their bodies and moved it to a new flower where it reached the ovule. The flower was fertilized and grew fruit.

HANDS-ON Apply What You Know
Pollination Models

For the models, students will need clear plastic cups, cotton balls to represent flowers, different color powders to represent pollen, and pipe cleaners to represent a bee's leg. Students will use the pipe cleaner to show how pollen is spread from one flower to another. Guide students to understand that the colored powder on the cotton ball fastens onto the bristles on the pipe cleaner, similar to how real pollen attaches itself to a bee's bristly legs. Challenge students to think how else the colored pollen could become transferred to another cotton ball.

Assessment Rubric

Students' should follow through with setting up two flower models, one bearing pollen, and then suggest using a fan or other force to move the model pollen.

LESSON 2 Engage • **Explore/Explain** • Elaborate • Evaluate

EXPLORATION 1 *Why Do Plants Have Flowers?, continued*

CCC Systems and Models

Work with students to help them recall what is happening in each image. Then have them number their labels 1 through 4 to show the order of events that must take place for a flower to reproduce.

> ### Differentiate Instruction
> **RTI/Extra Support** To aid students' understanding of the sequencing of pollination and reproduction, have students draw each labeled step in a circular diagram using arrows.

FORMATIVE ASSESSMENT
Putting It Together

Explain that a *system* is a group of interrelated parts or elements that form a complex whole, such as the *reproductive system*. In the reproductive system of a plant, the different structures (anther, ovule, etc.) work together to form a particular function, such as reproducing.

Discuss with the class how the different parts of a plant work together to form a reproductive system.

Ask: What would happen if one or more parts of the system wasn't doing its job? *The plant would not be able to reproduce.*

Have students write their thoughts independently in Item 7.

The Steps of Reproduction

6. You have now learned the steps of pollination and fertilization. Label what is happening in each image, and number the images in the correct order.

④ Seeds have developed inside the ripe fruit in the reproduction cycle

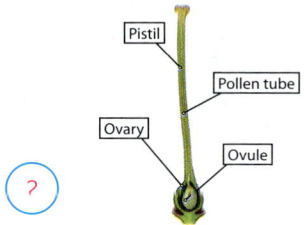

② Pollen from another flower moves down the pollen tube to the ovule.

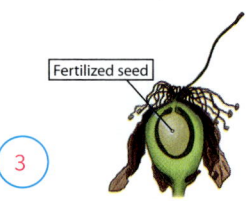

③ After pollen reaches the ovule, seeds become fertilized and ready to make more plants.

① Insects move pollen from one plant to another as they gather nectar to feed themselves.

Putting it Together

7. Look at the photos above. How do all these parts involved in reproduction form a system? What would happen if one or more parts of the system wasn't doing its job?

Possible answer: The flower attracts pollinators who move pollen from one flower to the ovule of another flower. All these parts work together to reproduce new flowers. If something fails, the plant will not reproduce.

Unit 4 Plant Structure and Function

EXPLORATION 2 What If Plants Don't Produce Flowers?

EXPLORATION 2
What If Plants Don't Produce Flowers?

Flowerless

Not all plants produce flowers. The fern and the pine tree shown in the images are examples of plants that do not produce flowers. They have different ways to reproduce.

A fern has spores.

A pine tree has cones.

8. How do you think plants reproduce without flowers?

Possible answer: Pinecones are like flowers, with ovules contained inside, and pollen must have some way of getting to the ovules.

 HANDS-ON Apply What You Know

Pinecone Parts

9. Get a pinecone from your teacher, and put it on a paper plate. Explore the pinecone to see its different structures. Draw what you see in detail. Dissect some of the seeds, and draw the structures you see inside. Is the pinecone male or female? What evidence do you see to support your decision?

Student responses should be based on observable evidence from their cones.

3D Learning Objective

Analyze the **structure and function** of non-flowering plants, and **collect evidence** to understand how they form a **reproductive system**.

CCC Systems and System Models

Explain that not all plants produce flowers, but that they can still reproduce. Plants such as ferns and pine trees don't have flowers.

Discuss with the class possible ways ferns and pine trees might reproduce. Have students write their thoughts independently before having them perform the following hands-on activity.

HANDS-ON Apply What You Know
Pinecone Parts

SEP Obtaining, Evaluating, and Communicating Information

Bring in several pinecones and paper plates. Separate the class into pairs and give each pair a pinecone on a paper plate. Challenge students to explore and dissect the pinecone. Have them draw what they see in detail and label what they think are the different parts.

Explain that there are male and female pinecones. Female pinecones are what we normally think of when we think of pinecones. They are larger (wider) and woodier than their male counterparts. Each woody scale contains ovules that when fertilized produce seeds. The male pinecone is usually longer and thinner and produces pollen.

Assessment Rubric

Students should reason that observing seeds in the dissected scales of the cone suggests the cone is female, and lack of seeds—or presense of pollen—suggests a male cone.

Lesson 2 How Do Plants Grow and Reproduce?

LESSON 2   Engage • **Explore/Explain** • Elaborate • Evaluate

EXPLORATION 2 *What If Plants Don't Produce Flowers?, continued*

Differentiated Instruction

Extension Both male and female pinecones are on the same tree. Male pinecones tend to be on the lower branches. Have students research why the tree is structured this way. **Answer: This way pollen doesn't normally fall on the female cones on the same tree. This promotes fertilization with other pine trees, which leads to genetic variation.**

 LS1.A Structure and Function

Have students study the labeled images on the timeline and find the male and female pinecones and their parts.

Ask: How do pinecone eggs become fertilized? **In the spring, pollen from the male pinecones is released and carried by the wind. If the pollen lands on a female cone of a similar type of tree, the egg can be fertilized and a seed can develop.**

Connection to Math

Have students study their pinecone from their hands-on activity. Have them place a string through the middle of the pinecone from top to bottom. Then have them observe the left and right sides.

Ask: What do you observe? **The two sides match; they look the same.**

Tell students that pinecones have symmetry. The two sides are mirror images of each other. Many things in science and math have symmetry. Ask students to draw the pinecone in their notebooks and draw the line of symmetry.

4.G.A.3 Recognize a line of symmetry

Ladies and Gentlemen

The pine tree you just saw does not produce flowers to reproduce. Instead, it produces cones. View the timeline to learn more about how pine trees and other trees like it, such as fir trees, reproduce.

1. Female / Male

Fir trees and other cone-bearing trees produce male and female cones. Male cones produce pollen and female cones contain many ovule.

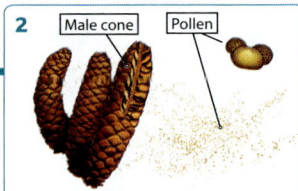

2. Male cone / Pollen

In the spring, pollen is released from the male cone. The pollen is carried by the wind.

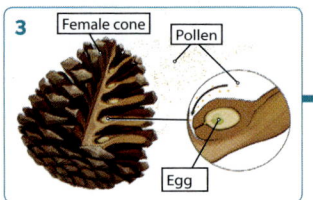

3. Female cone / Pollen / Egg

If pollen from a male cone lands on a female cone of the same type of tree, the egg can be fertilized. A seed can develop from the fertilized egg. A **seed** is where the new plant is contained.

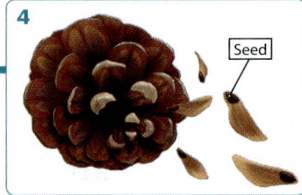

4. Seed

When the seed is fully developed, it will drop from the female cone to the ground.

5.

If the seed lands in a place with the right conditions, a new tree will begin to grow. That tree will also produce cones.

10. Which structure, or part, of a fir tree holds the pollen needed for reproduction?

   a. the female cone   **b. the male cone**   **c.** the male and female cones

262

262 Unit 4 Plant Structure and Function

How Unique!

Besides cones, there is another way that plants reproduce. They produce spores, which fall to the ground or are carried on the wind. **Spores** are the reproductive part of certain types of plants. If they land in a place where conditions are right, a new plant will begin to grow. View the timeline to learn more about this type of reproduction in plants.

1. Some plants, such as ferns, produce spores. These are stored on the underside of their leaves, or fronds. When released, they can be carried by the wind or fall onto the ground.

2. The new, small, heart-shaped structure starts to form. It grows and releases sperm cells and egg cells.

3. Using water, the sperm cells swim to the egg cells and fertilize them.

4. Once the egg is fertilized, it begins to grow into a young fern.

5. The young fern grows into a larger plant that looks like the ferns you have probably seen.

11. Choose the correct answer. What is the function of a spore?
    a. Spores fertilize eggs, which then make new ferns.
    b. Spores become structures that release sperm cells and eggs.
    c. Spores fertilize sperm cells, which then make new ferns.

263

 Systems and System Models

Ferns are similar to pine trees and fir trees in that they don't produce flowers, but they are also different from them because they don't produce cones either. So how do they reproduce?

To find out, have students study the labeled images on the timeline and discover the system by which ferns reproduce.

Ask: Instead of cones, what do ferns produce and where are they located? The undersides of their leaves produce spores.
Ask: How do the spores reach the ground? The leaves release the spores and they fall to the ground or are carried by wind or water.
Ask: How does the egg become fertilized? The sperm cells use water to swim to the egg cells and fertilize them.

Summarize the fern timeline by telling students that the fertilized egg begins to grow into a fern. It then matures and produces its own spores. Similar to the pine tree, the cycle repeats itself over and over.

 LS1.A Structure and Function

Review the information from Explorations 1 and 2 about flowering plants, pine/fir trees, and ferns. Have students answer the following questions and then have them fill out the chart on the next page independently.

Ask: In what way are the flowering and non-flowering plants alike? All three have male and female parts for reproduction.
Ask: Instead of flowers, what do non-flowering plants produce? Pine/fir trees produce cones and ferns produce spores.

Lesson 2 How Do Plants Grow and Reproduce? **263**

LESSON 2 Engage • **Explore/Explain** • Elaborate • Evaluate

EXPLORATION 2 *What If Plants Don't Produce Flowers?, continued*

Connection to Engineering

In the physical world, there are many types of systems with different structures, and those structures, as with those in flowering and non-flowering plants, have different functions. But like plants, physical systems such as electrical, plumbing, and mechanical systems have male and female parts that interact to create something. For example, an electrical connector consists of a plug (male part) that is put into a jack (female part) to produce an electrical circuit. In plumbing, male pipes fit into female parts to enable water to flow.

Ask: How are mechanical structures similar to living structures? *They have male and female parts.*

Ask: In an electrical system, what do the male and female parts do when connected? *They allow the flow of electricity.*

ETS1.A. Different solutions can be compared by how well they meet the criteria

Which Is true?

12. Look at the pictures of plants at the top of the chart and compare them. Put a check mark for each true statement about the plant.

Uses insects to pollinate		✓	
Produces a seed		✓	✓
Produces a spore	✓		
Produces a cone			✓
Has male and female structures	✓	✓	✓

 **EVIDENCE NOTEBOOK** Think about the images from the beginning of the lesson. What type of reproductive method and structure does the tree have? What evidence supports your answer?

13. **Language SmArts** A man wants to plant a garden with a few plants and let them reproduce to fill up his backyard. He lives in an environment that gets very little rain and is very windy at times. There are some birds but not many flying insects. Based on the scenario, Chantelle thinks plants that reproduce with spores would do well here but flowers and cones would not. Do you agree or disagree? Support your answer with evidence. Write your answers on the lines below. Then debate with your classmates.

Possible answer: Plants that produce spores will not grow well here. There is very little rain, and those plants need water to reproduce (sperm cell swims to egg cell for fertilization). The conditions are better for plants that produce cones (wind can pollinate) and possibly plants with flowers (birds can pollinate).

FORMATIVE ASSESSMENT

Language SmArts
ELA.W.4.9 Use Evidence for Support

Read and discuss the scenario presented. Consider the conditions that exist in Chantelle's environment: very little rain, but lots of wind. Ask students to determine whether Chantelle's plans for planting types are wise ones. Before agreeing or disagreeing with Chantelle's plan, review conditions needed for flowering and non-flowering plants to reproduce.

Based on the class review and student debate, have students independently write their answers and support them with evidence.

264 Unit 4 Plant Structure and Function

EXPLORATION 3 On the Move

EXPLORATION 3
On The Move

How Do Seeds Get Around?

When plants release seeds, it is best for the seeds to be moved away from the parent plant. Seeds cannot move on their own, so how do they get around? Some of the ways are the same ways that pollen gets moved from one flower to another.

Agents of Dispersal

14. Look at the three photos on the top row. Each of these structures either contains seeds or is a seed. Match the photo by drawing a line to the photo on the bottom row that shows how each seed is moved from one place to another.

15. Why is it important for seeds to spread out?

   Each new plant needs its own space to grow. If seeds fall only right next to their parent plant, the plants will be too crowded to get the light, water, and nutrients they need to survive.

265

3D Learning Objective

Understand that plants and animals have **external structures that function in survival, growth, and reproduction**. **Obtain information** about seed dispersal and come to an understanding of the **cause-and-effect** relationship of seeds and their method of dispersal.

DCI LS1.A Structure and Function

Help students identify the photos on the top row: image 1. blackberry bush bearing blackberry fruit; image 2. a dandelion with seeds; image 3. a burr.

Ask: What is a burr? **A rough barbed case that surrounds and protects the seeds of a plant such as the chestnut.**

Collaboration

Write, Pair, Share Have students complete this page, then have them explain their answers to a partner. As a class, discuss their answers, and then answer the questions below.

CCC Cause and Effect

Also help students make connections as to why seeds need to spread out.

Ask: How did you know how to match the seed with its method of dispersal? **I've seen birds eat berries. I've blown on a dandelion, and I've taken burrs off my dog.**

Ask: Why is it important for seeds to spread out? **This reduces competition and provides the seeds a better opportunity to grow.**

Lesson 2 How Do Plants Grow and Reproduce? 265

LESSON 2   Engage • **Explore/Explain** • Elaborate • Evaluate

EXPLORATION 3   On the Move, continued

DCI Structure and Function

Ask: Why are seeds from the sycamore tree easily moved by the wind? Why are they sometimes called helicopter seeds? **The wing shape of these seeds makes it easy for the wind to lift them. They are sometimes called helicopter seeds because as the wind moves them, they spin around like the blade on a helicopter.**

Ask: How do animals such as this squirrel help seeds move? **They eat fruits and nuts. These foods go through their digestive systems and are released wherever they make their droppings.**

Not all seeds are eaten by animals. Some are discarded after they eat the fruit around the seed. Some seeds have a tasty structure called an eliasome. Ants take the seeds back to the nest where they eat the tasty bit and discard the rest of the seed to germinate.

SEP Constructing Explanations

Ask: Why are some seeds, such as the coconut, carried far and easily by water? **They are light and float in the water to be delivered to a new location.**

Have students think of various reason why seeds would be carried away by water. Explain that heavy rain might carry them away, people or animals might drop them in bodies of water such as ponds, stream, lakes, etc. or in the case of a palm tree near the water, seeds (coconuts) might drop directly into the water.

> ## Differentiate Instruction
>
> **Extension** Challenge students to create a game to match seed types with their method if distribution. Remind them that games need written rules. These games may be useful in helping students that need extra support.

Seed Dispersal

When seeds spread out, it helps prevent overcrowding and competition for space, light, and other resources. Read to find out more about how seeds move.

The sycamore tree produces a seed that is sometimes called a helicopter seed, due to its winged shape. The seeds spin as the wind carries them away from the tree and onto the ground.

Some animals eat berries from trees. The fruits contain seeds, like the seed you find in the middle of an apple. After the fruit passes through an animal's digestive tract, the seeds are released in the animal's droppings elsewhere.

Some seeds have tiny hairs or bristles that cause them to stick to peoples' clothes or animals' fur when they brush up against the seeds. The seeds are then carried to a new location by the person or animal.

Some plants depend on water to move their seeds. Some seeds, including the coconut shown here, are light in weight and float in water. When the seeds are dropped in the water, they float to a new spot.

Some plants have a unique way of dispersing seeds. The seeds explode out of the seedpod and fly through the air. Seeds may fly several feet from the parent plant through this method.

16. Which methods can carry seeds far from the parent plant?

 **a.** animals    **b.** water   **c.** wind

 EVIDENCE NOTEBOOK You learned that apples grow from flowers. Construct an argument to prove that apples grow on apple trees as part of the tree's life cycle. Present the apple tree as a system. Identify the parts of the system and how they change during the life of the tree. Record your argument in your Evidence Notebook.

 Language SmArts
Summarize

You have read about several ways that seeds are dispersed. Answer the questions below to test your understanding.

Tip
The English Language Arts Handbook can provide help with understanding how to summarize.

17. The seeds of a milkweed plant are very light and have fluffy white hairs around them, similar to a dandelion seed. How do you think these seeds are dispersed? Explain your reasoning.

Possible answer: These seeds are dispersed by the wind. The
fluffy white hairs help them travel by catching the wind.

18. Explain how a deer eating a ripe tomato out of a garden might lead to the tomato plant's seeds being moved from one place to another.

Possible answer: The tomato seeds are moved from place to
place by the deer. Once the seeds move through the deer's
digestive tract, they would be deposited in another place.

Differentiate Instruction

RTI/Extra Support Bring in some seed pods and let students examine them. Break one open in front of students and have them observe the seeds inside. Explain that vegetables such as peas, have pods, and plants such as lilies and milkweed have pods. Share that milkweed pods have an unusual method of dispersing their seeds. Their pods dry out and they open up, dispersing their seeds. The seeds have silk hairs that look like parachutes. Wind moves these seeds to distant places.

 EVIDENCE NOTEBOOK

Students should note that apple trees produce flowers, the nectar of their flowers attracts bees, and as bees feed on their nectar, their bristly legs pick up pollen. The bees then land on the flowers of other trees and distribute pollen. When the pollen reaches the ovules, a seed develops. The surrounding tissue or fruit is the apple. Eventually, the seeds will reach the ground. In the right conditions, the seeds will grow into a tree, grow, thrive, and produce flowers of its own and the cycle begins all over again.

FORMATIVE ASSESSMENT

 Language SmArts
Summarize
W.4.9 Draw evidence from informational texts

Remind students that a good summary includes the most important ideas and details from a text. It also is a place to add some of your own experiences and knowledge of the topic. Before having students independently write summaries of the two scenarios, review what students have learned about the numerous ways seeds are scattered. Ask them to share and compare and contrast facts and details presented. Did any students include their own background knowledge or experiences?

LESSON 4   Engage • **Explore/Explain** • Elaborate • Evaluate

EXPLORATION 3   On the Move, continued

HANDS-ON ACTIVITY   Small groups   1 class period
Flying High

3D Learning Objective
Design and test a device that disperses seeds using wind.

 **Planning and Carrying Out Investigations**

Materials
Provide a variety of materials. If you add different materials, assign prices to them. All materials "purchased" must not exceed $10.

Preparation
Preassemble all materials. Place students into small groups. Consider assigning each student a role such as coordinator, recorder, materials manager, and timekeeper. Additional roles could be quality controller, reporter, and troubleshooter. Remind students that in addition to their role, they are all expected to participate with ideas. Remind students of appropriate group behavior.

 Cause and Effect

Before student groups begin, have them formulate a question to meet the objective, such as, *What materials can I use to build an effective device that uses wind to disperse seeds a good distance?*

Procedure

STEP 1 Give ample time to research how seeds are scattered by the wind. Provide library time and/or in-class time for Internet searches. Encourage students to take notes while they research.

STEP 2 Have students brainstorm to formulate plans for their devices, keeping the criteria and constraints in mind. Have them state the method of seed dispersal their model needs to show.

HANDS-ON ACTIVITY
Flying High

Objective

Collaborate to design and test a device that disperses a seed using wind.

A company has hired you to build a device to disperse a seed using wind. Use your knowledge of how seeds are dispersed by wind to design the device.

Find a Problem: What question will you investigate to meet this objective?
Possible answer: How can I move seeds through the air?

Materials
- corn kernels for seeds — $3
- balloons — $1 for 1 or $2 for 3
- box of tissues — $1 for 2 or $2 for 5
- paper clips — $1 per box
- rubber bands — $2
- straws — $1 for 3
- paper bag — $1
- yarn — $2
- ribbon — $1 per m
- aluminum foil — $1 per ¼ sq. m
- tape — $1
- cotton balls — $1 per 10
- popsicle sticks — $1 for 10
- pipe cleaners — $1 for 10
- fan — $0
- meter stick — $0

Procedure

STEP 1 Research with your group to find more information about how seeds are dispersed by wind.

STEP 2 Brainstorm ideas for your device. Keep in mind the criteria and constraints below.

Criteria	Constraints
☐ Seed must travel at least 30 cm through the air.	☐ Do not use the force of your hand to propel the seed forward.
☐ When device lands, seed must make contact with the ground to reproduce.	☐ Maximum device size: 15 x 15 x 15 cm.
	☐ Total budget $10.

What method of seed dispersal will your device model?
Responses should relate to the design plan.

268

STEP 3 **Plan** by making a drawing of your device. Write out the steps of your experiment to test your device.

Drawings and descriptions should reflect the built device.

STEP 4 Show your drawing and procedure to your teacher. Make any improvements suggested by your teacher. Have your teacher approve your final device and procedure.

STEP 5 **Build** a prototype of your device using the materials you selected.

STEP 6 **Test** your device. Carry out your experiment, and record your results.

Record Your Results

Record your results in the observation table.

Trial	Distance seed traveled (cm)	Other observations:
1		Check student data to see how far the seeds traveled in each trial.
2		
3		
4		

269

STEP 3 Have students draw a design of their device and then write a list of the steps they are going to use to test it. Monitor student pairs as they sketch designs, and challenge them in their thinking about the materials they plan on using and the feasibility of their design. As students work, ask questions to each group based off the criteria and constraints such as, "How will you ensure your seed touches the ground when it lands?"

STEP 4 Check designs and procedures and suggest helpful feedback. Encourage students to keep some money aside for unexpected things. As necessary, have students draw a new design and/or rewrite or revise procedures.

STEP 5 Before this step, students will need to "buy" materials. As students use materials to build their devices, they may experience problems and want to change their building materials. Assure students that this is acceptable and even encouraged to create better devices, but they still need to stay within budget.

STEP 6 Now is the time for students to test their designs. Suggest that one partner drop the seed device in front of the fan and the other measure the distance the seed travels, or that they alternate turns. Caution them that to get accurate distance results, they should drop the device at the same height and distance from the fan each time.

Encourage students to perform several test trials and measure accurately using the meter stick or tape measure. They should also note the seed distances in their observation table. Other observations should include the success on each criteria and constraint.

Lesson 2 How Do Plants Grow and Reproduce? **269**

LESSON 4 Engage • **Explore/Explain** • Elaborate • Evaluate

EXPLORATION 3 Hands-On Activity, continued

Analyze Your Results

SEP Analyzing and Interpreting Data

STEP 7 Ask questions to guide student thinking: **Do you think your device was too heavy, not heavy enough? Was its design one that enabled wind to lift it efficiently and carry the seed far?**

STEP 9 Have pairs discuss and then write why they think certain devices had better average dispersal lengths.

Draw Conclusions

STEPS 10–11 Helps students understand how to state their claim, such as **wind moves seeds**. Evidence could include: **My device, using wind from a fan, sent seeds on an average 25 cm.**

Claims, Evidence, and Reasoning

Have students work with a partner to critique each other's claims and evidence. Ask each pair to be prepared to share one way they changed or improved their claim or the evidence cited.

Scoring Rubric for Hands-On Activity	
3	meets all criteria and constraints; works collaboratively with group; keeps accurate data, analyzes all data for redesign improvements
2	meets most criteria and constraints; generally works collaboratively with group; keeps mostly accurate data, analyzes most data for redesign improvements
1	does not meet most criteria and constraints; has trouble working collaboratively; data is inaccurate, improvements are not based on data
0	little or no attempt to meet the requirements above

270 Unit 4 Plant Structure and Function

Analyze Your Results

STEP 7 **Evaluate** your test. What was the normal distance your seeds traveled? Do you think they could travel farther if you improved your device? Explain how you would improve your device.
Possible answer: The seeds could have traveled farther if we improved our device by making it weigh less and adding a larger parachute.

STEP 8 **Redesign** your device. What improvements could you make to your design? If time allows, redesign and retest your device.
Possible answer: We will use a fan instead of a balloon to propel our device so it will go farther.

STEP 9 **Communicate** to compare your device to other groups and their results. Did their seeds travel farther than yours? Why or why not?
Possible answer: Some of the other groups' seeds did travel farther than ours. They made devices that kept the seeds in the air longer.

Draw Conclusions

STEP 10 Make a claim based on the question you investigated. Cite evidence from your design and other designs to support your claim.
Possible answer: Using a parachute type device helped the seed travel in the wind. The devices that were lighter traveled farther than those that were heavy. The larger the opening in the parachute to catch wind, the farther it went.

STEP 11 Think of other questions you would like to ask about seed dispersal.
Possible answer: How does weight factor into how far seeds travel by wind?

270

LESSON 2 Engage • Explore/Explain • **Elaborate** • Evaluate

TAKE IT FURTHER Discover More

 **Explore Online** Students can explore all three Take It Further paths online.

TAKE IT FURTHER
Discover More

Check out this path . . . or go online to choose one of these other paths.

| Careers in Science | • Wait, There's More!
• It's What's on the Inside |

Pomologist

The science of growing fruit is known as *pomology*. Scientists who study how to grow fruits are known as *pomologists*.

Dr Janine Hasey is a pomologist and master gardener who specializes in finding better ways to grow fruits and nuts, such as kiwi and walnuts. Pomologists also perform tests to grow larger, better tasting fruits.

One thing that is essential to growing fruit is having a flower pollinated. In certain plants, after a flower is pollinated, it produces a fruit around the seeds. The fruit helps protect the seeds and also helps with seed dispersal.

Dr. Hasey researches ways to control pests and diseases that harm fruits and nuts. She studies the difference between animals that are pollinators and animals that are pests.

19. What does a pomologist do?

Pomologists perform tests to grow larger, better-tasting fruits.

271

Collaboration

Share Feedback You may chose to assign this activity or to direct students online to the Interactive Online Student Edition where they can explore and chose from all three paths. These activities can be assigned individually, to pairs, or to small groups.

Careers in Science: Pomologist

 LS1.A Structure and Function

Explain that there are many careers in the study of plants. One such career is pomology. Pomologists devote their time to the study of growing fruit. They research ways to control pests and diseases that harm fruits and nuts. Have students read about Dr. Hasey and pomology.

Ask: What kinds of tests does she perform? *She conducts tests to find better ways to grow larger, better-tasting fruits.*
Ask: What is essential to growing fruit? *pollinating flowers*

 Asking Questions

Connection to English Language Arts

Encourage students to research other sources to learn more about what pomologists do. First, have them write a list of questions they would want to ask a pomologist in an interview. Encourage them to write notes about the answers they found in their research. Ask students to write up their interview questions and answers.

ELA.W.3.7 Conduct short research projects that build knowledge about a topic.

Lesson 2 How Do Plants Grow and Reproduce? **271**

LESSON 2   Engage • Explore/Explain • **Elaborate** • Evaluate

TAKE IT FURTHER, *continued*

CCC Systems and System Models

Tell students that they are going to do independent research on four different pollinators and make a booklet illustrating the pollinator, including information about the types of plants each pollinator pollinates and its importance to the reproduction of those plants.

Consider assigning certain animals to encourage variety for interest.

Have students take notes as they research each pollinator. After their research, ask them to highlight and write the most important information in their booklets.

Ask: How do pollen and pollinators form a system? **Pollen relies on pollinators to aid in reproduction.**

SEP Engaging in Argument from Evidence

Have students draw information from their chart to summarize similarities and differences among the different pollinators.

Have students decide which pollinator they consider most important and back it up with evidence. For example, they may say a bee because it pollinates 70% of flowering plants. Have a friendly debate.

 Explore Online

Students can explore these additional topics online.

Wait, There's More!
Students explore how new plants can be produced from runners, gratings, and cuttings not seeds. *(No outside research required.)*

It's What's on the Inside
In this activity, students will learn more about what the inside of a seed looks like. *(Outside research required.)*

272   Unit 4 Plant Structure and Function

Pollinator Project

20. In this activity, you will research three or four pollinators. Make a booklet of your findings. Include a drawing or photo of the pollinator, the type of plants it pollinates, and its importance to the reproduction of plants. Then, compare them below. Submit your booklet to your teacher.

Comparing and Contrasting

Similarities	Differences
Possible answer: All of our pollinators fly.	Possible answer: Some of our pollinators, such as bees, fly. Others, such as deer, pollinate by eating and digesting.

21. Which pollinators were similar? What did they have in common?

Possible answer: The insects, such as bees and flies, pollinate by moving from plant to plant.

22. Compare and contrast your findings with your classmates. What similarities and differences did you observe?

Possible answer: We all found bees that pollinate by flying from flower to flower. Some found animals, like birds, that digest seeds. Others found animals, like raccoons, that spread seeds that attach to their fur.

272

LESSON CHECK

LESSON 2
Lesson Check

Name _____

Can You Explain It?

1. Look back at the images from the beginning of the lesson. Think about what you have learned about plant reproduction.
   - Explain how plants develop from seeds to a fully grown plant.
   - Explain the difference between flowering and nonflowering plants.
   - Describe how plants reproduce from seeds.
   - Identify other ways plants can be made without using seeds.

EVIDENCE NOTEBOOK Use the information you've collected in your Evidence Notebook to help you cover each point above.

Possible answer:
- Plants have life cycles, and they have individual parts that form a plant system.
- Flowering plants use pollination through flowers to reproduce, and nonflowering plants use structures such as cones and spores to reproduce.
- Plants reproduce from seeds when a female part is fertilized by a male part and the plant structure starts to grow.
- Some plants produce spores.

Checkpoints

2. Plant parts work together as a system for reproduction. Number the steps of the system in the correct order.
   - __4__ The seed develops and drops to the ground.
   - __3__ The egg is fertilized.
   - __5__ A new tree can begin to grow.
   - __2__ It lands on the female cone.
   - __1__ Pollen is released by the male cone.

Formal Assessment Go online for student self-checks and other assessments.

Can You Explain It?

> ### Collaboration
> **Discussion** You may wish to revisit the scenario of the flower becoming a fruit as a group activity to assess students' understanding of the material. Use the bulleted points in the student edition to lead the discussion.

EVIDENCE NOTEBOOK

Have students reread their answers to the Evidence Notebook prompts, and then use this evidence to justify their reasoning as they respond to the Can You Explain It question. Make sure that students understand that a complete response must address all bulleted points.

DCI LS1.A Structure and Function

Discuss each bullet point. Explain how plants develop from seeds to a fully grown plant: They have life cycles with parts that form a system. If students have a hard time addressing each bulleted item, suggest they revisit the Explorations in the lesson if needed.

SUMMATIVE ASSESSMENT
Engage in Argument from Evidence

2. Remind students that plants have parts (structures) that have different functions and work together as a reproductive system. The system has steps that happen in a particular order. Review those steps with students. (Pollen is released by the male cone, lands on the female cone, the egg is fertilized, the seed develops and drops to the ground, and a new tree can begin to grow.)

LESSON 2 Engage • Explore/Explain • Elaborate • **Evaluate**

LESSON CHECK, continued

3. This exercise prompts students to remember information from Explorations 2 about the various structures and functions of plants. Ask students to think about the types of images they viewed in the lesson and how those plant types reproduced.

4. Help student eliminate distractors by reviewing plant parts and categorizing them as reproductive or non-reproductive.

5. Have students read and think about the various evidence presented and review information in Explorations 1 and 2 to best summarize a proper claim. If students need help, have them think about what they all have in common.

6. Tell students that this exercise summarizes various ways seeds are dispersed from plants. Review information from Exploration 3 to refresh students' memories about the various methods of dispersal.

Choose the correct answer.

3. How does the plant in the picture reproduce?
   a. by producing flowers
   b. by producing cones
   c. by producing spores

4. Which plant structures are used in reproduction? Circle all that apply.
   a. leaves
   b. spores
   c. flowers
   d. wind
   e. cones

5. Read the evidence below, and then choose the best claim.
   • Wind blows pollen.
   • Flys can pollinate plants.
   • Some plants use cones to reproduce.
   • Spores contain egg and sperm cells.

   a. Pollinators are the best way to pollinate plants.
   b. There are many ways for plants to reproduce.
   c. Water is the quickest way for seeds to move.
   d. Spores use wind to reproduce.

6. Write the correct words to complete the sentences.

an animal	wind	water	burst from
stay inside	flowers	fruits	

   If a plant produces seeds that are sticky or bristled, __an animal__ most likely moves the seeds from one place to another. Some plants have seeds that __burst from__ a seedpod as a way of seed dispersal. A dandelion produces light, fluffy seeds that are carried by __wind__. Birds, bats, and monkeys are examples of animals that eat the __fruits__ of plants and disperse seeds in their droppings.

   274

LESSON 2

Lesson Roundup

A. Match each flower part to its description by filling in the blank.

stamen	anther	pollen
pistil	ovary	ovule

a. __stamen__ the part of a flower that contains the anther

b. __anther__ part of the flower where pollen is produced

c. __pollen__ When this comes into contact with the ovule, a seed is produced.

d. __pistil__ the part of the flower that contains the ovary

e. __ovary__ contains the ovule

f. __ovule__ If pollen reaches this structure, a seed is produced.

B. Study the illustrations below. Match each plant to the description of how it reproduces.

a

b

a. This plant produces spores that, if they land in the right place, grow into a heart-shape structure. This structure grows and releases sperm cells and egg cells.

b. This plant produces cones. In the spring, pollen is released from the male cone. If pollen from a male cone lands on a female cone of the same type of tree, the egg will be fertilized.

C. Choose the correct answer.
A plant produces berries that have seeds inside them. What is the most likely way that the seeds are moved from one place to another?

a. wind　　b. water　　**c. animals**

A plant produces fruit or seeds that float. Which is the most likely way its seeds are moved from one place to another?

a. wind　　**b. water**　　c. animals

Lesson Roundup

DCI LS1.A Structure and Function

This lesson summary enables students to quickly revisit key points in the lesson and prepare for tests.

A. Students may wish to revisit Exploration 1 and study the labeled illustration before answering this question. Make sure that they know and understand the different parts or structures of a plant and their roles, or functions. **LS1.A**

B. Clarify students' understanding of how some plants do not produce flowers to reproduce. Have them review the timelines of how a pine/fir tree reproduces and how a fern reproduces. Review the steps in each timeline to understand the steps in the reproductive system of both non-flowering plants. **LS1.A**

C. Have students revisit Exploration 3 to recall important information about seed dispersal by animals, people, wind, and water. Emphasize the advantage that parent plant has—in terms of being successful at reproduction—if its seeds can scattered far and wide: Better odds that some seeds will find the appropriate conditions in which to grow, and less competition for sun, water, and nutrients with the parent plants or others. **LS1.A**

Lesson 2 How Do Plants Grow and Reproduce?

UNIT 4 Performance Task

pairs · **2 class periods**

Flower Parts

3D Assessment Goal
Students **analyze flowers** to learn about the structures and parts of flowers. They will study how the **flower's parts function together as a whole** to demonstrate understanding of **LS1.A** in support of **4-LS1-1**.

Materials
- scissors or plastic knife
- flowers
- paper
- writing/drawing utensils (i.e., colored pencils or markers)
- hand lens

Preparation
Review safety protocols with students, as they will be using scissors or plastic knives to dissect their flowers.

CCC Systems and System Models
The various parts of a flower work together as part of a larger system.

Ask: How do the parts of the flower work together to allow the flower to reproduce?

Make a Plan

SEP Analyzing and Interpreting Data
Remind students that dissecting organisms, such as flowers, is something that scientists do to learn more about a species. Dissection involves collecting data obtained from the specimen, which can be used to analyze and interpret. **Ask:** Once you start dissecting the flower, what do you predict you will be able to learn about the flower?

UNIT 4 — UNIT PERFORMANCE TASK

Flower Parts

You work for a nursery that is putting together a botanist's handbook. Your team is tasked with creating an educational illustration of a specific flower. To do that, you'll need to dissect the flower and identify its individual parts. Then you'll need to draw those parts separately and write a caption for each that names it and explains its function.

A flower has many parts, and each has a function of its own.

DEFINE YOUR TASK: What will your completed assignment look like?

Sample answer: It will be a set of illustrations of flower parts. Each part will be labeled and have some text that explains its function.

Before beginning, review the checklist at the end of this Unit Performance Task. Keep those items in mind as you proceed.

RESEARCH: For this project, your teacher will play the role of your company's Project Coordinator, assigning your team its flower. Your team will be the only one in class with your specific flower. Use online or library resources to identify your flower and learn its parts. Cite your sources.

Student should name the flower and the parts that will be investigated. Student should also cite sources.

MAKE A PLAN: Consider the questions below as you plan your procedure for dissecting your flower and examining, illustrating, and describing its parts.

1. What tools and equipment will we need to dissect our flower?

   Scissors or a plastic knife.

2. What parts will we look for as we dissect our flower?

   leaves, petals, stem, sepal, pistils, anthers, seeds

3. What materials will we need to make our illustrations?
A hand lens, paper; colored pencils or markers

4. How large should we make our illustrations and how thoroughly should we describe the parts of our flower?
We should make our illustrations larger than many of the actual flower parts to show their tiny details.

These students are looking closely at the different parts of a flower.

5. How should we arrange our illustrations? Should we include one illustration of the complete flower?
Answers will vary. Students should support their decisions with reasoning.

DISSECT AND ILLUSTRATE: Dissect your flower. Draw, label, and describe each part of your illustrations as described in your plan.

COMMUNICATE: Give a short presentation to your class about your team's flower, what you learned from dissecting it, and what your team's illustrations teach the viewer. If there is time, the entire class can discuss similarities and differences among their different assigned flowers.

✓ Checklist

Review your project and check off each completed item.

____ All questions on the page are answered.

____ Includes an educational illustration of the parts of your team's flower.

____ Includes a demonstration and oral report about your team's procedures and illustration.

Dissect and Illustrate

Students may need to be reminded to dissect and study one part of the flower at a time. It is not a good idea for students to start cutting into the flower haphazardly or too quickly, as they may miss important information. Consider having student partners critique each other's dissections. Use sentence frames to guide their discussions:

- This part of the flower is interesting because _____.
- How will the _____ interact with the _____?
- What does the _____ do?
- Why is _____ this particular color?

CCC Cause and Effect

As students dissect the flowers, have them think about cause-and-effect relationships. **Ask: If a flower had no leaves, what could happen? What might happen if a flower's stem broke?**

Scoring Rubric for Performance Task	
3	• several resources, clear reasoning • complete, detailed, accurate educational illustration of the parts of the flower • demonstration and oral report engaging, accurate, supported by procedures and illustration
2	• a couple of resources, adequate reasoning • most parts present in the parts of the flower • demonstration and oral report mostly accurate, has an illustration and procedures
1	• one resource, simple reasoning • some description, mixed accuracy of educational illustration • demonstration and oral report inaccurate
0	• no resources, no reasoning • little description, inaccurate details of parts of the flower • demonstration and oral report incomplete

UNIT 4 Review

SUMMATIVE ASSESSMENT

1. Students can correctly answer this question by thinking about the vocabulary terms and their dissection of the plant. For a quick review, students can turn back to Lesson 1, Exploration 1.

2. To answer this question correctly, students need to know what all of the structures do. Then they need to determine which ones share a function. Students can recall the functions of seeds and spores by reviewing Lesson 1, Exploration 1.

3. Students need to study the image on the page, paying attention to the direction of the arrows. The arrows will help them understand what the question stem is hinting at. For a quick review, encourage them to turn to Lesson 1, Exploration 2.

UNIT 4

Unit Review

1. Describe the function of a leaf in detail?

   A leaf's function is to provide food for the plant by using sunlight.

2. Which two structures serve an identical function in plants? Circle both.
   a. roots
   b. stems
   c. seeds
   d. spores
   e. spines

3. Explain in detail how the food and water tubes work with other plant parts such as roots, stems, and leaves to provide a system.

   Water is taken in through the roots. The water tube carries that water up the stem to the other parts of the plant. The leaves use sunlight to make food, and the food tubes carry that food down the stem to different parts of the plant.

278

Unit 4 Plant Structure and Function

4. Place each term under the word that describes what it does. Some boxes have more than one word.

   roots   spore   bark   leaf   thorn

Growth	Protection	Reproduction
leaf; roots	bark; thorn	spore

5. Complete the sentences using the words in the word bank.

   bark   roots   spines   leaves   thorns

   Some trees and shrubs have thick __bark__ to protect them from animals. __thorns/spines__, along with __thorns/spines__, protect other plants by injuring animals that eat them.

6. Which of the following must combine for a seed to form? Circle all that apply.
   a. bark
   b. roots
   c. pollen
   d. ovule
   e. thorns

7. The pine tree is an example of a plant that reproduces using _____ instead of flowers.
   a. flowers
   b. cones
   c. spores
   d. ferns

---

4. Students are asked to recall the functions of several plant parts to categorize them according to what they do. Students should review Lessons 1 and 2 for a comprehensive refresher on the various structures of plants.

5. Students are asked to fill in the blanks using the words from the word bank. Have students do a comprehensive review of Lessons 1 and 2, as well as pay close attention to the sentences to arrive at the correct answers.

6. Students recall facts about plant reproduction, and they can turn back to Lesson 2, Exploration 3, for information to help them answer this question.

7. Students can refer back to Lesson 2, Exploration 2, to recall information about pine cones and plant reproduction.

UNIT 4 Review, continued

8. Students are asked to place the process in correct order from beginning to last. They can refer to Lesson 2, Exploration 1 for a brief refresher.

9. Plant movement and behaviors are covered in Lesson 1, Exploration 3. Students can also call upon personal experience to answer this question.

10. Spores and concepts of male and female plants are covered in Lesson 2, Exploration 2.

3D Item Analysis	1	2	3	4	5	6	7	8	9	10
SEP Engaging in Argument from Evidence	•		•							
DCI Structures and Function	•	•	•	•	•	•	•	•	•	•
CCC Systems and System Models		•			•		•			

8. Using the numbers 1–5, place the steps that led to the development of the fruit shown here.

   __2__ Flowers appeared.
   __5__ The oranges appeared.
   __1__ Buds appeared on the tree.
   __4__ Some of the flowers began to swell.
   __3__ Insects and birds began to visit the tree.

9. What are some behavior responses plants have? Circle all that apply.
   a. respond to light
   b. respond to touch
   c. respond to smells
   d. respond to gravity

10. Complete the sentences using the words in the word bank.

   | spores | flowers | male and female | animal |

   Ferns produce ____spores____ instead of seeds. All plants reproduce using ____male and female____ cells.

280

Unit 4 Plant Structure and Function

UNIT 5 Animal Structure and Function

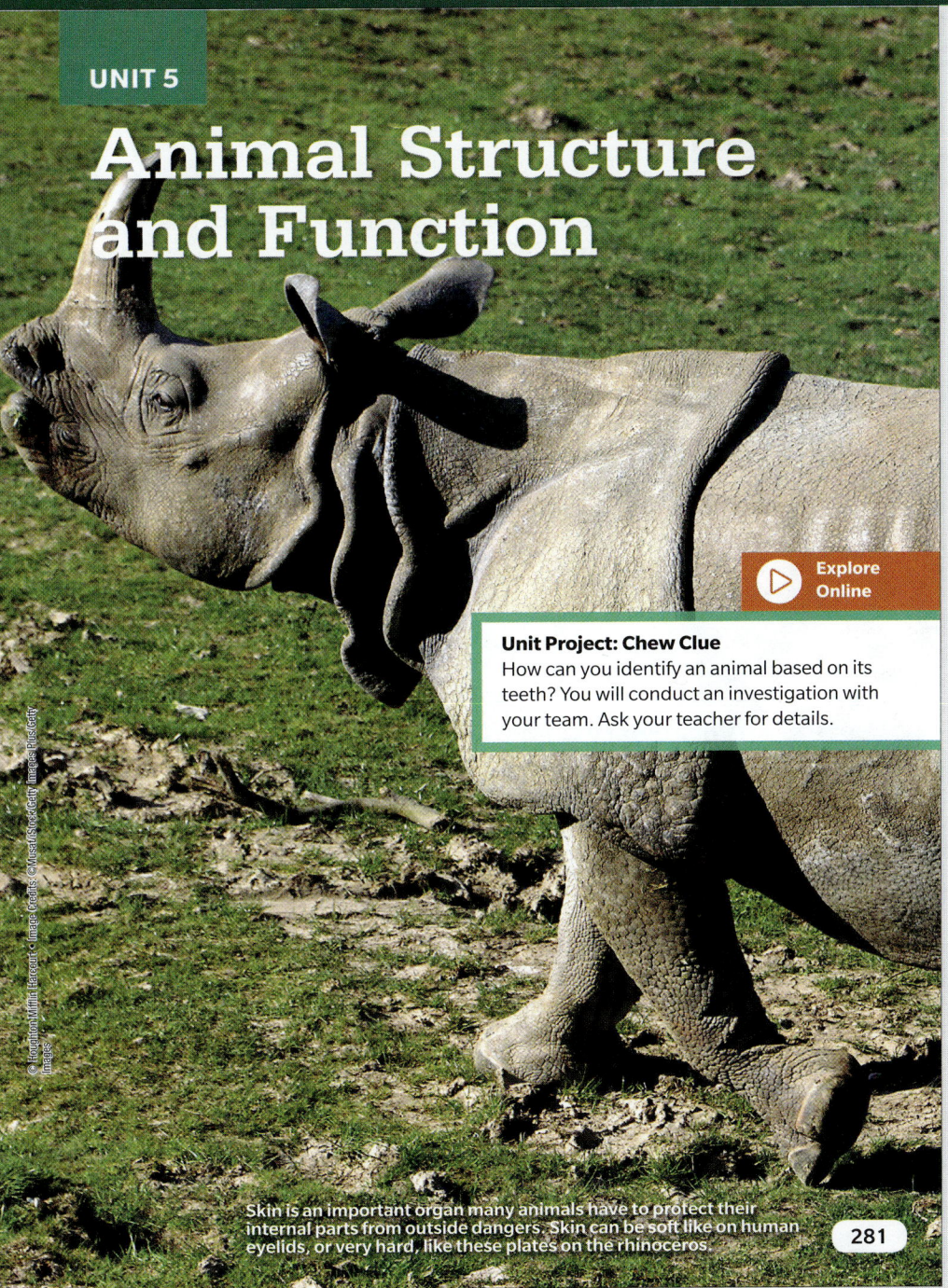

Unit Project: Chew Clue
How can you identify an animal based on its teeth? You will conduct an investigation with your team. Ask your teacher for details.

Explore Online

Skin is an important organ many animals have to protect their internal parts from outside dangers. Skin can be soft like on human eyelids, or very hard, like these plates on the rhinoceros.

Unit Overview
In this unit, children will . . .
- explore the internal and external structures of animals.
- learn about how different senses work.

About This Image
All animals have unique external features. Rhinos, for instance, have tough and wrinkly skin with large horns and flat, wide feet. Each of the rhinoceros's external parts plays an important role in sustaining life for the rhino. Its skin, for example, can help protect it against predators and harsh conditions. Its horn can be used in self defense against other animals. Although the rhinoceros may look tough on the outside, one thing that many people find surprising is that the rhinoceros is a vegetarian. That means rhinos only eat plants, and do not eat other animals.

Unit Project
As students work through the unit lessons, have them think about ways to identify an animal based on its teeth or its mouth. This type of observation will come in handy for the Unit Project.

To begin, draw students' attention to the picture of the rhinoceros, or challenge the class to use online or media center resources to find other types of animals to study for this project. More support for the Unit Project can be found on pp. 283I–283L.

UNIT 5 Animal Structure and Function

The learning experiences in this unit prepare children for the mastery of:

Performance Expectations

4-LS1-1 Construct an argument that plants and animals have internal and external structures that function to support survival, growth, behavior, and reproduction.

4-LS1-2 Use a model to describe that animals receive different types of information through their senses, process the information in their brain, and respond to the information in different ways.

> **Explore Online**

In addition to the print resources, the following resources are available online to support this unit.

Unit Pretest

Lesson 1 What Are Some External Structures of Animals?
- Online Student Edition
- Lesson Quiz

Lesson 2 What Are Some Internal Structures of Animals?
- Online Student Edition
- Lesson Quiz

Lesson 3 How Do Senses Work?
- Online Student Edition
- Lesson Quiz

You Solve It Break It Down!

Unit Performance Task

Unit Test

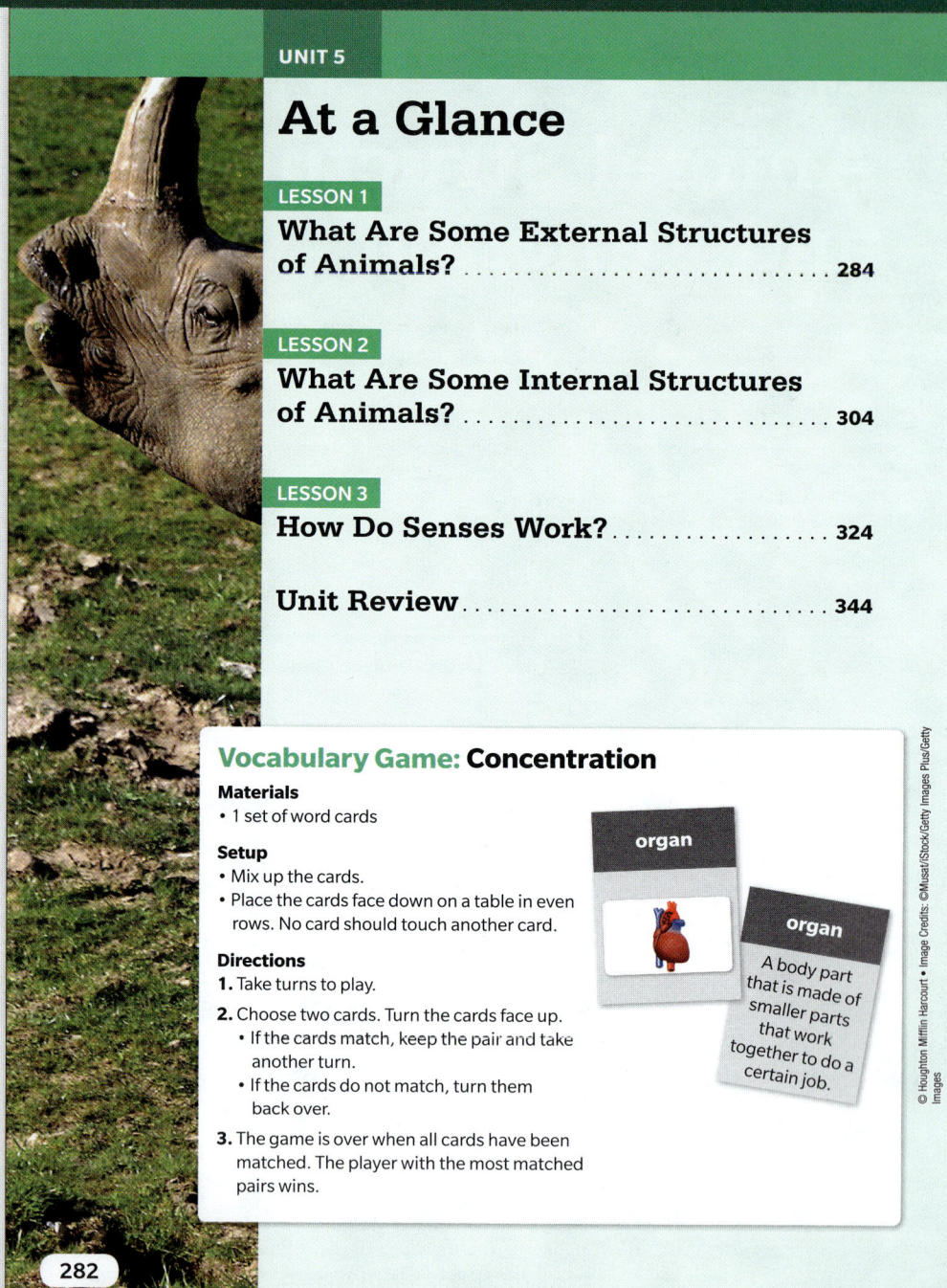

UNIT 5

At a Glance

LESSON 1
What Are Some External Structures of Animals? 284

LESSON 2
What Are Some Internal Structures of Animals? 304

LESSON 3
How Do Senses Work? 324

Unit Review 344

Vocabulary Game: Concentration

Materials
- 1 set of word cards

Setup
- Mix up the cards.
- Place the cards face down on a table in even rows. No card should touch another card.

Directions
1. Take turns to play.
2. Choose two cards. Turn the cards face up.
   - If the cards match, keep the pair and take another turn.
   - If the cards do not match, turn them back over.
3. The game is over when all cards have been matched. The player with the most matched pairs wins.

282 Unit 5 Animal Structure and Function

Unit Vocabulary

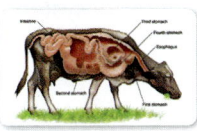
external structures: Those parts on the outside of a body or structure.

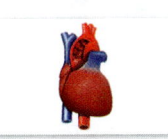
internal structures: Those parts on the inside of a body or structure.

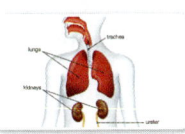
organ: A body part that is made of smaller parts that work together to do a certain job.

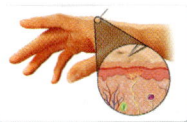
organ system: A group of organs that work together to do a job for the body.

receptors: Special structures that send information about the environment from different parts of the body to the brain.

Unit Vocabulary

Students can explore all lesson vocabulary terms in the **Online Glossary**.

Vocabulary Strategies

Have students review the terms individually. Then pair up and share an example of one term with their partner and tell why they think it's an example. Have each pair write down their examples to check during the unit.

Differentiate Instruction

RTI/Extra Support Have struggling readers find the vocabulary words within the unit. Have students use context clues to infer definitions and then share with a partner.

Extension Have students pick two terms and then work in small groups to illustrate and explain the terms for a third-grade student.

ELL Pronounce each term and have students repeat it. Then pair up students by native language and have them explain each term in their native language. Use realia wherever appropriate.

Vocabulary Game: Concentration

Preparation
Have the cards prepared and shuffled so that the pairs are not placed near each other.

Game Play
- The game is over when all cards have been matched. The player with the most matched pairs wins.

UNIT 5 Structure and Function in Animals
Integrating the NGSS* Three Dimensions of Learning

Building to the Performance Expectations

The learning experiences in this unit prepare students for mastery of the following Performance Expectations:

From Molecules to Organisms: Structures and Processes

4-LS1-1 Construct an argument that plants and animals have internal and external structures that function to support survival, growth, behavior, and reproduction.

4-LS1-2 Use a model to describe that animals receive different types of information through their senses, process the information in their brain, and respond to the information in different ways.

Waves and Their Applications in Technologies for Information Transfer

4-PS4-2 Develop a model to describe that light reflecting from objects and entering the eye allows objects to be seen.

Assessing Student Progress

After completing these lessons, the **Unit Project: Chew Clue** provides students with opportunities to practice aspects of and demonstrate their understanding of the Performance Expectation as they analyze teeth to identify the animal they belong to.

Additionally, students can practice or be assessed on aspects of the Performance Expectations by completing the **Unit Performance Task: Breathing In and Out**, in which they apply concepts of body systems to develop models of portable inventions.

Lesson 1
What Are Some External Structures of Animals?

In Lesson 1, students will learn and understand that plants have external and internal structures **(DCI Structure and Function)**. They will use evidence from the lesson to engage in arguments **(SEP Engaging in Argument from Evidence)**, and they will be able to describe the components of systems and their interactions **(CCC Systems and System Models)**.

Lesson 2
What Are Some Internal Structures of Animals?

In Lesson 2, students will gather evidence to support an argument **(SEP Engaging in Argument from Evidence)** regarding the importance of the internal structures of animals in growth, survival, behavior, and reproduction **(CCC Cause and Effect)**. They explore the components and functions of several body systems of animals **(CCC Systems and Systems Models)**. They also compare and contrast the systems to identify similarities and differences of the body systems in different groups of animals **(DCI Structure and Function)**.

Lesson 3
How Do Senses Work?

In Lesson 3, students will explore the ways in which people and animals use their senses. They will learn about the physical parts and unique structures **(LS1.A Structure and Function)** that make it possible for people and animals to analyze information through senses **(LS1.D Information Processing) (SEP Developing and Using Models)**, through which sensory information can be processed in the brain **(CCC Cause and Effect)**. Students will interpret sensory systems **(CCC Systems and System Models)** and apply what they learn to construct intelligent explanations using evidence and data **(SEP Engaging in Argument from Evidence)**.

*Next Generation Science Standards and logo are registered trademarks of Achieve. Neither Achieve or the lead states and partners that developed the Next Generation Science Standards were involved in production of, and does not endorse, these products.

NGSS Across the Unit

Explore Online!
Online only.

Next Generation Science Standards	Unit Project	Lesson 1	Lesson 2	Lesson 3	Unit Performance Task	You Solve It!
SEP Engaging in Argument from Evidence	•	•	•	•		•
SEP Developing and Using Models	•			•	•	
DCI LS1.A Structure and Function	•	•	•	•	•	•
DCI LS1.D Information Processing				•		
DCI PS4.B Electromagnetic Radiation				•		
CCC Systems and System Models	•	•	•	•	•	•

NGSS Across the Grades

Before
Waves and Their Applications in Technologies for Information Transfer
1-PS4-2

From Molecules to Organisms: Structures and Processes
1-LS1-1
1-LS1-2

Grade 4
From Molecules to Organisms: Structures and Processes
4-LS1-1
4-LS1-2

Waves and Their Applications in Technologies for Information Transfer
4-PS4-2

After
From Molecules to Organisms: Structures and Processes
5-LS1-1 Support an argument that plants get the materials they need for growth chiefly from air and water.

MS-LS1-3 Use argument supported by evidence for how the body is a system of interacting subsystems composed of groups of cells.

Waves and Their Applications in Technologies for Information Transfer
MS-PS4-2 Develop and use a model to describe that waves are reflected, absorbed, or transmitted through various materials.

Trace Tool to the NGSS™ Go online to view the complete coverage of these standards across this grade level and time.

Unit 5 Structure and Function in Animals 283B

UNIT 5 Structure and Function in Animals
3D Unit Planning

Lesson 1 What Are Some External Structures of Animals? pp. 284–303

Overview

Objective To identify the external parts animals have and how their parts are used for growth, survival, behavior, and reproduction.

SEP Engaging in Argument from Evidence
DCI **LS1.A** Structure and Function
CCC Systems and System Models
Math and **English Language Arts** standards and features are detailed on lesson planner pages.

	Print and Online Student Editions	▶ Explore Online!
ENGAGE	**Lesson Phenomenon** pp. 284–285 Can You Explain/Solve It? Why do you think the two lizards have different kinds of feet?	▶ Can You Explain It? Video
EXPLORE/ EXPLAIN	**Body Building** pp. 286–291 It's All In the Skin Apply What You Know Design to Survive **Inspired by Nature** pp. 292–298 Inspirations From Nature ENGINEER IT! Biomimicry Apply What You Know Find the Inspiration HANDS-ON Staying Warm	HANDS-ON Worksheet
ELABORATE	**Take It Further** pp. 299–300 Careers in Science & Engineering Careers in Engineering: Mimicking Animal Movement	**Take It Further** Balanced Parts **Take It Further** A Feat of Feet
EVALUATE	**Lesson Check** pp. 301–302 **Lesson Roundup** p. 303	Lesson Quiz

✋ HANDS-ON ACTIVITY PLANNING

Apply What You Know

Design to Survive ⏱ 20 minutes 👥 Pairs	**Materials** • poster board material • markers

Preparation/Tip Have students draw the animal in its natural environment.

Find the Inspiration ⏱ 1 class period 👥 Individuals	**Materials** • drawing paper • sketching utensils • pipe cleaner • glue & masking tape • plastic straws • cardboard & scissors • cotton balls • felt, fabric

Preparation/Tip Suggest that students keep their designs simple and limited to the materials that are available.

HANDS-ON

Staying Warm ⏱ 1 class period 👥 Small groups	**Materials** • vegetable shortening • spatula & duct tape • disposable gloves • resealable baggies • thermometer & timer • buckets or dish pans • water

Objective Students will discover how an animal's covering affects its survival by building and using a model.

Preparation/Tip Offer students an apron or smock in case they do not want to get wet using the water.

Lesson 2 What are Some Internal Structures of Animals? pp. 304–323

Overview

Objective To observe and describe some of the internal structures of animals, compare similar body parts that have similar and different uses from species to species or multiple uses within a species, and recognize that some animals have modified systems or don't have them at all.

SEP Engaging in Argument rom Evidence
DCI **LS1.A** Structure and Function
CCC Systems and System Models

Math and **English Language Arts** standards and features are detailed on lesson planner pages.

	Print and Online Student Editions	Explore Online!
ENGAGE	**Lesson Phenomenon** pp. 304–305 **Can You Explain/Solve It?** How does the body work differently when you sprint versus when you jog?	Can You Explain It? Video
EXPLORE/ EXPLAIN	**Pumping Parts** pp. 306–313 Take a Deep Breath **HANDS-ON** Pump It Up! **Food For Thought** pp. 314–318 It's Delicious! 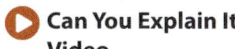 **Apply What You Know** All Systems Go	**HANDS-ON Worksheet**
ELABORATE	**Take It Further** pp. 319–320 People in Science: All About Anatomy	**Take It Further** Model Lungs **Take It Further** Support Your Statements
EVALUATE	**Lesson Check** pp. 321–322 **Lesson Roundup** p. 323	Lesson Quiz

HANDS-ON ACTIVITY PLANNING

Apply What You Know

All Systems Go

- 20 minutes
- Individuals

Materials
- poster board
- colored markers
- ruler or meterstick

Preparation/Tip Model how to create a chart for students.

HANDS-ON

Pump It Up

- 1 class period
- Small groups

Materials
- stopwatch or timer
- graph paper
- colored pencils

Objective Students will investigate to gather evidence about the relationship between exercise, heart rate, and breathing rate.

Preparation/Tip Make sure students perform the exercises safely and carefully.

Unit 5 Structure and Function in Animals 283D

UNIT 5 Structure and Function in Animals
3D Unit Planning, continued

Lesson 3 How Do Senses Work? pp. 324–343

Overview

Objective To construct an argument that animals receive different types of information through their senses, process the information in their brain, and respond to the information in different ways.

SEP Engaging in Argument from Evidence
SEP Developing and Using Models
DCI LS1.D Information Processing
DCI PS4.B Electromagnetic Radiation
CCC Systems and System Models
CCC Cause and Effect

Math and **English Language Arts** standards and features are detailed on lesson planner pages.

	Print and **Online** *Student Editions*	**Explore Online!**
ENGAGE	**Lesson Phenomenon** pp. 324–325 Can You Explain/Solve It? How can animals "see" without eyesight?	Can You Explain It? Video
EXPLORE/ EXPLAIN	**Touchy, Feely** pp. 326–332 Body Senses **HANDS-ON** Touch Test	**HANDS-ON Worksheet**
	Is That Something I Want to Eat? pp. 333–335 How the Nose Knows **Apply What You Know** Name That Scent! **Apply What You Know** No See, No Smell, No Taste?	
	Sights and Sounds pp. 336–338 Eye See! **Apply What You Know** Test It!	
ELABORATE	**Take It Further** pp. 339–340 Extreme Senses	**Take It Further** Eye Check **Take It Further** What Colors Do You See?
EVALUATE	**Lesson Check** pp. 341–342 **Lesson Roundup** p. 343	**Lesson Quiz**

HANDS-ON ACTIVITY PLANNING

Apply What You Know

Name That Scent! ⏱ 15 minutes 👥 Pairs	**Materials** • blindfold • assortment of items to smell • paper and pencil

Preparation/Tip Once the students are blindfolded, pass out the items that they will smell.

No See, No Smell, No Taste? ⏱ 15 minutes 👥 Pairs	**Materials** • blindfold • assortment of foods • paper and pencil

Preparation/Tip Make sure students do not have any allergies to the foods they will be tasting.

Test It ⏱ 10 minutes 👥 Pairs	**Material** • blindfold

Preparation/Tip Make sure students have enough space to participate in this activity.

HANDS-ON

Touch Test ⏱ 30 minutes 👥 Pairs **Objective** Students will develop a way to test the sense of touch by modeling how receptors in the body work.	**Material** • 2 paper clips, bent into a V-shape • metric ruler • pencil or pen

Preparation/Tip Model for students how to shape the paper clips into the V-shape properly.

UNIT 5 Animal Structure and Function

 **You Solve It** Go online for an additional interactive activity.

Break It Down

This virtual lab offers practice in support of **PE 4-LS1-1**.

SEP Engaging in Argument from Evidence
DCI **4-LS1.A** Structure and Function
CCC Systems and System Models

Use after Unit 5, Lesson 3—Can all animals digest and get nutrients and energy from the same foods? Do they all have the same structures to break down the food?

Objectives
1. Students identify the different structures animals have based on the foods they consume.
2. Students will compare and contrast two different animal digestive systems.

Activity Problem
You will identify foods that animals can digest with certain body structures. Your tasks will include:
1. identifying structures of animal digestive systems
2. choosing foods for animals that match their digestive body parts
3. observing and recording which foods match best with certain body parts

Interaction Summary
1. Students will select an animal out of the provided group.
2. They will choose a food that the chosen animal eats.
3. Students watch the simulation of the food going through the digestive system of the animal by clicking on different parts of the digestive system.
4. Notes and observations are recorded to conclude the best food suited for certain digestive systems.

Assessment

Pre-Assessment
Assessment Guide, Unit Pretest

The Unit Pretest focuses on prerequisite knowledge and is composed of items that evaluate students' preparedness for the content covered within this unit.

Formative Assessment
Student Edition, Apply What You Know, Lesson Check, and Self Check

Summative Assessment
Assessment Guide, Lesson Quiz
The Lesson Quiz provides a quick assessment of each lesson objective and of the portion of the Performance Expectation aligned to the lesson.

Student Edition, Performance Task pp. 344–345
The Performance Task presents the opportunity for students to collaborate with classmates in order to complete the steps of each Performance Task. Each Performance Task provides a formal Scoring Rubric for evaluating students' work.

Student Edition, Unit 5 Review pp. 346–348

Assessment Guide, Unit Test
The Unit Test provides an in-depth assessment of the Performance Expectations aligned to the unit. This test evaluates students' ability to apply knowledge in order to explain phenomena and to solve problems. Within this test, Constructed Response items apply a three-dimensional rubric for evaluating students' mastery on all three dimensions of the Next Generation Science Standards.

 **Assessment Online** Go online to view the complete assessment items for this unit.

UNIT 5 Animal Structure and Function
Differentiate Instruction

Leveled Readers

The **Science & Engineering Leveled Readers** provide additional nonfiction reading practice in this unit's subject area.

On-Level Reader • How Do Plants and Animals Reproduce and Adapt?
This reader reinforces unit concepts and includes response activities for your students.

Extra Support • How Do Plants and Animals Reproduce and Adapt?
This reader shares title, illustrations, vocabulary, and concepts with the On-Level Reader; however, the text is linguistically accommodated to provide simplified sentence structures and comprehension aids. It also includes response activities.

Enrichment • Exploring the Galapagos Islands
This high-interest nonfiction reader will extend and enrich unit concepts and vocabulary and includes response activities.

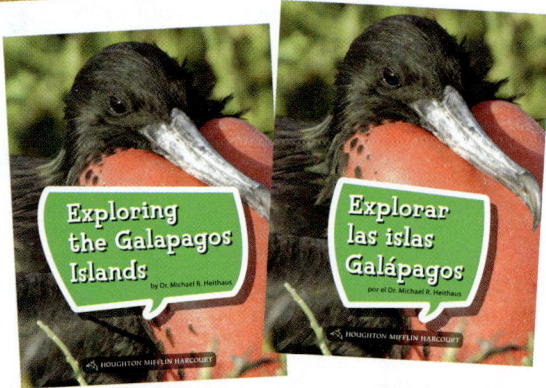

Teacher Guide

The accompanying Teacher Guide provides teaching strategies and support for using all the readers.

ELL

ELL teacher strategies in this unit:

Lesson 1: pp. 287, 289
Lesson 2: pp. 308, 317
Lesson 3: pp. 328, 331

RTI/Extra Support

Strategies for students needing extra support in this unit:

Lesson 1: pp. 286, 292, 294, 297
Lesson 2: p. 316
Lesson 3: pp. 326, 334, 336

Extension

Strategies for students who have mastered core content in this unit:

Lesson 1: pp. 288, 293, 299
Lesson 2: p. 315
Lesson 3: p. 338

 **Leveled Readers** All readers are available online as well as in an innovative, engaging format for use with touchscreen mobile devices. Contact your HMH Sales Representative for more information.

UNIT 5 Animal Structure and Function
Making Connections

Connections to the Community

Use these opportunities for informal science learning to provide local context and to extend and enhance unit concepts.

At Home

SEEING STRUCTURES Have students compare the external structures of two animals living in or near their home. The animals should be as different as possible, such as a mammal and a bird, fish, or insect. Students should write down how each animal's external structure may help it live. *Use with Lesson 1.*

DINNER TIME Tell students to take careful notes of their different senses one day before and during dinner time. They should write down what they are doing before dinner, noting what they experience through touch, taste, smell, hearing, and sight. Then they will describe their senses as they see and hear that dinner is ready, walk toward it, and smell, taste, and swallow it. Have students write down how they think this experience would be different without each of their senses. *Use with Lesson 3.*

In the Community

LOCAL WILDLIFE Tell students to think about the natural environment in the area where they live, such as temperature range, rain and snowfall, wind, bodies of water, and plant life. How does this connect to the external structures of animals that live in the area? *Use with Lesson 1.*

SUDDEN SPEED Have students watch a football game (or another sport suitable for this activity). An offensive player stands still until the ball is snapped. Suddenly that player bursts forward at full speed, racing to get in position to catch the ball. Have students describe changes in the motionless player's internal organ systems when he suddenly dashes forward to complete the pass and run for a touchdown *Use with Lesson 2.*

Home Letters Use these one-page letters to engage family members with unit concepts.

Collaboration

Opportunities for students to work collaboratively in this unit:

Build on Prior Knowledge
pp. 285, 305, 325

Pathways
p. 339

Discussion
pp. 301, 321, 341

Share Feedback
p. 293

Draw, Pair, Share
pp. 307, 315, 328

Think, Pair, Share
pp. 290, 306, 318, 335

Feedback
pp. 287, 300, 337

Write, Pair, Share
p. 288

Jigsaw
p. 309

Connections to Science

Opportunities to connect to other content areas in this unit.

Connection to Physical Science
Lesson 2, p. 315

Connection to Life Science
Lesson 3, p. 327

Connection to Earth and Space Sciences
Lesson 1, p. 286

UNIT 5 Animal Structure and Function
Unit Project

Unit Project: Chew Clue 👥 Small groups ⏱ 1 class period

For this task, groups of students of mixed ability will work together to identify various animals according to their teeth. Make sure students have pictures to use for this project to help them narrow down their choices.

3D Learning Objective

- Explore types of animals
- Analyze animal teeth
- Examine features of animal teeth

Skills and Standards Focus

This project supports building student mastery of **Performance Expectation 4-LS1-1**.

- **SEP** Developing and Using Models
- **SEP** Constructing Explanations and Designing Solutions
- **DCI** **LS1.A** Structures and Function
- **CCC** Cause and Effect

Suggested Materials

- Photos or molds of animal teeth
- Photos of animals
- Writing and drawing materials and utensils

Preparation and Planning Tips

Ensure that each group has a set of pictures to use for matching animal teeth to the correct animal. You might want to prepare this project by selecting different teeth and different animals for each small group, so that no two groups have the same teeth and animal samples. Make sure students understand that this is not a guessing game. The objective of the project is to use what they know about animal structure and function to identify the match between the teeth and the animal.

Differentiate Instruction

RTI/Extra Support For extra support, give students the same number of animal pictures as teeth pictures or teeth molds. That way, students have a more narrow selection of which animals to match with which teeth.

Extension Give students more pictures of animals than pictures or molds of teeth. This will require students to think more about the structure and function of the animal, so that the project is more challenging.

Name _____

UNIT PROJECT
Chew Clue

Chew on this! Each animal has a unique set of teeth. Teeth are structures that support the function of chewing and digesting foods. What are the different kinds of teeth animals have? How do their teeth look and function differently? For this project, you will perform an investigation to determine which teeth belong to which animal.

Write a question that you will investigate as you perform your analysis of animal teeth.

Students should write a question concerning how an animal can be identified by its teeth.

Materials

Think about how you will need to perform this investigation. What materials will you need?

Materials can include pictures of animals, pictures or molds of teeth, drawing paper, drawing utensils, and references (print or electronic).

To carry out this investigation, make a list of the characteristics you will focus on to match the teeth to the animal.

Shape of teeth
Size of teeth
Number of teeth
Arrangement of teeth (how many rows of teeth?)

283

UNIT 5 PROJECT
Chew Clue

 Cause and Effect

Before students begin, check their understanding of key underlying concepts.

Ask: How does an animal's teeth reflect the animal's environment? Animals have adapted to certain diets based on what they need to eat to survive. They have also adapted to certain diets according to what kinds of foods are available in their native lands. What animals eat is reflected in their teeth. Animals that have more vegetarian-based diets have flatter teeth. Animals that eat more meat have sharper teeth.

Refer students to Lesson 1, Exploration 1 for concept support.

ESSENTIAL QUESTIONS Ask the following questions before students begin to plan their activity.

- What are the different features of teeth?
- Do some animals have more teeth than other animals? Why or why not?
- What other external structures support the function of the teeth?

Remind students that an animal's mouth is specialized according to its teeth, as well as what the animal typically eats. In other words, its structure supports its function. This may help students as they match the animals to the teeth.

DCI LS1.A Structures and Functions

The structure of an animal part supports its function. It's important to remember that even internal structures and functions can be affected by the teeth.

Ask: Which internal structures are affected by an animal's teeth? organs of the digestive system: stomach, intestines

Unit 5 Animal Structure and Function 283J

Research and Plan

Students should carefully consider the features of the teeth they will focus on to identify the animal.

Ask: How will you study the teeth? **We will look at pictures of animals' teeth and study the characteristics of the teeth, including how many teeth there are, how they are aligned and shaped, and the size and shape of the mouth.**

Diagrams

Students should use pictures or molds of the animals' teeth to draw a diagram of how the teeth would look inside the animals' mouth. A diagram can help students visually observe how the teeth are placed in the mouth, which may lead them to identify the correct animal.

 Cause and Effect

Ask: What inferences can you make (besides diet) about an animal based on its teeth? **how the animal behaves, communicates, or protects itself**

Research and Plan

Make a plan for how you will carry out this investigation. As you make your plan, consider the following:

- whether the animal eats meat
- whether the animal eats plant-based foods
- how the animal uses the teeth, such as for protection
- the structure of the animal's mouth

Students should relate these considerations to the properties of teeth, demonstrating ability to connect structure and function.

Test your animal-to-teeth matches by uncovering the correct answers and seeing whether your plan for how to identify the animal based on its teeth worked well. Describe any modifications to your investigation that you would make for next time.

Students should explain whether or not they will modify their investigations to correctly match the teeth to the animal.

Analyze Your Results

Look for patterns in the data you used. Using your investigation, make two observations about animals and their teeth.

Students should explain that you can tell what an animal eats or how it protects itself according to its teeth.

Restate Your Question

Write the question you investigated.

Students should identify the question created at the beginning of the project.

Claims, Evidence, and Reasoning

Make a claim that answers your question.

Possible answers: Teeth can tell you a lot about an animal. They can clue you in as to what an animal eats, They can tell you how the animal might protect itself, and they can even serve as a guide to how an animal behaves.

Review your design. What evidence from your design supports your claim?

Students should cite evidence from their designs to support their claims. For example: more predatory animals have sharp teeth, because they eat other animals (meat) and need sharper teeth to shred into the flesh.

Discuss your reasoning with a partner.

283

Analyze Your Results

SEP Analyzing and Interpreting Data

Students should consider the following questions as they interpret their data: How do the teeth look? How are the teeth used? Do you think this animal has a lot of teeth?

SEP Engaging in Argument from Evidence

Review with students what it means to make a claim. Guide them to understand that they will be making claims about which animal they believe to be matched to the teeth.

Claims, Evidence, and Reasoning

Students should claim that certain animals have certain kinds of teeth.

Ask: What claim can you make? Answers will vary: The flat teeth in the picture belong to the rhinoceros. We know that the rhino eats a plant-based diet, so its teeth would be flatter and not jagged or sharp, like the meat-eating animals.

Ask: How does your evidence support your claim? The evidence is based on features of the teeth. The teeth are flat, which is not useful for tearing or shredding meat. Instead, flat teeth are useful for plant-based meals, which are easier to chew and digest.

Encourage students to discuss their reasoning.

Scoring Rubric for Hands-On Activity	
3	States a claim supported with ample, detailed evidence that certain teeth belong to certain animals.
2	States a claim that is somewhat supported with evidence that certain teeth belong to certain animals.
1	States a claim that is not supported by evidence.
0	Does not state a claim.

LESSON 1
What Are Some External Structures of Animals?

Building to the Performance Expectation

The learning experiences in this lesson prepare students for mastery of:

4-LS1-1 Construct an argument that plants and animals have internal and external structures that function to support survival, growth, behavior, and reproduction.

Trace Tool to the NGSS
Go online to view the complete coverage of these standards across this lesson, unit, and time.

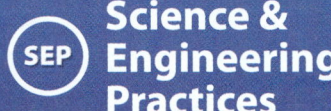

 Disciplinary Core Ideas

Engaging in Argument from Evidence
Construct an argument with evidence, data, and/or a model.

LS1.A Structure and Function
Plants and animals have both internal and external structures that serve various functions in growth, survival, behavior, and reproduction.

Systems and System Models
A system can be described in terms of its components and their interactions

 VIDEO System Models

 CONNECTIONS TO MATH

4.G.A.3 Recognize a line of symmetry for a two-dimensional figure as a line across the figure such that the figure can be folded across the line into matching parts. Identify line-symmetric figures and draw lines of symmetry.

 CONNECTIONS TO ENGLISH LANGUAGE ARTS

RI.4.3 Explain … scientific, or technical text… based on specific information in the text.

RI.4.7 Interpret information presented visually and explain how the information contributes to an understanding of the text in which it appears.

W.4.1 Write opinion pieces on topics or texts, supporting a point of view with reasons and information.

Supporting All Students, All Standards

Integrating the Three Dimensions of Learning

Students will learn and understand that animals have external and internal structures **(DCI LS1.A Structure and Function)**. They will use evidence from the lesson to engage in arguments **(SEP Engaging in Argument from Evidence)**, and they will be able to describe the components of systems and their interactions **(CCC Systems and System Models)**.

 **Professional Development** Go online to view **Professional Development videos** with strategies to integrate CCCs and SEPs, including the ones used in this lesson.

Extra Hands-On Activity: A Closer Look

What Protects Animals?

pairs
20–30 minutes

Have students conduct an investigation of the external structures of animals found in the schoolyard. Make sure each pair of students has a notebook, pencil, collection net, plastic gloves, a magnifying box, and hand lens. Give students 15 minutes to look for insects or make observations of other animals they find. Wearing gloves, they should use the collecting net to capture insects you determine are safe to collect, and gently place them in the magnifying box. Using the hand lens, they should record their observations of the insect's external features before releasing them back into the habitat.

Students could also observe animals such as birds, chipmunks, or squirrels from afar, recording observations of their external structures. Upon returning to class, make a class list of all the animals students observed and classify their external structures, such as feathers, shell, skin, fur. Discuss how the external structures help each animal survive in its habitat.

 This activity can support mastery of this Cross-Cutting Concept: Systems and Models

Preassessment

Have students complete the unit pre-test online or see the Assessment Guide.

Build on Prior Knowledge

Students should already know and be prepared to build on the following concepts:
- external structures of plants and their functions
- growth and reproduction of plants
- how organisms survive in their environments

Differentiate Instruction

Lesson Vocabulary
- external structure

The word *external* means "outer." Its antonym is *internal,* or "inner."

Ask: What other words start with *ex-*? exterior, exit, exclude, expire, exception

Ask: How are these words related in meaning? They are all related to something outside or out of the ordinary.

ELL/ELD Strategy
Review animal external structures with ELL/ELD students., including fur, hair, skin, feathers, shell, scales. Encourage them to translate some from English to their native language using images.

LESSON 1   **Engage** • Explore/Explain • Elaborate • Evaluate

ENGAGE: Lesson Phenomenon

Lesson Objective
To identify the external parts animals have and how their parts are used for growth, survival, behavior, and reproduction.

About This Image
A starfish, or sea star, isn't really a fish! It is an animal called an echinoderm. Sea stars live in all of Earth's oceans, but the North Pacific Ocean has the greatest variety. A sea star can lose one or more arms and grow them back. Though they look docile, sea stars hunt and eat a variety of marine organisms, including clams, mussels, and corals.

 LS1.A Structure and Function

Alternative Engage Strategy

A New Animal   small groups / 10 minutes

Ask students to pretend they are zoologists—scientists who study the animal kingdom. This zoologist has discovered a new animal. Have the student zoologist design a fact sheet documenting the animal's traits. They must include the animal's name, its needs, how it moves, and where it lives. Tell them to make connections between the animal's physical traits and its habitat and needs. Ask a volunteer from each group to share each group's results with the class.

LESSON 1

What Are Some External Structures of Animals?

Animals come in all different shapes and sizes. They move around in different ways, too. What kinds of parts does this starfish have for moving? How does it use those parts to accomplish what it needs to do?

By the end of this lesson . . .
you'll identify how external animal structures serve functions in growth, survival, behavior, and reproduction.

Unit 5 Animal Structure and Function

Explore Online Students can visit the lesson phenomenon online.

Can You Explain It?

Students are asked to explain how the gecko is climbing up the wall. Have them think about a way that things stick to a wall. Remind them that any answer they come up with now is okay because they will learn more about geckos in the Explorations, and they will have a chance to answer the question again at the end of the lesson.

Collaboration

Build on Prior Knowledge You may wish to have students discuss the images as a whole-class activity. In this way, you can more accurately gauge students' prior ability to make sense of the phenomenon by applying knowledge gained through previous experiences related to specific organisms and everyday interactions.

EVIDENCE NOTEBOOK

Encourage students to use an appropriate graphic organizer, such as main idea and supporting details, to set up their notebook for this lesson.

Find more strategies in the online ELA handbook.

Can You Explain It?

Lizards are excellent climbers, expertly moving around. Most lizards climb like the one on the left. The lizard on the red wall on the right is called a gecko. How are its feet different from the other lizard?

1. What did you observe about the two lizards in the photos? You can see how the lizard on the left is moving on the grass. But how is the surface the gecko is climbing different from the grass? How do you think the gecko's external structures are different?

   Students should respond based on the preliminary observations they can make of the images.

EVIDENCE NOTEBOOK Look for this icon to help you gather evidence to answer the question above.

Lesson 1 What Are Some External Structures of Animals? 285

LESSON 1 Engage • **Explore/Explain** • Elaborate • Evaluate

EXPLORATION 1 Body Building

3D Learning Objective

Students will develop an understanding that all animals have **external structures** that protect them from their environments and help them survive. They will **engage in an argument using evidence** to explain that where an animal lives and where it eats is related to the functions of its structures. Students will also study information to understand **animal interactions in a system**.

DCI LS1.A Structure and Function

Ask: If you wanted to know about where an animal lives, how would its skin covering help you know? If they have a lot of fur, they probably live in colder climates.

> ### Differentiate Instruction
>
> **Extra Support** Encourage a whole class discussion about cold and hot climates. Invite students who have visited such climates to describe them to peers.
>
> **Ask:** What are the challenges of living in a polar environment? not much sunlight in winter, a lot of snow, few plants

Connection to Earth Science

Some students may have seen news stories or conservation campaigns about climate change that feature swimming polar bears struggling to find sea ice from which to hunt seals. The polar bear is adapted to life on the ice. Discuss what it means for this species that the sea ice is melting due to a warming climate.
ESS3.C Human Impacts on Earth Systems

 EVIDENCE NOTEBOOK

Students may have observed facial features, such as eyes, nose, mouth. They may also note that the polar bear has cubs that she is caring for.

286 Unit 5 Animal Structure and Function

EXPLORATION 1

Body Building

It's All in the Skin

Animals that live in different environments have to deal with different conditions. These conditions can limit or control what characteristics animals that live in those environments can have to survive.

Body Coverings

2. Match each description with the animal covering it describes.

 a c    b d

a. Moisture and oxygen passes easily through the thin, moist skin. The animal needs to live in a wet and warm environment.

b. Thick hairs trap heat produced by the animal's body to keep the animal warm in cold environments.

c. A slimy substance produced by the skin keeps it from drying out in the warm environment.

d. Transparent, hollow hairs of the fur appear white so the animal can blend into its environment.

Animals have **external structures** that allow them to live, grow, reproduce, and survive. External structures are structures on the outside of an organism. The external structures of the frog wouldn't allow it to survive in the Arctic, but it can survive in a warmer, wetter environment.

A polar bear has external structures meant for an Arctic environment. Take a look at the polar bear picture again, and describe what you think an Arctic environment is like and how a polar bear would survive there.

 EVIDENCE NOTEBOOK Animals have many external structures that function to support survival, growth, behavior, and reproduction. Make a list of some of the other structures you see in the photos above.

286

> **Explore Online** Students can go online to watch videos of these animals using external features to move in their environments.

Moving Parts

3. Animals have structures that help them move. Look at the pictures below and record similarities and differences. Think about the way these animals move.

> **Explore Online**

An ant crawls along with its six legs.

The two, larger hind legs of the frog are strong, allowing it to jump far.

Alike:
Both have legs.

Different:
The ant crawls, and the frog jumps. The ant has six legs and the frog has four.

A bat's wings are thin, stretchy membranes made of skin that catch the air to fly.

A pigeon flaps its feathered wings to move it up in the air.

Alike:
Both have wings.

Different:
The bird wings are covered in feathers. The bat wings are thin skin membranes.

The tail of the shark pushes from side to side against the water, moving it along.

A dolphin pushes its tail up and down to move forward in the water.

Alike:
Both have fins and tails.

Different:
One moves its tail from side to side to propel through water. The other pushes up and down.

Collaboration

Feedback Have students answer item 3 on their own. Then have them share their answers as a class. Encourage students to give feedback containing evidence for any answer with which they disagree. Students should focus on evidence that is visible on the page rather than relying on prior knowledge of what the animals are or where and how they live.

CCC Systems and System Models

Discuss how different body parts allow these animals to move as shown on the page.

Ask: What structures do these different animals use to move? The dolphin and shark move using their fins because they live in the water. Because the bat and the pigeon mainly move by flying, they have wings. Frogs and ants have strong legs to move on land, but a frog also uses it's webbed feet and strong leg muscles to move in water.

Differentiate Instruction

ELL: Realia For students who have difficulty recognizing a specific animal type, bring in photos and fact sheets in their native language to help them understand each animal. It may also help to classify the animals into more general taxa, such as insects, amphibians, mammals, birds, fish, and marine mammals, to help ELL students recognize them.

Lesson 1 What Are Some External Structures of Animals?

LESSON 1 Engage • **Explore/Explain** • Elaborate • Evaluate

EXPLORATION 1 *Body Building, continued*

 SEP **Engaging in Argument from Evidence**

Discuss the differences among the legs of each of the animals pictured. Have students argue how the legs of the zebra are better adapted then those of the other two animals to land rather than air or water. For example, the thin long leg structures enable the zebra to move quickly on land but would not be useful for flying or swimming.

Collaboration

Write, Pair, Share Have students answer item 4 on their own. Then pair them in groups to share their answers. Encourage students to use evidence to support their arguments.

Differentiate Instruction

Extension Direct students' attention to the marine sponge on the bottom of the page. Have them research why animals such as sponges do not have to move.

Ask: How do sponges get their food? **Food and water flow through pores in the sponge. Food particles are trapped and ingested.**

 Language SmArts

RI.4.7 Interpret information presented visually.

Refer to the pictures to discuss how each animal is or is not adapted to live on land, water, or air.

Moving Through the Environment

Animals are adapted, or fit well, to the environments in which they live. They have external body parts that help them move about on land, in the air, or through the water.

Land, Water, or Air?

4. Based on your observations of the external structures of these animals, label whether the animal best moves on land, in air, or in water.

land — air — water

Although most animals have structures for moving in their environment, there are some animals that don't often move from place to place. Corals, sponges, and barnacles are animals that mostly stay in one place. These animals have structures that let them catch food even though they cannot move.

5. **Language SmArts** What do the animals moving about in each environment have in common? List similarities in structures you observe in the animals.

Possible answer: All of the animals have legs. The animal that mainly moves on land has 4 legs. The insect has legs and wings. The penguin has wings that it uses as flippers.

288

Unit 5 Animal Structure and Function

Time to Eat

Animals have external structures that they use to eat. Look at the photos to see how they get food.

 Explore Online

Mountain lions have powerful jaws with very sharp teeth inside their mouths.

Antelopes have mouths with flat teeth at the front. This allows them to bite grass close to the ground.

The female mosquito uses its tube-like mouth part to pierce skin and suck blood.

Eagles have very large, hooked beaks, that easily tear apart flesh.

The frog has a flexible jaw that allows it to open wide to snatch food and a long sticky tongue.

Giant tubeworms have no mouths! Instead of eating, they get nutrients from tiny organisms that live in them.

6. What do you think these animals eat, based on the structures of their mouth parts? What inferences can you make?

Animal	What does it eat?	What's your evidence?
mountain lion	meat	sharp teeth
antelope	plants	flat teeth
female mosquito	blood	piercing mouth part
golden eagle	meat	sharp beak
frog	any animal that fits in its mouth	wide jaw and sticky tongue
giant tubeworm	nutrients from organisms	no mouth

289

Explore Online Students can go online to view videos of animals mouth parts.

CCC Systems and System Models

Connect the specialized mouth parts (or lack thereof) among the six animals on the page with what they eat.

Ask: Which animals eat other animals? mountain lion, mosquito, eagle, frog

Ask: Can you compare the teeth of the two animals that have them? The mountain lion has sharp teeth that allows it to bite and tear meat. The antelope has flat teeth that allows it to pull on, and chew up, leaves and other vegetation.

Ask: How do the external structures help each animal survive? Possible answer: The mountain lion bites and tears meat. The antelope pulls and chews leaves and other vegetation. The tongue of the frog helps it catch insects moving by. These external structures allow these organisms to eat the kinds of foods they need to survive.

Differentiate Instruction

ELL Make a group list of words that describe how each animal eats. For example, bite, gnaw, peck, chew, suck, swallow, gulp. Compare and contrast the words by pantomime.

DCI LS1.A Structure and Function

Have students pantomime how each of the animals pictured catches and eats food. For example, the mountain lion bites and tears meat, the antelope pulls and nibbles vegetation, the eagle punctures and tears meat, the frog uses its quick tongue to catch insects. Discuss how each structure helps the animals survive in its habitat.

LESSON 1   Engage • **Explore/Explain** • Elaborate • Evaluate

EXPLORATION 1 Body Building, continued

DCI LS1.A Structure and Function

Discuss how the body covering of each pictured animal helps it survive in its habitat.

Ask: Which body coverings help the animal stay warm? *feathers and fur*

Ask: Which body coverings are best at protecting the animal from predators? *shell, spines, leathery skin*

> ## Collaboration
>
> **Think, Pair, Share** Have students look at and read the descriptions of all the animals on the page. Ask them to choose one that they would like to discuss based on interest or prior knowledge. Place students in pairs to share their ideas. Remind them to listen to opinions different from their own with an open mind.

Connection to English Language Arts

Have students compare two different animal coverings and argue for the best one. For example, fur keeps the animal warm, but it can be too hot and too dirty. Shells are good protection but they are heavy. Students should outline the advantages and disadvantages of each type and determine which is most effective. Have them share their opinion pieces with the class and identify the strongest arguments.

W4.1 Write opinion pieces supporting a point of view

Take Cover

Animals can be soft, hard, rough, slimy, or have spines. There are many kinds of coverings that protect the insides of an animal's body.

Fur helps insulate this alpaca, preventing heat loss in the cold mountains.

Birds have feathers to keep warm. They are also necessary for the bird to fly.

A snake's smooth scales help it grip and push against surfaces to move.

A hard shell covers some animals, such as tortoises, for protection.

Some animals have sharp spines on their skin to keep them safe.

A sea cucumber's leathery skin protects it from predators.

What's the Purpose?

7. Select the best answer from the word bank that describes each animal covering and completes the sentence.

| predators | body | scales | shells | spines |

_____Scales_____ cover the length of the fish's _____body_____.

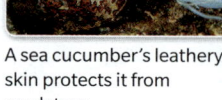
A sea urchin has _____spines_____ for protection from _____predators_____.

290 Unit 5 Animal Structure and Function

| feathers | fur | cool | warm | breathe |
| breathe | fat | wet | moist | flight |

Guinea pigs are covered with ___fur___. This helps keep them ___warm___.

A blue jay's ___feathers___ keep it warm. This kind of body covering is also required in birds for ___flight___.

The skin of a frog helps it ___breathe___ and stay ___moist___.

HANDS-ON Apply What You Know
Design to Survive

8. Pick an environment and describe the conditions in that environment. Then, select body parts from several animals to create a new animal that would survive there. Decide what your animal eats. Design your animal on a poster and label and describe your animal's body parts. Make sure to explain how the parts help the animal survive in its environment!

Putting It Together

9. What does an animal's external structure tell us about where it might live or eat? Suppose you encounter an animal that has a large mouth, scales, and fins. Based on this evidence about its structures, construct an argument about where the animal lives and what it eats.
The animal is probably a fish. Fish have scales for protection. Fins help a fish swim through the water. A fish's mouth may be large or small, depending on what it eats. A fish with a large mouth likely feeds on larger prey.

 Students can go online to take a closer look at the different coverings animals have.

CCC Systems and System Models

Explain to students that a given external structure can serve multiple purposes.

Ask: What are two functions of the blue jay's feathers?
insulation and flight

HANDS-ON Apply What You Know
Design to Survive

Be sure students answer these two questions: Where does your animal live? How do its body parts help it survive? It may help if they draw the animal's environment and label a specific interaction, such as a tail fin sweeping through water to propel the animal.

Scoring Guideline
An excellent response includes a full design of the animal and meets all criteria of the features to be included.

FORMATIVE ASSESSMENT
SEP Engaging in Argument from Evidence

Be sure students construct a meaningful argument where they back up their points and can prove their statements. Use questions to guide them.

Ask: Why don't we see many finned animals on land? Fins are most useful in water, where they can be used to propel or steer an organism.

LESSON 1   Engage • **Explore/Explain** • Elaborate • Evaluate

EXPLORATION 2 Inspired by Nature

3D Learning Objective

Students will develop an understanding that the animal world has led humans to some amazing inventions. They will learn that studying and mimicking the external coverings that protect animals may provide models of systems that can help humans in everyday life. They will evaluate data to explain animal parts and how they function in movement.

DCI LS1.A Structure and Function

Take time to look at the two photographs. The hook and loop tape was inspired by the burdock burr. It was believed that using the same idea, cloth could be hooked together.

Ask: On what clothing have you seen hook and loop tape?
sneakers, jacket, rip-away pants

SEP Engaging in Argument from Evidence

Discuss the different external structures of the animals in the pictures in item 10. Compare the different types of shells.

Ask: Based on the evidence, what argument can you form about how well a burr would stick to each covering?   *Possible answer: Because shells are smooth, the burr would not be able to attach.*

Differentiate Instruction

Extra Support Before answering item 10, review the animals with the students. They may not be familiar with the animals' traits, which means the students won't know which animal would be the best carrier of a burr.

Ask: Describe each type of covering in the pictured animals.
Possible answer: Shells are solid, smooth and bumpy. Some are thinner than others. Fur is flexible, layered, and stringy.

292   Unit 5 Animal Structure and Function

EXPLORATION 2

Inspired by Nature

Inspirations from Nature

The animal world often provides scientists with much inspiration. Scientists and engineers study how animals use their structures to move, eat, or protect themselves and then apply what they learn to the human world. They can design useful devices that mimic, or copy, animal structures and how they function.

hook and loop tape

a burdock burr

Living things have structures that function to support survival, growth, behavior, and reproduction in their environments. The burrs that cling to a person's clothes serve a purpose in plant reproduction. A burdock burr is a seed that has burrs on it. The burr's function is to catch on to passing animals. The seeds will then sprout and grow when they fall in a new place.

Hook and loop tape was designed to mimic the structure of a burdock burr on fur. The function of the hook tape is to stick to the loop tape!

10. Take a look at the pictures of the different animal body coverings. Circle the letter of the animal that the burdock burr would most likely stick to.

A. snail

B. alpaca

C. tortoise

D. beetle

292

Same but Different

As you have learned, animals use different structures for different functions. For example, different animal coverings help in protection, insulation, or communication. Sometimes body parts with different structures in different animals have similar functions.

Comparing Animal Parts

11. Examine the pictures. Then use your observations to compare and contrast each pair of animal parts in the boxes.  Explore Online

bat's wing | bird's wing

Compare and Contrast
Possible answer: Both are wing structures used for flight. The bird's has feathers. The bat's is made of a skin membrane.

eagle's beak | mountain lion's mouth

Compare and Contrast
Possible answer: Both animals have mouth parts for tearing flesh off their prey. The eagle has a sharp beak. The lion has sharp teeth.

frog's legs | dolphin's tail

Compare and Contrast
Possible answer: Both pictures show structures that allow animals to move. The frog jumps with legs. The dolphin swims propelled by its tail.

 Explore Online — Students can go online for a more interactive version of the matching activity.

Differentiate Instruction

Extension Some of the structures on the page are examples of analogous structures—features that have similar appearances and/or functions despite being from unrelated or distantly related organisms and having different developmental origins. For example, although bats and birds both have wings, bats are mammals, not birds. Have students research to write a comparison of each pair of animals to show how they are similar but different.

Systems and System Models

People who study animals use a system of animal classification according to things that animals have in common. These can be based on how the animals look but also on how they behave.

Ask: What are the different classifications of animals you see on these pages? birds, insects, reptiles, mammals, amphibians, mollusks

Collaboration

Share Feedback After students complete their comparisons of the animals, have them form pairs and review each other's work. Encourage a discussion between partners to talk about what they found similar or different about the animals being compared.

LESSON 1 Engage • **Explore/Explain** • Elaborate • Evaluate

EXPLORATION 2 Inspired by Nature, continued

Engineer It!
Biomimicry

DCI LS1.A Structure and Function

Bring student awareness to the structure and function of animal skins. Use the image of the sandfish lizard on the page as an example, but expand to include other examples of animals or organisms that are used in biomimicry. Explain that Geckskin™ uses the integration of the soft pad with a stiff skin. This allows the pad to drape over a surface for maximum contact and adhesiveness without leaving a residue. The low friction of the sandfish scales and it's shovel like head allow it to move as if it is swim through sand.

> ### Differentiate Instruction
> **RTI/Extra Support** Some students may have trouble with pronouncing the words *biomimetics* or *biomimicry*. Have them repeat each word after you until they can pronounce them with ease.

CCC Systems and System Models

Ask: How might scientists working with Geckskin continue to make it better? *They might improve it so it sticks on rough and bumpy surfaces.*

EVIDENCE NOTEBOOK

Students may want to brainstorm a list of animal features or some sort of human need or new technology before they design their model.

Engineer It!
Biomimicry

Scientists, engineers, and product designers may model everyday things after animal structures. This imitation of nature is called biomimetics or biomimicry.

Have you ever watched a gecko climb up a window? Gecko feet inspired the invention of Geckskin™. Most adhesives work by using something sticky, like glue, to attach things, and there is often residue left behind. Geckskin works differently. By using the full structure of a gecko's skin, scientists were able to develop an adhesive that functioned in a similar way as a gecko's feet.

A small piece of Geckskin can hold hundreds of pounds onto a smooth surface. It works by mimicking the adhesive properties of a gecko's foot and the gecko's skin's structure. This allows it to stick to a surface until it is pulled away in a certain direction.

This lizard is called a sandfish. Its body is structured to function as if it swims through sand. Scientists are trying to build robots that function in a similar way.

12. Identify two ways in which adhesives modeled after gecko feet are better than ordinary tape.

Possible answer: The adhesive is much stronger than regular tape, but it leaves no sticky residue.

13. How could having a robot mimic the sandfish's movement be useful to scientists and humans?

Possible answer: The robot might be able to find things underground or locate people in disaster situations.

 EVIDENCE NOTEBOOK Think about an animal structure that a human being could mimic. Design a model of how it could be used.

294

Unit 5 Animal Structure and Function

HANDS-ON Apply What You Know
Find the Inspiration

14. What do you think the device in the photo is? What is its function?

This device is a ornithopter. Do research to learn more about what an ornithopter is. Determine which animal structure inspired the engineering design.

Then, think of an animal that has an ability you think would be useful. Design a device that is similar in function to the ability of the animal. Then describe the function of your design and build a model of it to present to your class.

You have learned that different animals use various structures for surviving in their particular environments. Some structures may look very different but serve similar functions. For example, seal flippers and fish fins are structured differently, yet they have similar functions—swimming. Structures also may look similar but have different functions.

Language SmArts
Summarize

15. How might studying animal structures provide people with new invention ideas?

Scientists and engineers can study the structure and function of different animal parts to model the parts to serve similar functions for humans.

Tip
The English Language Arts Handbook can provide help with understanding how to summarize.

LESSON 1 Engage • **Explore/Explain** • Elaborate • Evaluate

EXPLORATION 2 Inspired by Nature, continued

HANDS-ON ACTIVITY Small groups   Partners 30 minutes
Staying Warm

3D Learning Objective
SEP Engaging in Argument from Evidence

Students will discover how an animal's covering affects its survival by building and using a model. They will evaluate evidence drawn from an experiment and describe how animal features function in survival.

Materials
The materials listed in the student edition are a starting point. Plastic gloves could themselves be used to make the mitts instead of the plastic baggies.

Preparation
Have all materials ready for students to use. Show them how to scoop the shortening. Also measure out the duct tape to the right size for students to use.

DCI LS1.A Structure and Function

Remind students that they are going to be working with the animals' internal and external structures and how they help them live in a particular environment. Hold up a spoon of the shortening.

Ask: What part of an animal do you think this represents? **fat**
Ask: How do you know? **because it is inside the skin and probably keeps the animal warm**

HANDS-ON ACTIVITY
Staying Warm

Skin, scales, feathers, shells, spines, and fur are different external structures of animals that help them survive.

Objective
Collaborate to investigate how an animal's covering affects its survival.

What question will you investigate to meet this objective?
How will an animal's skin or fur affect its chances for survival?

Materials
- vegetable shortening
- spatula
- duct tape
- disposable plastic gloves
- resealable plastic baggies
- thermometer
- timer
- buckets or dish pans
- ice water, room temperature water, warm water

Procedure

STEP 1 Make a blubber mitt. Start by scooping shortening into a plastic baggie. Spread it around all the sides of the baggie, but avoid getting it on the seals.

STEP 2 Turn a second baggie inside out. Insert it into the first bag, and zip the two bags together. Use duct tape to reinforce the seal so that water cannot get inside.

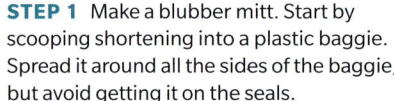

What type of animal covering does this model?
This models a layer of fat beneath an animal's outer skin.

STEP 3 Create a second mitt but without the "blubber" inside. This mitt will represent an animal's skin without a layer of fat and will be the control for the experiment.

Predict how the two models will differ in the three temperatures of water you are testing.
Students should predict differences in the way the water will feel through the two models.

296

Unit 5 Animal Structure and Function

STEP 4 Place one hand in each mitt. Stick both hands into the bucket of room temperature water for 1 minute. How does each hand feel? Record your observations in the table.

STEP 5 Take the temperature of the water outside the mitt with blubber, and then take the temperature inside the mitt while it is still inside the water. Record the data in the table.

STEP 6 Next, take the temperature of the water outside the mitt without blubber, and then take the temperature inside the mitt while it is still inside the water. Record your data in the table.

Temperature Inside Mitt (°F)				
Mitt	Room temp. water	Ice water	Warm water	Observations
Without shortening (control mitt)	Check student data. Temperatures should be more extreme in the control mitt.			
With shortening (blubber mitt)				

STEP 7 Repeat steps 4–6 in the warm water and then in the ice water. How did the blubber mitt feel in the ice water?
Possible answer: It felt harder or more solid.

Procedure

STEP 1 Monitor students as they scoop the shortening into the bag. It can be messy. Be sure they spread it evenly along the sides of the bag. The spatula can help with spreading.

STEP 2 Help students turn the bags inside out. It may be helpful to prepare pieces of duct tape beforehand.

STEPS 4–5 Circle the room and make sure students are collecting all data properly. Incorrect steps taken here can alter the observations.

STEP 6 Model for students how to fill in their data in the table provided. Review tables and make sure student data reflects temperatures becoming more extreme in the control mitt.

Differentiate Instruction

Extra Support If students have a hard time reading a thermometer, guide them as they read, helping if needed.

LESSON 1 Engage • **Explore/Explain** • Elaborate • Evaluate

EXPLORATION 2 HANDS-ON ACTIVITY, continued

STEP 8 Circulate to make sure students are referring back to the chart for their answers. Tell them that what they recorded in their charts can help them with the rest of the steps.

STEP 9 Students should look at their charts to answer this question.

Draw Conclusions
Invite students to work in pairs for this section of the activity. Students can share their responses with a partner.

STEP 11 Tell students this is what scientists do. They take one thing they know and apply it to similar things, in this case all Arctic animals.

SEP **Engaging in Argument from Evidence**

STEP 12 Remind students that they should be able to back up their arguments with their evidence, data, and model.

> ### Claims, Evidence, and Reasoning
> Have students work with partners to critique each other's claims and evidence in Step 12. Discuss whether hearing each other's responses led them to revise their own.

Scoring Rubric for Hands-On Activity	
3	completes the activity filling in all data and answering all questions demonstrating complete understanding of how a fat layer may help animals stay warm
2	completes the activity filling in some data and answering some questions demonstrating understanding of how a fat layer may help animals stay warm
1	completes the activity filling in little data and answering few questions demonstrating little understanding of how a fat layer may help animals stay warm
0	does not complete the activity or answers no questions

298 Unit 5 Animal Structure and Function

Analyze Your Results

STEP 8 Compare the results from the blubber mitt and control mitt. Compare your results with other groups results. What did you observe about each mitt? How did they feel in the different water temperatures? Were your results similar to those of different groups? Why do you think this is the case?

Student responses should indicate that in cooler water, the mitt without blubber was colder and that in the warmer water, the mitt without blubber was warmer. The results should be the same with other groups unless water temperatures were different.

STEP 9 Describe how your blubber mitt changed in the warm water.

Possible answer: It began to melt and started becoming softer.

Draw Conclusions

STEP 10 Which mitt provided better insulation against the cold?

Possible answer: The blubber filled mitt provided better insulation against the cold.

STEP 11 Polar bears have thick fur in addition to a thick layer of fat. What do you think happens to fur in water? What does this tell you about how polar bears and other Arctic animals, such as seals, survive the cold?

Possible answer: Polar bears and seals that live in the Arctic have a layer of fat under their skin to keep them warm. When fur gets wet, it loses its insulation properties, but the fat layer keeps the animals warm while swimming in ice cold water.

STEP 12 Based on your evidence, data, and model, write an argument for how an animal's covering affects its survival. What other questions would you like to ask about animal coverings?

Possible answer: A thick layer of fat will keep an animal warmer in cold environments. What kind of covering is best adapted to a hot, dry environment?

TAKE IT FURTHER Discover More

TAKE IT FURTHER

Discover More

Check out this path . . . or go online to choose one of these other paths.

Careers in Engineering → • Balanced Parts • A Feat of Feet

Mimicking Animal Movement

Biomimetics is the study of using the structures of living things to design human made devices. Researchers at Massachusetts Institute of Technology's (MIT) biomimetics lab study the natural movements of animals. They study horses, cheetahs, and antelopes, and other animals.

Researchers use their knowledge of biology and may use videos to understand how different body parts work together to produce the animals' unique walking, running, or jumping movement. Researchers then apply their understanding to design four-legged robots that move in ways similar to animals.

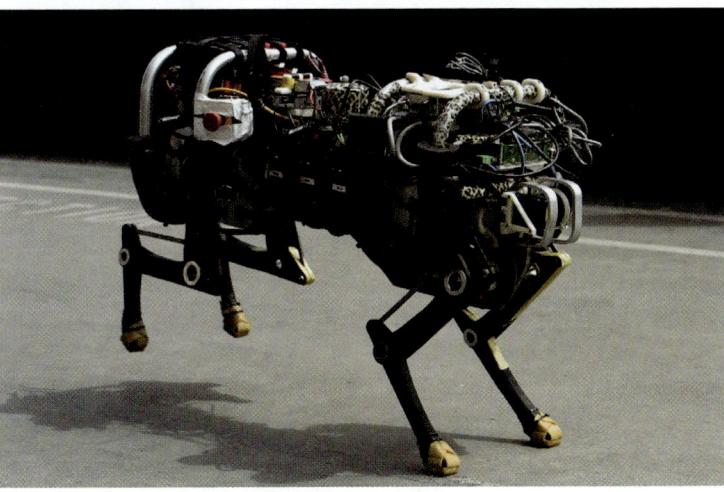

Walking may come naturally to people and animals, but it takes a great deal of coordination. It is challenging to program a robot to walk gracefully.

Collaboration

You may choose to assign this activity or to direct students online to the eSE where they can explore and choose from all three paths. These activities can be assigned individually, to pairs, or to small groups.

Careers in Engineering

DCI LS1.A Structure and Function

Engineers study nature to design things that are useful to humans, but they can also study nature to design things that can replace or replicate things in nature when the real things can't be used.

Ask: Have you seen any artificial organisms? What were they for? How did they compare to the real thing? **Answers may include fishing lures that look like prey, fake owls and eagles that scare pests away from gardens, and fake plants that don't need to be watered or placed in sunlight.**

Differentiate Instruction

Extension Have pairs of students conduct a formal argument about what animals would be best to study and mimic if the scientist wanted to create a specific robot built for speed. Have them continue the discussion about an animal that would be best to use if the scientist wanted something specific for digging.

Connection to Math

Observing and analyzing how four legged animals move has led to several discoveries.

Ask: Why is important to keep the legs symmetrical? **makes moving easier**

4.G.A.3 Recognize Lines of Symmetry

Lesson 1 What Are Some Internal Structures of Animals?

LESSON 1 Engage • Explore/Explain • **Elaborate** • Evaluate

TAKE IT FURTHER, continued

DCI LS1.A Structure and Function

Remind students that they should pay attention to detail when they sketch their ideas, that their ideas should be valid, and that if given the proper support and equipment, the ideas might even work.

CCC System and System Models

Have students describe the robot models they create. They should explain its function and how each part contributes to the whole.

Collaboration

Feedback After students have answered items 16 and 17, have them share their ideas with the class, and have students with the same ideas take a few minutes to collaborate together to describe the systems used in the design.

▶ Explore Online

Students can explore these additional topics online.

Balanced Parts
Students will see examples of radial and bilateral symmetry in animals. *(No outside research required.)*

A Feat of Feet
Students will watch a video about robots that are bipedal and quadrupedal. *(No outside research required.)*

---

16. Suppose you are a biomimetics engineer designing a device that can help humans perform various tasks. Think about the task you would like your robot to perform. What animal movements would be helpful to mimic? How could your device be built?

Do research to learn about other biomimetic projects. Your findings should explain the evidence you found, the kind of evidence, and where you found it. Apply your findings to help you design your device. Sketch your design below. Get your teacher's approval and build a model of your device.

17. What task will your biomimetic device complete? What animal movements did you find helpful in coming up with the idea of your device? What items would you use to build your device?

Student responses will vary based on which device they design and the animal(s) they have decided to mimic.

300 Unit 5 Animal Structure and Function

LESSON 1 Engage • Explore/Explain • Elaborate • **Evaluate**

LESSON CHECK

Explore Online — Students can revisit the lesson phenomenon online.

LESSON 1
Lesson Check

Name _____

Can You Explain It?

1. Think back to the lizards from the beginning of the lesson.
   - What structures do the animals have in common?
   - How do the structures function similarly?
   - How do the structures function differently?
   - Explain how the gecko climbs vertical surfaces.

 EVIDENCE NOTEBOOK Use the information you've collected in your Evidence Notebook to help you cover each point above.

Possible answer:
- Geckos and other lizards all have legs and feet.
- The foot structures allow them to climb and move.
- The first lizard wraps its toes on each foot tightly around the stems when climbing. The gecko, on the other hand, walks with its toes pressed to the surface.
- The gecko is able to climb straight up a wall because it's feet and skin have special structures that make its feet adhesive.

Checkpoints

2. An octopus can change the color and pattern of its skin to match the environment while hunting prey. How does this help the animal?
   a. to swim
   b. **to feed**
   c. to play
   d. to breathe

301

Formal Assessment Go online for student self-checks and other assessments.

Can You Explain It?

> ### Collaboration
> **Discussion** You may wish to revisit and discuss the image as a group to assess students' understanding of the material. Use the bulleted points in the student edition to lead the discussion.

 EVIDENCE NOTEBOOK

Have students reread their answers to the Evidence Notebook prompts, and then use this evidence to justify their reasoning as they respond to the Can You Explain It? question. Make sure students understand that a complete response must address all bulleted points.

 LS1.A Structure and Function

Remind students that when they are answering the Can You Explain It questions, they should look back at the lesson opener to see what they thought about the gecko and how their structures functioned before reading through the lesson.

SUMMATIVE ASSESSMENT

 Systems and System Models

Relate Cause and Effect

2. Students can refer back to what they already know about animals changing color and ways they survive in their environments.

Lesson 1 What Are Some Internal Structures of Animals? **301**

LESSON 1 Engage • Explore/Explain • Elaborate • **Evaluate**

LESSON CHECK, continued

3. Have students relate each situation to themselves. If they were trying to protect themselves, what would be the best way?

4. Encourage students look at the animals' mouths to determine what kind of food they eat. They can refer back to Exploration 2 for more help.

5. Remind students that to answer this question, they should know that the left side of the question will have one line coming from it, but the right side of the question should have several lines going toward it.

6. Remind students to review the *Inspired by Nature* section to answer this question.

Answer the following questions about animal structures and functions.

Choose the best answer.

3. Which of the following structures best functions to protect an animal from predators?
   a. sharp spines
   b. short legs
   c. colorful feathers
   d. thick fur

4. Label each animal feeding structure with what it most likely eats.

   nectar   fish   grass

   fish   nectar   grass

5. Draw lines to connect the structures on the left to the functions they perform on the right.

   A seagull's wings
   A snake's fangs
   An ant's mouthparts —— Feeding
   A tiger's padded feet —— Movement
   A frog's tongue
   An ostrich's long legs

6. Choose the best answer to complete the sentence. Biomimetics is the study of animals to
   a. help animals feed themselves.
   b. help protect animals from predators.
   c. help scientists design things to help people.
   d. help scientists change animal behavior.

302

302 Unit 5 Animal Structure and Function

LESSON 1

Lesson Roundup

A. Label the structures with whether they function in movement, eating, or covering the animals.

movement

covering

movement

eating

covering

eating

B. Write all the correct words to complete the sentences. Some sentences may need more than one word to complete them.

| legs | fur | nature | insects | small animals |

External structures for movement, include wings, fins, and ___legs___.

An animal's mouth shape is adapted to what it eats. A frog's large flexible mouth and sticky tongue are suited for catching any ___insect, small animals___ fit in their mouths.

In biomimetics, people design things that imitate ___nature___.

Lesson Roundup

DCI LS1.A Structure and Function

This lesson summary enables students to quickly revisit key points and prepare for tests.

A. Allow students to scan Explorations 1 and 2 to review what they learned about how the external structures of animals allow them to survive in their habitats.

Remind students of the different animal coverings (shell, scales, spines, fur, feathers, skin) that provide warmth, protection, and ability to move. Remind them of the different structures that allow animals to take in nutrients (mouth, beak, teeth, tongue) Remind them of the different external structures that allow animals to move on land (legs), in the air (wings), or in water (fins, tails).

If students struggle with this setup, write the words movement, covering, and eating on the front board and tell students to use those terms for the activity. **LS1.A**

B. You may wish to remind students that this question covers the entire lesson, and if they are stuck, they should take the time to find the answers in the lesson pages.

Review the concept of biomimicry, reminding students of the GeckSkin™ developed from studying geckos.

If students get stuck, let them know that four of the five terms in the word bank will be used, and that for one fill in the blank option, there are two correct answers. **LS1.A**

LESSON 2
What Are Some Internal Structures of Animals?

Building to the Performance Expectation

The learning experiences in this lesson prepare students for mastery of:

4-LS1-1 Construct an argument that plants and animals have internal and external structures that function to support survival, growth, behavior, and reproduction.

Trace Tool to the NGSS
Go online to view the complete coverage of these standards across this lesson, unit, and time.

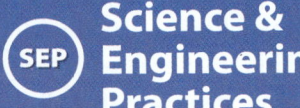 **Science & Engineering Practices**

Engaging in Argument from Evidence
Construct an argument with evidence, data, and/or a model.

 Disciplinary Core Ideas

LS1.A Structure and Function
Plants and animals have both internal and external structures that serve various functions in growth, survival, behavior, and reproduction.

 Crosscutting Concepts

Systems and System Models
A system can be described in terms of its components and their interactions.

▶ **VIDEO** Systems

▶ **VIDEO** System Models

Cause and Effect
Cause-and-effect relationships are routinely identified.

 CONNECTIONS TO MATH

4.OA.A.3 Solve multistep word problems posed with whole numbers and having whole-number answers using the four operations, including problems in which remainders must be interpreted. Represent these problems using equations with a letter standing for the unknown quantity. Assess the reasonableness of answers using mental computation and estimation strategies including rounding.

 CONNECTIONS TO ENGLISH LANGUAGE ARTS

RI.4.1 Refer to details and examples in a text when explaining what the text says explicitly and when drawing inferences from the text.

RI.4.7 Describe the overall structure (e.g., chronology, comparison, cause/effect, problem/solution) of events, ideas, concepts, or information in a text or part of a text.

RI.4.9 Integrate information from two texts on the same topic in order to write or speak about the subject knowledgeably

W.4.2.A Introduce a topic clearly and group related information in paragraphs and sections; include formatting (e.g., headings), illustrations, and multimedia when useful to aiding comprehension.

Supporting All Students, All Standards

Integrating the Three Dimensions of Learning

Gather evidence to support an argument **(SEP Engaging in Argument from Evidence)** regarding the importance of the internal structures of animals in growth, survival, behavior, and reproduction **(DCI Structure and Function).** Explore the components and functions of several body systems of animals **(CCC Systems and Systems Models).** Also compare and contrast the systems to identify similarities and differences of the body systems in different groups of animals.

 **Professional Development** Go online to view **Professional Development videos** with strategies to integrate CCCs and SEPs, including the ones used in this lesson.

Extra Hands-On Activity: Different Animals, Same Structures

How Are the Same Structures in Different Animals Alike and Different?

 Individuals
40–50 minutes

Using classroom and media resources, have students plan and conduct online research on similar systems, such as the circulatory, digestive, or respiratory systems, in two or more different animals.

As part of their research, students should identify the average weight and size of each animal as well as the environment that each animal lives in. They should also identify the system they will be researching as well as any structures related to that system. Any lines of symmetry in each of the systems should also be identified. Students should then create life-size models of the system, with each system's animal and related data affixed to the model in some fashion.

 This activity can support mastery of this Crosscutting Concept: Systems and Systems Models

Preassessment

Have students complete the unit pre-test online or see the Assessment Guide.

Build on Prior Knowledge

Students should already know and be prepared to build on the following concepts:
- Plants have internal and external parts that are essential for life functions.
- Animals have external parts that serve essential functions.
- There are differences in the external parts of different groups of animals.

Differentiate Instruction

Lesson Vocabulary
- internal structures
- organ
- organ system

Ask: Based on what you already know about systems, what is an *organ system*? An organ systems is a group of organs that together carry out a function.

Use students' responses to emphasize the relationship between the terms *organ* and *organ system*.

RTI/Extra Support
Have a discussion about other systems students encounter in their everyday lives. For example, a bicycle is a system made up of parts.

Ask: What is the relationship between the parts of a system? The parts of a system work together, or interact.

Connect students' responses to organs and organ systems.

Lesson 2 What Are Some Internal Structures of Animals? **304B**

LESSON 2   Engage • Explore/Explain • Elaborate • Evaluate

ENGAGE: Lesson Phenomenon

Lesson Objective

Observe and describe some of the internal structures of animals, compare similar body parts that have similar and different uses from species to species or multiple uses within a species, and recognize that some animals have modified systems or don't have them at all.

About This Image

Living things have both internal and external structures that carry out important life functions. External features can be examined by simple observation. Internal structures, such as the heart, must be assessed in different ways. The doctor's stethoscope allows heart rhythms to be observed and assessed. The heart, which is part of the circulatory system, serves the vital function of pumping blood through the body. The structure of the heart varies between different species.

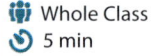 **Engaging in Argument from Evidence**

Alternative Engage Strategy

Inside Out	👥 Whole Class ⏱ 5 min

Before class, prepare two flashlights: one with batteries and one without. Demonstrate to students that you have two flashlights but only one works. Encourage students to identify possible problems with the flashlight that does not work. When students correctly infer that the flashlight has no batteries,

Ask: How are internal parts related to the function of the flashlight? *Without the internal structures that are needed, the flashlight cannot carry out its function of producing light.*

Ask: How are the batteries of a flashlight similar to the internal structures of animals? *Possible answer: Even though they cannot be seen, they carry out important functions.*

LESSON 2

What Are Some Internal Structures of Animals?

Living things have many internal structures that have specific functions. Veterinarians use a stethoscope to listen to the heartbeat of an animal.

By the end of this lesson . . .
you'll be able to provide evidence that animals have internal parts with many functions.

Unit 5 Animal Structure and Function

Can You Explain It?

a person jogging

a person sprinting

The person on the left is casually jogging while the person on the right is sprinting in a race. Think about when you jog and when you sprint. How does your body feel differently when you sprint compared to when you jog?

1. What did you observe about the runners in the photos? How do you think their internal structures are similar and different?

Students should answer based on the preliminary observations they can make of the images.

Tip
Learn more about how other animal structures work in What Are Some External Structures of Animals?

EVIDENCE NOTEBOOK Look for this icon to help you gather evidence to answer the questions above.

305

Can You Explain It?

Students are asked to record their initial thoughts about differences in internal structures of an individual who is jogging and an individual who is sprinting. To do so, students must begin to think about the internal structures of animals and their functions. Encourage students to record the first thoughts that come into their minds. Point out that their ideas might change as they work through the Explorations and Hands-On Activities. Explain that they will have another opportunity to answer the same questions at the end of the lesson.

Collaboration

Build on Prior Knowledge Activate students' knowledge of the external structures of animals that were discussed in the previous lesson.

Ask: What are some external structures of animals that are used for movement? Possible answers: legs, wings, fins

Ask: What are some external structures of animals that are used for protection? Possible answers: shells, fur

Point out that the external structures cannot carry out their functions without the internal structures that will be introduced and discussed in this lesson.

EVIDENCE NOTEBOOK

Encourage students to use an appropriate graphic organizer, such as main idea and supporting details, to set up their notebook for this lesson.

Find more strategies in the online ELA handbook

Lesson 2 What Are Some Internal Structures of Animals? 305

LESSON 2   Engage • **Explore/Explain** • Elaborate • Evaluate

EXPLORATION 1 Pumping Parts

3D Learning Objective
Observe the structures of the circulatory and respiratory systems and describe ways that these systems vary among different types of animals. Students explore the **structures and functions** of body **systems** to obtain **evidence to construct an argument** that internal structures function to support survival, growth, behavior, and reproduction.

Collaborate

Think, Pair, Share Challenge students to think about the internal parts of animals that play a role in running. Then pair students and have them discuss the internal parts they identified. Have each pair of students jot down a list of the internal parts they identify and discuss. Call on several pairs of students to share their lists. Then tell students that many internal structures play important roles in everyday functions of the body, such as movement. Explain to students that they will explore many of these structures and their functions as they read through the lesson.

CCC Systems and Systems Models

Students are introduced to the term *organ system* on this page. To enhance their understanding of the term, review some basic characteristics of systems. Point out that a system is a group of related parts that can carry out a function the individual parts cannot.

Ask: What are the parts that make up an organ system? Organ systems are made up of organs.

Ask: What are two examples of organs systems? Possible answers: respiratory system, circulatory system

---

EXPLORATION 1
Pumping Parts

Take a Deep Breath
When you ride your bike or do other kinds of exercise, what happens to your breath? You might breathe faster. You might notice that you take bigger breaths, too. Take a breath right now. Think about what happens. You take air into your body. Which **internal structures**, or parts inside your body, fill with air? And what happens to the air after that?

Have a Heart
The respiratory and circulatory systems are how your body moves oxygen and blood around. Oxygen is a gas in air that your body needs for its basic functions. When you breathe, air enters through your mouth or nose. The air then moves along the trachea to the lungs. From there, oxygen moves into the bloodstream. The oxygen-rich blood is then pumped throughout the body through a system of tubes called veins and arteries.

2. Which is the main organ that pumps blood carrying oxygen through the body? Circle the best answer.

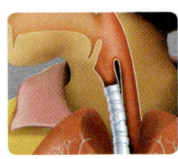
a. trachea

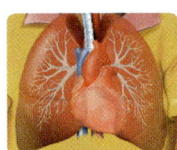
b. lungs

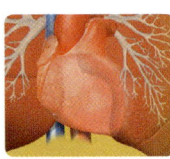
c. heart

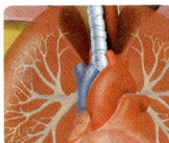
d. veins and arteries

The heart and lungs are organs. An **organ** is a body part that performs a function. An **organ system** is a group of organs that work together to do a job for the body. The lungs are the main organs of the respiratory system. The heart is the main organ of the circulatory system and is a muscular organ that can be made stronger through exercise. The respiratory system and circulatory system work together to deliver the oxygen needed in the bodies of many animals.

306

---

306   Unit 5   Animal Structure and Function

Explore Online — Students can explore online to find out about the movement of air through the respiratory system.

Breathe In, Breathe Out

3. Draw lines showing the movement of air in and out of the respiratory system.

Explore Online

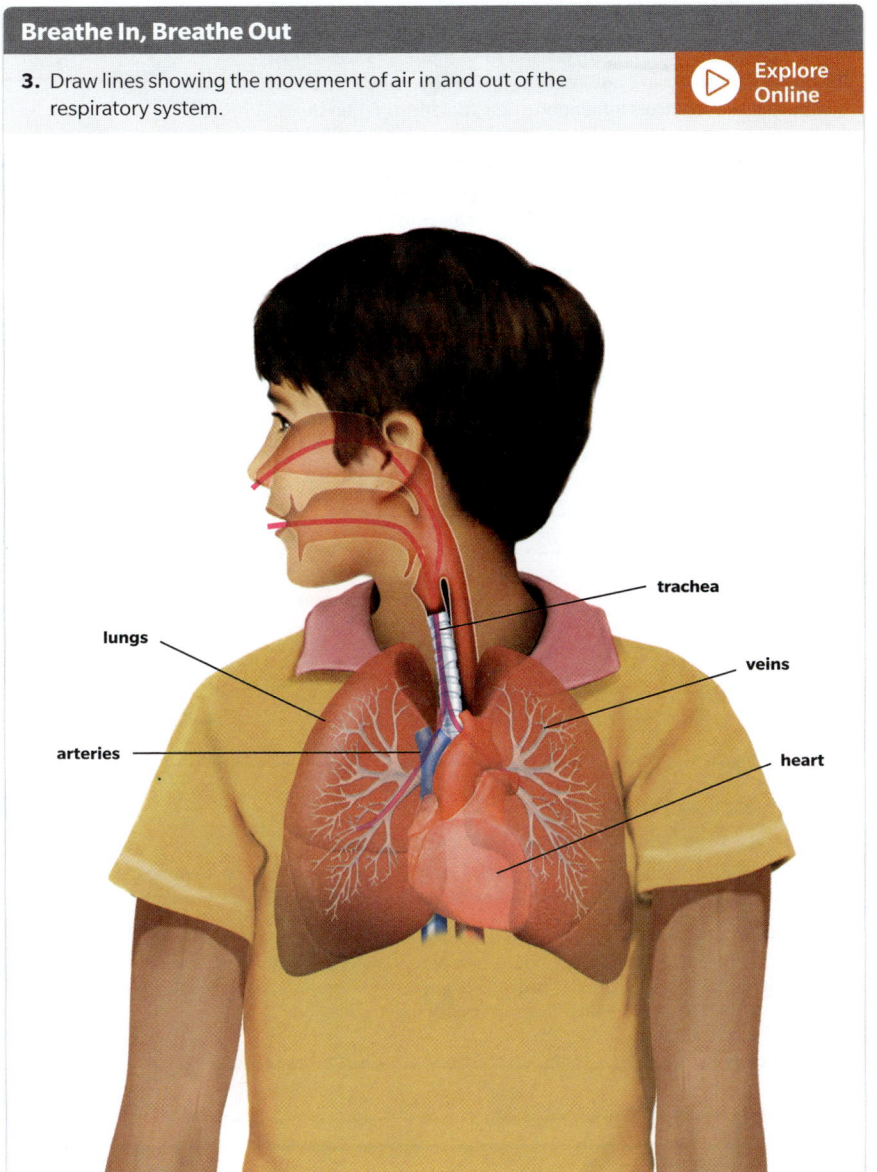

DCI LS1.A Structure and Function

The image on this page helps illustrate the relationship between the internal structures of animals and their functions.

Ask: How is the structure of the lungs related to their function? *Lungs are balloon-like, and their function is to take in air.*

Connection to English Language Arts

As students read the paragraph under the heading *Have a Heart*, have them describe the text structure and phrasing that indicate the order in which a series of steps happens.

RI.4.5 Describe the overall structure (e.g., chronology, comparison, cause/effect, problem/solution) of events, ideas, concepts, or information in a text or part of a text.

Collaboration

Draw, Pair, Share Give students 2–3 minutes for a quick partner discussion to review the arrows they drew to show the movement of air through the respiratory system. Encourage them to make any needed revisions after their discussion.

SEP Engaging in Argument from Evidence

Encourage students to use evidence from the image on this page to construct an argument that the respiratory system and circulatory system are both required for movement of air throughout the body.

Ask: What organs and organ systems are involved in moving oxygen through the body? *Possible answer: The circulatory system that has the heart, veins, and arteries, and the respiratory system that has the lungs and trachea are all involved in moving air throughout the body.*

Lesson 2 What Are Some Internal Structures of Animals?

LESSON 2 Engage • **Explore/Explain** • Elaborate • Evaluate

EXPLORATION 1 *Pumping Parts, continued*

 SEP **Engaging in Argument from Evidence**

The information on this page presents evidence that the heart plays an important role in survival.

Ask: Why is the heart important for survival? *Possible answer: The heart pumps the blood carrying oxygen around the body; oxygen is needed for most animals to survive.*

Differentiate Instruction

ELL: Organize Information Have students make a two-column table, with one column labeled Respiratory System and the other Circulatory System. As students read the information on this page, have them jot down names of structures in the correct columns.

 Do the Math
Breathing Rate

4.OA.A.3 Solve multistep word problems

Have students write out an equation to be solved for each of the two steps of this problem. To help students visualize a liter of air, show them an empty clear plastic one-liter bottle. Encourage students with respiratory conditions to assume the role of timekeeper for this activity.

Ask: How would you calculate the number of breaths you take in a day? *Possible answer: I would multiply the breaths per hour by 24 (the number of hours in a day).*

It Takes Teamwork!

Inhalation, or breathing in, causes air to move into the lungs. Exhalation, or breathing out, makes air leave the lungs. The diaphragm is a muscle that controls inhalation and exhalation. When the diaphragm contracts, it pulls downward. Air moves into the lungs. When the diaphragm relaxes, it moves upward, and air is pushed out of the lungs.

The heart then moves blood to the lungs, where the blood picks up oxygen. The heart then pumps the blood carrying oxygen around the body. Almost all animals need oxygen to survive. Birds, reptiles, and mammals get their oxygen from the air and their respiratory system includes the a heart and lungs. Fish use oxygen dissolved in water and their respiratory system typically includes a heart and gills.

4. Choose the correct answer from the word bank to complete each sentence.

arteries	lungs	circulatory
respiratory	heart	lungs

In birds, reptiles, and mammals, the ___**lungs**___ take in air. These organs are part of the ___**respiratory**___ system. Oxygen is carried by blood to the cells of the body. The blood is pumped by the ___**heart**___, which is part of the ___**circulatory**___ system.

 Do the Math
Breathing Rate

5. With a partner, count and record how many times you breathe in per minute. Take turns using the stopwatch to measure time for your partner. Record the number of breaths you take in one minute.

There are 60 minutes in one hour. Calculate and record how many times you breathe in one hour. Next, calculate and record how many liters of air pass through your lungs in an hour if each breath brings 1 liter of air into the body.

breaths per hour: ___Possible answer: 600___

liters of air per hour: ___Possible answer: 600___

What's the Difference?

There are similarities and differences in the internal structures of animals. Let's explore some of the ways that the circulatory and respiratory systems of animals differ.

 Explore Online

Birds and mammals have lungs and hearts with four chambers. Birds have structures called air sacs to store extra air in their respiratory systems. This makes breathing more efficient when flying.

Crocodiles have a four-chambered heart. Their systems interact in a similar way to those of birds and mammals. Other reptiles and adult amphibians have three-chambered hearts.

Most fish breathe through organs called *gills*. As water passes over the surface of the gills, oxygen is transferred to the fish's blood. Fish have a heart with two chambers.

Some invertebrates that live in water do not have respiratory or circulatory systems. In other invertebrates, air moves through a system of tubes in their bodies as they move.

Language SmArts
Compare and Contrast

6. Which of the animals above have respiratory and circulatory systems most similar to those of humans? Describe the features that make them similar.

Possible answer: Birds have four-chambered hearts and lungs like people do.

309

 Explore Online Have students go online to find out about similarities and differences of the circulatory and respiratory systems of animals.

DCI LS1.A Structure and Function

There are similarities and differences between the internal organs and systems of different types of animals.

Ask: What is a difference between a fish's heart and a mammal's heart? A fish's heart has two chambers and a mammal's has four.

CCC Systems and System Models

Explain that there may be differences in the parts of body systems of different animals, but the interactions between the systems are similar.

Ask: Describe how the heart and blood interact in most of the animals pictured. The heart pumps the blood through the body.

Collaboration

Jigsaw Have students form four groups. Assign each group one of the following: birds and mammals, reptiles, amphibians, fish, or invertebrates. Have each group research to learn more about the respiratory and circulatory systems (or equivalent) in their group. Regroup students into groups of four; one from each original group. Then have each student share information with the others.

Language SmArts
Compare and Contrast

RI.4.1 Refer to details and examples in a text when explaining what the text says explicitly and when drawing inferences from the text.

Have students review the information in the image captions on this page and explicitly refer to specific details as they develop their answer.

LESSON 2   Engage • **Explore/Explain** • Elaborate • Evaluate

EXPLORATION 1 Pumping Parts, continued

 Systems and Systems Models

For mammals, blood is essential for survival.

Ask: What is one way that blood interacts with the body? **Blood removes wastes from certain parts of the body.**

 EVIDENCE NOTEBOOK

Students should note ways that the circulatory and respiratory systems interact in the bodies of both runners. They should then apply what they know about the structures and functions of the circulatory and respiratory systems to identify problems that could occur if either of these systems is not working well. For example, a runner might not be able to run quickly if his or her heart does not efficiently pump blood containing oxygen to the body's cells.

Connection to Math

For a challenge, tell students that a typical adult heart pumps 4.7 liters of blood each minute. Using this information, have them calculate the amount of blood pumped in an hour and then in a 24-hour day. (5 × 60 × 24 = 7200)
4.OA.A.3 Solve multistep word problems using whole numbers

FORMATIVE ASSESSMENT

 Engaging in Argument from Evidence

After students have completed the table, have them write a brief summary statement that compares and contrasts the systems of these different groups of animals.

Ask: Do the structures of these systems vary between animal groups more than the functions of these systems vary between animal groups? Explain. **Yes, the structures vary between animal groups; for example, heart structure is different in each of these groups. However, the function of the heart (to pump blood) is the same.**

Special Delivery

We do not often see the blood that is in our bodies. It is usually in the veins and arteries of the circulatory system. Although we might not see the blood in our bodies, it has many important jobs.

You've discovered that blood delivers oxygen to different parts of the body in many kinds of animals. It also carries nutrients and energy from food. Blood takes wastes away, too!

While blood is very important to many animals, not all animals have blood. Some invertebrates have a different but similar fluid that moves oxygen, nutrients, and energy around their bodies.

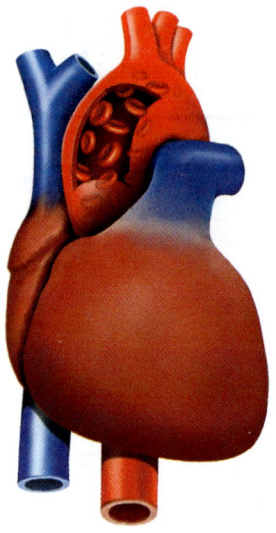

 EVIDENCE NOTEBOOK Think about the images of the runners at the beginning of this lesson. How do the circulatory and respiratory systems of these runners work together? List some problems that might happen if a person's circulatory or respiratory system isn't working well.

Putting It Together

7. Complete the table to classify the circulatory and respiratory systems of mammals, reptiles, and fish.

Compare/Contrast	Heart chambers	Respiratory system
Mammals	4	lungs
Reptiles	3 or 4	lungs
Fish	2	gills

310

310   Unit 5   Animal Structure and Function

HANDS-ON ACTIVITY
Pump It Up!

Objective
Collaborate to investigate the relationship between exercise and breathing rate. Your body uses oxygen for its basic functions. When you exercise, your body needs more oxygen.

Materials
- stopwatch or timer
- graph paper
- colored pencils

What question will you investigate to meet this objective?
Possible question: How do my breathing and pulse change when I exercise?

Procedure

STEP 1 Work in a group. Think of three kinds of exercise you could do in the classroom. Record your list. Show the list to your teacher for approval.
Possible answer: jumping jacks, touch your toes, sit-ups

STEP 2 Set the timer for 15 seconds. Count your own pulse at your wrist or at your neck for 15 seconds. Multiply this number by 4. This is your heart rate in beats per minute. Record your results in the table.

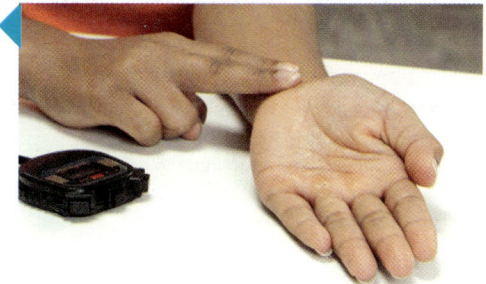

Why did you multiply the number of heart beats you counted in 15 seconds by 4?
Possible answer: Because I only counted for 15 seconds and there are 60 seconds in a minute.

HANDS-ON ACTIVITY — small groups — 1 class period
Pump It Up!

3D Learning Objective
SEP Engaging in Argument from Evidence

Students investigate to gather evidence about the relationship between exercise, heart rate, and breathing rate.

Materials
The colored pencils and graph paper in the materials list are used to extend the activity. Students will make a graph of how different types of exercise affect pulse (heart) rate.

Preparation
Divide the students into groups. Have students practice using the stopwatch. Encourage the students in each group to preview and discuss the steps of the activity.

Safety
Students with asthma, respiratory conditions, or other physical conditions that preclude exercise should be cautioned before this activity. Encourage these students to assume the role of time keeper or data recorder as necessary.

Procedure
STEP 1 Circulate among the groups. Be certain students have selected forms of exercise that can be carried out safely in the classroom.

STEP 2 Assist students as needed in finding their pulse in their wrist. Encourage students to practice counting their pulse rate for several 15-second intervals.

Lesson 2 What Are Some Internal Structures of Animals?

LESSON 2   Engage • Explore/Explain • Elaborate • Evaluate

EXPLORATION 2   HANDS-ON ACTIVITY, continued

STEP 3 Remind students to carefully record data after each form of exercise. Emphasize the importance of resting between exercises so the pulse rate can return to the resting rate.

STEP 4 Have students note differences between the different types of exercise and how they affected pulse rate.

DCI LS1.A Structure and Function

This activity helps students make the connection between the internal structures of organisms and their functions.

Ask: When you exercise, your body needs more oxygen. How does this relate to the heart? *One of the heart's functions is to pump blood containing oxygen through the body.*

CCC Cause and Effect

Point out that exercise causes a change in pulse rate and breathing rate.

Ask: What does an increase in pulse rate indicate? *that the heart is beating faster.*

Ask: What does an increase in breathing rate indicate? *that the body is taking in more oxygen.*

Analyze Your Results

STEP 5 Encourage students to review their data tables and to develop a statement that summarizes the data.

STEP 6 Have a class discussion in which each group shares its response to step 5. Students can then compare their results to those of other groups.

STEP 3 Do one of the exercises your group selected for one minute. After the minute is up, immediately count your pulse for 15 seconds and multiply by 4. Record your heart rate and the type of exercise you did in the table.

		Heart rate (beats per minute)		
Group member	Resting	After Exercise 1:	After Exercise 2:	After Exercise 3:
		Check student data for reasonable results.		

STEP 4 Repeat step 3 for the other two kinds of exercise. Make sure to wait until your pulse is back to its resting rate between exercises. Use coloring pencils and graph paper to make a bar graph.

Was your pulse rate different for different exercises? If so, why?
Possible answer: Yes, my pulse rate changed from exercise to exercise. Some exercises were more difficult than others. During the more difficult exercises, my heart had to work harder to pump blood through my system. When my heart worked harder, my pulse rate went up.

Unit 5 Animal Structure and Function

Analyze Your Results

STEP 5 How did exercise change your heart rate or the heart rates of your group members?

Possible answer: Exercise made my heart rate increase.

STEP 6 Compare your results to the results of other groups. Describe any similarities or differences you notice.

Possible answer: The other groups also noticed that exercise increases heart rate.

STEP 7 This activity measured change in heart rate due to exercise. How do you think your results would be similar or different if you measured breathing rate instead of heart rate?

Possible answer: My breathing rate would also increase after exercise because the cells of the body need more oxygen.

STEP 8 Usually, when a person exercises regularly, or at a higher intensity, his or her heart rate and breathing rate won't increase as much during exercise. Consider the runners in the beginning of this lesson. Which runner's heart and breathing rate probably increased the most due to exercise?

Possible answer: The jogger who was not a professional athlete would have a greater increase in heart rate and breathing rate when running due to not exercising as much.

Draw Conclusions

STEP 9 Make a claim about exercise, breathing, and heart rate. Cite evidence from your investigation to support your claim.

Possible answer: When a person exercises, his or her body needs more oxygen. The lungs need to take in more air to get enough oxygen. The heart needs to pump more often to move blood carrying oxygen around faster.

STEP 10 What other questions do you have about the effect of exercise on heart rate?

Possible question: Do different kinds of animals with different internal structures also have changes in heart rate or breathing rate when they move around quickly?

STEP 7 Have students recall the interactions of the circulatory and respiratory systems described in Exploration 1 as they respond to this question.

STEP 8 Have students review the information about the runners at the beginning of the lesson. Have them apply what they have learned in this activity to explain differences between the runners.

Draw Conclusions

STEP 9–10 Remind students that claims must be supported by evidence. Encourage students to ask additional questions about the topic.

> **Claims, Evidence, and Reasoning**
> Review with students the relationship between claims, evidence, and reasoning. Remind students that logical reasoning should connect the evidence to the claim.

Scoring Rubric for Hands-On Activity	
3	investigation completed as described, results recorded carefully and thoroughly, analysis and conclusions are detailed and logical, evidence and reasoning used to support claims
2	investigation carried out correctly, data recorded, analysis and conclusions lack logical connection to data, claims and evidence are not tightly connected
1	Procedure not carefully followed, data recorded incompletely or incorrectly, analysis and conclusions are incorrect or incomplete.
0	Student did not participate or follow the procedure as described

LESSON 2 Engage • **Explore/Explain** • Elaborate • Evaluate

EXPLORATION 2 Food for Thought

3D Learning Objective

Observe and describe the structures of the digestive and excretory systems and explore ways that these systems vary among different types of animals. Explore the **structures and functions** of body **systems** to obtain **evidence to construct an argument** that internal structures function to support survival, growth, behavior, and reproduction.

 Systems and Systems Models

As students read the text on this page, remind them that the digestive system is made up of components, or parts, that have individual functions. Together, the components carry out a function that the individual parts alone could not.

Ask: What is the function of the stomach? It mashes and mixes food with substances that break it down.

Ask: What is the function of the digestive system as a whole? to break down food so the body can use the nutrients and energy it contains

 Engaging in Argument from Evidence

Like all body systems, the digestive system carries out a vital function.

Ask: What evidence supports the claim that the digestive system is important for survival? Animals need the nutrients and energy in food to survive. The digestive system is the body system that makes the nutrients and energy in food available for use in the body. Therefore, the digestive system is important for survival.

 LS1.A Structure and Function

Before students start item 8, have them review the terms in the word bank. Have them look back in the reading and identify a function of each structure listed. Then have students apply this information and complete the item.

314 Unit 5 Animal Structure and Function

EXPLORATION 2

Food for Thought

It's Delicious!

When you take a bite of food, you might think about how delicious it is. But have you ever thought about why your body needs food? Animals need the nutrients and energy in food. They have internal parts that help them take in food and break it down.

Digestive System

Food enters the body through the mouth. Chewing helps break down the food before it's swallowed. When you swallow, food moves down a tube called the *esophagus* and into the stomach. The stomach is a muscular bag that mashes and mixes the food with substances that help break it down. By the time the food leaves the stomach, it is a liquid.

In the small intestine, chemicals made and stored by other organs, such as the liver, pancreas, and gallbladder, help break down food. The small intestine is the longest organ in the digestive system. There, nutrients and energy from food are absorbed by the body and move into the blood.

After the small intestine, the remaining material moves to the large intestine, where water and minerals are absorbed by the body. Solid waste is formed and then passes out of the body.

8. Choose the correct answer to complete each sentence.

stomach	small intestine	esophagus
large intestine	liver	gall bladder

In humans, food enters the body through the mouth and then moves through the __esophagus__. It then moves to the __stomach__. In the small intestine, food is mixed with substances produced by the __liver/gall bladder__, __liver/gall bladder__ and the pancreas. Nutrients are absorbed by the body in the small intestine. The remaining material moves to the __large intestine__ where water and minerals are absorbed before moving out of the body as waste.

314

Breaking It Down

9. Draw a line showing the path food takes through the digestive system.

▶ Explore Online

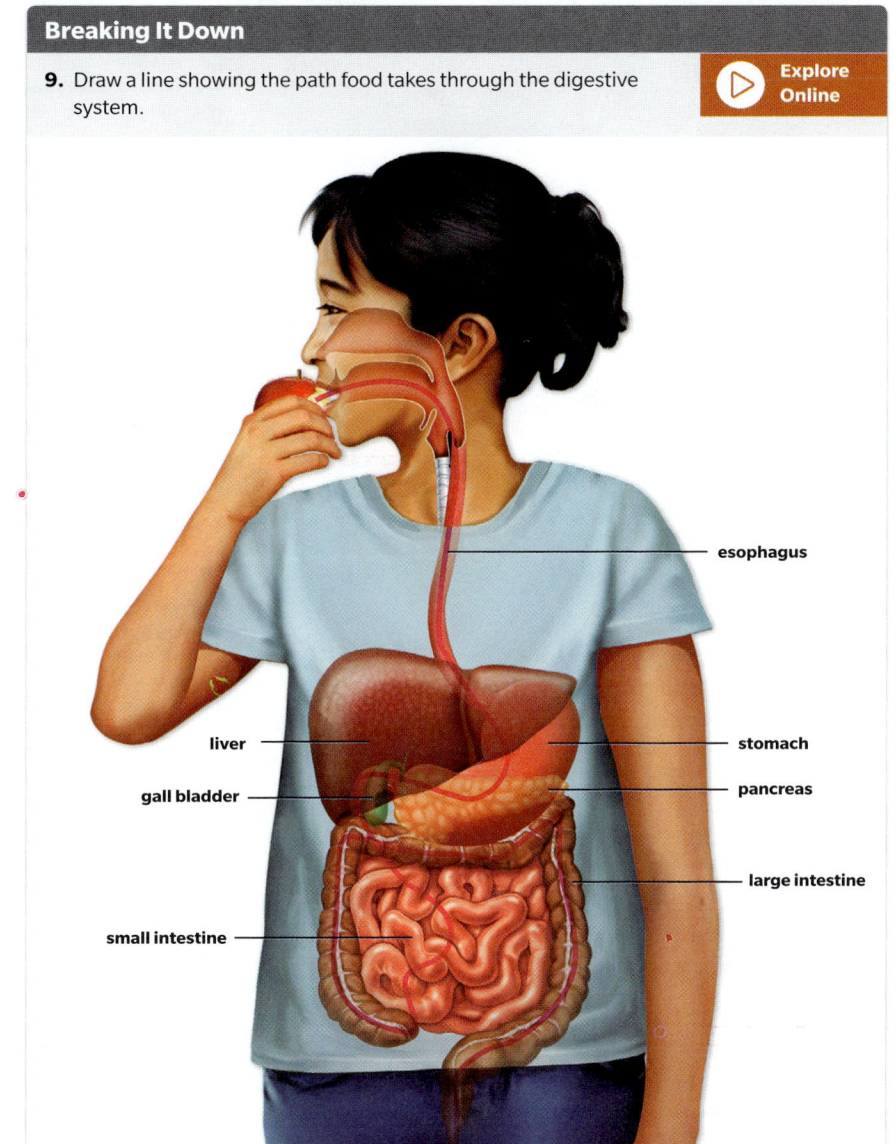

- esophagus
- liver
- gall bladder
- small intestine
- stomach
- pancreas
- large intestine

315

Connection to Physical Science

The energy in food is stored energy. This energy is stored during the processes of photosynthesis, during which energy from the sun is converted to energy in the chemical bonds of food. Animals need the energy in food to survive. Reactions that happen in the cells of animals' bodies allow this stored energy to be released in a controlled way and used by the body.

PS3.D Energy in Chemical Processes and Everyday Life

Differentiate Instruction

Extension Have students do some extra research on food labels, which provide information about the nutrients and energy (measured in calories) in different foods. Then have students select one specific food label to analyze. Have them share their analysis with the class. In their presentation, students should describe what nutrients and how much energy are provided by that specific food.

Collaboration

Draw, Pair, Share After students have completed item 9, have them form pairs. Have each pair of students compare and discuss the arrows they drew. Then have students make revisions or modifications as necessary based on their discussions.

Lesson 2 What Are Some Internal Structures of Animals? **315**

LESSON 2   Engage • **Explore/Explain** • Elaborate • Evaluate

EXPLORATION 2 Food for Thought, continued

DCI **LS1.A Structure and Function**

Have students look at the diagram and read the captions in item 10.

Ask: What kind of waste is released by the lungs?
carbon dioxide

Ask: What kind of waste is released by the skin? excess salt

> ## Differentiate Instruction
>
> **RTI/Extra Support** For item 10, pair students who struggle with reading with a partner who is a fluent reader. Have the students work as a team to complete item 10. One student can read aloud the captions. The other can draw the lines matching the organs to their descriptions.

EVIDENCE NOTEBOOK

Students should note that the lungs are components in two different body systems; they serve a function in each. Students might note that lungs can be part of two body systems based on their interactions with other body parts and their functions. Then students should provide an explanation for the role of the respiratory system and the excretory system in survival and growth.

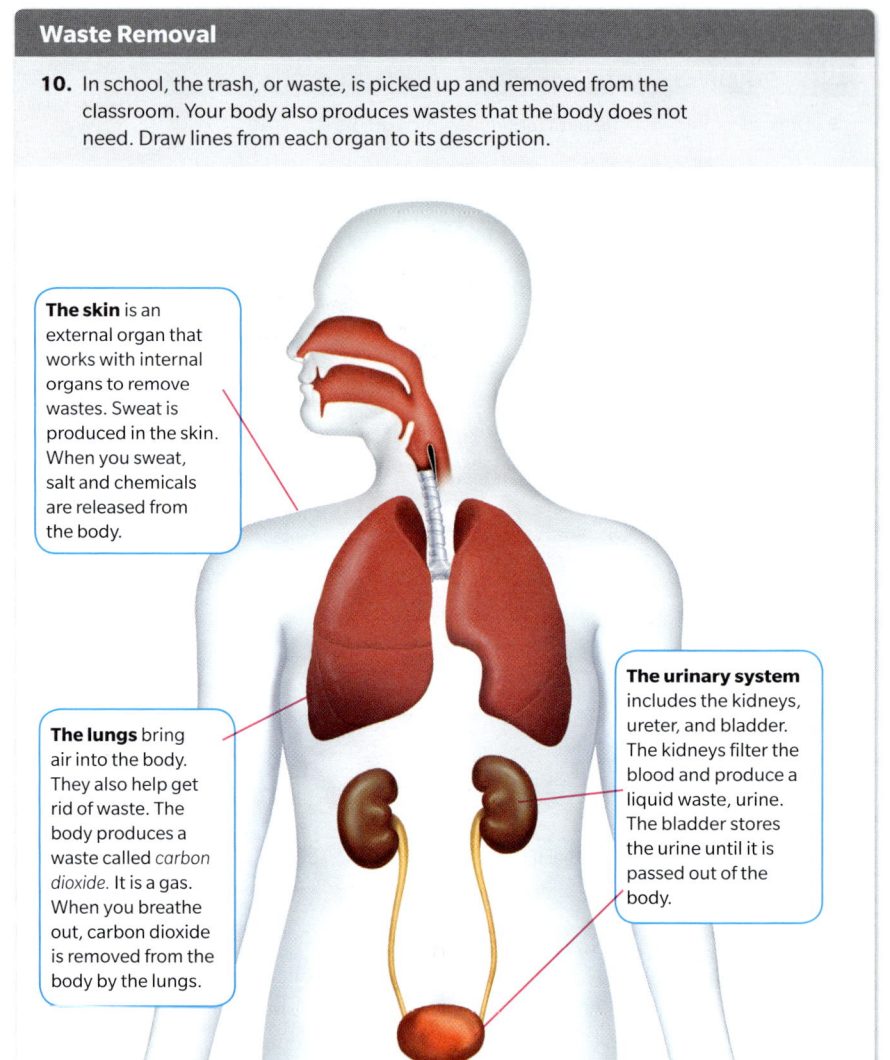

Waste Removal

10. In school, the trash, or waste, is picked up and removed from the classroom. Your body also produces wastes that the body does not need. Draw lines from each organ to its description.

The skin is an external organ that works with internal organs to remove wastes. Sweat is produced in the skin. When you sweat, salt and chemicals are released from the body.

The lungs bring air into the body. They also help get rid of waste. The body produces a waste called *carbon dioxide*. It is a gas. When you breathe out, carbon dioxide is removed from the body by the lungs.

The urinary system includes the kidneys, ureter, and bladder. The kidneys filter the blood and produce a liquid waste, urine. The bladder stores the urine until it is passed out of the body.

 EVIDENCE NOTEBOOK In your Evidence Notebook, explain how the lungs can be part of two different body systems: the respiratory system and the excretory system. Then describe how these two body systems work together to help people grow and survive.

316

316 Unit 5 Animal Structure and Function

Breaking It Down

11. For each image, draw a star on the esophagus, a square on to the stomach, and a triangle on the intestines.

Explore Online

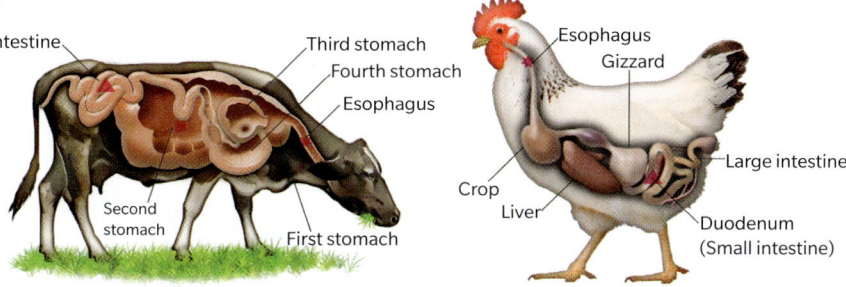

Although cows and humans are both mammals, their digestive systems have big differences. Cows have stomachs with four compartments. A cow needs to chew and swallow its food several times during digestion.

Birds have an organ called a gizzard. Some birds also have an organ called a crop that holds food until it can be sent through the digestive system. The gizzard is an organ in which food is ground up by little stones the bird has swallowed.

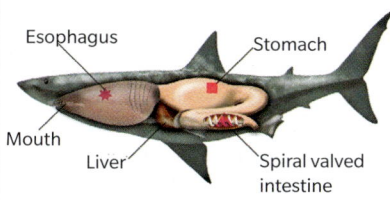

A shark's digestive system needs to break down food that is often swallowed whole! Sharks have intestines shaped like a spiral and a stomach shaped like a U. This provides more surface through which the body can absorb needed materials from food.

This jellyfish is an invertebrate that does not have a digestive system. Food enters through the mouth and is broken down inside the body. There, nutrients are absorbed. Waste then leaves the jellyfish's body through its mouth.

As you can see, there are many differences among the internal structures used for digestion in animals. The functions of the digestive structures and systems are the same: to take in food, break it down to release energy and nutrients, and to absorb the nutrients and energy for use by the body.

CCC Systems and Systems Models

Have students review the information in the captions under each image in item 11. Point out that these systems have similarities and differences.

Ask: What is a similarity of the digestive systems of birds, sharks, and cows? **Possible answers: All of these digestive systems include an intestine. All of the digestive systems function to break down foods.**

> ### Differentiate Instruction
>
> **ELL: Using Realia** Show students an example of a star, a square, and a triangle to be sure they understand the instructions for item 11. You might want to write a key on the board showing the shapes and naming the organ each shape is associated with.

SEP Engaging in Argument from Evidence

After students have completed item 11,

Ask: What evidence would you use to support the claim that the structures in a specific type of animal's digestive system are related to the type of food that animal eats? **Possible answers: I would use the evidence that sharks have digestive organs with large surface areas that help them digest food that is swallowed whole.**

Explore Online Have students explore online to find out more about the digestive systems of different types of animals.

LESSON 2   Engage • **Explore/Explain** • Elaborate • Evaluate

EXPLORATION 2 Food for Thought, continued

HANDS-ON Apply What You Know
All Systems Go

Students will need access to research materials or Internet access if they are allowed to select any animals for this activity. If time or resources are limited, have students use the animals described in this Exploration. Before students begin researching, ask them to plan and develop their chart. Then information can be recorded directly into the chart as students work.

Scoring Guideline
Exemplary charts will include four animals and accurately describe similarities but also identify at least a few differences.

> ## Collaboration
> **Think, Pair, Share** Pair students. Have them spend 1 or 2 minutes reviewing and discussing the body systems that were described in the lesson. Then have them work together to complete item 13.

FORMATIVE ASSESSMENT
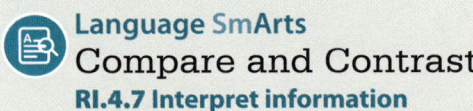
RI.4.7 Interpret information

Check to be sure that students correctly interpret the information in the text describing the digestive system and the excretory system. Their response should identify and describe a difference between the human digestive and excretory systems.

318   Unit 5 Animal Structure and Function

 HANDS-ON Apply What You Know
All Systems Go

12. Choose four animals or kinds of animals. They can be the animals in the illustrations, or you can research other animals. Make a chart that compares and contrasts the digestive systems of the animals you chose. Make sure to include both similarities and differences in your chart. Submit your chart to your teacher.

13. Draw a line from the organs and body structures to the system or systems to which they belong in the human body. Some body structures may be used in more than one system.

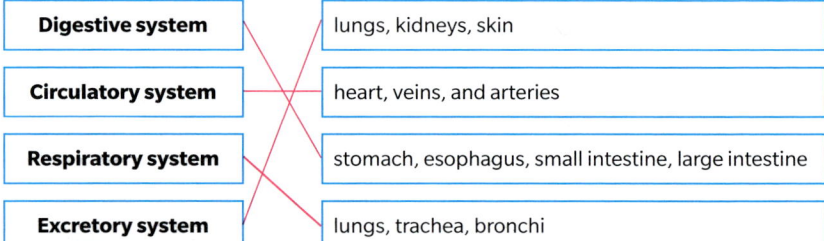

 Language SmArts
Compare and Contrast

14. The systems in the human body have similarities. For example, the function of each system supports survival and growth. The systems have differences, too. Explain one difference between the digestive system and the excretory system.

Possible answer: The digestive system and excretory system carry out different processes. The digestive system breaks down food, while the excretory system gets rid of wastes. The organs in each system are also different. The digestive system it also contains the stomach, gall bladder, liver and intestines while the excretory system contains the lungs, kidneys, bladder, and skin.

Tip
The English Language Arts Handbook can provide help with understanding how to compare and contrast topics and ideas.

318

LESSON 2   Engage • Explore/Explain • **Elaborate** • Evaluate

TAKE IT FURTHER Discover More

▶ **Explore Online**   Students can explore all three Take It Further paths online.

TAKE IT FURTHER

Discover More

Check out this path . . . or go online to choose one of these other paths.

| People in Science | • Model Lungs • Support Your Statements |

All About Anatomy

Henry Gray is famous for publishing a book titled *Gray's Anatomy* in 1858. In the book, Henry Gray gave detailed written descriptions of human body structures and systems. The book also included many illustrations. The illustrations, which were drawn by Henry Vandyke Carter, showed human body systems in a detailed way. The book is still used as a medical reference today.

Henry Gray was an English doctor who studied anatomy.

Vanessa Ruiz is a medical illustrator and artist who combines medical illustration and contemporary art. Her images of human body structures and systems are published and shown in public spaces. She hopes to show people that medical art can be interesting. She also hopes to increase people's awareness of the structures of the human body.

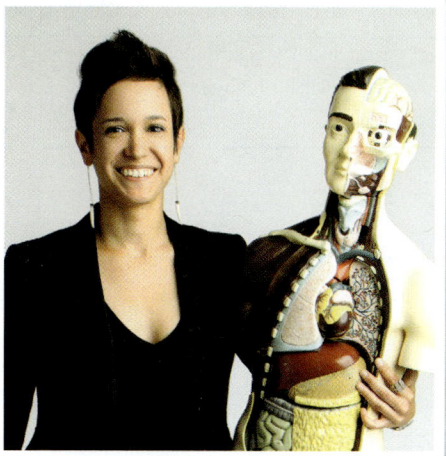

Vanessa Ruiz is an artist known for her work in anatomy.

Collaboration

You may choose to assign this activity or to direct students online to the eSE where they can explore and choose from all three paths. These activities can be assigned individually, to pairs, or to small groups.

People in Science: All About Anatomy

Both of the scientists highlighted effectively communicate information about anatomy; Henry Gray and Henry Vandyke Carter through their detailed descriptions and illustrations, and Vanessa Ruiz through her innovative artwork. *(Outside research required.)*

CCC Systems and Systems Models

Humans, like all animals, have many internal structures that cannot be seen. These structures serve important functions in growth, survival, behavior, and reproduction. Communicating this information by using models and illustrations can allow people to learn about the internal structures of their body. Understanding the components of body systems and how they interact can lead to better health decisions by individuals.

LESSON 2 Engage • Explore/Explain • **Elaborate** • Evaluate

TAKE IT FURTHER, continued

Connection to English Language Arts

As students research the structure of two-, three-, and four-chambered hearts, they can record basic information in the table on this page. Encourage them to take detailed notes from at least two sources on a separate sheet of paper to use as they prepare their "Anatomy of Animal Systems" booklet. As students prepare their booklet, have them group the information for each animal into sections that include headings and illustrations.

RI.4.9 Integrate information from two texts on the same topic in order to write or speak about the subject knowledgeably.

W.4.2.A Introduce a topic clearly and group related information in paragraphs and sections; include formatting (e.g., headings), illustrations, and multimedia when useful to aiding comprehension.

> ▷ **Explore Online**
>
> Students can explore these additional topics online.
>
> ### Model Lungs
>
> In this activity, students make a model of a human lung, using everyday materials. The completed model can be used to explore the function of the lung and the interaction between the diaphragm and the lung. Students then answer a series of questions about their model. *(No outside research required.)*
>
> ### Support Your Statements
>
> Students will research the body systems of an invertebrate that was not described in the lesson. Then they will make a model or drawing to convey information about the animal's body systems. Finally, they will present evidence to support a claim about the efficiency of the invertebrate's body systems as compared to a human's body systems. *(Outside research required.)*

Animal Anatomy

15. Research the structure of different animal hearts. Find information about the structure of two-, three-, and four-chambered hearts. Then research the circulatory and respiratory systems of at least six different animals. When you have completed your research, write and illustrate a booklet titled "Anatomy of Animal Systems." Include detailed written descriptions and accurate illustrations. Be sure to list your name as author and illustrator!

Animal	Number of chambers
Check student animal lists for a variety of mammals, amphibians, birds, reptiles, and fish. Mammals, birds, and some reptiles have four-chambered hearts, amphibians and most reptiles have three-chambered hearts, and fish have two-chambered hearts.	

LESSON 2   Engage • Explore/Explain • Elaborate • **Evaluate**

LESSON CHECK

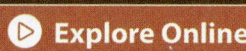 **Explore Online**   Students can revisit the lesson phenomenon online.

LESSON 2
Lesson Check

Name _____

Can You Explain It?

1. Remember the runners? What parts inside their bodies do they use while running? How are these runners similar? How are they different? Consider:
   - Which systems do they use while exercising?
   - What happens to the body during exercise?
   - How does frequent exercise change people's body systems?

 EVIDENCE NOTEBOOK Use the information you've collected in your Evidence Notebook to help you cover each point above.

Possible answer:
- The runners use the structures of the respiratory system, circulatory system, and excretory system while running. At all times, the respiratory and circulatory systems work together to deliver oxygen to parts of the body and the excretory system releases sweat and carbon dioxide.
- During exercise, the body needs more oxygen. In both of the runners' bodies, the circulatory and respiratory systems work at a higher rate.
- In people who exercise often, like the professional runner, the body systems become better able to deliver the extra oxygen needed during exercise.

Checkpoints

2. What would be the result of a person getting a disease that affected the lungs?
   a. blood would not be pumped through the body
   b. (it would be hard to breathe.)
   c. food would not be broken down
   d. wastes would not be filtered from the blood

 Formal Assessment Go online for student self-checks and other assessments.

Can You Explain It?

Collaboration

Discussion You may wish to revisit the image of the runners as a group activity to assess students' understanding of internal structures of animals. First, divide the class into three groups. Assign each group one of the bulleted questions. Have each group spend about 5 minutes developing a carefully thought out response to the questions using information from the lesson. Use the bulleted points in the student edition to lead the discussion, asking each group to contribute its response. Encourage members of other groups to offer constructive feedback on other groups' responses.

 EVIDENCE NOTEBOOK

Have students reread their answers to the Evidence Notebook prompts and then use this evidence to justify their reasoning as they respond to the Can You Explain It? Make sure students understand that a complete response must address all bulleted points.

 DCI LS1.A Structure and Function

Focus students on the internal structures of animals as they analyze the image of the runners.

SUMMATIVE ASSESSMENT
Checkpoints

2. This item requires students to apply the information they learned in Exploration 1 about the function of the lungs.

LESSON 2 Engage • Explore/Explain • Elaborate • **Evaluate**

LESSON CHECK, continued

3. If students are having a difficult time selecting a response, have them review information about the differences among the systems of different animals.

4. Encourage students to look back at the information about the digestive system found in Exploration 2. Emphasize that the different components of the system have individual functions. The digestive system as a whole carries out functions that the individual components cannot carry out alone.

5. Students will need to incorporate information from both Exploration 1 and Exploration 2 to answer this question.

6. Remind students that the lungs are part of more than one body system. Their function is to take in oxygen and release carbon dioxide. However, some animals have different structures that function to take in oxygen.

---

3. Which of the following aid in breaking down food? Circle all that apply.
   a. stomach
   b. heart
   c. lungs
   d. small intestine

4. What is the function of this structure? Circle the best answer.
   a. to carry food from the mouth to the stomach
   b. to release the nutrients in food
   c. to release substances needed to break down food
   d. to allow nutrients from food to move into blood

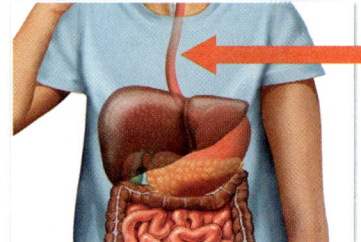

5. Draw a line from the system to the function it performs.

   digestive system — breaking down food
   circulatory system — moving materials through the body
   respiratory system — bringing in oxygen
   excretory system — removing wastes

6. Which statements correctly describe these organs? Circle all that apply
   a. part of the respiratory system
   b. found in all animals
   c. part of the excretory system
   d. take in oxygen

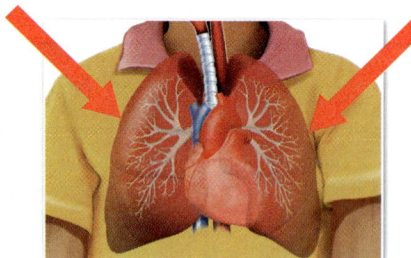

322

Unit 5 Structure and Function in Animals

LESSON 2

Lesson Roundup

A. Draw a line from the type of heart to the organism it belongs to.

four-chambered heart	—	fishes
three-chambered heart	—	mammals, birds
two-chambered heart	—	amphibians

(four-chambered heart → mammals, birds; three-chambered heart → amphibians; two-chambered heart → fishes)

B. Choose the correct answer for each sentence.

| excretory | respiratory | circulatory | digestive |
| kidney | stomach | gizzard | air sac |

In mammals, the ___digestive___ system breaks down food. Organs that are part of this system include the ___stomach___ and the small intestine. The ___excretory___ system removes wastes from the body. Other kinds of animals have different structures as parts of these systems. For example, birds have a ___gizzard___ in which food is broken down.

C. Draw a line from the organ to the system it belongs to. Some organs may belong to more than one system.

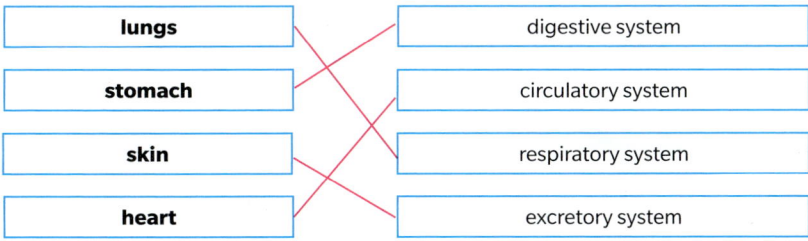

lungs	digestive system
stomach	circulatory system
skin	respiratory system
heart	excretory system

Lesson Roundup

DCI LS1.A Structure and Function

This lesson summary enables students to quickly revisit key points and prepare for tests.

A. Use this item to reemphasize the differences found in the internal structures of different kinds of animals. The information in Exploration 1 would be useful to review if students are having difficulty with this item. **LS1.A**

B. Have students review the information about the excretory and digestive systems of animals found in Exploration 2. Encourage them to review the word bank before they answer the question to be sure they are familiar with each term. **LS1.A**

C. This item asks students to develop a statement synthesizing what they have learned about the internal structures of animals and their functions. You might want to have a quick class discussion before students respond to review the information in the Explorations and activities. **LS1.A**

Lesson 2 What Are Some Internal Structures of Animals?

LESSON 3
How Do Senses Work?

Building to the Performance Expectations

The learning experiences in this lesson prepare students for mastery of:

4-LS1-1 Construct an argument that plants and animals have internal and external structures that function to support survival, growth, behavior, and reproduction.

4-LS1-2 Use a model to describe that animals receive different types of information through their senses, process the information in their brain, and respond to the information in different ways.

4-PS4-2 Develop a model to describe that light reflecting from objects and entering the eye allows objects to be seen.

Trace Tool to the NGSS
Go online to view the complete coverage of these standards across this lesson, unit, and time.

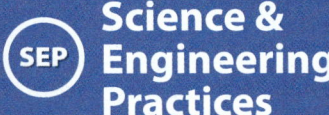

Science & Engineering Practices

 Disciplinary Core Ideas

Crosscutting Concepts

Engaging in Argument from Evidence
Construct an argument with evidence, data, and/or a model.

Developing and Using Models
Use a model to test interactions concerning the functioning of a natural system.

▶ **VIDEO** Developing and Using Models

LS1.A Structure and Function
Plants and animals have both internal and external structures that serve various functions in growth, survival, behavior, and reproduction.

LS1.D Information Processing
Different sense receptors are specialized for particular kinds of information, which may be then processed by the animal's brain. Animals are able to use their perceptions and memories to guide their actions.

PS4.B Electromagnetic Radiation
An object can be seen when light reflected from its surface enters the eye.

Systems and System Models
A system can be described in terms of its components and their interactions

▶ **VIDEO** System Models

Cause and Effect
Cause-and-effect relationships are routinely identified.

 CONNECTIONS TO MATH

MP.4 Model with mathematics.

 CONNECTIONS TO ENGLISH LANGUAGE ARTS

W.4.1 Write opinion pieces on topics or texts, supporting a point of view with reasons and information.

SL.4.5 Add audio recordings and visual displays to presentations when appropriate to enhance the development of main ideas or themes.

Supporting All Students, All Standards

Integrating the Three Dimensions of Learning

Explore ways in which people and animals use their senses. Learn about the physical parts and unique structures **(LS1.A Structure and Function)** that make it possible for people and animals to analyze information through senses **(LS1.D Information Processing)**, which allow sensory information, such as light **(PS4.B Electromagnetic Radiation)** to be processed in the brain **(CCC Cause and Effect)**. Interpret sensory systems **(CCC Systems and System Models)** and apply what is learned to construct intelligent explanations using evidence and data **(SEP Engaging in Argument from Evidence)**.

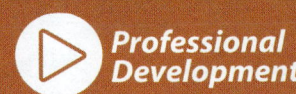 **Professional Development** — Go online to view professional development videos with strategies to integrate CCCs and SEPs, including the ones used in this lesson.

Extra Hands-On Activity: Catch Me If You Can

How Do Senses Help Us Learn?

pairs or small groups
30 minutes

Have students do this activity to help them understand how the senses work together to help us learn. Give each working group of students a meterstick.

Students take turns acting as the meterstick dropper and catcher. Catchers should be blindfolded or do their catching with their eyes closed. The dropper stands above the catcher on a chair. The catcher should stand with one hand open and the end of a meterstick dangling over the catcher's open hand. Students should note the starting measurement. The dropper should then tap or otherwise signal the drop of the meterstick. The catcher should close his or her hand, stopping the fall of the meterstick. Students should record the measurement on the meterstick, subtracting the two numbers to see how far the meterstick fell before being stopped. Each student should repeat this process five times. Students should find that the distance the meterstick falls goes down as they repeat the process.

 DCI **This activity can support mastery of this Disciplinary Core Idea: LS1.D Information Processing**

Preassessment

Have students complete the unit pre-test online or see the Assessment Guide.

Build on Prior Knowledge

Students should already know and be prepared to build on the following concepts:
- Humans and animals have sensory systems that are part of the neurological system. They allow people to interpret the world around them.
- A stimulus, such as pain or temperature, is something that triggers something else to happen.

Differentiate Instruction

Lesson Vocabulary
- receptors

Explain that species have their own unique sensory systems. For example, some animals are blind and rely on the sense of sound to navigate or to hunt for food.

ELL/ELD: Use Realia

Have students smell different scents, such as coffee beans, jelly beans, and refried beans.

Ask: How would you describe the aroma of all three scents? **The jelly beans smelled sweet; the coffee smelled strong or bitter; the refried beans smelled smoky.**

Ask: How do you react when your receptors receive a new smell? **It either makes me hungry or want to get away.**

LESSON 3   Engage • Explore/Explain • Elaborate • Evaluate

ENGAGE: Lesson Phenomenon

Lesson Objective
Construct an argument that animals have internal structures that support survival and behavior.

About This Image
The peacock mantis shrimp relies on its eyes to survive in the ocean. Being able to see many different colors and process them very quickly allows the peacock mantis shrimp to identify predators and prey so that it can safely swim the waters and feed on other organisms.

The depths of the ocean can be dark, as sunlight does not always reach certain parts of the water. By having such a powerful sense of sight, the peacock mantis shrimp may have an advantage over other species. It is adapted to the conditions of its environment over time.

 SEP Engaging in Argument from Evidence

Alternative Engage Strategy

Sensory Sensation!   👥 Pairs   ⏱ 15 min

Have students review the five basic human senses and the receptors/body parts that are related to them. **sight/eyes; hearing/ears; touch/fingers; smell/nose; taste/tongue**

Pair students and have them collaborate on listing their senses in order of importance. Then survey the groups and analyze their conclusions as a class. You may find that most students will say that "sight" is the number one important sense. Engage students in a whole-class discussion about the top three senses and why students have selected them.

LESSON 3
How Do Senses Work?

A peacock mantis shrimp has very complex eyes. Humans have three kinds of receptors to detect light. A peacock mantis shrimp has twelve! It uses its eyesight and other senses and traits to improve its chances of survival.

By the end of this lesson . . .
you'll be able to construct an argument that animals have internal structures to support survival and behavior.

Unit 5   Animal Structure and Function

Explore Online Students can view the lesson phenomenon online.

Can You Explain It?

Students are asked to study the image of the dolphin and explain how they think dolphins can find food in dark waters. To do so, students must have a basic understanding that not all animals use their sight for finding food, even though that's what humans do. They should expect their ideas to change as they progress through the Explorations. Students will have an opportunity to revise their answers when they revisit these questions at the end of the lesson.

Collaboration

Build on Prior Knowledge You may wish to spend a few minutes discussing the different animals and their primary senses as a whole class. In this way, you can gauge students' ability to make sense of the sensory system by applying knowledge learned through previous lessons and experiences.

 EVIDENCE NOTEBOOK

Encourage students to use an appropriate graphic organizer, such as main idea and supporting details, to set up their notebook for this lesson.

Find more strategies in the online ELA handbook.

Can You Explain It?

Animals use their senses to obtain and process information about their environment. Dolphins often swim and search for food in dark or murky water where they cannot see using their eyesight.

1. How do you think dolphins find food in dark water, especially if what they are looking for does not make any noise? What other sense might they use to "see" without using their eyesight?

   Students should respond based on the preliminary observations they can make of the image.

Tip

Learn more about parts animals use to move about in their environments in *What Are Some External Structures of Animals?*

 EVIDENCE NOTEBOOK Look for this icon to help you gather evidence to answer the questions above.

325

Lesson 3 How Do Senses Work? **325**

LESSON 3   Engage • **Explore/Explain** • Elaborate • Evaluate

EXPLORATION 1 Touchy, Feely

3D Learning Objective

Learn about the **human nervous and sensory systems,** and how they interrelate. Learn about the **structures and functions** of the integumentary system, and gain a deeper understanding about the ways in which **stimuli create reactions**. View **models of the body** to visualize how processes in the body work.

DCI LS1.D Information Processing

The information on the page gives an overview on information processing done by the nervous system.

Ask: How are the nervous system and skeletal system related? The skeletal system protects the nervous system.

Differentiate Instruction

RTI/Extra Support If the anatomical diagram confuses students, have other images ready to display for them. For (a), show pictures of the human skeleton and muscles. For (b), show pictures of the brain, spinal cord, and nerves. For (c), show pictures of a close-up of nerves. For (d), show pictures of bundles of nerve fibers.

---

326 Unit 5 Animal Structure and Function

EXPLORATION 1

Touchy, Feely

Body Senses

Have you ever touched something hot with your hand? How did you react? You probably responded by pulling your hand back very quickly!

The Skeletal and Nervous Systems

2. Look at the image showing systems in your body that work together, then match the description to the part it describes.    Explore Online

a. Humans and many other animals have a **skeletal system** mainly made of bones. The skeletal system gives structure, support, and protection to the softer parts of the body.

b. The nervous system contains some very important parts of the body—the **brain**, the spinal cord, and the nerves. The brain is the central processing organ and is protected by the skeletal system.

c. The nervous system contains two kinds of **nerves**: those that send information to the brain or spinal cord, and those that send information from the brain and spinal cord to the rest of the body.

d. The **spinal cord** is a bundle of special nerve fibers and tissue that connects almost all the parts of the body to the brain. It is protected by the backbone. The brain and the spinal cord make up the central nervous system.

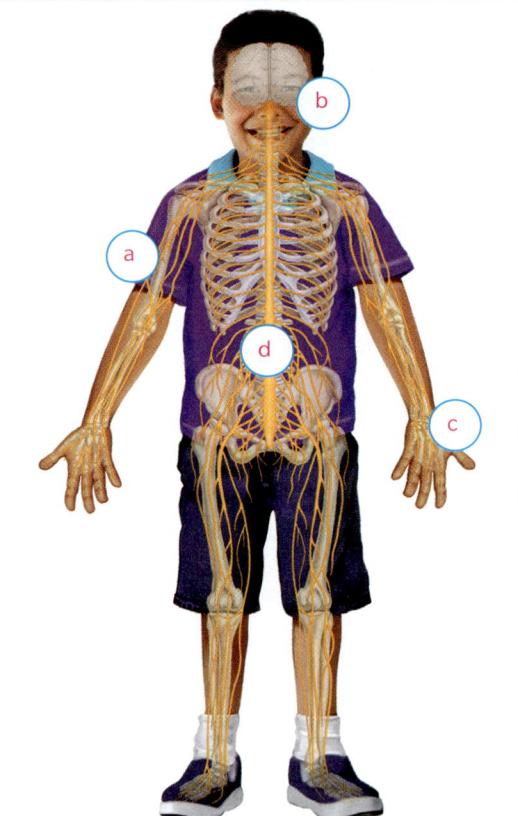

326

Skin Deep

The largest organ in your body is your skin. It provides protection by covering your entire body. Skin also contains special structures called **receptors.** Receptors respond to changes inside and outside the body and report them to your nervous system. Different parts of your body have different kinds of receptors.

There are three main types of skin receptors: touch, temperature, and pain. All three have free nerve endings, which can receive different kinds of information that comes to the skin from the environment.

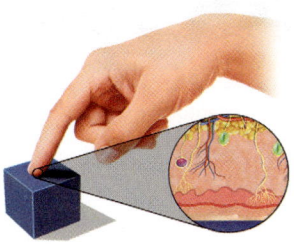

Touch and pressure receptors react to how hard, soft, rough, or smooth an object is. When you touch something like a wood block, the pressure receptors send nerve signals to your brain. The brain processes these signals so that you know what you are holding.

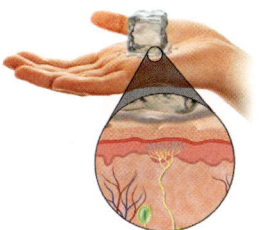

If you are holding an ice cube, you quickly realize that your hand is freezing! This is because temperature receptors in your skin react to the temperature of the ice cube and send nerve signals to the brain.

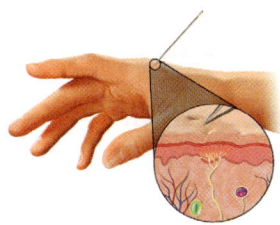

When the skin feels intense pressure or is injured, pain receptors send information about the pain to the brain. The brain processes the signals and causes the muscles to try to move away from the source of the pain. The body's reaction to pain is immediate.

Humans aren't the only organisms that have a central nervous system for controlling the body. All mammals, fish, insects, and birds rely on a central nervous system. Simpler animals have a more basic kind of nervous system.

327

Explore Online

Have students go online to view an animation about the human skeletal and nervous systems to learn more about senses.

CCC Systems and System Models

The skin may not look like much on the outside, but it is its own body system. The integumentary system includes skin, hair, and nails. The skin is the largest organ of the body.

Ask: Which skin receptor relays that a puppy is soft when you pet it? touch receptors

Ask: If you step into a bathtub, but the water is too cold, which skin receptor is responsible for telling your body to pull your foot out of the water? temperature receptors

SEP Engaging in Argument from Evidence

Explain that using facts, such as those presented on this page, can help students make claims about the human senses later on.

Ask: What is a fact that you learned from this page? Possible answer: The skin is the largest organ.

Connection to Life Science

Explain that animals and humans have adapted over the years, and our sensory systems have adapted with us. Scientists study the possibility of changing sensory systems; that is, sensory systems and structures that have had to adapt to new conditions based on changes in the planet over time. For example, it's possible that early mammals did not have as sophisticated sensory systems as mammals have today.

Ask: What evidence do you have that other animal senses are more or less sensitive than humans? Possible answer: Dogs can hear sounds we cannot hear and are more sensitive to smell.

Ask: How might human senses have changed over time? Possible answer: Early humans may have been more sensitive to sound because they relied on hunting and protecting themselves from other animals.

LS4.A Evidence of Common Ancestry and Diversity

LESSON 3 Engage • **Explore/Explain** • Elaborate • Evaluate

EXPLORATION 1 Touchy, Feely, continued

Differentiate Instruction

ELL Students learning English may struggle with the use of the term *feel* in the title of this page. Make sure students understand that "to feel" is different from "feelings" (or emotions). In this case, the pages are referring to the physical act of feeling things.

Collaboration

Draw, Pair, Share Place students into pairs and have them draw a diagram that depicts the sensory process and how information from outside the body is transferred to the brain. Once the drawings are complete, collect the pictures and post them around the room. Allow students to do a quick gallery walk of the drawings and then have a summary discussion as a whole class.

Language SmArts
Identifying Main Ideas and Details

W.4.1 Write opinion pieces on topics or texts

Forming an Explanation As students write about their opinions on stimuli, remind them that it's important to use facts and evidence, or details, to support their writing. Facts and evidence can help make opinions more valid.

Feel It

Test your understanding of how skin works by answering each of the questions below.

3. A friend places a warm rock in your hand. Which types of information about the rock will your skin receptors most likely receive? Circle all that apply.
   a. color
   b. taste
   c. weight
   d. temperature

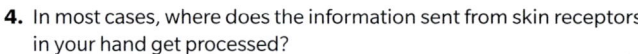

4. In most cases, where does the information sent from skin receptors in your hand get processed?
   a. in the brain
   b. in the hand
   c. in pain receptors
   d. in the tips of the fingers

5. Which kind of receptor do you think would relay the message to your brain if you were cut? Circle your answer.

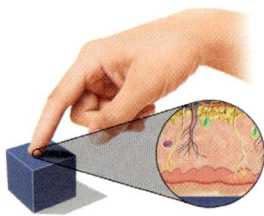 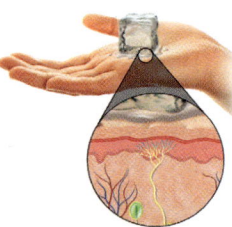 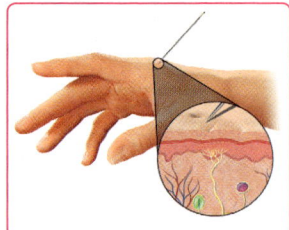

Language SmArts
Identifying Main Ideas and Details

6. How do your senses react to things in your environment?
   Possible answer: I use my senses to taste food, see where I am going, and experience temperature.

Knee-Jerk Response

Not all sensory information travels to the brain to be processed. Has your doctor ever checked your reflexes?

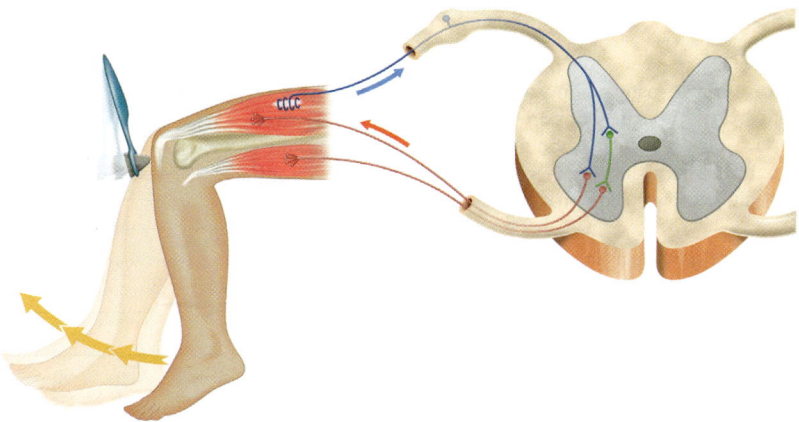

Certain body part have receptors that send information to the spinal cord. From the spinal cord, a response is immediately sent back to the muscles. The brain is not involved. These reactions are called reflexes. Reflexes are important to the survival of many animals because they allow animals to respond more quickly to their environment.

 EVIDENCE NOTEBOOK Think about how dolphins might use their sense of touch to catch food.

Putting It Together

Show what you've learned about the different kinds of sensory receptors.

7. Compare and contrast touch receptors, temperature receptors, and pain receptors.

Possible answer: Touch receptors send signals to the brain about how something feels against the skin (hard, smooth, rough). Temperature receptors send signals to the brain about how hot or cold something feels. Pain receptors send signals to the brain about injuries or pressure on the skin.

329

 SEP Developing and Using Models

Students view the model diagram on the page to learn about reflexes. Voluntary movements are those that people do while thinking about them. Involuntary movements, such as breathing, are things people do without thinking about them, or automatically.

Ask: Do you think reflexes are voluntary or involuntary?
involuntary

 EVIDENCE NOTEBOOK

Students have an opportunity to build on their initial responses to the issue involving how dolphins catch food in dark and murky waters.

 DCI LS1.D Information Processing

Misconception Alert Students may believe that there are only five senses. Sight, hearing, smell, touch, and taste are the five basic senses, but there are other senses, such as the sense of motion, equilibrium, and position in space that is controlled by the inner ear. People also have the ability to sense where their body parts are, so you can scratch an itch on your leg without looking. A sense of time, of thirst, and of hunger are also different types of senses that are in addition to the five basic senses.

FORMATIVE ASSESSMENT

 CCC Cause and Effect

The sensory system is a good example of biological cause and effect.

Ask: What is the cause and effect when you accidentally touch a hot plate and pull your hand away quickly? The cause is touching the hot plate. Pulling your hand away is the effect.

Lesson 3 How Do Senses Work? 329

LESSON 3   Engage • **Explore/Explain** • Elaborate • Evaluate

EXPLORATION 1   Touchy, Feely, continued

HANDS-ON ACTIVITY Pairs   30 minutes
Touch Test

3D Learning Objective

 **Developing and Using Models**

Students develop a way to test the sense of touch by modeling how receptors in the body work.

Materials
The materials listed in the student edition are a starting point. You could also use bendable wire instead of the paper clip, or toothpicks in modeling clay.

Preparation
Preassemble the materials to pass out to pairs of students.

CCC Cause and Effect

Introduce the activity to the student.

Ask: Can you predict what the cause and effect will be for this activity? **The cause will be the paper clip and the effect will be pain or sensation.**

Procedure
STEP 1 Monitor students to make sure they are preparing the paper clips correctly. This step will be more effective if you demonstrate for students how to reshape the paper clip correctly.

STEPS 2–3 Ensure students are performing the activity safely. Make sure to go over safety precautions before the activity and give reminders throughout the activity, as accidents can cause skin punctures from the paper clips.

HANDS-ON ACTIVITY
Touch Test

Objective

Collaborate to investigate how receptors work in your body. The sensory receptors in your skin are not arranged evenly across your body. Some parts of your body may have more of one kind of receptor but fewer of another. Find out which parts of your body are more sensitive to touch and pressure.

Materials
- 2 paper clips bent into a V-shape
- metric ruler
- pencil or pen

What question will you ask to meet this objective?
Possible question: How do I feel things differently when I touch them?

Procedure

STEP 1 Open and bend the paper clip into a V-shape so that its ends are about 2 cm apart. Use a metric ruler to measure the distance. Make sure the two halves of the V-shape are the same length.

STEP 2 Ask your partner to rest his or her hand, palm side down, on a flat surface. Tell your partner to look away.

STEP 3 Lightly press both ends of the paper clip into the back of your partner's hand. Do not press too hard! Make sure both ends touch the skin at the same times.

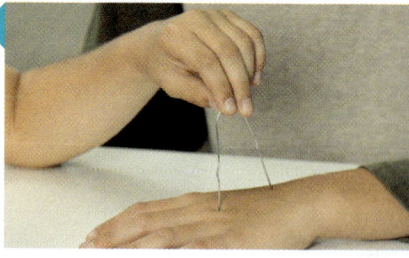

Why do you not want to press down too hard with the paper clip?
Possible answer: If I press down too hard, I may hurt my partner.

  Student Lab Worksheet and complete Teacher Support available online.

STEP 4 Ask your partner if he or she felt one or two pressure points. If your partner feels one point, spread the ends of the paper clip apart and test again. If your partner feels two points, push the ends a little closer together and try again. When your partner FIRST feels two points, record the distance between the paper clip's ends.

Think back to Step 1, in which you were instructed to make sure both halves of the V-shaped clip were the same length. Why was that important?

Possible answer: Making both halves the same length makes it easier to apply pressure evenly with both ends of the clip.

STEP 5 Repeat steps 2 and 3 three more times. Record your results in the second column of the data table by writing the smallest distance at which your partner reported feeling two points.

STEP 6 Repeat steps 2–5 on the right calf, the right shoulder, and the inside of the right forearm. You can use another data table and repeat steps 2–4 with your partner doing the testing using a new paper clip.

	Distance		
	Trial 1	Trial 2	Trial 3
Hand			
Shoulder			
Calf			
Forearm			

Analyze Your Results

STEP 7 What was the shortest distance record on your data table? What was the greatest distance?

Students' responses should be consistent with their recorded data.

STEP 8 On what part of the body were two points of the paper clip felt at the shortest distance?

Students' responses should be consistent with their recorded data.

STEP 9 On what part of the body were two points felt at the greatest distance?

Students' responses should be consistent with their recorded data.

DCI LS1.D Information Processing

Ask: What kind of skin sensory processing do you think this activity involves? touch sensation (do not accept the answer "temperature")

STEP 4 As students work to evaluate the pressure points, circulate the room and make sure students are applying strategic techniques to the test. Students should be calculating the measurement of the clips and carrying out the test in a controlled manner, rather than whimsically trying different approaches.

Ask: Why do you think it is important to record information about your test every step of the way? It can give you more accurate results or help you know how to repeat the test again next time to get the same results.

Ask: What is it called when something like a test result repeats itself over and over again? patterns

STEPS 5–6 You may need to demonstrate to students how to complete the table.

Differentiate Instruction

ELL/Use Realia If you have ELL students in your class, make sure it is clear which body parts are being used for this activity. You can do this by simply touching your own hand, shoulder, calf, and forearm as a demonstration.

Connections to Math

See what kinds of conclusions students can make regarding the data they put in the table. You can have students come up with the average distance and ask them what this information can tell them about the sense of touch and how mathematics can model their conclusions.

MP.4 Model with mathematics

LESSON 3   Engage • **Explore/Explain** • Elaborate • Evaluate

EXPLORATION 1   HANDS-ON ACTIVITY, continued

Analyze Your Results
STEPS 7–10 Answers may differ from student to student, but what you are looking for here is that the information matches what the students record in the data tables.

Draw Conclusions
Direct students to study their results in order to answer the questions.

Connections to English Language Arts
Remind students that when writing their opinions about test results, such as for this activity, it is important to support their opinions with data, facts, and observations. You may wish to encourage students to include at least two facts in their responses for steps 11–15.

W.4.1 Write opinion pieces on topics or texts

> ### Claims, Evidence, and Reasoning
> Have students cite evidence to support their claims in steps 11–15. Call on volunteers to share their explanations with the whole class.

	Scoring Rubric for Hands-On Activity
3	participates in the activity and completes all prompts, drawing evidence from the data table
2	participates in the activity and completes all prompts but does not draw evidence from the data table
1	participates in the activity but does not complete the prompts
0	did not participate or follow the procedure as described

STEP 10 On what part of the body did it take the most tries to feel two distinct points of the paper clip?

Students' responses should be consistent with their recorded data.

Draw Conclusions

STEP 11 How did your results compare to your partner's results?

Possible answer: My partner and I both had the shortest distances recorded for our hands. My partner's distance on his hand was smaller than mine, though.

STEP 12 Based on your results, which of the four parts of the body tested is the most sensitive on your partner? On you?

Students will likely discover that their hands are most sensitive.

STEP 13 Compare results with other groups in the classroom. How are they similar? How are they different?

Responses should reflect more similarities than differences.

STEP 14 Make a claim about senses. Support your claim with evidence from your observations in this activity.

Possible answer: Sensitivity varies throughout the body. I know this because I felt it during the investigation and recorded it in my table.

STEP 15 Think of other questions you would like to ask about senses.

Possible question: What are the most sensitive senses of some animals?

EXPLORATION 2 Is That Something I Want to Eat?

 **Explore Online** — Have students go online to learn more about the senses of smell and taste.

EXPLORATION 2
Is That Something I Want to Eat?

How the Nose Knows

You've learned about the receptors in your skin. But did you know that you also have receptors in your nose?

Every time you breathe air into your nose, receptors inside the nose sense different chemicals in the air. These smell receptors are attached to nerves that send signals to the brain about those chemicals. This is how you are able to smell odors and aromas in the air.

You probably think you have a strong sense of smell. But compared to other mammals, a human's sense of smell isn't very good. Mice have the second strongest sense of smell of all mammals.

8. Write the word that best completes each sentence.

   You are able to smell odors and aromas because you have smell receptors in your ___nose___. Elephants have the strongest sense of smell. The trunk of the elephant contains touch and ___smell___ receptors.

HANDS-ON Apply What You Know

Name That Scent!

Try a simple activity to test your sense of smell. Blindfold your partner and see how many smells he or she can identify correctly. Hold a scented item in front of your partner's nose. Keep track of your results. Switch with your partner and repeat.

9. Did your results surprise you? Why or why not? Which scents did you guess correctly?

   Answers will vary.
   _____
   _____
   _____

3D Learning Objective

Learn more about different senses; particularly the sense of smell and taste. Explore the fact that **sense and taste are interrelated systems,** and test this theory by participating in an activity that tests taste buds to gather information so they **can engage in arguments from evidence**. Gain a deeper understanding of how the **nose and tongue process information through sensory receptors** that are processed by the brain.

CCC Systems and System Models

The nose is an important part of the sensory system. But the nose is also part of its own system of the body, known as the olfactory system.

Ask: Why do you think the nose can trigger memories? *If you smelled something in the past and then smell it again, you may have a memory of what happened from back then.*

HANDS-ON Apply What You Know
Name That Scent!

Prepare for this activity by preassembling an assortment of things for students to smell. You might select things such as pencil erasers, flower petals, coffee beans, or blades of grass. Make sure that students do not see the assortment of things to smell prior to becoming blindfolded; otherwise, they will be able to guess.

Exemplary activity results would demonstrate awareness of the sense of smell and recognition of what the smell receptors can and cannot detect.

DCI LS1.A Structure and Function

Ask: Do you think the structure of the nose is related to its function? *Yes; the outside part of the nose protects all the receptors that are on the inside of it so it can smell things better.*

LESSON 3   Engage • **Explore/Explain** • Elaborate • Evaluate

EXPLORATION 2 *Is That Something I Want to Eat?*, continued

Differentiate Instruction

RTI/Extra Support If students are confused by the word bank and table, you can just use the table and have students come up with their own examples of each category: Taste, Touch, Temperature, and Pain.

CCC Systems and System Models

The skin and the tongue are both body parts full of receptors, but they have some differences.

Ask: What do the skin and the tongue have in common and how do they differ? *The skin and tongue are both able to sense temperature, pain, and touch. They are different because the tongue can taste while the skin cannot.*

Different sensory organs are interdependent. That is, one may not work as well without the other.

Ask: What other sensory organs do you think work better together? *nose and tongue; eyes and ears*

Need Salt?

Like your skin, your tongue has receptors to receive information from its environment: the mouth and whatever you may be drinking or chewing. The tongue has receptors that allow you to taste and feel what you eat and drink.

Which Receptor?

10. Explore how the sensory receptors of your tongue work. Then match the adjectives to the receptor they describe.

Taste isn't the only characteristic of food that's important. Touch receptors on your tongue let you know about the texture of what you eat and drink. Some things are smooth, some things are lumpy, and some things are rough.

It's also important to know the temperature of your food. When the temperature receptors of your tongue come into contact with what you are eating or drinking, they send signals to your brain letting you know how hot or cold it is.

The taste buds are the receptors on your tongue that sense salty, sweet, bitter, sour, and umami (savory) flavors. Every time you take a bite of something, taste buds send signals to the brain to let you know how your food tastes.

Occasionally, you might eat or drink something that's too hot, too spicy, too cold, or too sharp. The pain receptors on your tongue let your brain know when you're better off letting food cool off, warm up, or be avoided completely.

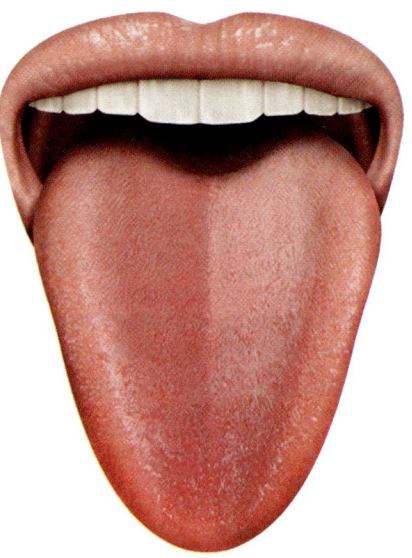

sour	smooth
sweet	cold
boiling	spicy
grainy	warm

Taste	Touch	Temperature	Pain
sweet	smooth	cold	spicy
sour	grainy	warm	boiling

334

334   Unit 5 Animal Structure and Function

HANDS-ON Apply What You Know
No See, No Smell, No Taste?

Your nose is more important than you might think, especially when it comes to tasting foods.

Surprisingly, much of your ability to taste comes from your smell receptors. Even though your taste buds react to salty, sour, sweet, savory, and bitter flavors, it's your smell receptors that allow you to specifically identify a particular food.

Blindfold a partner, then give him or her four different foods to eat. Have your partner hold his or her nose. Ask him or her to identify the food. Switch with your partner and repeat using four different foods.

11. What are your results? How do you think your daily life would change if you could not smell?

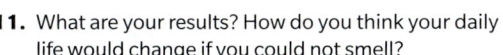
Possible answer: I wasn't very good at identifying tastes with no sense of smell. If I couldn't smell, my life would be different because my food wouldn't taste very good.

12. Discuss the results with your partner. Talk with your classmates about the ways we use smell in our daily lives.

 EVIDENCE NOTEBOOK Dolphins are mammals, just like us. However, they don't have a sense of smell. Why do you think the sense of smell wouldn't be useful to dolphins? Record your ideas in your notebook.

 Language SmArts
Cause and Effect

13. Is there a food you avoid because of the way it smells or tastes? How might an animal in the wild benefit from a strong smell or taste response?

Possible answer: I avoid sour milk because of its taste and smell. Animals benefit from their senses of taste and smell by identifying things that are rotten or poisonous from things that are safe to eat.

Tip
The English Language Arts Handbook can provide help with understanding how to make cause and effect connections.

335

HANDS-ON Apply What You Know
No See, No Smell, No Taste?

To prepare for this activity, you will need to have foods that students can eat/taste. Make sure that students do not have any food allergies or sensitivities to the foods selected for this activity. You may need to modify the food choices according to specialty diets.

Exemplary activity results would demonstrate awareness of the interaction of smell and taste and recognition of what the smell receptors can and cannot detect.

Collaboration

Think, Pair, Share Have students form pairs and discuss the activity they just performed. Guide them to discuss why they were or were not surprised by the results of the activity. Invite students to share their responses with the whole class.

 EVIDENCE NOTEBOOK

Students can build on their initial responses to the previous notebook prompts now that they have learned more about smell and taste.

FORMATIVE ASSESSMENT
 Language SmArts
Cause and Effect
W.4.1 Write opinion pieces on topics or texts

As students respond to these questions, remind them to include facts and examples that can support their opinions. It is important and helpful to get students into the habit of supporting their writing with facts and examples.

LESSON 3   Engage • **Explore/Explain** • Elaborate • Evaluate

EXPLORATION 3 Sights and Sounds

3D Learning Objective

Learn more about different senses, particularly the senses of sight and sound. Explore the fact that **sight and sound are sensory systems** that many animals use and rely on. Study **models of eyes and ears**, including their **structures and functions**, and participate in activities to test individual senses. Learn about some advanced senses, such as **echolocation and the ability to see ultraviolet light**.

> ### Differentiate Instruction
>
> **RTI/Extra Support** Students may be confused by the diagram of the eye. If possible, find alternative images of the eye and present them to students so they can see various angles of the eye and get a better sense of the structures and functions.

DCI   LS1.D Information Processing

Ask: What kind of information can the eyes process? color, shape, depth, dimension

CCC   Systems and System Models

Explain that not all animals "see" with their eyes. Other animals may have senses that are more sensitive than human senses, or that are stronger than their sense of sight. These senses may help them survive.

Connections to Physical Science

Discuss the process of seeing and that an object can be seen only when light reflected from its surface enters the eye.

Ask: What does a receptor need in order to be able to see? light

PS4.B   Electromagnetic Radiation

336 Unit 5 Animal Structure and Function

EXPLORATION 3

Sights and Sounds

Eye See!

Along with the skin, tongue, and nose, there are also sensory receptors in the eyes. Many animals have specialized receptors that receive different types of information through the eyes.

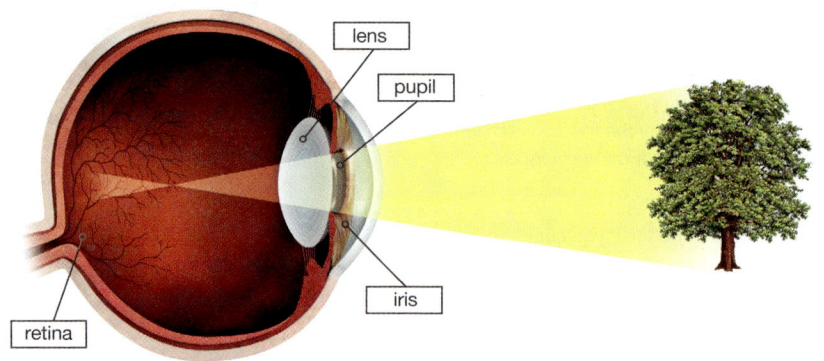

Light bounces off an object. It then enters the eye through an opening at the center of the iris called the *pupil*. The iris is the part of the eye that has color. After passing through the pupil, light strikes the back of the eye. At the back of the eye is an area called the *retina* where there are light receptors. These receptors react to the light and send nerve signals along a pathway to the brain, where the information is processed.

But How Does It See?

14. Circle the structures that allow each animal to "see."

Pigeons see color just like humans. But they can also see ultraviolet light, unlike humans.

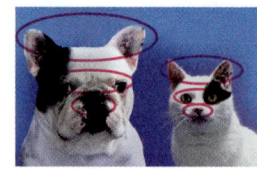
Dogs and cats can see with their eyes, but they rely more on scent and sound for their survival than on vision.

Some snakes see in two ways. They see color and have vision pits in their faces that allow them to *see* heat.

336

Here's to the Ears!

There are sounds everywhere, but you wouldn't be able to hear any of them without the hearing receptors in your ears. As you have learned, senses allow humans and other animals to receive different kinds of information. This information is carried by nerves to the brain. The brain processes the information, causing the body to react and respond to the information in different ways.

Animals have different levels of sensitivity to sound. Many animals are able to produce and hear lower or higher sounds than humans can hear.

All Ears

15. Explore the image that shows the parts of the ear and their functions. Match the caption to the part of the ear it describes.

a. The outer ear is the part of the ear you can see. The shape of the outer ear funnels sound into the ear, through the ear canal, and toward the middle ear.

b. The ear drum separates the outer ear from the middle ear. The middle ear is an air-filled area with three small bones: the hammer, the anvil, and the stirrup.

c. The inner ear contains the fluid-filled cochlea and the semicircular canals. The sound vibrations from the middle ear cause the fluid, and the thousands of tiny hairs inside the cochlea, to move.

d. Deep inside the ear are special sensory receptors that react to sound waves by turning them into nerve signals.

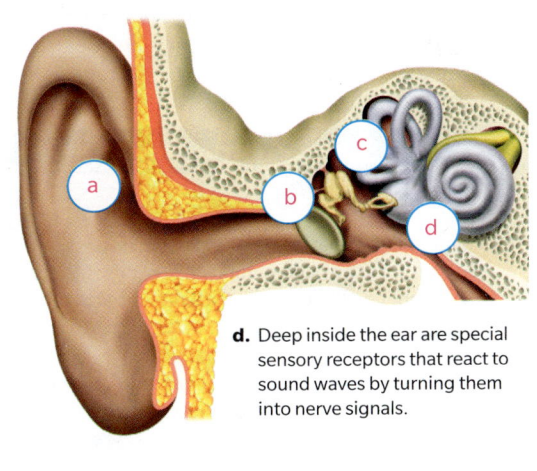

Language SmArts
Opinion

16. How do you feel when you hear music? Use words that describe music and sound to make connections between those words and words that describe feelings.

Students will respond from their own contexts and experiences.

337

DCI LS1.A Structure and Function

Ask: Where in the ear do you think sound is interpreted? inner ear; sensory receptors in the inner ear

Collaboration

Feedback After students work on matching the structure of the ear to the part of the ear diagram, have them work in pairs to critique each other's work and offer feedback. Conclude by bringing the whole class together and reviewing the structures of the ear and their functions.

SEP Engaging in Argument from Evidence

Ask: Do you think it could be true that if you injured your outer ear, you could lose your hearing? No, because the outer ear is not where hearing/the sense of sound occurs. Sound occurs in the inner ear. The outer ear is just to funnel sound into the ear.

Language SmArts
Opinion
W.4.1 Write opinion pieces on topics or texts

As students write their responses, remind them of the important of including examples and data and using the correct terminology whenever possible to strengthen their opinions. There are no right and wrong answers here, but you should "score" students according to their ability to use/incorporate data or examples.

Lesson 3 How Do Senses Work?

LESSON 3 Engage • **Explore/Explain** • Elaborate • Evaluate

EXPLORATION 3 Sights and Sounds, continued

Differentiate Instruction

Extension Challenge students further by having them do outside research on another animal that relies on echolocation. Students should summarize how echolocation has helped the animal survive and how the animal uses echolocation.

DCI LS1.A Structure and Function

Bat ears stand up straight. You might also notice that bats' ears are large in comparison to the rest of their bodies.

Ask: Do you think that if bats' ears were floppy, they would work the same way? No. If their ears were floppy, it might prevent the sound waves from entering the ear correctly, and then their echolocation would not work as well.

HANDS-ON Apply What You Know
Test It!

Make sure students conduct this activity safely in designated areas of the room. Tell students that once they are blindfolded, they should not move around. Exemplary activity results will demonstrate understanding of the capabilities of hearing receptors.

 EVIDENCE NOTEBOOK

Students should be able to use what they learned about echolocation for this notebook prompt.

FORMATIVE ASSESSMENT
Putting it Together

Ask: What are some animals that use their sense of smell more than other senses? dogs

Ask: Which animals rely mostly on their sense of sound? bats, dolphins, whales

Ask: Which animals use their eyes to see heat? snakes

---

338 Unit 5 Animal Structure and Function

"Seeing" By Hearing

Bats are the only flying mammals. As they fly at night, bats send out sounds through their mouth and nose. When the sounds hit an object, it bounces back, or echoes, and is funneled into the bat's ears. As in humans, the sound vibrations move through the ear and are converted to signals sent along nerves to the brain. There the information is processed. Bats use echolocation to locate food, navigate while flying, and find their way home.

17. How do you think bats use echolocation to tell the difference between small objects and large objects?

The echoes that bounce back from small objects are different from the echoes that bounce back from large objects. The bat's brain processes each kind of echo, so the bat knows what kind of object it is "seeing."

 HANDS-ON Apply What You Know

Test It!

18. Blindfold your partner. Make clicking noises in front of, to the left of, to the right of, and behind your blindfolded partner. Observe how your partner uses the clicking noises to locate your position.

 EVIDENCE NOTEBOOK How do you think dolphins might use sound to find their prey in murky water? Record your ideas in your notebook.

Putting It Together

Think about what you've learned about how animals see, hear, and smell.

19. Why is it important for their survival that animals see, hear, and smell in different ways?

Animals have different physical characteristics, eat different things, and live in different places. Therefore, they need to be able to see, hear, and smell different things in different environments.

TAKE IT FURTHER Discover More

Discover More

Check out this path . . . or go online to choose one of these other paths.

Extreme Senses
- Eye Check
- What Colors Do You See?

Extreme Senses

The greater wax moth is one of the favorite food sources of bats. Fortunately for the moth, it is often able to escape being eaten by using its extreme sense of hearing.

Greater wax moths can hear sounds in the same range as the bats who are trying to catch them. The moths then move in a way that makes it difficult for the bats to find them. This makes it much easier for the moths to avoid being eaten and survive.

Mantis shrimp are about four inches long but they are one of the strongest animals in the world. They use clubs to punch their prey at very high speeds. This incredible force is important for hunting food and to protect itself and its home.

The mantis shrimp is not a mantis, nor is it a shrimp. It is more closely related to lobsters and crabs. It has special structures in its eyes that scientists believe allow it to see and process information quickly.

Moth

Mantis shrimp

339

Collaboration

You may choose to assign this activity or to direct students to the eSE where they can explore and choose from all three paths. These activities can be assigned individually, to pairs, or to small groups.

Extreme Senses

Students explore more about the extreme senses of animals to gain a deeper understanding of some of the unusual sensory processing abilities that help animals survive in their environments. Encourage students to review each video online and to read detailed descriptions of the various species. *(No outside research required.)*

LS1.D Information Processing

DCI LS1.D Information Processing

Animals must adapt to their environments in order to survive. Adaptation can be both physical and behavioral. Over the years, certain animals have evolved in physical ways by developing extreme senses that help them navigate their environments. Animals use these extreme senses to hunt, eat, reproduce, and stay safe from predators. You might even think of these extreme senses as super powers!

LESSON 3 Engage • Explore/Explain • **Elaborate** • Evaluate

TAKE IT FURTHER, *continued*

 Language SmArts
Present It!

SL.4.5 Add audio recordings and visual displays to presentations when appropriate to enhance the development of main ideas or themes.

Have students work in pairs or small groups of mixed ability to perform outside research on other animals that have extreme senses. Encourage students to find and use audio clips and/or visual displays for their presentations. Remind students that multimedia engages audiences and keeps them interested in presentations. Make sure to leave enough time for all pairs or groups in the class to present their findings.

SEP Engaging in Argument from Evidence

Ask: What is an important thing to include in your presentations, besides pictures and audio clips? **data**
Ask: Why is data important to include? **It helps support claims about the information being presented.**

 Explore Online

Students can explore these additional topics online.

Eye Check
Students explore more about the structure and function of the eyes. *(Outside research required.)*

What Colors Do You See?
Students learn about the phenomenon of seeing colors. *(Outside research required.)*

 Language SmArts
Present It!

20. Research 5–10 other living things that have extraordinary senses. Find out how these senses are used for survival. Present your findings to the class in a multimedia presentation and submit your presentation to your teacher. Use the chart below to record your notes for your presentation.

Extreme Creatures

Organism	Extreme senses
Check students' charts for completion.	

21. What did you learn about extreme senses? Which was your favorite? If you could have an extreme sense, what would it be?

Check students answers for appropriateness.

340

340 Unit 5 Animal Structure and Function

LESSON 3 Engage • Explore/Explain • Elaborate • **Evaluate**

LESSON CHECK

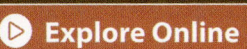 **Explore Online** Students can revisit the lesson phenomenon online.

LESSON 3
Lesson Check

Name _____

Can You Explain It?

1. Think back to how bats use their senses to receive and process information about their environment. How is the dolphin's environment like that of a bat's? How do you think a dolphin uses its senses to "see" its surroundings without using its eyes? Be sure to do the following:
   - Discuss the internal structures the dolphin might use.
   - Describe the receptors that might be involved.
   - Step through the whole process the dolphin uses, ending with it eating a fish.

 EVIDENCE NOTEBOOK Use the information you've collected in your Evidence Notebook to help answer these questions.

Possible answers:
- Like the bat, the dolphin makes sounds that go out into the environment.
- Some of the sounds bounce back from objects and are received by the dolphin's ears, where specialized receptors receive vibrations in the water.
- Sound information from the ears is sent to the brain.
- The brain processes the sound information, and the dolphin reacts by swimming toward the prey it located and eating it.

Checkpoints

2. Suppose you mistakenly rest your hand on a hot stovetop. What are some ways your nervous system will respond? Select all answers that are correct.
   a. Your brain will tell your arm muscles to pull the hand away.
   b. Your nervous system will wait for your muscles to respond.
   c. Your brain will remember that stovetops can be hot.
   d. Your pain receptors will send messages to the brain.

341

 Formal Assessment Go online for student self-checks and other assessments.

Can You Explain It?

> **Collaboration**
> **Discussion** You may wish to revisit the information covered in Explorations 1, 2, and 3 to ensure student understanding of the material. Use bulleted points in the student edition to lead the discussion.

EVIDENCE NOTEBOOK

Have students reread their answers to the Evidence Notebook prompts, and then use this evidence to justify their reasoning as they respond to the Can You Explain It? Make sure students understand that a complete response must address all bulleted points.

 LS1.D Information Processing

Now that students are more familiar with the different senses, draw their attention back to the image of the dolphin.

Ask: Do you think dolphins would be as able to find food in oceans without echolocation? Why or why not? No; echolocation is a sensory process that dolphins rely on to locate objects and orient themselves in water.

SUMMATIVE ASSESSMENT

2. To correctly answer the question, students must recall the facts they learned in Exploration 1, as well as understand the concept of cause and effect.

Lesson 3 How Do Senses Work? **341**

LESSON 3   Engage • Explore/Explain • Elaborate • **Evaluate**

LESSON CHECK, continued

3. Students may feel confused by the structure of this item. Help students by explaining that they can draw lines from one box to another (moving from left to right) to represent a "process." Explain to students that this question is asking them to understand what situation uses which receptor.

4. Students should be able to answer this question by studying the diagram of the eye. You can tell students that the answer for the second blank is one of the labels on the diagram if they struggle.

5. Students can recall their taste test of the food to answer this question.

6. Encourage students to use the diagram of the ear to answer the question.

---

3. Match each situation to the kind of receptor that reacts.

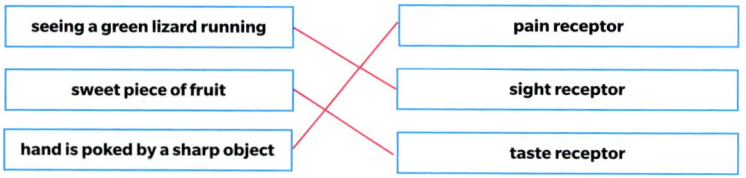

4. Use the image to help you choose the correct answer for each sentence.

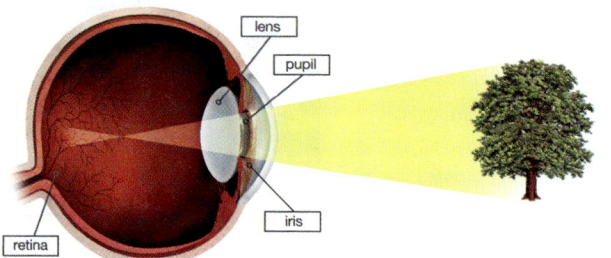

The eyes contain ____<u>light</u>____ receptors that react to light. Light passes through the ____<u>pupil</u>____ of the eye to reach the receptors.

5. What do you predict will happen if you hold your nose while eating your lunch? Circle the best answer.
   a. (My lunch won't taste as good.)
   b. I'll eat my lunch more quickly.
   c. My taste buds won't be able to function.
   d. The food in my lunch won't look the same.

6. How do sounds get from the inner ear to the brain?
   a. They pass through the eardrum.
   b. They make tiny hairs move in the cochlea.
   c. They are translated by receptors into nerve signals.
   d. They cause fluid to move in the outer and middle ear.

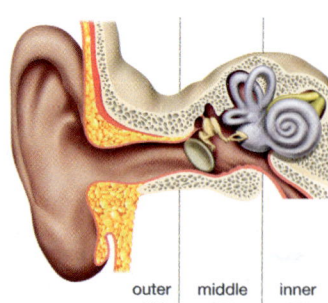

342

342   Unit 5   Animal Structure and Function

LESSON 3
Lesson Roundup

A. Choose the correct words that complete each sentence.

| skeletal system | nervous system |
| brain and spinal cord | central nervous system |

The _____nervous system_____ includes the brain, spinal cord, and all the nerves in the body. The central nervous system includes just the _____brain and spinal cord_____. Sensory receptors are constantly reacting to things inside and outside the body. The reactions are sent to the _____central nervous system_____ as nerve signals.

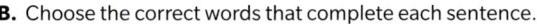

B. Choose the correct words that complete each sentence.

| taste | sight | smell | hearing | touch |

You use your sense of _____taste_____ to choose your favorite meal. A cheetah uses its sense of _____sight_____ to spot the weakest zebra in a herd. A bat uses its sense of _____hearing_____ to fly at night, searching for food. A hungry grizzly bear uses its sense of _____smell_____ to find the most fragrant berries to eat.

C. Choose the sense that reacts to each example. Place the example in the correct column.

| red | bumpy | spicy pepper | scent of pencil shavings |
| smooth | pin dropping | lion roar | sour cherry |

Touch	Taste	Smell	See	Hear
bumpy smooth	sour cherry spicy pepper	scent of pencil shavings	red	pin dropping lion roar

343

Lesson Roundup

**DCI LS1.A Structure and Function;
LS1.D Information Processing**

This lesson summary enables students to quickly revisit key points and prepare for tests.

A. To clarify students' understanding of the parts of the nervous system, have them revisit Exploration 1.

Alternatively, you can show students an unlabeled anatomical diagram that shows the nervous system to prompt their memories. **LS1.A, LS1.D**

B. Students may wish to scan Explorations 2 and 3 before responding. Remind students of the activities they participated in to test their senses. Students should be able to fill in the blanks even without reviewing the Explorations. **LS1.A, LS1.D**

C. Help students by letting them know that all of the terms in the word bank can be used for the categories in the table. Have students recall each of the senses and think carefully about the examples.

Alternatively, turn this item into a whole-class activity where you create a table with the same categories on the board, and fill in the examples as a group. **LS1.A, LS1.D**

▶ **Explore Online** Review the digital resource for additional source content.

UNIT 5 Performance Task

ENGINEER IT!  small groups · 1 class period
Breathing In and Out

3D Assessment Goal
Students **develop models of a portable invention** to come up with a design for a new product. They will apply concepts of **body systems** to demonstrate understanding of **LS1.A** in support of **4-LS1-1** and **4-LS1-2**.

Materials
- paper
- writing/drawing utensils

Preparation
For this activity, students will need access to computers to perform online research. Schedule class time in the computer lab or ensure all small groups have access to the computer in the classroom.

 Systems and System Models

The focus of this project is on lung capacity. **Ask: What system of the body is responsible for lung capacity? What other systems of the body are affected by lung capacity? Explain why.**

Research
Review how to properly cite resources.
Print: title, author, copyright date, page number
Online: webpage title, URL, date visited
If students are doing their own research on the Internet, remind them how to search for reliable sources that can be trusted.

Brainstorm/Assemble Data
Have students roll a number cube to choose a recorder, highest roll records. Remind students that the brainstorming group is just to come up with ideas. Each of them will be individually responsible for coming up with an idea of how to design a portable breathing device.

344 Unit 5 Animal Structure and Function

UNIT 5 · UNIT PERFORMANCE TASK

 ENGINEER IT!
Breathing In and Out

You work for a medical company that manufactures a product for those with asthma and other breathing difficulties. The portable invention is designed to fill its user's lungs with fresh air. The company has decided to develop a version of this product for young people. Your team is tasked with gathering data on the lung capacity of fourth-grade students.

How much air can this fourth-grader's lungs force into this balloon?

DEFINE YOUR TASK: What kind of data is it your goal to uncover?

Possible answer: We are trying to find the average lung capacity of fourth-graders.
_____

Before beginning, review the checklist at the end of this Unit Performance Task. Keep those items in mind as you proceed.

RESEARCH: Use online or library resources to learn about ways of measuring human lung capacity. If necessary, divide your research into two separate areas—ways to capture air from lungs and ways to measure that air. Examine multiple sources, and cite the ones you use.

Student should cite sources as instructed.
_____
_____
_____

BRAINSTORM/ASSEMBLE DATA: As a team, come up with at least two methods of safely gathering air from human lungs. Then discuss ways of accurately measuring that air once it is gathered.

Student should list possible methods of conducting their test.
_____
_____
_____

PLAN YOUR PROCEDURE: Consider the questions below as you plan your data-gathering procedure.

1. What materials, tools, and equipment will you need?
2. How will you gather air from your test subjects' lungs?
3. How will you measure the quantity of the air you gather?
4. How many test subjects will you use?
5. How will you record, graph, and present your results?
6. Will you express your final data as a single number or as a range? Why?

Student should describe the team's procedure, list the equipment that will be needed, and how it will be used. Students should also explain how results will be recorded, processed, and reported.

_____

PERFORM AND RECORD: Get your teacher's approval. Then, perform your procedure as you planned it. Examine your data, and summarize your results.

Student should summarize the results of the procedure performed.

_____

COMMUNICATE: Tell the class about your research, your procedures, and how you arrived at the data you were looking for. Display any graphs or charts that can help you communicate your results.

✅ Checklist

Review your project and check off each completed item.

_____ Includes a description of the data being sought.

_____ Includes a list of cited sources.

_____ Includes options considered for gathering and measuring air from lungs.

_____ Includes a thorough description of the test procedure, including materials used.

_____ Includes results expressed as written or charted data.

_____ Includes an oral presentation on your procedures, results, and conclusions.

345

Plan Your Procedure

 SEP **Developing and Using Models**

Students can use models of the human body to help them visualize and understand how their devices will work to help people who have trouble breathing. **Ask: For your own model, what are the criteria? What are the constraints?**

Perform and Record

Students must wait for approval before carrying out the procedure. Consider having student partners critique each other's summaries. Use sentence frames to guide their discussions:

- I don't understand why you chose _____.
- How will the _____ interact with the _____?
- Why did you choose _____ instead of _____?
- How will _____ help someone be able to breathe better?

Scoring Rubric for Performance Task	
3	• complete resources, clear reasoning, multiple sources • complete, detailed, accurate test procedure • presentation includes accurate procedures, results, and conclusions
2	• most resources, adequate reasoning and sources • most parts present in the test procedure • presentation includes mostly accurate procedures, results, and conclusions
1	• some key resources and reasoning, a few sources • some description, mixed accuracy of test procedure • presentation inaccurate
0	• few key resources, no reasons, minimal sources • little description, inaccurate details of test procedure • presentation incomplete

Unit 5 Animal Structure and Function 345

UNIT 5 Review

SUMMATIVE ASSESSMENT

1. Students can correctly answer this question by thinking about what it means to "mimic" something. They can refer back to Lesson 1, Exploration 2 for a refresher on biomimicry.

2. To answer this question correctly, students need to understand what adaptation means. They can find information on animal adaptation in Lesson 1, Exploration 1.

3. Students should be able to apply knowledge of animal structures to concepts of adaptation. Have them review Lesson 1, Exploration 1 if they get stuck.

4. Students are asked to classify physical structures. For extra support, it may be helpful to show students pictures of animals with fur, fins, legs, wings, shells, and spines. Using realia may help students apply knowledge. They can also turn back to Exploration 1, Lesson 1 for a quick review.

UNIT 5

Unit Review

1. An inventor develops an adhesive based on the substance a gecko uses to hold itself to glass. What term best describes how a design can imitate things found in nature? Circle the correct choice.

   a. biostructures
   b. adaptations
   c. camouflage
   d. **biomimicry**

2. Which of the following qualities demonstrates how a frog's skin is adapted to its environment? Circle all that apply.

   a. **It is thin.**
   b. **It is slimy.**
   c. It is warm.
   d. **It is moist.**

3. Use the word bank to complete the sentences.

   | animals   nectar   plants |

   The flat teeth of antelope are teeth suited to eating ___plants___.

   The sharp teeth and jaws of alligators are suited to eating ___animals___.

4. Classify each structure as helpful for protection (P) or motion (M):

   __P__ Fur
   __M__ Fins
   __M__ Legs
   __M__ Wings
   __P__ Shells
   __P__ Spines

346

Unit 5 Animal Structure and Function

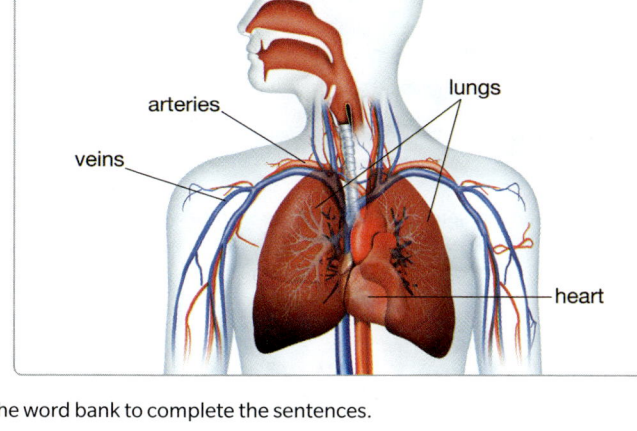

5. Use the word bank to complete the sentences.

| oxygen | circulatory | respiratory | excretory |

This drawing shows the ___respiratory___ and ___circulatory___ organ systems. These two systems work together to move ___oxygen___ and other gases through the body.

6. Why is the circulatory system considered a *system*? Explain the parts that work together and the function of those parts.

Possible answer: The circulatory system is considered a system because it has many components that interact. The heart, blood, veins, and arteries work together to move gases around the body.

7. Which of these are part of the human excretory system? Circle all that apply.
a. skin
b. lungs
c. heart
d. kidneys

---

5. Students should review the diagram to answer the question. They can refer back to Lesson 2, Exploration 1 to recall information about internal structures.

6. Students must make a connection between the various components of the body that work together to create a system. Systems are covered in Lesson 2, Explorations 1 and 2 if students need to review material to answer the question.

7. Students may need help remembering the meaning of *excretory system*. You can provide support by using images. Students can refer back to Lesson 2, Explorations 1 and 2 to recall information about systems.

UNIT 5 Review, continued

8. Students learned about sights and sounds in Lesson 3, Exploration 3. Remind students about the concept of "seeing by hearing," as was the example of the bat in Lesson 3, Exploration 3. Have them think about some of the similarities between bats and dolphins.

9. Students should make a comprehensive connection among the various senses and structures involved in managing movements. Students can turn back to Lesson 3, Explorations 1, 2, and 3 for a quick review.

10. Students should be able to answer this question by recalling personal experiences. They can also turn to Lesson 3, Exploration 1 for a review.

3D Item Analysis	1	2	3	4	5	6	7	8	9	10
SEP Developing and Using Models		•			•			•		
DCI Structures and Function	•	•	•	•	•	•	•	•	•	•
DCI Information Processing								•	•	•
CCC Cause and Effect				•	•		•	•	•	•
CCC Systems and System Models	•	•	•	•	•	•	•	•	•	•

348 Unit 5 Animal Structure and Function

8. Which sense does this animal sometimes use to "see" in murky water? Circle the correct choice.
   a. taste
   b. touch
   c. smell
   ⓓ. hearing

9. Sophia plays basketball at her elementary school. She uses her brain, eyes, and nerves to play the sport. Explain how these three parts of her body work together to manage her movements when she's trying to catch the ball.

Possible answer: Sophia's eyes will see the ball and send signals through her nerves to her brain. Her brain will interpret those images. As the ball gets closer, her eyes will continue to send messages to her brain. Her brain will send signals through her nerves to her arms and hands to catch the ball

10. Use the word bank to complete the sentence.

| touch | smell | temperature |
| sight | pain | taste |

There are three general types of receptors in human skin: _____touch_____ , _____temperature_____ , and _____pain_____ .

348

UNIT 6 Changes to Earth's Surface

UNIT 6

Changes to Earth's Surface

Unit Project: Nearby Weathering
What are some examples of weathering right near your school, and how can you affect them? You will conduct an investigation with your team. Ask your teacher for details.

Explore Online

The surface of our Earth changes constantly, in countless ways. Much of that change is gradual. Some of it, such as volcanic activity, is abrupt and violent.

349

Unit Overview

In this unit, children will . . .
- explore how Earth has been shaped by water and other factors.
- discover how people map Earth's surface.
- learn about the patterns we can see from maps.

About This Image

A volcanic eruption spurts lava and ash out of the volcano and into the atmosphere. Volcanic eruptions are factors that can shape the surface of Earth. The changes brought about by eruptions are sudden and can have many negative impacts on society and nature. In this image, the eruption seems to be isolated to an area where there are no nearby homes, but lava that runs down the volcano can destroy whatever is in its path, including wildlife, people, natural structures, and structures built by people.

Unit Project

To begin, draw students' attention to the details in the image, or challenge the class to use online or media center resources to identify other examples of volcanoes shaping Earth. Volcanoes make sudden changes to Earth's surface.

Even though many students don't live near volcanoes, they can see changes to Earth's surface right in their own neighborhoods. Tell students that volcanoes are one of many things that change Earth's surface. Many changes happen more slowly. As students work through the unit lessons, have them start to look around for examples of weathering at or near the school. More support for the Unit Project can be found on pp. 351K–351N.

UNIT 6 Changes to Earth's Surface

The learning experiences in this unit prepare children for the mastery of:

Performance Expectations

4-ESS2-1 Make observations and/or measurements to provide evidence of the effects of weathering or the rate of erosion by water, ice, wind, or vegetation.

4-ESS2-2 Analyze and interpret data from maps to describe patterns of Earth's features.

▶ Explore Online

In addition to the print resources, the following resources are available online to support this unit.

Unit Pretest

Lesson 1 How Does Water Shape Earth's Surface?
- Online Student Edition
- Lesson Quiz

Lesson 2 What Other Factors Shape Earth's Surface?
- Online Student Edition
- Lesson Quiz

Lesson 3 How Do People Map Earth's Surface?
- Online Student Edition
- Lesson Quiz

Lesson 4 What Patterns Do Maps Show Us?
- Online Student Edition
- Lesson Quiz

You Solve It Evidence of Change

Unit Performance Task

Unit Test

UNIT 6

At a Glance

LESSON 1
How Does Water Shape Earth's Surface? 352

LESSON 2
What Other Factors Shape Earth's Surface? 378

LESSON 3
How Do People Map Earth's Surface? 404

LESSON 4
What Patterns Do Maps Show Us? 428

Unit Review 448

Vocabulary Game: Guess the Word

Materials
- Kitchen timer or online computer timer

Directions
1. Take turns by choosing a word card. Do not tell others the word. Set the timer for one minute.
2. Point to another player, Give them a one-word clue to use to guess the word.
3. Repeat step 2 until the word is guessed or time runs out. Give a different clue each time.
4. One point is earned for guessing the word and 1 more point if they use the word in a sentence. That player gets the next turn choosing a word.
5. The first player to score 5 points wins.

desert An area of land that is very dry.

ocean trench A deep valley in the ocean floor.

Unit Vocabulary

 **continent:** One of the seven largest land areas on Earth.

 **ocean trench:** A deep valley in the ocean floor.

 **deposition:** The dropping or settling of eroded materials.

 **rain forest:** A dense forest found in regions with high heat and heavy rainfall.

 **desert:** An area of land that is very dry.

 **scale:** The part of a map that compares a distance on the map to a distance in the real world.

 **elevation:** The height of the land above sea level.

 **weathering:** The breaking down of rocks on Earth's surface into smaller pieces.

 **erosion:** The process of moving sediment from one place to another.

Unit Vocabulary

Students can explore all lesson vocabulary terms in the **Online Glossary**.

Vocabulary Strategies

Have students review the terms individually and come up with an example for each term. Then pair up and share an example of one term with their partner and tell why they think it's an example. Have each pair write down their examples to check during the unit.

Differentiate Instruction

RTI/Extra Support Have struggling readers find the vocabulary words within the unit. Have students use context clues to infer definitions and then share with a partner.

Extension Have students pick two terms and then work in small groups to illustrate and explain the terms for a third-grade student.

ELL Pronounce each term and have students repeat it. Then pair up students by native language and have them explain each term in their native language. Use realia wherever appropriate.

Vocabulary Game: Guess the Word

Preparation
Use a timer on your smartphone or tablet, if that is more convenient than a kitchen timer or online computer timer.

Game Play
- Students choose a word card and give clues about their word for other players to guess.

UNIT 6 Changes to Earth's Surface

Integrating the NGSS* Three Dimensions of Learning

Building to the Performance Expectations

The learning experiences in this unit prepare students for mastery of the following Performance Expectations:

Earth's Systems

4-ESS2-1 Make observations and/or measurements to provide evidence of the effects of weathering or the rate of erosion by water, ice, wind, or vegetation.

4-ESS2-2 Analyze and interpret data from maps to describe patterns of Earth's features

Assessing Student Progress

After completing these lessons, the **Unit Project: Nearby Weathering** provides students with opportunities to practice aspects of and demonstrate their understanding of the Performance Expectation as they investigate local examples of weathering.

Additionally, students can practice or be assessed on aspects of the Performance Expectations by completing the **Unit Performance Task: Model It, Map It**, in which they build and use a model to show how wind and water affect land.

Lesson 1
How Does Water Shape Earth's Surface?

In Lesson 1, students will identify and record evidence **(SEP Planning and Carrying Out Investigations)** of how water, weathering, erosion, and deposition shape Earth's surface **(DCI Earth Materials and Systems)**. Students will investigate how water impacts Earth and then examine the relationships between Earth's surface and the physical forces of weathering, erosion, and deposition **(CCC Cause and Effect)**.

Lesson 2
How Do Other Factors Shape Earth's Surface?

In Lesson 2, students will identify, explain, and record evidence **(SEP Planning and Carrying Out Investigations)** regarding how rainfall, weathering, erosion, and deposition **(DCI Earth Materials and Systems)** shape Earth's surface. Students will investigate how living things impact Earth and then examine and explain the relationships between them all **(CCC Cause and Effect)**.

Lesson 3
How Do People Map Earth's Surface?

In Lesson 3, students will **make observations and analyze data** about maps. Students will understand that maps can help locate the different land and water features of Earth (and reveal how **large-scale systems interact)**, as shown in the **patterns** of mountain ranges, ocean trenches, and other natural phenomena.

Lesson 4
What Patterns Do Maps Show Us?

In Lesson 4, Students will analyze and interpret data **(SEP Analyzing and Interpreting Data)** about the locations of mountain ranges, deep ocean trenches, ocean floor structures, earthquakes, and volcanoes **(DCI ESS2.B)** and use maps to identify the patterns **(CCC Patterns)** of the locations in which they appear on land and in the oceans.

*Next Generation Science Standards and logo are registered trademarks of Achieve. Neither Achieve or the lead states and partners that developed the Next Generation Science Standards Were involved in production of, and does not endorse, these products.

NGSS Across the Unit

Explore Online!
Online only.

Next Generation Science Standards	Unit Project	Lesson 1	Lesson 2	Lesson 3	Lesson 4	Unit Performance Task	You Solve It!
SEP Analyzing and Interpreting Data		•		•			•
SEP Asking Questions and Defining Problems	•			•			•
SEP Planning and Carrying Out Investigations	•		•		•	•	•
DCI ESS2.B Plate Tectonics and Large-Scale System Interactions				•			
DCI ESS2.A Earth Materials and Systems	•	•	•		•	•	•
DCI ESS2.E Biogeology			•				
CCC Patterns				•			
CCC Cause and Effect	•	•	•		•	•	•

NGSS Across the Grades

Before
Earth's Systems
3-ESS2-1
3-ESS2-2

Grade 4
Earth's Systems
4-ESS2-1
4-ESS2-2

After
Earth's Systems
MS-ESS2-2 Construct an explanation based on evidence for how geoscience processes have changed Earth's surface at varying time and spatial scales.

Trace Tool to the NGSS™ Go online to view the complete coverage of these standards across this grade level and time.

Unit 6 Changes to Earth's Surface 351B

UNIT 6 Changes to Earth's Surface
3D Unit Planning

Lesson 1 How Does Water Shape Earth's Surface? pp. 352–377

Overview

Objective To identify, explain, and record evidence about how water shapes Earth's surface and describe ways in which water causes weathering, erosion, and deposition to take place. They will also identify how the speed and volume of water affect these processes.

SEP Planning and Carrying Out Investigations
DCI ESS2.A Earth Materials and Systems
CCC Cause and Effect

Math and **English Language Arts** standards and features are detailed on lesson planner pages.

Print and Online Student Editions ▶ **Explore Online!**

ENGAGE
Lesson Phenomenon pp. 352–353
Can You Explain/Solve It? How did this cave form?
▶ Can You Explain It? Video

EXPLORE/ EXPLAIN
Making a Move pp. 354–357
Watery Trails
HANDS-ON Worksheet

 Apply What You Know Water Effects
Away It Goes! pp. 358–361
Vanishing Cottages
Cold Stuff! pp. 362–368
Water, Ice, and Water
 Apply What You Know Watching Water Grow
 HANDS-ON The Rate of Change
What About Us? pp. 369–372
At the Ranch
ENGINEER IT! Fighting Potholes

ELABORATE
Take It Further pp. 373–374
People in Science & Engineering: Anjali Fernandes
Take It Further Deposition Rate
Take It Further The Last Ice Age

EVALUATE
Lesson Check pp. 375–376
Lesson Roundup p. 377
Lesson Quiz

✋ HANDS-ON ACTIVITY PLANNING

Apply What You Know

Water Effects
⏱ 10 minutes
👥 Individuals

Materials
- images of flood damage

Preparation/Tip Prepare the images of flood damage ahead of time. Provide an assortment of different types of flood damage.

Watching Water Grow
⏱ 1 class period
👥 Individuals

Materials
- clear plastic cup
- water
- permanent marker
- freezer

Preparation/Tip Make sure to let someone at the school know that you will need to use a freezer for this activity.

HANDS-ON

The Rate of Change
⏱ 1 class period
👥 Partners

Objective Students will plan and conduct an investigation to model and observe the effect of slope on the erosion of Earth's surface.

Materials
- paper cup
- sharpened pencil
- plastic drinking straw
- scissors
- small piece of modeling clay
- piece of cardboard 31 cm square
- soil
- ruler
- large bottle filled with water (approx. 2 liters)

Preparation/Tip You might want to conduct the activity outside or in another area of the classroom, as students will be working with soil and water.

Lesson 2 How Do Other Factors Shape Earth's Surface? pp. 378–403

Overview

Objective To identify, explain, and record evidence about factors that shape Earth's surface, such as rainfall, organisms, weathering, erosion, and deposition.

SEP Planning and Carrying Out Investigations
DCI ESS2.A Earth Materials and Systems
DCI ESS2.E Biogeology
CCC Cause and Effect

Math and **English Language Arts** standards and features are detailed on lesson planner pages.

	Print and Online *Student Editions*	Explore Online!
ENGAGE	**Lesson Phenomenon** pp. 378–379 Can You Explain/Solve It? What are some natural processes that take place on Earth's surface?	Can You Explain It? Video
EXPLORE/ EXPLAIN	**Organisms and Environments** pp. 380–385 Water World Apply What You Know Dry Plants **Environments Change** pp. 386–394 Blast Off! ENGINEER IT! Blast It Off Apply What You Know A Slower Process HANDS-ON Finding Change **Always Changing** pp. 395–398 Evidence of Change	HANDS-ON Worksheet
ELABORATE	**Take It Further** pp. 399–400 Seeking Stability: No Disruptions ENGINEER IT! Slowing Change	Take It Further Extremes! Take It Further The Science of Slopes
EVALUATE	**Lesson Check** pp. 401–402 **Lesson Roundup** p. 403	Lesson Quiz

HANDS-ON ACTIVITY PLANNING

Apply What You Know

Dry Plants	Materials
⏱ 20 minutes 👥 Individuals	• pictures of saguaro cactus, or live baby cactus

Preparation/Tip If you bring in a live cactus, use caution with students. The needles are sharp!

A Slower Process	Materials
⏱ 10 minutes 👥 Pairs	• object, such as a piece of metal or wood • sandpaper • safety goggles • cloth or disposable dust masks • stopwatch or timer

Preparation/Tip Review safety precautions with students before they start sanding the object.

HANDS-ON

Finding Change	Materials
⏱ 1 class period 👥 Pairs **Objective** Students plan and conduct investigations to model and observe changes that occur on Earth's surface.	• 4 cookie sheets with raised edge • sand • fan • ice cubes • modeling clay • wooden stirring sticks • beaker or small jug of water • ruler

Preparation/Tip Assemble student stations in advance. Keep the ice cool so that it does not melt.

Unit 6 Changes to Earth's Surface 351D

UNIT 6 Changes to Earth's Surface
3D Unit Planning, continued

Lesson 3 How Do People Map Earth's Surface? pp. 404–427

Overview

Objective To interpret map contents that illustrate topographical features and use maps as sources of data about Earth's features.

SEP Analyzing and Interpreting Data
SEP Asking Questions and Defining Problems
DCI ESS2.B Plate Tectonics and Large-Scale System Interactions
CCC Patterns

Math and **English Language Arts** standards and features are detailed on lesson planner pages.

Print and Online Student Editions   ▶ **Explore Online!**

ENGAGE
Lesson Phenomenon pp. 404–405
Can You Explain/Solve It? What would you be able to see from certain vantage points, using a topographical map?
▶ Can You Explain It? Photo

EXPLORE/ EXPLAIN
What Is a Map? pp. 406–409
A History of Maps

How Do You Read a Map? pp. 410–414
Find Your Way
 Apply what you know Make a Map
What Can Maps Show Us? pp. 415–421
It's On the Map
 HANDS-ON Park Designer

HANDS-ON Worksheet

ELABORATE
Take It Further pp. 422–424
Careers in Science and Engineering: City Planner

Take It Further
Search Party
Take It Further
Build a Map

EVALUATE
Lesson Check pp. 425–426
Lesson Roundup p. 427

Lesson Quiz

HANDS-ON ACTIVITY PLANNING

Apply What You Know

Make a Map
⏱ 20 minutes
👥 Individuals

Materials
- drawing paper
- drawing utensils (crayons, colored markers, colored pencils)

Preparation/Tip Prompt students to be sure they include key features, such as exits, water fountains, etc.

HANDS-ON

Park Designer
⏱ 1 class period
👥 Pairs

Objective Students will design a park using what they have learned about maps, following specific criteria and constraints.

Materials
- printed park site map
- printed park material cutouts
- ruler
- glue
- scissors
- notebook

Preparation/Tip Review elements of a park so students are aware of what to plan and include.

351E Unit 6 Changes to Earth's Surface

Lesson 4 What Patterns Do Maps Show Us? pp. 428–447

Overview

Objective To identify and explain where on Earth's surface earthquakes, volcanoes, mountains, and ocean trenches can be found. They will also use maps to describe the patterns they observe in the locations of those land and water forms.

SEP Analyzing and Interpreting Data
DCI **ESS2.B** Plate Tectonics and Large-Scale System Interactions
CCC Patterns
Math and **English Language Arts** standards and features are detailed on lesson planner pages.

Print and Online Student Editions   ▶ Explore Online!

ENGAGE	**Lesson Phenomenon** pp. 428–429 Can You Explain/Solve It? How do the land and water change as the rift changes?	▶ Can You Explain It? Photo
EXPLORE/ EXPLAIN	**By Land or Sea** pp. 430–433 Ring of Fire ✋ Apply What You Know Earthquakes and Buildings ✋ Engineer It! Mapping the Ocean Floor **Can Maps Help Us See Patterns?** pp. 434–442 Finding Patterns on Land ✋ Apply What You Know Modeling Features of the Ocean Floor ✋ HANDS-ON Tracking Quakes	HANDS-ON Worksheet
ELABORATE	**Take It Further** pp. 443–444 People in Science & Engineering: Lewis and Clark ✋ Apply What You Know Making Mountains!	Take It Further Volcano Formation Take It Further Volcanic Islands
EVALUATE	**Lesson Check** pp. 445–446 **Lesson Roundup** p. 447	Lesson Quiz

✋ HANDS-ON ACTIVITY PLANNING

Apply What You Know

Earthquakes and Buildings ⏱ 20 minutes 👥 Small groups	**Materials** • toothpicks • modeling clay • 2 desks or tables • stopwatch • drawing paper • drawing utensils
Modeling Features of the Ocean Floor ⏱ 20 minutes 👥 Small groups	**Materials** • modeling clay • base (cardboard or plastic) • toothpicks • tape • scrap pieces of paper
Making Mountains ⏱ 20 minutes 👥 Pairs	**Materials** • paper plate • shaving cream • 2 small pieces of corrugated cardboard • bowl of water

HANDS-ON

Tracking Quakes ⏱ 1 class period 👥 Pairs **Objective** Students will analyze and interpret current data on earthquakes to identify patterns.	**Materials** • world map with country boundaries • data on earthquakes • data table • pencil

Preparation/Tip Build prior knowledge about earthquakes with students.

Unit 6 Changes to Earth's Surface   **351F**

UNIT 6 Changes to Earth's Surface
3D Unit Planning, continued

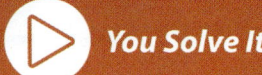 **You Solve It!** Go online for an additional interactive activity.

Evidence of Change

This virtual lab offers practice in support of **PE 4-ESS2-1**.

SEP Planning and Carrying Out Investigations
DCI 4-ESS2.A Earth Materials and Systems
CCC Cause and Effect

Use after Unit 6, Lesson 4—How does Earth's surface change over time?

Objectives
1. Students will determine the forces that cause changes to Earth's surface.
2. Students will describe cause-and-effect relationships between erosion and the change of the land.

Activity Problem
You will observe a certain scene of Earth's surface. Your tasks will include:
1. choosing a type of change
2. watching a video of the chosen change
3. comparing different changes to Earth's surface

Interaction Summary
1. Students select a type of change to Earth's surface.
2. Then they watch the animation of the chosen change.
3. Compare and contrast the before and after of the change.
4. Continue to repeat the process by choosing different changes and observing how they change Earth's surface.

Assessment

Pre-Assessment
Assessment Guide, Unit Pretest

The Unit Pretest focuses on prerequisite knowledge and is composed of items that evaluate students' preparedness for the content covered within this unit.

Formative Assessment
Student Edition, Apply What You Know, Lesson Check, and Self Check

Summative Assessment
Assessment Guide, Lesson Quiz
The Lesson Quiz provides a quick assessment of each lesson objective and of the portion of the Performance Expectation aligned to the lesson.

Student Edition, Performance Task pp. 448–449
The Performance Task presents the opportunity for children to collaborate with classmates in order to complete the steps of each Performance Task. Each Performance Task provides a formal Scoring Rubric for evaluating students' work.

Student Edition, Unit 6 Review pp. 450–452

Assessment Guide, Unit Test
The Unit Test provides an in-depth assessment of the Performance Expectations aligned to the unit. This test evaluates students' ability to apply knowledge in order to explain phenomena and to solve problems. Within this test, constructed response items apply a three-dimensional rubric for evaluating students' mastery on all three dimensions of the Next Generation Science Standards.

 **Assessment Online** Go online to view the complete assessment items for this unit.

Teacher Notes

UNIT 6 Changes to Earth's Surface
Differentiated Instruction

Leveled Readers

The **Science & Engineering Leveled Readers** provide additional nonfiction reading practice in this unit's subject area.

On-Level Reader • Earth's Changing Surface and Natural Resources
This reader reinforces unit concepts and includes response activities for your students.

Extra Support • Earth's Changing Surface and Natural Resources
This reader shares title, illustrations, vocabulary, and concepts with the On-Level Reader; however, the text is linguistically accommodated to provide simplified sentence structures and comprehension aids. It also includes response activities.

Enrichment • Conserving Earth's Resources
This high-interest nonfiction reader will extend and enrich unit concepts and vocabulary and includes response activities.

Teacher Guide

The accompanying Teacher Guide provides teaching strategies and support for using all the readers.

ELL

ELL teacher strategies in this unit:

Lesson 1: pp. 356, 360, 370
Lesson 2: pp. 382, 391, 393
Lesson 3: pp. 408, 410, 417, 423
Lesson 4: pp. 432, 437

RTI/Extra Support

Strategies for students needing extra support in this unit:

Lesson 1: pp. 358, 359, 365, 376
Lesson 2: pp. 380, 389, 398, 400
Lesson 3: pp. 406, 411, 413
Lesson 4: pp. 430, 434, 436

Extension

Strategies for students who have mastered core content in this unit:

Lesson 1: pp. 355, 375
Lesson 2: pp. 384, 386, 395
Lesson 3: pp. 408, 417, 423
Lesson 4: pp. 438, 441, 444

 **Leveled Readers** All readers are available online as well as in an innovative, engaging format for use with touchscreen mobile devices. Contact your HMH Sales Representative for more information.

UNIT 6 Changes to Earth's Surface
Making Connections

Connections to the Community

Use these opportunities for informal science learning to provide local context and to extend and enhance unit concepts.

At Home

DRAW A MAP Have students work with a responsible adult to look at an online map of the area near your home to observe the shape of nearby rivers. The area could include just a city, or it might include a section of a state. Have students draw a map of their own showing the rivers with labels for features as floodplains, deltas, and meanders. *Use with Lesson 1.*

LOOKING FOR CHANGES After students read about various factors that can change Earth's surface, have them walk around the area surrounding their home and list examples of ways the land has been changed. For each change they notice, have them list the factor they think caused the change and describe how their observations support their assumption. *Use with Lesson 2.*

In the Community

NEIGHBORHOOD MAP Have students work with a responsible adult to make a map of their neighborhood. Instruct students to include a compass rose on their map and to use a reasonable scale for the distances. Students should label locations that are important to them, such as their home, a friend's home, a local grocery store, and the school. *Use with Lesson 3.*

NEARBY QUAKES Arrange for a local geologist to give a presentation to the class about the closest areas where earthquakes have occurred. Suggest that the presentation include a discussion about why the nearby area is or is not prone to earthquakes. *Use with Lesson 4.*

 **Home Letters** Use these one-page letters to engage family members with unit concepts.

Collaboration

Opportunities for students to work collaboratively in this unit:

Build on Prior Knowledge
pp. 364, 366, 370, 382, 389, 407, 430, 440

Discussion
pp. 401, 425, 445

Draw, Pair, Share
pp. 375, 409

Feedback
p. 355

Share Feedback
p. 396

Think, Pair, Share
pp. 353, 362, 379, 388, 405, 407, 429, 437

Connections to Science

Opportunities to connect to other content areas in this unit:

Connection to Engineering and Design
Lesson 3, p. 417

Connection to Physical Science
Lesson 2, p. 385
Lesson 4, p. 433

Connection to Life Science
Lesson 1, pp. 354, 371
Lesson 2, pp. 381, 397
Lesson 3, pp. 416, 424

UNIT 6 Changes to Earth's Surface
Unit Project

Unit Project: Nearby Weathering 👥 Small groups ⏱ 2 class periods

For this task, each student will examine the outside of the school and school grounds for signs of weathering. You may wish to lead students around the school property as a group for safety purposes, though each student should come up with his or her own plan for dealing with the weathering he or she sees. Have students carry paper and writing utensils with them to record any weathering they see. They may use a disposable camera if they wish to record photographic evidence of the weathering.

3D Learning Objective

- Identify the differences between weathering and erosion
- Understand how weathering can affect property
- Design solutions to lessen, end, or reverse the effects of weathering

Skills and Standards Focus

This project supports building student mastery of **Performance Expectation 4-ESS2-1, 4-ESS2-2**

- **SEP** Analyzing and Interpreting Data
- **SEP** Asking Questions and Defining Problems
- **DCI** ESS2.A: Earth Materials and Systems
- **CCC** Cause and Effect

Suggested Materials

- Drawing paper
- Drawing utensils
- References—print (books, magazines), electronic (websites)
- Disposable camera (optional)

Preparing and Planning Tips

Ensure that each group has a set of print resources or list of URLs for websites you have previously reviewed. Also, as you lead students around the school grounds, be sure they have paper and utensils with them to record examples of the weathering they see. Explain the difference between weathering and erosion: weathering is the breaking down of material; erosion is the carrying of material from one place to another.

Differentiate Instruction

RTI/Extra Support Provide students with a list of the types of weathering that can occur, such as water and root damage, wind damage, freezing-thawing, and so on. Ask students to search for damage from each type of weathering on the school property and record it. Encourage them to ask questions as they search, and guide them toward the answers.

Extension Before taking students on a tour of the school grounds, have each one make a list of the different kinds of weathering. Ask them to write the definition of each type next to it. This will prepare them for what they will look for on the tour.

Name _____

UNIT PROJECT
Nearby Weathering

Have you ever left something out in the rain or sunshine for a long time and noticed that it changed how that object looked? For this project, you will investigate forms of weathering that happen at or near your school and decide what you can do to help prevent more weathering in the future.

Think about the last time you saw something that was weathered. What were the forces of weathering that you identified? Write a question that you will investigate as you perform your analysis of nearby weathering.

Students should write a question concerning which forces are causing

the weathering and how to prevent those factors.

_____

Materials

Think about how you will need to perform this investigation. What materials will you need?

Materials can include drawing paper, drawing utensils, and references

(print or electronic).

Optional: disposable camera

To carry out this investigation, go around your school with your team and teacher to locate evidence of weathering. Take pictures of, or draw, your observations. What kinds of things will you be looking for?

Overgrown roots

Water damage

Wind damage

Ice damage

Gravity

351

UNIT 6 PROJECT
Nearby Weathering

DCI ESS2.A Earth Materials and Systems

Before students begin the task, check their understanding of key concepts.

Ask: What is weathering? *the process by which the weather causes materials to break down*

Refer students to Lesson 1, Exploration 1 and Lesson 2, Explorations 1, 2, and 3 for concept support.

ESSENTIAL QUESTIONS Ask the following questions before students begin to plan their activity.

- How is weathering different from erosion?
- What are some effects of erosion?
- How can the effects of erosion be prevented, stopped, or reversed?

Provide students with a list of websites you have approved that will help them understand how each type of weathering can be prevented or reversed.

CCC Causes and Effects

Remind students that a cause is something that makes something else happen. An effect is what happens as a result. In weathering, wind, rain, ice, and plant roots are all causes. The damage that results is the effect. As students search the school grounds for examples of weathering, have them identify causes and effects.

Ask: Name one cause and one effect you have seen. *Possible answers: Water freezing and thawing in wintertime has caused the school's parking lot to develop potholes. Plant roots have damaged the hiking path next to the school.*

Research and Plan

Students should carefully consider each form of weathering they saw around the school and school grounds.

Ask: If you saw more than one type of weathering, which type will you develop a plan to prevent and reverse? **Possible answer: I will develop a plan to prevent and reverse damage from roots.**

Direct Observation

After students have taken a tour of the school grounds and made their lists, they will select one type of weathering from the list and research it online or in books. When they are finished, they will take what they have learned and develop a plan to combat the weathering.

Ask: How will you prevent or reverse the effects of the weathering you saw? **Possible answer: Remove the trees and cut out their roots to prevent future damage to pipes or trails.**

Brainstorming

Students may struggle to come up with a way to prevent or reverse the effects of the weathering they chose. Remind them to consult their research, which should contain a solution. Then have them brainstorm and write out a brief plan or design a model to carry out that solution. Once they are done, have them present their plans to the class. Invite the principal or superintendent to attend the class session to hear the solutions.

Research and Plan

Make a plan for how you will carry out this investigation and how you will be able to make changes so that weathering is reduced. As you make your plan, consider the following:

- What force(s) could have caused the weathering
- Whether that force(s) can be prevented
- How further weathering can be avoided
- How you will make a plan to affect weathering

Students should list the force or forces responsible for the type of weathering they identified at or around the school. They should indicate whether that force can be prevented. If it can, how? If the force cannot be prevented, then how can further weathering be avoided? They should then describe the overall plan for affecting weathering.

Develop your plan, and share your ideas with your team. As a group, vote on the plan that your group wants to present to the rest of the class. It's possible that you might want to take parts of different plans to make one master plan. Think about ways to improve your plan by looking for opportunities where your plan might not work. Can your plan be improved?

Possible response: Our plan can be improved by adding more to the section about removing the trees with the overgrown roots.

Analyze Your Results

Look for evidence of cause and effect in the data you found. Using your investigation, make a conclusive observation about weathering at or near your school.

Possible response: The school's main risk for weathering is overgrown roots from giant, old trees.

Restate Your Question

Write the question you investigated.

Students should identify the question created at the beginning of the project.

Claims, Evidence, and Reasoning

Make a claim that answers your question.

Possible answers: The trees should be removed so that their roots cannot do further damage. To prevent this in the future, giant trees should not be planted at the school. Instead, smaller trees, shrubs, or bushes can be planted.

Review your investigation. What evidence from your investigation supports your claim? Students should cite evidence from their investigation to support their claims. For example: The overgrown roots caused the ground to break open by the back fence.

Discuss your reasoning with a partner.

351

Analyze Your Results

Asking Questions and Solving Problems

Students should consider the following questions as they interpret their research data: What is the best way to prevent this type of weathering? What is the best way to fix damage already caused by this type of weathering?

Analyzing and Interpreting Data

Review with students what it means to make a claim. Guide them to understand that they will use their research to support their claims.

Claims, Evidence, and Reasoning

Students' claims should offer a helpful suggestion about how to prevent and/or fix damage from one type of weathering.

Ask: What claim can you make? Possible claim: Trees should be removed so that their roots cannot do further damage. To prevent this in the future, giant trees should not be planted. Instead, smaller trees, shrubs, or bushes can be planted.

Ask: How does your evidence support your claim? Students should cite evidence from their investigation.

Encourage students to discuss their reasoning.

Scoring Rubric for Hands-On Activity	
3	States a claim about how to fix and/or prevent damage from a certain type of weathering supported with ample, detailed evidence.
2	States a claim about how to fix and/or prevent damage from a certain type of weathering that is somewhat supported with evidence.
1	States a claim that is not supported by evidence.
0	Does not state a claim.

LESSON 1
How Does Water Shape Earth's Surface?

Building to the Performance Expectation

The learning experiences in this lesson prepare students for mastery of:

4-ESS2-1 Make observations and/or measurements to provide evidence of the effects of weathering or the rate of erosion by water, ice, wind, or vegetation.

Trace Tool to the NGSS
Go online to view the complete coverage of these standards across this lesson, unit, and time.

 Science & Engineering Practices

 Disciplinary Core Ideas

 Crosscutting Concepts

Planning and Carrying Out Investigations
Make observations and/or measurements to produce data to serve as the basis for evidence for an explanation of a phenomenon.

 VIDEO: Planning and Carrying Out Investigations

ESS2.A Earth Materials and Systems
Rainfall helps to shape the land and affects the types of living things found in a region. Water, ice, wind, living organisms, and gravity break rocks, soils, and sediments into smaller particles and move them around.

Cause and Effect
Cause-and-effect relationships are routinely identified, tested, and used to explain change.

 CONNECTIONS TO MATH

MP.2 Reason abstractly and quantitatively.
MP.4 Model with mathematics.
MP.5 Use appropriate tools strategically.
4.MD.A.1 Know relative sizes of measurement units within one system of units including km, m, cm; kg, g; lb, oz.; l, ml; hr, min, sec. Within a single system of measurement, express measurements in a larger unit in terms of a smaller unit. Record measurement equivalents in a two-column table.
4.MD.A.2 Use the four operations to solve word problems involving distances, intervals of time, liquid volumes, masses of objects, and money, including problems involving simple fractions or decimals, and problems that require expressing measurements given in a larger unit in terms of a smaller unit. Represent measurement quantities using diagrams such as number line diagrams that feature a measurement scale.

 CONNECTIONS TO ENGLISH LANGUAGE ARTS

W.4.8 Recall relevant information from experiences or gather relevant information from print and digital sources; take notes and categorize information, and provide a list of sources.

Supporting All Students, All Standards

Integrating the Three Dimensions of Learning

Students will identify, explain, and record evidence **(SEP Planning and Carrying Out Investigations)** of how water, weathering, erosion, and deposition shape Earth's surface **(DCI ESS2.A)**. Students will investigate how rivers, glaciers, ocean waves, and freezing and thawing impact the physical characteristics of Earth **(DCI ESS2.A)** and then examine and explain the relationships between Earth's surface and the physical forces of weathering, erosion, and deposition **(CCC Cause and Effect)**. By investigating a variety of specific phenomena that shape Earth's surface, students will develop an understanding of Earth's natural processes, thereby enabling them to apply their understandings to other patterns of change on Earth. Additionally, students will ask and answer questions, carry out investigations, and make connections to math, life science, and English language arts.

 **Professional Development** Go online to view **Professional Development videos** with strategies to integrate CCCs and SEPs, including the ones used in this lesson.

Extra Hands-On Activity: Where Has Water Been?

How Does Water Shape Earth's Surface

 Small groups
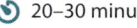 20–30 minutes

As a class, brainstorm what water does when it falls and flows on the ground. If possible, go outside your school and have students make careful observations of everyday examples of the changing nature of Earth's surface. Have them look for cracked or crumbling sidewalks, or places where bits of soil have been washed away from a garden bed. Have them look in dry places for evidence of where water has been. Suggest students take notes or make drawing of the evidence they find.

 This activity can support mastery of this Crosscutting Concept: Cause and Effect

Preassessment

Have students complete the unit pre-test online or see the Assessment Guide.

Build on Prior Knowledge

Students should already know and be prepared to build on the following concepts:
- Wind and water change the shape of the land.
- Water is found in many types of places and in different forms on Earth.
- Some events on Earth can occur very quickly; others can occur very slowly.

Differentiate Instruction

Lesson Vocabulary
- weathering
- erosion
- deposition

Before students begin the lesson, have them look up the vocabulary words in the dictionary and write down the definitions for **weathering**, **erosion**, and **deposition.**

Ask: Which term best describes the following events?
- a mudslide flowing down a steep hill **erosion**
- waves dropping sand on the beach **deposition**
- water getting into cracks, freezing, and breaking the rocks apart **weathering**

RTI/Extra Support Strategy
If students are having difficulty remembering the vocabulary words and definitions, have them use the acronym *WED*. **W**eathering: breaks it (down), **E**rosion: takes it (away), **D**eposition: drops it.

LESSON 1 **Engage** • Explore/Explain • Elaborate • Evaluate

ENGAGE: Lesson Phenomenon

Lesson Objective

Identify, explain, and record evidence about how water shapes Earth's surface, and describe ways in which water causes weathering, erosion, and deposition to take place; identify how the speed and volume of water affect these processes.

About This Image

The Grand Canyon is located in the northwest corner of Arizona. It is 277 miles long and up to 18 miles wide. It was formed by the Colorado River, which flows west through the canyon and averages 300 feet wide. It flows at an average speed of 4 miles per hour. The canyon's distinctive shape is due to how different rock layers in the canyon walls erode: some form slopes, and some form cliffs. The dramatic colors of rock layers along the canyon walls are due to small amounts of different minerals (mostly iron), which give them subtle shades of red, yellow, and green.

 SEP **Planning and Carrying Out Investigations**

Alternative Engage Strategy

Taking a Trip	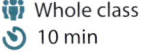 Whole class 10 min

Ask students to suppose they could take a trip to any place that was formed by water. Would they want to paddle in a canoe? Build sand castles? Look for seashells along the shoreline? Then have students write a brief description of where they would go, evidence that water formed that place, and a description of activities they would like to do once there. Call on volunteers to share their responses.

LESSON 1

How Does Water Shape Earth's Surface?

People from around the world come to visit the Grand Canyon. Look at the photo above. What are some features of the landscape that you notice?

By the end of this lesson . . .
you'll be able to explain how Earth processes shape the land.

352

352   Unit 6   Changes to Earth's Surface

 **Explore Online** Students can view the lesson phenomenon online.

Can You Explain It?

Students are asked to record their initial thoughts about how the different rock layers they see were formed. To do so, students must begin to think about how Earth's materials, such as sand and rock, are worn away from Earth's surface by water and wind. The river once flowed at the top layer, but now flows where we see it today. Encourage students to record the first thoughts that come into their minds. Point out that their ideas might change as they work through the Explorations and Hands-On Activities. Explain that they will have another opportunity to answer the same questions at the end of the lesson.

Cause and Effect

As students work to explain how the canyon formed, point out that natural cause-and-effect processes are constantly changing Earth's surface. Some happen slowly, and some happen very quickly.

Can You Explain It?

A river flows through the bottom of this canyon. Think about how the canyon may have formed. Imagine walking through the bottom of the canyon, near the river. What would you see and hear?

1. How do you think this canyon formed? What could have reshaped the rock?

Students should respond based on the preliminary observations they can make of the images. All reasonable answers should be accepted.

_____
_____
_____
_____

➡ **EVIDENCE NOTEBOOK** Look for this icon to help you gather evidence to answer the questions above.

Collaboration

Think, Pair, Share Show students photographs of other geologic landforms shaped by water, such as Badlands National Park, ND; Niagara Falls, NY; and Antelope Canyon, AZ. Pair students, and have them discuss how water is a sculptor of the land. Circulate to gauge students' prior knowledge about the ways in which flowing water has an effect on the landforms of Earth's surface. Call on students to share a one-sentence summary of the impact of water over time. Use this to gauge students' knowledge of the topic and to identify possible misconceptions they may have.

EVIDENCE NOTEBOOK

Encourage students to use an appropriate graphic organizer, such as Main Idea and Supporting Details, to set up their notebook.

Find more strategies in the online ELA handbook.

Lesson 1 How Does Water Shape Earth's Surface?

LESSON 1   Engage • **Explore/Explain** • Elaborate • Evaluate

EXPLORATION 1 Making a Move

3D Learning Objective

Investigate cause-and-effect relationships between water and the processes of weathering, erosion, and deposition that affect **the physical characteristics of Earth's surface**.

DCI ESS2.A Earth Materials and Systems

The text and images on these pages are about changes that take place in a river as it flows from its source to its mouth. Take time to guide students step-by-step through a river's journey.

Ask: How is a river like a sculptor? **Sample answer: A river carves out valleys and shapes Earth's surface like a sculptor carves out rock or clay and shapes that material into different forms.**
Ask: How would you describe the path of a river to the ocean? **Sample answer: In high areas, rivers flow through valleys and are somewhat straight. As land flattens, rivers widen and bend.**

CCC Cause and Effect

Emphasize the cause-and-effect relationship between elevation and the flow of a stream.

Ask: Why does a river often flow faster at its beginning? **The land is steep.**
Ask: Why might a river get wider farther downstream? **Other streams join it, bringing more water and sediment.**
Ask: Why do you think the banks of the river look this way in Step 3? **Fast-flowing water eroded the banks and deposited sediment.**
Ask: Do you think every delta looks the same? **No; every major river has these characteristics, but each river is different depending on the shape of the land.**

EXPLORATION 1

Making a Move

Watery Trails

A river is a stream of water that flows within a channel. A river starts at its source and ends at its mouth. In between these points, the width, volume, and flow of the river changes. These changes happen over time.

Hills and mountains are the source for many rivers. The riverbed has a steep slope, and its valley is narrow. As a result, the river flows downhill fast. The flowing river picks up small rocks and soil known as *sediment*. Other rivers may join the original river, making it wider. As a river nears its mouth, it slows down and drops sediment. A large area of flat land known as a *delta* may form here.

Step 1: The images on these pages show one way that a river can change through various processes.

Step 2: As it flows downstream, the river is forming curves and bends as sediment is picked up in one place and dropped in another. The dark areas show where sediment is being picked up. The lighter areas are where it is being dropped. These processes are changing the course of the river.

Step 3: Moving water continues to shape the river. It has nearly formed a loop. Look back at how the river began. Notice how much these processes have changed the river!

Step 4: Over time, this river has changed its course. Part of the old course has been cut off. The water left in the old path forms a lake known as an oxbow lake. Over time, it may dry up.

2. Choose the best word or phrase to complete each sentence.

| steep | flat | wider | narrower | banks |
| mouths | curves | meander | floodplain | deltas |

The slope of a river is often ____steep____ near its source. The river gets ____wider____ as other rivers and streams enter it. Rivers sometimes form ____curves____ as they flow through these flat areas. Rivers slow down near their mouths, dropping sediment to form ____deltas____.

EVIDENCE NOTEBOOK You've learned about some changes caused by rivers. In your Evidence Notebook, explain how this information might relate to the canyon you saw at the beginning of the lesson.

Connection to Life Science

Point out that rivers provide habitat to many organisms ranging from insects to plants to fish and mammals. Rivers and streams are often where species of plants and trees serve as homes to ducks, beavers, otters, and other creatures that build shelters along their shorelines.

LS4.D Biodiversity and Humans

Differentiate Instruction

Extension On separate index cards, write the name of one of the longest rivers in the world: the Mississippi, Nile, Amazon, Yangtze, and Mekong. Divide students into groups to research one river's journey from its source to its mouth. Have them gather information from print or digital sources about the width, volume, and flow of the river along its length. Ask each group to make a brief presentation to the class.

Collaboration

Feedback Have students work with partners to use the word bank to correctly match up words that describe the path of a river from its source to its mouth. Then bring the whole class together, and discuss answers. Did everyone agree?

EVIDENCE NOTEBOOK

It might be helpful for students to draw the path of a river from its source to its mouth in their notebooks, describing each image under the correct step. Students should be formulating accurate ideas about how the movement of the river slowly eroded the land, forming the canyon walls.

Lesson 1 How Does Water Shape Earth's Surface?

LESSON 1   Engage • **Explore/Explain** • Elaborate • Evaluate

EXPLORATION 1 *Making a Move, continued*

SEP Planning and Carrying Out Investigations

Provide time for pairs to research and come up with a list of the best ways to be prepared for a flood or flash flood. Ask volunteers to share their lists, and then discuss them as a whole class. Have students make posters with text and illustrations about flood preparedness.

CCC Cause and Effect

Explain that engineers sometimes build levees (embankments for preventing flooding) along the banks of rivers to keep them from overflowing. Demonstrate how levees work. Fill a long paint tray with sand, and make a shallow channel with flat banks in the sand. Pour a stream of water through the channel. Slowly increase the volume until the stream overflows its banks.

Ask: What caused the water to overflow? **Sample answer: an increase in the volume of water in the channel**

Rebuild the channel with mounds of sand along the banks, and repeat the demonstration.

Ask: What effect did the levee have? **It took longer for the river to overflow its banks.**

Differentiate Instruction

ELL: Modeling Students learning English may need extra help labeling the diagram. Pair them with strong English-language speakers who can model and convey the meaning of what each area on the diagram represents while reading the captions in English. Have the English-language learner repeat the key words from each caption to illustrate understanding.

---

356   Unit 6 Changes to Earth's Surface

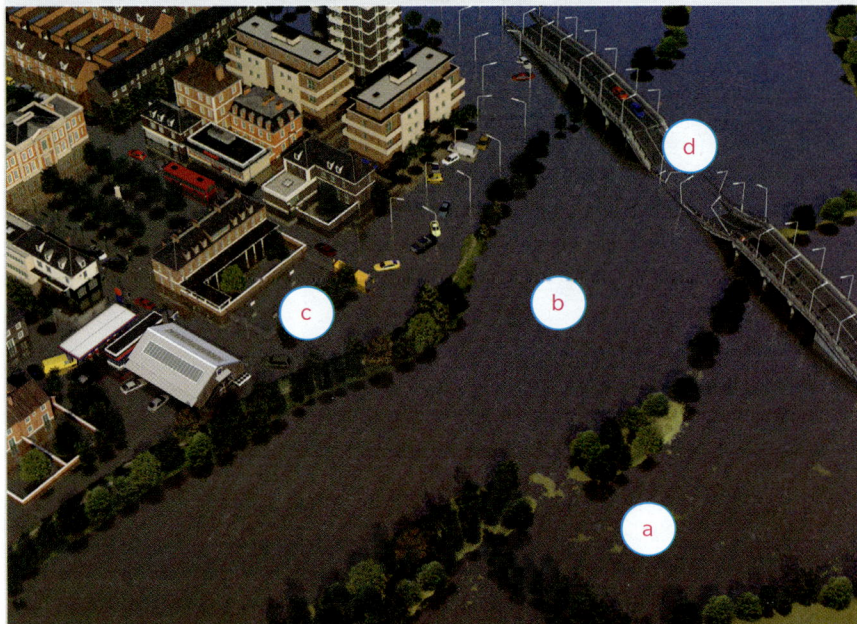

Over Its Banks

What happens to rain once it hits the ground? Some sinks in. Some runs into rivers, lakes, and the ocean. If rain is heavy, a river can flow over its banks. This causes flooding. Flooding can cause many things to happen.

Effects of a Flood

3. Read the descriptions and look at the picture. Then label the part of the picture that matches each description.

a. The flood has killed crops in this field, but the floodwaters also drop sediment that contains nutrients. This makes rich soil that is good for future crops.

b. Most of the time, this river flows between its banks where the trees are. When water flows over the banks, flooding occurs.

c. Floodwaters can cover roads and damage houses, schools, and other buildings. Water may enter basements and the first floor of some buildings.

d. In a flash flood, more water than normal rushes down a river. The rushing water is strong enough to damage low bridges over the river.

356

HANDS-ON Apply What You Know

Water Effects

4. Research to find images of ways that floods can damage roads. What do you notice about the roads and what they are made of? Do you think that floodwaters could break other things into pieces? Use evidence from your research to support your response.

Water has damaged this road.

Putting it Together

Select all the answers that apply for each question.

5. Why does the flow of a river slow down near its mouth?
   - **a. It flows over flat land.**
   - b. It is full of stones and gravel.
   - **c. It is entering a larger body of water.**
   - d. It is flowing through a steep channel.

6. When do bends form in a river?
   - a. when the river first forms
   - b. when the river flows very fast
   - **c. when the river is getting older**
   - **d. when the river flows over a broad, flat area**

7. What effects can flooding have?
   - **a. Streets are covered with water.**
   - **b. Floodwater enters houses.**
   - c. Rainfall is heavier than normal.
   - **d. Soil washes away.**

8. What are positive effects of flooding?
   - **a. Floodwaters drop sediment that is rich in nutrients.**
   - b. Curves form in a river.
   - c. Water flows very slowly down a river.
   - **d. Good farmland forms on floodplains.**

357

Connection to Math

Just 6 inches of fast-moving floodwater can knock down an adult. It takes only 12 inches of rushing water to carry away a small car and 2 feet of rushing water can carry away most vehicles. Remind students that there are 2.54 centimeters in 1 inch. Have students fold a piece of paper in half and record the metric equivalent of these measurements in a two-column table.

4.MD.A.1 Measurement and Data

HANDS-ON Apply What You Know
Water Effects

If students are having difficulty finding images of how floods can damage roads, you may want to show them some photographs that reinforce floods' enormous destructive power: Call on volunteers to describe what they see in each photo.

Ask: Why might bridges, houses, trees, and cars be picked up and carried off during a flood? **Sample answer: Many structures are unable to withstand the force of the water.**

Assessment Rubric

An excellent score on this activity involves thorough research and analysis of the images.

FORMATIVE ASSESSMENT
Putting It Together

 ESS2.A Earth Materials and Systems

Make certain students understand the concept of Earth's river systems by asking for different volunteers to describe one step in the sequence of a river's journey from its source to its mouth. Students should also understand the positive and negative affects of flooding.

Ask: How do floods affect the environment and people? **Possible answer: Floods erode the land and destroy vegetation, damage buildings, bridges, and other structures.**

Lesson 1 How Does Water Shape Earth's Surface? **357**

LESSON 1 Engage • **Explore/Explain** • Elaborate • Evaluate

EXPLORATION 2 Away It Goes!

3D Learning Objective

Students will **investigate** and gather evidence to explain the **cause-and-effect** relationship between floods, heavy rains, ocean waves, and swift currents and the impact they have on **Earth's surface**.

Differentiate Instruction

RTI/Extra Support Help students understand the sequence of events captured in the timeline.

Ask: What was the first year in which a record of erosion along the cliffs of Birling Gap began? **1905**

Ask: How many years are covered by this timeline? **110**

Ask: What do you predict the cliffs will look like in another 100 years? **Accept all reasonable responses.**

Language SmArts
W.4.8 Gather relevant information from print sources; take notes and categorize information.

DCI ESS2.A Earth Materials and Systems

Make sure students carefully observe and compare the distance from house to cliff in each photograph. Remind them that Earth's processes are continuously changing the shape of Earth's surface.

Ask: What happened to the soft rock and soil that appear to have disappeared from the cliffs? **Sample answer: During a storm, waves pounded the cliffs, causing weathering and erosion.**

EXPLORATION 2

Away It Goes!

Vanishing Cottages

These pictures show a seaside town in England named Birling Gap. The town is near cliffs by the sea. The cliffs are made of a very soft rock called chalk. Strong waves pound the cliffs, especially during storms.

1905: This picture shows several houses at Birling Gap. They are a short distance from a cliff that drops into the sea.

1930s: Compare this photo to the photo from 1905. You can see that some of the cliff has fallen away.

1970s: In this photo from the 1970s, more of the cliff has disappeared.

2015: Look at how the distance of the houses from the edge of the cliff has changed.

9. Language SmArts Use the images above to help you answer these questions. What happened to the distance between the houses and the cliff between 1905 and 2015? What do you think caused this change?

Possible answer: The distance between the houses and the cliff decreased. By 2015, some buildings had already fallen over the cliff. This happened because the waves wore away the chalk cliff.

358

358 Unit 6 Changes to Earth's Surface

Watch It Go!

Several processes constantly change Earth's surface. Three of these processes are described below.

- **Weathering** is the breaking down of rocks on Earth's surface into smaller pieces. Weathering occurs in rivers when the current causes rocks to bump against each other and break apart. Weathering can also occur in other ways.
- **Erosion** is the process of moving weathered rock and soil from one place to another. This happens when rivers move rock and soil downstream. Factors such as wind and gravity can also cause erosion.
- **Deposition** occurs when water slows down and drops the rocks and sediment it carries. This occurs at the mouth of rivers and anywhere water stops moving.

10. In the images below, circle where the change is taking place.

11. Choose the word or phrase to complete each sentence.

| erosion   weathering   deposition |

When rock from a cliff cracks, __weathering__ occurs. When the rock falls, __erosion__ occurs. Finally, the rock settles on the land below. This is called __deposition__.

SEP Planning and Carrying Out Investigations

Explain that it is hard to carry an object for a long time without putting it down. As water moves throughout a river system, it loses some of its energy of motion. The water can no longer carry some of its sediment, so it drops, or deposits, it along the bottom. Model this by creating a sedimentation tube. Fill a large-mouth, 2-liter water bottle with various sizes of sediments: gravel, sand, clay-sized particles, and soil. Fill the bottle with water, close the lid, and shake. Explain that materials in the tube are typical of materials found in a river.

Ask: What did you notice about the order in which the sediments settle? **Accept correct student observations**

Differentiate Instruction

RTI/Extra Support To help students understand what causes rocks to break down, place a handful of soft rocks, such as shale, limestone, or sandstone, into a coffee can with lid. Use pieces of chalk if rocks aren't available. Shake the can forcefully for two minutes. Put the rocks on a piece of paper, and have students observe and take notes on changes in their appearance.

DCI ESS2.A Earth Materials and Systems

While students match the images in item 10 to the processes that change Earth's surface, circulate to make sure they understand the differences between weathering, erosion, and deposition. Remind them of this mnemonic: weathering breaks, erosion takes, deposition drops.

Ask: What process provides the material that erosion can work with? **weathering**

LESSON 1   Engage • **Explore/Explain** • Elaborate • Evaluate

EXPLORATION 2 *Away It Goes!*, continued

CCC Cause and Effect

As students study the photographs, review the cause-and-effect relationships between water and weathering, erosion, and deposition and how these three natural processes affect the environment.

Ask: How does erosion and deposition occur in a stream? *Sample answer: The flowing water picks up and moves sediment. Some sediment gets deposited along the curves of the stream.*

Differentiate Instruction

ELL: Miming Students learning English may need extra help understanding the difference between erosion and deposition. Pair them with strong English-language speakers who can mime or draw pictures to convey the meaning of what each word means while saying the words in English. Have the English-language learner repeat the words to illustrate understanding.

Water Power

As you've seen, water helps shape the land through weathering, erosion, and deposition. Rivers change the areas they flow through. Flooding can move sediment. Waves can crumble cliffs.

There are many factors that can affect the rates of weathering, erosion, and deposition. The amount of water, the angle of a slope, and rate of the deposition can all affect how quickly these processes occur.

Changing the Shape of Land

12. Look at the images below, and label them with letters for the correct descriptions shown at the top of the next page.

Explore Online

a

d

c

b

360

360   Unit 6 Changes to Earth's Surface

a. Heavy rain can cause **mudslides,** or the quick movement of rain-soaked soil downhill. Mudslides are a type of erosion. When the ground is steep, water and mud can slide down faster. As a result, there is more erosion.
b. **Waves** cause both weathering and erosion on rocky beaches. The force of the pounding waves splits and chips rock. Then the water carries the pieces away.
c. A **swiftly flowing stream** causes erosion. The moving water carries sediment and rocks downstream.
d. **Falling water** weathers the stone under the falls. Erosion causes pieces of rock to drop away. Then deposition piles the rocks up under the falling water. When weathering happens quickly, erosion and deposition happen quickly, too.

 EVIDENCE NOTEBOOK You've learned about ways that water can cause weathering and erosion. In your Evidence Notebook, make a list that summarizes this information. Then write a sentence or two for each entry on your list, explaining how it provides evidence for how a canyon is formed.

 Language SmArts
Categorizing Information

13. Complete the table with these possible causes and effects: *waves, swift current, mudslide,* or *flooding.*

Cause	Effect
flooding	Sediment is deposited on farmland.
Heavy rain pours down a steep slope of bare soil.	mudslide
waves	Weathering splits and breaks the rock of a cliff.
swift current	Erosion occurs as rocks move downstream.

Tip The English Language Arts Handbook can provide help with understanding how to categorize information.

© Houghton Mifflin Harcourt

Explore Online Have students explore the power of water online to learn different ways in which this major force has shaped the land.

DCI ESS2.A Earth Materials and Systems

Students may need time to match the descriptions to the correct images in item 12.

Ask: How can water, a liquid, be strong enough to split and chip rocks on a beach? The force of the water is what is strong.

SEP Planning and Carrying Out Investigations

Bring in photographs, or have the Internet ready to show students some famous waterfalls, such as Niagara Falls, New York; Victoria Falls, Zimbabwe; or Iguazu Falls, Argentina. Have students work in groups to sketch their waterfall and research how the processes of weathering, erosion, and deposition play an important part in the formation and shape of their waterfall. When they are finished, pair groups to compare and contrast.

 EVIDENCE NOTEBOOK

Allowing students to make a list that summarizes the information in a way that will help them to remember how water can cause weathering and erosion will help build confidence in their ability to summarize in a way that is meaningful for them. Circulate as students write down their sentences, and note whether or not their sentences support how a canyon is formed.

FORMATIVE ASSESSMENT

 Language SmArts
Categorizing Information
W.4.8 Recall, categorize, and provide sources for information

As students fill in the table, remind them that water (*cause*) produces a certain outcome to shape and reshape Earth's surface and that outcome is the *effect*.

Lesson 1 How Does Water Shape Earth's Surface?

LESSON 1   Engage • **Explore/Explain** • Elaborate • Evaluate

EXPLORATION 3 Cold Stuff!

3D Learning Objective

Students will **make observations** of how **forces that break down rocks** have a **cause-and-effect relationship** with Earth's surface.

Build on Prior Knowledge

Have students recall ways in which rocks can be broken apart into smaller pieces. If students have trouble coming up with ideas, you may wish to have them look back at the examples of weathering and erosion in Exploration 1. Tell them in this Exploration, they will learn another way in which water can break down rocks into smaller pieces.

SEP Planning and Carrying Out Investigations

Students use evidence from the images and text on these pages to explain the weathering and erosion phenomena of ice wedging.

Ask: What happens when water freezes? **It expands.**

Collaboration

Think Pair Share Give students two or three minutes for a quick partner discussion to review the images and information on these pages. Encourage students to closely examine the images. It might be helpful for students to sketch and label the example shown in each image in their notebooks. The new concept can prompt students to ask questions as they draw.

DCI ESS2.A Earth Materials and Systems

Explain to students that water is a unique liquid. It gets bigger when it freezes. But freezing water can also pose problems at home. In winter, when the temperature falls below the freezing point of water (0°C), the water trapped inside an unheated water pipe can freeze and expand, causing burst pipes.

362 Unit 6 Changes to Earth's Surface

EXPLORATION 3

Cold Stuff!

Water, Ice, and Water

Explore Online

Liquid water becomes ice when its temperature drops to 0 °C or below. When its temperature rises above 0 °C, the ice thaws and becomes liquid water again. In nature, this cycle of freezing and thawing happens constantly. Can this pattern of freezing and thawing cause weathering and erosion? Look at the images on this and the next page to find out!

1 There are small cracks in the surface of this rock.

2 Precipitation fills cracks in the rock with water. This usually happens after rain falls or snow melts.

3 If the temperature falls below 0 °C, water in the cracks freezes. The liquid water becomes solid ice. What happens when the ice presses against the sides of the crack?

362

④
When the temperature rises above 0 °C, the ice melts. Compare the crack now to the original crack.

⑤
The crack is now wider than before. After this pattern repeats many times, pieces may break off and be carried away.

 HANDS-ON Apply What You Know
Watching Water Grow

14. Fill a clear plastic cup halfway with water. Use a permanent marker to make a line on the side of the cup where the top of the water is. Place the cup in the freezer overnight. The following day, take the cup out of the freezer. Observe the top of the water. Is it the same place where you drew the line? If not, can you explain why?

 Language SmArts
Recalling Information

15. Predict what will happen to the rock as the pattern of freezing and thawing continues. Use information from these pages or personal experience to support your prediction.

Possible answer: As the cycle continues, the cracks in the rock will widen, and the rock may break apart. Then the pieces may be carried away by water, wind, or ice. The images on these pages support the prediction by showing rock being broken apart by repeated freezing and thawing.

Differentiate Instruction

RTI/Extra Support Help students to understand the cause-and-effect relationship in the cycle of freezing and thawing by relating this concept to people who live in areas with a cold winter season. Explain that water turning to ice under roads sometimes causes the ice to push up the road and create a bump in the asphalt called a frost heave. As the cycle of freezing and thawing continues, it creates a pothole and sunken sections in a roadway. Reinforce that each time water freezes (cause), the crack in the rock gets bigger (effect).

HANDS-ON Apply What You Know
Watching Water Grow

By observing how water expands when it freezes, students will understand how ice can split rocks apart. Everyone knows that ice cubes float in water. Because of this, we can infer that ice is less dense than water. The water frozen in the plastic cup expanded.

Ask: What can you infer about the volume of ice as it went from liquid to solid? It increased. Make sure students conclude that water is a powerful force that can cause weathering and erosion.

Assessment Rubric
An exemplary response would include a detailed explanation on why the water expanded.

 Language SmArts
Recalling Information
W.4.8 Recall, categorize, and provide sources for information

Check to be sure that students identify the cycle of freezing and thawing as a natural force that breaks down rocks and has a cause-and-effect relationship with Earth's surface.

Lesson 1 How Does Water Shape Earth's Surface?

Build on Prior Knowledge

Students might not think of ice as something that moves. Have them recall what happens to an ice cube on a table.

Ask: What might happen as the ice cube begins to melt? **Sample answer: It makes a small puddle.**

Explain that the water under the cube makes the table surface slippery, which allows the ice cube to slide. Emphasize that a similar process to the ice cube melting on a table happens on a much larger scale with glaciers.

SEP **Planning and Carrying Out Investigations**

You may wish to demonstrate how moving ice erodes the land by conducting this simple activity. Take a small amount of modeling clay, a paper towel, and a pre-made ice cube that contains sand and gravel. Flatten the clay on top of a paper towel. Drag the ice cube across the clay. Have students record their observations. Leave the ice cube to melt on top of the clay.

Ask: What did you observe? **Sample answer: The sediment in the ice cube cut grooves in the clay. Some clay built up along the sides and at the end of the path. As the ice melted, sediment was deposited.**

Connection to Math

Currently, 10 percent of land area on Earth is covered with glacial ice. During the highest point of the last ice age, glaciers covered about 32 percent of the total land area. In order to grasp these quantities, have students draw two circle graphs showing each of these quantities.

MP.2 Reason abstractly and quantitatively

Pushing Through

A glacier is a river of ice moving downhill very slowly. Glaciers are found in the coldest parts of Earth—the cold polar zones or cold, high mountain valleys.

Glaciers look like they are standing still. But they are slowly moving—so slowly that you can't see the movement with your eyes alone. But as glaciers move, they can change the land—just like running water. Glaciers weather rock beneath them. They scrape and cut rock they slide over. They cause erosion by pushing the broken pieces of rock under them and on top of them as they move. Deposition occurs when glaciers melt and leave the rock they carried behind.

As this glacier moves, it pushes rocks along with it.

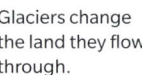

Glaciers change the land they flow through.

As the ice melts, glaciers also leave sediment behind.

364

364 Unit 6 Changes to Earth's Surface

16. The freezing and melting of water causes changes. The movement of glaciers does, too. Compare and contrast the two processes.

	Glacier	Freezing and thawing
Speed	Glaciers move slowly.	Freezing and thawing occurs quickly.
Effect	Erosion occurs slowly.	Erosion occurs rapidly.
Area covered	Glaciers cover a more limited space.	Freezing and thawing happens over large areas of land.

17. Use the evidence in your completed table to explain which process has a greater effect on the land.

Possible answer: Glaciers are big but affect isolated areas. The process of a glacier changing the land happens slowly. Freezing and thawing happens more quickly in many more places. So freezing and thawing might have a greater overall effect.

 EVIDENCE NOTEBOOK Think about what you've learned about how glaciers shape the land. Consider the canyon you saw at the beginning of the lesson. In your Evidence Notebook, explain whether or not the canyon could have been formed by glaciers. Support your explanation with evidence.

Putting it Together

18. The statements below describe some of the causes and effects of ice. Draw a line to match the causes in the left column to the correct effect in the right column.

- Glaciers move downhill.
- Glaciers scrape over rocks under them.
- Water freezes inside cracks in rock.
- Glacier ice melts.

- Erosion occurs as broken rocks are moved elsewhere.
- Weathering occurs as rocks crack and break.
- Deposition occurs as sediment is left behind.
- Weathering occurs as the water freezes and expands, making cracks bigger.

365

Differentiate Instruction

RTI/Extra Support Students might have difficulty understanding how such a giant mass of ice can "slide." Explain to them that the weight of a glacier and heat from Earth cause ice at the bottom of a glacier to melt.

DCI ESS2.A Earth Materials and Systems

Before students begin item 16, you may wish to have a quick whole-class discussion to summarize the different ways in which water and ice shape the land through the natural processes of weathering, erosion, and deposition. If students have trouble getting started with the table in item 16, have them work with a partner. Then, as they work on item 17, circulate to check that they used the evidence from their tables to justify their reasoning as they respond.

EVIDENCE NOTEBOOK

Students should note that water and ice share the same forces of weathering, erosion, and deposition. They should distinguish the ways in which water and ice change the land, and they should form accurate ideas about the formation of the Grand Canyon. Be sure they specifically say that the canyon is a product of the erosional force of the river water.

FORMATIVE ASSESSMENT
Putting it Together
Cause and Effect

Students should be able to correctly match up the cause-and-effect statements to identify how ice changes the shape of Earth's surface. When individuals are finished, allow time for pairs to discuss and analyze one another's reasoning for their answers. Then bring the whole class together, and discuss answers.

Lesson 1 How Does Water Shape Earth's Surface? 365

LESSON 1 Engage • **Explore/Explain** • Elaborate • Evaluate

EXPLORATION 3 *Cold Stuff!, continued*

HANDS-ON ACTIVITY Partners 1 class period

The Rate of Change

3D Learning Objective

SEP Planning and Carrying Out Investigations

Students plan and conduct an investigation to model and observe the effect of slope on the erosion of Earth's surface.

DCI ESS2.A Earth Materials and Systems

Flowing water is a an agent of erosion. The ability of water to erode rocks and soil is affected by the speed of the water. Moving water also picks up and carries particles of soil and rock.

Ask (before the activity): What might cause a river or stream to move faster? *steep landscape, such as mountain slope*

Materials

The materials listed are a starting point. You can use any kind of soil (from a yard or potting soil). You can use modeling dough instead of modeling clay. You may also wish to use plastic sheeting or plastic trash bags to cover the work area.

Preparation

Students will work with soil and water. Plan a space in the classroom where pairs can work without bumping into one another, or do the activity outside. Assemble the materials for each pair.

Procedure

STEP 1 As students prepare their cups, check to ensure the clay forms a tight seal around the straw.

STEP 2 As pairs work, be sure they are correctly interpreting the instructions. Remind them to make observations and answer the questions after each step.

366 Unit 6 Changes to Earth's Surface

HANDS-ON ACTIVITY

The Rate of Change

Objective
Collaborate with a partner to investigate the effect of slope on erosion.

What question will you investigate to meet this objective?
Possible question: How does slope affect erosion?

Materials
- paper cup
- sharpened pencil
- plastic drinking straw
- scissors
- small piece of modeling clay
- piece of cardboard 31 cm square
- soil
- ruler
- large bottle filled with water (approx. 2 liters)

Procedure

STEP 1 Working with a partner, carefully punch a hole near the bottom of the cup with the pencil. Use the scissors to cut a couple of inches from the straw. Push the straw into the hole. Press the clay around the straw to seal any openings around it.

Why is it important to seal the hole with clay?
Sealing the holes will prevent any leaks.

STEP 2 Place the piece of cardboard on the ground. Mound some dirt under one end of the cardboard to raise it about 2 inches off the ground so that the cardboard has a slight slope.

How would you describe the slope of the cardboard?
The cardboard is a slight, or moderate, slope.

366

  Student Lab Worksheet and complete Teacher Support available online.

STEP 3 Spread a thin layer of soil over the cardboard. Place the cup on the raised end of the cardboard, with the straw pointing downslope. Block the end of the straw with your finger, while your partner fills the cup with water.

What does the water in the cup model?
The water in the cup models rainwater or melting snow.

STEP 4 Take your finger off the straw, and allow the water to flow out. Observe how fast the water flows and the shape of the stream. Record your results in the box below.

How does the flow of the water affect the soil on the cardboard?
Possible answer: The water pushed the soil directly in front of the straw, but did not move soil farther from the straw.

Observations: Step 4	Check student observations to confirm that water flowed faster when straws were on a steeper slope.

STEP 5 Now raise the high end of the cardboard to about 6 inches so that it has a steeper slope than before. Repeat step 4 for this second trial. Record your results on the next page.

What does this set of steps model?
These steps model how the slope of land affects water erosion of soil.

367

STEP 3 Model how to spread a thin layer of soil over the cardboard so that the soil is evenly spread and does not go over the sides.

Ask (before they take their finger off the straw): What do you predict will happen when you remove your finger? Accept all reasonable answers.

SEP Planning and Carrying Out Investigations

Remind students that scientists make careful observations when conducting an investigation. Encourage students to accurately record what they observe. That way, others will know exactly what they observed and be able to compare their results.

STEP 4–5 Circulate to observe students as they record their results.

Ask: How did your observations compare to your predictions? Did anything about your observations surprise you? Accept all reasonable answers.

Connection to English Language Arts

Students will need time to process and record the information they collect during the activity and to categorize and organize it into the table of observations.

Ask: Did any of your observations surprise you, or were they all what you expected? Accept all reasonable answers.
W.4.8 Gather relevant information and categorize information

CCC Cause and Effect

Recall for students that in a cause-and-effect relationship, one event is the result of another.

Ask: How would the relative speed of the flow of water change if there were no slope, a slight slope, or a steep slope? Students should associate the slope (cause) with the amount of erosion (effect) as the water flows. More slope means higher speed.

Lesson 1 How Does Water Shape Earth's Surface? **367**

LESSON 1 Engage • **Explore/Explain** • Elaborate • Evaluate

EXPLORATION 3 HANDS-ON ACTIVITY, continued

Analyze Your Results

STEP 6–8 Discuss how the steepness of the slope affects erosion. Ask students to think about how modifying their investigation would yield different results and how variables in nature would cause changes.

Draw Conclusions

 Cause and Effect

Ask: What other variables might account for the rate at which the water flowed and for the shape of the stream? **Sample answer: the size of the soil particles and whether there was other material mixed in with the soil (vermiculite, pebbles, sand)**

STEP 9–10 Call on different pairs to share their conclusions, and be sure they cite evidence to support their claims.

> ## Claims, Evidence, and Reasoning
> Have each pair of students from the activity work with another pair to share their ideas about other factors that would change the rate at which the slope affects erosion.

Scoring Rubric for Hands-On Activity

3	investigation done correctly, results recorded accurately, analysis and conclusions reflect the results, claims follow logically from evidence, several questions for further study
2	like above, but analysis and conclusions are inadequate or incomplete, claims follow evidence loosely, few questions for further study
1	inadequate participation, results recorded but incomplete or unorganized, claims made but do not follow logically from evidence, few or no questions for further study
0	procedure not followed or did not participate, unorganized recording, claims have errors, no questions

368 Unit 6 Changes to Earth's Surface

Observations: Step 5	Check student observations to confirm that water flowed faster when straws were on a steeper slope.

Analyze Your Results

STEP 6 Did water flow over a steeper slope or a lower slope produce more erosion?
The water flow over the steeper slope caused more erosion.

STEP 7 Compare your results to the results of other groups. Describe any similarities or differences you notice.
Students' observations will vary from group to group, but all results should indicate that more erosion occurred with the steeper slope.

STEP 8 State a claim that is related to your question at the beginning of this activity.
Students should claim that the higher the slope, the more erosion occurs.

Draw Conclusions

STEP 9 Cite evidence to support your claim.
Students should cite the observations from their tables to support their claims.

STEP 10 What other questions do you have about the ways in which scientists study erosion?
Possible question: How do scientists study erosion caused by glaciers?

368

EXPLORATION 4 What About Us?

▶ **Explore Online** Students can go online to take a closer look at how weathering, erosion, and deposition change the shape of shorelines.

EXPLORATION 4
What About Us?

At the Beach

Look at the photos below. They show waves hitting a beach. Recall what you have learned about weathering, erosion, and deposition. Do you see any of these processes in the photos?

Waves in the ocean roll onto the shore. The waves move sand over the beach. They also bring with them bits and pieces of rocks and shells and leave them on the shore. Then the tide pulls the water back. Some of the material it deposited is washed back into the ocean. Erosion and deposition change the shape and slope of beaches.

Beach Weathering

19. Choose the word that correctly completes each sentence in the paragraph.

| erosion | deposition | weathering |

Beach sand forms from the ___weathering___, or breaking down, of rock.

Waves move sand along the beach, causing ___erosion___.

In some places, sand washes from the beach into the ocean. In other places, ___deposition___ leaves new sand on the beach.

3D Learning Objective

Students **observe** how **weathering, erosion, and deposition by water** have a **cause-and-effect relationship** on shorelines and roadways.

DCI ESS2.A Earth Materials and Systems

Explain that most of the erosion caused by waves occurs where the breaking waves interact with the land. As waves break on the shore, sediments are carried out to sea by the retreating water. Some of that sediment may later be deposited back on shore in the same location or a different one. Sediment from deep offshore can also be deposited on the shore.

Ask: Why would fossilized shark teeth be mixed with sand at the edge of the shore? Sample answer: Sand containing the teeth could be tossed onto shore by waves.

Connection to English Language Arts

Gather together six different photographs, slides, magazine cutouts, or pictures of different kinds of beach environments. Have students seated individually at their desks with a piece of paper divided into two columns: shores resistant to erosion and shores easily eroded. Show them the numbered pictures one by one. Ask them to write the number of the picture in the column they think correct and to write a few words explaining why each picture belongs in that category. Then have a whole-class discussion about their observations and responses.

W.4.8 Gather relevant information from print sources; take notes and categorize information.

CCC Cause and Effect

As students use the word bank to complete item 19, circulate to make sure they understand which event is the cause and which is the effect in each sentence.

LESSON 1   Engage • **Explore/Explain** • Elaborate • Evaluate

EXPLORATION 4 *What About Us?, continued*

Build on Prior Knowledge

Help students recall what they know about water when it changes from a liquid to a solid.

Ask: What happens to water when it freezes? **It expands.**

Explain that this Exploration builds on that information to show how the natural process of water freezing and thawing can cause the material in roads to erode.

 Cause and Effect

Before students work on item 20, explain that in some climates streets might seem to break out in potholes overnight. Explain there is a cause-and-effect relationship that can explain why. Water can get under the asphalt surface through cracks in the road.

Ask: In the colder winter climate, what will happen to the water under the road? **Sample answer: It will freeze and expand.**

Differentiate Instruction

ELL: Pantomime Pair English-speaking students with students acquiring English. Challenge each pair to pantomime or draw pictures to convey the meaning of *freeze* and *thaw*. The English-speaking student mimes or draws, and the student acquiring English mimes or draws in response to demonstrate understanding of the concept.

EVIDENCE NOTEBOOK

Superficially, the cracked asphalt road may resemble the Grand Canyon as seen from high altitude, but students should, at this point, understand that freeze-thaw action did not make the canyon.

On the Road

20. Look at the parts of two roads below. One road is in a place with a cold winter climate. The other road is in a place where the winter climate is warmer. Label the region each pair of images comes from.

colder winter climate

No matter how smooth pavement is, small cracks cover the surface of the road.

When precipitation falls, the small cracks fill with different forms of water: liquid or ice.

warmer winter climate

Small cracks cover the surface of the road.

When it rains, cracks in the road fill with water.

 EVIDENCE NOTEBOOK Study the surface of a sidewalk or road. Describe its surface in your Evidence Notebook. Explain how any cracks you observe may have occurred.

Unit 6 Changes to Earth's Surface

If the temperature drops below freezing, the water freezes and the cracks expand.

When temperatures rise and the ice melts, the cracks are wider than before.

The temperature stays above freezing so the water remains liquid.

The road is dry, and the cracks are the same size as before the rain.

21. Explain the reasoning you used to label the roads.

Possible answer: Water filled the cracks in both roads. But in the colder climate, the water froze into ice. When water freezes, it expands, causing cracks in rock to widen. These cracks could turn into potholes. This did not happen in the warmer climate because ice did not form.

SEP **Planning and Carrying Out Investigations**

To reinforce the freeze/thaw concept, provide time for students to research how potholes are formed. Have them create a diagram showing different stages.

Ask: If you see potholes with expanded cracks, what can you guess happened? Water was frozen between the cracks

Connection to English Language Arts

Asphalt covers more than 94 percent of the paved roads in the United States. It's a popular choice for driveways, parking lots, airport runways, racetracks, and tennis courts. Students might be more familiar with one of asphalt's other names: blacktop, tarmac, macadam, plant mix, and asphalt pavement.

RI.4.7 Interpret information and how it relates to understanding of the text

Connection to Life Science

Freezing and thawing temperatures affect more than just roads. For some plants, one night of temperatures below freezing could kill the plant completely—for example, citrus and avocado trees and succulent plants. Other plants—for example, trees such as conifers—have evolved the ability to survive in winter.

Ask: Can you think of a specific adaptation that a plant has to survive in a winter environment? Students may realize that some trees lose their leaves, while others keep theirs.

Have students research how plants that originated in cold climates have adaptations to survive typical winter conditions.

LS4.C Adaptation

Lesson 1 How Does Water Shape Earth's Surface?

LESSON 1 Engage • **Explore/Explain** • Elaborate • Evaluate

EXPLORATION 4 *What About Us?*, continued

Engineer It!
Fighting Potholes

DCI ESS2.A Earth Materials and Systems

The text and illustration provide information about how engineers use technology to lesson the impact of weathering and erosion to roads. Students find out information about how the sensors detect potholes.

Ask: How do you think sensors can tell civil engineers when potholes form? *by sensing a change in structure or height or temperature*

SEP Planning and Carrying Out Investigations

Engineers are finding new ways to prevent the weathering and erosion of roads. They are testing ways to pave roads, parking lots, sidewalks, and bike lanes with solar panels. The panels can melt snow or keep water from freezing. Sensors and solar panels are just two examples of products designed and built by engineers and scientists to solve the problem of erosion on roads and other important environments where people live, work, and play.

FORMATIVE ASSESSMENT
Putting It Together

CCC Cause and Effect

Before students work through items 23 and 24, discuss that each sentence has only one correct answer from the word bank.

Ask: How does understanding cause-and-effect relationships in the environment helps us better answer questions such as the ones shown here? *Accept all reasonable answers.*

Engineer It!
Fighting Potholes

Potholes are holes that form in roads due to weathering and erosion. One way that civil engineers might be able to stop potholes is by building smart roads. These roads are built with sensors in them. The sensors send information about traffic and road damage. When the information is received, needed repairs can take place before potholes get too big.

22. What other useful information could these sensors in the roads gather?

Possible answer: Sensors could send data about road conditions, such as snow or ice, that could affect driver safety.

Putting it Together

23. Choose the best word or phrase to complete the paragraph.

| weathering | erosion | deposition |

When waves move sand over beaches, _____*erosion*_____ occurs. Beaches also show _____*deposition*_____ when waves leave behind sand and bits of other material they carry. These processes change the shape and slope of beaches.

24. Choose the best word or phrase to complete the paragraph.

thaws	flows	freezes
closes	expands	melts
hot	mild	cold

Changing temperatures can affect the condition of roads. Water _____*freezes*_____ and thaws inside cracks in roads. Ice _____*expands*_____ in the cracks, just as it does in rock. As a result, roads in _____*cold*_____ climates often show winter damage.

372

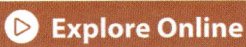 **Explore Online** Students can go online to take a closer look at how technology is helping to stop potholes before they start.

372   Unit 6 Changes to Earth's Surface

LESSON 1 Engage • Explore/Explain • **Elaborate** • Evaluate

TAKE IT FURTHER Discover More

 **Explore Online** — Students can explore all three Take It Further paths online.

TAKE IT FURTHER
Discover More

Check out this path . . . or go online to choose one of these other paths.

- People in Science
- Deposition Rate
- The Last Ice Age

Anjali Fernandes

Dr. Anjali Fernandes researches to learn how Earth's surface changes over different time periods. She studies how sediment is transported and where it is deposited in both land and water environments.

Dr. Fernandes specializes in the formation and changes of channels. A channel is a landform caused by water cutting into Earth. Channels can form over long periods of time by slow-moving water, or quickly by fast-moving floods.

One method Dr. Fernandes uses in her studies is field research. This means she goes to where channels exist and studies them. She also uses laboratory experiments to learn about the movement of sediments and how sediments are deposited in channels.

Dr. Anjali Fernandes studies Earth's changing surface.

25. Think of a question you would like to ask Dr. Fernandes about her work.
Possible question: How do you learn about erosion that happened a long time ago?

Collaboration

You may choose to assign this activity or to direct students online to the Interactive Online Student Edition where they can explore and choose from all three paths. These activities can be assigned individually, to pairs, or to small groups.

People in Science: Anjali Fernandes

DCI ESS2.A Earth Materials and Systems

Explain to students that field research is the collection of information outside of a laboratory, library, or workplace setting. Geoscientists might conduct field research to understand Earth's processes, such as floods, landslides, earthquakes, and volcanic eruptions. They also may study Earth's materials, such as rocks, water, metals, and oil. Some geoscientists conduct field research to study Earth's history to learn about plants and animals that lived on Earth in the past or what past climates of Earth were like and how they have changed across time.

SEP Planning and Carrying Out Investigations

Ask: If you wanted to know about how channels form, what would be the best way to find out? conduct field research

Differentiate Instruction

Extension Challenge interested students to find out more about geoscientists, for example: what background is necessary to become a geoscientist; special areas of study, such as geology, Earth's surface processes, Earth's history, geomicrobiology, and so on. Then have students make posters with text and illustrations about geoscientists.

Lesson 1 How Does Water Shape Earth's Surface? 373

LESSON 1 Engage • Explore/Explain • **Elaborate** • Evaluate

TAKE IT FURTHER, continued

Do the Math
Measuring Erosion

MP.5 Use appropriate tools strategically

MP.4 Model with mathematics

Explain to students that something that is constant occurs continuously and does not change. Call on volunteers to explain what is meant by the phrase *erosion was constant*. Then have students use pencil and paper or a calculator to determine the total number of meters (feet) that the cliff beneath Horseshoe Falls eroded between the years 1842 and 1905. **1905 − 1842 = 63 years; 63 × 1.16 m = 73.08 m (239.76 feet)**

Students might have difficulty grasping how long 73.08 m (239.76 feet) is. You can use the analogy of a football field, which is 300 feet long. Over the course of 63 years, the falls eroded about 80% of a football field.

Explore Online

Students can explore these additional topics online.

Deposition Rate!

Students will analyze the rate of deposition in the Mississippi River. *(No outside research required.)*

The Last Ice Age

Students will learn about the last ice age, which peaked around 20,000 years ago. *(Some outside research required.)*

---

26. Dr. Fernandes does both field work and laboratory experiments. If you were a scientist, do you think you would enjoy field work or laboratory work more? Why?

Students should state whether they prefer field or laboratory work and give the reasons why.

27. What kinds of changes in Earth's surface would you most like to study?

Possible answer: I would like to study how sediment becomes sedimentary rock.

Do the Math
Measuring Erosion

Each year, water erodes the cliff beneath Horseshoe Falls, Canada. Horseshoe Falls is part of the larger Niagara Falls. Between the years 1842 and 1905, erosion was constant at about 1.16 meters (3.8 feet) per year.

28. During the 63 years between 1842 and 1905, how much did Horseshoe Falls erode in meters? In feet?

73.08 meters; 239.4 feet

LESSON 1 Engage • Explore/Explain • Elaborate • **Evaluate**

LESSON CHECK

 **Explore Online** — Students can revisit the lesson phenomenon online.

LESSON 1
Lesson Check

Name _____

Can You Explain It?

1. Now that you've learned about how water shapes Earth's surface, explain how you think the canyon formed. Be sure to do the following:
   - Explain how the river is involved in the formation of the canyon.
   - Describe the role of weathering and erosion in the formation of the canyon.
   - Describe how weathering and erosion have changed the canyon over time.

EVIDENCE NOTEBOOK Use the information you've collected in your Evidence Notebook to help cover each point above.

- The river flows through the bottom of the canyon. It weathers and erodes rock as it flows.
- The weathering and erosion wears away rock and sediment at the bottom of the riverbed. The river also erodes rock and sediment along its banks.
- Weathering and erosion slowly cut deeper into the rock and sediment, forming a canyon.

Checkpoints

Answer the questions about how weathering, erosion, and deposition change Earth's surface. Choose the best answers to the questions.

2. Which of these would speed up erosion?
   a. warmer temperatures
   b. **steeper river channels**
   c. **a river with a fast current**
   d. deposition of sediment

375

Formal Assessment Go online for student self-checks and other assessments.

Can You Explain It?

Collaboration

Draw Pair Share Have students work in groups of four to create a sequence of drawings showing how the river cut through the rock layers over time. Students might want to show how other forces of weathering and erosion, such as rain, snowmelt, and small streams flowing into the river, caused the canyon to grow wider over time. Have them annotate and label their drawings with evidence of *weathering, erosion,* and *deposition.* When they are done, have a volunteer from each group explain their drawings.

EVIDENCE NOTEBOOK

Have students reread their answers to the Evidence Notebook prompts and then use this evidence to justify their reasoning as they respond to the Can You Explain It question. Make sure students understand that a complete response must address all bulleted points.

CCC Cause and Effect

Remind students that a cause is the reason something happened. An effect is what happened as a result.

Ask: What are some key words that help identify cause-and-effect relationships? *if, so, so that, because of, as a result of, since, in order to*

SUMMATIVE ASSESSMENT

2. Remind students of the climate where freezing and thawing are more likely to occur. Also remind them how the effect of water on sloping land differs from its effect on flat land.

Lesson 1 How Does Water Shape Earth's Surface? **375**

LESSON 1 Engage • Explore/Explain • Elaborate • **Evaluate**

LESSON CHECK, *continued*

3. This question asks students to think about which natural process—weathering, erosion, or deposition—is associated with the flooding of a river. Circulate to gauge if students can reason through each one of these answer choices correctly. For example, in the first answer choice, students should reason that a river flows between its banks and, when flooding occurs, the water overflows its banks. Talk through each answer choice if they get stuck.

4. If students are having difficulty choosing the correct answer for this question, encourage them to draw the path of a river from its source to its mouth. Help them recall that where the river spreads out and its volume increases, the river forms bends and curves.

5. It is sometimes difficult for students to distinguish between weathering, erosion, and deposition. If students are having difficulty with this question, remind them that the process of breaking down rock is weathering, when rocks, sediment, soil are transported, it is erosion, and when rocks, sediment, or soil are deposited, it is deposition.

6. Before students choose words from the word bank, suggest they read the sentences to look for key words that signal a cause-and-effect relationship. Then have them look at the word bank to choose the best answer to complete each sentence.

Choose the best answer to each question.

3. How do floods affect the environment? Select all that apply.
   - **a. Floods destroy buildings.**
   - **b. Floods create areas of more fertile soil.**
   - c. Floods speed up the weathering of rock.
   - d. Floods make riverbeds steeper.

4. Where does a river develop curves?
   - a. in places where there are big rocks
   - b. in places where it has the steepest slope
   - c. where sediment is dropped at its mouth
   - **d. in the flat, wide areas of its course**

5. Write the word in each blank that makes the sentences correct.

   | erosion | weathering | deposition |

   When a river moves rock downstream, the process is called __erosion__.

   Glaciers can grind over rock and break them in a process called __weathering__.

   In the process of __deposition__, water or ice drops rock or sediment that it has carried, causing landforms, such as deltas, to form.

6. Write the word in each blank that makes the sentences correct.

   | contracts | expands | |
   | erosion | weathering | deposition |

   Water __expands__ when it freezes. As a result, __weathering__ occurs when ice forms inside the cracks in rock. The ice widens cracks and often breaks the rock.

Unit 6 Changes to Earth's Surface

LESSON 1

Lesson Roundup

A. Write the word or phrase in each blank that makes the sentences correct.

| mountains | valleys | slowly |
| quickly | break apart | join together |

Many rivers have their source in ___mountains___. The riverbed has a steep slope. As a result, the river flows downhill ___quickly___ and in a straight path. As the river flows, it moves rocks and pebbles in the riverbed. The rocks ___break apart___ as they smash into each other and move downstream.

B. Describe one way that weathering, erosion, and deposition are similar.
___They all involve changes to rock.___

C. Write the word or phrase in each blank that makes the sentences correct.

| mountains | slowly | weathering |
| lakes | quickly | erosion | deposition |

Glaciers move ___slowly___ along the land. During their journey, they break up rock beneath them, which is called ___weathering___. They cause ___erosion___ as they move sand and rock along their path. In addition, glaciers leave mounds of dirt and rock behind in a process called ___deposition___.

D. Which of the statements about beach sand are correct? Choose all that apply.
- **a.** It is formed by the weathering of rock.
- **b.** Waves erode it and deposit it in new places.
- **c.** It is mostly eroded by glaciers.
- **d.** It is formed by freezing and thawing.

Lesson Roundup

DCI ESS2.A Earth Materials and Systems

This lesson summary enables students to quickly revisit key points and prepare for tests.

A. Most students will be able to recollect that a river's course begins at a higher altitude and is characterized by waterfalls and V-shaped valleys causing water to flow swiftly. Rushing water carries rocks that tumble and break apart as they are carried downstream. To clarify students' understanding of a river's journey from source to mouth, have them revisit Exploration 1. **ESS2.A**

B. Students may wish to scan Exploration 2 for the definitions of *weathering*, *erosion*, and *deposition* before responding. If students need scaffolded support, ask guiding questions to help them recognize that although the processes are different, they all affect the materials (rock) that Earth's surface is made from. **ESS2.A**

C. To clarify students' understanding of how glaciers slowly move downhill, causing erosion of the land they flow through by scraping, cutting, and pushing rock they slide over, have them revisit Exploration 3. **ESS2.A**

D. Students may wish to scan Exploration 4 before responding. If students need scaffolded support, begin by reminding them that weathering, erosion, and deposition affect beaches. If necessary, ask guiding questions to help students review which process causes the formation of beach sand and how it is transported by waves hitting the shore. **ESS2.A**

LESSON 2
How Do Other Factors Shape Earth's Surface?

Building to the Performance Expectation

The learning experiences in this lesson prepare students for mastery of:

4-ESS2-1 Make observations and/or measurements to provide evidence of the effects of weathering or the rate of erosion by water, ice, wind, or vegetation.

Trace Tool to the NGSS
Go online to view the complete coverage of these standards across this lesson, unit, and time.

Science & Engineering Practices

Planning and Carrying Out Investigations
Make observations and/or measurements to produce data to serve as the basis for evidence for an explanation of a phenomenon.

▶ **VIDEO** Planning and Carrying Out Investigations

Disciplinary Core Ideas

ESS2.A Earth Materials and Systems
Rainfall helps to shape the land and affects the types of living things found in a region. Water, ice, wind, living organisms, and gravity break rocks, soils, and sediments into smaller particles and move them around.

ESS2.E Biogeology
Living things affect the physical characteristics of their regions.

Crosscutting Concepts

Cause and Effect
Cause-and-effect relationships are routinely identified, tested, and used to explain change.

CONNECTIONS TO MATH

MP.2 Reason abstractly and quantitatively.

MP.4 Model with mathematics.

MP.5 Use appropriate tools strategically.

4.MD.A.1 Know relative sizes of measurement units within one system of units including km, m, cm; kg, g; lb, oz.; l, ml; hr, min, sec. Within a single system of measurement, express measurements in a larger unit in terms of a smaller unit. Record measurement equivalents in a two-column table.

4.MD.A.2 Use the four operations to solve word problems involving distances, intervals of time, liquid volumes, masses of objects, and money, including problems involving simple fractions or decimals, and problems that require expressing measurements given in a larger unit in terms of a smaller unit. Represent measurement quantities using diagrams such as number line diagrams that feature a measurement scale.

CONNECTIONS TO ENGLISH LANGUAGE ARTS

W.4.8 Recall relevant information from experiences or gather relevant information from print and digital sources; take notes and categorize information, and provide a list of sources.

RI.4.7 Interpret information presented visually, orally, or quantitatively (e.g. in charts, graphs, diagrams, time lines, animations, or interactive elements of Web pages) and explain how the information contributes to an understanding of the text in which it appears.

Supporting All Students, All Standards

Integrating the Three Dimensions of Learning

In this lesson, students will identify, explain, and record evidence **(SEP Planning and Carrying Out Investigations)** regarding how rainfall, wind, ice, and gravity shape Earth's surface **(DCI ESS2.A)**. Students will investigate how living things impact the physical characteristics of their regions on Earth **(DCI ESS2.E)**, and then examine and explain the relationships between Earth's surface, living organisms **(DCI ESS2.A)**, and the physical forces of weathering, erosion, and deposition **(CCC Cause and Effect)**. By investigating a variety of specific scenarios that shape Earth's surface, students will develop an understanding of core ideas, thereby enabling them to apply their understandings to other patterns of change on Earth. Students will ask and answer questions, carry out investigations **(SEP Planning and Carrying Out Investigations)**, analyze and interpret data, and communicate information.

 **Professional Development** Go online to view **Professional Development videos** with strategies to integrate CCCs and SEPs, including the ones used in this lesson.

Extra Hands-On Activity: Moving Soil

How Does Earth's Surface Change?

 Small groups
 20–30 minutes

Each group will need the following materials: ice cube (1 per group), modeling clay, tray, spoon, coarse sand or soil, and paper towels.

Line the trays with paper towels to absorb the water from melting ice.

Students should put a layer of coarse sand or soil on the tray. They should then prop the tray up on one end so the tray is tilted. The clay can be flattened or rolled into balls. The students should tilt the tray further until the clay moves down the tray. Students should observe that the clay eroded soil as it moved. The tray can then be lowered down and ice placed on the soil. Students should then raise the tray until the ice just starts to move. As the ice melts, it will then slide down. Melted ice should contain grains of sand and soil, more or less depending on the material, the shape of the ice cube, and the slope of the sand or soil.

 This activity can support mastery of this Crosscutting Concept: Cause and Effect

Preassessment

Have students complete the unit pre-test online or see the Assessment Guide.

Build on Prior Knowledge

Students should already know and be prepared to build on the following concepts:
- Wind and water change the shape of the land.
- Rocks are very hard, but they can change over time.
- Severe weather affects the surface of Earth.
- Four major Earth systems interact (land, water, air, living things).
- Plants and animals can change their local environment.

Differentiate Instruction

Lesson Vocabulary
- desert
- rain forest

Before students begin the lesson, write the vocabulary terms on the board and discuss their definitions. Then have students work in pairs to write sentences using the words, striving to use two or more of the words in each sentence.

Provide an example: *It is more difficult for organisms to survive in the <u>desert</u> than in the <u>rain forest</u> because there is more precipitation in the rain forest.*

Ask pairs to share their sentences with the group.

ELL/ELD Strategy
Point out cognates of key terms from students' home languages, for example, canyon/*cañón*, erosion/*erosión*, desert/*desierto*, to help bridge understanding of pertinent lesson vocabulary. Pronounce each word and spotlight the similarities. Ask other students to share the same words in their home languages.

LESSON 2 Engage • Explore/Explain • Elaborate • Evaluate

ENGAGE: Lesson Phenomenon

Lesson Objective
Identify, explain, and record evidence about factors that shape Earth's surface, such as rainfall, organisms, wind, ice, and gravity.

About This Image
A dune is a hill of sand built by either wind or water. Deserts often experience high winds that lead to the formation of sand dunes, such as the ones shown here. Many desert landscapes feature rocky surfaces. Rocks are extremely hard, but there are factors that can change the shape of rocks over long periods of time. Deserts cover about one-third of Earth's land surface. For dunes to persist, a sufficient amount of new sand must be provided from a source area, otherwise both wind and water will remove the sand faster than it can accumulate.

Planning and Carrying Out Investigations
Alternative Engage Strategy

Stay Out of My Sandbox!	Small group or whole class 10 min

Ask students to imagine that they are hired to create the perfect cover for a playground sandbox. Have students work in pairs or small groups to make a list of all the reasons that sandboxes need a cover. What should be kept out of the sand? What might happen to sand that is left uncovered? Ask students to plan and sketch a simple cover that will protect the sand. Now come back together as a class, and ask students to consider how these same factors relate to the sand on Earth's surface.

Ask a volunteer from each group to share their group's list of what factors affect sand, and then discuss them as a whole class.

LESSON 2

How Do Other Factors Shape Earth's Surface?

Rocks are very hard. You cannot mold them like clay, but they can change. Over long periods of time, weathering can break rock down into sand.

By the end of this lesson . . .
you'll identify, explain, and record evidence of weathering, erosion, and deposition.

378

Unit 6 Changes to Earth's Surface

Can You Explain It?

This rock is found in Bolivia. It is called Árbol de Piedra which means stone tree. The top of the rock is very large, but it sits firmly on a narrower column of rock.

1. How do you think natural processes on Earth's surface formed this rock? Why is it shaped this way?

Students should respond based on the preliminary observations they can make of the images.

Tip

Learn more about Earth's features and how they are shaped in How Does Water Shape Earth's Surface?

 EVIDENCE NOTEBOOK Look for this icon to help you gather evidence to answer the questions above.

379

▶ **Explore Online** Students can visit the lesson phenomenon online.

Can You Explain It?

Students are asked to record their initial thoughts about how natural processes on Earth's surface shape a rock such as the one shown in the photograph. To do so, students must begin to think about what factors cause change in rock. Remind students to consider the environment shown in the photograph and which factors would be present there. Point out that their ideas might change as they work through the Explorations and Hands-On Activities. Explain that they will have another opportunity to answer the same questions at the end of the lesson.

 Cause and Effect

As students work to explain the shape of the rock in the photograph, point out to them that they are finding natural cause-and-effect relationships on Earth's surface that lead to a variety of surface features.

Collaboration

Think, Pair, Share Gather together ten different photographs, slides, magazine cutouts, or pictures of different rock formations, each in a different environment. While students are seated individually at their desk with a piece of paper, show them the numbered pictures one by one. Ask them to make brief comments about what might have caused the rock formations to form in their current shape. Be sure that they number each rock formation on their piece of paper for later discussion. Then have students pair together and share their observations and predictions.

 EVIDENCE NOTEBOOK

Encourage students to use an appropriate graphic organizer, such as cause and effect, to set up their notebook for this lesson.
Find more strategies in the online ELA handbook.

Lesson 2 How Do Other Factors Shape Earth's Surface?   **379**

LESSON 2   Engage • **Explore/Explain** • Elaborate • Evaluate

EXPLORATION 1 Organisms and Environments

3D Learning Objective

Observe different organisms **to explain the phenomena** of why they live where they live, with water being a central focus. Determine **cause-and-effect relationships** between these organisms and their environment to determine how they **affect the physical characteristics of their regions**.

 Cause and Effect

Discuss the relationship between the amount of water in a given biome and how it relates to the number of organisms that live there.

Ask: Besides rain forests, can you think of another place on Earth that receives a lot of water each year? **wetlands such as swamps, bogs, and marshes**

Ask: Do wetlands have a lot of organisms that live there, or just a few? **Wetlands have a great number of aquatic plants and animals.**

Differentiate Instruction

RTI/Extra Support In pairs, give students a set of index cards with animals and plants on them. Include a wide variety of living things. Have students look at each organism and predict whether they think the organism lives in a habitat with a little water or a lot of water. Have them provide reasons for their thinking.

Connection to Math

Rainfall or precipitation is usually expressed in centimeters per year. Remind students that a centimeter is 1/100 of a meter. Fill a small container with a centimeter of water to demonstrate. Then fill a container with the average amount of rain per year in a desert (<25 cm). Explain that a rain forest gets so much rainfall (80–400 cm) that you'd need the deep end of a swimming pool to demonstrate that amount.

4.MD.A.1 Measurement & Data

380 Unit 6 Changes to Earth's Surface

EXPLORATION 1

Organisms and Environments

Water World

The presence and movement of water can change Earth's surface in direct ways, such as the sea eroding a sandy beach or a river carving a canyon into the land. But water can also allow organisms to live, grow, and thrive, and those organisms can change Earth's surface.

Deserts get less than 26 centimeters (10 inches) of precipitation per year. Since living things need water to survive and grow, this limits the number of plants, animals, and other organisms that can live here.

Rain forests get 203 centimeters (80 inches) or more of rain in a year. This allows a tremendous number of different organisms to live here. Think about how a single tree in the rain forest could itself be an environment for other organisms.

2. What differences did you notice between the rain forest and the desert? Why do you think the amount of water is such an important factor in determining the number of organisms in these environments?

Possible answer: The rain forest had more organisms, and most of the organisms were from a wider variety of types than those in the desert. Lack of water in the desert would make it more difficult for organisms to live there. Those that do live there are adapted to going without water for long periods of time.

380

Bactrian camels live in the rocky deserts of Central and East Asia. When water is scarce, the camel can convert the stores of fat in its two humps to water and energy. This allows Bactrian camels to live without access to drinking water for months if necessary. When drinking water is found, they can drink 135 liters (30 gallons) in just half an hour! They will also eat snow and ice and just about any plant life they can find.

The sambar deer is a large animal that lives in parts of South and Southeast Asia. It lives in a variety of different forests, from tropical dry forests to tropical rain forests. Sambars prefer to be near water, where they can find many different plants to eat.

3. How do you think the adaptations of these animals help them survive in the environment in which they live?
   The Bactrian camel can go much longer without water than the sambar deer, so it can survive and grow in areas without much rainfall. The sambar deer needs to live in an area with more regular rainfall.

 HANDS-ON Apply What You Know
Dry Plants

4. The saguaro is a type of cactus that lives in the southwest. Despite the extreme temperatures and dry weather of the desert, the saguaro can grow up to 70 feet tall! Do some research to find two key features that help the saguaro thrive in its environment.

DCI ESS2.A Earth Materials and Systems

Ask: Could the Bactrian camel and the sambar deer switch environments? Why or why not? No, the Bactrian camels have special features that allow them to live without water for months, so they can live in the desert. The sambar deer does not have the same adaptations, so it would not survive long in the desert.

Connection to Life Science

Point out that both animals and plants have adaptations that help them survive in the specific environment in which they live.

Ask: Can you think of a specific adaptation that an animal has to survive in its environment? Students may realize that some animals use camouflage to blend into their surrounding environment and avoid predators. Discuss examples, such as a walking stick insect that resembles a twig.
LS1.A Structure and Function

HANDS-ON Apply What You Know
Dry Plants
Show students a picture of a saguaro cactus, or bring in a small cactus to prompt discussion.

Assessment Rubric
Students should report that spines help cacti reduce water loss and survive hot temperatures and keep predators away because they are prickly. Spines also collect water from the air and let it drip down to the roots. Saguaro cacti have shallow roots that only go down in the ground 4 to 6 inches but spread out as wide as the cactus is tall. They also usually have one deep taproot that goes down 2 to 5 feet or more in search of groundwater. Saguaro cacti have a waxy coating to reduce water loss.

LESSON 2   Engage • **Explore/Explain** • Elaborate • Evaluate

EXPLORATION 1 *Organisms and Environments, continued*

Collaboration

Discussion Have students recall some ways they have observed humans affecting or changing the environment. If students have trouble coming up with ideas, give a few examples: using fertilizer, building bridges, fishing, pollution, clear cutting forests. Explain that this Exploration will build on that information to show how all living things (not just humans) impact the area in which they live.

DCI ESS2.E Biogeology

In the images on this page, you can see some examples of how plants and animals affect their environments.

Ask: How does a meerkat's burrowing behavior physically change the environment? It creates holes in the ground and transports dirt to the surface, where it may be carried elsewhere.

Ask: How do tree roots alter the environment? growing into and widening cracks in rock

Differentiate Instruction

ELL: Modeling Have student pairs fill a small clear container with pebbles or small rocks. One of the students pokes a pencil slowly down into the rocks as far as it will go. The other student counts how many rocks are moved or affected by the pencil. Explain to students that the pencil models a root growing down into rock to get water and that roots break apart rock in a process called *weathering*.

EVIDENCE NOTEBOOK

Students may speculate that burrowing animals may have dug around the base of the rock, exposing it to wind and other erosive forces over time.

Living Things Change Their Environments

Think about a ball field where kids play games, such as soccer or football. There may be patches of dirt where shoes have worn away the grass. Or perhaps you've walked on a trail through the woods and observed how it seems rockier and worn down after a rainstorm, while the surrounding area doesn't seem affected.

Animals, plants, and other organisms can have similar effects on the physical features of Earth's surface. Look at the images to see how organisms affect their environment.

This plant uses its roots to anchor itself in place and get water from the ground. As the roots grow, they can widen the cracks of the rock. Eventually, a chunk of rock may split off and fall.

Meerkats live in burrows. Digging a burrow creates a hole in the ground and moves dirt to the surface. This dirt may blow away, be carried by rainwater, or mixed with the dirt at the surface. It also exposes more rock that can then be weathered and eroded.

EVIDENCE NOTEBOOK Consider what you've learned about plants and animals. Is there any evidence that either played a role in the formation of the "stone tree"?

382

Unit 6 Changes to Earth's Surface

Ivy is a type of plant that grows up and around other objects, including rock walls, fences, telephone poles, statues, homes, and trees. As ivy climbs, it sends out small roots that change their shape to cling to the surface the ivy is climbing. These roots can push into cracks in rock.

The root hairs give off a glue-like substance and feature hook-like structures on their tips. The root hairs can also dry up and twist into shapes that anchor the roots more firmly into the surface cracks.

Select which processes are described in each example.
Circle all that apply.

5. An animal digging a burrow in the soil of a forest

   a. weathering   **b.** erosion   **c.** deposition

6. When a tree's roots grow in a crack of a boulder and the boulder breaks into two pieces

   a. weathering   **b.** erosion   **c.** deposition

7. Language SmArts Conduct research to learn more about how ivy affects its environment. Write your findings below.
Possible answer: The roots of ivy can grow into some rocks and cause weathering. Ivy can also become overgrown and kill plants.

383

CCC Cause and Effect

When vines and roots grow along and within other structures, they can cause *weathering*.

Ask: Have you ever seen vines growing along a wall like the image shown here? Accept all reasonable answers.

Ask: Why do you think vines grow on other surfaces? Vines save energy by growing on other surfaces to reach sunlight instead of growing a lot of their own support tissue. Growing as a vine also helps plants colonize large areas quickly, even without climbing high.

Misconception Alert Students may think that *weathering* and *erosion* are the same thing and can be used interchangeably. Be sure that students know that weathering is a physical or chemical breakdown of rock, but erosion is when sediment is moved or transported away from one location. Erosion moves the products of weathering. This differentiation will help them correctly answer the questions on this page. Students may also think erosion is bad. Explain that erosion can sometimes be good. River deltas are formed by sediments eroding and then flowing downstream. Without erosion and deposition, rich farming areas, such as the Nile River Delta, would not exist.

Language SmArts
W.4.8 Gather relevant information from print and digital sources

Have students research different plants to see if they cause weathering. After they have completed their research, have them share their notes with the class.

Ask: Do you think that all plants affect their environment? Why or why not? Yes. Even if a plant doesn't cause erosion, it may provide food, shelter, or some other need within the environment.

Lesson 2 How Do Other Factors Shape Earth's Surface? 383

LESSON 2 Engage • **Explore/Explain** • Elaborate • Evaluate

EXPLORATION 1 Organisms and Environments, continued

CCC Cause and Effect

The dams that beavers build have a major effect on the ecosystem. They can even affect neighboring ecosystems! Beavers create homes for other organisms by making quiet, still, sometimes deep pools of water that attract animals such as frogs, fish, and ducks. The dam also slows down the flow of the river to protect the beaver's home and gives them a place to hide from predators.

Ask: Can you think of a way that beaver dams cause harm? **Beaver dams can cause flooding, which can wipe out farmland and roads. Beavers also sometimes chew through trees that are important or rare.**

DCI ESS2.A Earth Materials and Systems

Beavers affect their environment by building dams, and termites affect their environment by building large mounds.

Ask: How do such tiny insects like termites build such large mounds? **In groups of a million or two, termites can build mounds that can reach 17 feet (5 meters) and higher. The 33 pounds (15 kilograms) of termites in a typical mound will move about 550 pounds of soil and several tons of water in an average year.**

Differentiate Instruction

Extension: Termite Trails There is a chemical in ballpoint pen ink that termites recognize. Some scientists think it is similar to a chemical that termites know and use in their communication. You can draw a design on paper and termites will follow the trail of the design. This is an excellent way to make observations and record data about the behavior of termites. Tell students to do some research online to find an experimental design, or work with a classmate to create their own.

Other Ways Organisms Change Environments

You've looked at how organisms can be forces of erosion, weathering, and deposition. Now it's time to see other impacts organisms can have on their environments.

Organism Cause and Effect

8. Look at the images to learn how some organisms change their environment. Then write the effects caused by these changes.

Beavers are dam builders. By toppling trees across streams, they cause the level of water behind the dam to rise.

Rising water causes a greater area of land to be covered by water.

This type of termite builds large mounds out of soil. The termites live and reproduce in the mounds, which can be tall and narrow or a hundred feet wide. When the mound erodes due to wind or rain, the termites deposit fresh soil to replace what was lost.

Termites move soil from one location to another, making large structures.

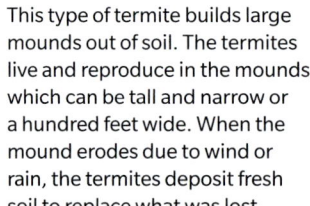

384

384 Unit 6 Changes to Earth's Surface

Prairie grasses cover the landscape in the Great Plains. When a river floods its banks, the grasses' roots help keep the wet soil in place.

Grass roots prevent erosion.

Language SmArts
Understand Cause and Effect

9. Think about the photos and information in this section. Fill in the chart below with the missing cause or effect.

Possible answers are shown.

Cause	Effect
The amount of water in an environment goes up.	The more water in an environment, the more organisms that can live there.
Growing ivy climbs rocks.	Ivy roots can cause weathering when they grow into rock.
Beavers build dams.	Dam building causes water to collect, resulting in once-dry land to be under water.

Tip
The English Language Arts Handbook can provide help with understanding how cause and effect works.

SEP Planning and Carrying Out Investigations

Grasslands contain more grass than trees. There are two different kinds of grasslands: temperate grasslands, which are mostly grasses, and tropical grasslands (savannas), which typically have some trees.

Ask: Use your observations of the image as evidence to explain how grasses can protect the soil from erosion? by keeping the wind and water from carrying it away

Connection to Physical Science

Here we have been looking at the relationship between living things and the changes they cause in their environments. There are cause-and-effect relationships that occur in every other branch of science as well.

Ask: One effect in physical science is our ability to see objects. What causes us to be able to see objects? We are able to see objects when light reflected from other surfaces enters our eyes.

PS4.B Electromagnetic Radiation

FORMATIVE ASSESSMENT

Language SmArts
Understand Cause and Effect

W.4.8 Gather relevant information from print sources; take notes and categorize information.

Ask students what wakes them up when they are sleeping. Tell them that if an alarm clock wakes them up, the alarm clock is the cause and waking up is the effect. As students fill in the table, remind them that living things produce (*cause*) a certain outcome in the environment (*effect*).

Lesson 2 How Do Other Factors Shape Earth's Surface?

LESSON 2   Engage • **Explore/Explain** • Elaborate • Evaluate

EXPLORATION 2 Environments Change

3D Learning Objective

Plan and conduct investigations and look at evidence to explain the **cause-and-effect relationship** between the forces of **wind and gravity and the rocks, soil, and sediments** they move around.

Engineer It!
Blast It Off

Cause and Effect

Like a sandblaster, there are weather events that blow sand around at high speeds and cause changes to Earth's surface.

Ask: Can you think of a weather phenomenon or weather event that causes sand to blow around at high speeds? tropical storms, hurricanes, sandstorms, dust storms

SEP Planning and Carrying Out Investigations

Ask: What kinds of things could you observe that would be evidence that a strong storm had just passed through an area? Bent street signs; broken traffic signals; damaged houses, cars, and sides of buildings would all be types of evidence.

After a storm, there is usually a lot of cleanup that needs to be done. After a hurricane, people have to clean up leaves and tree branches that were blown around their yards; after a sandstorm or a dust storm, there is lots of sweeping, vacuuming, and dusting to do.

Differentiate Instruction

Extension Have students research other ideas and inventions that came from natural disasters. Students will be surprised that there are many, including GPS (global positioning system).

---

386   Unit 6 Changes to Earth's Surface

EXPLORATION 2

Environments Change

Blast Off!

The photo shows a sandblaster in use. Think about what natural process may have inspired the invention of the first sandblaster.

Engineer It!
Blast It Off

Sandblasting is a technique for removing paint, rust, or other coatings from things such as cars, steel beams, pipes, and other objects. Sandblasting can smooth a rough surface or roughen a smooth surface. Compressed air is used to spray sand at an object at high speed. The friction from the sand hitting the object physically blasts particles off the object's surface.

10. How do you think the sandblaster compares to weathering and erosion?

The sandblaster blows sand with a strong force to remove material. Weathering and erosion also remove material.

HANDS-ON Apply What You Know
A Slower Process

11. With guidance from your teacher, use a piece of sandpaper to remove rust, paint, or some other substance from a piece of metal or wood. Keep track of how much time you spend actively sanding the material and how much debris ends up on the sandpaper or the table. Compare the results of your effort with what you saw in the sandblaster photo. Explain which factors might account for the differences between sandblasting and sanding by hand.

In places that receive very little precipitation, there isn't much erosion, weathering, or deposition that's caused by water or organisms. But rock and sediment in these places can still be eroded and weathered by other forces.

Desert Erosion

12. Look at the image below. Circle the spots where you think weathering and erosion may occur.

HANDS-ON Apply What You Know
A Slower Process

If you have students use sandpaper in the classroom, be sure to have safety goggles and cloth or disposable dust masks available. Sanding can be time consuming and requires patience. This activity works well when students work in pairs and switch off at a time interval (every 30 or 60 seconds). Cover the table with newspaper or butcher paper to collect the dust and debris. Tell students how long they will be sanding (5–10 minutes), and then tell them when there is 1 minute remaining. Students will compare their results with what they saw in the sandblaster video.

Scoring Guidelines

Students should attempt to remove paint or another substance from an object and quantify with some precision how much time it took and how much paint was removed. Explanations for the relatively low success compared to what the sandblaster can do should involve descriptions of power and force.

DCI ESS2.A Earth Materials and Systems

Gravity breaks rocks, soil, and sediments into smaller pieces and moves them around.

Ask: Think of a natural area around where you live. Have you seen a natural feature, such as a rock, a hillside, or a stream that was shaped by a force other than water? If so, what force changed the shape? **Accept all reasonable responses.**

SEP Planning and Carrying Out Investigations

As a whole class, brainstorm ways you could plan and carry out an investigation on how gravity moves sediment. Encourage students to start with a testable question and identify variables or factors in the investigation. When you uncover a good idea, ask what sort of data (observations, measurements) they will collect.

Lesson 2 How Do Other Factors Shape Earth's Surface?

LESSON 2   Engage • **Explore/Explain** • Elaborate • Evaluate

EXPLORATION 2 Environments Change, continued

DCI ESS2.A Earth Materials and Systems

The images on this page enable students to review some of the agents of change that contribute to weathering, erosion, and deposition on Earth's surface, regardless of the specific environment. Remind students that for erosion to occur, particles of sediment, sand, or rock must be moved or transported.

Ask: Why isn't weathering considered a type of erosion?
Sediment is not necessarily moved or transported; it is only broken apart.

> ## Collaboration
>
> **Think, Pair, Share** Give students 2–3 minutes for a quick partner discussion to review the answers they chose on this page and why they made the choices they did. In order to make connections, ask them to think about a time when they may have observed similar weathering and erosion patterns in their own local (and more familiar) environments. Encourage them to think about times when they may have seen a hole in a rock (at a beach), or an eroded hillside.

Connection to English Language Arts

Students use the images on this page to see specific examples of weathering, erosion, and deposition and to differentiate between them.

Have students list each of the processes (weathering, erosion, and deposition) in their notebooks, and then as they answer the questions, write or sketch the example shown in each image under the correct heading in their notebook. Later, they can add to these examples as their studies continue.

RI.4.7 Interpret information and how it relates to understanding of the text.
W.4.8 Recall, categorize, and provide sources for information.

388   Unit 6 Changes to Earth's Surface

The Sands of Time

Look at the images that follow. They show the results of weathering, erosion, and deposition over time. These factors contribute to changes in Earth's surface.

Changes Over Time

13. Choose the factor that is involved in each example.

a. Wind transports sand across the landscape. Some of the sand comes into contact with parts of a large boulder. Over time, the boulder becomes eroded.
   a. wind weathering the boulder
   b. windblown sand eroding the lower part of the boulder
   c. moving water eroding the lower part of the boulder

b. Wind can transport sand and other types of sediment from the base of a hill.
   a. wind erosion on the lower part of the slope
   b. deposition of sand at the top of the slope
   c. gravity pulling down on the rocks

388

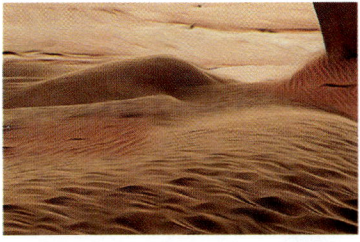 

c. As sand is transported across a landscape by wind, it can build up in certain areas.
   - **a. deposition of sand**
   - b. weathering of sand
   - c. moving water deposits sand and erodes dunes

14. You know that deserts are dry environments. Make a claim about whether or not you think water ever changes a desert landscape.

    Possible answer: I do think deserts are affected by water.

    a. Cite one piece of evidence to support your claim.
    Deserts do get some rain, and any rain would affect the sand and may weather some of the rock as it rains.

    b. Cite another piece of evidence to support your claim.
    Rain also can affect the desert indirectly by allowing certain organisms to live in the desert.

EVIDENCE NOTEBOOK Think about the ways the desert landscape changed. What ideas do you have about how the tree rock you saw at the beginning of this lesson formed? Record your ideas in your notebook.

389

Cause and Effect

Ask: What are some factors of the climate that help to reshape Earth's surface in a very cold place? wind, ice, snow

Ask: What are some factors that help to reshape Earth's surface if you live near the coast? waves, floods, and storms

Build on Prior Knowledge

Discuss where soil and sand comes from. Ask students to recognize that Earth is made up of rocks. Rocks are everywhere and come in many sizes and shapes. Point out that the type of parent material (rock) and how the soil is formed influences the properties of the soil.

ESS2.E Biogeology

Humans can also change the rate of weathering by contributing to the pollution that may cause landforms and nonnatural structures to break down.

Ask: Can you think of a way that human pollution affects rain so that it speeds up weathering? acid rain

Differentiate Instruction

RTI/Extra Support Have students research online to find pictures of weathering caused by acid rain. Then have them describe their findings to each other.

EVIDENCE NOTEBOOK

Students should note ways in which the desert landscape changes. They should also be formulating accurate ideas about the formation of a mushroom rock. Be sure they say specifically that the mushroom rock is a product of weathering and erosion. Wind weathers the whole boulder, but the wind near the ground contains more sand, which means there's weathering and erosion of the lower half of the boulder.

Lesson 2 How Do Other Factors Shape Earth's Surface? **389**

LESSON 2 Engage • **Explore/Explain** • Elaborate • Evaluate

EXPLORATION 2 *Environments Change, continued*

Misconception Alert Remind students that just as weathering and erosion are not the same, neither are erosion and deposition. Emphasize that erosion is the process by which weathered particles are moved or transported, but when they are deposited into a new location, that is called deposition.

Planning and Carrying Out Investigations

As world population continues to increase, many people build their homes in areas with steep slopes. The hazards of potential rock slides are becoming more of an issue. Flooding after a fire can also cause landslides. Luckily, scientists and engineers continue to collect data, plan, and work on keeping people and their homes safe.

Ask: What do scientists and engineers need to do to protect people from landslides and rockslides? *detect them before they happen, warn people*

Ask: Engineers build retaining walls. What do you think a retaining wall does? *It keeps the soil and rocks behind it from moving or falling.*

> **Language SmArts**
> **RI.4.7 Interpret information**
>
> Check to be sure that students correctly identified the formations affected by gravity. Be sure that they accurately deduced that sand can only affect the lower part of rocks since gravity pulls windblown sand downward.
>
> **Ask:** What is a landslide, and why does it happen? *A landslide is the sliding down of a mass of earth or rock from a mountain or cliff. Other names for landslides are rockslides, avalanches, or mudslides (depending on what is sliding). Gravity causes landslides when it pulls rocks down.*

Gravity and Weathering

Let's take a closer look at how wind and gravity can cause changes to the land.

A Closer Look

15. Use the descriptions below to label the desert scene after the processes of weathering, erosion, and deposition have changed the landscape.

a. Sand dunes build up where windblown sand was deposited in certain spots. The dunes act as a wall that catches some of the sand that's being blown around.

b. Over time, sand blown around the desert environment eroded the lower part of the rock. Gravity prevented much of the sand from rising high enough in the air to hit the higher part of the rock.

c. Wind eroded the lower portion of the hillside. Once the lower portion was gone, the force of gravity pulled the upper portion down into the empty space.

 16. Language SmArts Use information to identify which of these formations were affected by gravity. How did gravity affect these processes?

Gravity causes windblown sand to affect the lower places on the rock formation more than the higher places. Gravity also caused the rockslide.

Unit 6 Changes to Earth's Surface

17. Which of the following sentences best describes erosion caused by wind?
  a. Soot particles from a smokestack are carried through the air and deposited into the sea.
  b. Wind picks up particles of dry topsoil from a farm and carries them many miles away.
  c. A child shovels beach sand high into the air and watches it land on the sand dune.
  d. Arctic air moves in and freezes water in the cracks of a rock, causing the rock to break into small pieces.

18. Which of the following forms of erosion is caused by gravity?
  a. landslide after the lower hillside is eroded
  b. wind blowing against sandstone cliffs
  c. waves striking a sandy beach
  d. sand dune built up by sand deposition

Putting it Together

19. Read each sentence. Circle true or false.

a. Wind is a force that can build and move sand dunes.	**True**	False
b. If a large sand dune or other type of hill has part of the lower slope moved away, gravity will cause material higher on the slope to tumble down.	**True**	False
c. The sand tumbling down is called a sand dune.	True	**False**
d. When snow melts on a mountain, gravity pulls the meltwater downhill, which weathers sediment and carries it to a new place.	**True**	False
e. When the water reaches a relatively flat area, gravity causes the sediment to sink or settle in that new place.	**True**	False
f. Plants do not affect weathering.	True	**False**
g. Water in the process of carrying sediment is known as deposition.	True	**False**
h. Erosion can be caused by animal activity.	**True**	False

391

DCI ESS2.A Earth Materials and Systems

Point out that erosion occurs all throughout Earth's surfaces—in rocks, topsoil, beaches, farmland, and deserts. Make a connection between some of the factors studied previously—such as water and living organisms—which may help along gravity. For example, human disturbance or flooding can lead to a falling rock.

Differentiate Instruction

ELL: Modeling When water seeps into a rock and then freezes, it expands and causes cracks in the rock. Gather several different types of rock and model this process. Limestone is a good one to use because it is porous and will absorb water. Provide some magnifying lenses and allow students to look at rocks carefully and write down observations about each dry rock. Then soak the rocks in a container full of water and freeze the whole container. Take it out the next day, fully thaw it, and then freeze it again. Repeat several times and observe the rocks again with the magnifying lenses. See if the students can detect any splits, cracks, or pieces of broken rock.

FORMATIVE ASSESSMENT
CCC Cause and Effect

Practicing with cause-and-effect relationships in our natural world helps us better understand and answer questions.

Ask: If a soccer ball starts rolling and that is the effect, what was the possible cause? someone pushed it or kicked it

Ask: If you push on a gas pedal and that is the cause, what will be the effect? car speeds up

Ask: What can cause snow or rocks to start rolling down a mountainside? earthquake, volcanic eruption

Lesson 2 How Do Other Factors Shape Earth's Surface? **391**

LESSON 2 Engage • **Explore/Explain** • Elaborate • Evaluate

EXPLORATION 2 Environments Change, continued

HANDS-ON ACTIVITY Partners 1 class period
Finding Change

3D Learning Objective

 Planning and Carrying Out Investigations

Plan and conduct investigations to model and observe changes that occur on Earth's surface. Student observations are used as evidence for change to the models.

DCI ESS2.A Earth Materials and Systems

Changes that occur on Earth's surface are the result of many forces or factors that break apart rocks and sediment and move particles.

Ask: What forces should we include in this investigation to model what occurs on Earth? *gravity, ice, water, wind, organisms*

Materials
The materials listed in the student edition are a starting point. Have a small stack of books or magazines to elevate the cookie tray for the hillside model. You can substitute any kind of soil for sand. You can also use any small sticks or hay to build the beaver dam.

Preparation
Assemble each station ahead of time. At the glacier station, place a small bag of ice cubes in a cooler bag with ice packs so the students can take out ice when ready. Place a sign at the sand dune model that says, "Do NOT turn the fan on high."

 Cause and Effect

Remind students that to adequately conduct investigations to show all cause-and-effect relationships in this lesson, they should be sure to include *weathering*, *erosion*, and *deposition*. Have them jot down these terms each time they use them or model them occurring during the investigation.

HANDS-ON ACTIVITY
Finding Change

Materials
- 4 cookie sheets with raised edge
- sand
- fan
- ice cubes
- modeling clay
- wooden stirring sticks
- beaker or small jug of water
- ruler

Objective

Collaborate with your team to model processes that produce change on Earth's surface, and determine what kinds of evidence those processes leave behind.

What question will you investigate to meet this objective?
Students should frame a question that refers to weathering, erosion, and deposition.

Procedure

STEP 1 Go to the station your teacher assigns you to. Make observations of the model at your station. Record your observations. Then rotate through the other stations and record your initial observations. When done, return to your original station.

Why do you think there are four different stations?

to model different processes

STEP 2 Find your station below, and complete step 2 for that station.

- **Hillside model:** Use a small stack of thin books to slowly elevate the height of the sandy end of the cookie sheet. Watch the sand. When it begins to slide downhill, record the height of the higher end of the cookie sheet. Leave the cookie sheet in that position so other groups can observe the same results.

- **Sand dune model:** Turn on the lowest speed of the fan at one end of the cookie sheet, and observe what happens. Record your observations in the data table. Turn off the fan and leave the model so other groups can record their observations.

- **Glacier model:** Use a book to gently prop up the end of the cookie sheet nearest the ice cube. Firmly press the ice against the clay and slowly slide it down the slope. Record your observations in the data table. Leave the model alone so other groups can record their observations.

- **Beaver dam model:** Use the wooden stirrer or alternate materials to build a beaver dam across the middle of the river. Be sure that the dam is relatively watertight. Slowly add water to the river on just one side of the dam and observe what happens. Record your observations. Leave the model alone so other groups can record their observations.

Student Lab Worksheet and complete Teacher Support available online.

STEP 3 Rotate through the stations again, recording your observations. Compare your observations and experiences with the models as a class, and revise your data table, if needed.

List your comparisons below. How were your observations similar and different?

Students should note similar changes in each model.

___

___

___

Model	Initial observations	Observations after change
Hillside	Student observations should represent what the models show.	
Sand dunes		
Glacier		
Beaver dam		

393

Procedure

STEP 1 If there are student groups of 4 or more at each station, assign them individual roles: one student records observations for the group, one is in charge of keeping the station clean, and two complete the task at the station.

STEP 2 As students work, circulate and assist to be sure they are correctly interpreting the instructions at each station.

STEP 3 Students will need the opportunity to compare and refine their observations. This might be done in the following class period, if time does not allow. Remind students to bring their results tables or observations to class the following day. It may be beneficial to take photos of each station after the initial changes occur. This will provide students with a reference after the stations have been taken down.

Connection to English Language Arts

Students will need plenty of time to process the information they collect during the activity and to categorize and organize it into the table to include initial and final observations.

Ask: Did any of your observations surprise you, or were they all what you expected? Accept all reasonable answers.
W.4.8 Gather relevant information and categorize information.

Differentiate Instruction

ELL: Modeling Students learning English may need extra help doing this activity. Pair them with strong English language speakers who can mime or draw pictures to convey the meaning of what each model represents while saying the words in English. Have the English-language learner repeat the words to illustrate understanding.

Lesson 2 How Do Other Factors Shape Earth's Surface? **393**

LESSON 2   Engage • **Explore/Explain** • Elaborate • Evaluate

EXPLORATION 2   HANDS-ON ACTIVITY, continued

Analyze Your Results

STEP 4 During the investigation, students should have been directed to jot down each time they were modeling *weathering, erosion, or deposition*.

Draw Conclusions

STEP 5 Call on different pairs to share their conclusions. First, discuss how different student groups would model an earthquake triggering erosion. Then, encourage students to think about how modifying the models would yield different results. Discuss under what circumstances different outcomes would happen in nature.

> ## Claims, Evidence, and Reasoning
> Have each group of students from the activity work with another group to share their ideas about other factors that would change Earth's surface.
>
> **Ask:** What kinds of water-based processes affect coastlines?   *tidal action, waves, storms, tsunamis*

Scoring Rubric for Hands-On Activity	
3	investigation done correctly, results recorded accurately, analysis and conclusions reflect the results, claims follow logically from evidence, several ideas for further study
2	investigation and recording done correctly, but analysis and conclusions are inadequate or incomplete, claims follow evidence loosely, few ideas for further study
1	did not fully participate in activity, results recorded but incomplete or unorganized, claims are made but do not follow logically from evidence, few or no ideas for further study
0	procedure not followed or did not participate, unorganized recording, claims have errors, no ideas for further study

394   Unit 6 Changes to Earth's Surface

Analyze Your Results

STEP 4 Describe the changes to Earth's surface you modeled in this activity. Include the forces that caused these changes in your descriptions. Use the terms *weathering, erosion,* or *deposition* and other terms if they fit your results.
Possible answer: The tilting hillside modeled the erosion and deposition that can occur due to gravity on a slope with dry, sandy sediment. The fan created wind that eroded the front sides of the model dunes and deposited the sand on the downwind sides. The ice cube glacier modeled the erosion that a glacier can produce as well as the deposition that results. The model beaver dam and river showed the flooding and erosion that occur when a river becomes blocked. The water deposited some of the model soil of the riverbank on the land near the river.

Draw Conclusions

STEP 5 How could you modify one of the setups in this activity to model how earthquakes can trigger erosion? Suggest one modification of materials and one modification of how you physically handle the model.
Possible answer: I could shake the table that holds one of the models really hard. The model should contain loose material on the top layer to show how it would move.

STEP 6 Make a claim about factors that change Earth's surface.
Student claims should mention affects of wind, water, and/or ice on Earth's surface.

Cite evidence from the models to support your claim.
Students' evidence should include observations they made during the investigation

STEP 7 Think of other questions you would like to ask about factors that change Earth's surface.
Possible question: Are there places on Earth's surface that are not affected by the factors modeled in this activity?

EXPLORATION 3 Always Changing

▶ **Explore Online** — Have students explore the desert oasis online to learn more about evidence of change on Earth's surface.

EXPLORATION 3
Always Changing

Evidence of Change

The different processes you've learned about that change Earth's surface are happening all around the world. Some of these processes occur quickly, and others happen slowly. Explore the illustrated environments on this page and the next.

Desert Oasis

20. Observe and record the changes that have occurred and are occurring above. Include the force that caused the change.

Image	What's happening
a. Mushroom rock	Gravity has caused the mushroom rock's top to fall off the column, and some of it has broken off into smaller pieces.
b. Plant roots	The plant roots have grown into rock and caused cracks in the ground around it.
c. Waterfall	The waterfall is eroding the boulders, and some of the boulders have smoother surfaces.
d. Rocks at base of slope	A rockslide must have occurred due to gravity.
e. Digging animal	The digging animal is causing erosion and deposition.

3D Learning Objective

Make observations that will serve as the basis of an explanation of how **forces that break down rocks and move particles** have a **cause-and-effect relationship** with Earth's surface features.

> ## Differentiate Instruction
>
> **Extension** Plant roots are an agent of weathering. They grow down and among rocks and can break them into smaller pieces. Depending on the structure of your class, either have students do some research or discuss with them that roots from large trees can have an impact on urban planning and development.

SEP Planning and Carrying Out Investigations

Ask: The burrowing animal and tree are two organisms you can see in the image. Do you think other living things use this area? Why or why not? Usually you can find living things where there is water, so living things probably use the waterfall.

CCC Cause and Effect

Each part of the image—the rock, the plant roots, the waterfall, the rocks at the base of the slope, and the digging animal—is either a cause or an effect.

Ask: What caused the pileup of rocks in the middle of the right side of the image? Gravity caused loose rock to tumble and fall down from the land above, resulting in a pile of rocks on flatter ground.

LESSON 2   Engage • **Explore/Explain** • Elaborate • Evaluate

EXPLORATION 3 *Always Changing, continued*

DCI ESS2.A Earth Materials and Systems

Students have to thoroughly examine the image on this page to complete the table. Be sure students comment on the fact that glaciers weather and erode rocks as they move, and beaches are eroded by ocean waves.

Ask: How do you suppose the rocks in the photo cracked? freezing and thawing

Collaboration

Feedback Have students work together to compare their answers in both tables on these pages. Ask students to come up with one additional observation that is not listed in the table. If each group can add one observation that is not listed in the table, have them share with the class and celebrate their skills of observation with specific positive feedback. Encourage them to use the terms *weathering, erosion,* and/or *deposition* in their answers.

EVIDENCE NOTEBOOK

Students should note that even though the two environments are drastically different (desert oasis versus forces in the cold), they both share the same forces of weathering, erosion, and deposition that shape Earth's surface. Students should point out that water is visible in both—either in waterfalls, the ocean, or glaciers. Rocks appear to be shaped by wind and water in both images.

Forces in the Cold

Weathering occurs in cold places just as it does in warm places. Glaciers can move along the land, scraping up and grinding dirt and rock. Water can seep into rocks, freeze, melt, and freeze again until the rocks break apart.

21. Observe the image for signs of weathering, erosion, and deposition in the environment below.

22. Use your observations to complete the table below. One has been done for you.

Image	What's Happening
a. Glacier	The glacier has been weathering and eroding rocks and sediment as it moves downhill.
b. Moraine	A previous glacier moved rock and deposited it here as the glacier melted.
c. Beach	The beach sand is eroded by the ocean waves.
d. Cracked rock	The rocks are weathered by the freeze-thaw cycle.

EVIDENCE NOTEBOOK What similarities can you find in both tables? Make a list in your Evidence Notebook.

396

396   Unit 6 Changes to Earth's Surface

Rocks Crack Up

23. Look at the images below. Determine the cause and effect for each change shown. Some may have more than one cause or effect. Then give evidence for your answers.

 Explore Online

Causes: gravity   wind   water   plant growth   ice
Effects: weathering   erosion   deposition

Cause: plant growth

Effects: weathering

Evidence: plant roots cause cracks in rock

Cause: gravity

Effects: weathering, erosion, deposition

Evidence: trail of large sediment

Cause: ice

Effects: weathering

Evidence: large cracks in the rock

 **Explore Online** Students can go online to analyze the cause-and-effect relationships that alter Earth's surface.

CCC Cause and Effect

Discuss with students before they get started on Item 23 that some of the images may have more than one cause or effect, and that they should write each of their ideas down. Students should be able to use the word bank to correctly match up cause-and-effect words and then to provide evidence from the image to back up their choices.

Ask: Does gravity cause weathering, erosion, or deposition? Gravity may lead to all three of these answers, depending on the circumstance.

Connection to Life Science

Burrowing owls spend most of their time on the ground, where their sandy brown feathers provide camouflage from potential predators. They either dig their own burrows, or they will use a burrow from a prairie dog or gopher tortoise to roost in during the winter and raise their young in during breeding season.

Ask: What effect might burrowing owls have on Earth's surface? Burrowing animals dig holes that cause erosion.
LS1.A Structure and Function

SEP Planning and Carrying Out Investigations

Students use evidence from the images on this page to explain the phenomena of weathering (plant roots, ice, and gravity), erosion (gravity), and deposition (gravity) and to form complex cause-and-effect relationships. Check to be sure their connections are accurate.

Ask: How is the cracked rock evidence of weathering? Rocks do not form with cracks in them. The cracks are evidence that this rock has changed. Since weathering is the breaking down of rocks, this rock has been changed by weathering.

Lesson 2 How Do Other Factors Shape Earth's Surface?

LESSON 2   Engage • **Explore/Explain** • Elaborate • Evaluate

EXPLORATION 3 Always Changing, continued

 **Do the Math**
A Waterfall Over Time

MP.2 Reason abstractly and quantitatively.

MP.4 Model with mathematics.

Students should notice and be able to make sense of the quantitative pattern shown in the table.

Make sure students can explain that as the years increase, the amount of erosion by the waterfall increases. Help them understand that the rate of increase is 2 cm per year.

Differentiate Instruction

RTI/Extra Support Provide graph paper and a ruler so that students can draw along with you. Draw a line graph on the board so that students can visualize the change over time. Point out that every time two years pass, the area under the waterfall is eroded 2 centimeters.

EVIDENCE NOTEBOOK

In their notebook, students should have two columns: "Could Have Formed the Rock" and "Could Not Have Formed the Rock." Circulate as the students write down their answers. Check that they have placed the surface features changes in the correct columns.

FORMATIVE ASSESSMENT

Ask: Which forces act to weather and erode quickly and which happen more slowly? Roots weather rocks slowly as they grow; freezing and thawing of rocks can also be quite slow. But windblown sand can erode away rocks quickly if the wind is strong enough. Animals can burrow down and cause erosion somewhat quickly. Water can move either slowly in a gentle stream or quickly in a rushing river.

398   Unit 6 Changes to Earth's Surface

 Do the Math
A Waterfall Over Time

24. It took one year for 2 cm of rock to erode under a waterfall. Look at the table to see the effect of the waterfall over time. Fill in the table for the unknown amount of erosion.

2 years	50 years	100 years	1,000 years	10,000 years
4 cm	100 cm	200 cm	2,000 cm	20,000 cm

 EVIDENCE NOTEBOOK Think about all the ways the surface features of the desert environment changed. Consider which of those are similar to the rock you saw at the beginning of the lesson. List the causes in two columns titled: *Could have formed the rock* and *Could not have formed the rock*.

Putting it Together

25. Complete the sentences in the paragraph by selecting the correct words.

icebergs	glaciers	clouds
erosion	weathering	deposition
rockslide	waves	sandstorm

In cold locations, the slow downhill movement of large ___glaciers___ can erode the rock and sediment. In the same locations, the cycle of freezing and thawing in cracked rocks is a cause of ___weathering___. If enough rocks build up on a hill, they may tumble down as a ___rockslide___. The burrowing of animals causes ___erosion___ and ___deposition___. Liquid water in the form of waterfalls, rivers, rain, and ___waves___ can cause erosion.

398

LESSON 2   Engage • Explore/Explain • **Elaborate** • Evaluate

TAKE IT FURTHER Discover More

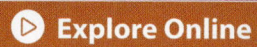 **Explore Online** Students can explore all three Take It Further paths online.

TAKE IT FURTHER
Discover More

Check out this path . . . or go online to choose one of these other paths.

| Seeking Stability | • Extremes!
• The Science of Slopes |

No Disruptions

 **Engineer It!**
Slowing Change

Floods, landslides, and other changes to Earth's surface can disrupt people's lives.

Engineers try to prevent some of these disruptions by designing and building structures such as wind barriers, levees, and sand fences. People can also help prevent erosion on hills by planting grasses, shrubs, and trees.

Look at the images here and on the next page. Then read about some of the ways engineers try to prevent disruptions.

Levees are long embankments or mounds of dirt along rivers or waterways that help prevent flooding.

Wind barriers are rows of trees that help prevent erosion by providing a natural barrier to blowing wind.

399

Collaboration

You may choose to assign this activity or to direct students online to the Interactive Online Student Edition where they can explore and choose from all three paths. These activities can be assigned individually, to pairs, or to small groups.

 **Engineer It!**
Slowing Change

Because weathering and erosion can present problems in people's lives, scientists and engineers work together to prevent or lessen the impact of some of these problems.

Ask: What factors might have an impact on people's homes? wind, water, and moving rock or soil

Engineers design wind breaks (shrubs or trees planted on a hillside), barriers, fences, levees, and walls to slow change and seek stability in the changing features on Earth's surface.

ESS2.A Earth Materials and Systems
W.4.8 Recall and categorize information from digital sources.

CCC Cause and Effect

When you think of a tree, you typically think of a tall, strong plant.

Ask: What do you think of as a plant that is the opposite of a tree (not tall and strong)? Student answers will vary, but you should try to lead their responses so that they identify plants that do not have woody stems but are soft and pliable and closer to the ground.

Wind barriers and windbreaks can be used to protect a given area from wind and are used a lot in agriculture to protect crops from wind damage. Explain that a windbreak is usually planted next to crops or along the side of them, such as a tall row of trees to protect the crops from wind.

Lesson 2 How Do Other Factors Shape Earth's Surface?   **399**

LESSON 2   Engage • Explore/Explain • **Elaborate** • Evaluate

TAKE IT FURTHER, continued

ESS2.A Earth Materials and Systems

A sand fence or sandbreak like the one shown here is a type of fence used to force windblown, drifting sand to pile up in a desired place.

Ask: Why would someone want to use a sand fence? *to control erosion, to help keep sand dunes intact, to keep sand off streets*

SEP Planning and Carrying Out Investigations

Have students research a force that they found most interesting in this lesson, such as rockslides or flooding. Students will come up with a plan to prevent damage from that force. The challenge will be to get them to create something new.

Differentiate Instruction

RTI/Extra Support You may need to review the concept of *pros* and *cons*. Students can work with a partner.

Ask: What are the pros and cons of a forest fire? *Pros: can help with infestations and disease, can provide nutrients for new generations of growth; Cons: can burn down valuable trees, move into developed areas and burn down homes, create smoke and soot in the air*

▶ Explore Online

Students can explore these additional topics online.

Extremes!

Students explore situations in which erosion and deposition happen very quickly, as in the case of extreme weather events such as flash flooding, hurricanes, earthquakes, and sinkholes. *(No outside research required.)*

The Science of Slopes

Students consider the rate at which erosion occurs in different scenarios. *(No outside research required.)*

400 Unit 6 Changes to Earth's Surface

Sand fences are used to force blowing sand to accumulate in a certain place. This helps prevent erosion of the sand.

Rooted plants help prevent topsoil erosion caused by wind or running water after rain or a storm.

26. Research one of the changes you've learned about in this lesson, such as erosion of beaches or rockslides. Come up with a plan to help prevent that change. Use the table below to describe your plan and list its pros and cons.

Plan
Possible answer: I will build a net to prevent rockslides from damaging or covering roads.
Pros
Possible answer: The net will keep boulders and other heavy rocks from damaging land or covering roads when they fall.
Cons
Possible answer: If the net were to break, the damage from the collected rocks could be worse than it would have been to begin with.

400

LESSON 2   Engage • Explore/Explain • Elaborate • **Evaluate**

LESSON CHECK

 **Explore Online**   Students can revisit the lesson phenomenon online.

LESSON 2

Lesson Check

Name _____

Can You Explain It?

1. Now that you've learned more about other factors that shape Earth's surface, explain how this rock formed. Be sure to do the following:
   - Describe what the rock probably looked like before it changed.
   - Explain what forces shaped the rock, and how much time they probably took.
   - Predict what might happen to the rock in the future, and how.
   - Use the terms *erosion*, *weathering*, and *deposition* in your answer.

 EVIDENCE NOTEBOOK   Use the information you've collected in your Evidence Notebook to help you cover each point above.

- The rock probably began as a boulder or slab of rock.
- Over hundreds or thousands of years, wind blew sand against the bottom of the rock. Over time, that part was eroded, while the top retained much of its width. The eroded material was deposited elsewhere as sand.
- Eventually the column of rock supporting the cap will become too weak or narrow, and the cap will fall and break. The cap could also be weathered by the freeze-thaw cycle of water.

Checkpoints

2. Which of the following is both a product of weathering and a factor that causes weathering?
   a. gravity
   b. water
   c. wind
   d. sand

401

Can You Explain It?

> **Collaboration**
>
> **Discussion** You may wish to revisit and discuss the image as a group to assess students' understanding of the material. Use the bulleted points in the Interactive Worktext to lead the discussion.

 EVIDENCE NOTEBOOK

Have students reread their answers to the Evidence Notebook prompts, and then use this evidence to justify their reasoning as they respond to the Can You Explain It? Make sure students understand that a complete response must address all bulleted points.

 Cause and Effect

Remind students that sometimes more than one force at a time is working to change an environment.

Ask: Which forces are most likely to cause changes in this environment? wind and gravity

Ask: How does the combination of these forces give this rock its shape? Wind blows the sand which causes the rock to weather. Gravity keeps the particles of sand near the ground so that more erosion occurs on the bottom part of the rock.

SUMMATIVE ASSESSMENT

2. Talk through with students that weathering is the breaking down of rock, and that it is possible that the very environmental factor that helps to break down the rock can also be the product of a rock being broken down!

 Formal Assessment   Go online for student self-checks and other assessments.

Lesson 2 How Do Other Factors Shape Earth's Surface?   **401**

LESSON 2 Engage • Explore/Explain • Elaborate • **Evaluate**

LESSON CHECK, continued

3. It is sometimes difficult for students to discern whether an animal digging a hole is causing weathering or erosion, because it is not always clear what happens to the sediment that is moved when the hole is being dug. If students have difficulty with this question, remind them that the very act of breaking down rock and soil is weathering, and when the sediment, soil, or rocks are transported across the landscape, it is erosion.

4. This question asks students to integrate the three processes of weathering, erosion, and deposition. Check in on students to be sure they reason through each one of these answer choices correctly.

5. While nonnatural structures can aid in deposition of sand, the correct answer to this question is a hiker that finds small, flat rocks stacked up. This was most likely not evidence of natural deposition but rather human intervention.

6. Encourage students to fill out this table with a pencil so that they have the option of changing an answer choice if need be. Tell them that a few of them can be more than one answer, but they should look for the best answer in each case.

Circle the correct answer or answers to each question below.

3. Which of the following factors contribute to weathering of rock?
   a. prairie dog digging burrows in the soil of a grassland
   b. the cycle of water freezing and thawing in cracks of exposed rock
   c. gravity causing rocks to tumble off cliffs or down hillsides
   d. a beaver building a dam across a stream
   e. plant roots growing into cracks of a cliff wall

4. Which of the following can be factors in weathering, erosion, and deposition. Choose all that apply.
   a. sand   **c. ice**
   b. wind   d. clouds

5. Which of the following most likely is not evidence of deposition?
   a. Damp sediment is piled up at the base of a mountain after the snow has melted.
   b. A river delta is broader and its water murkier after a flash flood has occurred upriver.
   c. A hiker finds small, flat rocks stacked at the peak of a mountain.
   d. A beach appears to have more sand after a large ocean storm.

6. Write the eight different terms to fill out four different sequences that begin with extreme events and cause changes to Earth's surface.

   | deposition of sand in city | earthquake | erosion of riverbanks | flash flood |
   | hurricane | large waves | loosened sediment | strong winds in desert |

hurricane →	large waves →	beach erosion
severe rain storm →	flash flood →	erosion of riverbanks
strong winds in desert →	sandstorm →	deposition of sand in city
earthquake →	loosened sediment →	erosion of hillsides

402

Unit 6 Changes to Earth's Surface

LESSON 2
Lesson Roundup

A. In the space below, describe how plants and animals can cause weathering or erosion. Give a real example of each organism and how it causes weathering or erosion.

Students might describe how ivy extends root hairs into cracks as it climbs a rock wall. The roots cause the cracks to expand, which can break off pieces of the wall. They might also described how a burrowing animal or mound-building termite erodes and deposits sediment in the process of making a home.

B. Write the correct words to complete the paragraph.

A hillside in a tropical rain forest is likely to have more erosion from _water_ than a desert because of the difference in _rainfall_. A desert is likely to have more erosion from _wind_ than a tropical rain forest because desert landscapes are more exposed. In many environments, plants prevent _erosion_ by holding soil, rocks, and sediment in place with their roots. However, plants can cause _weathering_ when their _roots_ grow and expand inside cracks of rocks.

word box:
water
wind
rainfall
temperature
deposition
weathering
erosion
trunks
leaves
roots

C. Circle the process or processes happening in each image.

flood
(weathering), (erosion), (deposition)

ivy
(weathering), erosion, deposition

delta
weathering, erosion, (deposition)

meerkat
weathering, (erosion), (deposition)

Lesson Roundup

DCI ESS2.A Earth Materials and Systems
ESS2.E Biogeology

This lesson summary enables students to quickly revisit key points and prepare for tests.

A. Most students can easily come up with an example to write about here, but some students may need prompting to give them an example of a plant or animal to use. It will help their writing if they have a solid understanding of the difference between weathering and erosion. Check to be sure that their writing shows an understanding of the difference between the two and that the correct cause-and-effect relationship is identified. **ESS2.E**

B. Encourage students to use pencil and to cross off the answer they chose once they fill in a blank. Point out to the students that four of the answers will not be used at all. The first two answers can be interchanged (water and rainfall), and students should therefore not worry which answer goes first in this case. **ESS2.A, ESS2.E**

C. Students connect with the concepts taught in this lesson by observing images that show the result of weathering, erosion, or deposition. Be sure that students are sure of their answer choice, and circulate and assist to help if there is any hesitancy to look for misconceptions. **ESS2.A, ESS2.E**

LESSON 3
How Can Maps Help Us Learn About Earth's Surface?

Building to the Performance Expectation

The learning experiences in this lesson prepare students for mastery of:

4-ESS2-2 Analyze and interpret data from maps to describe patterns of Earth's features.

Trace Tool to the NGSS
Go online to view the complete coverage of these standards across this lesson, unit, and time.

Science & Engineering Practices

Disciplinary Core Ideas

Crosscutting Concepts

Analyzing and Interpreting
Analyze and interpret data to make sense of phenomena using reasoning.
 **VIDEO** Analyzing Data

Asking Questions and Defining Problems
Asking progresses to defining a simple design problem that can be solved.
▶ **VIDEO** Asking Questions and Defining Problems

Developing and Using Models
Build and revise simple models for design solutions.
▶ **VIDEO** Developing and Using Models

ESS2.B Plate Tectonics and Large-Scale System Interactions
The locations of mountain ranges, deep ocean trenches, ocean floor structures, earthquakes, and volcanoes occur in patterns. Most earthquakes and volcanoes occur in bands that are often along the boundaries between continents and oceans. Major mountain chains form inside continents or near their edges. Maps can help locate the different land and water features of Earth. (4-ESS2-2)

Patterns
Patterns can be used as evidence to support an explanation.

 CONNECTIONS TO MATH

4.MD.A.2 Use the four operations to solve word problems including problems involving simple fractions or decimals, and problems that require expressing measurements given in a larger unit in terms of a smaller unit. Represent measurement quantities using diagrams such as number line diagrams that feature a measurement scale.

 CONNECTIONS TO ENGLISH LANGUAGE ARTS

RI.4.7 Interpret information presented visually, orally, or quantitatively and explain how the information contributes to an understanding of the text.

SL.4.5 Add audio recordings and visual displays to presentations when appropriate to enhance the development of main ideas or themes.

W.4.1 Provide reasons supported by facts and details.

Supporting All Students, All Standards

Integrating the Three Dimensions of Learning

Make observations and analyze data about maps to explain why people have developed them and how they use them. Understand that maps can help locate the different land and water features of Earth (and reveal how **large-scale systems interact**), as shown in the **patterns** of mountain ranges, ocean trenches, and other natural phenomena. They explore the advantages and disadvantages of different types of maps to show information.

 **Professional Development** Go online to view **Professional Development videos** with strategies to integrate CCCs and SEPs, including the ones used in this lesson.

Extra Hands-On Activity: Mapping Resources

What Other Things Do People Map?

Pairs
30–40 minutes

Have students research and generate a list of natural resources that are used in their area. They should determine the size of the area they are going to research, such as city, county, or state, as well as at least three natural resources that come from the area. Students should then generate a list of resource symbols such as trees for lumber, water drops for water, etc.

Students should then generate their own map using the symbols they have decided upon and placed in their map's legend. Finally, have students compare their resource map to a physical map that shows the general layout of the landforms.

 This activity can support mastery of this Crosscutting Concept: Patterns

Preassessment

Have students complete the unit pre-test online or see the Assessment Guide.

Build on Prior Knowledge

Students should already know and be prepared to build on the following concepts:
- People use maps for a variety of purposes.
- Maps can help people plan activities and find locations.
- Engineers, city planners, park rangers, and other professionals use maps as part of their jobs.

Differentiate Instruction

Lesson Vocabulary
- continent
- scale
- elevation

Students may need practice using the word *elevation* in a sentence.

Ask: What is an area in our state with a high elevation? **Possible answer: The top of a mountain has a high elevation.**

Connect students' knowledge of your state's geography to the term *elevation*.

ELL/ELD Strategy
Show a continent on a political map.

Ask: What are three countries that are in the continent of North America? **Possible answer: the United States, Canada, and Mexico**

A continent is any of the world's main continuous expanses of land, including Africa, Antarctica, Asia, Australia, Europe, North America, and South America. Have students identify and count the total number of continents on a political map or globe.

Lesson 3 How Can Maps Help Us Learn About Earth's Surface? **404B**

LESSON 3   **Engage** • Explore/Explain • Elaborate • Evaluate

ENGAGE: Lesson Phenomenon

Lesson Objective
To interpret map contents that illustrate topographical features and use maps as sources of data about Earth's features.

About This Image
The photo shows rocky mountain outcrops in the background with a flat, forested region at the foot of the mountain range. The lack of trees on the mountain slopes hints at their elevation. The trees in the foreground are clues that the elevation of that area is much lower.

 Planning and Carrying Out Investigations

Alternative Engage Strategy

Build It Up!   Small Group   ⏱ 10 min

Ask students to imagine Earth's surface, with areas of lower and higher elevation. Have small groups work together to cut out rounded shapes from craft materials to make mountains, such as the ones seen on the topographic map in this spread. The shapes should be of varying size. Students work together to stack shapes to create mountains, hills, plains, and valleys. Have volunteers explain their maps to the class.

Ask: How did you make the mountains? It is built up, with smaller shapes on top of larger ones.

LESSON 3

How Can Maps Help Us Learn About Earth's Surface?

Earth has many landforms such as mountains, valleys, and plains. Maps can model the surface features of Earth. Lines on a map can show the shape of the land. Numbers on the lines tell how high or low the land is.

By the end of this lesson . . .
you'll be able to use maps to learn about Earth's features.

Can You Explain It?

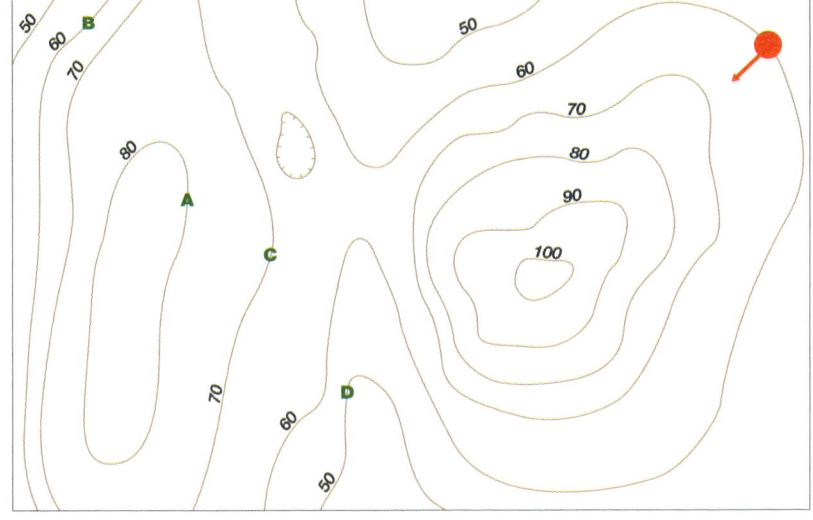

This is a topographical map. The lines and numbers tell the elevation, or height, of the land in different places.

1. Imagine standing at the placed marked by the red dot. What would you see if you looked in the direction of the arrow? How can you tell?

   Students should respond based on the preliminary observations they can make of the images.

   _____
   _____
   _____
   _____

   EVIDENCE NOTEBOOK Look for this icon to help you gather evidence to answer the questions above.

405

▶ **Explore Online** Students can view the lesson phenomenon online.

Can You Explain It?

Students record their thoughts about what they would see from certain vantage points, using a topographical map. Explain to students that the lines on a topographical map show the shape of the land while numbers show low and high points.

English-language learners may need help with comparative adjectives. Have them review a list of choices with a partner and order them: *highest, higher, high, lowest, lower, low,* and so on. You may also include nouns such as *height*.

 Patterns

As students explain the topographical variations in the map, point out that they are finding natural patterns and variations on Earth's surface. Mountains are the result of a chain of events starting with the movement of tectonic plates and are shown in various ways on different types of maps.

Collaboration

Think, Pair, Share Provide a variety of maps, including topographical maps. Have students work in pairs to examine the maps and identify the characteristics they have in common. Ask a few pairs to share their findings with the whole class, and ask for a show of hands to indicate which other pairs of students also identified those characteristics.

📓 EVIDENCE NOTEBOOK

Encourage students to use an appropriate graphic organizer, such as main idea and supporting details, to set up their notebook for this lesson.

Find more strategies in the online ELA handbook.

Lesson 3 How Can Maps Help Us Learn About Earth's Surface? **405**

LESSON 3   Engage • **Explore/Explain** • Elaborate • Evaluate

EXPLORATION 1 What Is a Map?

3D Learning Objective

Make observations about maps and their history **to explain** why people have developed them. Determine **cause-and-effect relationships** between maps and how they affect **our understanding of Earth's features**.

Asking Questions and Defining Problems

Prompt students to discuss types of maps on this page, using the images and descriptions. Students benefit from including the information in an organizer.

Ask: What are some advantages of having a printed map (not a cell phone or GPS map)? What are some disadvantages?

Printed Maps	
Advantages	**Disadvantages**
Possible answers: They are detailed and portable and can be carried in a vehicle. The work when technology is down.	Possible answers: When new roads are constructed, you need to get a new map; it does not show your location like GPS.

Differentiated Instruction

RTI/Extra Support If students have difficulty differentiating between the maps, have them work with a partner to highlight details in the book about each map's advantages.

EXPLORATION 1

What Is a Map?

A History of Maps

If you wanted to go somewhere you had never been before, how would you know how to get there? You would probably use a map. Over time, maps have been used by many different people in many different ways.

Photos taken from airplanes allowed for more accurate, or correct, representations of distances. They were better representations than the maps that were drawn from an on-the-ground perspective.

Hundreds of years ago, people walked the land or sailed the coast and drew what they saw to capture the overall shape of a place. The maps showed important roads, areas, landforms, and bodies of waters. The measurements were not always very accurate.

Printed road maps show not only major roads but also less traveled minor roads. Maps are changed and reprinted as new roads are constructed. Before smartphones or GPS, a family driving across the United States would carry a road map.

2. What is a disadvantage of a printed road map?
   a. Printed road maps cannot be used without a smartphone or GPS.
   b. They only show major roads and aren't very detailed.
   c. Printed road maps can be carried from place to place.
   d. When new roads are constructed or old roads are removed, a new road map needs to be printed.

406

Unit 6 Changes to Earth's Surface

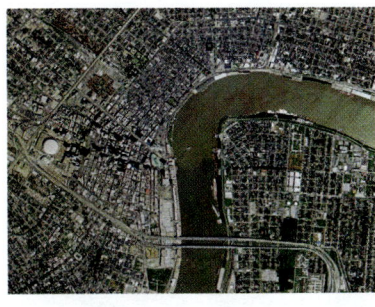

Satellites in space take photographs of locations all around Earth. This provides more detail of the area and can be sent electronically for use.

Global Positioning System (GPS) technology uses information from satellites. The GPS picks up information from satellites and uses it to determine your position on Earth. Using a map like this shows you exactly where you are while you are traveling.

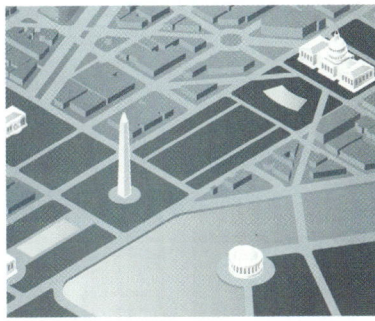

A 3D map shows the height and shape of land, buildings, and other features in a realistic way. Some 3D models are drawn by people with help from computers. There are also satellites that can record and analyze different images and piece them together into accurate 3D maps that a user can "fly through" on a computer or mobile device.

3. What are the benefits of using GPS? Circle all the answers that apply.
   a. It shows exactly where you are.
   b. It uses a 3D model.
   c. It can be used on a smartphone.
   d. It is very accurate.

Build on Prior Knowledge

Discuss students' experiences with cell phones, GPS technology, and online maps.

Ask: What types of maps do you and your family use? Which one is your favorite, and why? Answers will vary but should give insights about the topic.

Collaboration

Think, Pair, Share Have students review how GPS works. Student pairs discuss the advantages and disadvantages of GPS and complete an organizer similar to the one on the previous page. If necessary, provide prompts.

Ask: What are some disadvantages of GPS? For example, does GPS always work in all locations?

Using GPS	
Advantages	Disadvantages
Possible answers: It shows exactly where you are when traveling and is portable in a smartphone.	Possible answer: It does not always work as the signal might not reach a device; it's expensive; it depends on batteries that can run out.

LESSON 3 Engage • **Explore/Explain** • Elaborate • Evaluate

EXPLORATION 1 *What Is a Map?, continued*

> ## Differentiate Instruction
>
> **ELL: Partners** Students learning English may need support to comprehend the information on this page. Have English-language learners work with a student proficient in English to identify and discuss each type of map.
>
> **Ask:** Which map do you see at a shopping mall?
> locator map
>
> **Extension** Challenge interested students to draw a simple floor plan of where they live. They may include details such as the kitchen, bedrooms and living area. Provide pencils, rulers, and large sheets of paper. Volunteers share their plan with the class.

Connection to English Language Arts

Have students write note cards of each type of map: weather, road, locator, floor plan, world map, and topographical. They may include a short description or sketch. Then small groups work together to select and describe a type of map from the note cards.

Ask: What does the weather map show? How is it different from a road map? The weather map shows temperatures and other weather on a large outline. The road map shows roads and other details.

RI.4.7 Interpret information presented visually

How Many Maps

Different maps show different things. You choose a map depending on what you want to use it for. Explore the images to learn more about different types of maps.

4. What kind of maps have you used?
Possible answer: a road map or a GPS to help you get around.

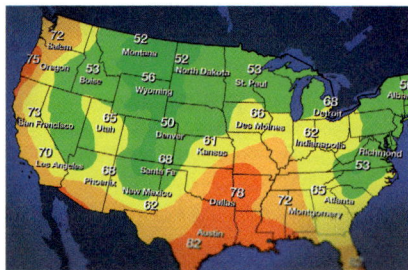 

Weather maps show rainfall, temperature, air pressure, and other types of weather. Data from satellites and tools on Earth's surface are used to make weather maps.

A **road map** shows all kinds of roads—from major to minor roads. When driving in a new area, road maps can help people figure out the best way to get to their destination.

Locator maps, such as this shopping mall map, help you find your way around a place. A *You Are Here* marker shows where you are standing compared to the rest of the mall stores. This way you can figure out how to get to certain stores.

A **floor plan** shows the relationship of the rooms in a building. It may show closets, doors, windows, and bedrooms. This map could help people who are looking for a new home figure out if the house has the features they need.

408 Unit 6 Changes to Earth's Surface

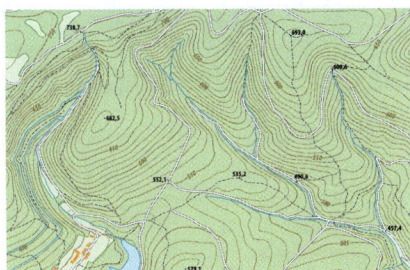
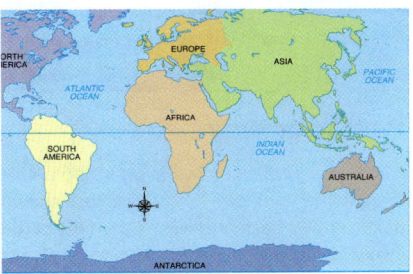

A **topographic map** shows features such as mountains or waterways. The features can be natural or man-made. Contour lines reveal the height and distances of these features in relation to each other.

A **world map** shows the **continents**, which are the major landmasses on Earth, and the oceans. Other features might be shown on a world map, too, such as country boundaries, islands, lakes, and mountains.

5. **Language SmArts** Compare and contrast two different maps on this spread.
A locator map and a floor plan are similar in that they show you where places are located. They differ in that one is used to find your way around a mall and the other one is used to see features of a home.

6. Which type of map would be the most helpful when going on vacation? Why?
Possible answer: a road map so you can find your way.

EVIDENCE NOTEBOOK Which type of map gives information most like the one you saw at the beginning of this lesson? What kinds of information does that type of map provide? Record your findings in your Evidence Notebook.

Putting it Together
All Kinds of Maps

7. Complete the sentences by choosing the best words or phrases.
Maps represent Earth's _**features**_. People use different maps for different needs. A _**weather**_ map shows how and where it is raining or snowing. A _**locator**_ map helps people get from one store to another store in a mall. Signals that travel from a satellite to a smartphone are used to show your place on a _**GPS**_ map.

| features |
| materials |
| road |
| 3D |
| weather |
| locator |
| topographic |
| GPS |

409

Language SmArts
W.4.1 Provide reasons supported by facts and details

Have students use supporting details as they compare both maps.

Ask: What details can you find on one map that help make it stand out from the other map? Possible responses: mountains and waterways can be found on the topographic map. The waterways are blue on the map.

EVIDENCE NOTEBOOK

Students should have said that the topographic map looks similar to the one at the beginning of the lesson. A topographic map shows the elevation of the land like mountain heights. The numbers show the height.

FORMATIVE ASSESSMENT

SEP **Analyzing and Interpreting Data**

Before students answer the question, pair students and provide each with one type of map. As you pose questions to the class, the student pair with an appropriate type of map stands up to answer the question.

Ask: What type of map can I use to find the fire exits in our school? floor plan of the school
Ask: What type of map can I use to find states bordering California? A political map shows that Arizona, Nevada, and Oregon border California.
Ask: What are several ways you could find directions from our school to your home? Accept all reasonable answers, including a road map, GPS on a smartphone, asking directions.

Lesson 3 How Can Maps Help Us Learn About Earth's Surface? **409**

LESSON 3 Engage • **Explore/Explain** • Elaborate • Evaluate

EXPLORATION 2 How Do You Read a Map?

3D Learning Objective

Students **analyze data** on maps in order to understand what information and **systems** the map is conveying. Students will apply these skills when reading maps about Earth's features to determine **patterns** of occurrences.

SEP Analyzing and Interpreting Data

Introduce students to finding direction with a compass by providing an actual compass, if available, or using an online compass or a compass rose. Point out and practice the directions, writing the full name and abbreviation (north, N; northeast, NE, and so on). As a class, take a tour around the room or school, calling out directions as you go.

Ask: What direction are we going? How do you know? **Possible answer: We are going south; the compass needle is pointing to S.**

Differentiate Instruction

ELL: Reading Pair students, and ask them to practice the names of directions and find places on the map of Washington, D.C. Point out that the term *direction(s)* can be used in several ways. For example:

- *Direction* can be the line or course on which something is moving or is aimed.

  Ask: Point the compass at the door. What direction is the compass pointing? **It is pointing north.**

- *Directions* can be a statement that tells a person what to do and how to do it, including going from one place to another.

  Ask: Can you give me directions from the school to the gas station? **Yes. You go down State Street and turn right.**

---

410 Unit 6 Changes to Earth's Surface

EXPLORATION 2

How Do You Read a Map?

Find Your Way

Knowing which direction on a map points north lets you use the map to find your way. A compass rose shows the cardinal directions—north, south, east, and west. Often the cardinal directions are indicated on the compass rose as N, S, E, and W. The points shown between two directions are called intercardinal directions. For example the mark between north and west is the northwest direction.

compass rose

A Map of Washington, D.C.

Use the compass rose and the map of Washington, D.C. to answer the questions.

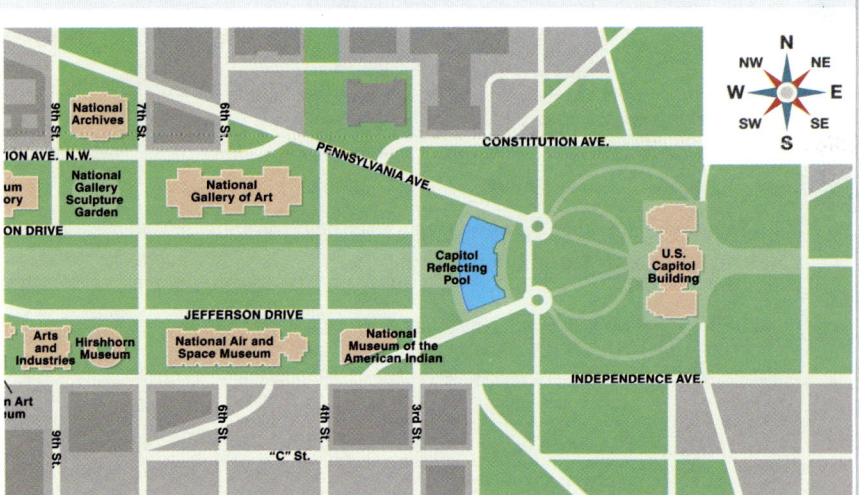

8. In what direction must you move from 6th St. to get to the U.S. Capitol Building?
   a. north
   b. northeast
   c. east
   d. **southeast**

9. Starting at the Hirshhorn Museum, travel east along Jefferson Drive. Turn north on 3rd St and look to your right. What do you see?
   a. National Gallery of Art
   b. National Air and Space Museum
   c. Constitution Ave.
   d. **Capitol Reflecting Pool**

It's Key!

An important part of any map is the key, or tool to unlock what the map shows. The key explains the meaning of the map's symbols, colors, and lines.

10. Why is a map key important?
Possible answer: The key helps you understand what the symbols, lines, and colors on a map mean.

11. How many lakes are located within the state of Nevada? Do not count lakes that border the state.
a. 1   b. 3   c. 5   d. 12

World Climate

12. This map shows Earth's climate. Use the key to answer the questions. Place an "x" on all the polar climates.

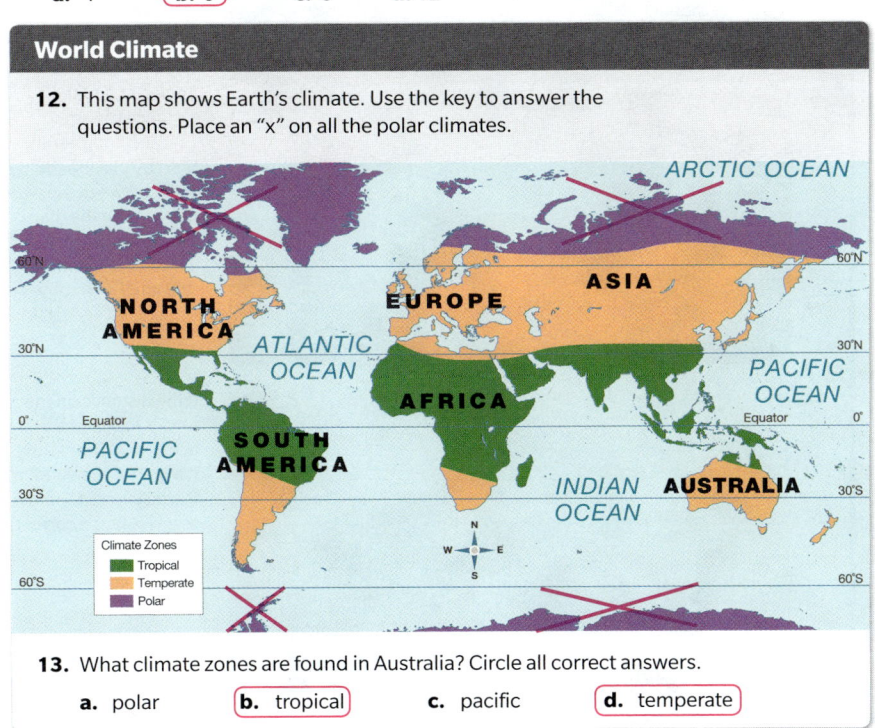

13. What climate zones are found in Australia? Circle all correct answers.
a. polar   b. tropical   c. pacific   d. temperate

411

DCI ESS2.B Large-Scale System Interactions

Point out the key on the top map. Discuss the elements featured within the key. Explain to students that keys can help locate different cities, as well as land and water features of Earth.

Ask: When might you want to study the key on a map? Possible response: when you are taking a trip or planning to go camping somewhere

Discuss the map at the bottom of the page. This map contains a different kind of key. This key doesn't have the names of cities or land features; instead, it indicates Earth's climates.

Ask: Why might people need to study a climate zone key? to better understand the natural landscapes, weather, ecosystems, and environments of specific regions on Earth

Differentiate Instruction

RTI/Extra Support Students may benefit from a step-by-step demonstration on using map keys. Model how to find information in the map by using the key to answer the question on this page. Make sure to point out what a border is.

Ask: Using the key, is Las Vegas the state capital or a city? city

Ask: Using the key, what climate zone is represented by the color green on this map? tropical

Lesson 3 How Can Maps Help Us Learn About Earth's Surface? 411

LESSON 3   Engage • **Explore/Explain** • Elaborate • Evaluate

EXPLORATION 2   How Do You Read a Map?, continued

Do the Math
Using a Map Scale

4.MD.A.2 Use operations to solve word problems involving distances.

SEP Analyzing and Interpreting Data

Read the page with the class to learn how to copy the scale onto an index card and use it to measure distance. There is a helpful video online if your students have access to the Internet.

Ask: How can you figure out what the tick marks in-between the numbers stand for? *You can skip count. This one is counting by 50.*

Ask: What can you do if the distance is longer than the map scale? *You can use your finger to mark the spot where the scale leaves off and move the scale over to continue to measure. At the end you add the numbers together.*

Do the Math
Using a Map Scale

Maps can be as small as the screen on a smartphone or as big as a dining room table. Most maps have a **scale**. The scale relates the distance on the map to the distance on Earth. Read below to learn how to use a map scale.

a.

Using the edge of a blank sheet of paper, copy the scale off the map.

b.

Use the scale you copied to find the distance between Chicago and Detroit. Start by placing the scale between the two city dots on the map. The distance from Chicago to Detroit is 450 km.

c.

If the distance on the map is longer than the actual scale, measure it in parts. Then add the distances together to arrive at the correct distance.

412

412   Unit 6 Changes to Earth's Surface

14. To find out how far away one city is from another, view the chart that measures the distance in centimeters. Multiply or add to find out how many kilometers that distance is on Earth's surface.

Rule: 1 cm = 5 km

Measure	Distance						
cm	1	2	3	4	5	6	7
km	5	10	15	20	25	30	35

15. The map below shows the state of Montana. The map scale shows the scaled distance on the map. Find the cities Big Timber and Roundup in the central, southern part of this state. The distance from the city Big Timber to Roundup is about 120 km. Try measuring it yourself. Then, work with a partner to find two cities that are about 60 km apart.

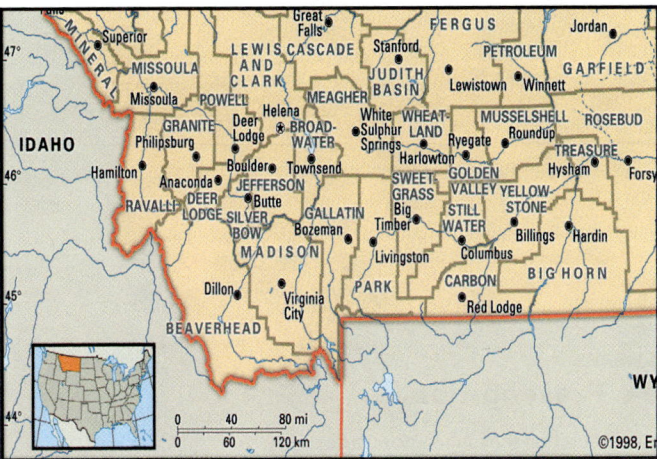

16. Pick two cities on the map and measure their distances using the map scale.

The distance from Dillon to Virginia City is about 90 km.

413

SEP Analyzing and Interpreting Data

Point out that maps are tiny compared to land area. The ratio is called the scale. 1 cm on a map may actually represent 5 km on Earth. Each map scale is different.

Discuss how some maps are measured with rulers instead of a premade map scale like on the prior page. To figure out the distance with a ruler, students must use multiplication.

- Elicit a starting unit such as 1 centimeter. As a class, decide what 1 centimeter represents. Then complete a chart as a class.

Scale 1 centimeter = 2 kilometer

Measure			
cm	1	5	10
km	2	10	20

Have students complete number 14.

Ask: Would a ruler work with maps found on the Internet? A ruler would not work because you can change the sizes of maps on the Internet, the ruler would not always be accurate. A map scale attached to the map that would also increase or decrease in size with the map would be accurate.

Differentiate Instruction

RTI/Extra Support Pair students of differing abilities. Have them work together on questions 15 and 16.

Ask: How did you find the distance? We used the method taught on the opposite page.

LESSON 3   Engage • **Explore/Explain** • Elaborate • Evaluate

EXPLORATION 2 *How Do You Read a Map?, continued*

HANDS-ON Apply What You Know
Make a Map
Show examples of floor plans, including plans of homes or schools. Note the features of the map, helping students to recall the goals of a floor plan.

Ask: What features do you see here? How are they shown?
Answers will vary but may show rooms, water fountains, exits using symbols.

Allow students who need extra support to use the example plans as they complete item 17.

Scoring Guidelines
An exemplary score should be given to students who draw maps of the school with main features labeled. Scores should not be based on artistic ability.

  EVIDENCE NOTEBOOK

Students should have observed that scales are used to help determine distance. Map keys help you know what the tiny symbols on a map stand for.

FORMATIVE ASSESSMENT

 Language SmArts
Create a Presentation
SL.4.5 Use Technology to Present Information

Review the ideas of a using a key, scale, and compass. If necessary, show a map as an example. **Ask:** How do we use a key? What does it show us? Keys help us understand symbols. Answers will vary but should address the topics.

Make sure that students understand the expectations of their presentations such as using multimedia. Have students add audio recordings to the presentation.

 HANDS-ON Apply What You Know
Make a Map

17. Draw a map of your school, including a map key that would help a map reader identify key features of the school, such as exits, water fountains, offices, and so on.

Students should represent key identifiable features of the school from their perspective.

 EVIDENCE NOTEBOOK Think about the different features of maps, such as keys and scale. In your Evidence Notebook, record how these features can be used to read a map.

 Language SmArts
Create a Presentation

Tip
The English Language Arts Handbook can provide help with understanding how to create a presentation.

18. Create a digital presentation that shows how to use a key, scale, and compass rose to read a map. List the parts of your presentation below.

Students should include at least three parts: key, scale, compass rose.

414

414   Unit 6 Changes to Earth's Surface

EXPLORATION 3 What Can Maps Show Us?

Explore Online — Have students explore the topic online to find out more about what maps show us.

EXPLORATION 3

What Can Maps Show Us?

It's On the Map!

You have learned about different types of maps, keys, compass roses, and scales. Now you will learn how scientists use maps to study Earth. View the different maps for details about each map.

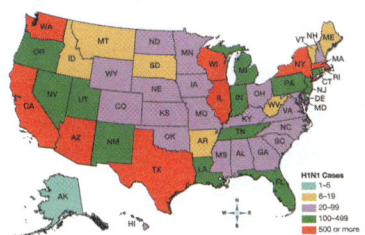

Medical Map Scientists use these maps to identify patterns, such as locations where certain diseases are more common.

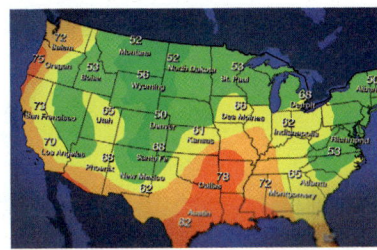

Weather Map This map shows rainfall, temperature, air pressure, and other parts of weather. A weather map usually applies to a few days.

Resource Map This map shows where resources such as gold, iron, and coal are found. Maps such as these help scientists determine patterns of where specific resources may be located.

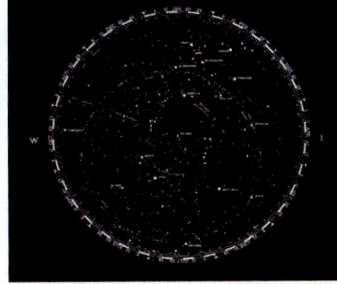

Star Map This map shows the positions of some of the stars and planets in the night sky. Star maps help scientists point their telescopes in the direction of the objects they want to observe.

19. What other ways do you think scientists use maps?

Possible answer: Wildlife biologists might use maps to know where certain animals live, or environmental scientists might use maps to see where wind farms are located in the country.

415

3D Learning Objective

Make observations and develop explanations about how maps show **patterns and variations in Earth's surface** and other types of information such as resources, climate, and the spread of disease.

CCC Patterns

Students use the maps on this page to observe patterns and variations that occur in a variety of information and that can be presented visually.

Ask: Why do scientists use maps? How does the map make it easier to see patterns? *Answers will vary but could include how diseases are common in some areas or the way they spread to areas.*

Connection to English Language Arts

Encourage students to consider how visual information helps them understand the ideas expressed on this page. Ask how the information contributes to an understanding of the text in which it appears in these examples.

RI.4.7 Integration of Knowledge and Ideas

Differentiate Instruction

RTI/Extra Support Provide students with specific scientific maps you have found online, such as maps showing the distribution of continents hundreds of millions of years ago or maps showing changes in weather patterns. Make a copy of each map, and pass it out to students, but remove their titles. Ask students what the maps show.

LESSON 3   Engage • **Explore/Explain** • Elaborate • Evaluate

EXPLORATION 3   What Can Maps Show Us?, continued

 Analyzing and Interpreting Data

Help students recall what they have learned about topographical maps. They will continue to analyze and interpret data in a topographical map to make sense of elevation.

Ask: What does a topographical map show? **high and low places, or elevation**

Ask: How does this map show us high places? **using contour lines and numbers**

Connection to Life Sciences

Challenge students to think about how the climate, flora, and fauna differ at certain elevations.

Ask: What is weather like at very high elevations? **It may be cold, windy, or snowy.**

Ask: What are some animals that live there? **Accept reasonable answers such as bighorn sheep, bears, mountain lions, and other animals adapted to cold conditions and scarce food.**

3-LS4.C Adaptation

Content Background

The word *topographic* refers to features of an entity or structure such as a land formation or a building. It also shows how those features are related. Elevation is one example. If the topographic map is of a mountain, it will show how each feature of the mountain relates to the others in terms of height. Explain to students that some topographic maps are three-dimensional, which means that you can see and feel the shape of what is being shown.

How High?

A topographical map uses contour lines to show a mountain's change in elevation. **Elevation** is the height above or below the level of the sea. The contour lines are marked in equal elevations on the map. The closer the lines are drawn, the steeper the mountain is.

 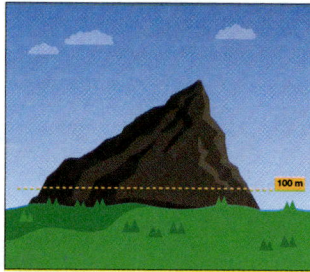

To make a topographic map of this mountain, we will begin by drawing the first contour line at 100 meters. The shape of the line shows the shape of the mountain at the given elevation.

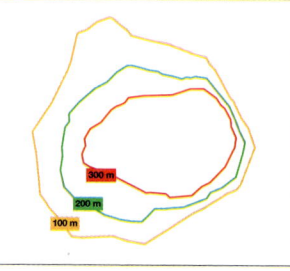 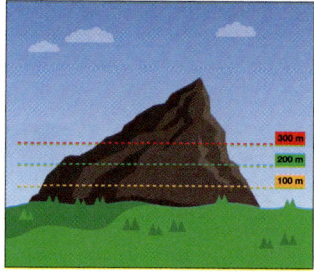

The shape of the mountain is marked every 100 meters as the elevation rises. Notice that the bands are drawn closer together on the right side and wider on the left. Discuss with a partner why it is drawn this way.

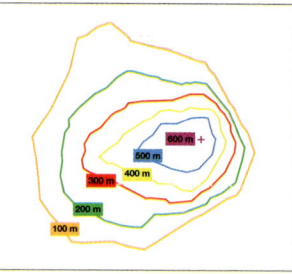 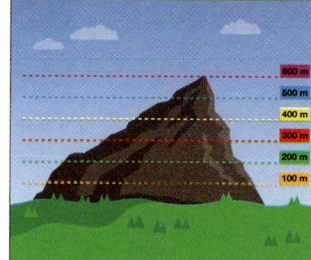

The contour lines continue every 100 meters until the summit, or the highest point of the mountain, is reached. The summit is shown with a cross. How can you tell by looking at the map, which side of the mountain is the steepest?

416

416   Unit 6   Changes to Earth's Surface

Navigation

Topographical maps are useful for planning buildings and roads. They have other uses too, such as for hiking.

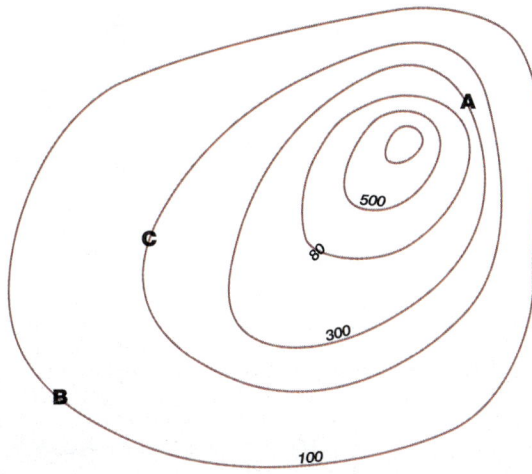

20. A group of hikers are planning to climb the mountain shown on the map. They would like to climb the part of the mountain that is the least steep. How should they plan their climb?
   a. Start below area B, then continue through area C to the top.
   b. Start below area A, then climb up through area A to the top.
   c. Start below area B, then cross to area A, and continue to the top.
   d. Start below area A, then cross to area C, and continue to the top.

21. Which of these points on the map has the highest elevation?
   a. A
   b. B
   c. C

417

Differentiate Instruction

Extra Support For students who require additional help, have them work with a partner to draw the hiker's path stated in each answer choice an determine which is the least steep. For question 21, have them use highlighters to trace the circular line for each letter. This will help them see which number goes with each line. As they answer the questions, monitor activity and provide additional support.

Extension Interested students can enlist an adult to take them on a hike. Students can use features they observe to draw a picture of their route to make a map.

Connection to Engineering

Students think about how a hiking trail can be designed to be safe and good for the environment. Point out that engineers and park designers create trails to withstand weather and prevent erosion.

Ask: What makes a hiking trail easy to hike on? **not too steep, good signs, rest stops**
ETS1.A Defining and Delimiting Engineering Problems

Lesson 3 How Can Maps Help Us Learn About Earth's Surface?   417

LESSON 3   Engage • **Explore/Explain** • Elaborate • Evaluate

EXPLORATION 3 What Can Maps Show Us?, continued

Differentiate Instruction

Extra Support To help support those students who are struggling with this lesson, have them make additional flashcards, similar to those they made in EE1, for the new maps introduced in this EE. Have them use the cards to answer question 22–24.

  EVIDENCE NOTEBOOK

Evidence should include observations about topographical lines. The numbers record height. Lines that are close together indicate steeper elevations.

FORMATIVE ASSESSMENT

 Language SmArts
Use Reasons and Evidence
W.4.1 Provide reasons supported by facts and details

Review the types of maps students have learned about by making a list. Include road maps, political maps, weather maps, and other types of maps. Have volunteers explain how each type would be useful or not useful for a road trip to a hiking destination. Check off maps that are not useful.

---

22. Write the words that complete the sentences.

topographic	resource	star
weather	medical	world

Maps provide many different kinds of useful information. A ___weather___ map is used to show where it is raining. To study the night sky, use a ___star___ map. Scientists use ___medical___ maps to identify patterns of the flu or other diseases in an area.

23. How can you tell how steep a mountain is by looking at the contour lines on a topographic map? Circle the best answer.
    a. The higher the elevation, the steeper the area.
    b. The lower the elevation, the steeper the area.
    c. The more space between the lines, the steeper the area.
    d. The less space between the lines, the steeper the area.

 EVIDENCE NOTEBOOK What do the lines and numbers on a topographic map indicate? What does it mean when the lines are close together or far apart? Record your answers to these questions in your Evidence Notebook.

 Language SmArts
Use Reasons and Evidence

24. You are planning a road trip across the country to do some hiking. What types of maps will be useful for your trip? Support your choices with reasons why you've chosen these maps.

Possible answer: I will use a road map to find the hiking spot, and a topographic map to plan my hiking route. The road map will help me get to my chosen spot, and the topographic map will help me understand how the land is elevated.

Tip The English Language Arts Handbook can provide help with understanding how to use reason and evidence.

418

418   Unit 6 Changes to Earth's Surface

HANDS-ON ACTIVITY
Park Designer

Objective
Collaborate to design a park. A park designer uses a map to plan where equipment and features go in the park. Think about how a park designer uses a map to do his or her job.

Materials
- printed park site map
- printed park material cutouts
- ruler
- glue
- scissors
- notebook

Find a Problem: What question will you investigate to meet this objective?

Possible answer: What is the best way to design a park for different purposes?

Procedure

STEP 1 Brainstorm: With your group, read through the criteria and constraints for this project. Brainstorm ideas with your group on how you can build the park and follow the requirements.

Think about the features in your park. To be successful, your park will meet certain criteria and constraints:

Criteria	Constraints
☐ Include a playground area.	☐ Your park can cost no more than $7,000.
☐ Include an eating area.	
☐ Include ways to protect the animals that live in and around the lake, such as ducks, raccoons, fish, and bats.	☐ Allow 90 centimeters minimum walking space between objects that people must walk around.
☐ Include several rest areas spread out in the park.	☐ Include a 240 × 240 cm garden.

Student Lab Worksheet and complete Teacher Support available online.

HANDS-ON ACTIVITY — Small groups — 2 class periods

Park Designer

3D Learning Objective
SEP Developing and Using Models

Students design a park using what they have learned about maps, following specific criteria and constraints.

Build on Prior Knowledge
Elicit students' thoughts and feelings about parks. Engage in a brief discussion about parks, asking whether students have ever been to one and, if so, what type. Have them share their experiences and knowledge.

Ask: What do you think makes a good park? What does it have?
Accept all reasonable answers.

Materials
Download and print the project sheets for each group (2 park site map pages and 1 materials cutout). Glue, scissors, and notebook paper help students complete the activity.

Preparation
In order for students to prepare for the activity, review elements of a park. Read through the criteria and constraints of the project as a class. Remind students that criteria determine success for a project and constraints are limits that need to be observed.

Procedure
STEP 1 Remind students that brainstorming means coming up with as many ideas as possible. Later, ideas are discussed and evaluated. Brainstorming often involves more than one person, who sit around a table or a room discussing their ideas, taking note of which ones are good and which ones won't work.

Lesson 3 How Can Maps Help Us Learn About Earth's Surface?

LESSON 3   Engage • **Explore/Explain** • Elaborate • Evaluate

EXPLORATION 3   HANDS-ON ACTIVITY, continued

SEP Developing and Using Models

Students plan and build the model of their park.

STEP 2 Monitor group activity. Encourage groups to discuss which of their brainstormed ideas will be most successful.

Ask: Why do you think this idea will be successful? What criteria are you using? Answers will vary but should include reasons.

STEP 3 Make sure groups cut their pieces, place them, and measure them before gluing the pieces down. Remind them of the distances listed in the criteria and constraints. Circulate among them, offering them assistance or answering questions as needed.

STEP 4 Point out that engineers frequently discuss, evaluate, and redesign based on initial results. Explain that planning and instituting a design is a process with many steps and some of those steps involve starting over or going back to an earlier idea. There's nothing wrong with testing a design, seeing that it doesn't work, and instituting a new one.

Ask: What parts do you think are successful? What things could you change or improve? Possible answer: We did not leave enough space around the benches, so we will move their location.

Analyze Your Results

STEPS 5–6 Students may be unfamiliar with how to cut costs of materials used in parks. Have students list the things that added that were not required for criteria and constraints, and also list the most expensive things they purchased. Have them decide if they could cut that item or replace it with something cheaper.

Ask: How could we make this part of the park less expensive? We could use cheaper materials or fewer playground pieces.

Ask: Why is it important to think about the animals while building? Because we changed part of their habitat, we need make sure their needs can be met for survival.

STEP 2 Plan: First, talk with your group about ideas that were brainstormed, and select those that seem most successful. Then, start drawing a rough draft of your park's design. Do not spend too much time on details. Last, make sure you are in budget by listing the items you need and the cost.

STEP 3 Build: Begin building your park on the provided map. Cut and lay out all your pieces first. Once you are happy with the placement, glue the pieces down. Use the scale to measure distances to be sure you meet the criteria and constraints. Make sure you add a key.

STEP 4 Evaluate and Redesign: Check to make sure you have met the criteria and the constraints. You might change your map several times before you have the most successful plan.

Analyze Your Results

STEP 5 How could you redesign the park at a lower cost?
You could use different, less expensive materials, or design on a smaller scale.

STEP 6 How does your park's design allow for the survival of the animals that live in and around the lake?
Possible answer: Signs are posted not to disturb the wildlife. A duck food vending machine is provided.

STEP 7 How did you make sure there was enough walking space for getting around the entire park?
Possible answer: We measured the spaces between objects.

Draw Conclusions

STEP 8 Communicate: Compare your park with your classmates. Name one thing you designed well and explain why you think so. Name one thing another group did well and explain why you think so.
Accept all reasonable answers.

STEP 9 In your opinion, what part or area of your park would you like to change? Why?
Possible answer: I would like to have a place for swimming.

STEP 10 Make a claim based on the question you investigated. Cite evidence from the activity to support your claim.
Possible answer: Scale should be set first so that all the pieces fit. We realized that we didn't have enough walking space and had to start all over again after the glue set.

STEP 11 Think of other questions you have about designing maps.
Possible answer: How do mapmakers draw areas too big for them to see?

STEP 7 Observe students closely as they answer the question. Provide assistance as needed, reminding students that they can look at the design of their parks and engage in a conversation with their group to arrive at an answer.

Draw Conclusions

STEPS 9–11 Remind students that a claim needs to be supported with solid reasons based on the investigation. Provide examples as necessary. For example: I think that the scale of the entire park should be set first because that determines how much space you have for each part of the park.

Claims, Evidence, and Reasoning

Have student pairs work with another pair to critique each other's claims and evidence. Ask each pair to share one way they would change or improve their claim. Discuss responses as a class.

Scoring Rubric for Hands-On Activity	
3	Meets all the criteria and constraints, makes a claim that is well supported by evidence and reasoning
2	Meets most of the criteria and constraints, makes a claim that is mostly supported by evidence and reasoning
1	Meets some of the criteria and constraints, makes a claim that is poorly supported by evidence and reasoning
0	Did not meet the criteria and constraints, makes no claim or does not support it with evidence or reasoning

LESSON 3   Engage • Explore/Explain • **Elaborate** • Evaluate

TAKE IT FURTHER Discover More

Collaboration

You may choose to assign this activity or to direct students online to the eSE where they can explore and choose from all three paths. These activities can be assigned individually, to pairs, or to small groups.

Careers in Science and Engineering: City Planner

City planners work to solve problems and design city spaces based on many criteria and constraints. Once a city is designed and built, city planners remain on staff to help plan future changes to the city, including those related to growth or to population movements and economic trends. Start a discussion based on student input.

Ask: What are some criteria a city planner might use for a new green space? Possible answer: Will it be useful and beneficial for many types of visitors?

Ask: What are some constraints? Possible answers: cost, time to plan and build, city regulations, safety

CCC Patterns

City planners follow established patterns in many aspects of their work. Elicit the ways in which patterns inform their work.

Ask: How do city planners help to design spaces? They study the designs of previous planners, evaluate them, and they suggest ways improve them. They may use what they learned to make a list of criteria for the person designing and building the space.

TAKE IT FURTHER

Discover More

Check out this path . . . or go online to choose one of these other paths.

| Careers in Science and Engineering | • Treasure Hunt
• Build a Map |

City Planner

To build a park, you would have worked with a city planner. City planners plan out city lands to suit the needs of the people living there.

City planners need to work and communicate well with others. They approve or deny plans to build in the city. They meet with the residents of the city, lawyers, builders, and politicians to decide what is best for the city.

City planners should have a good understanding of maps to help plan the layout of the city. Specific parts of land may be zoned, or set aside, for houses, businesses, retail stores, roads, public parks, and schools.

422

---

422   Unit 6 Changes to Earth's Surface

City planners must plan solutions to traffic and transportation problems. Buses and trains help reduce traffic and pollution in growing cities.

City planners help make laws about how land can be used. They make decisions about requirements for new buildings. For example, in an area with hurricanes, they may require buildings to withstand high winds.

City planners also must consider how to conserve, or protect, spaces for the local wildlife and plants. They may set aside a wooded area that cannot be developed or require a certain number of parks be built to preserve nature.

25. How do city planners use science and engineering in their job?

They need to be aware of newly engineered transportation systems. They need to know about animal habitats and weather hazards.

> **Explore Online** Students can explore all three Take It Further Paths Online.

SEP Obtaining and Communicating Information

Focus students' attention on each image, discussing the role of the city planner in these elements. Point out that city planners also help influence laws to regulate public spaces.

Ask: What are some solutions to traffic problems in our area? Carpool lanes were put on the highway to encourage people to drive together to work.

Ask: How did city planners protect spaces for wildlife in the last image? They created green spaces for wildlife.

Collaboration

Partners Have students work in pairs to research news articles on current city planning in your town. If you have trouble finding information on your town, use the closest urban city to your location. Have students present their findings to the class.

Ask: How was science and engineering involved in the city development you researched? Sample answer: A new traffic light was put in on Main Street and Easter Avenue after data was collected that numerous car accidents had occurred there. Because we live in an area with hurricanes, they have to engineer lights that can withstand strong winds.

LESSON 3 Engage • Explore/Explain • **Elaborate** • Evaluate

TAKE IT FURTHER, *continued*

SEP Obtaining and Communicating Information

Guide students to select a city map showing enough detail for them to decide on a location for a new park.

Ask: Where can you find a city or town map with a lot of detail? *Answers will vary but may include city hall, libraries, or online resources.*

Note that a map from a nearby city or small town would also work for schools in rural areas.

Connection to Life Sciences

Discuss plants and animals that are native to your area. Ask students what provisions need to be made to protect them.

Ask: How can we design a park to conserve wildlife? *It should have green spaces and regulations to keep wildlife protected.*
ESS3-1 Earth and Human Activity

Misconception Alert Some students may think that city planners work only in large cities. Although the majority do work in cities, small towns also have needs to be met and may have different criteria and constraints. City planners work in small towns as well.

Ask: What constraints could be different for a planner in a small town? *less money for public buildings*

 Explore Online

Students can explore these additional topics online.

Search Party
Students will use their map skills to follow a set of directions to find a missing dog. (*No outside research required.*)

Build a Map
Students produce a 3-D topographical model. (*Outside research required.*)

424 Unit 6 Changes to Earth's Surface

Improve Your City or Town

26. Suppose you want to add a new park to your city. You will have to decide what part of the city you can replace with a park. Do research to locate and print a map of your town. Use that map as a guide to draw a new map below that includes the location of your new park. Then answer the questions below.

27. About how big is the park you added? How did you decide on its size?
Possible answer: I looked at places in the city that could be changed into a park without hurting businesses or homes. Then I measured the space, which is about 3,000 square feet or 300 square meters.

28. What did you remove to make room for the park? Does this change cause other problems? If you were the city planner, how would you solve them?
Possible answer: I removed an abandoned building. We would have to get someone to tear it down and get rid of the materials.

LESSON CHECK

LESSON 3   Engage • Explore/Explain • Elaborate • **Evaluate**

Explore Online — Students can revisit the lesson phenomenon online.

LESSON 3
Lesson Check

Name _____

Can You Explain It?

1. Think back to the topographic map at the beginning of the lesson. What did it show? Then summarize what maps show and how they are useful. Be sure to include the following:
   - Names and descriptions of different types of maps.
   - Features that help you interpret a map's contents.
   - Descriptions of how maps can be used.

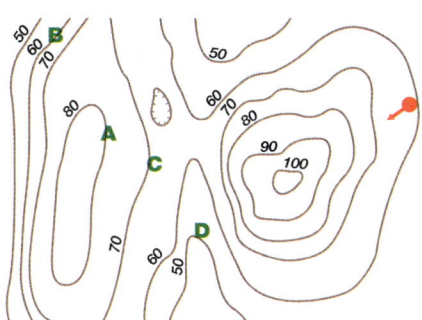

 EVIDENCE NOTEBOOK Use the information you've collected in your Evidence Notebook to help you cover each point above.

- The map shown is a topographic map of a mountain. The lines showed the different heights. I could tell by reading the map that the arrow was pointing at an increase in elevation.
- Weather maps show weather patterns.
- Star maps show the night sky.
- Road maps show roads, cities, and towns for traveling.
- A compass rose shows direction, a scale tells distances on the map, and the key tells what map symbols mean.

Checkpoints

2. How are maps useful to scientists in their work?
   a. Maps can be used to show data about weather or resources to make predictions.
   b. Maps can be used to show the location of rooms in a building.
   c. Maps can be used to show the state capital cities.
   d. Maps can be used to show the order of steps in an experiment.

Can You Explain It?

Collaboration

Discussion Have students work in small groups to recall information about different types of maps. Group students, and have them answer the following questions.

Ask: What does a topographical map show? elevation
Ask: What does a political map show? It shows cities, states, and political boundaries.
Ask: What is an advantage of using GPS? It shows your precise location on a map.

 **EVIDENCE NOTEBOOK**

Have students reread their answers to the Evidence Notebook prompts and then use this evidence to justify their reasoning as they respond to the Can You Explain It? Make sure students understand that a complete response must address all of the bulleted points.

Checkpoints

SUMMATIVE ASSESSMENT

2. Remind students that they may choose only one answer. Their task is to choose the ways scientists use maps. Explain to students that some of the choices deal with political boundaries or where places are. These are not examples of scientific maps.

Formal Assessment Go online for student self-checks and other assessments.

Lesson 3 How Can Maps Help Us Learn About Earth's Surface?

LESSON 3   Engage • Explore/Explain • Elaborate • **Evaluate**

LESSON CHECK, continued

3. You may need to review types of maps and information they contain. Model how to eliminate an incorrect answer choice, such as "the life cycle of a butterfly." Also invite students to revisit all three Explorations, as each gives examples of different types of maps.

4. Help students find points B and D if necessary. Remind them that the map they are looking at is known as a topographic map, which shows elevation ranges for a landform. The higher numbers denote a higher elevation. The lower numbers denote a lower elevation. To find a change in elevation, they will need to subtract one elevation from another.

5. Discuss the map of Nevada, pointing out cities and significant places listed on the map. Provide time for students to ask questions about locations on the map before they answer the question. Explain that the map contains a key, or legend, which tells readers what each symbol on the map means. For example, dots represent cities. Wavy blue lines represent rivers or bodies of water. Students can use the map key/legend to help answer the question.

6. Point out to students that, located along the bottom of the map, there is a scale. Scales show distance and allow readers to measure areas on the map. If they need further assistance, have them reread Exploration 2.

Answer each question below about maps and their uses.

3. Different maps show different kinds of information. Circle all the kinds of information a map can show.
   a. the elevation of the land
   b. the life cycle of a butterfly
   c. the location of stores
   d. the way to put together parts of a bicycle
   e. the way a rainbow forms
   f. the distance between two cities

4. What is the change in elevation between point B and point D?
   a. 10 m
   b. 20 m
   c. 30 m
   d. 40 m

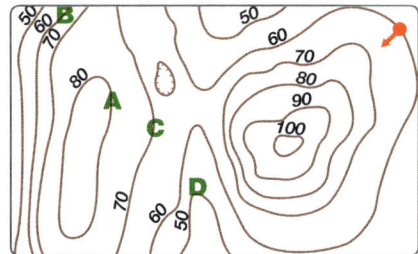

5. What is the capital of Nevada?
   a. Tonopah
   b. Carson City
   c. Las Vegas
   d. Wells

6. About how far across is the state of Nevada in kilometers?
   a. 100 km
   b. 300 km
   c. 500 km
   d. 600 km

426

Unit 6 Changes to Earth's Surface

LESSON 3
Lesson Roundup

A. Today, maps often show satellite images with roads or other kinds of information on them. Which of the following most likely describes a map from 250 years ago? Circle the correct answer.

a. a printed road map showing large highways

b. a 3D map showing all of the buildings in a city

c. a computer map showing large and small roads

d. a hand-drawn map showing the main roads in a town

B. Draw a line from each map part to match the correct description of how it is used.

a figure on a map that is used to show which way is north, south, east, and west

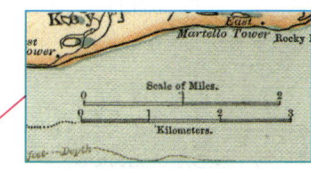

a figure on a map that shows the relationship between distances on the map and the distances on Earth's surface.

a figure on a map that explains the meaning of the map's symbols, colors, and lines

C. What else did you learn about the parts of a map?
Possible answer: Maps can show 3D features. GPS maps use satellites to locate exactly where you are. There are so many different kinds of maps.

Lesson Roundup

DCI ESS2-2 Analyze and interpret data from maps

This lesson summary enables students to quickly revisit key points and prepare for tests.

A. Recall that each type of map shows different information. Printed maps have advantages and disadvantages. Note that modern maps look much different from the maps of long ago. Older maps contained an artistic element that is usually missing from modern maps, such as sea serpents or flowery designs. They tended to present information in a slightly cruder way, sometimes with exaggerated features. **ESS2-2**

B. Students find out directions and other types of information using a key, scale, and compass rose. Have them think about the names of each figure: scales measure distance or size; compass roses show direction; and legends/keys offer a "key" to understanding the symbols on the map. **ESS2-2**

C. GPS (Global Positioning System) also have advantages and disadvantages. Encourage students to think about GPS and other types of maps as they answer the question. If students continue to struggle with the question, have them scan all three Explorations for information not found in the above two questions. **ESS2-2**

LESSON 4
What Patterns Do Maps Show Us?

Building to the Performance Expectation

The learning experiences in this lesson prepare students for mastery of:
4-ESS2-2 Analyze and interpret data from maps to describe patterns of Earth's features.

Trace Tool to the NGSS
Go online to view the complete coverage of these standards across this lesson, unit, and time.

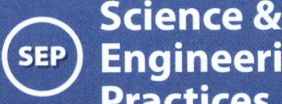 **Science & Engineering Practices**

 Disciplinary Core Ideas

 **Crosscutting Concepts**

Analyzing and Interpreting Data
Analyzing data in 3–5 builds on K–2 experiences and progresses to introducing quantitative approaches to collecting data and conducting multiple trials of qualitative observations.

Analyze and interpret data to make sense of phenomena using logical reasoning.

 **VIDEO** Analyzing Data

ESS2.B Plate Tectonics and Large-Scale System Interactions
The locations of mountain ranges, deep ocean trenches, ocean floor structures, earthquakes, and volcanoes occur in patterns. Most earthquakes and volcanoes occur in bands that are often along the boundaries between continents and oceans. Major mountain chains form inside continents or near their edges. Maps can help locate the different land and water features areas of Earth. (4-ESS2-2)

Patterns
Patterns can be used as evidence to support an explanation.

 CONNECTIONS TO MATH

4.MD.A.2 Use the four operations to solve word problems involving distances, intervals of time, liquid volumes, masses of objects, and money, including problems involving simple fractions or decimals, and problems that require expressing measurements given in a larger unit in terms of a smaller unit.

 CONNECTIONS TO ENGLISH LANGUAGE ARTS

RI.4.7 Interpret information presented visually, orally, or quantitatively (e.g., in charts, graphs, diagrams, time lines, animations, or interactive elements of Web pages) and explain how the information contributes to an understanding of the text in which it appears.

W.4.8 Recall relevant information from experiences or gather relevant information from print and digital sources; take notes and categorize information, and provide a list of sources.

RI.4.5 Describe the overall structure (e.g., chronology, comparison, problem/solution) of events, ideas, concepts, or information in a text or part of a text.

Supporting All Students, All Standards

Integrating the Three Dimensions of Learning

In this lesson, students will analyze and interpret data **(SEP Analyzing and Interpreting Data)** about the locations of mountain ranges, deep ocean trenches, ocean floor structures, earthquakes, and volcanoes **(DCI ESS2.B)** and use maps to identify the patterns **(CCC Patterns)** of the locations in which they appear on land and in the oceans. In using maps to identify locations of these phenomena, students will develop an understanding of what and where different land and water features appear on Earth.

Professional Development — Go online to view **Professional Development videos** with strategies to integrate CCCs and SEPs, including the ones used in this lesson.

Extra Hands-On Activity: Same Area, Different Map

How Do Maps Change?

 Pairs
45 minutes

Using classroom and media resources, have students investigate early world maps. Have students begin by searching for historical maps of the history of cartography, also known as mapmaking.

Once they have established a country or region to cover, they should locate the earliest version of a map available for that region. They should also locate an intermediate version, as well as a modern version. Each map they present should include the name of the map's author, the date it was made, as well as any other relevant information.

Students should note when the maps became more accurate and how technology influenced the maps. They should find that with time and improvements in measurement technologies, maps have improved in the accuracy of the landforms they represent.

 This activity can support mastery of this Science and Engineering Practice: Analyzing and Interpreting Data

Preassessment

Have students complete the unit pre-test online or see the Assessment Guide.

Build on Prior Knowledge

Students should already know and be prepared to build on the following concepts:
- Earth's surface changes.
- Different factors shape Earth's surface.
- Use map skills to read and interpret maps.

Differentiate Instruction

Lesson Vocabulary
- ocean trench

Students may know the words **ocean** and the word **trench**, but may not understand the open compound *ocean trench*.

Ask: What is a synonym for the word *ocean*? sea
Ask: What are the names of some of the oceans on Earth? Arctic, Atlantic, Indian, Pacific
Ask: What is a synonym for the word *trench*? ditch, channel, trough, rut, valley, dig, big crack

Ask: What would an *ocean trench* be? a long deep valley on the ocean floor

ELL/ELD Strategy
Show a picture of an ocean trench. Have students use adjectives to describe it. long, deep, underwater

Have students draw a picture of what they think an ocean trench is. Then, have them describe their pictures.

Lesson 4 What Patterns Do Maps Show Us? **428B**

LESSON 4 **Engage** • Explore/Explain • Elaborate • Evaluate

ENGAGE: Lesson Phenomenon

Lesson Objective

To identify and explain where on Earth's surface earthquakes, volcanoes, mountains, and ocean trenches can be found; to use maps to describe the patterns they observe in the locations of those land- and water forms.

About This Image

There are many different kinds of volcanoes such as: cinder cones, composite volcanos like Mount St. Helens, lava domes, and shield volcanoes such as the one shown here in Hawaii. Some students may have seen an actual volcano or a picture or a movie, or read about volcanoes. During a volcanic eruption, magma, or molten rock called lava, emerges from deep inside Earth. Pressure forces the lava to rise. Earthquakes often precede volcanic eruptions and gases and ash may be released.

Analyzing and Interpreting Data

Alternative Engage Strategy

Build it Up!	👥 Whole Class ⏱ 10 min

Assign pairs to look up the location of one earthquake or volcano. Use a world map to put one color of pushpins in the places where students know volcanoes exist or have erupted. Put another color of pushpins to identify locations students know earthquakes have occurred.

Ask: Is there any kind of pattern we can see in the placement of these pins? Students may or may not recognize that volcanoes and earthquakes occur along the edges of continents.

LESSON 4

What Patterns Do Maps Show Us?

An erupting volcano is a spectacular sight, especially at night. Volcanoes form when pressure below Earth's surface causes hot, melted rock called *lava* to flow onto the land. They also form when ash explodes onto Earth's surface. Volcanoes are found only in certain places on Earth. Do you know where?

By the end of this lesson . . .
you'll be able to describe patterns about the locations of earthquakes, volcanoes, mountains, and ocean trenches.

Unit 6 Changes to Earth's Surface

Can You Explain It?

In 2005, a huge crack began to form in the desert of eastern Africa. This giant crack is part of the Rift Valley. A rift is a large crack in Earth's surface where the top layers of Earth are being pulled apart.

1. The rift in Africa is getting bigger and deeper every year. Study the map. Predict how the land and bodies of water in this area of the world might change as the rift changes.

   Students should respond based on the preliminary observations they can make of the images.

   Tip

   Learn more about processes and things that can change Earth's rocks in *How Do Other Factors Shape Earth's Surface?*

   EVIDENCE NOTEBOOK Look for this icon to help you gather evidence to answer the question above.

▶ **Explore Online** — Students can view the lesson phenomenon online.

Can You Explain It?

Students are asked to study the map and make a prediction about how the land and bodies of water in this area of the world could change as the rift changes. Urge students not to worry about whether their answers are correct. They should expect their ideas and predictions to change as they progress through the Explorations. They will get to revise their answers at the end of the lesson.

Collaboration

Think, Pair, Share Provide students outlines of a world map. Have students locate the Rift Valley on the map. Ask them to predict what would have made a crack like this. Have them share their ideas with a partner and then with the class.

EVIDENCE NOTEBOOK

Encourage students to use an appropriate graphic organizer, such as main idea and supporting details, to set up their notebook for this lesson.

Find more strategies in the online ELA handbook.

Lesson 4 What Patterns Do Maps Show Us? 429

LESSON 4 Engage • **Explore/Explain** • Elaborate • Evaluate

EXPLORATION 1 By Land or By Sea

3D Learning Objective

Students **analyze and interpret data** to find **patterns** in where **mountain ranges, earthquakes, volcanoes, and ocean trenches** occur.

SEP Analyzing and Interpreting Data

Have students use a pencil to connect the dots and draw the Ring of Fire over the map in their books.

Ask: How can you describe the Ring of Fire? *A circle around the Pacific Ocean along the east coast of Asia and Australia and the west coast of North and South America.*

Differentiate Instruction

RTI/Extra Support If students are having trouble distinguishing between earthquakes and volcanic eruptions, it may be helpful to show them videos of volcanoes erupting and earthquakes shaking the ground.

DCI ESS2.B: Plate Tectonics and Large-Scale System Interactions

Discuss the differences between earthquakes and volcanoes and the different damage they can cause.

Ask: What do you think causes more damage, an earthquake or volcano? *Anything in the path of an erupting volcano would be destroyed and covered with rock and ash. Ash and gases could carry in the wind across wide areas. Earthquakes might be over in a few minutes but the collapsing buildings and bridges and loss of power can be devastating. Which is worse depends on the severity of the event.*

430 Unit 6 Changes to Earth's Surface

EXPLORATION 1

By Land or By Sea

Ring of Fire

Volcanoes form when lava flows onto Earth's surface. Some volcanoes form on land, some form under water. Earthquakes happen when large blocks of rock shift and release stored energy. Earthquakes happen on land and under water, too, and cause the ground to shake.

Thankfully, volcanic eruptions and earthquakes do not occur everywhere. But one area of Earth that does experience many volcanoes and earthquakes is along the edges of the Pacific Ocean. This region is called the Ring of Fire. Look at the map to locate this area that rings a large part of the Pacific Ocean.

Now look at the photos below. They are evidence of how earthquakes and volcanoes can change Earth's surface.

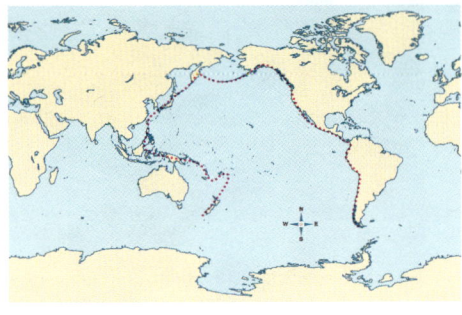

Earthquakes occur on land and under water. On land, they can cause the ground to crack.

The shaking of the ground during an earthquake can cause much damage. Sometimes, it makes buildings collapse.

Volcanoes can send lava, ash, smoke, and dust high into the air. Eruptions also add dangerous gases to the air.

Some volcanoes form tall mountains as the lava and other erupted materials cool and build up over time.

430

2. Language SmArts Compare and contrast earthquakes and volcanoes.

Both happen on land and under water. Both change Earth's surface. Volcanoes are cracks through which lava and other materials flow onto the surface. Earthquakes are movements of the ground.

3. Complete the sentences.

The Ring of Fire is an area with many ___volcanoes___ and ___earthquakes___.

It is located around the ___Pacific Ocean___.

4. Which are true of volcanoes? Circle all that apply.
  a. They always form tall mountains.
  b. They can pollute the air.
  c. Many form in the Ring of Fire.
  d. They cause the ground to crack.

 HANDS-ON Apply What You Know

Earthquakes and Buildings

Earthquakes can cause much damage to buildings. Work with two or three others to design and test a building that will survive a model earthquake.

Materials
- toothpicks
- modeling clay
- 2 desks or tables
- stopwatch

Procedure

1. With your team, brainstorm for 2 minutes to come up with a possible toothpick-clay building design. One design constraint is that the structure must be 4 stories high; 1 toothpick length equals 1 story height. Sketch your team's design on paper.
2. Construct your model building in 5 minutes or less.
3. Test your design, placing it over the space between two desks pushed together. Gently shake the desks or tables for 1 minute to simulate an earthquake.
4. With your team, spend 3 minutes discussing how well your design withstood the earthquake. Identify two or three ways to improve your design.

 EVIDENCE NOTEBOOK Do any of the images remind you of the African Rift? How does this help you begin to understand what is happening in the Rift Valley?

431

 Language SmArts
RI.4.5 Describe the overall structure of events

Ask: How are earthquakes and volcanoes the same? Both are results of underground energy and can cause damage. Both occur along the Ring of Fire.

Ask: How are they different? Volcanoes spurt out lava and ash. Lava can destroy whatever is in its path. Earthquakes shake Earth and may crack the surface.

 Patterns

Ask: What pattern does the Ring of Fire represent? A ring where earthquakes and volcanoes have occurred again and again.

HANDS-ON Appy What You Know
Earthquakes and Buildings
Review criteria and constraints with students.

Ask: Why is it important for buildings in earthquake zones to be structurally sound? They could collapse otherwise.

Scoring Guidelines
Exemplary activity results would demonstrate understanding of the construction of stable structures.

 EVIDENCE NOTEBOOK

Students should indicate that the image of the crack caused by the Earthquake is most similar ot the African Rift. The African Rift was likely caused by and Earthquake.

Ask: Is the Rift Valley photo more like the results of an earthquake or a volcano? earthquake

Lesson 4 What Patterns Do Maps Show Us? **431**

LESSON 4   Engage • **Explore/Explain** • Elaborate • Evaluate

EXPLORATION 1   By Land or Sea, continued

 Analyzing and Interpreting Data

Use the picture to discuss how mountains above and under the water might be the same and different.

Misconception Alert Some students may think that earthquakes and volcanoes are weather related, but they can occur in any type of weather because they occur as the result of underground energy, not atmospheric energy.

Ask: Are volcanoes and earthquakes caused by weather? **No. They are caused by the Earth's surface.**

 ESS2.B: Plate Tectonics and Large-Scale System Interactions

With the class, compare land holes with ocean trenches.

Ask: Why are ocean trenches called trenches and not holes? **They are not holes. They are very deep narrow valleys. They do not exist on land.**

Differentiate Instruction

ELL: Drawing Have students draw sketches and label a land mountain, an underwater mountain, and an ocean trench. Have them present and explain their pictures to the group.

Connection to Math

Ask: What is the difference between the the highest peak on land, Mt. Everest (8,848 meters high), and the deepest known part of the ocean, the Mariana Trench (10,994 meters deep)?
19,842

The word difference may confuse students into subtracting instead of adding. Have them work in small groups and encourage them to make a diagram to help see the difference in heights.

4.MD.A.2 Solve word problems including distances

432   Unit 6 Changes to Earth's Surface

Up and Down

Other features that can be found on Earth's surface are mountains and trenches. Study the drawing as you read about these two features of Earth's surface.

Mountains and Trenches

5. Use the information below to label the image. You may use a word more than once.

This drawing shows some land and ocean features. Drawing is not to scale.

 Mountains can form on land. Some are very tall and jagged, while others are smaller and rounded. Mt. Everest in the Himalayan Mountains is the tallest mountain on land. It is 8,848 meters high.

Mountains form under water, too. A huge mountain range called the Mid-Atlantic Ridge runs down the middle of the Atlantic Ocean.

 Trenches are long, deep, narrow valleys found on the ocean floor. The Marianas Trench in the Pacific Ocean is the deepest known part of the ocean. It is more than 10,994 meters deep!

6. Which is true of mountains? Circle all that apply.
   a. Some are rounded.
   b. Some are tall and jagged.
   c. They form only under water.
   d. They form on land and under water.

7. What is an ocean trench?
   a. an island that forms in the ocean
   b. a volcano with a jagged peak
   c. a round mountain on land
   d. a deep, narrow valley on the ocean floor

432

Engineer It!
Mapping the Ocean Floor

 Explore Online

The ocean floor has many interesting features—mountains, trenches, and volcanoes, just to name a few. But how do we know this?

Multibeam sonar is a technology that uses sound waves to determine how deep the ocean floor is. The signal is sent out from a ship in a fan like pattern, and it returns data about the features found on the ocean floor. This information is used to make ocean floor maps.

8. How is the ocean floor mapped?
The multibeam sonar uses sound waves to help make maps of the ocean floor.

Putting it Together

9. On each line, write whether the feature forms on *land*, *under water*, or *both*.

mountains
both

trench
under water

volcano
both

earthquake
both

 **Explore Online** Have students explore ocean features online.

 **Engineer It!**
Mapping the Ocean Floor

Connections to Physical Science

Refer to Unit 2, Lesson 2, How Is Energy Transferred? to refresh student knowledge about sound waves.

Ask: What is sound? Sound is energy that travels in vibrations, waves that come from an object that starts the vibration.

Ask: Do sound waves travel faster through water or air? water

Ask: How are sound waves able to help map the ocean floor? Sound waves are sent into the ocean at different locations. The equipment measures the length of time it takes for the sound to travel back from the sea floor as an echo. The longer the time, the deeper the ocean bottom.

PS4.A Wave Properties

 Patterns

Ask: How do people mapping the ocean floor rely on patterns? SONAR identifies elevation patterns on the bottom of the ocean.

FORMATIVE ASSESSMENT
Putting It Together

Review student answers as a class.

Ask: How do we know there are volcanoes and earthquakes both on land and under water? They can be measured and observed on land and also under water. Underwater volcanos build up and have even become islands.

Ask: Why would trenches like ocean trenches not occur on land? Possible answer: They are the deepest parts of Earth, so they are far below sea level.

Lesson 4 What Patterns Do Maps Show Us?

LESSON 4   Engage • **Explore/Explain** • Elaborate • Evaluate

EXPLORATION 2 Can Maps Help Us See Patterns?

3D Learning Objective

After learning about **mountains, deep ocean trenches, ocean floor structures, earthquakes, and volcanoes,** students **analyze and interpret data** to identify **patterns** of occurrence.

SEP Analyzing and Interpreting Data

For five minutes, have pairs of students compare the three maps to see how they are the same and different. Then have them identify the similarities and differences in the location of earthquakes, mountains, and volcanos on land as you record them on the board. For example:

Similarities	Differences
All three occur along the Ring of Fire.	Few volcanoes occur in the middle of continents. Many volcanoes are on islands.
All three occur on coastlines.	Mountains are found in the interior of continets.

Differentiate Instruction

RTI/Extra Support Have students compare the occurrences of earthquakes, volcanoes, and mountains continent by continent: Africa, Antarctica, Asia, Australia, North America, South America.

EXPLORATION 2

Can Maps Help Us See Patterns?

Finding Patterns on Land

You just learned that mountains, earthquakes, and volcanoes can occur in the ocean and on land. Are there particular places on Earth where they are more likely to occur? Look at these maps to help you answer this question.

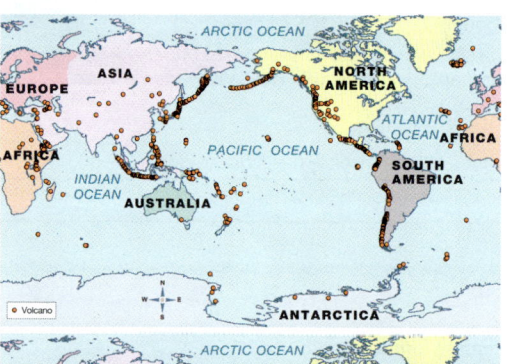

This map shows the locations of volcanoes that have formed on land.

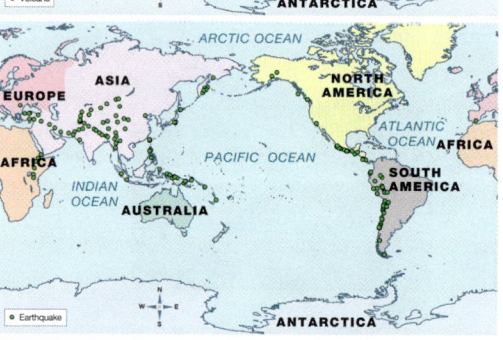

This map shows the locations of earthquakes that have occurred on land.

This map shows the locations of mountains that have formed on land.

434

434   Unit 6 Changes to Earth's Surface

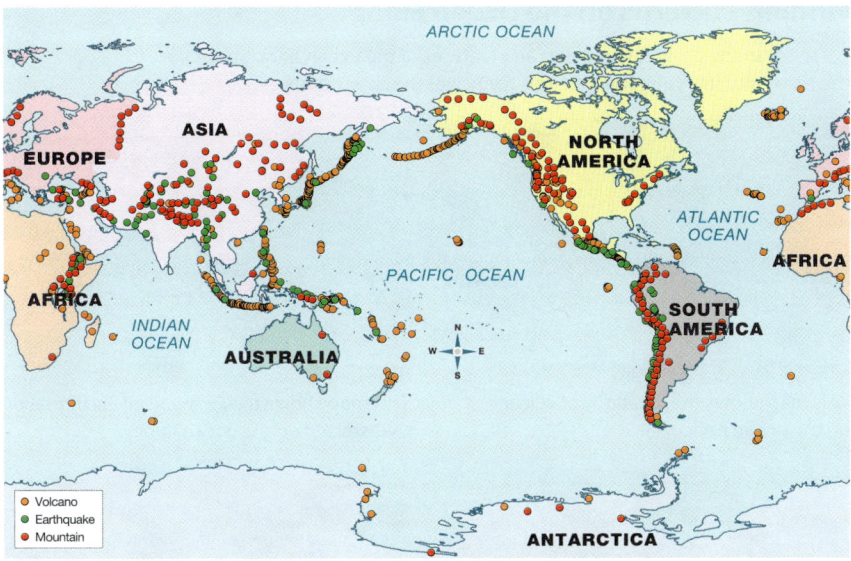

10. Based on your observations of the maps, what can you claim about mountains, volcanoes, and earthquakes?

Possible answer: I observed that most earthquakes, volcanoes, and mountain ranges on land are located near the edges of continents. Mountains can also be found in the center of continents. But some do not fit this pattern, as I also noticed that there are a few volcanoes, earthquakes, and mountains located in the interior of some continents.

11. Choose the words or phrases that correctly complete each sentence

| in the center | near the edges |

Earthquakes on land are most likely to occur __near the edges__ of continents.

Volcanoes on land often are located __near the edges__ of continents. Mountains on land are found __near the edges__ and __in the center__ of continents.

EVIDENCE NOTEBOOK How can these map patterns help you predict what is happening in the African Rift Valley?

CCC Patterns

Point out that the locations of mountain ranges, earthquakes, and volcanoes occur in patterns. Major mountain chains form inside continents or near their edges.

Ask: What is similar in the location patterns of mountains, earthquakes, and volcanoes on land? All three occur near the edges of continents.

DCI ESS2.B: Plate Tectonics and Large-Scale System Interactions

Ask: Why do you think earthquakes, mountains, and volcanoes occur in the same general locations in the world? There must be something that is causing disturbances in those locations that result in underground activity.

EVIDENCE NOTEBOOK

Have students locate the Rift Valley on these maps before they answer the question.

Ask: What do you notice about the location of the African Rift Valley? it is in the same place where numerous mountains, volcanoes and earthquakes occur.

Students should indicate that the location of the rift matches the location of earthquakes in Africa, which can cause breaks in the surface of Earth.

LESSON 4 Engage • **Explore/Explain** • Elaborate • Evaluate

EXPLORATION 2 Can Maps Help Us See Patterns?, continued

 Analyzing and Interpreting Data

For five minutes, have pairs of students compare the four maps to see how they are the same and different. Then have them identify the similarities and differences in the location of earthquakes, mountains, trenches, and volcanos found on the ocean floor as you record them on the board. For example:

Similarities	Differences
Ocean volcanoes, earthquakes, and trenches occur in about the same places.	Ocean mountains mainly occur away from continents.
Earthquakes also occur along with mountains in the middle of oceans.	There are more ocean earthquakes than volcanoes.
None of these occur in the Arctic Ocean.	

Differentiate Instruction

RTI/Extra Support Have students compare the occurrences of ocean earthquakes, volcanoes, trenches, and mountains ocean by ocean: Arctic, Atlantic, Indian, Pacific.

DCI ESS2.B: Plate Tectonics and Large-Scale System Interactions

Review student analysis.

Ask: What is the difference between land and ocean trenches? There are no land trenches.

Ask: How are land and ocean mountains alike? On land, they form on the edge and interior of continents. In the ocean, they occur in the interior.

Finding Patterns on the Ocean Floor

These maps show earthquakes and features of the ocean floor. Study the maps and use your observations to answer the questions below.

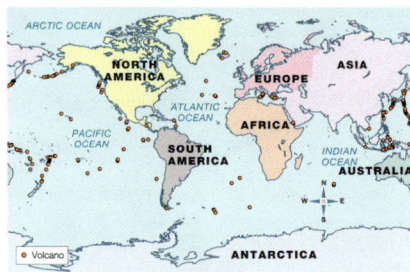

This map shows the locations of volcanoes on the ocean floor.

This map shows the locations of earthquakes that started on the ocean floor.

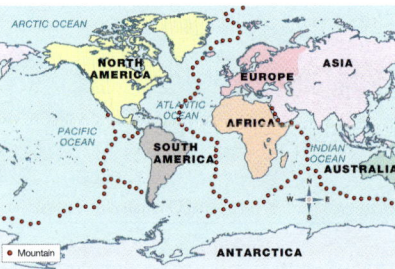 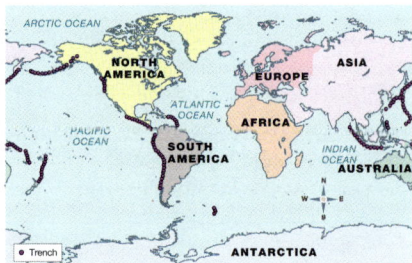

This map shows the mountains on the ocean floor.

This map shows trenches on the ocean floor.

12. Describe the pattern of ocean trenches.

Students likely said that many trenches occur in places where an ocean and continent meet.

13. Choose the words or phrases that correctly complete each sentence.

| the centers of oceans | coastlines | islands |

Most underwater volcanoes occur near ___coastlines___. Many underwater mountain ranges are found near ___the centers of oceans___. Ocean trenches are common near ___coastlines___.

436

436 Unit 6 Changes to Earth's Surface

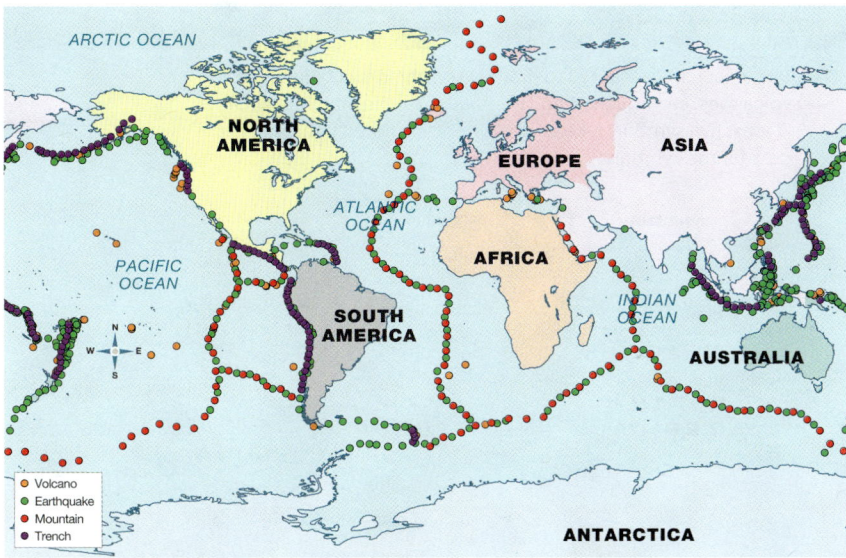

14. Compare the locations of earthquakes and volcanoes on land and the ocean floor. Use the map from the previous pages to compare.

Students might have stated that in the ocean, earthquakes and volcanoes occur near the oceans' edges as well as in the middle of the oceans, while on land, they mostly occur near the edges of continents.

15. Contrast the locations of mountains ranges on land and the ocean floor. Use the map from the previous pages to compare.

Students might have observed that mountain ranges on land occur at the edges of continents and near the centers of continents. By contrast, most underwater mountains are in the middle of oceans.

 **Patterns**

Ask: Do you see any patterns in the location of these ocean features? Many of them overlap.

Collaboration

Think, Pair, Share Have students compare the map here with the map on page 435. Have them make a similarities and differences chart comparing the ocean and land patterns of earthquakes, volcanoes, mountains and trenches.

Differentiate Instruction

Extension Have students research ocean trenches and make a presentation to share with the class.

LESSON 4   Engage • **Explore/Explain** • Elaborate • Evaluate

EXPLORATION 2 Can Maps Help Us See Patterns?, continued

Analyzing and Interpreting Data

In marking up the map, encourage students to analyze the locations of land and ocean earthquakes, volcanoes, and mountains from the maps on the previous pages.

Ask: What part of the Earth has the most earthquakes? Around Asia and the Pacific Ocean are the most earthquakes.

> ### Differentiate Instruction
> **Extension:** Have students add trenches to their maps.

HANDS-ON   Apply What You Know
Modeling Features of the Ocean Floor

Provide students with modeling clay and a base on which to work. You may wish to have different students create different features of the ocean floor instead of all the features. Have students complete their models and then present them to the class.

Scoring Guideline
Exemplary activity results will show all four features of the ocean floor in relative location.

DCI ESS2.B: Plate Tectonics and Large-Scale System Interactions

Have students compare the features they created and mapped. Explain how they occur in relation to one another.

Ask: What can you say about the relationship among earthquakes, volcanoes, and mountains? Answers may vary but should demonstrate that students recognize that earthquakes, volcanoes, and mountains mostly occur in similar locations in the world.

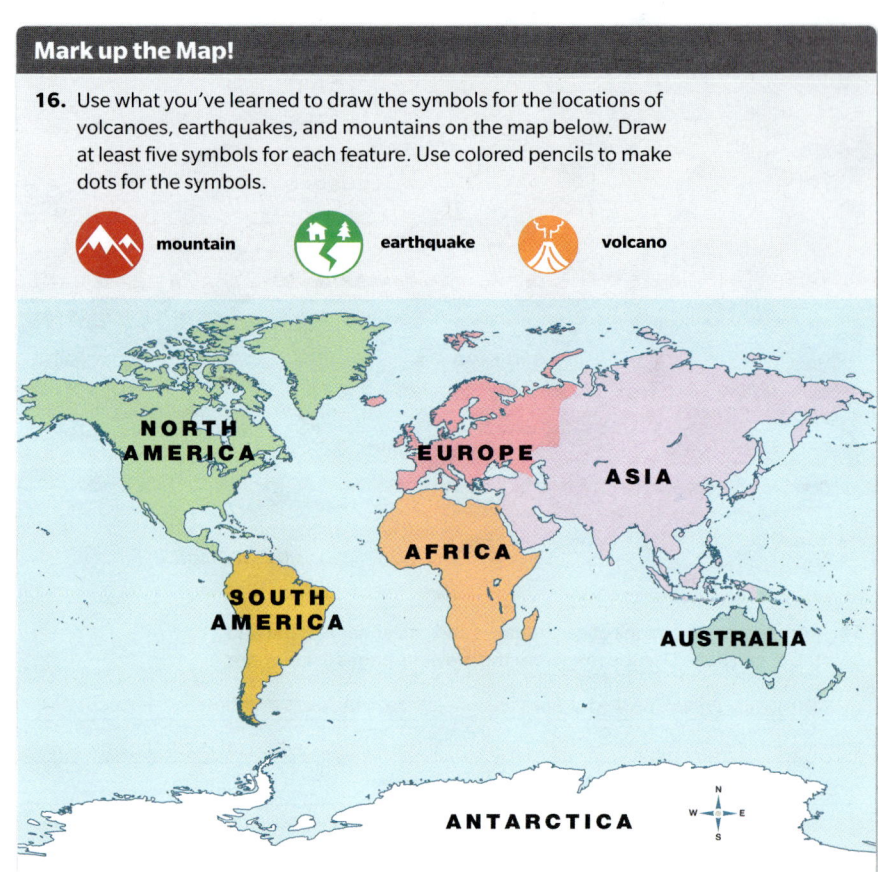

Mark up the Map!

16. Use what you've learned to draw the symbols for the locations of volcanoes, earthquakes, and mountains on the map below. Draw at least five symbols for each feature. Use colored pencils to make dots for the symbols.

HANDS-ON Apply What You Know

 Modeling Features of the Ocean Floor

17. Use modeling clay to make a 3D model of the features of the ocean floor. Include locations of volcanoes, mountains, trenches, and earthquakes. Label your model.

438

438 Unit 6 Changes to Earth's Surface

18. How would you describe the location of most underwater mountain ranges?
    a. They are at the edges of continents.
    b. **They are usually in the middle of oceans.**
    c. They are usually near large islands.
    d. They are always near the equator.

19. Where would volcanoes be most common?
    a. the central part of Asia
    b. **the edges of the Pacific Ocean**
    c. the North Pole
    d. the edges of the Atlantic Ocean

20. What is true of earthquakes?
    a. They only happen on land.
    b. Most happen at the edge of the Atlantic Ocean.
    c. They do not occur in any pattern.
    d. **Many occur near volcanoes.**

21. What is true of ocean trenches?
    a. They look exactly like underwater mountains.
    b. They are found in areas where water is shallow.
    c. They do not occur in any pattern.
    d. **They are mostly found near the edges of oceans.**

Language SmArts
Understand Graphics

22. Maps are visual models used to show information more easily. Choose one of the maps from this part of the lesson. Write a few sentences that explain what the map shows.

    Possible answer: One map shows where volcanoes occur on land. According to the map, most volcanoes on land are found along the edges of continents. In Asia, however, volcanoes are found within the interior of the continent.

Tip
The English Language Arts Handbook can provide help with how to understand graphics.

CCC Patterns

Ask: Locate Poland on a map. Use the patterns you studied to determine if you would likely find earthquakes there? No. It is in the interior of a continent and not in an active earthquake part of the world.

Ask: Locate Chili on a map. Use the patterns you studied to determine if you would likely find mountains there? Yes. It occurs on the coast in the Ring of Fire.

Ask: Locate Hawaii on a map. Use the patterns you studied to determine if you would likely find volcanoes there? Yes. It is an island located in the Ring of Fire.

DCI ESS2.B: Plate Tectonics and Large-Scale System Interactions

Ask: If you did not want to live in an earthquake or volcano zone, where would be the best place in the world to live? Students should compare the number of earthquakes and volcanoes in each continent. They might consider the east coasts of North and South America.

FORMATIVE ASSESSMENT

Language SmArts
Understand Graphics
RI.4.7 Understand Graphics

Discuss how maps are useful in showing patterns in Earth's surface.

Ask: How can maps of Earth's features lead to greater understanding of Earth processes? Recognizing the patterns of the locations of major events on Earth, helps people understand that the events are related and study why they occur in the places they do.

LESSON 4 Engage • **Explore/Explain** • Elaborate • Evaluate

EXPLORATION 2 *Can Maps Help Us See Patterns?*, continued

HANDS-ON ACTIVITY Small groups 1 class period
Tracking Quakes

3D Learning Objective
SEP Analyzing and Interpreting Data

Students analyze and interpret current data related to earthquakes to identify patterns of occurrence.

Preparation
Share with students that scientists detect about 50 earthquakes a day. Discuss the criteria and constraints of the project as a class. Remind students that criteria determine success for a project, and constraints are limits that need to be observed. In this activity, criteria are that students research earthquakes that have occurred in the past week. Constraints are limited to time and access to data available.

Materials
A world map is provided for you to download and print for your students. Provide access to data on earthquakes either on the Internet or in print form. Have students use the data table in the book to record their data.

Build on Prior Knowledge
Review what students already know about earthquakes.

Ask: Where have you learned that earthquakes occur? *at the edges of continents and some within the continent of Asia*

Procedures
STEP 1 There are several websites that report earthquakes. Students can search for earthquakes or go to the USGS site earthquake.usgs.gov/earthquakes/map/ to begin their investigations.

440 Unit 6 Changes to Earth's Surface

HANDS-ON ACTIVITY
Tracking Quakes

In this lesson, you learned that earthquakes happen all over the world. But they usually happen in predictable places. Now you have the chance to look for patterns with real earthquakes.

Materials
- world map with country boundaries
- data on earthquakes
- data table
- pencil

Objective
Collaborate to examine data to find out where most earthquakes occur. Scientists detect about 50 earthquakes each day. Most are mild and do not cause any damage, but they occur in the same *type* of area.

What question will you investigate to meet this objective?
Possible question: Is there a pattern to the location of earthquakes?

Procedure
STEP 1 With a partner, find data on 20 earthquakes that have occurred during the past week.

How did you decide which earthquakes to research?
Possible answer: We chose the strongest twenty earthquakes to research.

440

STEP 2 For each of the 20 earthquakes, record the date, the magnitude, and the location. Use additional paper as needed.

What does a quake's magnitude indicate? Research the term, if needed.
Magnitude is the strength of the event in terms of amount of energy released by a quake.

Earthquakes – Week of _____		
Date	Earthquake Magnitude	Location (city or country)

STEP 2 Tell students that magnitude is the amount of energy released during an earthquake. Earthquakes that are under a magnitude of five usually do not cause damage to property. People may not even feel earthquakes that are less then a magnitude of three.

Ask: What was the lowest and highest magnitude you recorded? answers will vary

> ### Differentiate Instruction
> **Extension** Have interested students use the Internet to research the Richter Scale, how it was developed, and how it is used to measure earthquake magnitude. Ask them to present their findings to the class.

SEP **Analyzing and Interpreting Data**

After students have collected data on about 20 earthquakes, have students rank the earthquakes in order of their magnitude.

Ask: Which earthquake was the strongest? Answers will vary based on the earthquake data collected by students.

DCI **ESS2.B: Plate Tectonics and Large-Scale System Interactions**

Ask: Which earthquakes are closest to us? Which are farthest away? Students may find that earthquakes have occurred nearby even if they live away from earthquake zones.

LESSON 4   Engage • **Explore/Explain** • Elaborate • Evaluate

EXPLORATION 2 HANDS-ON ACTIVITY, continued

Analyze Your Results
STEPS 3–4 As students plot the earthquakes they researched, check to see if they are plotting the correct locations.

Draw Conclusions

 Patterns

Ask: What patterns did you discover about the locations of earthquakes that have occurred recently? **Possible answer: They occur in places where other earthquakes occur but also in places we didn't expect.**

STEPS 7 Make a class list of questions students have. Brainstorm ideas for how their questions can be answered.

Claims, Evidence, and Reasoning
Have student pairs work with another pair to critique each other's claims and evidence. Ask each pair to share one way they would change or improve their claim. Solicit claims from all groups and make a class list.

Ask: How are these claims similar? How are they different? **Possible answer: All of us claimed that current earthquakes occur in places where earthquakes have occurred before.**

Scoring Rubric for Hands-On Activity	
3	follows procedure, gathers and records data accurately, and uses it to support a considered claim
2	most procedures are followed, data is recorded accurately with some errors or omissions, claim is supported by some evidence
1	there is an attempt at following procedures, but data is insufficient to support a claim
0	procedures are not followed, data is insufficient, and there is no claim given

442   Unit 6 Changes to Earth's Surface

Analyze Your Results

STEP 3 Plot the earthquake locations on your world map. You should have one symbol for each location of an earthquake. In which part of the world did most of the earthquakes occur? Did you see a pattern in the location of the earthquakes?

Students might have stated that they did see a pattern in the location of the quakes, and that many of them occurred in one part of the world.

STEP 4 Of the earthquakes you plotted, in what type of area did most occur?
Possible answer: Most of them occurred on land.

STEP 5 Compile the entire classes' results into one large data table. Each group should graph the results. What patterns do you see now, and how are those patterns different from the ones above? Did having more data help you see the patterns clearer?
Possible answer: I now see that most of the earthquakes happened on the edges of continents. The 20 we recorded were only on one continent. When it was just my group's data, it was unclear that they were mostly happening on the edges of continents all over the globe.

Draw Conclusions

STEP 6 Make a claim about earthquakes. What evidence do you have that most earthquakes occur in certain parts of the world?
Possible answer: Most of the earthquakes I recorded for this week occurred on land. Two of them occurred in the interiors of continents, but most occurred at the edges of continents.

STEP 7 What other questions do you have about the locations of most earthquakes?
Possible questions: Why do most earthquakes happen in certain places? Why are earthquakes in some places stronger than quakes in other places? Are earthquake locations related to the locations of volcanoes?

442

LESSON 4   Engage • Explore/Explain • **Elaborate** • Evaluate

TAKE IT FURTHER Discover More

Explore Online — Students can explore all three Take It Further paths online.

TAKE IT FURTHER
Discover More

Check out this path . . . or go online to choose one of these other paths.

- **People in Science & Engineering**
- Volcano Formation
- Volcanic Islands

Lewis and Clark

After the United States purchased the Lousianna Territory from the French in 1803, President Thomas Jefferson asked Meriwether Lewis and William Clark to find a water passage through the territory to make trade and commerce easier. The two men were also asked to create maps of the areas they traveled, including mountains and rivers, to make it easier for future explorers to find their way around. Crossing over steep mountains along their journey was quite a challenge.

Meriwether Lewis and William Clark

 HANDS-ON Apply What You Know

Making Mountains!

Procedure

1. Cover the bottom of the plate with a layer of shaving cream about 1 cm thick.
2. Dip the two pieces of cardboard in the bowl of water until they become soft.
3. Place the damp pieces of cardboard next to each other on top of the shaving cream.
4. Slowly push the pieces toward each other. Observe what happens to the cardboard at the edge where they smash together.
5. Draw a picture of your model and submit it to your teacher.

Materials
- paper plate
- shaving cream
- 2 small pieces of corrugated cardboard
- bowl of water

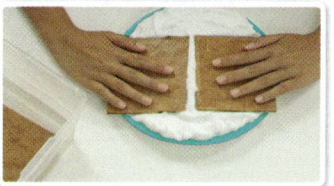

Collaboration

You may choose to assign this activity or to direct students online to the eSE where they can explore and choose from all three paths. These activities can be assigned individually, to pairs, or to small groups.

People in Science & Engineering: Lewis and Clark

 DCI ESS2.B: Plate Tectonics and Large-Scale System Interactions

The thirty-three members of the Lewis and Clark expedition were the first Americans to cross what is now the western United States. It took them over two years to travel from Saint Louis to the Pacific Ocean and back.

Ask: What would you need to do to draw a map of the trip from home to school? *Possible answer: a way to measure distances and a record of landmark observations*

HANDS-ON Apply What You Know
Making Mountains!

Discuss how students think mountains are created. Provide paper plates, shaving cream, cardboard, and bowls of water and have students follow the instructions. An alternative is to use whipped topping and graham crackers.

Ask: How does this show how mountains can be made? *If pieces of Earth's crust collide, they can rise up, like mountains.*

Scoring Guidelines

An excellent score involves participation and accurate observations.

LESSON 4   Engage • Explore/Explain • **Elaborate** • Evaluate

TAKE IT FURTHER, continued

 Analyze and Interpret Data

Study the three different pictures with students.

Ask: How do most mountains form? Two pieces of Earth's crust smash against each other. The edges of each piece crumple and fold. The collision can also shove one piece of crust over the other.

 Patterns

Ask: What patterns do you see in how mountains are formed? Major mountain ranges occur in the middle of continents.
Ask: If earthquakes and volcanoes occur along the boundaries of continents, why might mountain ranges occur in the middle of continents? The energy from the earthquakes and volcanoes might be pushing Earth's crust so that the pieces collide in the middle of continents.

Differentiate Instruction

Extension Have interested students research the elevations of mountain ranges over time to find out if there is evidence that some mountains are growing.

 Explore Online

Students can explore these additional topics online.

Volcano Formation
Students explore how different types of volcanoes occur. *(No outside research is required.)*

Volcanic Islands
Students learn about underwater volcanoes that rise from the ocean floor. *(Outside research is required.)*

Rising High

As you saw in the activity, some mountains form when two slabs of rock smash against each other. The edges of each slab crumpled and folded. Such a collision can also shove one slab of rock up over the other. This process produces some of the world's highest mountains.

Earth's crust is made up of plates, or slabs, that are always moving. Sometimes these slabs move toward each other.

When they meet, the slabs push against each other. This creates heat and pressure at the meeting point.

As the slabs continue to push against each other, mountains form and grow taller.

23. How do some of the world's highest mountains form?
Most of the world's highest mountains form when thick slabs of rocks smash into each other. This causes the rocks to crumple and fold to form mountains.

LESSON CHECK

LESSON 4
Lesson Check

Name _____

Can You Explain It?

1. Now that you've learned more about the features of Earth's surface, explain what is happening in the African Rift Valley. Be sure to do the following:
   - Explain what could have caused this crack.
   - Explain how you used patterns to determine what happened here.
   - Predict how the crack might change the nearby land over time.

EVIDENCE NOTEBOOK Use the information you've collected in your Evidence Notebook to help you cover each point above.

Possible answer:
- The rift was likely caused by an earthquake. I know this because earthquakes usually happen in patterns, near the edges of continents.
- It also looks similar to some photos of earthquake damage.
- I predict that the crack will become larger over time.

Checkpoints

2. You learned about several features found on the ocean floor. How do those compare with the ones on land?
   a. All of them are found on land.
   b. Most of them are found on land.
   c. They do not include volcanoes.
   d. They do not include mountains.

Formal Assessment Go online for student self-checks and other assessments.

Can You Explain It?

Collaboration

Discussion You may wish to revisit and discuss the images as a group to assess students' understanding of the materials. Use the bulleted points in the student edition to lead the discussion.

EVIDENCE NOTEBOOK

Have students reread their answers to the Evidence Notebook prompts, and then use this evidence to justify their reasoning as they respond to the Can You Explain It question. Make sure students understand that a complete response must address all of the bulleted points.

ESS2.B: Plate Tectonics and Large-Scale System Interactions

With students, compare the differences among earthquakes, volcanoes, trenches, and mountains. Then have them explain why the African Rift Valley is the result of an earthquake. Trenches only occur in oceans. There is no evidence of a volcanic eruption. The Rift is near the edge of a continent where earthquakes occur, so it follows that pattern.

Checkpoints
SUMMATIVE ASSESSMENT

2. Remind students to consider each answer choice based on their analysis of data from the maps and activities in the lesson. If students are having trouble, list all the features on paper and have them write land, ocean or both next to each.

LESSON 4 Engage • Explore/Explain • Elaborate • **Evaluate**

LESSON CHECK, continued

3. Discuss with students the characteristics of each of the answer options to help them discover that all of them can, in fact, exist in the ocean. If students continue to struggle, have them turn back to Exploration 1 for a review.

4. Have students recall what they learned about the Ring of Fire from this lesson. They can use the maps that they studied in Exploration 2 to help answer the question.

5. Have students focus on the patterns they notice in the map. Ask them to describe the kind of data they can get from these patterns. Encourage them to think about how these data and patterns can help answer the question.

6. Make sure students understand that some of the information in the chart is marked incorrectly. They must circle the correct answers to correct the chart. Students can think back to the maps they studied and the patterns they identified throughout the lesson.

---

3. Circle all the features that occur in the ocean.
   a. mountains   c. volcanoes
   b. ocean trenches   d. earthquakes
   (a, b, c, d all circled)

4. Circle the correct answer. Most volcanoes and earthquakes occur near the _____.
   a. middle of the Atlantic Ocean   c. coastlines of Africa
   b. near the Ring of Fire   d. the center of South America
   (b circled)

5. Study the map. Which statements describe the information shown? Circle all that apply.

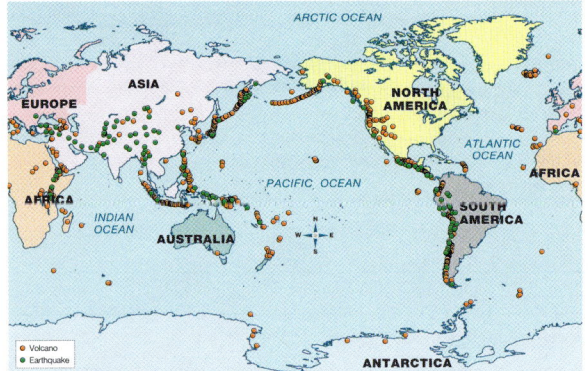

   a. It shows every volcano on Earth.
   b. It shows a pattern in the locations of volcanoes.
   c. It shows where every future earthquake will occur.
   d. It shows a pattern in the locations of past earthquakes.
   (b and d circled)

6. Look at the table. A student used Xs to mark the main locations of features on land. Some of his answers are incorrect. Help him by circling the correct answers.

Land patterns	On the edge of continents	In the middle of continents
earthquake	A) x	
volcano	B) x	E) x
trench	C) x	
mountain	D) x	F) x

(A, B, D, F circled)

446

Unit 6 Changes to Earth's Surface

LESSON 4

Lesson Roundup

A. What do volcanoes, mountains, and earthquakes have in common?
   a. They occur only on land.
   b. They occur in areas of the ocean far from land.
   c. They occur on land that is far from oceans.
   d. **They occur on land and in the ocean.**

B. Imagine you are piloting a submarine just above a somewhat flat area of the ocean floor. The ocean floor begins to slope downward. You cannot see the ocean floor any more. It's as though you've glided off the peak of a steep mountain. A few minutes later, the submarine's sensors tell you the ocean floor is now 5 kilometers deeper than your present depth. What are you and your submarine hovering over?
   a. a plain
   b. a mountain
   c. **an ocean trench**
   d. a volcano

C. What does this pattern in the Atlantic Ocean suggest?
   a. Slabs of rock are forming walls.
   b. The most common place volcanoes occur.
   c. **Mountains are common between continents.**
   d. There is an ocean trench between Europe and North America.

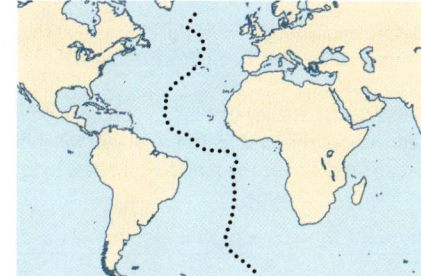

D. Why is the pattern shown on the map known as the Ring of Fire?
   a. Slabs of smashing rocks cause the Pacific Ocean to warm up.
   b. It shows a deep ocean trench, which causes warm water to rise.
   c. It is the site of earthquakes caused by volcanoes.
   d. **It shows volcanoes around the Pacific Ocean.**

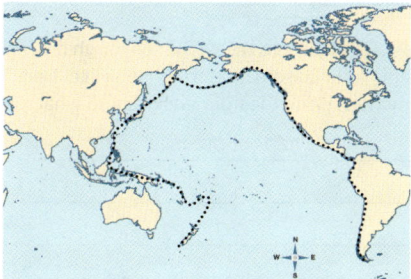

447

Lesson Roundup

DCI **ESS2.B: Plate Tectonics and Large-Scale System Interactions**

This lesson summary enables students to quickly revisit key points and prepare for tests.

A. Have students think about the characteristics of volcanoes, mountains, and earthquakes to answer the question. They should read each answer option to determine whether or not it makes sense based on what students know about earthquakes, volcanoes, and mountains. If students need additional help, have them review Exploration 1. **ESS2-2**

B. First, make sure students understand what a submarine is. If students get stuck on this question, draw out the scenario on the front board. As you draw out the scenario on the board, students should be able to recognize that you are drawing an ocean trench. Students can also review Exploration 1 to find the differences between ocean features to answer this question. **ESS2-2**

C. Allow students to review Exploration 2 before answering this question related to patterns of ocean features found in maps. Make sure students reach all answer choices to see which ones make the most sense. Ask students whether they have heard of walls forming between continents to eliminate option A. Have them also think about volcanoes and what they learned about the Ring of Fire to eliminate option B. For option C, ask students how ocean trenches are depicted on maps. **ESS2-2**

D. Students must recall what they learned about the Ring of Fire. Ask probing questions to get them to recall facts. They should easily recall that the Ring of Fire refers to volcanoes. Based on the location of the dots on the map, students should also see that this is the Pacific Ocean. Therefore, students should select option D. Information to answer this question is found in Exploration 1. **ESS2-2**

UNIT 6 Performance Task

👥 small groups   ⏱ 1 class period

Model It, Map It

3D Assessment Goal
Students **develop models** and **plan and carry out an investigation** to demonstrate **the effects of how a land feature is changed by wind or water** to demonstrate understanding of **ESS2.A** in support of **4-ESS2-1**.

Materials
- paper
- writing utensils
- sand
- water
- cardboard
- popsicle sticks
- eyedroppers

Preparation
Create your own model ahead of time so that you can demonstrate how to use the materials to put together the models.

 Cause and Effect

Depending on the land features the students choose to model, there will be different causes and effects. Circulate around the room and ask the following to each small group. **Ask: What do you think will be the factor that changes the land form?**

Plan Your Models

Each student on the team should submit a drawing of their idea for the model. The team can combine ideas or vote on the best drawing on which to base their model.

448   Unit 6 Changes to Earth's Surface

UNIT 6   UNIT PERFORMANCE TASK

Model It, Map It

A pair of three-dimensional models can contrast what something looks like before and after a change. Your team wil build two models that show how a land feature is changed by wind or water over a long period of time. Then you'll make topographic maps of your models. Your maps' keys will explain the processes that shaped the land features.

Imagine what this land area looked like before the river carved the canyon.

DEFINE YOUR TASK: Choose one of these land features to model: a changing coastline, a canyon, a winding river path, sand dunes. Write a brief description of factors that shape and change that type of land feature.

Students should identify moving water as the factor if they choose the coastline, canyon, or river path. They should iedntify wind as the agent that dunes.

Before beginning, review the checklist at the end of this Unit Performance Task. Keep those items in mind as you proceed.

RESEARCH: Review the lesson, and use online or library resources to learn about the land feature that you will model. Record notes about factors that shape the land feature how long it takes for such a feature to form and change.

Student should record facts they will include in the labels keyed to their maps..

PLAN YOUR MODELS: Sketch rough drawings of what your before and after land feature models will look like. Decide how big you will make the models. Write their dimensions and what materials you will use here.

Student should list practical dimensions and viable, available materials for models.

448

BUILD YOUR MODELS: Use materials provided by your teacher to build the before and after models of your selected land feature. Place at least three numbers on parts of each model you will explain in captions. What features did you number?

Students should identify features such as the elevation of canyon walls, the curves of a river, or the footprint of dunes.

MAP YOUR MODELS: Draw a topographical map of each model. Make a numbered key for each map. The numbers and features listed on your map key should match the numbers of the features on your models.

CAPTION YOUR MAPS: For each numbered feature on your models and map keys, write a corresponding caption. Each caption should describe a characteristic of the numbered part of the land feature and tell how it was formed or changed by wind or water.

COMMUNICATE: Display your models, maps, and captions for the class. Look at the models and maps made by other students. What do all the models and maps have in common? How do some of them differ?

Students should note that all the model pairs show the same land feature before and after a change caused by wind or water. Differences might be in the features selected or the process factors. Students also might note differences in techniques and materials used for the models.

 Checklist

Review your project and check off each completed item.

_____ Includes two three-dimensional models of a land feature.

_____ Models the same land feature before and after a change.

_____ Includes a topographic map corresponding to each model.

_____ Includes captions for at least three details on each model.

_____ Captions explain the processes and time involved in the change shown between the two models.

Map Your Models

SEP Developing and Using Models

Students use the models they developed to create maps. **Ask: Why is it important to map models of the topography? How can this help people who study Earth's surface?**

Communicate

Place the models and maps around the room on display and have the class do a gallery walk. Students should spend time at each exhibit, reviewing the details of the other teams' models and taking notes to answer the questions.

Scoring Rubric for Performance Task	
3	• complete resources, clear reasoning, multiple sources • two 3D models show the land feature before and after the change • numbered features and captions on the map correspond to the models
2	• most resources, adequate reasoning and sources • two 3D models somewhat show the land feature before and after the change • numbered features and captions on the map somewhat correspond to the models
1	• some key resources and reasoning, a few sources • 3D models do not show the land feature before and after the change • numbered features and captions on the map do not correspond to the models
0	• few key resources, no reasons, minimal sources • two 3D models incomplete • maps are incomplete

UNIT 6 Review

SUMMATIVE ASSESSMENT

1. Students should be able to recall facts about flooding to answer this question correctly. They can refer back to Lesson 1, Exploration 1 if they need a refresher on the effects of floods.

2. Students should say the sentences out loud, to themselves, to rule out obviously incorrect answer choices. Have students revisit Lesson 1, Exploration 3 for a review on glaciers.

3. Students may be able to answer this question correctly based on their own experiences in certain regions of the world, from watching movies or reading books, or by recalling information learned in Lesson 2, Exploration 1.

4. Students can answer this question by differentiating between weathering and erosion. Have them turn back to Lesson 1, Exploration 4 for a review.

UNIT 6

Unit Review

1. Which of these can be a positive effect of flooding? Circle the correct choice.
   a. It can enrich farm soil. *(circled)*
   b. It can protect roads from erosion.
   c. It can keep a river within its banks.
   d. It can keep a river from flowing too rapidly.

2. Complete the sentences using the words from the word bank.

slow-moving	flooding	freezing
fast-moving	erosion	deposition

   A glacier is a huge, __slow-moving__ block, or river, of ice.

   Glaciers cause __erosion__ when they are active and __flooding__ when they melt.

3. Indicate whether each phrase describes a desert (D), a rain forest (R), or both (B) by writing the letter on the line.

   __B__ Hot climate
   __D__ Low precipitation
   __R__ High precipitation
   __R__ Large variety of organisms
   __D__ Limited number of organisms

4. Complete the sentences using the words from the word bank.

weathering	erosion	sand	dirt	water	ice

   This photograph shows one common cause of __weathering__. Another is the freezing and expansion of __water__ during cold weather.

450

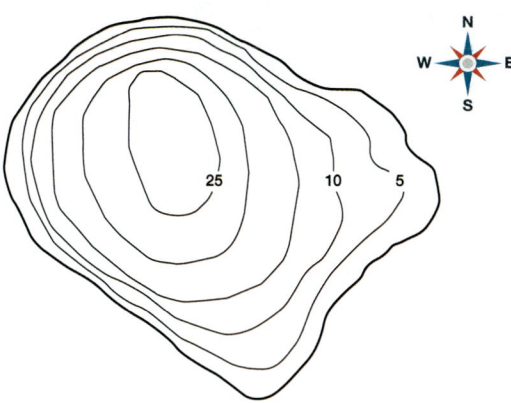

5. Use the map to answer the question. Which side of the mountain is the least steep?
   a. north
   b. south
   c. east
   d. west

6. Which choices name a specific type of map? Circle all that apply.
   a. key
   b. scale
   c. road
   d. weather
   e. topographical

7. Which landforms exist beneath the ocean but not on dry land? Circle the correct choice.
   a. hills
   b. valleys
   c. trenches
   d. mountains

5. Students need to recall how to read and use a map. They can turn back to Lesson 3, Exploration 2 for a refresher on reading and interpreting maps. They can also turn to Lesson 3, Exploration 3 for a similar looking map. You may need to remind them how to determine elevation by looking at a map.

6. Students should be able to recall the different kinds of maps. If you need to give them a clue, ask them to think about the features of a map versus types of maps. They can turn back to Lesson 3, Exploration 1 for a review.

7. Students should recall sorting Earth's features by their location on land, water or both, as described in Lesson 4, Exploration 1.

UNIT 6 Review, continued

8. Students may need to review Lesson 4, Exploration 1 in order to recall facts about volcanoes and earthquakes. Help students look for clue words in the answer choices that may give away an incorrect answer, such as "only" and "all over."

9. Students can review Lesson 4, Exploration 1 to refresh their memories of ocean trenches.

10. Students must study the image and determine the factors that shaped the landscape. They can turn back to Lesson 1, Exploration 4 for a review on weathering and erosion.

3D Item Analysis	1	2	3	4	5	6	7	8	9	10
SEP Analyzing and Interpreting Data					•					•
DCI Earth Materials and Systems	•	•	•	•			•	•	•	•
DCI Biogeology			•							
DCI Plate Tectonics and Large-Scale System Interactions						•	•	•	•	
CCC Cause and Effect	•	•			•					•
CCC Patterns		•	•	•	•		•	•	•	•

8. Where are volcanoes and earthquakes most likely to occur on land? Select all that apply
   a. near coasts
   b. all over a continent
   c. near the Ring of Fire
   d. in higher areas like mountains
   e. only in the ocean

9. Complete the sentences using the words from the word bank

   | earthquakes   continents   oceans   volcanoes   mountains |

   In general, ocean trenches form on the edges of ___oceans___ and ___continents___.

10. Which of the following played a role in the formation of the landscape shown here? Circle all that apply.
    a. erosion
    b. eruption
    c. elevation
    d. deposition
    e. weathering

UNIT 7 Rocks and Fossils

Unit Project: DinoZoo
What kind of zoo habitat would it take to house a dinosaur? You will research a dinosaur's needs and design a zoo space for it with your team. Ask your teacher for details.

Discoveries of fossil remains of extinct animals teach scientists about Earth's environmental past.

Unit Overview
In this unit, children will . . .
- explore the different layers of rocks and how they change.
- discover what we can learn about fossils and ancient environments.
- identify patterns in fossils.

About This Image
Fossils and rocks can tell us a lot about the past. They can teach us about the kinds of animals that used to roam Earth, what the weather may have been like back then, and what the environment might have been like. People, such as the person in this picture, make careers out of excavating, discovering, and interpreting fossils. It takes a lot of work to find and extract fossils from the ground. Delicate procedures need to be followed to make sure the fossil is not ruined when it's removed from the earth.

Unit Project
As students work through the unit lessons, have them start thinking of designs for zoo habitats that would house dinosaurs. They could include one type of dinosaur or several.

To begin, draw students' attention to the rocks in the image, or challenge the class to use online or media center resources to identify examples of fossils. More support for the Unit Project can be found on pp. 455I–455L.

UNIT 7 Rocks and Fossils

The learning experiences in this unit prepare children for the mastery of:

Performance Expectation
4-ESS1-1 Identify evidence from patterns in rock formations and fossils in rock layers to support an explanation for changes in a landscape over time.

▶ Explore Online

In addition to the print resources, the following resources are available online to support this unit.

Unit Pretest
Lesson 1 How Do Rock Layers Change?
- Online Student Edition
- Lesson Quiz

Lesson 2 What Do Fossils Tell Us About Ancient Environments?
- Online Student Edition
- Lesson Quiz

Lesson 3 What Are Some Patterns Fossils Show Us?
- Online Student Edition
- Lesson Quiz

You Solve It Layers of Change
Unit Performance Task
Unit Test

UNIT 7

At a Glance

LESSON 1
How Do Rock Layers Change? 456

LESSON 2
What Do Fossils Tell Us About Ancient Environments? 482

LESSON 3
What Are Some Patterns Fossils Show Us? 500

Unit Review 518

Vocabulary Game: Picture It

Materials
- Kitchen timer or online computer timer
- Sketch pad

Directions
1. Take turns to play.
2. To take a turn, choose a vocabulary word. Do not tell the word to the other players.
3. Set the timer for one minute.
4. Give clues about the word by drawing pictures on the sketch pad. Draw only pictures and numbers. Do not write words.
5. The first player to guess the word gets 1 point and the next turn. If that player can use the word in a sentence, he or she gets 1 more point.
6. The first player to score 5 points wins.

Unit Vocabulary

aquatic fossil: The remains or traces of an organism that lived in water long ago.

extinct: Describes a kind of thing that is no longer found on Earth.

fossil: The remains or traces of an organism that lived long ago.

relative age: The age of one thing compared to another.

terrestrial fossil: The remains or traces of an organism that lived on land long ago.

Unit Vocabulary

Students can explore all lesson vocabulary terms in the **Online Glossary**.

Vocabulary Strategies

Have students review the terms individually. Then pair up and share an example of one term with their partner and tell why they think it's an example. Have each pair write down their examples to check during the unit.

Differentiate Instruction

RTI/Extra Support Have struggling readers find the vocabulary words within the unit. Have students use context clues to infer definitions and then share with a partner.

Extension Have students pick two terms and then work in small groups to illustrate and explain the terms for a third-grade student.

ELL Pronounce each term and have students repeat it. Then pair up students by native language and have them explain each term in their native language. Use realia wherever appropriate.

Vocabulary Game: Picture It

Preparation
Use a timer on your smartphone or tablet, if that is more convenient than a kitchen timer or online computer timer.

Game Play
- Make sure students draw only pictures and numbers. Do not allow them to write words.

UNIT 7 Rocks and Fossils

Integrating the NGSS* Three Dimensions of Learning

Building to the Performance Expectation

The learning experiences in this unit prepare students for mastery of the following Performance Expectation:

Earth's Place in the Universe

4-ESS1-1 Identify evidence from patterns in rock formations and fossils in rock layers to support an explanation for changes in a landscape over time.

Assessing Student Progress

After completing these lessons, the **Unit Project: DinoZoo** provides students with opportunities to practice aspects of and demonstrate their understanding of the Performance Expectation as they design a zoo habitat that could safely house dinosaurs.

Additionally, students can practice or be assessed on aspects of the Performance Expectations by completing the **Unit Performance Task: Rocking the Layers**, in which they develop a models to demonstrate how patterns can occur in rock layers.

Lesson 1
How Do Rock Layers Change?

In **Lesson 1**, students will model rock layers to gather evidence about how they form and what information they contain about the history of planet Earth **(DCI The History of Planet Earth)**. They will look at examples of exposed layers in different formations and come up with explanations **(SEP Constructing Explanations and Designing Solutions)** for how these layers tell stories about the past and the Earth processes that shape and change rocks **(CCC Patterns)**.

Lesson 2
What Do Fossils Tell Us about Ancient Environments?

In **Lesson 2**, students examine fossils representing life from different periods in Earth's history **(DCI The History of Planet Earth)**, determine the habitats in which those fossils lived, and draw conclusions about what modern-day organisms the fossils may be related to **(SEP Constructing Explanations and Designing Solutions)**. By looking closely at the structures of fossils and living organisms, students see repeated forms and traits that helped these organisms survive in specific environments **(CCC Patterns)**.

Lesson 3
What Are Some Patterns Fossils Show Us?

In **Lesson 3**, students use evidence to determine what past environments were like, examine the fossils in different layers of rock to reveal the history of planet Earth **(DCI The History of Planet Earth)**, and construct explanations for how environments have changed over time **(SEP Constructing Explanations and Designing Solutions)**. Studying patterns in rocks and fossils, students learn how changes to Earth's surface have affected and will continue to affect rock layers **(CCC Patterns)**.

*Next Generation Science Standards and logo are registered trademarks of Achieve. Neither Achieve or the lead states and partners that developed the Next Generation Science Standards Were involved in the production of, and does not endorse, these products.

NGSS Across the Unit

Next Generation Science Standards	Unit Project	Lesson 1	Lesson 2	Lesson 3	Unit Performance Task	You Solve It!
SEP Constructing Explanations and Designing Solutions	•	•	•	•	•	•
DCI ESS1.C The History of Planet Earth	•	•	•	•	•	•
CCC Patterns	•	•	•	•	•	•

NGSS Across the Grades

Before
Biological Evolution: Unity and Diversity
3-LS4-1

Grade 4
Earth's Place in the Universe
4-ESS1-1

After
Earth's Place in the Universe
MS-ESS1-4 Construct a scientific explanation based on evidence from rock strata for how the geologic time scale is used to organize Earth's 4.6-billion-year-old history.

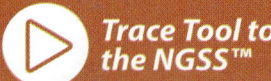

Trace Tool to the NGSS™ Go online to view the complete coverage of these standards across this grade level and time.

UNIT 7 Rocks and Fossils
3D Unit Planning

Lesson 1 How Do Rock Layers Change pp. 456–481

Overview

Objective Construct explanations for the ways in which rock layers reveal patterns and reflect the history of planet Earth.

SEP Constructing Explanations and Designing Solutions
DCI ESS1.C The History of Planet Earth
CCC Patterns

Math and **English Language Arts** standards and features are detailed on lesson planner pages.

Print and Online Student Editions

ENGAGE	**Lesson Phenomenon** pp. 456–457 **Can You Explain It?** How were these rock formations made?	▶ Can You Solve It? Video
EXPLORE/ EXPLAIN	**One Layer at a Time** pp. 458–461 Observing Rock Layers **Apply What You Know** Layered Landforms How Some Rocks Form **Layer on Layer** pp. 462–470 Telling a Story, Some Rocks and Fossils from Around the World, Patterns in Rock Layers **HANDS-ON** Modeling How Rocks Can Form **Not What It Used to Be** pp. 471–476 It's a Grand Canyon! **Apply What You Know** The Story of the Canyon Slow and Steady, In the Blink of an Eye **ENGINEER IT!** Measuring Earthquakes	HANDS-ON Worksheet
ELABORATE	**Take It Further** pp. 477–478 People in Science: Bernard Hubbard	Take It Further Rock Diversity Take It Further Why It's Grand
EVALUATE	**Lesson Check** pp. 479–480 **Lesson Roundup** p. 481	Lesson Quiz

HANDS-ON ACTIVITY PLANNING

Apply What You Know

Layered Landforms
⏱ 20 minutes
👥 Small groups

Materials
- clear jar
- three soil-like materials (sand, dirt, rice)

Preparation/Tip Students use a jar and three types of materials to model how rock layers form. Each material represents a different rock layer.

The Story of the Canyon
⏱ 15 minutes
👥 Individuals

Materials
- paper
- pens or pencils

Preparation/Tip Show an example of a three-panel comic strip.

HANDS-ON

Modeling How Rocks Can Form and Change
⏱ 1 class period
👥 Pairs

Materials
- modeling clay
- paper plate

Objective Model ways that rock layers form and the forces that can cause them to change.

Preparation/Tip Before students begin the project, make sure that each pair has enough clay to model six layers and that each has at least three colors of clay.

Lesson 2 What Do Fossils Tell Us About Ancient Environments? pp. 482–499

Overview

Objective Examine fossil evidence to determine how and in what environments organisms of the past lived, based on their physical traits and similarities to living organisms.

SEP Constructing Explanations and Designing Solutions
DCI **ESS1.C** The History of Planet Earth
CCC Patterns
Math and **English Language Arts** standards and features are detailed on lesson planner pages.

	Print and Online Student Editions	*Explore Online!*
ENGAGE	**Lesson Phenomenon** pp. 482–483 **Can You Explain It?** Can you figure out what type of environment the Petrified Forest used to be?	Can You Explain It? Video
EXPLORE/ EXPLAIN	**Clue from the Past** pp. 484–487 Check It Out!  **HANDS-ON** Old and New **Then and Now** pp. 488–491 Seeing the Past, Cousins? **Apply What You Know** Past Meets Present **Ancient Lands** pp. 492–491 Fossils and Environments, Identify Your Evidence	**HANDS-ON** Worksheet
ELABORATE	**Take It Further** pp. 495–496 Where Are They?	Take It Further Fossil Hangouts Take It Further How Do They Compare?
EVALUATE	**Lesson Check** pp. 497–498 **Lesson Roundup** p. 499	Lesson Quiz

HANDS-ON ACTIVITY PLANNING

Apply What You Know

Past Meets Present

⏱ 30 minutes
👥 Individuals

Materials
- reference materials or computer with Internet connection

Preparation/Tip You may want to provide students with research materials such as books from the library or Internet sites that feature fossils to help them find suitable material.

HANDS-ON

Old and New

⏱ 1 class period
👥 Small groups

Materials
- fossil kit
- classification chart
- magnifying glass

Objective Students examine fossils from a fossil kit to determine the kind of organism that each belonged to, how it lived, and in what environment it could be found.

Preparation/Tip Have a fossil identification book or other, similar resources ready, or have a computer available with a fossil identification website up. These are to be used only as a last resort for students who are struggling with identifying the fossils from the kit.

Unit 7 Rocks and Fossils 455D

UNIT 7 Rocks and Fossils
3D Unit Planning, continued

Lesson 3 What Are Some Patterns Fossils Show Us? pp. 500–517

Overview

Objective Examine fossils and other geologic evidence to understand what past environments were like, how they have changed over time, and how changes to Earth's surface have affected them.

SEP Constructing Explanations and Designing Solutions
DCI **ESS1.C** The History of Planet Earth
CCC Patterns

Math and **English Language Arts** standards and features are detailed on lesson planner pages.

	Print and Online *Student Editions*	Explore Online!
ENGAGE	**Lesson Phenomenon** pp. 500–501 **Can You Explain It?** How did a turtle fossil end up in a desert?	Can You Explain It? Video
EXPLORE/ EXPLAIN	HANDS-ON Layer by Layer pp. 502–504 **Evidence of Environments** pp. 505–508 Seeing History, Building the Story, Global Stories 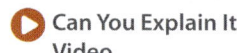 Apply What You Know Where Else? **More Changes** pp. 509–512 Consistent Patterns Apply What You Know Disordered Days When Things Change, Interpret Layers	HANDS-ON Worksheet
ELABORATE	**Take It Further** pp. 513–514 People in Science: Studying Evidence from the Past	Take It Further Changes in Environments Take It Further Careers in Science
EVALUATE	**Lesson Check** pp. 515–516 **Lesson Roundup** p. 517	Lesson Quiz

HANDS-ON ACTIVITY PLANNING

Apply What You Know

Where Else?
- 30 minutes
- Individuals

Materials
- computer with Internet access

Preparation/Tip Students should choose one of the following fossils: fern leaf, fish, snake, or crustacean. Research will show that these fossils have been found in formations all over the world, not just in the United States.

Disordered Days
- 10 minutes
- Individuals

Materials
- 10 sheets of paper
- pen or pencil

Preparation/Tip Limit this activity to weekdays (two sets of five sheets) per student. Assign pairs or small groups to use less paper.

HANDS-ON

Layer by Layer
- 1 class period
- Small groups

Materials
- nature magazines
- colored pencils
- scissors
- circular stencils
- construction paper
- white construction paper
- tape

Objective Students build a replica of rock layers, constructing an explanation for how fossil evidence can reveal much about the organisms and environment each layer represents.

Preparation/Tip Before you separate students into groups, have a bundle of images prepared for each group, as well as a place for the members of the group to work together.

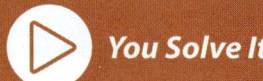 **You Solve It!** Go online for an additional interactive activity.

Layers of Change

This virtual lab offers practice in support of **PE 4-ESS1-1**.

SEP Constructing Explanations and Designing Solutions
DCI ESS1.C.1 The History of Planet Earth
CCC Patterns

Use after Unit 7, Lesson 3—How do rock layers indicate how and where the rock and fossils formed?

Objectives
1. Students will identify the environment in which fossils were deposited.
2. Students use the sequence of changes in rock type and fossils to identify a pattern.
3. Students use evidence to construct and support an explanation for changes in a landscape over time.

Activity Problem
You will assist a team of scientists studying rock layers in an area. Your tasks include:
1. analyzing the rock layers
2. deciding the environments in which the rocks likely formed
3. using the information to determine how the landscape changed over time

Interaction Summary
1. Students observe the rock layers and acknowledge the differences.
2. They use given data to identify the environment that matches each rock type in the layers.
3. Data and observations are recorded in a chart.
4. Students use the chart to identify patterns of change over time.
5. Explanations are constructed on how the landscape changed over time based on the pattern chart.

Assessment

Pre-Assessment
Assessment Guide, Unit Pretest

The Unit Pretest focuses on prerequisite knowledge and is composed of items that evaluate students' preparedness for the content covered within this unit.

Formative Assessment
Student Edition, Apply What You Know, Lesson Check, and Self Check

Summative Assessment
Assessment Guide, Lesson Quiz
The Lesson Quiz provides a quick assessment of each lesson objective and of the portion of the Performance Expectation aligned to the lesson.

Student Edition, Performance Task pp. 518–519
The Performance Task presents the opportunity for students to collaborate with classmates in order to complete the steps of each Performance Task. Each Performance Task provides a formal Scoring Rubric for evaluating students' work.

Student Edition, Unit 7 Review pp. 520–522

Assessment Guide, Unit Test
The Unit Test provides an in-depth assessment of the Performance Expectations aligned to the unit. This test evaluates students' ability to apply knowledge in order to explain phenomena and to solve problems. Within this test, constructed response items apply a three-dimensional rubric for evaluating students' mastery on all three dimensions of the Next Generation Science Standards.

 **Assessment Online** Go online to view the complete assessment items for this unit.

UNIT 7 Rocks and Fossils
Differentiate Instruction

Leveled Readers

The **Science & Engineering Leveled Readers** provide additional nonfiction reading practice in this unit's subject area.

On-Level Reader • Earth's Changing Surface and Natural Resources
This reader reinforces unit concepts and includes response activities for your students.

Extra Support • Earth's Changing Surface and Natural Resources
This reader shares title, illustrations, vocabulary, and concepts with the On-Level Reader; however, the text is linguistically accommodated to provide simplified sentence structures and comprehension aids. It also includes response activities.

Enrichment • Conserving Earth's Resources
This high-interest nonfiction reader will extend and enrich unit concepts and vocabulary and includes response activities.

Teacher Guide

The accompanying Teacher Guide provides teaching strategies and support for using all the readers.

ELL
ELL teacher strategies in this unit:
Lesson 1: pp. 459, 465, 474
Lesson 2: pp. 484, 494, 496, 498
Lesson 3: pp. 502, 510

RTI/Extra Support
Strategies for students needing extra support in this unit:
Lesson 1: pp. 460, 467, 474, 475
Lesson 3: pp. 503, 506

Extension
Strategies for students who have mastered core content in this unit:
Lesson 1: pp. 462, 472
Lesson 2: pp. 490, 492
Lesson 3: p. 505

 **Leveled Readers** — All readers are available online as well as in an innovative, engaging format for use with touchscreen mobile devices. Contact your HMH Sales Representative for more information.

UNIT 7 Rocks and Fossils
Making Connections

Connections to the Community

Use these opportunities for informal science learning to provide local context and to extend and enhance unit concepts.

At Home

FINDING FOSSILS Have students check the Internet or the public library to learn whether fossils have been found in your state. If so, students can learn more about those fossils. If not, have students search for the nearest state in which fossils have been identified. They can also look up whether your state has an official state fossil or dinosaur. *Use with Lesson 2.*

HOW IT WAS Have students use the Internet or public library to learn what the environment of their area was like at different prehistoric times and what forces caused it to change. *Use with Lesson 2.*

In the Community

NATURAL LANDSCAPE Have students think of natural landscape features in their area. These may be lakes, streams, waterfalls, hills, ravines, or plains. Tell students to visit one of these natural features with a adult family member and discuss possible ways it might have formed. *Use with Lesson 1.*

WHAT'S UNDERGROUND? Sometimes when builders excavate deeply before laying a foundation, they discover surprising things from the recent or distant past hidden in layers of soil or rock. Contact a builders' association or public library to ask about stories or photographs of what lies under the surface in your area or your state. Arrange for students to see any interesting material. *Use with Lesson 3.*

Home Letters Use these one-page letters to engage family members with unit concepts.

Collaboration

Opportunities for students to work collaboratively in this unit:

Build on Prior Knowledge pp. 489, 511	**Share Feedback** p. 472
Discussion pp. 466, 479	**Think, Pair, Share** pp. 457, 483, 497
Draw, Pair, Share pp. 474, 507	**Write, Pair, Share** pp. 488, 490
Feedback p. 501	

Connections to Science

Opportunities to connect to other content areas in this unit.

Connection to Nature of Science

Lesson 1, p. 459

Lesson 3, p. 503

UNIT 7 Rocks and Fossils
Unit Project

Unit Project: DinoZoo
Small Groups · 2 class periods

For this task, small groups of students will work together to come up with a design for keeping a dinosaur at a zoo. They will need to research the needs and habitat of dinosaurs and use this information to design a zoo that would allow dinosaurs to live there comfortably and safely. Students may have limited knowledge of dinosaur needs, so provide guidance and instruction as needed.

3D Learning Objective

- Explore the needs of dinosaurs
- Collect and analyze data about dinosaur habitats
- Study models of dinosaurs to understand how they could fit into a zoo environment

Skills and Standards Focus

This project supports building student mastery of **Performance Expectation 4-ESS1-1.**

- **SEP** Analyzing and Interpreting Data
- **DCI** ESS1.C History of Planet Earth
- **CCC** Patterns

Suggested Materials

- Drawing utensils (pencils, markers, pens)
- Drawing paper (construction paper, printer paper)
- Print and/or online reference materials

Preparing and Planning Tips

Ensure that each group has a set of print resources or a list of URLs for websites you have previously reviewed. Make sure students understand that in order to make their designs, they must understand the kind of environment a dinosaur could survive in. Specifically, students should take into consideration the temperature of the zoo space, what dinosaurs need to eat, and how much space they will need for roaming.

Differentiate Instruction

RTI/Extra Support Assign student groups a type of dinosaur to focus on for their zoo designs. This will help students know which dinosaur to research and collect information on to design a zoo habitat that will be successful.

Extension Challenge students to take this project one step further by incorporating two types of dinosaurs into one zoo exhibit. This will require students to do some extra research to agree on the two types of dinosaurs that can coexist peacefully with one another in a confined area.

Name _____

UNIT PROJECT
DinoZoo

What did dinosaurs look like? What did they used to eat? What kinds of behaviors did they have? For this project, you will design a zoo habitat that will be able to safely house dinosaurs.

Think about the last time you saw a dinosaur skeleton or a drawing of a dinosaur. It could be from a movie, a book, a magazine, or something you saw in a museum. Write a question that you will investigate as you design your zoo habitat.

Students should write a question concerning how a dinosaur could possibly live in a zoo.
_____

Materials

Think about how you will design your zoo habitat. What materials will you need?

Materials can include construction paper, drawing paper, drawing utensils, and references (print or electronic).
_____
_____

To make your zoo habitat designs, decide on the type of dinosaur that the exhibit will be for. There are many types of dinosaurs. The type of dinosaur you pick will determine the type of habitat it needs. It may help to create a list of different types of dinosaurs.

Land dinosaurs: *Tyrannosaurus rex, Brachiosaurus*
Flying dinosaurs: *Pterodactyl, Pteranodon*
_____
_____

UNIT 7 PROJECT
DinoZoo

 **DCI** **ESS1.C History of Planet Earth**

Before students begin, check their understanding of key concepts.

Ask: How can dinosaur bones be used to help scientists figure out facts about dinosaurs? They can tell scientists how big dinosaurs grew, what kinds of diets the dinosaurs may have had, what the dinosaurs looked like, and how they moved.

Refer students to Lesson 2, Exploration 1 for concept support.

ESSENTIAL QUESTIONS Ask the following questions before students begin to plan their activity.

- What do dinosaurs need to survive?
- What kinds of traits do dinosaurs have that will determine their habitat?

Provide students with different images of dinosaur bones and skeletons. Remind students that piecing together dinosaur bones is a visual and technical process. Scientists need to examine the bones visually to see patterns and other clues that will tell them more about the dinosaur's history.

CCC **Patterns**

Dinosaurs are extinct, but that doesn't mean that all animals related to dinosaurs are extinct, too. Some animals that may be related to dinosaurs still roam Earth today.

Ask: What kinds of animals may be related to dinosaurs? What features or traits do they share that lead you to this conclusion? Birds, because some dinosaurs used to fly; so they share the physical feature of wings in common with birds today.

Research and Plan

Students should carefully consider the criteria and constraints for a dinosaur habitat at the zoo.

Ask: What are some of the constraints of housing a dinosaur at a zoo? Space: the exhibit will need to be large enough to accommodate a dinosaur; safety: the exhibit will need to be secure enough to make sure the dinosaur cannot escape; food: the zoo will need to have enough food to feed the dinosaur, and this can be a lot!

Brainstorm

Students should brainstorm their ideas for a dinosaur exhibit at the zoo and present the ideas to the rest of the group. The group can vote on the exhibit that is the best and the safest and work on that model to design as a team.

Ask: What makes a good zoo habitat for a dinosaur? one that will prevent the dinosaur from getting loose; one that is temperature controlled so it is not too cold or too hot; one that has enough windows so people can see into the exhibit

Redesign

When students are finished with their designs, post them around the room and invite students to do a gallery walk. Encourage students to leave feedback cards for each group's design. Then, give teams a chance to review their feedback and make modifications to their designs to improve the zoo habitat for the dinosaurs.

Research and Plan

Make a plan for the research you will need to do and how you will create your design. As you make your plan, consider the following:

- Which dinosaur to focus on
- The behaviors and needs of that type of dinosaur
- The criteria and constraints for a zoo habitat
- How the dinosaur and the people will be safe

Students should indicate their selected dinosaur and provide researched facts regarding what the dinosaur eats, how it behaves, whether it flies, swims, or walks, etc.

Swap designs with another team, and provide constructive feedback for each other's designs. Describe any modifications you would make.

Students should explain whether or not they will modify their zoo habitat designs to improve the designs and indicate why they are or are not making these modifications.

Analyze Your Results

Look for patterns in your dinosaur data. Using your design, make two observations about dinosaurs and their needs.

Students should explain that dinosaurs need space, food, and a natural environment in order to survive well in a zoo habitat.

Restate Your Question

Write the question you investigated.

Students should identify the question created at the beginning of the project.

Claims, Evidence, and Reasoning

Make a claim that answers your question.

Possible answers: The zoo habitat would need to have the right conditions to keep a dinosaur there. Dinosaurs are large, they eat a lot, and they have different behaviors. The zoo design would need to make sure the dinosaur and people in the community are safe. The design would also need to make sure that the dinosaur gets fed properly and has enough space to wander around.

Review your design. What evidence from your design supports your claim?
Students should cite evidence from their designs to support their claims.

Discuss your reasoning with a partner.

455

Analyze Your Results

Analyzing and Interpreting Data

Students should consider the following questions as they interpret their data: Could a dinosaur survive in your group's zoo habitat? Why or why not?

Engaging in Argument from Evidence

Review with students what it means to make a claim. Guide them to understand that they will use the observations they made using their zoo designs as evidence to support their claim.

Claims, Evidence, and Reasoning

Students should claim that dinosaurs have very specific needs and a zoo habitat would not be like the ones we have today.

Ask: What claim can you make? Dinosaurs need very special kinds of zoo habitats, not like the ones we have now.

How does your evidence support your claim? My/our evidence supports this because dinosaurs are big and strong. We know this based on their skeletons. So they would need to be kept in special habitats that do not let them escape.

Encourage students to discuss their reasoning.

Scoring Rubric for Hands-On Activity	
3	States a claim supported with ample, detailed evidence that dinosaurs would need specialized zoo habitats to keep them and people safe.
2	States a claim that is somewhat supported with evidence that dinosaurs would need specialized zoo habitats to keep them and people safe.
1	States a claim that is not supported by evidence.
0	Does not state a claim.

Unit 7 Rocks and Fossils 455L

LESSON 1
How Do Rock Layers Change?

Building to the Performance Expectation

The learning experiences in this lesson prepare students for mastery of:

4-ESS1-1 Identify evidence from patterns in rock formations and fossils in rock layers to support an explanation for changes in a landscape over time.

Trace Tool to the NGSS
Go online to view the complete coverage of these standards across this lesson, unit, and time.

 **Science & Engineering Practices**

 Disciplinary Core Ideas

 Crosscutting Concepts

Constructing Explanations and Designing Solutions
Constructing explanations and designing solutions in 3–5 builds on K–2 experiences and progresses to the use of evidence in constructing explanations that specify variables that describe and predict phenomena and in designing multiple solutions to design problems.

- Identify the evidence that supports particular points in an explanation.

ESS1.C The History of Planet Earth
Local, regional, and global patterns of rock formation reveal changes over time due to earth forces, such as earthquakes. The presence and location of certain fossil types indicate the order in which rock layers were formed. (4-ESS1-1)

Patterns
Patterns can be used as evidence to support an explanation.

 CONNECTIONS TO MATH

MP.2 Reason abstractly and quantitatively.
MP.4 Model with mathematics.
MP.5 Use appropriate tools strategically.
4.MD.A.1 Know relative sizes of measurement units within one system of units including km, m cm; kg, g; lb, oz.; l, ml; hr, min, sec. Within a single system of measurement, express measurements in a larger unit in terms of a smaller unit. Record measurement equivalents in a two-column table.

 CONNECTIONS TO ENGLISH LANGUAGE ARTS

W.4.7 Conduct short research projects that build knowledge through the investigation of different aspects of a topic.

W.4.8 Recall relevant information from experiences or gather relevant information from print and digital sources; take notes and categorize information, and provide a list of sources.

W.4.9 Draw evidence from literary or informational texts to support analysis, reflection, and research.

456A Unit 7 Rocks and Fossils

Supporting All Students, All Standards

Integrating the Three Dimensions of Learning

Model rock layers to gather evidence about how they form and what information they contain about the history of planet Earth **(DCI ESS1.C)**. Look at examples of exposed layers in different formations, and come up with explanations **(SEP Constructing Explanations and Designing Solutions)** for how these layers tell stories about the past and the Earth processes that shape and change rocks **(CCC Patterns)**. By investigating a variety of formations, put together the pieces of a jigsaw puzzle that reveals how the land has changed over time, sometimes because of slow processes and other times because of quick and violent incidents on Earth's surface.

 **Professional Development** Go online to view **Professional Development** videos with strategies to integrate CCCs and SEPs, including the ones used in this lesson.

Extra Hands-On Activity: Folding Rocks

How Can You Model Changes in Rocks?

- Pairs
- 30–40 minutes

Using three or more colors of modeling clay, have students roll out model layers of sedimentary earth materials to approximately 1 cm thick. They should then stack the layers, placing dried beans or other similar materials to represent rock fragments. The stacked layers should be lightly rolled so the clay layers adhere to each other well. Have students make drawings to show what their layers looked like before they are folded. Students should then place the clay layers on a flat surface. Using two books wrapped in wax paper or plastic wrap, students place a book on opposite sides of the clay with the spine side facing the clay. Students should then slowly push the two books together, causing the layers to fold and reform. Have students compare the rock layers with the drawing they made to see how the layers have changed.

 This activity can support mastery of this Crosscutting Concept: Patterns

Preassessment

Have students complete the unit pre-test online or see the Assessment Guide.

Build on Prior Knowledge

Students should already know and be prepared to build on the following concepts:
- The movement of water and glaciers over Earth's surface affects the shape of the land.
- Other factors, such as earthquakes and volcanoes, also affect the shape of Earth's surface.
- By looking at maps, people can see patterns in Earth's surface that tell them about some of the planet's key features.

Differentiate Instruction

Lesson Vocabulary
- relative age

Students may be more familiar with each part of the term *relative age*.

Ask: What does the word *relative* mean? Possible answers: a person who is kin; something connected to something else
What does the word *age* mean? how old something is

Explain that relative age, then, is the age of one thing compared to another.

ELL/ELD Strategy
Show students images of people of various ages.

Ask: How old do you think the oldest person in these images is? Answers will vary based on the images.

Ask: How old do you think the youngest person in these images is? Answers will vary based on the images.

Explain to students that they are comparing ages. The youngest person's age is relative to the oldest person's age. Throughout this lesson, they will do the same thing with different layers of rock.

Lesson 1 How Do Rock Layers Change? **456B**

LESSON 1 **Engage** • Explore/Explain • Elaborate • Evaluate

ENGAGE: Lesson Phenomenon

Lesson Objective

To construct explanations for the ways in which rock layers reveal patterns and reflect the history of planet Earth.

About This Image

This mountain looks the way it does because of weathering and erosion. Elemental forces have caused the surface of the mountain to break down into small particles of rock, which have been moved by water and rain. As a result, the layers that make up the mountain can clearly be seen. Each horizontal line is a layer that represents a past period of time.

These layers were laid down over many years. Eventually they were covered by other layers, which pressed down on them, turning them into rock. Over millions to hundreds of millions of years, multiple layers were built up. The deeper down you go, the older the layers. So the layers at the base near the ground are the oldest, while those at the top are the youngest.

 **Constructing Explanations and Designing Solutions**

Alternative Engage Strategy

Books by Date Whole Class 10 minutes

Ask students to take five books from the classroom or their desks and look at the copyright date in each. Explain that the copyright date tells how old the book is. Have students stack the books from oldest (on the bottom) to newest (on the top), using the copyright dates as a guide. Explain that these books are like the layers of rock that can be found on Earth's surface. Ask how the books are similar to rock layers. Why is the oldest on bottom and the newest on top?

LESSON 1

How Do Rock Layers Change?

Rocks can give clues about things that happened on Earth long ago. They can also provide evidence of how our planet has changed over time. Some of these rocks formed in ancient oceans. Some of them formed on dry land. What else might rock layers tell us about the past?

By the end of this lesson...
you'll be able to determine the relative age of rock layers and explain how rock layers change.

456

Unit 7 Rocks and Fossils

 **Explore Online** Students can view the lesson phenomenon online.

Can You Explain It?

Students are asked to record their initial thoughts about how the rocks of the Niobrara chalk formation formed, as well as which layers are the oldest and which are the youngest. To do so, students must understand the basics of how rock layers form. Urge students not to worry about whether their answers are correct at this stage. They should expect their ideas to change as they progress through the Explorations. They will have an opportunity to revise their answers when they revisit these questions at the end of the lesson.

> ## Collaboration
>
> **Think, Pair, Share** You may wish to have students view the images individually and think about what they have seen. Then separate them into pairs, and encourage them to discuss what they saw. If you have assigned the activity with the books on the previous page, have them relate to each other how what they've seen is similar to what they did with their books. Then have them share their ideas in a whole-class discussion.

 EVIDENCE NOTEBOOK

Encourage students to use an appropriate graphic organizer, such as main idea and supporting details, to set up their notebook for this lesson.

Find more strategies in the online ELA handbook.

Can You Explain It?

Look at the photos. Rock like this can often contain fossils within its layers. Fossils form when ancient living things die and become preserved in rocks. Fossils are found in some types of rocks.

1. The rocks in the photos belong to a group of rocks called the Niobrara chalk formation. How do you think these rocks formed? Which rock layer is the oldest? Which is the youngest?

   Students should respond based on the preliminary observations they can make of the images.
   ___
   ___
   ___
   ___
   ___

Tip

Learn more about some of Earth's features in *How Does Water Shape Earth's Surface?* and *What Other Factors Shape Earth's Surface?*

 EVIDENCE NOTEBOOK Look for this icon to help you gather evidence to answer the questions above.

457

Lesson 1 How Do Rock Layers Change? **457**

LESSON 1   Engage • **Explore/Explain** • Elaborate • Evaluate

EXPLORATION 1 One Layer at a Time

3D Learning Objective

Develop an understanding of how rock layers form as older layers of sediment are compacted by new layers of sediment, which press the lower layers into rock. **Construct explanations** about how layers form by modeling the process with different materials. Look at the **patterns** that result, and then explain how the process reveals **the history of planet Earth**.

HANDS-ON Apply What You Know
Layered Landforms

Students use a clear glass jar and three types of materials to model how rock layers form. Each material represents a different rock layer. Students first place the three materials in the jar one by one, making note of the order. They then repeat the exercise, but this time placing the materials in a different order. Finally, they explain what the layers of material represent (rock layers) and how they can be laid down in different order.

Assessment Rubric	
3	understand that each material represents a different layer; a different order shows that patterns in layers can change; understand the order from oldest to youngest
2	understand that each material represents a different layer; a different order shows that patterns in layers can change; do not understand the order from oldest to youngest
1	understand that each material represents a different layer, but don't grasp that a different order shows that patterns in layers can change; also do not understand the order of the layers from oldest to youngest

458 Unit 7 Rocks and Fossils

EXPLORATION 1

One Layer at a Time

Observing Rock Layers

Have you ever seen layers of rocks along a highway or hillside? Have you ever wondered why they look the way they do? This activity will give you some answers to these questions.

 HANDS-ON Apply What You Know

Layered Landforms

2. Consider the rock layers you've seen. Different kinds of materials form layers that can become rock. Can you see patterns in rock layers?

Use the materials that your teacher has provided to follow the steps below.

Step 1: With your group, select one of the materials. This will be the first layer in your jar.

Step 2: Watch as your teacher shows how to pour the material into the jar.

Step 3: Pour the material you selected into the jar at a steady rate for 4 seconds.

Step 4: Repeat step 3 three times. Change the material and length of time you pour each time. Pour one time for 7 seconds, another time for 13 seconds, and another time for 10 seconds. However, always pour at the same rate.

Which rock layer in your model is the oldest? Which is the youngest? How did pouring the material for different amounts of time affect the layers? What can this tell you about rock layers in nature? What other factors could cause the same thing to happen?

Accept all reasonable answers.

458

 **Explore Online** Have students go online to learn more about what all rocks have in common.

Layer Upon Layer

These photos show rocks in places from different parts of the world. Yet all the rocks have something in common. Study the photos, and then answer the question.

Akaroa Head is in New Zealand, an island nation not far from Australia. These rock layers have been changed by the ocean and the wind.

The Alps are mountains that stretch across Europe. These mountains are made of many layers of different types of rocks.

Antarctica's Buckley Formation formed almost 300 million years ago! Some of the rocks in this formation include coal, a rock that formed in ancient swamps.

This the rock layers surrounding this waterfall are near Stoney Creek, Ontario. The rock layers show many different colors of rock.

3. Explain how all the rock layers shown on this page are the same.

Possible answer: Each layer sits on top of another layer. Most of the layers are fairly horizontal. The layers at the top of each sequence are younger than the layers at the bottom of the sequences.

Connection to Science

Natural systems have patterns that repeat over and over again. For example, organisms often develop similar traits to survive in similar environments. Rock layers form in similar ways to each other, whether under sediment, sand, or volcanic ash. Geologic processes often follow predictable patterns.

Ask: Why do scientists assume there is an order to natural processes? Possible answer: Scientists observe patterns that repeat over and over again.

4-ESS1.1 Earth's Place in the Universe

 **Patterns**

Ask: Are there patterns in rock layers shown in the images? Possible answer: Yes. The layers look like thin bands running horizontally through the rock. In each photo, they also have similar colors.

DCI ESS1.C The History of Planet Earth

No matter where layers of rock appear on Earth, they look similar, though they may tell very different stories.

Ask: Why might rock layers in different locations tell a different story? Possible answer: They were laid down in a different time and place, and they each tell about their own time and place.

Differentiate Instruction

ELL: Use Realia Locate and print images from the Internet that show exposed rock formations from the English-language learners' native areas. Explain where the images come from and what they show, and ask students whether they have heard of the places or been to them. Showing an interest in a student's home can help engage him or her in the learning process.

LESSON 1 Engage • **Explore/Explain** • Elaborate • Evaluate

EXPLORATION 1 *One Layer at a Time, continued*

Content Background

Some students may not have a recycling program in their area. Others may have such programs, but not understand what they are. Explain that paper products are made from trees, glass from sand, and plastic from fossil fuels. To conserve natural resources, we reuse as many products made from these as possible. That means sending them to a place where they can be made usable again. In some communities, residents are given a small red bin or a large blue bin, where they collect materials that can be recycled. Once a week, a truck comes around and collects the materials in the bin and then takes them to a recycling center, where they can be made usable again.

CCC Patterns

The reason we can use newspapers to model rock layers is that both follow a pattern.

Ask: What pattern do recycling newspapers in a bin and rock layers forming share? **Newer newspapers are piled on top of older newspapers, creating layers. Younger rock is piled on top of older rock, creating layers.**

Differentiate Instruction

RTI/Extra Support Model the activity for students. Have each student write his or her name on a sheet of paper. Then walk around the room with a container, asking each student to place his or her sheet into the container.

Ask: Which person's sheet will represent the oldest layer? **the person who was first to place a sheet in the container**

Ask: Which person's sheet will represent the youngest layer? **the person who was last to place a sheet in the container**

How Some Rocks Form

Many cities across the United States have recycling programs in which used items are collected and used to make new items. Read on to find out how recycling newspapers is similar to the way a series of rock layers can form.

Layer Over Layer

4. On Day 1, a family drops a newspaper into a large recycling bin. The newspaper falls to the bottom of the bin as it's thrown in. On Day 2, another paper is put into the bin. The family drops one newspaper into the bin each day. Label the missing days on the bins below.

Day 1   Day 5   Day 9

5. Think about the newspapers in the recycling bin. Which layer is the oldest? youngest? The image below shows the papers on Day 9. Circle the youngest layer and draw an arrow to the oldest layer. Put an X over the layers that are not the oldest or youngest.

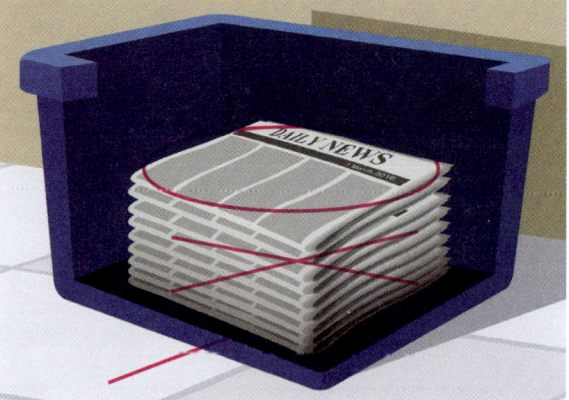

460

460 Unit 7 Rocks and Fossils

Scientists can tell the relative age of rocks by looking at where they fall in a sequence. **Relative age** is the age of one thing compared to another. Relative age explains things in terms of *older* and *younger*. For example, the newspaper from Day 1 is older than the newspaper from Day 3.

6. Look at your answers to question 5. How did you know which layer was the oldest? The youngest? Provide evidence to support your answer.

Possible answer: I knew that layer 1 was the oldest because it was the first newspaper put into the bin. I knew that layer 9 was the youngest because it was the last newspaper put into the bin. I knew that the other layers were put into the bin after layer 1 but before layer 9.

7. **Language SmArts** Research some rock layers near your house or in your state. Find evidence from informational texts to support that the oldest layers of rock are at the bottom of the sequence, and the youngest are at the top.

Students might suggest that the geologic ages of the rocks or any fossils that might be found in the rocks are evidence of the order in which the rocks formed.

 EVIDENCE NOTEBOOK Use what you've learned on these pages to help you explain how the Niobrara chalk may have formed.

Putting it Together

8. Choose the words or phrases that correctly complete each sentence.

at the top	at the bottom	in the middle
older	younger	

In a sequence of rock layers, the oldest layer of rock is ___at the bottom___ of the sequence. The youngest layer is ___at the top___. As the layers form, ___younger___ rock forms on top of ___older___ rock.

461

 **Explore Online** Have students go online to see how rock layers form.

 Language SmArts
W.4.8 Recall relevant information from experiences or gather relevant information from print and digital sources; take notes and categorize information, and provide a list of sources.

This activity is an opportunity to reinforce basic research skills. Remind students that good notetaking includes recording sources: the webpage URL and date visited; the book, author, and page number; encyclopedia volume and page number; and so on. You may wish to have students add this information to their data tables.

Ask: Why is it important to use information from informational texts? Using information from informational texts helps us to provide evidence for a claim.

 EVIDENCE NOTEBOOK

Students should relate the activity to what they observed at the beginning of the lesson. The rock layers they see in the Niobrara chalk formation were laid down one at a time with the oldest on bottom.

FORMATIVE ASSESSMENT

 ESS1.C The History of Planet Earth

Ask: What do the layers in rock represent? They represent different periods in Earth's history.

Lesson 1 How Do Rock Layers Change? **461**

LESSON 1   Engage • **Explore/Explain** • Elaborate • Evaluate

EXPLORATION 2 Layer on Layer

3D Learning Objective

Affirm understanding of rock layers through a group of exercises that show how those layers, or **patterns**, reveal **the history of planet Earth**. Learn that some layers contain fossils, and **construct explanations** for the age of some layers based on their fossils and relative ages.

DCI ESS1.C The History of Planet Earth

Each layer of rock was laid down over many thousands to hundreds of thousands of years, so multiple layers can represent millions of years.

Ask: What do the layers in rock represent? periods of time
Ask: If there are many layers of rock, what story is told in them?
what Earth was like during the time the layers were laid down

Patterns

Each layer of rock was laid down in a similar way. Sediment is deposited and covered in water. Over time, more sediment and water cover the original sediment and water. Eventually, the top layers get so heavy, they press the lower layers into rock.

Ask: Why is it possible to predict how future layers of sediment will become rock? The way sediment is laid down follows a pattern, which has been repeated many times in the past.

Differentiate Instruction

Extension Rock layers are often made of similar colors. For example, the layers in Mushroom Rock start out as red and gray in the lower layers before turning to brown or tan. The colors of a layer can tell us something about the rock itself. Have students research the colors of rock layers, explaining why they look the way they do.

---

462 Unit 7 Rocks and Fossils

EXPLORATION 2

Layer on Layer

Telling a Story

Mushroom Rock from South Africa, which is shown in the photo below, is made of many layers of rocks. Each rock layer formed in a certain way and gives clues about how this part of Earth changed over time.

A Long, Long Story!

9. Use a thin highlighter or a pen to trace the tops and bottoms of as many layers as you can pick out in this photo of Mushroom Rock. Then number the layers, marking the oldest layer as 1.

Some of the rocks that make up Mushroom Rock are millions of years old. The layers have been exposed through weathering and erosion.

10. How many rock layers did you count?

Students should count a minimum of 3 layers. Some may count more.

11. What number did you assign to the youngest layer in the rock?

Students' answers should reflect that they selected the largest number in their count as the youngest rock layer.

462

Do the Math
Canyon Clues

12. You have data about five rock layers labeled A through E. Use these clues to determine the relative ages of the rocks from youngest to oldest and complete the table.

- Layer A is 200 million years old, but it is 100 million years younger than Layer C.
- Layer B is the top layer of rock.
- Layer C has more layers above it than below it.
- Layer D is older than Layer B and younger than Layer A.
- Layer E is 480 million years old.

Youngest		
1	Layer	B
2	Layer	D
3	Layer	A
4	Layer	C
5	Layer	E
Oldest		

Language SmArts
Conducting Research

13. Many of the rock layers in Mushroom Rock are sedimentary rocks. Use informational texts to find out more about sedimentary rocks and how they form. Can you find a relationship between the types of rock and the color of the layers? Write your findings below.

Possible answer: Sandstone and limestone are two types of sedimentary rock that often form in the ocean. Sandstone is made of sand. Limestone is made of the mineral calcite. These rocks form as layers of sand and calcite collect on the ocean floor. When the sediment is cemented together and hardens, rocks form. Shale is sedimentary rock that forms in the ocean. It can be black, red, green, or tan and is made of very small bits of silt and mud.

 Patterns

Students can solve the Do the Math activity by looking at the patterns revealed in the descriptions.

Ask: What pattern can you find in the descriptions? **patterns related to age**

Do the Math
Canyon Clues
MP.2 Reason abstractly and quantitatively.

This activity requires students to think both abstractly and quantitatively and requires an understanding of relative age. Each layer of rock has an age relative to the other layers. Invite students to work out the problem on a separate sheet of paper. If they are struggling, guide them with the first few. Explain that because A is younger than C, it goes above C. Because B is covered in soil, it must be the youngest and goes on top.

Language SmArts
Conducting Research
W.4.7 Conduct short research projects that build knowledge through the investigation of different aspects of a topic.

This activity combines some of the things students are tasked with researching on the previous page. If they have been assigned those tasks, explain that they can build on research already completed. This is also an opportunity to reinforce basic research skills. Remind students that good notetaking includes recording sources: the webpage URL and date visited; the book, author, and page number; encyclopedia volume and page number; and so on.

LESSON 1   Engage • **Explore/Explain** • Elaborate • Evaluate

EXPLORATION 2 *Layer on Layer, continued*

Content Background

The Grand Canyon contains fossils mostly stretching from 1,200 million years ago to around 270 million years ago. That's a span of 930 million years. It is made up of layers of sedimentary rock, which is where fossils can be found. Many are from marine, or water, environments, though a few are from terrestrial, or land, environments. Fossils found in the Grand Canyon include trilobites, brachiopods, plant leaves, and proto-mammal tracks.

Ask: Why are most fossils found in sedimentary rock? *Sedimentary rock usually begins as mud or sand. When an animal dies in water or falls into water, it is sometimes covered by sand or mud. Over the years, this sand or mud is covered by other sand or mud and is eventually pressed into stone.*

DCI ESS1.C The History of Planet Earth

The Grand Canyon contains fossils that are 270 million years old and older. Dinosaurs lived between 230 and 65.5 million years ago.

Ask: Are the fossils in the Grand Canyon older or younger than dinosaur fossils? *older*

CCC Patterns

Many fossils can be found in places known as badlands. Badlands are areas where land is heavily eroded and there is sparse vegetation. Most dinosaur fossils have been found in badlands in such places as Alberta, Canada; Painted Desert, Arizona; the Badlands of South Dakota; and so on.

Ask: Why are badlands good areas for finding fossils? *Because the land is eroded, badlands feature rock layers visible to the naked eye.*

Some Rocks and Fossils From Around the World

Rock layers are found all over the world. Many of these rocks contain fossils. Fossils provide clues about the ages of the rocks in which they are found. Look at the map and photos and read the captions to learn about some rock formations around the world. Look for patterns in the rocks shown.

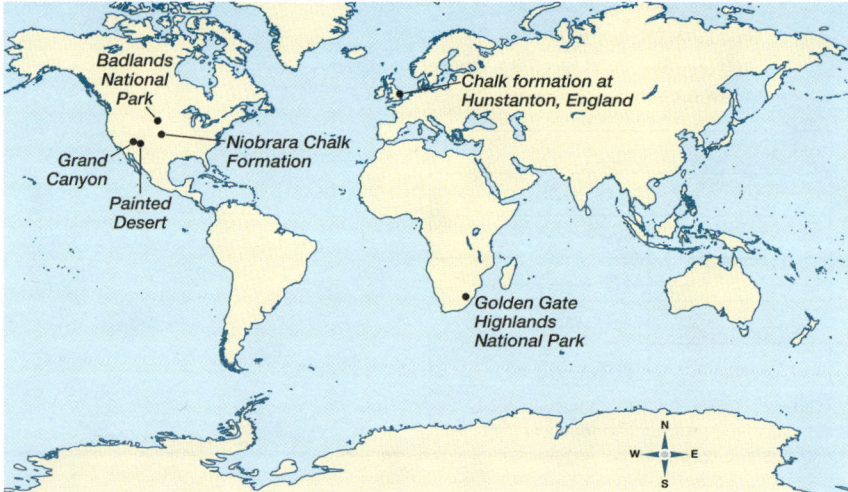

Some rocks in the Grand Canyon, in the southwestern United States, contain many fossils. But there are no dinosaur fossils. Why? The youngest fossils in the rocks are 270 million years old. Dinosaurs lived 230–65 million years ago.

Rocks in the Painted Desert in Arizona contain fossils from a time period spanning millions of years. The oldest fossils are older than dinosaurs, while the youngest are just a few thousand years old.

The Niobrara Chalk in Kansas, Nebraska and other states, is made of millions of fossils of marine algae. This means that Kansas and nearby states were once on the ocean floor!

The Badlands of South Dakota contain young fossils of the close relatives of modern deer, horses, mice, and turtles.

The Ferriby Chalk cliffs in England were part of the ocean floor about 100 million years ago. Fossils of many ocean plants and animals are embedded in this soft rock.

The Mushroom Rock formation in South Africa is home to the oldest fossilized dinosaur egg nest found to date. The nest is 190 million years old!

14. Look again at the photos of the rocks and reread the captions to complete the table below.

Location	Description of rocks/fossils
Grand Canyon in SW United States	red rocks; plants and animals older than the dinosaurs
Painted Desert in Arizona	gray and dark rocks; plants and animals older than the dinosaurs, dinosaurs, and more recent plants and animals
Niobrara Chalk in Kansas	gray; marine life
Badlands of South Dakota	gray and brown; ancestors of modern mammals and reptiles
Ferriby Chalk in England	white and red; marine life
Mushroom Rock in South Africa	tan, brown, red, and gray; dinosaurs

DCI ESS1.C The History of Planet Earth

Consider the photos in this spread and the kinds of fossils that can be found in them, based on their descriptions in the captions.

Ask: What span of Earth's history is represented in these photos? The Badlands of South Dakota contain fossils of recent life, such as deer, horses, mice, and turtles, while the Grand Canyon contains fossils that are older than 270 million years.

CCC Patterns

The Niobrara formation in Kansas and the Ferriby cliffs in England feature many fossils of marine organisms.

Ask: Why are the two areas white? They are both made of chalk, which is the microscopic fossils of marine organisms compacted together into rocky layers.

Differentiate Instruction

ELL: Matching Print a photo from each location that looks similar to those in the book. Then print images of the fossils found in each. Rather than have English-language learners write descriptions and match those descriptions to the names in the book, have them match the images of the fossils to the photos of their geographic location. Allow students to use the captions in the book to guide their choices.

Lesson 1 How Do Rock Layers Change?

LESSON 1   Engage • **Explore/Explain** • Elaborate • Evaluate

EXPLORATION 2 Layer on Layer, continued

 ESS1.C The History of Planet Earth

Have students reread the captions.

Ask: What evidence is there that each of these groups of rocks tells a story about the history of planet Earth? *Some of the rocks have very old fossils. Some have very young fossils. Fossils tell us about what life lived in a location at a certain time.*

CCC Patterns

Each photo on this page shows evidence of patterns.

Ask: What patterns do you see in the photos? *Possible patterns: Each layer is horizontal; most of the layers in each photo are the same or a similar color; each photo shows layer after layer stacked atop each other.*

> ## Collaboration
>
> **Class Discussion** Ask students whether they have seen any rock layers in their area. If not, have a list prepared of exposed rock layers near your school; these may be part of a badland, a mountain, a hill, a road cut, etc. Discuss the color of the rock layers and any fossils that may have been discovered in them. Engage students in a conversation about what the area might have been like before the layers became rock.

 EVIDENCE NOTEBOOK

Students should write that knowing what the rock layers are made of helps them understand how the layers formed. In this case, the layers are made of chalk, which is made up of the fossils of many tiny organisms that once lived in a sea or ocean. As the animals died, the hard parts of their bodies sank to the sea floor and piled up. Eventually, the layers above pressed them into rock.

Patterns in Rock Layers

You have learned that some rocks are very similar to one another, while other rocks are quite different. Some rocks contain fossils of similar ages. Other rocks contain fossils of different ages.

Patterns in Layers

15. Look again at these photos. Look for patterns from your observations to help you answer the question below.

Grand Canyon

Niobrara Chalk Formation

Ferriby Chalk Formation

16. Choose the words or phrases to correctly complete each sentence.

| flat | light | thinner | bent | black | thicker |

These rocks are made of layers that are _____*flat*_____. The layers in two of the photos are _____*light*_____ in color. The light layer in the Ferriby Chalk formation is _____*thicker*_____ than the other layers.

 EVIDENCE NOTEBOOK The rocks in these photos all contain layers. How do your observations here help you answer the questions from the beginning of this lesson?

466

466 Unit 7 Rocks and Fossils

Rocked and Rolled?

Forces and processes on Earth can cause rocks to change. What might happen to rocks when forces act on them?

Explore Online

Some rocks will bend due to temperature and pressure.

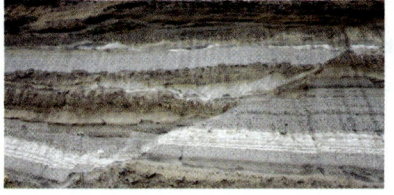
Others will break and crack during an earthquake.

17. Look again at the photos above. Compare them with the other photos you've seen so far in this lesson. Use your observations to complete each sentence with the correct word.

In rock layers that have not been disturbed, the ___oldest___ rocks are at the bottom and the ___youngest___ rocks are at the top. Due to heat and pressure, some rocks often ___bend___ and an earthquake may ___crack___ rocks.

| youngest |
| oldest |
| bend |
| crack |

18. How does finding rock layers made of different types of rock provide evidence that the landscape has changed over time?

Possible answer: Layers of different types and colors formed under different conditions.

Putting It Together

19. Choose the word that best completes each sentence.

| are layered | were bent by earthquakes | top |
| bottom | change | stay the same |

Rocks in the Grand Canyon ___are layered___. The oldest fossils in these rocks are found in the ___bottom___ layers. Broken rock layers show that forces have caused a ___change___ in the layers.

467

Explore Online Have students go online to learn more about how rock layers change.

CCC Patterns

Patterns can sometimes be deceptive. For example, throughout this lesson, students have learned that younger rock layers are on top and older ones on bottom. However, on rare occasions, pressure may cause rocks to rise and then fall over, reversing their order.

Ask: What can cause rock layers to change position in relation to each other? earthquakes

Ask: How is it possible to tell when rock layers may have changed position? Broken or bent rock layers would indicate that they have changed position.

SEP Constructing Explanations and Designing Solutions

Ask: What is one way to tell whether the layers in an exposed area of rock come from similar or different environments? Possible answer: If there are fossils, they may be the same, similar, or entirely different depending on the rock layer.

Differentiate Instruction

RTI/Extra Support Present students with two materials, one that is hard, but easy to break and one that is rubbery and bendable. Explain that your hand will apply pressure just as slabs of land apply when they push against each other. Break the first object, and then bend the second. When you are done, have students answer question 17 in their book.

FORMATIVE ASSESSMENT

DCI ESS1.C The History of Planet Earth

Ask: What is one way to tell whether rock layers from different areas represent the same time period? Possible answer: They contain the same fossils.

Lesson 1 How Do Rock Layers Change? 467

LESSON 1 Engage • **Explore/Explain** • Elaborate • Evaluate

EXPLORATION 2 Layer on Layer, continued

HANDS-ON ACTIVITY Pairs   1 class period
Modeling How Rocks Can Form and Change

3D Learning Objective

 Constructing Explanations and Designing Solutions

Model ways that rock layers form and the forces that can cause them to change.

Materials

Students will need writing utensils with which to draw their rock layers. Colored pencils or crayons may work best, as they will allow students to color the rock layers the same color as the layers of clay.

Preparation

Before students begin the project, make sure that each pair has enough clay to model six layers and that each has at least three colors of clay. Have the clay, along with the paper plates, ready for students.

 Patterns

Patterns will be obvious in the clay layers.

Ask: Why is it important for there to be different colors of clay?
The clay represents rock layers, and different colors are an easy way to tell the layers apart.

Procedure

STEPS 1–2 Circulate among the pairs as they lay down their first layers of clay, and answer any questions they may have.

Modeling How Rocks Can Form and Change

Objective

Collaborate with a partner to model how rock layers might form and how these layers can change.

Materials
- several colors of modeling clay
- paper plate

What question will you investigate to meet this objective?
Possible question: What can cause rock layers to change?

_____

_____

Procedure

STEP 1 Choose one lump of clay. Flatten it into a layer on the paper plate.

What can you say about this model rock layer?
Students should state that this piece of clay models the oldest rock layer that they will form.

_____

STEP 2 Choose another color of clay. Flatten it into a layer that sits on top of your first layer.

Why did you choose a different color of clay for this step?
It represents a different rock layer.

_____

468

  Student Lab Worksheet and complete Teacher Support available online.

468 Unit 7 Rocks and Fossils

STEP 3 Continue placing new layers of clay of different colors on top of each other until you have at least six layers. You may reuse colors as long as layers of the same color don't touch.

Why couldn't model rock layers of the same color touch?
Showing different colors makes it easier to distinguish each layer as they are manipulated.

STEP 4 As you build your model, think about how the model rock layers are like real rock layers. Draw a picture of your finished model in the box below.

STEP 5 Think about ways you can change your model to show how forces can change rock layers. Make the model look like one of the photos in this lesson. Explain how you will change it on the lines below.
Students might state that they will apply force to opposite ends of the stack of clay to bend the model rocks. Or they might pull the layers apart to break the model rock layers.

STEP 6 Share your results with other students. Discuss ways other types of changes can be represented. Then change your model. On a separate piece of paper, draw pictures of your before and after model. Label the drawings, and submit the paper to your teacher.

469

STEP 3 As you observe the student pairs, be sure that they are not placing same-colored clay in successive layers.

STEP 4 After students have finished making their models, walk among them as they draw the results. Their drawings should contain the same number of layers as their model and should be colored in the same way as the layers of clay.

STEP 5 Prompt students by reminding them what their clay layers represent.

Ask: What are some of the forces that can change rock? Possible answers: earthquakes, volcanoes, weathering
Ask: Which of these forces can cause instant changes to rock layers? earthquakes, volcanoes

STEP 6 Instruct students to look over the drawing of their previous clay layers.

Ask: What is one way you can change your second model so that it isn't like the first? change the order of the colors of the layers

Once they have made a new set of layers, they should draw and color it. Then have them apply force to the clay, after which they should draw and color what they see. Ask them to come up with a time period for each layer and label their drawings before they turn them in.

CCC Patterns

Ask: What do both models reveal about the clay layers? They look similar and break or bend in similar ways.

Lesson 1 How Do Rock Layers Change? **469**

LESSON 1 Engage • **Explore/Explain** • Elaborate • Evaluate

EXPLORATION 2 HANDS-ON ACTIVITY, continued

Analyze Your Results

STEP 7 Direct students to discuss with each other the similarities and differences between the models before and after they applied force. Then have them compare what happened to the two separate models by comparing their drawings.

STEPS 8–9 Be available to students, answering any questions they may have and guiding them to answer the questions correctly.

Draw Conclusions

Once the activity is completed, bring all students back together and lead a class discussion about what they learned.

> ### Claims, Evidence, and Reasoning
>
> Have students work with a partner to critique each other's claims and evidence in Step 10. Ask each pair to be prepared to share one way that they changed or improved their claim or the evidence decided. Discuss responses as a class.
>
> **Ask:** What is the most reliable evidence that rock layers can change? Why do you think so? **Students may cite that force or pressure caused the clay layers to bend or break and that this is similar to how force or pressure affects soft or hard layers of rock. Accept any reasonable answers.**

Scoring Rubric for Hands-On Activity	
3	Students understand what each layer of clay represents, what the order means, and how pressure can cause change.
2	Students understand two of the following: what each layer of clay represents, what the order means, or how pressure can cause change.
1	Students understand one of the following: what each layer of clay represents, what the order means, or how pressure can cause change.

Analyze Your Results

STEP 7 Compare and contrast the layers before and after you changed them.
Students should state that the model rocks were horizontal before they applied forces. After forces were applied, the rocks were bent or maybe even broken.

STEP 8 Did the order of the layers in your model change when you changed the model?
If students applied gentle compression or tensile forces to the models, the layers shouldn't have changed order.

STEP 9 Which rock layer in your model is the oldest? Which is the youngest?
The layer that was put down first is the oldest. The last layer to be added to the models is the youngest.

Draw Conclusions

STEP 10 Make a claim about rock layers.
Students might state that their models show what could happen to rock layers during an earthquake.

STEP 11 Cite evidence to support your claim.
Possible answer: My before and after drawings are evidence that the rock layers changed.

STEP 12 Write at least two more questions you would like to ask about how rock layers form and change.
Possible questions: How can rock layers change order? Do all rocks form in horizontal layers? Can rock layers tilt rather than bend? Can rock layers get thicker when forces are applied to them?

EXPLORATION 3 Not What It Used to Be

EXPLORATION 3
Not What It Used to Be

It's a *Grand* Canyon!

The layers of rock that make up the Grand Canyon formed over millions and millions of years.

HANDS-ON Apply What You Know

The Story of the Canyon

Look at these images of the Grand Canyon.

Dozens of rock layers can be seen in the Grand Canyon.

The Colorado River flows through the Grand Canyon.

20. Put on your creative cap! You're going to be a cartoonist! Draw a cartoon strip that shows how you think the Grand Canyon formed. Your strip should have at least three panels (boxes). Be sure to show what the land looked like before, during, and after formation of the canyon. Submit your cartoon to your teacher.

Once the layers were in place, the mighty Colorado River began to carve through them to create the long, deep canyon we see today.

21. In your own words, briefly explain how the Grand Canyon formed.

Possible answer: Many layers of rocks were laid down. The river carved out the canyon as it flowed over the rock layers.

471

3D Learning Objective

Students will **construct explanations** of how **patterns** in rock layers are caused by **slow or fast changes over time**.

 ESS1.C The History of Planet Earth

Over many thousands, hundreds of thousands, or millions of years, flowing water has the power to change the appearance and shape of Earth's surface.

Ask: What other examples of water changing Earth's surface can you think of? Possible answers: the badlands of Alberta; Gray Canyon, Utah; Bad Rock Canyon, Montana

Ask: What other natural processes can change Earth's surface?
Possible answers: wind, earthquakes, volcanoes, asteroid/meteor impacts

Explain that students will learn more about natural processes that can change Earth's surface in this Exploration.

HANDS-ON Apply What You Know
The Story of the Canyon

Student cartoons should be similar to the Explore Online video, showing water cutting into the surface of Earth until a canyon has formed. Students may choose to add a description to each box, explaining what is happening.

Assessment Rubric	
3	The first panel should show land with a thin river running over it. The second panel should show the river cutting into the land. The third panel should show a deep canyon or gorge.
2	The cartoons should illustrate at least two of the panels described above.
1	The cartoons should illustrate at least one example of the panels described above.

Lesson 1 How Do Rock Layers Change? 471

LESSON 1 Engage • **Explore/Explain** • Elaborate • Evaluate

EXPLORATION 3 Not What It Used to Be, continued

 DCI ESS1.C The History of Planet Earth

As students have learned, water can cut deep into layers of rock.

Ask: When water cuts into Earth's surface over long periods of time, what is left behind? *exposed rock*

Ask: What can be seen in this rock? *layers that have built up over time*

Ask: What can sometimes be found in these layers? *fossils*

Ask: How can these finds tell us about the history of planet Earth? *They can reveal past forms of life as well as information about past environments.*

SEP Constructing Explanations and Designing Solutions

Ask: What is the process that enables water to cut into Earth's surface? *weathering*

Differentiate Instruction

Extension Have students research a canyon near them and write a report about it. They should tell what span of years the canyon's rock layers cover and what fossils have been discovered there. They should describe how the area is similar to or different from what it was like in the past.

Collaboration

Share Feedback Have students as a group watch the video showing how canyons, such as the Grand Canyon, form. Then lead a class discussion. Point to other examples of canyons that have been formed by flowing water over time, such as those mentioned on the previous page.

Slow and Steady

Rivers are narrow bodies of water that flow over land. They can change the rocks beneath them by carving canyons. Look at the images and read the captions to find out how.

1. As a river flows over flat land, it slowly cuts down into the rocks.

2. Over time, the river cuts deeper and deeper into the rocks, making the riverbed's walls steeper.

3. After millions of years, a deep canyon with very steep walls can form.

22. How does a canyon such as the Grand Canyon form? Circle the best answer.

a. Earthquakes cause rocks to break and form a canyon.
b. Rock layers are put down in two places to form a canyon.
c. A river carves down into rocks to form a deep canyon.
d. Rain and snow cause rocks to dissolve to form a canyon.

You've just learned one way changes to a landscape can occur slowly over time. Other forces on Earth can change the land quickly. Look at the image on the next page to find out more.

In the Blink of an Eye!

Earthquakes can change the landscape very quickly. In fact, most earthquakes last for less than a minute! Look at the drawings to see what happens to rocks during these events.

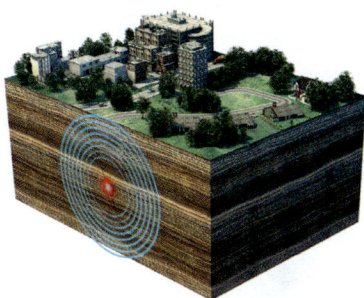
Over time, stored energy builds up in rocks.

During an earthquake, rocks move and the stored energy is released.

Earthquakes happen in many places around the world. But most, about 75%, occur along the edges of the Pacific Ocean. This active area is called the Ring of Fire. Many volcanoes are located there, too.

 Engineer It!
Measuring Earthquakes

23. Scientists use seismometers to detect and measure the energy released by earthquakes. The top image shows an early seismometer. The needle records the earthquake activity on the paper. The bottom photo shows a modern seismometer that uses digital technology to record the earthquake activity. What advantages might the modern way or recording data have over older ones?

<u>Possible answer: Recording the earthquake</u>
<u>activity digitally would allow for the information to</u>
<u>be shared more quilckly.</u>
_____
_____

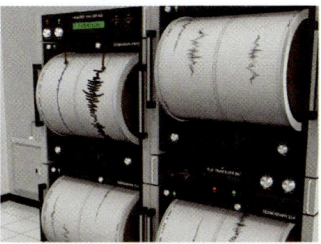
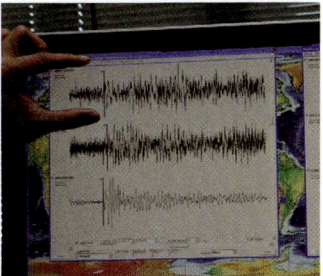

473

Content Background

In the early 1900s, a German scientist named Alfred Wegener proposed the theory that Earth's continents were drifting, some toward each other, others away from each other. By the 1950s, his theory was replaced by plate tectonics, or the theory that Earth's surface is made up of large plates floating on the planet's mantle. As these plates move, some crash into each other, pushing up mountains. Others pull apart, leaving behind rift valleys or deep ocean trenches.

 SEP **Constructing Explanations and Designing Solutions**

Earth's crust is made up of many plates that are slowly, almost imperceptibly moving. One of the planet's biggest plates is known as the Pacific plate. Where it meets other plates, geologic activity is occurring.

Ask: What evidence is there for where Earth's plates meet? The areas where the plates meet have more geologic activity than other areas.

 CCC **Patterns**

Ask: Why is the area around the Pacific Ocean known as the Ring of Fire? There are many volcanoes there.

 Engineer It!
Measuring Earthquakes

 SEP **Constructing Explanations and Designing Solutions**

Earthquakes occur on a daily basis.

Ask: How might detecting earthquakes help us in the future? Possible answer: If we know where they occur most often, someday we may be able to predict them.

▶ **Explore Online** Have students go online to watch the video of how canyons form.

Lesson 1 How Do Rock Layers Change? **473**

LESSON 1 Engage • **Explore/Explain** • Elaborate • Evaluate

EXPLORATION 3 *Not What It Used to Be, continued*

 **Patterns**

Ask: How do rivers, earthquakes, and pressures inside Earth act differently to change Earth's surface? Possible answer: Rivers change Earth's surface slowly, while earthquakes and pressures inside Earth can act quickly.

Differentiate Instruction

ELL: Use Realia Find a video online of someone heating steel. Explain that heating steel makes it bendable. If someone tried to mold cold, hard steel into something useful, the steel would break. However, by heating the steel first, it becomes pliant and bendable. Then it can be molded, or shaped, into something useful.

Ask: How is rock like steel? Rock is like steel in that when cold, it is hard and unbendable, but when heated, it is bendable.

RTI/Extra Support Direct students to look at the arrows in the image.

Ask: What do the arrows show? The arrows show forces pushing toward each other.

Collaboration

Draw, Pair, Share Invite students to draw an example of how geologic processes change Earth. They can draw the results of a river over a long period or an earthquake in a short period. When they have completed their drawings, have them add arrows to show the direction in which forces work to make the changes. Then separate the students into pairs, and have each pair trade their drawings and discuss.

What Else Can Change Rock Layers?

You've learned that rivers can slowly carve rock layers into deep canyons. You've also learned that earthquakes can cause rocks to quickly break. What other things can change the landscape? The layers of rocks in the drawing are under a lot of pressure from each side. Pressure and high temperatures deep below Earth's surface can cause rocks to slowly bend and change.

Temperature and pressure can change rocks.

24. Describe in your own words what is happening to the rock above.

Possible answer: Pressure coming from both sides of the rock layers is causing the layers to bend.

25. Choose the words or phrases to correctly complete each sentence.

bend	break	river
earthquake	slowly	quickly

The Grand Canyon formed as a(n) __river__ eroded rock layers. The changes happened __slowly__. Earthquakes change the land also. They can cause rocks to __break__.

High temperatures and pressures deep within Earth often cause rocks to __bend__.

474

474 Unit 7 Rocks and Fossils

Changing Landscapes

What are some other ways that processes and forces can change the landscape? Look at the images and read the captions to find out.

Rock layers can be changed by wind, water, and gravity. Natural bridges, such as this one, form when wind and water break rock into smaller pieces. Gravity causes the loose materials to fall to the ground. Eventually, an arch is carved into the rocks.

Glaciers are very large masses of ice and snow. Rocks frozen into the sides and bottoms of glaciers can carve deep grooves into the land as the ice slides over it. As a glacier slowly flows across the ground, rock layers can be weathered and eroded to form a canyon.

26. Explain two ways in which a glacier can change rock layers.

Rocks frozen in a glacier can scratch deep grooves into the rocks over which the glacier is moving. A glacier can also carve a canyon into the landscape as it freezes and thaws.

EVIDENCE NOTEBOOK Consider what you've learned about how landscapes change over time. Write your thoughts in your notebook.

475

Explore Online Have students go online to learn more about the processes that affect rock.

CCC Patterns

Weathering is a natural process in which wind and water break small pieces of rock off larger pieces of rock. Gravity causes the smaller pieces to fall to the ground, where erosion (also caused by wind or water) carries them elsewhere.

Ask: How can wind and water change Earth's surface? **They can break smaller pieces of rock off larger pieces and carry them away, causing a hole to form.**

SEP Constructing Explanations and Designing Solutions

Glaciers are giant mountains of frozen ice that flow like rivers across cold, snowy landscapes. They form at the North and South Poles and in surrounding areas.

Ask: How can glaciers alter Earth's surface? **As glaciers slide along, they can scrape away rocky surfaces and carve out the ground.**

Misconception Alert Students may believe that glaciers don't move. That's because we cannot see their movement with the naked eye. However, scientists who study glaciers use the latest equipment to measure their speed, and they say that glaciers can move anywhere from a few miles a year to over 7 miles a year.

Lesson 1 How Do Rock Layers Change? 475

LESSON 1   Engage • **Explore/Explain** • Elaborate • Evaluate

EXPLORATION 3 Not What It Used to Be, continued

 Patterns

Ask: How do earthquakes show patterns? When earthquakes occur, no matter where they occur, they have similar results, such as rocks breaking or shifting.

Ask: How do glaciers show patterns? Glaciers leave behind traces, such as torn-up tracks in the dirt or grooves in rock.

Ask: How does weathering show patterns? When rock is weathered, holes are often left behind.

Ask: How do rivers show patterns over time? Everywhere deep canyons have formed, there are rivers or evidence of past rivers running through them.

 ESS1.C The History of Planet Earth

Ask: How do most of the photos on this page reveal Earth's history? They reveal layers of rock that have built up over many millions of years. Each layer represents a different period in Earth's history and contains clues about what Earth was like during that time.

FORMATIVE ASSESSMENT

Language SmArts
Citing Evidence

W.4.9 Draw evidence from literary or informational texts to support analysis, reflection, and research.

Students should be reminded that when they write reports or answer science-related questions, they need to cite evidence to back up their claims. One way to do this is to quote an authority, book, or article on the subject. They should be careful to state exactly where they got their evidence.

Ask: Why is it important to cite evidence when making a claim? Citing evidence helps back up what is being claimed. It gives opponents an opportunity to research the same information to see whether it is true or false.

Patterns as Evidence

27. Many rocks form horizontal layers. But these layers can change over time. Use what you've learned to match each image to what changed the rocks.

28. Choose the word or phrase that best completes each sentence.

Changes to ____rock layers____ can be slow or fast.

____Rivers____ can slowly carve canyons into the land.

____Glaciers____ can carve deep grooves into rocks.

Rocks deep within Earth can be bent by ____pressure and temperature____.

____Earthquakes____ can cause rocks to break.

rock layers	rivers
earthquakes	glaciers
pressure and temperature	

Language SmArts
Citing Evidence

29. Many times, you can't see the processes that change rock layers. So what evidence do you have that a landscape has been changed?

Possible answer: Rock layers that are not flat provide evidence of earthquakes or changes caused by temperature and pressure. Canyons and natural bridges are evidence of slow changes due to weathering and erosion. Glacial grooves are evidence of bodies of ice once having moved over the land.

Tip
The English Language Arts Handbook can provide help with understanding how to cite evidence.

476 Unit 7 Rocks and Fossils

TAKE IT FURTHER Discover More

TAKE IT FURTHER
Discover More

Check out this path . . . or go online to choose one of these other paths.

- People in Science & Engineering
- Rock Diversity
- Why It's Grand

Bernard Hubbard

Bernard Hubbard was a geologist and explorer who led expeditions in Alaska from the late 1920s to the early 1960s. Not only did he explore glaciers and volcanoes as a scientist, he led expeditions for other people so they could see the geologic wonders in Alaska's remote wilderness, too.

Hubbard explored lakes in volcanic craters and other features that are very difficult to reach. He documented many geological features in Alaska with photographs.

Bernard Hubbard was a good writer and a skilled filmmaker in his time. He gave frequent public lectures, and he was an early producer of science and nature media programs before such programs were common. His photographs provide a record of the landscape around glaciers that today's scientists can look at to see how the glaciers have changed.

30. Imagine you are going to interview Bernard Hubbard. What questions would you ask? What answers would you expect him to give? Create a mock interview on the lines below. Write your questions and Mr. Hubbard's possible responses.

Possible questions: How many times did you explore glaciers? What did you find on your expeditions? Why did you become interested in exploring? How did you prepare for an expedition? Mock answers will vary based on the questions asked.

477

Collaboration

You may choose to assign this activity or to direct students online to the eSE where they can explore and choose from all three paths. These activities can be assigned individually, to pairs, or to small groups.

People in Science & Engineering: Bernard Hubbard

Students learn about Bernard Hubbard, who used his skills as an explorer, photographer, and filmmaker to study volcanoes, lakes, and glaciers in areas that were, and sometimes still are, difficult to get to. Encourage students to go online to learn more about Hubbard, his work, and how his work has influenced and taught other people.

ESS1.C The History of Planet Earth

W.4.9 Draw evidence from literary or informational texts to support analysis, reflection, and research.

DCI ESS1.C The History of Planet Earth

Hubbard's work has helped reveal the history of planet Earth by making others aware of how its natural processes occur. By comparing the photos he took of glaciers in the 1920s and 1930s to those same glaciers today, scientists can tell how they have changed. By examining the photos and film he shot of a volcano before and after it erupted, scientists were able to tell how long it took life to recover from such an eruption.

Ask: How have Hubbard's photos helped scientists studying Earth's processes? Possible answers: They provided evidence for what glaciers were like in the past, which scientists can compare to more recent evidence. They revealed how life recovered after a volcanic eruption.

Lesson 1 How Do Rock Layers Change? 477

LESSON 1 Engage • Explore/Explain • **Elaborate** • Evaluate

TAKE IT FURTHER, continued

Content Background

Moraines provide evidence for where glaciers have been. Scientists know that during the last glacial maximum (or period during the last Ice Age when ice sheets covered the largest area), glaciers reached as far south as Ohio, covering about two-thirds of the state. When the glaciers receded, they left behind moraines as evidence that they had been there. Moraines also appear in other states and have helped scientists know how far the ice sheets stretched.

SEP Constructing Explanations and Designing Solutions

When plows clear the streets, they push snow forward into a large mound. However, on each side of the plow, there is often a smaller ridge of snow that forms.

Ask: When a snow plow piles up snow, which are the lateral moraines? *The lateral moraines left by a snow plow are the two ridges on each side of where the plow has been.*

Ask: Which is the terminal moraine? *The terminal moraine is the large mound of snow that is piled in front of the plow.*

▶ Explore Online

Students can explore these additional topics online.

Rock Diversity
Students learn why rock layers are often made up of different colors and how these colors reflect their rich history. *(Outside research is required.)*

Why It's Grand
Students learn the measurements of the Grand Canyon and make calculations based on them. *(No outside research is required.)*

Moraines

A moraine is a landform or feature of sand, gravel, and rock that has been deposited by a glacier. Moraines can have features called kettles, which are dips that form when a large chunk of ice inside the debris pile melts and the surface of the moraine collapses into the hole.

As glaciers move, they weather rock. Some weathered pieces of rock become stuck in the ice. The rock is deposited as the glaciers move and melt.

Glaciers form moraines in these ways. The ridges that form to the sides of the glacier's path are called *lateral moraines*. A pile of debris that forms at the advancing end of a glacier is called a *terminal moraine*.

31. Diagram a glacier producing two lateral moraines and a terminal moraine in a wide valley.

Label the parts of your diagram. Write captions that tell which of the moraines is the oldest formation and why.

> *Student diagrams will vary but should show an understanding of moraines, how they look, and how they form.*

LESSON 1 Engage • Explore/Explain • Elaborate • **Evaluate**

LESSON CHECK

 **Explore Online**   Students can revisit the lesson phenomenon online.

LESSON 1
Lesson Check   Name _____

Can You Explain It?

1. Remember the Niobrara Chalk formation from the beginning of the lesson? Where do you think its rock layers came from? Which layer is the oldest? Explain your thinking below. Be sure to do the following:
   - Describe how the rocks might have formed.
   - Explain what you can conclude about their relative age.
   - Identify the oldest and youngest layers.

 EVIDENCE NOTEBOOK Use the information you've collected in your Evidence Notebook to help you cover each point above.

Possible answer:
- The layers of the Niobrara Chalk formation were formed over many millions of years. Each layer formed on top of the previous layer.
- The layer at the bottom formed first and is the oldest. The layer at the top formed last and is the youngest.

Checkpoints

2. Which of the following are examples of slow changes to rock layers?
   - **a. A river cuts a canyon into rock.**
   - **b. Rocks are broken by an earthquate.**
   - c. Glaciers carve a valley into the rock.
   - **d. Pressure from above presses sediment into rock.**

479

 Formal Assessment Go online for student self-checks and other assessments.

Can You Explain It?

> **Collaboration**
>
> **Discussion** You may wish to revisit the images as a group activity to assess students' understanding of the material. Use the bulleted points in the student edition to lead the discussion.

EVIDENCE NOTEBOOK

Have students reread their answers to the Evidence Notebook prompts and then use this evidence to justify their reasoning as they respond to the Can You Explain It question. Make sure students understand that a complete response must address all bulleted points.

DCI ESS1.C The History of Planet Earth

Have students reread the caption in the Engage at the beginning of the lesson. If students continue to struggle, have them create mock layers by labeling three sheets of paper and placing one on top of another.

Ask: Which sheet of paper was laid down first? This will represent the oldest rock layer.

Ask: Which sheet of paper was laid down next? This will represent the middle rock layer.

Ask: Which sheet of paper was laid down last? This will represent the youngest rock layer.

SUMMATIVE ASSESSMENT

2. If students have difficulty answering the question, prod them in the right direction by pointing out that fast changes tend to be related to outbursts of energy. Ask them what kind of geologic processes can result in a sudden outburst of energy.

Lesson 1 How Do Rock Layers Change?   **479**

LESSON 1   Engage • Explore/Explain • Elaborate • **Evaluate**

LESSON CHECK, continued

3. If you did not use the activity involving the three sheets of paper that appears on the previous page, you may wish to use it here. Or you may choose to model a similar exercise using something other than sheets of paper to model rock layers. Books would make a good alternative. If so, use three books with different publication dates, placing the one with the oldest date on bottom and the one with the most recent date on top.

4. Ask students which date for the newspaper would be on the bottom and which on top. The order of these dates will match the order in which the rock layers in the hillside were laid down.

5. Explain that not all processes act in the same way; some change Earth's surface slowly, while others change it very quickly. Slow changes tend to come from weathering and erosion. Faster changes tend to occur as a result of natural disasters or outbursts of energy. Ask students how weathering and erosion affects rock. Then ask them to name some natural disasters that can affect rock, and how those disasters make changes to the rock.

6. Help students understand that they can fill in the first blank by reflecting on what they saw in the various images of the Grand Canyon, including the one shown here. They can complete the next sentence by comparing the photos of the Grand Canyon to photos of other exposed rocky areas they have looked at. And finally, they can complete the last sentence by looking at what has happened to the rocks in the past.

---

3. In undisturbed rock layers, the youngest layer is always _____.
   a. on top   c. the thinnest
   b. on the bottom d. the thickest

   (a. on top is circled)

4. Your family is riding in a car. You see some rock layers in a hillside. Your little sister asks how the rocks got there. How can you best explain it to her? Circle the best answer.
   a. Tell her how earthquakes are measured.
   b. Remind her how your family puts newspapers into a recycling bin every day.
   c. Tell her about the Grand Canyon.
   d. Remind her how sand at the playground can be shaped into layers.

   (b. is circled)

5. Use the words in the bank to complete the sentences.

   | earthquakes | fossils | glaciers | rivers |

   Rivers and _glaciers_ can change rocks slowly while _earthquakes_ can change rock layers quickly.

6. Use the words in the bank to complete the sentences.

   | are layered | similar | different |
   | were bent by earthquakes | change | stay the same |

   Rocks in the Grand Canyon _are layered_. Rock layers around the world exhibit _similar_ patterns. All of the rocks in the canyon will _change_ over time.

480

Unit 7 Rocks and Fossils

LESSON 1

Lesson Roundup

A. Which of these is true of rock layers? Circle all that apply.
   a. They are always flat.
   (b.) They can be different ages.
   c. They can only change during earthquakes.
   (d.) They can change slowly or quickly.
   (e.) They can bend or break.
   f. They all contain the same type of rock.

B. On each line, write the word or phrase that best completes each sentence.

> at the top   Colorado River   slowly   near the bottom

The Grand Canyon is a landform in the southwestern United States. It formed as the __Colorado River__ flowed over rock layers. The oldest rocks in the canyon are __near the bottom__. The youngest rocks are __at the top__. The canyon formed very __slowly__.

C. Explain how pressure, temperature, wind, water, and gravity can change rocks.
Possible answer: Pressure and temperature can cause rocks deep within Earth to bend. Wind and water can break rocks into smaller pieces that can be moved by gravity.

Lesson Roundup

DCI ESS1.C The History of Planet Earth

This lesson summary enables students to quickly revisit key points and prepare for tests.

A. Allow students to revisit all three Explorations, doing a quick scan for information relating to the question. You may have students use the process of elimination to remove incorrect options. Instruct students to write the answer options on a separate sheet of paper and then examine each one. Have them recall the various images they saw of the rock layers, and ask how they were laid down. What processes have since resulted in changes to the layers, and did these happen quickly or slowly? How did they cause changes? **ESS1.C**

B. You may direct students to reread Exploration 3. If they continue to struggle to answer the question, engage in a short discussion about how changes in rock can occur, from slow changes wrought by weathering and erosion to fast changes wrought by natural disasters or outbursts of energy. Remind students of their various experiments with rock layers to determine which are the oldest and which are the youngest, depending on which were laid down first and which were laid down last. **ESS1.C**

C. Allow students to skim Exploration 3. Note that some changes happen over long periods of time while others happen relatively quickly. Also point out that water can change rocks in two different ways (one slowly, one quickly): as liquid and as ice. Pressure and temperature are related; as pressure builds, heat is generated. And finally, gravity is related to weathering and erosion. **ESS1.C**

LESSON 2
What Do Fossils Tell Us About Ancient Environments?

Building to the Performance Expectation

The learning experiences in this lesson prepare students for mastery of:

4-ESS1-1 Identify evidence from patterns in rock formations and fossils in rock layers to support an explanation for changes in a landscape over time.

Trace Tool to the NGSS
Go online to view the complete coverage of these standards across this lesson, unit, and time.

 **Science & Engineering Practices**

 Disciplinary Core Ideas

 **Crosscutting Concepts**

Constructing Explanations and Designing Solutions
Constructing explanations and designing solutions in 3–5 builds on K–2 experiences and progresses to the use of evidence in constructing explanations that specify variables that describe and predict phenomena and in designing multiple solutions to design problems.
- Identify the evidence that supports particular points in an explanation.

ESS1.C The History of Planet Earth
Local, regional, and global patterns of rock formation reveal changes over time due to earth forces, such as earthquakes. The presence and location of certain fossil types indicate the order in which rock layers were formed. (4-ESS1-1)

Patterns
Patterns can be used as evidence to support an explanation. (4-ESS1-1)

 CONNECTIONS TO MATH

MP.2 Reason abstractly and quantitatively. (4-ESS1-1)

MP.4 Model with mathematics. (4-ESS1-1)

MP.5 Use appropriate tools strategically. (4-ESS1-1)

4.MD.A.1 Know relative sizes of measurement units within one system of units including km, m, cm; kg, g; lb, oz.; l, ml; hr, min, sec. Within a single system of measurement, express measurements in a larger unit in terms of a smaller unit. Record measurement equivalents in a two-column table. (4-ESS1-1)

 CONNECTIONS TO ENGLISH LANGUAGE ARTS

W.4.7 Conduct short research projects that build knowledge through the investigation of different aspects of a topic. (4-ESS1-1)

W.4.8 Recall relevant information from experiences or gather relevant information from print and digital sources; take notes and categorize information, and provide a list of sources. (4-ESS1-1)

W.4.9 Draw evidence from literary or informational texts to support analysis, reflection, and research. (4-ESS1-1)

Supporting All Students, All Standards

Integrating the Three Dimensions of Learning

Examine fossils representing life from different periods in Earth's history **(DCI ESS1.C)**, determine the habitats in which those fossils lived, and draw conclusions about what modern-day organisms the fossils may be related to **(SEP (Constructing Explanations and Designing Solutions)**. By looking closely at the structures of fossils and living organisms, students see repeated forms and traits that helped these organisms survive in specific environments **(CCC Patterns)**. By comparing and contrasting fossils and living organisms, students are able to not only tell about the past environments in which the fossils lived, but also how those environments are similar to or different from the modern-day environments where the fossils were found.

 **Professional Development** Go online to view **Professional Development videos** with strategies to integrate CCCs and SEPs, including the ones used in this lesson.

Extra Hands-On Activity: Dino Pets

How Did It Change?

👥 Pairs
⏱ 30 minutes

Have students plan and conduct online research on how a modern animal has changed. They should identify an animal to research and then work backwards to identify how the species has changed over time. Alternately, students may choose a dinosaur and follow the evolutionary evidence to show how the dinosaur changed over millions of years. You may wish to model a research chain for students, such as identifying the ancestor for chickens, which is the Tyrannosaurus rex, which also shares unique genes with frogs and newts. As students research, ask them how the changes they see reflect the environment in which the ancestor animals lived.

 This activity can support mastery of this Cross-Cutting Concept: Patterns

Preassessment

Have students complete the unit pre-test online or see the Assessment Guide.

Build on Prior Knowledge

Students should already know and be prepared to build on the following concepts:
- Earth has many processes that affect the features of its surface, resulting in different environments and climates.
- Rock layers form in different ways, and these layers can be 'read' to determine their age and the order in which they were laid down.

Differentiate Instruction

Lesson Vocabulary
- fossil
- extinct
- aquatic fossil
- terrestrial fossil

Explain that the word **fossil** comes from a Latin word that means "dug up" or "taken from the ground."

Ask: Why do you think the word fossil comes from a word meaning "dug up" or "taken from the ground"?
Possible answers: Fossils are taken from the rocky Earth.

RTI/Extra Support
Point out that fossils are the remains of life that lived on Earth in the prehistoric past. Show students photos of the following items: the roots of a plant pulled out of the ground; a rock that has been dug out of the ground; an actual fossil such as a brachiopod or trilobite.

Ask: Which of the following are fossils?
the brachiopod or trilobite

Explain that fossils are the remains of things that lived so long ago they have turned to rock, but they still resemble the plant or animal they once were.

Lesson 2 What Do Fossils Tell Us About Ancient Environments? **482B**

LESSON 2 Engage • Explore/Explain • Elaborate • Evaluate

ENGAGE: Lesson Phenomenon

Lesson Objective
Examine fossil evidence to determine how and in what environments organisms of the past lived, based on their physical traits and similarities to living organisms.

About This Image
Everything we know about dinosaurs comes from their fossils. The fossil shown here is from a *Coelophysis*, a meat-eating dinosaur that was bipedal (walked on two legs). When the dinosaur died, its body was likely covered by water and sediment in a flash flood before it could be broken down by decomposers and its bones separated. Over millions of years, more water and sediment covered the dinosaur. The upper layers pushed down on the lower layers, pressing them into rock. Minerals seeped through the rock layers, replacing the original organic material from the dinosaur's body. Eventually, only a cast of the original dinosaur was left, and today that cast is this fossil.

SEP Constructing Explanations and Designing Solutions

Alternative Engage Strategy

Fossils or Not Fossils	👥 Small groups or whole class ⏱ 10 min

Distribute images of various organisms to students. Be sure to mix images of fossils with images of living organisms and skeletons. Remind students of the definition of *fossil*: the remains of ancient life that have been preserved over time. Have them draw two columns on a sheet of paper. The first column should be titled *Fossils*. The second column should be titled *Not Fossils*. Then ask them to identify which images are fossils and which are not by describing them in the correct column on the sheet.

LESSON 2

What Do Fossils Tell Us About Ancient Environments?

Fossils are the remains of ancient life that have been preserved over time. They can tell us much about how plants and animals of the past lived and died. They can also tell us about the environments in which those plants and animals lived.

By the end of this lesson . . .
you'll be able to make inferences about ancient environments and organisms from fossil evidence.

Can You Explain It?

This is Petrified Forest National Park. Imagine what it feels like to walk through the area. You can almost feel the heat and dryness of the desert just by looking at the photos.

1. Think about the type of environment this used to be. Was it like the present-day environment of the Petrified Forest? What can you infer about this area millions of years ago from the presence of fossil trees?

   Students should respond based on the preliminary observations they can make of the images. All reasonable answers are acceptable.

Tip

Learn more about rock layers in How Do Rock Layers Change?

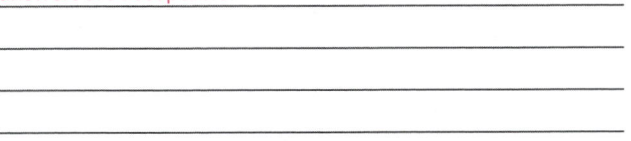

EVIDENCE NOTEBOOK Look for this icon to help you gather evidence to answer the questions above.

 **Explore Online** Students can view the lesson phenomenon online.

Can You Explain It?

Students are asked to examine the image, describe the present-day environment, and then infer what the environment was like when the fossil organism shown was alive. Some students will correctly ascertain that the present-day environment is a desert and is very dry, with few trees and little water. They should identify the fossil shown as a tree. From this, they may correctly infer that the environment in this place long ago was wetter and contained trees. It was possibly a forest. Urge students not to worry about whether their answers are correct. They should expect their ideas to change as they progress through the lesson. They will have an opportunity to revise their answers when they revisit these questions at the end of the lesson.

Collaboration

Think, Pair, Share Separate students into pairs, and have them examine the image. To help them understand what they're seeing, ask them to consider what they learned in the previous lesson about rock layers and how they form. Ask them to think about how the trees in Petrified Forest National Park became fossils. Direct them to discuss possible answers with each other, and then select one student to share each pair's ideas with the class as a whole. Remind them that at this stage, it's okay if they don't understand the process of fossilization, but as the lesson progresses, they will learn more.

 EVIDENCE NOTEBOOK

Encourage students to use an appropriate graphic organizer, such as main idea and details, to set up their notebook for this lesson.

Find more strategies in the online ELA handbook.

LESSON 2   Engage • **Explore/Explain** • Elaborate • Evaluate

EXPLORATION 1 Clues from the Past

3D Learning Objective

Develop an understanding of what fossils tell us about life in the distant past. **Construct explanations** for how animals lived to arrive at a greater understanding of the **history of planet Earth**, carefully examining **patterns** in the traits of extinct and living organisms. By looking at the body of an extinct reptile, determine how its features, or traits, affected its movement and indicate the kind of environment in which it lived.

SEP Construction Explanations and Designing Solutions

The image shows the fossil of a plesiosaur, or marine reptile. The first plesiosaur fossil was discovered by a young woman named Mary Anning in Lyme Regis, England, in 1821. At the time, very little was known about prehistoric life.

Ask: How might the discovery of a plesiosaur fossil in 1821 have helped our understanding of the past? **Possible answer: It helped us understand that there were once animals alive that aren't alive today.**

Differentiate Instruction

ELL: Drawing Some students may struggle with the word *infer*. Ask them to look at the image and then draw the animal as if it were alive, in the environment students believe it might have lived. If students are uncertain about where the animal lived, have them look closely at its limbs, which are paddle-like. Ask them to identify other animals that have paddle-like structures instead of hands and feet, and ask them to describe where these animals mostly live. Then have them draw that environment.

EXPLORATION 1
Clues from the Past

Check It Out!

Earth is billions of years old. Many types of plants and animals have lived on Earth during that time. But many of them, like the dinosaurs, died out long ago.

Even though dinosaurs aren't around now, we know they were once here. How? We can look at fossils. A **fossil** is the remains or traces of an organism that lived long ago.

Take a look at the fossil below. It is the fossil of a reptile that lived at the same time as the dinosaurs but is now extinct. **Extinct** organisms are no longer found on Earth. Think about the types of things you can learn by looking at the fossil.

Plesiosaur fossil

2. In the space below, record two observations about the fossil. What can you infer about the fossil from your observations?

Possible answer: This is the fossil of an animal that had long, sharp teeth for eating meat or fish. It also had flat, paddle-like limbs. I can infer that this animal lived in the water.

484

Unit 7 Rocks and Fossils

3. Circle all the statements about the fossil that are true. Go back and observe the fossil again if you cannot recall what you saw.
   a. This is a fossil of an animal.
   b. This organism had a long neck.
   c. This organism had a large, round head.
   d. The fossil bones show legs that look like flippers.
   e. This creature had no tail.

 EVIDENCE NOTEBOOK Take a look at the plesiosaur fossil. In your Evidence Notebook, write down all of the features that you can identify from the fossil. Infer what these features might have been used for.

 Language SmArts
Compare and Contrast

4. Think about the body shape of the plesiosaur. Compare it to something else that looks similar. It could be a vehicle or other object, or it could be a living thing. In the box below, draw the object you are comparing to the fossil. Circle similar structures in your drawing and the fossil on the previous page. Explain your comparison in the table that follows.

Tip
The English Language Arts Handbook can provide help with understanding how to compare and contrast.

Possible answer: Students may say the plesiosaur fossil is similar to a sea turtle and draw a sea turtle.

Fossil	Sample answer: Turtle
Possible answer: Both have round bodies. Both also have tails and four limbs.	Possible answer: The plesiosaur has a much longer neck and a longer tail than a turtle has.

485

 Explore Online Have students explore fossils online.

 Patterns

Remind students that living organisms have features, or traits, that help them to survive. These traits are adapted to where the organisms live. By comparing the traits of organisms that live in similar habitats, we can see patterns that we can apply to fossils. For example, we know that dolphins have flippers or paddle-like structures rather than hands and feet. These adaptations help the dolphins move in water.

Ask: Based on what we know about dolphins' paddle-like structures, what can we conclude about plesiosaurs? **They lived in water.**

 EVIDENCE NOTEBOOK

Students may observe that the fossil has a long neck, a long tail, a squat body, four paddles-like structures rather than hands and feet, a long head, and sharp teeth.

FORMATIVE ASSESSMENT
 Language SmArts
Compare and Contrast
W.4.8 Recall relevant information; take notes and categorize information

Explain to students that one way we develop a better understanding of an organism is by comparing it to other things that are similar. One of the best ways to compare and contrast is to write down the information we recall. How are the two things alike? How are they different? We can then list similarities together and differences together.

Ask: Why is it important to compare the body shape of a plesiosaur to other living things? **Possible answer: By comparing the plesiosaur to living things with a similar shape, we can better understand the environment in which it lived.**

Lesson 2 What Do Fossils Tell Us About Ancient Environments? **485**

LESSON 2   Engage • **Explore/Explain** • Elaborate • Evaluate

EXPLORATION 1   Clues from the Past, continued

HANDS-ON ACTIVITY   Small groups   1 class period
Old and New

3D Learning Objective
SEP Constructing Explanations and Designing Solutions

Students examine fossils from a fossil kit to determine the kind of organism that each belonged to, how it lived, and in what environment it could be found.

Materials
Because students may be unfamiliar with many or all of the fossils, have books or the Internet ready for students to use in their research. The magnifying glass will help students examine them.

Preparation
Find a place in the room for each fossil kit and chart. Separate students into groups, with each group being provided a fossil kit. Have a fossil identification book or other, similar resources ready; or have a computer available with a fossil identification webpage up. These are to be used only as a last resort for students who are struggling with identifying the fossils from the kit.

DCI ESS1.C The History of Planet Earth

Ask: Why is it important to examine fossils from different places and ages? They can tell us about the history of life on planet Earth, from the earliest life to the most recent.

Procedure
STEP 1–3 Circulate among groups, making sure that each student gets an opportunity to examine and discuss each fossil. Be available to answer any questions they may have, and gently steer them in the right direction if they are struggling to identify the fossils.

HANDS-ON ACTIVITY
Old and New

Objective
Collaborate with others in your group to identify the structures and features of fossils. You can then determine how and where the fossil lived.

Materials
- fossil kit
- magnifying glass
- classification chart

What question will you investigate to meet this objective?

Possible question: What evidence from a fossil tells us about the organism that left it and the environment it lived in?

STEP 1 With your group, place all the fossils from your fossil kit on a table in front of you. What do all the fossils have in common?

They are all hard, nonliving, and show us what an organism from the past looked like.

STEP 2 Observe each fossil one by one with the magnifying glass. Use your senses of sight and touch to determine the characteristics of each one. Why is using your sense of touch important?

The sense of touch can makes it easier to sense the shapes of the fossils.

STEP 3 Record your observations and conclusions about each fossil in the table at the top of the next page. Share your results with the class.

486

 Student Lab Worksheet and complete Teacher Support available online.

486   Unit 7   Rocks and Fossils

Fossil	What evidence tells us how this organism lived?	Did the organism live on land or in water?	What are some similar living things today?
Ammonite	has a shell	water	snail or nautilus
Bird	has wings and two legs	land	bird
Trilobite	has a shell and legs	water	horseshoe crab or pill bug
Fish	has fins and a tail	water	fish
Crinoid	has many tentacles or arms	water	crinoid or feather stars
Coral	has a hard covering with no limbs	water	coral

Analyze Your Results

STEP 4 What evidence did you use to determine whether an organism lived on land or in water?
Possible answer: The parts of the organisms indicated whether they lived on land or water.

STEP 5 Based on the data you collected, how many organisms lived on land and how many lived in water?
5 lived in water and 1 lived on land.

Draw Conclusions

STEP 6 Make a claim about the relationship between fossil animals and animals living today. Cite evidence to support your claim
Possible claim. Some fossils are related to animals living today. Most of the fossils look like similar organisms that are alive today.

STEP 7 What is one question you have about fossils?
Possible question: Why have many animals that are fossils gone extinct?

487

Analyze Your Results

 Patterns

Ask: What patterns do you seen in the chart? The organisms lived in water. Several had hard shells. They have some traits similar to organisms living in similar environments today.

Draw Conclusions

STEP 6–7 As students finish their task, be available to answer any questions they may have and to guide them to understanding that animal traits can tell us how animals lived, whether they lived long ago or are living today. As students write down any questions they may have, engage in a discussion about those questions, guiding students toward the correct answers.

Claims, Evidence, and Reasoning

Have students work with a partner to critique each other's claims and evidence in Step 6. Ask each pair to be prepared to share one way that they changed or improved their claim or the evidence used. Discuss responses as a class.

Ask: What is the most reliable evidence that animals living today can help us understand how animals lived in the past? Students may cite information that they researched or observations made during the activity. Accept any reasonable answer.

Scoring Rubric for Hands-On Activity	
3	correctly identifies all fossil organisms, their environment, and living organisms they are similar to
2	correctly identifies some fossil organisms, some environments, and some of the living organisms they are similar to
1	correctly identifies few to none of the fossil organisms, environments, and living organisms they are similar to

Lesson 2 What Do Fossils Tell Us About Ancient Environments? 487

LESSON 2   Engage • **Explore/Explain** • Elaborate • Evaluate

EXPLORATION 2 Then and Now

3D Learning Objective

By comparing anatomical traits, or physical structures, in organisms, learn how organisms of the past lived. Throughout the **history of planet Earth**, organisms have developed many of the same adaptations to specific environments. Compare these **patterns** in living organisms to patterns in fossil organisms to **construct explanations** about how the fossil organisms survived.

SEP Constructing Explanations and Designing Solutions

The images in this spread show the fossil organism followed by an artist's rendition of how it would have looked in life.

Ask: How do artists know what an organism looked like from its fossils? **Possible answer: Artists can look at organisms with similar structures today, compare them to the fossils, and determine what the fossils may have looked like from that.**

CCC Patterns

Direct students to examine the organisms in the images in the spread. All of them contain features that organisms living today have.

Ask: What are some of the features that these organisms share with similar living organisms? **Possible answers: leaves, antlers, eyes, noses, mouths, teeth, fins, legs, fur, skin, scales**

Collaboration

Write, Pair, Share Have students make a list of things the artist could illustrate from the fossils that isn't shown. For example, the fossils don't have skin, eyes, or fur. After students have completed their lists, separate them into pairs to compare and contrast their lists. Then have one member of each pair share his or her findings with the class.

---

488 Unit 7 Rocks and Fossils

EXPLORATION 2
Then and Now

Seeing the Past

We can use the structures of an organism's body to tell where it lived. But how similar to today's organisms are animals that lived millions of years ago?

The pairs of pictures below show fossils and illustrations of what the real organisms may have looked like. Observe each pair closely.

The fossil is of a plant called a fern. Ferns are ancient plants that were around hundreds of millions of years ago. There are many types of ferns today, too, but most of them grow in places that are warm and moist. It is easy to spot the delicate leaves, or fronds, of a fern plant.

The fossil skeleton is of an Irish elk. The Irish elk was the largest of an extinct type of deer that lived in Europe and Asia about 2.5 million years ago. You can see the elk's slender legs and massive antlers—up to 4 meters (13 feet) from tip to tip!

The fossil skeleton is of a mosasaur. The mosasaurs are an extinct group of reptiles. They had long, narrow bodies and long snouts. The mososaurs had short, flattened limbs that looked like paddles.

5. Complete each sentence using the best word or phrase from the bank.

land	underground	in the water	antlers	legs	flippers
the forest	water	the air			

Most plants, such as ferns, live on _____land_____. Deer and their relatives, such as the Irish elk, use their slender _____legs_____ to walk through forests and meadows. The paddle-like limbs of the mosasaur helped it move through _____water_____.

Language SmArts
Comparing Structures

6. Research two methods scientists use to learn about fossils. Write how each method helps scientists understand the environment the fossil came from.

Possible answer: Scientists study the area in which the fossils is found. They also compare the fossil to similar plants or animals alive today.

EVIDENCE NOTEBOOK In your Evidence Notebook, list the parts of the organisms that give clues to the environment where the organisms lived. Then identify the type of environment where organisms with those parts did live.

Content Background

In 1764, men working in a quarry on the Meuse River in Holland found a large skull in the rock. There was little interest in the skull until another, similar skull was found. When Napoleon's forces invaded the area, they took one of the skulls back to France, where the famous anatomist Baron Georges Cuvier determined that it came from an animal that was extinct.. Cuvier was the first scientist to suggest that extinction could happen and that the history of life on Earth was punctuated by mass extinctions.

Build on Prior Knowledge

Mosasaurus is just one genus in a family called *Mosasauridae*, or mosasaurs for short. Other genera include *Tylosaurus* and *Globidens*. Some students may have seen popular movies which feature a *Mosasaurus*. However, in real life, *Mosasaurus* was much smaller than the ones ususally shown in film, which is much closer in size and build to a mosasaur known as *Hainosaurus*.

Language SmArts
Comparing Structures

W.4.7 Conduct short research projects that build knowledge through the investigation of different aspects of a topic.

This activity can reinforce basic research skills. Remind students that good research includes recording sources: the webpage URL and date visited; book, author, and page number; and so on. This way, if the teacher needs to confirm the research, he or she has the tools with which to do it.

EVIDENCE NOTEBOOK

Students should list that the plant's leaves suggest it lived on land, the Irish elk's legs and antlers suggest it lived on land, and the *Mosasaurus*'s flippers suggest it lived in the water.

Lesson 2 What Do Fossils Tell Us About Ancient Environments?

LESSON 2 Engage • **Explore/Explain** • Elaborate • Evaluate

EXPLORATION 2 Then and Now, continued

 **Patterns**

Just because organisms have similar traits and body structures doesn't mean they're related to each other. Sometimes, different organisms can develop similar traits to live in the same or similar environments. For example, different kinds of animals might develop streamlined bodies and flippers.

Ask: Mammals such as manatees, marine reptiles such as mosasaurs, and fish such as the alligator gar have streamlined bodies and flippers or fins. Are they closely related to each other? **No**

Ask: If they aren't closely related, why do they have similar traits and body structures? **They developed these structures to live in the same environment: water.**

Differentiate Instruction

Extension Provide students with images of fossils that have not been discussed in class, and ask them to research organisms living today that have similar traits. Ask students to prepare a short presentation for each image, explaining why the organism may have developed the trait and what environment it lived in.

Collaboration

Write, Pair, Share Have students write their responses to the question, and then separate them into pairs. Ask each pair to trade their responses, discussing which traits helped them determine how the organisms in the images were connected. When they are finished, ask one member of each pair to share his or her pair's findings with the class. Encourage students to engage in a discussion, asking questions and sharing information to learn more.

Cousins?

Sometimes fossils can be the ancestors of modern-day organisms, or they can be similar-looking organisms.

Matching Fossils and Organisms

7. Draw a line from the image of the fossil in the first column to the image of the modern organism it most closely resembles in the second column.

8. What features helped you match them up?
Possible answer: I matched the fern to the fern based on similar structure and appearance. I matched the elk to the moose because they both have large heads and broad antlers. I matched the mosasaur to the fish based on similar skull shape and limbs.

HANDS-ON Apply What You Know
Past Meets Present

9. Look at the image in the amber fossil and describe what you see.

   You have learned that fossils can give clues about the environment in which the organism lived. Apply what you have learned.

   Research two fossils. For each fossil, find a related or similar modern-day organism and determine what type of environment it lives in. Infer whether the organisms that became fossils lived in similar environments.

Putting It Together

10. Read the paragraph. Choose the correct words to complete each sentence. Write the words on the lines.

    | photographs | fossils | skeletons |
    | remains | bones | shapes |
    | animals | related | infer |
    | the same | different | |

    We learn about the organisms of long ago from ___fossils___.

    They are the ___remains___, or traces, of organisms that lived in the past. Many animals alive today have structures that are similar to ___animals___ that lived in the past. The similarities suggest that the organisms are ___related___. When we study today's organisms, we can ___infer___ things about related organisms of the past.

HANDS-ON Appy What You Know
Past Meets Present

For this activity, which is similar to the Extension on the previous page, do not provide names or images of fossils for students to research. Students should come up with the fossils on their own, and they should be different from any that have already been discussed in class. You may want to provide students with research materials such as books from the library or Internet sites that feature fossils to help them find suitable material.

Ask: Which fossils did you choose? Possible answers: Tyrannosaurus rex, Triceratops, woolly mammoth

Ask: What organism living today is similar? Possible answers: The T. rex is similar to some birds. I found small reptiles that had horns on their faces and neck shields similar to Triceratops. The woolly mammoth is similar to modern-day elephants.

Content Background

Amber is a type of resin that comes from trees. When it leaks out, it can trap insects or small animals. Once the amber hardens, the organism inside is preserved. Thanks to amber, we know a great deal about insects of the past and how similar they are to insects of the present. Ants, scorpions, and even dinosaur feathers have been preserved in amber, adding to our knowledge of the past.

Ask: How can amber contribute to our knowledge of the past? It has helped preserve plants and animals of the past so that we can study them today.

FORMATIVE ASSESSMENT
SEP Constructing Explanations and Designing Solutions

Ask: How can living organisms help us understand the past? By studying modern organisms, we can learn what adaptations, or traits, help them survive in their environments.

Lesson 2 What Do Fossils Tell Us About Ancient Environments?

LESSON 2   Engage • **Explore/Explain** • Elaborate • Evaluate

EXPLORATION 3 Ancient Lands

3D Learning Objective

Observe that **patterns** in fossils can reveal much about the **history of planet Earth** through its many past environments. **Construct explanations** about how organisms' traits reflect the environments in which they lived. Understand that just as life has changed over time, so, too, have the planet's environments. What today is a desert may once have been a forest; what today is dry land may once have been a sea; what today is a mountain may have once been flat land.

SEP Constructing Explanations and Designing Solutions

The images in this spread contain fossils that easily reveal what type of environment they lived in.

Ask: If you want to know where a fossil organism lived, what traits should you look for? **Possible answer: traits that reveal how the organism moved or what it ate, as these can reveal what environment it lived in**

Differentiate Instruction

Extension Have students write a brief paragraph for each image, detailing the evidence for why it suggests a certain kind of environment.

DCI History of Planet Earth

The history of life on Earth goes back billions of years, but early forms were single-celled organisms. The available evidence suggests that life began in the oceans and spread to land. Have students look at the fossil images.

Ask: Which are similar to organisms that live in the ocean today, and which are similar to organisms that live on land today? **ocean: ammonites, fish, clams; land: ferns, snails, ants**

492 Unit 7 Rocks and Fossils

EXPLORATION 3

Ancient Lands

Fossils and Environments

We can learn a lot from fossils. Many times fossils can indicate the type of environment where the organism lived. Organisms that lived in water leave behind **aquatic fossils**. **Terrestrial fossils** are left behind by organisms that lived on land. The features of the fossil determine which type it is.

Fossils and Ancient Lands

11. Read the information about each organism and answer whether the fossil is an aquatic fossil or a terrrestrial fossil.  Explore Online

Ammonites were animals that lived in coiled shells. They moved by squirting jets of water from their bodies.

aquatic fossil

Ferns are plants that live in warm, moist environments such as rain forests. This fossil is an imprint of a fern leaf.

terrestrial fossil

Fish use their fins and tails to move. They often move in large groups, called schools.

aquatic fossil

Snails are small animals with coiled shells. They slide slowly along surfaces with one flat foot made of muscle.

aquatic or terrestrial fossil

492

Clams are soft animals that live inside shells. Clams have lived on Earth for millions of years.

aquatic fossil

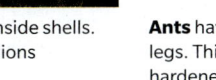

Ants have jointed body segments and six legs. This one was found inside a bubble of hardened amber.

terrestrial fossil

 Do the Math
Clues in Footprints

12. Dinosaurs that left behind three-toed footprints such as those shown in the photo include Tyrannosaurus and Allosaurus. At one time, scientists thought these dinosaurs walked upright with their tails dragging behind them and their heads high in the air. Today, we know that their upper bodies leaned forward and were balanced by their tails, which hovered over the ground. Their height is usually measured at their hips.

Did you know that scientists have a way of measuring a dinosaur's hip height? They do it by measuring the dinosaur's footprints. Hip height is four times the length of the footprint. The formula can be expressed this way: H = 4l

If a dinosaur's footprint is 35 cm in length, how tall would the dinosaur have been at the hip? Show your calculations

1.4m, or 55 inches 35cm x 4 = 1.4m

 EVIDENCE NOTEBOOK In your Evidence Notebook, compare the fossils you just saw to the fossils you observed at the start of the lesson. Which are most like those you observed at the beginning? What clues does this provide to where the fossils at the beginning lived? Record your ideas in your Evidence Notebook.

Content Background

Fossil trackways can tell us much about the animal that made them. Sometimes they tell us how tall an animal was or how much it might have weighed. They can tell us how fast the animal was moving or what its average rate of speed was. They can tell us whether the animal lived in groups or alone and whether it took care of its young.

Ask: Why is it important to study fossil trackways? Trackways can tell us how big or small an animal was, where it lived, how it moved, how much it weighed, whether it lived in groups, and what it ate.

 Do the Math
Clues in Footprints

4.MD.A.1 Know relative sizes of measurement units within one system of units including km, m, cm; kg, g; lb, oz.; l, ml; hr, min, sec. Within a single system of measurement, express measurements in a larger unit in terms of a smaller unit.

Students should understand that once they can solve a problem in meters, they can then convert those meters to feet. Scientists and people in technical fields use meters because they want to solve problems using the same mathematical units of measurement no matter where they are on Earth. This reduces problems and makes it easier for scientists the world over to share information.

EVIDENCE NOTEBOOK

Students should observe that the fern fossil is the most like the tree fossil they saw at the beginning of the lesson. Because ferns and modern trees live on land, they should conclude that the fossil in Petrified Forest also lived on land. But because most trees do not grow in deserts, the land in the park once must have been a forest.

LESSON 2 Engage • **Explore/Explain** • Elaborate • Evaluate

EXPLORATION 3 *Ancient Lands, continued*

 Patterns

In the activity, students are asked to identify the environments in which certain fossils lived by thinking about patterns. If most bipedal, or two-legged, animals walk on land, this is a pattern. If most animals with fins swim in water, this is a pattern. Once we know a pattern, we can make educated guesses about organisms that follow that pattern.

Ask: If you wanted to know where an organism lived, what would you look for? **Possible answer: patterns in its body structures or movements**

Differentiate Instruction

ELL: Use Realia For the Language SmArts activity, pair ELL students with a proficient English-speaking student. Have them work together to use images as a way of guiding the student whose primary language is not English through answering the questions.

FORMATIVE ASSESSMENT

 Language SmArts

W.4.8 Recall relevant information from experiences or gather relevant information from print and digital sources; take notes and categorize information, and provide a list of sources.

Students should draw on what they've learned to understand the connections between traits in organisms and the environments in which they lived.

Ask: Why is it important to learn about Earth's past environments? **Possible answer: By learning about how Earth's environments have changed in the past, we might be able to predict future changes, which could help us survive.**

Identify Your Evidence

Fossils are evidence of past organisms and past environments. On the last page, you identified fossils by their environment. Complete the section below to identify the evidence you used to determine where each fossil belonged.

13. Complete the paragraph by writing the correct words to complete each sentence.

leaves	arms	tentacles	shell	legs	ammonite
fish	dragonfly	clam	fern	walking stick	

The ___leaves___ of the fern fossil are evidence that it was a plant, and most plants live on land. The ___shell___ of the snail helps identify it. Some snails live on land. The shells of the ___ammonite___ and ___clam___ helped identify them as aquatic animals.

Language SmArts
Compare and Contrast

Tip: The English Language Arts Handbook can provide help with understanding how to compare and contrast.

14. Describe how you would determine where an organism lived by analyzing its fossil remains. What features would you look for? Think about the shapes of features and their sizes relative to the rest of the organism. Recall information from your experiences in this lesson as you develop your response.

Possible answer: You would look for different kinds of shells that are common in animals that live in water. Any feature that looks like a paddle or flipper is likely from an aquatic animal. Limbs with distinct toes or other parts used for walking are likely from a land-dwelling animal. To decide whether a flat limb was a wing and not a flipper or fin, the size should be compared to the whole animal. A large, flat limb about the same size as the rest of the animal was most likely a wing. A small, flat limb much smaller than the animal's body was most likely a flipper or fin.

LESSON 2   Engage • Explore/Explain • **Elaborate** • Evaluate

TAKE IT FURTHER Discover More

▶ **Explore Online**   Students can explore all three Take It Further paths online.

TAKE IT FURTHER
Discover More

Check out this path . . . or go online to choose one of these other paths.

- Where Are They?
- Fossil Hangouts
- How Do They Compare

Where Are They?

Take a look at the three fossils. Research each one, and identify four different places where each fossil has been found. Describe the current environment in these locations as well.

Ammonites were squid-like sea animals with coiled shells. They died out 65 million years ago, at the same time as the dinosaurs.

Polyps live inside a limestone skeleton that remains after they die and is called coral. The oldest coral fossils date back 500 million years.

The earliest jawed fishes appeared about 416 million years ago. They lived in many parts of ancient seas.

Collaboration

You may choose to assign this activity or to direct students online to the eSE where they can explore and choose from all three paths. These activities can be assigned individually, to pairs, or to small groups.

Where Are They?

Students research the areas in which the fossils shown in the images are found and describe their current environments. Most fossils are found in dry places where weathering and erosion are wearing away rocky surfaces to reveal the fossils inside them. Provide books from the school's library or a nearby public library, as well as access to the Internet, to help guide students' research.

DCI ESS1.C The History of Planet Earth

Ammonite fossils can be found in such places as Alberta, Canada, in North America and Madagascar off the west coast of Africa. Both have dry, rocky areas that were once covered by sea beds during the Mesozoic, when ammonites flourished. Fossil coral can be found in many parts of the world, including Kansas in the United States and Victoria, Australia. These, too, are often found in dry, rocky areas that were once covered by a sea bed. Fish such as the one shown in the photo are commonly found in the Green River Formation of Wyoming and Colorado. Unlike the other fossils shown here, the fish in Green River once lived in a group of large lakes in the area.

Ask: What pattern can you see in where these fossils are found? *Most of them are found in dry, rocky places that were once covered by water.*

Lesson 2 What Do Fossils Tell Us About Ancient Environments?

LESSON 2   Engage • Explore/Explain • **Elaborate** • Evaluate

TAKE IT FURTHER, continued

Differentiate Instruction

RTI/Extra Support Note that students shouldn't necessarily be required to mark really specific locations on the map (such as Alberta, Canada; Kansas, United States; Madagascar, Africa; or Victoria, Australia). Rather, they can mark the continents where the fossils were discovered.

 Constructing Explanations and Designing Solutions

Some students may believe that fossils only form in large bodies of water. However, fossils can also form on land when covered by sand or volcanic ash. For example, a famous fossil of a *Velociraptor* in battle with a *Protoceratops* was discovered in Mongolia. It is believed that a massive flow of sand, possibly caused by a collapsing sand dune, covered the animals while they were battling. Over many years, sand piled on sand, causing the layers below to become pressed into rock.

Ask: What are other ways ancient remains can become fossils?
They can be covered in sand or volcanic ash.

▶ **Explore Online**

Students can explore these additional topics online.

Fossil Hangouts
Students explore areas that are considered hotspots for fossils, or places where fossils are commonly found. *(No outside research is required.)*

How Do They Compare?
Students compare ichthyosaurs and dolphins, marine-based reptiles and mammals. *(No outside research is required.)*

---

15. On the map below, mark an *X* for the places where ammonite fossils have been found. Use a dot for coral. Mark a triangle for the locations of the jawed fishes.

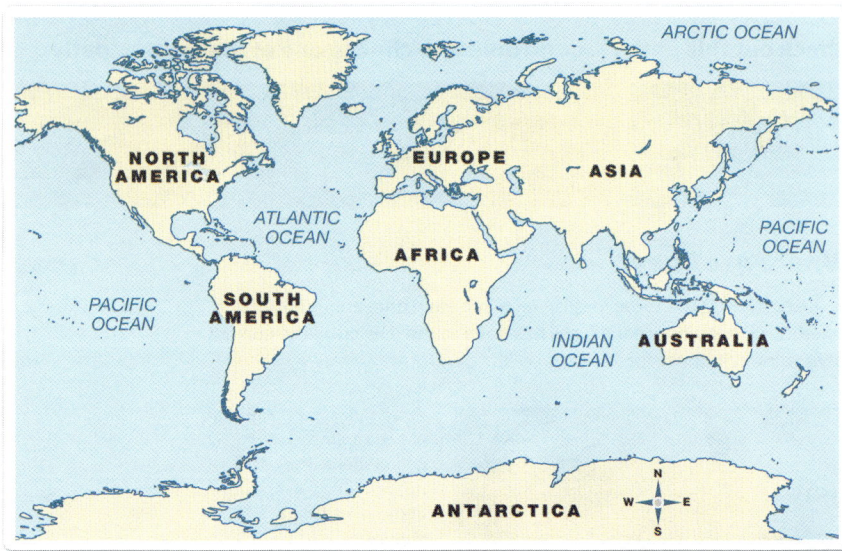

16. The three fossils were found on land. Consider the types of animals whose remains became the fossils. Were the areas where the fossils were found the same types of environments when the animals were alive? Include an explanation for your answer.

The areas were under water when the ammonite, coral, and fish lived there.

Therefore, the environments were different from what they are today. They are now on land.

17. What conclusions can you draw about the fact that aquatic fossils are often found in areas that are far away from today's seas? Circle all that apply.
a. Earth's surface was different long ago.
b. The world did not have land when fossils formed.
c. Some places that are dry land now were once covered by water.
d. Fossils never form on dry land.

496

496   Unit 7 Rocks and Fossils

LESSON 2   Engage • Explore/Explain • Elaborate • **Evaluate**

LESSON CHECK

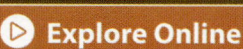 **Explore Online**   Students can revisit the lesson phenomenon online.

LESSON 2
Lesson Check

Name _____

Can You Explain It?

1. Think back to the fossil you saw at the beginning of the lesson. Explain what we can learn from the fossil. Be sure to do the following:
   - Explain how the fossil represents the original organism.
   - Identify similar structures found in organisms today.
   - Describe how the type of fossil and structures show where it lived.

 EVIDENCE NOTEBOOK   Use the information you've collected in your Evidence Notebook to help you cover each point above.

Possible answers:
- The Petrified Forest is in the desert now. That means the tree fossils were found in what is now a desert.
- You might have inferred that there was once an ancient forest the tree lived in, whereas that area is now a desert.
- Environments can change drastically. Fossils can tell us a lot about what the environment in the past was like.

Checkpoints

2. What do some fossils and modern-day organisms have in common? Circle all that apply.
   a. They are the same age.
   b. **They may be related.**
   c. **They may have similar body structures.**
   d. They all come from rock layers.

497

 Formal Assessment   Go online for student self-checks and other assessments.

Can You Explain It?

> ### Collaboration
> **Discussion**   You may wish to revisit the image as a group activity to assess students' understanding of the material. Use the bulleted points in the Student Edition to lead the discussion.

 EVIDENCE NOTEBOOK

Have students reread their answers to the Evidence Notebook prompts and then use this evidence to justify their reasoning as they respond to the Can You Explain It question. Make sure students understand that a complete response must address all bulleted points.

CCC **Patterns**

Ask: What structures show where the fossil in the photo lived?   The fossil was once a tree, which means that it had woody parts. These parts grow in soil. These trees appear to have been thick and tall, which suggests that they grew in a forest.

SUMMATIVE ASSESSMENT

2. While it's true that shared traits can sometimes indicate a close relationship between organisms, this is not always the case. Remind students that many organisms share traits because they are adapted for survival in similar areas. Because of these traits in living organisms, scientists can look at fossil organisms and tell what kind of environment they lived in, the types of food they ate, and so on.

Lesson 2   What Do Fossils Tell Us About Ancient Environments?   **497**

LESSON 2 Engage • Explore/Explain • Elaborate • **Evaluate**

LESSON CHECK, *continued*

3. Point out that evidence for how organisms become extinct comes from the geologic record rather than just from fossils. For example, we know that non-avian dinosaurs went extinct at the end of the Cretaceous Period because their fossils disappear at that time, but we know why because of other evidence, including an impact crater. This evidence helps us understand why non-avian dinosaurs went extinct.

4. Heads and tails can be found in animals that live on land and in the sea; therefore, they are not an indication of environment. On the other hand, legs and paddle-like tell us how an animal moved. If we know how an animal moved, we can usually tell where it most commonly lived.

> ## Differentiate Instruction
>
> 5. **RTI/Extra Support** Unless students live in an area where ferns are common, this might be a tricky question for some. Explain that ferns are adapted to areas where there is less direct sunlight, and then ask students where such areas can be found. This will help them answer the question.

6. Remind students that they can determine the environment in which an organism lived by considering the organism's physical traits. Have students examine each image carefully, making a list of the traits they can see.

---

3. Which statement is true about fossils?
   a. Fossils can tell us what animals looked like millions of years ago.
   b. Fossils are never organisms that lived in the sea.
   c. Fossils found today are always terrestrial fossils.
   d. Fossils can tell us how animals become extinct.

4. Which of the following would be evidence of the kind of environment a fossilized organism lived in? Circle all that apply.
   a. flat, paddle-like limbs and a broad tail with two fins
   b. jointed legs
   c. a long tail
   d. a small head

5. You are digging in a desert in the mountains and find fossil imprints of ferns. Based on this, which type of environment did the mountain used to be?
   a. a warmer and drier environment
   b. a colder and drier environment
   c. a warmer and moister environment
   d. a deep, watery environment

6. Write *aquatic* or *terrestrial* on each line to tell which type of environment the organism lived in.

terrestrial

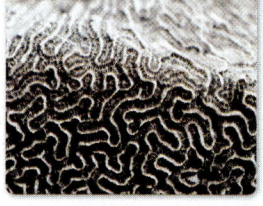
aquatic

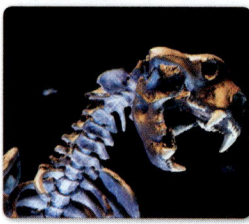
terrestrial

aquatic

LESSON 2
Lesson Roundup

A. Choose the answer that best completes each sentence.

| they died | they grew | they lived |

Observing the structures of fossils allows scientists to make inferences about the way __they lived__ .

| the same as | similar to | nothing like |

Fossils show us that many organisms alive today, such as corals, are __similar to__ organisms that lived millions of years ago.

| lake | desert | swamp |

The discovery of a fossil fern leaf means that the environment in that area was most likely a __swamp__ millions of years ago.

B. You see a fossil with a long, narrow skeleton. It has four limbs that look like flippers. What can you infer about the kind of animal this was and where it lived?

Possible answer: The animal's limbs are similar to those of aquatic animals such as a dolphin. I can infer that this is the fossil of an animal that lived in the water.

C. Scientists find a fossil that is millions of years old. Its body structure is similar to animals that are alive today. What can the scientist infer about the ancient animal and today's animal?

The scientists can infer that the animal from the past lived in a similar environment to the living animal, and they may be related.

D. Why are fossils important in understanding Earth's past?

Fossils tell us what kinds of organisms lived in the past. Knowing the kinds of organisms that existed in the past can tell us about the environments of the past as well.

499

Lesson Roundup

 ESS1.C The History of Planet Earth

 Patterns

This lesson summary enables students to quickly revisit key points and prepare for tests.

A. To help students better understand the ways that traits in organisms can determine how and where they lived, have them revisit all three Explorations. Also note that there are patterns to traits in living organisms and that these patterns can be observed in fossil organisms as well. Once you know how organisms use traits to survive today, you can look for those traits in fossil organisms to see how they survived in the past. **ESS1.C, Patterns**

B. If students are struggling with this item, point them to Exploration 1. Remind students that limbs are how many animals move. Different kinds of limbs are adapted for movement in specific environments. Ask students what kinds of limbs they have and what kind of environment they live in. Then have them compare their limbs to the limbs described in the item. How are they similar? How are they different? In what environment would the limbs described in the item help an organism move? **Patterns**

C. Some students may be tempted to write that having similar body structures makes organisms closely related. This is another opportunity to remind students that organisms with similar body structures certainly can be closely related but that isn't always true. Remind them that dolphins live in the water and have similar body structures to mosasaurs; one is a mammal, and the other is a reptile. **ESS1.C, Patterns**

D. To better understand this question, students may need to revisit all three Explorations, doing a quick scan of each. Also explain that looking at the entirety of the history of life on planet Earth can help us understand not only the past, but also the present and the future. For example, understanding what caused extinctions in the past can help us better prepare for extinction events in the future. **ESS1.C, Patterns**

Lesson 2 What Do Fossils Tell Us About Ancient Environments? **499**

LESSON 3
What Are Some Patterns Fossils Show Us?

Building to the Performance Expectation

The learning experiences in this lesson prepare students for mastery of:

4-ESS1-1 Identify evidence from patterns in rock formations and fossils in rock layers to support an explanation for changes in a landscape over time.

Trace Tool to the NGSS
Go online to view the complete coverage of these standards across this lesson, unit, and time.

 Science & Engineering Practices

Constructing Explanations and Designing Solutions
Constructing explanations and designing solutions in 3–5 builds on K–2 experiences and progresses to the use of evidence in constructing explanations that specify variables that describe and predict phenomena and in designing multiple solutions to design problems.

- Identify the evidence that supports particular points in an explanation.

Disciplinary Core Ideas

ESS1.C The History of Planet Earth
Local, regional, and global patterns of rock formation reveal changes over time due to earth forces, such as earthquakes. The presence and location of certain fossil types indicate the order in which rock layers were formed.

 Crosscutting Concepts

Patterns
Patterns can be used as evidence to support an explanation.

Scientific Knowledge Assumes an Order and Consistency in Natural Systems
Science assumes consistent patterns in natural systems.

CONNECTIONS TO MATH

MP.2 Reason abstractly and quantitatively.

4.MD.A.1 Know relative sizes of measurement units within one system of units including km, m, cm; kg, g; lb, oz.; l, ml; hr, min, sec. Within a single system of measurement, express measurements in a larger unit in terms of a smaller unit. Record measurement equivalents in a two-column table.

CONNECTIONS TO ENGLISH LANGUAGE ARTS

W.4.7 Conduct short research projects that build knowledge through the investigation of different aspects of a topic.

W.4.8 Recall relevant information from experiences or gather relevant information from print and digital sources; take notes and categorize information, and provide a list of sources.

W.4.9 Draw evidence from literary or informational texts to support analysis, reflection, and research.

Supporting All Students, All Standards

Integrating the Three Dimensions of Learning

Use evidence to determine what past environments were like. Examine the fossils in different layers of rock to reveal the history of planet Earth **(DCI ESS1.C)**, and construct explanations for how environments have changed over time **(SEP Constructing Explanations and Designing Solutions)**. Studying patterns in rocks and fossils, learn how changes to Earth's surface have affected and will continue to affect rock layers **(CCC Patterns)**. Build on knowledge learned from prior lessons to understand that fossils appear in specific layers of rock, that these rock layers were laid down in specific order, and that these layers present an incomplete but informative history of the life and geologic processes of the planet.

Professional Development Go online to view **Professional Development videos** with strategies to integrate CCCs and SEPs, including the ones used in this lesson.

Extra Hands-On Activity: Footprints in the Sand

What Can We Learn From Fossil Footprints?

- Small groups
- 45 minutes

Identify an outdoor location such as a volleyball court, a long-jump pit, or the infield of a baseball field that will give students room to spread out. If you have limited space, secure a rack and smooth out the soil or sand prior to each team's use. Test the consistency of the soil or sand to make sure footprints will be visible.

Instruct students to wear or bring shoes that can get sandy. Provide old towels for students who choose to conduct this activity barefoot.

Have groups do test measurements of their own length of stride and height to develop a correlation between stride and height. Each group should then make a set of footprints for another group to analyze. After swapping footprint sites, students should use their measurements of the stride and what they have studied as methods to help them determine the height and movement pattern, such as walking or running, of the person who made the prints.

Students will find that an organism's height and gait are reflected in the tracks they make.

 This activity can support mastery of this Crosscutting Concept: Patterns

Preassessment

Have students complete the unit pre-test online or see the Assessment Guide.

Build on Prior Knowledge

Students should already know and be prepared to build on the following concepts:
- Internal and external structures of organisms help determine their survival in specific environments.
- The structures of living animals can help determine the environments of fossil animals.

Differentiate Instruction

Lesson Vocabulary
Students likely will be more familiar with the everyday meaning of *formation*.

Ask: What are some examples of a formation in nature? Possible answer: a mushroom rock; a hoodoo; a mesa; a peak; a cliff

Connect students' answers to a larger exposure of rock in which fossils may be found.

RTI/Extra Support
The word *formation* comes from a shorter word, *form*.

Ask: What does the word *form* mean? Possible answer: the shape of something

Terms such as *mushroom rock*, *hoodoo*, *mesa*, *peak*, and *cliff* all refer to the shape of specific rocks. A formation, then, can refer to a large area of exposed rocks.

Lesson 3 What Are Some Patterns Fossils Show Us? **500B**

LESSON 3   **Engage** • Explore/Explain • Elaborate • Evaluate

ENGAGE: Lesson Phenomenon

Lesson Objective
To examine fossils and other geologic evidence to understand what past environments were like, how they have changed over time, and how changes to Earth's surface have affected them.

About This Image
The mangrove trees you see in the image are part of a warm, watery environment, but that doesn't mean this area was always warm and watery. Mangrove trees grow along coastlines, specifically in low intertidal zones such as the coast of Florida in the United States.

The mangrove trees and water in this photo cover a layer of sand, dirt, and mud that in turn covers a layer of rock. Below that layer of rock is another layer, and so on. Each layer of rock may represent a different period in Earth's history, each with unique species of plants and animals.

The environment in each layer may have been similar to or different from the environment in other layers. Only by studying each layer can we tell what each period in Earth's history was like in that area.

SEP **Constructing Explanations and Designing Solutions**

Alternative Engage Strategy

Environment Then, Environment Now 👥 Whole class 🕐 10 min

Show students an image of a fossil from their area. Then ask them what kind of environment the area had when the fossil was alive based on what they learned in the previous lesson. Give students an opportunity to study the image of the fossil. Then ask them how the area at the time the fossil was alive was different from the area today.

LESSON 3
What Are Some Patterns Fossils Show Us?

Today, these mangrove trees grow near a watery environment. Do you think this environment has always looked like this?

_____

By the end of this lesson . . .
you'll be able to use information from fossils and rock layers to describe how an environment has changed over time and determine the relative ages of those fossils and rock layers.

500

500 Unit 7 Rocks and Fossils

> **▶ Explore Online** Students can view the lesson phenomenon online.

Can You Explain It?

Students are asked to explain how the fossil of a turtle that lived at sea got into the interior of a desert, where there is no water around for many kilometers. To answer the questions, students must apply what they learned in the previous two lessons, that environments today are not necessarily indicative of environments in the past in the same area. Encourage students not to get too caught up in finding the correct answer. They should expect their ideas to change as they progress through the Explorations in the lesson. They will have an opportunity to revise their answers when they revisit the questions at the end of the lesson.

Collaboration

Feedback Have students engage in a whole-class discussion about the image. Lead the discussion, asking guiding questions and encouraging students to give each other positive and constructive feedback as they share their thoughts on how environments change over time and how fossils tell a story about those changes.

EVIDENCE NOTEBOOK

Encourage students to use an appropriate graphic organizer, such as main idea and supporting details, to set up their notebook for this lesson.

Find more strategies in the online ELA handbook.

Can You Explain It?

Scientists found this fossilized sea turtle in a desert. Like sea turtles today, ancient sea turtles moved by using powerful flippers to swim through the water. Their bony shells offered some protection against large predators.

1. How did this fossilized sea turtle end up in the desert? What can fossils like this tell us about the past?

   Students should respond based on the preliminary observations they can make of the images.
   _____
   _____
   _____

   Tip
   Learn more about rock layers and fossils in How Do Rock Layers Change? and What Do Fossils Tell Us About Ancient Environments?

EVIDENCE NOTEBOOK Look for this icon to help you gather evidence to answer the questions above.

Lesson 3 What Are Some Patterns Fossils Show Us?

LESSON 3   Engage • **Explore/Explain** • Elaborate • Evaluate

EXPLORATION 1 Evidence of Environments

HANDS-ON ACTIVITY   Small groups   1 class period
Layer By Layer

3D Learning Objective

SEP **Constructing Explanations and Designing Solutions**

Students build a replica of rock layers, constructing an explanation for how fossil evidence can reveal much about the organisms and environment each layer represents.

Materials
If you do not have enough magazines or other materials, you may ask students to bring materials from home. However, some students may not be in a position to furnish materials; if this is the case, use the classroom or library computer to print out images from the Internet.

Preparation
Before you separate students into groups, have a bundle of images prepared for each group, as well as a place for the members of the group to work together.

Procedure
STEPS 1–3 Circulate among the groups, observing carefully to ensure that each understands how to complete the task and what its purpose is. Be available to answer any questions students may have, and gently offer guidelines or suggestions to get them back on track if they become confused.

HANDS-ON ACTIVITY
Layer By Layer

Objective
Collaborate with your group to investigate how to use evidence to determine what an environment was like.

What question will you investigate to meet this objective?
Possible question: How can I figure out the relative ages of different environments?

Materials
- nature magazines
- colored pencils
- scissors
- circular stencils
- construction paper
- white construction paper for drawing
- tape

Procedure

STEP 1 Your teacher will provide you with magazines or other sources of images of present-day environments. Individually, each person in your group will choose a specific environment, such as a desert, swamp, or underwater environment. From the materials provided, select an image that best represents your environment. It should show animals and plants that live there.

STEP 2 Use a stencil to cut out two to three round holes in a sheet of construction paper. The round holes will be windows that show some but not all of the organisms in your environment. After cutting the holes, place the construction paper over your drawing paper. Trace the cut out circles on your drawing paper.

What do you think you are modeling by using paper to block portions of the images?
the relative scarcity of fossils or other clues about what an environment looked like or what organisms lived in it

STEP 3 Draw or cut out a picture of the environment and its plants and animals. Be sure one plant or animal is in each circle you drew in step 2.

What do you think the climate is like in the environment you chose?
Possible answer: The climate for my environment would be very hot and dry.

502

502   Unit 7 Rocks and Fossils

STEP 4 Place the construction papers on top of your environment. Make sure you can see plants and animals through the windows. Tape the pages together.

STEP 5 With your group, layer all the environments by stacking them one on top of the other.

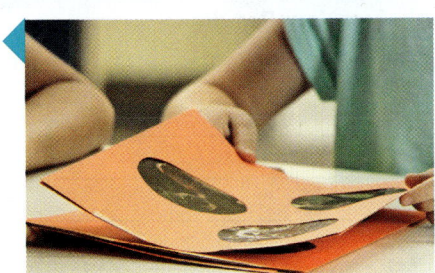

What are you modeling when you layer the different pictures on top of each other? What does the stack represent?

layers of rock that form over time

STEP 6 Trade your layers with another group.

STEP 7 Look at each layer of your new stack. Use the images you can see through the windows of each layer to identify each environment.

STEP 8 Talk with other members of your group about which environment came first and which came later.

List the environments in the chart, layer by layer, from oldest to youngest. Include observations that helped you identify the environments.

Possible answers:

Relative Age	Observations	Type of Environment
1st environment	fish, frogs, aquatic plants	lake
2nd environment	bald cypress trees and alligators	swamp
3rd environment	pine trees, arctic hare	cold plains
4th environment	tall grasses, deer, foxes	prairie
5th environment	maple trees, squirrels	deciduous forest

Connection to Nature of Science

Ask: Why do scientists assume there is an order to natural processes? They observe patterns that repeat over and over.
4-ESS1-1 Natural systems have patterns that repeat over and over again.

STEPS 4–5 Direct students to make a list of each layer they have made. This can act as a checklist for other groups after they have completed the activity and allow each group to compare and contrast their layers with the layers they have traded from others.

CCC Patterns

Ask: Are there patterns in rock layers? Possible answer: Yes and no. Rock layers are formed one on top of the other, regardless of where they are formed. However, not every group of rock layers includes the same environments or the same order.

STEPS 6–8 Note that each group's layers will be different from the other groups, resulting in each group filling out the chart differently. Walk among students as they complete the chart based on the evidence they have from the model environments/rock layers. Answer any questions they may have, and nudge them in the right direction if they are having difficulties.

Differentiate Instruction

RTI/Extra Support Some students may have a difficult time grasping what they are recording in the chart. Explain that each line of the chart represents a different layer in the model, which in turn represents a different environment, in the same way that each layer of rock does.

Lesson 3 What Are Some Patterns Fossils Show Us?

LESSON 3   Engage • **Explore/Explain** • Elaborate • Evaluate

EXPLORATION 1 *Evidence of Environments, continued*

Analyze Your Results

STEPS 9–10 Help students connect their models to the real world. Explain that fossils are only one way to know what environment a rock layer once was.

Ask: What is another way to tell what environment a rock layer used to be? **Possible answer: Scientists study what kind of particles the rock is made of. These particles can tell a lot about what the environment used to be like.**

Draw Your Conclusion

STEP 11 Make sure students are drawing upon facts and evidence they find to determine the newest environment.

Claims, Evidence, and Reasoning

Ask: If you couldn't see any fossils in a layer, does that mean it came from an environment where there were no living organisms? **no**
Why or why not? **Possible answer: For an organism to become a fossil, very specific conditions must be met. It must be covered in sediment, sand, or volcanic ash. Over time, layers must build up over it, pressing the lower layers into rock. Water carrying minerals must seep through the rock layers, replacing the original organism's parts.**

Scoring Rubric for Hands-On Activity	
3	Students understand what each layer of paper represents, what the order means, and what the missing sections stand for.
2	Students understand two of the following: what each layer of paper represents, what the order means, or what the missing sections stand for.
1	Students understand one of the following: what each layer of paper represents, what the order means, or what the missing sections stand for.

504   Unit 7 Rocks and Fossils

Analyze Your Results

STEP 9 By covering up most of the picture and leaving only a small window to see what lived in that environment, what do you think you modeled?
Covering up most of the picture was like what happens to environments over time when they change and are turned into layers of rock and fossils. The few organisms visible through the window are like fossils, which can be hard to find.

STEP 10 Compare your results with those from another group? How are they similar and different?
Students may find that the order of the environments are different among different groups, and the organisms found in each will vary. The oldest layer will still be on bottom and the youngest on top.

Draw Your Conclusion

STEP 11 Based on where each layer is in the stack, which environment came first in this area? Which is the newest environment?
The oldest environment is on the bottom of the stack. The age of the environments decreases as you move up toward the top of the stack. The newest environment is the top layer.

STEP 12 Make a claim about fossils and environments, and cite evidence to support it.

Claim	Evidence
Possible claim: Fossils give us incomplete glimpses into what an environment was like a long time ago.	Possible evidence: The fossil record, as well as the model we created today, are evidence of how incomplete that glimpse is.

STEP 13 What is one question you have about fossils and environments?
Possible question: When there are no fossil plant or animal remains in a rock layer, how can you tell what the environment was like?

504

EXPLORATION 1

Evidence of Environments

Seeing History

Many locations around the world are rich with fossils. Some of these places have rock layers where fossils from many types of organisms can be found. The fossils below were all found in one of these locations.

Identify the Fossil

2. Look at the fossils. Match each description to the correct fossil.

a. This fossil is a snake. You can see its backbone, skull, and ribs.
b. Small fossil shrimp are common in the Green River formation. This is one example.
c. The leaf of a plant clearly shows in this fossil. It is the leaf of a willow tree. Plants give scientists important clues to past environments.
d. Some rock layers at Green River are full of fish fossils. Consider the types of environment where fish were common.

Explore Online Have students go online to learn more about fossils and past environments.

3D Learning Objective

Examine **patterns** of fossil distribution, and **construct an explanation** for why fossils appear in the order they do in rock layers to learn about **the history of planet Earth**.

SEP Constructing Explanations and Designing Solutions

Snakes first appear in the fossil record between 112 and 94 million years ago. Because they typically have been small animals with fragile bodies, the likelihood of fossilization when they die decreases.

Ask: If a snake is found in a layer of rock, what can we conclude about the age of the layer? The rock layer was likely laid down within the last 112 million years.

Ask: Why are so few snakes found in the fossil record? They're small and fragile and don't fossilize as often as bigger organisms.

Differentiate Instruction

Extension Assign students two of the fossils shown in the images, and ask them to write a short research paper about each one. Each paper should be about one page in length and should describe when the first fossils of that organism were found and where and how old they are.

DCI ESS1.C The History of Planet Earth

Some fossils can only be found in certain layers of rock because the animals they belong to went extinct. For example, most proto-mammals went extinct at the end of the Permian Period.

Ask: How can we tell a rock layer's age by looking at the fossils in it? Some organisms only lived during certain periods. If those animals are found in the layer, we can tell when the layer formed.

Lesson 3 What Are Some Patterns Fossils Show Us?

LESSON 3   Engage • **Explore/Explain** • Elaborate • Evaluate

EXPLORATION 1   *Evidence of Environments, continued*

Misconception Alert The location of fossils in a rock layer can sometimes be deceptive. Some species of organisms, such as turtles and snakes, might live on land while others might live in water. Sometimes wind, a flash flood, or scavenging animals might move an organism from one environment to another, where parts of it might then fossilize. For these reasons, we have to look for additional evidence about a rock layer's former environment.

Connection to Math

Have students examine the layers of rock in the image.
Ask: Are all the layers the same thickness? **No.**
Which layers do you think took longer to form? **The thicker layers.**

Tell students that rock layers do not form at a consistent rate. Some thick layers may have formed very quickly, while thinner layers may have taken longer to form.
Ask: Suppose you were exploring rock layers and found a set of rock layers with three layers. One layer was 3 meters thick, one layer was 1 meter thick, and one layer was 5 meters thick. How many centimeters thick was the entire rock formation? **900 centimeters**

Remind students that they can make a table to change units from meters to centimeters.
4.MD.A.1 Know relative sizes of measurement units.

Differentiate Instruction

RTI/Extra Support While most students will know what type of environments these fossils come from, a few students may need help, particularly in the case of the snake, which can be found in more than one type of environment. Print out a modern living image of each, and cut the organism out of the image. Then print out an image of the environment in which each organism lives. Have students match the organism to its environment.

Building the Story

Take a look at the picture. It shows several rock layers.

3. Analyze the picture to describe the fossils in the rock layers and the types of environments they would have lived in.

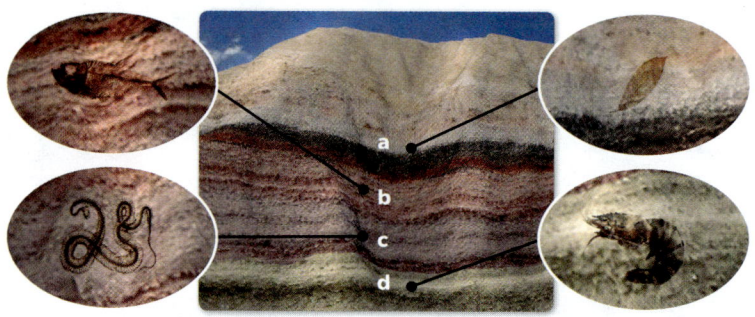

	Type of Fossil	Where Organism Lived
Layer A	leaf	land
Layer B	fish	water
Layer C	snake	land
Layer D	shrimp	water

Choose the correct answer for each question.

4. Which rock layer is the oldest?
   a. Layer A   c. Layer C
   b. Layer B   **d. Layer D**

5. How do you know the layer you chose is the oldest?
   a. The oldest layer is usually on top.
   b. The oldest layer usually has land animals.
   c. The oldest layer is usually on the bottom.
   d. The oldest layer is between layers of limestone.

6. Use the evidence to identify the oldest type of environment represented in these rock layers.
   a. desert   c. forest
   b. sea   d. mountain

506

506   Unit 7 Rocks and Fossils

EVIDENCE NOTEBOOK Make a statement about the type of environment one rock layer indicates. Use evidence to support your statement. Record any ideas you may have about how the sea turtle fossil shown at the beginning of the lesson ended up in a desert.

7. Look at the four environments below and read their descriptions. Use the rock layers on the previous page as evidence to number the environments in order of age, with 1 being the oldest.

This area was once covered by a freshwater lake. Many fish, turtles, and other aquatic animals lived here at that time. Terrestrial animals also lived on the land around the lake. They used the lake as a drinking source.

Willow trees once grew here. During this time, the climate was much warmer than it is today. It had a temperate to sub-tropical environment, unlike today. Summers were hot and humid, and winters were mild but sometimes cool. Some trees lost their leaves in the winter.

The area was also once covered by a saltwater sea. Many saltwater animals lived in the water including clams, shrimp, sharks and other fish.

At another time, the area was covered by a cypress forest. The ground was moist. Once in awhile, organisms might become trapped in the mud in this environment.

EVIDENCE NOTEBOOK

Students should pick a layer and provide evidence for why they think it came from a certain environment. For example, they may pick a layer and claim that it was once a lake or river, with the fish fossil as evidence.

DCI ESS1.C The History of Planet Earth

Students have learned over the past lessons that much of Earth's history can be found in rock layers. Some layers have fewer fossils than others. This may be because conditions weren't right for fossilization to occur or because organisms were smaller and fragile, leading to fewer of them becoming fossils.

Ask: Why do some rock layers have fewer fossils than others? Conditions may not have been right for fossilization, or the organisms may have been too small and fragile to fossilize often.

Collaboration

Draw, Pair, Share Ask students to draw a picture of things from our time that might be found in rock layers 50 million years from now and explain why. Separate them into pairs. Have each member trade drawings and respond. Then call the class together and discuss what they drew.

CCC Patterns

Note that rock layers themselves present a visual pattern that can be seen with the naked eye. Show students an image of exposed rock, with layers that are clearly different colors. Point out that each thin band of color is actually a different layer, which has been deposited at a different time from all the rest. If scientists were to look at an exposed outcropping of rock, they may see these different layers. Some layers would be thinner, some thicker.

LESSON 3   Engage • **Explore/Explain** • Elaborate • Evaluate

EXPLORATION 1 Evidence of Environments, continued

HANDS-ON Apply What You Know
Where Else?

Students should choose one of the following fossils: fern leaf, fish, snake, or crustacean. Research will show that these fossils have been found in formations all over the world, not just in the United States. In fact, except for the snake, these fossils are fairly common.

Assessment Rubric	
3	Students name multiple places where the fossil has been discovered and mark them on a map.
2	Students name one place where the fossil has been discovered and mark it on a map.
1	Students name one or more places where the fossil has been discovered but don't mark it/them on a map.

Language SmArts
W.4.9 Draw evidence from literary or informational texts to support analysis, reflection, and research.

This item is an opportunity to reinforce what students have learned so far. Remind them that when they make inferences, they are looking at evidence and using reason to draw a conclusion from it. In this case, they are making inferences based on what they have read and learned in the Hands-On Activity and this Exploration.

FORMATIVE ASSESSMENT
Putting it Together

 CCC Patterns

Ask: What patterns are revealed in evidence for environments?
Possible answer: Fossil location is a pattern of evidence for environments.

Global Stories

The types of fossils found in any given location, may also be found in other parts of the world. And the order in which fossils are found in rock layers is often the same at different locations around the globe.

 HANDS-ON Apply What You Know
Where Else?

8. Choose a fossil from this lesson that interests you. Research to find out where else in the world it has been found. List those places on a sheet of paper. Use a world map and colored pencils to mark where similar fossils have been found.

9. **Language SmArts** You now have some idea of the types of environments that were available to organisms millions of years ago. What can you infer about how Earth's surface has changed?

Students should note that there were aquatic environments and areas of land that were warm and moist. Some of these places are now cooler or drier than before.

Putting It Together

10. How can fossils serve as evidence of specific events and environments in Earth's history? How can they show patterns in that history?

The order of fossils and the rock layers that contain them can reveal the order in which environments existed. If the same fossils are found in multiple locations around the world, that can show a pattern of global environmental change.

11. Choose the correct words to complete the sentences.

| shrimp | aquatic | plants |

The rock layers from the previous pages show change over time. The first animals there were ___shrimp___. This shows that the environment at the time was ___aquatic___. Over time, most of the water disappeared. A forest formed. The forest had many types of ___plants___ that are common in warm climates.

EXPLORATION 2 More Changes

More Changes

Consistent Patterns

The pattern in which rock layers are laid down and evidence of how environments and organisms are preserved can be affected by events at Earth's surface.

> **HANDS-ON** Apply What You Know
>
> **Disordered Days**
>
> 12. You have seen rock layers that lay flat, one on top of the other. But some rock layers are not quite so neat.
>   a. Label five pieces of paper with the days of the week, starting with Monday.
>   b. Stack the papers one on top of the other in the order of the days, with Monday at the bottom.
>   c. Before putting Thursday on the pile, remove Wednesday. Then put Thursday on top of Tuesday.
>   d. Finish by adding Friday.
>   e. Create a second set of layers by repeating the first two steps. Do not remove the Wednesday layer this time.
>
> Compare and contrast the two sets of layers. Think about what the missing layer could represent if the layers were made of rock. What could cause a layer to be missing? Answer the questions below.

13. Circle the correct answer. How does the first stack model erosion?
    a. It has several layers.
    b. One layer was removed.
    c. One layer was broken.
    d. The layers are all rock.

14. Circle the correct answer. Which layer(s) can be eroded?
    a. The top layer
    b. The bottom layer
    c. One of the middle layers
    d. Both the top and bottom layers

15. Circle the correct answer. What would happen if erosion removed the third layer before the fourth layer formed?
    a. The third layer would form again.
    b. The second layer would be larger.
    c. The fourth layer would be on top of the second.
    d. There would be two third layers.

3D Learning Objective

Understand how **patterns** in rock layers can be affected by events at Earth's surface, **constructing explanations** for these events and their effects. These events, which are part of **the history of planet Earth**, include earthquakes, weathering, and erosion.

HANDS-ON Apply What You Know
Disordered Days

Before the activity begins, make sure that each student has enough sheets of paper: 10 sheets each. This activity can be done from students' desks, with each student conducting the activity on his or her own.

Assessment Rubric	
3	Students understand that the missing sheet of paper represents missing layers of rock in the geologic record and can name an event at Earth's surface that caused the layers to disappear.
2	Students understand that the missing sheet of paper represents missing layers of rock in the geologic record and understand that events at Earth's surface caused the layers to disappear, but they cannot name which event(s) caused the missing layers.
1	Students understand that the missing sheet of paper represents missing layers of rock in the geologic record but don't understand why the layers are missing.

SEP Constructing Explanations and Designing Solutions

Ask: Why might there not be a fossil record for some parts of the past in certain rock layers? Possible answer: Weathering and erosion removed those layers before they could become rock or sometimes even after they became rock.

LESSON 3   Engage • **Explore/Explain** • Elaborate • Evaluate

EXPLORATION 2 *More Changes, continued*

 **Patterns**

Ask: Why might some layers not contain fossils? **Possible answer: The environment may not have contained the right conditions for fossilization to occur.**

Differentiate Instruction

ELL: Modeling Some students for whom English is a second language may not understand what the word *earthquake* means. Model an earthquake by placing dirt in a pan. On top of the dirt, place toy figures, vehicles, and/or homes and buildings. Shake the pan hard enough that the ground, figures, vehicles, and buildings move. Explain that this is like what happens during an earthquake. Earth's surface moves, or quakes, sometimes causing vehicles to move or buildings to collapse.

Ask: What is an earthquake? **An earthquake is movement of the ground at Earth's surface.**

DCI ESS1.C The History of Planet Earth

Ask: How do rock layers reveal the history of planet Earth? **Possible answer: Each layer shows what Earth was like during a specific period of time. Sometimes fossils of once-living organisms tell us what life was like or what kind of environment existed in a certain place at a certain time. As you move through layers, you go further back in time.**

When Things Change

Look at the rock layers below. Notice that some of the layers have fossils in them.

This column of rock has five layers. Three of the layers contain fossils.

16. Using the rock layer image above as a reference, assign layer numbers to the area of rock that was offset by the earthquake. The older layer should be labeled *1*, the youngest *5*.

17. What did the earthquake do to the order of the rock layers? Circle the best answer.
   a. It did not change the order of the layers.
   b. It reversed the order of layers.
   c. It removed several of the layers.
   d. It created one new layer.

510

18. Sometimes, layers of rock break down through weathering and erosion. Think back to the activity you did on page 509. Then look at the rock layers below. Suppose these layers are part of the same rock layers as the those on the previous page, but at a different location. Again, label each layer, starting with *1* for the oldest layer.

19. Compare your numbering here to your numbering in question 16. Is each layer given the same number in both images? Why or why not?

No. These layers are missing a layer. The missing layer probably eroded from this section of rock while it was the top layer, before the younger layers formed.

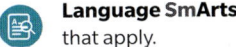 **Language SmArts** Answer the questions below. Circle all that apply.

20. What evidence did you use to number the layers?
    a. the color of each rock layer
    b. the fossils in each rock layer
    c. the fact that layers get older as you move down from the surface
    d. the fact that an earthquake occurred
    e. the fact that erosion occurred

21. How do the rock layers show changes in the land over time?
    a. They have the same number of layers.
    b. The type of fossils found in them change from aquatic to terrestrial.
    c. The type of fossils found in them were all aquatic.
    d. There are fossils in almost every layer.
    e. Disruption to the layers shows change over time.

511

Build on Prior Knowledge

As a reminder, explain to students that weathering and erosion are not the same thing. Weathering occurs when wind, water, plants, and other things break small pieces of rock from larger pieces of rock. Erosion occurs when wind, water, or animals move the weathered rock from its original position to a new position.

Ask: How can weathering and erosion affect rock layers? Weather can break apart the rock, while erosion can move the particles to a new location.

ESS1.C History of Planet Earth

Weathering and erosion can happen not only to rock layers, but also to fossils. In 1922, American explorer Roy Chapman Andrews and his team discovered the partial remains of a giant mammal. But all they found of one specimen were four legs. The legs were standing upright in the rock layer, indicating that the animal had died in quicksand before becoming fossilized.

Ask: What do you think happened to the rest of the animal's body? It weathered and eroded from the rock layer.

Ask: Why did this not happen to the legs? Possible answer: The weathering and erosion began at the top of the layer of rock and worked its way down. The legs were in the lower part of the layer. The legs were discovered before weathering and erosion could destroy them.

Language SmArts
W.4.9 Draw evidence from literary or informational texts to support analysis, reflection, and research.

Explain to students that when they research topics, they are searching for evidence in informational texts. This evidence can be used to support student analysis of a problem and help students construct an explanation or design a solution.

Lesson 3 What Are Some Patterns Fossils Show Us? 511

LESSON 3 Engage • **Explore/Explain** • Elaborate • Evaluate

EXPLORATION 2 More Changes, continued

Content Background

Most coal comes from the Carboniferous Period. Note the word *Carbon* in *Carboniferous*. *Carboniferous* means that there was a great deal of carbon on Earth surface at that time. The world was full of large, swampy forests with lots of trees. When these trees died and were covered by sediment and water, they were eventually pressed into coal. When coal is burned, it releases carbon into the atmosphere.

Ask: Why is coal known as a fossil fuel? Coal is the fossil remains of ancient plants.

 EVIDENCE NOTEBOOK

Students should write that, in most cases, the oldest layers were those lowest in the rock layers, while the newest layers were on top. The fossil record is one piece of evidence for this. Scientists have analyzed fossils such as the sea turtle at the beginning of the lesson, compared them everywhere they've been found, and determined what period in Earth's history the rocks that contain them come from. Once they have done this with many different kinds of fossils, they can determine the age and order of rock layers.

FORMATIVE ASSESSMENT

 Language SmArts
Refer Explicitly to Text
W.4.9 Draw evidence from literary or informational texts to support analysis, reflection, and research.

Have students read back over this Exploration.

Ask: What kind of events at Earth's surface can disrupt rock layers or destroy them altogether? Possible answer: earthquakes, weathering and erosion (Note that, though this is not covered in the Exploration, volcanoes and other events can affect rock layers as well. Accept any reasonable answer.)

Interpret Layers

Use what you've learned about rock layers to answer the questions.

22. Circle the correct answer.

The oldest fossil is the fossil shrimp.
a. I agree because the shrimp fossil is in the oldest layer.
b. I disagree because the leaf fossil is in the oldest layer.

23. Circle the correct answer.

The snake lived after the leaf but before the shrimp.
a. I agree because the snake fossil is in a younger rock layer than the leaf fossil, but in an older layer than the shrimp fossil.
b. I disagree because the snake fossil is in an older rock layer than the leaf fossil and in a younger layer than the shrimp fossil.

 EVIDENCE NOTEBOOK How did you determine which layers were oldest and which were youngest? What evidence did you use? How does analyzing rock layers like these help explain why a sea turtle fossil might be found in a desert?

 Language SmArts
Refer Explicitly to Text

24. How could fossils in the rock layers help you determine their age if the layers were moved out of their original order?

Two layers are the same age if they have the same fossils, even if they are split by some type of disruption.

Tip
The English Language Arts Handbook can provide help with understanding how to refer explicitly to text.

LESSON 3 Engage • Explore/Explain • **Elaborate** • Evaluate

TAKE IT FURTHER Discover More

 **Explore Online** Have students go online to learn more about the people who study the ancient past.

TAKE IT FURTHER
Discover More

Check out this path . . . or go online to choose one of these other paths.

People in Science & Engineering → • Changes in Environments
• Careers in Science

Studying Evidence from the Past

Read these profiles of important people in science. The field of paleontology has changed over time.

 Explore Online

Edward Cope was a paleontologist who lived in the 1800s. He discovered the fossils of 1,000 species of extinct animals. Many of his discoveries were made during the 1860s. At that time, there was little technology to assist in locating fossils and recovering them.

Mary Higby Schweitzer is a modern paleontologist who studies the hidden interiors of fossilized bones. By breaking parts of some specimens down and examining their material under a microscope, she has made new discoveries about dinosaur tissues.

> **Collaboration**
> You may choose to assign this activity or to direct students online to the eSE where they can explore and choose from all three paths. These activities can be assigned individually, to pairs, or to small groups.

People in Science & Engineering: Studying Evidence from the Past

Students learn that paleontologists are people who study the life of the ancient past. Since the early 1800s, men and women have been making new fossil discoveries and writing about them. From these, we know much about different forms of life.

Misconception Alert Because many students will have heard the word *paleontologist* in connection to people who study dinosaurs, they may believe that a paleontologist is a person who studies dinosaurs alone. However, these scientists study all ancient life, from single-celled organisms to more recent extinct mammals. Students may also mistakenly believe that only men are paleontologists. In fact, there are many women in the field, some of whom students will learn about here.

CCC Patterns

We know that dinosaurs first appeared in the late Triassic Period around 230 million years ago and disappeared at the end of the Cretaceous Period around 65.5 million years ago. Before them, proto-mammals and many forms of sea life went extinct. After them, many kinds of mammals have gone extinct.

Ask: What is one pattern the fossil record reveals about life on Earth? Possible answer: Life on Earth has been punctuated by mass extinctions.

Lesson 3 What Are Some Patterns Fossils Show Us? 513

TAKE IT FURTHER, continued

Content Background

When Baron Georges Cuvier first proposed the notion that mass extinctions had occurred, he believed they had been caused by catastrophes such as the Great Flood. This notion was known as catastrophism. Over the years, as scientists learned more and more about ancient life on Earth, they came to believe that mass extinctions were long, drawn-out, slow affairs caused by long-term changes to the environment. When the Alvarezes first proposed their theory that the dinosaurs had been wiped out as a result of an asteroid impact, many scientists scoffed. They said it was a return to catastrophism. Today, however, scientists have found a great deal of evidence to bolster the Alvarezes' theory—and the idea that catastrophes sometimes can cause mass extinctions has returned to favor.

▶ Explore Online

Students can explore these additional topics online.

Changes in Environments

Students learn about fossils from Antarctica and how the environment there has changed over millions of years. *(Outside research required.)*

Careers in Science

Students read an interview with a museum director and then ask questions of their own. *(No outside research required.)*

In 1980, **Luis Alvarez,** along with his son, **Walter** proposed a new explanation for the extinction of the dinosaurs. They claimed an asteroid hit Earth 65 million years ago. It threw up dust that blocked the sun for months and caused massive wildfires. The result was the extinction of many species, including the non-avian dinosaurs.

Patricia Vickers-Rich is a paleontologist. She studies the fossils of animals that lived in Australia and, with her husband, has discovered several new species of dinosaur. They named two of these after their children. She has written many books. In 1993 she won awards for a book she wrote about her work studying fossils.

Dong Zhiming is a paleontologist. A paleontologist is someone who studies fossils to learn about life long ago. He studies the fossils of dinosaurs. He wrote an important book on the dinosaur fossils of China in 1988.

25. Choose the correct words to complete the sentences.

beaks	teeth	footprint	asteroid	outbreak of disease
drought	Chile	China	Iran	Austria
Afghanistan	Australia	fossils	tissue	bones

Edward Cope discovered many species of extinct animals before technology existed to locate _____fossils_____. Luis and Walter Alvarez proposed the idea that many dinosaurs were wiped out by an _____asteroid_____. Dong Zhiming is a paleontologist who wrote a book about the dinosaur fossils found in _____China_____. Patricia Vickers-Rich's work has focused on animals whose fossils have been found in _____Australia_____.

LESSON CHECK

LESSON 3 Engage • Explore/Explain • Elaborate • **Evaluate**

> **Explore Online** — Students can revisit the lesson phenomenon online.

LESSON 3
Lesson Check

Name _____

Can You Explain It?

1. Take another look at the turtle from the beginning of the lesson. How did this turtle end up in the desert? What can this fossil tell us about the land around it? In your answers to these questions, be sure to do the following:
   - Identify where sea turtles live, how they move, and what this information tells you about the history of this environment.
   - Discuss how the turtle fossil may have become exposed over time.

EVIDENCE NOTEBOOK Use the information you've collected in your Evidence Notebook to help you cover each point.

Possible answer:
- Sea turtles of today live in the ocean, using flippers to swim.
- What is now desert must have been ocean when the turtle died.
- If the turtle fossil was found at or near the surface, erosion may have removed other ancient rock layers that were laid on top of the turtle's layer

Checkpoints

2. Choose the word or words to complete the sentence.

   A ___fish fossil___ indicates an aquatic environment once existed in an area.

wolf fossil	disrupted
rock formation	fish fossil
layer that is eroded	

Formal Assessment Go online for student self-checks and other assessments.

Can You Explain It?

> **Collaboration**
> **Discussion** You may wish to revisit the image as a group activity to assess students' understanding of the material. Use the bulleted points in the student edition to lead the discussion.

EVIDENCE NOTEBOOK

Have students reread their answers to the Evidence Notebook prompts and then use this evidence to justify their reasoning as they respond to the Can You Explain It question. Make sure students understand that a complete response must address all bulleted points.

DCI ESS1.C The History of Planet Earth

Direct students to consider the prehistoric sea turtle found in a modern-day desert environment. Some may struggle to connect the ideas they've learned in the Exploration to the image they see.

Ask: How might the environment in the image be different from what it used to be when the sea turtle was alive? *It used to be water but today is desert.*

Ask: What does that mean for the history of the planet in this area? *It means that environments changed in this area over long periods of time.* This should lead to students understanding how the fossil of a marine reptile got into the middle of a desert.

SUMMATIVE ASSESSMENT

2. Only one of the choices in the word bank is of an organism that indicates a watery environment through limbs adapted for swimming. If students have a difficult time answering the question, point them to Exploration 1 or 2; either should help students understand how to connect an organism's movement to its environment.

Lesson 3 What Are Some Patterns Fossils Show Us? 515

LESSON 3 Engage • Explore/Explain • Elaborate • **Evaluate**

LESSON CHECK, continued

3. Direct students to revisit Exploration 1 or 2, as both can help them understand which layers of rock are the oldest (those laid down first) and which are the youngest (those laid down most recently).

4. Remind students that disruptions can come in the form of earthquakes or other processes at Earth's surface. If they cannot grasp how to order the rock layers, have them revisit Exploration 2, which focuses on disruptions to rock layers and the results.

5. To answer this question, students must understand that the history of planet Earth is long and features many changes in weather and environment. They must also understand that each layer of rock represents a different period in that long history and that fossils in each layer can help them know what kind of environment existed there when the layer was laid down. If they need a refresher, have them scan Exploration 1.

Differentiate Instruction

6. **ELL** English-language learners may have difficulty with the word infer. Explain that it means to look at the evidence and draw a conclusion about what it means. In this example, students have to explain why the same fossil may be found in different rock layers in different locations. If necessary, direct students to Exploration 2, where they learn about what type of disruptions can change or destroy rock layers.

---

3. Choose the correct word to complete the sentence.

   | youngest | thickest | oldest |

   If there are four rock layers, the layer at the bottom is most likely the ___oldest___.

4. Examine the rock layers. Then answer the question.

   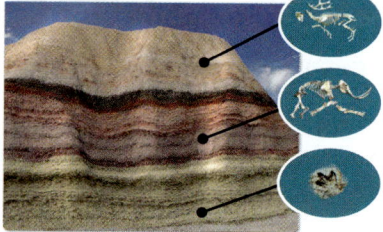

   Consider what you can observe in the image. Is there evidence in the image that this environment has changed over time? Make a claim by circling yes or no.

   Yes (No)

   Support your claim by selecting the accurate evidence below.
   a. The fossils are all terrestrial, so there is no evidence that an aquatic environment once existed here.
   b. There are only five rock layers. This does not provide enough evidence to state whether or not the environment changed.
   c. The layers are made of different types of rock. This shows that the environment changed over time.
   d. The three fossils shown are different types of animals. This shows that the environment changed over time.

5. What can show that the type of environment in an area has changed over time? Circle all that apply.
   a. many fossils in different layers of rock
   b. fossils from different climates in different layers of rock
   c. no fossils in any layers of rock
   d. land and water fossils in two layers of rock near each other

6. Infer why it could be possible to find the same type of dinosaur fossil in the third rock layer from the top layer in Spain, but in the fifth rock layer from the top layer in England. Select all that apply.
   a. It is not be possible for one type of fossil to be in different layers.
   b. Some rock layers may have eroded in Spain but not England.
   c. Dinosaurs are extinct in Spain, but they are not extinct in England.
   d. The environments changed at different rates in both locations.

LESSON 3

Lesson Roundup

A. Choose the answer that correctly orders the environments represented by the rock layers to the right in order from oldest to youngest.
   a. **lake, swamp, grassland, forest**
   b. lake, grassland, swamp, forest
   c. forest, grassland, swamp, lake
   d. forest, swamp, lake, grassland

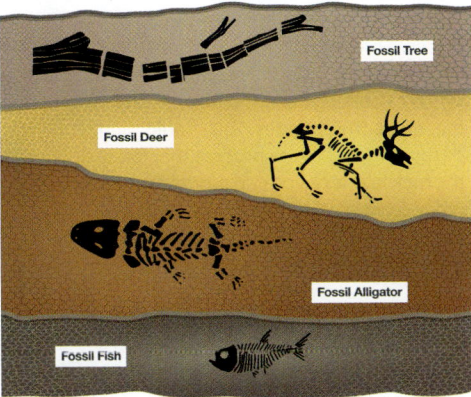

B. What are some limitations of using fossils to learn about past environments? Select all that apply.
   a. **Fossils are not common in many places.**
   b. **Fossils might indicate more than one type of environment.**
   c. Fossils do not show enough detail to identify an environment.
   d. There are many different types of fossils.
   e. **Fossils are often missing pieces**

C. Choose the correct word that completes each sentence.

| earthquakes | fossils | erosion | climate | position |

Rock layers can be disrupted when rock is worn away by **erosion**.

Rock layers have been disrupted. But you can use **fossils** to tell when two disrupted layers are the same age.

Lesson Roundup

DCI ESS1.C History of Planet Earth

This lesson summary enables students to quickly revisit key points and prepare for tests.

A. Students learn about the order of fossil layers in both Exploration 1 and Exploration 2 and may be invited to scan them if they are having difficulty answering this question. The top layer represents a forest (as shown by the large tree fossil), the second a grassland (as shown by the deer fossil), the third a swamp (as shown by the alligator fossil), and the fourth a lake (as shown by the fish fossil). **ESS1.C**

B. Invite students to scan both Explorations for clues to the answers. Remind them that different rock layers represent different periods and environments. Also note how difficult it is for some organisms to fossilize and the specific conditions required for fossilization. **ESS1.C**

C. Students may wish to scan Exploration 2 to help them answer the question. When disruptions occur, this means that a rock layer (or layers) is missing from a certain place in the geologic record. By examining the order of rock layers elsewhere, scientists can determine not only which layer is missing, but also what fossils are likely to belong in that layer. **ESS1.C**

UNIT 7 Performance Task

 small groups   1 class period

Rocking the Layers

3D Assessment Goal
Students **provide explanations** and **develop models** to demonstrate **rock processes and patterns** to demonstrate understanding of **ESS1.C** in support of **4-ESS1-1**.

Materials
- paper
- writing utensils
- drawing utensils

Preparation
Students will need access to online sources to research various types of rock layers.

CCC Patterns

The patterns on rocks can be used to learn more about Earth's history. **Ask:** What kinds of patterns will you look for on the rocks to come up with information about Earth's history?

Research

Review how to properly cite resources.
Print: title, author, copyright date, page number
Online: webpage title, URL, date visited
If students are doing their own research on the Internet, remind them how to search for reliable sources that can be trusted.

Brainstorm

Have students roll a number cube to choose a recorder, highest roll records. Remind students that the brainstorming group is just to come up with ideas. Each of them will be individually responsible for coming up with an idea of how to model the rock layer change.

518 Unit 7 Rocks and Fossils

UNIT 7   UNIT PERFORMANCE TASK

Rocking the Layers

Observe the way the rock layers shown have changed. Your task is to research how rock layers can change and identify the processes that made the changes. You should then design a model of the process that formed the rock layers or you can model one of the other processes that change rock layers. As part of your model, you may wish to show how rock layers are formed.

DEFINE YOUR TASK: What main question will you need to research?

Sample answer: What process caused the rock layers to change in the images?

How have the rock layers changed?

Review the checklist at the end of this Unit Performance Task. Keep those requirements in mind as you proceed.

RESEARCH: Use online and library sources to research how rock layers form and are changed. Identify at least three ways rock layers can change. List your findings, and cite your sources.

Student should reference at least three ways rock layers change and cite their sources.

BRAINSTORM: With your team, brainstorm ways to model the rock layer change. Identify three or more ways, then evaluate the ways and choose the best.

Sample answer: We decided to show how rock layers change as mountains are made. We will model the way the layers move and fold up so they run up and down instead of across.

518

PLAN YOUR PROCEDURE: Consider the questions below as your group prepares its model. Write a few sentences below to briefly summarize your strategy.

1. What type of model will be used?
2. What type of materials should be used in the model to best represent the natural world?
3. What would the area the rock formation is in look like before and after the changes?
4. Does our model properly represent the area it can be found in?
5. How will the model illustrate the changes in the rock layers?
6. What other areas is this pattern of change in rock layers seen?

Student strategies for modeling should reference researched information and appropriate modeling techniques.

_____
_____
_____
_____
_____

MAKE YOUR MODEL: Use the materials available to make your model. Label any important information other people might need to see.

COMMUNICATE: Present your model to the class. Cite evidence to explain how the rock formation changes over time.

 Checklist

Review your project and check off each completed item.

_____ Includes evidence that show how rock layers change over time.
_____ Includes any patterns of change seen and how they relate to how rock layers change.
_____ Includes evidence you have found in your research.
_____ Includes a model that shows the way rock layers change.
_____ Includes evidence in the model that supports proof of the changes in the rock layers.

Plan Your Procedure

SEP **Constructing Explanations and Designing Solutions**

Students research information about rock formation to come up with explanations that can then be used to create their models.

Ask: How does the area in which the rock was found affect the formation of the rock?

Make Your Model

Students only need to design two-dimensional renderings of their models.

Scoring Rubric for Performance Task	
3	• complete resources, clear reasoning, multiple sources • models are detailed and support proof of the changes in the rock layers • presentations are engaging and accurate
2	• most resources, adequate reasoning and sources • models are somewhat detailed and support proof of the changes in the rock layers • presentations are somewhat engaging and accurate
1	• some key resources and reasoning, a few sources • models are detailed but do not support proof of the changes in the rock layers • presentations are engaging or accurate but not both
0	• few key resources, no reasons, minimal sources • models are not detailed and do not support proof of the changes in the rock layers • presentations incomplete

UNIT 7 Review

SUMMATIVE ASSESSMENT

1. Students can correctly answer this question by recalling their Performance Task activity. They can also review information about rock layers in Lesson 1, Exploration 1.

2. Students must study the image to answer the question correctly. They can also review information about rock layers in Lesson 1, Exploration 1.

3. Students should take time to answer this question by saying the sentences aloud to themselves, using the different answer choices from the word bank. Students can deduce which terms make sense in the context of the sentence. They can also refer back to Lesson 1 for a review.

UNIT 7

Unit Review

1. What is the most reliable way to judge the age of a rock layer? Circle the correct choice.
   a. **The lower the layer, the older the rock.**
   b. The higher the layer, the older the rock.
   c. The darker the layer, the older the rock.
   d. The lighter the layer, the older the rock.

2. Which of the following may have caused the formation shown here? Circle all that apply.
   a. **an earthquake**
   b. delta formation
   c. **volcanic activity**
   d. glacier movement
   e. **underground pressure**

3. Choose the word that best completes each sentence.

   | fossils | glaciers | formations | layers |

   Scientists can determine the age of a rock layer by studying the _____fossils_____ found in that layer.

   _____Layers_____ of rock can show how an environment has changed over time.

4. Indicate whether each sentence applies to glaciers (G), or natural bridges (NB).

   __NB__ Gravity forms rock into an arch.

   __G__ Gravity causes huge ice formations.

   __NB__ Loose material inside them erodes away.

   __G__ Downhill movement creates large grooves.

5. Choose from the word bank to complete the sentence.

   | ice | sand | water | wildlife |

   The petrified trees in this desert are evidence that there was once far more ____water____ in the area.

6. Which present-day organism has also been found in fossilized form? Circle the correct choice.

   a. ferns
   b. Irish elk
   c. mosasaurs
   d. giant short-faced bears

7. You find a four legged fossil. In what type of environment did it most likely live? What evidence from the fossil would support your answer.

   Sample answer: The legs of the fossil would indicate that it spent the majority of its time in a terrestrial environment.

---

4. Students are asked to categorize the answer choices. They can be directed back to Lesson 1, Exploration 3 for a quick refresher.

5. Students need to use the image to answer the question correctly. Have them pay close attention to the appearance of the petrified trees.

6. Students should recall learning about ferns in Lesson 2, Exploration 3.

7. Students learn about terrestrial fossils in Lesson 2, Exploration 3. Check responses for rational connections and application of knowledge.

UNIT 7 Review, continued

8. Lesson 2 provides a good general overview for students on fossils, particularly Exploration 2. If students struggle to answer this correctly, encourage them to take time to study the image. Have them identify what kind of shape this is. You may even want to have images of animals ready to show students to have them pick out the one they think is shown in the image. This can help them connect the dots to the correct answer.

9. Students should be able to arrive at the correct answers by reading the sentences aloud to themselves and checking for sense. Have students use the process of elimination based on what does or does not make sense in the sentences. They can review Lessons 2 and 3 on fossils for additional support.

10. Students can answer this question through their collective knowledge gained from Lessons 1, 2, and 3 in this unit.

This fossil was found in rock high in the mountains.

8. What is **most likely** to be true of the region in which this fossil was found?
   a. It was once frozen.
   b. It was once a desert.
   c. It was once a lake.
   d. It was once temperate.

9. Choose the word that best completes each sentence.

   | insects   mammals   fish   snails   ferns |

   Fossils with fins and scales prove that _____fish_____ have existed for millions of years.

   Ammonites are extinct, but their fossils show us that they had shells similar to _____snails_____ .

   | water   air   environment |

10. A large variety of fossils are found in a region's different rock layers. This indicates that the region's _____environment_____ has changed several times.

522

3D Item Analysis	1	2	3	4	5	6	7	8	9	10
SEP Constructing Explanations and Designing Solutions			•				•			•
DCI The History of Planet Earth		•	•	•	•	•	•	•	•	•
CCC Patterns		•	•	•	•	•	•	•		•

522 Unit 7 Rocks and Fossils

UNIT 8 Natural Resources and Hazards

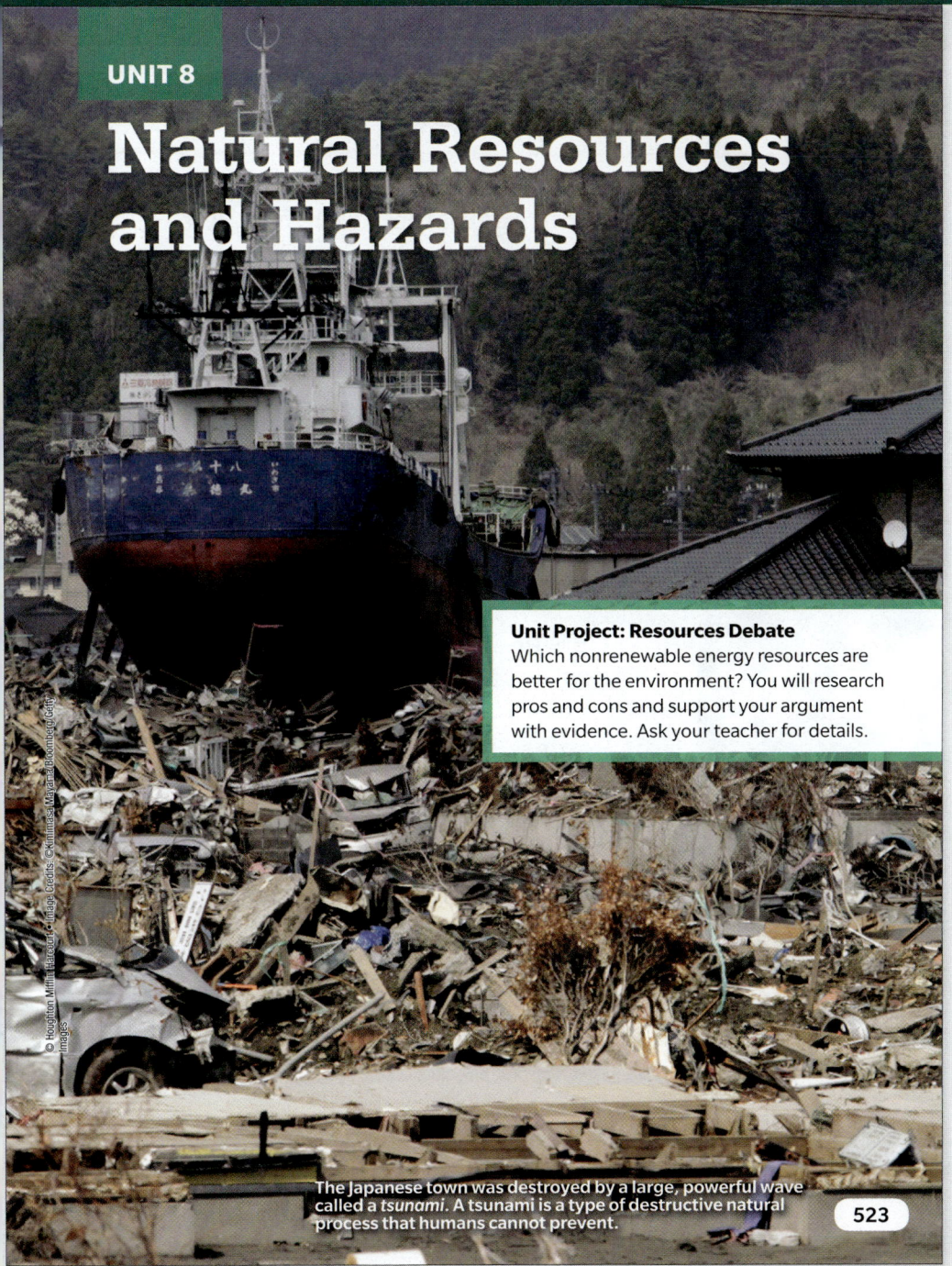

UNIT 8

Natural Resources and Hazards

Unit Project: Resources Debate
Which nonrenewable energy resources are better for the environment? You will research pros and cons and support your argument with evidence. Ask your teacher for details.

The Japanese town was destroyed by a large, powerful wave called a *tsunami*. A tsunami is a type of destructive natural process that humans cannot prevent.

Unit Overview

In this unit, students will . . .
- explore how renewable and nonrenewable resources are used for energy.
- discover how people can reduce land- and water-based hazards and their impacts.

About This Image

A Japanese town by the water was destroyed. A large ship sits in what used to be the middle of the town. Buildings, structures, and cars are in ruins, and people were likely harmed. In the background, a large hill with green trees stands tall. All of this destruction is because of a tsunami, which is a large and powerful wave. Tsunamis can have severe impacts on society as well as the natural environment.

Unit Project

As students work through the unit lessons, have them research, plan, and write down the pros and cons of nonrenewable energy sources. They will need to identify the ones that are better for the environment.

To begin, draw students' attention to the details in the image, or challenge the class to use online or media center resources to identify other examples of natural hazards. More support for the Unit Project can be found on pp. 525K–525N.

Unit 8 Natural Resources and Hazards   523

UNIT 8 Natural Resources and Hazards

The learning experiences in this unit prepare students for the mastery of:

Performance Expectations

4-ESS3-1 Obtain and combine information to describe that energy and fuels are derived from natural resources and their uses affect the environment.

4-ESS3-2 Generate and compare multiple solutions to reduce the impacts of natural Earth processes on humans.

▶ Explore Online

In addition to the print resources, the following resources are available online to support this unit.

Unit Pretest
Lesson 1 What Nonrenewable Resources Are Used for Energy?
- Online Student Edition
- Lesson Quiz

Lesson 2 What Renewable Resources Are Used for Energy?
- Online Student Edition
- Lesson Quiz

Lesson 3 How Can People Reduce the Impact of Land-Based Hazards?
- Online Student Edition
- Lesson Quiz

Lesson 4 How Can People Reduce the Impact of Water-Based Hazards?
- Online Student Edition
- Lesson Quiz

You Solve It Solutions for Natural Hazards
Unit Performance Task
Unit Test

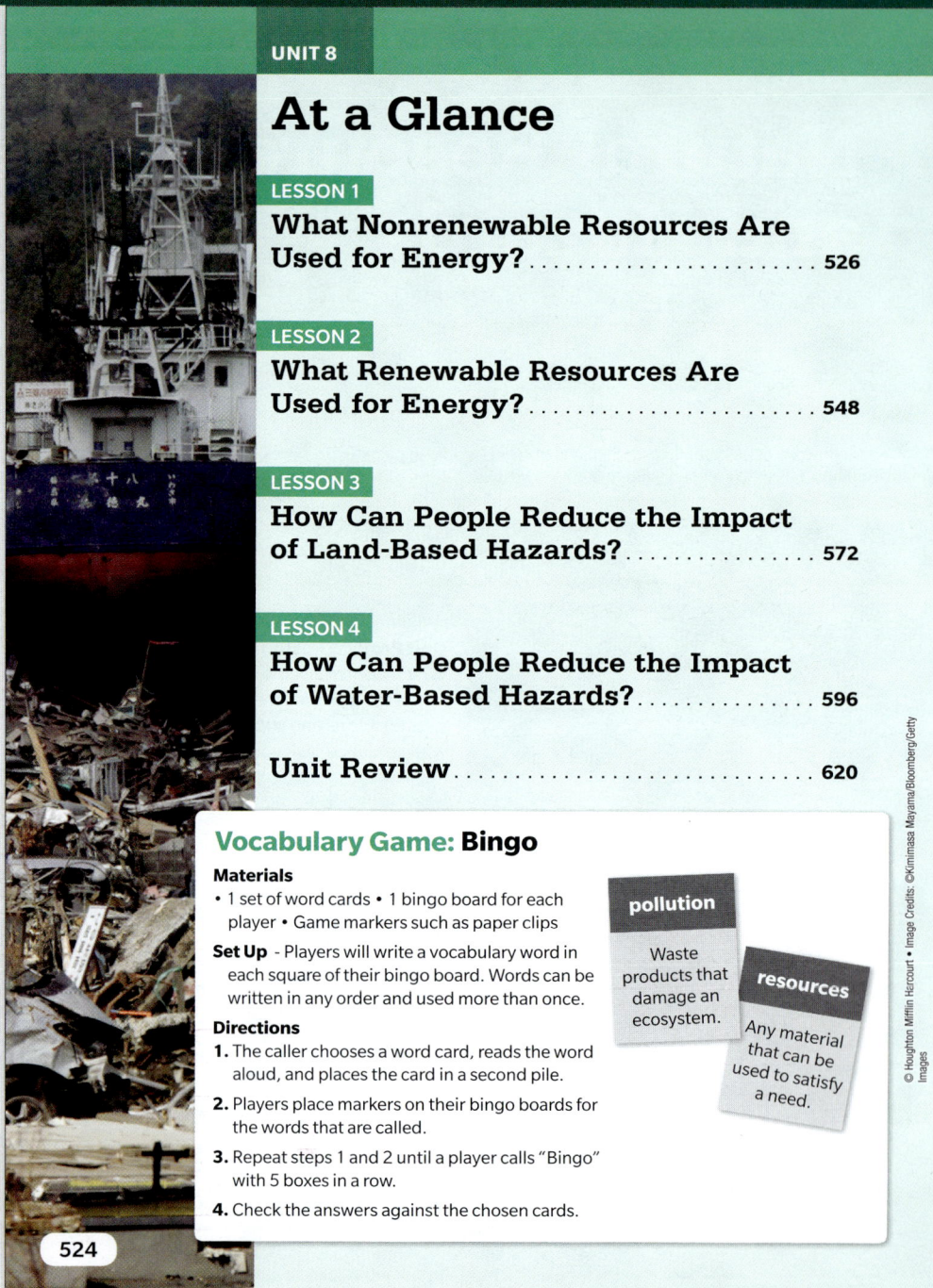

UNIT 8
At a Glance

LESSON 1
What Nonrenewable Resources Are Used for Energy? 526

LESSON 2
What Renewable Resources Are Used for Energy? 548

LESSON 3
How Can People Reduce the Impact of Land-Based Hazards? 572

LESSON 4
How Can People Reduce the Impact of Water-Based Hazards? 596

Unit Review 620

Vocabulary Game: Bingo

Materials
- 1 set of word cards • 1 bingo board for each player • Game markers such as paper clips

Set Up - Players will write a vocabulary word in each square of their bingo board. Words can be written in any order and used more than once.

Directions
1. The caller chooses a word card, reads the word aloud, and places the card in a second pile.
2. Players place markers on their bingo boards for the words that are called.
3. Repeat steps 1 and 2 until a player calls "Bingo" with 5 boxes in a row.
4. Check the answers against the chosen cards.

pollution
Waste products that damage an ecosystem.

resources
Any material that can be used to satisfy a need.

Unit Vocabulary

drawback: A disadvantage or problem.

natural hazard: An earth process that threatens to harm people and property.

natural resource: Materials found in nature that people and other living things use.

nonrenewable resource: A resource that once used cannot be replaced in a reasonable amount of time.

pollution: Waste products that damage an ecosystem.

renewable resource: A resource that can be replaced within a reasonable amount of time.

resource: Any material that can be used to satisfy a need.

Unit Vocabulary

Students can explore all lesson vocabulary terms in the **Online Glossary**.

Vocabulary Strategies

Have students review the terms in pairs and share an example of one term with their partner and tell why they think it's an example.

Differentiate Instruction

RTI/Extra Support Have struggling readers find the vocabulary words within the unit. Have students use context clues to infer definitions and then share with a partner.

Extension Have students pick two terms and then work in small groups to illustrate and explain the terms for a fourth-grade student.

ELL Pronounce each term and have students repeat it. Then pair up students by native language and have them explain each term in their native language. Use realia wherever appropriate.

Vocabulary Game: Bingo

Preparation
Have the Bingo cards and markers prepared ahead of time.

Game Play
- Players put a marker on the word box each time they find it on their bingo boards.
- First player to have markers on the word boxes in a row wins.

UNIT 8 Natural Resources and Hazards
Integrating the NGSS* Three Dimensions of Learning

Building to the Performance Expectations

The learning experiences in this unit prepare students for mastery of the following Performance Expectations:

Earth and Human Activity

4-ESS3-1 Obtain and combine information to describe that energy and fuels are derived from natural resources and their uses affect the environment.

4-ESS3-2 Generate and compare multiple solutions to reduce the impacts of natural Earth processes on humans.

Assessing Student Progress

After completing these lessons, the **Unit Project: Resources Debate** provides students with opportunities to practice aspects of and demonstrate their understanding of the Performance Expectation as they debate which nonrenewable energy sources are better for our environment.

Additionally, students can practice or be assessed on aspects of the Performance Expectations by completing the **Unit Performance Task: Avoiding Disaster**, in which they apply to concepts of weather patterns to analyze the risk of weather-related hazards in the local area.

Lesson 1
What Nonrenewable Resources Are Used for Energy?

In **Lesson 1,** students will obtain, evaluate, and communicate information **(SEP Obtaining, Evaluating, and Communicating)** about nonrenewable resources, protecting and reducing the use of nonrenewable resources **(DCI Natural Resources).** They will learn how people's need and wants change over time as they demand new and better technologies **(CCC Influence of Engineering, Technology, and Science on Society and the Natural World).**

Lesson 2
What Renewable Resources Are Used for Energy?

In **Lesson 2,** students will learn about renewable energy resources **(DCI Natural Resources),** including how we make use of them **(CCC Interdependence of Science, Engineering, and Technology).** They will evaluate the benefits and drawbacks of renewable resources **(SEP Obtaining, Evaluating, and Communicating Information).**

Lesson 3
How Can People Reduce the Impact of Land-Based Hazards?

In **Lesson 3,** students learn about natural hazards that take place on land, such as volcanic eruptions, earthquakes, landslides, and wildfires **(DCI Natural Hazards).** They explore the causes and effects of these events **(CCC Cause and Effect)** and analyze information **(SEP Obtaining, Evaluating, and Communicating Information)** about how maps can be used to assess the risk of natural hazards.

Lesson 4
How Can People Reduce the Impact of Water-Based Hazards?

In **Lesson 4,** students will study a variety of water-based Earth processes **(DCI Natural Hazards)** that can be hazardous to humans and design and test multiple solutions **(SEP Constructing Explanations and Designing Solutions)** to lessen the impacts of these processes on humans **(CCC Influence of Engineering, Technology, and Science on Society and the Natural World)**

*Next Generation Science Standards and logo are registered trademarks of Achieve. Neither Achieve or the lead states and partners that developed the Next Generation Science Standards Were involved in production of, and does not endorse, these products.

NGSS Across the Unit

Explore Online! Online only.

Next Generation Science Standards		Unit Project	Lesson 1	Lesson 2	Lesson 3	Lesson 4	Unit Performance Task	You Solve It!
SEP	Obtaining, Evaluating, and Communicating Information	•	•	•	•		•	
SEP	Constructing Explanations and Designing Solutions				•	•		
SEP	Developing and Using Models				•			
DCI	ESS3.A Natural Resources	•	•	•	•	•	•	
DCI	ETS1.B Developing Possible Solutions				•	•	•	
CCC	Cause and Effect		•	•	•			
CCC	Interdependence of Science, Engineering, and Technology		•	•				
CCC	Influence of Engineering, Technology, and Science on Society and the Natural World	•	•	•	•	•	•	

NGSS Across the Grades

Before
Earth and Human Activity
3-ESS3-1

Grade 4
Earth and Human Activity
4-ESS3-1
4-ESS3-2

After
Earth and Human Activity
5-ESS3-1 Obtain and combine information about ways individual communities use science ideas to protect the Earth's resources and environment
MS-ESS3-1 Construct a scientific explanation based on evidence for how the uneven distributions of Earth's mineral, energy, and groundwater resources are the result of past and current geoscience processes.

Trace Tool to the NGSS™ Go online to view the complete coverage of these standards across this grade level and time.

UNIT 8 Natural Resources and Hazards
3D Unit Planning

Lesson 1 What Nonrenewable Resources Are Used for Energy? pp. 526–547

Overview

Objective To understand that humans use energy and fuels derived from natural resources. Students will rely on books and other media to explain the use and reuse of natural resources as well as gaining the knowledge that human needs change over time.

SEP Obtaining, Evaluating, and Communicating Information
DCI ESS3.A Natural Resources
CCC Cause and Effect
CCC Interdependence of Science, Engineering, and Technology
CCC Influence of Engineering, Technology, and Science on Society and the Natural World

Math and **English Language Arts** standards and features are detailed on lesson planner pages.

	Print and Online Student Editions	Explore Online!
ENGAGE	**Lesson Phenomenon** pp. 526–527 **Can You Explain/Solve It?** What do designers and engineers consider when designing cars that do not run on gasoline?	Can You Explain It? Image
EXPLORE/ EXPLAIN	**Materials We Use** pp. 528–533 Resources Around You Apply What You Know The School's Energy **Search and Find** pp. 534–542 Digging a Little Deeper Apply What You Know Mining Challenge Engineer It! Hybrid Cars HANDS-ON Catch That Dirt	HANDS-ON Worksheet
ELABORATE	**Take It Further** pp. 543–544 Careers in Science & Engineering: Types of "ISTs"	Take It Further What's Around You? Take It Further On a Mining Mission
EVALUATE	**Lesson Check** pp. 545–546 **Lesson Roundup** p. 547	Lesson Quiz

HANDS-ON ACTIVITY PLANNING

Apply What You Know

The School's Energy
- 20 minutes
- Pair

Materials
- computers for Internet access
- print sources on school electricity
- paper and pencil

Preparation/Tip Prepare by making a list of websites to direct students to for their research.

Mining Challenge
- 1 class period
- Pairs

Materials
- 1 spoon, 1 pan
- birdseed
- beads
- sunflower seed

Preparation/Tip Students can mine at the same time if the pan is large enough.

HANDS-ON

Catch That Dirt
- 1 class period
- Pairs

Objective Students will evaluate the air quality around the school.

Materials
- 4 small plastic containers with lids
- petroleum jelly
- plastic spoon
- hand lens

Preparation/Tip Cover the workspace with newspaper to keep the area easy to clean up.

Lesson 2 What Renewable Resources Are Used for Energy? pp. 548–571

Overview

Objective To understand that humans use energy and fuels derived from natural resources. Students will learn about renewable resources and apply what they know about the interdependence of science and technology to evaluate the benefits and drawbacks of renewable resources.

SEP Obtaining, Evaluating, and Communicating Information
DCI **ESS3.A** Natural Resources
CCC Cause and Effect
CCC Interdependence of Science, Engineering, and Technology
CCC Influence of Engineering, Technology, and Science on Society and the Natural World

Math and **English Language Arts** standards and features are detailed on lesson planner pages.

Print and Online Student Editions — Explore Online!

ENGAGE	**Lesson Phenomenon** pp. 548–549 **Can You Explain/Solve It?** What are some forms of energy that power a house?	Can You Explain It! Image
EXPLORE/ EXPLAIN	**Exploring Renewable Resources** pp. 550–553 Use It Again **Engineer It!** Tidal Energy **Renewable Natural Resources** pp. 554–566 Cloudy Days, No Wind, Little Water 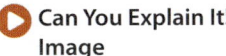 **Apply What You Know** Plastics From Plants **HANDS-ON** Running on Sunshine	HANDS-ON Worksheet
ELABORATE	**Take It Further** pp. 567–568 People in Science & Engineering: Elon Musk	Take It Further Sort It Out Take It Further The Hoover Dam
EVALUATE	**Lesson Check** pp. 569–570 **Lesson Roundup** p. 571	Lesson Quiz

HANDS-ON ACTIVITY PLANNING

Apply What You Know

Plastics From Plants

- 20 minutes
- Pairs

Materials
- zip top plastic bag
- measuring spoons
- 2 drops food coloring
- 2 drops corn oil
- 1 tablespoon cornstarch
- 1 tablespoon water
- microwave oven

Preparation/Tip The materials used in this activity are nontoxic, and edible, but do not allow students to eat or taste the ingredients.

HANDS-ON

Running on Sunshine

- 3 class periods
- Small groups

Objective Students have to stay within a budget to design a solar hot water heater.

Materials
- water container
- scissors
- tape
- thermometer
- timer or watch
- measuring cup

Preparation/Tip Show students how they can reuse the materials from this activity. The materials are available at grocery or convenience stores.

UNIT 8 Natural Resources and Hazards
3D Unit Planning, continued

Lesson 3 How Can People Reduce the Impact of Land-Based Hazards? pp. 572–595

Overview

Objective To describe a variety of Earth processes on land that can be hazardous to humans, and how the impact of these processes can be lessened.

SEP Constructing Explanations and Designing Solutions
SEP Obtaining, Evaluating, and Communicating Information
SEP Developing and Using Models
DCI ESS3.B, ETS1.B
CCC Cause and Effect
CCC Influence of Science, Engineering, and Technology on Society and the Natural World

Math and **English Language Arts** standards and features are detailed on lesson planner pages.

	Print and Online *Student Editions*	Explore Online!
ENGAGE	**Lesson Phenomenon** pp. 572–573 **Can You Explain/Solve It?** How can people reduce the impact of land-based natural hazards?	Can You Explain It! Video
EXPLORE/ EXPLAIN	**Land-Based Natural Hazards** pp. 574–579 Apply What You Know Make Your Own Seismometer **Reducing the Impacts of Land-Based Hazards** pp. 580–590 Apply What You Know Disaster Supply Kit ENGINEER IT! Earthquake Resistant Buildings ENGINEER IT! Reducing Impacts With Technology Apply What You Know Make a Plan HANDS-ON Reduce the Risk	HANDS-ON Worksheet
ELABORATE	**Take It Further** pp. 591–592 Careers in Science and Engineering	Take It Further Hawaii Island Lava Hazard Zone Maps Take It Further Debate About a Volcano Solution
EVALUATE	**Lesson Check** pp. 593–594 **Lesson Roundup** p. 595	Lesson Quiz

HANDS-ON ACTIVITY PLANNING

Apply What You Know

Make Your Own Seismometer
- 1 class period
- Small groups

Materials
- shoebox without lid
- ruler
- pointed-tip scissors
- construction paper
- clear adhesive tape
- two rubber bands
- fine line marker
- yarn or string

Disaster Supply Kit
- 20 minutes
- Individuals

Materials
- drawing paper
- drawing utensils
- paper and pencil

Make a Plan
- 20 minutes
- Small groups

Materials
- paper and pencil
- video/digital camera
- video/digital software
- props

HANDS-ON

Reduce the Risk
- 1 class period
- Pairs

Objective Students will develop a plan to reduce the impact of a landslide.

Materials
- large shallow container (painting tray or bin)
- mixture of soil, sand, gravel, and rocks
- toy cars and milk carton houses
- 1 liter of water
- newspapers
- 1 liter bottle with small holes on the bottom

525E Unit 8 Natural Resources and Hazards

Lesson 4 How Can People Reduce the Impact of Water-Based Hazards? pp. 596–619

Overview

Objective To analyze and describe a variety of water-based processes that can be hazardous to humans and design and test multiple solutions to lessen the impacts of these natural Earth processes on humans.

SEP Constructing Explanations and Designing Solutions
DCI ESS3.B Natural Hazards
DCI ETS1.B Developing Possible Solutions
CCC Influence of Engineering, Technology, and Science on Society and the Natural World

Math and **English Language Arts** standards and features are detailed on lesson planner pages.

	Print and Online *Student Editions*	Explore Online!
ENGAGE	**Lesson Phenomenon** pp. 596–597 **Can You Explain/Solve It?** How can water-based hazards be prevented or reduced by using sandbags?	Can You Explain It! Video
EXPLORE/ EXPLAIN	**Water-Based Natural Hazards** pp. 598–603 Water, Water, Everywhere **Apply What You Know** Take Action	HANDS-ON Worksheet
	Reducing the Impacts of Water-Based Hazards pp. 604–614 Think Ahead! **ENGINEER IT!** Using Technology to Reduce Impacts **ENGINEER IT!** Improving Levees **HANDS-ON** Is It Safe?	
ELABORATE	**Take It Further** pp. 615–616 Hurricanes and Their Effects	Take It Further Careers in Science & Engineering Take It Further Make It Safer
EVALUATE	**Lesson Check** pp. 617–618 **Lesson Roundup** p. 619	Lesson Quiz

HANDS-ON ACTIVITY PLANNING

Apply What You Know

Take Action
- 20 minutes
- Small groups

Materials
- poster board
- name tags
- markers
- notepaper

Preparation/Tip Encourage students to write a script for each of the roles they will play in their group.

HANDS-ON

Is It Safe?
- 1 class period
- Small groups

Materials
- large shallow container (tub or pan)
- water
- stiff, flat piece of cardboard to make waves

Objective Students will develop a design solution to reduce the impact of a tsunami.

Preparation/Tip Come up with a way for students to track their budgets.

Unit 8 Natural Resources and Hazards 525F

UNIT 8 Natural Resources and Hazards
3D Unit Planning, continued

 **You Solve It!** Go online for an additional interactive activity.

Solutions for Natural Hazards

This virtual lab offers practice in support of **PE 4-ESS3.2.**

SEP Constructing Explanations and Designing Solutions
DCI 4-ESS2.A.1 Natural Hazards
CCC Cause and Effect

Use after Unit 8, Lesson 4—How can natural hazards be prevented?

Objectives
1. Students will identify preparation and protection strategies against the hazards of floods.
2. Students develop a workable solution and stay within a budget.

Activity Problem
You will observe an animation of a flood to a town. Your tasks will include:
1. collecting information on the causes and effects of floods
2. identifying preparation solutions that have worked well for floods
3. devising a solution within budget that minimizes the effects of a flood

Interaction Summary
1. Students view an animation of a river running through a town.
2. They observe the changes in the animation and note the time frame of the changes.
3. Students choose different flood damage prevention solutions from a given menu.
4. Solutions are changed and adjusted based on how well they prevent floods and keep within the budget.
5. Photos are taken for evidence.
6. Students use evidence to construct an explanation of the best prevention to use and stay within budget.

Assessment

Pre-Assessment
Assessment Guide, Unit Pretest

The Unit Pretest focuses on prerequisite knowledge and is composed of items that evaluate students' preparedness for the content covered within this unit.

Formative Assessment
Student Edition, Apply What You Know, Lesson Check, and Self Check

Summative Assessment
Assessment Guide, Lesson Quiz
The Lesson Quiz provides a quick assessment of each lesson objective and of the portion of the Performance Expectation aligned to the lesson.

Student Edition, Performance Task pp. 620–621
The Performance Task presents the opportunity for children to collaborate with classmates in order to complete the steps of each Performance Task. Each Performance Task provides a formal Scoring Rubric for evaluating students' work.

Student Edition, Unit 8 Review pp. 622–624

Assessment Guide, Unit Test
The Unit Test provides an in-depth assessment of the Performance Expectations aligned to the unit. This test evaluates students' ability to apply knowledge in order to explain phenomena and to solve problems. Within this test, Constructed Response items apply a three-dimensional rubric for evaluating students' mastery on all three dimensions of the Next Generation Science Standards.

 **Assessment Online** Go online to view the complete assessment items for this unit.

Teacher Notes

UNIT 8 Natural Resources and Hazards
Differentiate Instruction

Leveled Readers

The **Science & Engineering Leveled Readers** provide additional nonfiction reading practice in this unit's subject area.

On-Level Reader • Earth's Changing Surface and Natural Resources
This reader reinforces unit concepts and includes response activities for your students.

Extra Support • Earth's Changing Surface and Natural Resources
This reader shares title, illustrations, vocabulary, and concepts with the On-Level Reader; however, the text is linguistically accommodated to provide simplified sentence structures and comprehension aids. It also includes response activities.

Enrichment • Conserving Earth's Resources
This high-interest, nonfiction reader will extend and enrich unit concepts and vocabulary and includes response activities.

Teacher Guide

The accompanying Teacher Guide provides teaching strategies and support for using all the readers.

ELL

ELL teacher strategies in this unit:
Lesson 1: pp. 531, 532, 538, 541
Lesson 2: pp. 550, 558
Lesson 3: p. 579
Lesson 4: p. 605

RTI/Extra Support

Strategies for students needing extra support in this unit:
Lesson 1: pp. 531, 536, 544, 546
Lesson 2: p. 562
Lesson 3: pp. 576, 584
Lesson 4: pp. 599, 602, 610, 616

Extension

Strategies for students who have mastered core content in this unit:
Lesson 1: pp. 528, 534
Lesson 2: pp. 554, 568
Lesson 3: pp. 574, 588
Lesson 4: pp. 601, 606, 609

 **Leveled Readers** All readers are available online as well as in an innovative, engaging format for use with touchscreen mobile devices. Contact your HMH Sales Representative for more information.

UNIT 8 Natural Resources and Hazards
Making Connections

Connections to the Community

Use these opportunities for informal science learning to provide local context and to extend and enhance unit concepts.

At Home

ELECTRIC METER Describe to students what an electric meter is and how it records a home's electrical usage. Have students work with an adult family member to read their electric meter each day for a week and make a table showing the days, meter readout, and total usage for each day and for the week. *Use with Lesson 1.*

ENERGY SOURCES Have students work with an adult family member to research online the types of generating stations that supply their local electric company. Have them find the percentages of various types of energy sources, such as nuclear, gas, hydro, and coal, the company uses. Then have students make a circle graph showing the percentages. *Use with Lesson 1 or Lesson 2.*

In the Community

LEARN ABOUT LOCAL HAZARDS Arrange for an emergency management professional to visit the class and talk about local land and water hazards. Before the presentation, have each student write two or three questions they have about the topic. Provide an opportunity for students to ask the professional their questions. *Use with Lesson 3 or Lesson 4.*

HAZARD PREPARATION Identify one or more land or water hazards in your community, and lead students in discussing it and the types of preparations people might make for it. Have students work with a responsible adult to survey people in their neighborhood to see if they know about the problem and make reasonable preparations for it. Have students present their results to the class. *Use with Lesson 3 or Lesson 4.*

Home Letters Use these one-page letters to engage family members with unit concepts.

Collaboration

Opportunities for students to work collaboratively in this unit:

Build on Prior Knowledge
pp. 530, 549, 562, 576, 602

Share Feedback
pp. 527, 589, 611

Discussion
pp. 569, 604, 608

Think, Pair, Share
pp. 530, 535, 536, 597

Draw, Pair, Share
p. 573

Write, Pair, Share
p. 607

Jigsaw
p. 603

Connections to Science

Opportunities to connect to other content areas in this unit:

Connection to Physical Science
Lesson 1, p. 539

Lesson 2, pp. 550, 558

Connection to Life Science
Lesson 3, p. 585

Lesson 4, p. 600

Connection to Earth and Space Sciences
Lesson 2, p. 557

UNIT 8 Natural Resources and Hazards
Unit Project

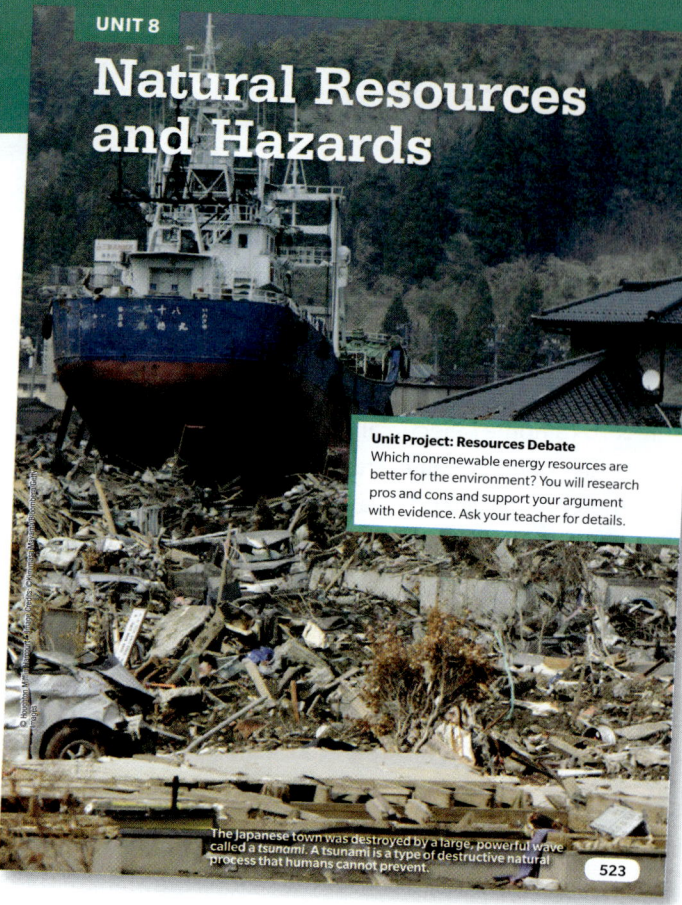

Unit Project: Resources Debate   👥 Small groups   ⏱ 3 class periods

For this task, small groups of students will work together to come up with a presentation that they will use in a classroom debate. Students will debate which nonrenewable energy resources are better for the environment. Make sure students are familiar with the types of renewable and nonrenewable resources.

3D Learning Objective

- Explore nonrenewable energy resources
- Collect and analyze data
- Analyze data to reveal the pros and cons of nonrenewable energy resources

Skills and Standards Focus

This project supports building student mastery of **Performance Expectation 4-ESS3-1.**

SEP Obtaining, Evaluating, and Communicating Information
DCI ESS3.A Natural Resources
CCC Influence of Engineering, Technology, and Science on Society and the Natural World

Suggested Materials

- writing utensils
- writing paper
- poster board
- drawing utensils
- print and/or online reference materials

Preparation and Planning Tips

Ensure that each group has a set of print resources or a list of URLs for websites you have previously reviewed. Make sure students understand that there are three parts of this project: (1) writing a speech for their debate; (2) creating visual aids to support their speeches; and (3) participating in a debate.

Differentiate Instruction

ELL/ELD Students who are learning English may not feel comfortable participating in the debate. Pair students into small teams of mixed ability. Recommend that different people in the team be responsible for different parts. For example, the English language learner may be comfortable putting together the visual aids, while another student recites the speech and participates in the debate.

Extension Have students research real debates that have happened in the legal system over the use of nonrenewable energy sources. Instruct students to cite these in their speeches, visual aids, and debates as evidence to support their claims.

Name _____

UNIT PROJECT
Resources Debate

Are all resources the same? Are all nonrenewable resources bad for society and the environment? For this project, you will prepare a speech and visual aids to use in a classroom debate to argue that one kind of nonrenewable energy source is better than other kinds.

Think about the kinds of nonrenewable and renewable energy sources you use on a daily basis. Write a question that you will investigate as you write your speech and develop your presentation for the debate.

Students should write a question concerning the points for why a nonrenewable energy source may have its benefits.

_____

Materials

Think about how you will put your speech and visual aids together. What materials will you need?

Materials can include writing utensils, paper, drawing utensils, poster board, and online/print resources.

_____

_____

Think about how you will organize your speech. Develop an outline that includes the important points you wish to discuss. Then, come up with the visual aids to support those arguments. It can help to map this out ahead of time.

Fossil fuels are cheaper – use a graph that shows the cost of fossil fuels compared to other sources

Fossil fuels are more available – use a map that shows how many countries have access to fossil fuels compared to other sources

525

UNIT 8 PROJECT
Resources Debate

Influence of Engineering, Technology, and Science on Society and the Natural World

Before students begin, check their understanding of key underlying concepts.

Ask: What are some ways that nonrenewable energy sources are bad for people and the environment? **They can cause pollution; they can damage the ozone.**

Ask: What are some ways that nonrenewable energy sources are good for people and the environment? **Some are readily available and cheap, meaning more people have access to them.**

Refer students to Lesson 1, Exploration 1 for concept support.

ESSENTIAL QUESTIONS Ask the following questions before students begin to plan their activity.

- What are some of the advantages of nonrenewable energy sources?
- What are some of the disadvantages of nonrenewable energy sources?

If too many teams are using the same source, then it will not make for an effective or lively debate. Encourage students to try to use different nonrenewable energy sources.

DCI ESS3.A Natural Resources

Students may not think that nonrenewable energy sources can have advantages. Remind students that nonrenewable energy sources have different kinds of advantages than renewable sources.

Ask: How are the advantages of nonrenewable sources different than renewable sources? **They focus more on convenience than on what's good for the environment.**

Research and Plan

Students should carefully consider the advantages of the nonrenewable energy source they selected.

Ask: What are some things you will include in your debate? **We will focus on convincing the audience that nonrenewable energy sources are plentiful and easy to get. (Answers will vary based on students' plans.)**

Students will need to research data and facts to use for their debates. Be prepared to provide students with resources they can use for print and electronic sources.

Brainstorm

Students should brainstorm and share ideas for components of the visual aids and debate speeches. Have groups develop an outline of what they want to discuss, and use that logical order for developing their speeches.

Ask: What makes an effective speech? **one that gets the audience engaged; one that uses facts and data as evidence**

Debate

During the final class period, when students are finished with their speeches and visual aid presentations, have the class participate in a debate. Give each team a chance to present their nonrenewable energy source to the rest of the class and make sure the debate stays friendly and respectful.

Research and Plan

Make a plan for the research you will need to do. As you write your speech, consider the following points:

- Can your claims be supported by facts and data?
- Can you show those facts and data graphically or on your visual aids?
- What might your opponent say during the debate? How can you prepare yourself for what the opponent might say?

For each claim students make, they should support their statements with as much data as possible. Students can have more than one visual aid if it will help them make stronger points. Students should not just focus on the advantages of the energy source; they should also understand the disadvantages, as their opponent will likely focus on the disadvantages in order to prove their opposing claim. Part of being prepared for a debate means understanding what other people can say negatively about the claim.

Rehearse the speech using visual aids. Describe any modifications you would make.

Students should explain whether or not they will modify their speeches and visual aids.

Analyze Your Results

Analyze your speech by focusing on how many of your claims are supported by facts and examples.

Students should explain that the more facts and examples they have, the better their speeches are.

Restate Your Question

Write the question you investigated.

Students should identify the question created at the beginning of the project.

Claims, Evidence, and Reasoning

Make a claim that answers your question.

Answers will vary depending on the selected nonrenewable energy source. Possible answer: Students can provide a percentage of other form of data as to the usage of their energy source.

Review your plan. What evidence from your plan supports your claim?

Students should cite evidence from their plans to support their claims.

Discuss your reasoning with a partner.

Analyze Your Results

SEP Analyzing and Interpreting Data

Students should consider the following questions as they interpret their data: Does the speech describe why this is the best nonrenewable energy source? Does the visual aid support the claims of the speech?

SEP Engaging in Argument from Evidence

Review with students what it means to make a claim. Guide them to understand that they will be making and presenting their claims during their debate.

Claims, Evidence, and Reasoning

Students should claim that their selected nonrenewable energy source is the best, as far as nonrenewable energy sources go.

Ask: What claim can you make? Answers will vary: People have more access to this energy source, and it is cheaper.

Ask: How does your evidence support your claim? We have data and facts that show how widely used the energy source is.

Encourage students to discuss their reasoning.

Scoring Rubric for Hands-On Activity	
3	States a claim supported with detailed evidence; participates in a debate discussion and uses visual aids to support claim.
2	States a claim that is somewhat supported with evidence; somewhat participates in a debate discussion and uses visual aids to support claim.
1	States a claim that is not supported by evidence; does not adequately participate in a debate discussion; presentation is incomplete.
0	Does not state a claim; does not participate in the debate; presentation is incomplete.

LESSON 1
What Nonrenewable Resources Are Used for Energy?

Building to the Performance Expectations

The learning experiences in this lesson prepare students for mastery of:

4-ESS3-1 Obtain and combine information to describe that energy and fuels are derived from natural resources and their uses affect the environment.

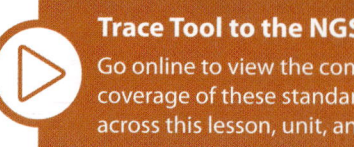
Trace Tool to the NGSS
Go online to view the complete coverage of these standards across this lesson, unit, and time.

 Science & Engineering Practices (SEP)

 Disciplinary Core Ideas (DCI)

 **Crosscutting Concepts** (CCC)

Obtaining, Evaluating, and Communicating Information
Obtain and combine information from books and/or other reliable media to explain phenomena or solutions to a design problem.

 VIDEO Obtaining, Evaluating, and Communicating Information

ESS3.A Natural Resources
Energy and fuels that humans use are derived from natural sources, and their use affects the environment in multiple ways. Some resources are renewable over time, and others are not. (4-ESS3-1)

Cause and Effect
Cause-and-effect relationships are routinely identified, and used to explain change.

Interdependence of Science, Engineering, and Technology
Knowledge of relevant scientific concepts and research findings is important in engineering.

Influence of Engineering, Technology, and Science on Society and the Natural World
People's needs and wants change, as do their demands for new and improved technologies.

 CONNECTIONS TO MATH

MP.2 Reason abstractly and quantitatively.
MP.4 Model with mathematics.

 CONNECTIONS TO ENGLISH LANGUAGE ARTS

RI.3.9 Compare and contrast the most important points and key details presented in two texts on the same topic.

W.4.8 Recall relevant information from experiences or gather relevant information from print and digital sources; take notes and categorize information, and provide a list of sources.

Supporting All Students, All Standards

Integrating the Three Dimensions of Learning

Obtain, evaluate, and communicate information **(SEP Obtaining, Evaluating, and Communicating)** about protecting and reducing the use of nonrenewable resources and coming up with alternative resources that are renewable **(DCI ESS3.A)**. Understand the causes and effects **(CCC Cause and Effect)** of human use when mining nonrenewable resources, recognizing the pros and cons **(CCC Interdependence of Science, Engineering, and Technology)** and understanding how over time people's needs and wants change as they demand new and better technologies **(CCC Influence of Engineering, Technology, and Science on Society and the Natural World)**.

 **Professional Development** — Go online to view **Professional Development videos** with strategies to integrate CCCs and SEPs, including the ones used in this lesson.

Extra Hands-On Activity: Personal Energy Sources

What sources of energy did you use today?

 Pairs
30-40 minutes

Have students make a list of all of the different types of energy they used today. For example, they may have used electric lights, a battery operated cell phone, gas stove, microwave, gas powered bus, stop lights, air conditioner, heater, and so on. Encourage them to list at least 10 different types of energy.

Have them attempt to identify the source for each type of energy they listed by asking them to think about where the energy for things such as lights, or heat came from. Then have them choose one type of energy and draw a diagram of its sources. Have them write if they think that type of energy harms the environment or not. Revisit this activity at the end of the lesson to have students re-evaluate their assumptions.

 This activity can support mastery of this Crosscutting Concept: Influence of Engineering, Technology, and Sceince on Society and the Natural World

Preassessment

Have students complete the unit pre-test online or see the Assessment Guide.

Build on Prior Knowledge

Students should already know and be prepared to build on the following concepts:
- Living things live in places where they can get what they need.
- Humans use natural resources for everything they do.
- The energy and fuels humans use are derived from natural resources.

Differentiate Instruction

Lesson Vocabulary
- drawback
- natural resource
- nonrenewable resource
- pollution
- resource

Before students begin the lesson, review the definitions of **resource** and **natural resources**. Have students identify examples of each so you know they understand the difference.

ELL: Use Realia
Point out cognates of key terms from students' home languages, for example, *resource/rescurso, natural resource/rescurso natural,* to help bridge understanding of pertinent lesson vocabulary. Pronounce each word, and spotlight the similarities. Ask other students to share the same words in their home languages.

LESSON 1 **Engage** • Explore/Explain • Elaborate • Evaluate

ENGAGE: Lesson Phenomenon

Lesson Objective
Understand that humans use energy and fuels derived from natural resources. Rely on books and other media to explain the use and reuse of natural resources as well as gain the knowledge that human needs change over time.

About This Image
An oil rig is equipped to drill and service an oil well. A well provides access to an oil "field" that is underground or beneath the ocean floor. The oil that is removed from the ground can be sent through a pipeline or transferred to ships.

 Planning and Carrying Out Investigations

Alternative Engage Strategy

| **All That Plastic** | 👥 Small group or whole class
⏱ 10 min |

Ask students to think about all the ways you can use plastic. Ask students if they know what plastic is made from. Ask students if plastic can be easily replaced or if it is limited? Give them two minutes to list all the plastic items they can see right now. Have students work in small groups to think of ways to conserve plastic. Are there any materials other than plastic that can be used more than once or many times? Ask students to share their ideas with the class.

LESSON 1

What Nonrenewable Resources Are Used for Energy?

Oil is buried deep within Earth's surface. In order to remove it, big drills have to dig down into the ground, or even into the ocean floor. Many cars use oil and gasoline, as fuel. Look at the image to learn more.

By the end of this lesson . . .
you'll be able to describe nonrenewable resources and explain the effects of using them.

526

Unit 8 Natural Resources and Hazards

Can You Explain It?

The look of cars has changed a lot over time. The way cars run is also starting to change. Many of the first cars were fueled by gasoline, and many of today's cars still are.

1. The cars in these photos differ. What factors do you think car designers consider when designing a car that doesn't run on gasoline? What might be a problem of designing such a car?

   Students should answer based on the preliminary observations they can
   make of the images.
   _____
   _____

EVIDENCE NOTEBOOK Look for this icon to help you gather evidence to answer the questions above.

527

Explore Online Students can view the lesson phenomenon online.

Can You Explain It?

Students are asked to look at cars and to observe how they have changed over the years. Have a class discussion on the cars in the photographs. Have children tell you whether they have ever heard of or ridden in a hybrid car.

Ask: What are all the ways you know that cars can run? List ways people can travel without using up nonrenewable resources? Answers may vary. Point out that their ideas might change throughout the lesson. Explain that they will have another opportunity to answer the same questions at the end of the lesson.

CCC Cause and Effect

Explain to students that nonrenewable resources cannot be easily replaced. Tell them that most would take millions of years to replace.
Ask: What will happen if we use up all the oil? What will scientists and engineers have to do? Many technologies that rely on petroleum would need to be re-engineered to use alternative energy sources.

Collaboration

Share Feedback In teams, have students think about what they know about the use of oil. List on the board the following items that use oil: gasoline, plastic water bottles, plastic grocery bags, shower curtains, bandages. Have a discussion with them about how we can use fewer of these items or even eliminate them altogether. Allow volunteers to share replacement items they can use instead of the ones listed.

EVIDENCE NOTEBOOK

Encourage students to use an appropriate graphic organizer, such as main idea and supporting details, to set up their notebook for this lesson.
Find more strategies in the online ELA handbook.

Lesson 1 What Nonrenewable Resources Are Used For Energy? **527**

LESSON 1   Engage • **Explore/Explain** • Elaborate • Evaluate

EXPLORATION 1 Materials We Use

3D Learning Objective

Evaluate information about resources. Recognize that **some resources are renewable and others are not**. Analyze how **people's wants and needs change** due to the environment and other circumstances.

SEP Obtaining, Evaluating, and Communicating Information

After students have evaluated the illustration on the page and the descriptions, discuss the following questions.

Ask: Are there items shown on this page that you see at home or in other places? *Possible answer: Yes, I see water bottles and garbage bins at home.*

Ask: Can you list five resources you use at home? *garbage bins, food containers, picture frames, toys, computer*

Differentiate Instruction

Extension Have pairs of students use reliable webpages or books and magazines to come up with alternative materials to use for the items on the page that would be less harmful to the environment and use up less space in our landfills. Provide students with index cards. Have them list the item from the page on one side and then the alternative materials on the other side. Encourage them to find alternatives for at least three items.

EXPLORATION 1

Materials We Use

Resources Around You

A **resource** is anything that helps you live. Your house is a resource because it gives you shelter. The clothes you wear are a resource because they help keep you warm. A **natural resource** is a material from nature that people can use. Water, air, trees, wind, fossil fuels, and sunlight are examples of natural resources.

Match the text to the picture above by writing in the correct letter in each circle.

a. The water you drink comes from a river, a lake, or an underground well.

b. The part of the pencil that writes is made of graphite, a mineral.

c. Most paper is made from the mashed up wood of trees.

d. Metals are found in Earth's rocky layers.

e. Cotton is often used to make curtains. Cotton comes from a plant.

f. Plastic is made from petroleum. Petroleum is also known as crude oil, a fossil fuel.

2. Explain how three different items you see in your classroom are made from materials found in nature.

Possible answer: Bulletin board is made of cork, a plant. Wallboard is made of plaster, which comes from rocks and minerals. Metal chair legs are stainless steel, which comes from different metals.

528

528   Unit 8 Natural Resources and Hazards

Limited Supply

A <mark>nonrenewable resource</mark> is a resource that, once used, cannot be replaced in a reasonable amount of time. Fossil fuels, such as crude oil, coal, and natural gas, are nonrenewable resources. They are nonrenewable because they take hundreds of millions of years to form.

Use It, You Lose It

Crude oil is the remains of ancient organisms that were buried under mud. Oil fuels vehicles. It is an ingredient of many products, like plastics.

Coal is the buried remains of huge plants that died millions of years ago. Burning coal generates electrical energy.

Natural gas is the remains of ancient plants and tiny sea animals. Less harmful to the air than crude oil, it is used for heat and as a fuel source for buses

Uranium is a natural element not from plants but found in rocks formed billions of years ago. Uranium is used to develop nuclear energy.

3. How do these nonrenewable resources help people in their daily lives?

Possible answer: Crude oil and natural gas provide heat and fuel for vehicles. Plastic materials are also made from petroleum, also known as crude oil.

Language SmArts
Compare and Contrast

4. How are crude oil, coal, and natural gas different from uranium?

Crude oil, coal, and natural gas all come from once living material. Uranium is the only one of the four that does not come from once living material.

529

DCI ESS3.A Natural Resources

Natural resources are found in nature. Some, such as water and lumber, renew after relatively short periods of time, but others, such as oil and gas, take many years to renew. They are called *nonrenewable*.

Ask: Read about the nonrenewable resources. Do you use any of these in your home? Possible answer: Yes, we use natural gas.

Ask: How? Possible answer: Natural gas is used in our stove and oven, as well as the furnace and hot water heater.

CCC Cause and Effect

Point out to students that the world is running out of some of these nonrenewable resources. Gasoline, made from oil, is one example.

Ask: Can you think of a way that we can all use less gasoline? Students may suggest riding on buses or trains, carpooling, walking more, or riding a bicycle.

Language SmArts
Compare and Contrast
RI.3.9 Compare and Contrast

Check to be sure the students have read the captions carefully and that they know what nonrenewable resources are.

Ask: How are coal, oil, and natural gas alike and different? They all come from the remains of organisms that died long ago, but they are found in different states: oil is a liquid, natural gas is gaseous, and coal is a solid.

Lesson 1 What Nonrenewable Resources Are Used For Energy? 529

LESSON 1   Engage • **Explore/Explain** • Elaborate • Evaluate

EXPLORATION 1 Materials We Use, continued

Build on Prior Knowledge

With students, think of ways they have conserved natural resources.

Ask: Did you ever cut back on using things such as electricity or water? **Possible answer: Yes, we turned off house lights not in use.**

Collaboration

Think, Pair, Share Have students look at the photographs and read the captions. Give them time to think about the kinds of materials used to process the nonrenewable resources. Have them discuss with a partner some ways they have tried to reduce their use of nonrenewable resources.

Ask: How can you reduce coal and gasoline use? **Possible answer: Use solar energy as a source of electricity; rely less on automobiles and more on walking or bicycling.**

HANDS-ON Apply What You Know
The School's Energy

Materials

computers for research, energy source pamphlets, poster board, markers

Remind students that the school may use a different energy source than their homes. In school, there are more rooms, a bigger kitchen, and more people to serve and keep comfortable. Many schools were built over 40 years ago, when energy supplies were different and there was less interest in renewables.

Ask: Do you think our school is using the most effective source of energy? Why or why not? **Possible answer: No, because it uses oil, a nonrenewable resource instead of a renewable resource.**

Scoring Guideline

Exemplary activity results and posters identify and describe the school's energy generating station.

530   Unit 8 Natural Resources and Hazards

Collecting and Processing

Each picture shows an example how nonrenewable energy sources are collected or processed. Fossil fuels such as crude oil, coal, and natural gas are first removed from Earth's crust. Then they can be used by electricity generating plants to provide electricity to homes and businesses.

It took millions of years for fossil fuels to form. Once these nonrenewable energy sources are used up, it will take millions of years for a new supply to form. To make sure people have enough energy for current and future needs, efforts have been made to conserve fossil fuels and use them wisely. The effects of carbon dioxide emissions are another reason why these efforts have been made.

Coal, which is mined from deposits in layers of rocks, is taken to electricity generating plants to be burned and converted to electrical energy. Some early trains and ships ran on coal.

Uranium is mined from rocks and is used to create large amounts of energy, which is then provided to homes and businesses for heat and electricity.

Gasoline used as fuel in vehicles comes from crude oil, which is drilled from underground wells, including wells that are under water. Crude oil is used to make paints and plastics.

Natural gas is extracted from rock formations deep underground and then transported by pipeline for use in electricity generation.

 HANDS-ON Apply What You Know

The Schools Energy

5. Do research to find out about the energy generating station that supplies electricity to your school. How does it generate electricity? Make a poster about your findings. Compare your findings with your classmates.

530

What Do They Use?

6. Draw lines to connect the nonrenewable resources with the facilities that use them.

7. Choose between natural gas or coal. Describe how this energy source is used in your daily life?

Anno: The nonrenewable energy source I chose is natural gas. I have seen people cook on natural gas stoves.

 EVIDENCE NOTEBOOK What kinds of vehicles can you think of that do not run using one of these nonrenewable sources of energy? List your ideas in your Evidence Notebook.

531

Differentiate Instruction

ELL: RTI/Extra Support Some students may have difficulty identifying the objects on the pages. Go over each photograph with students so they understand what each shows. Encourage students to think about things from their home country that are similar to those shown.

SEP Obtaining and Evaluating Information

As students begin to answer item 5, have them look back at the previous pages to help them match the objects correctly.

Ask: Where have you ever seen the objects on the left and right? Students may have seen objects on the right but not on the left.

Misconception Alert Students may think that renewable energy sources such as solar and wind power work all the time. Yet solar power only works when the sun is shining, and wind power only works when the wind is blowing. However, this doesn't mean that the electricity will go out if the sun isn't shining or there isn't any wind. There is a backup.

Ask: What is one drawback of solar and wind energy? They do not work all the time.

CCC Interdependence of Science, Engineering, and Technology

Discuss the role of science, engineering, and technology in converting energy resources to energy we can use.

Ask: What must happen in a power plant to produce electricity in your home? Fuel like coal must be burned and then converted to electrical energy, which is transmitted through wires.

EVIDENCE NOTEBOOK

Remind students to think of all vehicles that they can operate using their own muscles or that can be operated by wind or solar energy.

Lesson 1 What Nonrenewable Resources Are Used For Energy? **531**

LESSON 1   Engage • **Explore/Explain** • Elaborate • Evaluate

EXPLORATION 1   Materials We Use, continued

Do the Math
Calculate Energy Units

MP.2 Reason abstractly and quantitatively

MP.4 Model with mathematics

Students should be able to make sense of the information in the graph.

Students should understand the connection between Btu and population size. They should also note that while at first when the population went up, so did the nonrenewable energy use. But eventually the nonrenewable energy use went down and the renewable energy use went up even as the population continued to increase.

Ask: What operations should you use when comparing one year in the graph to another year? subtraction

ccc Cause and Effect

Between 1990 and 1995, all of the energy used in the United States went up by at least 1 quadrillion BTU, with natural gas use alone going up 3 quadrillion BTU. Look at the population in both years.

Ask: Did the population increase or decrease? increase

Ask: How did a population increase cause the energy use to increase? There were more people, so they need more energy.

Differentiate Instruction

ELL: Use Primary Languages Make language connections by pointing out the similarities in the words *population* (English), *populasyon* (Tagalog), and *población* (Spanish). You can also introduce the term *gasoline* (English), or *gasolina* (Spanish and Tagalog).

Do the Math
Calculate Energy Units

7. Do you think energy usage changed in the United States in the 20 years between 1990 and 2010? Use the timeline below and find out.

The amount of energy used is expressed in Btu. Btu stands for British Thermal Unit. Amounts of energy can be measured in Btu. A quadrillion is a huge number. It is 1 followed by 15 zeros. An 100 square meter home needs around 24,000 BTUs to heat in winter.

1995
U.S. population = 261 million
Petroleum use = 35 quadrillion Btu
Natural gas use = 23 quadrillion Btu
Coal use = 20 quadrillion Btu
Nuclear energy use = 7 quadrillion Btu
Other renewable energy use = 2 quadrillion Btu

2005
U.S. population = 296 million
Petroleum use = 40 quadrillion Btu
Natural gas use = 23 quadrillion Btu
Coal use = 23 quadrillion Btu
Nuclear energy use = 8 quadrillion Btu
Other renewable energy use = 2 quadrillion Btu

1990
U.S. population = 249 million
Petroleum use = 34 quadrillion Btu
Natural gas use = 20 quadrillion Btu
Coal use = 19 quadrillion Btu
Nuclear energy use = 6 quadrillion Btu
Other renewable energy use = 1 quadrillion Btu

2000
U.S. population = 281 million
Petroleum use = 38 quadrillion Btu
Natural gas use = 24 quadrillion Btu
Coal use = 22 quadrillion Btu
Nuclear energy use = 5 quadrillion Btu
Other renewable energy use = 2 quadrillion Btu

2010
U.S. population = 309 million
Petroleum use = 36 quadrillion Btu
Natural gas use = 24 quadrillion Btu
Coal use = 21 quadrillion Btu
Nuclear energy use = 8 quadrillion Btu
Other renewable energy use = 4 quadrillion Btu

532

Unit 8 Natural Resources and Hazards

8. Choose one of the resources from the timeline and graph how its use changed over time.

Students should draw a bar graph for the data set of one type of energy resources.

Units of Resources Used

Year

9. Does the data in the timeline support the statements below? If it does, circle *true*. If it doesn't, circle *false*.

   Coal use in the United States decreased about 2 quadrillion Btu between 2005 and 2010.
   (true)   false

   Renewable energy use increased steadily between 1990 and 2010.
   (true)   false

Putting it Together

10. Write the word or phrase that correctly completes each sentence.

| fossil fuels | nonrenewable | electricity generating plants |
| resources | renewable | generators |

All living things need __resources__ in order to live. Some of these exist naturally all around us and are called natural resources. Some natural resources are considered __nonrenewable__ because they cannot be replaced in a reasonable amount of time. Examples of nonrenewable resources include __fossil fuels__, such as coal, crude oil, and natural gas

533

Collaboration

Partners Model for students how to create a graph using one energy source from the timeline. Then place students in pairs, and have them create their own graphs using alternate energy resources from the timeline. Be sure they have enough graph paper to complete the activity. When they are done, have them share their graphs with the class.

SEP Obtaining and Evaluating Information

Have the students evaluate the timeline before answering item 8.

Ask: How much coal was used in the United States in 2005? 23 quadrillion BTU

Ask: How much coal was used in the United States in 2010? 21 quadrillion BTU

Ask: What was the difference between coal use in 2005 and in 2010? 2 quadrillion BTU less

Use the same technique to help students answer item 9.

FORMATIVE ASSESSMENT
Putting it Together

Review all the words in the box with students before they fill in the answers to item 10. Remind them that they may look back in Exploration 1 for help with the words and where they belong in the sentences.

Ask: What are some fossil fuels? coal, oil, and natural gas

Ask: What do we call resources that cannot be replaced easily? nonrenewable

LESSON 1   Engage • **Explore/Explain** • Elaborate • Evaluate

EXPLORATION 2 Search and Find

3D Learning Objective

After learning about nonrenewable resources, evaluate the pros and cons of using them by studying causes and effects of using nonrenewable resources.

Cause and Effect

Many years ago, mining nonrenewable resources was easier because the resources were closer to the ground. Today big drills that dig deeper into Earth are needed to reach the resources.

Ask: What do you think could be a danger for the men and women who work in mines today? **Being deep underground can lead to collapses and expose them to other dangers.**

To avoid disasters in mines, many safety measures are in place. A miner wears a belt that allows him or her to carry a battery pack, a self-rescuer, and other supplies. It also come with a reflective strip so the miner can be highly visible. Protective head gear is another safety device.

Ask: Try to think of ways the safety measures have helped save lives in case of a disaster. Why does a reflective strip help the miners? **They can be seen from farther away or in dimmer light.**

Point out that in addition to personal equipment, mines have equipment and supplies to benefit everyone, such as ventilation fans. When working deep in the earth, air can become sparse, so fans are brought in to provide fresh air.

Differentiate Instruction

Extension Have students research other safety measures used in mining. Have them make a drawing of a typical mine showing at least five safety measures.

EXPLORATION 2

Search and Find

Digging a Little Deeper

Nonrenewable resources are being used at a much faster rate than they can be replenished, or replaced. Today, there is more demand for coal and crude oil than there was before. Due to crude oil being used up, big drills called oil rigs dig deeper into the ground to find crude oil. People now need to dig deep or strip away the surface of the earth to reach coal.

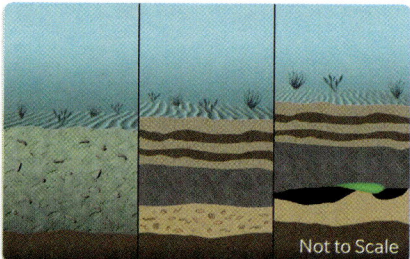

Crude oil and natural gas were formed from small sea animals that died million years ago. Pressure and heat from rock layers above the buried sea animals formed crude oil.

Today, mechanical drills dig deep into Earth's rock layers to remove crude oil and natural gas. Both are used to generate electricity and as fuel sources.

Coal formed from plants that died millions of years ago. Over time, the plants were squeezed and heated by the layers of rock pushing down from above.

Today, surface and underground mines are used to remove the coal. Once removed, coal is burned to provide heat and electricity.

Uranium is an element found in certain rocks and rock layers. It is removed by strip-mining from the surface of the earth or by deep underground mining.

It can also be removed from rocks by leaching, fusing water and chemicals to release it from underground. Nuclear-fueled plants use uranium to make electricity.

534

534   Unit 8   Natural Resources and Hazards

Before the 20th century, people relied mainly on wood and some coal for heating and cooking. Burning coal started the industrial age with the development of steam engines that fueled trains and other machines and electricity generating plants. Cars and other engines increased the use of crude oil as a source of energy. As technology improved, people found ways to mine and use natural gas and nuclear energy.

How to Get It

11. Identify how each type of nonrenewable resource is mined. Write the letters on the lines. Some lines will contain more than one letter.

a, b

c

c

a, b, d

a. underground mines
b. surface mines
c. drilling
d. leaching

Language SmArts
Summarize

12. What do the methods of extracting these fuels all have in common?

They all require digging into Earth's surface in some way.

Tip
The English Language Arts Handbook can provide help with understanding how to summarize.

535

SEP Obtaining and Evaluating Information

Students will need to review the previous pages to properly identify each type of fuel. Remind them that they can have more than one letter and that letters may be used more than once.

DCI ESS3.A Natural Resources

Natural gas isn't the only natural resource used to generate electricity.

Ask: Think about other natural resources you have learned about. Which might be used to generate electricity? **Possible answer: wind**

Collaboration

Think, Pair, Share Give students two or three minutes for a quick partner discussion to review the answers they chose for item 11 and why they made the choices they did. In order to make connections, ask them to think about a time when they may have seen some of these resources in their everyday life.

Ask: Did you ever see coal being used to cook? **Possible answer: when grilling outside**

Language SmArts
Summarize

W.4.8 Recall relevant information

Check to be sure that students correctly identify how the methods for extracting the fuels are all the same. Be sure they summarize how the fuels are extracted today and not when they were first discovered.

Ask: Where do miners find these fuels? **deep in the ground**

Lesson 1 What Nonrenewable Resources Are Used For Energy? **535**

LESSON 1   Engage • **Explore/Explain** • Elaborate • Evaluate

EXPLORATION 2 Search and Find, continued

 Obtaining and Evaluating Information

Have students study the map and read the information below it.

Ask: What fossil fuels can be found in Kansas? oil
Ask: Which two fossil fuels can be found in Texas? oil and natural gas
Ask: Which fossil fuels, if any, are mined in our state? Answers will vary.

 ESS3.A Natural Resources

Some natural resources are rarer than others.

Ask: According to the map, which natural resource is the rarest, and where can it be found? [Uranium; Wyoming and Utah]

Collaboration

Think, Pair, Share As students study the map, have them think about the parts of the country where there is a lot of nonrenewable resource extraction. Then have pairs of students list states where more than two fossil fuels are extracted. Have students share their lists with the class.

Differentiated Instruction

RTI/Extra Support For students who may have difficulty completing item 13, review all the words in the box, leading them to where they can find them in the lesson. Then have pairs do the page together before you review it.

Where Are They Found?

Scientists and engineers use special fossil fuel technology to locate, remove, and process coal, crude oil, natural gas, and uranium. Each of these methods has certain benefits and risks. Some create **pollution**, or waste products that damage an ecosystem.

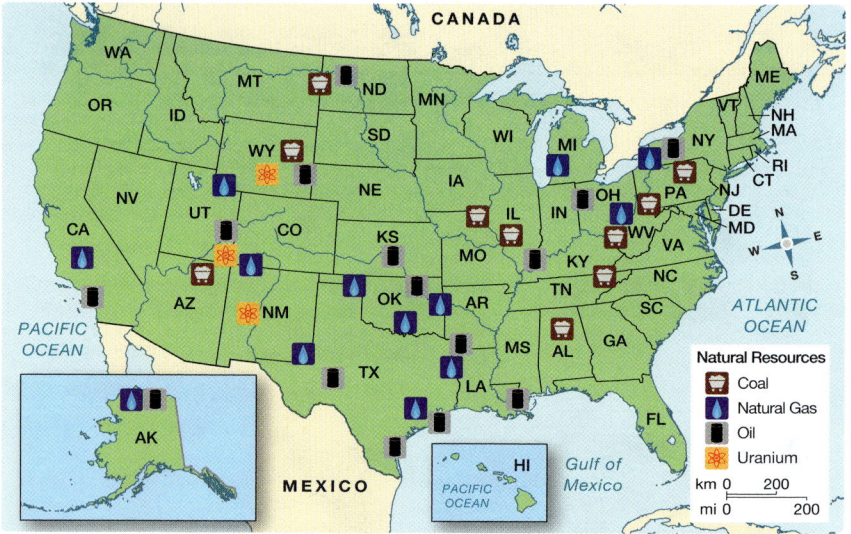

 In the United States, crude oil is found mostly in the Midwest, South, Southwest, Alaska, and around Pennsylvania.

 The Midwest, Montana, Wyoming, and Pennsylvania are the main sources of coal in the United States.

 Natural gas is found mostly in Alaska, Texas, Oklahoma, New Mexico, Wyoming, and Louisiana.

 The United States was once the leader in uranium mining. Today, however, uranium is mined in only a few places, including Utah and Wyoming.

13. Choose the word or phrase that correctly completes each sentence.

| crude oil | coal | natural gas | uranium | Alaska | Montana |
| Wyoming | heat | plastic | cooking | Pennsylvania | |

Both ___crude oil___ and coal can be found in the Midwest. Natural gas and uranium are found in New Mexico and ___Wyoming___. Oklahoma has both ___natural gas___ and crude oil. Pennsylvania is one of the main sources of ___coal___ in the United States.

536

Unit 8 Natural Resources and Hazards

What Does It Use

14. Write **u** for uranium, **o** for oil, **c** for coal or **g** for gas to identify the nonrenewable resource shown being used in each picture below.

Many kitchen stoves cook food with an open flame. A fossil fuel is piped into the stove, where it ignites and heats up the food.

Early trains had steam engines. A fire heated up water, which turned to steam. The steam then helped the trains to move.

Paint is a product of fossil fuels. The same product that is used in paint is also used in plastic, rubber, and soap.

kitchen stove — g

train — c

paint — o

HANDS-ON Apply What You Know
Mining Challenge

Model a mining operation by tallying up the value of the minerals mined and subtracting the costs of mining. Your teacher will supply a pan with birdseed and beads in it and will give you futher directions. The birdseed represents minable earth, and the beads represent different minerals and costs associated with mining. Each minute you use will cost $10 in reclamation fees. Using only a single spoon to pick up materials, you have up to 10 minutes to mine beads out of the birdseed. You must also use only the spoon to return any birdseed removed back into the pan. Subtract your costs from the value of what you mined. Did you make a profit?

Student answers will be based on the results from their activity.

Materials
- 1 spoon
- 1 pan
- birdseed
- beads:
  - gold bead = $5
  - silver bead = $4
  - Blue Bead = $3
- Sunflower Seed = $2

Influence of Engineering, Technology, and Science on Society and the Natural World

Remind students that over time, people's wants and needs change. Their need for better and improved technology changes also.

Ask: Look at the pot on the stove. What kind of nonrenewable resource is being used? **natural gas**

Ask: What is causing the food in the pot to cook? **heat from the combustion of the gas (fire)**

Ask: What renewable sources can people use to generate heat? Possible answer: **wood, sun, wind**

HANDS-ON Apply What You Know
Mining Challenge

Materials: a pan with birdseed and beads in it and a spoon for every 2 students, a stopwatch or other timing device, paper and pencil to record their work

Safety: Students may need safety goggles to avoid getting any small particles in their eyes.

Have students complete the activity in pairs. If the pan is only big enough for one person at a time, have students switch off every 30 seconds or 1 minute. Tell students how long they will be mining (10 minutes), and then tell them when there is 1 minute remaining. Be sure that students understand the value of the beads and how that relates to minerals that people mine in real life.

Ask: Is mining easier by hand or by machine? **machine**
Ask: Did you make a profit? **Answers will vary.**

Scoring Guideline
Exemplary activity results would show a clear relationship between the cost and the amount of beads mined.

Connection to Math

Discuss how the Mining Challenge represents the choices mining companies must make in exploring new energy sources.
MP.2 Reason abstractly and quantitatively

Lesson 1 What Nonrenewable Resources Are Used For Energy?

LESSON 1   Engage • **Explore/Explain** • Elaborate • Evaluate

EXPLORATION 2 *Search and Find, continued*

DCI ESS3.A Natural Resources

Natural resources have plenty of benefits, and life would be very different if we didn't have ways to mine fossil fuels and obtain other resources.

Ask: Can you think of a product in your home made from fossil fuels? Name one positive thing about the product and one negative thing. Possible answer: Trash bags (plastic made from petroleum) are good because they help keep my house clean, but they are also bad because they can get in the oceans and hurt marine organisms, and the oil industry is a major polluter.

SEP Evaluating and Communicating Information

As a whole class, have students brainstorm ways they can reduce their use of fossil fuels. Start out by suggesting they try giving up or cutting back on one each week. Encourage students to begin by asking their families to walk to places that are close instead on driving.

Ask: What ways of reducing natural resources did you brainstorm? Possible answers: use less electricity in summer; use less heat in winter

CCC Cause and Effect

A cause is what makes something happen. An effect is what happens as a result.

Ask: What would happen if we used more renewable resources and fewer nonrenewable resources? Possible answer: There would be less pollution.

Differentiated Instruction

ELL Remind students that some causes and effects are listed in the chart. Help students identify which letter choices are causes and which are effects. Then have pairs of students finish the chart together.

Pros and Cons

The pros and cons of something are similar to its benefits and risks. The pros are the positive things about it and the cons are the negative things, or **drawbacks**. Using fossil fuels has some pros and some cons. A *pro* is that they give us affordable fuel. A *con* is that using them often causes pollution, or harmful substances mixed with water, air, or soil.

Humans have used coal for energy for thousands of years. Some forms of strip-mining for coal harm ecosystems.

Many vehicles run on gasoline. Hazardous oil spills have occurred when transporting crude oil.

Airplanes use fossil fuel to run their engines. This fuel is expensive and also adds pollution to the air.

Burning fossil fuels in cars and at electricity generating plants generates energy, but it also creates pollution and harmful gases in Earth's atmosphere.

Burning natural gas and using nuclear energy produce less pollution than other fossil fuels, but transporting uranium is dangerous.

15. Write the letter of the sentence that completes the chart.

Cause	Effect
b.	Pollution and greenhouse gases are added to the air.
New nuclear plants are built.	a.
d.	Habitats and farmland are lost.
Crude oil is transported.	c.

a. Uranium is rare and must be moved long distances.
b. Fossil fuels are burned.
c. Oil spills pollute water and destroy wildlife.
d. Resources are surface mined.

538 Unit 8 Natural Resources and Hazards

Engineer It!
Hybrid Cars

Hybrid cars use two or more different methods to generate energy to run the car. This hybrid uses gasoline as a partial source of fuel.

Many gasoline/electric hybrids have brakes that are set up like an electrical generator. When they are applied, the electrical charge generated is stored in the battery.

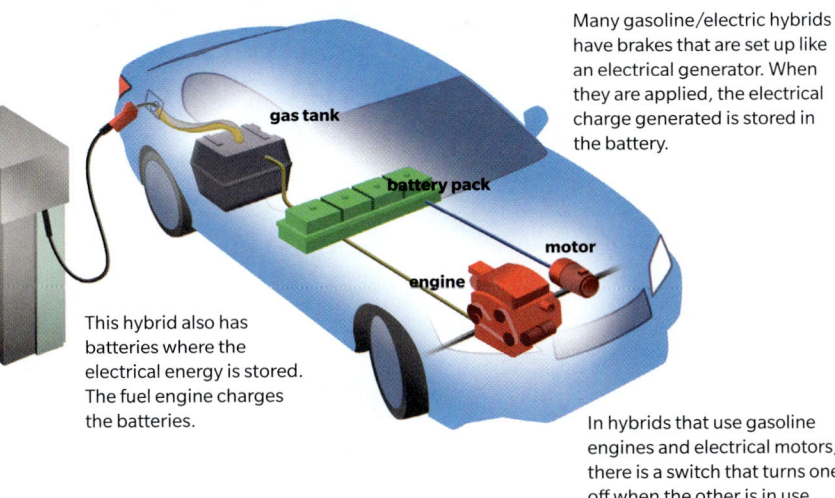

This hybrid also has batteries where the electrical energy is stored. The fuel engine charges the batteries.

In hybrids that use gasoline engines and electrical motors, there is a switch that turns one off when the other is in use.

16. How does a hybrid car such as the one in the diagram help with some of the cons of fossil fuel use?

It runs partially on electricity, so it uses less fossil fuel and pollutes less.

Language SmArts
Making Inferences

17. Some cars run entirely on electric energy. How do you think their batteries might be recharged with electricity?

They need to be plugged into an electrical outlet regularly.

Tip

The English Language Arts Handbook can provide help with understanding how to make inferences.

Engineer It!
Hybrid Cars

Influence of Engineering, Technology, and Science on Society and the Natural World

There are many different types of hybrid cars. Have students research and compare different types of hybrid car technologies.

Ask: What does hybrid mean? **Possible answer: A thing made by combining two different elements. In this case, the car uses both electric and gas power.**

Connection to Physical Science

Energy comes in many forms: sound, light, heat, and electric current. Fossil fuels such as coal, oil, and gas are used to generate electricity.

Ask: What is one way you can reduce your electricity use? **Possible answer: Turn off lights and appliances when I leave.**
PS3.2 Energy Make observations to provide evidence that energy can be transferred from place to place by sound, light, heat, and electric currents.

FORMATIVE ASSESSMENT

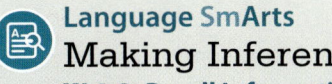

Language SmArts
Making Inferences
W.4.8 Recall Information

Collaboration

Feedback As students answer the question, have small groups discuss any toys or household appliances that may have rechargeable batteries.

Ask: What devices with rechargeable batteries have you used or seen? **Possible answers: cell phones, tablets, video games, vacuum cleaner**

Ask: How do you or other members of your family charge the rechargeable batteries? **They are placed in a battery charger.**

LESSON 1   Engage • **Explore/Explain** • Elaborate • Evaluate

EXPLORATION 2   Search and Find, continued

HANDS-ON ACTIVITY  Partners   1 class period
Catch That Dirt

3D Learning Objective
SEP **Obtaining and Evaluating Information**

Evaluate the air quality in four different places around the school.

Materials
The materials listed in the student edition are a starting point. You may wish to provide gloves so students' hands don't get dirty. You may wish to cover the workspace with newspapers. You may also wish to include permanent markers so students can mark their names on their containers. A microscope may take the place of a hand lens to more closely observe the particles in the air.

Preparation
In order for this activity to run smoothly, have all the supplies ready for each pair of students. Set up containers with lids. Set up petroleum jelly and spoons so students can easily scoop the jelly into the jars. Make sure students know how to use the hand lens.

Procedure
STEP 1 To save time, you may want to give each student a spoon to scoop the petroleum jelly. If using only one spoon, be sure students take turns.

HANDS-ON ACTIVITY
Catch That Dirt

Tiny dirt and dust particles are floating in the air around us. Some places have more of these tiny particles than others. Perhaps the air inside your classroom is cleaner than the air outside. Maybe the air outside is cleaner.

Materials
- 4 small plastic containers with lids
- petroleum jelly
- plastic spoon
- hand lens

Objective
Collaborate to investigate pollution in the air.
What question will you investigate to meet this objective?
Possible question: Is the air inside my classroom cleaner than the air outside?

Procedure
STEP 1 Gather your materials. Use the plastic spoon to spread petroleum jelly inside each container. Cover the sides and bottom with a thin layer. Label the containers 1–4 and place a lid on each.

Why do you think you have prepared more than one container?
Possible answer: to be able to compare differences

STEP 2 Look closely at all four containers. Describe what the inside surface of the containers looks like.
Possible answer: slippery and shiny

540

Student Lab Worksheet and complete Teacher Support available online.

540   Unit 8 Natural Resources and Hazards

STEP 3 Place two containers indoors. Remove the lids.

Place the other two containers outdoors. Remove the lids. Leave the containers in place for two hours. Write the location of each container.
Students should record the location where they placed each container.

STEP 4 After two hours, use a hand lens to study the inside of each container.

Describe what you see on the insides of the containers.

Container 1: Students should observe particles of dirt and dust on the surfaces of the container interiors.

Container 2: _____

Container 3: _____

Container 4: _____

STEP 2 As students work, circulate and assist to be sure they are correctly interpreting the instructions at each station. Make sure they are filling all four containers with an equal amount of petroleum jelly.

STEP 3 Allow students to place their containers without other students knowing where they are. This will help when comparing information at the end of the experiment. Students should record their locations.

CCC Cause and Effect

Remind students that after they check their containers, they will be able to record the dirt and dust particles that are part of the air around them.

Differentiate Instruction

ELL Students learning English may need extra help doing this activity. Pair them with strong English-language speakers who can mime or draw pictures to convey the meaning of what is happening in each step. Have the English-language learner repeat the words to illustrate understanding.

STEP 4 Students may have a hard time waiting the two hours. Be sure to have an activity on hand to fill the time while waiting. Another option would be to complete the activity right before a break time, such as lunch.

Lesson 1 What Nonrenewable Resources Are Used For Energy?

LESSON 1   Engage • **Explore/Explain** • Elaborate • Evaluate

EXPLORATION 2 HANDS-ON ACTIVITY, continued

Analyze Your Results

STEP 5 Remind students to look at their recordings for Step 4 before answering the questions. Remind them that their observations should be consistent throughout the experiment.

STEP 6 Students should use their hand lenses to get a good picture of what they are seeing. If there are microscopes available, have students observe the particles with them.

Draw Conclusions

STEPS 7–10 Call on different pairs to share their conclusions. Remind them that their conclusions should be consistent throughout the experiment.

Claims, Evidence, and Reasoning

Have each pair of students from the activity work with another pair to share their ideas about what may be causing the air to be dirty. Be available for any questions or concerns that might arise.

	Scoring Rubric for Hands-On Activity
3	experiment set up correctly, results recorded accurately, analysis and conclusions reflect the results
2	experiment and recording done correctly but analysis and conclusions are inadequate or incomplete, conclusions follow evidence loosely
1	did not fully participate in activity, results recorded but incomplete or unorganized, conclusions are made but do not follow logically from evidence
0	procedure not followed or did not participate, unorganized recording, conclusions have errors or don't exist

Analyze Your Results

STEP 5 Did you notice differences between the containers? If you did, describe them.

Descriptions should be consistent with what students recorded in step 4.

STEP 6 Share and compare your results with other students. Discuss how you could explain the differences you observed.

Students should speculate about the origins of the particles they observe.

Draw Conclusions

STEP 7 Based on your observations, which containers were left to sit in the cleaner air?

Conclusions should be consistent with what students recorded in step 4.

STEP 8 Make a claim about the air inside your classroom and the air outside. Cite evidence to support your claim.

Students should claim that the air in one place is dirtier than the other and should use their observations of the containers as evidence to support their claims.

STEP 9 What does this investigation tell you about the environment?

Possible answer: There are particles in the air that you can see if you look closely enough. Just because air looks clean at first doesn't mean that it is clean.

STEP 10 Think of other questions you want to ask about air quality.

Possible question: How can I tell whether any of the particles I observed are from fossil fuels?

542

542   Unit 8 Natural Resources and Hazards

LESSON 1   Engage • Explore/Explain • **Elaborate** • Evaluate

TAKE IT FURTHER Discover More

▶ **Explore Online**   Students can explore all three Take It Further paths online.

TAKE IT FURTHER
Discover More

Check out this path . . . or go online to choose one of these other paths.

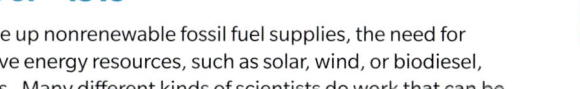

Careers in Science & Engineering
- What's Around You?
- On a Mining Mission

Types of "-ISTs"

As we use up nonrenewable fossil fuel supplies, the need for alternative energy resources, such as solar, wind, or biodiesel, increases. Many different kinds of scientists do work that can be related to fossil fuels. Some discover. Some invent.

▶ **Explore Online**

A petroleum geologist locate and discover places where new fossil fuel deposits can be found.

A chemist might investigate how chemicals found in fossil fuels can be used as fuel and to make products.

18. Decide if each description is a discovery or an invention. Match each to the scientist who was most likely responsible for it.

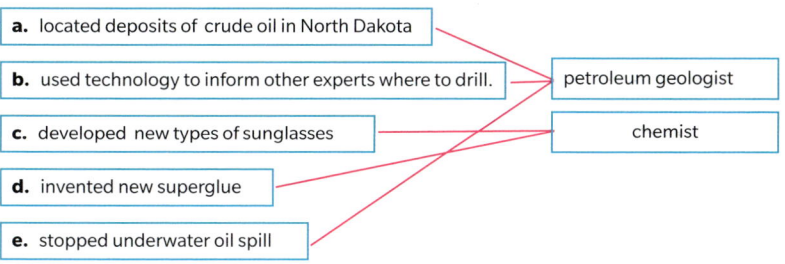

a. located deposits of crude oil in North Dakota
b. used technology to inform other experts where to drill.
c. developed new types of sunglasses
d. invented new superglue
e. stopped underwater oil spill

petroleum geologist
chemist

543

Collaboration

You may choose to assign this activity or to direct students online to the eSE where they can explore and choose from all three paths. These activities can be assigned individually, to pairs, or to small groups.

Careers in Science & Engineering: Types of "-ISTs"

Scientists and engineers work to solve problems. We need to reduce our use of nonrenewable resources, but at the same time, there are ways we can't live without them. Some scientists look for places we can find new fossil fuels?

Ask: How might a scientist who finds new fossil fuels help us? New fuels would keep us from completely depleting the old ones.

CCC Cause and Effect

Some chemists investigate how we can better use fossil fuels.

Ask: Why does a chemist try to investigate how fossil fuels can be used as fuel? How can they help the environment? Students should include how scientists are trying to make the environment a safer place by investigating better ways to use fossil fuels.

SEP Obtaining and Evaluating Information

Inventing new technologies, investigating safer uses for fossil fuels, and preventing mining disasters from happening are just a few examples of what chemists do.

Ask: How are the chemists helping Earth? Can we call them heroes? Student answers will vary, but they should say chemists are making the world a safer place, and yes, they can be called heroes because like people we traditionally call heroes, such as firefighters and police officers, these chemists are helping us be safe.

Lesson 1 What Nonrenewable Resources Are Used For Energy?   543

TAKE IT FURTHER, continued

DCI ESS3.A Natural Resources

Look at the two scientists on the page.

Ask: What natural resources would these scientists deal with in their jobs? **Samples answers: Climatologists work with snow, rain, sun, precipitation, and wind. Marine biologists work with fish, water, and plants.**

> ### Differentiate Instruction
> **RTI/Extra Support** If students have difficulty with comparing and contrasting the scientists, create a chart on the board, listing what they do.

Connection to English Language Arts

As students complete items 21 and 22, be sure they are using appropriate and trustworthy sources. Any books or webpages they use should be documented, and remind them that they shouldn't copy directly from the source. Everything they write should be in their own words.
W.4.7 Writing

 Explore Online

Students can explore these additional topics online.

What's Around You
Students research nonrenewable resources in their state or town. *(Outside research required.)*

On a Mining Mission
Students explore removing nonrenewable resources from the earth. *(Outside research required.)*

A climatologist studies long-term changes in climate. These changes are related to use of fossil fuels.

Marine biologists describe the effects of fossil fuel pollution on the plants and animals living in the ocean.

19. Describe a similarity and difference among the four different types of scientists.

Possible answer: Similarity: They all use science to study fossil fuels. Difference: Geologists look for places fossil fules can be found. Chemists study how chemicals in fossil fuels can be used.

20. Pick your favorite type of scientist from the ones described here. Research interesting facts about that type of scientist's job.

Which type of scientist did you choose and why?

Students should identify a type of scientist and what makes that type of science appealing.

21. Describe where that type of scientist does most of his or her work.

Student answers should reflect understanding of the different types of scientists.

22. Compare your research with that of a classmate who researched a different type of scientist's job.

Which job would you rather have? Why?

Students should include information about the scientist that relates to the study of fossil fuels.

544

Unit 8 Natural Resources and Hazards

LESSON 1   Engage • Explore/Explain • Elaborate • **Evaluate**

LESSON CHECK

▶ Explore Online Students can revisit the lesson phenomenon online.

LESSON 1
Lesson Check

Name _____

Can You Explain It?

1. Think back to the cars at the beginning of the lesson. Now that you've learned about resources, explain how vehicles in use today relate to the available fuel resources. Be sure to do the following:
   - Identify the types of fuel source.
   - Tell whether fuel sources are renewable or nonrenewable.
   - Identify technologies that engineers build into things to replace fossil fuels.
   - Identify the benefits and drawbacks of each fuel source used.

 EVIDENCE NOTEBOOK Use the information you've collected in your Evidence Notebook to help you cover each point above.

- Modern vehicles are relying less on fossil fuels, which are nonrenewable. Some cars are more fuel efficient. Some hybrid cars use both gas and electricity. Cars in the future may use renewable sources like solar power.
- When engineers design a car that doesn't run on gasoline, they need to be sure that the car can get refueled easily and as often as needed. For example, electric cars don't pollute, but if drivers can't get access to charging stations, the cars aren't useful. Cars that run on solar energy will be useful in sunny areas but not practical in places that don't get enough sunlight to refuel the car.

Checkpoints

2. Which of the following is a nonrenewable resource not made from fossil fuels?
   a. natural gas   **c. uranium**
   b. oil   d. coal

545

Formal Assessment Go online for student self-checks and other assessments.

Can You Explain It?

> ### Collaboration
> **Discussion** You may wish to revisit the image as a group to asses students' understanding of the material. Use the bulleted points in the Interactive Worktext to lead the discussion.

ESS3.A Natural Resources

As students complete item 1, remind them of the resources they have learned about. Allow them to look back at the beginning of Lesson 2. Tell them they will need to review the whole lesson to answer the questions. This includes nonrenewable resources in Exploration 1 and pros and cons of fossil fuels in Exploration 2.

Ask: What are fossil fuels? Fossil fuels are nonrenewable energy sources that come from past life.

EVIDENCE NOTEBOOK

Have students reread their answers to the Evidence Notebook prompts and then use this evidence to justify their reasoning as they respond to the Can You Explain It? Make sure students understand that a complete response must address all bulleted points.

SUMMATIVE ASSESSMENT

2. Students distinguish between types of nonrenewable reources. Refer them to Exploration 2 if they have difficulty with this question, specifically the map of the United States showing where nonrenewable resources are mined or sourced.

Lesson 1   What Nonrenewable Resources Are Used For Energy?   545

LESSON 1   Engage • Explore/Explain • Elaborate • **Evaluate**

LESSON CHECK, continued

3. Students may have to look back to Exploration 1 to identify the nonrenewable resources shown in the images.

> ## Differentiate Instruction
>
> 4. **RTI/Extra Support** This question has students using new vocabulary to fill in answers. Review all vocabulary with students before they answer the question, and remind them that they can cross out the choices as they fill in the answers, and if they don't know what goes in the blank, they can skip over it for later. Also, not all word choices will be used. Depending of the ability of the students, you may wish to give them a head start by telling them some or all of the unused words.

5. Remind students that use of fossil fuels should also decrease as people try to use less of them using alternate renewable sources instead.

6. Encourage students to review Exploration 1 if they have difficulty answering this question.

---

3. Write the letter that identifies each nonrenewable energy resource.

   a. natural gas
   b. coal
   c. uranium
   d. crude oil

 c

 d

 a

 b

4. Write the words or phrases that make each sentence correct.

difficult	inexpensive	dangerous
decreasing slowly	decreasing quickly	increasing quickly
increasing slowly	hundreds of thousands	hundreds of millions

   Fossil fuels were once easy to find and __inexpensive__ to use because there was so much of each available. But today, we are using so much that supplies are __decreasing quickly__. It took __hundreds of millions__ of years for fossil fuels to form, so there will be no more when our current supply is gone.

5. What will most likely cause our fossil fuel use to decrease over the next hundred years?
   a. smaller supply; higher prices
   c. less need; larger supply
   b. lower prices; less need
   d. larger supply; lower prices

6. Write renewable or nonrenewable to complete the sentence.

   Fuels that takes millions of years to develop are __nonenewable__.

546

546 Unit 8 Natural Resources and Hazards

LESSON 1
Lesson Roundup

A. Write the letter for each nonrenewable resource by its description.

> **a.** solid fossil fuel   **b.** nonrenewable   **c.** produces heat when burned

a, b, c   b, c   b, c   a, b

B. Which statement describes a benefit of buying an electric car instead of a gasoline-fueled car? Circle the correct answer.
- **a.** Electric cars are bigger.
- **b.** Electric cars are easier to drive.
- **c.** Electric cars are less expensive.
- **(d.** Electric cars do not pollute the air.**)**

Extraction of Fossil Fuels

C. What could explain why an oil rig is no longer able to get crude oil from an area?
- **a.** The oil has become solid.
- **(b.** All the oil has been removed.**)**
- **c.** The drill needs to be replaced.
- **d.** The oil has moved to a different area.

D. Keep track of anything else you learned about extracting fossil fuels here!
Student answers will vary. Accept all reasonable responses.

E. Circle the sources of energy that are are the remains of ancient plants and animals.
- **a.** uranium
- **(b.** coal.**)**
- **(c.** natural gas**)**
- **(d.** crude oil**)**

547

Lesson Roundup

DCI ESS.3.A Natural Resources

This lesson summary enables students to quickly revisit key points and prepare for tests.

A. Students need to be reminded that the resources can often fill more than one description. It is important they look at each nonrenewable resource and each of the descriptions before they settle on an answer. **ESS.3.A**

B. Encourage students to first cross out the answers they know are incorrect. As they do that, the correct answer should be easier to find. **ESS.3.A**

C. Be wary of questions that may have two answers. If a student has a good argument for why an answer is correct, allow them to state their case, and if it makes sense, give them the credit. **ESS.3.A**

D. Allow students to look back at the lesson and at their Evidence Notebook to answer the question. **ESS.3.A**

E. Students need to be reminded that although they learned about nonrenewable resources, not all of those resources are fossil fuels. Students also need to be reminded that not all nonrenewable resources were formed the same way. Students may wish to review Exploration 2 before responding. **ESS.3.A**

Lesson 1 What Nonrenewable Resources Are Used For Energy?   547

LESSON 2
What Renewable Resources Are Used for Energy?

Building to the Performance Expectation

The learning experiences in this lesson prepare students for mastery of:

4-ESS3-1 Obtain and combine information to describe that energy and fuels are derived from natural resources and their uses affect the environment.

Trace Tool to the NGSS
Go online to view the complete coverage of these standards across this lesson, unit, and time.

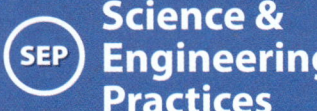 **Science & Engineering Practices**

 Disciplinary Core Ideas

 **Crosscutting Concepts**

Constructing Explanations and Designing Solutions
Generate and compare multiple solutions to a problem based on how well they meet the criteria and constraints of the design problem

 **VIDEO** Constructing Scientific Explanations

Obtaining, Evaluating, and Communicating Information
Obtain and combine information from books and other reliable media to explain phenomena.

 **VIDEO** Obtaining, Evaluating, and Communicating Information

ESS3.A Natural Resources
Energy and fuels that humans use are derived from natural sources, and their use affects the environment in multiple ways. Some resources are renewable over time, and others are not.

Cause and Effect
Cause-and-effect relationships are routinely identified and used to explain change.

Interdependence of Science, Engineering, and Technology
Knowledge of relevant scientific concepts and research findings is important in engineering.

Influence of Engineering, Technology, and Science on Society and the Natural World
Over time, people's needs and wants change, as do their demands for new and improved technologies.

 CONNECTIONS TO MATH

MP.2 Reason abstractly and quantitatively.

MP.4 Model with mathematics.

4.OA.A.1 Interpret a multiplication equation as a comparison, e.g., interpret $35 = 5 \times 7$ as a statement that 35 is 5 times as many as 7 and 7 times as many as 5. Represent verbal statements of multiplicative equations.

 CONNECTIONS TO ENGLISH LANGUAGE ARTS

W.4.7 Conduct short research projects that build knowledge through investigation of different aspects of a topic.

W.4.8 Recall relevant information from experiences or gather relevant information from print and digital sources; take notes and categorize information; provide a list of sources.

W.4.9 Draw information from literary or informational texts to support analysis.

Supporting All Students, All Standards

Integrating the Three Dimensions of Learning

In this lesson, students will learn about renewable and nonrenewable energy resources **(DCI ESS3.A)**. They will learn how we make use of them **(CCC Interdependence of Science, Engineering, and Technology)**, and they will evaluate the benefits and drawbacks of both types of resources **(Obtaining, Evaluating, and Communicating Information)** to see how they affect society and the environment **(CCC Influence of Engineering, Technology, and Science on Society and the Natural World and Cause and Effect)**.

 **Professional Development** Go online to view **Professional Development videos** with strategies to integrate CCCs and SEPs, including the ones used in this lesson.

Extra Hands-On Activity: Local Energy

What Are Some Local Energy Sources?

👥 Pairs
🕐 30–40 minutes

Students assume the role of executives with an energy company. They have to find the types of energy sources, both renewable and nonrenewable, that are acquired locally. They should then consider options for ways other renewable and nonrenewable resources could be added to the area. Pairs create a poster of the possible acquisition of additional energy sources, and describe the effects of those sources on the community (health, economy, etc).

You can provide info about what's currently used in the area so students can devote more time to researching other possibilities, such as new wind farms, hydropower, and solar, and working on their posters.

 This activity can support mastery of this Science and Engineering Practice: Obtaining, Evaluating, and Communicating Information

Preassessment

Have students complete the unit pre-test online or see the Assessment Guide.

Build on Prior Knowledge

Students should already know and be prepared to build on the following concepts:
- Living things need water, air, and resources from the land, and they live in places that have the things they need.
- Humans use natural resources for everything they do.

Differentiate Instruction

Lesson Vocabulary
- renewable resource

ELL/ELD Strategy
Break down the vocabulary term *renewable resource*.

Ask: What does it means to renew something? Make it new again.

Ask: What is a resource? Something we can use.

Tell students that a renewable resource is one that can be made new again, or replenished. It doesn't get totally used up.

Extension
The subject of this lesson, as well as Lesson 1, is natural resources.

Ask: What shorter word do you see in *resource*? *Source* is part of *resource*.

A source is a place where you can get something to use, and resource is something to use. Natural resources are things in nature that we can put to use.

LESSON 2   Engage • Explore/Explain • Elaborate • Evaluate

ENGAGE: Lesson Phenomenon

Lesson Objective
Obtain and evaluate information about renewable resources. Apply knowledge of the interdependence of science and technology to draw conclusions about electrical energy systems.

About This Image
Wind turbines are an alternative way to harvest energy. They collect energy from wind. As such, they are usually installed in places where there is a lot of wind, such as open landscapes or by the ocean.

Obtaining, Evaluating, and Communicating Information

Alternative Engage Strategy

Vroom, Vroom!	Whole class 15 minutes

Discuss with students how transporation relies heavily on types of fuel to power cars, buses, trains, and planes.

Ask: Where do gasoline and diesel fuel come from? Are they renewable? They're made from crude oil, which is not renewable.

If students do not recognize the difference between *renewable* and *nonrenewable*, have a volunteer give a short explanation. Then show the class a photo or video of a biodiesel car.

Ask: What does *biodiesel* mean? It's diesel fuel made from substances that came from the remains of organisms.

Ask: Would we need much land to grow enough oil to replace gasoline and diesel fuel with biofuels? Yes, we would need a lot of land.

Ask for a volunteer to research and present a short report to the class on biofuels.

548   Unit 8 Natural Resources and Hazards

LESSON 2

What Renewable Resources Are Used for Energy?

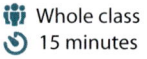

A wind farm is a place where several turbines are installed to convert wind to electrical energy.

By the end of this lesson . . .
you'll be able to explain the potential risks and benefits of using wind, water, and solar energy compared to fossil fuels.

548

Explore Online ▶ Students can view the lesson phenomenon online.

Can You Explain It?

Look carefully at this house. Even though it's not close to any town, it still has electricity. When you look at most houses, you see wires connected to them. Wires bring electricity to the house so the refrigerator, lights, TV, heating and cooling system, and other electric appliances work. Some houses have underground wires, while others get their electricity from other sources.

1. This home has plenty of electricity day and night. How does it get most of its electricity?

Students should respond based on the preliminary observations they can make of the images.

Tip
To recall what you have read about energy, read What Is Energy? and How Is Energy Transferred?

 EVIDENCE NOTEBOOK Look for this icon to help you gather evidence to answer the question above.

549

Can You Explain It?

Students are asked to think what provides electricity to the house. If students do not recognize the solar panels on the roof (some may think they are large skylights), ask whether the roof looks unusual. Once they recognize the solar panels, they need to think a step further.

 DCI ESS3.A Natural Resources

A natural resource does not necessarily mean that it is renewable or nonrenewable.

Ask: Is the energy from solar panels renewable or nonrenewable? renewable

 CCC Energy and Matter

Most houses have electrical lines connected to them.

Ask: How does the energy get from the electrical lines to the toaster in your kitchen? There are wires in the walls.

Collaboration

Build on Prior Knowledge Have students discuss what things in their houses use energy. They know that appliances use electricity, but they may not know that many houses use fuels for heating.

Ask: If the house used natural gas, how would the gas get to the house? through a pipe

 EVIDENCE NOTEBOOK

Encourage students to use an appropriate graphic organizer, such as main idea and supporting details, to set up their notebook for this lesson.

Find more strategies in the online ELA handbook.

Lesson 2 What Renewable Resources Are Used for Energy? **549**

LESSON 2   Engage • **Explore/Explain** • Elaborate • Evaluate

EXPLORATION 1 Exploring Renewable Resources

3D Learning Objective

Explore the nature of **renewable energy resources** to **evaluate information** about their **influence on society and the world**.

Connection to Physical Science

Review different forms of energy: energy of motion, chemical energy, nuclear energy, electrical energy, light, and heat.

Ask: What is energy? **ability to move something or cause change**

Ask: How do wind and water transfer energy? **by pushing against turbine blades**

PS3.A Definitions of Energy
PS3.B Conservation of Energy and Energy Transfer

Differentiate Instruction

ELL: Use Realia Use objects such as a ball, a battery, and a light bulb to demonstrate energy of movement, electrical energy, light, and other forms of energy.

EXPLORATION 1

Exploring Renewable Resources

Use It Again

As you have learned, nonrenewable resources, cannot be replaced in a reasonable amount of time. However, **renewable resources** are resources that can be replaced within a reasonable amount of time. They were the main forms of energy used before the 20th century.

2. Read below to learn more about renewable energy sources. Then, match the text to the picture by writing the correct letter in each circle.

   a. Using wind as an energy source does not produce pollution. It has low or no cost. Because we will never run out of wind, it is renewable.

   b. Solar energy is clean, renewable energy from the sun. When solar panels capture energy from the sun and change it to electricity, no pollution is given off.

   c. The energy of water flowing through a dam is called hydroelectricty. Hydroelectric dams uses water, which is a renewable resource.

   d. Geothermal-fueled plants use the heat below Earth's surface to produce electricity. Earth's heat is a renewable resource.

   e. Biomass is fuel that comes from dead organisms. The most common type is wood. Other types include cornstalks and animal waste.

3. What is the difference between a renewable and a nonrenewable resource?
   Renewable resources do not run out or can be replaced in a short time.
   Nonrenewable resources are used up and can't be replaced fast enough to be useful.

How Does That Work?

4. When you turn on the TV or a light bulb in a lamp, you're using electricity. Draw a line to match the electricity-producing device to the natural resource.

 EVIDENCE NOTEBOOK Do any of the nonrenewable resources you have learned about seem as if they might be what's providing electricity to the house you saw at the beginning of the lesson? Record your thoughts and observations in your Evidence Notebook.

 Language SmArts
Making Connections

5. Describe two renewable and two nonrenewable resources where you live. What are the natural resources and the electricity-producing devices?
Possible answer: solar panels using the sun; local dam using water energy; cars using gasoline; traffic lights using electricity from a coal burning plant

 Interdependence of Science, Engineering, and Technology

Ask: Which power sources have turbines that spin? wind turbines, dams, and fossil fuels plants Which do not? solar cells

 ESS3.A Natural Resources

Ask: Which of the three energy sources show here are renewable? All of them.

Point out to students that although electrical lines are not shown with any of these three energy sources, lines would be necessary to transmit power to homes and other buildings.

 EVIDENCE NOTEBOOK

Evidence should include the fact that the solar panels resemble the structure on the roof in the Can You Explain It? image.

SEP Obtaining Information

Natural gas and coal may be important sources of energy locally.

Ask: Where did the oil and gas come from? Answers will vary, but fossil fuels may travel hundreds of miles on their way to a power plant.

 Language SmArts
Making Connections
W.4.8 Recall relevant information from experiences

Ask students if they have heard the phrase "oil patch" in reference to the oil-producing region of Texas and nearby states. Ask if they have heard of any other regions known for energy production. Examples: Kentucky produces coal, while California and Texas have wind farms. States in the Southwest have solar farms.

Lesson 2 What Renewable Resources Are Used for Energy?

LESSON 2 Engage • **Explore/Explain** • Elaborate • Evaluate

EXPLORATION 1 *Exploring Renewable Resources, continued*

SEP Obtaining Information

Have students perform outside research on how energy is generated and to obtain statistics.

Ask: What are the major sources of energy for electric energy, and what are those percentages? Answers may vary. For 2015, coal and natural gas were the largest with about 33% each; nuclear was about 20%, hydroelectrcity 6%, other renewables 7%, and oil 1%.

CCC Cause and Effect

Renewable energy sources are not always available in every location, or in adequate supply to provide energy to people. Discuss the conditions that are optimal for harnessing the four types of renewable energy. Use questions to lead the discussion.

Ask: Would it be better to build a solar power plant in a sunny area or an area that is usually cloudy? A sunny area would be better, because the solar panels would receive direct sunlight. However, solar panels will still work even when the light is reflected or partially blocked by clouds.

Connection to English Language Arts

Consider having groups of students research real-world examples of the four types of energy-harnessing facilities or structures shown on the page, and write short reports on what they learn.

W.4.7 Conduct short research projects

Differentiate Instruction

Extension Some renewable energy sources still work in places where you might not expect them to work. Germany and Ohio aren't places you think of as being very sunny. However, solar panels can be a great source of renewable energy in these places. Ask students to research how much of Germany's electricity comes from solar energy. Have them research and discuss how it is possible for solar energy to work in cloudy places.

Energy Plants

Each photo shows one type of renewable energy, and how it is used to produce electricity that people can use instead of nonrenewable resources for energy needs.

Wind energy does not pollute the air. Wind spins the blades of huge turbines. The spinning blades turn a device, called a generator, inside the turbine. The generator spins to produce electricity.

Hydroelectric energy is fueled by water, a clean energy source. Hydroelectric plants are dams with machinery inside. Water flows through the dam, turning the blades of a turbine. The turbine then spins a generator, producing electricity.

Geothermal energy is heat from the earth. Geothermal plants use steam from underground to spin the blades of a turbine. The turbine spins a generator that makes an electric current. It is considered a clean fuel source, because once the steam is used, it is pumped back into the ground.

Solar energy is considered to be clean energy. Each solar panel contains several dozen solar cells. These are devices that turn the sun's energy into electricity though a chemical reaction.

6. Choose two energy sources from the ones you learned about. How are the processes to produce energy alike? How are they different?

I chose hydroelectric energy and wind energy. They are both clean energy fuel sources. They both have a turbine that spins a generator to produce electricity. One works with wind and one works with steam from underground.

Engineer It!
Tidal Energy

Scientists and engineers are working on tapping other sources of renewable energy. Tidal energy is one example.

Gravity helps produce tides—the predictable rise-and-fall action of the ocean. Huge amounts of seawater flow over the ocean floor in between tides. By anchoring turbines in areas of the ocean floor where tidal flow is especially strong, electricity can be produced.

AK1000 is the world's largest tidal turbine. Its rotors have a diameter of 18 meters (60 feet) and will harness enough tidal energy to generate electricity for more than 1,000 homes.

7. What do you think the engineering challenges are in building turbines that operate in the sea?

Turbines in the ocean need to be strong to handle storms and strong tides. It would be a challenge to connect the turbine to land with a strong transmission cable to carry the electricity.

 EVIDENCE NOTEBOOK Have you identified any sources of energy that could provide electricity to the house without being visible from the outside? Record your findings in your Evidence Notebook.

Putting it Together

8. Test your knowledge of renewable resources by completing the questions below.

burned	replaced	used	solar	biomass	geothermal
dams	generators	turbines	water	wind	ice

Choose the correct words that complete each sentence.

Renewable energy sources are those that can be ___replaced___ in a reasonable amount of time. Energy from the sun is called ___solar___ energy. Machines called ___turbines___ use the wind to produce energy. Hydroelectricity uses moving ___water___ to produce electricity.

553

 Have students go online to learn more about how renewable energy sources can help harness electricity that people can use for their energy needs.

 **Engineer It!**
Tidal Energy

 Interdependence of Science, Engineering, and Technology

Tides reverse direction twice a day as they move in and out.

Ask: Would it be harder or easier to design a turbine working in both directions than one in a dam, where the water flows one way? A tidal turbine would be harder to design.

 ESS3.A Natural Resources

Discuss how long it takes for some renewables to renew, and the original source of energy for most types of energy found on Earth.

Ask: How quickly does wood renew itself? Trees take years to grow.

Ask: What is the source of energy for trees and most other renewables? the sun

 EVIDENCE NOTEBOOK

Students should reply that there's no way for solar panels to be invisible outside the house, as they need full exposure to the sun in order to function. Wind turbines would also need to be visible.

FORMATIVE ASSESSMENT
Putting it Together

Ask: Which sources of energy are energy of motion? wind and hydropower

Ask: Which are chemical energy? coal, oil, gas, and biomass

Lesson 2 What Renewable Resources Are Used for Energy? 553

LESSON 2 Engage • **Explore/Explain** • Elaborate • Evaluate

EXPLORATION 2 Renewable Natural Resources

3D Learning Objective

Explore the advantages and disadvantages of **renewable energy resources** to **evaluate information** about their **influence on society and the world**.

SEP Obtaining and Communicating Information

Discuss with students the kind of information they can obtain by looking at the images on the page.

Ask: What can you determine about the image on the right? more clouds mean less energy

> ### Differentiate Instruction
>
> **Extension** Have students research and report on the cost of electric power from different sources as part of this exploration. They should search for costs in kilowatt hours.

DCI ESS3.A Natural Resources

Misconception Alert Some students may think that a home with solar panels or a wind turbine can meet all of its energy needs through those technologies. This is rarely the case, unless the home always receives a lot of wind or sunlight and it has large batteries for storing electricity that can be tapped at night or when the wind is weak.

Ask: What happens when wind and solar energy are unavailable? Nonrenewable energy must be used instead because the energy will be inadequate to meet people's needs.

EXPLORATION 2

Renewable Natural Resources

Cloudy Days, No Wind, Little Water

If you stand in the middle of a vegetable farm, you'll see rows of crops. If you stand in the middle of a wind farm, you'll see rows of wind turbines. Wind farms are built in very windy areas. The wind makes the turbines spin, which produces electricity. Moving water can also make turbines spin, which produces electricity. The electricity from these devices goes to an electricity generating plant and then to homes and businesses.

Electricity from solar energy can come from large fields of solar panels and through an electricity generating plant, too. Solar panels can also be installed directly onto houses.

Energy can be stored for use at times when the wind dies down or there is no sun, or other forms of energy can be used. When there's no wind or sun, backup sources of energy are used to meet people's energy needs. That way, no one is left without electricity.

Solar, Wind, and Water Energy

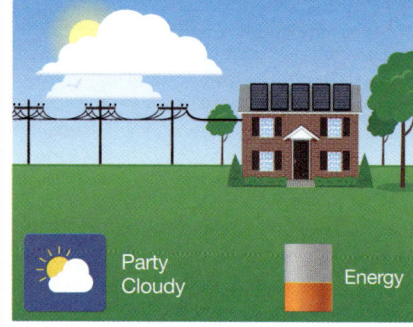
solar panels

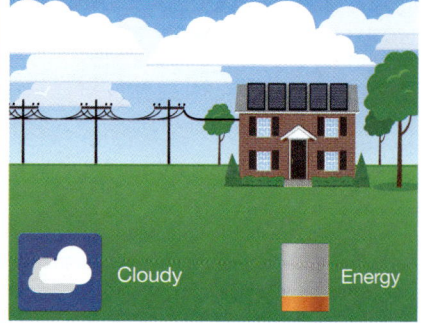
solar panels

9. What can you conclude from the images of solar panels?
Possible answer: Solar panels get their energy from sunlight. Therefore, they work better on days when there is more sunlight. On days when there is less sunlight, they are less efficient.

554

---

554 Unit 8 Natural Resources and Hazards

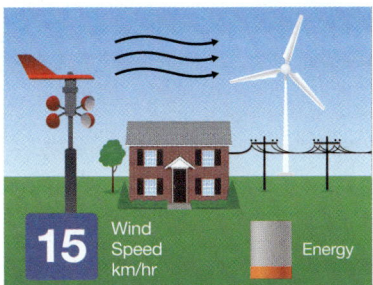
wind turbine

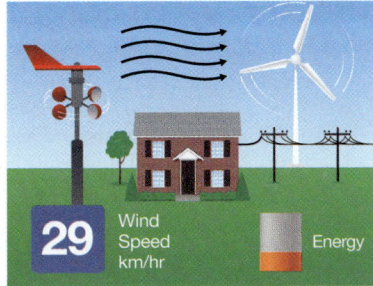
wind turbine

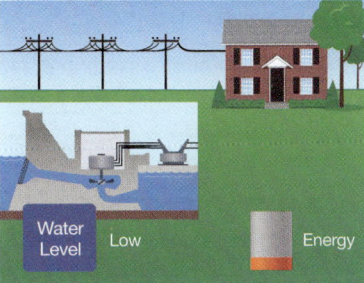
hydroelectric dam

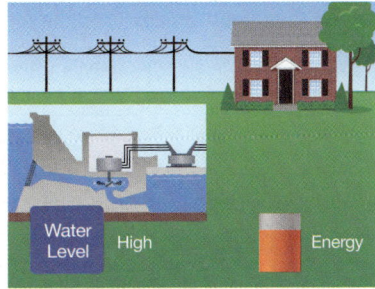
hydroelectric dam

10. Which of the following best describe the relationship between water and energy in a hydroelectric dam? Circle all that apply.

   a. More water moving through the dam means less energy.
   c. Less water moving through the dam means more energy.
   b. More water moving through the dam means more energy.
   d. Less water moving through the dam means less energy

11. Based on the pictures you see here and on the previous page, what do you think are the benefits and drawbacks of using renewable energy sources?

   The energy sources may not run out, but they are not always available at the same level.

   EVIDENCE NOTEBOOK Do you think renewable sources of energy can generate electricity for a house by themselves, or are other sources of energy necessary? Record evidence in your Evidence Notebook.

555

Cause and Effect

Review the types of locations and conditions that are conducive to harnessing renewable energy such as hydelectric, wind, and solar.

Ask: Would it be more effective to have a wind farm in a coastal area or in a city? Explain. It would be more effective to have a wind farm in a coastal area. The wind is strong and steady in coastal areas.

Ask: What are other ideal locations to have a wind farm in? Other ideal locations for wind farms include open plains, gaps in mountains, and at the tops of rounded hills.

EVIDENCE NOTEBOOK

Students may suggest that wood may be stored for heating. If there are batteries in the house, then the solar panels may be enough. Otherwise, an outside source of energy is necessary. It probably would not be renewable.

Ask: Would it make snse to build a dam in a desert? On a flat plain? Explain. No, in a desert there would be no water, and on a plain the water would only move slowly.

Collaboration

Share Feedback Allow students to work in pairs to review each other's answers. They should compare the benefits and drawbacks of using renewable energy sources. Have them see which of their answers are similar and which are different, and encourage a discussion

Lesson 2 What Renewable Resources Are Used for Energy? **555**

LESSON 2   Engage • **Explore/Explain** • Elaborate • Evaluate

EXPLORATION 2 Renewable Natural Resources, continued

 Influence of Technology on Society

Sometimes the best place to set up a large-scale solar farm or wind farm may also be the best place to grow crops, have recreational facilities, or serve some other purpose. People have to consider what's the best use of an area.

Ask: Is it wise to set up solar panels on land that is farmed? Explain. **No, it would be bad for crops, since solar panels would block the sunlight that plants need to grow.**

Connection to English Language Arts

Point out to students that they do not need to guess to fill in the table. Tell them to look for phrases that relate to particular resources. For instance, "floods valuable land" must relate to water. They should look at benefits as well as drawbacks.

W.4.9 Draw information to support analysis

 ESS3.A Natural Resources

Wood or other biomass can be used to generate electricity.

Ask: What solid waste product is produced from burning wood? **ash**
Ask: What can it be used for? **as fertilizer**

Benefits and Drawbacks

Renewable energy resources have benefits, especially when compared with nonrenewable energy sources. They will never be used up and do not pollute the air. However, there are some drawbacks to using renewable energy sources.

Solar panels, hydroelectric dams, and geothermal plants can be expensive to build or set up. Both wind turbines and hyroelectric dams can harm wildlife. Biomass plants and geothermal plants can cause some pollution the air. Hyroelectric dams can cause habitat loss and even flood valuable land. However, they still cause less pollution to the air in comparison to nonrenewable energy sources and they will never run out.

12. The table below shows the benefits and drawbacks of five different types of renewable energy sources. Fill in the source for each type of energy.

hydroelectric dam   solar panels   biomass plant   wind turbines   geothermal plant

Source	Benefits	Drawbacks
hydroelectric dam	• clean energy source • will never be used up	• habitat loss • can harm wildlife • floods valuable land • expensive to build or set up
wind turbines	• clean energy source • will never be used up	• can harm wildlife • can be noisy and unattractive • only works well on windy days
solar panels	• clean energy source • will never be used up	• expensive to build or set up • only works well on sunny days
geothermal plant	• will never be used up	• can be used in a limited number of places • can pollute air • expensive to build or set up
biomass plant	• will never be used up • reduces waste that goes to landfills	• can pollute air

13. Which benefits do all renewable sources of energy share? Select all that apply.
   a. Their waste is easy to clean up.
   b. Energy from renewable sources is cleaner than energy from nonrenewable resources.
   c. They will never be used up.
   d. They work well in all environments.

556

556   Unit 8   Natural Resources and Hazards

Going Green Debate

Energy efficiency means to use products or technologies that perform the same fuction but consume less energy. For example, a compact fluorescent bulb is more energy efficient than a traditional incandescent bulb. It uses much less electrical energy to produce the same amount of light. How do you think renewable and nonrenewable resources compare? Which one do you think is more energy efficient?

14. Consider both types of energy resources, then fill out the table below.
    - Under *Claim,* fill in either "renewable" or "nonrenewable" to complete the sentence.
    - Then under *Evidence,* give three facts that support your claim.
    - Use facts from this lesson and the previous one. Research any other facts you need to use as evidence.

Claim
I think that _____*Student choice of*_____ energy is the most efficient type of energy.
Evidence
a. _Students should cite facts about energy sources in support of their claims._   b. _____   c. _____

15. Discuss your answer with a classmate. Do you agree or disagree with his or her answer? Explain why or why not.

    Students should provide information-based defenses where their opinions differ.

557

Collaboration

 Obtaining and Communicating Information

Debate Have a class discussion and come to a consensus on the Going Green debate questions. If that is not possible, clearly formulate different answers to the question that factions of the class agree with.

You may want to have an actual class debate on the questions, but that is a very large time commitment. If the class goes ahead with the debate, it is probably wise to focus on benefits and drawbacks apart from the greenhouse effect.

Connection to Earth Science

Ask: What are greenhouse gases? carbon dioxide, water vapor, and other gases that trap heat near Earth's surface.

Ask: Does biomass release greenhouse gases when it is burned? yes

ESS3.C Human Impacts on Earth Systems

LESSON 2   Engage • **Explore/Explain** • Elaborate • Evaluate

EXPLORATION 2 *Renewable Natural Resources, continued*

Do the Math
Bright Savings

MP.2 Reason Abstractly and Quantitatively

Discuss the information in the table to help students infer what generates the typical yearly cost figures for the different bulbs.

Ask: The incandescent bulb uses 45 watts of electricity. The CFL uses 15 watts. How do you think these numbers relate to the typical yearly costs of these bulbs? *15 watts is just over one third of 43 watts, and $1.20 is just over one third of $3.50.*

Differentiate Instruction

ELL: Making Connections Ask: Do you know a shorter word that is similar to *incandescent*? Give students time to research if needed. What is the connection between the two words? *Yes, a* candle *also means something that glows.*

Connection to Physical Science

Ask: Why is a fluorescent bulb more efficient than an incandescent bulb? Does an incandescent bulb get hotter than a CFL? *An incandescent bulb gives off heat energy as well as light, so it is less efficient.*

PS3.B Conservation of Energy and Energy Transfer

Do the Math
Bright Savings

16. Think about the light bulbs in your home. Chances are, you'll see a variety of types. The most common are called incandescent light bulbs. Newer types, such as compact fluorescent bulbs, are more efficient and use less energy.

Use the chart to learn more.

	High-efficiency incandescent 43 watt	Compact fluorescent 15 watt
Average number of hours it lasts	2,000	10,000
Typical yearly cost	$3.50	$1.20
Benefits	• Uses less electricity than regular incandescent bulbs • Less air and water pollution from fossil fuel plants that supply most electricity • Last longer than regular incandescent bulbs, so less use of resources to make them.	• Uses less electricity than eco incandescent bulbs, which means less use of fossil fuels that produce most electricity • Less air and water pollution from electricity generating plants
Drawbacks	• Burn hotter than regular incandescent bulbs.	• Compact fluorescent bulbs contain a small amount of poisonous mercury that they can release when broken or thrown out in regular garbage.

558

558 Unit 8 Natural Resources and Hazards

17. Have you seen high-efficiency, incandescent, or compact fluorescent bulbs in your home? Which would you choose to use?

Possible answer: There are both types of bulbs in my house. I think compact fluorescent bulbs are the better choice. They last longer and cost less to use.

18. Compare the cost of a high-efficiency incandescent bulb and a compact fluorescent bulb. Use the space above to solve the problem, and then select the best answer.
   a. The high-efficiency incandescent bulb costs two times as much as the compact fluorescent bulb.
   c. The high-efficiency incandescent bulb costs almost five times as much as the compact fluorescent bulb.
   b. The high-efficiency incandescent bulb costs about three times as much as the compact fluorescent bulb.
   d. The high-efficiency incandescent bulb costs six times as much as the compact fluorescent bulb.

19. How many hours longer will the compact fluorescent last compared to the high-efficiency incandescent bulb? Use the space above to solve the problem, and then select the best answer.
   a. The compact fluorescent bulb will last 2,000 hours longer.
   c. The compact fluorescent bulb will last 8,000 hours longer.
   b. The compact fluorescent bulb will last 4,000 hours longer.
   d. The compact fluorescent bulb will last 10,000 hours longer.

559

SEP Obtaining Information and Presenting

Students probably know about LED bulbs, which are more efficient than CFLs.

Ask: What is an LED? **It is a light-emitting diode.**
Ask: Is an LED bulb more expensive to buy than a CFL? **Yes, but it is more efficient.**

You can tell interested students to investigate costs and subsidies for CFL and LED bulbs. A starting point is the U.S. Energy Information Administration.

Connection to Math

For Item 18, students can write an equation to relate the costs of the two bulbs. $1.20 \times 2.92 = $3.50

4.OA.A.1 Interpret a Multiplication Equation

CCC Influence of Technology on Society

Some people have emergency generators in their houses. Have students reasearch some pros and cons of generators.

Ask: Why doesn't everybody have a generator at home that runs all the time? **They are not convenient; they are expensive and noisy; they must operate outside the home**

Lesson 2 What Renewable Resources Are Used for Energy? 559

LESSON 2   Engage • **Explore/Explain** • Elaborate • Evaluate

EXPLORATION 2 Renewable Natural Resources, continued

HANDS-ON Apply What You Know
Plastics from Plants

Materials
The materials for this activity are nontoxic, but you should tell students never to eat anything they use in an activity. Make sure they wash their hands after the activity.

 ESS3.A Natural Resources

Some resources or technologies that are not renewable can be replaced by others that are.

Ask: Why might it be better to make plastics from corn than from oil? Corn is a renewable resource.

Ask: How might the use of corn and other plants for producing plastic affect the production of food? Answers will vary, but some students may infer that foods could become more expensive or scarce if farmers grow plants for use in plastics instead of food.

CCC Influence of Technology on Society

Students may already know that plastics don't break down quickly in landfills.

Ask: Is there a way to keep plastics out of landfills? Yes, we can recycle them. We can also avoid using them in the first place.

Scoring Guidelines
Excellent performance in this activity involves students working through all the steps in the procedure and providing thorough answers at the end.

 HANDS-ON Apply What You Know

In the previous lesson, you learned about typical plastics such as PET, or polyethylene terephthalate, which are made from petroleum (oil), a fossil fuel. PET is the most common type of plastic. Did you know we now have ways to make plastics from plants?

Materials
- zip-top plastic bag
- measuring spoons
- 2 drops of food coloring
- 2 drops of corn oil
- 1 tablespoon of cornstarch
- 1 tablespoon of water
- microwave oven

Procedure
a. Place 1 tablespoon of cornstarch in the plastic bag.
b. Add 1 tablespoon of water.
c. Add 2 drops of corn oil.
d. Add 2 drops of food coloring.
e. Seal the bag almost completely closed. Tilt the bag so the contents settle in one corner, then squish them together to mix.
f. Your teacher will place the bag in a microwave oven with the bag's seal slightly open. Microwave for 20 seconds.
g. Your teacher will remove the bag from the oven and let it cool before removing the contents.
h. Shape the "plastic" with your fingers.
i. After working with the plastic for a few minutes, dip it in water.

20. Think about how simple it was to take a few different corn-based ingredients and turn them into a substance you could work into different shapes. Think also about what happened when you dipped the corn plastic into water. How do you think corn plastic compares to petroleum-based plastics in terms of environmental impact?

Possible answer: Corn plastic is less harmful to the environment than typical plastic because it will biodegrade in a landfill while typical petroleum-based plastics take thousands of years to break down.

Solar Energy!

21. Solar energy has many different uses. Write what solar energy is being used for on the line below each picture.

heats houses/water

powers cars

cooks food

charges batteries

 Language SmArts
Cause and Effect

Tip
The English Language Arts Handbook can provide help with understanding cause and effect.

22. Choose the best words to complete each sentence.

> microwaves   pollution   electricity   generator   turbine   fan

Most renewable energy sources do not cause __pollution__.

Rooftop solar panels turn sunlight into __electricity__. Wind spins the blades of a __turbine__ to make electricity.

561

SEP **Obtaining and Communicating Information**

Have students study the photos to review how solar energy is being used in each example.

Ask: What is happening to solar energy in the solar cooker? *It's being reflected to a clear container so the sunlight heats the food inside.*

Ask: What is happening to solar energy in the solar panels on the house? *It's being converted to electricity.*

FORMATIVE ASSESSMENT

 Language SmArts
Cause and Effect
W.4.9 Draw Information to Support Analysis

Ask: If you charge an electric car with electricity generated by a coal-burning power plant, aren't you still polluting the air? *Yes, the pollution is emitted at the power plant, not at the car.*

Ask: How can you rewrite the last sentence of item 22 using the word *biomass*? *Biomass is burned in a boiler and makes steam that spins a turbine to make electricity.*

Lesson 2 What Renewable Resources Are Used for Energy? **561**

LESSON 2 Engage • **Explore/Explain** • Elaborate • Evaluate

EXPLORATION 2 Renewable Natural Resources, continued

HANDS-ON ACTIVITY Small groups 3 class periods
Running on Sunshine

3D Learning Objective
SEP Constructing Explanations and Designing Solutions

Students must work within a budget to determine the materials they can bring with them on a camping trip.

Materials
Materials are available at grocery stores or discount stores. Stores may be willing to give you empty boxes and packing peanuts without charge. Some of the materials for this activity can be reused and most can be recycled.

Preparation
Make sure all the group members participate in brainstorming. For the construction and testing, you may want to assign roles to particular students, for instance drawing, cutting out, and assembling parts; reading the thermometer and keeping time.

> ### Differentiate Instruction
> **RTI/Extra Support** To focus on the criteria of the design problem, have students ignore the cost constraint.

Procedure
STEP 1 Make sure students focus on the criteria and constraints when brainstorming the materials they will want to use for the activity.

HANDS-ON ACTIVITY
Running on Sunshine

Objective
Imagine you are going on a camping trip. It is a remote spot. You don't have a battery-powered stove. The weather has been very dry, and the park has banned campfires. You are not allowed to make a cooking fire. You remember that the sun gives off light that generates heat and decide to build a solar hot water heater to bring on the trip. You have a budget of $10.

Materials	Budgeted materials
• water container	• cardboard box—$5
• scissors	• black paint—$3
• tape	• black construction paper—$2
• thermometer	• plastic wrap—$1
• timer or watch	• packing peanuts—$2
• measuring cup	• newspaper—$1
	• cotton balls—$1
	• aluminum foil—$3
	• wax paper—$2
	• paper plates—$1
	• plastic shopping bags—$1
	• paper towels—$1

Collaborate to design a solar hot water heater.

Find a Problem: What question will you investigate to meet this objective?

How can we use solar energy to heat water?
_____
_____

Procedure
STEP 1 Brainstorm: Think about which materials you can use that will help you capture solar energy. Think about how the color and texture of the materials affects your design. Brainstorm as many ideas as you can think of. Keep in mind your criteria and constraints:

Criteria	Constraints
☐ Your solar heater should be able to heat at least one cup of water at least 2 °C.	☐ You may only use the materials your teacher provides.
☐ The heater has to stay warm when it is out of the sunlight, too.	☐ Your design must be built in the time given.
☐ The heater has to use sunlight to heat the water.	☐ You must stay within the $10 budget.

562

 Student Lab Worksheet and complete Teacher Support available online.

562 Unit 8 Natural Resources and Hazards

STEP 2 Plan: With your group, plan your design. Work together to draw a model of your solar water heater on a separate sheet of paper, and make a materials list suited to your design. Have your teacher approve your design. Gather your materials. What is the problem you need to solve?

Possible answer: I need to figure out how to heat water using the energy of the sun instead of fire.

STEP 3 Build: Build your solar water heater. Draw the finished solar water heater in the box below and label each of its parts. Explain what it does on the lines below.

Possible answer: My solar water heats water up with the sun's energy. We used dark materials to help it absorb the heat.

Students drawings should show a usable water heater with its parts labeled. Each part should have a short explanation written for it.

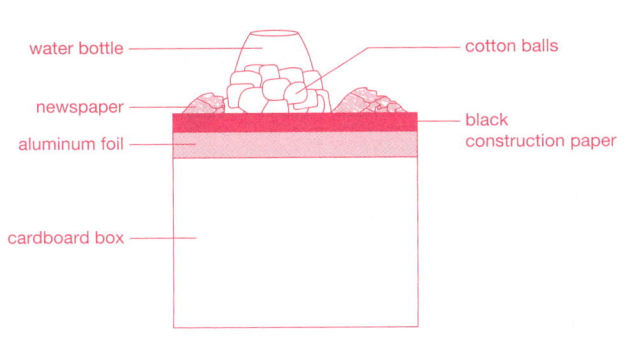

563

Constructing Explanations and Designing Solutions

SEP

STEPS 2–3 Circulate and remind students to focus their designs on the goal of what they want it to do. All designs have a purpose.

Ask: What will you do with the collecting surface? **Cover it with foil, because foil reflects light.**

ETS1.A Defining and Delimiting Engineering Problems

DCI

Remind students that engineers use criteria and constraints to design solutions to solve problems.

Ask: What are the criteria for a problem? **Criteria tell what needs to be done.**

Ask: What are the constraints for a problem? **Constraints tell how to do it.**

Science Is a Human Endeavor

CCC

Discuss the concept of brainstorming with students. Explain how different teams work together, such as engineering teams, research and development teams, quality control teams, etc.

Ask: Does working in a group help to solve design problems? **Yes, with more people, there are more ideas.**

Differentiate Instruction

Extension For a challenge, have students draw a mirror focusing light to a point (a circle representing a cross section that focuses parallel rays).

Ask: What is this mirror doing with the light? **It is focusing the light.**

Lesson 2 What Renewable Resources Are Used for Energy? **563**

LESSON 2   Engage • **Explore/Explain** • Elaborate • Evaluate

EXPLORATION 2   HANDS-ON ACTIVITY, continued

SEP Planning and Carrying Out Investigations

STEPS 4–5 Make sure that there is a safe, reserved area for students to take their tests outside. Students must be accompanied by adults when working on Step 4.

Ask: When you measure the temperature of the cup, are you checking the criteria or the constraints of the design problem? **We are measuring temperature to see if the design meets the criteria.**

DCI PS3.B Conservation of Energy and Energy Transfer

Students should already understand that the cooker converts light to heat.

Ask: What is heat? **energy of moving particles.**
Ask: When something cools off, what is happening? **Energy is moving from a warmer to a cooler temperature.**

CCC Influence of Technology on Society

You have built a light solar cooker for a camping trip. Now suppose that you live in a remote village that needs to use solar cookers every day because there are few other sources of energy.

Ask: Would your cooker last long? Explain. **No, it is made out of cardboard.**
Ask: How could you make a cooker that would last longer? **I would use metal and other stronger materials.**
Ask: Would your improved cooker be more expensive? **Yes, the new materials would cost more, and they would take more time to put together.**

STEP 4   Test: Test your heater outside. Fill a cup with water. Use the thermometer to record the starting temperature of the water. Record the temperature in the table on the next page, in the "Temperature in the sun" row under 0. Place the heater in bright sunlight. Place the water in the heater. Record the temperature of the water every 5 minutes for 20 minutes in the "Temperature in the sun" row of the table.

How will you know whether your results are accurate? What steps can you take to assure your measurements are accurate?

Possible answer: I compared my results to those of other students using different thermometers, and they were the same. I can repeat the experiment to see whether my results will be similar.

STEP 5 Take the heater inside. Measure the temperature of the water right away. Then record it in the "Temperature when not in the sun" row under 0. Then measure and record the water temperature every 5 minutes for the next 20 minutes.

What differences do you notice when moving the heater inside?

Possible answer: When not in the sun, the temperature of the water began to drop.

STEP 6 Record the temperatures measured during the investigation in the table below.

Solar Water Heater Results						
Time (min)	0	5	10	15	20	
Temperature in the sun (°C)						
Temperature when not in the sun (°C)						

Temperatures will vary depending on time of day, time of year, and location.

Analyze Your Results

STEP 7 What was the highest water temperature you recorded? What was the difference between that temperature and your starting temperature?

Student responses should indicate that the highest temperature came at the end of the water's time in the sun. That temperature should be warmer than the temperature at the beginning of the experiment.

STEP 8 Did your heater maintain its temperature when you took it inside? How much did the temperature drop in the 20 minutes it was out of sunlight?

Student responses should indicate that the temperature began to cool shortly after the water heater was removed from the sun, though by how much will vary from student to student.

Analyze Your Results

Connection to Math

STEPS 7–8 Point out to students that working with science means solving word problems. The following is a one-step word problem: *What is the difference between your starting and ending temperatures?*

Ask: If you drew a line graph of the temperature in the cup, what would it look like? The line would rise quickly for 10 minutes while the water was heating. Then it would drop more slowly while the water cooled.

Ask: If you improved your cooker design, what would a graph of the temperature look like? The line would rise more quickly and then drop more slowly.
MP.2, MP.4, 4.MD.B.4

Help students record the temperatures accurately. Model for them how to take the values from the thermometer to record them on the chart.

Lesson 2 What Renewable Resources Are Used for Energy?

LESSON 2   Engage • **Explore/Explain** • Elaborate • Evaluate

EXPLORATION 2   HANDS-ON ACTIVITY, continued

Draw Conclusions

 **PS3.B and ETS1.C**

Discuss with students how certain materials serve as insulation. Define insulation and explain how it works.

Ask: How could you make the cup cool more slowly? **I could use more insulation.**

Claims, Evidence, and Reasoning

 Constructing Explanations and Designing Solutions

After the class has compared designs, have the entire class brainstorm an improved design for the cooker. They should critique each other's claims and evidence for answers related to their designs.

Ask: Can you think of improvements that would need materials not on the list? **Accept reasonable answers that involve affordable and readily available materials.**

Scoring Rubric for Hands-On Activity	
3	cooker completed and tested; criteria met
2	cooker completed and tested poorly, or criteria not met
1	plan completed, but cooker not completed
0	plan not completed

Analyze Your Results

STEP 9 Evaluate and Redesign: Why did you choose the materials you used? Do you think they helped your heater work? If not, which materials could you use instead? What would you do differently to improve your design?

Student responses should explain why they chose their materials and whether they worked. If they didn't work, students should be able to explain what materials they think would work and why. Students should explain how they can improve their design.

STEP 10 Can you claim that your design met the criteria? Why or why not?

Possible answer: Yes, my design heated the water by the minimum requirement, though I wish it had heated it more.

Draw Conclusions

STEP 11 What evidence do you have that your solar water heater was successful? Did it hold in heat? Explain your answer.

Possible answer: Yes, it heated the water, and the water held the heat for about 15 minutes. I would like to design a heater that holds heat longer.

STEP 12 How do you think you could have made your heater better? What other materials would you have chosen instead?

Possible answer: I could have selected materials that held heat longer and made my heater better. (Students should then name these materials.)

STEP 13 Communicate: Compare your results to those of the other groups in your class. Did their heaters work better than yours? Why or why not?

Possible answer: Some groups' water heaters worked better, while others didn't work as well. Those that worked better had better design and materials.

STEP 14 What questions do you have about using solar energy for heat?

Possible answer: How do different materials affect the amount of heat that can be generated? Could I capture enough energy to start a fire?

LESSON 2   Engage • Explore/Explain • **Elaborate** • Evaluate

TAKE IT FURTHER Discover More

 **Explore Online**   Students can explore all three Take It Further paths online.

TAKE IT FURTHER
Discover More

Check out this path . . . or go online to choose one of these other paths.

People in Science & Engineering → • Sort It Out
• The Hoover Dam

Elon Musk

Elon Musk is a successful businessman and physicist who has founded several companies. He is known for the compny Tesla Motors. In 2003, the company began work on producing electric cars. The cars run on lithium ion batteries and go about 250 miles before needing to be recharged.

In 2013, Musk announced a new idea called the Hyperloop. The Hyperloop is a transportation idea in which people ride in pods through interconnected tubes. The Hyperloop would run on solar energy and move at speeds of 700 miles per hour.

The Tesla Powerwall is a rechargable lithium-ion battery made for home use. It stores electricity and can provide backup electricity in case of an outage. It can save up to 20 percent on a home's electric bill.

Elon Musk

A Tesla car

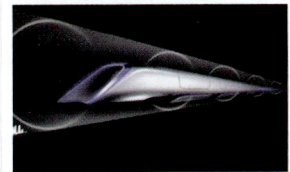
The Hyperloop

A Tesla powerwall

23. The batteries for electric cars need to be plugged into a source of electricity to be recharged. Which type of energy resource would be better to use to recharge an electric car battery—nonrenewable energy resources or renewable energy resources?

Possible answer: Renewable energy sources would be better because they don't pollute like nonrenewable resources do. They also can be replaced.

Collaboration

You may choose to assign this activity or to direct students online to the Interactive Online Student Edition where they can explore and choose from all three paths. These activities can be assigned individually, to pairs, or to small groups.

People in Science & Engineering: Elon Musk

CCC Interdependence of Science, Engineering, and Technology

Ask: Are there limits on electric cars? Yes, they have to stop to recharge after a few hundred miles.

Ask: Does cold weather affect them? (Prompt students by asking what it is like to start a gasoline car in cold weather.) Yes, batteries are weak in the cold.

Ask: What advantage would there be to recharging cars at night? Late at night, people don't need as much power. There would be more electricity available for recharging. You can tell students it might be possible for car owners to get cheaper power at night (off-peak rates).

DCI ESS3.A Natural Resources

Ask: Does recharging at night work with solar power? No, solar panels don't work at night. To rely only on solar power to recharge a car at night, batteries would need to store the solar energy collected during daylight hours and then transfer that energy to the car's battery.

LESSON 2 Engage • Explore/Explain • **Elaborate** • Evaluate

TAKE IT FURTHER, continued

SEP Obtaining, Evaluating, and Communicating Information

Have students reseach the differences between diesel and gasoline used as fuels for cars. Diesel automobiles get better mileage than gasoline automobiles. Have students research and report on the subject.

Ask: How is diesel fuel different from gasoline? It has more energy than gasoline.

Ask: How are engines different? They burn fuel at a higher temperature, so they are more efficient.

Differentiate Instruction

Extension The text tells students about advances in battery technology. Ask them to go a step further.

Ask: Will people be willing to drive a car that will not travel 300 or 500 miles on a charge? Yes, people drive Teslas.

Point out to students that most car trips are short. Since many families own two cars, one car could be electric without inconveniencing people.

▶ Explore Online

Students can explore these additional topics online.

Sort it Out

Students analyze and classify renewable and nonrenewable resources. *(Outside research required.)*

The Hoover Dam

Students learn about the Hoover Dam, a hydroelectric dam that provides power to the Southwest. *(Outside research required.)*

568   Unit 8   Natural Resources and Hazards

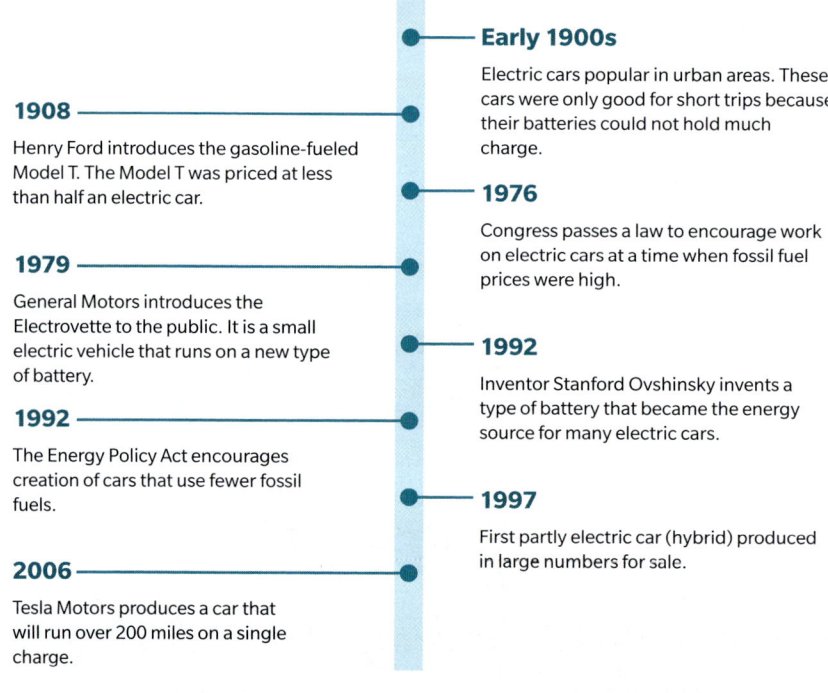

The History of Cars and Batteries

Most cars today run on fossil fuels such as gasoline and diesel fuel. It is possible, however, for cars to run on electricity alone. Electric cars are not common, but they are becoming more popular.

This timeline shows some important events in the development of electric cars and the batteries that help them run.

Development of Electric Car Batteries and Cars

1908 — Henry Ford introduces the gasoline-fueled Model T. The Model T was priced at less than half an electric car.

1979 — General Motors introduces the Electrovette to the public. It is a small electric vehicle that runs on a new type of battery.

1992 — The Energy Policy Act encourages creation of cars that use fewer fossil fuels.

2006 — Tesla Motors produces a car that will run over 200 miles on a single charge.

Early 1900s — Electric cars popular in urban areas. These cars were only good for short trips because their batteries could not hold much charge.

1976 — Congress passes a law to encourage work on electric cars at a time when fossil fuel prices were high.

1992 — Inventor Stanford Ovshinsky invents a type of battery that became the energy source for many electric cars.

1997 — First partly electric car (hybrid) produced in large numbers for sale.

24. What is one thing that has changed about electric car batteries between the early 1900s and 2006? Support your answer with evidence from the timeline.

Possible answer: Early electric cars didn't a hold charge very long. They could only go short distances on their charge. Newer electric cars can go much farther.

568

LESSON CHECK

LESSON 2
Lesson Check

Name _____

Can You Explain It?

1. Remember the house you saw at the start of the lesson? Most houses have wires connected to them that bring electricity for people to use day and night. How does this house gets its electricity? Consider the following:

   - Evidence of how the house is getting energy in the form of electricity.
   - Wires and other things that are necessary to send electricity to a house from an electricity generating plant.
   - Potential downsides to how this house gets its electricity.

> **EVIDENCE NOTEBOOK** Use the information you've collected in your Evidence Notebook to help you cover each point above.

- The house has solar panels on the roof. These panels can help convert sunlight into electrical energy.
- It's also possible the house is getting electricity from underground wires.
- One downside to solar energy is that on dark, cloudy days, the lack of sunlight might result in less electricity. The house will get energy from another source though.

Checkpoints

Choose the correct answer.

2. A family wants to use a renewable energy resource to help provide electricity to their house. Which of these energy resources should they use?
   a. oil   **b. solar**   c. coal   d. natural gas

569

 Formal Assessment Go online for student self-checks and other assessments.

Can You Explain It?

> ### Collaboration
> **Discussion** You may wish to revisit the house without power lines as a group activity to assess students' understanding of the material. Use the bulleted points in the student edition to lead the discussion.

 EVIDENCE NOTEBOOK

Have students reread their answers to the Evidence Notebook prompts and then use that evidence to justify their reasoning as they respond to the Can You Explain It question. Make sure students understand that a complete response must address all bulleted points.

SUMMATIVE ASSESSMENT
Engage in Argument from Evidence

DCI ESS3.A Natural Resources

Students should be able to recall the difference between renewable and nonrenewable energy sources. Remind them, if they get stuck, that renewable and nonrenewable can both be "natural."

1. **Ask:** What other renewable energy might be available? *They might use wood for heat or perhaps a small wind turbine for electricity.*

2. **Ask:** Name one resource that was produced long ago by living things? *natural gas*

Lesson 2 What Renewable Resources Are Used for Energy?   569

LESSON 2   Engage • Explore/Explain • Elaborate • **Evaluate**

LESSON CHECK, *continued*

 Influence of Technology on the Natural World

As students answer these questions, emphasize that even the cleanest, "greenest" renewable energy technology involves some effect on nature.

3. This is a good opportunity to remind students that *natural* does not imply renewable. Fossil fuels are natural, but they are nonrenewable.

4. Give examples of places where certain renewables are unavailable or inadequate, such as the Arctic in winter.

5. If students cannot answer, refer them back to the description of drawbacks at the beginning of Exploration 1. Reiterate the point made above about how all renewable energy technologies involve some impact on Earth, in some form, such as mining for metals and other materials that are needed for the turbines.

Ask: Is it true that renewables cannot harm the environment? **No, most renewables can harm the environment. However, in comparison to nonrenewable, renewable is less harmful to the environment.**

6. Discuss what forms biomass takes (wood, plant remains, animal waste), and how the energy it contains is converted to a form that an electricity generating station can use (usually burned).

3. A new electricity generating plant wants to avoid using any nonrenewable energy resources to produce electricity. Which energy resource should the plant not use?
   a. solar
   b. geothermal
   c. hydroelectric
   d. natural gas ✓

4. Read the sentence below. Choose the best word or phrase to complete the sentence.

   | it is available everywhere |
   | it never harms wildlife |
   | it will never run out |
   | it produces little or no pollution |

   There are many benefits to using renewable energy sources. One of the benefits of using renewable energy sources is that ___it will never run out___. Another benefit is that ___produces little or no pollution___.

5. Read the sentence below. Choose the best word or phrase to complete the sentence.

   | heat | pollution |
   | harm wildlife | cause droughts |

   One drawback of hydroelectric energy is that dams can ___harm wildlife___.
   Geothermal energy comes from ___heat___. Solar energy does not result in ___pollution___.

6. Choose the correct answer. An electricity generating plant doesn't want to use biomass to produce electricity due its drawbacks. Which of these is a drawback of using biomass to produce electricity?
   a. It is nonrenewable.
   b. It is very costly to use.
   c. It can be used in few places.
   d. It can produce air pollution. ✓

570

570   Unit 8   Natural Resources and Hazards

LESSON 2

Lesson Roundup

A. Choose the correct words to complete each sentence.

coal	pollution	natural gas	biomass
oil	severe weather	radiation	

One example of a renewable energy resource is __biomass__. One drawback of nonrenewable energy resources is that they produce __pollution__.

B. Fill in the term of the renewable resource to the row that features the benefits and drawbacks.

| hydroelectric | solar | biomass | wind | geothermal |

Renewable Resource	Benefits	Drawbacks
solar	• renewable • clean energy	• needs sun to work • equipment is expensive
wind	• renewable • clean energy	• long spinning blades can hurt birds • turbines are loud • large area of land is needed
hydroelectric	• renewable • clean energy	• dams are expensive • reservoirs flood valuable land • dams can harm fish and other life by changing depth and temperature of rivers • reservoirs take away wildlife habitat
geothermal	• renewable • low pollution	• only available in certain areas • some processes release water containing chemicals that can pollute the air
biomass	• renewable • less polluting than fossil fuels	• burning the material can produce air pollution

C. What other information did you learn about the benefits or drawbacks of using renewable resources for energy?

Student responses will vary but should not repeat what is written in the table.

Lesson Roundup

DCI ESS3.A Natural Resources

This lesson summary enables students to quickly revisit key points and prepare for tests.

A. The prefix *bio-* in the word *biomass* should remind students that biomass comes from living things, and so it is renewable. Biomass is derived from solar energy. Having eliminated biomass from their choices by completing the first sentence, students should recognize that pollution has been a topic in this lesson, but radiation and severe weather have not. **ESS3.A**

B. The table presents a useful summary of benefits and drawbacks. Students may refer to Exploration 2 to refresh their memories. Certain phrases will help them to recognize each resource: *needs sun*, *long spinning blades*, *reservoirs flood*, and *burning the material* should be firmly linked to the appropriate renewable resources. **ESS3.A**

C. Students may wish to refer to item B or scan Exploration 2 before responding. If they need scaffolded support, begin by reminding them that they may need to combine information to find the answer. Make sure students recognize that society is not choosing between renewable and nonrenewable resources. It is not possible at present to stop using nonrenewable resources. Also, nonrenewable resources have harmful effects that must be dealt with. **ESS3.A**

Lesson 2 What Renewable Resources Are Used for Energy?

LESSON 3
How Can People Reduce the Impact of Land-Based Hazards?

Building to the Performance Expectation

The learning experiences in this lesson prepare students for mastery of:

4-ESS3-2 Generate and compare multiple solutions to reduce the impacts of natural Earth processes on humans.

Trace Tool to the NGSS
Go online to view the complete coverage of these standards across this lesson, unit, and time.

 Science & Engineering Practices

Constructing Explanations and Designing Solutions
Generate and compare multiple solutions to a problem based on how well they meet the criteria and constraints of the design solution.

Obtaining, Evaluating, and Communicating Information
Obtain and combine information from books and other reliable media to explain phenomena.

 **VIDEO** Obtaining, Evaluating, and Communicating Information

Developing and Using Models
Develop a model using an example to describe a scientific principle.

 **VIDEO** Developing and Using Models

Disciplinary Core Ideas

ESS3.B Natural Hazards
A variety of hazards result from natural processes (e.g., earthquakes, tsunamis, volcanic eruptions). Humans cannot eliminate the hazards but can take steps to reduce their impacts. (4-ESS3-2)

ETS1.B Designing Solutions to Engineering Problems
Testing a solution involves investigating how well it performs under a range of likely conditions. (4-ESS3-2)

 Crosscutting Concepts

Cause and Effect
Cause-and-effect relationships are routinely identified, tested, and used to explain change.

Influence of Science, Engineering, and Technology on Society and the Natural World
Engineers improve existing technologies or develop new ones to increase their benefits, to decrease known risks, and to meet societal demands.

CONNECTIONS TO MATH

MP.2 Reason abstractly

MP.4 Model with mathematics.

4.OA.A.1 Interpret a multiplication equation as a comparison, e.g., interpret $35 = 5 \times 7$ as a statement that 35 is 5 times as many as 7 and 7 times as many as 5. Represent verbal statements of multiplicative comparisons as multiplication equations.

CONNECTIONS TO ENGLISH LANGUAGE ARTS

RI.4.1 Refer to details and examples in a text when explaining what the text says explicitly and when drawing inferences from the text.

RI.4.9 Integrate information from two texts on the same topic in order to write or speak about the subject knowledgeably.

Supporting All Students, All Standards

Integrating the Three Dimensions of Learning

In this lesson, students learn about natural hazards that take place on land, such as volcanic eruptions, earthquakes, landslides, and wildfires **(DCI ESS3.B)**. They explore the causes and effects of these events **(CCC Cause and Effect)** and obtain and communicate information **(SEP Obtaining, Evaluating, and Communicating Information)** about how maps can be used to assess the risk of natural hazards. Students learn how land-based natural hazards are predicted using technology, mapping, and observations in the field **(CCC Influence of Science, Engineering, and Technology on Society and the Natural World) (DCI ETS1.B)**. They investigate how engineers and scientists develop strategies to reduce the impacts of these events, and they design their own solutions to mitigate the effects of a landslide **(SEP Constructing Explanations and Designing Solutions)**.

Professional Development Go online to view **Professional Development** videos with strategies to integrate CCCs and SEPs, including the ones used in this lesson.

Extra Hands-On Activity: Shakeproof, Quakeproof

What Makes a Building Earthquake Proof?

 Small groups
45 minutes

Have students design an earthquake-proof building that they will test. Provide each group with building materials such as straws or toothpicks for model beams and clay for joining the beams. To test each building, place the building on an upside-down aluminum cake pan. Tap the cake pan for 10 to 30 seconds to model the compression waves that are felt at the beginning of an earthquake. After that, lightly shake the cake pan side to side to model the secondary waves that follow the compression waves of an earthquake.

After every group's models have been tested, have students revisit their designs. They should list the elements that worked in their design as well as the elements of the design that failed to withstand the forces of the model earthquake. Once every group is done redesigning their buildings, retest the buildings using the same testing method from their initial design.

 This activity can support mastery of this Crosscutting Concept: Influence of Science, Engineering, and Technology on Society and the Natural World

Preassessment

Have students complete the unit pre-test online or see the Assessment Guide.

Build on Prior Knowledge

Students should already know and be prepared to build on the following concepts:
- Natural hazards are events caused by natural processes such as severe weather, earthquakes, or volcanoes.
- Living things can affect their environment in many ways.

Differentiate Instruction

Lesson Vocabulary
- natural hazard

Ask: What do you think of when you hear the word natural? **Sample answer: something found in nature**

Explain that natural hazards are events that happen in the natural world. They are mainly caused by natural processes, but some natural hazards can be triggered by human activities.

ELL/ELD Strategy
Model Have students preview at the types of land-based natural hazards in Exploration 1. Model how to use the captions and diagrams to define each hazard.
Say: I'm not sure what an earthquake is. But when I look at the diagram of an earthquake on this page, I see a large crack in the ground. The caption tsays the ground shakes violently during an earthquake. So an earthquake must be a hazard that makes the ground move.

LESSON 3   **Engage** • Explore/Explain • Elaborate • Evaluate

ENGAGE: Lesson Phenomenon

Lesson Objective

Describe a variety of Earth processes on land that can be hazardous to humans and how the impact of these processes can be lessened.

About This Image

Volcanic eruptions can emit large amounts of gases and debris. Following an exceptionally violent eruption, volcanic gases in the atmosphere can lower global temperatures for several years by partially blocking sunlight. Volcanic eruptions can cause deadly mudslides as hot lava mixes with snow or ice as it flows down the mountainside. Other volcanic hazards include ash that can cover large areas surrounding the volcano. Ash clouds can impact air travel and damage infrastructure.

Alternative Engage Strategy

Modeling Faults

Pairs
15 minutes

Explain that earthquakes occur along faults, or breaks in rocks. Tell students that there are three main kinds of faults: strike-slip, normal, and reverse. In strike-slip faults, two chunks of rock slide past one another in opposite directions. In normal faults, two chunks of rock move away from each other, with one chunk shifting downward. In reverse faults, two chunks of rock push together, with one chunk shifting upward.

Give pairs of students two wooden blocks, and have them model the movement of rocks along the different types of faults.

Ask: Do you think powerful earthquakes are associated with large shifts in rocks or small shifts in rocks? Explain. Powerful earthquakes are associated with large shifts in rocks because large shifts release more energy.

LESSON 3

How Can People Reduce the Impact of Land-Based Hazards?

A picture of a volcanic eruption is amazing. You can see the hot lava and billowing ashes and gases the volcano releases. How can people stay safe when a volcanic eruption happens?

By the end of this lesson . . .
You'll be able to describe some natural hazards and tell how people can stay safe when they occur.

572

Unit 8 Natural Resources and Hazards

 **Explore Online** Students can view the lesson phenomenon online.

Can You Explain It?

Can You Explain It?

At the University of California, San Diego, engineers construct buildings to test their ability to withstand earthquakes. The buildings sit on a giant "shake table" that models how Earth moves during an earthquake.

1. In what ways can people reduce the impact of land-based natural hazards, such as earthquakes?
   <u>Students should respond based on the preliminary</u>
   <u>observations they can make of the images.</u>
   _____
   _____
   _____

Tip Learn more about ways that people can design solutions to problems in *How Do Engineers Define Problems?* and *How Do Engineers Design Solutions?*

 EVIDENCE NOTEBOOK Look for this icon to help you gather evidence to answer the question above.

573

Students are asked to identify ways that people can reduce the impacts of natural hazards, such as earthquakes. Point out that the "shake table" represents one way to lessen the impact of natural hazards by helping engineers design and test buildings that can withstand the vibrations of an earthquake. As students think about their preliminary answer to the question, tell them not to limit their thinking to earthquakes. They may want to focus their ideas on land-based natural hazards that affect their own area, such as volcanoes, landslides, or wildfires.

Collaboration

Draw, Pair, Share Have partners each draw a picture that shows the effects of a land-based natural hazard of their choice. Then have pairs work together to come up with captions describing their drawings. Display students' work around the classroom. Refer to the drawings as students progress through the lesson.

 EVIDENCE NOTEBOOK

Encourage students to use an appropriate graphic organizer, such as main idea and supporting details, to set up their notebook for this lesson.
Find more strategies in the online ELA handbook.

Lesson 3 How Can People Reduce the Impact of Land-Based Hazards? **573**

LESSON 3   Engage • **Explore/Explain** • Elaborate • Evaluate

EXPLORATION 1 Land-Based Natural Hazards

3D Learning Objective

Learn about <mark>natural hazards that take place on land</mark>, such as volcanic eruptions, earthquakes, landslides, and wildfires, explore the <mark>causes and effects of these events</mark>, and learn how scientists measure the intensity of earthquakes. They will <mark>obtain and communicate information</mark> about how maps can be used to assess the risk of natural hazards.

DCI ESS3.B Natural Hazards

Tell students that human activities can help prevent or reduce some natural hazards. Have students research how people can reduce the effects of land-based hazards. Discuss as a class.

Ask: Which land-based natural hazards can people prevent or reduce? *Possible answer: landslides and wildfire*

Differentiate Instruction

Extension Have students research different types of landslides, including rockslides, mudslides, avalanches, creeps, and slumps. Tell them to download images that show each type of landslide. They can use the images as visual aids as they share what they learned with the class.

Ask: What role does gravity play in landslides? *It pulls material on slopes downward, resulting in landslides.*

HANDS-ON Apply What You Know
Make Your Own Seismometer

You may find it helpful to use rolls of parchment paper or wrapping paper and have students cut the paper into long strips rather than taping short strips of construction paper together. Also, cut the slits in the boxes for students ahead of time. Tell students to pull the paper through the box at a slow but steady rate.

Ask: What do the peaks and valleys of your reading represent? *vibrations (tremors) from an earthquake*

574 Unit 8 Natural Resources and Hazards

EXPLORATION 1
Land-Based Natural Hazards

Our Active Earth

Earth has many process that help shape its surface. But these can also cause natural hazards. A **natural hazard** is an earth process that threatens people and property.

Types of Land-Based Hazards

Use the images and captions to learn about land-based hazards.

 When a volcano erupts, it can release lava, rocks, ash, and poisonous gases. These can be dangerous to people and surrounding property.

 Landslides can be falling or flowing soil, mud, rocks, or snow. They can knock down trees and bury homes and other property.

 In an earthquake, the ground shakes violently. This shaking can collapse buildings and bridges. Roads and walkways can crack and crumple.

 During a wildfire, an area of forest, shrub, or grassland burns out of control. Buildings can be completely destroyed and people have to leave.

2. Why is it important for people to be warned about natural hazards?
Possible answer: We cannot stop natural hazards, but when we know about them, we can take steps to be safe.

 HANDS-ON Apply What You Know

Make Your Own Seismometer

3. A seismometer detects and measures ground movement. In this interaction you will make a seismometer.

Materials
- shoebox without lid
- ruler
- pointed-tip scissors
- construction paper
- clear adhesive tape
- two rubber bands
- fine line marker
- yarn or string

574

Procedure:

a. Working in a team of two or three, use a ruler to measure a 10 cm cutting line along the bottom edge of each long side of the box.
b. Cut a slit along each cutting line.
c. Cut the paper into strips slightly less than 10 cm wide.
d. Attach the pieces together with clear adhesive tape to form one long strip.
e. Insert the strip of paper into the slits so the ends of the strip extend out of the slits.
f. Attach two rubber bands so the bands are stretched wide to the sides of the two box slits.
g. Cut two pieces of yarn or string and tie the marker into place between the rubber bands so the tip lightly rests on the strip of paper in the box.
h. Working together, one partner jiggles the box while the other pulls the paper through to get a continuous reading of the magnitude of the simulated earthquake.

4. Identify and describe a problem or difficulty you noticed while using the seismometer.
Possible answer: I noticed that when the box was jiggled very hard, the marker went off the paper.

5. Describe one way your seismometer could be improved.
Possible answer: by using wider strips of paper so that a wider range of simulated earthquake intensities could be recorded

6. Think about your model and how it works. Which part(s) remain relatively stationary during an earthquake, and how does this make the seismometer work?
The marker remains relatively stationary, while everything else moves with the earthquake. By having the marker be independent, it captures the movement of everything around it.

7. What would an Earth scientist need to do to be able to interpret a seismometer such as yours? How would he or she "read" it?
The sizes or shapes of the scribbles of the marker would need to represent the intensity of the earthquake in specific units.

575

Influence of Science, Engineering, and Technology on Society and the Natural World

Tell students that a seismometer measures seismic waves released during an earthquake. By tracking the paths of the waves as they move within Earth, scientists can pinpoint the focus of the earthquake, or its point of origin. They can also locate the epicenter, or place on Earth's surface directly above the earthquake's focus. Have students find out more about seismometers.

Ask: Why might it be helpful to know the point of origin of an earthquake? You can map the point of origin and monitor it for signs of future earthquakes.

Constructing Explanations and Designing Solutions

Review students' suggestions for improving their models. If time permits, have teams redesign their models and retest them.

Ask: Did your redesign improve your model? Why or why not? Answers will vary depending on students' models.

Scoring Guideline

A strong performance in this activity will involve complete setup of a functional seismometer, so the marker shakes in rhythm with the movement the students provide."

LESSON 3 Engage • **Explore/Explain** • Elaborate • Evaluate

EXPLORATION 1 *Land-Based Natural Hazards, continued*

DCI ESS3.B Natural Hazards

Tell students that melted rock beneath Earth's surface is called magma. Magma that flows onto Earth's surface through a crack in Earth's crust is called lava.

Ask: How can one natural hazard, such as a volcanic eruption, cause other natural hazards? Hot lava from a volcano can cause a wildfire. Falling ash can cause landslides.

> ### Differentiate Instruction
>
> **RTI/Extra Support** Tell students that a cause makes something happen. An effect is what happens because of a cause. Give them the following example: I missed the bus because I woke up late.
>
> **Ask:** What is the cause? What is the effect? waking up late; missing the bus

CCC Cause and Effect

Have students make graphic organizers to show the causes and effects of each natural hazard. Show them an example of a simple cause-and-effect graphic organizer to get them started.

Build on Prior Knowledge

Ask students if they have ever watched a movie about a natural hazard. Have them describe its effects.

Ask: What are some ways that people stay safe during a natural hazard? Sample answer: They leave the area until it is safe to return.

Cause and Effect

The cause of every natural hazard is related to an Earth process. The effects of these events can be very destructive.

Causes and Effects of Land-Based Hazards

8. Read about each of the land-based hazards shown here. Then complete the table.

Volcanic eruptions occur when melted rock bursts through an opening in Earth's crust. The hot lava can cause wildfires. Falling ash can cause landslides.

Sometimes enormous pieces of Earth's crust suddenly grind against each other, causing an earthquake. The ground shakes so hard that buildings can collapse.

Landslides can be triggered by volcanic eruptions or earthquakes. Rock slides and snow avalanches occur on steep slopes, but mud can flow on even a gentle slope.

Wildfires are caused by human activities, volcanic eruptions, and lightning. They can destroy natural environments and homes and cause landslides.

Natural hazard	Cause and effect
volcanic eruption	Cause—Melted rock bursts through a crack in Earth's crust.
wildfire	Effect— Trees and homes are burned up, and there is risk of landslides.
earthquake	Cause—Earth's enormous rock plates grind against each other.
landslide	Cause— A volcano or earthquake loosens the soil or turns it to mud.

576

Do the Math
Richter Scale

Magnitude	Ground shaking
1–3	not felt
3–4	weak
4–5	light/moderate
5–6	strong/very strong
6–7	very strong/severe
7+	severe/violent/extreme

The Richter scale can be used to measure and compare strength of earthquakes. Each magnitude on the Richter scale is 10 times greater than the one before it. So a magnitude 3 earthquake is 10 times stronger than a magnitude 2 earthquake and 100 times stronger than a magnitude 1 earthquake.

9. Use the table to determine the magnitude of an earthquake in which you felt the ground shake.

Possible answer: The earthquake must have had a magnitude greater than 3.

10. How much stronger is an earthquake that measures 7 on the Richter scale than an earthquake that measures 5 on the Richter scale?

   a. 2 times as strong
   c. 100 times stronger
   b. 10 times stronger
   d. 1,000 times stronger

11. If you use the number 1 to represent the strength of a magnitude 1 earthquake, explain what number would be used to represent the strength of a magnitude 5 earthquake.

Possible answer: 10,000; If 1 represents a magnitude 1 earthquake, then 2 would be 10, 3 would be 100, 4 would be 1,000, and 5 would be 10,000.

Language SmArts
Drawing Examples from Text

12. Use examples from the text to explain why an understanding of the causes and effects of land-based hazards is important to helping people stay safe.

Possible answer: Knowing the causes and effects of earthquakes can help people know where earthquake-resistant buildings would be most useful.

 EVIDENCE NOTEBOOK In your Evidence Notebook, identify three specific facts about natural hazards that would be important to engineers who are designing ways to keep people safe. Explain why you included each fact.

 Have students explore the causes and effects of land-based hazards online to learn more about natural hazards.

Do the Math
Richter Scale
4.OA.A.1 Interpret a multiplication equation as a comparison

Use multiplication equations to help students understand magnitude on the Richter scale. For example, for item 11, write the following equations on the board: $1 \times 10 = 10$; $10 \times 10 = 100$; $100 \times 10 = 1,000$; $1,000 \times 10 = 10,000$.

Ask: Using the same formula from item 11, what magnitude earthquake would be represented by the number 100,000? **magnitude 6 earthquake**

Obtaining, Evaluating, and Communicating Information

Have interested students research other ways to measure earthquakes, such as the moment magnitude scale or the Mercalli scale. Ask them to share their findings with the class.

Language SmArts
Drawing Examples from Text
RI.4.1 Refer to details and examples in a text

Ask students to refer to specific examples in the text in their answers, such as the connection between earthquakes and damage to buildings in zones that are earthquake prone.

Ask: In addition to words, how else is information presented in the text? **It is presented visually in the form of photos and diagrams.**

 EVIDENCE NOTEBOOK

Students might include the following facts and reasons: engineers need to know where the hazard occurred so it can be monitored and how intense or widespread the hazard was so the damage can be assessed.

LESSON 3   Engage • **Explore/Explain** • Elaborate • Evaluate

EXPLORATION 1 *Land-Based Natural Hazards, continued*

Connection to Math

Help students understand the concept of "average." Tell them that average describes the central or most typical value in a set of data. It can be found by dividing the sum of all the values in a data set by the number of values in the set. For example, there are 10 values listed in the interactive for item 14. Have students add the values together and then divide the answer by 10 to find the average number of earthquakes experienced by the 10 states over 29 years.

$38 + 34 + 32 + 24 + 22 + 21 + 20 + 17 + 17 + 16 = 241 \div 10 = 24.1$

MP.4 Model with mathematics

DCI ESS3.B Natural Hazards

Direct students' attention to the first map on the student page.

Ask: Based on what you have learned about how earthquakes happen, what can you infer about the rock that makes up the western part of the United States? *It is made up of pieces of rock that grind against each other.*

CCC Influence of Science, Engineering, and Technology on Society and the Natural World

Ask: Where would you expect the most earthquake-proof buildings in the United States? Explain. *in the western part of the country, because that area experiences the most earthquakes*

Hazards Here and There

Some natural hazards occur more frequently in some places than in others. Maps can be used to show this information.

Earthquake Maps

These maps provide information about the number of earthquakes of magnitude 3.5 or greater in different states from 1974–2003. Use the information in the maps to answer the questions.

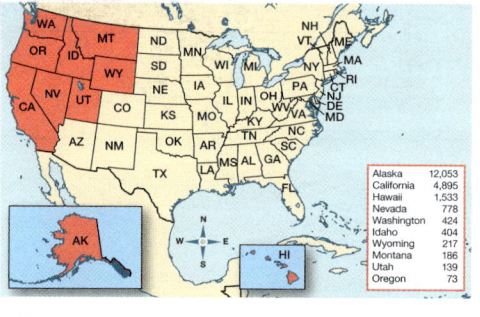

Alaska	12,053
California	4,895
Hawaii	1,533
Nevada	778
Washington	424
Idaho	404
Wyoming	217
Montana	186
Utah	139
Oregon	73

This map shows the ten states that experienced the greatest number of earthquakes.

13. Other than Alaska, how would you describe the location of the states in the "top ten" earthquake list?

Possible answer: They are in the western part of the United States.

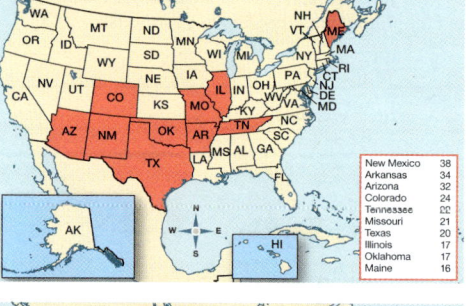

New Mexico	38
Arkansas	34
Arizona	32
Colorado	24
Tennessee	22
Missouri	21
Texas	20
Illinois	17
Oklahoma	17
Maine	16

This map shows the states ranked 11 through 20 based on the number of earthquakes.

14. Which states in this list had more than one earthquake per year during the 29 years shown?

New Mexico, Arizona, and Arkansas

New York	16
Alabama	15
Kentucky	15
South Carolina	10
South Dakota	10
Virginia	10
Nebraska	8
Ohio	8
Georgia	7
Indiana	6
New Hampshire	6
Pennsylvania	6
Kansas	4
North Carolina	3
Massachusetts	2
Michigan	2
Minnesota	2
Mississippi	2
New Jersey	2
Louisiana	1
Rhode Island	1
West Virginia	1

This map shows all the remaining states that experienced at least one earthquake.

15. How does the location of the states shown here compare to the location of the states that had the most earthquakes?

Possible answer: These states are farther east on the map.

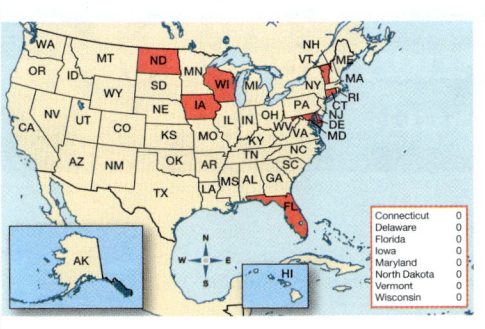

This map shows which states did not experience an earthquake.

16. How would you describe the possibility of an earthquake in the states shown in this map?

Possible answer: These states have a low possibility of earthquakes.

17. Locate your state on one of the maps. What can you infer about earthquakes in your state based on the information in the maps?

Possible answer: My state has a medium risk of earthquakes.

18. Using the maps, choose the state that makes each sentence most correct.

| Vermont | Minnesota | Illinois | New York |
| North Carolina | California | Nebraska | New Mexico |

Among the states listed above, the most earthquakes happen in ___California___. Of the states listed, the smallest number of earthquakes happen in ___Vermont___.

Putting It Together

19. Choose the correct word to complete each sentence.

| landslides | earthquakes | volcanic eruptions | wildfires |

Two hazards caused by natural processes that occur under Earth's surface are ___earthquakes/volcanic eruptions___ and ___earthquakes/volcanic eruptions___. Processes occurring on Earth's surface are the direct cause of ___landslides/wildfires___ and ___landslides/wildfires___.

Obtaining, Evaluating, and Communicating Information

Tell students that there are also maps that show risk of landslides and volcanic eruptions. Have them search for maps online and assess the risk in their area for landslides and volcanic eruptions.

Ask: Based on the maps you found, which type of natural hazard is more common? **landslides**

Differentiate Instruction

ELL: Build Background Point out that each pair of letters on the maps is an abbreviation that represents the name of a state. The abbreviations for states are sometimes the first two letters in the state's name or, if the state's name is made up of two words, the first letter of each word.

Ask: What does OH stand for on the map? **Ohio**

Ask: What are some examples of abbreviations for states that are not made up of the first two letters in the states' names? **MO for Missouri, KS for Kansas, VT for Vermont, AK for Alaska**

FORMATIVE ASSESSMENT

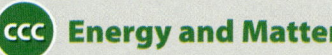 **Energy and Matter**

Tell students that each term is used only once. They may find it helpful to review the information about the causes and effects of natural hazards.

Ask: What causes volcanoes? **Melted rock bursts through an opening in Earth's crust.**

Ask: What causes earthquakes? **Huge pieces of Earth's crust grind against each other.**

Ask: What causes landslides? **earthquakes and volcanoes**

Ask: What causes wildfires? **human activities, volcanic eruptions, and lightning**

LESSON 3   Engage • **Explore/Explain** • Elaborate • Evaluate

EXPLORATION 2 Reducing the Impacts of Land-Based Hazards

3D Learning Objective

Discover how **land-based natural hazards** are predicted using **technology, mapping, and observations in the field**. **Obtain information and communicate** how engineers and scientists develop strategies to reduce the impacts of natural hazards. Work together to create plans about how individuals and families can stay safe during a natural hazard.

DCI ESS3.B Natural Hazards

Human activities can increase the severity or frequency of some natural hazards. We can take measures to lessen the impact. Tell students that building houses on steep slopes can make the slopes more vulnerable to landslides because construction weakens rock layers and removes vegetation that "anchors" earth materials.

Ask: What is one measure we can take to reduce this problem?
Sample answer: Replant vegetation on steep slopes, or limit construction on steep slopes.

SEP Obtaining, Evaluating, and Communicating Information

Students might have said that they could prepare for an earthquake by having a plan of where the family should gather if an event occurred while everyone was out of the house.

Ask: How might technology help you carry out your family plan?
Sample answer: answers may vary

Differentiate Instruction

Extension More than one factor can cause a land-based hazard. Lightning strike involves high temperatures and can cause fires. Lack of rain at times can cause wild fires. Have students research other factors that can cause wildfires and possible ways to help prevent wildfires. Discuss as a class.

---

580 Unit 8 Natural Resources and Hazards

EXPLORATION 2
Reducing the Impacts of Land-Based Hazards

Expect the Unexpected

You can't prevent natural hazards from happening. They're results of Earth's processes. However, you can prepare for natural hazards and plan for how to be safe when they do occur.

Preparation and Response

20. For each natural hazard shown, research to find out how to prepare ahead of time and respond while it is happening.

Hazard	Preparation	Response
Volcanic eruption	Student responses should reflect information from reliable sources about how to prepare and respond to different types of land hazards.	
Earthquake		
Landslide		
Wildfire		

21. Circle the pictures that represent a way to stay safe during an earthquake.

  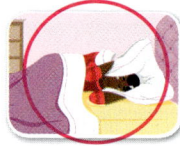 

580

HANDS-ON Apply What You Know
Disaster Supply Kit

22. Select one type of natural hazard. Brainstorm and research what supplies would be important to include in a disaster supply kit for this type of hazard. Draw a diagram of your supply kit. Identify the type of hazard it is designed for. List the things you will include, and write an explanation of why each item is important.

Engineer It!
Earthquake Resistant Buildings

23. How would you design an earthquake-resistant building? When engineers design buildings to be resistant to earthquakes, they consider many factors. Look at the picture to learn more.

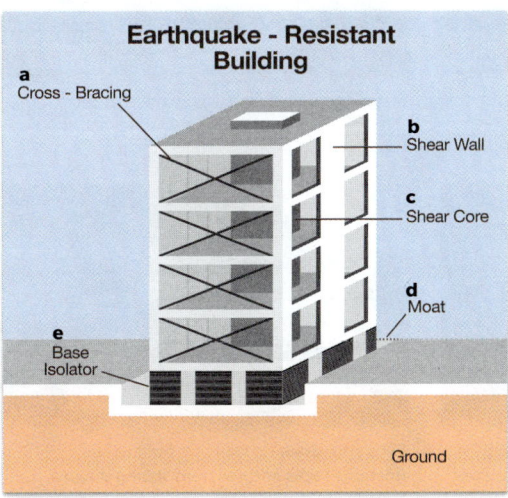

a. Cross-braces are diagonal. They help reinforce the building and increase its stability.

b. Shear walls are vertical walls. They help make the building solid and stiff. They increase the ability of the structure to withstand rocking.

c. In the middle of a building, you might find a shear core. This is an inside structure made out of shear walls. You might find a shear core around an elevator.

d. A moat is an area around the outside of a building. This helps keep the building from being damaged by nearby buildings that might not be earthquake resistant.

e. A base isolator separates the building from the ground. A base isolator is made to absorb the movement of the earthquake.

24. Describe two specific ways that engineers make buildings earthquake resistant.

Possible answer: Cross-braces and shear walls are two ways that engineers make buildings more stable, increasing their safety during an earthquake.

581

HANDS-ON Apply What You Know
Disaster Supply Kit

Tell students that government agencies are helpful online resources for information about disaster supply kits.

Scoring Guidelines

An excellent score consists of an appropriately drawn diagram with the hazard type identified and a comprehensive explanation of the items.

Engineer It!
Earthquake Resistant Buildings

Go over each element of the building to be sure that students understand its function.

Ask: How does a moat help a building stay safe during an earthquake? A moat keeps a building from being damaged by the potential collapse of other buildings that are close by.

Have partners quiz one another about the purpose of other elements in the diagram.

Have students use multiple sources to look for pictures and diagrams of earthquake resistant buildings.

Influence of Science, Engineering, and Technology on Society and the Natural World

Tell students that engineers have designed buildings that can hold up under the ash and smaller debris from a volcanic eruption but that the buildings cannot withstand a lava flow.

Ask: Why do you think this is so? The lava from a volcanic eruption is extremely hot and difficult to control. It can destroy everything in its path.

Lesson 3 How Can People Reduce the Impact of Land-Based Hazards? **581**

LESSON 3   Engage • **Explore/Explain** • Elaborate • Evaluate

EXPLORATION 2 *Reducing the Impacts of Land-Based Hazards, continued*

Engineer It!
Reducing Impacts with Technology

Tell students that a firebreak may be bare ground, a road, or low plants that are kept short by regular mowing.

Ask: Can you think of any firebreaks that occur in nature?
Sample answer: lakes and rivers

Connection to English Language Arts

Direct students' attention to the photo of piles and retaining walls. Explain that piles are a row of upright metal beams pushed downward until they anchor into a sturdy rock base. A retaining wall is made by stacking metal, concrete, or wooden beams on top of each other, usually across the piles. Point out also that the photo shows a drainage pipe that diverts water away from the hillside.

Ask: Infer how a drainage pipe can help prevent landslides. Water makes earth materials more prone to slippage, so diverting water increases the stability of the hillside.

RI.4.1 Refer to details and examples in a text when explaining what the text says explicitly and when drawing inferences from the text.

DCI ESS3.B Natural Hazards

Explain that when melted rock moves upward through the inside of a volcano, it causes the volcano to swell. The swelling causes the angle of the ground around the volcano to change.

Ask: What do you think scientists do after they find a large change in the angle of the ground around a volcano? They issue warnings to the public.

Engineer It!
Reducing Impacts with Technology

Earth's natural processes create quite a few hazards. Humans cannot prevent earthquakes, volcanic eruptions, or other natural hazards. The good news is that technology can help us be safer from natural hazards.

25. Use the pictures and captions to identify the hazard for each technology in the first column. Then research other technology that helps keeps us safe. Write these in the third column labeled AdditionalTechnologies.

When melted rock moves upward, it tilts the ground around it. A tiltmeter records these changes, helping scientists predict eruptions.

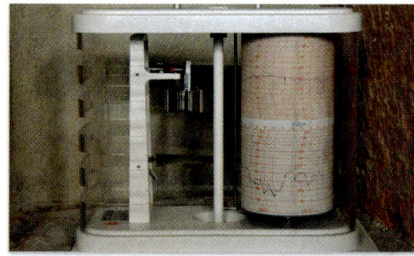
Seismograph readings show the size and location of an earthquake's source, including how deep underground it is.

Firebreaks prevent wildfires from spreading. A firebreak is a strip of land that does not provide fuel for the fire, so the fire usually cannot move past it.

Piles and retaining walls are built to keep unstable rocks and soil from sliding down a hillside.

Hazard	Technology	Additional Technologies
wildfire	Firebreaks	
volcanic eruption	Tiltmeter	
landslide	Piles and retaining walls	
earthquake	Seismograph	

HANDS-ON Apply What You Know

Make a Plan

26. For every natural hazard, there are ways to plan ahead to be safer. With a team of three or four students, choose a land-based natural hazard. Using what you learn during your research, create a safety video about that hazard. Submit your video to your teacher.

27. **Language SmArts** For the natural hazard you chose above, make a plan for each member of your family should that hazard occur. Carry out research if necessary, then write your plan below.

Possible plan: My sister will keep track of the flashlight. My brother will grab extra blankets. My mother will put a bag of nonperishable groceries together. My father will be responsible for getting us out of the house and to safety.

28. Volcanic eruption can cause other land-based hazards to occur. Identify one of these and describe preparation for that hazard.

Possible answer: Volcanic eruptions can cause wildfires. Preparation for wildfires might include having a firebreak around the edge of a property and keeping a family emergency kit available in case a family needs to leave quickly to escape.

29. A safety warning on the evening news based on results of tiltmeter readings would indicate that a family needed to prepare for
    a. a volcanic eruption.
    b. an earthquake.
    c. a storm.

 EVIDENCE NOTEBOOK Engineers are designing technology to keep people safe during an earthquake. How might seismographs and maps showing the history of earthquakes in an area help them? Write your answer in your Evidence Notebook.

583

HANDS-ON Apply What You Know
Make a Plan

As a class, agree upon criteria for the video before students begin researching. For example, you may want to place a three-minute time limit on each video. You may want to assign each team member a role to ensure that all students participate in the activity.

Ask: What new information did you learn about your natural hazard? Answers will vary depending on the natural hazard students researched.

 Language SmArts
RI.4.9 Integrate information from two texts on the same topic

Communicate a Plan Invite students to present their plans to the class.

Ask: After listening to other students' plans, how would you revise your own family plan? Sample answer: I would calculate the amount of food and water each family member would need for one week and make sure that we had that amount safely stored in the house.

SEP **Constructing Explanations and Designing Solutions**

Give students maps of their area. Have them work in pairs to develop an evacuation route for a local natural hazard, such as a flood or landslide.

 EVIDENCE NOTEBOOK

Students might note that areas that experienced an earthquake in the past are likely to experience an earthquake in the future. So mapping where earthquakes occur and monitoring earthquake activity are crucial to assessing earthquake risk and designing technology to keep people safe.

LESSON 3 Engage • **Explore/Explain** • Elaborate • Evaluate

EXPLORATION 2 Reducing the Impacts of Land-Based Hazards, continued

 ESS3.B Natural Hazards

Note that earthquakes are signs that a volcanic eruption may occur.

Ask: What does this tell you about the natural processes that cause earthquakes and volcanic eruptions? **If earthquakes are signs of an impending volcanic eruption, then these events are likely caused by similar processes.**

Explain that volcanic eruptions and earthquakes are both related to the movement of the large chunks of rock that make up Earth's crust. For this reason, these two natural hazards often occur in the same general regions.

Differentiate Instruction

RTI/Extra Support Tell students that a pattern is something that occurs regularly, such as the thunder that accompanies lightning. When we hear thunder, we know that a storm is likely on the way. In a similar fashion, each time a volcano gives off gases, it's a sign that an eruption could occur. Emphasize that scientists use a combination of signs to assess whether an eruption will happen.

Ask: In addition to the release of gases, what other patterns indicate that a volcanic eruption might occur? **earthquakes and movement of the ground**

What's the Pattern?

Since we can't prevent natural hazards, it's important to have some idea about when they might happen so that people can get to safety or at least be prepared. Scientists try to know a hazard is coming by watching for patterns in nature that serve as warning signs.

Patterns that are Warning Signs

30. Use the pictures and captions to list warning signs for each hazard.

Natural hazard	Volcano	Earthquake	Landslide	Wildfire
Warning signs	earthquakes, volcanic gas	pattern of earthquakes, measurements	earthquakes, volcanos, wildfires	dry conditions

Scientists can predict a volcanic eruption if they see a pattern of movement of the ground, earthquakes, and release of volcanic gases.

Earthquakes are more likely in areas that have had earthquakes in the past and have strain in Earth's crust. Earth movement and strain are measured using seismometers, creepmeters, strainmeters, tiltmeters, and lasers.

Landslides happen suddenly, with little warning, often triggered by earthquakes, volcanoes, and wildfires.

Under dry conditions, once a wildfire has started, satellites or aircraft can find it. Then people are alerted and take action.

31. Imagine that scientists are monitoring an area using a seismometer. They notice patterns of small movements of Earth's surface, and they know this is an area where there is strain in Earth's crust. Based on the patterns you know, which of these natural hazards could happen soon? Circle all that apply.

   a. lava erupting from volcano
   b. landslide
   c. wildfire
   d. earthquake

32. Individual landslides cannot be predicted, but scientists know occurrence of certain hazards can make a landslide more likely. Identify one of those hazards, and explain how it can trigger a landslide.

   Possible answer: An earthquake can cause a landslide because it moves and shakes Earth's surface. Materials on hillsides and slopes might get shaken free of their positions, starting a landslide.

33. What pattern of events is most likely to indicate that a wildfire might occur in an area?

   a. low rainfall amounts
   b. small movements of Earth's surface
   c. change in the tilt of the land in an area
   d. shifts in Earth materials on a hillside

Language SmArts
Summarizing Information

35. Choose the correct words to complete each sentence.

   | watch | patterns | prevent | future | warning |

   You cannot __prevent__ natural hazards, but you can plan what you will do during one. Natural hazards can't be predicted far in advance, but studying __patterns__ makes some advance warning possible.

   Technology helps keep people safe by giving a __warning__ that a hazard has begun or by reducing the impact of the hazard in another way.

Tip
The English Language Arts Handbook can provide help with understanding how to summarize information.

Connection to Life Science

Tell students that many people have reported that their animals acted oddly before an earthquake occurred. Scientists in Japan and China in particular are investigating whether animal behavior can be used to predict earthquakes. So far, the research is inconclusive. Have students conduct their own research about this topic and make charts listing evidence that supports and refutes the hypothesis that animal behavior can be used to predict earthquakes.

LS1.D Information Processing

 ## Constructing Explanations and Designing Solutions

Explain that wildfires can be caused by human activities, such as leaving hot coals or ashes in a campfire. Wind can spread the hot coals or ashes over dry leaves and other forest debris, causing a wildfire. Have students work in groups to create posters to help educate others on how to help prevent wildfires.

FORMATIVE ASSESSMENT

 Language SmArts
Summarizing Information
RI.4.9 Integrate information from two texts

 ## Influence of Science, Engineering, and Technology on Society and the Natural World

Tell students that public officials often issues warnings in advance of a natural hazard.

Ask: Why is it important to follow directions given by public officials when a warning is given about a natural hazard?
Fewer people will be injured if everyone follows directions given by public officials during a natural hazard.

Lesson 3 How Can People Reduce the Impact of Land-Based Hazards?

LESSON 3 Engage • **Explore/Explain** • Elaborate • Evaluate

EXPLORATION 2 *Reducing the Impacts of Land-Based Hazards, continued*

HANDS-ON ACTIVITY Small groups 35 min
Reduce the Risk

3D Learning Objective
CCC Influence of Science, Engineering, and Technology on Society and the Natural World
Students collaborate to develop a plan to reduce the impact of a landslide.

Materials
Preview the lab activity. After you have selected the trays or bins that will be used to construct and test design solutions, evaluate the amount of materials that will be used by most students, based on the size and depth of the bins. Depending on the size of the hill, you may choose to modify the amount of water used in this hands-on acitivty. However, make sure that each group gets the same amount of water. Each group should get about the same amount of the mixture of soil, sand, gravel, and rocks.

Preparation
Remind students that aisde from that they have already learned, heavy rainfalls can also cause landslides. Show students a video of a landslide before they begin the activity. Connect objects seen in the video, such as trees and large rocks, to the materials that are available in this activity.

DCI ETS1.B Developing Possible Solutions

Discuss that testing a solution involves investigating how well it performs under a range of likely conditions.

Ask: What conditions are associated with a landslide? **Sample answers: steep slope, unstable materials, heavy rainfall**

HANDS-ON ACTIVITY
Reduce the Risk

Landslides are land-based natural hazards that can damage property and injure people and animals. They occur when materials such as soil and rocks slide down a slope. Earthquakes and human activity can cause landslides. For example, building roads and homes can change the slope of an area.

Scenario: Imagine you have been hired by an engineering firm to develop a way to reduce the impact of landslides on a specific slope.

Materials provided
- large shallow container (painting tray or bin)
- mixture of soil, sand, gravel, and rocks
- toy cars and milk carton houses
- 1 liter of water
- newspapers
- 1 liter bottle with small holes on the bottom

Materials from your budget
- 5 units per popsicle stick
- 5 units per "tree" (twigs)
- 5 units per of piece of cardboard
- 5 units per medium rock
- 5 units per piece of netting
- 1 unit per wire twist tie

Objective
Collaborate with a group to develop a plan to reduce the impact of a landslide.

Find a Problem: What question will you investigate to meet this objective?
Possible question: How can I reduce the impact of a landslide?

Procedure
STEP 1 Brainstorm: Discuss criteria for a successful design to reduce the impact of a landslide. Consider constraints on your design.

Criteria	Constraints
☐ Reduce the amount of materials that moves to the bottom of the slope	☐ Uses available material
☐ Reduces damage to houses and or cars	☐ Stays within a budget of 100 units.
	☐ Stays within the alloted time set by the teacher.

586

Student Lab Worksheet and complete Teacher Support available online.

586 Unit 8 Natural Resources and Hazards

STEP 2 Research: Research landslides and methods used to reduce their impact, such as retaining walls, piles, and buttress walls. Brainstorm ideas for designs that could reduce the impact of a landslide. Record at least three ideas here.

Possible answer: I could use popsicle sticks to build a retaining wall. I could add plants to stabilize the materials on the slope. I could add netting to the surface of the slope.

STEP 3 Build a hillside of earth materials in the bin or tray. Build houses or a road with cars at the bottom of the slope. Simulate a landslide with your water bottle, by sprinkling a liter of water over your hillside. Carefully observe and record the impact of the landslide. Describe the amount of Earth materials that move down the slope and the impact on the cars or houses.

Possible answer: After the landslide, there was about 4 cm of Earth materials at the base of the slope. The toy car on the road was buried in rocks and damaged.

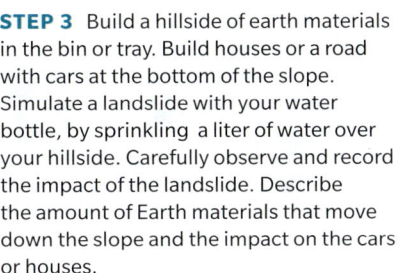

STEP 4 Plan: Review the materials available for your design and their "costs." Review the budget of 100 units. Choose one design to develop as a prototype. Identify the design chosen to develop, and explain why your group chose this design.

Possible answer: We have chosen a design that uses popsicle sticks to construct a retaining wall. It should reduce the impact of the landslide and can be built with the amount of money in the budget.

Procedure

STEP 1 Review that criteria are goals that must be met in order for a design to be considered successful. Constraints are like rules that must be followed in order for a design to be considered successful.

Ask: Why do you think that engineers use criteria and constraints in their work? Sample answer: Criteria and constraints are similar to the steps of a scientific procedure in that they help guide engineers as they design solutions.

STEP 2 At this point in the activity, students should not be overly concerned about constraints. They should record the ideas they find most feasible and will later decide if these ideas are doable given the project's constraints.

SEP Developing and Using Models

STEP 3 Monitor students as they build their model hillsides and simulate a landslide.

Ask: How will you model your landslides? Sample answer: We will shake the bin becaue earthquakes can create landslides. We will pour water to represent rain because heavy rains can cause landslides.

Plan

STEP 4 Place the materials in a central location, and give students ample time to examine them. You may want to make a simple poster that shows the cost of each material; hang the poster above the materials.

LESSON 3 Engage • **Explore/Explain** • Elaborate • Evaluate

EXPLORATION 2 HANDS-ON ACTIVITY, continued

Differentiate Instruction

Extension Allow interested students to use computer graphics programs to draw their designs. Students can print out their designs to share with the group.

Build

DCI ETS1.B Developing Possible Solutions

STEP 6 Have students take careful notes about any modifications they make. This will impact their budget going forward.

Ask: How do your modifications affect your budget? Answers will vary depending on students' modifications.

Test

STEP 7 Suggest that students use the same method for simulating a landslide as they used in Step 3. Explain that this will help them to control variables.

STEP 5 Use the space below to draw a model of your design.

Sketches will vary but should show key aspects of the design plan.

STEP 6 Build: Using your group's model and your available budget, build a design solution for reducing the impact of landslides. Describe any modifications you needed to make as you built your design solution.

Possible answer: As we built our design, we used fewer popsicle sticks than we had shown in the model.

STEP 7 Test: Carry out a test of your design by simulating conditions that could start a landslide. Record the results of your test here. Be sure to describe any damage to the houses or cars.

Possible answer: When we carried out our first test, the homes in the model were damaged.

STEP 8 Evaluate and Redesign: Explain how you will modify your design based on the results of your test. You will need to stay within your budget.

Possible answer: I will make the retaining wall stronger by adding supports.

STEP 9 Modify your design and make any necessary improvements. Keep in mind, you will need to stay within your budget. The slope, road, and houses need to be placed the same in all trials. Test your modified prototype. Describe what happened.

Possible answer: The modifications improved the design. There was less damage to the houses at the base of the slope. There was much less material at the base of the slope as well; only about 1 cm.

STEP 10 Communicate: In the space below, write a summary to communicate the details of your final design.

Possible answer: Our final design was a retaining wall made of popsicle sticks that was reinforced with the addition of vertical supports (also made of popsicle sticks, attached using wire ties.)

589

Evaluate and Redesign

Collaboration

Share Feedback Have each group member suggest a way to modify their design. As a group, students should decide upon the best method to use to improve their models.

SEP Constructing Explanations and Designing Solutions

STEP 9 Again, students should use the same method for simulating a landslide as they used in Steps 3 and 7.

Ask: Why is it important to use the same method for simulating a landslide in each test? If you use different methods for simulating a landslide, then the results are not comparable.

CCC Influence of Science, Engineering, and Technology on Society and the Natural World

STEP 10 Ask: Why is it important that scientists and engineers communicate their results? Communication helps scientists and engineers evaluate one another's work and build on one another's advances. It also informs the public of new discoveries and technologies.

You may want to discuss how scientists and engineers can communicate the results of investigations, or new designs, through journal articles, patent applications, or other forms of communication.

Lesson 3 How Can People Reduce the Impact of Land-Based Hazards? 589

LESSON 3   Engage • **Explore/Explain** • Elaborate • Evaluate

EXPLORATION 2 HANDS-ON ACTIVITY, continued

Analyze Your Results

DCI **ETS1.B Developing Possible Solutions**

STEPS 11–13 Tell students that engineers often revise and retest their designs multiple times before deciding upon a final solution.

Ask: What improvements would you make to your design?
Sample answer: Use several methods of reducing landslide effects.

Draw Conclusions

SEP **Developing and Using Models**

STEP 14 Have students also evaluate their work.

Ask: Were you able to meet all the criteria for this activity? Why or why not? Answers will vary depending on students' designs.

Claims, Evidence, and Reasoning

Have groups exchange lab reports and read each other's answers to each question. On a scale of 1 to 5, have groups assess the other group's evidence and reasoning, with 1 being the lowest ranking and 5 being the highest.

	Scoring Rubric for Hands-On Activity
3	Designs, constructs, and tests a prototype that reduces the impact of a simulated landslide; design meets all criteria and constraints
2	Designs, constructs, and tests a prototype that reduces the impact of a simulated landslide; meets most criteria and constraints
1	Designs, constructs, and tests a prototype intended to reduce the impact of a simulated landslide; meets one or two criteria and constraints for the design
0	Does not design, construct, or a prototype to reduce the impact of a simulated landslide

Unit 8 Natural Resources and Hazards

Analyze Results

STEP 11 Compare your team's results with those of a different team. Describe how and why your results were similar to or different from the other team's results.

Possible answer: Our results were less successful than the other team's; they had less damage to their houses.

STEP 12 What method did you use to determine whether your design reduced the impact of a landslide?

Possible answer: We analyzed the amount of damage to the houses and cars to determine whether our design reduced the impact of the landslide.

STEP 13 Describe a specific aspect of your design that helped reduce the impact of a landslide.

Possible answer: The supports strengthened the retaining wall and helped reduce the impact of the landslide.

Draw Conclusions

STEP 14 Make a claim about the success of your design. Cite evidence to support your claim.

Possible answer: I would classify our design as successful. It greatly reduced the impact of the landslide.

STEP 15 What other questions do you have about ways that engineers can design devices to reduce the impact of landslides?

Possible answer: How do engineers reduce the impact of landslides when they cannot build a retaining wall?

TAKE IT FURTHER Discover More

TAKE IT FURTHER
Discover More

Check out this path . . . or go online to choose one of these other paths.

People in Science & Engineering
- Hawaii Island Lava Hazard Zone Maps
- Debate About A Volcano Solution

Dr. Lucy Jones was world famous as a seismologist, an earthquake scientist. She was an expert at understanding, predicting, and preparing for earthquakes.

Dr. Jones studied small earthquakes that are sometimes followed by a bigger, more damaging one. Dr. Jones developed a way to predict how likely it is that a small earthquake will be followed by a bigger one.

Lucy Jones did even more. She worked to improve how we prepare for natural hazards. She recommended that people keep fire extinguishers in their homes and know how to use them. She believesd that homes in areas of high earthquake risk could be fixed in important small ways to make them safer.

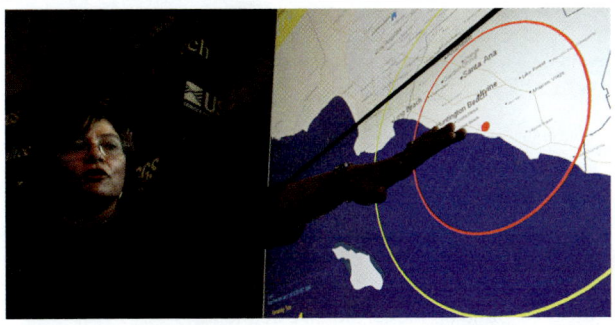

Dr. Lucy Jones' at work.

36. Which of the following is not a job of Dr. Lucy Jones?
- a. understanding earthquakes
- **b. stopping earthquakes**
- c. predicting earthquakes
- d. preparing for earthquakes

591

LESSON 3 Engage • Explore/Explain • **Elaborate** • Evaluate

TAKE IT FURTHER, continued

SEP **Obtaining, Evaluating, and Communicating Information**

Tell students to imagine that they live in an area at risk of earthquakes.

Ask: What question would you like to ask Dr. Jones? **Sample answer: How should my family prepare for an earthquake?**

> **Differentiate Instruction**
>
> **RTI/Extra Support** Discuss the meaning of "frequency" in the data table.
>
> **Ask:** How could you revise the heading at the top of the second column to make it more clear what "frequency means"? **Add "number of quakes in the last year" in parentheses.**

▶ Explore Online

Students can explore these additional topics online.

Hawaii Island Lava Hazard Zone Maps

Students interpret a lava hazard zone map of Hawaii to assess the risk of areas near an active volcano. They also role-play engineers who must design a school in the safest location on the island. *(No outside research required.)*

Debate About a Volcano Solution

Students research two proposed methods of reducing the impact of volcanic eruptions by using cold ocean water to stop the flow of lava or by building barrier walls to divert the flow of lava. They then conduct a debate about which method is better suited for a hypothetical town. *(Outside research required.)*

37. Go online to the US Geological Survey website and gather data about earthquakes of magnitude 2.5 or greater in the past year. Determine the five states that had the most earthquakes, and list the states and the number of earthquakes in the table.

State	Frequency
Student responses should reflect current earthquake data.	

38. Use the information from the US Geological Survey to plot the location of the five most recent earthquakes in the United States on the map.

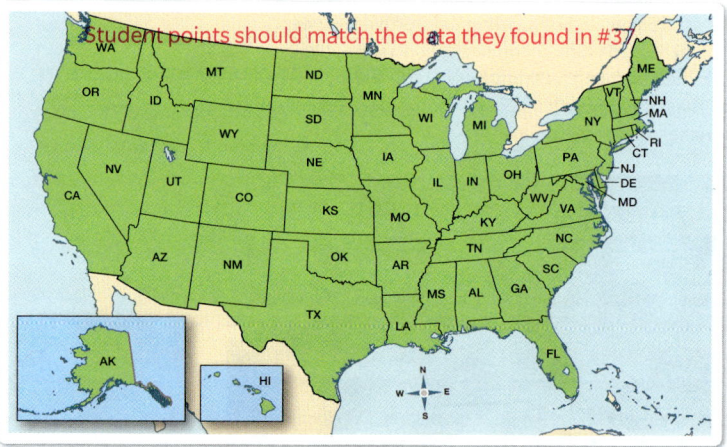

Student points should match the data they found in #37.

39. Compare your data to the data found on the earthquake frequency map shown earlier in the lesson. Explain how your results are similar to or different from the information shown in those maps.

Possible answer: My data shows that many earthquakes occurred in Alaska, which is similar to the information shown on the maps.

592

Unit 8 Natural Resources and Hazards

LESSON CHECK

LESSON 3
Lesson Check

Name _____

Can You Explain It?

1. What are some ways people can reduce the impact of land-based natural hazards such as earthquakes? Be sure to do the following:
   - Describe several land-based natural hazards.
   - Describe ways that the impact of natural hazards can be lessened.
   - Explain how engineering processes can reduce the impact of natural hazards.
   - In particular, describe how the impacts of earthquakes could be reduced.

EVIDENCE NOTEBOOK Use the information you've collected in your Evidence Notebook to help you cover each point.

Possible answer:
- Earthquakes, volcanic eruptions, wildfires, and landslides are land hazards and a description of each.
- by watching for patterns that can predict the upcoming occurrence of a natural hazard, and by engineering solutions to decrease the impact of the hazard
- Testing and improving helped us find out what parts of the solution worked and what parts didn't work, and fix them.
- by not building or living in areas with history of strong, destructive earthquakes, and by using earthquake monitoring technology and construction practices

Checkpoints

2. Which of these is a sign that a volcano will probably erupt soon? Circle all that apply.
   a. **ground movement**
   b. increasing mudslides
   c. **earthquakes**
   d. **changes in volcanic gases**

Formal Assessment Go online for student self-checks and other assessments.

Can You Explain It?

Collaboration

Discussion You may wish to revisit the beginning of the lesson as a group activity to assess students' understanding of the material. Use the bulleted points in the Interactice Worktext to lead the discussion.

DCI ESS3.B Natural Hazards

Have students go back and reread the caption about the shake table at the beginning of this lesson.

Ask: What is the function of the shake table? Buildings are placed on the table, and then the table shakes to model how Earth moves during an earthquake. Observations of the buildings are used to help engineers design structures that can withstand earthquakes.

EVIDENCE NOTEBOOK

Have students reread their answers to the Evidence Notebook prompts and then use this evidence to justify their reasoning as they respond to the Can You Explain It question. Make sure students understand that a complete response must address all bulleted points.

SUMMATIVE ASSESSMENT
Engage in Argument from Evidence

2. Caution students not to confuse the effect of a volcanic eruption with its cause.

   Ask: Which of the answer options only occurs after an eruption? increasing landslides

LESSON 3   Engage • Explore/Explain • Elaborate • **Evaluate**

LESSON CHECK, continued

3. Have volunteers identify each type of technology shown in the question. If students need further guidance, have them revisit Exploration 2.

4. Suggest that students review the information about patterns that can lead up to a natural hazard in Exploration 2.

Using Representations to Assess Proficiency

In this lesson, students learned about land-based natural hazards, such as volcanic eruptions, earthquakes, landslides, and wildfires. They also explored methods to predict these hazards and lessen their effects.

5. Students may find it helpful to look at photos of the damage caused by earthquakes and volcanoes.

   Ask: Which of the effects is most likely to happen when the ground shakes? **Roads will crumble, and buildings will collapse.**
   Which of the effects is most likely to happen when ash and debris are released into the air? **Houses will be buried.**

6. **Ask:** Which of the natural hazards are associated with high temperatures that can cause fires? **volcanic eruptions and lightning strike**

---

3. Draw lines to match each word with the correct picture of a technology that can reduce the impact of that type of hazard.

Natural Hazards

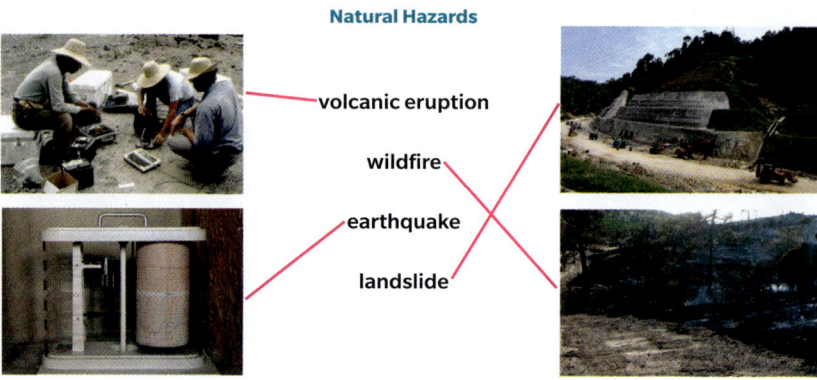

- volcanic eruption
- wildfire
- earthquake
- landslide

4. The risk of which land-based natural hazard is increased during time periods when there is not much rain?
   a. volcanic eruption
   b. landslide
   c. earthquake
   d. wildfire

5. Use the word bank to write the most likely cause of each of these effects.

   | earthquake   volcano |

   a. landslide _____earthquake_____
   b. crumpled roads _____earthquake_____
   c. building collapse _____earthquake_____
   d. release of poisonous gases _____volcano_____

6. Which natural hazards are most likely to be the direct cause of a wildfire? Circle all that apply.
   a. earthquake
   b. volcano
   c. landslide
   d. lightning strike

594

594   Unit 8   Natural Resources and Hazards

LESSON 3

Lesson Roundup

A. Choose the correct words to complete each sentence.

| volcanic eruption |
| earthquake |
| landslide |
| wildfire |

When melted rock and gases burst through an opening in Earth's crust, a(n) __volcanic eruption__ occurs. Sudden movement of the rocky plates that form Earth's crust result in a(n) __earthquake__.

A(n) __landslide__ happens when materials slide down a slope.

What else have you learned about natural hazards in this lesson?
Possible answer: I have learned that patterns can be used to predict some natural hazards.

B. Choose a technology from the word bank that can lessen the impact of each natural hazard.

| earthquake resistant building | firebreak | retaining wall | tiltmeter |

 tiltmeter

 earthquake resistant building

 firebreak

 retaining wall

What else have you learned about natural hazard safety in this lesson?
Possible answer: I have learned that technology can be applied to reduce the damage from a natural hazard but that natural hazards cannot be contained.

Lesson Roundup

DCI ESS3.B Natural Hazards
ETS1.B Designing Solutions to Engineering Problems

This lesson summary enables students to quickly revisit key points and prepare for tests.

A. Have students review the causes and effects of land-based hazards in Exploration 1. Stress that there are no wrong answers to the questions about what they learned in this lesson.

Ask: What questions do you still have about natural hazards? Sample answer: How do places recover from natural hazards?
Ask: How could you go about finding the answers to these questions? Sample answer: Conduct research, or ask an expert. ESS3.B

B. Have students review the technology used to lessen the impact of land-based hazards in Exploration 2.

Ask: What questions do you still have about staying safe during a natural hazard? Sample answer: What plans are in place in my community for helping people stay safe during a natural hazard? ESS3.B, ETS1.B

LESSON 4
How Can People Reduce the Impact of Water-Based Hazards?

Building to the Performance Expectation

The learning experiences in this lesson prepare students for mastery of:

4-ESS3-2 Generate and compare multiple solutions to reduce the impacts of natural Earth processes on humans.

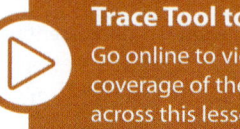

Trace Tool to the NGSS
Go online to view the complete coverage of these standards across this lesson, unit, and time.

 Science & Engineering Practices

Constructing Explanations and Designing Solutions
Generate and compare multiple solutions to a problem based on how well they meet the criteria and constraints of the design problem.

 Disciplinary Core Ideas

ESS3.B Natural Hazards
A variety of hazards result from natural processes (e.g., earthquakes, tsunamis, volcanic eruptions). Humans cannot eliminate the hazards but can take steps to reduce their impacts. (4-ESS3-2)

ETS1.B Designing Solutions to Engineering Problems
Testing a solution involves investigating how well it performs under a range of likely conditions. (secondary to 4-ESS3-2)

 **Crosscutting Concepts**

Cause and Effect
Cause and effect relationships are routinely identified, tested, and used to explain change.

Influence of Engineering, Technology, and Science on Society and the Natural World
Engineers improve existing technologies or develop new ones to increase their benefits, decrease known risks, and meet societal demands.

 CONNECTIONS TO MATH

MP.2 Reason abstractly and quantitatively.
MP.4 Model with mathematics.

 CONNECTIONS TO ENGLISH LANGUAGE ARTS

W.4.7 Conduct short research projects that build knowledge through investigation of different aspects of a topic.

RI.4.9 Integrate information from two texts on the same topic in order to write or speak about the subject knowledgably

Supporting All Students, All Standards

Integrating the Three Dimensions of Learning

Students will analyze and describe a variety of water-based Earth processes **(DCI ESS3.B)** that can be hazardous to humans and design and test multiple solutions **(SEP Constructing Explanations and Designing Solutions) (DCI ETS1.B)** to lessen the impacts of these processes on humans **(CCC Influence of Engineering, Technology, and Science on Society and the Natural World)**.

 **Professional Development** Go online to view **Professional Development videos** with strategies to integrate CCCs and SEPs, including the ones used in this lesson.

Extra Hands-On Activity: Soaking-Wet Mud

How Can Water Make a Building Fall?

- Small groups
- 30-45 minutes

Soil liquefaction occurs when water in the soil pushes the particles of soil apart, effectively turning the soil into a solution and making it so that the soil can no longer support weight. Quicksand in an example of soil liquefaction. Anything in the soil can sink into or rise out of the soil because of liquefaction. In this activity, students will model liquefaction.

Each group of students should have a pan containing a lightly moistened mix of sand and soil roughly an inch deep with a model building on top of the soil. Using a spray bottle of water set to wide spray, students should spray the soil until they see little puddles form on top.

They should then lightly shake the pan for 30 seconds, recording anything they see. They should then repeat this process until the building starts to sink into the soil.

Have students discuss what role they think water played in the sinking of the building. They should also consider the role that vibrations, such as those representing earthquakes, played in the sinking of the building. Have students discuss some possible solutions to this problem in their groups.

 This activity can support mastery of the Disciplinary Core Idea: Natural Hazards

Preassessment

Have students complete the unit pre-test online or see the Assessment Guide.

Build on Prior Knowledge

Students should already know and be prepared to build on the following concepts:
- How to design solutions that address natural problems.
- Natural hazards impact humans.

Differentiate Instruction

Lesson Vocabulary
In this lesson, students are introduced to the terms *hurricane*, *drought*, *tsunami*, and *flood*. Have students make a three-column table, with the columns labeled "Term," "Definition," and "Picture." Have them write the terms that appear in the lesson in the left column and their definitions in the middle column. Finally, have them add a small drawing to the third column to help them remember the definition.

ELL/ELD Strategy
Have English-language learners add fourth and fifth columns to their tables. In those columns, have them add the term and definition in their primary language.

Ask: Can you notice any similarities in the terms between your primary language and the English version? Answers will vary.

LESSON 4   **Engage** • Explore/Explain • Elaborate • Evaluate

ENGAGE: Lesson Phenomenon

Lesson Objective
To analyze and describe a variety of water-based processes that can be hazardous to humans and design and test multiple solutions to lessen the impacts of these natural Earth processes on humans.

About This Image
Drought is a hazard that occurs when an area receives very little rain over a long time period. Drought is a water-based hazard that has far-reaching impacts on humans. For example, crops and livestock can be damaged or destroyed by drought conditions. Humans have designed multiple solutions that can lessen the impact of drought on humans.

 **Constructing Explanations and Designing Solutions**

Alternative Engage Strategy

What's the Impact? 👥 Whole class ⏱ 5 min

Two weeks before introducing this lesson, obtain an inexpensive small potted plant or potted seedling. You will be using this plant to show the impact of drought, so do not water the plant. On the day you introduce the lesson, display the plant. Encourage students to closely observe the plant and the soil.

Ask: How would you describe this plant? **Possible answers: wilted, dried out, droopy, dead**

Ask: How would you describe the soil? **dry, cracked**

Explain that water-based hazards include those that result from too little water as well as those involving too much water.

LESSON 4

How Can People Reduce the Impact of Water-Based Hazards?

The land in this picture is dry and cracked. Many plants probably cannot grow here. What causes conditions like this? And how does it impact people?

By the end of this lesson . . .
you'll be able to describe some water-based hazards and tell how people can stay safe when they occur.

596

Unit 8 Natural Resources and Hazards

Can You Explain It?

These people are placing bags full of sand along a river. They know that lots of rain is expected, and the river might overflow its banks.

1. How will these actions help reduce the impact of a water-based hazard? What else could reduce the impact of this hazard?

Students should respond based on the preliminary observations they can make of the images. Accept all reasonable answers.

_____
_____
_____
_____

Tip

Learn more about the affects of water on Earth's surface in How Does Water Shape Earth's Surface?

EVIDENCE NOTEBOOK Look for this icon to help you gather evidence to answer the questions above.

▶ **Explore Online** Students can view the lesson phenomenon online.

Can You Explain It?

Students are asked to record their initial thoughts about ways that the impact of this water-based hazard can be lessened. To do so, students must begin to think about design solutions related to flooding. Encourage students to record the first thoughts that come into their minds. Point out that their ideas might change as they work through the Explorations and Hands-On Activities. Explain that they will have another opportunity to answer the same questions at the end of the lesson.

> ## Collaboration
>
> **Think, Pair, Share** Challenge students to think about other water-based hazards. Then, pair students and have them jot a list of the water-based hazards they identified. Finally, have students think about ways that the impacts of each hazard could be lessened. Call on several pairs of students to name a hazard and a possible solution.

EVIDENCE NOTEBOOK

Encourage students to use an appropriate graphic organizer, such as main idea and supporting details, to set up their notebook for this lesson.

Find more strategies in the online ELA handbook.

LESSON 4 Engage • **Explore/Explain** • Elaborate • Evaluate

EXPLORATION 1 Water-Based Natural Hazards

3D Learning Objective

Students explore **causes and effects** of water-based **natural hazards** including hurricane, drought, tsunami, and flood. They consider how **designing solutions** could help lessen their impact.

DCI ESS3.B Natural Hazards

Discuss the different water-based natural hazards.

Ask: How would you describe a hurricane? *strong ocean storm with high wind and heavy rain*

Ask: How do hurricanes, tsunamis, and floods differ from droughts? *Hurricanes, tsunamis, and floods all result in an area having too much water, while a drought occurs when there is too little water in an area.*

CCC Cause and Effect

Point out that water-based hazards can be thought of in terms of their causes and their effects. Tell students to watch for more information about the causes and effects of water-based hazards on the upcoming pages.

Ask: Why is it important to understand both the causes and the effects of natural hazards? *Possible answer: If people understand the causes, they might be able to predict when a hazard might happen. If they understand the effects, they might be able to prepare for the impacts.*

SEP Constructing Explanations and Designing Solutions

After students have read the descriptions of water-based hazards on this page, **ask:** What are some ways a design solution to tsunamis might lessen their impact? *Possible answer: A design solution might be designed to prevent flooding from moving inland from the ocean shore.*

598 Unit 8 Natural Resources and Hazards

EXPLORATION 1

Water-Based Natural Hazards

Water, Water, Everywhere

Some of the natural processes of Earth's surface, its oceans, and its atmosphere can produce water-based hazards. Deep below Earth's surface, pieces of the crust can suddenly move, producing waves that are unusually large and dangerous. Above Earth's surface, great storms can produce heavy rain and wind so strong that it destroys buildings.

Types of Water-Based Hazards

Use the images and captions to learn about some kinds of water-based hazards.

 A hurricane is a strong storm with devastating winds and heavy rains. It is not safe to be outdoors during a hurricane.

 A tsunami is a powerful type of wave. It rushes onto the ocean shore like a high flood. It can have enough force to smash buildings.

 During a drought, there is much less water than usual. People and animals struggle to have enough water.

 During a flood, water covers the land and may flood homes as well. Floodwater can ruin property and threaten people's safety.

2. What are some impacts of water-based hazards?
Possible answer: Some of the impacts of water-based hazards include damage to homes and property and injuries or harm to people and animals.

3. Which water-based hazard's impacts are caused by a lack of water?
 a. hurricane
 b. tsunami
 c. drought
 d. flood

598

Do the Math
Classifying Hurricanes

Wind speeds are used to assign hurricanes to categories. Category 1 storms have the lowest wind speeds. Category 5 storms have the highest wind speeds. Scientists can use these classifications to compare hurricanes and tell people the strength of the hurricane they have to prepare for.

Category	Sustained Winds (km/hr)	Sustained Winds (mph)
1	119 to 153 km/hr	74-95 mph
2	154 to 177 km/hr	96-110 mph
3	178 to 208 km/hr	111-129 mph
4	209 to 251 km/hr	130-156 mph
5	252 km/hr and greater	157 mph or higher

2015 Atlantic Hurricanes		
Hurricane	Maximum Sustained Winds (km/hr)	Maximum Sustained Winds (mph)
Danny	185 km/hr	115 mph
Fred	140 km/hr	85 mph
Joaquin	250 km/hr	155 mph
Kate	120 km/hr	75 mph

4. Complete the sentence and expression for each hurricane. The first one has been completed as an example.

   A. Hurricane Danny is a Category __3__ hurricane because its winds were greater than __178 km/hr__ but less than __208 km/hr__.

   B. Hurricane Fred is a Category __1__ hurricane because its winds were greater than __119 km/hr__ but less than __153 km/hr__.

   C. Hurricane Joaquin is a Category __4__ hurricane because its winds were greater than __209 km/hr__ but less than __251 km/hr__.

5. Forecasters predict the strength of hurricanes so people can prepare for them. What category is Hurricane Kate and how would knowing that help someone prepare?

   Possible answer: Hurricane Kate is a Category 1 hurricane. Knowing the strength of Category 1 winds means people can make preparations, such as boarding up windows but not evacuating an area.

Do the Math
Classifying Hurricanes
MP.2 Reason abstractly and quantitatively
MP.4 Model with mathematics

Explain that scientists place hurricanes into categories based on wind speed. By categorizing hurricanes, scientists can compare one hurricane season to another. Point out that the top table contains the information about the categories into which hurricanes are classified, and explain that the *Sustained Winds* column provides a range of wind speeds. The table on the bottom contains information about specific hurricanes that occurred in the 2015 hurricane season. Explain that the category of each of the hurricanes can be determined by comparing its wind speed to the ranges for each category.

Ask: In what category would scientists classify a hurricane with a wind speed of 165 km/hr? **Category 2**

Ask: Why is it important to know the category of a hurricane? **It is important because people can know what type of storm they are preparing for and they can estimate potential property damage.**

Differentiate Instruction

RTI/Extra Support Make a number line that is marked in increments of 50 and extends from 100 to 300. Then, divide or shade the number line into segments representing each range listed in the table. For example, shade the segment from 119 to 153 and label it Category 1. Shade the segment from 154 to 177 as Category 2 and so on. Then have students use the labeled number line as they work through the activity.

LESSON 4 Engage • **Explore/Explain** • Elaborate • Evaluate

EXPLORATION 1 Water-Based Natural Hazards, continued

CCC Cause and Effect

The information on this page gives students the opportunity to focus on the causes and effects of water-based natural hazards.

Ask: How are the effects of tsunamis and hurricanes similar?
Sample answer: They both involve water damage to the shore.
Ask: How are the effects of tsunamis and hurricanes different?
Sample answer: Hurricanes cause wind damage; tsunamis don't.

DCI ESS3.B Natural Hazards

As students read about the effects of natural hazards, encourage them to think about how these effects impact humans.

Ask: How does one of the effects described on this page impact people? Sample: Flooding can wash away roads that people need to get from one place to another.

Connection to Life Science

As students analyze the causes and effects of water-based hazards, have them also consider the effect these hazards can have on the structures and functions of plants in the affected area. Point out that plants are the base of most food chains, so any event that impacts plants also affects the other living things in the area.
LS1.A Structure and Function

SEP Constructing Explanations and Designing Solutions

Although technological solutions to water-based hazards are more deeply explored in the next Exploration, this is a good opportunity to activate students' interest in the topic. Have students consider how possible solutions to a hazard are related to the causes and/or the effects of the hazard.

Ask: How are solutions to a hazard related to its effects?
Solutions are likely designed to minimize a particular effect of a hazard, such as building damage by water and winds.

Connecting Cause and Effect

Hazards have causes and effects. If people know the causes of a hazard, it can help them make predictions. If they know the effects of a hazard, it can help them prepare.

Causes and Effects of Water-Based Hazards

6. Read about each of the water-based hazards shown here. Then complete the table. 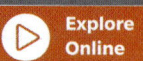 Explore Online

A hurricane forms as the energy in warm ocean water fuels strong winds and heavy rains. It causes storm surges, flooding, landslides, and wind damage.

Droughts are caused by long dry periods. Droughts can last years. A drought's effects are related to a lack of water. Dried up plants burn easily, so droughts can lead to wildfires.

Tsunamis are a series of giant waves, caused by undersea earthquakes, landslides, or volcanic eruptions. Tsunamis move onto shore, washing away almost anything in its path.

River flooding is caused by heavy rain or snow melt. Coastal flooding is caused by storm surges. Floodwater can damage structures and cause landslides.

Natural hazard	Cause and effect
hurricane	Effect—Strong winds, storm surge, heavy rain, and coastal landslides.
flood	Cause—Heavy rainfall, melting snow, or a storm surge raises the water level.
tsunami	Effect—A series of waves that demolish almost everything in its path.
drought	Effect—Plants, animals and people do not have enough water, and the wildfire danger is high.

HANDS-ON Apply What You Know

Take Action

7. Imagine you and your family live in a region called Watertown. Your region is currently being impacted by a drought. Carry out one activity from the list below to show your understanding of the impact of a drought and how the effects of a drought can be lessened.

   - Create a poster informing the residents of Watertown what they can do to help reduce the impacts of a drought. You will need to identify two specific impacts of the drought, and tell how the effects of those two impacts could be decreased.
   - Write a letter to the editor of *Watertown Newspaper* that draws attention to the need for residents to take actions to reduce the impact of a drought. Include evidence to support your claim.
   - In a group, role play a meeting of interested community members about what action can be taken to offset the impact of the drought that has hit the Watertown region. Assume specific roles, such as farmer, truck driver, and mayor. Each person should present information specific to his or her assigned roles.
   - In a group, brainstorm and come up with ways you can help members of Watertown save water in their house, in their backyard, and at their school. Present your ideas in the form of a three-column table.

8. What information about the causes and effects of drought did you apply to complete the activity you chose?

   Possible answer: I know that the cause of drought is lack of rain for a long time period, so I applied that information and thought of ways in which people can conserve water.

 EVIDENCE NOTEBOOK In your Evidence Notebook, identify how information about the causes and effects of water-based hazards can be used to lessen their impacts.

 Have students explore online to find out more about the causes and effects of hazards.

HANDS-ON Apply What You Know
Take Action

Materials
Required materials will vary based on the activity selected by each group. Possible materials include poster board and name tags

Preparation
You might choose to divide the class into four groups and assign one of the activities to each of the groups. Plan in advance for students to have access to computers to do some research related to the topic as they complete their projects. Groups that are carrying out the role-play should develop a script so their role-play can be performed for the class. Have each group share its results or completed project with the remainder of the class. Then, have students work with their groups to develop a response for item 8.

Scoring Guidelines
An excellent student score consists of students completing the activities thoroughly and with accurate information.

> ## Differentiate Instruction
>
> **Extension** Have students research information about cloud-seeding and share what they learn with the remainder of the class. Encourage them to make and support a claim based on their research about the effectiveness of cloud-seeding as a means of reducing the impact of drought.

EVIDENCE NOTEBOOK

Students should record evidence about ways that information about causes and effects of hazards can be applied to lessen their impacts.

LESSON 4   Engage • **Explore/Explain** • Elaborate • Evaluate

EXPLORATION 1 *Water-Based Natural Hazards, continued*

Build on Prior Knowledge

Prompt students to recall the earthquake maps that were part of the previous lesson. Those maps showed the amount of earthquakes that had occured in each state. There are other types of natural hazard-related maps identify areas where different kinds of hazards might be more or less likely to occur. Point out that the drought maps on this page are similar in that they show how different areas are affected by droughts during a specifc period of time.

 ESS3.B Natural Hazards

Point out that different types of hazards occur in different locations. For example, hurricanes affect coastlines more than inland areas. The maps on this page provide information about areas that are experiencing drought. Remind students that as natural hazards occur, or as patterns change, scientists update maps to be able to provide people with the most current information.

Ask: What information can be gathered by looking at these maps? Sample answer: states suffering most from droughts

Cause and Effect

Ask: What area might be experiencing the greatest impact due to drought? Possible answer: I think the Southwest, because it is the only part of the United States experiencing extreme and exceptional drought.

Differentiate Instruction

RTI/Extra Support Some students may have difficulty analyzing the maps to respond to the items on this page. Point out that each of the three maps shows the same area. Tell them that the shaded area on each map shows areas experiencing drought. Point out the key in the corner of each map, and then show students where on the page they can find the caption for each image.

Where Are There Droughts?

Some water-based hazards, such as droughts, occur more frequently in some places than in others. Drought monitor maps can be used to show this information.

Drought Maps

The maps provide information about areas experiencing drought. Use the information in the maps to answer the questions.

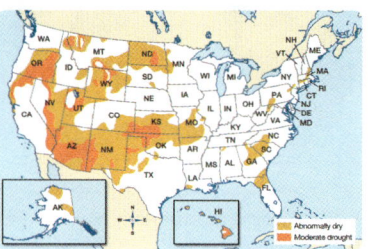

The areas shown on this map are experiencing abnormally dry conditions to moderate drought conditions. This level of drought has some effect on crops, and water-use restrictions are voluntary, not required.

9. What conditions could cause these areas to change classification to severe drought?

Possible answer: A continued lack of rain would cause these areas to change to a classification of severe drought.

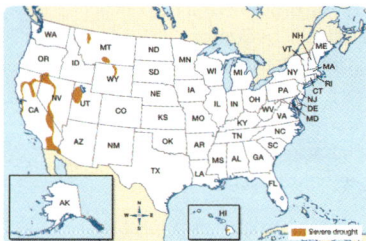

The areas shown on this map are experiencing severe drought conditions. In these areas, crops are strongly affected and water-use restrictions and water shortages are common.

10. How does the size of the area experiencing severe drought compare to the size of the area experiencing abnormally dry or moderate drought conditions?

The area experiencing severe drought is smaller.

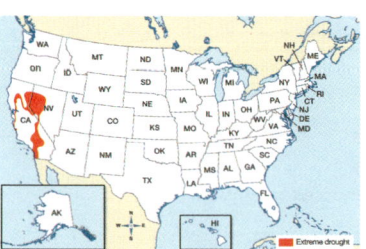

The areas shown on this map are experiencing extreme drought conditions. These areas experience substantial crop losses and extreme water shortages.

11. In which geographic portion of the United States are there extreme drought conditions?

Extreme drought conditions are found in the southwest portion of the United States.

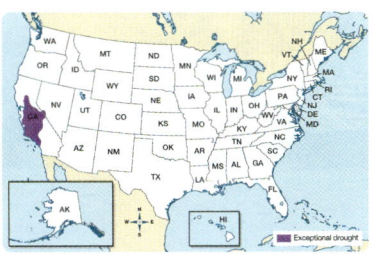

The areas shown on this map are experiencing exceptional drought conditions. Drought of this level results in widespread crop loss and reduced water levels in streams, lakes, and reservoirs.

12. What is one way that exceptional drought conditions in part of the United States could affect other parts of the country?

Possible answer: Crops that are usually grown in this area will not be available to people anywhere in the country.

13. Locate your state on one of the drought monitor maps. What drought conditions, if any, are being experienced in your state?

Possible answer: Based on the information in the map, my state is not currently experiencing any drought conditions.

14. Using the drought monitor maps, choose the state that makes each sentence most correct.

| Pennsylvania | Ohio | Illinois | New York |
| North Carolina | California | Kansas | |

There are exceptional drought conditions in _California_.

There are abnormally dry and moderate drought conditions but no exceptional drought conditions in _Kansas_.

Language SmArts
Analyze and Evaluate Internet Information

15. What are some ways that people can apply information about water-based natural hazards to help them stay safe?

Possible answer: People can apply information about risks in different areas to think about safety plans they should have in place.

Tip
The English Language Arts Handbook can provide help with understanding how to analyze and evaluate Internet information.

603

Collaboration

Jigsaw Divide the class into five groups. Assign one specific drought level (abnormally dry, moderate drought, severe drought, extreme drought, exceptional drought) to each group. Have each group use the map, caption, and if time permits, outside resources to learn about that specific level of drought and where it is being experienced. Then have students reform groups (one student from each original group). Within their groups, have each student share a summary about the specific level of drought they researched.

SEP Obtaining, Evaluating, and Communicating Information

Emphasize that there are many ways to gather information about water-based natural hazards.

Ask: Why are maps an effective way of communicating the information about different levels of drought? **Sample answer: Maps allow information about the locations experiencing each level of drought to be visualized.**

FORMATIVE ASSESSMENT
Language SmArts
Analyze and Evaluate Internet Information
RI.4.9 Integrate information from two texts on the same topic in order to write or speak about the subject knowledgably

Check to be sure that students have analyzed and evaluated information from two or more texts or sources to develop their response. As students research, encourage them to evaluate the reliability of the information they obtain.

Lesson 4 How Can People Reduce the Impact of Water-Based Hazards? 603

LESSON 4   Engage • **Explore/Explain** • Elaborate • Evaluate

EXPLORATION 2 Reducing the Impacts of Water-Based Hazards

3D Learning Objective

Students explore how information about the causes and effects of **natural hazards** can be used to reduce the impacts of hazards and applied to **constructing explanations and designing solutions** to minimize the impact of the hazards. As they do, they will consider the **influence of science, engineering, and technology on society and the natural world**.

DCI ESS3.B Natural Hazards

Inform students that nature, as well as manmade solutions, can be used to protect people and property from natural hazards. Wetlands and forests along rivers help buffer from floods. Coral reefs provide natural barriers. Have students research other forms of nature that help protect against water-based hazards.

Ask: What other forms of nature help protect against water-based hazards? **Possible answers: Mangroves and coral reefs can help buffer from tsunamis and storm surges. Restoring wetlands and flood plains can reduce the impact of tsunamis and floods.**

> ## Collaboration
> **Think, Pair, Share** In pairs, have students discuss responses to item 16. Have the students in each group work as a team to complete the table. Then, call on each group to share one or more responses. Use each response to launch a short class discussion of preparation and response to various hazards.

CCC Cause and Effect

Ask: What are some effects of hurricanes? **Possible answer: heavy rain and high wind, coastal flooding**

Ask: Based on those effects, what are some ways to stay safe during hurricanes? **Possible answers: stay away from windows, prepare a home emergency kit**

604   Unit 8 Natural Resources and Hazards

EXPLORATION 2

Reducing the Impacts of Water-Based Hazards

Think Ahead!

Most water-based hazards cannot be prevented. That's why it's important to know how to prepare for and respond to a variety of hazards.

Staying Safe

16. For each natural hazard shown in the chart, research to find out how to prepare ahead of time and how to respond while it is happening.

Hazard	Preparation	Response
Hurricane		
Tsunami	Student answers will vary but should present common-sense approaches to preparing and staying safe during crises, such as evacuating or boarding up windows and staying indoors during a hurricane; evacuating or seeking higher ground before a tsunami or flood; stocking up on water before a drought and conserving it during a drought.	
Flood		
Drought		

17. Select which pictures represent a way to stay safe during a hurricane. Circle all the pictures that apply.

604

Understanding Tsunamis

Water from a powerful tsunami can travel as far as 16 km inland if the shoreline is not elevated much above sea level. A tsunami can devastate the area. Learn more about tsunamis.

A tsunami begins with an underwater disturbance, such as an earthquake.

When the first wave reaches shallow water, it slows down. Its height increases.

A tsunami harms people and property by both the force of its impact and the amount of water it moves onto land.

After the water has drained away, many people find their homes, schools, and businesses are destroyed.

After a tsunami, people need to clean up and rebuild.

18. Natural hazards, such as tsunamis, are triggered by Earth processes. They can harm many people, homes, and property, as well as animals and their habitats. What is one way people can reduce the impact of a tsunami?

Possible answer: An early warning system could allow people to move to safety before the tsunami hits land.

605

Connection to English Language Arts

Have students establish the chronology of the information presented in the five images and their captions on this page. Encourage them to note that the captions, when read in order, describe a sequence of events from the origin of the tsunami to the cleanup and rebuilding stages. The images show the same sequence of events.

RI.4.5 Describe the overall structure (e.g., chronology, comparison, cause/effect, problem/solution) of events, ideas, concepts, or information in a text or part of a text.

Differentiate Instruction

ELL: Language Explain that the word *tsunami* is Japanese. Like many words used in English, it has been "borrowed" from another language. Have students note that very few words in English begin with the letter combination *ts*. Point out that in English, the word *tsunami* is pronounced with the leading *t* sound. Encourage students to identify examples of words from their primary language that are "borrowed" by, or used in, American English.

SEP Constructing Explanations and Designing Solutions

Have students construct an explanation of ways that people can reduce the impact of a tsunami as a response to item 18.

Ask: Is the solution you suggested related to the cause of tsunamis or the effects? Explain. Possible answers: My solution, an early warning system that is activated by the occurrence of an undersea earthquake, is related to the cause of tsunamis. My solution, a levee that reduces flooding, is related to the effect of tsunamis.

LESSON 4   Engage • **Explore/Explain** • Elaborate • Evaluate

EXPLORATION 2 Reducing the Impacts of Water-Based Hazards, continued

CCC **Influence of Science, Engineering, and Technology on Society and the Natural World**

Remind students that technologies such as the ones they will be reading about, are developed to help people stay safe. Over time, such technologies are improved to increase their benefits or reduce their risks.

Ask: Which of the technologies described on the page could be used to lessen the impact of a drought? reservoir

Collaboration

Partners   In groups, have students read and discuss the information on this page. Have groups develop two quiz-show style questions about the information on the page. Then have the groups take turns asking the class their questions.

Differentiate Instruction

Extension   Have students carry out brief research to identify and gather information about another technology that is used to lessen the impact of a water-based hazard. Have them obtain an image and write a brief caption. Have them share their information with the remainder of the class.

 ETS1.B Designing Solutions to Engineering Problems

Remind students that we can also use nature (forests, coral reefs, restore wetlands and flood plains) to reduce the impacts of water-based hazards. Ask students to compare and contrast the technology on this page to the solutions from nature. Discuss as a class.

Ask: What can engineers learn from nature when it comes to designing solutions for protecting against hazards? how natural barriers work to keep areas safe from water-based hazards

606   Unit 8 Natural Resources and Hazards

 Engineer It!
Using Technology to Reduce Impacts

Geostationary operational environmental satellites (GOES) move so that they hover above the same place on Earth. Information collected helps predict hurricanes and other severe weather events. They are used to warn people about hurricanes, tornadoes, and flash floods and can help reduce the impact of a drought.

Deep-ocean tsunami detection buoys measure the height of the water's surface. If a tsunami wave passes under a buoy, the buoy transmits that information to the tsunami warning center via satellite. The network of buoys can help scientists predict when tsunami waves might reach shore.

A levee is like a wall alongside a river or other waterway to help keep floodwater from spilling onto nearby land. Levees are usually made of packed dirt. Sandbags can be stacked to build walls that are similar to levees.

Reservoirs are usually constructed by building a dam on a river. Water collects in the reservoir, making it available during drier times. Sometimes, plastic balls are put over the reservoir to prevent evaporation. They also protect the water from dust, rain, chemicals and wildlife.

606

19. Identify the hazard for each technology in the first column. Then research other technology that helps keep us safe. Write these in the third column labeled Additional Technologies.

| hurricane | flood | tsunami | drought |

Technology	Hazard	Additional Technologies
reservoirs	drought	Students should suggest technology that helps to protect against the hazards they identified.
deep ocean buoys	tsunami	
levees and sandbags	flood	
geostationary operational environmental satellites	hurricane	

20. **Language SmArts** Choose a water-based natural hazard that occurs in your state, and describe a family emergency plan that would help keep you safe if you got a warning the hazard might occur. Carry out research if necessary to write your answer.

Possible answer: Hurricanes can happen in my state. Our family has emergency supplies, such as food, water, and batteries. We also have a list of things we will take if we need to evacuate to avoid a hurricane.

21. How do reservoirs reduce the impact of a drought?

Possible answer: Reservoirs allow water to be stored when it is available. The stored water can then be used if a drought should occur.

22. Choose the correct response. A geostationary operational environmental satellite can

   a. prevent a tsunami
   b. reduce the impact of a drought
   c. prevent a flood
   d. reduce the impact of a hurricane

607

Constructing Explanations and Designing Solutions

Remind students that different hazards require different solutions.

Ask: Tsunamis can cause flooding at the shore. Do you think solutions for flooding could be effectively used to reduce the impact of a tsunami? Why or why not? **Answers will vary. Students might note that locations of tsunamis are difficult to predict in advance, so building levees might not be practical. However, with enough warning, sandbags might be able to be used to reduce the impact of coastal flooding.**

Collaboration

Write, Pair, Share Have students write a response for item 21. Pair students, and have them quickly discuss their responses. Encourage students to modify their responses as necessary after their discussions.

ESS3.B Natural Hazards

Discuss the answer choices for item 22 with students. Reiterate that hazards cannot be prevented but impacts can be reduced.

Ask: How can a satellite reduce the impact of a natural hazard? **Sample answer: By providing advance warning of a possible hazard, people can make preparations.**

Language SmArts
W.4.7 Conduct short research projects

Encourage students to research a water-based hazard that occurs in the state in which they live. After the specific hazard has been identified, students can research and develop emergency plans specific to the identified hazard.

Lesson 4 How Can People Reduce the Impact of Water-Based Hazards? 607

LESSON 4 Engage • **Explore/Explain** • Elaborate • Evaluate

EXPLORATION 2 Reducing the Impacts of Water-Based Hazards, continued

Influence of Science, Engineering, and Technology on Society and the Natural World
CCC

Remind students that levees are a solution that can reduce the impact of floods. Explain that engineers always look for ways to improve existing solutions. Identifying potential problems helps engineers recognize needed improvements.

Ask: Choose one of the solutions on the page, and explain how it increases the benefits or decreases the risks of a levee. **Sample answer: A seepage cutoff wall reduces the known risk of water flow under or through a levee.**

Constructing Explanations and Designing Solutions
SEP

Point out that each of the three potential problems with levees shown on this page and the next page has multiple solutions presented. Emphasize that engineers compare multiple solutions based on how well they meet the criteria and constraints of the design solution.

Ask: Do you think there is one best solution for all levee problems? Why or why not? **Answers will vary. Students should recognize that different areas might have different problems and different criteria for success. The best solution in one location might not be the best solution in another location.**

Collaboration

Partners Have students form small groups. Assign the groups one of the problems shown on this page or the next page. Have the groups analyze the problem and the two associated solutions that are presented. Have students discuss and evaluate the two solutions and choose the solution they think is best. Have each group share and justify its response.

Engineer It!
Improving Levees

Engineers inspect, maintain, and improve levees. Here are some examples of ways in which engineers reduce the impact of floods.

Problem: Seepage

When water flows under or through a levee, it is called *seepage*. Engineers use several solutions to prevent seepage.

Seepage Cutoff Wall

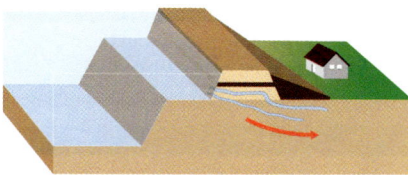
Seepage Berm

Solution: A seepage cutoff wall is an effective solution to seepage, but this solution cannot be used in all places.

Solution: Seepage berms are also used as a solution to seepage.

Problem: Erosion

Levees are used to contain flowing water, so erosion of levees is a major problem.

Widening and Flattening Slopes

Rock Layer

Solution: One solution to erosion is widening and flattening the slope of the levee walls.

Solution: Adding a layer of rock over the levee materials is also a solution to the problem of erosion.

23. You are an engineer and have been contacted to design an alternative solution to the erosion of levees. What materials would you use? Describe what your solution would look like and how it would improve levees.

Accept all reasonable answers.

Problem: Water Flows Over Levee

Sometimes water flows over the top of levees that have been built.

Increase Height

Flood Wall

Solution: One solution for water that flows over a levee is to increase the height of the levee. That can lead to other problems, however, such as increased erosion.

Solution: Flood walls are made of concrete instead of clay, soil, and rock. They can be taller than many levees, so a flood wall can be a solution to water flowing over a levee.

24. Which best describes how flood walls and seepage cutoff walls are similar? Choose the correct response.

    a. Both prevent water from moving.
    b. Both prevent water from moving under and through a levee.
    c. Both prevent erosion that can occur on levees.
    d. Both are designed solutions to problems with levees.

25. How do well-maintained levees help reduce the impact of a water-based natural hazard?

    Possible answer: Well-maintained levees can keep water from spilling out of a river and into the surrounding area.

EVIDENCE NOTEBOOK In your Evidence Notebook, describe a variety of methods that can be used to reduce the impact of flooding.

609

Differentiate Instruction

Extension Have students find out more about the history of levees. Encourage them find information about ways that levee technology has changed over time. Have these students share a brief summary of what they learn with the remainder of the class.

ETS1.B Designing Solutions to Engineering Problems

Have students discuss the problems and solutions shown on this page and the previous page. Have them think about ways these solutions could be tested.

Ask: Why might engineers use models or prototypes to test solutions to reduce the impact of flooding? **Sample answer: Building the actual solution before testing with a model could result in an expensive failure. If a solution fails because it was not tested, damage to homes and building could result.**

EVIDENCE NOTEBOOK

Students should note that levees and sandbags are two methods that can be used to reduce the impact of flooding. There are advantages and disadvantages associated with both of these solutions.

Lesson 4 How Can People Reduce the Impact of Water-Based Hazards? **609**

LESSON 4 Engage • **Explore/Explain** • Elaborate • Evaluate

EXPLORATION 2 *Reducing the Impacts of Water-Based Hazards, continued*

CCC Patterns

Remind students that patterns of change can be used to make predictions. The warning signs of different hazards are related to patterns of change that can be identified. Explain that some hazards, such as hurricanes, can be predicted well in advance. Others, such as tsunamis, give little time for preparation.

Ask: What patterns of change might a scientist look for to make a prediction that a hurricane might occur? **Possible answers: rising air temperature above warm ocean water; a storm forming over the ocean**

Differentiate Instruction

RTI/Extra Support Provide support to help students understand the format of the information on this page and the next page. First, explain that item 26 provides a place to record a summary of what they will learn by looking at each image and reading the caption. Explain that each image shows a different kind of water-based hazard and the captions provide a written description. Have students cover all but the first image and caption (about tsunamis) with blank paper. Have them study the image and caption. Have them repeat this method for each of the four hazards described.

DCI ESS3.B Natural Hazards

Encourage students to think back to the information about the causes and effects of hazards that was presented earlier in the lesson.

Ask: Why is knowing the cause of a hazard important for making predictions? **Sample answer: Predictions cannot be made without knowing what causes a specific hazard to happen.**

Hazards and Patterns

Advance preparation can reduce the impact of water-based hazards. By identifying patterns of events that lead up to water-based hazards, scientists can warn people that a hazard might occur in the near future.

Identifying Warning Signs

26. Use the pictures and captions to list warning signs for each hazard.

Natural hazard	tsunami	flood	hurricane	drought
Warning signs	earthquake, ground shaking, rise or fall of water level	intense rainfall, levee or dam failure, early snow melt	increase in ocean swell, wave frequency, wind and rain	lack of rain, climate patterns

Earthquakes may cause Tsunamis. If an earthquake moves a large volume of water above it, a tsunami could form. It might also travel thousands of kilometers across the ocean and cause devastation on distant shores. A noticeable fall or rise in the water level is another warning sign. An international warning system tells other countries whether their coasts are in danger.

Common warning signs for floods are intense rainfall, levee or dam failure, and even early snow melt. Flood warnings are given based on past patterns of flooding, readings from sensors placed in rivers, and information from weather satellites.

Until a hurricane has gotten close to making landfall, hurricane warning signs are not clearly visible. Some warning signs include an increase in ocean swell, wave frequency, wind speed, and rainfall. Scientists can track hurricanes using satellites and radars. This helps them warn people in areas that might be damaged.

Information about weather and climate patterns can be used to determine what areas might be at risk for droughts. Droughts happen when surface or underground water is greatly reduced. Knowing if a drought will affect an area is dependent on weather conditions, such as rainfall and temperature.

27. Circle the correct answer. Information about patterns in the location and intensity of earthquakes is most useful in helping people prepare for

   a. droughts
   b. river flooding
   c. hurricanes
   d. **tsunamis**

Putting It Together

28. Choose the correct words to complete each sentence. Use each word only once. Not all words will be used.

| patterns | flooding | future |
| drought | tsunamis | warning |

Technology and information about ___patterns___ in nature can be used to help lessen the impact of water-based hazards. For example, levees can be used to lessen the impact of ___flooding___, and data about weather patterns can be used to predict areas where a ___drought___ is possible.

SEP Obtaining, Evaluating, and Communicating Information

Have students read the question for item 26.

Ask: What are some questions a scientist might ask about patterns of earthquakes to help people prepare for tsunamis? Sample answer: What are some places where earthquakes occur underwater? Is there a strength or magnitude of an earthquake that is more likely to cause a tsunami? What is the relationship between an earthquake's distance from shore and the speed of a tsunami?

Collaboration

Share Feedback Have students form groups and share feedback as they complete item 27. Ask them to discuss with their groups the relationship between earthquakes and tsunamis.

FORMATIVE ASSESSMENT

DCI ETS1.B Designing Solutions to Engineering Problems

Ask: Do you think that government funding is better used to develop methods of *preventing* water-based hazards or *predicting* water-based hazards? Justify your response. Sample answer: I think that funding is better used for methods of predicting water-based hazards because natural hazards cannot be prevented. Spending money on predicting hazards allows the impact of the hazard to be lessened.

Lesson 4 How Can People Reduce the Impact of Water-Based Hazards?

LESSON 4 Engage • **Explore/Explain** • Elaborate • Evaluate

EXPLORATION 2 Reducing the Impact of Water-Based Hazards, continued

HANDS-ON ACTIVITY Small groups 1 class period
Is It Safe?

3D Learning Objective

 Constructing Explanations and Designing Solutions

Students perform an investigation and develop a design solution to reduce the impact of a tsunami.

Materials
The materials listed in the student edition are a starting point. By extending the materials list, students can explore a wider range of solutions.

Preparation
Before launching the activity, develop a way for students to track their budgets for the project. Each group has 500 units to work with, which they will need to spend to buy materials. You might want to use sticky notes, paper clips, or index cards to represent currency. Gather the milk cartons and other materials. Designate student groups for the activity. Plan for Internet access or access to other appropriate resources for the research required in Step 3.

Safety
Be sure students immediately clean up any spills to prevent slip and fall risks.

Procedure
STEP 1 Circulate among the groups to be sure students' discussions are on topic. If necessary, review the definitions of the terms *criteria* and *constraints* with students.

 **HANDS-ON ACTIVITY**
Is It Safe?

Scenario: Imagine a company called Wave Good-bye has hired you to build a small family neighborhood in a town on the seacoast. Part of your job is to make this small neighborhood as safe as possible from tsunami damage.

Objective

Collaborate with your team to figure out how to reduce the damage a tsunami might do to a small neighborhood. Identify a solution to help reduce the impact. Use materials to design and build a model of your solutions. You have a budget of 500 units in local currency to build this small neighborhood.

Materials provided by "nature"	Materials from your budget
• large shallow container (tub or pan) • water • stiff, flat piece of cardboard to make waves	• 0 units per milk carton (house) • 25 units per tree or plant • 25 units per cup of gravel • 10 units per newspaper page (land, when wadded into a ball) • 10 units per cup of dirt • 5 units per medium rock • 5 units per cup of sand • 5 units per craft stick

Find a Problem: What question will you investigate to meet this objective?

Possible question: How can we reduce the impact of the tsunami using the materials and budget we have?

Procedure

STEP 1 Brainstorm: Discuss criteria for a successful design to reduce the impact of a tsunami. Consider constraints on your design. Write your ideas below.

Accept all reasonable responses.

Criteria	Constraints
☐ Reduce the damage done by the tsunami ☐ Reduce damage to houses	☐ Use available material ☐ Stay within the budget ☐ Stay within the alloted time set by your teacher.

612

 Student Lab Worksheet and complete Teacher Support available online.

Unit 8 Natural Resources and Hazards

STEP 2 Research: Research tsunamis and methods used to reduce their impact. Brainstorm ideas for designs that could reduce the impact of a tsunami.

List and describe some of your ideas.
Possible answer: I could use trees to protect land from eroding. I could use a floodwall to block inland flooding. I could build a hill to place houses.

STEP 3 Plan: Choose one design to develop as a prototype. Sketch it on a separate sheet of paper. Remember to keep the budget in mind.

Identify the design chosen and explain why your group chose it.
Possible answer: We have chosen a design that uses materials to increase the elevation of the neighborhood. It should reduce the impact of the tsunami.

STEP 4 Build: Make your model. Scrunch up newspaper and use it to make land on one half of the container. Flatten mud onto the newspaper, covering the land and sloping down to the sea. Add the features you have planned, including houses. Pour water into the empty side of the container.

STEP 5 Test: Test your prototype. Thrust a piece of cardboard through the water with a rapid force to make a wave. Repeat two additional times. After your test, identify and make any needed improvements in your design. Keep the budget in mind. You must keep the same amount of houses in the same location. You will be re-testing your prototype in step 6.

What did you observe from your test? What improvements did you make in your design?
Possible answer: The waves did some damage. We made the elevation of the neighborhood even higher and added rocks and vegetation.

STEP 2 Have students research possible design solutions that could be used to lessen the impact of tsunamis. Remind students to evaluate the reliability of any sources they use for research.

Before moving forward, be sure that the models constructed include at least one house. Students should keep track of the materials they use to help them analyze their results and compare to other groups. Point out that the materials used to construct the model shore will likely have an impact on their results. Remind each group to keep track of its budget of currency.

STEP 3 Based on the results of their research, each group will choose a design to develop as a prototype. Circulate among the groups, and evaluate each groups' choice of design. Approve their choices before they begin.

STEP 4 Circulate to make sure students are constructing their models correctly, and using their materials appropriately.

STEP 5 Remind students to evaluate the results of their testing by comparing to the criteria they developed in Step 1. Encourage them to carefully observe and record the damage to the shoreline and the homes.

DCI ESS3.B Natural Hazards

The arrival of digital video capability in mobile devices and other cameras has allowed a number of recent tsunamis to be captured on video as they occurred. You may want to show some videos to your students before they embark on this activity. The tsunami that struck Japan in 2011, for example, can be seen in multiple videos, some of which may dispel the misconception that a tsunami resembles a wind-driven wave or a computer-generated tsunami from a movie. Exercise caution in vetting videos, as they can be disturbing.

Lesson 4 How Can People Reduce the Impact of Water-Based Hazards? 613

LESSON 4   Engage • **Explore/Explain** • Elaborate • Evaluate

EXPLORATION 2 HANDS-ON ACTIVITY, *continued*

STEP 6 If possible, have students create a video of their redesigned prototype and the test they performed on it.

Analyze Your Results

STEP 7 Call on each group to share a summary of its results. After each group has shared, students will have the information they need to complete Step 7. If students created a video, have them share it during their s

STEPS 8–9 Circulate among the groups to be sure that students have identified a logical improvement and a valid method of evaluating their design.

Draw Conclusions

STEPS 10–11 Circulate among students to be sure their claims are supported.

> ### Claims, Evidence, and Reasoning
> Remind students that there should be a clear connection between their evidence and claims.

	Scoring Rubric for Hands-On Activity
3	Design is constructed carefully, criteria and constraints are considered, design is tested, and claims are well-supported by evidence.
2	Design is constructed with some regard to criteria and constraints, design is tested, and claims are supported by evidence.
1	Designs are constructed but criteria and constrains are not considered, testing might be limited in scope, claims might be unrelated to evidence.
0	Student did not participate in activity

STEP 6 Now that you have redesigned your prototype, test it again following the same steps.

Record your observations. How do your results compare to the results from your first prototype?

The second test caused less damage and less erosion. I think it is because we added more plants.

Analyze Your Results

STEP 7 Communicate: Compare your team's results with those of a different team. Describe how and why your results were similar to or different from the other team's results.

Possible answer: Our results were less successful than the other team's results; they had less damage to their houses.

STEP 8 Evaluate and Redesign Based on your two prototype designs, how could you improve your design further?

Possible answer: We could have designed a higher hill to limit the damage.

STEP 9 What method did you use to determine whether your design reduced the impact of the tsunami?

Possible answer: We analyzed the amount of damage to the houses to see whether our design reduced the impact of the tsunami.

Draw Conclusions

STEP 10 Make a claim about the success of your design? Cite evidence to support your claim.

Possible answer: I would classify our design as successful because it greatly reduced the impact of the tsunami. (Students should cite the results of their test for evidence.)

STEP 11 What other questions do you have about ways that engineers can design devices to reduce the impact of tsunamis?

Possible answer: I wonder how engineers stop flooding from tsunamis without building a structure that keeps people from accessing the beach.

LESSON 4 Engage • Explore/Explain • **Elaborate** • Evaluate

TAKE IT FURTHER Discover More

▶ **Explore Online** Students can explore all three Take it Further paths online.

TAKE IT FURTHER
Discover More

Check out this path . . . or go online to choose one of these other paths.

- **Hurricanes and Their Effects**
- Careers in Engineering
- Make It Safer

Hurricanes form in warm ocean waters. When the moist air above the sea surface reaches 28 °C, it rises toward the cooler air above. When conditions are right, the moving air develops into a thunderstorm with strong winds and heavy rains. The storm gets larger as more warm, moist air rises up. The clouds begin moving in a circular pattern. The winds increase as the storm turns into a hurricane. Hurricanes cause flooding, heavy rains, damages property and loosens soil and rocks, which can trigger landslides.

▶ **Explore Online**

29. How could knowing where hurricanes and storms appear help you reduce the effects of hazardous weather? Use the map to your right and what you have read to support your answer.

Accept all reasonable answers.

Hurricane and Tropical Storm frequency map

30. What conclusions can you draw from the Hurricane and Tropical Storm frquency map?

Students might say that coastal areas are more prone to hurricanes.

615

Collaboration

You may choose to assign this activity or to direct students online to the Interactive Online Student Edition where they can explore and choose from all three paths. These activities can be assigned individually, to pairs, or to small groups.

Hurricanes and Their Effects

DCI ESS3.B Natural Hazards

This feature provides additional information about hurricanes and their impacts on people. Have students read the information and examine the map. Have them recall other maps they have viewed as a part of this lesson and the previous lesson.

Ask: Why are maps, such as the ones in this lesson, a valuable tool for engineers working on solutions to lessen the impact of hazards? Design solutions for a particular type of hazard should be focused on areas most likely to be impacted by that type of hazard.

CCC Cause and Effect

Students can gain an in-depth look at the causes and effects of hurricanes in this feature.

Ask: Identify one fact about the cause of hurricanes described on this page. Sample answer: Warm air over the ocean rises and develops into a storm that grows into a hurricane.

Ask: Identify one fact about the effects of hurricanes described on this page. Sample answer: Hurricanes can cause a storm surge that leads to flooding.

Lesson 4 How Can People Reduce the Impact of Water-Based Hazards? 615

LESSON 4 Engage • Explore/Explain • **Elaborate** • Evaluate

TAKE IT FURTHER, continued

SEP Constructing Explanations and Designing Solutions

Have students think about the information provided in the timeline. Encourage them to think about ways that information about past events can be applied by those who are designing solutions to help lessen the impact of future events.

Ask: What data shown here would be particularly useful to those designing solutions to reduce the impact of hurricanes? Explain your response. *Sample answer: I think the locations of the hurricanes' landfalls would be very useful to engineers as they decide where design solutions to reduce the impact of hurricanes should be located.*

Differentiate Instruction

RTI/Extra Support Some students will need extra support to understand the format of this page. Point out the timeline at the center of the page. Explain that it is used to show the years in which certain hurricanes occurred and the order in which they occurred. Emphasize that many other hurricanes occurred in this time period but the hurricanes featured are examples of hurricanes that had a major impact on humans.

▷ Explore Online

Students can explore these additional topics online.

Careers in Engineering

Students research diverse careers in water engineering, especially those that focus on reducing the impact of water-based hazards. *(Outside research required.)*

Make It Safer

Students carry out a Hands-On Activity to further explore ways that the impact of natural hazards can be reduced. *(No outside research required.)*

The timeline shows seven different hurricanes that have occurred in this century.

Hurricanes can have a large impact.

2004
Hurricane Charley
- August 13, 2004
- Category 4 at landfall
- Landfall along west coast of Florida
- Damage: $11 billion

2005
Hurricane Katrina
- August 29, 2005
- Category 1 at 1st landfall, Category 3 at 2nd landfall
- First landfall near Miami, Florida Second landfall near Buras, Louisiana
- Damage: $100+ billion

2005
Hurricane Wilma
- October 24, 2005
- Category 5 at 1st landfall, Category 3 at 2nd landfall
- First landfall near Mexican Yucatan Peninsula Second landfall near Naples, Florida
- Damage: $21 billion

2012
Hurricane Sandy
- October 22–29, 2012
- Category 1 at 1st landfall Category 3 at 2nd landfall
- First landfall in Jamaica Second landfall in Cuba Final landfall in Brigantine, New Jersey
- Damage: $62 billion in the United States and at least $315 million in the Caribbean.

2004
Hurricane Frances
- September 5–6, 2004
- Category 2 at landfall
- Landfall near Stuart, Florida
- Damage: $9 billion

2005
Hurricane Rita
- September 24, 2005
- Category 3 at landfall
- Landfall near Johnson's Bayou, Louisiana
- Damage: $10 billion

2008
Hurricane Ike
- September 1–14 2008
- Category 4 at first landfall
- Category 2 at final landfall
- First landfall in Cuba
- Final landfall in Galveston Island, TX
- Damages: 29.5 billion in the United States and $7.3 billion in Cuba

31. Use the information in the timeline to make a bar graph. Number the *y*-axis 1 through 5 and label it *Category*. Make a labeled bar for each hurricane to show the category at landfall. Make a bar for each landfall. Analyze your graph to see whether you notice any relationship between a hurricane's category and the amount of damage it caused. Submit your bar graph to your teacher.

LESSON 4
Lesson Check

Name _____

Can You Explain It?

1. Look back at the image at the beginning of the lesson. What are some ways people can reduce the impact of a flood? Be sure to do the following:
   - Describe several water-based natural hazards that can affect humans.
   - Describe ways that the impact of water-based natural hazards, such as floods, can be lessened and people in a community can prepare for them.
   - Explain how testing, improving, and retesting design solutions can lead to ways that will help reduce the impact of water-based natural hazards.

 EVIDENCE NOTEBOOK Use the information you've collected in your Evidence Notebook to help you cover each point.

Possible response:
- Water-based natural hazards include floods, tsunamis, hurricanes, and droughts.
- The impacts of water-based natural hazards can be reduced by watching for patterns that can predict future occurrences of the hazard and by engineering solutions to decrease their impacts. (Students should give examples.)
- Testing and improving helped us find out what parts of the solution worked and what parts didn't work and fix them.

Checkpoints

2. Choose the correct response. Which of these would show you whether your state is experiencing drought conditions?
   a. daily weather report
   b. road map
   c. drought monitor map
   d. deep ocean buoy

Formal Assessment Go online for student self-checks and other assessments.

Can You Explain It?

Collaboration

Discussion You may wish to revisit the image of the people placing sandbags as a group activity to assess students' understanding of water-based hazards and solutions that can lessen their impacts. Use each of the bulleted questions as a prompt for class discussion. Encourage students to cite evidence from the text to support their responses.

 EVIDENCE NOTEBOOK

Have students reread their answers to the Evidence Notebook prompts and then use this evidence to justify their reasoning as they respond to the Can You Explain It question. Make sure students understand that a complete response must address all bulleted points.

DCI **ESS3.B Natural Hazards**

Focus students on water-based natural hazards as they analyze the image of the steps being taken to reduce the impact of a flood.

SUMMATIVE ASSESSMENT
Engage in Argument From Evidence

2. This item requires students to apply the information they learned in Exploration 1 about droughts. Students may think that the correct answer is "A" for "daily weather report," but explain to students why this would not provide the necessary information. Students should easily be able to tell that answers "B" and "D" are incorrect.

LESSON 4 Engage • Explore/Explain • Elaborate • **Evaluate**

LESSON CHECK, continued

3. If students are having a difficult time selecting a response, have them review information in Exploration 2 related to technologies used to lessen the impact of specific hazards. You may even have students think back to the types of natural barriers that trees and coral reefs provide, and how engineers and scientists use similar methods for constructing manmade design solutions.

4. Make sure students read the question stem correctly, understanding that the this is asking the question in the negative form. It may be helpful to rephase the question in the positive form, and then have students answer it, identifying "A", "B", and "D" as the correct answers. Then, flip the question back to the negative form, and have stuents select the correct answer "C". Information about the causes of each type of hazard can be applied to answer this item. If students need to review, encourage them to look back to Exploration 1.

5. A review of the information about patterns of events that can be used as warning signs of natural hazards in Exploration 2 will help students select the correct response to this question. If students struggle with this item, tell them that each word will be used only once, so each box will have one word for them to write.

6. Students can synthesize the information in Exploration 1 and Exploration 2 to answer item 6. Let students know that there is more than one correct answer to this question. Help students by asking them probing questions about the characteristics of each answer choice, until they arrive at the correct answers.

3. Draw lines to match each word with the correct picture of a technology that can reduce the impact of that type of hazard.

   Natural Hazard
   - hurricane
   - flood
   - tsunami
   - drought

4. The risk of which water-based natural hazard is increased during time periods when there is NOT much rain?
   a. tsunami
   b. flood
   c. drought
   d. hurricane

5. Complete the table by writing the hazard from the word bank in the box with its possible warning signs.

A pattern of very dry weather	An earthquake under the ocean
drought	tsunami
A storm starting to develop over warm ocean water	A pattern of rapid temperature increase leading to snow melt near a river
hurricane	flooding

Word bank: drought, tsunami, flood, hurricane

6. Which of these form in or over the ocean before causing damage on land? Select all that apply.
   a. tsunami
   b. flood
   c. drought
   d. hurricane

618

618 Unit 8 Natural Resources and Hazards

LESSON 4

Lesson Roundup

A. Choose the correct words to complete each sentence.

Weather conditions over warm ocean water can cause a ___hurricane___ to form, which can lead to a ___flood___ near the coast. A ___drought___ is a natural hazard that can lead to water-use restrictions being put in place to conserve water.

> drought
> tsunami
> flood
> hurricane

What else have you learned about water-based natural hazards in this lesson?

Possible answer: I have learned that patterns can be used to predict some water-based natural hazards.

B. For each water-based natural hazard shown here, identify a technology and how it can lessen its impact.

Possible answer: Deep ocean buoys detect tsunamis in advance so people can be warned.

Possible answer: Sandbags or levees control flood waters.

Possible answer: Geostationary satellites track hurricanes so people can be prepared.

Possible answer: Reservoirs store water for times of drought.

Lesson Roundup

 ESS3.B Natural Hazards
ETS1.B Designing Solutions to Engineering Problems

This lesson summary enables students to quickly revisit key points and prepare for tests.

A. Use this item to reemphasize the causes and effects of water-based natural hazards. Have students review the information in Exploration 1 to help them complete the paragraph using the words in the word bank. Then, encourage students to skim Exploration 1 to identify at least one additional fact about water-based hazards for the second part of this item. **ESS3.B**

B. Suggest that students review the information in Exploration 2 to help them recall the technologies used to lessen the impacts of specific types of natural hazards. This is also a good time to remind students that there are natural barriers that provide protection from water-based hazards, too, such as coral reefs, mangrove trees, etc. **ESS3.B, ETS1.B**

UNIT 8 Performance Task

👥 small groups   🕐 2 class periods

Avoiding Disaster

3D Assessment Goal
Students **obtain information** and **develop solutions** to demonstrate **minimize the risk of flood hazards in the community** to demonstrate understanding of **ESS3.A** in support of **4-ESS3-2**.

Materials
- paper
- writing utensils

Preparation
Students will need access to online sources to research the weather patterns in their cities.

CCC Influence of Engineering, Technology, and Science on Society and Natural World

Students attempt to come up with solutions for preventing severe hazards to society and the environment caused by rainfall and flooding. **Ask:** What are some effective flood prevention methods that you have researched so far?

Research
Review how to properly cite resources.
Print: title, author, copyright date, page number
Online: webpage title, URL, date visited
If students are doing their own research on the Internet, remind them how to search for reliable sources that can be trusted.

Brainstorm
Each student will be individually responsible for coming up with flood prevention strategies.

620   Unit 8 Natural Resources and Hazards

UNIT 8   UNIT PERFORMANCE TASK

Avoiding Disaster

You are a small-town mayor in the midwestern United States. Last summer, your town experienced record rainfall and flooded for the first time in history. Nobody was hurt, but there was a lot of damage. This year, you and a group of volunteers are tasked with planning strategies to minimize the danger and damage of flooding.

It is your job as mayor to keep this from happening again.

DEFINE YOUR TASK: How will you know if your project is successful?

If we can minimize the threat posed by heavy rains and flooding, then we will know that our project was successful.

Before beginning, review the checklist at the end of this Unit Performance Task. Keep those items in mind as you proceed.

RESEARCH: Use online or library resources to learn about flood prevention methods. A good place to start is the Federal Emergency Management Agency (FEMA) website (http://www.fema.gov). Find out how other communities have successfully prevented flooding. Note which methods seem the best. Cite your sources.

Student should note their research and cite sources.

BRAINSTORM: Brainstorm three or more flood strategy ideas with your volunteers. Use what you have learned about natural disasters to identify what your strategy must achieve to be effective.

Students should note that natural disasters cannot be prevented. Strategies to deal with them center on prevention of injury and damage.

PLAN YOUR PROCEDURE: Consider the questions below as your group plans its flood strategy. Be sure to address the resources you will need and your overall goals and limits. Write a few sentences below to briefly summarize your strategy.

1. What kind of flood-control structures should we build, and where should we build them?
2. What other precautions should we take now?
3. How can we know if a flood threat is near?
4. What plan should be in place to react to a flood threat?
5. How can we educate the community about our plans?
6. How can we alert the community in the event of a threat?
7. What is our budget?
8. Will we need to raise more money, and if so, how and how much?

Student should use the questions to summarize the various goals and aspects of the group's flood strategy.

REPORT: Create a document that details your flood strategy. Describe the precautions to be put in place. List steps to be carried out during a flood emergency. Be specific and complete.

COMMUNICATE: Present your flood plan to your class orally and with multimedia. Explain the reasoning behind your plan and discuss possible ways to revise and improve it.

✓ Checklist

Review your project and check off each completed item.

_____ Includes a statement defining your group's task.

_____ Includes research into and consideration of various flood-control strategies with sources cited.

_____ Includes a list of flood-plan precautions to be taken.

_____ Includes a description of flood-control structures with a list of materials needed to build them.

_____ Includes a plan of action to be followed during a flood.

_____ Includes an explanation of how the flood plan will be paid for.

_____ Includes an oral presentation with multimedia support.

Plan Your Procedure

 Constructing Explanations and Designing Solutions

Students can come up with solutions once they have identified where and what the problems or weak areas are. For instance, poor drainage on the roads could be an example of an infrastructural weakness. **Ask: What are some of the problems, or weaknesses, in the area that make flooding more likely in this town?**

Report

Students should design their reports as if they were going to present the information to a committee of volunteers to help prepare the town.

Scoring Rubric for Performance Task	
3	• complete resources, clear reasoning, multiple sources • flood plan precautions are detailed with descriptions of structures and materials • presentation includes plan of action and is supported by multimedia
2	• most resources, adequate reasoning and sources • flood plan precautions are somewhat detailed with some descriptions of structures and materials • presentation includes plan of action and is somewhat supported by multimedia
1	• some key resources and reasoning, a few sources • flood plan precautions lack detailed descriptions of structures and materials • presentation lacks plan of action or multimedia
0	• few key resources, no reasons, minimal sources • flood plan precautions incomplete • presentation incomplete

UNIT 8 Review

SUMMATIVE ASSESSMENT

1. Students can correctly answer this question by recalling facts about nonrenewable resources. They can refer back to Lesson 1, Exploration 1.

2. Students must first study the image to understand what is being depicted. It is a gas station. Then students must apply their knowledge of gas stations and the energy source used to arrive at the correct answers. Have students revisit Lesson 1, Exploration 1 for additional help.

3. Suggest that students apply what they know about these elements to answer this question correctly. Encourage students to say the sentences out loud, to themselves, to hear which options make the most sense. Students can also refer back to Lesson 1, Exploration 1.

4. Students can answer this question by differentiating between renewable and nonrenewable energy sources. Have them refer back to Lessons 1 and 2 for a quick review.

UNIT 8

Unit Review

1. Which fuel source is made entirely of long-dead plants? Circle the correct choice.
   a. oil
   b. coal
   c. uranium
   d. natural gas

2. Which of the following is true of the product sold here? Circle all that apply.
   a. It is a natural resource.
   b. Its use creates pollution.
   c. It is a renewable resource.
   d. It is a nonrenewable resource.

3. Use the word bank to complete the sentences.

   | Oil | Uranium | Coal | Natural Gas |

   _____Natural Gas_____ and oil are the remains of plants and tiny sea creatures that died millions of years ago.

   _____Uranium_____ does not come from once living material.

4. Indicate whether each type of energy is nonrenewable and causes pollution (NP) or renewable and non-polluting (RN).

   Coal ___NP___
   Wind ___RN___
   Solar ___RN___
   Water ___RN___
   Natural Gas ___NP___

622

Unit 8 Natural Resources and Hazards

5. Use the word bank to complete the sentences.

   | stored | created | reduced | increased |

   Energy from this source can be __stored__ for times when it is not being produced.

6. The methods used to generate electricity from both wind and water are similar. Explain how they are alike.

   Both moving air and moving water can spin a turbine to produce electricity. Both methods are clean methods of generating electricity, and both are renewable resources.

7. Which of these are known to trigger tsunamis? Circle all that apply.
   a. wildfires
   b. **landslides**
   c. **volcanoes**
   d. hurricanes
   e. **earthquakes**

---

5. Students need to use the image to answer the question correctly. Have them pay close attention to the energy source in the picture. They can refer back to Lesson 2, Exploration 1 to recall information about renewable energy sources.

6. Students need to recall the ways in which both wind and water generate electricity in order to compare their similarities. More on this can be found in Lesson 2.

7. Make sure students recall the meaning of a tsunami. They can also refer back to the unit photo or water-based natural hazards in Lesson 4, Explorations 1 and 2.

UNIT 8 Review, continued

8. Students need to study the image to arrive at the correct answer. They need to not only see the tree, but also study the environment as a whole. Land-based natural hazards can be reviewed with students in Lesson 3.

9. Students can review Lesson 3, Exploration 1 to refresh their memories of the Richter scale and other land-based natural hazards.

10. Hurricanes are water-based natural hazards. Suggest students recall characteristics of hurricanes to provide proper descriptions for item 10. Students can turn to Lesson 4 for a quick review of this material.

3D Item Analysis	1	2	3	4	5	6	7	8	9	10
SEP Obtaining, Evaluating, and Communicating Information						•				
DCI Natural Resources		•	•	•	•	•	•	•	•	•
CCC Influence of Engineering, Technology, and Science on Society and the Natural World		•	•	•	•	•	•	•		•

---

8. What long-term natural disaster is pictured here?

Circle the correct choice.
a. a flood
b. **a drought**
c. a tsunami
d. a hurricane

9. Use the word bank to complete the sentences.

hurricanes	half as strong as	twice as strong as
earthquakes	volcanoes	ten times stronger than

The Richter scale is used to measure the strength of _____earthquakes_____

Each level of the Richter scale is _____ten times stronger than_____ the previous level.

10. Air and water at different temperatures can produce violent storms such as hurricanes. Explain how temperature, water, and air are related to a hurricane.

A hurricane can form where cooler air moves over warmer water. The moving air develops into a thunderstorm. The storm gets larger as more warm, moist air rises up. The clouds move in a circular pattern. Wind increases as the storm turns into a hurricane.

Resources

Reading in the Science Content Area **TR2**

English Language Arts Correlation **TR6**

Math Correlation **TR10**

ScienceSaurus Correlation **TR12**

Student Edition Interactive Glossary **TR16**

Index **TR24**

Reading in the Science Content Area

Integrating Reading and Science Instruction

This listing compiles readers and trade books that align with the topical organization of the Performance Expectations and Disciplinary Core Ideas for Grade 4 of the NGSS, and the units contained within the **HMH Science Dimensions™** program. Titles are arranged according to their approximate Guided Reading Levels.

As with all materials you share with your class, we suggest you review the books first to ensure their appropriateness. While titles are available at time of publication, they may go out of print without notice.

Energy (Units 1–2)

Level M
Experiments with Heat and Energy by Magloff, Lisa (GarethStevens)

Level N
Energy for the Future by Rigby Staff (Rigby/Steck-Vaughn)
What Are Some Forms of Energy? by Rigby Staff (Houghton Mifflin Harcourt Publishing)

Level O
How Do We Generate and Use Electricity? by Rigby Staff (Houghton Mifflin Harcourt Publishing)
How Do We Use Forms of Energy? by Rigby Staff (Houghton Mifflin Harcourt Publishing)

Level P
Bridging The Energy Gap by Langley, Andrew (Capstone Press)
Power Partners: Electricity And Magnetism by Rigby Staff (Rigby/Steck-Vaughn)

Level Q
Nuclear Energy by Saunders, Nigel (GarethStevens)

Level R
All About Energy by Herweck, Don (Shell Educational Publishing/TCM)
Geothermal Energy: Using Earth's Furnace by Gleason, Carrie (Crabtree Publishing Company)

Level S
Conservation of Energy by Barchers, Suzanne (Shell Educational Publishing/TCM)
Hydroelectric Power: Power from Moving Water by Rodger, Marguerite (Crabtree Publishing Company)
Power on Demand: Making Electricity by Rigby Staff (Houghton Mifflin Harcourt Publishing)
The Scientists Behind Energy by Solway, Andrew (Capstone Press)

Level T
Energy by Mullins, Matt (Grolier/Scholastic Library Publishing)
Transfer of Energy by de Pinna, Simon (GarethStevens)

Level U
The History of Energy by Landau, Elaine (Lerner Publishing Group)
Wind Power by Allen, Kathy (Cherry Lake Publishing)

Waves: Waves and Information—Unit 3

Level N
What Are Patterns in Space? by Rigby Staff (Houghton Mifflin Harcourt Publishing)

Level O
Sounds All Around by Pfeffer, Wendy (Harper Collins)

Level Q
All About Light and Sound by Jankowski, Connie (Shell Educational Publishing/TCM)
Music Technology by Rigby Staff (Rigby/Steck-Vaughn)
Patterns Around Us by Hyland, Tony (Shell Educational Publishing/TCM)
Telegraph And Telephone Networks: Ground Breaking Developments In American Communications by Jarnow, Jesse (Rosen Publishing)

Level R
Inventing the Computer by Groves, Marsha (Crabtree Publishing Company)
Making Noise!: Making Sounds by Spilsbury, Louise (Capstone Press)
Samuel Morse And The Telegraph by Seidman, David (Capstone Press)
The Terrific Tale of Television by Enz, Tammy (Capstone Press)

Structure, Function, and Information Processing—Units 4-5

Level N
How And Why Animals Hatch From Eggs by Pascoe, Elaine (Creative Teaching Press)
How And Why Plants Eat Insects by Pascoe, Elaine (Creative Teaching Press)
How And Why Seeds Travel by Pascoe, Elaine (Creative Teaching Press)
Investigating Invertebrates by Hammonds, Heather (Rigby/Steck-Vaughn)
Mammal Mania by Housel, Debra (Shell Educational Publishing/TCM)
Plant Classification by Gray, Leon (GarethStevens)
Power Packed Plants by Rigby Staff (Rigby/Steck-Vaughn)

Level O
A World Of Fish by Hammonds (Rigby/Steck-Vaughn)
Adaptation and Survival by Spilsbury, Richard (Crabtree Publishing Company)
Amazing Dolphins! by Thomson, Sarah L. (Harper Collins)
Amazing Gorillas! by Thomson, Sarah L. (Harper Collins)
Amphibians by Hammonds, Heather (Rigby/Steck-Vaughn)
Bats by Gibbons, Gail (Holiday House)
Bird Fact File by Rigby Staff (Rigby/Steck-Vaughn)
Carnivorous Plants by Rigby Staff (Rigby/Steck-Vaughn)
How A Plant Grows? by Kalman, Bobbie (Crabtree Publishing Company)
How And Why Animals Hide by Pascoe, Elaine (Creative Teaching Press)
How Do Living Things Change and Grow? by Rigby Staff (Houghton Mifflin Harcourt Publishing)
How Do Organisms Interact With Their Environment? by Rigby Staff (Houghton Mifflin Harcourt Publishing)
The Life Cycle Of A Sea Turtle by Kalman, Bobbie (Crabtree Publishing Company)
What is a Living Thing? by Kalman, Bobbie (Holiday House)

Level P
Animal Senses: Sight and Hearing by Rigby Staff (Rigby/Steck-Vaughn)
Animal Senses: Smell, Taste, Touch by Rigby Staff (Rigby/Steck-Vaughn)
Behavior of Living Things by Bright, Michael (Capstone Press)
How And Why Animals Are Poisonous by Pascoe, Elaine (Creative Teaching Press)
How Do Animals Adapt? by Kalman, Bobbie (Crabtree Publishing Company)
How Do Plants and Animals Reproduce and Adapt? by Rigby Staff (Houghton Mifflin Harcourt Publishing)
Invasive Plant Species by Spilsbury, Richard (Rosen Publishing)
Plant Discoveries by Rigby Staff (Rigby/Steck-Vaughn)
The Largest Living Things by Rigby Staff (Rigby/Steck-Vaughn)
The Magic School Bus Plants Seeds: A Book About How Living Things Grow by Relf, Patricia (Scholastic, Inc.)

Level Q
Albatross, The Survivor by Rigby Staff (Rigby/Steck-Vaughn)
Deadliest Creatures by Rigby Staff (Rigby/Steck-Vaughn)
How do animals find food? by Kalman, Bobbie (Crabtree Publishing Company)
Mudskippers and Other Extreme Fish Adaptations by Rake, Jody (Capstone Press)
Odd Bods by Rigby Staff (Rigby/Steck-Vaughn)
Surprising Adaptations by Rigby Staff (Houghton Mifflin Harcourt Publishing)

Reading in the Science Content Area

Level R
Cane Toads by Rigby Staff (Rigby/Steck-Vaughn)
Designed for Living by Rigby Staff (Rigby/Steck-Vaughn)
Mammals Under Water by Rigby Staff (Rigby/Steck-Vaughn)
Structures of Life: What is this Fossil? by Sohn, Emily (Norwood House)

Level S
Extreme Animals by Davies, Nicola (Candlewick Press)
Frogs: Fascinating...and Fragile by Rigby Staff (Rigby/Steck-Vaughn)
Vampire Bats, Giant Insects, and Other Mysterious Animals of the Darkest Caves by Rodríguez, Ana María (Enslow Publishers, Inc.)
Vampires and Light by Jensen-Shaffer, Jodeen Marie (Capstone Press)

Level T
North America's Most Amazing Animals by Ganeri, Anita (Capstone Press)
Plant Cells by Dowdy, Penny (Crabtree Publishing Company)
Wild Planet by Rigby Staff (Rigby/Steck-Vaughn)

Level U
Monkeys, Diverse Animals by Rigby Staff (Rigby/Steck-Vaughn)
Science Lab: The Life Cycles of Plants by Hirsch, Rebecca (Cherry Lake Publishing)

Earth's Systems: Processes that Shape the Earth—Units 6–8

Level O
Earthquakes by Branley, Franklyn M. (Harper Collins)
Earthquakes and Tsunamis by Draper, Mary (Rigby/Steck-Vaughn)
Water and Wind by Draper, Mary (Rigby/Steck-Vaughn)
Weathering and Erosion by Hoffman, Steven (Shell Educational Publishing/TCM)
What Are Natural Resources? by Rigby Staff (Houghton Mifflin Harcourt Publishing)

Level P
An Encyclopedia Of Rocks by Rigby Staff (Rigby/Steck-Vaughn)
Climate Change by Spilsbury, Richard (Crabtree Publishing Company)
Earth's Changing Surface and Natural Resources by Rigby Staff (Houghton Mifflin Harcourt Publishing)
Fossils by Rigby Staff (Rigby/Steck-Vaughn)
My Search For Fossils by Rigby Staff (Rigby/Steck-Vaughn)
Our Ever-Changing Environment by Buchanan, Shelly (Shell Educational Publishing/TCM)
Rock Hunters by Rigby Staff (Rigby/Steck-Vaughn)
Soil Erosion and How to Prevent It by Hyde, Natalie (Crabtree Publishing Company)
The Magic School Bus At The Water Works by Cole, Joanna (Scholastic, Inc.)
The Magic School Bus Inside The Earth by Cole, Joanna (Scholastic, Inc.)
Water All Around The Earth by Rigby Staff (Rigby/Steck-Vaughn)
Why is there Life on Earth? by Solway, Andrew (Capstone Press)

Level Q
Fossils: Pictures From The Past by Rigby Staff (Rigby/Steck-Vaughn)
Natural Disasters by Noonan, Diana (Shell Educational Publishing/TCM)
Nature's Power (Earth's Odditites) by Kummer, Patricia K. (Rigby/Steck-Vaughn)
Water: A Natural Resource by Rigby Staff (Rigby/Steck-Vaughn)

Level R
Aliens From Earth: When Animals And Plants Invade Other Ecosystems by Batten, Mary (Peachtree Publishers)
Examining Erosion by Riley, Joelle (Lerner Publishing Group)
How Do Humans Depend On Earth? by Lundgren, Julie (Rourke Publishing)
Maps by Rigby Staff (Rigby/Steck-Vaughn)
The Explosive World of Volcanoes with Max Axiom, Super Scientist by Harbo, Christopher (Capstone Press)
Understanding Global Warming with Max Axiom, Super Scientist by Martin, Cynthia (Capstone Press)
Volcanoes And Other Natural Disasters by Griffey, Harriet (DK Publishers)

Level S
Conservation Area Maps by Gillett, Jack (Rosen Publishing)
Earth's Core and Crust by Davis, Brangien (GarethStevens)
Earth's Cycles by Dakers, Diane (Crabtree Publishing Company)
Natural Resource Maps by Gillett, Jack (Rosen Publishing)
The Scientists Behind Earth's Processes by Solway, Andrew (Capstone Press)

Level T
Global Warming by Buchanan, Shelly (Shell Educational Publishing/TCM)
Ocean Maps by Wall, Julia (Shell Educational Publishing/TCM)
Our Footprint On Earth by Sturm, Jeanne (Rourke Publishing)

Level U
STEM Guides To Maps by Robertson, Kay (Rourke Publishing)
Sustaining Our Natural Resources by Green, Jen (Capstone Press)
The Appalachians by Aloian, Molly (Crabtree Publishing Company)
The Rocky Mountains by Aloian, Molly (Crabtree Publishing Company)

English Language Arts Correlations ▷ Explore Online

Common Core State Standards for English Language Arts

A correlation to the Next Generation Science Standards is located in the front of this Teacher Edition. Correlations to the Common Core State Standards for English Language Arts are provided on these pages.

Grade 4	Units/Lessons
RI.4.1 Refer to details and examples in a text when explaining what the text says explicitly and when drawing inferences from the text.	Unit 3 Lesson 3
	Unit 5 Lesson 2
	Unit 8 Lesson 3
RI.4.3 Explain events, procedures, ideas, or concepts in a historical, scientific, or technical text, including what happened and why, based on specific information in the text.	Unit 2 Lesson 3
	Unit 3 Lesson 2
	Unit 3 Lesson 3
	Unit 4 Lesson 1
	Unit 5 Lesson 2
	Unit 8 Lesson 1
	Unit 8 Lesson 4
RI.4.7 Interpret information presented visually, orally, or quantitatively (e.g., in charts, graphs, diagrams, time lines, animations, or interactive elements on Web pages) and explain how the information contributes to an understanding of the text in which it appears.	Unit 3 Lesson 1
	Unit 3 Lesson 3
	Unit 5 Lesson 2
	Unit 6 Lesson 1
	Unit 6 Lesson 2
	Unit 6 Lesson 3
	Unit 6 Lesson 4

English Language Arts Correlations

Grade 4	Units/Lessons
RI.4.9 Integrate information from two texts on the same topic in order to write or speak about the subject knowledgeably.	Unit 2 Lesson 2
	Unit 3 Lesson 1
	Unit 3 Lesson 3
	Unit 4 Lesson 1
	Unit 5 Lesson 2
	Unit 8 Lesson 3
	Unit 8 Lesson 4
W.4.1 Write opinion pieces on topics or texts, supporting a point of view with reasons and information.	Unit 3 Lesson 3
	Unit 4 Lesson 1
	Unit 4 Lesson 2
	Unit 5 Lesson 1
	Unit 5 Lesson 3
	Unit 6 Lesson 3
W.4.2 Write informative/explanatory texts to examine a topic and convey ideas and information clearly.	Unit 2 Lesson 3
	Unit 5 Lesson 2

English Language Arts Correlations ▷ Explore Online

Grade 4	Units/Lessons
W.4.7 Conduct short research projects that build knowledge through investigation of different aspects of a topic.	Unit 1 Lesson 2
	Unit 1 Lesson 3
	Unit 2 Lesson 1
	Unit 2 Lesson 2
	Unit 4 Lesson 1
	Unit 4 Lesson 2
	Unit 7 Lesson 1
	Unit 7 Lesson 2
	Unit 7 Lesson 3
	Unit 8 Lesson 1
	Unit 8 Lesson 2
	Unit 8 Lesson 4
W.4.8 Recall relevant information from experiences or gather relevant information from print and digital sources; take notes and categorize information, and provide a list of sources.	Unit 1 Lesson 1
	Unit 1 Lesson 3
	Unit 2 Lesson 1
	Unit 2 Lesson 2
	Unit 2 Lesson 3
	Unit 4 Lesson 1
	Unit 6 Lesson 1
	Unit 6 Lesson 2
	Unit 6 Lesson 4
	Unit 7 Lesson 1
	Unit 7 Lesson 2
	Unit 7 Lesson 3
	Unit 8 Lesson 1
	Unit 8 Lesson 2

English Language Arts Correlations

Grade 4	Units/Lessons
W.4.9 Draw evidence from literary or informational texts to support analysis, reflection, and research.	Unit 1 Lesson 1
	Unit 1 Lesson 2
	Unit 1 Lesson 3
	Unit 7 Lesson 1
	Unit 7 Lesson 2
	Unit 7 Lesson 3
	Unit 8 Lesson 1
	Unit 8 Lesson 2
SL.4.5 Add audio recordings and visual displays to presentations when appropriate to enhance the development of main ideas or themes.	Unit 3 Lesson 1
	Unit 3 Lesson 2
	Unit 5 Lesson 3

Math Correlations

Common Core State Standards for Mathematics

A correlation to the Next Generation Science Standards is located in the front of this Teacher Edition. Correlations to the Common Core State Standards for Mathematics are provided on these pages.

Grade 4	Units/Lessons
4.OA.A.1 Interpret a multiplication equation as a comparison, e.g., interpret $35 = 5 \times 7$ as a statement that 35 is 5 times as many as 7 and 7 times as many as 5. Represent verbal statements of multiplicative comparisons as multiplication equations.	Unit 8, Lesson 1 Unit 8, Lesson 2 Unit 8, Lesson 3
4.OA.A.2 Multiply or divide to solve word problems involving multiplicative comparison, e.g., by using drawings and equations with a symbol for the unknown number to represent the problem, distinguishing multiplicative comparison from additive comparison.	Unit 1, Lesson 2 Unit 2, Lesson 1 Unit 4, Lesson 2 Unit 8, Lesson 3
4.OA.A.3 Fluently multiply and divide within 100, using strategies such as the relationship between multiplication and division (e.g., knowing that $8 \times 5 = 40$, one knows $40 \div 5 = 8$) or properties of operations. By the end of Grade 3, know from memory all products of two one-digit numbers.	Unit 1, Lesson 1 Unit 2, Lesson 2 Unit 2, Lesson 3 Unit 4, Lesson 1 Unit 4, Lesson 2 Unit 5, Lesson 2 Unit 8, Lesson 3
4.OA.C.5 Generate a number or shape pattern that follows a given rule. Identify apparent features of the pattern that were not explicit in the rule itself.	Unit 2, Lesson 2 Unit 3, Lesson 3
4.NBT.B.4 Fluently add and subtract multi-digit whole numbers using the standard algorithm.	Unit 1, Lesson 1 Unit 3, Lesson 1 Unit 4, Lesson 1 Unit 4, Lesson 2 Unit 6, Lesson 4 Unit 8, Lesson 3

Math Correlations

Grade 4	Units/Lessons
4.NBT.B.6 Find whole-number quotients and remainders with up to four-digit dividends and one-digit divisors, using strategies based on place value, the properties of operations, and/or the relationship between multiplication and division. Illustrate and explain the calculation by using equations, rectangular arrays, and/or area models.	Unit 1, Lesson 2 Unit 2, Lesson 1
4.MD.A.1 Know relative sizes of measurement units within one system of units including km, m, cm; kg, g; lb, oz.; l, ml; hr, min, sec. Within a single system of measurement, express measurements in a larger unit in terms of a smaller unit. Record measurement equivalents in a two-column table.	Unit 2, Lesson 3 Unit 3, Lesson 1 Unit 3, Lesson 2 Unit 6, Lesson 1 Unit 6, Lesson 2 Unit 7, Lesson 1 Unit 7, Lesson 2 Unit 7, Lesson 3
4.MD.A.2 Use the four operations to solve word problems involving distances, intervals of time, liquid volumes, masses of objects, and money, including problems involving simple fractions or decimals, and problems that require expressing measurements given in a larger unit in terms of a smaller unit. Represent measurement quantities using diagrams such as number line diagrams that feature a measurement scale.	Unit 6, Lesson 1 Unit 6, Lesson 2 Unit 6, Lesson 3 Unit 6, Lesson 4
4.MD.B.4 Make a line plot to display a data set of measurements in fractions of a unit (1/2, 1/4, 1/8). Solve problems involving addition and subtraction of fractions by using information presented in line plots.	Unit 8, Lesson 2
4.G.A.1 Draw points, lines, line segments, rays, angles (right, acute, obtuse), and perpendicular and parallel lines. Identify these in two-dimensional figures.	Unit 3, Lesson 1 Unit 3, Lesson 2 Unit 5, Lesson 3
4.G.A.2 Recognize a line of symmetry for a two-dimensional figure as a line across the figure such that the figure can be folded along the line into matching parts. Identify line-symmetric figures and draw lines of symmetry.	Unit 4, Lesson 1 Unit 4, Lesson 2 Unit 5, Lesson 1

Correlations to ScienceSaurus

ScienceSaurus, A Student Handbook, is a "mini-encyclopedia" children can use to explore more about unit topics. It contains numerous resources including concise content summaries; an almanac; many tables, charts, and graphs; a history of science and a glossary. *ScienceSaurus* is available from Houghton Mifflin Harcourt.

Science Dimensions Grade 4	*ScienceSaurus* Topic
Unit 1 Engineering and Technology	
Lesson 1 Engineer It • How Do Engineers Define Problems? How Do We Define a Problem?	Science, Technology, and Engineering, Science and Engineering
People in Science and Engineering: Marion Down	Science, Technology, and Engineering, Science and Engineering
	Science, Technology, and Engineering, Science and Society
	Yellow Pages: History of Science, Science Time Line, Famous Scientists & Inventors
Lesson 2 Engineer It • How Do Engineers Design Solutions?	Science, Technology, and Engineering, Science and Engineering
Careers in Science and Engineering: Acoustic Engineer	Science, Technology, and Engineering, Science and Engineering
	Science, Technology, and Engineering, Science and Society
Lesson 3 Engineer It • How Do Engineers Test & Improve Prototypes?	Science, Technology, and Engineering, Science and Engineering
Unit 2 – Energy	
Lesson 1 What Is Energy?	Physical Science, Energy
	Physical Science, Heat
	Physical Science, Light and Sound
People in Science and Engineering: Mary Artiles	Science, Technology, and Engineering, Science and Engineering
	Science, Technology, and Engineering, Science and Society
	Yellow Pages: History of Science, Science Time Line, Famous Scientists & Inventors
Lesson 2 Engineer It • How Is Energy Transferred?	Physical Science, Energy
Career in Science and Engineering: HVAC Tech	Science, Technology, and Engineering, Science and Engineering
	Science, Technology, and Engineering, Science and Society
Lesson 3 How Do Collisions Show Energy?	Physical Science, Energy
People in Science and Engineering: Amanda Steffy	Science, Technology, and Engineering, Science and Engineering
	Science, Technology, and Engineering, Science and Society
	Yellow Pages: History of Science, Science Time Line, Famous Scientists & Inventors

Correlations to *ScienceSaurus*

Science Dimensions Grade 4	*ScienceSaurus* Topic
Unit 3 – Waves and Information Transfer	
Lesson 1 What Are Waves?	Physical Science, Energy
	Physical Science, Light and Sound
People in Science and Engineering: Christian Doppler, Debra Fischer	Science, Technology, and Engineering, Science and Engineering
	Science, Technology, and Engineering, Science and Society
	Yellow Pages: History of Science, Science Time Line, Famous Scientists & Inventors
Lesson 2 How Does Light Reflect?	Physical Science, Energy
	Physical Science, Light and Sound
Careers in Science and Engineering: Optics Researcher	Science, Technology, and Engineering, Science and Engineering
	Science, Technology, and Engineering, Science and Society
Lesson 3 How Is Information Transferred from Place to Place?	Physical Science, Energy
	Physical Science, Light and Sound
	Science, Technology, and Engineering, Science and Society
Unit 4 – Plant Structure and Function	
Lesson 1 What Are Some Plant Parts and How Do They Function?	Life Science, Characteristics of Living Things
	Life Science, Cells, Tissues, Organ Systems
People in Science and Engineering: Clayton Anderson	Science, Technology, and Engineering, Science and Engineering
	Science, Technology, and Engineering, Science and Society
	Yellow Pages: History of Science, Science Time Line, Famous Scientists & Inventors
Lesson 2 Engineer It • How Do Plants Grow and Reproduce?	Life Science, Characteristics of Living Things
	Life Science, Cells, Tissues, Organ Systems
Careers in Science and Engineering: Pomologist	Science, Technology, and Engineering, Science and Engineering
	Science, Technology, and Engineering, Science and Society
Unit 5 – Animal Structure and Function	
Lesson 1 Engineer It • What Are Some External Structures of Animals?	Life Science, Characteristics of Living Things
	Life Science, Cells, Tissues, Organ Systems
	Life Science, Human Body Systems
Careers in Science and Engineering: Mimicking Animal Movement	Science, Technology, and Engineering, Science and Engineering
	Science, Technology, and Engineering, Science and Society

Correlation to ScienceSaurus

Science Dimensions Grade 4	ScienceSaurus Topic
Unit 5 – Animal Structure and Function (continued)	
Lesson 2 What Are Some Internal Structures of Animals?	Life Science, Characteristics of Living Things
	Life Science, Cells, Tissues, Organ Systems
	Life Science, Human Body Systems
People in Science and Engineering: Henry Gray, Venessa Ruiz	Science, Technology, and Engineering, Science and Engineering
	Science, Technology, and Engineering, Science and Society
	Yellow Pages: History of Science, Science Time Line, Famous Scientists & Inventors
Lesson 3 How Do Senses Work?	Life Science, Characteristics of Living Things
	Life Science, Cells, Tissues, Organ Systems
	Life Science, Human Body Systems
Unit 6 – Changes to Earth's Surface	
Lesson 1 How Does Water Shape Earth's Surface?	Earth Science, Earth's Changing Surface
People in Science and Engineering: Anjali Fernandes	Science, Technology, and Engineering, Science and Engineering
	Science, Technology, and Engineering, Science and Society
	Yellow Pages: History of Science, Science Time Line, Famous Scientists & Inventors
Lesson 2 What Other Factors Shape Earth's Surface?	Earth Science, Earth's Changing Surface
Lesson 3 Engineer It • How Can Maps Help Us to Learn About Earth's Surface?	Earth Science, Earth's Structure
	Almanac, Maps
Careers in Science and Engineering: City Planner	Science, Technology, and Engineering, Science and Engineering
	Science, Technology, and Engineering, Science and Society
Lesson 4 What Patterns Do Maps Show Us?	Earth Science, Earth's Structure
	Earth Science, Earth's Changing Surface
	Almanac, Maps
People in Science and Engineering: Lewis and Clark	Science, Technology, and Engineering, Science and Engineering
	Science, Technology, and Engineering, Science and Society
	Yellow Pages: History of Science, Science Time Line, Famous Scientists & Inventors

Correlation to ScienceSaurus

Science Dimensions Grade 4	ScienceSaurus Topic
Unit 7 – Rocks and Fossils	
Lesson 1 How Do Rock Layers Change?	Earth Science, Earth's Changing Surface
People in Science and Engineering: Bernard Hubbard	Science, Technology, and Engineering, Science and Engineering
	Science, Technology, and Engineering, Science and Society
	Yellow Pages: History of Science, Science Time Line, Famous Scientists & Inventors
Lesson 2 What Do Fossils Tell Us About Ancient Environments?	Earth Science, Earth's Changing Surface
Lesson 3 What Are Some Patterns Fossils Show Us?	Earth Science, Earth's Changing Surface
People in Science and Engineering: Edward Cope, Mary Ann Mantell, Louis and Walter Alverez, Patricia Vickers-Rich, Don Zhiming	Science, Technology, and Engineering, Science and Engineering
	Science, Technology, and Engineering, Science and Society
	Yellow Pages: History of Science, Science Time Line, Famous Scientists & Inventors
Unit 8 – Natural Resources and Hazards	
Lesson 1 What Non-Renewable Resources Are Used for Energy?	Natural Resources and the Environment, Natural Resources
	Natural Resources and the Environment, Pollution
	Natural Resources and the Environment, Conserving Resources
Careers in Science and Engineering: Geologist, Chemist, Climatologist, Marine Biologist	Science, Technology, and Engineering, Science and Engineering
	Science, Technology, and Engineering, Science and Society
Lesson 2 Engineer It • What Renewable Resources Are Used for Energy?	Natural Resources and the Environment, Natural Resources
	Natural Resources and the Environment, Pollution
	Natural Resources and the Environment, Conserving Resources
Lesson 3 Engineer It • How Can People Reduce the Impact of Land-Based Hazards?	Earth Science, Earth's Changing Structure
People in Science and Engineering: Lucy Jones	Science, Technology, and Engineering, Science and Engineering
	Science, Technology, and Engineering, Science and Society
	Yellow Pages: History of Science, Science Time Line, Famous Scientists & Inventors
Lesson 4 Engineer It • How Can People Reduce the Impact of Water-Based Hazards?	Earth Science, Earth's Changing Structure
	Earth Science, Water on Earth

Interactive Glossary

Teacher Notes

_____

_____

_____

_____

_____

_____

_____

_____

_____

_____

_____

_____

_____

_____

Interactive Glossary

As you learn about each item, add notes, drawings, or sentences in the extra space. This will help you remember what the terms mean. Here is an example:

 **fungi** (FUHN•jee) A group of organisms that get nutrients by decomposing other organisms

hongos Un grupo de organismos que obtienen sus nutrientes al descomponer otros organismos.

Mushrooms are a type of fungi.

Glossary Pronunciation Key

With every glossary term, there is also a phonetic respelling. A phonetic respelling writes the word the way it sounds, which can help you pronounce new or unfamiliar words. Use this key to help you understand the respellings.

Sound	As in	Phonetic Respelling	Sound	As In	Phonetic Respelling
a	bat	(BAT)	oh	over	(OH•ver)
ah	lock	(LAHK)	oo	pool	(POOL)
air	rare	(RAIR)	ow	out	(OWT)
ar	argue	(AR•gyoo)	oy	foil	(FOYL)
aw	law	(LAW)	s	cell	(SEL)
ay	face	(FAYS)		sit	(SIT)
ch	chapel	(CHAP•uhl)	sh	sheep	(SHEEP)
e	test	(TEST)	th	that	(THAT)
	metric	(MEH•trik)		thin	(THIN)
ee	eat	(EET)	u	pull	(PUL)
	feet	(FEET)	uh	medal	(MED•uhl)
	ski	(SKEE)		talent	(TAL•uhnt)
er	paper	(PAY•per)		pencil	(PEN•suhl)
	fern	(FERN)		onion	(UHN•yuhn)
eye	idea	(eye•DEE•uh)		playful	(PLAY•fuhl)
i	bit	(BIT)		dull	(DUHL)
ing	going	(GOH•ing)	y	yes	(YES)
k	card	(KARD)		ripe	(RYP)
	kite	(KYT)	z	bags	(BAGZ)
ngk	bank	(BANGK)	zh	treasure	(TREZH•er)

R1

A

amplitude (AM•pluh•tood) A measure of the amount of energy in a wave. p. 156

amplitud Medida de la cantidad de energía en una onda.

aquatic fossil (uh•KWAH•tik FAHS•uhl) The remains or traces of an organism that lived in water long ago. p. 492

fósil acuático Restos o vestigios de un organismo que vivió en el agua hace mucho tiempo.

C

collision [kuh•LI•shuhn] The result of two objects bumping into each other. p. 128

colisión Resultado del choque entre dos objetos.

constraint (kuhn•STRAYNT) Something that limits what you are trying to do. p. 9

restricción Algo que limita lo que se está tratando de hacer.

continent (KON•tn•uhnt) One of the seven largest land areas on Earth. p. 409

continente Una de las siete áreas terrestres más grandes de la Tierra.

crest (KREST) The top part of a wave. p. 156

cresta Parte superior de una onda.

criteria (kry•TEER•ee•uh) The desirable features of a solution. p. 8

criterios Características deseables de una solución.

D

deposition (dep•uh•ZISH•uhn) The dropping or settling of eroded materials. p. 359

deposición Caída o asentamiento de materiales erosionados.

Interactive Glossary **TR17**

D

desert (DEZ•ert) An area of land that is very dry. p. 380

desierto Superficie de tierra muy seca.

design process (dih•ZYN PRAHS•es) A series of steps that engineers can follow to make solutions that meet a need or want.

proceso de diseño Serie de pasos que los ingenieros pueden seguir para desarrollar soluciones que cumplan con un requisito o una necesidad.

drawback (DRAW•bak) A disadvantage or problem. p. 528

inconveniente Desventaja o problema.

E

electric current (ee•LEK•trik KER•uhnt) The flow of electric charges along a path. p. 72

corriente eléctrica Flujo de cargas eléctricas a lo largo de una trayectoria.

elevation (el•uh•VEY•shuhn) The height of the land above sea level. p. 416

elevación Altura de la tierra sobre el nivel del mar.

energy (EN•er•jee) The ability to do work and cause changes in matter. p. 70

energía Capacidad de realizar una tarea y causar cambios en la materia.

energy transfer (EN•er•jee TRANZ•fuhr) The movement of energy from place to place or from one object to another. p. 78

transferencia de energía Movimiento de energía de un lugar a otro o de un objeto a otro.

energy transformation (EN•er•jee TRANZ•fuhr•may•shuhn) A change in energy from one form to another. p. 78

transformación de la energía Cambio en la energía, de una forma a otra.

R4

R5

TR18 Interactive Glossary

E

erosion (uh•ROH•zhuhn) The process of moving sediment from one place to another. p. 359

erosión Proceso de mover el sedimento de un lugar a otro.

external structures (EX•tuhr•nuhl STRUK•churs) Those parts on the outside of a body or structure. p. 286

estructuras externas Partes que se encuentran fuera de un cuerpo o estructura.

extinct (ex•STINGT) Describes a kind of thing that is no longer found on Earth. p. 484

extinto Describe cierto tipo de ser vivo que ya no se encuentra en la Tierra.

F

fertilization (fur•tl•uh•ZEY•shuhn) The process when male and female reproductive parts join together. p. 257

fertilización Proceso en el que se unen los órganos reproductivos del macho y la hembra.

fossil (FAHS•uhl) The remains or traces of an organism that lived long ago. p. 484

fósil Restos o vestigios de un organismo que vivió hace tiempo.

H

heat (HEET) The energy that moves between objects of different temperatures. p. 90

calor Energía que se mueve entre objetos con temperaturas distintas.

I

internal structures (IN•tuhr•nuhl STRUK•churs) Those parts on the inside of a body or structure. p. 306

estructuras internas Partes que se encuentran dentro de un cuerpo o estructura.

L

leaf (LEEF) The part of a plant that makes food, using air, light, and water. p. 235

hoja Parte de la planta que es capaz de generar alimento usando aire, luz y agua.

Interactive Glossary **TR19**

N

natural hazard (NACH•er•uhl HAZ•urd) An earth process that threatens to harm people and property. p. 574

peligro natural Proceso terrestre que amenaza con dañar a personas y bienes

natural resource (NACH•er•uhl REE•sawrs) Materials found in nature that people and other living things use. p. 528

recurso natural Materiales que se encuentran en la naturaleza y que las personas y otros seres vivos utilizan.

nonrenewable resource (nahn•rih•NOO•uh•buhl REE•sawrs) A resource that, once used, cannot be replaced in a reasonable amount of time. p. 529

recurso no renovable Recurso que, después de haber sido utilizado, no podrá ser reemplazado en un tiempo razonable.

O

ocean trench (OH•shuhn TRENCH) A deep valley in the ocean floor. p. 432

fosa oceánica Valle profundo en el suelo del océano.

opaque (oh•PAYK) Not allowing light to pass through. p. 175

opaco Que no permite que la luz lo atraviese.

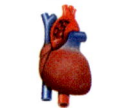
organ (AWR•guhn) A body part that is made of smaller parts that work together to do a certain job. p. 306

órgano Parte del cuerpo conformada por otras partes más pequeñas que trabajan juntas para cumplir una función determinada.

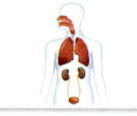
organ system (AWR•guhn SIS•tuhm) A group of organs that work together to do a job for the body. p. 306

sistema de órganos Grupo de órganos que trabaja en conjunto para realizar una tarea en el cuerpo.

P

pollination (pol•uh•NEY•shuhn) The transfer of pollen in flowers or cones. p. 257

polinización Transferencia del polen en flores o conos.

P

pollution (puh•LOO•shuhn) Waste products that damage an ecosystem. p. 536

contaminación Todo desperdicio que daña un ecosistema.

prototype (PROH•tuh•typ) A working model used for testing a solution.

prototipo Modelo de trabajo que se utiliza para probar una solución.

R

rain forest (RAYN FOR•est) A dense forest found in regions with high heat and heavy rainfall. p. 380

bosque lluvioso Bosque denso que se encuentra en regiones de altas temperaturas y fuertes lluvias.

receptors (ree•SEP•turs) Special structures that send information about the environment from different parts of the body to the brain. p. 327

receptores Células nerviosas especiales que envían información acerca del ambiente desde la piel hasta el cerebro.

reflection (rih•FLEHK•shuhn) The bouncing of light waves when they encounter an obstacle. p. 176

reflejo Rebote de las ondas de luz cuando encuentran un obstáculo.

relative age (REL•uh•tiv AYJ) The age of one thing compared to another. p. 463

edad relativa Edad de una cosa al compararla con otra.

renewable resource (rih•NOO•uh•buhl ree•SAWRS) A resource that can be replaced within a reasonable amount of time. p. 550

recurso renovable Recurso que puede ser reemplazado en un tiempo razonable.

reproduction (ree•pruh•DUHK•shuhn) To have young, or more living things of the same kind. p. 257

reproducción Tener cría o generar más seres vivos del mismo tipo.

R

resource (ree•SAWRS) Any material that can be used to satisfy a need. p. 528

recurso Cualquier material que pueda ser utilizado para satisfacer una necesidad.

root (ROOT) A plant part that is usually underground and absorbs water and minerals from the soil. p. 235

raíz Parte de la planta que usualmente es subterránea y que absorbe agua y minerales del suelo.

S

scale (SKEYL) The part of a map that compares a distance on the map to a distance in the real world. p. 408

escala Parte de un mapa que compara la distancia en el mapa con la distancia en el mundo real.

seed (SEED) The part of a plant that contains a new plant. p. 262

semilla Parte de la planta que contiene una nueva planta.

spore (SPOR) A reproductive structure of some plants, such as mosses and ferns, that can form a new plant. pp. 235, 263

espora Estructura reproductiva de algunas plantas, como los musgos y los helechos, que puede generar una nueva planta.

stem (STEM) The part of a plant that holds it up and has tubes that carry water, minerals, and nutrients through the plant. p. 235

tallo Parte de la planta que la sostiene y que tiene conductos que llevan agua, minerales y nutrientes a través de toda la planta.

T

terrestrial fossil (tuh•RES•tree•uhl FAHS•uhl) The remains or traces of an organism that lived on land long ago. p. 492

fósil terrestre Restos o vestigios de un organismo que vivió en la tierra hace mucho tiempo.

translucent (trahns•LOO•suhnt) Letting some light through. p. 175

translúcido Que deja pasar parte de la luz.

R12

R13

TR22 Interactive Glossary

T

transparent (trahns•PAIR•uhnt) Letting all light through. p. 175

transparente Que deja pasar toda la luz.

trough (TROF) The bottom part of a wave. p. 156

depresión Parte inferior de una onda.

V

vibrate (VY•brayt) To move back and forth. p. 102

vibrar Moverse hacia delante y hacia atrás.

volume (VAHL•yoom) How loud or soft a sound is. p. 158

volumen Cuán alto o bajo es un sonido.

W

wave (WAYV) The up-and-down movement of surface water. It can also be a disturbance that carries energy through space. p. 149

ola Movimiento hacia arriba y hacia abajo de la superficie del agua.

onda Alteración que lleva energía por el espacio.

wavelength (WAYV•length) The distance between a point on one wave and the identical point on the next wave. p. 156

longitud de onda Distancia entre un punto en una onda y ese mismo punto en la próxima onda.

weathering (WETH•er•ing) The breaking down of rocks on Earth's surface into smaller pieces. p. 359

desgaste Descomposición de las piedras de la superficie terrestre en piezas más pequeñas.

Index

Note: Page numbers in plain type refer to the Student Edition. Page numbers in **boldface** indicate pages in the Teacher's Edition.

3D Item Analysis, 20, 42, 58, 64, 86, 112, 134, 140, 168, 198, 222, 228, 252, 274, 280, 302, 322, 342, 348, 376, 402, 426, 446, 452, 480, 498, 516, 522, 546, 570, 594, 618, 624

3D Learning Objective, **3I,** 6, 9, 14, 24, 28, 31, 34, 46, 49, 52, **67I,** 70, 76, 78, 90, 95, 99, 102, 116, 122, 125, 128, **143I,** 146, 149, 156, 161, 172, 174, 182, 185, 202, 208, 210, **231I,** 234, 239, 243, 246, 256, 261, 265, 268, **283I,** 286, 292, 296, 306, 314, 326, 330, 336, **351K,** 354, 358, 362, 369, 380, 386, 395, 406, 410, 415, 430, 434, 440, 458, 462, 468, 484, 488, 492, 502, 505, 509, 528, 534, 548, 550, 554, 574, 580, 586, 598, 604

3D Unit Planning, **3C–3F, 67C–67F, 143C–143F, 231C–231E, 283C–283F, 351C–351G, 455C–455F, 525C–525G**

A

About This Image, 1, 65, 141, 229, 281, 349, 453, 523
acoustic engineers, 38–39
aerial photo, 406
air pollution, 73, 540–542
Akaroa Head (New Zealand), 459
algae farming, 73
Alps, 459
Alternative Engage Strategy, **4, 22, 44, 68, 88, 114, 144, 170, 200, 232, 254, 284, 304, 324, 352, 378, 404, 428, 456, 482, 500, 526, 548, 572, 596**
Alvarez, Luis and Walter, 514
amber, 493
amplitude, 156–158, 162–163
Analyze Your Results, **3L,** 12, 33, 48, **67L,** 77, 101, **143L,** 148, 173, 184, 209, **231L,** 245, 270, **283L,** 312–313, 332, **351N,** 368, 394, 420, 442, **455L,** 470, 487, 504, **525N,** 542, 565, 590, 614
Anderson, Clayton, 249
anechoic chamber, 34, 36–37
animals
  adaptations to environment, 381
  alpaca, 290
  ammonite, 492, 495
  antelope, 289
  ants, 287, 493
  archerfish, 186
  Bactrian camel, 381
  bat, 287, 338, 339
  beaver, 384
  birds, 290, 309, 317
  body coverings, 286, 290–292, 296–298
  cat, 336
  circulatory system, 306, 308–310
  clam, 493
  corals, 493, 495
  cow, 317
  crocodile, 309
  crustaceans, 505
  digestive system, 314–318
  dog, 336
  dolphin, 287, 325
  dragonfly, 493
  eagle, 289
  elephant, 219–220, 333
  fish, 186, 309, 492, 495–496, 505
  frog, 287, 289
  gecko, 285, 294
  greater wax moth, 339
  Irish elk, 488
  jellyfish, 317
  lizards, 285, 294
  meerkat, 382
  mosasaur, 489
  mosquito, 289
  mountain lion, 289
  mouse, 333
  mouth parts, 289, 293
  peacock mantis shrimp, 324, 339
  pigeon, 287, 336
  plesiosaur, 484
  polyp, 495
  respiratory system, 306–309
  sambar deer, 381
  sandfish, 294
  sea cucumber, 290
  shark, 287, 317
  snail, 492
  snakes, 152, 290, 336, 505
  sounds of, 155, 219–220
  structures for movement, 287–288, 293, 295
  termite, 384
  tubeworm, 289
  turtles and tortoises, 290, 501
anther, 256
anvil (ear), 337
aquadynamic testing, 35
arch, rock, 475
argument, 50, 267, 291, 298
argument from evidence, 232, **232A,** 234, 237, 241, 242, 247, 248, 250, 251, 254, **254A,** 272, **284A,** 287, 288, 291, 292, 296, 298, 304, **304A,** 307, 308, 310, 311, 314, 317, 324, 593
Arrange Your Information, **225, 344**
artery, 306, 310
Artiles, Mayra, 83
asking questions, 4, **4A,** 6, 9, 11, 15, 18, 70, 76, 80, 114, **114A,** 122, 124, **254A,** 265, 271, **404A**
Assessing Student Progress, **3A, 67A, 143A, 231A, 283A, 351A, 455A, 525A**
Assessment
  Formative, **3F, 67F, 143F, 231E, 283F, 351G, 455F, 525G**
  Pre-Assessment, **3F, 67F, 143F, 283F, 342E, 351G, 455F, 525G**
  Summative, **3F,** 19–20, 41–42, 57–58, 62–64, **67F,** 85–86, 111–112, 133–134, 138–140, **143F,** 167–168, 197–198, 221–222, 226–228, **231E,** 251–252, 273–274, 278–280, **283F,** 301–302, 321–322, 341–342, 346–348, **351G,** 375–376, 401–402, 425–426, 445–446, 450–452, **455F,** 479–480, 497–498, 515–516, 520–522, **525G,** 545–546, 569–570, 593–594, 617–618, 622–624

B

Badlands of South Dakota, 464–465
bark (tree), 235, 237
base isolator, 581
batteries, 74, 78–79, 82–83, 567–568
beach erosion, 151, 358, 369, 396
beak, 293
beats (tuning), 164
binary code, 210–211, 214–215

Index

binoculars, 189
biomass fuel, 73, 550
biomimicry (biomimetics), 292, 294–295, 299–300
Birling Gap, England, 358
bits (in binary code), 210, 212–213
bladder, 316
Block, Adrienne, 442
blood, 306–310
brain, 190–191, 326, 337
brainstorm, 60, 136, 344, 518, 601, **620**
breathing, 306–307, 308, 311–313
bridge (rock formation), 475
British Thermal Unit (BTU), 532
Buckley Formation (Antarctica), 459
buffering, electronic, 212–213
Build, 588
Building to the Performance Expectations, 3A, 4A, 22A, 44A, 67A, 68A, 88A, 114A, 143A, 144A, 170A, 200A, 231A, 232A, 254A, 283A, 284A, 304A, 324A, 351A, 352A, 378A, 404A, 428A, 455A, 456A, 482A, 500A, 525A, 526A, 548A, 572A, 596A
Build on Prior Knowledge, 4B, 5, 22B, 44B, 53, 68B, 88B, 114B, 144B, 170B, 174, 200B, 232B, 254B, 284B, 304B, 306, 324B, 352B, 362, 364, 366, 370, 378B, 382, 389, 404B, 407, 419, 428B, 430, 440, 456B, 482B, 489, 500B, 511, 526B, 530, 548B, 562, 572B, 576, 596B, 602
buoy, 150–151, 606
burr, 292
burrow, 382

C

cable, telegraph, 204–205
camera lens, 188
canyon formation, 462, 471–472, 475
Can You Explain It?, 57, 69, 85, 89, 111, 115, 133, 145, 167, 171, 201, 221, 233, 251, 255, 285, 301, 305, 321, 325, 341, 353, 375, 379, 401, 405, 429, 457, 479, 483, 501, 515, 527, 545, 549, 573, 597, 617
Can You Solve It?, 5, 19, 23, 41, 45
carbon dioxide, 90, 316
cardinal directions, 410
Careers in Science
  acoustic engineer, 38–39
  astronaut, 249
  astrophysicist, 166
  audiologist, 17
  car engineer, 83
  chemist, 543
  city planner, 422–423
  climatologist, 544
  geologist, 477
  HVAC technician, 109–110
  marine biologist, 544
  medical illustrator, 319, 320
  optical engineer, 195–196
  petroleum geologist, 543
  pomologist, 271
  seismologist, 591
  veterinarian, 304
cars
  design of, 527, 539, 567
  electric, 539, 567–568
  history of cars and batteries, 568
  hybrid, 539, 568
  side mirrors on, 194
Carter, Henry Vandyke, 319
catastrophism, 514
cell phone, 82, 212–213, 216–217
cell tower, 216–217
Celsius (C), 91
central nervous system, 326–329
channel (river), 354–355, 360, 373
chemical energy, 74
chemists, 543
circuit, 76
circulatory system, 306, 308–310
claim
  in *Hands-On Activity*, 33, 48, 101, 124, 148, 173, 184, 245, 270, 313, 332, 368, 394, 421, 442, 470, 487, 504, 542, 566, 590, 614
  in lessons, 238, 242, 389, 435, 476, 557, 601
Claims, Evidence, and Reasoning, 3L, 12, 33, 48, 67L, 77, 101, 124, 143L, 148, 173, 184, 209, 231L, 245, 270, 283L, 313, 332, 351N, 368, 394, 421, 442, 455L, 470, 487, 504, 525N, 542, 590, 614
climate map, 411
climatologists, 544
coal
  deposit locations, 459, 536
  formation of, 72, 507, 529, 534
  strip mining of, 538
  uses of, 72, 532, 538
coastal erosion, 151, 358, 369, 396
coastal flooding, 600, 615
cochlea, 337
cochlear implant, 17
codes
  binary code, 210–211, 214–215
  examples of, 206–207
  Internet transmission of, 212–215
  Navajo code talkers, 206
Collaboration
  brainstorm, **55, 94,** 566
  build on prior knowledge, **5, 23, 69,** **145, 325, 549**
  class discussion, **466, 557**
  discussion, **19, 41, 57, 85, 111, 133, 197, 219, 221, 251, 273, 301, 303, 321, 341, 401, 425, 443, 445, 479, 515, 569, 604, 606, 617**
  draw, pair, share, **89, 102, 115, 129,** 171, 189, 205, 211, 241, 285, 307, 315, 328, 375, 409, 474, 507, 573
  energy, **533**
  feedback, **7, 29, 35,** 70, 75, 80, 118, 150, 157, 166, 179, 196, 203, 215, 234, 287, 293, 300, 337, 355, 396, 472, 501, 527, 539, 589, 611
  jigsaw, **309, 603**
  online, **131, 165, 195, 249, 271, 299,** 319, 373, 399, 422, 443, 477, 495, 513, 543, 567, 591, 593, 615
  opportunities for, **3H, 67H, 143H, 231H, 283H, 351J, 455H, 525J**
  partners, **15,** 159
  pathways, **17,** 38, 83, 339
  small groups, **606, 608**
  think, pair, share, **25, 37, 39,** 84, 92, 106, 109, 163, 187, 201, 217, 233, 236, 239, 246, 290, 305, 318, 335, 353, 362, 379, 388, 405, 407, 429, 437, 457, 483, 497, 530, 535, 536, 597
  use realia, **287**
  write, pair, share, **51, 98, 212, 218,** 255, 288, 488, 490, 607
College and Career, T46–T48
collisions, 120–121, 128–130
color, 177, 181, 185
communicate, 137, 449
communication
  binary code, 210–211, 214–215
  cell phones, 212–213
  codes, 206–207, 210–211, 214–215
  electronic signals, 212
  elephant stomp sounds, 219–220
  emojis, 206
  engineering in, 52–53
  flags, 207
  hieroglyphics, 202
  Internet, 214–215
  lanterns, 203
  modems, 214

Index

pictographs, 202
pixels in, 218
scytales, 207
smoke signals, 203
talking drums, 203
telegraph using Morse code, 204–205
telephone game, 216
communication optical cables, 196
Community Connections, 3H, 67H, 143H, 231H, 283H, 351J, 455H, 525J
compact fluorescent light bulbs, 558–559
compass rose, 410
computers, 196, 210–211, 214–215
concave lens, 192
concave mirror, 194
cone (tree), 237, 261
Connections
  Community, **3H, 67H, 143H, 231H, 283H, 351J, 455H, 525J**
  Home, **3H, 67H, 143H, 231H, 283H, 351J, 455H, 525J**
constraints
  in *Hands-On Activity*, 9–12, 31, 33, 243, 245, 268, 419, 562, 586, 612
  as part of engineering, 14–16, 23, 39, 212, 250, 419, 431
Content Background, 96, 107, 119, 460, 464, 472, 478, 489, 491, 493, 506, 512, 514, 548B
continents, 409
contour lines (on maps), 416–417
convex lens, 192
convex mirror, 194
Cope, Edward, 513
Correlations
  English Language Arts, **TR6–TR9**
  Math, **TR10–TR13**
  NGSS, **T22–T29**
  ScienceSaurus, **TR14–TR17**
creepmeter, 584

crest (wave), 156
criteria
  definition, 8
  in engineering problems, 15, 18, 20, 34, 39, 49, 54, 59, 212, 250, 419
  in *Hands-On Activity*, 9–11, 31–32, 46, 99, 243–245, 268, 419–420, 562, 586, 612
crop (bird), 317
cross-brace, 581
Cross-Curricular Connections
  Earth Science, **16, 54, 78, 186, 286, 557**
  Engineering Design, **417**
  English Language Arts, **4A, 7, 22A, 44A, 53, 68A, 73, 88A, 114A, 144A, 158, 170A, 189, 192, 200A, 205, 212, 220, 232A, 235, 254A, 284A, 290, 304A, 307, 320, 324A, 352A, 367, 369, 371, 378A, 388, 393, 404A, 408, 415, 428A, 456A, 482A, 500A, 526A, 544, 548A, 556, 572A, 582, 596A, 605**
  Language Arts, **332, 563**
  Life Science, **26, 56, 72, 151, 190, 219, 327, 354, 371, 381, 397, 416, 424, 585, 600**
  Math, **4A, 14, 22A, 44A, 50, 68A, 74, 88A, 114A, 123, 144A, 147, 170A, 173, 183, 200A, 206, 232A, 243, 254A, 262, 284A, 299, 304A, 310, 324A, 331, 352A, 357, 358, 364, 378A, 380, 404A, 413, 428A, 432, 456A, 482A, 500A, 526A, 548A, 559, 565, 572A, 578, 596A**
  Nature of Science, **459, 503**
  Physical Science, **203, 236, 264, 315, 336, 385, 433, 539, 550, 558**
  Reading Language Arts, **271**
  Science, **3H, 67H, 143H, 231H, 283H, 351J, 455H, 525J**
Crosscutting Concepts (CCC)

cause and effect, **143J, 170A, 175, 176, 179, 181, 183, 185, 186, 188, 190, 192, 194, 197, 254A, 265, 266, 268, 277, 283J, 283K, 312, 324A, 329, 330, 335, 351L, 352A, 353, 354–355, 356, 360, 363, 365, 367, 369, 370, 372, 375, 376, 378A, 379, 380, 383, 384, 386, 389, 391, 393, 395, 397, 399, 401, 403, 448, 526A, 527, 529, 532, 534, 538, 541, 543, 548A, 552, 555, 572A, 576, 598, 600, 602, 604, 615**
energy and matter, **67J, 68A, 71, 78, 88A, 91, 101, 114A, 118, 122, 126, 129, 130, 549**
how society uses new design technologies, **49**
influence of science, engineering, and technology on society and the natural world, **3J, 3K, 4A, 7, 10, 11, 16, 17, 22A, 24, 26, 28, 32, 33, 34, 36, 40, 44A, 47, 56, 57, 60, 68A, 72, 81, 83, 88A, 91, 95, 97, 114A, 120, 526A, 537, 539, 548A, 558, 560, 564, 567, 570, 572A, 575, 578, 581, 585, 586, 589, 591, 596A, 606, 608, 620**
interdependence of science, engineering, and technology, **200A, 204, 214, 526A, 548A, 551, 553, 558**
patterns, **144A, 147, 148, 150, 152, 153, 157, 158, 160, 162, 164, 166, 200A, 203, 208, 211, 215, 216, 219, 404A, 405, 415, 422, 428A, 431, 433, 435, 437, 439, 442, 444, 455J, 456A, 459, 460, 462, 463, 464, 465, 467, 468, 469, 473, 474, 475, 476, 481, 482A, 485, 487, 488, 490, 494, 497, 499, 500A, 503, 507, 508, 510, 513, 517, 518, 610**
relate cause and effect, **301–302**
science is a human endeavor, **68A, 88A, 94, 104, 110, 114A, 117, 563**
systems and system models, **231J, 232A, 234, 237, 238, 239, 240, 242, 245, 246, 250, 254A, 260, 261, 263, 272, 276, 284A, 287, 289, 291, 293, 294, 297, 304A, 306, 309, 310, 314, 317, 319, 324A, 327, 333, 334, 336, 338, 344**

D

decibel, 40
defining problems, 4, 4A, 6, 8, 9, 11, 14, 15, 17, 18, 19, 21, 70, 76, 80, 82, 88A, 109, 114, 114A, 122, 124, 254A, 265, 271, 404A, 563
degree (temperature), 91
delta (river), 355
Demonstration Preparation, 224
deposition
  on beaches, 369
  definition, 359
  from flowing water, 355–356, 360–361
  from glaciers, 364–365, 478
  of sand, 369, 389
deserts, 380–381, 387, 390–391, 395, 464
design, 16, 34, 54, 527
diaphragm (muscle), 308
Differentiate Instruction
  different cultures, different tastes, **13**
  ELL/ELD, **3, 3G, 10, 26, 44B, 50, 67, 67G, 67I, 81, 88B, 91, 96, 110, 118, 128, 143, 143G, 149, 170B, 175, 176, 180, 186, 191, 200B, 206, 210, 214, 231, 231G, 232B, 247, 254B, 255, 283, 283G, 284B, 289, 308, 317, 324B, 328, 331, 351, 351I, 356, 360, 370, 378B, 382, 391, 393, 408, 410, 417, 423, 428B, 432, 437, 455, 455G, 456B,**

Index

459, 465, 474, 475, 484, 494, 502, 510, 516, 525, 525I, 525K, 526B, 531, 532, 538, 541, 550, 558, 572B, 579, 596B, 605

extension, 3, 3G, 3I, 13, 25, 29, 36, 52, 67, 67G, 67I, 79, 82, 92, 104, 105, 108, 114B, 117, 119, 125, 127, 132, 143, 143G, 143I, 151, 156, 158, 177, 188, 193, 204, 215, 220, 231, 231G, 231I, 244, 247, 249, 262, 283, 283G, 283I, 288, 293, 299, 315, 338, 351, 351I, 351K, 355, 373, 384, 386, 395, 408, 417, 423, 438, 441, 444, 455, 455G, 455I, 462, 472, 490, 492, 505, 525, 525I, 525K, 528, 534, 548B, 554, 568, 574, 588, 601, 606, 609

extra support, 4B, 6, 22B, 32, 35, 36, 39, 68B, 90, 94, 97, 102, 103, 106, 108, 116, 143I, 144B, 147, 154, 162, 178, 183, 202, 207, 213, 214, 217, 235, 237, 239, 241, 246, 256, 260, 267, 286, 292, 294, 297, 304B, 316, 326, 334, 336, 352B, 358, 359, 363, 365, 376, 380, 389, 398, 400, 404B, 406, 411, 413, 430, 434, 436, 531, 536, 544, 546, 562

lesson vocabulary, 4B, 22B, 44B, 68B, 88B, 114B, 144B, 170B, 200B, 232B, 254B, 284B, 304B, 324B, 352B, 378B, 404B, 428B, 456B, 482B, 500B, 526B, 548B, 572B, 596B

Leveled Readers, 3G, 67G, 143G, 231G, 283G, 351I, 455G, 525I

RTI/extra support, 3, 3G, 3I, 32, 35, 36, 39, 67, 67G, 143, 143G, 202, 207, 213, 214, 217, 231, 231G, 231I, 283, 283G, 283I, 351, 351I, 351K, 455, 455G, 455I, 460, 467,

474, 482B, 496, 498, 500B, 503, 506, 525, 525I, 576, 584, 599, 602, 610, 616

using realia, 70, 74, 84, 126, 153, 154

digestive system, 314–318

Digital Activities. *see* You Solve It

digital code, 212

dinosaur fossils, 464–465

disaster supply kit, 581

Disciplinary Core Ideas (DCI)

analyze and interpret data from maps, **427**

biogeology, **378A, 382, 389, 403**

conservation of energy and energy transfer, **67J, 68A, 71, 78, 80, 85, 87, 88A, 91, 95, 103, 104, 105, 108, 113, 114A, 120, 122, 130, 131, 564**

defining and delimiting engineering problems, **3J, 4A, 8, 9, 11, 14, 15, 17, 19, 21, 76, 82, 83, 88A, 100, 109, 563**

definitions of energy, **68A, 70, 74, 88A, 93, 96, 97, 104, 108, 111, 113, 114A, 119, 129, 132, 133**

designing solutions to engineering problems, **572A, 595, 606, 611, 619**

developing possible solutions, **3K, 22A, 24, 27, 28, 30, 31–32, 34, 36, 38, 41, 43, 44A, 45, 46–47, 51, 52, 55, 59, 586, 588, 590, 596A**

draw on information from multiple print or digital sources, **109, 131**

Earth materials and systems, **351L, 352A, 354, 359, 361, 362, 365, 366, 369, 371, 372, 373, 377, 378A, 381, 384, 387, 388, 391, 392, 396, 399, 400, 403**

electromagnetic radiation, **143J, 170A, 172, 174, 177, 178, 180, 183, 185, 186, 188, 190, 192, 195, 224, 324A, 336**

energy in chemical processes and everyday life, **68A, 72, 88A, 92, 98, 109, 113, 114A, 117, 123**

the history of planet Earth, **455J, 456A, 459, 461, 462, 464, 465, 466, 467, 471, 472, 476, 477, 479, 481, 482A, 486, 492, 495, 499, 500A, 502, 505, 507, 510, 511, 515, 517**

influence of science, engineering, and technology on society and the natural world, **49**

information processing, **324A, 326, 331, 336, 339, 341, 343, 585**

information technologies and instrumentation, **200A, 201, 202, 205, 210, 213, 217, 218, 221, 223**

large-scale system interactions, **411**

natural hazards, **572A, 574, 576, 578, 580, 582, 584, 591, 593, 595, 596A, 598, 600, 602, 604, 607, 610, 613, 615, 617, 619**

natural resources, **526A, 529, 530, 533, 535, 536, 538, 544, 545, 547, 548A, 549, 551, 553, 554, 556, 560, 567, 569**

optimizing the design solution, **44A, 48, 53, 57–58, 59, 200A, 206, 218, 565**

plate tectonics and large-scale system iterations, **404A, 428A, 430, 432, 434, 436, 438, 441, 443, 445, 447**

relationship between energy and forces, **114A, 121, 122, 131, 135, 136**

structure and function, **231J, 232A, 233, 235, 236, 238, 240, 242, 244, 247, 249, 251, 253, 254A, 256, 257, 259, 262, 263, 265, 266, 271, 273, 275, 283J, 284, 284A, 286, 288, 290, 292, 294, 296, 299, 300, 301, 303, 304A, 307, 309, 312,**

314, 316, 321, 323, 324A, 333, 337, 338, 343

wave properties, **144A, 146, 149, 153, 155, 156, 159, 160, 161, 163, 164, 165, 167, 169**

Dissect and Illustrate, 277

dog whistle, 159

Doppler, Christian, 165–166

Doppler effect, 165, 165–166

Doppler radar, 166

Do the Math

binary code, 211

breathing rate, 308

canyon clues, 463

energy units, 75, 532–533

hurricane classification, 599

light bulb comparison, 558–559

measuring erosion, 374

measuring sound, 40

Richter scale, 577

speed of sound, 106

units of time, 185

using a map scale, 412–413

waterfall erosion, 398

Downs, Marion, 17

Draw Conclusions, 12, 33, 48, 77, 101, 124, 148, 173, 184, 209, 245, 270, 298, 313, 332, 368, 394, 421, 470, 487, 504, 542, 565, 590, 614

drought, 598, 600–604, 611

drums, 154, 203

dry ice, 90

E

ear canal, 337

ear drum, 337

ear plugs, 18

ears, 337–338

earthquakes

building design and, 431, 573, 581

causes and effects, 576

Index **TR27**

Index

destruction from, 574
landscape changes from, 473, 584
mapping locations of, 434, 438, 578–579, 592
measuring, 473, 574–575, 577, 582
predicting, 584, 591, 610
in the "Ring of Fire," 430, 473
rock layer changes from, 467, 473, 510
tracking, 440–442, 610
tsunamis and, 605, 610
waves in, 155

Earth Science Connection, 16, 54, 78, 186, 286, 557
ear trumpet, 28
echolocation, 325, 338
Editing and Revision, 225
egg (plant), 256, 262
electrical circuit, 76
electrical energy, 72, 78–81, 84, 88
electric cars, 539, 567–568
electric current, 72, 88
electricity from renewable energy sources, 70, 176, 549–555
electromagnet, 204–205
electronic tuner, 164
Electrovette, 568
elevation, on maps, 416–417
ELL. see **English Language Learners**
email, 214
emojis, 206
energy. see also **nonrenewable energy resources; renewable energy resources**
   from algae farming, 73
   amplitude and, 156–157, 162–163
   in batteries, 74, 78–79, 82–83, 567–568
   chemical energy, 74
   from coal, 72, 532, 536, 538
   in collisions, 120–121, 128–130
   conservation of, 82, 241
   definition, 70

   electrical energy, 72, 78–81, 84, 88
   heat energy, 70, 72, 79, 90–94, 130
   household energy source, 72–73, 549
   light energy, 70, 78
   mass and, 126
   motion energy, 79, 88, 116–121
   in ocean waves, 84, 150–152, 553
   solar energy, 79, 95, 99–101, 176, 549, 552, 561–566
   sound energy, 78, 88, 103–107, 154
   speed and, 118–119, 128–129
   in springs, 122–124, 125–127
   stored, 74, 75, 98, 122–124
   transfer of, in waves, 149–151, 156
   units of, 75, 532–533
   in waves that move side to side, 153–154
   wind energy, 70, 208, 545, 555
energy rays, 96
energy transfer
   in car design, 83
   in collisions, 118–120, 128–130
   by contact, 92
   definition, 78
   at a distance, 93
   examples of, 78–81, 108, 128
   as heat, 90–93
   on Mars, 131–132
   of sound energy, 88, 103–107
   in vibrations, 102–103
   in waves, 149–151, 156
engineering
   biomimicry, 292, 294–295, 299–300
   communication in, 52–53
   constraints in, 14–16, 23, 39, 212, 250, 419, 431
   criteria in, 8, 15, 18, 20, 34, 39, 49, 54, 59, 212, 250, 419
   earthquake resistant buildings, 431, 573, 581
   failure analysis, 49–51
   menu planning, 9–13

   optimization in, 53
   problems and solutions in, 6, 8, 38–39, 49, 54, 56, 241, 249, 552, 575, 608–609
   prototypes and models in, 34
   reducing tsunami impact, 612–614
   testing in, 34–38
Engineering, 3K
Engineering, Technology, and Applications of Science Connections, 179
Engineering Design Connections, 417
Engineer It!
   algae energy, 73
   biomimicry, 294
   device to grow plants upside down, 250
   earthquake resistant buildings, 581
   green roofs, 241
   hybrid cars, 539
   improving levees, 608–609
   mapping the ocean floor, 433
   measuring earthquakes, 473
   pothole prevention, 372
   reducing impacts with technology, 582
   sandblasting, 386
   side mirrors on cars, 194
   slowing changes in Earth's surface, 399–400
   springs in off-road trucks, 127
   thermal imaging, 94
English Language Arts Connections, T43–T45, 4A, 7, 22A, 44A, 53, 68A, 73, 88A, 114A, 144A, 158, 170A, 189, 192, 200A, 205, 212, 220, 232A, 235, 254A, 284A, 290, 304A, 307, 320, 324A, 352A, 367, 369, 371, 378A, 388, 393, 404A, 408, 415, 428A, 456A, 482, 500A, 526A, 544, 548A, 556, 572A, 582, 596A, 605

English Language Arts Correlation, TR6–TR9
English Language Learners (ELL), 3, 3G, 44B, 67, 67G, 128, 143, 143G, 175, 231, 231G, 255, 283G, 324B, 328, 331, 351, 351I, 356, 360, 378B, 455, 455G, 516, 525, 525I, 525K
   build background, 579
   causes and effects, 538
   cognates, 200B, 232B, 255
   comparisons, 149
   demonstrating concepts, 170B, 331, 370
   drawing and describing pictures, 428B, 432, 475
   inferring, 484
   labeling diagrams, 356
   Latin roots of words, 88B
   life cycle diagrams, 254B
   matching, 465
   meaning of words, 360
   mirroring, 50
   modeling, 180, 191, 210, 247, 382, 391, 393, 510, 572B
   multiple meanings, 410
   organizing information, 308
   partners, 408, 417, 423, 494, 502, 541
   reading, 206, 214
   role playing, 289
   showing images, 81, 284B, 531
   synonyms, 558
   timelines or scales, 96–97
   translating foods, 10
   using a map, 437
   using primary language, 532, 596B, 605
   using realia, 26, 91, 110, 118, 175, 186, 287, 324B, 459, 474, 526B, 550
   visual references, 317
   word discovery, 176

Index

Enigma machine, 206
environments
  animal adaptations to, 381
  changes from living things, 382–384
  effect of water on, 380
  evidence of change in, 395–398
  modeling processes of change, 392–394
EQuIP Rubric, T50–T53
erosion
  coastal, 151, 358, 369, 396
  definition, 359
  in deserts, 387
  effect of slope on rate of, 366–368
  by freezing and thawing, 362–363, 365, 370–371
  by glaciers, 364–365
  of landforms, 151, 358–361, 366–368, 459, 471–472, 475
  of levees, 608
  measuring, 358, 374
  by mudslides, 361
  by oceans, 151, 358, 360–361, 369
  preventing, 399–400
  by rivers, 354–355
  of roads, 370–371, 372
  of rocks, 151, 459, 471–472, 475, 511
  by waterfalls, 361, 398
  by wind-blown sand, 388–391
esophagus, 314, 317
Essential Questions, 3J, 67J, 143J, 231J, 283J, 351L, 455J, 525L
Evaluate and Redesign, 61, 589
Everest, Mount, 432
Every Student, Every Standard, T49
evidence
  in *Hands-On Activity,* for example, 33, 48, 101, 124, 173, 184
  in *Language SmArts,* for example, 8, 16, 148, 155, 238
  in lessons, for example, 95, 97, 98, 108, 149

Evidence Notebook, T40–T42
  Multiple assignments are given in every lesson. Example references follow, 5, 8, 16, 19, **23**, 69, 73, 79, **97**
excretory system, 316
exhalation, 308
explanation
  in *Can You Explain It?,* for example, 69, 89, 115, 145, 171
  in *Hands-On Activity,* for example, 33, 48, 173, 244, 270
  in *Language SmArts,* for example, 54, 121, 155, 267
  in *Lesson Check,* for example, 85, 111, 133, 167, 197
  in lessons, for example, 8, 15, 18, 25, 37, 73, 98, 119
Explore Online, 2, 66, 84, 142, 230, 282, 350, 454, 524
Extra Hands-On Activity, 404B
  build a better bookshelf, **4B**
  catch me if you can, **324B**
  cold as ice, **284B**
  crash bang boom, **114B**
  create a code, **200B**
  defining sound constraints, **22B**
  different animals, same structures, **304B**
  dino pets, **482B**
  finding out about flowers, **254B**
  folding rocks, **456B**
  footprints in the sand, **500B**
  hot and cold, **88B**
  how are variables controlled?, **44B**
  hybrid car case study, **68B**
  local energy, **526B**, **548B**
  looking around a corner, **170B**
  moving soil, **378B**
  plant parts, **232B**
  same area, different map, **428B**
  shakeproof, quakeproof, **572B**
  slowing waves, **144B**
  soaking wet mud, **596B**
  where has water been?, **352B**
eyeglasses, 192
eyepiece (telescope), 193
eyes
  lenses in, 190–191
  light and, 180
  in peacock mantis shrimp, 324, 339
  structure of, 336
eye-tracking device, 35

F

Fahrenheit (F), 91
failure analysis, 49–51
fair test, 36
feathers, 290
Fernandes, Anjall, 373–374
Ferriby Chalk Formation (England), 464–466
fertilization (plants), 257, 258–260
field research, 373–374
firebreak, 582
fireworks, 154
Fischer, Debra, 166
fish, 186, 309, 492, 495–496, 505
flags (communication), 207
flexible glass, 196
floods
  causes and effects, 598, 600
  flash floods, 356
  in hurricanes, 615
  improving levees, 608–609
  landform changes from, 360–361
  plant roots and, 385
  preparation and response, 604
  in rivers, 356–357, 360, 608–610
  warnings, 610
floor plan, 408
flowers, 234, 237, 256–260
focal point, 190–191
Formative Assessment, 3F, 67F, 143F, 231E, 283F, 351G, 455F, 525G

fossil fuels, 529. *see also* coal
  energy from, 530, 532–533
  extraction of, 534–535
  formation of, 72, 534
  gasoline, 526, 530, 538
  historical use of, 532–533
  hydraulic fracturing, 535
  natural gas, 529–530, 532, 535–536, 538
  as nonrenewable resource, 529
  oil, 526, 529–530, 534–536
  pollution from, 538
  pros and cons of use, 538–539, 556–557
fossils
  in amber, 493
  consistent patterns of, 508–509
  definition, 482, 484
  dinosaur fossils, 464–465
  examining, 486–487
  footprints, 493
  illustrations of, 488–489
  inferring environments for, 464–465, 491–496, 502–505, 507
  information from, 484–485, 506–507
  leaf fossils, 488, 492, 505, 507
  marine fossils in dry environments, 501
  modern animals compared with, 490
  in rock layers, 464
freezing and thawing, 362–363, 365
friction, 386

G

Galileo, 193
gallbladder, 314
Gamburtsev Mountains (Antarctica), 443
gases, 106–107, 430
gasoline, 526, 530, 538
Geckskin, 294

Index **TR29**

Index

generator, 72, 552
geostationary operational environmental satellites (GOES), 606
geothermal power plants, 550, 552
gizzard, 317
glacier, 364–365, 396, 475, 478
glassblowing, 90
Global Positioning System (GPS), 407, 407
Glossary, TR18–TR25
GOES (geostationary operational environmental satellites), 60
Grand Canyon, 462–463, 466, 471
gravity
   erosion and weathering, 390, 475
   plant growth direction and, 247, 249–250
   tides and, 553
Gray, Henry, 319
Gray's Anatomy (Gray), 319
Great Rift Valley, 429, 445
Green River formation, 505–507
green rooftops, 241
guitar, electric, 88

H

hammer (ear), 337
Hands-On, Apply What You Know
   bang a gong, 118
   biomimicry, 295
   bobbing and waving, 151
   body coverings of animals in survival, 296–298
   compare and contrast digestive systems, 318
   compare and contrast rock layers, 509
   design a battery test, 75
   design an animal for survival, 291
   design and test a building for earthquake survival, 431

disaster supply kit, 581
draw a cartoon strip, 248, 471
echolocation, 338
find energy examples, 71
find engineering products, 7
flood damage, 357
fossils and their environment, 491
hearing experiment, 30
knots, 49
layered landforms, 458
light and dark, 180
make a map, 414
make a plan, 583
make a scytale, 207
make a seismometer, 574–575
make mountains, 443
make vibrations, 103
make your own code, 210
mark a map with fossil locations, 508
measure height of bouncing ball, 130
model a mining operation, 537
model features of the ocean floor, 438
model pollination, 259
model water flow in plants, 242
motion energy, 121
name the scent, 333
observe volume change with freezing, 363
paper folding, 15
pinecone parts, 261
plastics from plants, 560
read through convex and concave lenses, 193
research power stations, 530
research saguaro cactus, 381
sanding compared with sandblasting, 387
share feedback, 54
take action in a drought, 601
taste without smelling, 335
test how sound travels in different materials, 107

Hands-On Activity. *see also* Extra Hands-On Activity
   build a circuit to light a light bulb, 76–77
   build a system to grow plants in water, 243–245
   design and test a hearing-enhancement device, 46–48
   design and test a seed dispersal device, 268–270
   design and test a solar cooker, 99–101
   design a solar hot water heater, 562–566
   disappearing coins in water, 172–173
   examine fossils, 486–487
   exercise and breathing rate, 311–313
   funhouse mirrors, 182–184
   investigate air pollution, 540–542
   investigate effect of slope on erosion, 366–368
   make waves, 146–148
   menu planning, 9–13
   model how rocks can form and change, 468–470
   model processes of change in Earth's surface, 392–394
   park designer, 419–421
   pixels to pictures, 208–209
   reduce the impact of landslides, 586–590
   reduce tsunami damage, 612–614
   scoring rubrics for, **12, 33, 48, 77, 101, 124, 149, 173, 209, 245, 270, 298, 313, 332, 368, 394, 421, 442, 470, 487, 504, 542, 566, 590, 614**
   stored energy in a spring, 122–124
   touch test, 330–332
   track quakes, 440–442
   use evidence to determine fossil environment, 502–504
Hands-On Activity Planning, **3C–3E, 67C–67E, 143C–143E, 231C–231D,** **283C–283E, 351C–351F, 455C–455E, 525C–525F**
harmony, 161
Hasey, Janine, 271
HD (high-definition) TV, 218
headphones, noise-canceling, 163
hearing, 17–18, 28–30, 337–338
hearing aids, 17–18, 28–29, 46–48
heart, 306, 308–309
heart rate, 311–313
heat, 90–91, 474, 550
heat energy, 70, 72, 79, 90–94, 130
heating, venting, and air conditioning (HVAC) system, 109–110
helicopter seeds, 266
hieroglyphics, 202
Himalayan Mountains, 432
Home Connections, **3H, 67H, 143H, 231H, 283H, 351J, 455H, 525J**
Home Letters, **3H, 67H, 143H, 231H, 283H, 351J, 455H, 525J**
hook and loop fasteners, 179
hot air balloon, 93
Hubbard, Bernard, 477
humans
   circulatory system, 306, 308–310
   digestive system, 314–316
   nervous system, 326–329
   respiratory system, 306–309
   in seed dispersal, 266, 268–270, 292
hurricanes
   causes and effects, 600, 615, 617
   classifying by strength of, 599
   description of, 598
   predicting and tracking, 599, 606, 611, 615
   preparation and response, 604
   timeline of, 616–617
HVAC (heat, venting, and air conditioning) system, 109–110
HVAC technicians, 109–110
hybrid cars, 539, 568

Index

hydraulic fracturing, 535
hydroelectric dam, 550, 552
hydroelectric plant, 552
hydrophone, 55
hydroponics, 243
hydropower, 550, 552
Hyperloop, 567

I

incandescent light bulb, 558–559
information transfer. *see also* communication
  binary code, 210–211, 214–215
  cell phones, 212–213
  codes, 206–207
  by elephants, 219–220
  email, 214
  emojis, 206
  flags, 207
  hieroglyphics, 202
  lanterns, 203
  modem, 214
  pictographs, 202
  pixel, 218
  scytales, 207
  smoke signals, 203
  talking drums, 203
  telegraph using Morse code, 204–205
  telephone game, 216
infrasonic sounds, 220
infrasounds, 219
inhalation (breathing), 306–307, 308, 311–313
inner ear, 337
Integrating the Three Dimensions of Learning, 3A–3B, 4B, 22B, 44B, 67A–67B, 68B, 88B, 114B, 143A–143B, 144B, 170B, 200B, 231A–231B, 232B, 254B, 283A–283B, 284B, 304B, 324B, 351A–351B, 352B, 378B, 404B, 428B, 455A–455B, 456B, 482B, 500B, 525A–525B, 526B, 548B, 572B, 596B
International Space Station, 170, 249
Internet, 212–213
invertebrates, 309–310, 317
iris (eye), 336

J

Jones, Lucy, 591

K

kettle (landform), 478
key (map), 411
kidneys, 316

L

laboratory safety, T62–T64, 311, 612, XVIII
LAN (local area network), 214–215
land-based hazards. *see also* earthquakes; volcanoes
  causes and effects of, 576
  landslides, 361, 574, 576, 584–585, 615
  mapping locations of, 578–579, 592
  preparation and response, 580–581, 583, 591
  reducing impacts with technology, 582, 586–590
  types of, 574–575
  warning signs of, 584–585, 591
  wildfire, 574, 576, 582, 584–585
landforms. *see also* volcanoes
  canyons, 462, 471–472, 475
  channels, 354–355, 360, 373
  erosion of, 151, 358–361, 366–368, 459, 471–472, 475
  freezing and thawing of, 362–363, 365
  glaciers and, 364–365, 396, 475, 478
  kettles, 478
  moraines, 478
  mountains, 432, 434, 438, 443–444
  rift valleys, 429, 445
  rock arches, 475
  trenches, 432, 436
landslides, 361, 574, 576, 584–585, 615
land use planning, 423
language, 204–206, 603. *see also* communication
Language Arts Connections, 332, 563
Language SmArts
  analyze and evaluate Internet information, **603**
  asking questions, **94**
  categorizing information, 361, **361, 399**
  cause and effect, 93, **93,** 128, **128, 329,** 335, **335,** 363, 385, **385, 577**
  citing evidence, 8, **8,** 476, **476**
  classifying, 155
  classifying information, **155**
  compare and contrast, **27, 240,** 309, **309,** 318, **318,** 431, **431,** 485, **485,** 494, **494,** 529, **529**
  comparing structures, 489, **489**
  conducting research, 463, **463, 607**
  creating a presentation, **414**
  criteria and constraints in surfing the Internet, 212
  describing, **128**
  describing a family emergency plan, 607
  describing energy transfer, 79
  describing music effects, 337
  describing the effect the energy causes, 71
  drawing evidence from informational texts, 461, **461, 511**
  drawing examples from text, 577, **577**
  explaining how weight affects collisions, 121
  forming an explanation, **79, 121**
  gathering relevant information from print sources, **358, 385, 477**
  identifying main ideas and details, 194, **194,** 328, **328**
  inferring changes in Earth's surface, 508
  influence of science, engineering, and technology on society and the natural world, **585**
  interpreting photographs, 358
  making a plan, 583
  making connections, 551, **551**
  making inferences, **202,** 508, **539,** 539
  organizing work, **288**
  planning and communicating, **583**
  political maps, 409
  presentation, 340, **340,** 414
  recalling from experience, 127
  recalling information, 54, **54, 71, 79, 127,** 363, **399, 535, 539**
  recounting details, 16, **16**
  refer explicitly to text, 512, **512**
  research electrical energy transformation, 81
  rewriting, **561**
  sequencing, **215**
  short research projects that build knowledge, **81**
  steps in computer messages, 215
  summarizing information, 257, 267, **267,** 295, **295,** 535, **535,** 585
  taking notes and categorize information, **358, 385**
  understanding graphics, 156, 439, **439**
  using evidence to support a position, 264, 511
  using images for letters, 202
  using information to identify effects, 390, **390**

Index TR31

Index

using multiple sources, **248**
using reasons and evidence, 418, **418**
using word parts, 187, **187**
write, pair, share, **212**
writing opinion pieces, 238, **238**, **264**, **332**, **337**
lanterns (communication), 203
large intestine, 316
laser, 195, 584
lateral moraine, 478
lava, 428, 430
leaf, plant, 234–236
legs, 287, 293
Lehmann, Marcus, 84
lenses (singular, *lens***)**
  convex and concave, 192
  in eyeglasses, 192
  in eyes, 190–191, 336
  in telescopes, 193
  in tools, 188–189
Lesson Check, 19–20, 41–42, 57–58, 85–86, 111–112, 133–134, 167–168, 197–198, 221–222, 251–252, 273–274, 301–302, 321–322, 341–342, 375–376, 401–402, 425–426, 445–446, 479–480, 497–498, 515–516, 545–546, 569–570, 592–594, 617–618
Lesson Objective, 4, 22, 44, 68, 88, 114, 144, 170, 200, 232, 254, 284, 304, 324, 352, 378, 404, 428, 456, 482, 500, 526, 548, 572, 596
Lesson Roundup, 21, 43, 59, 87, 113, 135, 169, 199, 223, 253, 275, 303, 323, 343, 377, 403, 427, 447, 481, 499, 517, 547, 571, 595, 619
levee, 399, 597, 606, 608–609
Leveled Readers, 3G, 67G, 143G, 231G, 283G, 351I, 455G, 525I
Life Science Connections, 26, 56, 72, 151, 190, 219, 327, 354, 371, 381, 397, 416, 424, 585, 600

light
  absorption of, 170, 181, 185
  colors 181, 170, 185
  Doppler effect in, 166
  energy, 70, 78
  eyes and, 180, 190–191, 336
  lasers, 195
  light waves, 153
  reflection of, 170, 176–181
  refraction of, 172–173, 185–194
  speed in air and water, 185
  in transparent, translucent, and opaque materials, 174–175, 180
  visible, 96
  wave interactions in, 161
  white, 185
light bulb, 558–559
light microscope, 55, 189
listening post, 28
liver, 314
local area network (LAN), 214–215
locator map, 408
lungs, 306–308, 316

M

magnifying glass, 189
Make a Plan, 61, 276
Mantell, Mary Ann, 513
maps
  in city planning, 422
  direction on, 410
  drawing symbols on, 438
  of droughts, 603
  of earthquakes, 434, 438, 578–579
  elevation on, 416–417
  finding patterns on land, 434–437
  history of, 406–407
  of hurricane risk, 615
  key on, 411
  scale on, 408, 412–413
  types of, 407, 408–409, 415

Map Your Models, 449, 519
Mariana Trench, 432
marine biologists, 544
mass and energy, 126
Materials, 3I, 60, 67I, 99, 136, 143I, 224, 231I, 276, 283I, 344, 351K, 448, 455I, 518, 525K, 620
Math Connections, 4A, 14, 22A, 44A, 50, 68A, 74, 88A, 114A, 123, 144A, 147, 170A, 173, 183, 200A, 206, 232A, 243, 254A, 262, 284A, 299, 304A, 310, 324A, 331, 352A, 357, 358, 364, 378A, 380, 404A, 413, 428A, 432, 456A, 482A, 500A, 526A, 548A, 559, 565, 572A, 578, 596A
Math Correlation, TR10–TR13
matter, 150, 152, 154, 155
medical map, 415
menu planning, 9–13
microscope, 55, 189
microwaves, 96
Mid Atlantic Ridge, 432
middle ear, 337
military technology, 205, 206
mining, 534, 537–538
mirror, 176, 182–184, 188, 194
Misconception Alert, 30, 132, 176, 181, 216, 235, 246, 383, 390, 424, 432, 475, 506, 513, 531
moat, 581
model
  with computers, 196
  in engineering design process, 34
  in *Hands-On Activity,* for example, 146, 268, 296, 298, 367, 392–394
  in lessons, for example, 34, 196, 242, 259, 294, 300, 407
modem, 214–215
moraine, 478
Morse, Samuel, 204–205
Morse code, 204–205

motion energy
  examples of, 79, 88, 116–117
  size and, 120–121
  speed and, 118–119, 128–129
  in springs, 122–124, 125–127
mountains, 432, 434, 437–438, 443–444
movement (animals), 287–288
mudslide, 361
Mushroom Rock (South Africa), 464–465
music, 88, 103, 161–162, 164
Musk, Elon, 567

N

Native Americans, 203
natural gas, 529–530, 532, 535–536, 538
natural hazards. *see also* earthquakes; floods; volcanoes
  causes and effects of, 576, 600
  drought, 598, 600–604, 611
  hurricanes, 598–600, 604, 606, 611, 615–616
  improving levees, 608–609
  landslides, 574, 576, 584–585, 615
  mapping locations of, 578–579, 592, 602–603
  preparation and response, 580–581, 583, 591, 604
  reducing impacts with technology, 582, 586–590, 606–609, 612–614
  tsunamis, 598, 600, 604–606
  types of, 574–575
  warning signs of, 584–585, 591, 610–611
  wildfire, 574, 576, 582
natural resources, 528–534. *see also* nonrenewable energy resources; renewable energy resources
Nature of Science Connection, 459, 503
Navajo code talkers, 206

Index

nebula, 171
needles (tree), 236
nerves, 326
nervous system, 326–329
Niobrara Chalk Formation (Kansas), 457, 464–465, 466
noise-canceling headphones, 163
nonrenewable energy resources
    definition, 529, 550
    fossil fuels as, 529–530
    natural gas, 529–530, 532, 535–536, 538
    oil, 526, 529–530, 534–536
    renewable sources compared with, 556–557
    uranium, 529–530, 534, 536, 538
    uses of, 530–531
nuclear energy, 532, 534

O

ocean
    erosion by, 151, 358, 360–361, 369
    mapping earthquakes and volcanoes in, 436–437, 438
    mapping the ocean floor, 433, 436–437
    mountains and trenches in, 432, 436–437, 438
    power generation from, 84, 553
    "Ring of Fire," 430–431, 473
    tsunamis, 598, 600, 604–605
ocean waves, 150–151, 156, 160
oil, 526, 529–530, 534–536
oil spills, 538
opaque materials, 175
optical cables, 196
optimization, 53
organs, 306
organ system, 306
outer ear, 337
Ovshinsky, Stanford, 568

ovule (plant), 256
oxygen
    circulation in the body, 306–308, 310
    exercise and need for, 311–313
    gills and, 309

P

Pacific Ocean, 430, 432, 473
Pacing, T32–T33
pain receptors, 327, 334
Painted Desert (Arizona), 464
pancreas, 314
papyrus, 202
parks, 419–421, 422–423
People in Science and Engineering
    Alvarez, Luis and Walter, 514
    Anderson, Clayton, 249
    Artiles, Mayra, 83
    Block, Adrienne, 442
    Carter, Henry Vandyke, 319
    Cope, Edward, 513
    Doppler, Christian, 165–166
    Downs, Marion, 17
    Fernandes, Anjall, 373–374
    Fischer, Debra, 166
    Gray, Henry, 319
    Hasey, Janine, 271
    Hubbard, Bernard, 477
    Jones, Lucy, 591
    Lehmann, Marcus, 84
    Mantell, Mary Ann, 513
    Musk, Elon, 567
    Ovshinsky, Stanford, 568
    Ruiz, Vanessa, 319
    Steffy, Amanda, 131–132
    Vickers-Rich, Patricia, 514
    Zhiming, Don, 514
Performance Expectations, 2, 4A, 22A, 44A, 66, 68A, 88A, 114A, 142, 144A, 170A, 200A, 230, 232A, 254A, 282, 284A, 304A, 324A, 350, 352A, 378A, 404A, 428A, 454, 456A, 482A, 500A, 524, 526A, 548A, 572A, 596A
Performance Task, 60–61, 136–137, 224–225, 276–277, 344–345, 448–449, 518–519, 620–621
petal, 256
Petrified Forest National Park, 483
petroleum, 529
petroleum geologists, 543
phenomena, 88A, 128, 144A, 170A, 186, 254A, 255, 340, 352A, 362, 378A, 380, 386, 404A, 428A, 428B, 456A, 484A, 500A, 526A, 548A, 572A
Physical Science Connections, 203, 236, 264, 315, 336, 385, 433, 539, 550, 558
piano tuner, 164
pictograph, 202
piles (erosion control), 582
pinecone, 237, 261
pistil, 256
pixel, 208, 218
plant reproduction
    in cone-bearing trees, 261–262
    flowers, 234, 237, 256–260
    pollen, 237, 257–258
    pollination, 257–259
    seed dispersal, 237, 258, 262, 265–270, 292
    spores, 235, 237, 263
    steps in, 260
plants. *see also* plant reproduction
    coal formation from, 507, 529, 534
    in erosion control, 400
    ferns, 263, 488, 492
    functions of parts of, 234–238
    growth direction, 246–248, 250
    hydroponics, 243–245
    ivy, 383
    palm tree, 505, 507

    pine tree, 237, 261–262
    plastics from, 560
    prairie grasses, 385
    skunk cabbage, 258
    in space, 249
    sycamore tree, 266
    Venus flytrap, 247
    water and food transport in, 239–240
Plan Your Models, 448
Plan Your Procedure, 137, 345, 519, 621
plastics from plants, 560
political map, 409
pollen, 237–258, 257–258, 262
pollinator, 257–259
pollution, 73, 536, 538, 540–542
pomologists, 271
pothole prevention, 372
power plants
    coal-burning, 72, 532, 538
    nonrenewable resources in, 530
    renewable resources in, 552
Preassessment, 3F, 4B, 22B, 44B, 67F, 68B, 88B, 114B, 143F, 144B, 170B, 200B, 232B, 254B, 283F, 284B, 304B, 324B, 342E, 351G, 352B, 378B, 404B, 428B, 455F, 456B, 482B, 500B, 525G, 526B, 548B, 572B, 596B
pressure receptor, 327
prism, 185
Probing Question, 435, 439
problem (engineering)
    defining, 5, 6, 8, 14, 19
    in *Hands-On Activity*, 9, 46, 99, 101, 243, 250, 419, 563, 586, 612
    researching, 24–25
    in science and engineering, 38–39, 49, 54, 56, 241, 249, 552, 575, 608–609
Professional Development, 4B, 22B, 44B, 68B, 88B, 114B, 144B, 170B, 200B, 232B, 254B, 284B, 304B,

Index

324B, 352B, 378B, 404B, 428B, 456B, 482B, 500B, 526B, 548B, 572B, 596B
Projects, 1, 3I–3L, 65, 67I–67L, 141, 143I–143L, 229, 231I–231L, 281, 283I–283L, 349, 351K–351N, 453, 455I–455L, 523, 525K–525N
prototype, 34
pulse (heart rate), 311–313
pupil (eye), 336
Putting It Together, 30, 37, 51, 75, 82, 94, 98, 108, 121, 127, 130, 181, 207, 218, 242, 248, 260, 291, 310, 329, 338, 357, 365, 372, 391, 398, 409, 433, 461, 467, 491, 508, 533, 553, 579, 611

Q

questions (in investigations)
in *Hands-On Activity*, for example, 31, 46, 76, 101, 146

R

radio wave, 96, 216–217
rainbow, 181
rainforest, 380–381
Reading in the Science Content Area, TR2–TR5
Reading Language Arts Connections, 271
reasoning, 33, 267, 371
receptors
in ears, 337–338
in eyes, 336
in noses, 333
pain, 327, 334
pressure, 327
temperature, 327, 334, 336
in tongues, 334
touch, 327, 334
Record Your Results, 77, 269, 345, 367, 393, 541
reflection
angles of, 182–184
in cameras, 188
color and, 177, 181
eyes and, 180, 190–191
in mirrors, 176, 182–184, 188, 194
reflectors and, 176–177, 180
surface properties and, 178–179
reflexes, 329
refracting telescope, 55, 193
refraction of light
definition, 186
examples of, 186–187
in eyes, 190–191
lenses and, 188–193
magnification of images in, 188
speed of light and, 185
in telescopes, 193
in tools, 188–189
in water, 173, 186
Remotely Operated Vehicle (ROV), 433
renewable energy resources
algae farming, 73
for batteries, 567–568
biomass fuel, 73, 550
for cars, 527, 539, 567–568
definition, 550
energy plants using, 552, 554–557
geothermal, 550, 552
historical use of, 532
hydropower, 550, 552, 555
nonrenewable resources compared with, 556–557
ocean waves, 84
solar, 79, 99–101, 176, 549–550, 552, 561–566
tidal, 553
wind, 548, 550, 552
Report, 621
Research, 3K, 60, 67K, 136, 143K, 224, 231K, 283K, 344, 351M, 455K, 518, 525M, 620
reservoir, 606
resource, 528. *see also* nonrenewable energy resources; renewable energy resources
resource map, 415
respiratory system, 306–309
retaining wall, 582
retina, 336
Revere, Paul, 203
Richter scale, 577
Rift Valley (Africa), 429, 445
"Ring of Fire", 430, 473
ripples, as waves, 149
rivers
canyon formation by, 462, 471–472, 475
channel formation by, 354–355, 360, 373
deposition from, 355–356, 359–360
floods, 356–357, 360, 608–610
weathering and erosion by, 359–361
road map, 407, 408
roads, 370–372
robots, 299–300
rock layers
canyon formation in, 462, 471–472, 475
consistent patterns in, 466–467, 509
earthquakes and, 467, 473, 510
Earth's history from, 458–459, 462
fossils in, 464
inferring environments in, 465, 506–507
interpreting, 458, 464, 512
modeling, 458, 468–470
pressure and heat in, 458, 474
relative age of, 460, 462–463, 506–507
weathering and erosion of, 459, 471–472, 475, 511
rocks. *see also* rock layers
formation of, 460
in freezing and thawing, 362–363, 396
in glaciers, 364–365, 475
plant roots and, 382
pressure and heat and, 474
sedimentary, 463
weathering and erosion of, 151, 459, 471–472, 475, 511
role playing, 601
root hairs, 383
roots, 234–236, 238, 240, 247, 382, 385
ROV (Remotely Operated Vehicle), 433
RTI/Extra Support, 3, 3G, 3I, 32, 35, 36, 39, 67, 67G, 143, 143G, 202, 207, 213, 214, 217, 231, 231G, 231I, 283, 283G, 283I, 351, 351I, 351K, 455, 455G, 455I, 460, 467, 474, 482B, 496, 498, 500B, 503, 506, 525, 525I, 576, 584, 599, 602, 610, 616
Ruiz, Vanessa, 319

S

safety
disaster supply kit, 581
family emergency plan, 607
fire extinguishers, 591
laboratory, XVIII
thermal imaging devices, 94
Safety in Science, T62–T64, 311, 612
sandbag, 597, 606
sandblasting, 386
sand dune, 390, 396
sand fence, 399–400
sand transport, 388–391
satellites
in flood prediction, 610
in hurricane detection, 606
maps from, 407
photographs from, 407, 606

Index

signals from, 153, 200, 212, 217
in wildfire detection, 584
scale (maps), 408, 412–413
schools of fish, 492
science, 55–56, 544
Science Connections, 3H, 67H, 143H, 231H, 283H, 351J, 455H, 525J
Science & Engineering Practices (SEP)
  analyzing and evaluating data, **258**
  analyzing and interpreting data, **231L, 254A, 276, 283L, 351N, 404A, 410, 412, 416, 428, 428A, 430, 432, 434, 436, 438, 441, 444, 445, 455L**
  asking questions and defining problems, **3K, 4, 4A, 6, 9, 11, 15, 18, 61, 67L, 70, 76, 80, 84, 114, 114A, 122, 124, 254A, 265, 271, 351N, 404A**
  constructing explanations and designing solutions, **3L, 22, 22A, 25, 29, 31, 35, 37, 39, 68A, 73, 79, 82, 88A, 105, 114A, 116, 125, 129, 132, 143L, 200, 200A, 202, 204, 207, 212, 216, 266, 456, 456A, 467, 472, 473, 475, 478, 482, 482A, 484, 486, 488, 491, 492, 496, 500, 500A, 502, 509, 519, 563, 566, 572A, 575, 583, 585, 589, 596, 596A, 598, 600, 605, 607, 608, 612, 616, 621**
  developing and using models, **12, 144, 144A, 146, 148, 150, 152, 154, 156, 159, 164, 170, 170A, 172, 175, 177, 178, 181, 182, 187, 189, 191, 193, 196, 225, 324A, 329, 330, 334, 345, 449, 572, 572A, 587, 590**
  engaging in argument from evidence, **231L, 232, 232A, 234, 237, 241, 242, 247, 248, 250, 251, 254, 254A, 272, 283L, 284A, 287, 288, 291, 292, 296, 298, 304, 304A,** 307, 308, 310, 311, 314, 317, 324, 324A, 327, 337, 340, 455L, 593
  obtaining, evaluating, and communicating information, **261, 406, 423, 424, 526A, 528, 531, 533, 535, 536, 538, 540, 543, 548, 548A, 551, 552, 554, 557, 559, 561, 568, 572A, 577, 579, 580, 592, 603, 611**
  planning and carrying out investigations, **44, 44A, 46, 49, 50, 56, 67L, 68, 68A, 88, 88A, 90, 99, 137, 268, 352, 352A, 356, 359, 361, 362, 364, 366, 367, 368, 371, 372, 373, 378, 378A, 383, 385, 387, 390, 392, 395, 397, 400, 404, 419, 420, 526, 564**
ScienceSaurus Correlation, TR14–TR17
scientific explanations, 22, 22A, 25, 29, 31, 35, 37, 39, 68A, 73, 79, 82, 88A, 105, 114A, 116, 125, 129, 132, 200, 200A, 202, 204, 207, 212, 216, 266, 456, 456A, 467, 472, 473, 475, 478, 482, 482A, 484, 486, 488, 491, 492, 496, 500, 500A, 502, 509, 563, 566, 572A, 575, 583, 585, 589, 596, 596A, 598, 600, 605, 607, 608, 612, 616
scytale, 207
secret codes, 206–207
sediment, 355–356, 359, 364, 388
sedimentary rocks, 463
seeds, 237, 258, 262, 265–267, 268–270, 292
seeing, 324, 336, 339
seismograph, 473
seismometer, 473, 574–575, 582, 584–585
self-pollination, 259
semi-circular canal (ear), 337
senses
  echolocation, 325, 338
  extreme, 339
  nervous system, 326–329
  reflexes, 329
  sight, 324, 336, 339
  smell, 333
  taste, 334–335
sepal, 256
shear core, 581
shear wall, 581
skeletal system, 326
Skills and Standards Focus, 3I, 67I, 143I, 231I, 283I, 351K, 455I, 525K
skin, 286, 290–291, 316, 327–328
slithering, 152
small intestine, 314
smart roads, 372
smell receptor, 333
smoke signal, 203
solar energy
  solar cells, 79, 561
  solar cooker, 99–101, 561
  solar hot water heater, 562–566
  solar panels, 95, 176, 549, 552, 554, 561
  solar rays, 96
solution (to problem)
  in *Can You Solve It?*, for example, 5, 19, 23, 41, 45
  in *Hands-On Activity*, for example, 9, 31, 46, 99
  in lessons, for example, 17, 24–25, 38, 49–51, 217
SONAR technology, 433
sound energy, 78, 88, 103–107, 154
sound waves
  amplitude of, 156–158, 162–163
  in anechoic chambers, 34, 36–37
  canceled, 163
  in cell phones, 216–217
  direction of motion in, 154–155
  Doppler effect, 165
  from elephant stomps, 219–220
  hearing, 18, 337–338
  infrasounds, 219
  in matter, 155
  measuring, 40
  in SONAR technology, 433
  from vibrations, 102–103
  wavelength of, 159
space exploration
  astronauts, 249
  energy transfer on Mars, 131–132
  International Space Station, 170, 249
  waves in, 153, 155
speakers, 103
speed and energy, 118–119, 128–129
spinal cord, 326, 329
spines (animal), 290
spines (plant), 235, 237
spores (plants), 235, 237, 263
spring energy, 122–124, 125–127
stamen, 256
star map, 415
Steffy, Amanda, 131–132
stem, plant, 234, 236, 247
stethoscope, 28, 304
stirrup (ear), 337
stomach, 314, 317
strainmeter, 584
Summative Assessment, 3F, 19–20, 41–42, 57–58, 62–64, 67F, 85–86, 111–112, 133–134, 138–140, 143F, 167–168, 197–198, 221–222, 226–228, 231E, 251–252, 273–274, 278–280, 283F, 301–302, 321–322, 341–342, 346–348, 351G, 375–376, 401–402, 425–426, 445–446, 450–452, 455F, 479–480, 497–498, 515–516, 520–522, 525G, 545–546, 569–570, 593–594, 617–618, 622–624
sunlight
  characteristics of, 96, 185
  solar energy from, 79, 95, 99–101, 176, 549, 552, 561–566
surfing, 145, 151, 160

Index

sweat, 316
systems
 audio, 36–38
 audio-testing, 36–38
 circulatory, 306, 308–310
 digestive, 314–318
 drainage, 241
 heating, venting, and air conditioning, 109–110
 hydroponic, 243–245
 nervous, 326–329
 organ, 306
 respiratory, 306–309

T

tails, 287, 293
talking drum, 203
taproot, 236
taste, 334–335
taste buds, 334
Teacher Guide, 3G, 67G, 143G, 231G, 283G, 351I, 455G, 525I
technology
 engineering of, 6–8
 Enigma machine, 206
 Global Positioning System, 407
 hearing aids, 17–18
 hook and loop tape, 292
 natural hazard impact reduction, 582, 586–590, 606–609, 612–614
 noise-canceling headphones, 163
 ROV, 433
 smart roads, 372
 SONAR, 433
 telegraph, 204–205
 thermal imaging, 94, 130
 tire design for Mars, 132
telegraph, 204–205
telephone game, 216
telescope, 171, 193
television (TV), 212–213, 218

temperature, 90–91
temperature receptors, 327, 334
terminal moraine, 478
Tesla Motors, 567–568
text message, 206, 214
thermal energy (heat energy), 70, 72, 79, 90–94, 130
thermal imaging, 94, 130
thermographic camera, 56
thermometer, 91
thorn, 235, 237
thunderstorm, 615
tidal power, 553
tiltmeter, 582, 584
timelines
 of electric car batteries and cars, 568
 of energy use, 532
 of hurricanes, 616–617
tongue, 334
tools for science, 55–56
topographical map, 417–418
touch, 247, 327, 330–332, 334
trachea, 306
translucent materials, 175
transparent materials, 175
trench, 432, 436
trough (wave), 156
tsunami, 598, 600, 604–606, 612–614
tuning, in music, 164
tuning fork, 107, 164
turbines, 548, 552–553

U

ultrasound, 155
ultraviolet light, 97
Unit Overview, 1, 65, 141, 229, 281, 349, 453, 523
Unit Projects. see Projects
Unit Review, 62–64, 138–140, 226–228, 278–280, 346–348, 450–452, 520–522, 622–624

Unit Vocabulary, 3, 67, 143, 231, 283, 351, 455, 525
uranium, 529–530, 534, 536, 538
ureter, 316
urinary system, 316
urine, 316

V

veins, 306, 310
vertical collisions, 130
vibrations, 102–103, 106–107
Vickers-Rich, Patricia, 514
vision pits, 336
Vocabulary Games
 Bingo, 525
 Concentration, 231, 283
 Guess the Word, 3, 67, 351
 Picture It, 143, 455
Vocabulary Strategies, 3, 67, 143, 231, 283, 351, 455, 525
volcanoes
 causes and effects of eruptions, 576
 eruptions, 428, 430, 572, 574, 576
 formation of, 428
 landslides from, 584–585
 mapping locations of, 434, 438
 in the "Ring of Fire," 430, 473
 warning signs, 584
volume (of sound), 158

W

water. see also ocean; rivers
 aquadynamic testing, 35
 in canyon formation, 462, 471–472, 475
 in deserts and rainforests, 380–381
 erosion from, 358–361, 366–368, 459, 475
 freezing and thawing, 362–363, 365, 370–371

 hydropower from, 550
 reflection of light from, 176
 in seed dispersal, 266
 water cycle, 95
 in waves, 150–151, 156, 160
 weathering by, 360–361, 398
water-based natural hazards
 causes and effects of, 600
 drought, 598, 600–604, 611
 hurricanes, 598–600, 604, 606, 611, 615–616
 levees and, 608–609
 mapping occurrences, 602–603
 predicting, 610–611
 preparation and response, 604, 607
 technology to reduce impacts of, 606–609, 612–614
 tsunami, 598, 600, 604–606
 types of, 598
waterfall, 361, 398
"the wave", 153
wavelength, 156–157, 159, 181
waves. see also sound waves
 amplitude, 156–158, 162–163
 in crowds of people, 153
 definition, 149
 energy transfer in, 149–151, 156
 erosion from, 151, 358, 360–361, 369
 harmony and, 161
 interactions in, 161–164
 light waves, 153
 making, 146–148
 neutral, 163
 ocean waves, 150–151, 156, 160
 parts of, 156–157
 power from, 84
 radio waves, 96, 216–217
 size of, 149
 that move side to side, 152–153
 tuning instruments, 164
weather forecasts, 166, 606
weathering of landforms

Index

definition, 359
in deserts, 387
by living things, 382–383
rate of change, 366–368
by water, 360–361, 398
weather maps, 408, 415
Why NGSS?, T34–T39
wildfire, 574, 576, 582, 584–585
wind
    energy from, 70, 548, 550, 552
    in hurricanes, 615

plant reproduction and, 237, 258, 266
rock erosion from, 388–391, 475
sand transport, 388–391
solar energy and, 95
waves from, 151
wind barrier, 399
wind farm, 548, 554
window blinds, 174–175
wind turbine, 554–555
wings, 287, 293
wood, energy from, 550

world map, 409
World Wide Web, 215

X

X-rays, 56, 96–97

Y

You Solve It, 3F, 67F, 143F, 231E, 283F, 351G, 455F, 525G

Z

Zhiming, Don, 514